▲ INDIVIDUAL INCOME TAX FORMULA

Income (broadly conceived)	$XX,XXX
Less: Exclusions	(X,XXX)
Gross income	$XX,XXX
Less: Deductions for adjusted gross income	(X,XXX)
Adjusted gross income	$XX,XXX
Less: Deductions from adjusted gross income—	
The greater of—	
The total itemized deductions	
or standard deduction	(X,XXX)
Personal and dependency exemptions	(X,XXX)
Taxable income	$XX,XXX

▲ BASIC STANDARD DEDUCTION AMOUNTS

	Standard Deduction Amount	
Filing Status	1995	1994
Single	$3,900	$3,800
Married, filing jointly	6,550	6,350
Surviving spouse	6,550	6,350
Head of household	5,750	5,600
Married, filing separately	3,275	3,175

▲ AMOUNT OF EACH ADDITIONAL STANDARD DEDUCTION FOR AGE & BLINDNESS

	Standard Deduction Amount	
Filing Status	1995	1994
Single	$ 950	$ 950
Married, filing jointly	750	750
Surviving spouse	750	750
Head of household	950	950
Married, filing separately	750	750

▲ PERSONAL AND DEPENDENCY EXEMPTION AMOUNT

1995:	$2,500	
1994:	$2,450	

CONCEPTS IN FEDERAL TAXATION

1996
EDITION

CONCEPTS IN FEDERAL TAXATION

1996
EDITION

KEVIN E. MURPHY
Oklahoma State University

CONTRIBUTING AUTHORS:

RICK L. CROSSER
Weber State University

MARK HIGGINS
University of Rhode Island

WEST PUBLISHING COMPANY
Minneapolis/St. Paul   New York   Los Angeles   San Francisco

Copyediting: Polly Kummel
Composition: Parkwood Composition, Inc.
Index: Terry Casey
Chapter opening art and writing assignment icons: Randy Miyake, Miyake
    Illustration.
Cover Image: Randy Miyake, Miyake Illustration.

Production, prepress, printing, and binding: West Publishing Company.

WEST'S COMMITMENT TO THE ENVIRONMENT

In 1906, West Publishing Company began recycling materials left over from the
production of books. This began a tradition of efficient and responsible use of
resources. Today, up to 95 percent of our legal books and 70 percent of our college
and school texts are printed on recycled, acid-free stock. West also recycles nearly 22
million pounds of scrap paper annually—the equivalent of 181,717 trees. Since the
1960s, West has devised ways to capture and recycle waste inks, solvents, oils, and
vapors created in the printing process. We also recycle plastics of all kinds, wood,
glass, corrugated cardboard, and batteries and have eliminated the use of Styrofoam
book packaging. We at West are proud of the longevity and the scope of our
commitment to the environment.

 TEXT IS PRINTED ON 10% POST CONSUMER RECYCLED PAPER   PRINTED WITH SOY INK™

COPYRIGHT © 1994   By WEST PUBLISHING COMPANY
COPYRIGHT © 1995   By WEST PUBLISHING COMPANY
COPYRIGHT © 1996   By WEST PUBLISHING COMPANY
                     610 Opperman Drive
                     P.O. Box 64526
                     St. Paul, MN 55164–0526

Printed in the United States of America

02 01 00 99 98 97 96 95   8 7 6 5 4 3 2 1 0

Library of Congress Cataloging-in-Publication Data

Murphy, Kevin E.
     Concepts in federal taxation, 1996 edition / Kevin E. Murphy.
        p.   cm.
     Includes index.
     ISBN 0-314-04532-5 (hard) ISSN 1081-1338
     1. Taxation—Law and legislation—United States.   I. Title.
KF6289.M87   1996a
343.7304—dc20
[347.3034]   95-47062
                                                          CIP

▲ BRIEF TABLE OF CONTENTS ▲

Preface   xxiii

Introduction   xxix

▲ **PART I**
CONCEPTUAL FOUNDATIONS OF THE TAX LAW   1

CHAPTER 1   Federal Income Taxation—An Overview   2

CHAPTER 2   Income Tax Concepts   48

▲ **PART II**
GROSS INCOME   87

CHAPTER 3   Income Sources   88

CHAPTER 4   Income Exclusions   137

▲ **PART III**
DEDUCTIONS   177

CHAPTER 5   Introduction to Business Deductions   178

CHAPTER 6   Business Expenses   222

CHAPTER 7   Losses: Deductions and Limitations   269

▲ **PART IV**
INCOME TAX ENTITIES   315

CHAPTER 8   Taxation of Individuals   316

CHAPTER 9   Income Tax Entities   373

▲ **PART V**
PROPERTY TRANSACTIONS   423

CHAPTER 10   Acquisitions of Property   424

CHAPTER 11   Cost Recovery on Property: Depreciation,
Depletion, and Amortization   471

CHAPTER 12   Property Dispositions   538

CHAPTER 13   Nonrecognition Transactions   582

▲ PART VI
TAX CONSIDERATIONS 625

CHAPTER 14 Other Factors Affecting Tax Liability 626

CHAPTER 15 Tax Research 672

APPENDIX A Tax Rate Schedules and Tax Tables A-1

APPENDIX B Tax Return Problem B-1

APPENDIX C Tax Forms C-1

APPENDIX D Statements on Responsibilities in Tax Practice D-1

GLOSSARY G-1
INDEX I-1

▲ TABLE OF CONTENTS ▲

Preface xxiii

▲ **INTRODUCTION xxix**
Why Study Federal Income Taxation xxix
  Significance of Tax Costs xxx
  Conservation of Wealth xxxii
  Taxes Influence Routine Decisions xxxiii
  Self-Protection xxxiii

PART I
CONCEPTUAL FOUNDATIONS OF THE TAX LAW 1

▲ **CHAPTER 1**   Federal Income Taxation—An Overview 2
Introduction 3
Definition and Evaluation of a Tax 3
  Definition of a Tax 3
  Standards for Evaluating a Tax 5
  Tax Rates and Structures 7
    Tax Rate Definitions 7
    Tax Rate Structures 8
Major Types of U.S. Taxes 11
  Income Taxes 11
  Employment Taxes 12
    Social Security Taxes 13
    Unemployment Taxes 14
  Sales Tax 15
  Property Taxes 15
  Other Taxes 16
    Excise Taxes 16
    Wealth Transfer Taxes 16
Sources of Federal Income Tax Law 18
Federal Income Tax Terminology 19
  Income 19
  Deductions 21
  Income Tax Rates 21
  Tax Prepayments 23
  Tax Credits 24
  Filing Returns 24
Individual Income Tax Calculation 25
  Deductions for Adjusted Gross Income 26
  Deductions from Adjusted Gross Income 27
  Personal and Dependency Exemptions 29

Tax Planning 29

  Mechanics of Tax Planning 29

    Timing Income and Deductions 30

    Income Shifting 33

  Tax Evasion and Tax Avoidance 34

Ethical Considerations in Tax Practice 35

Summary 38

Key Terms 38

Primary Tax Law Sources 39

Discussion Questions 40

Problems 42

Discussion Case 1–1 45

Discussion Case 1–2 46

Tax Planning Case 1–3 46

Ethics Discussion Case 1–4 47

▲ **CHAPTER 2**   Income Tax Concepts   48

Introduction 49

General Concepts 50

  Ability-to-Pay Concept 50

  Administrative Convenience Concept 51

  Arm's-Length Transaction Concept 52

  Pay-as-You-Go Concept 53

Accounting Concepts 54

  Entity Concept 54

    Assignment-of-Income Doctrine 57

  Annual Accounting Period Concept 58

    Accounting Method 58

    Tax Benefit Rule 59

    Substance-over-Form Doctrine 60

Income Concepts 61

  All-Inclusive Income Concept 61

  Legislative Grace Concept 62

  Capital Recovery Concept 63

  Realization Concept 63

    Claim-of-Right Doctrine 64

    Constructive Receipt Doctrine 65

    Comparing Claim of Right and Constructive Receipt 66

  Wherewithal-to-Pay Concept 67

Deduction Concepts 68

  Legislative Grace Concept 68

  Business Purpose Concept 68

  Capital Recovery Concept 71

Summary 73

Key Terms 74

Primary Tax Law Sources 74

Discussion Questions 76

Problems 77

Discussion Case 2–1 84

Tax Planning Case 2–2 84

Ethics Discussion Case 2–3 85

PART II
GROSS INCOME 87

▲ **CHAPTER 3**　　Income Sources　　88

Concept Review 89

Introduction 89

What Constitutes Income 90

　Income Is Derived from Labor and Capital 91

　Income as an Increase in Wealth 92

　What Constitutes Income: Current View 93

Common Income Sources 94

　Earned Income 94

　Unearned Income 96

　　Rental and Royalty Income 96

　　Annuities 97

　　Calculation of Gain/Loss on Sale of Investments 99

　　Income from Conduit Entities 100

　Transfers from Others 100

　　Prizes and Awards 101

　　Unemployment Compensation 101

　　Social Security Benefits 101

　　Alimony Received 105

　Imputed Income 106

　　Below Market-Rate Loans 107

　　Payment of Expenses by Others 111

　　Bargain Purchases 111

Capital Gains and Losses—An Introduction 112

　Capital Gain-and-Loss Netting Procedure 113

　Tax Treatment of Capital Gains 115

　Tax Treatment of Capital Losses 115

　Capital Gains and Losses of Conduit Entities 116

Effect of Accounting Method 117

　Cash Method 117

　　Exceptions Applicable to the Cash Method 118

　Accrual Method 119

　　Exceptions Applicable to the Accrual Method 120

　Hybrid Method 121

　Exceptions Applicable to All Methods 121

　　Installment Sales 121

　　Long-Term Construction Contracts 122

Summary 122

Key Terms   124

Primary Tax Law Sources   124

Discussion Questions   126

Problems   127

Discussion Case 3–1   135

Discussion Case 3–2   135

Tax Planning Case 3–3   135

Ethics Discussion Case 3–4   136

▲ **CHAPTER 4**   Income Exclusions   137

Concept Review   138

Introduction   138

Donative Items   139

   Gifts   140

   Inheritances   141

   Life Insurance Proceeds   141

   Scholarships   143

   Certain Death Benefits   144

Employment-Related Exclusions   144

   Foreign Earned Income   145

   Payments Made on Behalf of an Employee   145

      Payments to Qualified Pension Plans   146

      Group Term Life Insurance   147

      Health and Accident Insurance Premiums   148

      Meals and Lodging Provided by the Employer   149

      General Fringe Benefits   150

      Other Benefits Paid by an Employer   151

   Employer Benefit Plans   151

Returns of Human Capital   153

   Workers' Compensation   153

   Damage Payments for Personal Injury or Sickness   154

   Payments from Health and Accident Policies   155

Investment-Related Exclusions   156

   Municipal Bond Interest   156

   Stock Dividends   158

   Discharge of Indebtedness   158

   Improvements by a Lessee   161

Summary   161

Key Terms   163

Primary Tax Law Sources   163

Discussion Questions   165

Problems   166

Integrative Problems   172

Discussion Case 4–1   175

Tax Planning Case 4–2   175

Ethics Discussion Case 4–3   175

PART III
DEACTIONS 177

▲ **CHAPTER 5** Introduction to Business Expenses   178

Concept Review   179

Introduction   179

Reporting Deductions   182

Conduit Entity Reporting   183

Classification of Deductions   185

   Profit-Motivated Expenditures   185

   Trade or Business or Production-of-Income Expenses?   186

     Trade or Business Expenses   187

     Expenses for the Production of Income   188

   Rental Activity   189

   Personal Expenditures   191

   Mixed Business and Personal Expenditures   191

     Mixed-Use Assets   191

     Mixed-Use Expenditures   192

Tests for Deductibility   193

   Ordinary, Necessary, and Reasonable in Amount   193

     Ordinary Expense   193

     Necessary Expense   194

     Reasonable in Amount   195

   Not a Personal Expense   195

   Not a Capital Expenditure   196

     Repair-and-Maintenance Expense   198

     Start-up Costs   198

   Not Frustrate Public Policy   199

     Expenses of an Illegal Business   200

     Lobbying Expenses and Other Political Activities   200

   Not Related to Tax-Exempt Income   201

   Expenditure Must Be for Taxpayer's Benefit   202

Timing of Deductions—Effect of Accounting Method   202

   Cash Method   203

   Accrual Method   205

   Financial and Taxable Income Differences   208

Summary   210

Key Terms   211

Primary Tax Law Sources   211

Discussion Questions   213

Problems   214

Comprehensive Problem   219

Discussion Case 5–1   220

Discussion Case 5–2   220

Tax Planning Case 5–3   221

Ethics Discussion Case 5–4   221

▲ **CHAPTER 6**   Business Expenses   222

Concept Review   223
Introduction   223
Business Expenses   224
  Entertainment, Auto, Travel, Gift, and Education Expenses   224
    Meals and Entertainment   224
    Auto Expenses   228
    Travel Expenses   230
    Business Gifts   232
    Substantiation Requirements   233
    Education Expenses   233
  Compensation of Employees   234
  Bad Debts   236
  Related Party Accrued Expenses   239
  Other Business Expenses   240
    Insurance Expense   241
    Taxes   241
    Rental Payments   243
    Legal Fees   244
Limited Mixed-Use Expenses   245
  Hobby Expenses   245
  Vacation Home Expenses   247
  Home Office Expenses   250
Summary   252
Key Terms   253
Primary Tax Law Sources   253
Discussion Questions   254
Problems   255
Integrative Problem   264
Discussion Case 6–1   266
Discussion Case 6–2   267
Discussion Case 6–3   267
Tax Planning Case 6–4   267
Ethics Discussion Case 6–5   268

▲ **CHAPTER 7**   Losses—Deductions and Limitations   269

Concept Review   270
Introduction   270
Annual Losses   272
Net Operating Losses   273
Tax-Shelter Losses: An Overview   275
  The At-Risk Rules   277
  Passive Activity Losses   279
    Passive Activity Definition   279
    Types of Income   282
    Taxpayers Subject to the Limits   283
    General Rule for Passive Activities   284

Dispositions of Passive Activities 284

Exceptions for Rental Real Estate 287

Transaction Losses 290

Trade or Business Losses 291

Business Casualty and Theft Losses 291

Investment-Related Losses 295

Capital Losses 295

Specially Treated Investment Losses 296

Personal Use Losses 299

Summary 301

Key Terms 302

Primary Tax Law Sources 303

Discussion Questions 304

Problems 305

Comprehensive Problem 312

Discussion Case 7–1 312

Discussion Case 7–2 312

Tax Planning Case 7–3 313

Ethics Discussion Case 7–4 313

PART IV
INCOME TAX ENTITIES 315

▲ **CHAPTER 8** Taxation of Individuals 316

Concept Review 317

Introduction 317

Personal and Dependency Exemptions 318

Dependency Requirements 319

Gross Income Test 319

Support Test 319

Relationship or Member of Household Test 320

Citizen or Residency Test 320

Joint Return Test 321

Filing Status 321

Married, Filing Jointly 321

Married, Filing Separately 322

Single 322

Head of Household 323

Deductions for Adjusted Gross Income 324

Reimbursed Employee Business Expenses 325

Accountable Reimbursement Plans 325

Nonaccountable Reimbursement Plans 326

Deductions for Self-Employed Taxpayers 328

Retirement Plan Contribution Deductions 329

Individual Retirement Accounts 330

Moving Expenses 331

Deductions from Adjusted Gross Income   332

Standard Deduction   332

Itemized Deductions   334

Medical Expenses   334

Taxes   337

Interest Expense   338

Charitable Contributions   340

Miscellaneous Itemized Deductions   342

**Itemized Deductions and Exemptions—Reductions
by High-Income Taxpayers   344**

Exemption and Standard Deduction Restrictions on Dependents   346

Calculating Tax Liability   346

Tax on Unearned Income of a Minor Child   347

Filing Requirements   348

Summary   348

Key Terms   349

Primary Tax Law Sources   349

Discussion Questions   351

Problems   352

Integrative Problems   359

Discussion Case 8–1   364

Discussion Case 8–2   364

Tax Planning Case 8–3   364

Ethics Discussion Case 8–4   365

APPENDIX TO CHAPTER 8
Comprehensive Tax Return Illustration   367

▲ **CHAPTER 9**   Other Tax Entities   373

Concept Review   374

Introduction   374

Corporations   375

Income Tax Considerations   376

Tax Rate Differentials   376

Personal Service Corporations   379

Owner-Employee Status   379

Special Rules for Corporations   381

Dividends-Received Deduction   381

Passive Activity Losses   383

Capital Loss Limitations   384

Charitable Contribution Limitations   385

Organizational Costs   387

Calculation of Taxable Income   387

Accounting Periods and Methods   388

Distributions to Shareholders   389

Multiple Corporations   390

Controlled Groups   390

Fiduciaries 392

  Estates 392

  Trusts 392

  Income Taxation of Fiduciaries 393

    Charitable Contributions 394

    Accounting Periods 395

    Exemption Amounts 395

  Income Tax Calculation 395

Conduit Entities 396

  Accounting Periods 396

  Accounting Methods 397

  Basis in Partnerships and S Corporations 397

  Sole Proprietorships 399

  Partnerships 400

    Legal Characteristics 401

    Partners Are Not Employees 401

    Basis of Partnership Interest 402

    Partnership Distributions 403

    Partnership Terminations 404

    Limited Liability Companies (LLCs) 404

    Limited Liability Partnerships (LLPs) 405

  S Corporations 405

    Qualification Requirements 405

    Revocation of the S Election 406

    Change from C Corporation to S Corporation 406

    Employee Status of Stockholders 407

    Distributions and Basis Adjustments 407

Uses of Entities 408

  Income Splitting 408

Summary 410

Key Terms 412

Primary Tax Law Sources 412

Discussion Questions 414

Problems 415

Discussion Case 9–1 420

Discussion Case 9–2 420

Tax Planning Case 9–3 420

Tax Planning Case 9–4 421

Ethics Discussion Case 9–5 421

PART V
PROPERTY TRANSACTIONS 423

▲ **CHAPTER 10** Acquisitions of Property 424

Concept Review 425

Introduction 425

Classes of Property 426

The Property Investment Cycle 427

    Adjusted Basis 428

        Increases in Basis 429

        Decreases in Basis 430

    Basis in Conduit Entities 432

    Property Dispositions 433

Initial Basis 435

Purchase of Assets 435

    Determining the Amount Invested 435

    Basis of a Bargain Purchase 437

    Purchase of Multiple Assets 437

    Purchase of a Business 438

        Purchase of the Assets of a Business 438

        Purchase of Corporate Stock 440

    Constructed Assets 440

Specially Valued Property Acquisitions 441

Basis of Property Acquired by Gift 441

    General Rule for Gift Basis 442

    Split Basis Rule for Loss Property 443

        Special Sales Price Basis 444

    Holding Period 444

Basis of Property Acquired by Inheritance 444

    Primary Valuation Date 445

    Alternate Valuation Date 445

    Distribution Date 446

    Other Considerations 446

Property Acquired from a Spouse 448

Personal Use Property Converted to Business Use 449

    General Rule for Basis 449

    Split Basis Rule 449

Basis in Securities 451

    Stock Dividends 451

        Taxable Stock Dividends 452

    Transfers of Assets to a Controlled Corporation 453

    Wash Sale Stock Basis 453

Summary 455

Key Terms 457

Primary Tax Law Sources 458

Discussion Questions 459

Problems 459

Integrative Problem 467

Discussion Case 10–1 468

Discussion Case 10–2 468

Discussion Case 10–3 469

Tax Planning Case 10–4 469

Tax Planning Case 10–5 469

Ethics Discussion Case 10–6 470

▲ **CHAPTER 11**   Cost Recovery on Property:
                    Depreciation, Depletion, and Amortization   471

Concept Review   472

Introduction   472

Property Subject to Periodic Capital Recovery   474

Basis Subject to Periodic Capital Recovery   476

Capital Recovery from Depreciation or Cost Recovery   476

Depreciation before 1981   477

    Facts and Circumstances Method   477

    Class Life Asset Depreciation Range (ADR)   478

Cost Recovery in General   479

    Property Subject to Cost Recovery   480

    Basis Subject to Cost Recovery   480

    Class Lives   481

    Depreciation Methods   481

    Conventions   481

    IRS Percentage Tables   482

Section 179 Election to Expense Assets   482

    Qualified Taxpayers   483

    Qualified Property   483

    Limitations on Deduction   484

        Annual Deduction Limit   *484*

        Annual Investment Limit   *486*

        Active Trade or Business Income Limit   *486*

Accelerated Cost Recovery System (ACRS)   487

    ACRS Real Property Recovery Periods   488

    Use of ACRS Percentage Tables   489

    ACRS Depreciation Methods   489

    ACRS Conventions   490

    ACRS Straight-Line Election   490

Modified Accelerated Cost Recovery (MACRS)   491

    Using MACRS Percentage Tables   494

    MACRS Depreciation Methods   495

    MACRS Conventions   496

    Alternative Depreciation System (ADS)   499

    Limitations on Listed Property   499

    Listed Property in General   500

        Limitation on Passenger Autos   *501*

        Adequate Record Keeping   *502*

Depletion   502

    Depletion Methods   503

    Cost Depletion   503

    Percentage Depletion   504

Intangible Assets   505

Summary   507

Key Terms   509

Primary Tax Law Sources   509

Discussion Questions   510

Problems   510

Integrative Problems   516

Discussion Case 11–1   517

Discussion Case 11–2   518

Tax Planning Case 11–3   518

Tax Planning Case 11–4   518

Ethics Discussion Case 11–5   519

APPENDIX TO CHAPTER 11
MACRS Class Lives, ACRS Real Property
Depreciation Schedules, MACRS Depreciation Schedules   521

▲ **CHAPTER 12**   Property Dispositions   538

Concept Review   539

Introduction   539

Realized Gain or Loss   541

  Amount Realized   542

  Effect of Debt Assumptions   543

Character of Gain or Loss   545

Capital Gains and Losses   545

  Capital Asset Definition   546

  Long-Term versus Short-Term Classification   546

  Capital Gain-and-Loss Netting Procedure   547

    Capital Gain Exclusion on Qualified Small Business Stock   551

  Capital Gains and Losses—Planning Strategies   552

    Net Capital Gain Position   552

    Net Capital Loss Position   553

    Short Sales   553

    Worthless Securities   555

    Basis of Securities Sold   556

Section 1231 Gains and Losses   557

  Definition of Section 1231 Property   557

  Section 1231 Netting Procedure   557

  Dispositions of Rental Activities   561

Depreciation Recapture   561

  Section 1245 Recapture Rule   563

  Section 1250 Recapture Rule   563

    Installment Sales of Depreciable Assets   565

  Section 1245 and Section 1250 Properties   566

Summary   567

Key Terms   569

Primary Tax Law Sources   569

Discussion Questions   569

Problems   571

Integrative Problem   577

Comprehensive Problems   578

Discussion Case 12–1 579

Discussion Case 12–2 580

Tax Planning Case 12–3 580

Tax Planning Case 12–4 581

Ethics Discussion Case 12–5 581

▲ **CHAPTER 13** Nonrecognition Transactions 582

Concept Review 583

Introduction 583

Rationale for Nonrecognition 584

Commonalities of Nonrecognition Transactions 584

Like-Kind Exchanges 589

  Exchange Requirement 589

  Like-Kind Property Requirements 591

  Effect of Boot 594

    Receipt of Boot 594

  Related Party Exchanges 598

  Carryover of Tax Attributes 599

Involuntary Conversions 599

  Treatment of Involuntary Conversion Gains and Losses 600

  Qualified Replacement Property 602

Sale of a Principal Residence 603

  Principal Residence 603

  Replacement Period 604

  Deferral of Gain 605

Sale of a Principal Residence—Taxpayers Older Than 55 607

  Gain Exclusion Requirements 607

  One-Time Exclusion of Gain 607

  Interaction of Deferral and Exclusion Provisions 608

Summary 609

Key Terms 611

Primary Tax Law Sources 611

Discussion Questions 612

Problems 612

Comprehensive Problem 618

Discussion Case 13–1 619

Discussion Case 13–2 619

Discussion Case 13–3 619

Tax Planning Case 13–4 619

Tax Planning Case 13–5 620

Ethics Discussion Case 13–6 620

APPENDIX TO CHAPTER 13
Selected SIC Product Classes 621

PART VI
TAX CONSIDERATIONS 625

▲ **CHAPTER 14**   Other Factors Affecting Tax Liability   626
Concept Review 627
Introduction 627
Accounting Periods 627
    Limitations on Choice of Taxable Year   629
        Partnership Limitations   629
        S Corporation Limitations   631
Accounting Methods 632
    Restrictions on Use of the Cash Method   633
    Long-Term Construction Contracts   634
        The Lookback Method   635
        Taxpayers Exempt from Percentage-of-Completed-Contract Method   637
    Accounting for Inventories   637
        Determining Inventory Cost   638
        Inventory Flow Assumptions   640
        Electing LIFO   641
Income Tax Credits 642
    Business Tax Credits   642
        Investment Tax Credit   642
        Foreign Tax Credit   642
        Research and Experimental Credit   644
        Rehabilitation Tax Credit   645
    Individual Tax Credits   646
        Earned Income Credit   647
        Child and Dependent Care Credit   648
The Alternative Minimum Tax 650
    Basic AMT Computation   651
        AMT Adjustments   653
        AMT Preferences   657
        AMT Exemptions   658
        AMT Tax Credits   658
        Tax Planning and the AMT   660
Key Terms 661
Primary Tax Law Sources 661
Discussion Questions 662
Problems 664
Discussion Case 14–1 670
Discussion Case 14–2 670
Tax Planning Case 14–3 670
Ethics Discussion Case 14–4 671

▲ **CHAPTER 15**   Tax Research   672
Introduction 673

Primary Sources of Federal Income Tax Law   673

Legislative Sources   673

The U.S. Constitution   673

Internal Revenue Code of 1986   675

Tax Treaties   679

Administrative Sources   679

Treasury Regulations   679

Revenue Rulings and Procedures   680

Acquiescence and Nonacquiescence   680

Other Pronouncements   681

Judicial Sources   681

Trial Courts   682

Appellate Courts   683

Supreme Court   683

Citations to Primary Authorities   683

Committee Reports   683

Code and Regulations   684

Other IRS Pronouncements   685

Court Decisions   685

Secondary Sources of Federal Income Tax Law   686

Tax Services   686

Citators   687

Tax Periodicals   688

Computer-Assisted Tax Research   688

Tax Research   689

Tax Compliance versus Tax Planning   689

Step 1: Establish the Facts and Determine the Issues   689

Step 2: Locate the Relevant Authorities   690

Step 3: Assess the Importance of the Authorities   690

Code and Regulations   690

Pronouncements   691

Court Decisions   691

Step 4: Reach Conclusions, Make Recommendations, and Communicate the Results   692

Comprehensive Research Example   692

Step 1: Establish the Facts and Determine the Issues   692

Step 2: Locate the Relevant Authorities   692

Step 3: Assess the Importance of the Authorities   693

The Code   693

Regulations   694

Court Decision   695

Step 4: Reach Conclusions, Make Recommendations, and Communicate the Results   695

The Audit and Appeal Process within the IRS   695

Tax Return Selection Processes   696

Types of Examinations   696

Settlement Procedures   697

Administrative Appeals   697
Summary   698
Key Terms   698
Primary Tax Law Sources   699
Discussion Questions   699
Research Problems   701
Income Problems   701
Deduction Problems   702
Loss Problems   705
Property Problems   706
Accounting Methods/Procedure Problems   707

▲ **APPENDIX A**   Tax Rate Schedules and Tax Tables   A-1

▲ **APPENDIX B**   Tax Return Problem   B-1

▲ **APPENDIX C**   Tax Forms   C-1

▲ **APPENDIX D**   Statements on Responsibilities
in Tax Practice   D-1

Glossary   G-1
Index   I-1

Concepts in Federal Taxation is designed for use in an introductory tax course. The textbook provides a conceptual approach that is new to teaching introductory tax materials. The book is sufficiently rigorous for those students who will go on to specialize in the area of taxes but is unlikely to intimidate those who plan to pursue other areas of accounting and business.

The 1996 edition has been revised to make it easier to implement the teaching objectives of the Accounting Education Change Commission. The revised text places more emphasis on the transactions that are common to all entities. This edition has been enhanced by the inclusion of more visual presentations (exhibits, figures, tables) of crucial information and additional critical thinking problems in each chapter, as well as an expanded set of writing assignment problems. All chapters in this edition have discussion cases, tax planning cases, and ethics discussion cases. The upgraded solutions manual offers suggestions about integrating group assignments for each chapter in the course.

The Conceptual Approach

This textbook evolved as a solution to a problem that has frustrated academicians for many years in teaching the first tax course at the undergraduate level. The problem is what I refer to as the "technical approach." The technical approach treats income tax in such great depth that the first-time tax student has difficulty understanding the myriad rules, exceptions to the general rule, and exceptions to the exceptions. As a result, students tend to view the first tax course as a long string of unrelated topics that they must memorize in order to pass the course. The premise of the conceptual approach is that what is important at the introductory level is that students gain a conceptual view of income tax law and be able to relate the concepts to basic aspects of everyday economic life. In the long run, all students taking the course will benefit from gaining more general knowledge than an introductory tax course usually provides.

Chapter 2 develops the conceptual framework and uses it to explain the operation of the tax system in general. Each subsequent chapter begins with a brief review of the concepts used in that chapter's discussion. Students are encouraged to return to Chapter 2 and to review the concepts whenever they are uncertain about the application of a particular concept. Each chapter presents the tax law in terms of the appropriate concepts.

The approach of this textbook is consistent with the way real learning takes place. Real learning is the ability to store information in long-term memory (called *propositions*). As new information arrives in short-term memory, it combines with stored propositions to form new propositions. It is this linkage of prior memory with new information that is the key to learning. Providing the conceptual framework up front creates in long-term memory basic propositions about income tax law. The brief review of these propositions at the beginning of each chapter further stimulates the memory. As new information is introduced in the chapter, it combines with the stored concepts—which makes it easier to learn the material. In addition, using each chapter's material to link the concepts highlights the integrative nature of tax law and dispels the notion that tax law is a subject that can be mastered only through memorization.

Chapter Pedagogy

The decision to use the conceptual approach in this textbook was based on the desire to make the text more "student friendly" by providing many examples that use familiar situations. The literature of cognitive psychology tells us that extensive elaborations lead to greater recall. Elaboration is the process of adding something to new information to make it more meaningful. The examples in this book are elaborations designed to add substance to the tax law being discussed, which is why this book has many more examples than other textbooks. The examples are presented in a question-and-discussion format that fully explains the question being asked.

The textbook also takes a different approach to footnotes. Rather than interrupt the text with extensive footnoting of specific subsections or paragraphs of the Internal Revenue Code, the primary tax law sources appear at the end of each chapter with explanatory notations. This approach uses more references to Treasury regulations, Revenue rulings, and court cases than usually appear in an introductory tax book. This allows the student who wishes to explore a topic further to find the primary tax law sources, which are more explanatory than the Internal Revenue Code.

End-of-Chapter Material

Problems.   Many end-of-chapter problems do not call for mathematical solutions. Rather, they require the student to explain the appropriate treatment, based on the concepts. The problems are a valuable learning tool that encourages students to apply the concepts in order to arrive at a solution. More traditional problems are also provided; all can be solved by reference to the examples in the chapter and they address every aspect of the chapter. The problems take advantage of the richness and vastness of income tax to show students how the concepts apply in practice. In most cases, two or more problems are provided for each aspect. This allows the instructor to choose problems of varying levels of difficulty, based on the instructor's desired level of emphasis for each topic.

Other Features.   In addition to discussion questions and problems covering the material in each chapter, various other material is provided. *Tax planning cases* require students to use the materials in the chapter to devise an optimal tax plan for the facts given. *Discussion cases* are used to stimulate thinking about issues raised in the chapter. *Ethics discussion cases* provide ethical dilemmas related to the chapter material that the student must resolve according to the Statements on Responsibilities in Tax Practice of the American Institute of Certified Accountants (AICPA). Chapter 1 includes a discussion of the ethical considerations in tax practice, particularly with regard to the AICPA's Statements. The complete set of AICPA statements appears in Appendix D. All case material can be used to emphasize writing in the tax curriculum. As a further aid to those who wish to integrate writing assignments in their courses, problems that are amenable to such use have been designated with a writing assignment icon (see margin). The instructor's manual (discussed later) provides specific suggestions on use of the various materials to emphasize writing and group work in the introductory tax course. *Comprehensive problems* cover a number of issues discussed within the chapter. *Integrative problems* require the student to bring together material learned in previous chapters and combine it with information in the current chapter. Integrative problem 63 in Chapter 4 provides the information necessary to calculate the gross income of a married couple. Integrative problem 74 in Chapter 8 follows up by providing the information necessary to complete the tax return for the married couple. This approach allows the student to do a fairly complex tax return in two stages, spreading the work out over the semester rather than preparing it for a single due date. This two-stage tax return problem has been recast in the instructor's manual with the appropriate tax-reporting documents for those who would like to assign a tax return problem but find the problem in Appendix B unsuited to their needs.

The tax return problem in Appendix B is presented in three phases, which correspond to the organization of the text. Each phase presents some information in actual tax documents that a taxpayer might receive from commonplace third-party sources. Upon working through Appendix B, the student will have completed a fairly complex tax return. The problem can be worked with tax preparation software or manually. This approach familiarizes students with tax reporting and tax compliance forms and relates to the material as it is being covered, rather than in one burst at the end of the semester.

Organization

The entire textbook can be covered in one semester, although some instructors will find it convenient to skip selected chapters. For example, Chapter 15 discusses the basic aspects of tax research. This chapter can be omitted by those who would like to spend more time on other aspects of the course. Instructors who have their students engage in tax research during the first tax course will want to use Chapter 15 early in the course.

By its very nature, the introductory tax course contains much material that relates almost solely to individual taxpayers. I have tried to deemphasize the individual aspects of taxation and focus on transactions common to all tax entities. In this regard, the mechanics of the individual tax calculation are not discussed in depth until Chapter 8. Chapter 1 introduces the individual tax formula and briefly discusses the for versus from adjusted gross income distinction that is unique to individuals. This allows the text to focus more on the overall scheme of taxation—what is income, what is a deduction, and so on—with individual tax return preparation a secondary issue. Further, itemized deductions are not accorded the traditional in-depth treatment. Again, the focus is on the more common itemized deductions, and elaborate technical detail is omitted for the more unusual items.

The text is organized into five parts, each of which contains chapters of related materials. The flow of the material is designed to lead the student into the calculation of taxable income and the problems associated with various aspects of the calculation.

Part I introduces the student to the conceptual foundations of tax law. Chapter 1 provides an overview of the tax system, briefly discusses other types of taxes, outlines the general income tax calculation, discusses the nature of tax planning, and introduces ethical considerations of tax practice. Chapter 2 develops the conceptual foundation of the income tax system, using a framework that discusses and illustrates the underlying concepts.

Part II addresses the calculation of gross income. Chapter 3 classifies various sources of income and explains the common problems encountered within each income classification. Its overview of property transactions differentiates the taxation of capital gains and losses from other sources of income. Accounting methods that affect the recognition of income are introduced at the end of the chapter.

Chapter 4 classifies allowable exclusions from income according to the purpose of the exclusion and discusses the problems commonly encountered with exclusions in each category.

Part III discusses the deductions that are allowed in computing taxable income. Chapter 5 provides an overview of the general criteria necessary to obtain a tax deduction. The chapter concludes with a discussion of the effect of a taxpayer's accounting method on the timing of deductions. Chapter 6 addresses specific business expense deductions that are subject to special rules and/or limitations. Deductions for losses are covered in Chapter 7. Annual losses are distinguished from transaction losses, and the limitations on the deductibility of the two types of losses are discussed. This includes the treatment of net operating losses, the at-risk rules, passive losses, capital losses, and casualty and theft losses.

Part IV provides an overview of the taxation of various types of income tax entities. The unique features of the individual income tax calculation and deductions of individual taxpayers are discussed in Chapter 8. Chapter 9 introduces the general tax treatment of other types of income tax entities, including corporations, estates, trusts, partnerships, limited liability entities, and S corporations.

Part V covers property transactions. The property investment cycle is introduced in Chapter 10, and common acquisition problems are discussed. Chapter 11 provides the allowable deductions for property expenditures. This includes the MACRS depreciation system, depletion deductions, and allowable amortization deductions. Dispositions of property are discussed in Chapter 12. The calculation of the gain or loss from a disposition of property is explained, and the classification of gains and losses from property is discussed. Chapter 13 covers the common nonrecognition situations related to property dispositions, including exchanges, involuntary conversions, and sales of a principal residence.

Part VI considers other aspects of the income tax law. Chapter 14 provides an overview of other items that affect tax liability. Accounting periods and methods are discussed in more detail in this chapter. The chapter also discusses the general operation of the alternative minimum tax and tax credits. Chapter 15 provides the mechanics of tax research. As mentioned earlier, instructors wishing to introduce their students to tax research will want to introduce this chapter early in the course.

Supplementary Materials

Materials have been specifically developed to aid the instructor in teaching this new approach to the introductory course. This includes an instructor's manual, a solutions manual, transparency masters, a test bank, and a reader. In addition, other West supplementary materials are available to adopters.

Instructor's Manual.   The *Instructor's Manual* includes suggested syllabi for a one-semester course and a two-quarter course. Syllabi of several adopters of the 1995 edition are provided so that users can see how other instructors are using the material in their courses. In addition, the materials include suggestions for incorporating writing and group assignments in the income tax curriculum. Each chapter begins with an overview of the chapter and specific teaching tips related to the chapter. Each chapter also presents specific ideas for writing and group assignments in that chapter. This is followed by a set of lecture notes for the chapter. The lecture notes are designed to assist the instructor in organizing classroom activities and include suggestions for incorporating material from the problems in the instructor's lecture. Each chapter also features an annotated bibliography on selected topics from each chapter for instructors who wish to have their students explore additional aspects of these topics. The instructor's manual is available on floppy disk to allow instructors to easily edit the material for their specific classroom needs.

Solutions Manual.   The *Solutions Manual* provides in-depth discussions of the solutions to the end-of-chapter material. The actual text of each discussion question and problem are reproduced with the solution. This makes it easier for instructors to integrate the problem material in their lecture notes.

Transparency Masters.   A separate set of *Transparency Masters* provides overheads of solutions to all problems and cases for use in the classroom.

Test Bank.   The *Test Bank* that accompanies this book includes a variety of testing approaches. The material is designed to help instructors fashion exams that are consistent with a conceptual teaching approach. This includes matching questions, multiple choice questions, short answer questions, and comprehensive problems. Part of the package accompanying this book is *WESTEST*™ 3.1, software for producing tests and examinations.

Reader.   *Insights: Readings in Federal Taxation* provides articles from leading tax and popular journals that instructors can use to enhance students' appreciation of the importance of taxation. There are several articles for each chapter. The articles present additional background and interesting applications of the chapter material to real situations. This item is for sale at a nominal charge.

Other Supplementary Materials.   In addition to the materials developed specifically for this textbook, the following West Publishing products are available:

- *West® CD-ROM Federal Tax Library*™ (Compact Disc with Read-Only Memory). The library provides a complete desktop tax research library. Qualified adopters receive one subscription to the complete *Federal Tax Library* through August 31, 1995.
- *WESTLAW®.* WESTLAW is a computer-assisted tax and legal research service that provides access to hundreds of valuable information sources. Qualified adopters receive six free hours of WESTLAW during unrestricted hours (restricted hours are 12:30 P.M. to 5:00 P.M. EST).
- *Tax Legislation Update.* If necessary, a tax update covering new tax laws enacted since the publication of the last edition of the book will be sent to adopters.
- *Electronic Update.* An electronic bulletin board puts the latest tax legislation in instructors' hands within days of its passage. Adopters will be able to log on to the bulletin board, download, and print out the latest tax updates.
- *TurboTax®.* The tax preparation software by Chipsoft, Inc., is a best-selling tax preparation software package. *TurboTax* can be used to solve the comprehensive problems and the problems in Appendix B. The *TurboTax* package, available for student purchase, includes disks bound with a workbook by Sam Hicks. *MacIntax®* and *TurboTax® for Windows®* are also available.

Acknowledgments

The completion of this project required the help of many individuals. I am deeply indebted to my colleague, John Wilguess, who provided valuable insight and overview throughout. Will Yancey, Texas Christian University, and Rick Walter, University of Louisville, have made significant suggestions for improving the text and related materials. Joseph P. Matoney, University of Rhode Island, assisted in the design of the tax return problem. Rosa Murphy and Doug Laufer, Weber State University, assisted in the preparation of the instructor's manual and the test bank.

The following reviewers gave freely of their time and their suggestions and comments improved the text: Susan Anderson, University of North Carolina at Greensboro; Bart Basi, Southern Illinois University at Carbondale; Alan Campbell, Arkansas State University; Barbara Cassidy, St. Edward's University; Roberta Chambers, Drake University; Andy Cuccia, Louisiana State University; James Fellows, University of South Florida; Ronald Flinn, Creighton University; Daniel Fulks, University of Kentucky; Leslie Grow, Central Missouri State University; Bob Kilpatrick, Northern Arizona University; Kwangok Kim, University of Southern Indiana; Bill Lathen, Boise State University; Doug Laufer, Weber State University; Roland Lipka, Temple University; Suzanne Luttman, University of Santa Clara; Richard Mark, University of Texas at Arlington; James Pattilo, University of Indiana at South Bend; Ian Redpath, Canisius College; W. Eugene Seago, Virginia Polytechnic Institute and State University; Keith Sellers, University of Arkansas; Paul J. Streer, University of Georgia; Victor Tidwell, Arizona State University; Vicky Vorrell, Cuyahoga Community College; Tom White, University of Charleston; and Betsy Willis, Baylor University.

The following reviewers provided valuable suggestions about the revisions for the 1996 edition: Charles Christian, Arizona State University; James Fellows, University of South Florida; Carol Fischer, Saint Bonaventure University; Sanjay Gupta, Arizona State University; Sue Porter, University of Texas at Austin; John Robinson, University of Texas at Austin; Donald Samelson, Moorhead State University; Bill Samson, University of Alabama; and George Violette, University of Southern Maine.

Secretarial assistance was provided by Lois Pazienza, Kristi Chase, Cherry Brown, Saundra Manzer, and Cindy Conway.

Suggestions

Concepts in Federal Taxation will be revised annually. I encourage all adopters to participate in the continuing development of the book by providing comments and/or suggestions for improving the textbook and supplementary materials. Please address these comments to me at Oklahoma State University or to Rick Leyh, Editor, West Educational Publishing Company, 1515 Capital of Texas Highway South, Suite 402, Austin, Texas 78746.

Kevin E. Murphy

If you are beginning the study of the federal income tax law and plan to become a tax attorney or accountant, why you are taking this course is obvious. But if you want to become a management accountant or auditor, why should you study federal income taxation? Don't accountants rely on tax specialists to do tax research and prepare tax returns? Better yet, why should a business executive, an attorney, a physician, or a farmer take a tax course? They too can, and often do, have professional tax advisers to take care of their tax problems. The heart of the answer lies in the fact that most economic transactions have an income tax effect.

The income tax law influences personal decisions of individuals. The decision to buy a house instead of renting one may depend on the after-tax cost of the alternatives. Although the payment of rent reimburses the owner of the dwelling for mortgage interest and property tax, a tenant cannot deduct the cost of renting a home. However, a homeowner can save income tax by deducting home mortgage interest and property tax and perhaps reduce the after-tax cost of buying relative to renting.

> ▲ **EXAMPLE 1** Zola lives in an apartment she rents for $700 per month. She is considering purchasing a house, which will require an initial cash outlay of $5,000 and monthly payments of $850. Although none of the $5,000 initial down payment is deductible, $800 of the monthly payment is deductible as interest expense. Assuming that Zola earns 6% on her investments and is in the 28% tax rate bracket, what is the after-tax monthly cost of purchasing the house?
>
> *Discussion:* Assuming that Zola itemizes her deductions, the $800 interest payment will be deductible. Her taxable income will be reduced by $800 per month, resulting in tax savings of $224 ($800 × 28%). This leaves her with a net after-tax house payment of $626. However, she will lose interest income on the $5,000 investment of $25 per month [$5,000 × (6% × 1/12)]. She will not have to pay any tax on the lost interest, resulting in an after-tax interest loss of $18 [$25 − ($25 × 28%)]. Her net after-tax monthly cost of purchasing the house is $644 ($626 + $18). Because this is less than her rent of $700, Zola will come out ahead by $56 per month by purchasing the house.
>
> This analysis of Zola's investment in a house considers only the tax aspects of the investment. Clearly, other factors influence the decision to purchase a house—potential appreciation in value, the intangible value of owning your own home, and so on. The point is that the tax consequences are one objective factor to consider when making various decisions, but they are rarely the sole and/or controlling factor.

Other personal decisions are often influenced by tax savings. For example, a taxpayer may decide to accelerate or defer charitable donations or elective medical treatment to claim the deductions in the year that results in the most significant tax savings. Even child-care decisions may be based on the availability of tax savings in the form of a child-care tax credit.

> ▲ **EXAMPLE 2** On January 1 of each year, Steve gives $2,000 to his church. For 1995, Steve's income is more than double its usual amount because of a one-time gain from a sale of stock. In a typical year, Steve is in the 28% tax rate bracket. Because of his increased income in 1995, Steve estimates that he will be in the 36% tax rate bracket, but his income will return to normal in 1996. What steps might Steve take to reduce his tax bill?

Discussion: Instead of waiting until January 1, 1996, to make his regular $2,000 donation, which will reduce his tax by $560 ($2,000 × 28%), Steve could pay the contribution in 1995. By taking the deduction in 1995 when he is in the 36% tax rate bracket, Steve saves $720 ($2,000 × 36%) in tax. By accelerating his $2,000 charitable contribution by a few days, he saves an extra $160 in tax ($720 − $560).

From these examples, you can see that income taxes can and do have an influence on routine decisions. However, the cost of the income tax is more than just the outlay for the tax liability. A knowledge of the income tax laws enables taxpayers to make decisions that can reduce these other costs. By being familiar with the tax laws, an individual can enter into transactions that will provide the best tax result for both the taxpayer and the taxpayer's family. By minimizing the income tax burden, taxpayers conserve wealth that can be put to other uses. Last, taxpayers are responsible for reporting their correct taxable income to the government. Knowing the tax laws protects against audits by the IRS that could result in additional tax owed and penalties for improper reporting of the tax liability.

Significance of Tax Costs

Keeping records and filling out forms to comply with the tax law can consume a substantial amount of time. Table I–1 presents the IRS's estimates of the time involved in record keeping, learning about the tax law, preparing a return, and assembling the various commonly filed tax forms. As you can see, the IRS estimates that completing and filing the basic tax return form (Form 1040) requires

▲ **Table I–1**

ESTIMATED TAX RETURN PREPARATION TIME, INTERNAL REVENUE SERVICE—1994

SOURCE: Internal Revenue Service, Form 1040 Instructions, 1994.

Estimated Preparation Time

The time needed to complete and file the following forms will vary depending on individual circumstances. The estimated average times are

Form	Record Keeping	Learning About the Law or the Form	Preparing the Form	Copying, Assembling, and Sending the Form to the IRS
Form 1040	3 hr., 8 min.	2 hr., 53 min.	4 hr., 41 min.	53 min.
Sch. A (1040)	2 hr., 32 min.	26 min.	1 hr., 10 min.	27 min.
Sch. B (1040)	33 min.	8 min.	17 min.	20 min.
Sch. C (1040)	6 hr., 26 min.	1 hr., 10 min.	2 hr., 5 min.	35 min.
Sch. C-EZ (1040)	46 min.	4 min.	18 min.	20 min.
Sch. D (1040)	51 min.	42 min.	1 hr., 1 min.	41 min.
Sch. E (1040)	2 hr., 52 min.	1 hr., 7 min.	1 hr., 16 min.	35 min.
Sch. EIC (1040)		2 min.	4 min.	5 min.
Sch. F (1040):				
Cash Method	4 hr., 2 min.	35 min.	1 hr., 14 min.	20 min.
Accrual Method	4 hr., 22 min.	25 min.	1 hr., 19 min.	20 min.
Sch. R (1040)	20 min.	15 min.	22 min.	35 min.
Sch. SE (1040):				
Short	20 min.	13 min.	11 min.	14 min.
Long	26 min.	22 min.	34 min.	20 min.

more than 11 hours on average. When you consider that many taxpayers file a multitude of forms and schedules to detail their tax affairs, the time involved in complying with the tax law is quite substantial.

Tax compliance also may cost a taxpayer money. Taxpayers must weigh the cost of the time and investment needed to prepare their own tax returns, the out-of-pocket cost of hiring a tax preparer to prepare the return, and the risk of additional time and monetary costs for any errors. Thus, taxpayers need to choose whether to save money and spend the time to prepare their own tax returns or to pay to have someone else help to determine the proper amount of income tax.

When deciding whether to prepare their own returns, taxpayers should be aware that the amount of income tax shown on the return may contain errors or differences of opinion that may be found in an IRS audit. These differences of opinion can result from a taxpayer's or the tax preparer's lack of familiarity with the tax law and how it applies to the taxpayer. Similarly, the IRS agent performing the audit may not fully understand the law as it applies to a particular situation. In addition to clerical mistakes, tax return errors can be the result of inadequate communication between a taxpayer and tax preparer. A tax audit may reveal that the taxpayer either is entitled to a refund or owes more tax. If you are entitled to a refund, you have lost the use of the money while it was held by the U.S. Treasury. If you have to pay more tax, you will probably have to pay extra costs in the form of penalties and interest on the tax you owe. An audit of your return will require an additional investment of your personal time and quite likely additional out-of-pocket costs for professional tax advice. In addition, many taxpayers are intimidated when facing an income tax audit.

As your involvement in professional activities increases, taxes and the costs of compliance grow in importance. If you are like most taxpayers, you will want to pay the least tax required by the law. You will also want to spend as little time and money as possible to satisfy the compliance requirements. As Table I–2 shows, in 1970 an average taxpayer worked approximately 116 days to pay federal, state, and local taxes. By 1994, the time a person had to work to pay taxes had increased by 7.8 percent, to 125 days. In 1994, a taxpayer worked about one-third (34.2 percent) of the year to pay taxes. Figure I–1 divides an eight-hour work day into the minutes necessary to pay typical expenses. An average person worked 1 hour and 48 minutes each day to pay federal taxes and 57 minutes a day to pay state and local taxes during 1994. Thus, 2 hours and 45 minutes of each working day are devoted to the payment of taxes. The time worked to pay taxes is almost the same as the time worked to pay for household, food and tobacco, and health care

Tax Year	Freedom Day	Number of Days	Increase in Days	% of Year
1950	April 3	93		25.5
1960	April 16*	107	13	29.3
1970	April 26	116	10	31.8
1980	May 1*	122	6	33.3
1991	May 3	123	-0-	33.7
1992	May 2*	123	-0-	33.6
1993	May 3	123	-0-	33.7
1994	May 5	125	2	34.2

▲ Table I–2

TAX FREEDOM DAY

*Leap year caused Tax Freedom Day to appear one day early.
SOURCE: Tax Foundation, *Tax Features*, April 1994, p. 1.

▲ **Figure I–1**

TAX BITE IN THE
EIGHT-HOUR DAY

SOURCE: Tax Foundation, *Tax
Features*, April 1994, p. 27.

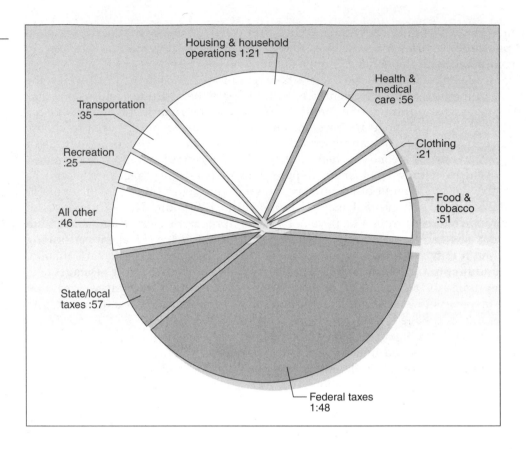

costs, 3 hours and 8 minutes. As Table I–2 and Figure I–1 demonstrate, the amounts paid for taxes represent major expenditures for the typical taxpayer.

Conservation of Wealth

An understanding of basic tax concepts and planning can often help conserve wealth by reducing taxes. To reduce taxes, you need to be able to recognize potential planning situations and problems. Because you know your financial affairs better than anyone else, you are in the best position to spot potential tax-saving opportunities. You should never wait for your tax adviser to find new ways to save you taxes. Although a competent tax adviser will know about tax-planning techniques and current tax developments, you will be more familiar than an adviser is with your financial affairs and objectives. A tax adviser is best used in the same way you use other professionals. When you visit your physician, you usually describe the symptom that brought you to the office to help the doctor identify the proper treatment. When you visit your attorney for a legal problem, you take along the information necessary to help the lawyer identify the legal issues. In both instances, you evaluate information and decide when you need professional assistance. Likewise, you will need to evaluate information, based on your understanding of the tax laws, to determine when you need to consult a professional tax adviser.

▲ **EXAMPLE 3**   Gwen, 19, is a full-time student at State University. Her parents pay all her expenses, which total $12,000 a year. Gwen does not have any other source of support, and she does not pay any income tax. Gwen's father, Marty, owns a substantial portfolio of stock that earns $12,000 in income each year. Marty is in the 31% tax rate bracket.

Discussion: A tax plan could save Marty money by transferring ownership of the stock portfolio to Gwen, who is in a lower tax bracket. Marty pays $3,720 ($12,000 $\times$ 31%) in tax on the investment income. The amount of income left after paying tax is $8,280 ($12,000 $-$ $3,720).

If Marty gave the stock portfolio to Gwen as a gift (which is not subject to income tax), Gwen would be taxable on the income at a lower tax rate than her father. Assuming the $12,000 in investment income is taxed at 15%, Gwen's tax on the income would be $1,800. The family could save $1,920 ($3,720 $-$ $1,800) in tax by shifting the income to Gwen. The amount of income left after paying tax is increased to $10,200 ($12,000 $-$ $1,800).

Taxes Influence Routine Decisions

An auditor, management accountant, attorney, physician, or a farmer may never prepare a business tax return. Yet, they need a general understanding of the tax effects of their daily business decisions. For example, an auditor might find that an improperly recorded transaction results in an undisclosed tax liability or refund. A managerial accountant may need to consider the tax effects of buying or selling plant assets or acquiring a new business. To provide reliable advice to clients, lawyers often need a general understanding of how the tax laws apply to different types of entities. A doctor may need a general understanding of fringe-benefit plans that can be set up to keep highly qualified nurses and medical technicians as employees. A farmer can benefit from familiarity with the complex rules that govern reporting of income from farm production and the deduction of farm expenses. Individuals can also benefit from a knowledge of the tax laws in their everyday decisions.

▲ **EXAMPLE 4**   Isaac wants to buy a new car. During a special promotion, the dealer will finance the purchase with a 6% loan. Isaac knows that he can obtain a home equity loan from his bank at 8% interest. If Isaac is in the 28% tax bracket, which loan should he use to finance his new car?

Discussion: Interest paid on personal loans is not deductible. However, interest paid on a home equity loan is deductible. If Isaac itemizes his deductions, the interest on the home equity loan is deductible. This makes the real after-tax cost of the home equity loan 5.76% [8% $-$ (8% $\times$ 28%)]. Therefore, the home equity loan actually offers a lower after-tax cost than the dealer loan.

However, note that if Isaac does not itemize deductions (i.e., he uses the standard deduction), he receives no benefit from the deduction for home equity loan interest. In this case, the dealer loan would have a lower after-tax cost, because neither loan would produce deductible interest.

Self-Protection

Another reason for being aware of the federal income tax law is self-protection. Perhaps you have heard others say that all they have to do is give a list of income and deduction items to their tax return preparer. When they get the completed tax return back and pay the tax due, their responsibility for complying with the tax law is finished. If any mistakes are made, it is the preparer's problem. This assumption is erroneous and can lead to disaster.

Taxpayers are fully liable for additional tax, interest, and penalties due because of an error on their tax return. If a person paid to prepare a return misinterprets the information and/or makes a mistake that results in an underpayment of tax, the taxpayer will have to pay any additional amounts owed to the government. Whether the preparer will reimburse the taxpayer for the penalties and interest depends on the agreement with the preparer. Legal recourse against the preparer is available in certain circumstances, but the cost of obtaining reimbursement (e.g., legal fees, court costs) from the preparer may be prohibitive. For your own protection, you should always examine the completed return. Before you sign and file the return, thoroughly review it with your preparer and be sure you understand any entries that do not seem to be correct. Again, a knowledge of the tax law can help you catch errors or other misrepresentations made by a tax preparer before the return is filed.

▲ **EXAMPLE 5**   Raul gave his tax return preparer a list of income and deduction items to be reported on his tax return. The income items totaled $50,000, and the deduction items totaled $14,000. When the preparer put the information on the return, he omitted $10,000 of the income and reported only $40,000 ($50,000 − $10,000) in income. In addition, the preparer included a $2,000 deduction twice so that total deductions were reported as $16,000. As a result, Raul understated his taxable income by $12,000 ($36,000 correct taxable income − $24,000 reported taxable income).

Discussion: If the IRS detects the errors on the return, Raul will have to pay the IRS the additional tax due on the $12,000 understatement plus penalties and interest. Depending on their agreement for preparing the return, Raul may or may not recover part of his costs from the preparer. If the preparer does not agree to reimburse Raul for his mistakes, Raul may take legal action to obtain the amount due from the preparer. However, this can be a costly process and may not be worth the additional tax and penalties and interest due.

Clearly, all taxpayers can benefit from a basic knowledge of the tax law. Although the federal income tax is only one of many taxes that government bodies use to raise revenue, it is by far the most important in terms of revenue produced and the number of taxpayers affected. Therefore, this book focuses on federal income tax law.

Federal income tax law is a complex array of statutory, administrative, and judicial authorities. Because of its ability to affect taxpayers' decisions, lawmakers frequently make changes in the tax law to achieve economic, social, and/or political objectives. This causes the tax law to be in constant evolution. Professional tax advisers spend a significant portion of their time maintaining their knowledge of this changing body of law. Fortunately, many aspects of the tax law have remained stable over time. The approach used in this book is to provide a conceptual framework for analyzing how particular transactions should be treated for federal income tax purposes. The book then presents the general operation of the tax law and explains it in terms of the basic concepts. Throughout the book, the focus of the discussion is on those aspects of the federal income tax that have remained stable over time. A knowledge of the basic operation of the tax law will enhance your ability to make the best decisions for your individual situation.

CONCEPTUAL FOUNDATIONS OF THE TAX LAW

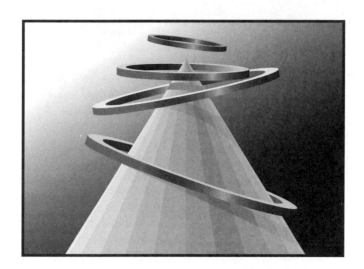

CHAPTER 1
FEDERAL INCOME TAXATION—AN OVERVIEW

CHAPTER 2
INCOME TAX CONCEPTS

Federal Income Taxation— An Overview

▲ CHAPTER LEARNING OBJECTIVES

■ Discuss what constitutes a tax and the various types of tax rate structures that may be used to calculate a tax.

■ Introduce the major types of taxes in the United States.

■ Identify the primary sources of federal income tax law.

■ Define *taxable income* and other commonly used tax terms.

■ Introduce the calculation of taxable income for individual taxpayers and the unique personal deductions allowed to individuals.

■ Develop a framework for tax planning and discuss the effect of marginal tax rates and the time value of money on tax planning.

■ Make the distinction between tax avoidance and tax evasion.

■ Introduce ethical considerations related to tax practice.

We have all heard the adage, "There's nothing certain but death and taxes." However, equating death and taxes is hardly a fair characterization of taxation. It is often stated that taxes are the price we pay for a civilized society. An early decision of the U.S. Supreme Court described a tax as "an extraction for the support of the government." Regardless of your personal view of taxation, society as we know it could not function without some system of taxation. People constantly demand that the government provide them with various services, such as defense, roads, schools, unemployment benefits, medical care, and environmental protection. The cost of providing the services that the citizens of the United States demand is principally taxation. People are introduced to taxation at an early age. Remember the candy bar that had a price sticker of 25 cents yet its actual cost was 27 cents? The tax collector is all around us. Upon receiving their first paycheck, many are surprised that the $100 they earned resulted in a check of only $80 after taxes were deducted. The point is that taxes are a fact of life. Learning to deal with taxes, and perhaps using them to your advantage, is an essential element of success in today's world.

The federal income tax is a sophisticated and complex array of laws that imposes a tax on the income of individuals, corporations, estates, and trusts. Current tax law has developed over a period of more than 80 years through a dynamic process involving political, economic, and social forces. At this very minute, Congress is considering various changes in the tax law; the Internal Revenue Service (IRS) and the courts are issuing new interpretations of current tax law, and professional tax advisers are working to obtain the meaning of all these changes.

The purpose of this book is to provide an introduction to the basic operation of the federal income tax system. However, before looking at some of the specifics, it is helpful to have a broad understanding of taxes and how the federal income tax fits into the overall scheme of revenue production. Toward this end, this chapter briefly discusses what constitutes a tax, how taxes are structured, and the major types of taxes in the United States before considering the federal income tax. Next, the primary sources of tax law authority are introduced. These sources provide the basis for calculating the tax and the unique terminology of federal income taxation. This chapter also introduces the tax calculation for individuals, the discussion of which serves as a reference for discussion in succeeding chapters. The next section of the chapter provides a framework for tax planning and a discussion of tax avoidance and tax evasion.

Because ethics has become an important issue in the accounting profession in recent years, the chapter concludes with a brief discussion of the ethical considerations related to tax practice. The discussion provides the background that will help you detect ethical issues that you will face if you go on to practice in the tax area.

▲ INTRODUCTION

Because this is a tax text, one starting point is to define what is meant by the term *tax*. Particular types of taxes and tax rules are often criticized as being loopholes, unfair, or creating an excessive burden on a particular group of taxpayers. The discussion that follows presents the four criteria commonly used to evaluate these criticisms. In addition, three different types of tax rate structure are presented as an aid in evaluating whether a particular tax is "good" or "bad."

▲ DEFINITION AND EVALUATION OF A TAX

Definition of a Tax

What is a tax? The Internal Revenue Service defines a tax as "an enforced contribution, exacted pursuant to legislative authority in the exercise of the taxing power, and imposed and collected for the purpose of raising revenue to be used for public or governmental purposes. Taxes are not payments for some special privilege granted or service rendered and are, therefore, distinguishable from various other charges imposed for particular purposes under particular powers or functions of government."[1]

A tax could be viewed as an involuntary contribution required by law to finance the functions of government. The amount of the contribution extracted from the taxpayer is unrelated to any privilege, benefit, or service received from the government agency imposing the tax. According to the IRS definition, a tax has the following characteristics:

1. The payment to the governmental authority is required by law.

2. The payment is required pursuant to the legislative power to tax.

3. The purpose of requiring the payment is to provide revenue to be used for public or governmental purposes.

4. Special benefits, services, or privileges are not received as a result of making the payment. The payment is not a fine or penalty that is imposed under other powers of government.

Although the IRS definition states that the payment of a tax does not provide the taxpayer with directly measurable benefits, the taxpayer does benefit from, among other things, military security, a legal system, and a relatively stable political, economic, and social environment. Payments to a government agency that relate to the receipt of a specific benefit—in privileges or services—are not considered taxes; they are payments for value received or are the result of a regulatory measure imposed by the government agency.

▲ **EXAMPLE 1**   Keith lives in Randal County. Randal County enacted a law setting a 1% property tax to provide money for county schools. The 1% tax applies to all property owners in Randal County. All school children in the county will benefit from the tax, even if their parents do not own property or pay the tax. Is the 1% property tax a tax according to the definition?

Discussion: The property tax is a tax. The tax is a required payment to a government unit. The payment is imposed by a property tax law. The purpose of the payment is to finance public schools. The tax is levied without regard to whether the taxpayer receives a benefit from paying the tax.

▲ **EXAMPLE 2**   Assume that in example 1 the tax is imposed on a limited group of property owners to finance the construction of new sewer lines to their properties. Is the 1% tax a tax as defined by the IRS?

Discussion: Each payer of the tax receives a direct benefit—a new sewer line. Therefore, the 1% tax payment is considered a payment to the government unit to reimburse it for improvements to the taxpayer's property. The taxpayers would treat the payment as an investment in their property and not as a tax. The 1% tax in this case is a special assessment for local benefits. An assessment differs from a tax in that an assessment is levied only on specific groups of taxpayers who receive the benefit of the assessment.

Certain payments that look like a tax are not considered a tax under the IRS definition. For example, an annual licensing fee paid to a state to engage in a specific occupation such as medicine, law, or accounting is not a tax, because it is a regulatory measure that provides a direct benefit to the payer of the fee. A fee paid for driving on a toll road, the quarter deposited in a parking meter, and payments to a city for water and sewer services are payments for value received and are not taxes according to the IRS's definition. Fines for violating public laws and penalties on tax returns are not taxes. Fines and penalties are generally imposed to discourage behavior that is harmful to the public interest and not to raise revenue to finance government operations.

Standards for Evaluating a Tax

In *The Wealth of Nations*, Adam Smith identified four basic requirements for a good tax system. Although other criteria can be used to evaluate a tax, Smith's four points are generally accepted as valid and provide a basis for discussion of the primary issues regarding taxes. These requirements are equality, certainty, convenience, and economy. Although Smith clearly stated the maxims, taxpayers have different opinions as to whether the federal income tax strictly satisfies the four requirements.

> 1. **Equality**—A tax should be based on the taxpayer's *ability to pay*. The payment of a tax in proportion to the taxpayer's level of income results in an equitable distribution of the cost of supporting the government.

The concept of equality requires consideration of both horizontal and vertical equity. **Horizontal equity** exists when two similarly situated taxpayers are taxed the same. **Vertical equity** exists when taxpayers with different situations are taxed differently but fairly in relation to each taxpayer's ability to pay the tax. This means that those taxpayers who have the greatest ability to pay the tax should pay the greatest proportion of the tax. These equity concepts are reflected to a great extent in the federal income tax. Certain low-income individuals pay no tax. As a person's taxable income level increases, the tax rate increases from 15 percent to 28 percent to 31 percent to 36 percent to 39.6 percent.

▲ **EXAMPLE 3**   Tom and Jerry each earn $15,000 a year and pay $1,500 in tax.

Discussion: The two taxpayers pay the same amount of tax on the same amount of income. Because they are treated the same, based on the facts given, horizontal equity exists.

Discussion: A slight change of facts provides a different result. If Tom is married and supports his wife and 5 children and Jerry is single with no one else to support, the tax appears unfair and not horizontally equitable. The lack of horizontal equity exists because the taxpayers' situations are no longer the same, yet they pay the same amount of tax on the same income.

▲ **EXAMPLE 4**   Assume that because of the size of his family Tom (example 3) pays $500 in taxes. Jerry still pays $1,500.

Discussion: In this situation, vertical equity is considered to be present. Because he presumably has a greater ability to pay tax, Jerry pays a larger amount of tax than Tom—Jerry's income, although equal to Tom's, supports fewer people.

Some taxpayers consider inequitable the tax law provisions that treat similar income and deductions differently. For example, a person investing in bonds issued by a city does not have to pay tax on the interest income. In contrast, interest income earned on an investment in corporate bonds is taxed. People who operate proprietorships may deduct the cost of providing their employees with group term life insurance but may not deduct the cost of their own group insurance premium. If the proprietor incorporates, the cost of the insurance for both the shareholder-employee (owner) and employees can be deducted. Thus, the perception of equality often depends on the taxpayer's personal viewpoint. Because the concepts of equity are highly subjective, a tax rule considered equitable by one taxpayer is often considered unfair by a taxpayer who derives no benefit. Often, when evaluating the equality of a tax provision, taxpayers do not consider—or are not aware of—the economic, social, and administrative reasons for what may seem to be an inequity in the tax law.

▲ **EXAMPLE 5**   Karen is a single mother who earns $10,000 a year. Jane and her husband Ben earn $75,000 a year. Karen and Jane each pay Neighborhood Day Care $2,000 per year for taking care of 1 child while they work. Because the payment is for qualified child care, Karen is entitled to a $600 reduction in her income tax because of her low income level. Because of their high income level, Jane and Ben receive only a $400 reduction in their income tax. Who is more likely to view this treatment as being inequitable?

Discussion: Jane and Ben may view the tax rule as unfair, because Karen receives a larger reduction in tax for the same amount of payment for day care. However, there is increasing emphasis on tax relief for families. Congress has decided that it is important that children be adequately cared for while parents are at work. Thus, Karen's family is given a larger tax break to help provide child care. Without the larger tax reduction, Karen might not be able to afford to pay child-care costs. The difference in treatment could also be based on the ability to pay child-care costs. In addition, the difference in treatment depicts a situation of vertical equity. Because Jane and Ben have higher incomes, vertical equity requires that they pay a higher tax (through receiving a smaller tax credit).

2. **Certainty**—A taxpayer should know when and how a tax is to be paid. In addition, the taxpayer should be able to determine the amount of tax to be paid.

Certainty in the tax law is necessary for tax planning. An individual's federal income tax return is due on the fifteenth day of the fourth month (usually April 15) after the close of the tax year. A corporation's return is due on the fifteenth day of the third month after the close of its tax year.[2] The balance of tax due with the return is usually paid by check to the IRS. However, determining the amount of tax due may not be so simple. When planning an investment that will extend over several tax years, the ability to predict with some degree of certainty how the results of the investment will be taxed is important to the investment decision. Frequent changes in the tax law create uncertainty for the tax planner. In its 1990 *Annual Report*, the IRS stated that the Internal Revenue Code had been changed more than 100 times since 1980. In addition to these legislative amendments to the tax law, the IRS and the courts issue a constant stream of decisions and interpretations on tax issues, which results in a tax law that is in a continual state of refinement. However, for the average individual taxpayer, who has wages subject to withholding, receives some interest income, owns a home, pays state and local taxes, and perhaps donates to a church or other charities, there is little complexity and a great deal of certainty in the tax law despite the numerous changes to the tax system.

3. **Convenience**—A tax should be levied at the time it is most likely to be convenient for the taxpayer to make the payment. The most convenient time for taxpayers to make the payment is as they receive income and have the money available to pay the tax.

Most taxpayers would argue that it is not convenient to keep records, determine the amount of tax due, and fill out complex forms. However, certain aspects of the income tax law make it more convenient than it might be otherwise. Based on the **pay-as-you-go concept,** taxes are paid as close to the time the income is earned as is reasonable. The pay-as-you-go system results in the collection of the tax when the taxpayer has the money to pay the tax. This tax payment system applies to all taxpayers, including the self-employed and those who earn their income from investing activities. This system is discussed in more detail later in this chapter.

The federal income tax is based on **self-assessment** and **voluntary compliance** with the tax law. Taxpayers determine in privacy the amount of their income, deductions, and tax due. The tax calculated by the taxpayer is considered correct unless the IRS detects an error and corrects it or selects the return for an audit. The federal income tax system relies on the honesty and integrity of taxpayers in determining their tax payments. This system of self-assessment and voluntary compliance promotes convenience for taxpayers.

> 4. **Economy**—A tax should have minimum compliance and administrative costs. The costs of compliance and administration should be kept at a minimum so that the amount that goes to the U.S. Treasury is as large as possible.

The IRS operates on a budget of about one half of 1 percent of the total taxes collected. However, the IRS's budget does not reflect the full cost of administering the tax law. A taxpayer's personal cost of compliance can be substantial. Taxpayers often need to maintain accounting records for tax reporting in addition to those that are necessary for business decisions. A corporation, for example, might use different depreciation methods and asset lives for financial reporting and for income tax. The taxpayer's personal cost also includes fees paid to attorneys, accountants, and other tax advisers for tax-planning, compliance, and litigation services.

Tax Rates and Structures

Tax rates are often referred to as a *marginal rate, an average rate*, or an *effective rate.* In addition, a tax rate structure is frequently described as being *proportional, regressive,* or *progressive.* Because a tax rate structure indicates how the average tax rate varies with changes in its tax base, examining a rate's structure helps in understanding and evaluating the effect of a tax.

To compute a tax it is necessary to know the tax base and the applicable tax rate. The tax is then computed by multiplying the tax base by the tax rate:

$$\text{Tax} = \text{Tax base} \times \text{Tax rate}$$

A **tax base** is the value that is subject to tax. The tax base for the federal income tax is called **taxable income.** Other common tax bases include the dollar amount of a purchase subject to sales tax, the dollars of an employee's wages subject to payroll tax, and the assessed value of property subject to property tax.

Tax Rate Definitions.   When working with the federal income tax, different measures of the rate of tax paid from one year to the next are often compared in order to evaluate the effectiveness of tax planning and to help make decisions about future transactions. Three different rates are commonly used for these comparisons:

- The marginal tax rate
- The average tax rate
- The effective tax rate

The **marginal tax rate** is the rate of tax that will be paid on the next dollar of income or the rate of tax that will be saved by the next dollar of deduction. The marginal tax rate is used in tax planning to determine the effect of reporting additional income or deductions during a tax year. One objective of tax planning is to minimize the marginal rate and to keep the marginal rate relatively constant from one year to the next. The marginal tax rates for an individual taxpayer are 15 percent, 28 percent, 31 percent, 36 percent, and 39.6 percent.[3] If you know a person's taxable income (the tax base), you can find the marginal tax rate by looking it up in the tax rate schedules in Appendix A.

▲ **EXAMPLE 6**   Don has an asset he could sell this year at a $10,000 profit, which would increase his marginal tax rate from 15% to 28%. If he waits until next year to sell the asset, he is sure his other income will be less and the $10,000 gain will be taxed at 15%. Should Don sell the asset this year or wait until next year?

Discussion: By waiting until next year to sell the asset, Don's tax savings on the sale are $1,300 [$10,000 × (28% − 15%)]. In addition, he will postpone the payment of the tax interest free for a year (a time value of money savings). Assuming that he can sell the asset early in the next year and does not need the proceeds from the sale before next year, he should wait until next year to sell the asset to take advantage of the lower marginal tax rate and the time value of money savings on the tax to be paid on the gain.

The **average tax rate** is the total federal income tax divided by taxable income (the tax base). This is the average rate of tax on each dollar of income that is taxable. The **effective tax rate** is the total federal income tax divided by the taxpayer's economic income (the tax base plus nontaxable income). Economic income is a broader base; it includes all the taxpayer's income, whether it is subject to tax or not. The effective tax rate is the average rate of tax on income from all taxable and nontaxable sources.

▲ **EXAMPLE 7**   Assume that in example 6 Don sells the asset in 1995 and reports taxable income of $40,000. Also, Don collects $50,000 on a life insurance policy that is not taxable income. Don's tax on $40,000 is $8,165 (using the tax rate schedules in Appendix A). In addition, the only difference between Don's economic income and his taxable income is proceeds from the life insurance policy. What are Don's marginal, average, and effective tax rates?

Discussion: Based on the facts given, Don's marginal tax rate is 28% (from the tax rate schedules). His average tax rate is 20.41% ($8,165 ÷ $40,000). The effective tax rate on his economic income of $90,000 ($40,000 in taxable income + $50,000 in nontaxable income) is 9.07% ($8,165 ÷ $90,000) and is much less than both the marginal and average tax rates.

Tax Rate Structures.   Tax rate structures are described as being proportional, regressive, or progressive. The structures explain how the tax rates vary with a change in the amount subject to the tax (the tax base).

PROPORTIONAL RATE STRUCTURE.   A **proportional rate structure** is defined as a tax for which the average tax rate remains the same as the tax base increases. This rate structure is also referred to as a *flat tax*. If you charted a proportional tax rate structure on a graph, it would look like the first chart in Figure 1–1.

If a tax rate is proportional, the marginal tax rate and the average tax rate are the same at all levels of the tax base. As the tax base increases, the total tax paid will increase at a constant rate. Examples of proportional taxes are sales taxes, real estate and personal property taxes, and certain excise taxes, such as the tax on

▲ **Figure 1–1**

TAX RATE STRUCTURES

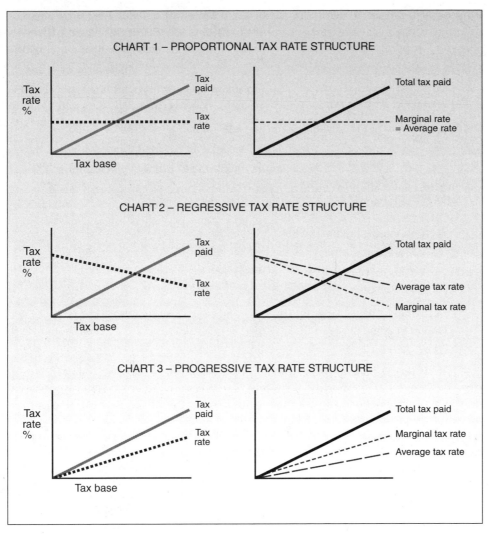

gasoline. The sales tax is a fixed percentage of the amount purchased, property tax is a constant rate multiplied by the assessed value of the property, and the gas tax is a constant rate per gallon purchased.

▲ **EXAMPLE 8** Betsy bought a new suit for $350. The sales tax at 7% totaled $24.50. Steve bought a new lawn tractor for $3,500. At 7%, the sales tax he paid came to $245. Is the sales tax proportional?

Discussion: Betsy's and Steve's marginal tax rate is 7%. In addition, Betsy's average tax rate is 7% ($24.50 ÷ $350), the same as Steve's (7% = $245 ÷ $3,500). The sales tax is proportional, because the marginal and average tax rates are equal at all levels of the tax base (the selling price).

REGRESSIVE RATE STRUCTURE.   A **regressive rate structure** is defined as a tax in which the average tax rate decreases as the tax base increases. On a graph, a regressive tax rate structure would look like chart 2 in Figure 1–1.

If a tax rate structure is regressive, the marginal tax rate will be less than the average tax rate as the tax base increases. Note that although the average tax rate and the marginal tax rate both decrease as the tax base increases, the total tax paid will increase. As a result, a person with a low tax base will pay a higher average and a higher marginal rate of tax than will a person with a high tax base. The person with the high tax base will still pay more dollars in total tax. Although a pure regressive tax rate structure (as defined earlier) does not exist in the United States, example 9 illustrates a regressive tax.

▲ **EXAMPLE 9**   Each year, Alan purchases $4,000-worth of egg rolls and Tranh purchases $17,000-worth of egg rolls. A tax is levied according to the dollar value of egg rolls purchased per the following tax schedule:

Tax Rate Schedule		Alan		Tranh	
Base	Rate	Purchases	Tax	Purchases	Tax
$-0- < $5,001	10%	$4,000	$400	$ 5,000	$ 500
$5,001 < $10,001	7%			5,000	350
More than $10,000	5%			7,000	350
Totals		$4,000	$400	$17,000	$1,200
Marginal tax rate			10%		5.0%
Average tax rate			10%		7.1%

Discussion: This tax rate schedule is regressive. The average tax rate applicable to Alan (10%) is greater than the average tax rate for Tranh (7.1%), even though Tranh's tax base is higher. Note that Tranh pays more total tax ($1,200) than Alan ($400).

If a different base is used to evaluate the tax rate structure, the same tax that may be viewed as proportional by one taxpayer may be considered regressive by another taxpayer. For example, using total wages as the tax base for evaluation, a person who spends part of her wages for items subject to sales tax would pay a lower average rate of tax than the person who spends all of his wages on taxable items.

▲ **EXAMPLE 10**   Judy earns $25,000 a year and spends it all on items subject to sales tax. Guillermo earns $30,000 a year and is able to save $5,000 of his earnings. He spends the remaining $25,000 on purchases subject to sales tax. If the sales tax rate is 10% of purchase price, is it a regressive tax?

Discussion: Judy and Guillermo pay the same total sales tax ($2,500). Thus, the tax is proportional when evaluated by using purchases as the tax base. However, Guillermo's average tax rate based on wages [8.3% = ($2,500 ÷ $30,000)] is less than Judy's [10% = ($2,500 ÷ $25,000)]. Thus, the sales tax is regressive when using wages to evaluate the tax.

Although property taxes are a proportional tax according to these definitions, an investor in property subject to property taxes might consider the effect of the tax on investments regressive compared to investments in stocks and bonds, which are not subject to property taxes. Similarly, low-income wage earners who pay Social Security tax on all their wages may consider this tax regressive compared to a person whose wages exceed the amount subject to the tax.

PROGRESSIVE RATE STRUCTURE.   A **progressive rate structure** is defined as a tax in which the average tax rate increases as the tax base increases. On a graph, a progressive tax rate structure would look like chart 3 in Figure 1–1.

If a tax rate structure is progressive, the marginal tax rate will be higher than the average tax rate as the tax base increases. The average tax rate, the marginal tax rate, and total tax all increase with increases in the tax base. A person with a low tax base will pay both lower average and marginal rates of tax than will a person with a high tax base.

The progressive tax rate structure reflects the embedding in the federal income tax rates of Adam Smith's equality criterion. Recall that according to this criterion, taxpayers should pay tax according to their ability to pay the tax. The use of progressive rate structures, wherein higher taxable income levels pay higher marginal tax rates, promotes equality.

▲ **EXAMPLE 11**   Doug reports $16,000 a year in taxable income from wages he earns watering the greens at the Hot Water Golf Course. Shawana earns $28,000 in annual taxable income as a first grade teacher.

Discussion: Doug's and Shawana's 1995 income taxes using the single taxpayer rates are as follows:

	Doug's Tax (income: $16,000)	Shawana's Tax (income: $28,000)
Tax on income below $23,350 @ 15%	$2,400	$3,503
Tax on income above $23,350 @ 28%	-0-	1,302
Total tax	$2,400	$4,805
Marginal tax rate	15%	28%
Average tax rate	15%	17%

Discussion: As a result of Shawana's larger tax base and the progressive tax rates, her marginal and average tax rates are higher than Doug's. Thus, the tax rate structure of the federal income tax promotes equality among taxpayers.

▲ MAJOR TYPES OF U.S. TAXES

The federal, state, and local governments use a variety of taxes to fund their operations. Figure 1–2 depicts tax revenues generated by federal, state, and local government bodies by source for 1993. An examination of the sources of tax revenue shows that the bulk of the federal government's revenues is derived from the income tax. State governments also receive a substantial portion of their revenues from a tax on income, with the sales tax also providing significant revenue. Local governments rely heavily on the property tax for their financing. In terms of overall taxes collected in the United States, the federal income tax produces almost as much revenue as all other forms of state and local taxes combined. The amount of Social Security tax collected by the federal government is the second-largest source of government revenue, surpassing the total revenue intake of all state and local governments combined. Although this text covers the basic operation of the federal income tax, it is helpful to have a basic understanding of the other taxes levied by governments. As will be seen throughout the text, many taxes affect and interact with the rules for the federal income tax. Each major type of tax is discussed briefly in turn. Do not be concerned with the mechanics of the taxes at this point. Focus only on their general nature.

Income Taxes

The federal government levies a tax on the income of individuals, corporations, estates, and trusts. Most states also tax the income of these taxpayers, and a few local governments also impose an income tax on those who work or live within their boundaries. The income tax is levied on a *net* number—taxable income. In its simplest form, taxable income is the difference between the total income of a

▲ **Figure 1–2**

1993 GOVERNMENT
REVENUES BY SOURCE
(ESTIMATED IN BILLIONS)

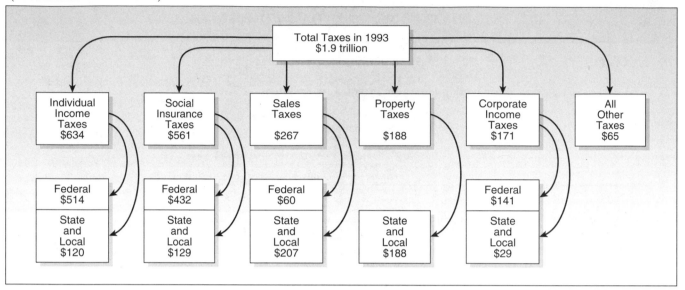

SOURCE: Tax Foundation, Inc., *Tax Features,* February 1994, p. 8, based on data from U.S. Bureau of the Census. Figures may not add because of rounding.

taxpayer and the deductions allowed that taxpayer. Thus, the study of income taxation is really the study of what must be reported as income and what is allowed as a deduction from that income to arrive at taxable income.

Each of the three government units that impose an income tax has its own set of rules for determining what is included in income and what is deductible from income to arrive at taxable income. However, because most state and local governments begin their taxable income calculation in relation to the federal income tax computation, an understanding of the federal income tax rules is essential for calculating most income taxes. This book makes no attempt to cover the myriad state and local income tax rules.

Income taxes are determined on an annual basis. However, the United States uses a pay-as-you-go collection system under which taxpayers pay an estimate of their tax as they earn their income. Employers must withhold income taxes from wages and salaries of their employees and remit them on a timely basis to the appropriate government body.[4] When taxpayers file their tax returns, these prepaid amounts are credited against their actual tax bill, resulting in either a refund of taxes, if the prepaid amount is greater than the actual tax, or an additional tax due, if the prepaid amount is deficient.[5] Self-employed taxpayers and those with other sources of income that are not subject to withholding (e.g., dividend and interest income) must make quarterly estimated tax payments that are applied against their tax bills upon filing of the return.[6]

Employment Taxes

All employees and their employers pay taxes on the wages earned by employees. Employees pay **Social Security taxes** that are matched by their employers.[7] Self-employed individuals pay the equivalent of both halves of the Social Security tax by paying the **self-employment tax.**[8] In addition to the Social Security tax, employers pay unemployment compensation taxes to both the federal and state government.

Social Security Taxes.   Under the Federal Insurance Contribution Act (FICA), a tax is levied on wages and salaries earned. The Social Security system was originally designed to provide retirement benefits to all individuals who contributed to the system. This function has been expanded to include many other social programs, such as medical insurance, disability benefits, and survivor's benefits. The result of this expansion of coverage has been a great increase in the amount of Social Security taxes paid by workers and employers. It should be stressed that the Social Security system is not a "funded" system. Current payments into the system are used to pay current benefits; technically, any excess is placed in a fund. However, the federal government often borrows against this "fund" to pay general government expenses. Thus, there is no absolute guarantee that the amounts paid by current taxpayers will actually be available to them when they are eligible to receive their benefits.

The Social Security tax is imposed on employees and self-employed individuals. Employers are required to match employees' payments into the system.[9] Because a self-employed person is both an employee and an employer, the self-employment tax rate is twice the employee tax, resulting in an equivalent payment of tax by employee/employer and the self-employed.[10] The tax on employees and employers is a constant percentage of wages up to a maximum wage base. Both the percentage and the maximum wage base have been raised over time. As Table 1–1 shows, the tax has two components. In 1995, a tax of 6.2 percent is levied on the first $61,200 of wages for Old Age, Survivors, and Disability Insurance (OASDI). A tax of 1.45 percent on all wages pays for Medical Health Insurance (MHI). Note that before 1994, the MHI portion was subject to a maximum wage base. This established a maximum amount of Social Security tax that any taxpayer would pay. However, the abolition of the maximum MHI wage base for tax years after 1993 effectively eliminated the ceiling on Social Security tax.

Year	OASDI[1]	MHI[2]	Total	Maximum Wage Base	Maximum Tax Paid
1991	6.20		6.20	$ 53,400	$3,311
		1.45	1.45	$125,000	$1,812
			7.65		$5,123
1992	6.20		6.20	$ 55,500	$3,441
		1.45	1.45	$130,200	$1,888
			7.65		$5,329
1993	6.20		6.20	$ 57,600	$3,571
		1.45	1.45	$135,000	$1,958
			7.65		$5,529
1994	6.20		6.20	$ 60,600	$3,757
		1.45	1.45	Wages earned	No maximum
			7.65		
1995	6.20		6.20	$ 61,200	$3,794
		1.45	1.45	Wages earned	No maximum
			7.65		

▲ **Table 1–1**

SOCIAL SECURITY TAX RATES FOR EMPLOYEES AND EMPLOYERS

[1]Old Age, Survivors, and Disability Insurance
[2]Medical Health Insurance

▲ **EXAMPLE 12**   Jenny earned $2,000 during February 1995 in her job as a carpenter for Acme Construction Co. How much Social Security tax must be paid by Jenny and Acme on her February earnings?

Discussion: Jenny must pay 6.2% (OASDI) and 1.45% (MHI) on the first $61,200 of income earned in 1995. Thus, Jenny must pay $153 [($2,000 × 6.2%) + ($2,000 × 1.45%)] in Social Security taxes on her wages. Acme must match the $153 in Social Security taxes Jenny paid on the wages.

▲ **EXAMPLE 13**   Chandra earned $85,000 as the administrator of the Local Accounting Program in 1995. How much Social Security tax does Chandra pay in 1995?

Discussion: Chandra pays the maximum OASDI of $3,794 (6.2% × $61,200) and $1,233 (1.45% × $85,000) of MHI for a total Social Security payment of $5,027. Her employer is required to pay the same amount on Chandra's behalf.

As with income taxes, Social Security taxes are withheld from the employee's pay by employers and remitted to the federal government with the employer's Social Security payment and other federal tax withholdings.

▲ **EXAMPLE 14**   Assume that in example 12 Acme also withheld $312 in federal income tax and $87 in state income tax from Jenny's February earnings. What is Jenny's actual take-home pay for February?

Discussion: Jenny's February take-home pay is $1,448 after withholding for income tax and Social Security. Out of her earnings of $2,000, $153 is withheld for payment of Social Security tax, $312 for federal income tax, and $87 for state income tax. Acme must pay these taxes to the appropriate government unit on a timely basis. Acme will also remit its $153 in Social Security taxes on Jenny's wages when it makes Jenny's payments.

Self-employed individuals pay a tax equal to the sum of the employee's and employer's payments. Thus in 1995, self-employment income is subject to a tax of 12.4 percent (6.2% × 2) on the first $61,200 of income for OASDI and 2.9 percent (1.45% × 2) on all self-employment income for MHI. Because employees are not taxed on the Social Security contribution made on their behalf by their employers, self-employed taxpayers are allowed to deduct one-half of their self-employment tax as a business expense to equalize the tax treatments of employees and the self-employed.

▲ **EXAMPLE 15**   Assume that in example 13 Chandra's $85,000 in earnings constitute self-employment income rather than wages as an employee. How much self-employment tax must Chandra pay on her self-employment income?

Discussion: Chandra pays $7,589 (12.4% × $61,200) of OASDI and $2,465 (2.9% × $85,000) of MHI, for a total self-employment tax of $10,054. Note that this is equal to the total tax paid by Chandra and her employer ($5,027 × 2) in example 13. Because Chandra is self-employed, she must pay the equivalent of the employee's and employer's tax.

Unemployment Taxes.   Employers must also pay state and federal unemployment taxes on wages paid to employees to fund unemployment benefits. The Federal Unemployment Tax (FUTA) is 6.2 percent of the first $7,000 in wages paid to each employee. Unemployment taxes do not have to be paid for employees who earn less than $1,500 per calendar quarter and certain classes of agricultural workers. Because each state also levies an unemployment tax, employers are allowed a credit of up to 5.4 percent for the state unemployment taxes they pay. Thus, the minimum FUTA tax rate is 0.8 percent (6.2% − 5.4%).

Sales Tax

Most state and local governments raise significant amounts of revenue from a sales tax. A sales tax is based on a flat percentage of the selling price of a product or service. In contrast to income and employment taxes, which are based on the income of taxpayers, a sales tax is based on a taxpayer's consumption of goods and services. The business that sells the goods or services subject to the tax collects the tax for the government. However, the tax is still paid by the taxpayer purchasing the goods or services. Each government unit that imposes a sales tax determines which goods and/or services are subject to the tax. Thus, not all goods and services are subject to a sales tax. For example, medical services are typically exempted from the tax. Other items that are often exempted from the sales tax are food, farm equipment, and sales to tax-exempt organizations.

Property Taxes

A tax on the value of property owned by taxpayers is called a *property tax*. In general, **real property** is land and any structures that are permanently attached to land, such as buildings. All other types of property are referred to as **personal property.** Because real property is immobile and difficult to conceal from tax assessors, local governments such as cities, counties, and school districts prefer it as a revenue source.

Property taxes are referred to as **ad valorem taxes,** because they are based on the value of the property being taxed. However, most property taxes are not based on the true fair market value of the property. Rather, the assessed value of the property is used to determine the tax. The *assessed value* of property varies widely but is typically 50 to 75 percent of the estimated market value of the property. Market values are determined by the designated assessment authority (e.g., the county assessor) based on various factors such as recent comparable sales, replacement cost per square foot, and other local market conditions. The assessed value is then computed as the predetermined percentage of the assessor's valuation.

> ▲ **EXAMPLE 16**   Maria Corporation owns a piece of land that it purchased for $6,000 in 1989. In 1995, the county tax assessor determines that the fair market value of the land is $8,000. In the county in which the land is located, assessed values are 50% of the fair market value. What is the assessed value of Maria Corporation's land?
>
> *Discussion:*   Maria Corporation's assessed value is $4,000 ($8,000 × 50%). Note that the local authority can increase or decrease property taxes on the land by varying the percentage of fair market value that is subject to tax. Thus, if the county raised the percentage to 75%, the corporation would pay property tax based on an assessed value of $6,000 ($8,000 × 75%).

Taxes on personal property are not as common as real property taxes. The mobility and ease of concealment of personal property make the collection of a personal property tax administratively difficult. However, many local governments continue to selectively impose personal property taxes on types of property that are easier to track. Because of the relatively small number of establishments, property taxes on business property are still widely used. In addition, automobiles and boats are often assessed a personal property tax as part of their annual licensing fee.

▲ **EXAMPLE 17**   Oklahoma imposes an annual tag fee on automobiles. The licensing fee is $18. A personal property tax is also levied, based on the initial selling price of the automobile and its age. During 1995, Darla paid a $94 tag fee on her automobile. How much of the fee is a personal property tax?

Discussion: Darla's personal property tax on the automobile is $76 ($94 − $18). The $18 licensing fee is not a tax.

Other Taxes

Income taxes, employment taxes, sales taxes, and property taxes are the primary revenue producers for the various forms of government. However, businesses and individuals pay a number of other taxes. The most important of these are excise taxes and wealth transfer taxes. In addition, state and local governments impose taxes on certain occupations (e.g., liquor dealers) and franchise taxes for the privilege of doing business within their jurisdiction.

Excise Taxes.   Excise taxes are imposed on various products and services. The federal government imposes excise taxes on a vast array of products and some services. Many states also levy excise taxes on the same products and services. An excise tax differs from a sales tax in that it is not based on the sales value of the product. Rather, an excise tax is typically imposed on a quantity, such as a gallon of gasoline or a pack of cigarettes. Some products subject to excise taxes include

Alcohol	Guns
Coal	Shells
Diesel fuels	Telephone services
Fishing equipment	Tires
Gasoline	Tobacco

In addition to these excise taxes, in 1990 Congress added a 10-percent luxury tax on certain items. The 10-percent luxury tax applied to the purchase price of automobiles, boats, airplanes, jewelry, and furs that exceeded a set price for the items. Congress repealed the luxury tax on all items except automobiles, effective for 1993. The tax on automobiles is imposed on the purchase price in excess of $32,000 for automobiles purchased in 1994.

Wealth Transfer Taxes.   Transfers of wealth between taxpayers are taxed by the federal gift tax and the federal estate tax. Most states also impose taxes on the value of an estate. These taxes are essentially a tax on the right to transfer property to another. Gift taxes are paid by the donor of property—the person making the gift. The person who receives the gift, the donee, is not subject to either the gift tax or income tax on the gift. The estate tax is paid by the administrator (called the *executor*) of a deceased taxpayer's estate from the assets of the estate. Both the gift tax and the estate tax are based on the fair market value of the property being transferred. In addition, there are numerous exclusions from both taxes, the effect of which is to tax only relatively large gifts and estates. Although gift and estate taxes are vaguely familiar to many people, they are relatively minor revenue producers. However, a basic understanding of the operation of the two taxes will aid in understanding some of the income tax issues related to gifts and estates that are discussed later in the text.

FEDERAL GIFT TAX.   A gift tax is imposed on the fair market value of gifts made between individuals.[11] Neither the donor nor the donee is subject to income tax on gifts. The donor of the gift property is responsible for reporting and paying the gift tax. The gift tax has several exclusions, the most basic of which is an annual exclusion of $10,000 per donee.[12] Under this provision, taxpayers can give as many individuals as they wish as much as $10,000 a year each and pay no gift tax. A married couple can use this exclusion to make tax-free gifts of up to $20,000 per person per year. Taxpayers are also allowed to make unlimited gifts to their spouses and to charities without payment of gift tax.

> ▲ **EXAMPLE 18**   Ansel and Hannah gave their daughter a new car for graduation. The car cost $18,000. Is the gift subject to the gift tax?
>
> *Discussion:*   Ansel and Hannah each are entitled to give $10,000 to any person each year. Therefore, they may make gifts of up to $20,000 to an individual without incurring any gift tax. Because the fair market value of the car is less than $20,000, it is not subject to gift tax.
>
> ▲ **EXAMPLE 19**   On their 25th wedding anniversary, Ansel gave Hannah a diamond ring that cost $30,000. Is the gift subject to the gift tax?
>
> *Discussion:*   Gifts to a spouse are not subject to gift tax, regardless of the value transferred. Therefore, the ring is not subject to the gift tax.

As these examples illustrate, the most common forms of gifts, such as those for birthdays, graduations, weddings, and anniversaries are not subject to the gift tax. However, when a gift is made that is not totally excludable under one of these provisions, the taxpayer may use the unified donative-transfers credit to avoid payment of the gift tax.[13] The **unified donative-transfers credit** allows a lifetime credit of $192,800 against gift and estate taxes. The credit is equivalent to being able to exclude $600,000 in property from the gift and/or the estate tax.

FEDERAL ESTATE TAX.   The estate tax is levied on the fair market value of the assets a taxpayer owned at death.[14] The executor of the estate is responsible for valuing the assets of the estate, administering the assets before their distribution to the heirs, paying the estate taxes, and distributing the assets to the estate's beneficiaries. As with the gift tax, several exclusions and the unified donative-transfers credit serve to limit taxation of estates to those estates that are fairly substantial.[15] The fair market value of the estate's assets is reduced by funeral and administrative costs, debts owed by the taxpayer, amounts bequeathed to charities, and the marital deduction for property passing to the surviving spouse. The marital deduction is unlimited—all amounts that pass to a surviving spouse are exempt from the estate tax. Judicious use of the marital deduction and the donative-transfers credit allow the value of most estates to go untaxed at the death of the first spouse. Because the unified donative-transfers credit is a cumulative lifetime amount that applies to both gifts and property passing through the estate, careful planning is required in order to minimize the lifetime tax on gifts and property held at death. Suffice it to say that the gift and estate tax provisions can be quite complex. Taxpayers with substantial assets should seek competent professional advice in planning their estates to minimize the liability for these taxes.

Although the transfer of property from an estate to the heirs of the decedent has no income tax effect, the estate itself is subject to income tax while it holds the assets of the decedent. The executor of the estate must file an income tax return that reports the income and the deductions related to the assets of the decedent for the period between the date of death and the final distribution of the estate's assets. The taxable income calculation of an estate is discussed in Chapter 9.

▲ SOURCES OF FEDERAL INCOME TAX LAW

This text contains a general discussion of the federal income tax and by itself should not be considered a substitute for the original sources of the tax law. Before making a final decision about a tax issue, you should review the appropriate original source of the tax rule on which you are going to rely. Thus, it is important to be aware of the legislative, administrative, and judicial sources of tax law. These sources are frequently referred to as *primary sources* of tax law. The discussion that follows briefly outlines the primary sources. A more detailed discussion of the primary authorities is contained in Chapter 15, Tax Research. The remainder of this text generally will not make specific references to sources of tax law. Instead, this book makes generic reference to ''tax law'' in order to simplify the discussion.

The end of each chapter includes a list of applicable sources keyed to footnote numbers in the chapter and a brief summary of each source. For those who wish to read the primary sources, they are available in most university and public libraries. Briefly, our citations follow common tax practice, with deference to *The Bluebook: A Uniform System of Citation* (Harvard Law Review Association) and the *Chicago Manual of Style* (University of Chicago Press). For example, *Sec. 61* refers to Section 61 of the Internal Revenue Code of 1986 as amended. *Reg. Sec. 1.61-2* refers to the second Treasury regulation issued that interprets Section 61. *Helvering v. Gregory*, 69 F.2d 809 (2d Cir. 1934), is a citation to a 1934 court case that was decided by the U.S. Court of Appeals for the Second Circuit. The case is located in volume 69 of the *Federal Reporter* case series, beginning at page 809. A complete explanation of all citations and how to locate the primary sources can be found in Chapter 15.

The federal income tax law dates to 1913 and has been amended, revised, and reworked numerous times since. The current statutory source of federal income tax law is the **Internal Revenue Code of 1986,** as amended (referred to as the *Code*). The tax law is laid out in the Code by section number. Thus, the basic reference to a particular tax law provision is to the section of the Code in which the law is stated. Often, particular tax treatments are referred to by their Code section number. For example, Section 179 allows a taxpayer to elect to deduct up to $17,500 of the cost of qualifying depreciable property in the year of acquisition (rather than depreciating it over its tax life). Tax practitioners refer to this election as the *Section 179 election*. Therefore, when appropriate, references to Code sections will include the popular terminology associated with that section.

The Internal Revenue Service is the branch of the Treasury Department that is responsible for interpreting and administering the tax law. The Treasury provides overall interpretive guidance on the Code by issuing **Treasury regulations.**[16] Regulations undergo an intensive review and public comment process before they are issued. Because of this intensive review, interpretations of regulations generally carry considerable authority, sometimes approaching that of the Code.

In fulfilling its administrative function, the IRS issues revenue rulings, revenue procedures, and a variety of other pronouncements that provide guidance on the interpretation of the Code. Because the IRS issues several hundred rulings each year, they do not undergo the extensive review process accorded regulations. As such, they are given less weight as an authority than a Treasury regulation.

In addition to providing interpretive guidance, the IRS has responsibility for ensuring taxpayers' compliance with the tax law. During 1993, the IRS processed 207 million tax returns, provided tax preparation assistance to 65.3 million taxpayers, and audited 0.92 percent of the individual tax returns filed by individual taxpayers in 1992. When audited by the IRS, taxpayers are allowed to present their reasoning for the items in question on their return. As might be expected, disputes often arise between taxpayers and the IRS concerning its interpretations and enforcement of the tax law. Most disputes are resolved through the IRS appeals process. However, taxpayers who are dissatisfied with the result of the appeals process are entitled to take their disputes to court for settlement.

Court decisions establish precedent in the interpretation of the tax law. Taxpayers and the IRS are generally bound by the interpretation of a court on a particular issue. However, the loser of an initial court case may choose to appeal the decision to a U.S. Circuit Court of Appeals. A loss at the appellate level may be further appealed to the U.S. Supreme Court. However, the Supreme Court limits its review of tax cases to those of major importance (e.g., a constitutional issue) or to resolving conflicting decisions in the appellate courts. A Supreme Court decision is not subject to review—it is the final interpretation of the law. Only Congress can override an interpretation of the Supreme Court by amending the Code section in question.

Tax information is also published in a variety of secondary sources. These sources include tax reference services, professional tax journals, tax newsletters, and textbooks. Secondary sources are useful when researching an issue, and they often are helpful for understanding the primary sources. However, you should exercise care when using secondary sources, because their interpretations are not authoritative.

Individuals, corporations, and certain estates and trusts are subject to tax on their federal taxable income. Federal taxable income is defined by the tax law and differs from both financial accounting and economic measures of income. The general computational framework for determining the taxable income of all taxpayers is shown in Exhibit 1–1. Both the terms used in the computations and the order of the computational framework are prescribed in the tax law.

▲ FEDERAL INCOME TAX TERMINOLOGY

Income

The term *income* is used in several different ways. Therefore, always be sure you understand the context in which the term is used. As broadly defined, income includes both taxable and nontaxable types of income. This definition includes all income that belongs to the taxpayer. *Gross Income* is a more restrictive term. As

	Income "Broadly Defined" (includes income from all sources)
Minus:	Excluded income
Equals:	Gross income
Minus:	Deductions and exemptions
Equals:	Taxable income
×	Tax rate (schedule of rates)
Equals:	Income tax
Minus:	Tax prepayments Tax credits
Equals:	Tax (refund) due with return

▲ Exhibit 1–1

INCOME TAX COMPUTATIONAL FRAMEWORK

Exhibit 1–1 shows, **gross income** is income broadly defined minus income items that are excluded from taxation.[17] Items of gross income are included in the computation of taxable income. Generally, gross income is the starting point for reporting income items on a tax return. Chapter 3 discusses the most commonly encountered gross income items.

A fundamental rule to observe in regard to income is that an item is included in gross income unless it is specifically excluded by the tax law. **Exclusions** represent increases in a taxpayer's wealth and recoveries of the taxpayer's capital investment that Congress has decided should not be subject to income tax. Thus, income exclusions are not counted as gross income. Common income exclusions include inheritances, gifts, and interest on certain municipal bonds. Exclusions are discussed in Chapter 4.

Although not an explicit part of the income tax computation, deferrals of income and deductions are also found in the tax law. A **deferral** is an item that does not affect the current period's taxable income but will affect taxable income in some future tax year. Thus, a deferral is like an exclusion in that it does not have a current tax effect. However, it differs in that an exclusion is *never* subject to tax, whereas a deferral *will* be subject to tax at some point in the future.

Taxable income is a net number and is the tax base. Taxable income is determined by subtracting deductions and exemptions from gross income. Taxable income is the tax base that is multiplied by the applicable tax rate schedule to compute the federal income tax. Taxable income is usually different from financial accounting income computed by using generally accepted accounting principles.

The differences between financial accounting income and taxable income generally arise because taxable income is computed according to the rules prescribed by the tax law. Tax accounting rules are not based on generally accepted accounting principles (GAAP). GAAP are concerned with determining the "true income" for an annual period. The income tax is geared to producing and collecting tax revenues and providing incentives for particular economic and social transactions. An important difference between the two objectives is that the income tax system attempts to collect the tax on income in the period during which the taxpayer has the resources to pay the tax. Under GAAP, having the resources to pay taxes is of no concern. As a result, specific income and deduction items may be accelerated, deferred, or permanently excluded from the current year's taxable income computation versus the GAAP treatment. For example, prepaid rental income may be amortized over the lease period for financial reporting but must be reported in full in the year it is collected for tax reporting. Another example is the treatment of depreciable property. For tax purposes, assets must be depreciated by using a statutorily determined recovery period, without regard for its actual useful life. For financial reporting, the same asset is depreciated over its useful life. These are but two examples of income and deduction items that are different for financial and taxable income and that will be discussed throughout the text.

Income is also referred to as *ordinary income*. **Ordinary income** is the recurring income earned by a taxpayer for a tax year.[18] It is the common type of income that people and businesses expect to earn. Ordinary income typically includes business profits, rent from property, interest on investments, dividend income, and wages. Ordinary income is subject to tax using regular tax rates and computations explained in later chapters. That is, ordinary income receives no special treatment under the tax laws.

Income also results from gains. A **gain** is the difference between the selling price of an asset and its tax cost and is the result of disposing of the asset.[19] Usually, a gain will be the result of a sale of a single asset. Most gains produce ordinary income. However, gains on the sale of certain types of assets receive special treatment in the determination of taxable income and the tax liability. These gains are called *capital gains* and result from the sale of a capital asset.

Deductions

Deductions are amounts that the tax law specifically allows as subtractions from gross income. Deductions are a matter of legislative grace. The concept of legislative grace gives us a basic rule to follow in order to determine items that qualify for deduction. The rule is that an item may not be deducted unless the tax law specifically permits it. Deductions are characterized as *expenses*, *losses*, and *exemptions*.

An **expense** is a current period expenditure that is incurred in order to earn income. Deductions for expenses are limited to those incurred in a trade or business,[20] in an income-producing activity (investment activity),[21] and certain specifically allowed personal expenses of individuals. Trade or business expenses and income-producing expenses must be ordinary, necessary, and reasonable in amount in order to be deductible. Allowable personal expenses are deductible as itemized deductions and are subject to strict limitations.

The term **loss** refers to two distinctly different types of events. A loss occurs when an asset is disposed of for a selling price that is less than its tax cost. This type of loss is referred to as a **transaction loss** and represents a loss of capital invested in the asset. In later chapters, it will be necessary to apply limits to the amount of a loss that can be deducted in a tax year. To apply the limits, losses are characterized as personal, business, or capital. These limits deny deductions for most personal losses, place a cap on the amount of capital losses that may be deducted in the year of the loss, and allow business losses to be fully deducted as incurred.

The second type of loss is an annual loss. An **annual loss** results from an excess of allowable deductions for a tax year over the reported income for the year. The treatment of the annual loss depends on the activity in which the loss is incurred. Chapter 7 discusses the limitations on and treatment of all losses, transaction and annual.

Individuals, trusts, and estates may subtract predetermined amounts called **exemptions** to determine their taxable income. The exemption deduction for individuals is, in effect, Congress's recognition that people need a minimum amount of income to provide for their basic living expenses. Thus, this minimum amount of income is deducted as an exemption and is not subject to tax. The deduction for individual exemptions is reduced for high-income taxpayers. Apparently, the reduction is Congress's way of saying that these taxpayers have enough income to support themselves and that the ability-to-pay concept should prevail. Because the minimum basic costs of living increase each year due to inflation, the exemption amounts are indexed to inflation and increase each year to reflect the increased costs individuals incur.

Income Tax Rates

The 1995 tax rate schedules for two classes of individual taxpayers and corporations are reproduced in Table 1–2.[22] A full set of tax rates for individuals, corporations, estates, and trusts for 1994 and 1995 is reproduced in Appendix A. The income tax is calculated by multiplying taxable income by the applicable tax rates. Each year, the IRS publishes new tax rate schedules that are adjusted for cost-of-

▲ Table 1–2

1995 TAX RATE
SCHEDULES

Single Taxpayers			
If taxable income is over	**But not over**	**The tax is**	**Of the amount over**
$ -0-	$ 23,350	...............15%	$ -0-
23,350	56,550	$ 3,502.50 + 28%	23,350
56,550	117,950	12,798.50 + 31%	56,550
117,950	256,500	31,832.50 + 36%	117,950
256,500	....	81,710.50 + 39.6%	256,500

Married Taxpayers Filing Jointly and Surviving Spouse			
If taxable income is over	**But not over**	**The tax is**	**Of the amount over**
$ -0-	$ 39,000	...............15%	$ -0-
39,000	94,250	$ 5,850.00 + 28%	39,000
94,250	143,600	21,320.00 + 31%	94,250
143,600	256,500	36,618.50 + 36%	143,600
256,500	....	77,262.50 + 39.6%	256,500

Corporate Tax Rate Schedule			
If taxable income is over	**But not over**	**The tax is**	**Of the amount over**
$ -0-	$ 50,000	...............15%	$ -0-
50,000	75,000	$ 7,500 + 25%	50,000
75,000	100,000	13,750 + 34%	75,000
100,000	335,000	22,250 + 39%	100,000
335,000	10,000,000	113,900 + 34%	335,000
10,000,000	15,000,000	3,400,000 + 35%	10,000,000
15,000,000	18,333,333	5,150,000 + 38%	15,000,000
18,333,333	....	6,416,667 + 35%	18,333,333

living increases. Adjusting the tax rate schedules for changes in the cost of living helps to minimize a hidden tax that results from inflation.

Assume the following information (shown in Exhibit 1–2): A single taxpayer's taxable income in 1994 was $55,000. The rate of inflation in 1994 was 2.63 percent, and the taxpayer was able to keep up with inflation by increasing her income. Her taxable income goes up by $1,447 to $56,447 ($55,000 × 1.0263%) in 1995. At this point, the taxpayer is no better or worse off in 1995 than in 1994. Her income increase merely kept up with the rate of inflation. The top panel of Exhibit 1–2 shows that failure to adjust the 1995 tax rates for the 2.63 percent inflation rate results in $445 in additional tax. The increased tax is attributable to two sources. First, the increased income results in an additional $405 (28% × $1,447) in tax, even if the marginal rate stays the same from the first to the second year. Second, the problem worsens when the inflated income pushes the taxpayer into a higher marginal tax bracket (tax bracket creep) causing an additional $40 in tax [(31% − 28%) × ($56,447 − $55,100)]. Thus, the taxpayer is worse off, because she pays $445 more tax on the same deflated income when tax rates are not adjusted for inflation. The net result is an increase of after-tax income of only $1,002 ($1,447 − $445), which is less than the rate of inflation.

The bottom panel of Exhibit 1–2 calculates the tax using the actual 1995 rates, which are adjusted for the 2.63 percent inflation rate. The tax on a 1995 taxable

	Tax Year	
	1994	1995
Taxable income	$55,000	$55,000
Increase in taxable income due to 2.63% inflation	-0-	1,447
Inflation-adjusted taxable income	$55,000	$56,447
Tax using 1994 single taxpayer rates:		
Tax on base amount	$ 3,413	$12,471
Excess taxed at marginal rate		
28%	9,030	
31%		417
Total tax	$12,443	$12,888
Additional tax resulting from inflation		$ 445
Tax on $56,447 at 1995 tax rates		
Tax on $23,350		$ 3,503
Tax on income in excess of $23,350		
($56,447 − $23,350) × 28%		9,267
Tax at 1995 rates		$12,770
1994 After-tax income ($55,000 − $12,443)		$42,557
1994 Inflation rate adjustment		× 1.0263
1995 Real after-tax income		$43,676
Actual 1995 after-tax income ($56,447 − $12,770)		$43,677 *

*The $1 difference is due to rounding in the calculation of the inflation-adjusted amounts.

▲ **Exhibit 1–2**

The Hidden
Inflation Tax

income of $56,447 is $12,770. This is a reduction of $118 ($12,888 − $12,770) over the tax calculated using 1994 rates on the same income. The adjustment for inflation in the tax rate brackets leaves the taxpayer with the same inflation-adjusted after-tax income in 1995 [($55,000 − $12,443) × 1.0263% = $43,676 = ($56,447 − $12,770)] that the taxpayer had in 1994. Thus, the adjustment of the tax brackets for inflation each year ensures that taxpayers whose income merely keeps pace with inflation will not realize a decrease in real after-tax income.

Tax Prepayments

The pay-as-you-go system requires the payment of tax as the income is earned and when the taxpayer has the resources available to pay the tax. Tax prepayments are subtracted from the income tax liability to determine whether the taxpayer has underpaid and owes additional tax with the return (tax due) or is entitled to a refund of overpaid taxes (refund due). Employees prepay taxes on wages through payroll-tax withholding. Other types of income, such as pensions and some gambling winnings, are also subject to the withholding of tax by the payer. The employer or other person withholding the tax pays the tax withheld to the IRS, to be credited to the taxpayer's account with the government.

Self-employed people and taxpayers with income not subject to withholding (trade or business income, interest income, dividend income, gains from sales of assets, etc.) are required to make quarterly payments of their current-year estimated tax payments. An individual usually makes quarterly payments on April 15, June 15, and September 15 of the tax year and on January 15 of the next year. This corresponds to the fifteenth day of the fourth, sixth, and ninth months of the tax year and the fifteenth day of the first month of the following year. A corporation makes its estimated tax payments on the fifteenth day of the fourth, sixth, ninth, and twelfth months of its tax year. Estates and trusts follow the estimated tax schedule used by individuals. Estimated tax payments, like withheld amounts, are subtracted as credits for the prepayment of tax.

Tax Credits

A **tax credit** is a direct reduction in the income tax liability. In effect, tax credits are treated like tax prepayments. As Exhibit 1–1 shows, a credit is not deducted to arrive at taxable income but is instead subtracted directly from the tax due. Thus, a tax credit is more valuable than a deduction of an equal amount, because the credit yields a larger reduction in the total tax due. Tax credits are often used as incentives to encourage taxpayers to enter into specific types of transactions that Congress feels will further some public purpose.

If a taxpayer's marginal tax rate is 31 percent, a $5,000 tax deduction has the same value as a $1,550 tax credit ($5,000 × 31%). Likewise, a $1,000 tax credit has the same value as a $3,226 deduction if the marginal rate is 31 percent ($1,000 ÷ 31%).

> ▲ **EXAMPLE 20**   Ron and Martha, whose marginal tax rate is 31%, paid $1,000 for child care.
>
> *Discussion:*   If the expenditure is treated as a credit, the tax they owe for the year will be reduced by the full $1,000. If the expenditure is treated as a deduction, their tax would be reduced by $310 ($1,000 × 31% marginal rate). Treatment of the expenditure as a credit would save them $690 more than treatment as a deduction.

Filing Returns

In general, all income tax entities must file an annual tax return (see Chapter 8 for individual filing requirements). Returns for individuals, estates, trusts, and partnerships must be filed on or before the fifteenth day of the fourth month following the close of the entity's tax year (April 15 for calendar-year taxpayers). Corporate tax returns are due on or before the fifteenth day of the third month following the close of a corporation's tax year (March 15 for calendar-year corporate taxpayers). Taxpayers who cannot complete and file their returns by the regular due date can apply for extensions for filing the return. Individuals are granted an automatic four-month extension by applying for the extension by the due date of the return. Corporations are allowed an automatic six-month extension; partnerships and trusts can automatically extend their filing date by three months. Filing an extension does not extend the time for paying the tax. Applications for automatic extensions must show and include payment of the estimated amount due with the final return.

> ▲ **EXAMPLE 21**   Thelma procrastinates about preparing her tax return and determines that she cannot complete the return by April 15. She has withholdings and estimated tax payments totaling $8,600 and estimates that her total tax liability for the year will be $8,950. What must Thelma do to extend the date for filing her return?
>
> *Discussion:*   Thelma can extend the period for filing her return to August 15 (four months from April 15) by filing the application for automatic extension by April 15. This only grants Thelma permission to delay the filing of the return. She must pay the $350 ($8,950 − $8,600) estimated tax she owes when she applies for the extension.

Taxpayers and the government can correct errors on returns within a limited time period called the **statute of limitations.** Generally, once the statute of limitations has expired, corrections cannot be made. The general statute of limitations is three years from the due date of the return, not including extensions. The three-year statute of limitations has several exceptions, the most important of which deal with fraudulently prepared returns. The statute of limitations runs for six years when a taxpayer omits gross income in excess of 25 percent of the gross income reported on the return. The government can bring charges of criminal fraud against a taxpayer at any time. That is, neither the three-year nor the six-year statute of limitations protects a taxpayer who willfully defrauds the government.

The government corrects errors on taxpayers' returns through its audit process (discussed in Chapter 15). Taxpayers correct errors on prior year returns by filing amended returns. Amended returns are not used to adjust returns for previous years (see discussion of the tax benefit rule in Chapter 2). An amended return should be filed only when a taxpayer finds that an item of income that should have been included in gross income was omitted in the original filing or if the taxpayer improperly included an item of income in income in a prior year. Tax-payers also should file amended returns if they find that they failed to take an allowable deduction or if they find that they took an improper deduction on an earlier return.

▲ **EXAMPLE 22**   Geraldo Corporation incurred a net operating loss in 1994, its first year of operation. Because the controller knew that Geraldo was going to suffer a loss, he took no deductions for depreciation for 1994. Geraldo's independent auditor came upon the error in 1995 and advised Geraldo that it must take all allowable deductions in the proper year. Should Geraldo file an amended return for 1994?

Discussion: Because the depreciation was not treated properly on the 1994 tax return, Geraldo should file an amended return that takes the proper depreciation deduction for 1994.

▲ **EXAMPLE 23**   Walstad Corporation is an accrual basis taxpayer. In 1994, Walstad determined that one of its customers with an accounts receivable balance of $40,000 was in bankruptcy. After conferring with the customer's lawyers, Walstad determined that it would be able to collect only $15,000 of the account and deducted the $25,000 uncollectible amount as a bad debt expense. In 1995, the customer's bankruptcy was settled, and Walstad received $10,000 as a final settlement of the account it had written off. Should Walstad file an amended return for 1994 and correct the bad debt deduction?

Discussion: The actual bad debt is $30,000 ($40,000 − $10,000). The $25,000 bad debt deduction that Walstad took in 1994 was an estimate of the amount of the bad debt. Therefore, the deduction was not incorrect at the time the return was filed. Walstad should deduct the additional $5,000 ($30,000 − $25,000) of actual bad debt in 1995 to adjust the estimate. Amended returns are not filed to adjust estimates on prior year returns. Adjustments to estimates are made on the return for the year in which the actual amount of the deduction becomes known.

The general tax calculation presented in Exhibit 1–1 applies to all taxpayers. However, the tax law modifies this calculation for individuals in order to take into account the unique characteristics of individual taxpayers.

The calculation of an individual's taxable income is outlined in Exhibit 1–3. Note that the general flow remains the same—deductions are subtracted from gross income to arrive at taxable income. Gross income is determined under the

▲ INDIVIDUAL INCOME TAX CALCULATION

		$ XXX
	All sources of income (broadly defined)	$ XXX
Minus:	Exclusions from income	(XXX)
Equals:	Gross income	$ XXX
Minus:	Deductions *for* adjusted gross income	
	Trade or business expenses	
	Rental and royalty expenses	
	Other specifically allowable deductions	(XXX)
Equals:	**ADJUSTED GROSS INCOME**	$ XXX
Minus:	Deductions *from* adjusted gross income	
	Personal deductions: the greater of	
	1. itemized deductions (allowable personal expenses and certain other allowable deductions)	
	OR	
	2. individual standard deduction	(XXX)
Minus:	Personal and dependency exemptions	(XXX)
Equals:	Taxable income	$ XXX

general tax formula. The distinguishing feature of the individual taxable income calculation is that deductions are broken into two classes—deductions for adjusted gross income and deductions from adjusted gross income. This dichotomy of deductions results in an intermediate income number called the **adjusted gross income (AGI)**.[23] As will become clear in the discussion that follows, this is a very important income number, because it is used to provide limitations on the deductions from adjusted gross income of an individual taxpayer. Deductions are discussed in more detail in later chapters. However, at this point a general knowledge of the computational form and allowable deductions of individuals is necessary. Both types of deductions are discussed in turn.

Deductions for Adjusted Gross Income

Individuals are always allowed to deduct the qualified expenses they incur as **deductions for adjusted gross income.** In contrast to deductions from adjusted gross income, deductions in this class are not subject to reduction based on the income of the taxpayer. That is, once the allowable amount of an expenditure in this category has been determined, it is not subject to further reduction based on the income of the taxpayer. The allowable deductions for adjusted gross income are generally those that are incurred in a trade or business of the taxpayer or that are related to the earning of other forms of income. In addition, several other specifically allowed items are deductible for adjusted gross income. Deductions for adjusted gross income include

Trade or business expenses
Rental and royalty expenses
Capital loss deduction
Alimony paid
Contributions to individual retirement accounts (IRAs)
Moving expenses
Reimbursed employee business expenses

One-half of self-employment taxes paid

A percentage of self-employed medical insurance premiums

Although these expenditures are not limited by the income of the taxpayer, other limitations in the tax law may serve to reduce the current period's tax deduction. For example, the allowable deductions for rental properties may be limited by either the vacation home rules or the passive activity loss rules. Losses on the sale of capital assets are deductible but are first netted against capital gains. If the result is a net capital loss, the current year's deduction is limited to a maximum of $3,000.[24] These losses and other limits are covered in the chapters on deductions and losses. The important point to remember for now is that once the allowable amount of a deduction for adjusted gross income has been determined, it is not subject to further reduction. In addition, there is no preset minimum allowable amount of deductions for adjusted gross income.

Deductions from Adjusted Gross Income

Individuals are allowed to deduct certain personal expenditures and other specified nonpersonal expenditures as **deductions from adjusted gross income.** These deductions are commonly referred to as **itemized deductions.** Note in Exhibit 1–3 that individuals deduct the greater of their allowable itemized deductions or the standard deduction.[25] The **standard deduction** is an amount that Congress allows all taxpayers to deduct, regardless of their actual qualifying itemized deduction expenditures. Thus, taxpayers itemize their deductions only if their total allowable itemized deductions exceed the standard deduction. For 1995, the standard deduction for a single individual is $3,900 and $6,550 for a married couple.

▲ **EXAMPLE 24**   Festus is a single taxpayer with total allowable itemized deductions of $1,800 in 1995. What is Festus's allowable deduction from adjusted gross income?

Discussion: Festus deducts the larger of his $1,800 in itemized deductions or the $3,900 standard deduction for a single individual. In this case, Festus deducts the $3,900 standard deduction.

▲ **EXAMPLE 25**   Assume that in example 24, Festus's total allowable itemized deductions are $6,700 in 1995. What is his allowable deduction from adjusted gross income?

Discussion: Festus would deduct the $6,700 in actual itemized deductions because it exceeds his $3,900 standard deduction.

As these examples illustrate, just because a particular expenditure is allowed as an itemized deduction does not necessarily mean that a taxpayer incurring the expense will actually deduct it. Itemized deductions reduce taxable income only when a taxpayer's total itemized deductions exceed the allowable standard deduction.

In addition to providing all taxpayers with some minimum amount of deduction, the standard deduction eliminates the need for every taxpayer to list every qualifying personal expenditure. This makes it easier for taxpayers with small amounts of qualifying expenditures to comply with the tax law and relieves the government from having to verify millions of deductions that would have been claimed as a result of itemizing. Thus, the standard deduction is an important tool that the government uses to promote income tax law compliance by removing the burden of record keeping and reporting for relatively small amounts of deductible items.

In the deduction classification scheme, specifically allowed personal expenditures are classified as itemized deductions.[26] In addition to personal expenditures, investment expenses and certain other employment-related expenses are deductible as itemized deductions. Many allowable itemized deductions are subject to an income limitation. That is, the amount of the qualifying expenditure must be reduced by a percentage of the taxpayer's adjusted gross income to determine the actual deduction. The effect of using this type of income limitation is to disallow deductions for amounts that are small in relation to the taxpayer's income.

▲ **EXAMPLE 26**   Qualifying medical expenses are deductible to the extent that they exceed 7.5% of a taxpayer's adjusted gross income. During the current year, Li has an adjusted gross income of $40,000 and incurred $4,200 in qualified medical expenses. What is Li's itemized deduction for medical expense?

Discussion: Li must reduce the $4,200 of qualified medical expenses by $3,000 ($40,000 × 7.5%), resulting in deductible medical expenses of $1,200.

Note that the effect of the limitation is to allow larger deductions for taxpayers with smaller incomes. Another taxpayer incurring the same $4,200 in expenses and who had an adjusted gross income of only $25,000 would be allowed to deduct $2,325 [$4,200 − ($25,000 × 7.5% = $1,875)] of the medical expenses.

The following list is intended to acquaint you with the categories of itemized deductions available to individuals. At this point, you should note the types of personal expenses that are allowed as a deduction. Do not be concerned about the detailed deduction requirements and limitations. These issues are explained in more detail in Chapter 8.

MEDICAL EXPENSES—Unreimbursed medical expenses are deductible to the extent that they exceed 7.5 percent of adjusted gross income. Medical expenses include the cost of medical insurance, physicians, hospitals, glasses and contact lenses, and a multitude of other items. Because of the AGI limit, many taxpayers benefit from these deductions only when there is a major illness in the family.[27]

TAXES—State, local, and foreign income taxes, real estate taxes, and state and local personal property taxes may be deducted.[28]

INTEREST—An individual's deduction for personal interest expense is limited to the following:[29]

- Home mortgage interest related to the acquisition of a home or to a home equity loan
- Investment interest expense

CHARITABLE CONTRIBUTIONS—Gifts to qualified charitable organizations may be deducted. Generally, the deductible contribution may not exceed 50 percent of the taxpayer's adjusted gross income.[30]

PERSONAL CASUALTY AND THEFT LOSSES—Deductions are allowed for losses of property from casualty or theft, subject to two limitations. Because of the limitations, most taxpayers must have a large total loss for the year to get a deduction for a personal casualty or theft loss.[31]

MISCELLANEOUS ITEMIZED DEDUCTIONS—This is a broad category of deductions that includes most expenses related to the production of investment income. The following list of miscellaneous deductions illustrates the types of items deducted in this category:

- Business expenses of an employee not reimbursed by an employer
- Investment-related expenses
- Expenses related to tax return preparation, planning, and examination

Generally, the deduction allowed for miscellaneous itemized deductions must be reduced by 2 percent of the taxpayer's adjusted gross income.[32]

Personal and Dependency Exemptions

Individuals are allowed to deduct a predetermined amount for each qualifying exemption.[33] In 1995, individuals deduct $2,500 for each qualifying personal and dependency exemption. The intention is to exempt from tax a minimum amount of income that is used to support the taxpayer and those who are dependent on that taxpayer. Because support costs increase with inflation, the exemption amounts are increased each year to account for the prior year's inflation. **Personal exemptions** are allowed for the taxpayer and the taxpayer's spouse. **Dependency exemptions** are granted for individuals who are dependent on the taxpayer for support. Although there are five technical tests (discussed in Chapter 8) that must be met to qualify as a dependent, the underlying reasoning is that the dependent must rely on the taxpayer for basic living costs. Thus, children of a taxpayer and other relatives, such as parents and grandchildren who live with the taxpayer, are the most common dependents.

> ▲ **EXAMPLE 27**   John and Nancy are married and have 3 small children who live with them and depend on them for their support. What is John and Nancy's 1995 exemption deduction?
>
> *Discussion:*   John and Nancy are entitled to 2 personal exemptions and 3 dependency exemptions. Their deduction is $12,500 ($2,500 × 5 exemptions).

▲ TAX PLANNING

The objective of tax planning is to maximize after-tax wealth. An effective tax plan results in a reduction of taxes for the planning period. Because a planning period may be two or more years, focusing on reducing tax for one year without considering any offsetting effects for other years can lead to excessive tax payments. The traditional planning technique of deferring income and accelerating deductions may not always be the best tax plan. The traditional technique considers only the time value of money savings that can be obtained from delaying tax payments on income or receiving tax savings from deductions sooner. Although the time value of money must always be considered, changes in marginal tax rates from one year to the next can have effects that offset the time value of money. Thus in many cases, changes in both the marginal tax rate and the time value of money must be considered when developing a tax plan. The mechanics of tax planning demonstrate basic techniques that can be used to help make tax-planning decisions. The planning discussion concludes by pointing out that tax avoidance is acceptable but tax evasion is not.

Mechanics of Tax Planning

The mechanics of tax planning focus on the issues of timing and income shifting. The timing question to be answered is when income and deductions should be claimed to save the most *real tax*. To make decisions involving timing, it is necessary to compare the tax effects of changes in marginal tax rates and the time value of money. To make the optimal choice among different alternatives, it is necessary to do the calculations to determine the *real* after-tax cost of each alternative. Income shifting involves moving income among related taxpayers to achieve the lowest marginal taxes (and lowest total tax) on the entire income of the related taxpayers. Shifting is commonly done by transferring income-producing property between family members and by using corporations that taxpayers control to shift income into the lowest marginal tax rates.

Timing Income and Deductions.   A taxpayer's marginal tax rate and the time value of money must be considered in tax planning. The traditional technique of deferring income and accelerating deductions relies solely on the time value of money savings from delaying the tax payment or receiving the tax deduction savings earlier. For example, a taxpayer who expects to be in a 28-percent marginal tax bracket for the next several years might be indifferent about reporting $1,000 in extra income in 1995 or 1996. Regardless of which year the income is reported, the taxpayer pays $280 in tax and keeps $720 ($1,000 − $280) in after-tax income. When the present value of the tax payment is considered (see Table 1–3 for present values factors), it becomes clear that choice of years does make a difference. If the taxpayer's applicable interest rate is 10 percent and the marginal rate is expected to remain the same, deferring payment of the tax until 1996 results in an interest-free loan. The present value of the tax savings is $25:

Tax paid in 1996	$280
10% present value factor	× 0.909
Present value of tax paid in 1996	$255
Present value of tax paid in 1995	280
Real tax savings by deferring income	$ 25

If the marginal rate is expected to decrease to 15 percent in 1996, the taxpayer has a greater incentive to defer the income. By deferring the income to 1996, the taxpayer receives the benefit of an interest-free loan for one year plus the benefit of the lower marginal tax rate. Deferring the income to 1996, would result in a real tax benefit of $144:

Tax paid in 1996 ($1,000 × 15%)	$150
10% present value factor	× 0.909
Present value of tax paid in 1996	$136
Present value of tax paid in 1995	280
Real tax savings by deferring income	$144

Table 1–3 shows how much $1 to be paid at a future date is worth today at the discount rate indicated.

If the taxpayer expects the marginal tax rate to increase to 31 percent next year, the income should be reported in 1995. Deferring the income to 1996 would have a real tax cost of $2:

Tax paid in 1996 ($1,000 × 31%)	$310
10% present value factor	× 0.909
Present value of tax paid in 1996	$282
Present value of tax paid in 1995	280
Real tax cost of deferring income	$ 2

The same approach can be used to determine the best timing for a deduction. However, keep in mind that deductions are the opposite of income—they reduce

Present Value of a Single Payment							
Year	5%	6%	7%	8%	9%	10%	12%
1	0.952	0.943	0.935	0.926	0.917	0.909	0.893
2	0.907	0.890	0.873	0.857	0.842	0.826	0.797
3	0.864	0.840	0.816	0.794	0.722	0.751	0.712
4	0.823	0.792	0.793	0.735	0.708	0.683	0.636
5	0.784	0.747	0.713	0.681	0.650	0.621	0.567
6	0.746	0.705	0.666	0.630	0.596	0.564	0.507
7	0.711	0.665	0.623	0.583	0.547	0.513	0.452
8	0.677	0.627	0.582	0.540	0.502	0.467	0.404
9	0.645	0.592	0.544	0.500	0.460	0.424	0.361
10	0.614	0.558	0.508	0.463	0.422	0.386	0.322

taxes paid. Therefore, the optimal choice for deductions is to maximize the real after-tax reduction in taxes paid. In many situations, it may be necessary to compare the offsetting effects of income and deduction items.

▲ **EXAMPLE 28**   Ann Corporation owes a $2,000 expense that may be paid and deducted on the cash basis of accounting in either 1995 or 1996. The applicable interest rate is 10%. In which year should Ann Corporation take the deduction if its 1995 marginal tax rate is 25%?

Discussion: The optimal year for taking the deduction depends on Ann Corporation's expected marginal tax rate in 1996. The following schedule calculates the real tax savings (real tax cost) of deducting the expenses in 1995 as compared to deferring the deduction until 1996 at different assumed marginal tax rates:

	Assumed 1996 Marginal Tax Rates		
	15%	25%	34%
Tax saved by 1996 deduction	$ 300	$ 500	$ 680
Present value @ 10%	× 0.909	× 0.909	× 0.909
Present value of tax savings	$ 273	$ 455	$ 618
Less: Tax savings of deduction in 1995 @ 25% marginal tax rate	(500)	(500)	(500)
Deduction in 1995 will result in:			
Tax savings	$(227)	$ (45)	
Tax cost			$ 118

Discussion: Ann Corporation should claim the deduction in 1995 if it expects the marginal tax rate to remain at 25% or decrease to 15%. If the corporation expects its marginal rate to increase to 34%, it should defer the deduction to 1996 to save $118.

▲ **EXAMPLE 29**   Lanny's marginal tax rate for 1995 is 28%. Lanny has $20,000 in income and $10,000 in deductions that could be reported in 1995 or deferred to 1996. Lanny expects his 1996 marginal tax rate to be 31% and the applicable interest rate to be 10%. When should the items be reported if both the income and deductions must be reported in the same year?

Discussion: The result of reporting both the income and the deductions in 1995 as compared to 1996 is as follows:

	1995	1996
Increase in income	$ 20,000	$ 20,000
Less: Increase in deductions	(10,000)	(10,000)
Net increase in taxable income	$ 10,000	$ 10,000
Marginal tax rate	× 28%	× 31%
Tax on net increase in income	$ 2,800	$ 3,100
Present value factor		× 0.909
Present value of tax in 1995	$ 2,800	$ 2,818

Discussion: Lanny should report the items in 1995 to save $18 in real tax cost.

▲ **EXAMPLE 30**   If Lanny could report the income or deductions separately, when should the income and the deductions be reported to maximize the tax savings?

Discussion: The tax cost of reporting each item must be considered separately and the total result compared to reporting both items in 1995 (which was previously determined to be the optimal same-year reporting).

Income

	Report income in	
	1995	1996
Increase in taxable income	$20,000	$20,000
Marginal tax rate	× 28%	× 31%
Increase in tax	$ 5,600	$ 6,200
Present value factor		× 0.909
Present value of tax in 1995	$ 5,600	$ 5,636
Net tax savings from reporting in 1995	36	

Deductions

	Report deductions in	
	1995	1996
Decrease in taxable income	$10,000	$10,000
Marginal tax rate	× 28%	× 31%
Tax savings from deduction	$ 2,800	$ 3,100
Present value factor		× 0.909
Present value of tax savings	$ 2,800	$ 2,818
Net tax savings from reporting in 1996		18

Discussion: If Lanny reports the $20,000 of income in 1995, he has a real tax savings of $36. Deferring the reporting of the $10,000 in deductions until 1996 results in a real tax savings of $18. Thus, by reporting each item separately in the period that is optimal, he saves $54. This compares to a savings of $18 when both income and deductions are reported in the same tax year.

In summary, there are four general rules of thumb to follow when planning the timing of income and deductions; two are based on time value of money propositions, and two are based on marginal tax rate considerations:

Time Value of Money
1. Defer recognition of income.
2. Accelerate recognition of deductions.

Type of Item	Marginal Tax Rate		
	Increasing	**Decreasing**	**Unchanged**
Income	Calculate	Defer	Defer
Deduction	Calculate	Accelerate	Accelerate

▲ **Table 1–4**

Summary of Tax-Planning Rules

Marginal Tax Rate

3. Put income into the year with the lowest expected marginal tax rate.
4. Put deductions into the year with highest expected marginal tax rate.

These general rules of thumb can be used in most situations. However, if there is a conflict between the time value rule and the marginal tax rate rule, the only way to determine the optimal strategy is to calculate the real tax cost of each. Table 1–4 summarizes the rules of thumb and indicates when calculation of the real tax cost is necessary.

Income Shifting.   Income shifting is a method commonly used to reduce taxes. The basic idea behind income shifting is to split a single stream of income between two or more taxpayers to lower the total tax paid. The total tax paid is lower because of the progressive tax rate structure. For example, if a taxpayer in the 31-percent marginal tax rate bracket can shift $1,000 in income to another taxpayer who is in the 15-percent marginal tax rate bracket, $160 [$1,000 × (31% − 15%)] of tax will be saved on the $1,000 in income. Obviously, taxpayers shifting income will want the income to go to taxpayers whom they want to benefit, such as children or grandchildren.

▲ **EXAMPLE 31**   A married taxpayer has $100,000 in taxable income in 1995. The taxpayer has 2 children who have no taxable income. What are the tax savings if the taxpayer can legally shift $10,000 in income to each of her children?

Discussion: The taxpayer saves $2,773 in tax by shifting $10,000 in taxable income to each child. Using the rates for married taxpayers, the tax on $100,000 in taxable income is $23,103:

$$\$21,320 + 31\% (\$100,000 - \$94,250) = \$23,103$$

By splitting the income into 3 streams, the taxpayer pays tax on $80,000, and each child pays tax (at single taxpayer rates) on $10,000. This results in a tax of $20,330:

Tax on $80,000 for a Married Couple
$$\$5,850 + 28\% (\$80,000 - \$39,000) = \$17,330$$

Tax on $10,000 for a Single Person
$$\$10,000 \times 15\% = \$1,500 \times 2 = \underline{3,000}$$
$$\text{Total tax paid} \qquad \underline{\$20,330}$$

The result of the income shift to the children is a reduction in the total tax paid on the $100,000 in taxable income of $2,773 ($23,103 − $20,330).

It should be noted that numerous provisions in the tax law make it difficult to get the full advantage of income shifting. For example, merely directing some of your income to be paid to your children will not shift the income for tax purposes. In order to shift income to family members, you will generally need to transfer ownership of income-producing property to the children in order to shift the income from the property. Unless the parents are willing to give up ownership of income-producing property, income shifting to children is difficult to achieve. Even if a valid transfer of property ownership is made, if the child is younger than 14, provisions exist to take away much of the marginal rate advantage of such a shift.

Another popular income-shifting technique used by owners of a business is to incorporate the business and split income between themselves and the corporation. A review of the corporate tax rates (see Table 1–2) shows that the first $50,000 in taxable income of a corporation is taxed at 15 percent. The owners can split the income by paying themselves salaries, which are deductible by the corporation, and reduce the corporation's taxable income to the lower tax brackets.

▲ **EXAMPLE 32**   Assume that the $100,000 in taxable income in example 31 comes from a business owned by the taxpayer. If the taxpayer incorporates the business and pays herself a salary of $50,000, what is the tax savings?

Discussion: Splitting the income between the taxpayer and a corporation results in a tax savings of $6,673. The taxpayer pays tax on $50,000, and the corporation pays tax on $50,000 ($100,000 income − $50,000 salary). This results in a tax of $16,430:

Tax on $50,000 for a Married Couple

$$\$5,850 + 28\% (\$50,000 - \$39,000) = \$8,930$$

Tax on $50,000 for a Corporation

$$\$50,000 \times 15\% = \underline{\quad 7,500}$$

$$\text{Total tax paid} \qquad \underline{\underline{\$16,430}}$$

Before incorporation, the tax paid by the married couple was $23,103. The incorporation and split of the income saves $6,673 ($23,103 − $16,430) in tax.

Numerous other income-shifting techniques can be used by owners of a business. These include shifting income by employing children and using fringe-benefit packages to get tax-subsidized health care. It should be noted that careful planning is required in order to gain the optimal tax advantage from such shifting plans. The tax law contains many provisions that are designed to block blatant shifting schemes that lack economic substance. These provisions are discussed throughout the remainder of the text as they apply to the study of income and deductions.

Tax Evasion and Tax Avoidance

Taxpayers do not have to pay more income tax than is required by the tax law. In fact, taxpayers may plan transactions to make their tax bills as low as possible. In this regard, Judge Learned Hand stated: "[A] transaction, otherwise within an exception of the tax law, does not lose its immunity, because it is actuated by a desire to avoid, or, if one choose, to evade, taxation. Any one may so arrange his affairs that his taxes shall be as low as possible; he is not bound to choose that pattern which will best pay the Treasury; there is not even a patriotic duty to increase one's taxes."[34]

Tax evasion occurs when a taxpayer uses fraudulent methods or deceptive behavior to hide the actual tax liability. Tax evasion usually involves three elements:

■ Willfulness on the part of the taxpayer

- An underpayment of tax
- An affirmative act by the taxpayer to evade the tax

Tax evasion often involves rearranging the facts about a transaction in order to receive a tax benefit. An intentional misrepresentation of facts on a tax return to avoid paying tax is not acceptable taxpayer behavior. Tax evasion is illegal and is subject to substantial penalties. Note that unintentional mathematical or clerical errors on the return are not generally considered tax evasion.

Tax planning uses tax avoidance methods. **Tax avoidance** is the use of legal methods allowed by the tax law to minimize a tax liability. Tax avoidance generally involves planning an intended transaction to obtain a specific tax treatment. Further, tax avoidance is based on disclosure of relevant facts concerning the tax treatment of a transaction.

▲ **EXAMPLE 33** Ted, an accountant, uses the cash method of accounting. To avoid reporting additional income in 1995, he does not send his December bills to clients until January 2, 1996.

Discussion: The income was properly reported when collected in 1996. Under the cash method of accounting, Ted properly reported income when his clients paid him. Ted's activity involved permissible tax avoidance.

▲ **EXAMPLE 34** Ken, a painter, spent all the cash he received for his art work. He deposited payments he received by check to his business bank account. When he filed his tax return, he intentionally did not report the cash receipts as income.

Discussion: Ken is engaged in tax evasion. Ken's method of reducing his tax is illegal, and he is subject to substantial penalties.

At this point, you are probably wondering, "How will the IRS ever know?" Most people are aware that it is almost impossible for the government to track every cash receipt of income. In fact, the probability that the IRS will detect underreporting of cash income is quite low. This has led many taxpayers to play the "audit lottery," omitting cash income or overstating deductions, because they know that they probably will not be caught. The IRS estimates that this behavior results in a loss of nearly $100 billion per year in tax revenue. This loss must be made up through higher taxes on wage earners and honest taxpayers. It is clear that if taxpayers were more honest in their reporting of income and deductions, everyone's taxes could be lowered. There is no clear-cut, cost-efficient solution to the evasion problem. However, as future professionals and taxpayers, you should recognize your obligations to your profession and the country when it comes to tax evasion situations. Only through education and ethical taxpayer behavior will the tax evasion problem be resolved. Keep in mind that avoiding detection by the IRS does not somehow magically transform a fraudulent act into allowable behavior. The idea that something is not illegal unless one is caught is an idea that should have died ages ago.

▲ ETHICAL CONSIDERATIONS IN TAX PRACTICE

The field of tax practice is virtually unregulated—anyone who wishes to can prepare tax returns for a fee. However, anyone who prepares tax returns for monetary considerations, or who is licensed to practice in the tax-related professions, is subject to various rules and codes of professional conduct. For example, the Internal Revenue Code contains provisions (see Exhibit 1–4 for a list of preparer penalties) that impose civil and criminal penalties on tax return preparers for various improprieties.

Understatement of taxpayer's liability due to unrealistic positions

Understatement of taxpayer's liability due to willful or reckless conduct

Failure to furnish a copy of a return to the taxpayer

Failure to sign a return

Failure to furnish identifying information

Failure to retain a copy or a list of returns prepared

Failure to file correct information returns

Negotiation of tax refund check

Improper disclosure or use of information on taxpayer's return

Organizing (or assisting in doing so) or promoting and making or furnishing statements with respect to abusive tax shelters

Aiding and abetting an understatement of tax liability

Aiding or assisting in the preparation of a false return

All tax practitioners are subject to the provisions of *IRS Circular 230*, "Regulations Governing the Practice of Attorneys, Certified Public Accountants, Enrolled Agents, and Enrolled Actuaries Before the Internal Revenue Service." Tax attorneys are subject to the ethical code of conduct adopted by the state(s) in which they are licensed to practice. Certified Public Accountants (CPAs) who are members of the American Institute of Certified Public Accountants (AICPA) are governed by the institute's Code of Professional Conduct. The AICPA's Statements on Responsibilities in Tax Practice provide eight advisory guidelines for CPAs who prepare tax returns. Although tax practitioners who are not members of the AICPA are not bound by the Code of Professional Conduct and the Statements on Responsibilities in Tax Practice, the rules and guidelines contained in them provide useful guidance for all return preparers.

The AICPA Code of Professional Conduct is a set of rules that set enforceable ethical standards for members of the institute. The standards are broad and apply to all professional services that a CPA may render, including tax advice and tax return preparation. For example,

1. Rule 102 requires CPAs to perform professional services with objectivity and integrity; they should avoid any conflict of interest. CPAs should neither knowingly misrepresent facts nor subordinate their judgment to that of others in rendering professional advice.

2. Rule 202 requires compliance with all standards that have been promulgated by certain bodies designated by the AICPA's governing council.

3. Rule 301 states that CPAs will not disclose confidential client data without the specific consent of the client, except under certain specified conditions.

The eight Statements on Responsibilities in Tax Practice (SRTP) provide guidance on what constitutes appropriate standards of tax practice. The statements are intended to supplement, not replace, the Code of Professional Conduct. Because they specifically address the problems inherent in tax practice, each statement is briefly described here. The full text of the SRTP is reproduced in Appendix D.

SRTP No. 1: *Tax Return Positions.* CPAs should not recommend that a position be taken on a return unless they believe that, if the position is challenged, it is likely to be sustained, which is known as the *realistic possibility standard.* CPAs should not prepare a return or sign as preparer of a return if they know that the return takes a position that could not be recommended because it does not meet the realistic possibility standard. However, a CPA may recommend any return position that is not frivolous, so long as the position is adequately disclosed on the return. SRTP Interpretation No. 1-1 (reproduced in Appendix D) contains the AICPA interpretation of the realistic possibility standard.

SRTP No. 2: *Answers to Questions on Returns.* A CPA should make a reasonable effort to obtain from the client and provide appropriate answers to all questions on a tax return before signing as preparer. Where reasonable grounds exist for omission of an answer, no explanation for the omission is required, and the CPA may sign the return unless the omission would cause the return to be considered incomplete.

SRTP No. 3: *Procedural Aspects of Preparing Returns.* A CPA may in good faith rely upon, without verification, information furnished by the client or third parties. Reasonable inquiries should be made if the information furnished appears to be incorrect, incomplete, or inconsistent. The CPA should make use of previous years' returns whenever possible in order to avoid omissions. In addition, the CPA may appropriately use information from the tax return of another client if the information would not violate the confidentiality of the CPA-client relationship and is relevant to and necessary for proper preparation of the return.

SRTP No. 4: *Use of Estimates.* A CPA may prepare returns using estimates provided by the taxpayer if it is impracticable to obtain exact data and the estimates are reasonable, given the facts and circumstances.

SRTP No. 5: *Departure from Previous Position.* If a CPA follows the standards in SRTP No. 1, the result of an administrative proceeding or court decision with respect to a prior return of the taxpayer does not bind the CPA as to how the item should be treated in a subsequent year's return.

SRTP No. 6: *Knowledge of Error: Return Preparation.* A CPA who becomes aware of an error in a previous year's return—or of the client's failure to file a required return—should promptly inform the client and recommend measures to be taken to correct the error. The CPA may not inform the IRS of the error except when required to do so by law. If the client does not correct the error, the CPA should consider whether to continue the professional relationship and must take reasonable steps to ensure that the error is not repeated if the relationship is continued.

SRTP No. 7: *Knowledge of Error: Administrative Proceedings.* When a CPA becomes aware of an error in a return that is the subject of an administrative proceeding, the CPA should promptly inform the client of the error and recommend measures to be taken. The CPA should request the client's consent to disclose the error to the IRS but should not disclose the error without consent unless required to do so by law. If the client refuses disclosure, the CPA should consider whether to withdraw from representing the client in the administrative proceeding and whether to continue a professional relationship with the client.

SRTP No. 8: *Form and Content of Advice to Clients.* A CPA should use judgment to ensure that advice given to a client reflects professional competence and appropriately serves the client's needs. For all tax advice given to a client, the CPA should adhere to the standards of SRTP No. 1, pertaining to tax return positions. A CPA may choose to notify a client when subsequent developments affect advice previously given on significant tax matters but is under no strict obligation to do so.

▲ SUMMARY

Taxes are a fact of everyday life. Taxes are levied on income, products, property holdings, and transfers of wealth. The federal income tax is the largest revenue producer of all the taxes currently in use in the United States. Therefore, a solid understanding of the basic rules of the income tax system is essential to maximize your after-tax income.

The term *tax* has been defined, and concepts have been examined that will help you reach your own conclusions about whether a tax is "good" or "bad." Keep these evaluations in mind as you continue through the text and as you read articles on proposed tax legislation.

The income tax law is a complex body of constantly changing information that is issued by legislative, administrative, and judicial sources. When evaluating a particular tax rule, it may be necessary to consult resources in all three areas.

Tax terms used in income tax computation have been defined in this chapter. Subsequent chapters explain the terms and build on the basic information. When you encounter a new term in later chapters, do not hesitate to refer to this chapter to see how the new term fits into the computational framework.

The study of federal income taxation will help you evaluate how business and personal financial decisions influence the amount of income tax you will have to pay. Awareness of basic income tax concepts will help you recognize opportunities to minimize compliance costs, save taxes, avoid IRS penalties, and make more informed business decisions.

The practical approach to tax planning discussed in this chapter does not require you to be a tax specialist to become an effective tax planner. In later chapters, you will be asked to solve tax-planning problems that require you to make decisions about when an item of income or deduction should be reported. When solving these problems, you will need to consider the effects of changes in the marginal tax rate and the time value of money.

Finally, always be aware of the difference between tax evasion and tax avoidance. Avoid tax evasion—it is illegal. Tax avoidance is legal and is expected of taxpayers.

▲ KEY TERMS

ad valorem tax (p. 15)	deductions for adjusted gross income (p. 26)	equality (p. 5)
adjusted gross income (AGI) (p. 26)	deductions from adjusted gross income (p. 27)	estate tax (p. 16)
annual loss (p. 21)	deferral (p. 20)	exclusion (p. 20)
average tax rate (p. 8)	dependency exemption (p. 29)	exemption (p. 21)
certainty (p. 6)	economy (p. 7)	expense (p. 21)
convenience (p. 6)	effective tax rate (p. 8)	gain (p. 20)
deduction (p. 21)		gift tax (p. 16)
		gross income (p. 20)

horizontal equity (p. 5)
Internal Revenue Code of 1986
    (p. 18)
itemized deduction (p. 27)
loss (p. 21)
marginal tax rate (p. 8)
ordinary income (p. 20)
pay-as-you-go concept (p. 7)
personal exemption (p. 29)
personal property (p. 15)
progressive rate structure (p. 10)

proportional rate structure
    (p. 8)
real property (p. 15)
regressive rate structure (p. 9)
self-assessment (p. 7)
self-employment tax (p. 12)
Social Security taxes (p. 12)
standard deduction (p. 27)
statute of limitations (p. 24)
taxable income (p. 7)
tax avoidance (p. 35)

tax base (p. 7)
tax credit (p. 24)
tax evasion (p. 34)
transaction loss (p. 21)
Treasury regulations (p. 18)
unified donative-transfers credit
    (p. 17)
vertical equity (p. 5)
voluntary compliance (p. 7)

▲ PRIMARY TAX LAW SOURCES

[1] Rev. Rul. 77-29.

[2] Sec. 6072—Specifies the general rules for due dates of tax returns.

[3] Sec. 1—Imposes a tax on the taxable income of different classes of individual taxpayers; provides tax rates by class of taxpayer and requires adjustment of rate schedules each year for inflation; limits the tax rate on net long-term capital gains to 28%.

[4] Sec. 3402—Requires employers to withhold estimates of taxes on wages and salaries paid to employees.

[5] Sec. 31—Provides that amounts withheld as tax from salaries and wages are allowed as credits against that year's tax liability.

[6] Sec. 6654—Provides that all individuals must pay estimated taxes when their tax liability is expected to be greater than $500; imposes a penalty for not paying the proper amount of estimated tax.

[7] Sec. 3101—Imposes the Social Security tax on employees; provides rates of tax to be paid.

[8] Sec. 1402—Defines *self-employment income* and provides for the tax to be paid on base amounts as specified in the Social Security Act for each tax year.

[9] Sec. 3111—Imposes the Social Security tax on employers for wages paid to employees.

[10] Sec. 1401—Provides the tax rates for self-employment taxes.

[11] Sec. 2501—Imposes a gift tax on transfers of property by gift.

[12] Sec. 2503—Allows exclusion from gift tax of gifts up to $10,000.

[13] Sec. 2505—Allows unified credit against taxable gifts.

[14] Sec. 2001—Imposes a tax on the assets of an estate. Provides tax rates on estate assets and for unlimited marital exclusion.

[15] Sec. 2010—Provides for unified tax credit against tax liability of an estate.

[16] Sec. 7801—Directs the secretary of the Treasury to issue the regulations necessary to implement and interpret the tax law.

[17] Sec. 61—Provides the general definition of *gross income* as all income from whatever source derived.

[18] Sec. 64—Defines *ordinary income* as income that does not result from the sale or exchange of property that is not a capital asset or an asset described in Sec. 1231.

[19] Sec. 1001—Prescribes the calculation of gains and losses for dispositions of property; defines *amount realized* for purposes of determining gain or loss for dispositions.

[20] Sec. 162—Allows the deduction of all ordinary and necessary expenses incurred in a trade or business of the taxpayer.

[21] Sec. 212—Allows the deduction of all ordinary and necessary expenses incurred in a production-of-income activity of the taxpayer.

[22] Sec. 11—Imposes an income tax on corporations and provides the applicable tax rate schedules.

[23] Sec. 62—Defines *adjusted gross income* for individual taxpayers and specifies the deductions allowed as deductions for adjusted gross income.

[24] Sec. 1211—Sets forth the limit on deductions of capital losses of corporations and individuals.

[25] Sec. 63—Defines *taxable income*. Allows individual taxpayers to deduct the greater of their allowable itemized deductions or the standard deduction. Standard deduction amounts are specified and are required to be adjusted annually for inflation.

[26] Sec. 211—Generally allows specific personal expenditures as itemized deductions of individuals.

[27] Sec. 213—Allows the deduction of medical expenses as an itemized deduction for individual taxpayers; defines *medical expenses* and prescribes limitations on the amount of the deduction.

[28] Sec. 164—Specifies the allowable deductions for taxes.

[29] Sec. 163—Specifies the allowable deductions for interest.

[30] Sec. 170—Allows the deduction of contributions to qualified charitable organizations.

[31] Sec. 165—Specifies the allowable deductions for losses.

[32] Sec. 67—Limits the allowable deduction for miscellaneous itemized deductions to the excess of 2% of adjusted gross income.

[33] Sec. 151—Allows an exemption deduction for the taxpayer, the taxpayer's spouse, and for each qualifying dependent.

[34] Helvering v. Gregory, 69 F.2d 809 at 810 (2d Cir. 1934).

▲ DISCUSSION QUESTIONS

1. Briefly state Adam Smith's four requirements for a good tax system.

2. Based on the discussion in the chapter, evaluate how well each of these taxes meets Adam Smith's four requirements:
   a. Income tax
   b. Employment taxes

3. Based solely on the definitions in the chapter, is the Social Security tax a proportional, regressive, or progressive tax? Explain, and state how the tax might be viewed differently.

4. Based solely on the definitions in the chapter, is the sales tax a proportional, regressive, or progressive tax? Explain, and state how the tax might be viewed differently.

5. As stated in the text, the federal income tax is the largest revenue-producing tax currently in use in the United States. Why do you think that the income tax produces more revenue than any other tax?

6. How are federal, state, and local income taxes collected by the government? Consider the cases of an employee and a self-employed taxpayer.

7. How is a sales tax different from an excise tax?

8. Who is responsible for collecting sales and excise taxes? Who actually pays the tax?

9. Why is a tax on real property used more often than a tax on personal property?

10. The gift tax is supposed to tax the transfer of wealth from one taxpayer to another. However, the payment of gift tax on a transfer of property is relatively rare. Why is gift tax not paid on most gifts?

11. The estate tax is a tax on the value of property transferred at death. Why is payment of the estate tax not a common event?

12. What is the basis for valuing assets transferred by gift and at death?

13. Who is responsible for reporting and paying gift taxes? estate taxes?

14. Identify three primary sources of tax law.

15. Explain why the following statement is not necessarily true: "If the IRS disagrees, I'll take my case all the way to the Supreme Court."

16. What is the federal income tax base?

17. What is an exclusion?

18. How is a deferral different from an exclusion?

19. How is gross income different from income?

20. What are the three basic tests that an expense must satisfy in order to be deductible?

21. What is the difference between an expense and a loss?

22. How is a transaction loss different from an annual loss?

23. How does the legislative grace concept help identify amounts that qualify for deduction?

24. What is the purpose of the exemption deduction?

25. Based on the example in Exhibit 1–2, explain how inflation can have two effects that result in a hidden tax.

26. Explain the pay-as-you-go system.

27. What is a tax credit?

28. How is a tax credit different from a tax deduction?

29. If you were in the 31% marginal tax bracket and you could choose either a $1,000 tax credit or a $2,500 tax deduction, which would give you the most tax saving? Why?

30. What is the statute of limitations, and what role does it play in the filing of tax returns?

31. How is the calculation of taxable income for an individual different from the calculation of a corporation's taxable income?

32. How do deductions for adjusted gross and deductions from adjusted gross income of an individual differ?

33. What is the purpose of the standard deduction for individuals?

34. Randy is studying finance at State University. To complete the finance major, he has to take a basic income tax course. Because Randy does not intend to be a tax expert, he considers the course a waste of his time. Explain to Randy how he can benefit from the tax course.

35. Since graduating from college, Mabel has used the firm of R&P to prepare her tax returns. Each January, Mabel receives a summary information sheet, which she fills out and sends to R&P along with the appropriate documentation. Because she has always received a refund, Mabel feels that R&P is giving her good tax advice. Explain why Mabel may not be getting good tax advice from R&P.

36. Evaluate the following statement: "The goal of good tax planning is to pay the minimum amount of tax."

37. It has often been said that only the rich can benefit from professional tax planning. Based on the information presented in this chapter, why is this statement at least partially true?

▲ PROBLEMS

38. State whether each of the following payments is a tax. Explain your answers.
    a. A $5 fee paid to the city to license the family pet.
    b. The Department of Motor Vehicles charges $295 for a current auto license tag for your car. The fee is made up of two parts: a $15 basic fee for all registered autos and a fee ($280) determined by the current value of the auto.
    c. Postage of $3.75 to mail a package to San Jose.
    d. The city put in sewer lines and assessed each property owner $6,000 for his or her share of the cost.
    e. Bella withdrew $12,000 from her individual retirement account (IRA). In addition to paying the regular income tax on the withdrawal, she had to pay an additional 10% ($1,200) early distribution penalty to the IRS. The penalty is imposed to discourage withdrawal of funds before retirement.

39. Explain why each of the following payments does or does not meet the IRS's definition of a tax:
    a. Jack is a licensed beautician. He pays the state $45 each year to renew his license to practice as a beautician.
    b. Polly Corporation pays state income taxes of $40,000 on its $500,000 of taxable income.
    c. Winona pays $15 annually for a safety inspection of her automobile that is required by the state.
    d. The Judd Partnership owns land that is valued by the county assessor at $30,000. Based on this valuation, the partnership pays county property taxes of $800.
    e. Andrea failed to file her income tax return on time. She filed the return late, and the IRS assessed her $25 for the late filing and $5 for interest on the tax due from the due date of the return until the filing date.

40. Susan is single with a gross income of $72,000 and a taxable income of $48,000. In calculating taxable income, she properly excluded $2,000 of tax-exempt interest income. Using the tax rate schedules in the chapter, calculate Susan's
    a. Total tax   c. Average tax rate
    b. Marginal tax rate   d. Effective tax rate

41. A taxpayer has $58,000 of taxable income for the current year. Determine the total tax, the marginal tax rate, and the average tax rate if the taxpayer is a
    a. Single individual
    b. Married couple
    c. Corporation

42. Paul earns $33,000 per year as a maintenance man. Latesia is a marketing executive with a salary of $190,000. With respect to the Social Security tax, what are Paul's and Latesia's
    a. Total taxes?   c. Average tax rates?
    b. Marginal tax rates?   d. Effective tax rates?

43. For each of the following, state whether the tax rate structure is progressive, proportional, or regressive:
    a. Ripley County imposes a 3% sales tax on all retail sales made within the county.
    b. Vigo County imposes a county income tax using the following tax rate schedule:

Taxable Income	Tax Rate
-0- to $5,000	No tax
$5,001 to $25,000	6%
$25,001 and above	8%

    c. Rhonda's total income is $75,000 per year. She spends $50,000 on living expenses and saves the rest. Lou uses his total income of $15,000 to support his family and saves no part of his earnings. Lou considers the 3% sales tax charged in Ripley County unfair.

44. The country of Boodang is the leading producer of sausage. Boodang imposes three different taxes on its citizens and companies. The taxes are designed to encourage production of sausage and discourage its consumption. Each tax applies as follows:
    - Income tax—Rates apply to each taxpayer's total income:

$-0-$50,000	5% of total income
$50,000–$200,000	$2,500 + 10% of income in excess of $50,000
$200,000–$500,000	$17,500 + 20% of income in excess of $200,000
$500,000 or more	40% of all income

    In calculating total income, sausage workers are allowed to deduct 25% of their salary. Companies that produce sausage are allowed to deduct 50% of their sales. No other deductions are allowed.
    - Sausage tax—All sausage purchases are subject to a 100% of purchase price tax. Citizens who consume less than 10 pounds of sausage per year are given a 50% rebate of the sausage tax they paid.
    - Property tax—Taxes are based on the distance of a taxpayer's residence from state-owned sausage shops per the following schedule:

0–2 miles	$15,000 per mile
2 miles–5 miles	$ 5,000 per mile
5 miles or more	$ 2,000 per mile

    Given the definitions in the chapter, are Boodang's taxes progressive, proportional, or regressive? Evaluate and discuss each tax and the aspect(s) of the tax that you considered in making your evaluation.

45. Joe Bob is an employee of Rollo Corporation, and he receives a salary of $7,000 per month. How much Social Security tax will be withheld from Joe Bob's salary in
    a. March?
    b. November?

46. Return to the facts of problem 45. Assume that each month Joe Bob has $2,000 in federal income tax and $800 in state income tax withheld from his salary. What is Joe Bob's take home pay in
    a. March?
    b. November?

47. Pedantic Corporation has 3 employees. During the current year, Larry earned $42,000, Harry earned $60,000, and Moe earned $150,000. How much Social Security tax will Pedantic have to pay on the salaries earned by Larry, Harry, and Moe?

48. Eric is a self-employed financial consultant. During the current year, Eric's self-employment income was $63,000. What is Eric's self-employment tax?

49. Darrell is an employee of Whitney's. During the current year, Darrell's salary is $70,000. Whitney's self-employment income is also $70,000. Calculate and compare the Social Security and self-employment taxes paid by Darrell and Whitney.

50. Classify the following items as ordinary income, a gain, or an exclusion:
    a. An employee's salary
    b. Interest on Kansas City bonds
    c. Interest on AMOCO bonds
    d. Sale for $6,000 of Pactel stock that cost $5,000
    e. Rental income from an office building

51. Explain why each of the following expenditures is or is not deductible.
    a. Alfredo, Inc., pays $300,000 in salaries to employees. The $300,000 is deductible.
    b. Winona sells furniture at a garage sale for $200. She paid $800 for the furniture. The $600 loss is not deductible.
    c. Rangoon Corporation sells office equipment for $2,300. The tax cost of the equipment was $3,200. Rangoon can deduct the $900 loss on the sale of the equipment.
    d. Inga owns an apartment complex. During the current year, the apartments are painted at a cost of $4,000. Inga can deduct the $4,000 painting cost.
    e. Mark paints his personal residence at a cost of $600. The painting cost is not deductible.

52. Based on the following information, what are the taxable income and tax liability for a single individual?

Total income	$88,000
Excludable income	800
Deductions for adjusted gross income	2,200
Deductions from adjusted gross income	5,000

53. Based on the facts in problem 52, calculate the taxable income and the tax liability for a married couple.

54. Reba's 1995 income tax calculation is as follows:

Gross income	$120,000
Deductions for adjusted gross income	(3,000)
Adjusted gross income	$117,000
Deductions from adjusted gross income:	
Standard deduction	(3,900)
(Total itemized deductions are $2,000)	
Personal exemption	(2,500)
Taxable income	$110,600

Before filing her return, Reba finds an $8,000 deduction that she omitted from these calculations. Although the item is clearly deductible, she is unsure whether she should deduct it for or from adjusted gross income. Reba doesn't think that it matters where she deducts the item, because her taxable income will decrease by $8,000 regardless of how the item is deducted. Is Reba correct? Calculate her taxable income both ways, and explain why the placement of the deduction does or does not make a difference.

55. Ruby has an opportunity to earn a $5,000 bonus. She can receive the bonus in either 1995 or 1996. When she receives the bonus, she intends to invest it in a certificate of deposit (CD). What additional information does she need in order to decide whether to take the bonus in 1995 or 1996?

56. Art is in the 28% marginal tax bracket for 1995. He owes a $10,000 bill for business expenses. Because he reports taxable income on a cash basis, he can deduct the $10,000 in either 1995 or 1996, depending on when he makes the payment. He can pay the bill at any time before January 31, 1996, without incurring the normal 8% interest charge. If he expects to be in a 31% marginal tax bracket for 1996, should he pay the bill and claim the deduction in 1995 or 1996?

57. Elki would like to invest $100,000 in tax-exempt securities. He now has the money invested in a certificate of deposit that pays 5.75% annually. What rate of interest would the tax-exempt security have to pay to result in a greater return on Elki's investment than the certificate of deposit? Work the problem, assuming that Elki's marginal tax rate is 15%, 28%, 31%, and 39.6%.

58. Talisa and Curan are married and have 3 dependent children. They estimate their 1995 taxable income will be $148,000. They would like to lower their overall tax liability on the income. Talisa owns $30,000 face value of 10% taxable bonds. Curan thinks that they can save some taxes either by transferring ownership of the bonds to their children

or by selling the bonds and reinvesting in tax-exempt bonds. Which of the following strategies provides the highest after-tax return?

a. The ownership of the bonds is legally transferred to their children. Each child will receive $10,000 face value of the bonds.

b. The bonds are selling for $62,000. Talisa purchased them for $58,000. If they sell the bonds, they will reinvest the proceeds in tax-exempt municipal bonds yielding 4%.

59. For each of the following situations, state whether the taxpayer's action is tax evasion or tax avoidance:

a. Tom knows that farm rent received in cash or farm produce is income subject to tax. To avoid showing a cash receipt on his records, he rented 50 acres for his choice of 5 steers to be raised by the tenant. He used 2 of the steers for food for his family and gave 3 to relatives. Because he did not sell the livestock, he did not report taxable income.

b. Betty applied for and received a Social Security number for Kate, her pet cat. Surprised by how easy it was to get a Social Security number, she decided to claim a dependent exemption on her tax return for Kate. Other than being a cat, Kate met all the tests for a dependent.

c. Glen has put money in savings accounts in 50 different banks. Glen knows a bank is not required to report to the IRS interest it pays him that totals less than $10. Because the banks do not report the payments to the IRS, Glen does not show the interest he received as taxable income. Although Glen's accountant has told him all interest he receives is taxable, Glen insists that the IRS will never know the difference.

d. Bob and Sue entered a contract to sell their home at a $25,000 gain in 1994. To avoid reporting the gain in 1994, they closed the sale and delivered possession of the home to the buyers on January 2, 1995.

e. Asha's taxable income for 1995 puts her in the 31% marginal tax bracket. Asha has decided to purchase new equipment for her business some time during 1996. A special election allows Asha to treat $17,500 of the cost of the equipment as a current period expense. Because she expects to be in a lower tax bracket next year, Asha buys and begins using $17,500-worth of the equipment during December 1995. She claims a $17,500 expense deduction under the special election for 1995.

60. In each of the following situations, explain why the taxpayer's action is or is not tax evasion:

 a. Jamal owns an electrical appliance repair service. When a client pays him in cash, he gives the cash to his daughter Tasha. Jamal does not report the cash he gave to Tasha in his business income. Tasha has no other income, and the amount of cash that she receives from Jamal is small enough that she is not required to file a tax return.

 b. Roberta and Dudley are married. Roberta usually prepares their tax return. However, in 1994 she is in the hospital and is unable to prepare the return, so Dudley does it. In preparing their 1995 return, Roberta notices that Dudley included $2,000 of tax-exempt municipal bond interest in their 1994 gross income. To correct this mistake, Roberta takes a $2,000 deduction on the 1995 return.

 c. In 1995, Hearthome Corporation receives notice that the IRS is auditing the corporation's 1993 return. In preparing for the audit, Hearthome's controller, Monique, finds a mistake in the total for the 1993 depreciation schedule that resulted in a $5,000 overstatement of depreciation expense.

 d. In the process of preparing his 1995 return, Will becomes unsure of the treatment of a deduction item. He researches the issue and can find no concrete tax law authority pertaining to the particular item. Will calls his buddy Dan, an accounting professor, for advice. Dan tells Will that if the law is unclear, he should treat the deduction in the most advantageous manner. Accordingly, Will deducts the full amount of the item, rather than capitalizing and amortizing it over 5 years.

 e. Sonja is a freelance book editor. Most companies for which she works pay her by check. In working out the terms of a job for a new client, the client agrees to pay her by giving her a new computer valued at $3,600. In preparing her tax return, Sonja notes that the client failed to report to the IRS the value of the computer as income for Sonja. Aware that her chances of getting caught are small, Sonja does not include the $3,600 value of the computer in her gross income.

▲ DISCUSSION CASE 1–1

A value-added tax has been the subject of much debate in recent years as a tax to use to help reduce the deficit. Various forms of value-added taxes are used throughout Europe, Canada, and in many other countries. To acquaint yourself with the basic operation of a value-added tax, read the following article:

Peter Chin and Joel G. Siegel, "What the Value Added Tax Is All About," *TAXES—The Tax Magazine*, January 1989, pp. 3–13.

After reading the article consider the following circumstances:

Joe is married and has 2 children. Joe, a brain surgeon, earns about $300,000 annually from his medical practice and averages about $250,000 in investment income. Jane, Joe's wife, spends most of her time doing volunteer work for charitable organizations. Tom is also married and has 5 children. Tom earns $20,000 per year working as a maintenance man for Joe.

While Joe was working late one night, he and Tom had a serious disagreement about two new tax bills recently introduced to help reduce the deficit. The first bill would levy a 10% value-added tax on all goods and services. A second bill introduced at the same time would add an additional 10% tax to each of the five current tax rate brackets (i.e., 15% would become 25%, 28% would become 38%, 31% would become 41%, 36% would become 46%, and 39.6% would become 49.6%.

Joe is concerned that the imposition of a value-added tax would mean that fewer people could afford medical treatment. Both his patients and his practice would suffer from the tax. Tom strongly disagrees with Joe. He thinks that Joe does not want to pay his fair share of taxes. Tom charges that Joe can afford to hire tax accountants to help him avoid paying higher income taxes, even with the higher tax rates. By enacting a value-added tax, Tom believes that high-income taxpayers like Joe will have to pay up. He thinks it is the only fair way to raise taxes to bring down the deficit.

After several hours of arguing, neither could convince the other that he was wrong. Joe finally ended the discussion by saying that he would get an independent person knowledgeable in tax law to decide who is right.

REQUIRED: You work for the firm that prepares Joe's tax return and advises him on managing his finances. The tax partner of your firm asks you to prepare a memorandum discussing the merits and the deficiencies of the two proposals as they apply to Joe and Tom. In your memorandum, you are directed to specifically consider the following and provide a response:

a. What is a value-added tax, and how does it work?

b. Evaluate the rate structures of the two proposed taxes. Are they proportional, progressive, or regressive?

c. What, if anything, is wrong with Tom's and/or Joe's point of view? Be sure to explain this part in depth.

Norman and Vanessa are married and have 2 dependent children. This is a summary of their 1994 tax return:

▲ **DISCUSSION CASE 1–2**

Adjusted gross income	$53,850
Deductions from adjusted gross income:	
Standard deduction	(6,350)
Exemptions ($2,450 × 4)	(9,800)
Taxable income	$37,700
Tax liability	$ 5,655

a. Assuming that Norman and Vanessa's 1995 adjusted gross income will increase at the 2.63% rate of inflation and that the standard deduction and exemption amounts do not change, calculate their 1995 taxable income. Calculate the tax liability on this income using the 1994 tax rate schedules (Appendix A).

b. Calculate Norman and Vanessa's projected 1995 taxable income and tax liability, assuming that their adjusted gross income will increase by 2.63% and that all other inflation adjustments are made. Compare these calculations with those in part a, and explain how the inflation adjustments preserve Norman and Vanessa's after-tax income.

Bonnie is married and has 1 child. She owns Bonnie's Rib Joint, which produces a taxable income of approximately $120,000 per year.

▲ **TAX PLANNING CASE 1–3**

a. Assume that Bonnie's taxable income is $40,000 without considering the income from the rib joint. How much tax will she pay on the $120,000 of income from the rib joint?

b. What actions might Bonnie take to lower her overall taxes on the $120,000? Present two alternatives and the calculations that show the tax savings from each alternative.

Return to the facts of problem 59. Assume that you are the CPA in charge of preparing the tax return for each of the taxpayers in the problem. Based on the Statements on Responsibilities in Tax Practice (Appendix D), explain what you should do in each case. Your discussion should indicate which, if any, of the eight statements is applicable and your obligations with regard to each applicable statement. If the facts are not sufficient to determine whether a statement applies to a situation, discuss the circumstances in which the statement would apply.

▲ **ETHICS DISCUSSION CASE 1–4**

Income Tax Concepts

▲ CHAPTER LEARNING OBJECTIVES

■ Discuss the operation of the U.S. income tax as a system and how concepts, constructs, and doctrines provide overall guidance in the tax treatment of items that affect taxable income.

■ Identify the general concepts that underlie the tax system and explain how the concepts affect taxation.

■ Explain the effect of accounting concepts, how such concepts provide guidance in determining when an item of income should be included in gross income, and when an expense item is deductible.

■ Describe income concepts and explain how they aid in determining which items constitute gross income for tax purposes.

■ Discuss deduction concepts and how such concepts affect what may be deducted for income tax purposes.

The federal income tax is based on a system of rules and regulations that determine the treatment of various items of income and expense. The key point to be made is that federal income taxation is based on a *system*. As such, it shares the characteristics of any type of system. We are all familiar with systems; our society is organized by systems of rules. Some systems are natural and afford us little leeway in abiding by them. For example, gravity is part of the environmental system in which we live and a force that cannot be overcome without great difficulty. Because of our knowledge of and experience with the concept of gravity, we have learned that we must be aware of its effects on our behavior. For example, because of the effect of gravity you cannot walk off a cliff without suffering grave consequences.

Most of the legal and social systems we deal with every day are artificial. That is, people make rules and prescribe actions to enforce them. In these systems, detailed rules are developed for general concepts. For example, all states have testing requirements that must be met in order to get a driver's license. A person who moves from one state to another generally has no problem passing the test in the new state, because the general concepts involved in driving an automobile do not change from location to location.

Artificial systems are distinguished from natural systems by exceptions to the general rules of the system. These exceptions are necessary in order to meet specific needs. Returning to our driving example, we know that most states permit you to make a right turn at a red light after making a complete stop (i.e., the general rule). However, traffic experts have determined that some intersections are so hazardous that the general rule cannot be followed. The result is an exception to the law—we cannot make a right turn on red after a complete stop at some intersections. How do we identify those instances in which we may not make a right turn on red? Simple—the rules provide that an appropriately labeled sign be posted to alert us to the exception.

As with all artificial systems, the federal income tax system has been developed around general concepts that guide us in its application to various types of transactions. There are, of course, exceptions that do not follow from the application of the general concepts. These exceptions generally stem from the desire to use the tax system to promote some social, economic, or political goal. For example, the income tax law provides an exclusion from income for employer-provided health insurance policies. This payment of the employee's expenses by the employer could be taxed. However, in order to encourage employers to provide health-care coverage for their employees (a social goal), Congress has excluded such payments from the employee's income. Another example of an exception involves losses on the sale of stocks. Net loss deductions on the sale of stocks by individuals are limited to $3,000 per year. However, to encourage investment in small companies (an economic goal), a special provision in the tax law allows the deduction of up to $50,000 in losses from an investment in the stock of a new company. The only effective way to learn the exceptions in the tax law is through experience and study. That is, there are no explicit "no right turn on red" signs in the tax law. The major exceptions to the general concepts of taxation are presented in this book, but the focus is on developing the ability to determine the treatment of transactions by applying the general concepts of taxation.

This chapter groups income tax concepts by their major function(s) within the income tax system. The four major groupings for discussion purposes are *general concepts*, *accounting concepts*, *income concepts*, and *deduction concepts*. Throughout the remaining chapters, the text constantly refers to these concepts to help explain

▲ INTRODUCTION

the tax treatments being presented. You must understand these concepts, so we suggest that you return to this chapter and review the applicable concepts before you begin reading a new chapter. To help you, each chapter begins with a summary of the concepts applicable to the chapter's material.

Before beginning the discussion of the concepts, it is necessary to introduce a bit of terminology used throughout the remainder of the book. A **concept** is a broad principle that provides guidance on the income tax treatment of transactions. Because a specific concept covers many transactions, concepts are broad. A **construct** is a mechanism that has been developed to implement a concept. A **doctrine** is a construct that has been developed by the courts. Thus, constructs and doctrines are the interpretive devices necessary to apply a concept. When this book refers to a concept, the text includes all its related constructs and doctrines. An example of a concept is the annual accounting period concept; it requires all income tax entities to report their results on an annual basis. In order to properly identify the income of each annual period, each entity must select an accounting method. In this example, *annual accounting period* is the concept, and *accounting method* is the construct necessary to implement the concept. Thus, when we talk about the annual accounting period concept, the construct accounting method is implicitly a part of the concept.

This chapter introduces and discusses the fundamental concepts of income taxation. The discussion of each concept includes the fundamental constructs and doctrines necessary to begin the study of income taxation.

▲ GENERAL CONCEPTS

General concepts provide guidance on the overall operation and implementation of the income tax system. As such, these concepts apply to almost every aspect of the system, be it an accounting issue, an income issue, or a deduction issue.

Ability-to-Pay Concept

A fundamental concept underlying the income tax structure is the **ability-to-pay concept.** This concept states that the tax levied on a taxpayer should be based on the amount that the taxpayer can afford to pay. The first result of this concept is that the income tax base is a *net* income number (i.e., income minus deductions and losses) rather than a gross figure such as total income received. Therefore, the tax base recognizes different deduction levels incurred by taxpayers as well as different levels of income.

> ▲ **EXAMPLE 1**   Jerry and Jody each have a total income of $65,000. Jerry's allowable deductions are $20,000, and Jody's allowable deductions are $35,000.
>
> *Discussion:*   Although Jerry and Jody have identical total incomes, Jerry's allowable deductions are $15,000 less than Jody's. Thus, Jerry has a greater ability to pay taxes than does Jody. Allowing deductions in the income tax base recognizes taxpayers' varying abilities to pay.

The example of Jerry and Jody illustrates that the notions of *income* and *deduction* are fundamental constructs that are used to implement one aspect of the ability-to-pay concept. Losses and tax credits also reduce the amount of tax due and are related to a taxpayer's ability to pay tax. These constructs were defined and discussed in Chapter 1, and we will not elaborate further at this juncture. However, we would note that the study of income taxation is essentially the study of what comprises these constructs. It is important to remember that these constructs are really the basic elements of the system.

A second aspect of the ability-to-pay concept is the use of a progressive tax rate structure. Recall that a progressive tax is one in which higher levels of the tax base are subjected to increasingly higher tax rates. Individuals with large taxable incomes pay a higher marginal tax rate than do individuals with small taxable incomes. Thus, both the tax base—taxable income—and the tax rate applied to the base are determined by the taxpayer's ability to pay tax. It should be noted that the ability-to-pay concept is undermined by provisions that exclude certain types of income from the tax base. That is, to the extent that a taxpayer has income that is not subject to tax because of an allowable exclusion, the taxpayer is being taxed at less than her or his ability to pay.

▲ **EXAMPLE 2**   Dewitt and Gloria are a retired couple with a taxable income of $32,000. The primary source of their taxable income is Gloria's pension and taxable dividends and interest. In addition, Dewitt and Gloria own municipal bonds that pay annual interest of $14,000 that is not included in their taxable income. What is the effect of the exclusion of the bond interest on the ability-to-pay concept?

Discussion: Because the $14,000 in interest income from the bonds is available to pay Dewitt and Gloria's taxes, the exclusion of the interest from the tax base allows them to pay less tax than they could afford to pay. This effect is somewhat mitigated by the lower interest rates found on tax-exempt bonds versus taxable bonds. That is, by investing in municipal bonds, Dewitt and Gloria have accepted a lower interest rate than they could have obtained by investing in taxable bonds. Thus, they have paid some implicit tax (although nothing goes to the federal government) on the bonds by accepting the lower tax-exempt bond rate.

Administrative Convenience Concept

Throughout the discussion of the income tax a particular item often is not treated consistently with the basic concept applicable to the situation. Many of these treatments result from the **administrative convenience concept.** This concept states that items may be omitted from the tax base whenever the cost of implementing a concept exceeds the benefit of using it. The cost is generally the time and effort for taxpayers to accumulate the information necessary to implement the concept as well as the cost to the government of ensuring compliance with the concept. The benefit received from implementation is generally the amount of tax that would be collected. Thus, many items that meet the definition of *income* are not taxed, because the costs of collecting the information necessary to ensure compliance are greater than the tax produced by the income.

▲ **EXAMPLE 3**   Bravo Co. provides a break room for its employees. Free coffee is provided to the employees in the break room at a cost to Bravo of 10 cents per cup. Leroy is an employee of Bravo Co. who drinks 3 cups of coffee in the break room on an average day. Is Leroy taxed on the free coffee he receives from Bravo Co.?

Discussion: Under general concepts of income recognition (discussed later in this chapter and in depth in Chapter 3), Leroy is in receipt of income when he drinks the free coffee provided by his employer. This is, in effect, a form of compensation Bravo provides to its employees. However, the cost of each employee's tracking his or her consumption of coffee, as well as the cost of the government's ensuring that all employees include the cost of their free coffee in their income, exceeds the additional tax that would be collected. Thus, under the administrative convenience concept, Leroy is not taxed on the free coffee.

Another aspect of this concept relates to deductions for individuals. The tax law allows individuals to take deductions for certain personal expenditures (e.g., medical expenses, charitable contributions). However, many individuals incur only small amounts of these allowable personal deductions. In these situations, the tax law allows a taxpayer to take a standard deduction in lieu of accumulating the information necessary to deduct the actual allowable deductions. This treatment saves taxpayers' time in accumulating and reporting deduction information and the government's time in ensuring the accuracy of the information reported (i.e., the standard deduction does not need to be audited).

▲ **EXAMPLE 4**   Tara believes that she probably does not have a significant amount of allowable personal deductions in 1995. Even if she searches her records, she figures it's unlikely she can document more than $3,900, the 1995 standard deduction for a single taxpayer.

Discussion: Tara may elect to deduct the $3,900 standard deduction. This relieves her of having to document her small amount of allowable personal deductions, and the government incurs no costs to ensure that her deductions are correct. When taxpayers' allowable personal deductions are close to the amount of their allowable standard deduction, it is more convenient for them to deduct the allowable standard deduction than spend a lot of time trying to document deductions that may provide very little tax savings.

Arm's-Length Transaction Concept

In seeking to pay the minimum amount of tax, taxpayers often structure transactions that may not reflect economic reality. In many such cases, the transaction is not given any tax effect, because the transaction is deemed not to conform with the **arm's-length transaction concept.** An arm's-length transaction is one in which all parties to the transaction have bargained in good faith and for their individual benefit, not for the benefit of the transaction group. Transactions that are not made at arm's length are generally not given any tax effect or are not given the intended tax effect.

▲ **EXAMPLE 5**   Bo is the sole shareholder of Shoe Co. Bo owns a shoe-stretching machine for which he paid $15,000 and that is worth $18,000. Bo sells the machine to Shoe Co. for $5,000. Can Bo deduct the loss on the sale of the machine to Shoe Co.?

Discussion: Because Bo was, in effect, negotiating with himself when he sold the machine to Shoe Co., the transaction was not made at arm's length, and Bo will not be allowed to deduct the loss on the sale. NOTE: Bo can deal at arm's length with Shoe Co. However, the tax law assumes that related parties (defined subsequently) do not transact at arm's length. One effect of this assumption is that losses on sales to related parties are always disallowed, even if the transaction is made at arm's length and the price reflects fair market value.

As example 5 shows, transactions that are not made at arm's length generally involve an element of self-dealing. The tax law has formally incorporated the notion of self-dealing through a set of **related party provisions.**[1] Some of the more common related party relationships (depicted in Figure 2–1) are

1. Individuals and their families. Family members include a spouse, brothers, sisters, lineal descendants (children, grandchildren), and ancestors (parents, grandparents).

2. Individuals and a corporation if the individual owns more than 50 percent of the stock of the corporation.

3. A corporation and a partnership if the same person owns more than 50 percent of both the corporation and the partnership.

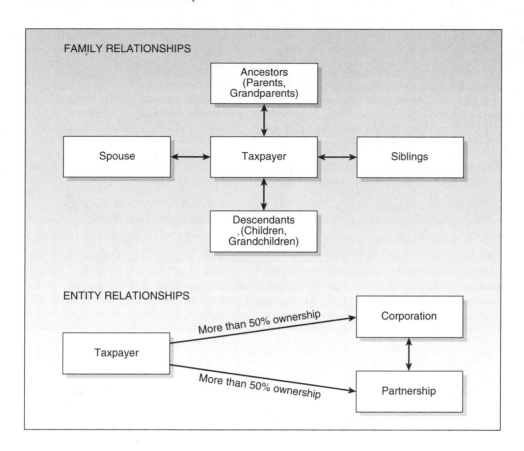

Note that all these relationships have the potential for self-dealing, either because of family relationships or a substantial ownership interest in an entity. The more-than-50-percent test for corporations and partnerships is based on the level of ownership necessary to control the actions of these entities. In example 5, Bo and Shoe Co. are related parties, because Bo owns more than 50 percent of Shoe Co. and effectively controls Shoe Co.'s actions. Thus, when Bo deals with Shoe Company, he really deals with himself. In trying to circumvent the related party rules, individuals might attempt to reduce their direct ownership in a corporation or a partnership by distributing ownership among family members, other corporations, or partnerships that they control. This effort is stymied by the **constructive ownership rules,** which state the relationships within which an individual is deemed to indirectly own an interest actually owned by another person or entity. These rules can be complex and are beyond the scope of this text.

Pay-as-You-Go Concept

The U.S. income tax system is one in which voluntary compliance is essential to the operation of the system. Most taxpayers comply with the requirement that they file a return each year and pay the tax due on their taxable income. However, the payment of the entire tax bill at the end of the year could be unduly burdensome for those taxpayers who do not have the foresight to save money for the payment of the tax or who do not have the ability to adequately estimate the amount of the tax they owe. To alleviate situations in which taxpayers are faced with a huge tax bill at the end of the year, the pay-as-you-go concept requires taxpayers to pay tax as they generate income. This concept is implemented through withholding and estimated tax payment requirements. The withholding provisions require employers to withhold amounts from each employee's paycheck to pay the tax on the income in that check. The withheld amounts are remitted to the government, and taxpayers receive credit on their tax returns for the tax paid through withholding. This minimizes the probability of the taxpayer's facing a huge tax bill at the end of the year. Note that the taxpayer might pay too much tax through this process. In such cases, the government simply refunds the excess tax that has been paid.

> ▲ **EXAMPLE 6**   Giovanna is a machinist who works for Adilia Co. During the current year, Giovanna earned $32,500 and had $3,450 federal income tax withheld from her paycheck. In filing her return, Giovanna's actual tax was determined to be $3,675. How much tax must Giovanna pay when she files her return for the current year?
>
> *Discussion:*   Although Giovanna's actual tax is $3,675, she has already paid in $3,450 through withholding. Therefore, she has to pay only $225 ($3,675 − $3,450) when she files her current year's return. NOTE: The withholding provisions ease for Giovanna the burden of having to come up with the full $3,675 when she files her tax return. By having Giovanna pay as she goes (her employer withholds tax payments), the tax system encourages voluntary compliance; it spreads the burden of taxes over the period of time during which the income is being earned.

Although salaries paid by employers constitute a large percentage of the income taxed in the United States, it is by no means the only source of income for individual taxpayers. That is, taxpayers often earn income independent of any employee-employer relationship. Many people are their own bosses (i.e., self-employed), others earn income from investments such as savings accounts, dividends from stock, and sales of assets, and retired individuals collect pensions, Social Security benefits, and income from investments. To ensure that such taxpayers have the means to pay the tax due on these various sources of income, all individual taxpayers are required to make quarterly estimated tax payments—to meet the estimated tax payment requirements—when their estimated tax due for the year is at least $500.[2] Corporations also must file quarterly estimated tax payments. Thus, taxpayers who have significant amounts of income that are not subject to withholding by employers are also required to adhere to the pay-as-you-go concept. Failure to make the required estimated tax payments will result in a penalty for underpayment of estimated taxes.

▲ ACCOUNTING CONCEPTS

Accounting concepts guide the proper accounting for and recording of transactions that affect the tax liability of taxpayers. In order to determine the treatment of a transaction, we must first identify the appropriate taxpaying unit. Next, we must ascertain the rationale that controls its tax treatment in order to record it. Finally, the transaction must be reported in the correct tax period. These ideas appear to be rather simplistic and part of basic bookkeeping. That is partly true. However, without these basic accounting concepts, the tax system could not function in an orderly and efficient manner. Perhaps even more important, without these concepts taxpayers could manipulate their affairs so as to avoid paying taxes for many years.

Entity Concept

The most basic accounting concept is the entity concept. According to the **entity concept,** each tax unit must keep separate records and report the results of its operations separate and apart from other tax units. The tax law requires that all tax units be classified as one of two basic entity types: taxable and conduit. The characteristics and unique features of each of the taxable and conduit entities are discussed in detail in Chapters 8 and 9.

Taxable entities are those that are liable for the payment of tax. That is, taxable entities must pay a tax based on their taxable income. The four entities responsible for the payment of income tax are individuals; regular, or C corporations; estates; and some trusts.

Conduit entities are nontaxable reporting entities. A conduit entity is one in which the tax attributes (income, deductions, losses, credits) of the entity flow through the entity to the owner(s) of the entity for tax purposes. The entities record transactions undertaken by the entity and report the results to the government. However, these entities pay no tax on the results of their operations. Rather, the tax characteristics (i.e., the income, deductions, losses, tax credits, etc.) of the operating results are passed through the conduit entity and are taxed to its owners. NOTE: All conduit entities are owned by one or more taxable entities. Two types of conduit entities authorized by the tax law are partnerships and subchapter S corporations.[3,4] Hereafter, any reference to a corporation means a taxable C corporation. Conduit corporations are referred to as *S corporations*.

Trusts are a mixture of taxable and conduit entities. A trust is an arrangement in which a trustee manages assets for the benefit of another, referred to as the *beneficiary*. The trust reports the results of its operations to the government (a conduit characteristic). Any income distributed by the trust to the beneficiary is taxable to the beneficiary. However, the trust must pay income tax on any income that is earned but not distributed to the beneficiary (a taxable entity characteristic). Thus, trusts are both taxable and conduit entities in that they are taxed on income that is retained and are not taxed on income that is distributed. The calculation of the taxable income of a trust is discussed in Chapter 9.

To illustrate the relationship between the two basic types of entities, consider a 100-percent owner of a corporation. The corporation is recognized as an entity separate from its owner for purposes of recording transactions. That is, the owner cannot commingle personal transactions with those of the corporation for tax purposes. All income, deductions, losses, and credits attributable to the operation of the business are identified and recorded on the books of the corporation. The summarized results of these transactions are then reported on the corporation's tax return, and a tax is paid on the corporate taxable income. The owner of the corporation only includes as income on an individual tax return any salary or dividends she or he receives from the corporation. However, a different result is obtained if the corporation is organized as an S corporation. As a conduit entity, the S corporation still identifies and records on its books only those items that are attributable to the operation of the corporation. The summarized results of the transactions are reported to the government, but the S corporation pays no tax on its income. Rather, the income of the S corporation is reported on the tax return of the owner, along with the owner's other items of income and deductions, and a tax is paid based on the owner's taxable income.

▲ **EXAMPLE 7**   Martina and Fran each own 50% of the stock of Card Corporation. During the current year, Card Corporation had a taxable income of $80,000 and paid a total of $20,000 in dividends. What are the tax effects of Card Corporation's income and dividend distributions?

Discussion: As a separate and distinct taxable entity, Card Corporation must pay the tax on its $80,000 in taxable income. Martina and Fran each must include the $10,000 in dividends she received from Card Corporation in her calculation of taxable income. Note that the dividends are being taxed twice—once when included as income by the corporation and again when distributed to the shareholders.

▲ **EXAMPLE 8**   Assume the same facts as in example 7, except that Card Corporation is an S corporation. What are the tax effects of Card Corporation's income and dividend distributions?

Discussion: An S corporation is a conduit entity. Therefore, the $80,000 in taxable income flows through to the owners and is included on their tax returns. Card Corporation pays no income tax. Martina and Fran each must include $40,000 in income on her individual tax return. Because the $80,000 is being taxed to the owners, the dividends paid are not taxed again to the owners. Rather, the dividends are considered a repayment of their investment that reduces the amount invested in the stock of the corporation.

The distinction between entities becomes blurred when a business is owned as a sole proprietorship. Although not technically a conduit entity, the sole proprietorship does not pay tax on its income. The books of the sole proprietorship are kept separate and distinct from the personal transactions of the owner. However, the income tax attributes of the business are reported on the owner's return, in much the same manner as a conduit entity.

▲ **EXAMPLE 9**   Karina is a machinist for Silver Marine Co. At nights and on weekends, Karina repairs washing machines and dryers. During the current year, Karina's income from her repair business was $10,000, and she incurred $3,500 in expenses to produce this income. She also earned a salary of $30,000 from Silver Marine Co. and had $400 in interest income from a savings account. How should Karina treat these items on her tax return?

Discussion: Karina's repair business is a sole proprietorship, which is similar to a conduit entity. In accounting for the repair business, she must keep the results of the repair business separate from her other taxable transactions. The business income of $10,000 and business expenses of $3,500 result in an income of $6,500 from the repair business. The $6,500 in business income is then added to her salary and interest income on her individual return, and Karina pays tax on the sum of all her income.

The result for our sole proprietor appears to be much ado about nothing. However, two important aspects of this entity treatment prevent income manipulation. First, by not allowing the commingling of business and personal transactions, owners cannot turn nondeductible personal items into deductible business expenses. The classic example of this separation is interest expense. As we shall see in Chapter 5, all interest paid on debt incurred in a trade or business (i.e., the sole proprietorship) is fully deductible, whereas interest paid on debt used for personal purposes (other than qualified home mortgage interest) is not deductible. The entity concept requires the owner to identify these two types of interest for each entity and deduct them according to the rules for each entity. Without such a split, business owners would effectively be allowed to deduct all their interest, and basic wage earners would get no deduction for interest on their personal debts. This treatment would result in an inequity most taxpayers would not tolerate.

▲ **EXAMPLE 10**   In example 9, assume that Karina owns a van that she uses on repair calls. Karina also drives the van to work at Silver Marine and for various other personal purposes such as trips to the store, taking the kids to school, and so on. How should Karina account for the van and its operating costs?

Discussion: For tax purposes, the van is viewed as two distinct assets. One asset is used in her repair business, whereas the other asset is used as a personal vehicle. Karina must keep records that adequately document the use of the van in her repair business. She can deduct the costs incurred in using the van in her repair business. The costs incurred for her personal use of the van are not deductible. This separation of business and personal use is required by the entity concept.

The second major aspect of the reporting of a conduit entity's income on the return of the owner of the entity is that conduit entities are not useful in income-shifting strategies. This results from the progressive nature of the federal income tax. Recall that in a progressive tax rate structure, the higher your taxable income is, the greater your marginal tax rate becomes. If each conduit entity paid tax on its separate income, taxpayers would be able to arrange their affairs into a multitude of conduit entities, all of which are taxed at the lowest marginal income tax rate. Under such circumstances, the income tax would effectively become a flat tax at the lowest tax rate instead of the progressive rate desired. By passing the income through to the owners of the conduit entity, income shifting by using such entities is not an effective tax-planning strategy. As an aside, it should be noted that the tax laws' requirement that taxable entities aggregate results from all their income-producing activities also contains a positive element. That is, if the conduit entity posts a loss from its operations, the taxable entity or entities that own the conduit are generally allowed to use this loss to offset income from other sources.

▲ **EXAMPLE 11**   Assume the same facts as in example 9, except that Karina's repair income was $8,000 and her expenses for producing this income were $11,000. How should Karina treat this on her tax return?

Discussion: The loss from the repair business flows through to Karina's individual return. The $3,000 loss is deductible on Karina's individual tax return, reducing the tax she would have paid on her other income.

Assignment-of-Income Doctrine.

Assignment-of-Income Doctrine.   One corollary of the entity concept is the judicially developed **assignment-of-income doctrine**.[5] According to this doctrine, all income earned from services provided by an entity are to be taxed to that entity, and income from property is to be taxed to the entity that owns the property. Merely directing payment of income (i.e., assigning income) that has been earned by one entity to another, although legal, does not relieve the owner of the income from paying tax. Thus, it is not possible to avoid the payment of tax on wages earned by simply having them paid to someone else. Although you may legally assign the right to receive income to another, the income tax is imposed on the person who earns the income.

▲ **EXAMPLE 12**   Sharon owns a landscaping business. Sharon has a two-year-old son, Jeffrey. To provide funds for Jeffrey's college education, Sharon has every tenth customer make her or his check payable to Jeffrey. Sharon deposits the checks in a savings account in Jeffrey's name. Is Sharon taxed on the amounts paid to Jeffrey?

Discussion: Under the assignment-of-income doctrine, Sharon cannot escape taxation on the income from her labor by directing the payments to Jeffrey. Sharon is taxed on all income earned by the landscaping business, regardless of who receives payment for the services.

Similarly, the owner of a building cannot escape taxation on the income from the building by having the rents paid to another entity. The only legal way for the building owner to pass the taxability of the income to the other entity is to legally transfer ownership of the building to that entity.

▲ **EXAMPLE 13**   Andrea owns a house that she rents out to college students attending State University. Her grandson Andy is a college student who goes to school at State University. To help Andy with his college expenses, Andrea has her tenants pay the rent to Andy. Is Andrea taxed on the rental income?

Discussion: Because Andrea is the owner of the rental property, she is taxed on all rents, whether she or Andy receives the payments. Under the assignment-of-income doctrine, the owner of property is taxed on the income of the property, regardless of who actually receives the income.

Discussion: In order for Andrea to avoid payment of tax on the rental income, she would have to make a valid gift of the house to Andy. This would make Andy the owner of the property and thus taxable on the rental income. Andy would pay no income tax on the receipt of the gift property. Andrea may or may not have to pay a gift tax on such a transfer.

Annual Accounting Period Concept

The second accounting concept is that of an annual accounting period. The **annual accounting period concept** states that all entities must report the results of their operations on an annual basis and that each taxable year is to stand on its own, apart from other tax years.[6] The most basic result of this concept is that all entities must choose an annual accounting period for reporting their results to the government. The two basic types of accounting periods are calendar years, which end on December 31, and fiscal years, which can end on the last day of any other month the taxpayer chooses. Although all entities are allowed to choose their accounting period, most individuals elect to be calendar-year taxpayers. This book assumes the taxpayer is using the calendar year unless otherwise noted. The election of a fiscal year carries some important restrictions, the most important of which are discussed in Chapter 14.

Accounting Method.   An important outgrowth of the annual accounting period requirement is that each taxpayer must select an **accounting method** to determine the year(s) in which taxable transactions are to be reported.[7] The two basic allowable methods are the **cash basis of accounting** and the **accrual basis of accounting.** Taxpayers using the cash basis are taxed on income as it is received and take deductions as they are paid. In contrast, accrual basis taxpayers report their income as it is earned and take deductions as they are incurred, without regard to the actual receipt or payment of cash. At this point, a simple example will illustrate the basic differences between the two methods of accounting.

▲ **EXAMPLE 14**   Steen, Inc., is in the carpet-cleaning business. In December 1995, Steen cleans Gary's business office and bills him $200. Gary pays Steen in January 1996.

Discussion: Assume that both Steen, Inc., and Gary are cash basis taxpayers. Although Steen earns the $200 during 1995, it is not taxed on the $200 until payment is received in 1996. Similarly, Gary takes the deduction for the carpet-cleaning expense in 1996 when he makes the payment.

▲ **EXAMPLE 15**   Assume that in example 14 both Steen, Inc., and Gary are accrual basis taxpayers.

Discussion: Steen must include the $200 in the year in which it was earned, 1995, and Gary takes his deduction in the year the carpet-cleaning expense is incurred, 1995.

Discussion: Assume that Steen, Inc., is on the cash basis and Gary is on the accrual basis of accounting. Steen does not include the $200 in income until it is received in 1996. Gary deducts the carpet-cleaning expense in the year incurred, 1995.

Note that the use of the cash method is a violation of generally accepted accounting principles (GAAP), which require books to be kept using the accrual method. The accrual method used for tax purposes is generally the same as that used in financial accounting under GAAP. However, various limitations and exceptions apply to the application of each method. The most important of these are discussed as they apply to income recognition in Chapter 3 and to deductions in Chapter 5. Some additional special accounting methods are covered in Chapter 14.

Tax Benefit Rule.   The requirement that each tax year stand on its own, apart from other tax years, leads to some problems when circumstances arise in which one transaction could affect more than one year. This has led to development of the **tax benefit rule.** Under this rule, any deduction taken in a prior year that is recovered in a subsequent year is reported as income in the year it is recovered, to the extent that a tax benefit is received from the deduction.[8] The tax benefit received means the amount by which taxable income was actually reduced by the deduction recovered. Consider the following examples:

▲ **EXAMPLE 16**   Rayson Corporation is an accrual basis taxpayer selling widgets for cash and on account. Late in 1993, Rayson sells $500-worth of widgets on account to Tom. In 1994, before any payment is made to Rayson, Tom is sentenced to 20 years in prison for embezzlement. How should the corporation account for this series of events?

Discussion: Because Rayson Corporation is on the accrual basis, it includes the $500 sale to Tom as income in the year of the sale, 1993. The tax law does not generally allow taxpayers to use the allowance method of accounting for bad debts, so Rayson must wait until it determines that Tom's debt is worthless to take a bad debt deduction. Going to jail for 20 years is enough evidence that Tom won't repay the debt, so Rayson should take a bad debt deduction of $500 in 1994. The recognition of the bad debt in 1994 stems from the requirement that the events of each tax year stand alone. Rayson Corporation does not go back to amend the income reported in 1993.

▲ **EXAMPLE 17**   While Tom is in prison, his aunt dies and leaves him a considerable inheritance. He had always felt badly about not paying Rayson Corporation for the widgets, so in 1995 he sends Rayson a check for the $500. How should Rayson account for the $500?

Discussion: Because Rayson Corporation took a deduction for Tom's bad debt in 1994, the tax benefit rule requires it to include the $500 in its 1995 income. Note again that there is no attempt to adjust the prior year's income. The events of each tax year stand apart from each other under the annual accounting period concept.

As these examples demonstrate, the tax benefit rule has its most common applications in situations in which an annual accounting period and an accounting method interact. It is necessary to put accrual basis and cash basis taxpayers in the same position after accounting for all years involved. In example 16, if Rayson Corporation had been a cash basis taxpayer, it would have recognized no income from the initial sale to Tom, because it never received payment. However, when Rayson received the $500 payment in 1995, it would have been included in income under the cash basis. Thus, over the three-year period, both a cash basis and an accrual basis taxpayer would have recognized income of $500 from the transactions in examples 16 and 17.

Substance-over-Form Doctrine. The accounting concepts, constructs, and doctrines presented to this point require that all transactions be traced to and recorded by the entity responsible for that transaction in accordance with the method of accounting selected by that entity. Occasionally, the basis for recording the transaction is not clear. That is, taxpayers attempting to avoid taxation sometimes carefully sculpt transactions that are unrealistic in the ordinary sense.

▲ **EXAMPLE 18**   Bill is the sole proprietor of Bill's Sub Shop. In order to lower his tax on the income from the sub shop, Bill ''employs'' his 3-year-old daughter as a janitor at a salary of $200 per week. Is Bill's employment of his daughter unrealistic?

Discussion: Because it is unlikely that a 3-year-old could perform such services, Bill's characterization of his daughter as an employee is unrealistic.

Although the courts have consistently held that taxpayers are under no legal obligation to pay more tax than the law prescribes (i.e., tax avoidance is a legal activity), the courts have also said that transactions must bear some semblance to reality. This judicially created concept is referred to as the **substance-over-form doctrine.** The doctrine states that the taxability of a transaction is determined by the reality of the transaction, rather than some (perhaps contrived) appearance.[9] This is generally interpreted to mean that a transaction is to be taken at its face value only when it has some business or economic purpose other than the avoidance of tax.

▲ **EXAMPLE 19**   In example 18, should Bill be allowed to deduct the salary paid to his daughter?

Discussion: Because the payment of the salary to the daughter is unrealistic under the circumstances, Bill would not be allowed a deduction for the salary paid to her. This arrangement lacks economic substance and is solely for the purpose of tax avoidance. Thus, the form of the arrangement (daughter as an employee) is ignored, and the tax treatment is based on the substance of the transaction (a gift to his daughter, which is not deductible).

When might substance over form apply? This is a difficult and subjective question that has no hard-and-fast answers that apply in every situation. However, a few factors should alert us to the possibility of this doctrine's being invoked by the IRS. The major element to look for is whether the transaction has economic substance. Most legitimate business transactions are made at arm's length between two parties, neither of which stand to benefit by mutual manipulation of the transaction. Consider the following examples:

▲ **EXAMPLE 20**   Selma is the president and chief executive officer of Megainternational Corporation. Megainternational is a large, publicly held corporation that operates in more than 50 countries around the world. During the current year, Selma receives a salary of $1,000,000 and a bonus of $2,000,000. The bonus is based on a percentage of Megainternational's profits. Can Megainternational deduct the $3,000,000 salary and bonus paid to Selma?

Discussion: Megainternational can deduct the entire $3,000,000 in salary and bonus paid to Selma. The salary-and-bonus contract was negotiated at arm's length between Selma and Megainternational. Because Megainternational is a publicly held corporation, Selma is not able to exert undue influence over her contract, and the salary and bonus paid to her would be typical of such a position.

▲ **EXAMPLE 21**   Eugene is the president and chief executive officer of Florence Dunes Co. Florence is a closely held corporation that is wholly owned by Eugene and his wife

Dahlia. Florence pays Eugene a salary of $300,000 during the current year and a bonus of $200,000. The bonus is paid even though Florence has only $250,000 in income. Although Florence has been in business for more than 10 years, it has never paid a dividend. Can Florence deduct the $500,000 in salary and bonus it pays to Eugene?

Discussion: Because Florence is wholly owned by Eugene and Dahlia, salary payments to the owners are subject to extra scrutiny. All deductions are subject to the requirement that they be reasonable under the facts and circumstances. In Eugene's case, the first question is whether the $300,000 salary is reasonable when compared with the salaries paid by other, comparable companies to executives who do not control the corporation. Any portion of the salary that is unreasonable is considered a dividend paid to the owner. Dividends are not deductible expenses of a corporation.

Eugene's bonus payment is suspicious under the circumstances. Because Florence has never paid a dividend, the payment of such a large bonus relative to the income of the corporation to a 100-percent owner appears to be more in the nature of a dividend distribution. Thus, although the *form* of the payment is a salary bonus, the *substance* of the payment is that of a dividend distribution under the facts presented. It is unlikely that the bonus can be deducted as a salary payment by Florence.

In many situations, the tax law itself specifies that certain transaction forms be treated according to their underlying substance. For example, in the area of alimony and child support, the tax law specifies that the amount of an alimony payment that varies according to some contingency related to a child is treated as a child support payment. This distinction is critical, because alimony is taxable to the receiver and deductible by the payer, whereas child support payments have no effect on the taxable income of either party.[10]

▲ **EXAMPLE 22**   Dick and Jane divorce in the current year. They have 2 children who are in Jane's custody throughout the year. The divorce decree specifies that Jane will receive $100 per month per child for child support and $2,000 per month as alimony. However, the alimony will be reduced by $600 per month per child when the child reaches age 18, marries, or if the child dies. How much of the $2,000 payment is alimony, and how much is child support?

Discussion: Because the alimony is reduced when an event related to the children occurs, the tax law treats the reduction in alimony related to the contingency as child support. That is, the agreed-upon alimony will ultimately be reduced by $1,200 per month, at which time Jane will receive only $800. The $800 is considered the true alimony payment to Jane, and the remaining $1,200 is child support for income tax purposes. From the $2,200 Jane receives each month, $1,400 [$1,200 + (2 × $100)] is child support, and $800 is alimony.

Income concepts determine what constitutes taxable income, explain why one type of income is taxed differently than other income, and establish the period in which income is to be reported.

▲ INCOME CONCEPTS

All-Inclusive Income Concept

The broadest income concept is the **all-inclusive income concept.** Under this concept, all income received is considered taxable unless some specific provision can be found in the tax law that excludes the item in question from taxation. Income can be received in any form: cash, property, services, and so on. Thus, the tax law always starts with the proposition that anything of value received is taxable.[11]

Many situations dealing with income recognition are covered in Chapter 3, so we are using only one example here to illustrate the pervasive nature of this concept.

> ▲ **EXAMPLE 23**   Felicia is a tax accountant with Oil Rich Co. Alice is a plumber. Both are cash basis taxpayers. Felicia had a problem with her plumbing that Alice fixed. The normal charge for this service would have been $300. However, Alice agreed to waive her fee in exchange for some tax advice from Felicia relating to her business. Do either Felicia or Alice have taxable income from this agreement?
>
> *Discussion:*   Both Felicia and Alice have income from rendering services, Alice from the plumbing repair and Felicia from the provision of tax advice. Although income was never reduced to cash by either party, both received something of value in exchange for their services. Alice should report the $300 as income when she receives the promised tax advice. Felicia should report $300 of income when Alice fixes her plumbing.

We noted earlier that certain items of income are not subject to tax. How do we know which items are taxable and which are not? As with all exceptions to the general concepts, only study and experience in working with the tax laws provide answers. Chapter 4 discusses some major income items that are excluded from taxation.

Legislative Grace Concept

Exclusions are based on the **legislative grace concept.** This concept states that any tax relief provided to taxpayers is the result of specific acts of Congress that must be applied and interpreted strictly. Note that relief from taxes on income received can take several forms. Income can be either permanently excluded from tax, or it may be deferred for taxation in a future period (resulting in a time value of money savings). *Legislative grace* means that only Congress can grant an exclusion from income, and the exclusion must be taken in its narrowest sense. An example illustrates these two related notions.

> ▲ **EXAMPLE 24**   Jorge received 200 shares of MNO Corporation common stock as a gift from his grandfather. At the date of the gift, the shares had a fair market value of $20,000. During the current year, Jorge received dividends totaling $2,000 on the stock. Recall that the tax law excludes the value of a gift from the gross income of the recipient. What are the tax effects for Jorge of the gift from his grandfather?
>
> *Discussion:*   The receipt of the stock as a gift from the grandfather is specifically excluded from Jorge's income by the tax law. However, the exclusion applies only to the value of the gift received and does not exclude from tax any subsequent income Jorge receives on the gift property.[12] Therefore, Jorge will be taxed on the $2,000 in dividends received on the stock.

One other form of tax relief that Congress has provided is special treatment for certain types of income. Most income received and allowable losses incurred by taxpayers are simply added to (deducted from, in the case of losses) the income tax return of the taxpayer and taxed according to the taxpayer's marginal tax rate. In tax jargon, this is referred to as *ordinary income (loss).* Congress has created a special class of income treatment for gains and losses arising from the sale of capital assets. A **capital asset** is generally defined as any asset that is *not* a receivable, inventory, real or depreciable property used in a trade or business, and certain intangible assets, such as copyrights.[13] Thus, capital assets primarily consist of stocks, bonds, and other investment-related assets. In addition, all personal use assets (home, furniture, clothing, automobile, etc.) of individual taxpayers are capital assets.

The gains and losses from the sale of capital assets, known as **capital gains** and **capital losses,** must be separated from other gains and losses and aggregated through a prescribed netting procedure before they enter into the taxpayer's income calculation. Net long-term capital gains are currently given preferential treatment through a cap on the tax rate that must be paid on this type of income. Currently, the maximum tax rate paid on net long-term capital gains is 28 percent, versus the top marginal tax rate of 39.6 percent for individual taxpayers. If the netting procedure results in a net capital loss for the year, only $3,000 of the net capital loss can be deducted from an individual's tax return per year.[14] Chapter 3 provides an overview of capital gains, and Chapter 12 covers capital gains and losses in more detail. For now, just remember that capital gains and losses are treated differently than all other types of income and losses.

Capital Recovery Concept

Once it has been determined that an item of taxable income has been received, the next logical step is to determine the amount of the income that belongs in the calculation of taxable income. In most cases, this is straightforward. However, sales of investment and/or business assets require more guidance. The **capital recovery concept** states that no income is taxed until all capital previously invested in the asset is recovered.[15] That is, on any asset purchased, all investment in that asset must be recorded in order to determine the amount of profit (or loss) made upon disposition of the asset. The amount invested in an asset is referred to as its **basis.**[16]

> ▲ **EXAMPLE 25**   Earl purchased 100 shares of ABC Co.'s common stock at a total cost of $1,000. When he sold the stock, 1 lot of 50 shares was sold for $600 and the other 50 shares were sold for $300. What are the tax effects of these sales?
>
> *Discussion:*   Because there are 2 separate sales of the stock at different prices, each sale must be considered separately. Each 50-share lot has a basis of $500 (half the $1,000 purchase price). The lot sold for $600 results in a $100 ($600 − $500) taxable gain. That is, Earl has recovered $100 more than he had invested in the 50 shares.
>
> The 50 shares sold for $300 result in a loss of $200 ($300 − $500). Note that a loss is nothing more than invested capital that has not been recovered. Because of the capital recovery concept, we recognize gains only when the recovery from the disposition of an asset is greater than the amount invested in the asset. A loss results when all the capital invested in an asset is not recovered upon its disposition.

Realization Concept

A crucial question regarding income items is when to recognize the income (i.e., in which accounting period it should be taxed). In this regard, the taxpayer's accounting method resolves many of the problems. However, some general concepts provide additional guidance. The most basic recognition concept is the **realization concept.** This concept states that no income is recognized for tax purposes (i.e., is included in taxable income) until it has been realized by the taxpayer. In most cases, realization occurs when an arm's-length transaction takes place: Goods are sold, services are rendered, and so on. Mere changes in value without the advent of a realization event—in which the taxpayer receives the change in value—do not result in a taxable recognition.[17]

▲ **EXAMPLE 26**   Assume that in example 25 Earl purchases the 100 shares of ABC common stock on July 2, 1995. On December 31, 1995, the 100 shares have a fair market value of $1,200. The first lot of 50 shares is sold on February 5, 1996. As of December 31, 1996, the remaining 50 shares have a fair market value of $400. What is Earl's recognized income from the stock in 1995? in 1996?

Discussion: Although the shares gain $200 in value as of December 31, 1995, Earl still holds the shares and has not realized the increase in value. Therefore, the change in value does not result in a recognition of income in 1995. He realizes the $100 gain from the sale of the first 50 shares in 1996 and reports it in that year. The loss in value of $100 as of December 31, 1996, has not been realized, so Earl cannot deduct this loss in value until he realizes it through sale.

Claim-of-Right Doctrine.

To aid in determining when a realization has occurred, the **claim-of-right doctrine** states that a realization occurs whenever an amount is received without restriction as to its disposition.[18] An item is received without restriction when the receiver has no definitive obligation to repay the amount received. Income received under a claim of right is reported in the year of receipt. If income is realized under a claim of right and a repayment of part or all of the receipt occurs in a later year, it is accounted for as a deduction in the year of repayment because of the annual accounting period concept. When a taxpayer receives amounts, but their use is restricted in some substantial manner, those amounts are not realized until the restriction is removed.

▲ **EXAMPLE 27**   Sadie, a landlord and a cash basis taxpayer, enters into a 1-year lease agreement with Bob, as tenant, on December 1, 1995. The lease agreement calls for a monthly rent of $500, with payment of first and last months' rents upon signing. In addition, Bob is required to pay a $100 cleaning deposit that is to be returned at the end of the lease if the property is returned in good condition. What are tax effects for Sadie of receiving the $1,100?

Discussion: The first and last months' rents are taxable when received. Sadie is on the cash basis and has an unrestricted right to the use of the rent payments. However, she must return the cleaning deposit at the end of the lease if Bob abides by its terms. Because of this restriction, Sadie does not have a claim of right to the cleaning deposit when she receives it, and it is not taxed at that time. If Sadie keeps all or a part of the deposit at the end of the lease, it is included in her income at that time.

▲ **EXAMPLE 28**   Assume that in example 27 Sadie sells the building in 1996 before the end of the lease term. Because of the sale, Sadie returns the last month's rent prepayment to Bob. How should Sadie account for the repayment of the last month's rent?

Discussion: Because Sadie had previously included the last month's rent in her 1995 income, she is allowed to deduct the repayment in 1996. NOTE: The mere possibility that a repayment might be required does not negate Sadie's unrestricted use of the rent prepayment when she received it.

Note that the claim-of-right doctrine applies when something of value has been received by the taxpayer. The question to be answered in such cases is whether the receipt has resulted in a realization of income. If the taxpayer has a clear obligation to repay the amount received, the taxpayer does *not* have a claim of right to the amount and is not taxable on the receipt. However, if there is no clear and definitive obligation to repay, the taxpayer is deemed to have received income.

▲ **EXAMPLE 29**   Herbert Corporation borrowed $10,000 from Local Bank to purchase a stamping machine. Herbert will repay the $10,000 by making monthly payments with interest at 14% over the next 6 years. Does Herbert Corporation have income from the receipt of the $10,000 it borrowed from Local Bank?

Discussion: Because Herbert Corporation is obligated to repay the $10,000 loan, it does not have a claim of right and is not required to recognize the $10,000 as income.

Constructive Receipt Doctrine.   Accrual basis taxpayers recognize income when it has been earned, whereas a cash basis taxpayer recognizes income when it is received. Whether a receipt has occurred is not critical for accrual basis taxpayers. However, a major question for cash basis taxpayers is when is income received? That is, is income received only when it has been physically received in the form of cash? The all-inclusive income concept tells us that income can be received in any form—cash, property, or services. Thus, it is not necessary for a cash basis taxpayer to reduce the income to cash to be in receipt of income. A more fundamental problem is what constitutes a receipt. Based on the **constructive receipt doctrine,** cash basis taxpayers are deemed to be in receipt of income when it is credited to their accounts or otherwise made unconditionally available to the taxpayers.[19] For example, interest income is taxed on the day it is credited to a savings account, regardless of when the taxpayer actually withdraws it. That is, the interest income is available for use by the taxpayer when it is credited to the account and is taxed at that time. Physical possession of the interest income is not required for it to be taxed. Note that this is not a problem for an accrual basis taxpayer—the interest income would be taxed in the period in which the income was earned, regardless of when the actual payment was received. Once income has been made unconditionally available, taxpayers cannot turn their back on the income and thus select the year for taxation.[20] To be considered unconditionally available, the taxpayer must be aware that the income is available for use.

▲ **EXAMPLE 30**   At the December 12, 1995, meeting of the board of directors of Gould Co., the board awards bonuses to all officers in the amount of 5% of their annual compensation. The bonuses are to be paid in December. Samantha, the controller of Gould Co., requests that her bonus not be paid until January 1996. In what year is Samantha taxed on the bonus?

Discussion: Because the board made the bonus unconditionally available to Samantha in December, she is in constructive receipt of the bonus in 1995 and is taxed as if she received the bonus in that year.

However, income is *not* constructively received if the taxpayer's control of its receipt is subject to substantial limitations or restrictions.

▲ **EXAMPLE 31**   Aardvark Corporation mails its annual dividend checks to shareholders on December 31, 1995. Alana receives her dividend check on January 4, 1996. In what year is the dividend taxable to Alana?

Discussion: Because Alana does not have any control over the dividend check and does not have unrestricted use of the check until she receives it on January 4, 1996, she is taxed on the dividend in 1996. Although she knows that the check is coming, it is not available for use as of December 31, 1995.

▲ **EXAMPLE 32**   Assume that Aardvark Corporation policy is to mail its annual dividend checks to shareholders so that the checks arrive on or before December 31 of each year. Alana has been a shareholder of Aardvark for 5 years. Alana's dividend check arrives in her mailbox on December 31, 1995. However, Alana is out of town to visit relatives for the holiday and does not return until January 4, 1996, at which time she deposits the check in her checking account. In what year is the dividend taxable to Alana?

Discussion: Because the dividend is made annually, Alana is aware that the check is coming. She is taxed on the dividend in 1995, because it is available to her on December 31 and she knew that the check was coming.

▲ **EXAMPLE 33**   Paul is selected the outstanding player in the Super Bowl on December 31, 1964. He is awarded a car worth $10,000, which he picks up 3 days later at the dealer that supplied the car. When is Paul taxed on the award?

Discussion: As long as Paul could not have picked up the car under any condition on December 31, it is not made unconditionally available to him until the first date on which he can pick it up. Therefore, he is taxed on the value of the car in 1965.[21]

These are just a few applications of the constructive receipt doctrine. More detail on different types of restrictions and conditions is covered in the discussion of income sources in Chapter 3. At this point, the important point to remember is that cash basis taxpayers do not have to actually receive cash to trigger income recognition; the only requirement is that the income be unconditionally within their control.

▲ **Figure 2–2**

CONSTRUCTIVE RECEIPT
AND CLAIM OF RIGHT

Comparing Claim of Right and Constructive Receipt.   One of the most difficult problems encountered by beginning tax students is determining when the claim-of-right and constructive receipt doctrines apply. Figure 2–2 presents a time

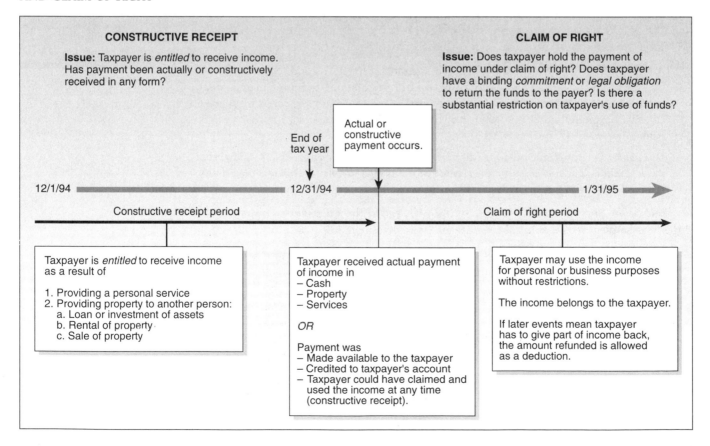

line that differentiates the two doctrines. In Figure 2–2, note that the constructive receipt doctrine applies when an item of income has not yet been physically received by the taxpayer. The question to be answered in determining whether the item is currently taxable is whether the taxpayer has the income within his or her control. This is in contrast to the claim-of-right doctrine where an amount has been received. The question in this case is whether the amount received is currently taxable.

Wherewithal-to-Pay Concept

The income tax system is philosophically based on the ability-to-pay concept. Features such as progressive tax rates and taxation based on the net income of a taxpayer are derived from the concept that the amount of tax paid should be in relationship to the ability of the taxpayer to pay the tax. Ability to pay the tax in the current tax year is also important for income-recognition purposes. To distinguish general ability-to-pay principles and income-recognition applications, we use the **wherewithal-to-pay concept.** This concept states that income should be recognized and a tax paid on the income when the taxpayer has the resources to pay the tax. Although this would generally require that the transaction in question provide cash to pay the tax, the receipt of other asset forms and relief from debts are considered forms of receipt with which tax can be paid.[22] NOTE: The concept applies equally to both cash and accrual basis taxpayers.

The wherewithal-to-pay concept provides the rationale for the deferral of recognition on several types of realized gains.

> ▲ **EXAMPLE 34**   Mike exchanged a computer with a basis of $600 that he used in his dental practice for a new computer. The new computer cost $3,000, but Mike was given a trade-in value of $1,000 for his old computer and had to pay only $2,000 out of pocket for the new computer. Has Mike realized a gain from the exchange? If so, is the gain available to pay tax?
>
> *Discussion:*   An exchange does constitute a realization. Mike has disposed of the computer in an arm's-length transaction and converted its value toward the purchase of the new computer. The substance of the transaction is a sale of the old computer for $1,000 and the purchase of the new computer for $3,000.
>
> Although Mike has realized a gain of $400 ($1,000 - $600) on the exchange, all the gain has been reinvested in the purchase of the new computer, and none of the $1,000 he received for his old computer is available to pay the tax on the $400 gain.

Mike's computer transaction is an example of a like-kind exchange. Because Mike exchanged business property that is of like kind (in this case, one computer for another computer), the tax law allows him to defer recognition of the gain until he disposes of the new computer in a transaction that gives him cash (or other assets) with which to pay the tax. Like-kind exchanges and other types of transactions in which gains are deferred under the wherewithal-to-pay concept are discussed in Chapter 13.

Another important application of this concept is the acceleration of income recognition by accrual basis taxpayers on advance receipts for goods and services. In general, accrual basis taxpayers recognize income in the tax year in which the income is earned, without regard to when cash payment is actually received. However, when an accrual basis taxpayer receives an advance payment for goods and services, the IRS takes the position that the taxpayer is in the best position to pay the tax in the period in which the cash is received rather than when it is earned.[23]

▲ **EXAMPLE 35**   Return to the facts of example 27. Assume that Sadie, the landlord, is an accrual basis taxpayer. She receives the first and last months' rent on the 1-year lease in December 1995. In which year(s) should the $1,000 first and last months' rent receipts be taxed?

Discussion: Under the accrual method of accounting used in financial accounting, Sadie is deemed to have earned only the December rent in 1995; the $500 advance receipt for the last month's rent is not recognized until it is earned in 1996.

Application of the wherewithal-to-pay concept would cause the entire $1,000 received in December to be taxed in 1995. That is, the $500 advance receipt for the last month's rent that will not be earned until next year is available for Sadie to use to pay her taxes and should be taxed at the time she receives it.

The income concepts discussed here apply to income-recognition problems. No attempt has been made to cover every situation in which these concepts might apply. Rather, throughout the remaining chapters these concepts serve as the basis for discussing the treatment of income items.

▲ DEDUCTION CONCEPTS

The federal income tax is based on the general proposition that taxpayers will pay tax according to their ability to pay. This results in the tax being assessed on the income net of the costs of producing that income. The tax law provides for this through the allowance of deductions (and losses) in computing a taxpayer's taxable income. The fundamental questions that need to be answered in regard to deductions are what types of expenditures are deductible, how much is deductible, and when the deduction can be taken. **Deduction concepts** provide the basis for resolving these issues.

Legislative Grace Concept

The most fundamental deduction concept is that of legislative grace. Applied to deductions, this concept means that deductions are allowed only as a result of a specific act of Congress and that any relief granted in the form of a deduction must be strictly interpreted. In contrast to the all-inclusive income approach to the recognition of income—where we assume that everything is taxable unless we can find a provision exempting an item from tax—deductions must be approached with the philosophy that nothing is deductible unless a provision in the tax law allows the deduction.

Business Purpose Concept

The allowance of deductions is governed by the **business purpose concept.**[24] This concept means that a deduction is allowed only for an expenditure that is made for some business or economic purpose that exceeds any tax avoidance motive. This concept has been interpreted to mean that the expenditure was made in connection with a profit-seeking activity.[25] Note that a transaction may be entered into for a profit and for the additional profit from the tax savings associated with the deductibility of the expenditures related to the transaction. Two general types of expense deductions in the tax law embody this profit motive requirement: expenses incurred in a trade or business and those related to the production of income (investment activity).[26,27] These two general types of expenses are commonly referred to as **trade or business expenses** and **investment expenses.**

A third category of expenses that is specifically disallowed (with a few specific exceptions) are those expenses that are personal in nature, known as **personal**

expenses.[28] As stated in Chapter 1, the tax law does allow individuals to deduct certain personal expenditures from adjusted gross income. The list of deductible personal expenses includes medical expenses, home mortgage interest, income and property taxes, personal casualty losses, and charitable contributions. Recall that these expenses are deductible only if they exceed the taxpayer's allowable standard deduction amount. In addition, many of the expenses are limited to a percentage in excess of the individual's adjusted gross income.

In order to determine the tax treatment of any expenditure, the motive behind the transaction must be determined. Based on the motive—profit or personal purposes—it is categorized in one of these general classes:

1. Trade or business expenses
2. Investment expenses
3. Personal expenses

Distinguishing a personal expenditure (category 3) from a profit-motivated activity (i.e., categories 1 and 2) is generally a fairly easy task.

▲ **EXAMPLE 36**   Peter paid $1,000 for a new couch for his home. Is this a personal expenditure?

Discussion: As long as the couch is not used in Peter's trade or business or is not held as an investment by Peter, its use is personal and no deduction would be allowed for the purchase of the couch.

▲ **EXAMPLE 37**   Peter purchased a couch for the reception area of his optometry practice. What is the proper treatment of the couch?

Discussion: Because providing a place for clients to sit while they wait is something that businesses normally do, the couch is properly classified as related to his trade or business of optometry. Peter can therefore take the deductions allowed for the couch.

A more difficult task is distinguishing a trade or business activity from an investment activity. This is covered in depth in Chapter 5, but consider the following examples:

▲ **EXAMPLE 38**   Roger owns Gould Trucking Co. The physical layout of the company includes an office building, a parking lot for his trucks, and a maintenance shop. During the current year, Roger purchased the house next door to his trucking company and rented it out to individuals unrelated to the trucking company. Is the house an investment activity or part of his trucking business?

Discussion: Because Roger purchased the house to produce rents, which is an investment activity unrelated to his trucking business, it is considered an investment activity. He must account for the house and any related expenses under the rules for investments, not as part of his trade or business of trucking.

▲ **EXAMPLE 39**   Assume that instead of renting the house out, Roger allows his drivers to stay in the house during rest periods between trucking runs. How should the house be treated?

Discussion: In this case, the use of the house is related to his trucking business. Therefore, the house is considered a trade or business asset and is accounted for under the rules for trade or business assets.

Once the general category to which an expenditure belongs has been determined, the tax law provides specific rules regarding deductibility for each category. For example, business expenses are generally limited only by the reasonableness (i.e., what a prudent businessperson would pay in the same circumstances) of their amount, whereas deductions for investment expenses of individuals are often subject to a limitation based on the income of that taxpayer. Losses incurred in a trade or business are fully deductible, but losses from the sale of personal use assets (automobile, furniture, clothing, personal residence, etc.) are generally not deductible. These are just a few general examples of the importance of distinguishing the activity in which an expenditure has been incurred. Chapters 5 through 7 discuss the specifics of differences in deductions and losses in the three classes of expenditures. For now, consider the following treatments of the sale of an automobile:

▲ **EXAMPLE 40**   Jill owns an automobile that has a basis of $8,000. She sells the automobile for $5,000. How much of the $3,000 loss can Jill deduct on her tax return?

Discussion: The deductibility of the loss depends on the use of the automobile. If Jill uses the automobile in a business, the loss would be fully deductible. However, if the use of the automobile was purely personal, no loss on the sale would be allowed.

▲ **EXAMPLE 41**   Assume that Jill sold the automobile for $9,000, resulting in a $1,000 gain. Is the gain taxable in all cases?

Discussion: Yes, the gain would be taxed even if it were used for purely personal purposes. Remember that the all-inclusive income concept requires that all income be taxed unless specifically excluded by the tax law. There is no exclusion in the tax law for income from the sale of personal use assets.

Although the tax law provides a general disallowance of deductions for personal expenditures of individuals, some specific deductions are allowed for personal expenditures. Based on the ability-to-pay concept, the tax law allows individuals to take personal and dependency exemption deductions. That is, each individual is allowed to deduct a predetermined amount for herself or himself and for each person who is dependent on that person for their living expenses. This deduction recognizes that a basic cost of living must be paid in order to live and that this money is not available for the payment of taxes.

Certain personal expenditures, referred to as *itemized deductions*, for medical care, charitable contributions, home mortgage interest, casualty losses, and other miscellaneous types of personal expenses are also allowed as deductions.[29] As with exemptions, these are items that Congress feels are necessary living expenditures that are not available for the payment of tax. In order to create some equity for taxpayers of different means and for administrative convenience, a minimum deduction for these types of expenditures (itemized deductions) is allowed to all individual taxpayers through the provision of a standard deduction.

▲ **EXAMPLE 42**   Mary and Tom are both single taxpayers. Mary makes a salary of $50,000 and Tom makes $20,000. Mary has total allowable itemized deductions of $8,000 for 1995. Tom's total allowable itemized deductions are $2,000. The standard deduction for a single taxpayer in 1995 is $3,900, and the personal exemption deduction amount is $2,500. Given these facts, what are Mary's and Tom's total allowable deductions for 1995?

Discussion: Each is entitled to the $2,500 personal exemption deduction. Because Mary's itemized deductions exceed the standard deduction, she is allowed to deduct her actual $8,000 in expenditures, for a total deduction of $10,500. Tom's itemized deductions are less than the minimum allowable standard deduction, so he is allowed to deduct the $3,900 standard deduction in lieu of his $2,000 in actual expenditures, for a total deduction of $6,400.

The allowance of a standard deduction is unique to individual taxpayers. Individuals, estates, and trusts are allowed to take exemption deductions. The constructs of exemptions and standard deduction amounts do not apply to other tax entities, which may take only those deductions that are based on the business purpose concept in connection with a profit-motivated activity.

Capital Recovery Concept

After establishing the category of an expenditure, the next question to be answered is how much of the expenditure can be deducted. In general, the amount of a deduction can never exceed its cost. This is derived from the capital recovery concept discussed earlier. Under this concept, no income is realized until the amount invested has been recovered. The amount of investment in an asset is referred to as the asset's *basis*. Thus, the amount invested in an item, its cost, is the maximum amount that can be deducted in determining taxable income.

▲ **EXAMPLE 43**   Wojo's Warblers, Inc., sells miniature porcelain birds. Wojo's purchased a shipment of the birds several months ago at a per-unit cost of $45. Wojo's recently sold the entire shipment for $65 per unit. It will cost $50 per unit to replace the birds sold. How much income does Wojo's, Inc., have from the sale of each bird?

Discussion: Although it will cost Wojo's $50 to replace each porcelain bird, its income calculation is based on the amount actually invested in each bird. Therefore, the per-bird profit is $20 ($65 − $45).

The year(s) in which expenditures may be deducted is generally determined by the taxpayer's accounting method. However, even cash basis taxpayers cannot deduct capital expenditures in total in the period in which they are paid.[30] The main characteristic of a **capital expenditure** is that its usefulness extends substantially beyond the end of the tax year in which the expenditure is made.[31] The classic example of a capital expenditure is the purchase of a long-lived asset such as a building.

▲ **EXAMPLE 44**   In 1995, Amy Corporation, a cash basis taxpayer, purchases a computer to use in its consulting business. Amy pays $15,000 for the computer, which it expects to be able to use in its business for at least 5 years. When can Amy Corporation deduct the $15,000 investment in the computer?

Discussion: Because the use of the computer extends beyond the end of 1995, Amy cannot deduct the entire $15,000 in 1995, even though it is on the cash basis. Amy Corporation must capitalize the $15,000 cost and deduct it over its tax life through depreciation deductions. Specific rules for depreciating property for tax purposes are covered in Chapter 11.

In example 44, the computer would have an original basis equal to its cost, $15,000. As depreciation deductions are taken on the computer, the investment is being recovered against current period income. Therefore, the basis must be reduced whenever part of the investment is recovered through a tax deduction. To understand why basis is reduced for recoveries, consider the following example:

▲ **EXAMPLE 45**   Amy Corporation took depreciation on its computer at $3,000 per year. At the end of 5 years, when total depreciation taken amounted to $15,000, it sold the computer for $5,000. What is Amy Corporation's gain (loss) on the sale of the computer?

Discussion: Amy Corporation's gain is $5,000. When the computer was sold, it had no capital investment remaining in the computer, because it had deducted the entire $15,000 cost against income during the 5 years it used the computer.

Note that if basis was not reduced for the depreciation deductions taken, Amy Corporation would have a loss of $10,000 ($5,000 − $15,000) on the sale. Allowing the corporation to deduct a $10,000 loss and $15,000 of depreciation would result in a total deduction of $25,000. This would be a violation of the capital recovery concept, which limits deductions to the amount invested in an asset.

Similarly, any additional capital expenditures pertaining to the computer would be added to the computer's basis for recovery over the remaining tax life. Because the amount of capital invested in a long-lived asset varies throughout its tax life because of these adjustments to basis, the investment in an asset is more appropriately referred to as its *adjusted basis*.[32] An asset's **adjusted basis** is the amount of unrecovered investment in the asset after considering increases and decreases in the original amount invested in the asset.[33]

For any given expenditure, a deduction for the expenditure can take place at three points in time:

- In the period paid or incurred
- Over the useful life of the expenditure
- Upon disposition of the asset created by the expenditure

When the benefit of expenditures does not extend beyond the end of the current tax year, the expenditures are deducted in the year in which they are incurred (accrual basis) or paid (cash basis). These are the normal, recurring expenditures commonly made to produce the income being generated. Examples of currently deductible expenditures include salaries, rental payments, supplies, bank charges, and utilities.

Expenditures that benefit more than the current tax year must be capitalized. If the asset created by the expenditure is depreciable in nature, its cost is recovered by depreciation deductions over its useful tax life.[34] Long-lived assets that do not depreciate are recovered through amortization over the useful life of the asset. In order to be depreciable or amortizable, the asset must have a determinable life or period of usefulness to which the cost can be attributed.

▲ **EXAMPLE 46**   Joe, a cash basis taxpayer, prepays the rent on his business building for 3 years on July 1, 1995. The monthly rental is $1,000, resulting in a $36,000 prepayment. How much rent can Joe deduct in 1995 through 1998?

Discussion: Although Joe uses the cash method of accounting, the rent prepayment benefits tax years 1995, 1996, 1997, and 1998 and must be capitalized and amortized according to the number of rental months in each year. In 1995, the building is rented for 6 months, resulting in a $6,000 deduction. In 1996 and 1997, Joe can deduct 12 months of rent, $12,000, with the remaining $6,000 deductible in 1998.

Assets such as land and common stock that do not have determinable lives are neither depreciable nor amortizable. Capital recovery on this type of asset does not take place until there is a disposition of the asset.

▲ **EXAMPLE 47**   The Stephanie Partnership purchases some land in 1992 for $20,000. The land is held until 1995, when it is sold for $30,000. What deductions can the partnership take on the land and when can it take them?

Discussion: Land is not a depreciable asset, because it has no determinable life, so no capital recovery deductions are allowed until the land is sold. In 1995, Stephanie recognizes a gain of $10,000 from the sale of the land. That is, the $20,000 basis is deducted from the $30,000 selling price.

It is possible for capital recovery to occur at more than one point in time for any given asset.

▲ **EXAMPLE 48**   Raul purchases a heavy-duty truck for use in his construction business in 1993 at a cost of $30,000. He uses the truck until 1995, when it is sold for $6,000. How much can Raul deduct in 1993, 1994, and 1995 for use of the truck, and what is his gain or loss on the sale of the truck?

Discussion: The heavy-duty truck is eligible for a special-election-to-expense (the Section 179 election to expense, discussed in Chapter 11) deduction of $17,500 in the year of purchase, 1993.[35] In addition, the remaining $12,500 of cost can be depreciated over 5 years for tax purposes. Under the rules for straight-line depreciation (discussed in Chapter 11), Raul is allowed a depreciation deduction of $1,250 in 1993, $2,500 in 1994, and $1,250 in 1995. This leaves him an adjusted basis of $7,500 at the date of the sale and a loss on the sale of $1,500:

Calculation of Adjusted Basis

Original basis	$ 30,000
Less: Amounts recovered (deducted) against income	
First year election to expense	(17,500)
Depreciation	
1993	(1,250)
1994	(2,500)
1995	(1,250)
Total recovered through deductions against income	$(22,500)
Adjusted basis at date of sale	$ 7,500

Calculation of Loss on Sale

Selling price	$ 6,000
Less: adjusted basis	(7,500)
Loss on sale	$ (1,500)

Discussion: In this example, Raul recovers his $30,000 investment in the truck as follows: (1) $17,500 in the year of purchase through the election to expense, (2) $5,000 in depreciation during the period he uses the truck, and (3) $7,500 recovered against the $6,000 selling price when the truck is sold.

These deduction concepts are applicable to all deduction situations. As with the other concepts presented, this chapter does not attempt to cover all applications of the deduction concepts. Throughout the remaining chapters, the discussion of deductions is presented with reference to the applicable deduction concepts.

▲ **SUMMARY**

The federal income tax is based on a system of rules and regulations. These rules and regulations are based on general concepts that can be used to determine the income tax treatment of most transactions. As with all systems devised by human beings, the federal income tax system contains exceptions to the treatments prescribed by the system's concepts. Throughout the remaining chapters, the treatment of various transactions is developed by reference to the applicable concepts. In order to deal with the federal income tax system effectively, knowledge of the

▲ Table 2–1

INCOME TAX CONCEPTS
WITH RELATED
CONSTRUCTS AND
DOCTRINES

General Concepts	Income Concepts	Accounting Concepts	Deduction Concepts
Ability to Pay Income, exclusions, deductions, losses, tax credits Progressive rate structure **Administrative Convenience** Standard deduction **Arm's-Length Transaction** Related party Constructive ownership **Pay as You Go** Withholding Estimated tax payments	**All-Inclusive Income** **Legislative Grace** Capital asset— Capital gains and losses **Capital Recovery** Basis **Realization** Claim of right Constructive receipt **Wherewithal to Pay**	**Entity** Taxable/Conduit Assignment of income **Annual Accounting Period** Accounting method Tax benefit rule Substance over form	**Legislative Grace** **Business Purpose** **Capital Recovery** Basis Capital expenditure

concepts on which it is based is essential. This chapter has presented the basic tax concepts and categorized them according to their use within the tax system: general, accounting, income, and deduction concepts. For reference purposes, each category is summarized in Table 2–1.

▲ KEY TERMS

ability-to-pay concept (p. 50)
accounting method (p. 58)
accrual basis of accounting (p. 58)
adjusted basis (p. 72)
administrative convenience concept (p. 51)
all-inclusive income concept (p. 61)
annual accounting period concept (p. 58)
arm's-length transaction concept (p. 52)
assignment-of-income doctrine (p. 57)
basis (p. 63)

business purpose concept (p. 68)
capital asset (p. 62)
capital expenditure (p. 71)
capital gain (p. 63)
capital loss (p. 63)
capital recovery concept (p. 63)
cash basis of accounting (p. 58)
claim-of-right doctrine (p. 64)
concept (p. 50)
conduit entity (p. 55)
construct (p. 50)
constructive ownership rules (p. 53)
constructive receipt doctrine (p. 65)

deduction concepts (p. 68)
doctrine (p. 50)
entity concept (p. 54)
investment expense (p. 68)
legislative grace concept (p. 62)
personal expense (p. 68)
realization concept (p. 63)
related party provisions (p. 52)
substance-over-form doctrine (p. 60)
taxable entity (p. 55)
tax benefit rule (p. 59)
trade or business expense (p. 68)
wherewithal-to-pay concept (p. 67)

▲ PRIMARY TAX LAW SOURCES

[1] Sec. 267—Defines related parties and provides limits on deductibility of certain transactions between related parties.

[2] Sec. 6654—Provides that all individuals must pay estimated taxes when their tax liability is expected to be greater than

$500; imposes a penalty for not paying the proper amount of estimated tax.

[3] Sec. 701—Provides that partners, not the partnership, are responsible for payment of tax on the income of the partnership.

[4] Sec. 1336—Prescribes the taxation of income by S corporations.

[5] Lucas v. Earl, 281 U.S. 111 (1930)—Established the assignment-of-income doctrine in holding that salaries and fees earned by the taxpayer but paid to his wife under a valid agreement were still income to the taxpayer who earned the income.

[6] Burnet v. Sanford & Brooks Co., 282 U.S. 359 (1931)—Held that the transactions of each tax year should stand separate and apart from transactions of other tax years.

[7] Sec. 446—Sets general rules for methods of accounting, including the allowance of the cash and accrual methods; requires that the method selected by a taxpayer clearly reflect income.

[8] Sec. 111—Establishes the tax benefit rule.

[9] U.S. v. Phellis, 257 U.S. 156 (1921)—Made the first application of the substance-over-form doctrine; held that the substance of a transaction should be considered and the form of a transaction can be disregarded in applying the provisions of the tax law.

[10] Sec. 71—States that alimony received is taxable; defines *alimony*.

[11] Sec. 61—Provides the general definition of *gross income* as all income from whatever source derived.

[12] Willcuts v. Bunn, 282 U.S. 216 (1931)—Determined that gain on the sale of tax-exempt securities is taxable income.

[13] Sec. 1221—Defines *capital assets*.

[14] Sec. 1211—Sets forth the limit on deductions of capital losses of corporations and individuals.

[15] Sec. 1001—Prescribes the calculation of gains and losses on dispositions of property; defines *amount realized* for purposes of determining gain or loss on dispositions.

[16] Sec. 1012—Defines *basis of property*: The general rule for the initial basis of a property is its cost.

[17] Eisner v. Macomber, 252 U.S. 189 (1920)—In holding that a stock dividend did not constitute gross income, determined that increases in value that have not been realized are not subject to tax.

[18] North American Oil Consol. v. Burnet, 286 U.S. 417 (1932)—Established the claim-of-right doctrine in holding that an amount received under the clear control of the taxpayer was income even if some portion of the amount received might have to be repaid in the future.

[19] Reg. Sec. 1.446-1—Requires all items that constitute gross income be included in gross income in the tax year in which the item is actually or constructively received.

[20] Hamilton National Bank of Chattanooga v. CIR, 29 B.T.A. 63 (1933)—Held that ''a taxpayer may not deliberately turn his back upon income and thus select the year for which he will report it.''

[21] Hornung v. CIR, 47 T.C. 428 (1967)—Held that the value of an automobile received by a football player as most valuable player in championship game was not included in income until the player had actual possession made available to him.

[22] Reg. Sec. 1.61-1—States that income can be realized in any form, including cash, services, and property received.

[23] Reg. Sec. 1.61-8—States that advance receipts of rents are included in gross income in the year of receipt, regardless of the taxpayer's accounting method.

[24] Helvering v. Gregory, 293 U.S. 465 (1935)—Originated the business purpose concept; held that the transaction in question had no business purpose, therefore the applicable tax law did not apply.

[25] CIR v. Transport Trading & Terminal Corp., 176 F.2d 510 (2d Cir. 1949)—Expanded the application of the business purpose concept enunciated in *Helvering v. Gregory* to include any tax law provisions pertaining to commercial transactions.

[26] Sec. 162—Allows the deduction of all ordinary and necessary expenses incurred in a trade or business of the taxpayer.

[27] Sec. 212—Allows the deduction of all ordinary and necessary expenses incurred in a production-of-income activity of the taxpayer.

[28] Sec. 262—Sets the general rule for the disallowance of deductions for personal expenditures by individuals.

[29] Sec. 211—Generally allows specific personal expenditures as itemized deductions of individuals.

[30] Sec. 263—Provides the general rule that disallows current period deductions for capital expenditures.

[31] Reg. Sec. 1.461-1—Specifies that expenditures that create an asset with a life expectancy that extends substantially beyond the end of the tax year must be capitalized.

[32] Sec. 1011—Provides general rules for determining the adjusted basis of property.

[33] Sec. 1016—Provides the general rules for adjustments to basis of property for capital expenditures and recoveries of capital subsequent to purchase.

[34] Sec. 167—Allows a depreciation deduction for property subject to exhaustion and wear and tear on property used in a trade or business or held for the production of income.

[35] Sec. 179—Provides an election to expense of up to $17,500 of the cost of depreciable tangible personal property in the year of purchase for tax years after 1992.

▲ DISCUSSION QUESTIONS

1. This chapter compared the operation of the income tax system to the operation of other systems we have devised to govern our everyday lives. Choose an example of a system you deal with in your everyday life, and explain part of its operation in terms of concepts, constructs, and exceptions to the general concepts and constructs.

2. The chapter stated that the ability-to-pay concept is fundamental to the operation of the income tax system. What is the ability-to-pay concept, and what are the two basic aspects of the income tax system that are derived from the concept? What might the tax system be like without this concept?

3. What is an arm's-length transaction? What is its significance to income taxation?

4. Explain how the related party construct and the arm's-length transaction concept interact.

5. Why is the pay-as-you-go concept important to the successful operation of the income tax system? What other types of taxes are based on this concept?

6. What is the difference between a taxable entity and a conduit entity?

7. Why is the tax benefit rule necessary? That is, which concept drives the need for this construct? Explain.

8. What are the two basic methods of accounting that may be used by taxpayers? How do the two basic methods differ?

9. What is the effect of the capital recovery concept on income recognition?

10. Chapter 1 discussed how gross income is equal to all income received, less exclusions. Which concepts form the basis for this calculation of gross income? Explain.

11. What is capital gain income? How is it different from ordinary income?

12. Why does the doctrine of constructive receipt apply only to cash basis taxpayers?

13. How is the wherewithal-to-pay concept different from the ability-to-pay concept?

14. Explain how the business purpose concept provides the basis for determining which expenses are deductible.

15. What is a capital expenditure?

16. The legislative grace concept is both an income concept and a deduction concept. Explain how the application of the concept differs for income items and deduction items.

17. The capital recovery concept is both an income concept and a deduction concept. Explain how the application of the concept differs for income items and deduction items.

18. Which of the following are based on an ability-to-pay concept? Explain.   ▲ **PROBLEMS**
    a. State Y collects a sales tax of 5% on all purchases of goods and services.
    b. State X collects a sales tax of 5% on all purchases of goods and services but gives low-income families a tax credit for sales taxes.
    c. Students at State University are given free parking in designated lots. Faculty and staff must pay $125 per year for parking at State University.
    d. Barton City charges all customers a flat monthly rate of $10 for garbage pickup.

19. Sheila, a single taxpayer, is a retired computer executive with a taxable income of $40,000 in the current year. Sheila receives approximately $30,000 per year in tax-exempt municipal bond interest. Adam and Tanya are married and have no children. Adam and Tanya's $40,000 taxable income is comprised solely of wages they earn from their jobs. Calculate and compare the amount of tax Sheila pays versus Adam and Tanya's tax. How well does the ability-to-pay concept work in this situation?

20. Andrew and Barbara each receive a salary of $80,000. Neither Andrew nor Barbara has any other source of income. During the current year, Barbara paid $800 more in tax than Andrew. What might explain why Barbara paid more tax than Andrew when they both have the same income?

21. Which of the following are related parties:
    a. Eric and his uncle Bob?   d. Eric and his sister Zelda?
    b. Eric and his grandfather Richard? e. Eric and his nephew Dwayne?
    c. Eric and his girlfriend Louise?

22. In each of the following cases, determine whether Inez is a related party:
    a. Inez owns 500 shares of XYZ Corporation's common stock. XYZ has 50,000 shares of common stock outstanding.
    b. Inez owns a 40% interest in the Tetra Partnership. The other 60% interest is owned by 3 of Inez's friends.
    c. Inez owns 40% of the stock in Alabaster Co. Her husband Bruce owns 30% and her brother-in-law Michael owns the remaining 30%.
    d. Inez is a 100% owner of Nancy Corporation.

23. Junior bought some stock several years ago for $6,000. He is thinking of selling the stock and has 2 offers. His broker told him he could sell the stock for $6,600 and he would have to pay a $900 commission, for a net realization of $5,700. His sister Bonnie offered to pay Junior $5,700 with no commissions paid on the transaction. What is the potential problem with the sale of the stock to Bonnie? Explain.

24. Doiko Corporation owns 90% of the stock in Nall, Inc. Trebor owns 40% of the stock of Doiko. Trebor's sister owns the remaining 60% of Doiko. During the current year, Trebor purchased land from Nall for $43,000. Nall had purchased the land for $62,000. Based on the income tax concepts, what are the likely tax effects of Trebor's purchase of the land?

25. Ed runs an auto repair business out of the garage attached to his personal residence. How should Ed account for each of the following items?
    a. Cash received from repair services, $28,000.
    b. Interest paid on his home mortgage, $7,300.
    c. Power jack hoist purchased at a cost of $12,000.
    d. Electricity bills, $3,600 (Ed does not have separate electricity service to the garage).
    e. Checks received from customers that were returned by bank, $1,600. The bank charged Ed's account $35 for processing the bad checks.
    f. Telephone bill for phone in the garage, $420 (Ed has a separately listed phone in his house).
    g. Advertising in the local newspaper, $800.
    h. Interest paid on home furniture loan, $600.

26. Henrietta is the president and sole shareholder of Clutter Corporation. In 1993, Henrietta transferred ownership of her personal residence to the corporation. As part of the transfer, Clutter Corporation assumed Henrietta's mortgage on the house. At the same time, she and the corporation entered a lease agreement that allows Henrietta to lease the property for as long as she wants at an amount approximating the monthly mortgage payments on the house. During the current year, Clutter paints the house at a cost of $5,000, makes other repairs totaling $3,000, and adds an entertainment room at a cost of $30,000. Current-year property taxes and interest paid by Clutter on the house are $1,400 and $18,000, respectively. Henrietta paid $18,000 in rent to Clutter. Based on the income tax concepts, discuss the tax effects this arrangement could have for Henrietta and Clutter Corporation.

27. Amanda, Barney, and Carla own the ABC Partnership, sharing profits and losses 50:30:20. During the current year, ABC had total gross income of $60,000 and total allowable deductions of $20,000. How should each of the following taxpayers account for ABC's results? Explain.
    a. ABC Partnership   c. Barney
    b. Amanda   d. Carla

28. Alicia owns 40% of the common stock of Dahl Co. During the current year, Dahl reported a taxable income of $60,000 and paid $15,000 in cash dividends. What are the income tax effects for Alicia of her investment in Dahl Co. if Dahl is organized as
    a. A corporation?
    b. An S corporation?

29. Zelda owns 3 separate businesses. The total income generated by all 3 businesses puts her in the highest marginal tax rate bracket. In order to lower her overall tax on this income, Zelda organized each business into a separate S corporation. Why will this plan not lower Zelda's taxes? Suggest an alternative plan that might lower her tax on the income from the 3 businesses.

30. Christie purchases a one-third interest in the Corporate Capital Partnership (CCP) in 1994 for $35,000. During 1994, CCP suffers a loss of $15,000, and Christie withdraws $5,000 in cash from the partnership. In 1995, CCP earns an income of $60,000, and Christie withdraws $12,000.
    a. What are the tax consequences for Christie of this investment in 1994 and 1995?
    b. What is Christie's basis in the partnership investment at the end of 1994 and 1995?

31. Elroy is a self-employed electrician. Whenever a customer pays him in cash, he gives the cash to his son, Errol. Because he does not actually have use of the cash, Elroy thinks that he should not be taxed on the amounts he gives to Errol. What are the tax effects of this arrangement? Explain.

32. Milton is an inventor who has also written several successful mystery novels. Because he didn't really need the income from the novels, Milton wrote the novels under an assumed name and had the royalties from the novels paid to Hammer Corporation. When Milton incorporated Hammer, he gave all the stock to his three sons. The sons

are employed by the corporation. The salaries paid to the sons are approximately equal to the royalties earned each year from the novels. What is the likely tax treatment of this arrangement?

33. Esmeralda is an attorney. Before 1995, she is employed by the law firm of Ellis and Morgan (E&M). Esmeralda is not a partner in E&M; her compensation consists of a fixed salary and a percentage of any fees generated by clients she brings or refers to the firm. In January 1995, she becomes a partner in the law firm of Thomas, Gooch, and Frankel (TGF). As a partner, Esmeralda agrees to turn over to TGF any income from the practice of law from the date of her admittance to the practice. In leaving E&M, it is agreed that she will continue to receive her percentage of fees from clients she referred to E&M during her employment there. In return, Esmeralda agrees that, upon request, she will consult E&M attorneys regarding those clients. During 1995, she consults with 2 of her former E&M clients and receives $12,000 from E&M per their agreement. The $12,000 consists of $10,000 as a percentage of fees for client referrals after she left E&M and $2,000 as a percentage for work done before she left E&M. Esmeralda turns the $12,000 over to TGF per her partnership agreement. Is Esmeralda taxed on the $12,000 she receives from E&M? Explain.

34. For each of the following situations, determine the proper year for recognition of the income or deduction if the taxpayer is (1) a cash basis taxpayer and (2) an accrual basis taxpayer:
   a. Harry does some legal work for Janet in December 1995. Janet pays Harry's bill in January 1996.
   b. Ruben sells land to Mark on July 1, 1994, for $30,000. The terms of the sale call for Mark to pay Ruben $10,000 on July 1, 1994, and $10,000 on July 1 of 1995 and 1996.
   c. Acme Hardware Co. purchases new counters for the store on October 4, 1995, at a cost of $6,500. The counters have an estimated useful life of 20 years, but the tax life is 7 years.
   d. Odakota pays his employee, Sally, $13,480 in salary up to December 22, 1995. As of December 31, Odakota owes Sally $390 for the period of December 22 through December 31. The $390 is to be paid on the next pay date, which is January 5, 1996.
   e. Judy purchases office supplies costing $800 on December 28, 1995. Judy pays for the office supplies on January 28, 1996.

35. Tim has state income taxes of $3,800 withheld from his salary during 1994. On his 1994 federal income tax return, Tim properly deducts the $3,800 as state taxes paid. Upon filing his 1994 state income tax return, he determines that his actual state income tax for 1994 is only $3,000, and the state sends him an $800 refund. What are the tax consequences of the refund? Explain in terms of the concepts presented in the chapter. How would your answer change if Tim's actual state income tax is $4,100 and he has to pay $300 with his state return?

36. Jamal Corporation is an accrual basis taxpayer. In 1994, Jamal writes off a $400 account receivable from a customer who has died. In 1995, the former customer's estate sends Jamal a check for $250. What are the tax effects of the receipt of the $250 in 1995? Explain. How would your answer be different if Jamal Corporation is a cash basis taxpayer?

37. Jerry and his wife Joanie own a successful concrete company that is organized as a corporation. Jerry spends all his time running the company, whereas Joanie has a full-time job as a legal secretary. The corporation pays Joanie a salary of $45,000 a year as vice president. What tax problem might Jerry and Joanie have with this arrangement? Explain.

38. The Prevetti Partnership is engaged in the purchase and management of apartment complexes. The partnership entered into an agreement with Parsnip Development Co. on July 1 of the current year to purchase the Perry Apartments. The sales agreement stated the purchase price of $5,000,000. It also provided for "other payments to seller," composed of a $500,000 payment for a covenant not to compete, $50,000 for the seller's management advice during the period of ownership transition, and a financing fee of $100,000. In addition, the seller is to receive the first $400,000 of the rent collected by Prevetti. The purchase was completed on August 5. Monthly rentals on the property are $90,000. Prevetti paid Parsnip the first $400,000 of rent it collected per the purchase agreement. How much rental income does the Prevetti Partnership have for the current year? Explain.

39. For each of the following tax treatments, determine the concept, construct, or doctrine that provides the rationale for the treatment:

  a. Lester purchases some stock for a total cost of $2,500. On December 31, 1994, the stock is worth $2,800. In August 1995, he sells the stock to his brother Rufus for $2,000. Lester has no income from the stock in 1994, and he is not allowed to deduct the $500 loss on the sale of the stock to Rufus in 1995.

  b. Kerry is an employee of Ross Co. During the year, Ross withheld federal income taxes of $3,500 from her salary. Her tax liability for the year was only $3,200, so she received a refund of $300.

  c. Catherine is a city government employee. She often uses the city's photocopier to make personal photocopies and has her secretary type an occasional personal letter. The value of these services for the current year was approximately $55 but is not included in Catherine's gross income.

  d. Dante's allowable personal deductions were only $2,800 this year, so he deducted the standard deduction of $3,900 in computing his taxable income.

40. EAL Corporation purchases a delivery truck costing $33,000 for use in its floral business in 1993. It deducts $3,300 in depreciation on the truck in 1993, $6,600 in 1994, $6,600 in 1995, and $3,300 in 1996. It sells the truck in 1996 for $22,000. What is its gain (loss) on the sale of the delivery truck?

41. George purchases stock in Dodo Corporation in 1992 at a cost of $40,000. In 1995, he sells the stock for $26,000. What is the effect of the sale of stock on George's 1995 taxable income? Assume that George sells no other assets in 1995.

42. Chelsea, who is single, purchases land for investment purposes in 1992 at a cost of $43,000. In 1995, she sells the land for $57,000. Chelsea's taxable income without considering the land sale is $96,000. What is the effect of the sale of the land on her 1995 taxable income, and what is her 1995 tax liability? Would your answer change if Chelsea were married?

43. Determine whether the taxpayer in each of the following situations has realized income. Explain why there has or has not been a realization, and determine the amount of income to be reported.

  a. Ward owns 300 shares of Montezuma common stock. During the current year, Montezuma splits the stock 2 for 1. As a result of the split, Ward receives an additional 300 shares of stock.

  b. Shannon is the sole shareholder of Bubbles, Inc., a corporation. During the current year, Bubbles has taxable income of $80,000.

  c. Bob's Balloon Flights owes Kona Bank $100,000. Bob's is having cash-flow problems because of a decline in tourism and cannot make full payment on its loan from Kona. Rather than foreclose on the loan, Kona reduces the debt to $60,000 so that Bob's can stay in business.

  d. Alfredo runs a ballet studio. He charges customers $50 per month for lessons. Alternatively, customers can pay a lump sum of $480 for 1 year of lessons. During the current year, Alfredo receives $11,000 in monthly payments and $18,000 in 1-year prepayments.

44. Ayah signs a contract to write a book for East Publishing Co. in 1995. Under the terms of the contract, she receives a $5,000 advance against future royalty payments upon signing the contract. The contract stipulates that if Ayah does not write a suitable book or if the royalties from the book are insufficient to cover the advance, she must repay any portion not earned. Does Ayah have any income from the receipt of the royalty advance? Explain in terms of the income tax concepts presented in the chapter.

45. Determine whether the taxpayer in each of the following situations has a claim of right to the income received:

   a. Trigger, Inc., received a $5,000 stud fee for services rendered by one of its prized horses. Under its standard contract, Trigger will return the fee if a live foal is not born.

   b. Orville works as a salesman for Brewster Co. He receives a travel allowance of $1,000 at the beginning of each quarter. At the end of each quarter, he must make a full accounting of his travel expenses and reimburse Brewster for any of the $1,000 not spent on approved travel.

   c. Assume that in part b, Orville is not required to account for his actual travel expenses for Brewster and is not required to return unused portions of the travel advance.

   d. Arco Architecture, Inc., received $10,000 from a client for work done by a subcontractor on the client's project. Arco, in turn, paid $10,000 to the subcontractor.

46. Consider the following two situations. Although they are similar, their treatments are exactly opposite. Identify the concept underlying both treatments, and explain why the concept treats the two situations differently.

   a. Sam is an employee of Dunbar Co. The company regularly mails salary checks to employees to arrive on or before the last day of each month. Sam's regular paycheck arrives at his house on December 31, 1995, but Sam is away on a ski trip and does not return until January 2, 1996. Sam deposits the check in his bank account the following day. The check is included in Sam's 1995 income. *Constructive receipt.*

   b. Percy is an employee of Daly Co. In November 1995, Percy's position is eliminated in a "streamlining" of company costs. As part of the cost reduction program, Percy is entitled to severance pay; however, his boss tells him that it will be 3 or 4 months before the severance payments are made. The check arrives by mail on December 31, 1995, while Percy is away on a ski trip. He returns on January 2, 1996, and deposits the check in his bank account the following day. The severance pay check is not taxable until 1996. *Constructive Receipt*

47. Determine whether the taxpayer in each of the following situations is in constructive receipt of income. If not, explain when the income will be constructively received.

   a. Morton earns a salary of $5,000 per month from Shipley Co. In December, Morton is notified that Shipley is unable to meet its December payroll obligation until sometime in January.

   b. Constancia works as an agent for Wesellum Realty. During 1995, Constancia borrows $10,000 from Wesellum. Wesellum deducts amounts against the loan from Constancia's commission checks. Constancia actually receives $17,000 in commissions during 1995, and an additional $5,000 in commissions is applied against her loan.

   c. Mikhail is the president of Boris Manufacturing, Inc. His employment contract entitles him to a bonus each year based on that year's profitability. The bonus is not payable until February 15 of the following year. In December 1995, he receives a $25,000 advance on his 1995 bonus. The following February, the actual amount of the bonus is determined to be $40,000, and Mikhail receives the remaining $15,000 on February 15, 1996.

48. Using the income concepts presented in this chapter, discuss whether the taxpayer has realized income in each of the following situations:

    a. Adco Corporation pays the health insurance premiums for all its employees. Adrian is an employee of Adco. Health insurance premiums Adco paid for Adrian cost $1,150 for the current year.

    b. The Sung Partnership bought a parcel of unimproved land for $32,000. Sung spent an additional $22,000 to put in roads and sewerage and to grade the property for subdividing. The property was subdivided into 15 lots and offered for sale at $10,000 per lot.

    c. Doctors and nurses at Valley View Hospital are allowed to eat free of charge in the hospital cafeteria during their shifts. Sue, a doctor, ate meals valued at $1,900 during the current year.

    d. Wayman won the golf championship at his country club. In addition to a handsome trophy, he received merchandise worth $500 for winning the tournament.

    e. Rock signed a contract to play football for the Rangers. In addition to a salary of $1,000,000 per year for 5 years, Rock is to receive a signing bonus of $5,000,000 to be paid 10 years from the date the contract was signed.

49. Elmo Corporation leased land to Valerie for $1,000 per month under a 30-year lease. The terms of the lease provided that any improvements to the land made by Valerie would revert to Elmo upon termination of the lease. Valerie constructed a building on the property at a cost of $12,000. At the end of the lease, the fair market value of the land was $60,000, and the fair market value of the building was $30,000. Elmo Corporation sold the property 2 years later for $105,000.

    a. List three points at which Elmo Corporation might recognize income from the improvements made by Valerie.

    b. According to the income concepts presented in the chapter, when should Elmo Corporation recognize income from the lease? Explain.

    c. Would your answer to part b be different if the lease provided that any improvements made by Valerie could be deducted from the rental payment made to Elmo Corporation?

50. For each tax treatment described, determine the applicable income tax concept(s), and explain how it forms the basis for the treatment:

    a. Jackson owned some coupon bonds with detachable interest coupons. He detached coupons worth $5,000 and gave them to his son to buy a car. Jackson is taxed on the $5,000 of interest, even though he never actually received the interest.

    b. Joan's barn on her ranch was destroyed by a tornado. The barn had an adjusted basis of $24,000. Joan received insurance proceeds of $35,000 and built a new barn costing $40,000. Joan does not have to recognize the gain realized on the barn in the current period.

    c. Elvis borrowed $30,000 from University Credit Union to purchase a new X car. He is not taxed on the receipt of the $30,000.

    d. Kelley lost the diamond ring she received from her husband Ian. The ring had a basis of $2,000, and she received $3,000 from her insurance company. Kelley used the money to pay off some medical bills. Kelley must recognize a $1,000 gain on the loss of her diamond.

51. Seymour is a salesman who travels extensively to see clients. In 1995, Seymour buys a new car costing $24,000. Seymour uses the car primarily to travel to see clients during the week. On weekends, he uses the car to run personal errands. What is the tax problem Seymour faces regarding the new car? Explain.

52. Arnold is a college professor specializing in robotics. During the current year, he attended a meeting on robotics in San Diego. Because of the desirable location of the meeting, he took along his wife Hortense and their 2 children. The meeting lasted for 3 days, but Arnold and his family stayed for 2 weeks. What tax problem is posed by this situation? Explain in terms of the concepts presented in the chapter.

53. For each of the following situations, determine the deduction concept(s) involved, and explain how it forms the basis for the tax treatment described:

   a. Individuals are allowed to deduct medical expenses.

   b. Happy Burgers, Inc., owns a chain of drive-in restaurants in California. Seeking to expand its operations, Happy spent $90,000 investigating locations in Oregon. Happy decided that expanding into Oregon was not a wise move at the time, but it is allowed to deduct the $90,000.

   c. Lage's Licorice Co. suffered a fire in one of its warehouses. Equipment that had cost $40,000 and that had been depreciated $15,000 was destroyed. The equipment, which cost $50,000 to replace, was uninsured. Lage is allowed to deduct a loss of $25,000 on the equipment.

   d. While Ray was out to dinner one night, someone broke into his personal car. The thief stole his stereo and his golf clubs. The fair market value of the items stolen was $300. Because he had a $500 deductible on his insurance policy, he received no reimbursement from his auto insurance. To make matters worse, no tax deduction for his loss was allowed.

54. Sidney lives in Hayes, Kansas. He owns some land in Cotulla, Texas, that he inherited from his father several years ago. The land is unimproved and has never produced income. On January 26, 1995, Sidney receives a statement of delinquent taxes on the property for 1992, 1993, and 1994 for $120. On February 10, 1995, Sidney and his wife Ellen start to drive to Cotulla; they arrive on February 20 and pay the taxes on the same day. The cost of the trip for Sidney and Ellen is $450. Can Sidney and Ellen deduct the cost of the trip? Explain in terms of the deduction concepts.

55. Doris purchased a ski cabin in Montana during the current year. Doris has hired a real estate management company to rent out the cabin on a daily basis. The real estate management company told Doris to expect an average of 70 rental days per year. Doris intends to use the cabin for her vacation 3 weeks during the year. What tax problem is posed by the ski cabin? Explain.

56. Explain why the legal fees paid in the following three situations are treated differently for income tax purposes:

   a. Jim paid $10,000 in legal fees in obtaining a divorce. None of the $10,000 is deductible.

   b. Camella invented and patented a device that shells nuts. When she learned that another company was selling copies of her device, she paid an attorney $10,000 to enforce her patent. The $10,000 is fully deductible.

   c. Melody paid $10,000 in legal fees for advice relating to various investments she owns. Only $6,000 of the fees is deductible.

57. A truck owned by Duster Demolition Services was involved in an accident. The truck had originally cost $30,000, and $10,000 of depreciation had been taken on the truck as of the date of the accident. The cost of repairing the truck was $3,000, for which the insurance company reimbursed Duster $2,000.

   a. How much of a loss, if any, is Duster entitled to deduct as a result of the accident?

   b. What is the adjusted basis of the truck after the accident?

58. Determine the taxpayer's adjusted basis in each of the following situations. If any changes are made in the original basis of the asset, explain why they are necessary.

   a. Simone purchases 300 shares of Wilguess, Inc., stock in 1993 for $6,300. In 1993 and 1994, Wilguess pays cash dividends of $2 per share. In 1995, Wilguess pays a 40% stock dividend (nontaxable), and Simone receives an additional 120 shares of stock.

   b. Chasteen Corporation purchases a building in 1992 at a cost of $240,000. Annual maintenance costs on the building are $80,000. In 1994, Chasteen adds a wing to the building at a cost of $60,000. In 1995, the building is painted at a cost of $25,000. Chasteen deducts $4,800 in depreciation in 1992, $7,300 in 1993, and $8,100 in 1994 and 1995.

   c. Lorissa purchases land as an investment in 1993 for $33,000. Property taxes on the property are $400 per year. In 1994, Lorissa is assessed $2,000 by the county assessor for her share of a sidewalk that the county builds adjacent to the land. Lorissa pays the assessment in 1995.

   d. The Barton Brothers Partnership purchases a computer in 1993 for $8,000. The partnership elects to deduct the entire cost of the computer in 1993. In 1995, Barton Brothers spends $300 to repair the computer.

59. Wiggins, Inc., is a manufacturer of fire extinguishers. The fire extinguishers come with a 2-year warranty. Wiggins engineers estimate that approximately 2% of the extinguishers will be defective and require payment under the warranty. Discuss the propriety of allowing Wiggins a deduction in the current year if

   a. Wiggins is a cash basis taxpayer.

   b. Wiggins is an accrual basis taxpayer.

▲ DISCUSSION CASE 2–1

The controller of Newform Oil Co. has come to you for advice. Newform recently cleared a forested area and began drilling an oil well on the site. The well was a gusher, and Newform's geologists estimate that it will produce for at least 10 years. Environmental restoration laws will require Newform to completely reforest and restore the oil well site when the well is taken out of production. An engineering firm hired by Newform estimates that the cost of complying with the environmental requirements will be $8,000,000. For financial accounting purposes, Newform intends to amortize the estimated cost over the 10-year expected life. In addition, it plans to put $500,000 per year into an account that should provide the $8,000,000 necessary to perform the restoration.

The controller would like your advice on the deductibility of the costs of restoration. That is, when can Newform deduct the costs and how much can it deduct? Based on the concepts discussed in this chapter, write a memorandum to the controller detailing what you think is the proper treatment of the restoration costs for tax purposes.

▲ TAX PLANNING CASE 2–2

Biko owns a snowmobile manufacturing business, and Miles owns a mountain bike manufacturing business. Because each business is seasonal, their manufacturing plants are idle during their respective off-seasons. Biko and Miles have decided to consolidate their businesses as one operation. In so doing, they expect to increase their sales by 15% and cut their costs by 30%. Biko and Miles own their businesses as sole proprietors and provide the following summary of their 1994 taxable incomes:

	Biko	Miles
Business income		
Sales	$ 600,000	$ 450,000
Cost of goods sold	(400,000)	(300,000)
Other expenses	(100,000)	(75,000)
Business taxable income	$ 100,000	$ 75,000
Other taxable income		
(net of allowable deductions)	20,000	35,000
1994 taxable income	$ 120,000	$ 110,000

Biko and Miles don't know what type of entity they should use for their combined business. They would like to know the tax implications of forming a partnership versus a corporation. Under either form, Biko will own 55% of the business and Miles will own 45%. They each require $60,000 from the business and would like to increase that by $5,000 per year.

Based on the information provided, do a three-year projection of the income of the business and the total taxes for a partnership and for a corporation. In doing the projections, assume that after the initial 30% decrease in total costs, their annual costs will increase in proportion to sales. Also, assume that their nonbusiness taxable income remains unchanged. Use the 1995 tax rate schedules to compute the tax for each year of the analysis.

You are a CPA who has been preparing tax returns for Sign, Seal, and Deliver, a mid-size CPA firm, for the last 5 years. During the current year, you are assigned the individual return of a new client, Guadalupe Piaz. Guadalupe has completed and returned the tax return questionnaire that the firm sent to her.

In reviewing the questionnaire, you notice that Guadalupe has included an entry for $10,000 in cash dividends received from Quinn Corporation. However, there is no supporting documentation for the dividend payment in the information Guadalupe provided.

What concerns you is that until this year you had prepared the tax return for Quinn Corporation (it was reassigned to another firm member when you were promoted late last year). You know that Quinn Corporation was organized as an S corporation during the years that you prepared the return. During that period, Quinn was equally owned by 3 shareholders and Guadalupe was not among them. In addition, the corporation was highly profitable, averaging approximately $6,000,000 per year in taxable income. Given this information, what are your obligations under the Statements on Responsibilities in Tax Practice (Appendix D)?

▲ **ETHICS DISCUSSION CASE 2–3**

GROSS INCOME

CHAPTER 3
INCOME SOURCES

CHAPTER 4
INCOME EXCLUSIONS

Income Sources

▲ CHAPTER LEARNING OBJECTIVES

■ Discuss the historical development of what constitutes gross income and how it affects the current view of gross income.

■ Distinguish earned income from unearned income, and discuss the tax problems associated with each type of income.

■ Identify sources of income that result from transfers from others and discuss the tax rules for each type of income.

■ Discuss imputed income and identify the common sources of such income and their tax treatments.

■ Provide an overview of the tax treatment of capital gain income.

■ Describe the primary accounting methods used for tax purposes and how income is recognized under each method: the cash method, the accrual method, and the hybrid method.

■ Discuss the exceptions to the general rules of income recognition for each of the accounting methods.

▲ CONCEPT REVIEW ▲

Ability to pay   A tax should be based on the amount that the taxpayer can afford to pay, relative to other taxpayers.

Administrative convenience   Those items for which the cost of compliance would exceed the revenue generated are not taxed.

All-inclusive income   All income received is taxable unless a specific provision can be found in the tax law that either excludes the income from taxation or defers its recognition to a future tax year.

Annual accounting period   All entities must report the results of their operations on an annual basis (the tax year). Each tax year stands on its own, apart from other tax years.

Arm's-length transaction   A transaction in which all parties to the transaction have bargained in good faith and for their individual benefit, not for the benefit of the transaction group.

Assignment of income   The tax entity that owns the income produced is responsible for the tax on the income, regardless of which entity actually receives the income.

Capital recovery   No income is realized until the taxpayer receives more than the amount invested to produce the income. The amount invested in an asset represents the maximum amount recoverable.

Claim of right   A realization occurs whenever an amount is received without any restriction as to its disposition.

Constructive receipt   Income is deemed to be received when it is made unconditionally available to the taxpayer.

Legislative grace   Any tax relief provided is the result of a specific act of Congress that must be strictly applied and interpreted. All income received is taxable unless a specific provision can be found in the tax law that excludes the income from taxation. Deductions must be approached with the philosophy that nothing is deductible unless a provision in the tax law allows the deduction.

Realization   No income (or loss) is recognized until it has been realized. A realization involves a change in the form and/or the substance of a taxpayer's property rights that results from an arm's-length transaction.

Related party   Family members, corporations that are owned by family members, and certain other relationships between entities in which the power to control the substance of a transaction is evidenced through majority ownership.

Tax benefit rule   Any deduction taken in a prior year that is recovered in a subsequent year is income in the year of recovery, to the extent that a tax benefit was received from the deduction.

Wherewithal to pay   Income is recognized in the period in which the taxpayer has the means to pay the tax on the income.

The first step in calculating the taxable income for any tax entity is determining its gross income. Gross income equals all income received, less exclusions from income. Therefore, all items of income realized during the period under consideration must first be identified. Next, the income items are analyzed and segregated into those that are taxable and those that are excluded from taxation. Finally, the proper tax year for recognition of the income items must be determined. The purpose of this chapter is to introduce the basis for identifying income sources and to discuss those sources that present particular problems. In addition, a brief overview of the tax treatment of capital gains and losses is presented. The chapter also considers the effect of an entity's accounting method on the recognition of income and exceptions to the general methods of accounting. Exclusions from income tax are discussed in Chapter 4.

▲ INTRODUCTION

▲ WHAT CONSTITUTES INCOME

The all-inclusive income concept provides the basis for calculating gross income. Under this concept, any income received is assumed to be taxable unless some provision in the tax law allows its exclusion. This concept is the basis of the Internal Revenue Code's definition of *gross income*:

SECTION 61 GROSS INCOME DEFINED
(a) General Definition.—Except as otherwise provided in this subtitle, gross income means all income from whatever source derived, including (but not limited to) the following items:
> (1) Compensation for services, including fees, commissions and similar items;
> (2) Gross income derived from business;
> (3) Gains derived from dealings in property;
> (4) Interest;
> (5) Rents;
> (6) Royalties;
> (7) Dividends;
> (8) Alimony and separate maintenance payments;
> (9) Annuities;
> (10) Income from life insurance and endowment contracts;
> (11) Pensions;
> (12) Income from discharge of indebtedness;
> (13) Distributive share of partnership gross income;
> (14) Income in respect of a decedent; and
> (15) Income from an interest in an estate or trust.

The phrase "all income from whatever source derived" is the statutory equivalent of the all-inclusive income concept's requirement that any income received is initially considered taxable. This phrase has been part of the income tax law since the Sixteenth Amendment to the Constitution empowered Congress in 1913 to "lay and collect taxes on *incomes, from whatever source derived*" [emphasis added]. In Section 61 of the Code, the phrase "except as otherwise provided" allows for items to be excluded from gross income, provided that the specific exclusion is found within the Internal Revenue Code.

The realization concept requires that income be realized before it is included in gross income. However, nothing in the definition of gross income in the Internal Revenue Code requires that income be *realized* before it is *recognized*. Although absent from the Internal Revenue Code, the realization concept was developed primarily by the courts in response to cases requiring an interpretation of the statutory definition of *income*. As a result, the concept has been adopted by the Internal Revenue Service in the regulation that interprets the definition of gross income:

(a) General Definition. Gross income means all income from whatever source derived unless excluded by law. Gross income includes income *realized* in any form, whether in money, property, or services. Income may be *realized*, therefore, in the form of services, meals, accommodations, stock, or other property, as well as in cash.[1]

Thus, a better working definition would be that gross income includes all income realized from whatever source derived, unless specifically excluded.

At first glance, the statutory and administrative definitions of income appear to be quite simplistic and straightforward. However, a linguist would no doubt be bothered by the circular nature of the definition: Gross income means all income. In fact, no definition of the term *income* exists in the Internal Revenue Code. Thus, the threshold question of whether a particular item is or is not income is not answered by these definitions of gross income. Perhaps wisely, Congress has never seen fit to attempt to define the term *income*. Do you think that drafters of tax legislation in 1913 could have foreseen the complexities of business in the 1990s and been able to draft a precise definition of income to cover such items as incentive stock options and gains from currency translations? By not providing a precise definition, what constitutes income evolves with changes in society. In this regard, the courts have played a major role in guiding taxpayers on the treatment of various transactions in which it is not clear whether the statutory definition of income has been met.

Income Is Derived from Labor and Capital

In 1920, the U.S. Supreme Court considered the first case addressing the concept of income. In determining that specific provisions in the tax law that included stock dividends as taxable income were unconstitutional, the Supreme Court said, "Income may be defined as the gain derived from capital, from labor, or from both combined, provided it be understood to include profit gained through sale or conversion of capital assets." [2]

This initial attempt at defining income implies that income could be generated from only two sources: capital and labor. The Court also emphasized the necessity of a realization as a precondition to the existence of income:

> Here we have the essential matter: *not* a gain *accruing* to capital, not a *growth or increment of value in* the investment; but a gain, a profit, something of exchangeable value *proceeding from* the property, *severed from* the capital however invested or employed, and *coming in*, being *"derived"*—that is, *received* or *drawn by* the recipient (the taxpayer) for his *separate* use, benefit and disposal; *that* is income derived from property. Nothing else answers the description. [Court's emphasis][3]

In fact, a vast majority of items we commonly think of as income fit nicely into this definition: wages, income from a sole proprietorship (income from labor), interest, dividends, rental income, and royalty income (income from capital). However, this definition did not contemplate sources of income that were not returns from labor or capital, such as windfalls. Consider the following examples:

▲ **EXAMPLE 1**   Lee was playing golf one day and hit an enormous hook into the woods. While searching for his ball, Lee found a tattered sack full of $100 bills. The police were never able to locate the owner, and Lee was allowed to keep the money, which totaled $50,000. Does Lee have income from finding this money?

Discussion: Given the Supreme Court's definition, it would seem that such a windfall would not be considered as "derived from capital, from labor, or from both combined." However, it would appear that such a "treasure trove," as it is referred to in income tax jargon, would fit the statutory definition of "income from whatever source derived." In fact, the courts have said that such treasure troves do constitute income. [4]

▲ **EXAMPLE 2**   Johnson, Inc. leased a lot and a building to Wenona Corporation under a 99-year lease that permitted Wenona to remodel the building at its own cost. The lease provided that all improvements would be Johnson's property upon termination of the lease. Twenty years after remodeling the original building, Wenona defaulted on the lease payment, and Johnson repossessed the property. The net increase in the value of the property from the remodeling of the building was $50,000. Does Johnson, Inc., have taxable income when it retakes possession of the building?

Discussion: On similar facts, in 1940 the Supreme Court held that Johnson, Inc. was taxable on the increase in the value of the property attributable to the remodeling of the building at the time it repossessed the property. [5]

Although the Court's decision on the facts in example 2 would appear to fit the notion of income "derived from capital," it does not square with the requirement that income be realized by "severing" it from the capital investment and that it be *received* or *drawn* by the recipient (the taxpayer) for his *separate* use, benefit and disposal." In addressing this issue, the Court said:

> While it is true that economic gain is not always taxable as income, it is settled that the realization of gain need not be in cash derived from the sale of an asset. Gain may occur as a result of exchange of property, payment of the taxpayer's indebtedness, relief from a liability, or other profit realized from the completion of a transaction. The fact that the gain is a portion of the value of property received by the taxpayer in the transaction does not negative its realization.[6]

This decision severely weakened the earlier realization requirement by suggesting that any definitive event could be properly considered a realization of income. At this point, there was no requirement that the income be severed from the capital and available for use by the taxpayer. However, in reaction to this decision, in 1942 Congress adopted a provision that excluded from gross income such increases in the value of property upon termination of a lease, to the extent that the lessee's improvements did not constitute a payment in lieu of rent.[7] This exclusion is discussed in Chapter 4.

Income as an Increase in Wealth

As can be seen from the discussion of court cases that define income, the courts increasingly diluted the original judicial requirement that income be derived from capital or labor and that recognition of the income required a realization. In 1955, the Supreme Court closed the circle on its original definition in a case involving the taxability of punitive damages awarded in an antitrust action. In finding that such windfall profits were taxable income, the Court did not even attempt to reconcile its decision with the earlier "gain derived from capital or labor" requirement. Rather, the Court relegated this concept to minor status in determining that *any* increase in the wealth of the taxpayer that has been realized is subject to income tax:

> But it [income derived from capital or labor] was not meant to provide a touchstone to all future gross income questions. . . . Here we have instances of *undeniable accessions to wealth, clearly realized* and over which the taxpayers have *complete dominion*. The mere fact that the payments were extracted from the wrongdoers as punishment for unlawful conduct cannot detract from their character as taxable income to the recipients . . . We find no . . . evidence of intent to exempt these payments. [emphasis added][8]

Thus, the Court adopted a much broader concept of income, "undeniable accessions to wealth," as its interpretation of "income from whatever source derived." The notion of income as an increase in wealth is not new or, for that matter, surprising. Economists have long argued that the true measure of income is the change in wealth for the period under consideration. Using the economist's definition of income, all gains received during the period, whether realized or not, are considered income. Where the tax law deviates from the economists' notion of income is in the requirement that the increase in wealth be "clearly realized." Note also that the tax law definition of income not only requires a realization but also that the taxpayer have "complete dominion" over the realized income. The requirement of complete dominion means that the taxpayer must have a claim of right to the income. Recall that the claim of right doctrine says that any amount received without restriction as to its disposition is income in the period received.

What Constitutes Income: Current View

Given this brief historical account of how the concept of income developed, what is considered income today? Although the courts continue to consider the issue, no significant developments have occurred since the Supreme Court determined that any increase in wealth that has been realized constitutes income. Thus, it is safe to say that the first requirement is that the taxpayer experiences an increase in wealth. An increase in wealth can be through an increase in net worth or through consumption.

> ▲ **EXAMPLE 3**   Janet purchases 100 shares of XYZ Co. stock during 1995 at a cost of $2,000. As of December 31, 1995, the shares of stock are worth $2,500. Does Janet experience an increase in wealth during 1995 as a result of this stock purchase?

> *Discussion:*   Janet's wealth increases during 1995 as a result of the stock purchase. Her net worth increases by $500 over what it was before she purchased the stock.

> ▲ **EXAMPLE 4**   Cara's car needed new spark plugs. She called Local Service Station and found out that it would cost $50 to get the job done. Rather than pay the $50, Cara purchased the spark plugs for $15 and installed them herself. Has Cara's wealth increased as a result of installing the spark plugs herself?

> *Discussion:*   Cara's wealth has increased by the $35 she saved by doing the job herself. Through consumption of the labor and overhead involved in the $50 charged by Local, her net worth has increased by the $35 she saved.

Although an increase in wealth is a necessary condition for the recognition of income, it alone is not sufficient to trigger taxation. Before an increase in wealth becomes taxable (i.e., is recognized income), it must also be realized. As stated previously, realization is not an explicit statutory requirement for the recognition of income; however, over the years the concept has become so basic to the structure of the tax system that the general premise of the requirement is simply not challenged. What typically is challenged by taxpayers is what constitutes a realization. A reasonable working definition contains the following two elements:

- A change in form and/or substance of the taxpayer's property (or property rights)
- The involvement of a second party in the income process

The most common forms of income realization involve the receipt of something of value (cash, stock, services) for a service rendered or the sale, exchange, or lease of a property.

> ▲ **EXAMPLE 5**   Return to the facts of example 3. Does Janet realize any income from her dealings in XYZ Co.'s stock?

> *Discussion:*   Although Janet's wealth increases through the increase in the value of the stock, she has not realized that wealth through sale, exchange, or other disposition of the stock. That is, the form of her property (stock) has not been changed through a transaction with another party.

> ▲ **EXAMPLE 6**   Return to the facts of example 4. Has Cara realized the increase in wealth she obtained by repairing the car herself?

> *Discussion:*   Cara has had a change in the form of her property through the repairs but because no second party was involved, she would not be considered to have a realization of income.

In general, any increase in wealth that has been realized by a taxpayer must be recognized (i.e., included in gross income) for tax purposes in the period in which the realization occurs. However, this general rule has several exceptions. As previously stated, some income realizations are excluded by law and therefore are never recognized for tax purposes. The tax laws also provide for deferral of gains on certain types of property transactions in which the wherewithal to pay tax from the transaction is lacking. The recognition of gains from this class of transactions is deferred to a future period when a transaction occurs that provides the cash to pay the tax.

> ▲ **EXAMPLE 7**   Duc's business automobile, which had an adjusted basis of $2,000, was destroyed in a tornado. Duc received a check for $6,000 from his insurance company. Duc used the $6,000 as a down payment on a new business automobile costing $30,000. Has Duc realized a gain from the destruction of his old automobile? If so, must he recognize the gain in the period of the trade-in?
>
> *Discussion:*   Duc has realized a gain of $4,000 ($6,000 in insurance proceeds − the adjusted basis of $2,000) on the destruction of his automobile. He realized a gain because he received something of value, $6,000 in cash, for his old automobile in a transaction with another party.
>
> Duc will not have to recognize the gain (include the gain in gross income) on the destruction of his automobile in the current period. When the entire proceeds from the casualty are reinvested in a qualifying replacement asset, the tax law allows the deferral of gains from casualties on business property that has been replaced. In this case, Duc reinvested the entire $6,000 he received for his old automobile and has no cash remaining to pay the tax on the gain.
>
> Although Duc does not have to pay tax on the gain in the current period, he will pay tax on the gain when he disposes of the new business automobile in a taxable transaction. Chapter 13 discusses the rules for deferrals of gains and the mechanics of the calculations to ensure that the tax is eventually paid on the gain.

▲ COMMON INCOME SOURCES

This chapter discusses four categories of income sources to provide a framework for working with income sources. The first two categories are based on the Supreme Court's early definition of income as being derived from labor, which is referred to as *earned income*, and income derived from capital, referred to as *unearned income*. The third category consists of transfers from others. The fourth category considers taxable sources of imputed income.

Earned Income

The most common form of income for individuals is compensation paid for their services. That is, individuals provide their labor for the production of goods and services. In return for their labor, they are compensated by the entity for which they are performing the work. Providing labor for compensation produces **earned income.** All amounts paid by an employer to or on behalf of an employee are taxable unless specifically excluded by law. In addition, income generated from the operation of a business is considered earned by the owner. Income from illegal activities (gambling, drugs, extortion, etc.) is also considered earned and subject to tax.[9] The most common forms of earned income are

1.   Wages, salaries, tips, bonuses and commissions
2.   Income from the active conduct of a trade or business

3. Income from the rendering of services

4. Income from the performance of illegal activities

The taxability of earned income sources is undisputed. However, two problems often arise with this type of income. The first problem stems from a desire to take advantage of the progressive nature of the tax rate schedules by transferring income earned by a high marginal tax rate payer to a family member who is in a lower tax bracket. These attempts are foiled by the assignment-of-income doctrine, which requires the entity earning the income to pay the tax on the income, regardless of who actually receives the income.

▲ **EXAMPLE 8**   Thelma has a successful carpet-cleaning business. In order to lower her taxes, she instructs every fifth client to make the check out to Thelma's son. Her son is a college student who does not work and uses the checks received from Thelma's business to pay for his college expenses.

Discussion: Because the payments made to the son were earned by Thelma, she must include the payments in her taxable income. Therefore, this scheme results in no tax savings to Thelma. NOTE: There are legal ways for Thelma to transfer taxability of the income earned from her carpet-cleaning business to her son. The simplest method would be to employ her son in the business and pay him a reasonable salary for his labor. This would lower Thelma's taxable income through a deduction for compensation and transfer the income to her son for taxation at a lower marginal tax rate.

Taxpayers may also attempt to transfer income to establish a basis for taking business deductions.

▲ **EXAMPLE 9**   Michael has a computer in a separate room of his house that he uses to perform work related to his employment as an engineer for Ajax Corporation as well as for personal purposes. Because he is not considered to be in a trade or business, the tax law does not allow a deduction for either the office or the computer. Michael's wife Daniela does the bookkeeping and payroll work for several small businesses. In order to establish a trade or business for himself, Michael has the payments for Daniela's bookkeeping services made out to him.

Discussion: No marginal tax rate savings result from the transfer of income from Daniela to Michael, because Michael and Daniela commingle their respective incomes on their joint tax return. The tax benefit to be derived from such a scheme would be the additional deductions Michael could take for the office and the computer, if he can establish their use in the business of bookkeeping. However, under the assignment-of-income doctrine, Daniela would still be deemed to have earned the payments for her services, and Michael could not claim the checks he receives as income he earned in a trade or business. Thus, he could not take any deductions for the office or the computer.

The second concern with earned income is what constitutes a receipt of income. Typically, earned types of income are received in cash. However, if receipts of cash were the sole source of earned income, clever taxpayers could arrange their affairs to receive significant amounts of their income in other forms, thus avoiding tax. To counter such tax avoidance schemes, a **cash-equivalent approach** is used to measure receipts of income. Under this approach, the receipt of anything with a fair market value will trigger recognition of income. Thus, income can be realized in the form of property, services, meals, lodging, stock, and so on.

▲ **EXAMPLE 10**   Betty agreed to clean Shiro's house once a week, in return for which Shiro agreed to mow Betty's lawn once a week. Betty usually charges $20 to clean a house, which is what Shiro charges to mow a lawn. Do Betty and/or Shiro have taxable income from this arrangement?

Discussion: Yes, both have income of $20 per week from this arrangement. Each receives something of value in return for her or his services. Therefore, they are taxed as if they had paid each other cash.

Under the constructive receipt doctrine, a cash basis taxpayer does not have income until there is an actual or constructive receipt of the income earned. Therefore, a cash basis taxpayer who sells merchandise or performs services on general account does not recognize income until the account is paid with something of value. However, if the customer of such a taxpayer gives the taxpayer a promissory note for the amount due, the fair market value of the note is considered a receipt of property and is taxable when received.

▲ **EXAMPLE 11**   Farnsworth, a cash basis taxpayer, put a new roof on Emma Corporation's warehouse in late November and billed it $3,000. Emma paid the bill in January. When is Farnsworth taxable on the $3,000 roofing job?

Discussion: Because Farnsworth did not receive anything of value until January, the $3,000 is not included in his taxable income until that time.

▲ **EXAMPLE 12**   Assume that in example 11 Emma Corporation had given Farnsworth a valid note payable for $3,000 when it completed the roofing job in November. Farnsworth did not discount the note, although local banks typically discount such personal notes by 30%. Emma paid the note in full in January. How does this affect Farnsworth's recognition of income?

Discussion: Because Farnsworth could have converted the note to cash upon receipt, the amount of cash he could have received from discounting the note, its fair market value, is taxable upon receipt. Therefore, $2,100 [$3,000 − (30% × $3,000)] is taxable in the year Farnsworth received the note. The remaining $900 is taxable when he receives full payment on the note the following January.

Unearned Income

The **unearned income** category of income includes the earnings from investments and gains from the sale, exchange, or other disposition of investment assets. The distinguishing feature of this type of income is that it constitutes a return on an investment and producing the income does not require any labor by the owner of the investment. The most common forms of unearned income are

1.   Interest income
2.   Dividend income
3.   Income from rental and royalty-producing activities
4.   Income from annuities
5.   Income from conduit entities
6.   Gains from the sale of investments producing any of the five forms of unearned income

As with earned sources of income, the inclusion of unearned types of income in the tax base is not controversial. However, a few practical difficulties do arise.

Rental and Royalty Income.   The first problem deals with the definition of *rental and royalty income.* Technically, the tax law defines these two types of income as gross income from the property, less the related expenses to produce the income.

▲ **EXAMPLE 13**   Ali Corporation owns an apartment building and rents the units. During 1995, Ali receives total rents of $15,000 and incurs costs of $13,000 related to the apartments. What is Ali Corporation's rental income for 1995?

Discussion: Ali Corporation has rental income of $2,000 ($15,000 − $13,000).

▲ **EXAMPLE 14**   Assume that because utility and maintenance costs are higher than expected, Ali's total expenses related to the apartments are $18,000 in 1995. What is Ali's rental income for 1995?

Discussion: Ali Corporation does not have any rental income in 1995. Rather, it has a rental loss of $3,000, the deduction of which is subject to the rules for deducting losses, discussed in Chapter 7.

Annuities.   The second item to consider is the taxation of annuities. An **annuity** is a string of equal payments received over equal time periods for a determinable period. The purchase of annuity contracts has become increasingly popular in recent years as a way to guarantee income during a taxpayer's retirement years. A typical annuity is illustrated in the top panel of Exhibit 3–1. In the typical annuity situation, an individual pays a certain sum now, in return for which the seller of the annuity promises to make set payments for a period of time in the future. The payments are calculated to provide the purchaser with a predetermined rate of return on the investment. The problem with these arrangements is determining how much of each payment is a return *of* the original capital investment and how much is a return *on* the investment. Recall that the capital recovery concept exempts returns of capital from taxation; only returns on capital are taxable sources of income.

▲ **EXAMPLE 15**   Susan, 40, purchased an annuity contract for $25,000. Under the contract, when Susan reaches 62, she is to receive $5,000 per year until she dies. Actuarial tables indicate that Susan is expected to live until she is 77. How much income will Susan earn in total from this investment?

Discussion: Because we do not know precisely how long Susan will live, it must be assumed that she will live until she is 77, the average life expectancy. Under this assumption, she will receive payments totaling $75,000 ($5,000 × 15) from the contract, resulting in a total profit of $50,000 ($75,000 − $25,000).

In example 15, the major tax problem is determining when to recognize the $50,000 in earnings from her investment. Although it is clear that she will not

General Operation of an Annuity		▲ **Exhibit 3–1**

ANNUITIES

realize any income until she begins receiving payments on the contract, taxation once the payments begin is more controversial. A strict application of the capital recovery concept would exempt the first $25,000 as a repayment of capital investment. However, the tax law views the amounts paid out under the contract as being partly a return *of* her original capital investment (excluded) and partly a return *on* her capital investment (taxable income).[10] The general formula for determining the amount of each payment that is a return of capital and therefore excluded from income, called the **annuity exclusion ratio,** is shown in the lower panel of Exhibit 3–1.

The taxable and excluded portions of any annuity payment can easily be determined by using the annuity formulas in Exhibit 3–1.

▲ **EXAMPLE 16**   How much of each $5,000 payment that Susan receives from the annuity contract is taxable?

Discussion: The exclusion ratio on the contract is $25,000 ÷ $75,000 = 1/3. Therefore, one-third of each $5,000 payment, $1,667, is not taxable, because it is considered a return of her $25,000 investment. The remaining $3,333 is taxed as a return on capital.

To make the annuity calculations, you must assume that a fixed number of payments is to be made under the contract. For payments that continue until the death of the taxpayer, the number of payments is determined by the life expectancy of the annuitant at the date the annuity commences. However, life expectancies are merely averages. As such, few people die at their average life expectancy: Some people die before the average, whereas others outlive their life expectancies. Therefore, in most cases adjustments are required to ensure that proper capital recovery of the annuity investment is made.

▲ **EXAMPLE 17**   Assume that Susan lives for 20 years and receives payments totaling $100,000 under the annuity contract. How is Susan taxed on these payments?

Discussion: Because we do not know how long Susan will live when the payments start, we figure the annual exclusion and income as in example 16. That is, she will exclude $1,667 per year.

After she receives the 15th payment (i.e., the expected number of payments used in the exclusion calculation), Susan will have excluded her entire $25,000 investment ($1,667 × 15 = $25,000). At that time, her capital investment will have been fully recovered. Therefore, payments 16 through 20 will be fully taxable.

Note that during the 20 years of payments, Susan will recognize $75,000 ($100,000 received − the $25,000 investment) in income.

Years 1–15:	$50,000 ($3,333 × 15)
Years 16–20:	$25,000 ($5,000 × 5)

What happens when an annuity owner dies before her life expectancy? In this case, her capital recovery is incomplete; she has not fully recovered her capital investment through an exclusion. To allow full recovery of capital in this situation, the tax law permits a deduction in the year of death for the unrecovered portion of the annuity investment.

▲ **EXAMPLE 18**   Assume that Susan dies in the 10th year of the annuity contract. How would this be treated on her year-10 tax return?

Discussion: The $5,000 received in year 10 would be reported as all other annuity payments were reported: $3,333 would be taxable, and $1,667 would be excluded.

After 10 years, Susan would have excluded a total of $16,670 ($1,667 × 10 years) of her $25,000 investment. The remaining $8,330 ($25,000 − $16,670) of her original investment, which was not recovered, is deductible on her year-10 tax return. Therefore, over the 10-year period she will have recovered her $25,000 capital investment through $16,670 of excluded income and a deduction of $8,330 in the year of death.

Note the effect of the annual accounting period concept on the reporting of annuities. This concept requires not only an annual reporting of income but also embodies the notion that the events of each tax year are to stand apart from each other. Thus, we do not go back and adjust the annuity calculations on prior years' returns when we know the true number of payments. Rather, we apply the capital recovery concept as it applies to the individual year in question.

As a final note on annuities, the exclusion ratio is used when the taxpayer receives amounts that represent both a return of investment in the contract and a return on the investment in the contract. Many pension plans are structured so that amounts paid into the plan by the employee and the employer are excluded from current taxation. Such plans are called *qualified plans* and allow the deferral of tax on payments into the plan and earnings on the plan's assets until they are withdrawn. As such, the taxpayer has no previously taxed capital investment in the plan. Therefore, all amounts paid from the plan are subject to tax.

▲ **EXAMPLE 19** Agatha worked for Crystal Co. for more than 30 years. As part of her employment contract, Crystal matched contributions Agatha made to a qualified plan. None of the payments to the plan or the earnings on the plan investment was subject to tax. Over the years, Agatha accumulated $420,000 in her pension plan. At retirement, she will receive $850 per month from the plan. How much of the monthly payment is subject to tax?

Discussion: Because the $420,000 in the pension plan is income that has not been taxed, the full amount of each payment is subject to tax. Agatha must include all payments she receives from the plan in her gross income in the year she receives the payments.

Calculation of Gain/Loss on Sale of Investments. Another aspect related to unearned income is the calculation of gains (losses) from sales, exchanges, or other dispositions of investment property. Again, this is not a particularly perplexing problem. However, you should keep in mind what constitutes a gain. A gain is the result of a realization in excess of capital investment.[11] The amount of unrecovered capital investment in a property is its adjusted basis.[12] More formally,

	Proceeds from sale of property
Less:	Selling expenses
Equals:	Amount realized from sale of property
Less:	Adjusted basis of property sold
Equals:	Gain (loss) on sale

▲ **EXAMPLE 20** The Alima Partnership buys a rental property in 1993 for $70,000. In 1995, after deducting depreciation of $5,000, Alima sells the rental property for $90,000 and pays a $6,000 commission on the sale. What is Alima's gain (loss) on the sale of the rental property?

Discussion: The Alima Partnership realizes $84,000 ($90,000 − the $6,000 commission) from the sale. Because Alima has already recovered $5,000 of its investment through depreciation deductions, the adjusted basis for the rental property is $65,000 ($70,000 − $5,000). This results in a gain of $19,000 ($84,000 − $65,000).

Note that property dispositions can also result in losses. A loss results when a property is disposed of at less than its adjusted basis. That is, a loss represents incomplete capital recovery.

▲ **EXAMPLE 21**   Assume that in example 20 the Alima Partnership is able to sell its rental property for only $60,000 and pays a $3,000 commission on the sale. What is Alima's gain (loss) on the sale of the rental property?

Discussion: In this case, the Alima Partnership realizes only $57,000 ($60,000 − $3,000) on the sale, resulting in a loss on the sale of $8,000 ($57,000 − $65,000). Note that the $8,000 loss represents Alima's unrecovered investment in the rental property. Allowing Alima to deduct the $8,000 loss fully recovers its original $70,000 investment:

Capital deducted as depreciation	$ 5,000
Capital deducted against sales price	57,000
Capital deducted as a loss	8,000
Total amount invested	$70,000

Income from Conduit Entities.   The last consideration related to unearned forms of income is the recognition of income from conduit entities (primarily S corporations and partnerships). Recall that a conduit entity is not taxed on its income; rather, the income from the conduit flows to the owner(s) of the entity for taxation. Thus, taxpayers who own investments in such entities must recognize their share of the conduit's income on their tax return.[13] Conversely, distributions from a conduit entity are not taxed; they are merely a return of capital investment in the entity.

▲ **EXAMPLE 22**   Ansel owns a 20% interest in Forrest, Inc. Forrest is organized as an S corporation and had a taxable income of $80,000 in the current year. Forrest also distributed $20,000 in dividends. What amount of income must Ansel recognize from his ownership in Forrest Inc.?

Discussion: Ansel must recognize his proportionate share of Forrest's income, $16,000 (20% × $80,000). Because he is taxed on his share of Forrest's income, the $4,000 in dividends (20% × $20,000) received is not taxed; it is considered a return of his investment, which reduces the basis of his investment in Forrest.

▲ **EXAMPLE 23**   Assume that in example 22 Forrest, Inc., is a corporation. What amount of income must Ansel recognize from his ownership in Forrest, Inc.?

Discussion: As a corporation, Forrest is taxed on the $80,000 in income it earned; it does not flow to the owners. Ansel is taxed on the $4,000 in dividends he receives from Forrest.

Transfers from Others

As the discussion of what constitutes income indicated, not all income is the result of labor or capital. Tax entities, particularly individuals, sometimes receive amounts that are neither earned nor unearned, yet they constitute realizations of increases in wealth and as such are taxable to the recipient. In this area, there are four common sources of taxable transfer income:

- Prizes and awards
- Unemployment compensation
- Social Security benefits
- Alimony received

Prizes and Awards.   With two exceptions, any prizes or awards received are taxable to the recipient.[14] One way to avoid tax on the receipt of a prize or award is to immediately transfer the prize or award to a government or other qualified charitable organization such as a church, school, charity, and so on. This exclusion is available only for certain awards, such as those for literary, scientific, and charitable achievements for which the taxpayer did not take action to obtain the award and for which no future services must be performed as a condition of receiving the award. Thus, winnings on game shows cannot be excluded, even if they are immediately transferred to a local charity, because the contestant voluntarily entered the contest.

> ▲ **EXAMPLE 24**   Letisha received the outstanding teacher award at State University. The award included a cash prize of $5,000. Is the $5,000 taxable to Letisha?
>
> *Discussion:*   If Letisha keeps the $5,000, she will have to include it in her gross income. However, if she was chosen from among all teachers at State University and the award does not require her to perform a specific future service, she can avoid taxation by transferring the check to a government body or charitable organization.

The second class of awards that may be excluded is employee achievement awards that are paid in the form of property and are based on length of service or on safety achievements. The maximum dollar exclusion for such awards is $400 per employee per year. However, if the award comes from a qualified plan, the individual limit is raised to $1,600. A qualified plan is a formal written plan or program to award all employees who qualify under the plan's requirements. The plan must not discriminate in favor of highly compensated employees.

> ▲ **EXAMPLE 25**   At her retirement party, Tova received a Rolex watch worth $1,200 in recognition of her 30 years of service to her employer. Is the receipt of the watch taxable to Tova? If so, how much income must she recognize?
>
> *Discussion:*   Because the watch is an award of property that was given in recognition of length of service, at least $400 of the $1,200 fair market value of the watch may be excluded. If Tova's watch was given as part of a qualified plan, she may exclude the entire $1,200 from her taxable income, because it is worth less than the $1,600 limit for such plans.

Unemployment Compensation.   Amounts received from state unemployment compensation plans are considered substitutes for earned income and are always taxable to the recipient.[15] Unemployment compensation is designed to aid individuals who become unemployed until they can find new employment. A similar type of benefit paid by states to individuals is workers' compensation. Workers' compensation is paid to employees who are injured on the job and cannot continue to work as a result of their injuries. A specific exclusion from income is provided for workers' compensation payments and is discussed in Chapter 4.

Social Security Benefits.   Before 1983, Social Security benefits were excluded from taxation. The exclusion was evidently based on administrative convenience because the tax law contained no specific exclusion for such payments. This made some sense, because the payments made by an employee into the fund are not exempt from tax. However, the matching portion paid by the employer is not taxable to the employee. Thus, under the capital recovery concept, it could be said that half of each payment received from Social Security represented a return of the taxpayer's investment and was therefore excluded, much like the annuities discussed earlier. However, when Congress decided to begin taxing Social Security benefits in 1984, politicians were concerned about taxing those whose main source of income came from Social Security. That is, Congress questioned the ability of lower-income taxpayers to pay the tax. To negate this possibility, Congress used a lesser-of formula to determine the amount of Social Security to include in gross income; the formula allows lower-income taxpayers to escape taxation on Social Security benefits.[16] Calculation of the taxable portion of Social Security benefits before 1994 is presented in Exhibit 3–2.

Although the second formula seems unduly complex, modified adjusted gross income serves as a "floor" value under which no Social Security benefits are taxed. Note that as long as the taxpayer's modified adjusted gross income is less than the base amount, none of the Social Security benefits is subject to tax. Thus, people with relatively modest incomes are not taxed on Social Security benefits.

Recall from Chapter 1 that adjusted gross income (AGI) is defined as gross income less deductions for adjusted gross income. Deductions allowable for AGI include trade or business expenses, rental and royalty expenses, reimbursed employee business expenses, payments into pension accounts (IRAs), and certain other business- and investment-related expenses. As such, adjusted gross income provides a measure of the individual's ability to pay tax. In the second formula, the two major additions to AGI, for the foreign earned income exclusion and tax-exempt interest (both exclusions are discussed in Chapter 4), are there to ensure that individuals with large, untaxed economic incomes pay some tax on Social Security benefits.

▲ **EXAMPLE 26**   Judith is a single individual who receives $4,000 in Social Security benefits during 1993. Her adjusted gross income before considering the taxability of the Social Security benefits is $10,000. How much of the $4,000 is taxable?

Discussion: None of the $4,000 is included in Judith's gross income, because her modified adjusted gross income falls below the $25,000 floor value for taxation of unmarried taxpayers. Per the formulas in Exhibit 3–2, Judith includes in income the *lesser* of

$$1/2(\$4,000) = \$2,000$$
$$\text{OR}$$
$$1/2(\$10,000 + \$2,000 - \$25,000) < 0$$

▲ **EXAMPLE 27**   Jack and Bettina received the following income during 1993:

Retirement pay	$23,000
Tax-exempt bond interest	$10,000
Social Security benefits	$6,000

How much of the $6,000 must be included in their gross income?

▲ **Exhibit 3–2**

CALCULATION OF TAXABLE PORTION OF SOCIAL SECURITY BENEFITS RECEIVED

The taxable portion of Social Security is equal to the lesser of

1. one-half of the Social Security benefits received during the year,

OR

2. one-half of the amount by which modified adjusted gross income exceeds the base amount,

Where

Modified adjusted gross income = Adjusted gross income + one-half the Social Security benefits received during the year + any foreign earned income exclusion + any tax-exempt interest

And

Base amount = $25,000 for an unmarried individual
$32,000 for a married couple, filing jointly
$ -0- for all others

Discussion: Social Security benefits of $2,000 are taxable per the following formulas:

The lesser of

$$1/2(\$6,000) = \$3,000$$
OR
$$1/2(\$23,000 + \$3,000 + \$10,000 - \$32,000) = 1/2(\$36,000 - \$32,000) = \$2,000$$

Note that if Jack and Bettina were not required to include their tax-exempt interest in the Social Security benefits calculation, their income ($26,000) would have fallen below the base amount for a married couple ($32,000) and no part of their benefits would have been taxed. Thus, the adjustment for tax-exempt interest has made a portion of their benefits taxable in accord with Congress's intent: to apply the tax to individuals with large economic incomes.

▲ **EXAMPLE 28**   Ruth is a retired executive whose adjusted gross income for 1993 is $80,000. In addition, Ruth receives $5,000 in Social Security benefits. How much of the $5,000 must be included in Ruth's gross income?

Discussion: Ruth must include $2,500 in her gross income per the following formula:

The lesser of

$$1/2(\$5,000) = \$2,500$$
OR
$$1/2(\$80,000 + \$2,500 - \$25,000) = \$28,750$$

Example 28 illustrates how, once a taxpayer's modified adjusted gross income reaches the level at which formula 2 exceeds one-half of the Social Security benefits, the maximum amount of Social Security subject to tax is one-half of the benefits received, no matter how much the taxpayer's income increases. Thus, formula 1 establishes a "ceiling" value for the taxation of Social Security benefits received before 1994.

The Omnibus Budget Reconciliation Act of 1993 created a second tier of Social Security benefit inclusion for higher-income taxpayers. The second tier applies to unmarried individuals with modified adjusted gross incomes greater than $34,000 and married couples filing joint returns with modified adjusted gross incomes exceeding $44,000. The rules discussed earlier (which the act refers to as *present law*) remain in effect for taxpayers with modified adjusted gross incomes that are less than these amounts.

For tax years after 1993, taxpayers with modified adjusted gross incomes above the threshold levels of $34,000 and $44,000 have to make an additional computation to determine the amount of Social Security benefits that they must include in gross income. As outlined in Exhibit 3–3, the new second-tier rule increases the taxable portions in the original Social Security formulas from 50 percent to 85 percent. In addition, formula 2 is increased by the amount of Social Security included under present law or a fixed amount ($4,500 for single individuals, $6,000 for married taxpayers filing joint returns), whichever is less. This change in formula 2 requires taxpayers subject to the second-tier rules to calculate the amount of Social Security they would have included in their gross income under present law.

▲ **EXAMPLE 29**   Assume the same facts as in example 26, except that the tax year is 1995. How much of the $4,000 in Social Security benefits is included in Judith's gross income?

Discussion: None of the $4,000 is included in Judith's gross income, because her modified adjusted gross income is below the $25,000 floor value for unmarried individuals. Note that the new second-tier rule does not apply to Judith, and her Social Security benefits will not be subject to tax.

CALCULATION OF SECOND
TIER FOR INCLUSION OF
SOCIAL SECURITY
BENEFITS RECEIVED AFTER
1993

The taxable portion of Social Security is equal to the lesser of
  1. 85% of the Social Security benefits received during the year,
OR
  2. The sum of
    a. 85% of the amount by which modified adjusted gross income exceeds the base amount
    PLUS
    b. The smaller of
        the amount of Social Security benefits included in gross income under present law,
      OR
        $4,500 for an unmarried individual
        $6,000 for a married couple filing jointly
Where

Modified adjusted gross income = Adjusted gross income +
one-half of the Social Security benefits received during the year +
any foreign earned income exclusion + any tax-exempt interest

And

Base amount $34,000 for an unmarried individual
$44,000 for a married couple filing jointly
$ -0- for all others

▲ **EXAMPLE 30**   Assume the same facts as in example 27, except that the tax year is 1995. How much of the $6,000 in Social Security benefits received by Jack and Bettina is included in their gross income?

Discussion: Jack and Bettina's modified adjusted gross income is $36,000 ($23,000 + $3,000 + $10,000). Because their modified adjusted gross income is less than $44,000, Jack and Bettina's Social Security benefits are taxed as under present law. They include $2,000 in Social Security benefits in their gross income.

▲ **EXAMPLE 31**   Dieter and Luann are a married couple whose adjusted gross income for 1995 is $42,000. In addition, they received $10,000 in Social Security benefits. How much of the $10,000 must be included in Dieter and Luann's 1995 gross income?

Discussion: Dieter and Luann's modified adjusted gross income is $47,000 [$42,000 + $5,000 (1/2 × $10,000)]. Because their modified adjusted gross income exceeds the $44,000 base amount, they are subject to the second-tier rule. Under present law, their taxable Social Security is $5,000:

The lesser of

$$1/2(\$10,000) = \$5,000$$
$$\text{OR}$$
$$1/2(\$47,000 - \$32,000) = \$7,500$$

Under the second-tier rule, Dieter and Luann must include $7,550 of the Social Security benefits in gross income:

The lesser of
1.   85% × $10,000 = $8,500
OR
2.   The sum of
    a.   85% × ($47,000 − $44,000) = $2,550
    b.   the smaller of
            $5,000 (amount included under present law)
      OR
            $6,000   5,000
Equals $7,550

▲ **EXAMPLE 32**   Camilla is a single individual whose adjusted gross income for 1995 is $33,000. In addition, she receives $6,000 in Social Security benefits and has tax-exempt municipal bond interest income of $2,000. How much of the $6,000 must be included in Camilla's 1995 gross income?

Discussion: Camilla's modified adjusted gross income is $38,000 [$33,000 + $3,000 (1/2 × $6,000) + $2,000], and she is subject to the second-tier rule. Under present law, her taxable Social Security is $3,000:

The lesser of

$$1/2(\$6,000) = \$3,000$$
$$\text{OR}$$
$$1/2\ (\$38,000 - \$25,000) = \$6,500$$

Under the second-tier inclusion rule, Camilla must include $5,100 of the Social Security benefits in gross income:

The lesser of

1.   85% × $6,000 = $5,100

OR

2.   The sum of
   a.   85% × ($38,000 − $34,000) = $3,400
   b.   the smaller of
               $3,000 (amount taxable under present law)

   OR

               $4,500   3,000

Equals $6,400

Example 32 illustrates how the modification of formula 2 invokes the new ceiling of 85 percent of Social Security benefits received sooner than under present law. That is, if she had not had to add to formula 2 the $3,000 of Social Security included under present law, Camilla would have had to include only $3,400 of Social Security benefits in her gross income.

Alimony Received.   In divorce situations, one spouse often makes payments to a former spouse. These payments may be to provide for the support of children (called **child support payments**), they may be simply a sharing of income between the two parties (called **alimony**), or they may constitute a division of marital property **(property settlement).** Child support payments are not taxable to the recipient, regardless of how the recipient actually spends the money.[17] However, payments that are a sharing of current income (alimony) are taxable to the recipient and deductible for adjusted gross income by the payer. That is, alimony is an allowable transfer of income from one former spouse to another. In order to be considered alimony, all the following conditions must be met:

1.   The payment must be in cash

2.   The payment must be in a written agreement (either a separation or divorce agreement)

3.   The written agreement does not specify that the payments are for some other purpose (i.e., child support)

4.   The payer and the payee cannot be members of the same household at the time of the payment

5.   There is no liability to make payments for any period after the death of the payee.[18]

These requirements are intended to ensure that both parties to the agreement concur on the amount of alimony being paid. One controversial tax aspect of divorce involves property settlements. Payments and transfers pursuant to property settlements between spouses do not have any income tax consequences.

▲ **EXAMPLE 33**   Walt and Janice were divorced during the current year. As part of the divorce settlement, Walt paid Janice $100,000 for her interest in their home (the home had a fair market value of $200,000) and agreed to pay Janice $12,000 per year in alimony. The home had an adjusted basis to Walt and Janice of $120,000. What are the tax effects of the payments Walt makes to Janice?

Discussion: The $100,000 payment to Janice is not a taxable disposition by Janice, and no deduction is allowed to Walt, because it is a property settlement payment. The $12,000 per year of alimony is included in Janice's gross income and is deductible for adjusted gross income by Walt.

This treatment of property settlements may tempt the spouse making a property settlement to try to disguise the settlement as deductible alimony payments. A complex set of "recapture" rules has been designed to stop this so-called front loading of property settlements disguised as alimony payments during the first three years of separation. The recapture rules require the spouse making the alimony payment (and taking the alimony-paid deduction) to include in income the excess deductions taken when the property settlement has been disguised as alimony. The spouse receiving the disguised payments is allowed a deduction to offset the overstated alimony. These recapture rules have removed the incentive to disguise property settlements as alimony.

▲ **EXAMPLE 34**   In example 33, assume that instead of specifying the $100,000 as a property settlement in their divorce decree, Walt agreed to pay Janice alimony of $112,000 in the first year and $12,000 per year for every year after the first year. What are the tax effects of the payments Walt makes to Janice?

Discussion: The large payment in the first year relative to the other years (front loading) will trigger the alimony recapture rules. The net effect of the recapture rules will be to treat the additional $100,000 in the first year as a property settlement. That is, the net tax treatment is identical to that in example 33.

The final problem in the alimony area is the attempt to disguise child support payments as alimony. To counter this problem, the tax law requires that any reductions in alimony payments that are the result of a contingency related to a child are classified as child support payments.[19]

▲ **EXAMPLE 35**   Ben and Diane were divorced in the current year. As part of their divorce agreement, Ben is to pay Diane alimony of $500 per month until their son reaches age 18, at which time the payments will be reduced to $200 per month. What are the tax effects of the payments Ben makes to Diane?

Discussion: Because the payments are to be reduced to $200 when their child reaches age 18 (a contingency related to a child), only $200 per month of all payments made are considered alimony. The remaining $300 is a nondeductible child support payment.

Imputed Income

Two major sources of income that are untaxed under current law are the goods and services produced by individuals for personal consumption and individuals' use of their personal residence and other durable goods. To understand why these items constitute income under the principles described earlier in the chapter, consider the following example:

▲ **EXAMPLE 36**   Jana has a garden in which she grows tomatoes for her personal consumption. The full cost of producing the tomatoes amounts to $40. At current prices, it would have cost $100 to purchase the tomatoes. Does Jana have income from growing and consuming her tomatoes?

Discussion: Although Jana's wealth has increased by $60 from growing and consuming her own tomatoes rather than purchasing them, she does not have to recognize the $60 as income. The key factor in the nonrecognition of the income is that the $60 increase in wealth was not realized in an arm's-length transaction with another party. Note that if Jana had sold the tomatoes for $100 and used the money for other purposes, she clearly would have realized the income, and the $60 increase in wealth would be subject to tax.

This example of income from in-kind consumption is but one of many types of **imputed income** from which taxpayers profit on a daily basis but is not subject to taxation. The primary reason that these kinds of income are not taxed is that there is no realization of the income. In addition, even if in-kind consumption were considered a realization, such income would not be taxed, because it would be administratively inconvenient: Imagine the nightmare of having to keep track of all the tasks you perform for yourself rather than hire someone else to do the work! How could the government audit this type of income?

Although the vast majority of imputed income is not taxed, the tax law does identify several specific items of imputed income that must be taxed. The three most common forms of imputed income subject to tax are

- Below market-rate loans
- Payment of expenses by others
- Bargain purchases

Below Market-Rate Loans.   Before 1984, a common tax-planning technique that taxpayers used to shift income from high marginal tax rate taxpayers to low marginal tax rate taxpayers was the use of an interest-free loan, called a **below market-rate loan.** The savings that could have been realized from such a plan are illustrated in the following example:

▲ **EXAMPLE 37**   Binh, who is in the 36% marginal tax rate bracket, lent his son Chee $50,000 interest free. Chee, who is a 15% marginal tax rate payer, put the money in a savings account earning 10%. How much tax does the family save through this arrangement?

Discussion: If Binh invested the $50,000 at the same earnings rate, the tax savings would be $1,050. That is the difference between the tax Binh would have paid on the $5,000 in interest, $1,800 ($5,000 × 36%), and the tax paid by Chee on the $5,000 in interest, $750 ($5,000 × 15%).

In 1984, Congress curtailed some advantages of interest-free loans by enacting provisions that consider such loans as consisting of two transactions: a normal interest-bearing loan (at the current federal rate of interest) and an exchange of cash between the lender and the borrower to pay the interest on the loan. The imputed exchange of cash is the amount of cash necessary for the borrower to pay the lender the interest on the loan. A conventional interest-bearing loan and an interest-free loan are compared in Figure 3–1.

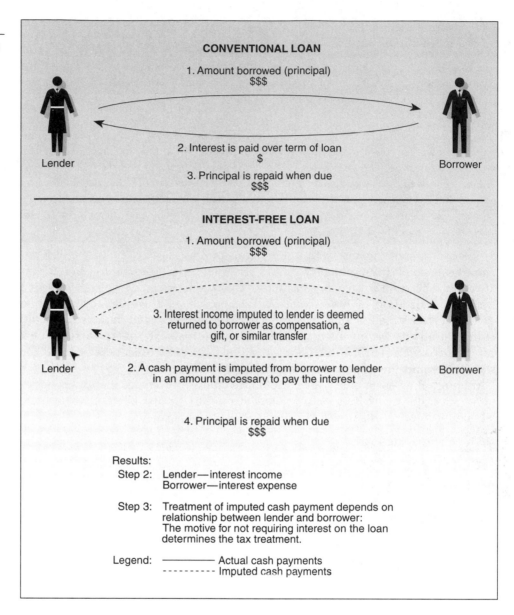

Under the imputed interest rules,[20] the lender is deemed to have interest income at the federal rate of interest, whereas the borrower is deemed to have made a payment (first imputed cash payment) of the interest (step 2 at the bottom of Figure 3–1). The imputed payment of cash (second imputed cash payment) from the lender to the borrower to pay the interest (step 3 at the bottom of Figure 3–1) may also produce income taxable income to the borrower, depending on the type of loan.

The three basic types of loans are

- Gift loans
- Employment-related loans
- Corporation/shareholder loans

A gift loan is one made between family members. The imputed cash exchange on these loans is considered a gift from the lender to the borrower and is not subject to tax (the exclusion for gifts is covered in Chapter 4).

▲ **EXAMPLE 38**   What is the tax treatment of the loan Binh made to Chee in example 37 if the federal rate of interest is 8%?

Discussion: The first step in accounting for an interest-free loan is to determine the amount of imputed interest on the loan using the applicable federal rate of interest. In this case, the amount of imputed interest is $4,000 ($50,000 × 8%). This is the amount of interest income the lender is deemed to have earned (and the borrower is deemed to have paid) from the making of the loan. In this case, interest income of $4,000 is imputed to Binh, and interest expense of $4,000 is imputed to Chee. Binh therefore includes $4,000 of interest in his gross income. Chee has interest expense of $4,000, the deductibility of which depends on how he uses the money (interest deductions are discussed in Chapter 5). NOTE: Because this is a gift loan of less than $100,000, the amount of interest imputed may be less than the $4,000 federal rate. See examples 41–43.

The second step is to give effect to the motive for the nonpayment of interest on the loan. This is done by assuming that the lender gave the borrower the cash with which to pay the interest imputed on the loan in the first step. This imputed payment of cash is then taxed as any payment of cash would be taxed. In this case, Binh is deemed to have made a gift to his son of the $4,000 in interest. The receipt of the gift is not taxable to Chee, nor is it deductible by Binh.

When a loan is made to an employee by an employer, the imputed exchange of cash in the second step is deemed to be compensation paid to the employee and thus is taxable to the employee and deductible by the employer.

▲ **EXAMPLE 39**   In the previous example, assume that Binh lent the $50,000 to Celine, an employee of his roofing business. What is the tax treatment of the loan?

Discussion: As in the gift loan, Binh is assumed to have received (and Celine is assumed to have paid) interest income of $4,000. The imputed payment of cash for the interest is considered a payment for compensation. Therefore, Binh is deemed to have paid Celine $4,000 in compensation, which is taxable to Celine and deductible by Binh.

Note that the net effect of this arrangement for Binh is zero. That is, he has an increase in his income of $4,000 because of the imputation to him of the interest income on the loan, which is counterbalanced by the compensation payment deduction of $4,000. Whether the same is true for Celine depends on whether she can deduct the interest expense imputed on the loan. For example, if Celine used the $50,000 for a purely personal purpose such as the payment of a personal debt, the interest would not be deductible. In that case, the net effect for Celine would be an increase in taxable income of the $4,000 in imputed compensation.

When an interest-free loan is made to a shareholder of a corporation, the imputed exchange of cash is deemed to be a dividend paid to the shareholder and thus is taxable to the shareholder. A corporation is not allowed a deduction for dividends paid to shareholders.

▲ **EXAMPLE 40**   In example 39, assume that Celine is a shareholder of Binh's roofing business, which is organized as a corporation. The loan is made from the corporation to Celine. What is the tax treatment of the loan?

Discussion: The $4,000 in interest is imputed to the corporation and Celine, as in the previous example. The $4,000 imputed exchange of cash to pay the interest is deemed a dividend paid to Celine and is taxable to her as dividend income. Binh's corporation is deemed to have paid a dividend of $4,000, which is not deductible by the corporation.

A summary of the treatments of the second imputed cash payment for the three types of loans is presented in Table 3–1.

EXCEPTIONS TO IMPUTED INTEREST RULES.   There are two exceptions to the rules for interest-free loans. First, any loan of $10,000 or less is exempted from the imputed interest rules. This exception is for administrative convenience; it would be very costly to keep track of all small loans that people make to friends and relatives. Therefore, a small amount of income can still be shifted through the use of $10,000 interest-free loans.

The second exception is for gift loans of $100,000 or less. On such loans, the imputed interest on the loan cannot exceed the borrower's net investment income (investment income less the costs of producing the income) for the year. Further, if the borrower's net investment income for the year does not exceed $1,000, the imputed interest is deemed to be zero; the loan has no tax effect. Therefore, gift loans that do not produce much income for the borrower or that are used for in-kind consumption by the borrower escape the imputed interest rules.

▲ **EXAMPLE 41**   Allegra lent her daughter Elena $50,000, which she used to purchase a new house. The loan was interest-free, the federal rate of interest was 8%, and Elena had $600 in investment income for the year. What are the tax consequences of the loan?

Discussion: Because this was a gift loan of less than $100,000, the imputed interest is limited to Elena's net investment income for the year. However, because Elena's investment income is less than $1,000, no interest is imputed on the loan. Therefore, the loan has no income tax effects for either Allegra or Elena.

▲ **Table 3–1**

TREATMENT OF SECOND
IMPUTED CASH PAYMENT

Type of Loan	Lender	Borrower
Gift loans	Imputed payment is a gift made to the borrower—*no income tax effect.*	Imputed payment is a gift received from the lender—*no income tax effect.*
Employment-related loans	Imputed payment is compensation paid to the borrower—*lender gets a deduction for compensation paid.*	Imputed payment is compensation received by the borrower—*borrower has compensation income.*
Shareholder loans		
1. **Loan to a shareholder**	1. Imputed payment is a dividend paid to the borrower—*lender gets no deduction for dividends paid.*	1. Imputed payment is a dividend received from the lender—*borrower has dividend income.*
2. **Loan to the corporation**	2. Imputed payment is a contribution to corporate capital—*no deduction allowed to lender (added to basis in stock).*	2. Imputed payment is receipt of contributed capital—*no income imputed to the borrower.*

▲ **EXAMPLE 42**   Assume the same facts as in example 41, except that Elena's investment income was $2,500.

Discussion: In this case, interest on the gift loan would be imputed at $2,500, Elena's investment income. Allegra would have interest income of $2,500, and Elena would have interest expense of $2,500.

▲ **EXAMPLE 43**   Assume the same facts as in example 41, except that Elena's investment income was $6,000.

Discussion: In this case, interest at the federal rate of $4,000 ($50,000 × 8%) is less than Elena's investment income of $6,000. Therefore, interest of $4,000 is imputed on the loan. That is, none of the special exceptions for gift loans is applicable. NOTE: Interest is never imputed at a rate greater than the applicable federal interest rate.

Payment of Expenses by Others.   Whenever one taxpayer pays another taxpayer's expenses, the taxpayer who received the benefit of the payment has realized an increase in wealth and is taxed on the payment, unless the payment constituted a valid gift (gifts are excluded from income).[21] The more common situations involve payments of expenses of an employee by an employer, taxes of the lessor paid by the lessee of property, and the payment of the personal expenses of the principal shareholder of a closely held corporation (a closely held corporation is one in which five or fewer shareholders own more than 50 percent of the stock of the corporation).

▲ **EXAMPLE 44**   Ramona is the president of DEF, Inc. Ramona's employment contract states that DEF is to pay Ramona a salary of $100,000 and the federal income tax due on the salary. In the current year, the tax on Ramona's DEF salary totals $27,000, which is paid by DEF. What is Ramona's gross income from DEF?

Discussion: The payment of the $27,000 of tax on Ramona's salary is considered compensation income paid to Ramona. Therefore, her gross income from DEF is $127,000.

▲ **EXAMPLE 45**   Joe lost his job this year. Because he was having trouble paying all his bills, his grandfather agreed to pay Joe's home mortgage until he could find a new job. His grandfather made payments on Joe's mortgage totaling $10,000 during the current year. What are the tax effects of the payment of Joe's mortgage by his grandfather?

Discussion: The payment of the mortgage is not meant to be compensation from grandfather to Joe; rather, it is in the nature of a gift from grandfather to Joe to help him through his tough economic times. Therefore, the payments are not taxable to Joe (gifts are excluded from income).

These two examples illustrate the key consideration in determining whether the payment of an expense by another is taxable: intent to compensate. That is, when payments are made on behalf of another in an employment or other business-related context, they are generally taxable. Payments made on behalf of family members that are unrelated to employment or other business matters are generally considered nontaxable gifts.

Bargain Purchases.   Ordinarily, when taxpayers astutely purchase property for less than it is worth, they are not taxed immediately on the increased wealth resulting from the purchase. Any such gain will be reflected when the property is sold. However, a true **bargain purchase** is taxable to the buyer. Such a purchase occurs when the difference between the purchase price and the fair market value represents an effort by the seller to confer an economic advantage to the buyer.[22] That is, the purchase price does not result from an arm's-length transaction. As such, bargain purchases are typically found in employer/employee purchases and other instances in which the seller perceives some ultimate advantage in selling the property to a particular taxpayer at less than fair market value.

▲ EXAMPLE 46   Sterling is an employee of Shelf Road Development Co. The company recently subdivided some property and offered lots for sale at a price of $50,000. Shelf sold Sterling a lot for $20,000. How much gross income does Sterling have from the purchase of property?

Discussion: The difference between the $50,000 fair market value and the $20,000 purchase price—$30,000—is taxable to Sterling as compensation. The purchase price, an attempt to compensate Sterling, was not the result of an arm's-length bargain.

▲ EXAMPLE 47   Karolina wanted to purchase a new Bugatti roadster. She knew that such cars usually sell for about $50,000. However, she found a dealer who was having financial difficulties and was able to purchase a Bugatti for only $40,000. Does Karolina have gross income from the purchase of the Bugatti?

Discussion: Because the dealer gained no long-term benefit from selling the car to Karolina for $40,000, her astute purchase is not considered a bargain purchase for tax purposes. Further, the purchase price was the result of an arm's-length transaction. Therefore, she is not taxed on the $10,000 below market-value purchase.

▲ CAPITAL GAINS AND LOSSES—AN INTRODUCTION

Whenever a property is sold, exchanged, or otherwise disposed of, a realization occurs, and the entity owning the property must calculate the gain (loss) resulting from the disposition of the property. The income tax provisions governing property transactions are an important part of the income tax system. Chapters 10 through 13 discuss in detail various aspects of income tax accounting for the acquisition, use, and disposition of property. However, because of their importance in the income tax system, we briefly discuss capital gains and losses at this point.

A capital gain or a capital loss results from the sale or other disposition of a capital asset. As discussed in Chapter 2, a capital asset is any asset that is not a receivable, an item of inventory, depreciable property used in a trade or business, or real property used in a trade or business.[23] Thus, the most common capital assets are investment assets (stocks, bonds, rental property held for investment) and assets used for personal use purposes (home, furniture, clothing, personal automobile, etc.) by individuals.

Since 1921, the tax law has provided some form of preferential tax treatment for capital gains. For example, until 1987, individuals were allowed to deduct 60 percent of any net long-term capital gains. This meant that only 40 percent of net long-term capital gains was subject to tax. During most of this time, the top marginal tax rate was 50 percent, resulting in a maximum tax rate on long-term capital gains of 20 percent (50% × 40%). Although the 60-percent capital gains deduction was repealed in 1986, all the mechanisms for accounting for capital gains and other limitations were left in place. Therefore, although the tax savings may not be as great as they once were, accounting for capital gains and losses remains an important aspect of our tax system. The basic aspects of accounting for capital gains and losses are discussed in the sections that follow. More detailed analysis is provided in Chapter 12.

Capital Gain-and-Loss Netting Procedure

The income tax law determines the treatment of capital gains and losses on an annual basis. That is, all capital gains and losses occurring during a tax year are aggregated through a prescribed netting procedure to determine the net effect of all capital asset transactions for the year.[24] The special tax treatments (if any are applicable) are applied only to the net results for the year, not to individual transactions.

Exhibit 3–4 outlines the procedure for determining the net long-term capital gains or losses for the year. The first step requires segregation of the year's gains into long-term and short-term gains and losses. Whether a gain (loss) is short term or long term depends on its holding period. As the phrase indicates, the **holding period** is how long the taxpayer owned the asset that was sold. Assets held for more than one year produce **long-term capital gains** and **long-term capital losses.** Assets held for one year or less produce **short-term capital gains** and **short-term capital losses.**[25] The distinction is important, because preferential treatment is accorded only to net *long-term* capital gains.

The second step in the netting procedure is to reduce the gains and losses for the year into one net long-term position (either a gain or a loss) and one net short-term position (either a gain or a loss). At this stage, all capital gains and losses for the year have been reduced to two numbers—one for the effect of long-term gains and losses and another for short-term gains and losses.

▲ **EXAMPLE 48**   Astrid had the following capital gains and losses for the current year:

Long-term capital gain	$13,000
Long-term capital loss	($ 4,000)
Short-term capital gain	$ 8,000
Short-term capital loss	($10,000)

What are Astrid's net long-term and net short-term capital gain (loss) positions for the year?

Discussion: Astrid has a net long-term capital gain of $9,000 and a net short-term capital loss of $2,000 for the current year:

Long-term Gain/Loss Netting	
Long-term capital gain	$13,000
Long-term capital loss	(4,000)
Net long-term capital gain	$ 9,000

Short-term Gain/Loss Netting	
Short-term capital gain	$ 8,000
Short-term capital loss	(10,000)
Net short-term capital loss	$(2,000)

After the capital gain-and-loss transactions for the year have been reduced to a long-term and a short-term position for the year, the next step is to reduce the capital gain position for the year to either a gain or a loss on capital asset transactions for the year. Thus, if the short- and long-term positions are opposite (one is a gain and one is a loss), the two positions must be netted together to determine whether a gain or a loss has resulted from the taxpayer's capital asset transactions for the year.

▲ Exhibit 3–4
_____

Capital Gain-and-Loss
Netting Procedure

Step 1	Segregate all capital gains and losses occurring during the year into short-term gains and losses and long-term gains and losses.	
Step 2	Combine all long-term gains and losses to determine a net long-term position for the year. Combine all short-term gains and losses to determine a net short-term position for the year.	

Long-term gains	$XXX	
Long-term losses	(XXX)	
Net long-term gain (loss)		$XXX or $(XXX)
Short-term gains	$XXX	
Short-term losses	(XXX)	
Net short-term gain (loss)		$XXX or $(XXX)

Step 3	If the positions determined in step 2 are opposite (i.e., one is a gain and one is a loss), net the two positions together to obtain either a gain or a loss position for the year.
	If the positions determined in step 2 are the same (i.e., either both are gains or both are losses), no further netting is necessary.
Step 4	Capital gain-and-loss treatments (individuals)
	Short-term capital gain—no special treatment
	Long-term capital gain—taxed at a maximum rate of 28%
	Capital losses—Individuals may deduct only $3,000 in net capital losses per year. Any excess loss is carried forward to the next year's capital gain-and-loss netting. In determining the $3,000 deduction, short-term capital losses are deducted before long-term losses.

▲ **EXAMPLE 49**   Return to the facts of example 48. What is Astrid's net capital gain or loss for the year?

Discussion: Astrid has a net long-term capital gain of $7,000 for the year. Because the first netting resulted in a long-term capital gain and a short-term capital loss, one more netting is necessary to determine Astrid's net capital gain position for the year:

Net long-term capital gain	$9,000
Net short-term capital loss	(2,000)
Net long-term capital gain	$7,000

Note that the effect of the netting procedure is to summarize all of Astrid's capital gains and losses for the year in a net gain position. This is the purpose of the procedure—to reduce all capital gains and losses occurring during the year into either a net gain or a net loss position.

If the first netting produces short- and long-term positions that are the same (both are gains or both are losses), the taxpayer's gain or loss position for the year is known and no further netting is necessary.

▲ **EXAMPLE 50**   Milton had the following capital gains and losses for the current year:

Long-term capital gain	$3,000
Long-term capital loss	($1,000)
Short-term capital gain	$6,000
Short-term capital loss	($2,000)

What is Milton's net capital gain (loss) position for the current year?

Discussion: The first netting results in a net long-term capital gain of $2,000 and a net short-term capital gain of $4,000:

Long-term Gain/Loss Netting	
Long-term capital gain	$3,000
Long-term capital loss	(1,000)
Net long-term capital gain	$2,000

Short-term Gain/Loss Netting	
Short-term capital gain	$6,000
Short-term capital loss	(2,000)
Net short-term capital gain	$4,000

Because both the long- and short-term positions are gains, it is clear that Milton has a gain in his capital asset transactions for the year. Therefore, no further netting is necessary. He will report a long-term capital gain of $2,000 and a short-term capital gain of $4,000 on his current year's tax return.

After the net capital gain (loss) position for the year has been determined, each of the four types of gains and losses is subject to special rules in the calculation of taxable income. These rules are outlined in step 4 of Exhibit 3–4 and discussed in the next section. One thing you should note is that the tax treatments are applied to the net gain (loss) for the entire tax year, not for individual gains and losses occurring during the year.

Tax Treatment of Capital Gains

The only current tax relief is for **net long-term capital gains.** Net short-term capital gains receive no tax relief and are merely added to gross income. Net long-term capital gains are also added to gross income. However, the tax law provides that net long-term capital gains cannot be taxed at a marginal tax rate greater than 28 percent. This provision provides tax savings only to taxpayers whose marginal tax rate is greater than 28%. Taxpayers in the 15- and 28-percent brackets receive no benefit from having net long-term capital gains.

▲ **EXAMPLE 51**   Assume that in example 50 Milton is a single individual with taxable income of $80,000, not including capital gains. What is the tax on his net capital gains?

Discussion: Milton would pay a tax of $560 ($2,000 × 28%) on his net long-term capital gain and a tax of $1,240 ($4,000 × 31%) on his net short-term capital gain. In 1995, single individuals began paying a 31% marginal tax rate at a taxable income of $56,550. Because Milton's taxable income is greater than this amount, his marginal tax rate is 31%. The short-term capital gain is added to his gross income and taxed at his marginal tax rate. The net long-term capital gain is taxed at the 28% capital gain rate, not his actual marginal tax rate. Milton saves $60 [$2,000 × (31% − 28%)] because of the provision limiting capital gains to 28%.

Tax Treatment of Capital Losses

Net capital losses of individuals are deductible up to an annual limit of $3,000.[26] Capital losses are deductible as a deduction *for* adjusted gross income. Any capital loss in excess of the $3,000 limit is carried forward to the next year and is used in the next year's capital gain-and-loss netting.[27]

▲ **EXAMPLE 52**   Chalmer had a net long-term capital gain of $6,000 and a net short-term capital loss of $17,000 in the current year. What is the effect of Chalmer's capital asset transactions on his taxable income?

Discussion: Because the long- and short-term positions are opposite, they are netted together, resulting in a net short-term capital loss of $11,000 ($6,000 − $17,000). Chalmer can deduct $3,000 of the loss as a deduction for adjusted gross income in the current year. The remaining $8,000 loss is carried forward to next year as a short-term capital loss and used in next year's capital gain-and-loss netting.

When an individual has both a net short-term capital loss and a **net long-term capital loss** in the same year, the short-term loss must be used toward the $3,000 annual limit before any long-term loss is deducted.[28]

▲ **EXAMPLE 53**   During the current year, Cara had a $2,000 net short-term capital loss and a $5,000 net long-term capital loss. What is the effect of Cara's capital asset transactions on her taxable income?

Discussion: Because the long- and short-term positions are both losses, no netting is necessary. Cara deducts $3,000 of the total loss as a deduction for adjusted gross income. The $3,000 loss deduction is composed of the $2,000 short-term loss and $1,000 of the long-term loss. The remaining $4,000 ($5,000 − $1,000) of the long-term loss is carried forward to the next year as a long-term capital loss and used in next year's capital gain-and-loss netting.

One thing to remember when dealing with personal use assets (which are capital assets) is that gains on the sale of personal use assets are taxable under the all-inclusive income concept. However, losses on personal use assets are disallowed. Therefore, if a personal use asset is sold at a gain, the gain is a capital gain and subject to the rules for capital gains. A loss on the sale of a personal use asset is not deductible and does not enter into the capital gain netting procedure.

▲ **EXAMPLE 54**   Morgan sold for $3,400 a diamond necklace she had purchased in 1975 at a cost of $2,000. Larry sold his personal truck, for which he had paid $12,000, for $5,000. What are the effects of the sales on Morgan's and Larry's incomes?

Discussion: Morgan has a long-term capital gain of $1,400 ($3,400 − $2,000) from the sale of her necklace. The $1,400 gain must be combined with her other capital gains and losses in the capital gain-and-loss netting procedure. Larry's loss of $7,000 ($5,000 − $12,000) on the sale of his truck is a nondeductible personal use loss. Therefore, the loss has no effect on his taxable income.

Capital Gains and Losses of Conduit Entities

All items of income—gains, losses, deductions, and credits—of a conduit entity flow through the entity and are reported directly by the owners of the conduit. However, many items realized at the conduit level receive special treatment on the owners' tax returns. To provide owners with the information necessary to prepare their returns properly, a conduit entity is required to report each owner's share of the "ordinary" taxable income or loss separately from those items that receive special treatment.[29] The ordinary taxable income or loss is the income that results from income, gains, losses, and deductions that receive no special treatment. Because capital gains and losses are aggregated in the netting process on an owner's return, they must be allocated to each owner.

▲ **EXAMPLE 55**   Parnell and Isis are equal partners in the Steiner Partnership. Steiner has total income of $70,000, consisting of the following items in the current year:

Gross income from sales	$120,000
Trade or business expenses	90,000
Ordinary income	$ 30,000

Long-term gain on investment property	50,000
Short-term loss on Webto stock	(10,000)
Total income	$ 70,000

How do Steiner's results affect Parnell and Isis?

Discussion: As equal partners, Parnell and Isis share the partnership items equally. Each reports $15,000 (50% × $30,000) in ordinary income from the partnership. In addition, each will have a long-term capital gain of $25,000 and a short-term capital loss of $5,000 that each must include in his or her capital gain-and-loss netting.

▲ **EXAMPLE 56**   Assume that in addition to the items reported to her in example 55, Isis had the following income items:

Salary from Webto Corporation	$64,000
Dividend income	4,000
Long-term capital loss	(14,000)

What is Isis's adjusted gross income?

Discussion: Isis's adjusted gross income is $89,000:

Salary from Webto Corporation	$64,000
Dividend income	4,000
Ordinary income from Steiner Partnership	15,000
Net long-term capital gain ($25,000 − $14,000 − $5,000)	6,000
Adjusted gross income	$89,000

Note that if the Steiner Partnership were not required to report its capital gains and losses separately, Isis's adjusted gross income would have been $100,000 [(1/2 × $70,000) + $64,000 + $4,000 − $3,000] because of the limitation on capital loss deductions. Because capital gains and losses are reported separately from the partnership's ordinary income, Isis's $14,000 long-term capital loss is deducted against the $25,000 long-term capital gain from the partnership and is not subject to the capital loss limitations.

Once an income item has been identified as taxable, the tax year for recognition must be determined. In general, the taxpayer's accounting method dictates the proper period for inclusion. The two basic accounting methods allowed for tax purposes are the cash method and the accrual method.[30] We will discuss each method and its general income-recognition criteria in turn. Within each of the two basic accounting methods are exceptions to the treatments prescribed by the methods. These exceptions are generally designed to either discourage tax avoidance schemes or are based on the wherewithal-to-pay concept, which states that income should be taxed when the taxpayer has the means to pay the tax. More detailed accounting methods requirements are covered in Chapter 14.

▲ **EFFECT OF ACCOUNTING METHOD**

Cash Method

Taxpayers using this method of accounting recognize income when it is actually or *constructively* received. Recall that reduction to cash is not necessary to trigger income recognition because of the cash-equivalent approach to income recognition under the cash method of accounting. All that is required is that something with a fair market value (property, services, etc.) be received. Under the constructive receipt doctrine, income is received when it is made unconditionally available to the taxpayer and is subject to the taxpayer's complete control.

Because of its simplicity (a checkbook is all the record keeping that is required), most individuals use the cash method. In addition, this method gives taxpayers a somewhat limited ability to determine the year of taxation by accelerating or deferring cash receipts.

> ▲ **EXAMPLE 57**   Harold is a cash basis taxpayer who repairs and maintains air conditioners and heating units in his spare time. The current year has been a good one for Harold, and he expects to be in the top marginal tax bracket. Next year, he plans to expand his business with a resulting increase in expenses and a drop in his marginal tax rate. What can Harold do to lower his tax bill?
>
> *Discussion:*   To lower his taxes, Harold should defer receipt of some of his repair and maintenance income until next year, when his marginal tax rate will be lower. This can be accomplished by delaying billings to customers until next year or by easing any credit terms he extends to customers.

Because of this ability to determine the year of taxation using the cash method, several restrictions are placed on the use of the method by certain types of taxpayers. These restrictions are discussed more fully in Chapter 14. The most basic restriction on the use of the cash method is that taxpayers who sell inventories must account for sales, purchases, and inventories using the accrual basis.[31]

Exceptions Applicable to the Cash Method.   The major income-recognition exception for cash basis taxpayers is for investments in **original issue discount (OID) securities.** An OID security is a debt instrument that has interest payable at maturity rather than throughout the life of the debt. Before the OID rules were codified, cash basis taxpayers could defer interest income by purchasing OID instruments.

> ▲ **EXAMPLE 58**   First Financial, Inc., loaned Heywood $10,000 on an interest-only basis, with interest payable annually at 10% for 3 years. Under the agreement, Heywood paid $1,000 in interest at the end of each year for 3 years. The $10,000 loan balance was repaid at the end of the third year. How much income does First Financial recognize each year?
>
> *Discussion:*   This is a conventional debt situation wherein interest is received throughout the term of the loan and is recognized accordingly. The $1,000 in interest received each year would be included in First Financial's gross income.
>
> ▲ **EXAMPLE 59**   As an alternative, First Financial could lend the money on a discount basis. As an OID debt, the face amount of the debt would be $13,310, payable at the end of 3 years, and Heywood would still receive the $10,000 at the inception of the loan. If First Financial is a cash basis taxpayer, how would it recognize the interest under the general rules for the cash method?
>
> *Discussion:*   Under the cash method, First Financial would recognize no income until it receives payment at the end of the third year. At that time, First Financial would recognize the difference between the amount received at maturity and the amount Heywood actually received as income, $3,310 ($13,310 − $10,000). Note that First Financial receives slightly more interest under this arrangement, because interest is being earned on the annual interest payment that is not being made throughout the 3 years.

Current tax law requires that all OID securities with a maturity of more than one year be accounted for on the accrual basis, using the effective interest method.[32] The intent of this provision is to discourage cash basis investors from deferring income using OID instruments.

▲ **EXAMPLE 60**   What is the proper income recognition for First Financial in example 59?

Discussion: Because the loan is made on an OID basis and has a term of more than one year, First Financial must recognize the interest annually, using the effective interest method. Under this method, the book value of the debt is increased each year for the prior year's interest, which was accrued but not paid. Interest is calculated as the product of the book value outstanding throughout the year and the rate of interest charged on the loan.

Year 1	$10,000 × 10% =	$1,000
Year 2	($10,000 + $1,000) × 10% =	$1,100
Year 3	($10,000 + $1,000 + 1,100) × 10% =	$1,210
	Total income recognized =	$3,310

Series E and EE **savings bonds** issued by the U.S. government are OID securities that are exempt from the OID rules.[33] Taxpayers purchasing these bonds are not required to amortize interest income during the life of the bonds, although they may elect to amortize all such bonds they hold currently. If such an election is made, they must amortize interest on any bonds they purchase in the future.

▲ **EXAMPLE 61**   Henry purchased for $650 a Series EE savings bond with a face value of $1,000 in the current year. The savings bond matures in 10 years and was priced to yield a 6% annual return. How should Henry account for the interest income related to the savings bond?

Discussion: Because Series EE savings bonds are exempted from the OID rules, Henry will not have to recognize interest on the bond until he cashes in the bond. If Henry cashes in the bond at maturity, he will receive the $1,000 face value of the bond. At that time, he would recognize $350 ($1,000 − $650) in interest income. NOTE: Henry may elect to amortize the interest earned on the bond each year, using the effective interest method. However, if he makes this election, any other Series EE bonds he owns, as well as any others he may purchase in the future, must also be amortized. That is, you must use the same accounting method for all such bonds.

Accrual Method

Taxpayers using this method recognize income when it is *earned*, regardless of the actual period of receipt. Income is considered earned when (1) all events have occurred that fix the right to receive the income, and (2) the amount of income earned can be determined with reasonable accuracy.[34] In the majority of cases, these recognition criteria parallel the recognition rules for financial accounting. Some significant differences between the two are discussed later.

Two important aspects of the accrual method should be noted at this point. First, the checkbook approach commonly used by cash basis taxpayers is not sufficient to account for the many accruals and deferrals of income required by the accrual method. Thus, this is a more costly method. Second, accrual basis taxpayers have little control over the timing of their income, because the earning of the income, not the receipt of payment, is the critical recognition event.

▲ **EXAMPLE 62**   Assume the same facts as in example 57, except that Harold has elected to be an accrual basis taxpayer.

Discussion: Harold must recognize the income from the performance of his repair and maintenance services in the year in which they are performed, not when he receives payment for them. Therefore, he has little ability to control the timing of his income recognition to take advantage of marginal rate differences between tax years.

Exceptions Applicable to the Accrual Method.

The receipt of prepaid income by accrual basis taxpayers is generally taxable in the tax year in which payment is received (under the wherewithal-to-pay concept). Thus, advance receipts of rent, interest, royalties, payments for goods, and payments for services are taxable when the cash payment is received, even for accrual basis taxpayers.[35]

There are two exceptions to the general rule for prepayments received for goods and services. For service prepayments, the accrual method may still be used if the services will be performed before the end of the tax year following the year of receipt.[36] This is referred to as the **one-year rule for services.**

▲ **EXAMPLE 63**   On July 1, 1995, Toy's Termite Service, Inc., receives $1,200 on a one-year service contract. Under the contract, Toy's is to perform pest control once per month. Assuming that Toy's uses the accrual method of accounting, when should the $1,200 be recognized for tax purposes?

Discussion: The services are to be performed before December 31, 1996 (the end of the tax year following the year of receipt). Therefore, under the one-year rule for services, Toy's may use the accrual method to recognize income from the contract. Six months of services are to be performed in 1995 and 1996, resulting in the recognition of $600 in income in each year. NOTE: If Toy's uses the cash method of accounting, the entire $1,200 is taxable in the year of receipt. The one-year rule is an exception for accrual basis taxpayers.

▲ **EXAMPLE 64**   Assume the same facts as in example 63, except that the $1,200 advance receipt is for a two-year service contract. When should Toy's recognize the income from the contract?

Discussion: Because the contract continues past December 31, 1996 (the end of the tax year following the year of receipt), the one-year rule for services does not apply. Toy's must recognize the entire $1,200 in 1995. NOTE: A one-year prepayment contract always meets the one-year rule requirement, but a two-year prepayment contract never meets the one-year rule requirement.

It should be noted that the one-year rule applies only to advance receipts for services. Advance receipts for rents and interest are never deferred under the one-year rule for services; they are always taxable in the year of receipt.

The second exception to the general rule for prepayments is for prepaid receipts received for goods. In order to use the accrual method to account for advance receipts for goods, the prepayment must be less than the cost of the goods and the prepayment must be deferred for financial accounting purposes.[37]

▲ **EXAMPLE 65**   Anne wants to buy a new car, but none of the dealers in her area has the exact car she wants. Local Car Sales, Inc., agrees to order the car she wants from the factory. The agreed-upon price for the car is $17,500, and Anne agrees to give Local a $500 deposit on the order, the balance to be paid upon delivery. Local receives the deposit on December 27, 1995. The car arrives the following February, and Anne pays Local the $17,000 balance due on the car. How should Local Car Sales, Inc., account for the $500 deposit received in 1995?

Discussion: Assuming that the $500 deposit is less than the cost of the car to Local, Local may defer recognition of the deposit until 1996, provided that it also defers recognition for financial accounting purposes.

Hybrid Method

The **hybrid method of accounting** allows the taxpayer to account for sales of merchandise and the related cost of goods sold on the accrual basis and all other items of income and expense on the cash basis. Thus, the hybrid method is mixture of the accrual and cash methods. This method is most commonly used by taxpayers who have inventories and therefore must use the accrual method to account for sales and the cost of goods sold from inventories. Such taxpayers must still use the cash method to account for other revenues and must use the cash method for all other expenses.

▲ **EXAMPLE 66**   Sunshine is a cash basis taxpayer who repairs and maintains hot tubs in her spare time. She also sells hot tubs. How must Sunshine account for sales of the hot tubs?

Discussion: Sunshine must use the accrual method to account for sales and calculate cost of goods sold for the hot tubs. However, she may elect to use the hybrid method of accounting, which would allow her to use the cash method for her service income and for all other expenses.

Exceptions Applicable to All Methods

Certain taxpayers must use two major income-recognition methods, regardless of their accounting methods. These methods relate to installment sales of property and accounting for long-term construction contracts.

Installment Sales.   An **installment sale** occurs whenever property is sold and at least one payment is received in a tax year subsequent to the year of sale. Taxpayers who are not dealers in the particular type of property but who make casual sales of property must recognize income from the sale by using the installment method, unless they elect to recognize the entire gain in the year of the sale.[38] The installment method is based on the wherewithal-to-pay concept and recognizes income proportionally as the selling price is received.[39]

▲ **EXAMPLE 67**   Lene purchases a tract of land in 1991 at a cost of $20,000 as a speculative investment. In 1995, she sells the land for $50,000. The terms of the sale require the buyer to pay Lene $10,000 in 1995, $20,000 in 1996, and $20,000 in 1997 with interest at 8% on the outstanding balance. How much income must Lene recognize in 1995 through 1997?

Discussion: Because Lene is not a dealer in property, she must use the installment method, unless she elects to recognize the entire $30,000 ($10,000 + $20,000 + $20,000 − $20,000) gain in 1995. Under the installment method, the gain is recognized proportionately as the $50,000 selling price is received.

1995	$10,000 × ($30,000 ÷ $50,000) = $ 6,000
1996 & 1997	$20,000 × ($30,000 ÷ $50,000) = $12,000

In addition, Lene has interest income of $3,200 ($40,000 × 8%) on the outstanding balance in 1996 and $1,600 ($20,000 × 8%) in 1997.

The use of the installment method by other taxpayers (i.e., dealers in property generally cannot use the installment sales method) has been severely restricted in recent years.

Long-Term Construction Contracts.   Taxpayers in the construction industry typically undertake projects that span a number of years. In the past, the income recognition on contracts spanning more than one tax year could be deferred until the completion of the contract. Although this method is still allowable in greatly restricted circumstances (see Chapter 14), most long-term construction contracts must be accounted for by using the **percentage-of-completed contract method.**[40] As the name of the method implies, income is recognized according to the amount of work completed on the contract each year. The work completed must be based on costs incurred during the year in relation to the estimated total costs of the project.

> ▲ **EXAMPLE 68**   Acme Construction Corporation enters into a contract in 1995 to construct a bridge for Garden City. The contract price for the bridge is $10,000,000, and Acme estimates its total cost of building the bridge to be $8,000,000. In 1995, Acme's actual costs were $2,000,000. How much gross income from the contract must Acme report in 1995?
>
> *Discussion:*   Using the percentage-of-completion method, Acme reports gross income from the contract of $2,500,000 in 1995.

$$\text{Work completed} = (\$2,000,000 \div \$8,000,000) = 25\%$$
$$\text{Gross income} = 25\% \times \$10,000,000 = \$2,500,000$$

To ensure that contractors do not manipulate their income by inaccurately estimating contract costs, a look-back rule is applied at the completion of the contract, and interest is charged on any deficient income reporting. This rule and other aspects of the method are discussed more fully in Chapter 14.

▲ SUMMARY

This chapter focused on the determination of taxable income sources. In general, a taxpayer is in receipt of income when an increase in wealth is realized. Realization requires a change in the form or substance of a taxpayer's property or property rights and the involvement of a second party in an arm's-length transaction.

The four primary sources of income are earned income (income from labor), unearned income (income from investments), transfers from others (increases in wealth that are not the result of either labor or investment), and imputed income (increases in wealth realized because another party confers an economic advantage). Within each of these categories are various problems of realization and recognition. In most instances, application of the income tax concepts provides a solution to the problem. In other cases, the treatment is prescribed by law and must be learned through study and experience. To aid you in reviewing these sources of income, Table 3–2 classifies the income items discussed in this chapter and summarizes the major problems within each category of income.

Capital gains and losses are subject to special reporting rules. All capital gains and losses for a tax year are segregated from other forms of income and subjected to the capital gain-and-loss netting procedure. The purpose of the capital gain-and-loss netting procedure is to reduce a taxpayer's capital gain and loss trans-

	Income Sources	Major Problems
Earned Income	Wages and salaries Tips, commissions, bonuses Income from sole proprietorship—either the active conduct of a trade or business or the rendering of services Income from illegal activities—gambling, drug dealing, racketeering, etc.	Assignment of income What is a receipt?
Unearned Income	Income from investments—interest, dividends, rental income, royalty income, income from annuities, gains (losses) from the sale of investments Income from investment in conduit entities	Definition of income from rents and royalties Capital recovery on annuities Calculation of gain (loss) Income from conduit entity
Transfers from Others	Prizes and awards Unemployment compensation Social Security benefits Alimony received	Exception for prizes and awards given to charity Exception for employee awards for length of service or safety Calculation of taxable portion of Social Security benefits Front loading of alimony payments to disguise a property settlement Child support payments disguised as alimony
Imputed Income	Below market-rate loans Payment of expense by others Bargain purchases	Exceptions for below-market rate loans Gift vs. compensation for payment of expenses by others Compensatory nature of bargain purchase

actions for the tax year to a net figure that represents the gain or loss for the year. Net long-term capital gains of individuals are taxed at a maximum rate of 28 percent. Up to $3,000 of net capital losses of individuals are deductible for adjusted gross income. Any excess losses are carried forward to the next year's netting.

The period in which an item of income is recognized is determined by the taxpayer's method of accounting. The two basic accounting methods are the cash method and the accrual method, although some taxpayers may use a combination of the two methods called the *hybrid method*. Exceptions to the general recognition rules exist for certain installment sales and long-term construction contracts. Other specific recognition exceptions exist for both the cash and the accrual methods.

▲ Key Terms

alimony (p. 97)
annuity (p. 105)
annuity exclusion ratio (p. 98)
bargain purchase (p. 111)
below market-rate loan (p. 107)
cash-equivalent approach (p. 95)
child support payment (p. 105)
earned income (p. 94)
holding period (p. 113)
hybrid method of accounting (p. 121)

imputed income (p. 107)
installment sale (p. 121)
long-term capital gain (p. 113)
long-term capital loss (p. 113)
net long-term capital gain (p. 115)
net long-term capital loss (p. 116)
one-year rule for services (p. 120)
original issue discount security (OID) (p. 118)
percentage-of-completed contract method (p. 122)

property settlement (p. 105)
savings bond (U.S. government-issued) (p. 119)
short-term capital gain (p. 113)
short-term capital loss (p. 113)
unearned income (p. 96)

▲ Primary Tax Law Sources

[1] Reg. Sec. 1.61-1—States that income can be realized in any form, including cash, services, and property received.

[2] Eisner v. Macomber, 252 U.S. 189 at 207 (1920)—In holding that a stock dividend did not constitute gross income, determined that income is derived from labor and capital.

[3] Eisner v. Macomber at 207.

[4] Cesarini v. Comm., 428 F.2d 812 (6th Cir. 1970)—In determining that cash found in a purchased piano was included in gross income, established that "treasure troves" constitute gross income.

[5] Helvering v. Bruun, 309 U.S. 461 (1940)—Held that a landlord realized gain on the forfeiture of a leasehold for the nonpayment of rent and that the increase in the value of the property was taxable even though the gain was not severed from the property. (Subsequently overturned by enactment of Sec. 109).

[6] Helvering v. Bruun at 469.

[7] Sec. 109—States that gross income does not result from increases in the value of a property at the termination of a lease.

[8] Glenshaw Glass v. Comm., 348 U.S. 426 at 430–431 (1955)—Determined that income consists of undeniable accessions to wealth that are completely controlled by the taxpayer.

[9] Reg. Sec. 1.61-14—States that income from illegal activities is included in gross income.

[10] Sec. 72—Describes the general rules for the taxation of annuities and presents the

formula for determining the amount of each payment that is taxable.

[11] Sec. 1001—Prescribes the calculation of gains and losses on dispositions of property; defines *amount realized* for purposes of determining gain or loss on dispositions.

[12] Sec. 1016—Provides the general rules for adjustments to basis of property for capital expenditures and recoveries of capital subsequent to purchase.

[13] Reg. Sec. 1.61-13—States that a partner's share of the partnership's income is included in the gross income of the partner.

[14] Sec. 74—States that prizes and awards are taxable; details situations under which a qualified prize or award may be excluded from income.

[15] Sec. 85—States that unemployment compensation payments received are taxable.

[16] Sec. 86—States that Social Security payments received are taxable for high-income taxpayers; provides the formula for determining the taxable portion of Social Security payments.

[17] Reg. Sec. 1.71-1—States that child support payments are not taxable.

[18] Sec. 71—States that alimony received is taxable; defines *alimony* and presents the required recapture for front loading of alimony payments.

[19] Reg. Sec. 1.71-1T—Discusses what constitutes a contingency related to a child.

[20] Sec. 7872—Prescribes the treatment of below market-rate (interest-free) loans and

the exceptions to the below market-rate rules.

[21] Old Colony Trust Co. v. CIR, 279 U.S. 716 (1929)—Determined that the payment of a corporate officer's state and federal taxes by the corporation constituted gross income to the officer; established that payment of another's expense in an employment-related setting is compensation that is included in gross income.

[22] CIR v. Smith, 324 U.S. 695 (1945)—Held that selling stock to an employee at less than its fair market value constituted compensation received by the employee; established that a "bargain purchase" in an employment-related setting is included in gross income.

[23] Sec. 1221—Defines *capital assets*.

[24] Sec. 1222—Defines *short-term and long-term capital gains and losses*; prescribes the netting procedure used for capital gains and losses.

[25] Sec. 1223—Defines *holding period* for purposes of determining short-term and long-term classification of capital gains and losses.

[26] Sec. 1211—Sets forth the limit on deductions of capital losses of corporations and individuals.

[27] Sec. 1212—Allows the carryforward of disallowed capital losses by individuals.

[28] Reg. Sec. 1.1211-1—Requires the deduction of short-term capital losses before long-term capital losses in determining the current year's capital loss deduction.

[29] Sec. 703—Requires a partnership to state separately the items of income, gain, losses, deductions, and credits provided in Sec. 702 in computing its taxable income. Sec. 702 requires partners to separately account for their share of capital gains and losses, gains and losses on the sale of certain types of business property, charitable contributions, foreign taxes, and other items as prescribed by the secretary of the Treasury. Sec. 1366 contains similar provisions for S corporations.

[30] Sec. 446—States general rules for methods of accounting, including the allowance of the cash and accrual methods.

[31] Reg. Sec. 1.446-1—Requires the use of the accrual method for sales and cost of goods sold for sales of inventories; allows accounting of other income and expenses with the cash basis (the hybrid method is an acceptable accounting method).

[32] Sec. 1273—Prescribes the methods for determining the amount of original issue discount to include in gross income.

[33] Sec. 1272—Provides for the inclusion of original issue discount on debt instruments in gross income. Allows the exclusion of U.S. savings bonds from the OID rules.

[34] Sec. 451—Sets forth general rules for taxable year of inclusion of gross income items.

[35] Reg. Sec. 1.61-8—States that gross income includes rental and royalty income and that advance receipts of rent are included in gross income in the year of receipt, regardless of the taxpayer's accounting method.

[36] Rev. Proc. 71-21—Prescribes the conditions under which an accrual basis taxpayer may defer an advance receipt for services (one-year rule for services).

[37] Reg. Sec. 1.451-5—Specifies the conditions under which an accrual basis taxpayer can defer recognition of income from an advance receipt for goods.

[38] Sec. 453—Prescribes the required treatment of installment sales of property.

[39] Temp. Reg. Sec. 15a.453-1—Provides the calculations for determining the amount of income to be recognized under the installment method of accounting.

[40] Sec. 460—Requires the use of the percentage-of-completed-contract method of accounting for long-term construction contracts.

▲ **DISCUSSION QUESTIONS**

1. How is the definition of *income* for income tax purposes different from the definition used by economists to measure income?

2. One of Adam Smith's four criteria for evaluating a tax is certainty. Does the income tax definition of *gross income* promote certainty in the U.S. tax system? Explain.

3. What is the difference between realized income and recognized income?

4. Buford purchased a new automobile in March for $23,000. In April, Buford receives a $500 rebate check from the manufacturer. The rebate was paid to all customers who purchased one of the manufacturer's automobiles in March. Should Buford include the $500 rebate in his gross income? Explain.

5. During her vacation, Janita found a gold bar from a sunken ship while she was scuba diving off the coast of Texas. Is Janita taxed on her find? If so, when is she taxed, and how much should she include in her income?

6. What is a cash equivalent? How does a cash equivalent affect the reporting of income?

7. What type of income does a sole proprietor of a business receive?

8. What is the difference between earned income and unearned income?

9. How is the gross income from a rental property or a royalty property determined?

10. Explain how the capital recovery concept applies to the taxation of annuities. Consider both purchased annuities and pension payments in your answer.

11. Explain the difference in determining the amount of income recognized from a conduit entity versus a taxable entity.

12. What effect does an asset's adjusted basis have in determining the gain or loss realized upon its sale?

13. This chapter noted that returns on investment are taxable, whereas returns of investment are not taxable. What is the conceptual basis for this treatment? Cite examples of each type of return, and explain why they are or are not taxable.

14. Prizes and awards are generally taxable. Under what conditions is the receipt of a prize or award not taxable?

15. Are Social Security benefits taxable? Explain.

16. How is the taxation of an alimony payment different from the taxation of a child support payment?

17. What incentive does a taxpayer have to disguise a property settlement as an alimony payment?

18. Does the tax treatment of below market-rate loans violate any income tax concepts? If so, how? Explain.

19. Evaluate the following statement:

    Whenever another person pays an expense for you, you are in receipt of taxable income.

20. What is a bargain purchase?

21. How is capital gain income treated differently from other forms of income?

22. What is the purpose of the capital gain-and-loss netting procedure?

23. Are all losses realized on the sale of capital assets deductible?

24. Why is it important that a conduit entity separate the reporting of its capital gains and losses from its report of other forms of income?

25. Detail any significant differences in the recognition of income using the cash method and using the accrual method of accounting.

26. Explain the hybrid method of accounting.

27. How does the wherewithal-to-pay concept affect the tax treatment of prepaid income?

28. Under what circumstances can the following taxpayers defer recognition of prepaid income beyond the year of receipt?
   a. A cash basis taxpayer
   b. An accrual basis taxpayer

29. What is an installment sale?

30. How is the degree of completion of a long-term construction contract determined?

31. Mitch travels extensively in his job as an executive vice president of Arthur Consulting Co. During the current year, Mitch used frequent flier miles that he had obtained during his business travel to take his family on a vacation to Europe. The normal airfare for the trip would have been $6,000.
   a. Discuss whether Mitch has realized income from the use of the frequent flier miles for personal purposes.
   b. Do you think that Mitch will have to recognize any income from the use of the frequent flier miles? Explain.

▲ PROBLEMS

32. In 1989, Awnings, Inc., issues $200,000 of 15%, 20-year bonds payable at par. During 1995, when Awnings' bonds are trading at 93, Awnings purchases and retires $100,000 par value of the bonds. Does Awnings have income from the retirement of the bonds? Explain.

33. Heidi sold her carpet-cleaning business to Elki. As part of the sales agreement, Elki paid Heidi $3,000 for her agreement not to open another carpet-cleaning business in the area for three years. Is Heidi taxed on the $3,000? Explain.

34. Yung is the sole owner of Southern Hills Insurance Agency. Yung's primary business is the sale of fire and casualty policies. He has recently expanded his business by selling life insurance policies. Under his agreement with Heart Life Insurance Co., he receives a basic commission on each policy he sells. The basic commission is equal to the cost of the insurance minus the first year's premium. Under the agreement, Yung collects the cost of the insurance policy and remits the first-year premium to the company. He is also entitled to an override commission, which is paid on subsequent years' premiums. To build up his life insurance business, Yung enters into separate contracts with clients in which he agrees to act as an insurance consultant for a fee that is equal to the first-year premium. The client pays Yung the fee, which he remits to Heart Life. This contract effectively waives Yung's basic commission and offers the insurance at a discounted price, a practice that is illegal under state law. During the current year, Yung sold policies that had a cost of $50,000 and first-year premiums of $18,000 (which were remitted to Heart Life). He also received $11,000 in override commissions from policies sold in previous years. How much income must Yung report from the life insurance policies in the current year? Explain.

35. How much gross income does each of the following taxpayers have for the current year?
   a. Doris is employed as a plumber by Paloma Corporation. She received wages of $17,000 from Paloma during the current year. At nights and on weekends, Doris does freelance plumbing repairs. During the current year, her total revenues were $6,200, and she incurred $2,800 of allowable expenses.
   b. Athony runs a gambling operation in the basement of his home. During the current year, his total revenue from the gambling operation was $78,000, and he incurred allowable expenses of $36,000.

36. In each of the following cases, determine who is taxed on the income:

   a. For $200, Lee purchased an old car that was badly in need of repair. Lee worked on the car for 3 months and spent $300 on parts to restore the car. Lee's son Jason needed $2,000 to pay his college tuition. Lee gave the car to Jason, who sold it for $2,000 and used the money to pay his tuition.

   b. Erica loaned a friend $20,000. The terms of the loan require the payment of $2,000 in interest each year to Erica's daughter. At the end of 4 years, the $20,000 loan principal is to be repaid to Erica. Erica's daughter will use the $2,000 to pay her college tuition.

37. Determine whether Frank or Debra, his daughter, is taxable on the income in each of the following situations:

   a. Frank owns 10% bonds with a face value of $10,000 that pay interest annually on December 31. On April 1, Frank makes a valid gift of the bonds to Debra.

   b. Several years ago, Frank wrote a book for which he still receives royalty payments. On July 1, Frank directs the publisher of the book to pay all future royalties to Debra.

   c. Frank owns U.S. Series E savings bonds with a face value $10,000 that he had purchased many years ago for $4,000. On November 18, 1995, Frank makes a valid gift of the bonds to Debra. The bonds mature on December 31, 1995, and Debra receives the $10,000 face value of the bonds at that time.

   d. Frank owns 100 shares of ABC common stock. On April 15, ABC declares a $5 per share cash dividend payable to shareholders of record as of May 1. On April 20, Frank makes a valid gift of the shares to Debra. Debra receives the $500 dividend in May.

38. Determine whether any income must be recognized in each of the following situations, as well as who must report income, how much that person should report, and when that person will report the income:

   a. Merlene Corporation owns a chain of bookstores. The bookstore in Austin needs repainting, but the manager of the Austin store is short of cash to hire a painter to do the job. Fred is a painter who enjoys fine mystery novels. The Austin manager makes a deal with Fred to have him paint the bookstore for any thirty mystery novels Merlene has in stock. Fred paints the store and selects novels that had a cost to Merlene of $250 and a retail selling price of $480.

   b. Julie owns a pastry shop in California that specializes in home delivery of exotic pastries and unique cakes. For her parents' 50th anniversary, Julie spends an entire day making a special 10-layer cake for their anniversary party. Because her parents live in Florida, Julie buys 2 first-class tickets costing $1,100 (one for herself and one for the cake) and flies the cake to Florida. The cake would normally have sold for $400.

   c. Jerry is an accountant who builds model airplanes in his spare time. Jerry enjoys taking the airplanes he builds to various collectors' shows around the country at which airplanes are displayed and sold by model airplane enthusiasts. During the current year, Jerry sells 5 planes for a total of $1,700 (the cost of the planes to Jerry is $1,200). In addition, Jerry exchanges 1 plane for another airplane worth $500 (the cost of the plane to Jerry is $300).

39. You have been assigned to prepare the tax return for a new client, Thuy Griswold. Her husband Jerry died during the current year, and Thuy came to your firm for assistance, because Jerry had always done their taxes. Thuy has provided you with last year's return. After reviewing the return, only one item is unclear to you. Jerry reported $550 of income from an annuity purchased from New Bradenton Life Insurance. You are going to call Thuy about the annuity. What type of information must Thuy provide so that you can determine the tax treatment for the annuity?

40. Several years ago, Minnie purchased an annuity for $102,000. The annuity is to pay Minnie $20,000 per year for life after she reaches age 65. Minnie turns 65 in 1995, at which time her life expectancy is 17 years.

   a. How should Minnie treat the $20,000 payment she receives in 1995?
   b. Shortly after receiving her payment for the year 2001, Minnie is killed in an auto-mobile accident. How does the executor of Minnie's estate account for the annuity on her return for the year 2001?
   c. Assume that the accident does not occur until 2016. How does the executor of Minnie's estate account for the annuity on her 2016 return?

41. Hank retired this year after working 30 years for Local Co. Per the terms of his employment contract, Hank is to receive a pension of $600 per month for the rest of his life. During the current year, he received 7 pension payments from Local. At the time of his retirement, his life expectancy was 15 years.
   a. How much taxable income does Hank have if his employer's plan was noncontributory (i.e., Local Co. paid the entire cost of the plan; Hank made no contributions to the plan)?
   b. How would your answer change if Hank had contributed $27,000 to the pension plan? Assume that the $27,000 had been included in Hank's income (i.e., he has already paid tax on the $27,000).
   c. What if Hank had contributed $27,000 to the plan and none of the $27,000 was taxed (i.e., the tax law allows certain pension contributions to go untaxed during the contribution period)?

42. The Rosco Partnership purchases a rental property in 1990 at a cost of $120,000. From 1990 through 1995, Rosco deducts $14,000 in depreciation on the rental. The partnership sells the rental property in 1995 for $138,000 and pays $7,000 in expenses related to the sale. What is Rosco's gain (loss) on the sale of the rental property?

43. Reddy owns some common stock with a market value of $15,000. The stock currently pays a cash dividend of $1,200 per year (an 8% annual yield). Reddy is considering selling the stock, which she purchased 13 years ago for $5,000, and using the proceeds to purchase stock in another company with a 10% annual dividend yield. If Reddy's goal is to maximize future dividends on her common stock investments, should she make the sale and purchase the new shares? Assume that Reddy is in a 28% marginal tax rate bracket.

44. How much income should the taxpayer recognize in each of the following situations? Explain.
   a. Julius owns a 25% interest in the Flyer Co., which is organized as a partnership. During the current year, Julius is paid $14,000 by Flyer as a distribution of earnings. Flyer's taxable income for the year (calculated without any payments made to partners) is $40,000.
   b. Felix owns 1,000 shares of Furr Co., which is a publicly traded corporation. Furr has 1,000,000 shares of stock outstanding during the current year. Furr has a net income of $2,500,000 and pays out a $2 per share dividend during the current year.
   c. Andrea is the sole proprietor of Andrea's Art Shop. During the current year, Andrea's has total revenue of $160,000 and total expenses of $115,000. Andrea draws a monthly salary of $2,500 from the shop that is not included in the $115,000 in expenses.
   d. Maryanne owns 60% of the stock of Sterling Safe Co., an S corporation. During the current year, Sterling has a taxable income of $200,000 and pays out dividends of $100,000 to its shareholders.
   e. Assume the same facts as in part d, except that Sterling incurs a loss of $40,000 during the current year.

45. DeWitt is the president of Weaver Co. and owns 20% of the common stock of the company. During the current year, DeWitt was paid a salary of $160,000 and received a $20,000 bonus. Weaver had taxable income of $450,000 and paid cash dividends of $150,000. How much gross income does DeWitt have if
   a. Weaver is a corporation?
   b. Weaver is an S corporation?

46. Pablo won a new automobile on a television game show. The car had a listed sticker price of $32,500. How much income does Pablo have from the receipt of the car? Explain.

47. Has the taxpayer in each of the following situations received taxable income? If so, when should the income be recognized? Explain.

    a. Charlotte is a lawyer who specializes in drafting wills. Charlotte wants to give her husband a new gazebo for Christmas. In November, she makes a deal with Joe, a local handyman, to build a gazebo. In return, Charlotte is to draft a last will and testament for Joe's father. The gazebo normally would cost $3,000, which is approximately what Charlotte would charge for drafting the will. Joe builds the gazebo in time for Christmas. Charlotte drafts the will and delivers it to Joe the following January.

    b. Ed buys 500 shares of Northstar stock in January 1994 for $4,000. On December 31, 1994, the shares are worth $4,600. In March 1995, Ed sells the shares for $4,500.

    c. Dayo is the director of marketing for Obo, Inc. In December, the board of directors of Obo votes to give Dayo a $10,000 bonus for the excellent work she had done throughout the year. The check is ordered and written on December 15 but is misplaced in the mail room and is not delivered to Dayo until January 5.

    d. John is unemployed. During the current year, he receives $4,000 in unemployment benefits. Because the unemployment is not enough to live on, John sells drugs to support himself. His total revenue for the year is $120,000. The cost of the drugs is $60,000.

48. Elwood had to retire early because of a job-related injury. During the current year, he received $13,000 in Social Security benefits. In addition, he received $4,000 in cash dividends on stocks that he owned and $8,500 in interest on tax-exempt bonds. Assuming that Elwood is single, what is his gross income if

    a. He received no other sources of income?

    b. He also received $9,000 in unemployment compensation?

    c. He sold some land he owned for $80,000? He had paid $50,000 for the land.

49. Hermano and Rosetta are a retired couple who received $16,000 in Social Security benefits during the current year. They also received $10,000 in interest on their savings account and taxable pension payments of $28,000. What is their gross income if

    a. They received no other sources of income?

    b. They received $12,000 in interest from tax-exempt bonds they own?

50. Upon returning from lunch, you find the following message on your voice mail:

> This is Jarrett Ogilvie. I'm not one of your clients, but I need some advice. I received a statement in the mail from the Social Security Administration reporting the eighty-five hundred dollars I received from them last year. It says that a portion of my Social Security may be taxable. Last year was the first year I ever received Social Security and I'm confused. I thought Social Security wasn't taxable. Could you call me and explain this?

What facts will you need from Jarrett to determine what portion, if any, of the $8,500 of Social Security benefits are taxable? In your answer, explain how different facts may lead to different taxable amounts.

51. Albert and Patricia were divorced during the current year. As part of their divorce agreement, Patricia agreed to pay Albert alimony of $85,000 in the current year and $5,000 per year in subsequent years. What tax problem is presented by this agreement? What will be the ultimate tax treatment of the alimony payments?

52. Will and Janine were divorced during the current year. Will is to have custody of their two children and will receive their house as part of the divorce settlement. The house, which Will and Janine bought for $60,000, is worth $90,000. Janine is to receive one of their automobiles, for which they paid $21,000 and is now worth $9,000. Will will get the other automobile, which cost $6,000 and is worth $2,000. Janine is to pay Will alimony of $400 per month. However, the alimony payment is to be reduced by $100 per month as each child reaches age 18 or if a child should die or marry before reaching age 18. What are the tax effects of the divorce settlement for Will and Janine?

53. Simon and Sherry were divorced during the current year. As part of their property settlement, Simon gave Sherry 25% of the stock in his 100% owned corporation, Hobday, Inc. The stock had a fair market value of $80,000. Rather than pay Sherry alimony, Simon agreed to make Sherry a vice president of Hobday with an annual salary of $70,000. In her position, Sherry has no responsibilities and no involvement in the company. What are the tax implications of this arrangement? Explain.

54. Laura made the following interest-free loans during the current year. Discuss the income tax implications of each loan for both Laura and the borrower. In all cases, the applicable federal interest rate is 8%.
   a. On April 15, Laura loaned $20,000 to her brother Hyun to pay his income taxes. Hyun is financially insolvent and has no sources of investment income.
   b. On March 1, Laura loaned $15,000 to her secretary George. George used the money as a down payment on a new house.
   c. On July 1, Laura loaned her father $200,000. Her father used the money to buy a franchise to open a yogurt store. He made $5,000 on the yogurt store during the current year.
   d. On January 1, Laura loaned $50,000 to Lotta, Inc. Laura is the sole shareholder of Lotta, Inc., which is organized as a corporation.

55. On January 1, Wilton loaned Andy $75,000. The loan is to be repaid in 5 years with no interest charged. The applicable federal rate is 6%. Discuss the treatment of the loan for both Wilton and Andy in each of the following independent situations:
   a. Andy is Wilton's son, and he used the loan to purchase a new home. Andy had no sources of investment income during the year.
   b. Andy is Wilton's son, and he used the loan to purchase some investment property. Andy's net income from all investments for the year was $3,000.
   c. Assume the same facts as in part b, except that Andy is an employee of Wilton's.
   d. Assume the same facts as in part b, except that Andy is a shareholder in Wilton's corporation, which made the loan to Andy.

56. Determine whether the following taxpayers have taxable income from the payment of their expenses:
   a. Julia's mother, Henrietta, was short of cash when it came time to pay her property taxes. Julia paid Henrietta's property taxes of $350.
   b. Kurt fell sleep at the wheel one night and crashed his car into a telephone pole. Repairs to the car cost $600. Kurt wasn't covered by insurance and didn't have the cash to pay the repair shop. Because he needed his car in his job as a salesman, his employer paid the repair bill.
   c. Leonard leased a building from the PLC Partnership for $800 per month. The lease agreement required Leonard to pay the property taxes of $1,100 on the building.
   d. On July 1, Gino bought some land from Harco Corporation for $14,000. As part of the sales agreement, Gino agreed to pay the property taxes of $700 for the year. Harco had paid $10,000 for the land.

57. Randy worked during the summer for Yardco Yard Service. Randy was paid $3,400 in cash compensation by Yardco. In addition to the cash payments, Yardco gave Randy a truck worth $800 and agreed to pay Randy's college tuition of $1,300 as part of his compensation package. How much gross income does Randy have from this arrangement?

58. Determine whether the taxpayer has income that is subject to taxation in each of the following situations:
  a. Capital Motor Co. was going out of business. As a result, June was able to purchase a car for $13,000; its original sticker price was $22,000.
  b. Chuck is the sole owner of Patz, Inc., a corporation. Chuck purchased a machine from Patz for $8,000. Patz had paid $44,000 for the machine, which was worth $30,000 at the time of the sale to Chuck.
  c. Gerry is an elementary school teacher. She received the Teacher of the Month Award for the month of February. As part of the award, she gets to drive a new car supplied by a local dealer for a month. The rental value of the car is $350 per month.
  d. Payne has worked for Stewart Co. for the last 25 years. On the 25th anniversary of his employment with Stewart, he received a set of golf clubs worth $900 as a reward for his years of loyal service to the company.
  e. Anna entered a sweepstakes contest that was advertised on the back of a cereal box. She was recently informed that she had won $20,000 in the contest. The prize will be paid out in 10 annual installments of $2,000. She received her first check this year.
  f. Terry bought an antique vase at an estate auction for $780. Upon returning home, she accidentally dropped the vase and found that a $100 bill had been taped inside it.

59. Pedro purchases 50 shares of Piper Co. stock on February 19, 1993, at a cost of $4,300. Pedro sells the 50 shares on July 2, 1995, for $8,200. On March 14, 1995, Pedro purchases 100 shares of Troxel stock for $9,700. He sells the Troxel shares on December 18, 1995, for $6,600. What is the effect of the stock sales on Pedro's 1995 income?

60. Jawan has the following capital gains and losses for 1995:

Short-term capital gain	$ 500
Short-term capital loss	2,000
Long-term capital gain	6,000
Long-term capital loss	10,000

What is the effect of the capital gains and losses on Jawan's 1995 income?

61. Refer to problem 60. In 1996, Jawan has the following capital gains and losses:

Short-term capital gain	$3,200
Long-term capital gain	7,300
Long-term capital loss	6,000

What is the effect of the capital gains and losses on his 1996 income?

62. Clark and Jill are married and have an eight-year-old daughter. During the current year, they sold land for $135,000. They had purchased the land as an investment three years ago for $85,000. Their other income and deduction items for the current year are

Jill's salary	$96,000
Clark's salary	67,000
Interest and dividend income	6,000
Short-term loss on sale of White, Inc., stock	(13,000)
Deductions for adjusted gross income	4,500
Total itemized deductions	18,500

Calculate Clark and Jill's taxable income and income tax liability for the current year. Do they obtain any tax relief on the sale of the land?

63. Ozzello Property Management is organized as a partnership. The owners, Lorenzo, Erwin, and Michelle, share profits and losses 20:30:50. Ozzello had the following results for the current year:

Management fees	$230,000
Long-term gain on sale of investments	22,000
Short-term loss on sale of investments	(4,000)
Salaries paid to employees	67,000
Office rent	43,000
Office expenses	19,000

Determine each partner's share of Ozzello's taxable income for the current year.

64. Ramona owns 20% of the stock of Miller, Inc. Miller reports the following items for the current year:

Sales	$3,400,000
Gain on sale of stock held for 2 years	250,000
Cost of goods sold	1,800,000
Operating expenses	900,000
Dividends paid to stockholders	180,000

What are the effects on Ramona's taxable income if Miller, Inc., is organized as
a. a corporation?
b. an S corporation?

65. Caine opens a consulting business after leaving his previous employer in September. During the remainder of 1995, he records the following:

	Amount Earned	Cash Received	Liability Incurred	Cash Paid
Consulting revenue	$35,000	$25,000		
Supplies, utilities, etc.			$14,000	$12,000
Wages of secretary			5,600	5,000
Equipment purchased			15,000	6,000

The allowable depreciation on the equipment for tax purposes is $3,000.
a. What is Caine's taxable income if he elects the cash method of accounting?
b. What is Caine's taxable income if he elects the accrual method of accounting?
c. Which method would you recommend that he elect? Why?

66. Bonnie opens a computer sales and repair service during 1995. Her records show the following for 1995:

	Sales Made	Cash Received	Liability Incurred	Cash Paid
Repair revenue	$21,000	$17,500		
Computer sales	18,000	11,500		
Computer purchases			$45,000	$20,000
Employee wages			13,000	12,000
Supplies, utilities, etc.			7,000	6,500

Bonnie has computers on hand on December 31 that cost $36,000 and have a retail selling price of $49,000.

Bonnie needs help figuring her taxable income for 1995. Is more than one income figure possible for 1995? If so, explain why, and compute taxable income under the various methods.

67. Arlene is a lawyer. She began the current year with $8,000 in accounts receivable from customers. During the year, she billed customers $180,000 in fees and received $140,000 in payments on account. During the year, she wrote off $12,000 of the receivables as being uncollectable, leaving her a year-end receivable balance of $36,000. What is Arlene's gross income if
a. She uses the cash basis of accounting?
b. She uses the accrual basis of accounting?

68. Determine how much interest income Later Federal Loan Co., a cash basis taxpayer, must recognize on each of the following loans in 1995:
a. A $10,000, 8.5%, 6-month loan made on October 1, 1995. The principal and interest are due on April 1, 1996.
b. A $10,000, 6-month loan, discounted at 8% on October 1, 1995. Later gives the borrower $9,615, and the borrower must repay the $10,000 face amount on April 1, 1996.
c. A $10,000, 2-year loan, discounted at 6% on October 1, 1994. Later gives the borrower $8,900; the $10,000 face amount is to be repaid on October 1, 1997.

69. In January 1995, Conan, a cash basis taxpayer, purchases for $4,000 a Series EE savings bond with a maturity value of $4,800 (a 6% annual yield). At the same time, he also purchases for $5,000 a 3-year bank certificate of deposit with a maturity value of $6,650 (a 10% annual yield). Both securities mature in 1997. Must Conan recognize any income in 1995? How much income must Conan recognize in 1997?

70. Lorene, Inc., owns an apartment complex. The terms of Lorene's lease agreement require new tenants to pay the first and last month's rent as well as a cleaning deposit at the inception of the lease. The cleaning deposit is returned when tenants move out and leave their apartment in good condition. If the apartment is not in good condition, Lorene hires a cleaning company and uses the tenant's deposit to pay the cleaning bill, with any excess deposit returned.

    During 1995, Lorene receives monthly rents totaling $38,000, last month's rent deposits from new tenants of $14,000, and security deposits of $7,000. Lorene keeps $5,000 in cleaning deposits to pay the cleaning company bill on apartments that are not left in good shape (the $5,000 is the actual cost that is paid in cash to the cleaning company) and returns $4,000 in deposits. Lorene's expenses (other than the cleaning costs) related to the rental property are $28,000. What is Lorene, Inc.'s 1995 gross income from the rental property if Lorene is a cash basis taxpayer? an accrual basis taxpayer?

71. The A.B. Partnership constructed a commercial building at a cost of $320,000. A.B. rented the building to Harko Storage Co.. Harko signed a 20-year lease that required Harko to pay $33,000 per year in rent. In addition, Harko was required under the lease to pay A.B.'s annual property taxes on the building. The property taxes were estimated at $5,500 per year. The terms of the lease also stipulated that any permanent improvements to the building would remain A.B.'s, and Harko would not be reimbursed for any such expenditures. Harko installed carpeting, fixtures, and other improvements costing $30,000. How much income must the A.B. Partnership recognize from the lease in the first year? the last year?

72. How much income would an accrual basis taxpayer report in 1995 in each of the following situations?
    a. Toby's Termite Services, Inc., provides monthly pest control on a contract basis. Toby sells a 1-year contract for $600 and a 2-year contract for $1,100. In October, Toby sells 10 one-year contracts and 5 two-year contracts.
    b. John's Tractor Sales receives a $150 deposit from a customer for a new tractor that the customer orders in December. The tractor arrives the following February, at which time the customer pays the remaining $9,800 of the agreed-upon sales price.
    c. A customer of First Financial Lending sends First Financial two $600 checks in December in payment of December and January interest on a loan.
    d. First Financial Lending receives interest payments totaling $8,400 in January 1996 in payment of December 1995 interest on loans.

73. Daryl purchases some land in 1991 at a cost of $75,000. In 1995, he sells the land for $120,000.
    a. How much gain (loss) does Daryl realize on the sale of the land?
    b. Assume that the sales contract on the land calls for the buyer to pay Daryl $40,000 at the time of sale and $20,000 per year for the next 4 years with interest on the unpaid balance at 8%. How much income must Daryl recognize in 1995? in 1996?

74. In 1992, Patricia purchases a rental property as an investment at a cost of $66,000. From 1992 through 1995, she takes $6,000 in depreciation on the property. In 1995, she sells the property for $50,000.
    a. How much gain (loss) does Patricia realize on the sale of the rental property?
    b. Assume that the sales contract on the rental property calls for the buyer to pay Patricia $10,000 per year for 5 years with interest on the unpaid balance at 10%. How much income (loss) must Patricia recognize in 1995?

75. Assume the same facts as in problem 74, except that Patricia sells the rental property for $80,000, payable at $20,000 per year for 4 years with interest on the unpaid balance at 10%. How much income (loss) must Patricia recognize in 1995?

Assume that in addition to the sale of the rental property, Patricia sells other capital assets that result in a loss of $26,000. What would you recommend that Patricia do regarding the gain on the sale of the rental property?

76. In 1995, Big Builders, Inc., enters into a contract with Layne County to build a bridge for $20,000,000. Completion of the bridge is expected to take 3 years and cost Big Builders $15,000,000. During 1995, Big Builders incurs $4,500,000 in costs on the bridge and receives $5,000,000 in progress payments from Layne County. How much income must Big Builders recognize in 1995 from work done on the bridge?

77. Quapaw Construction Co. entered into an agreement with Paine County to resurface 30 miles of highway. The contract was for $600,000. Quapaw estimated its total cost of the project to be $450,000. During the current year, Quapaw completed 12 miles of resurfacing, incurred $150,000 in actual costs, and received $300,000 in advance payments on the project. How much income will Quapaw have to recognize during the current year?

Many tax theorists feel that homeowners should be required to include the rental value of their homes in gross income. Discuss why, in theory, the rental value of a home should be included in gross income. In your discussion, consider the cases of Taxpayer A who invests $100,000 in securities that pay annual dividends of $10,000 and Taxpayer B who invests $100,000 in the purchase of a residence. In addition, discuss why you think that Congress has chosen not to tax the rental value of homes.

▲ **DISCUSSION CASE 3–1**

Kerry is employed as a ticket vendor at an off-track betting parlor in New York. No credit is extended to customers, and employees are not allowed to bet on races. Kerry is a compulsive gambler and occasionally places bets without paying for them. In the past, she has always managed to cover her bets without being detected by her employer. Earlier this year, Kerry ran up $80,000 in bets that she did not pay for and won only $33,000. She was unable to cover this large loss and turned herself in to her employer. Kerry was convicted of grand larceny and sentenced to five years of probation, required to perform 200 hours of community service, and pay a $500 fine. Her employer was liable to the racetrack for the bets she made and obtained a judgment against her for the $47,000 shortfall it had to pay because of her indiscretions. How much, if any, gross income must Kerry recognize from her illegal betting?

▲ **DISCUSSION CASE 3–2**

Nick and Jolene are married. Nick is 61 and retired in 1993 from his job with Amalgamated Co. Jolene is 56 and works part time as a special education teacher. Nick and Jolene have a substantial amount of investment savings and would like to reorganize it to achieve the best after-tax return on their investments. They give you the following list of projected cash receipts for 1995:

▲ **TAX PLANNING CASE 3–3**

Jolene's salary	$13,000
Nick's pension—fully taxable	11,000
Interest income	4,000
Dividend income	4,000
Social Security benefits	7,000
Farmer's Fund annuity	6,000

In addition, Nick tells you that he owns a duplex that he rents out. The duplex rents for 1995 are $18,000, and Nick estimates expenses of $22,000 related to the duplex. The annuity was purchased 18 years ago for $20,000. The annuity pays $500 per month for 10 years.

Nick and Jolene's investments consist of the following:

6-month certificates of deposit (CD)	$100,000
1,000 shares of Lardee's common stock (current market value = $7 per share, projected 1995 dividend = $1 per share)—cost	10,000
2,000 shares of Corb Co. common stock (current market value = $40 per share, projected 1995 dividend = $1.50 per share)—cost	20,000

1. Assuming that Nick and Jolene have total allowable itemized deductions of $7,300 in 1995 and that they have no dependents, determine their 1995 taxable income and tax liability based on the projections they gave you.

2. The 6-month CDs consist of two separate $50,000 certificates, both of which yield 4% interest. One CD matures on January 3, 1995. Nick's banker tells him that he can renew the CD for one year at 4%. Nick's stockbroker tells him that he can purchase tax-exempt bonds with a yield of 3%. Nick would like you to determine whether the tax-exempt bonds provide him a better after-tax return than the CD.

3. Jolene is concerned that they are not getting the best return on their Corb Co. stock. When they purchased the stock in 1984, the $1 per share dividend at that time was yielding 10% before taxes. However, the rise in market value has far out-paced the dividend growth, and they are yielding only 3.75%, based on the current market value. Jolene thinks they should sell the stock and either purchase the 3% tax-exempt securities or the 4% CD, if it would be a better deal from an income tax viewpoint. Calculate the tax effect on their 1995 income of selling the shares, and determine whether they should sell the shares and invest the after-tax proceeds in tax-exempt securities or the 4% CD. Do this calculation after you have determined the best option regarding the CD that matures in January.

▲ ETHICS DISCUSSION CASE 3–4

The Gallery is an indoor recreational facility. It employs 95 minimum-wage employees and 7 management-level staffers. During the past month, all employees participated in a promotion to enhance sales by distributing discount coupons to potential customers. The employee who had the most coupons redeemed was to receive a $150 credit toward the purchase of a mountain bike. The general manager won the coupon promotion. After accepting the $150 credit, he instructed the controller, Aretha, not to include the $150 on his pay stub or on his Form W-2. Aretha is a CPA and a member of the AICPA. Explain what Aretha should do, according to the Statements on Responsibilities in Tax Practice.

Income Exclusions

▲ CHAPTER LEARNING OBJECTIVES

■ Discuss the requirements for the exclusion of an item of income.

■ Explain the rationale for excluding items from gross income.

■ Identify the allowable exclusions for donative items of income: gifts, inheritances, life insurance proceeds, scholarships, and certain death benefits.

■ Describe the effect of employment-related exclusions on the after-tax compensation of employees.

■ Discuss the nontaxable fringe benefits that a business may provide to its employees.

■ Identify payments that represent returns of human capital and are excluded from income as capital recoveries: workers' compensation, damage payments for personal injuries, and medical expense reimbursement payments.

■ Discuss the exclusions from income allowed for investment-related items: municipal bond interest, stock dividends, discharge of indebtedness, and improvements by a lessee.

▲ CONCEPT REVIEW ▲

Administrative convenience   Those items for which the cost of compliance would exceed the revenue generated are not taxed.

All-inclusive income   All income received is taxable unless a specific provision can be found in the tax law that either excludes the income from taxation or defers its recognition to a future tax year.

Basis   This is the amount of unrecovered investment in an asset. As amounts are expended and/or recovered relative to an asset over time, the basis is adjusted in consideration of such changes. The **adjusted basis** of an asset is the original basis, plus or minus the changes in the amount of unrecovered investment.

Capital recovery   No income is realized until the taxpayer receives more than the amount invested to produce the income. The amount invested in an asset represents the maximum amount recoverable.

Claim of right   A realization occurs whenever an amount is received without any restriction as to its disposition.

Legislative grace   Any tax relief provided is the result of a specific act of Congress that must be strictly applied and interpreted. All income received is taxable unless a specific provision can be found in the tax law that excludes the income from taxation. Deductions must be approached with the philosophy that nothing is deductible unless a provision in the tax law allows the deduction.

Realization   No income (or loss) is recognized until it has been realized. A realization involves a change in the form and/or the substance of a taxpayer's property rights that results from an arm's-length transaction.

Substance over form   Transactions are to be taxed according to their true intention rather than some form that may have been contrived.

Tax benefit rule   Any deduction taken in a prior year that is recovered in a subsequent year is income in the year of recovery, to the extent that a tax benefit was received from the deduction.

Wherewithal-to-pay   Income is recognized in the period in which the taxpayer has the means to pay the tax on the income.

▲ INTRODUCTION

After identifying all the sources of income received during an accounting period, the next step in calculating taxable income is determining which, if any, of the income sources do not have to be included in the current period's gross income. This step requires identification of income items that are subject to exclusion or deferral. The all-inclusive income concept considers taxable any income received unless a specific provision can be found that exempts the item from taxation. Under the legislative grace concept, only Congress can provide such tax relief. In addition, tax relief provisions are strictly applied and interpreted, thereby explicitly limiting the scope of any tax relief provision to that which Congress intended.

Congress has chosen to exempt certain items that meet the definition of *gross income* for several reasons. Some of the relief provisions are designed as equity measures that relieve the item from double taxation. Other provisions are meant as incentives for taxpayers to engage in the activity. Most incentive provisions have as their goal some social objective, such as encouraging firms to provide medical coverage for their employees. As the provisions are introduced, the chapter states the rationale for providing the relief.

This chapter discusses the most common exclusions found in the tax law. Because they represent exceptions to the general concepts of income recognition, exclusions are an area of the tax law that can be mastered only through exposure and study. The more you encounter and work with these items, the more familiar they will become. In addition, this chapter introduces several common deferral provisions. Recall from Chapter 1 that the difference between an exclusion and a deferral of income is that an exclusion is permanent—it is never subject to taxation.

On the other hand, a deferral is not taxed in the current period but will be taxed in some future period(s). Most deferrals are a result of the wherewithal-to-pay concept and are not taxed currently, because the transaction has not produced the cash with which to pay the tax.

Exhibit 4–1 lists the titles of the Internal Revenue Code sections that allow the various exclusions. As you can see from the list, the number of exclusions and the topics they cover is formidable. The discussion in this chapter focuses on those exclusions that have the widest application. To provide a frame of reference for your study of exclusions, they are grouped into four categories: donative items, employment-related exclusions, returns of human capital, and investment-related exclusions.

Items in this category are receipts of wealth that the receiver has not earned and for which no future services are to be rendered as a result of the transfer, nor are they the result of an investment. Because they represent realized increases in

▲ **DONATIVE ITEMS**

▲ **Exhibit 4–1**

INCOME EXCLUSIONS BY INTERNAL REVENUE CODE SECTION

Sec. 101	Certain death benefits
Sec. 102	Gifts and inheritances
Sec. 103	Interest on state and local bonds
Sec. 104	Compensation for injuries or sickness
Sec. 105	Amounts received under accident and health plans
Sec. 106	Contributions by employer to accident and health plans
Sec. 107	Rental value of parsonages
Sec. 108	Income from discharge of indebtedness
Sec. 109	Improvements by lessee on lessor's property
Sec. 111	Recovery of tax benefit items
Sec. 112	Certain combat pay of members of the armed forces
Sec. 115	Income of states, municipalities, etc.
Sec. 117	Qualified scholarships
Sec. 118	Contributions to the capital of a corporation
Sec. 119	Meals or lodging furnished for the convenience of the employer
Sec. 120	Amounts received under group legal services plans
Sec. 121	One-time exclusion of gain from sale of principal residence by individual who has attained age 55
Sec. 122	Certain reduced uniformed services retirement pay
Sec. 123	Amounts received under insurance contracts for certain living expenses
Sec. 125	Cafeteria plans
Sec. 126	Certain cost-sharing payments
Sec. 127	Educational assistance programs
Sec. 129	Dependent care assistance programs
Sec. 130	Certain personal injury liability assignments
Sec. 131	Certain foster care payments
Sec. 132	Certain fringe benefits
Sec. 133	Interest on certain loans used to acquire employer securities
Sec. 134	Certain military benefits
Sec. 135	Income from United States savings bond used to pay higher education tuition and fees
Sec. 136	Energy conservation subsidies provided by public utilities

wealth, items in this class fit the definition of *income*. However, Congress has determined that such items should not be taxed either for equity or incentive reasons. Donative items include gifts and inheritances, life insurance proceeds, scholarships, and certain death benefits.

Gifts

The value of property acquired by **gift** has been excluded from income taxation since 1913. Gifts received are not subject to income taxation;[1] however, the donor (person making the gift) is subject to the gift tax rules on the making of a gift. Thus, the exclusion of gifts from income tax is an equity measure that prevents a double tax on a gift. However, neither Congress nor the Treasury has ever attempted to provide a strict definition of what constitutes a gift. The most authoritative definition was developed by the U.S. Supreme Court in 1960:

> A gift in the statutory sense, . . . proceeds from a detached and disinterested generosity, . . . out of affection, respect, admiration, charity, or like impulses, . . . And in this regard, the most critical consideration, as the Court was agreed in the leading case here, is the transferor's "intention." . . . What controls is the intention with which payment, however voluntary, has been made.[2]

In the majority of situations, the intention to make a gift is clear. People make gifts to friends and relatives all the time "out of affection, respect, admiration, charity, or like impulses" with no expectation of any consideration in return.

▲ **EXAMPLE 1**   Odom gave his daughter Althea a new car worth $21,000 when she graduated from college. Does Althea have taxable income from the receipt of the car?

Discussion: It is unlikely that Odom is attempting to compensate his daughter; he gave her the car out of affection and respect for her accomplishments, and it therefore constitutes an excludable gift.

Recall that the legislative grace concept requires a strict application and interpretation of the exclusion for gifts. Thus, only the receipt of a gift is a nontaxable event; any subsequent earnings from property received as a gift are subject to taxation. Subsequent earnings may be in the form of income flows from the property (interest, dividends, rents, royalties, etc.) or gains from the sale of the property.

▲ **EXAMPLE 2**   For Christmas, Zane's uncle Bob gave him 100 shares of ABC Co. stock that had a fair market value of $200. Sometime later, Zane received a cash dividend of $50 on the stock. Does Zane have any taxable income from the stock?

Discussion: The receipt of the stock is a gift, the value of which is excluded from Zane's income. However, the exclusion applies only to the receipt of the gift; any subsequent earnings on the gift property are subject to tax. Thus, Zane must include the $50 dividend in his taxable income. NOTE: If the dividend had already been declared when Bob made the gift, Bob would have been taxed on the dividend under the assignment-of-income doctrine. Under such circumstances, the cash dividend would have been an additional gift.

The major problem with gifts involves gifts made in a business setting. Per the standard outlined, the donor's intent in making the gift is controlling. That is, if the gift was meant to be compensation for past, present, or future services, the gift is not really a gift but is taxable as compensation.

▲ **EXAMPLE 3**   Over the years, Albert has provided Phillip with the names of many potential customers. Albert has never asked Phillip for anything but his friendship in return. In 1995, Phillip has a particularly good year and decides to give Albert a new automobile worth $20,000 for being such a good friend through the years. Does Albert have income from the receipt of the automobile?

Discussion: On similar facts, in 1960 the Supreme Court held that the automobile did not constitute a gift, although both parties testified that nothing was owed between the two and that the automobile was meant to be a present. The Court felt that the nature of their past relationship indicated that the automobile was either compensation for past customer leads or an inducement to Albert to continue providing such information in the future.

As example 3 illustrates, gifts between individuals who also engage in business with one another are always suspect. In most cases, such "gifts" have some compensatory element to them and as such do not meet the income tax definition of a gift. Note that the treatment of business gifts is an application of the substance-over-form doctrine, which taxes transactions according to their true intention rather than their technical form.

Inheritances

As with gifts, the value of property received by **inheritance** has been excluded from taxation since 1913. The rationale for exclusion also follows that for a gift—property held in an estate is subject to an estate tax; thus, the income tax exclusion for inheritances avoids a double taxation of the property of a deceased taxpayer. There are no particular problems in this area. Remember, the legislative grace concept requires that exclusions be strictly applied. In the case of inherited property, the exclusion is limited to the value of property received. Any subsequent earnings from the inherited property are not excludable.[3]

▲ **EXAMPLE 4**   Elinor received 100 shares of Pleasing Pools common stock worth $6,000 from the estate of her uncle Frank. She subsequently received dividends totaling $200 on the stock. What are the tax effects for Elinor of receiving the stock?

Discussion: Elinor is not taxed on the $6,000 value of the stock received from the inheritance. However, she is taxed on the income received from the stock subsequent to its receipt and must include the $200 dividend in her gross income.

▲ **EXAMPLE 5**   Elinor held the stock she received from her uncle's estate for two years, at which time she sold it for $8,500. Does Elinor have a taxable gain from the sale of the stock?

Discussion: Elinor is taxed on the gain from the sale of the stock. Her taxable gain is $2,500 ($8,500 − $6,000). Note that the $6,000 fair market value of the stock received from the estate becomes Elinor's basis. Because the value of the inheritance (in this case $6,000) must never be taxed, it is permanently excluded from income. Therefore, under the capital recovery concept, Elinor does not have income unless she receives more than $6,000 for the stock upon disposition.

Life Insurance Proceeds

Payments from life insurance upon the death of the insured are generally excluded from income tax,[4] although **life insurance proceeds** may be included in the decedent's gross estate and subject to the estate tax. Life insurance proceeds resemble inheritances, which are excluded from taxation. Thus, the exclusion of life insurance proceeds provides equity with other forms of inherited property.

▲ **EXAMPLE 6**   Alice's husband Ralph dies this year. Ralph has a $200,000 life insurance policy that names Alice as the beneficiary. Alice invests the $200,000 in a certificate of deposit that earns 6% annually. What are the tax effects of the receipt of the $200,000 for Alice?

Discussion: The receipt of the $200,000 face value of the policy is excludable under the provision for receipt of life insurance proceeds. However, the subsequent earnings on the proceeds, $12,000 per year, are subject to tax.

The life insurance proceeds exclusion applies to such payments even if the payments are received in installments, although any earnings included in the installment payments are taxable.

▲ **EXAMPLE 7**   Assume the same facts as in example 6, except that Alice elects to take the proceeds in installments of $32,000 per year for 10 years. What are the tax consequences of the receipt of the annual installments?

Discussion: The $200,000 face value of the policy is excludable. However, Alice will receive a total of $320,000 under the installment plan. Thus, she must recognize the $120,000 ($320,000 − $200,000) in earnings as they are received. The payments are in the form of an annuity, so the annuity formula described in Chapter 3 is used to determine the taxable portion of each payment:

Annuity Exclusion Formula

$$\text{Amount excluded} = \frac{\text{Cost of contract}}{\text{Expected return}} \times \text{Payment received}$$

$$\text{Amount excluded} = \frac{\$200,000}{\$320,000} \times \$32,000 = \$20,000$$

$$\text{Taxable amount} = \$32,000 - \$20,000 = \$12,000$$

Note that this treatment is consistent with the treatment in example 6. In both cases, Alice invests the $200,000 proceeds at a 6% annual return. In example 7, the fact that she makes the investment with the insurance company does not provide her with any tax relief. It is taxed as any investment of the proceeds would be taxed.

An exception to the exclusion for life insurance proceeds is made for amounts paid to the owner of a policy that was obtained for a consideration (i.e., purchased). That is, if a taxpayer purchases or otherwise obtains for some valuable consideration a policy on the life of another, the receipt of the insurance proceeds is considered the realization of an investment.

▲ **EXAMPLE 8**   Athena owned a life insurance policy on herself that had a face value of $50,000. During a financial crisis, she assigned the proceeds of the policy to Helena for $10,000. Helena subsequently paid premiums on the policy totaling $20,000 before Athena died. What is the tax effect of Helena's receipt of the $50,000 life insurance proceeds?

Discussion: Because Helena purchased the policy for a consideration, she is taxable on the receipt of the $50,000. Under the capital recovery concept, she is allowed to recover her $30,000 investment in the policy before she recognizes any income. Therefore, she has a realized and recognized gain of $20,000 on the receipt of the life insurance proceeds.

This exception to the life insurance exclusion provisions does not apply to policies owned by partners or partnerships in which the insured is a partner or a corporation in which the insured is an officer or a shareholder. Payments on such contracts are excluded, because they are deemed to be for legitimate business purposes rather than for speculative gain. This type of life insurance is usually used to fund buy-out agreements on the death of a partner or a key employee and are necessary to ensure continuation of the business in most cases.

▲ **EXAMPLE 9**   Nina and Chen are partners in a consulting business. The business has been highly profitable, and each has a considerable equity interest in the partnership. When they realize that paying off each other's estate in the event of death would drain the business of all its resources, the partnership purchases life insurance payable to the partnership for $500,000 on both Nina and Chen. After several years, Chen dies in an automobile accident, and the partnership receives the $500,000. At that time, Chen's equity in the partnership is $400,000, which is paid to his estate. Is the partnership in receipt of taxable income?

Discussion: Because the partnership is the owner of the policy that was taken out for legitimate business reasons (to ensure continuity of the business), the $500,000 received by the partnership is excluded from taxation. Note that this is the case even though only $400,000 was required to settle Chen's account. The $100,000 windfall for the partnership remains tax free.

Scholarships

A college student who is a candidate for a degree may exclude the value of a **scholarship**, provided that the award does not require the student to perform any future services such as teaching, grading papers, or tutoring.[5] That is, the scholarship must be gratuitous in nature and not merely a form of compensation for past, present, or future services.

▲ **EXAMPLE 10**   Diane received a $1,000 scholarship to the College of Agriculture. The college gives such scholarships annually to students in the top 10% of their class. There are no other criteria or obligations for the receipt of the scholarship. Is the scholarship eligible for exclusion?

Discussion: Because the scholarship is based solely on merit and does not require Diane to provide any services to the college, it is eligible for the exclusion for scholarships.

▲ **EXAMPLE 11**   Peggy received a graduate assistant scholarship from the School of Accounting to aid her in her graduate studies. As part of the scholarship, which pays $300 per month, she is to work for an accounting professor for 10 hours per week, grading papers and assisting the professor in her duties. Is the scholarship eligible for exclusion?

Discussion: Because Peggy is required to perform services in return for her scholarship, the $300 per month that she receives is not eligible for exclusion as a scholarship.

The amount of the exclusion is limited to the direct costs of the student's college education. Direct costs consist of the student's tuition, fees, books, supplies, and other equipment required for the student's course of instruction.[6] Amounts received in excess of the direct costs of the education are taxable. This puts students receiving scholarships on an equal footing with nonstudents regarding personal living expenses. That is, individuals are not allowed to deduct personal living expenses. Therefore, students who receive amounts for personal living expenses must include such amounts in income in order to provide equity with nonstudents, who are effectively taxed on income they spend for personal living expenses. Thus, scholarships that are specified as being for the payment of a student's room and board are fully taxable.

▲ **EXAMPLE 12**   Henrietta received a scholarship for $10,000 to attend Local University. The cost of her tuition, books, fees, and supplies totaled $9,000 for the year. How much of the $10,000 scholarship is taxable?

Discussion: Henrietta may exclude only the $9,000 she spent on the direct costs of her college education. The remaining $1,000 is included in her gross income.

Certain Death Benefits

When an employee dies, the employer often makes payments to surviving dependents to help them out financially while they adjust to life without the income of the deceased. As such, the payments may constitute an excludable gift. However, it is often difficult to determine whether such payments meet the income tax definition of a gift. In order to eliminate some of the uncertainty surrounding **death benefit payments,** the tax law allows one $5,000 exclusion for death benefits paid to a deceased employee's beneficiaries. In order to qualify for this exclusion, the payment must be made solely because of death and cannot represent payment for services performed before the employee died.[7] If more than $5,000 is paid to more than one beneficiary, the $5,000 exclusion must be taken pro rata among the beneficiaries.[8] That is, the total amount of excludable death benefit payments cannot exceed $5,000.

▲ **EXAMPLE 13**   Shiro was an agent for All Farmers Insurance Co. until his death in 1995. Shortly after his death, All Farmers paid his widow Yoko $2,000 in commissions he had earned before he died and $5,000 as a death benefit. In addition, each of his 2 children was paid $2,500 in death benefits. How much of the $12,000 ($2,000 + $5,000 + $2,500 + $2,500) paid as a result of Shiro's death may be excluded from income of the beneficiaries?

Discussion: The $2,000 in commissions was earned by Shiro before he died and is not a payment made because of his death. Therefore, the $2,000 is not eligible for exclusion. The $5,000 death benefit exclusion must be allocated pro rata among the 3 beneficiaries. Yoko will exclude $2,500, and each of their children will exclude $1,250:

$$\text{Total death benefits paid} = \$5,000 + \$2,500 + \$2,500 = \$10,000$$

Pro Rata Allocation of $5,000 Exclusion	
Wife	($5,000 ÷ $10,000) × $5,000 = $2,500
Each child	($2,500 ÷ $10,000) × $5,000 = $1,250

Yoko is taxed on the remaining $2,500 of the payment she receives, and each child is taxed on the remaining $1,250 of the payment that each receives. NOTE: The total amount excluded cannot exceed $5,000, regardless of how much is paid out or to how many beneficiaries the payments are made.

▲ EMPLOYMENT-RELATED EXCLUSIONS

The largest class of exclusions is certain payments made to or on behalf of an employee by an employer. This category of exclusions is costly in terms of the tax revenue lost to the government, because these payments are deductible by the employer and yield no tax revenue because of the exclusion from income granted the employee. These relief provisions are intended to provide equity in cases of double taxation and act as incentives to employers and employees to engage in the specified activity.

Foreign Earned Income

U.S. citizens are subject to tax on all income they receive, regardless of the source. Thus, taxes are levied on worldwide income. To provide relief from double taxation for U.S. citizens working in foreign countries, the tax law allows individuals two options. First, taxpayers may include the **foreign earned income** in their taxable income, calculate the U.S. tax on the income, and take a tax credit for any foreign taxes paid.[9] The amount of the allowable tax credit is the lesser of (1) the actual foreign taxes paid, or (2) the U.S. tax that would have been paid on the foreign earned income. Under the second option, individuals may exclude up to $70,000 in foreign earned income for each full year they work in a foreign country.[10] In order to take advantage of these options, an individual must be either a bonafide resident of the foreign country or must be present in the foreign country for 330 days in any 12 consecutive months. Selection of the most tax-advantageous option will depend on the amount of income earned abroad as well as the relative marginal tax rates between the foreign country and the United States. Thus, in order to select the optimal choice in a given situation, both options must be calculated to determine which option results in the lower net tax payable.

> ▲ **EXAMPLE 14**   Rollie works on a drilling rig in South America during all of the current year. He earns $80,000 from this job and pays $20,000 in tax to the appropriate South American government. Should he elect the tax credit or the exclusion option? Assume that he has sufficient other income from U.S. sources to make him a 31% marginal tax rate payer.
>
> *Discussion:*   Rollie should elect the option that minimizes the amount of U.S. tax paid on the foreign income. Under the tax credit option, the gross tax on the $80,000 would be $24,800 (31% × $80,000), and he would receive a tax credit for the $20,000 of foreign tax paid, resulting in a net U.S. tax of $4,800 ($24,800 − $20,000). Under the exclusion option, he pays no tax on $70,000 of excluded income. The remaining $10,000 of income not eligible for exclusion produces a tax of $3,100 (31% × $10,000). Therefore, the exclusion option results in a tax savings of $1,700 ($4,800 − $3,100).

Payments Made on Behalf of an Employee

Recall from the discussion of income sources in Chapter 3 that when one person pays the expenses of another in an employment setting, the person whose expenses were paid generally has taxable income. However, the tax law does exempt from taxation the payment of the following employee expenses by an employer:

- Payments to qualified pension plans
- Group term life insurance
- Health and accident insurance premiums
- Meals and lodging provided by the employer

The favorable tax treatment accorded these items has encouraged employers to provide more and more of an employee's compensation in the form of excludable fringe benefits. This is quite advantageous to the employee, as the following example illustrates:

▲ **EXAMPLE 15**   Lacy Corporation offers its employees various fringe-benefit package options. Under one of Lacy's options, the employee may participate in the company's accident and health insurance plan or may take the cost of the plan, $1,200 per year, in cash.

Discussion: As discussed later, health and accident insurance premiums paid by an employer on behalf of an employee are excludable from income. Assuming that an employee would ordinarily purchase such insurance, selection of this option effectively increases that person's after-tax compensation from Lacy Corporation by $1,200. An employee who elects to take the $1,200 in cash will be taxed on the receipt of cash. Assuming a 28% marginal tax rate, an employee taking the cash option would have only $864 [$1,200 − (28% × $1,200)] to purchase insurance after paying the tax. In most cases, the employee could not purchase a comparable insurance plan for this amount and would be worse off by electing the cash option.

This example illustrates the tremendous advantage of employer-provided benefits. Employees get benefits at no tax cost that they would otherwise purchase. This use of before-tax compensation can greatly increase the employee's effective pay rate. If the benefit is clear for the employee, what is the incentive for the employer to provide these tax-free benefits? The employer realizes a tax savings from a deduction for the payment of the tax-free benefit as an ordinary and necessary business expense, but it would get the same deduction for any form of compensation paid to the employee. The key for the employer is that the market for employees demands that each employee be paid a certain wage. Thus, the employer will pay the same price for labor, whether the payment is totally in cash or a combination of cash and tax-free benefits. Thus, it makes sense for firms to increase their effective compensation to employees by providing the tax-free benefits: $1,000 in cash compensation is not worth as much after taxes as the same $1,000 in compensation paid in the form of tax-free benefits. In this way, employers are able to increase their employees' real after-tax compensation without an increase in cash outflow. In addition, the tax-free fringe benefits are generally not subject to payroll taxes (e.g., Social Security, unemployment tax), reducing the cost of compensation for the employer.

Although some qualifications for exclusion are quite complex, the discussion that follows is designed to provide an overview of the tax-free benefits that an employer can provide to an employee. Therefore, most of the complexities involved in the exclusions are omitted.

Payments to Qualified Pension Plans.   The income tax law provides many different ways for individuals to provide for their retirement on a tax-deferred basis. Individuals who are not covered by an employer-provided pension plan can set up an individual retirement account (IRA) and deduct contributions made to the account for adjusted gross income.[11] Self-employed individuals are allowed to establish either an IRA or what is referred to as a *Keogh plan* and deduct amounts paid into the plan for adjusted gross income.[12] In addition to the tax deductions allowed for payments into such plans, any earnings on the assets in the plans are not subject to tax as the income is earned. Rather, the retirement plan is taxed when amounts are drawn from the plan. Thus, retirement plans defer current income until the taxpayer retires. The operation of IRAs and the deduction limits are discussed in Chapter 8.

Many companies provide pension plans for their employees. Several allowable variations of such plans permit employers and employees to make payments into the plans and receive the same tax treatment as IRA and Keogh plans. Such plans are referred to as **qualified pension plans.**[13] Payments made by an employer to an employee's account in a qualified pension plan are not taxable in the period in which the payments are made. The tax on such payments is deferred until the employee actually withdraws the payments from the plan.[14] As such, this is not a true exclusion on which a tax is never paid but a deferral of income-recognition to a future period. An added benefit of a qualified pension plan is that the *earnings* on amounts paid into such plans are not taxed until they are withdrawn by the employee. The deferral of income through pension plan payments is mentioned in this chapter because of the growing popularity of employer-sponsored pension plans as an employee fringe benefit.

▲ **EXAMPLE 16**   Linda is an employee of Ross Co. Ross has a qualified pension plan for its employees under which it contributes 5% of each employee's salary to the plan each year. Linda's salary for the current year is $30,000, resulting in a pension plan payment of $1,500. How is Linda taxed on the $1,500?

Discussion: Because Ross Co.'s plan is qualified, the $1,500 payment is not taxed to Linda in the current period. When Linda withdraws the $1,500 from the plan (either at retirement or when she leaves the company), she will be taxed on amounts paid into the plan by Ross as well as any earnings on the amounts in her pension plan.

In addition to the deferral of amounts paid into qualified pension plans by employers, employees may defer taxation of any amounts that they pay into such plans until they withdraw amounts from the plan.

▲ **EXAMPLE 17**   Assume that in example 16 Ross Co.'s pension plan allows employees to contribute up to 5% of their annual earnings to the plan. What is the tax effect to Linda if she contributes the maximum allowed under the plan?

Discussion: Linda can contribute a maximum of $1,500 of her $30,000 salary. Because Linda is not taxed on the contribution now, her gross salary from Ross Co. is reduced to $28,500 ($30,000 − $1,500) by the contribution to the plan. As with the employer's contribution, Linda will be taxed on her contribution when she withdraws it from the plan.

What is the benefit derived from payments to pension plans? First, by deferring tax on payments to the plan until a future period, a time value of money savings is effected on the tax being deferred. A second benefit is that the earnings in the plan accumulate tax free, allowing a larger buildup of funds at retirement than if the earnings were taxed as they were earned. Last, employees often have less income when they retire, resulting in a tax on the deferred income at a lower marginal tax rate.

Group Term Life Insurance.   One of the most popular employee benefits is the exclusion of the premiums paid by an employer on the first $50,000 face amount of **group term life insurance.** This exclusion is available only for term insurance that is provided to a group of employees on a nondiscriminatory basis.[15] Payments made on whole life policies, term insurance purchased for individuals (not a group policy), or plans that discriminate in favor of highly compensated individuals are not eligible for exclusion. The intention of this provision is to encourage employers to provide life insurance to all their employees so that their families have a cushion if the employee dies while still working (a social goal). If an employee's qualified group term policy has a face value greater than $50,000, the premiums paid on the coverage in excess of $50,000 are taxable to the employee. That is, only the premiums paid on $50,000 of group term life insurance are excludable from the employee's income. To calculate the income from premiums paid in excess of the $50,000 exclusion, use a prescribed table of premium values.[16] This table is reproduced in Table 4–1. Note that the premium cost is related to the employee's age and is stated per $1,000 of coverage.

▲ **EXAMPLE 18**   Jim is an employee of Panko Builders with an annual salary of $40,000. Panko provides group term life insurance to all its employees at twice their annual salaries. Jim's $80,000 of group term life insurance cost Panko $400 during the current year. How much taxable income does Jim receive from the provision of the life insurance if he is 33?

Discussion: Jim is allowed to exclude the premiums paid on the first $50,000 of the group term life insurance. The premiums paid on the $30,000 of excess coverage must be included in his gross income as compensation from Panko. Using Table 4–1, the amount of the premiums taxed to Jim is $32 (rounded):

Cost per $1,000 of coverage for 33-year-old	$1.08
Coverage in excess of $50,000	× 30
Gross income from excess coverage	$ 32

▲ **EXAMPLE 19**   Assume that Panko also provides $100,000 of whole life insurance to all management-level employees. Jim is in a management-level position. The cost of his $100,000 policy to Panko was $1,800. How much taxable income does Jim receive from the provision of the whole life insurance?

Discussion: There is no exclusion for the provision of whole life insurance to employees. Therefore, Jim must include the $1,800 cost of the policy in his gross income as compensation from Panko.

Health and Accident Insurance Premiums.   Premiums paid by an employer to purchase **health and accident insurance** coverage for employees (and their dependents) are excluded from the employee's income.[17] The exclusion also applies to companies that choose to "self-insure" by making payments to a fund that is used to pay employees' medical expenses. However, if **a self-insured medical plan** discriminates in favor of highly compensated employees, the amounts paid for medical expenses of highly compensated employees covered by the plan are included in the individual's taxable income.

▲ Table 4–1

GROSS INCOME FROM GROUP TERM LIFE INSURANCE IN EXCESS OF $50,000

	Includable Income per $1,000	
Employee's Age	**Monthly**	**Annually**
Under 30	$ .08	$ .96
30 to 34	.09	1.08
35 to 39	.11	1.32
40 to 44	.17	2.04
45 to 49	.29	3.48
50 to 54	.48	5.76
55 to 59	.75	9.00
60 to 64	1.17	14.04
65 to 69	2.10	25.20
70 and older	3.76	45.12

▲ **EXAMPLE 20**   Rory is an employee of Royce Co. Royce provides health and accident insurance for all its employees. During the current year, Royce pays $1,300 for each employee for coverage under the plan. Does Rory have taxable income from the payment of the premiums?

Discussion: The $1,300 is not taxable to Rory, because it is a payment for a health and accident insurance plan premium that is not discriminatory.

▲ **EXAMPLE 21**   Cory is a senior vice president of Discriminator Corporation. The corporation has a self-insured health and accident plan that covers only executive officers of the corporation. Discriminator makes monthly payments to a fund that is used to reimburse the executives for any medical expenses they incur. During the current year, Cory incurs $3,700 in medical expenses, all of which are reimbursed by the plan. Does Cory have taxable income from the payment of her medical expenses by the plan?

Discussion: Because the plan discriminates in favor of highly compensated employees (only executive officers are covered), all payments from the plan are taxable to Cory. Thus, Cory must include the $3,700 reimbursement in her gross income.

Note that the exclusion is allowed only for the premiums paid by an employer for the purchase of health and accident insurance on a nondiscriminatory basis. The taxation of payments made to the employee from such plans is discussed in the section on returns of human capital.

Meals and Lodging Provided by the Employer.   The value of meals provided to an employee free of charge may be excluded from the employee's income if the meals are provided on the employer's business premises and the provision of the meals is "for the convenience of the employer."[18] Note that the exclusion is for the **meals provided by the employer;** cash meal allowances are generally taxable, because they are not meals provided by the employer.[19] To satisfy the convenience-of-the-employer requirement, the provision of the meals must have a substantial noncompensatory business purpose.

▲ **EXAMPLE 22**   Hilda waits tables at Jiffy Fast Foods. To encourage employees to stay on the premises during their food breaks, Jiffy allows employees to eat one free meal per shift. Is Hilda taxable on the value of the meals she receives from Jiffy's?

Discussion: Because the provision of the meals serves a business purpose (keeping employees close at hand during their meal breaks), the value of the meals is excluded from Hilda's income. Note that this is the case even if Hilda eats her free meal before or after her shift starts.

▲ **EXAMPLE 23**   Blue Trucking Co. gives all its drivers meal vouchers that are honored at various truck stops on the company's trucking routes. The drivers pay for their meals with the vouchers, which are then billed to Blue Trucking Co. Brian is a driver for Blue; he consumed meals costing a total of $3,900 during the current year. Can Brian exclude the value of the meals provided by Blue?

Discussion: Because the meals were not provided on Blue's business premises, they are taxable as compensation to Brian. Brian must include the $3,900-worth of meals in his gross income.

In order to exclude the value of **employer-provided lodging,** the lodging must meet an additional requirement: The acceptance of the lodging must be a condition of employment. That is, the employee has no choice but to live in the employer-provided housing.

▲ **EXAMPLE 24**   Rona is an employee of Arctic Pipeline Co. Because the construction site of a new pipeline is in a remote area, all employees are required to live in temporary quarters erected at the construction site by Arctic. The cost of the lodging to Arctic is estimated at $7,200 per employee per year. Does Rona have taxable income from the provision of the lodging?

Discussion: Because the lodging on the employer's business premises (the job site) is for the convenience of the employer (employees can work more hours if they don't have to make a long commute), and is required as a condition of employment, it is not taxable to the employee. Therefore, Rona may exclude the $7,200 of employer-provided housing from her gross income.

General Fringe Benefits.   The tax law also allows the exclusion of four general types of employment-related fringe benefits:

- No additional cost services
- Employee discounts
- Working-condition fringes
- De minimis fringe benefits[20]

No additional cost services and **employee discounts** must be made available to employees on a nondiscriminatory basis and must also be in the same line of business in which the employee works. For example, a hotel chain may allow hotel employees to stay free at any of its hotels on a space-available basis with no tax consequences to the employee. However, if the hotel chain also allows free hotel rooms to employees of its rental car business, the fair market value of the hotel room is taxable to the employee. Reciprocal agreements between companies in the same line of business are allowed.

▲ **EXAMPLE 25**   Marshall is an employee of Deloitte Airlines. Deloitte and Arthur Air have a reciprocal agreement under which their employees may fly free of charge on each other's airlines on a space-available basis. Marshall used the agreement to take 2 free flights on Arthur Air that would have cost him $880 if he had paid the regular fare. Is Marshall taxed on the value of the free flights?

Discussion: Because Marshall is an airline employee and the free flights are available to all employees, he is allowed to exclude the value of any flights on either Deloitte or Arthur as a no additional cost service. Therefore, the free flights are not taxable to Marshall.

▲ **EXAMPLE 26**   Assume that Deloitte also owns a finance company. Employees of the finance company are allowed to take free flights only on Deloitte Airlines on a space-available basis. Janelle is a financial analyst with Deloitte's finance company. She took 2 free flights on Deloitte that would have cost $1,060 if she had paid the regular fare. Is Janelle taxed on the value of the free flights?

Discussion: Because Janelle does not work in the same line of business as the free service, she is not allowed to exclude the value of the free flights. She must include the $1,060 value of the flights in her gross income.

In order to exclude employee discounts, the discount must be made available to all employees on a nondiscriminatory basis and the goods and/or services provided must be in the same line of business. Note that the exclusion for discounts would ordinarily constitute a bargain purchase. The distinguishing feature between a valid employee discount and a taxable bargain purchase is that employee discounts must be made available to all employees in order to be excluded.

Bargain purchases are essentially employee discounts that are made available only to select employees. The excludable discount on goods is limited to the gross profit percentage on the goods purchased (i.e., employees can't buy goods below the employer's cost tax free). Excludable service discounts are limited to 20 percent. Any employee discount on services in excess of 20 percent is taxable to the employee (the first 20 percent of the discount is excludable).

> ▲ **EXAMPLE 27**   All-City Hardware allows all its employees to buy its products at a 25% discount. All-City marks up all its products by a minimum of 100% of its cost. Arnold is a store employee who bought various tools that normally retail for $200 (cost to All-City of $100) for $150 during the current year. Is Arnold taxed on the $50 discount?
>
> *Discussion:*   Because the discount is available to all employees and the discount does not exceed All-City's gross profit percentage (100% markup on cost equals a gross profit percentage of 50%), the discount is excludable from Arnold's gross income.
>
> ▲ **EXAMPLE 28**   In addition to the tools, Arnold bought a used delivery truck from All-City. The truck was worth $8,000, but All-City sold the truck to Arnold for $5,000, because he has been such a good employee through the years. Is Arnold taxed on the $3,000 discount?
>
> *Discussion:*   Because the discount on the truck is not available to all employees, Arnold is taxed on the $3,000 as a bargain purchase.

A **working-condition fringe benefit** is any item provided to the employee that would have been deductible by the employee as an employee business expense if the employee had paid for the item. This class of fringe benefits includes dues to professional organizations, professional journals, uniforms, and so on.[21] Although not normally deductible as an employee business expense, the payment of parking by an employer is designated as a working-condition fringe benefit. Since 1993, employer-provided parking is excludable only up to $155 per month. In contrast to discounts on goods and services, working-condition fringes can be given on a discriminatory basis. For example, a company can provide free parking only to officers of the company, and the fringe benefit will remain tax free—up to the $155 per month maximum exclusion.

De minimis fringes are those items that are too small to permit a reasonable accounting.[22] This would include such items as personal use of the office photocopier and free coffee in the employees' break room. Also included in this category would be employee parties and small holiday gifts, such as a Christmas ham. This exclusion is based on administrative convenience—the cost of accumulating the information necessary to tax such items would exceed the revenue derived from taxing the items.

Other Benefits Paid by an Employer.   Several other employer-paid fringe benefits are also excludable from income. An employee may exclude up to $5,000 per year of employer-provided **child and dependent care services.**[23] The value of the use of an **employer's athletic facility** may also be excluded, provided that the facility is on the employer's premises and substantially all use of the facility is by employees and their families. In addition, up to $5,250 in payments made for such costs as tuition and books is excludable if the payments are made from a nondiscriminatory **educational assistance program.**[24]

Employer Benefit Plans

As the number of tax-free benefit options proliferated in the late 1970s and early 1980s, employers began to realize that they could not afford to offer all benefits to all employees. Further, every employee did not derive the maximum benefit from every type of benefit. For example, single individuals with no dependents receive no benefit from employer-provided child and dependent care. In response to this situation, firms developed cafeteria plans. In a **cafeteria plan,** a menu of tax-free benefits is offered at the employer's cost. The rules for cafeteria plans allow employers to offer any benefit that is specifically excluded by the tax law in their plans.[25] Each employee is allowed to choose a certain dollar amount of benefits from the menu or may choose to take the cash cost of the benefit. That is, employees who do not want to take all their allowable dollar amount in tax-free benefits are allowed to take the cash equivalent of the benefits. Employees who choose the tax-free benefits are not taxed on the value of the benefit; however, those who elect to receive cash are taxed on the amount of cash received. In order to receive this favorable treatment, the employer must make the benefits of the plan available to all employees on a nondiscriminatory basis. All benefits received from a plan that discriminates in favor of highly compensated employees are included in gross income.

▲ **EXAMPLE 29**   Theodore is the chief financial officer of CEO Corporation. CEO has a cafeteria plan that allows all employees to select from a menu of tax-free benefits a total of 5% of their annual compensation. Theodore's annual salary is $100,000, allowing him to select $5,000 in benefits from the plan. Under the plan, he selected $50,000-worth of group term life insurance and health and accident insurance at a cost to the company of $4,000. He took the remaining $1,000 of allowable benefits in cash. What are the tax consequences to Theodore of the cafeteria plan?

Discussion: The plan is nondiscriminatory, because it covers all employees and allows benefits in proportion to their salaries. Therefore, Theodore can exclude the value of the tax-free benefits (group term life insurance and health insurance) he selected. He must include in his gross income the $1,000 of benefits he took in cash.

Another type of plan that has gained popularity is the **flexible benefits, or salary reduction, plan.**[26] With this type of plan, the employee has an annual amount withheld from his or her salary that is used to pay medical care expenses or child-care costs. As the costs are incurred, the employer reimburses the employee from the account. Amounts paid into the account by the employee are not included in the employee's gross income, thus the term *salary reduction plan.* These plans allow employees to pay for medical costs and child care with before-tax dollars rather than after-tax dollars.

▲ **EXAMPLE 30**   Bale Corporation has a flexible benefits plan that allows employees to have amounts withheld from their salaries to pay for unreimbursed medical costs and child-care costs. Melchior is an employee of Bale whose annual salary is $45,000. Melchior has Bale withhold $8,000 under the plan to pay for health and accident insurance, dental costs, eyeglasses, and so on for his dependents. During the year, Melchior incurs $9,500 in such costs, and Bale reimburses him the $8,000 that had been withheld. What is the tax effect on Melchior of the flexible benefits plan?

Discussion: Melchior's salary is reduced by the $8,000 he paid into the plan, leaving him with a gross income of $37,000. He is not taxed on the amounts he is paid for reimbursements from the plan ($8,000 in this case).

Note that Melchior has been able to pay for $8,000 of his costs with before-tax dollars. Without such a plan, Melchior still would have spent the $8,000, but the income would have been subject to tax. Therefore, he would have had to make more than $8,000 before taxes to have $8,000 after taxes to pay for these expenses.

One final note on this type of plan: The regulations governing these plans do not allow the company to return unused payments to the employee. The employee makes an annual election of the amount she or he wants put into the plan. Any amounts put into a flexible benefits or salary reduction plan that are not spent during the year are retained by the plan and are not available to the employee in subsequent years. That is, the employee loses any payments that are not reimbursed during the plan year.

▲ **EXAMPLE 31**   Assume that in example 30 Melchior spent only $7,500 of the $8,000 he paid in during the year. What is the effect on Melchior?

Discussion: Melchior is still allowed to exclude the $8,000 he paid into the plan, reducing his gross income to $37,000. However, the plan would keep the $500 he paid in but did not spend. It would not be available for Melchior to use to pay his expenses in the next plan year.

Individuals often receive payments that are intended either to reimburse them for the costs of injuries or to compensate them for injuries in such a way as to "make them whole." Such payments are not deemed to increase wealth; rather, they are viewed as a return of human capital lost because of injury or sickness. As such, they are treated as a capital recovery that is not subject to tax. However, payments that are meant to replace lost income do not constitute returns of human capital and are generally taxable. Various types of payments received as compensation for injury or sickness are excluded from gross income. The list of excluded payments includes

▲ **RETURNS OF HUMAN CAPITAL**

■ Workers' compensation payments received as compensation for personal injury or sickness

■ Damage payments received on account of personal injury or sickness

■ Payments received for personal injuries or sickness that are paid from health and accident policies purchased by the taxpayer

■ Payments received from employer-provided health and accident insurance if the payments

   1.   Are made for the permanent loss or loss of use of a member or function of the body, or for permanent disfigurement of the body; or

   2.   Are based on the nature of the injury and are computed without reference to the period of time the employee is absent from the workplace; or

   3.   Are payments received to reimburse the taxpayer for expenses incurred for medical care.

Workers' Compensation

Payments from a state **workers' compensation** fund are excluded from taxation. These payments are made to workers who become unable to work as a result of a work-related injury. Although the payments are somewhat of a substitute for earned income, Congress has provided relief from taxation for such payments, because they are related to an injury suffered on the job and help taxpayers through the period they are recovering from their injuries. As such, they help to restore the human capital of the individual. Note that this is not true for unemployment compensation benefits. Unemployment compensation is meant to be a substitute for income and is therefore subject to tax.

Damage Payments for Personal Injury or Sickness

Damage payments for personal injury or sickness are excluded from taxation.[27] The courts have interpreted **personal injury** to include any personal wrong committed against the taxpayer, such as libel, slander, breach of promise to marry, invasion of privacy, assault, and battery. The exclusion also applies to loss-of-income payments that result from the personal injury.[28]

▲ **EXAMPLE 32**   Rose was hit by an automobile while riding her bicycle to work. Although she was not hospitalized, her injuries prevented her from working for two weeks. The insurance company of the driver of the automobile paid Rose $2,000 for her pain and suffering and reimbursed her $650 for the wages she lost when she was unable to work. How much of the $2,650 Rose received is included in her gross income?

Discussion: None of the $2,650 is taxable. The $2,000 payment for pain and suffering is an excludable damage payment. In addition, because the loss-of-income payment is related to the personal injury, it is excluded from income.

▲ **EXAMPLE 33**   Elliot works as a corner grocer. A feature on the local news about organized crime portrayed Elliot as having links to organized crime. Elliot was outraged, the allegation was false, and he sued the television station for libel and slander. The court awarded Elliot $5,000 for the public humiliation he suffered and $60,000 for loss of his business reputation. How much of the $65,000 is included in Elliot's gross income?

Discussion: The $5,000 payment for his public humiliation is a personal injury and therefore excluded from gross income. Although the $60,000 payment for loss of business reputation is based on estimated lost income, the courts have held that such payments are for a personal injury and thus are excludable.[29]

The treatment of other payments made in connection with a personal injury is more controversial and has resulted in much litigation. In addition to payments for pain and suffering (which are excluded as damages), the courts often award **punitive damages** and/or **loss-of-income damages** in personal injury actions. Damage payments made to replace lost income are generally taxable as a replacement of taxable income unless they are related to a personal injury. Punitive damages are meant to punish the offender in a personal injury case for gross negligence or the intentional infliction of harm to the other party. Punitive damages are included in gross income unless they are the result of a claim for physical injury or physical sickness.[30]

▲ **EXAMPLE 34**   Assume that in example 32 Rose had sued the driver of the automobile. In addition to the payments for pain and suffering, the courts awarded her $10,000 in punitive damages for the gross negligence exhibited by the driver. Are the punitive damages included in Rose's gross income?

Discussion: Because the punitive damages relate to a physical injury, they are excluded from Rose's gross income.

▲ **EXAMPLE 35**   Assume that in example 33 the court found that the television station intentionally harmed Elliot, and he was awarded $30,000 in punitive damages. Are the punitive damages included in Elliot's gross income?

Discussion: Because the punitive damages do not result from a physical injury or physical sickness, they are included in Elliot's gross income.

Payments from Health and Accident Policies

Health and accident insurance policies may be provided by an employer to an employee, or they may be purchased separately by the taxpayer. In either case, payments for medical expenses from such policies are excluded, because they make the taxpayer whole.[31]

An important distinction between employer- and taxpayer-purchased policies is that all health and accident insurance payments from policies purchased by an individual taxpayer are excluded from taxation. The exclusion for payments from employer-provided policies is limited to those for medical care, loss of body parts, or payments made for specific types of injuries. Thus, amounts received as **disability payments** (sick pay or wage-continuation plans) from an employer-provided health and accident plan would be included in gross income. However, the same payments made from a plan purchased by the individual taxpayer would be excluded from gross income. The disparity in treatment is apparently an additional incentive Congress has provided to individuals to purchase adequate health insurance. Figure 4–1 summarizes the tax treatment of payments received from health and accident policies.

▲ **EXAMPLE 36** Sean was involved in an automobile accident in which he sustained severe injuries. The costs of his medical care totaled $8,000. His employer-sponsored plan paid $6,400 of the medical costs and $2,200 in sick pay. In addition, a policy that he had purchased separately paid the remaining $1,600 of his medical costs and an

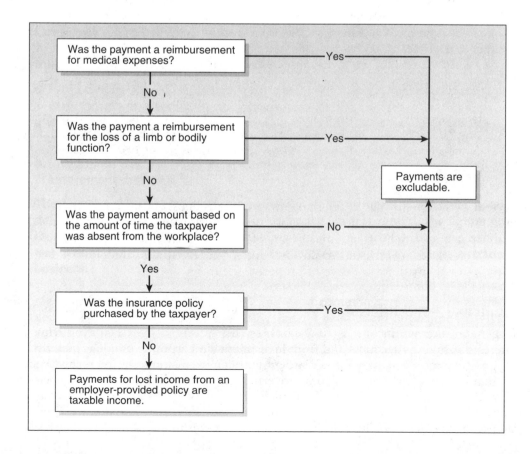

▲ **Figure 4–1**

TAXABILITY OF PAYMENTS
RECEIVED FROM HEALTH
AND ACCIDENT POLICIES

additional $1,000 for income lost while he was unable to work. What are the tax consequences of the receipt of the payments from the two plans?

Discussion: The $8,000 in reimbursed medical care expenses is excludable. The $6,400 payment from his employer-provided plan was for medical expenses and is excludable. The remaining $1,600 of medical expense payments came from a plan that Sean purchased and is also excludable. The $1,000 lost-income payment from his personal plan is also excludable, because Sean purchased the policy. However, the $2,200 in sick pay from his employer's plan is not excludable and must be included in his gross income. Payments for loss of income are excluded only if the payment comes from a policy that the taxpayer purchased. All other payments for loss of income are included in gross income.

A problem sometimes arises with reimbursements for medical care when an individual takes an allowable medical deduction for unreimbursed medical expenses in one tax year and then is reimbursed for those expenses in a subsequent year. Individuals are allowed to deduct unreimbursed medical expenses but only to the extent that they exceed 7.5 percent of the individual's adjusted gross income (the specifics of this deduction are covered in Chapter 8). Under the tax benefit rule, any reimbursed amount that was deducted in a prior year must be included in taxable income in the year of the reimbursement, to the extent that a tax benefit was received from the deduction.

▲ **EXAMPLE 37** Jo is seriously injured in a ski accident late in 1994. The cost of her medical care, which she pays in cash, is $5,000. Thinking that her insurance would not reimburse her for these costs, she correctly includes the $5,000 in medical costs as a deduction on her 1994 tax return, which she files in February 1995. Because of the limitations on medical deductions, her actual medical deduction is for only $1,000 of the $5,000. In May 1995, her insurance company reimburses her for $4,500 of the medical costs. What is the proper treatment of the $4,500 reimbursement?

Discussion: Because the medical costs she deducted on her 1994 return are reimbursed in 1995, Jo must include the reimbursement in her 1995 gross income to the extent she received a tax benefit from the deduction. In this case, her actual deduction is only $1,000 because of the medical deduction limitations. Therefore, she includes only the amount deducted on her 1994 tax return, $1,000, in her 1995 gross income.

▲ INVESTMENT-RELATED EXCLUSIONS

Several exclusions in the income tax law provide relief from taxation on certain investment-related transactions. These include exclusions from income for certain municipal bond interest and the receipt of a stock dividend. Other provisions allow deferral of income in certain discharge-of-indebtedness situations and for improvements made by a lessee of property.

Municipal Bond Interest

In general, interest income is fully taxable when received by a taxpayer. Thus, interest on savings accounts and from investments in corporate bonds is included in gross income. However, the tax law provides an exclusion from interest earned on bonds issued by state and local governments (cities, counties, state agencies such as turnpike authorities) of the United States as well as those of U.S. possessions (Guam, Puerto Rico),[32] called **municipal bond interest.** Note that the exclusion from tax does not include interest on U.S. government obligations such as

Treasury bills, nor does it apply to interest received on foreign government obligations.

▲ **EXAMPLE 38** During the current year, Jorge received the following interest payments:

General Motors bonds	$ 350
Province of Ontario bonds	220
State of Oklahoma bonds	330
Puerto Rico Port Authority bonds	100
Total interest received	$1,000

How much of the $1,000 in interest is taxable to Jorge?

Discussion: Only interest on the debt obligations of state and local governments of the United States and its possessions is excluded from gross income. This would include the interest Jorge received on the state of Oklahoma bonds and the Puerto Rico bonds, a total of $430. The interest on the General Motors bonds and the Ontario bonds is fully taxable. Thus, Jorge has taxable interest income of $570.

Municipal bond interest is excluded because it allows municipalities to raise money for projects at lower interest rates than comparable taxable bonds.

▲ **EXAMPLE 39** ALF Corporation is considering investing in some bonds. ALF's broker has told the company that it can buy City of Nashville tax-exempt bonds at a yield of 6%. Assuming that ALF is in the 34% tax bracket, what would a fully taxable bond of the same risk have to yield to provide an equivalent return?

Discussion: Because tax will have to be paid on the taxable bond, it will have to have a higher before-tax yield to provide the same 6% after-tax return on the City of Nashville bonds. To find the after-tax equivalent return, equate the 6% return to the after-tax return, X, and solve:

$$
\begin{aligned}
0.06 &= X - 0.34X \\
0.06 &= X(1 - 0.34) \\
0.06 &= X(0.66) \\
0.06 \div 0.66 &= X \\
0.0909 &= X
\end{aligned}
$$

Therefore, any taxable bond with a pretax yield greater than 9.09% will provide ALF with a higher after-tax return than the Nashville bonds.

Proof: Assume that ALF invests $1,000 in the City of Nashville bonds yielding 6% and another $1,000 in Togoto, Inc., bonds yielding 10%. Which bond investment has the greater after-tax return?

Discussion: The Togoto, Inc., bonds have a greater after-tax return. This is shown by computing the after-tax income from each $1,000 investment:

City of Nashville interest ($1,000 × 6%)	$ 60
Income tax	(-0-)
After-tax income	$ 60
Togoto, Inc., interest ($1,000 × 10%)	$100
Income tax ($100 × 34%)	(34)
After-tax income	$ 66

Stock Dividends

The Supreme Court ruled in 1920 that the receipt of a **stock dividend** does not constitute a realization of income.[33] That is, a dividend paid in stock of the same company (either a stock dividend or a stock split) is merely "slicing the pie" into smaller ownership units, with no resulting increase in shareholder wealth. The value of a shareholder's interest does not change; it is merely spread over more ownership units.

▲ **EXAMPLE 40**   Imelda owns 100,000 shares of Smith common stock, for which she paid $1,200,000 several years ago. During the current year, when Smith had a total of 1,000,000 shares outstanding, Smith declared and distributed a 20% stock dividend. Imelda received 20,000 new shares (of the 200,000 total dividend issued) from the dividend. What are the tax consequences for Imelda from the receipt of the dividend?

Discussion: Imelda's wealth has not increased from the receipt of the shares. Before the dividend, she owned 10% (100,000 ÷ 1,000,000) of Smith. After the dividend, she still owns 10% (120,000 ÷ 1,200,000). Therefore, she has not realized an increase of wealth from the dividend and is not taxed on the value of the 20,000 shares received. NOTE: Imelda's original 100,000 shares had a basis of $12 per share ($1,200,000 ÷ 100,000). She now owns 120,000 shares with a total basis of $1,200,000. Thus, her basis per share is now $10 ($1,200,000 ÷ 120,000).

▲ **EXAMPLE 41**   After making the stock dividend, Smith paid a cash dividend of $2 per share on the 1,200,000 shares outstanding. Imelda received $240,000 from the dividend. What are the tax effects of the dividend for Imelda?

Discussion: The exclusion from tax is only for the shares of stock received from a stock dividend. Any subsequent cash dividends received on the stock are fully taxable. Imelda must include the $240,000 cash dividend in her gross income.

However, if the receiver of the stock dividend has the option to receive cash in lieu of stock, the dividend is taxed as if the cash option had been selected.[34] In this case, the shares of stock are deemed to have a cash equivalent and thus are taxable.

▲ **EXAMPLE 42**   Opubco, Inc., a public utility, declares a 10% stock dividend when its stock is selling for $50 per share. Stockholders have the option of receiving $5 cash per share in lieu of the stock. Ginny owns 1,000 shares of Opubco stock. She elects to take the 100 additional shares of Opubco stock. What is the tax effect of the receipt of the stock dividend for Ginny?

Discussion: Because Ginny could have received cash instead of the shares of stock, she is taxed on the fair market value of the shares received, resulting in taxable income of $5,000 (100 × $50). Her basis in the 100 shares she actually received is the taxable income reported, $5,000.

Discharge of Indebtedness

Under the general principles of income recognition, the borrowing of money is not a taxable event, because the borrower is under an obligation to repay the loan. Similarly, the repayment of the loan principal does not generate taxable income. However, if a lender forgives all or a portion of the debt of the borrower, the borrower realizes an increase in wealth from the reduction of the liability. That is, the borrower who is relieved of a debt has obtained a claim of right to the amount of debt forgiven. This increase in wealth, known as a **discharge of indebtedness,** is generally taxable to the borrower.

▲ **EXAMPLE 43**   Leonard borrowed $17,000 from his employer to purchase a new car. Several years later, when Leonard had paid the debt down to $3,000, his employer told Leonard he no longer owed the debt as a bonus for Leonard's hard work and devotion to the company. Is Leonard taxed on the forgiveness of the $3,000 owed on the loan?

Discussion: Leonard is taxed on the $3,000. His wealth has increased as a result of the extinguishment of the liability, and he now has obtained a claim of right to the $3,000, because he is no longer under any obligation to repay.

The tax law provides an exception to the general rule of taxability of a discharge of indebtedness when the borrower is insolvent (liabilities exceed assets), both before and after the forgiveness of the debt.[35] This exception includes any debt reductions as a result of a bankruptcy proceeding.

▲ **EXAMPLE 44**   Because of a slump in the real estate market, Koka Properties, Inc., was having trouble paying its debts. The value of Koka's assets was $400,000, and its liabilities were $600,000. In order to help Koka restore stability, its bank forgave a $100,000 line of credit loan it had made to Koka several years earlier. What are the tax effects of the $100,000 forgiveness of debt?

Discussion: Because Koka is still insolvent ($400,000 − $500,000) after the debt reduction, it does not have to recognize the $100,000 forgiveness as income.

However, if the discharge makes the debtor solvent, the debtor must recognize income to the extent that the debtor is solvent after the debt reduction. That is, if the taxpayer has a positive net worth after the forgiveness of debt, he or she is deemed to have the wherewithal to pay, up to the amount of the solvency.

▲ **EXAMPLE 45**   In example 44, what would the tax effects be if Koka's bank line of credit, which was forgiven, had been $250,000?

Discussion: The tax law provides that income from the discharge of indebtedness is excluded only if the borrower is insolvent after the discharge. Therefore, income must be recognized to the extent that the borrower is solvent after the debt reduction. Applying this to Koka, its net worth after the discharge is $50,000 ($400,000 − $350,000), which must be included in its gross income.

When a taxpayer is allowed to exclude discharge of indebtedness income because of insolvency, any tax attributes the taxpayer has in relation to the debt must be reduced by the amount of the exclusion. Tax attributes that must be reduced include net operating loss carryforwards, capital loss carryforwards, and the basis of property purchased with the debt.

A second exception to the taxability of debt discharges applies to taxpayers who have been negatively affected by depressed real estate markets. Taxpayers other than corporations can elect to exclude from income some cancellation of "qualified real property business indebtedness." **Qualified real property business indebtedness** is debt incurred or assumed in connection with real property used in a trade or business that is secured by that real property. Only debt incurred before 1993 qualifies for the exclusion, unless it is incurred to refinance previously incurred qualified debt or is qualified acquisition debt. Qualified acquisition debt is debt incurred to acquire, construct, or substantially improve real property that is secured by such debt.

The amount of the exclusion for qualified real property debt is the lesser of (1) the property's adjusted basis or (2) the excess of the principal amount of the debt immediately before the discharge over the fair market value of the property that secures the debt. Note that part 2 of the exclusion formula effectively restricts application of this relief provision to those situations in which the amount of debt on the property is greater than the property's fair market value. The adjusted basis of the property must be reduced by any amounts excluded under this provision.

▲ **EXAMPLE 46**   In 1991, the Felicia Partnership purchased a building that now has a fair market value of $120,000; Felicia uses the building, secured by a mortgage of $160,000, in its insurance business. Felicia negotiates a reduction in the mortgage debt to $100,000. If the partnership's adjusted basis in the building is $70,000, how much of the $60,000 debt reduction must Felicia include in its gross income?

Discussion: The debt is qualified real property business indebtedness, because the debt is secured by real property that the partnership uses in its insurance business. Felicia may exclude $40,000 of the $60,000 debt reduction:

The lesser of
1. $70,000 (adjusted basis)
OR
2. $40,000 ($160,000 indebtedness before the discharge − $120,000 fair market value of the building)

Felicia must include $20,000 ($60,000 − $40,000) of the discharged debt in gross income. The adjusted basis of the building is reduced by the $40,000 of excluded discharge of indebtedness income, leaving an adjusted basis after the discharge of $30,000 ($70,000 − $40,000). Note that the basis reduction will reduce the amount of Felicia's subsequent depreciation deductions on the building. This ultimately results in Felicia's recognizing the debt discharge through higher taxable incomes in the future as a result of the smaller depreciation deductions.

▲ **EXAMPLE 47**   Assume the same facts as in example 46, except that Felicia's adjusted basis in the building is $25,000.

Discussion: In this case, Felicia's exclusion is limited to its $25,000 adjusted basis:

The lesser of
1. $25,000
OR
2. $40,000

Felicia will have to include $35,000 ($60,000 − $25,000) of the debt discharge in gross income. The adjusted basis in the building is reduced to zero ($25,000 - $25,000).

If the qualified property is secured by more than one qualified real property indebtedness, the fair market value of the property must be reduced by the outstanding principal amount of the other indebtedness in calculating the amount of the exclusion.

▲ **EXAMPLE 48**   Heinrich owns a building with a fair market value of $200,000 that he has used in his floral design business since 1989. The building is secured by two mortgages: The first mortgage is for $150,000, and the second mortgage is for $80,000. The lender on the first mortgage agrees to reduce the debt to $100,000. If Heinrich's adjusted basis in the building is $140,000, how much of the $50,000 discharge of indebtedness income must Heinrich include in his gross income?

Discussion: The debt is qualified real property business indebtedness. In calculating the amount of the exclusion, the $200,000 fair market value must be reduced by the $80,000 second mortgage to a net fair market value of $120,000. Heinrich can exclude $30,000 of the debt discharge:

The lesser of
1. $140,000 (his adjusted basis)
OR
2. $30,000 ($150,000 indebtedness before the discharge − $120,000 net fair market value of the building).

Heinrich must include $20,000 ($50,000 − $30,000) of the debt discharge in his gross income. The adjusted basis of the building is reduced to $110,000 ($140,000 − $30,000).

Improvements by a Lessee

The tax law provides that a property owner does not have income when a lessee makes improvements to the owner's property or when such improvements revert to the property owner at the termination of the lease.[36] This allows the property owner to defer the gain in the value of the property from the improvements until the property is sold, at which time the owner will have the wherewithal to pay the tax on the increased value from the **improvements by a lessee.**

▲ **EXAMPLE 49**   Natasha leased a building from Rudy Corporation under a 10-year lease that provided that any improvements made by Natasha would revert to Rudy at the expiration of the lease. Natasha added a wing to the building at a cost of $40,000. When the lease ended, the new wing increased the value of the property by $75,000. Does Rudy Corporation have any income from the addition of the new wing by Natasha?

Discussion: Rudy will not be taxed on the increased value of the property until it sells or otherwise disposes of the property in a taxable transaction. At that time, the $75,000 increase in value will be reflected in any gain from the property's disposition.

The exclusion from income for improvements by a lessee does not apply when the improvements are made in lieu of rent. When that is the case, the lessee is paying the rent in the form of the improvement rather than in cash. Under the cash-equivalent approach to income recognition, the value of such improvements is included in income.[37]

▲ **EXAMPLE 50**   Andrea leased a building from Petros for $2,000 per month. The bathroom was in need of repair, so Petros agreed to reduce Andrea's rent by the cost of repairing the bathroom. Andrea paid $1,800 to have the bathroom repaired and paid Petros only $200 for the next month's rent. What are the tax effects to Petros of the payment of the repairs by Andrea?

Discussion: Because the repair improvement was made in lieu of a rental payment, the $1,800 is considered a rental payment received by Petros. It is not excludable as an improvement by a lessee.

Although Petros recognizes income from the repairs, he is allowed a deduction for the repair cost as an ordinary and necessary expense. The net effect of this situation for Petros is no increase in his income. This effect follows from the substance of the transaction: If Andrea had paid Petros the $2,000 monthly rent and Petros then reimbursed Andrea for the repairs, Petros would include the repairs in income through the rent payment and deduct the repair expense payment.

All income received by a taxpayer is taxable unless specifically excluded by the tax law. Excludable forms of income must be identified in order to determine a taxpayer's gross income. Exclusions from income are a result of the legislative

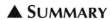

▲ **SUMMARY**

grace concept. Under this concept, only Congress can provide relief from tax. Any relief provided must be strictly applied and interpreted. As applied to exclusions, this means that a specific provision must be found in the tax law before an income item can be excluded from taxation. Exclusions from income are usually meant to avoid double taxation or to provide incentive for taxpayers to enter into a tax-favored transaction. Often, amounts are excluded from taxation based on the

▲ **Table 4–2**

INCOME EXCLUSIONS BY
CATEGORY

	Exclusions	Major Problems
Donative Items	Gifts Inheritances Life insurance proceeds Scholarships Death benefits	What is a gift? No exclusion for future earnings on amounts excluded for gifts, inheritances, life insurance proceeds Only direct costs of education excludable for scholarships

Employment-related Exclusions	Foreign earned income
	Employer-provided benefits
	  Pension plan payments
	  Group term life insurance
	  Health/accident insurance
	  Meals and lodging
	  No additional cost services
	  Employee discounts
	  Working-condition fringes
	  De minimis fringes
	  Child care
	  Athletic facilities
	  Educational assistance
	Employee benefit plans
	  Cafeteria plans
	  Flexible benefits/salary reduction plans
		Nondiscrimination requirement for most benefits
		Each benefit has specific requirements and/or limitations

Returns of Human Capital	Workers' compensation Damages for personal injury Payments from employee-purchased health/accident plan Payments from employer-provided health/accident insurance for medical expenses	Payments for lost income—wage continuation/disability payments Payments for punitive damages Tax benefit rule for medical expenses reimbursed in a year subsequent to deduction
Investment-related Exclusions	Municipal bond interest Stock dividends Discharge of indebtedness—insolvent debtor Discharge of indebtedness—qualified real property business indebtedness Improvements by a lessee	Taxability of gain on disposition of tax-exempt securities/nontaxable dividend shares Cash option on stock dividend Insolvent debtors who become solvent after discharge of debt Improvements made in lieu of rent

wherewithal-to-pay concept, under which amounts are taxed when the means are available to pay the tax.

This chapter identified and discussed four general classes of exclusions: donative items, employment-related exclusions, returns of human capital, and investment-related exclusions. Because all these exclusion items represent departures from the general concepts of income recognition, there is no hard-and-fast method for learning the various types of exclusions. To aid you in your study of exclusions, Table 4–2 summarizes by category the exclusions discussed in this chapter and points out the major problems involved within each category. At the completion of this chapter, you should be able to compute the gross income for most common situations faced by taxpayers.

▲ KEY TERMS

cafeteria plan (p. 152)
child and dependent care services (p. 151)
damage payments (p. 154)
death benefit payment (p. 144)
de minimis fringe benefit (p. 151)
disability payment (p. 155)
discharge of indebtedness (p. 158)
educational assistance program (p. 151)
employer's athletic facility (p. 151)
employee discount (p. 150)
employer-provided lodging (p. 149)
flexible benefits plan (p. 152)

foreign earned income (p. 145)
gift (p. 140)
group term life insurance (p. 147)
health and accident insurance (p. 148)
improvements by a lessee (p. 161)
inheritance (p. 141)
life insurance proceeds (p. 141)
loss-of-income damages (p. 154)
meals provided by employer (p. 149)
municipal bond interest (p. 156)
no additional cost services (p. 150)

personal injury (p. 154)
punitive damages (p. 154)
qualified pension plan (p. 147)
qualfied real property business indebtedness (p. 159)
salary reduction plan (p. 152)
scholarship (p. 143)
self-insured medical plan (p. 148)
stock dividend (p. 158)
workers' compensation (p. 153)
working-condition fringe benefit (p. 151)

▲ PRIMARY TAX LAW SOURCES

[1] Sec. 102—States that the value of property received by gift or inheritance is excluded from gross income.

[2] Comm. v. Duberstein, 363 U.S. 278 at 283 (1960)—Held that a Cadillac received by a taxpayer from a businessman to whom he occasionally gave names of potential customers was not a tax-free gift.

[3] Reg. Sec. 1.102-1—States that property received by gift or inheritance is not subject to income tax, but income earned on such property subsequent to receipt is not excluded.

[4] Sec. 101—States that life insurance payments and $5,000 in death-benefit payments paid are excluded from gross income.

[5] Sec. 117—States that qualified scholarships are excluded from gross income and the amount of the exclusion is limited to qualified tuition and related expenses.

[6] Prop. Reg. Sec. 1.117-6—Defines *scholarships* and discusses the types of expenditures that are excludable as direct education costs.

[7] Rev. Rul. 62-102—Assumes that voluntary payments made by an employer to a deceased employee's family are compensation for past services.

[8] Reg. Sec. 1.101-2—Explains the allocation of the $5,000 per employee death-benefit exclusion among beneficiaries.

[9] Sec. 901—Allows a tax credit for foreign taxes paid on earned income.

[10] Sec. 911—Allows the exclusion of up to $70,000 of foreign earned income from gross income in lieu of the tax credit provided by Section 901.

[11] Sec. 219—Allows a deduction for adjusted gross income for up to $2,000 in contributions to qualified retirement accounts.

[12] Sec. 401—Allows self-employed individuals to establish retirement accounts that allow deductions for contributions comparable to those provided by employer-sponsored pension plans.

[13] Sec. 401—Prescribes the requirements for a qualified employer-provided retirement plan.

[14] Sec. 402—Prescribes the tax treatment of qualified employer-provided pension plans.

[15] Reg. Sec. 1.79-4T—Discusses the nondiscrimination rules as they apply to the provision of group term life insurance to employees.

[16] Reg. Sec. 1.79-3—Specifies the taxability of premiums paid on group term life insurance in excess of $50,000.

[17] Sec. 106—States that gross income does not include payments for health and accident insurance coverage by an employer for an employee.

[18] Sec. 119—Provides an exclusion from gross income for meals and lodging provided by an employer to an employee.

[19] Reg. Sec. 1.119-1—Defines terms for purposes of the exclusion for meals and lodging provided by an employer.

[20] Sec. 132—Excludes no-additional-cost services, qualified employee discounts, working-condition fringes, and de minimis fringe benefits from gross income; also provides that employer-provided parking and on-premises athletic facilities are excludable fringe benefits.

[21] Reg. Sec. 1.132-5—Discusses working-condition fringes and gives examples of qualifying working-condition fringe benefits.

[22] Reg. Sec. 1.132-6—Discusses de minimis fringe benefits and provides examples of such benefits.

[23] Sec. 129—Excludes up to $5,000 per year for employer-provided dependent care.

[24] Sec. 127—Excludes up to $5,250 in reimbursements to an employee from an employer's qualified educational assistance plan. This exclusion was set to expire on December 31, 1994, and had not been renewed when this book went to press.

However, it also expired in 1992 and was reinstated retroactively in 1993. Therefore, Congress is likely to renew the exclusion for payments made in 1995.

[25] Sec. 125—Provides an exclusion for benefits selected under a cafeteria plan; defines a *cafeteria plan* and describes the types of benefits the plan may offer.

[26] Prop. Reg. Sec. 1.125-1—Provides information about cafeteria plans in a question-and-answer format; question 7 answers questions relating to what constitutes a flexible benefits (salary reduction) plan.

[27] Sec. 104—States that amounts received for workers' compensation and damages for personal injuries are excluded from gross income.

[28] Rev. Rul. 85-97—Allows the exclusion of loss-of-income payments resulting from a personal injury.

[29] Roemer, Jr. v. Comm., 716 F.2d 693 (6th Cir. 1983)—Held that damages paid for injury to professional reputation are excludable as payments for personal injury. The IRS said in Revenue Ruling 85-143 that it would not follow *Roemer* and would continue to tax such damage payments. However, in *Threlkeld v. Comm.*, 848 F.2d 81 (6th Cir. 1988), the court rejected the IRS's position in Revenue Ruling 85–143.

[30] Glenshaw Glass v. Comm., 348 U.S. 426 (1955)—Held that punitive damage payments constitute gross income and are not excludable. Sec. 104 excludes punitive damage payments that are the result of a physical injury or physical sickness.

[31] Sec. 105—States that payments for medical expenses from an employer-provided plan are excluded from gross income.

[32] Sec. 103—States that interest received on state or local government bonds is excluded from gross income.

[33] Eisner v. Macomber, 252 U.S. 189 (1920)—Held that a stock dividend did not constitute gross income.

[34] Sec. 305—States that stock dividends with a cash option are taxable.

[35] Sec. 108—Provides an exclusion from gross income for the discharge of indebtedness of an insolvent taxpayer and for

discharges of indebtedness on qualified real property indebtedness.

[36] Sec. 109—States that the value of improvements made to a lessor's property by a lessee are not income to the lessor at the termination of the lease.

[37] Reg. Sec. 1.109-1—States that improvements made by a lessee to a lessor's property that are in lieu of rental payments are included in gross income as income from rents.

▲ DISCUSSION QUESTIONS

 1. What are the two reasons most commonly advanced for excluding items from income? Give examples of each, and explain how they accomplish the purpose of the exclusion.

2. What is the difference between an exclusion of income and a deferral of income?

3. How can gifts be used to lower the overall tax paid by a family?

4. Why are life insurance proceeds excluded from the gross income of the beneficiary of the policy?

5. Are all scholarships excluded from tax? Explain the circumstances under which a scholarship would not be excluded from gross income.

6. What is the purpose of the death benefit exclusion?

7. What tax relief is provided to U.S. citizens who earn income in a foreign country and pay taxes in that country?

8. How do employees benefit from payments made into a qualified pension plan on their behalf?

9. Distinguish group term life insurance from whole life insurance.

10. What is the difference in the tax treatment of a medical insurance plan that is purchased from a third-party insurer and a self-insured medical reimbursement plan?

11. What is the difference between a qualified employee discount and a bargain purchase by an employee?

12. What is the difference between a cafeteria plan and a flexible benefits (salary reduction) plan?

13. Why are workers' compensation payments treated differently than unemployment compensation payments for tax purposes?

14. What is a personal injury for purposes of excluding damage payments received?

15. Are punitive damages taxable? Explain.

16. Are payments for loss of income taxable? Explain.

17. Discuss the difference in the tax treatment of payments received from an employer-provided health and accident insurance policy and a health and accident insurance policy purchased by the taxpayer.

18. What is the purpose of excluding municipal bond interest from gross income?

19. Are all stock dividends received excluded from gross income?

20. In 1993, Bud borrows $20,000 from a friend. Before Bud can repay any of the loan, the friend dies. His friend's last will and testament provides that any amounts owed to him are to be forgiven upon his death. Does Bud have gross income from the forgiveness of debt?

▲ PROBLEMS

21. Throughout the textbook, it has been stated that tax relief can come in several forms. Assuming that the taxpayer in question is in a 28% marginal tax rate bracket and the time value of money is 6%, determine the tax value of the following forms of relief:
    a. A $1,000 item of income that is excluded from income
    b. A $1,000 expenditure that is deductible in computing taxable income
    c. A $1,000 expenditure that is eligible for a 10% tax credit
    d. A $1,000 item of income that is deferred for five years (assume no change in the marginal tax rate)

22. A tornado did extensive damage in the community in which Bodine Co. had its primary manufacturing facilities. Bodine gave $1,000 to each household that suffered damage from the tornado to help residents while repairs were being made. Some (but not all) payments were made to Bodine employees. What are the tax consequences of the receipt of the $1,000 by Bodine employees? Explain.

23. On May 1, Raisa received a $1,000, 6% bond of Altomba Corporation as a graduation present from her aunt Lenia. The bond pays interest semiannually, on June 30 and December 31. What are the tax effects of this transfer for Raisa and Lenia for the current year?

24. During the current year, Alexis gave her daughter Tabatha stocks worth $100,000 on the condition that she pay her son Rory the first $6,000 in dividends on the stock each year. Discuss the taxability of this arrangement in each of the following cases:
    a. The stocks pay total dividends of $8,000. Tabatha pays Rory $6,000 under the agreement.
    b. The stocks pay total dividends of $4,500. Tabatha pays Rory $4,500 under the agreement.

25. Hersh inherits $50,000 from his grandfather. Hersh receives the $50,000 on January 1 and immediately invests $25,000 in General Motors bonds that pay 8% annual interest and $25,000 in Lane County highway improvement bonds with a 6% annual interest rate. How much gross income does Hersh have from these transactions?

26. Binh met Anika 10 years ago at a cocktail party. Anika was a wealthy investor with extensive holdings in the oil and gas industry. Binh was a real estate agent earning about $35,000 a year. Several months after they met, Binh proposed marriage and Anika accepted. Just before the wedding, Anika told Binh that she had a "mental hangup" about marriage, and Binh agreed to live with her without benefit of matrimony. In return, Anika promised to leave Binh her entire estate. In the ensuing years, they had an intimate marriagelike relationship, attending social, business, and family functions together. Anika died in 1994. No will was found immediately. A few months after Anika's death, her sister found a one-page paper signed by Anika. The paper left Anika's entire estate to her brothers and sisters and named her sister as executor of the estate. Binh sued Anika's estate and won a judgment of $2,000,000 for sevices rendered to Anika during their relationship. The estate appealed the decision, which was affirmed as to liability but reversed and remanded for a new trial on the amount of the judgment. Binh and the estate subsequently worked out an agreement in which the estate paid Binh $1,200,000 in settlement of his claim. Can Binh exclude the $1,200,000 payment as an inheritance? Discuss, and explain why you think the payment is (or is not) an excludable inheritance.

27. Allison died during the current year. She was covered by a $250,000 life insurance policy that was payable to her husband Bob. Bob elected to receive the policy proceeds in 10 annual installments of $32,000. How much income does Bob have to recognize during the current year?

28. Earl is a student at Aggie Tech. He received a $5,000 general scholarship for his outstanding grades in previous years. Earl is also a residence hall assistant, for which he receives free room and board worth $6,000 per year. Earl's annual costs for tuition, books, and supplies are $8,000. Does Earl have any taxable income from the scholarship or the free room and board?

Do this one **29.** Assume the same facts as in problem 28, except that Earl was not a residence hall assistant and his general scholarship was for
   a. $5,000 *NO*
   b. $10,000 *2,000*

30. Fawn received a $2,500 scholarship to State University. Discuss the taxability of the scholarship under each of the following assumptions:
   a. The scholarship is paid from a general scholarship fund and is awarded to students with high academic potential. Recipients are not required to perform any services to receive the scholarship.
   b. The scholarship is paid by the finance department. Recipients are required to work 10 hours per work for a professor designated by the department.

31. Determine whether the taxpayers in each of the following situations have realized taxable income:
   a. Alexander inherited a tract of land from his uncle who died during the current year. A friend of Alexander's who is a petroleum engineer told him he thought there might be oil on the land. Alexander had the land surveyed, and an oil deposit worth an estimated $5,000,000 was discovered on the property.
   b. Mickey was given two tickets to the World Series by a friend. Mickey sold the tickets for $500 apiece.
   c. Hannah is the purchasing agent for Slim Diet Centers. Harold, a salesman who does considerable business with Hannah, gave her a set of golf clubs worth $750. Harold told Hannah that he was giving her the clubs to show his appreciation for being such a good friend throughout their business dealings.
   d. Melanie's father died during the current year. Melanie was the beneficiary of a $200,000 life insurance policy on her father's life. She received the proceeds on August 1 and immediately invested in a bank certificate of deposit with a 9% annual earnings rate.

32. Jobe works as a sales agent for Wegotcha Marketing, Inc. Jobe dies on October 12 of this year. Wegotcha pays Ellen, Jobe's wife, $2,200 in salary and commissions Jobe had earned before he died. In addition, Wegotcha pays $3,000 each to Ellen and the 2 children (a total of $9,000). What are the tax consequences of the payments to Ellen and the children?

33. Lucinda is a welder for Big Auto Co., Inc. Lucinda dies in an automobile accident on March 14 of this year. Big Auto has a company policy of paying $4,000 to the spouse of any employee who dies. In addition to the $4,000 payment, Big Auto pays Harvey, Lucinda's husband, $1,800 in salary and $1,300 in vacation pay Lucinda had earned before her death. Harvey also collected $90,000 from a group term life insurance policy Big Auto provided as part of Lucinda's compensation package. Lucinda had contributed to a qualified employer-sponsored pension plan. Big Auto had matched Lucinda's contributions to the plan. The plan allows the beneficiary of an employee who dies before payments begin to take the plan balance as an annuity or in a lump sum. Harvey elects to take the $210,000 plan balance in a lump sum. Discuss the taxability of each payment that Harvey received as a result of Lucinda's death.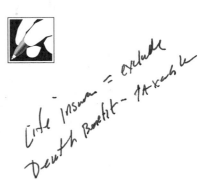

Life Insurance = exclude
Death Benefit - taxable

34. Gregorio is a single individual who works for Olive Importers, Inc. During all of 1995, he is stationed in Italy. He pays Italian taxes of $30,000 on his Olive salary of $120,000. His taxable income without considering his salary from Olive is $50,000. How should Gregorio treat the salary he receives from Olive on his 1995 U.S. tax return?

35. Assume that in problem 34, Gregorio pays only $20,000 in Italian taxes. Would your answer change? Explain.

36. Ariel works for Sander Corporation for 30 years. Sander has a pension plan in which it matches employee contributions by up to 5% of the employee's salary. Ariel retires during the current year. Her pension plan contains payments and earnings of $300,000, half of which are attributable to payments made by Ariel and half attributable to payments made by Sander. Under the plan, Ariel is to receive $2,000 per month until she dies (her estimated life expectancy is 20 years). What is the tax treatment of each $2,000 payment under each of the following assumptions?
    a. The plan is a qualified pension plan. Therefore, no tax has been paid on any of the contributions or earnings in the plan.
    b. The plan is not a qualified plan. Therefore, Ariel has paid tax on all contributions and earnings in the plan.

37. Erwin works for Close Corporation for 24 years. Close has a qualified, noncontributory pension plan that pays employees with more than 5 years of service $75 per month per year when they reach age 65. Erwin turns 65 in February of this year and retires in June. Payments from Close's plan begin in July. In preparing for his retirement, Erwin had purchased an annuity 15 years ago for $18,000. The annuity pays $150 per month for life beginning at age 65. Erwin begins receiving the annuity payments in March, at which time his life expectancy is 15 years. How much gross income does Erwin have from the receipt of the payments from Close and the annuity in the current year?

38. Deirdre, 47, is the vice president of marketing for Holland Co. and receives an annual salary of $100,000. As part of her compensation package, Deirdre receives life insurance at twice her annual salary. Determine the taxability of the payment of the life insurance premiums by Holland under each of the following circumstances:
    a. The insurance is term insurance and is available to all employees. The annual cost of Deirdre's premiums is $600.
    b. The insurance is whole life insurance and is available to all employees. The annual cost of Deirdre's premiums is $1,800.
    c. The insurance is term insurance and is provided only to employees who make at least $100,000 per year. The annual cost of Deirdre's premiums is $600.

39. Bear Co. provides all its employees with a $10,000 group term life insurance policy. Elk Co. does not provide any life insurance but pays $10,000 to survivors of employees who die. Jackie, an employee of Bear Co., dies during the current year. Joan, an employee of Elk Co., dies during the current year. What is the difference (if any) in the tax treatment of the $10,000 payments their families receive upon their deaths?

40. Horace is an employee of Ace Electric Co. Ace provides all employees with group term life insurance equal to twice their annual salary. How much gross income does Horace have under each of the following assumptions?
    a. Horace is 28 and earns $22,000 per year.
    b. Horace is 28 and earns $42,000 per year.
    c. Horace is 67 and earns $33,000 per year.
    d. Horace is 55 and earns $100,000 per year.

41. Abe is an employee of Haddock, Inc. Haddock provides basic health and accident insurance to all its employees through a contract with Minor Accident Insurance Co. Because the Minor policy does not cover 100% of medical costs, Haddock provides all executive officers with a self-insured plan to pay any medical costs not covered by Minor's policy. Abe is eligible for both plans. During the current year, premiums on the Minor policy for Abe were $1,450. Abe also received reimbursements from the self-insured plan of $1,900.
    a. What are the tax consequences for Abe of the payments made by Haddock?
    b. What difference would it make if all employees were covered under both plans?

42. Adam works during the summer as a fire watcher for the Oregon forest service. As such he spends three weeks in the woods in a forest service watchtower and then gets a week off. Because of the remoteness of the location, groceries are flown in by heli-

copter to Adam each week. Does Adam have any taxable income from this arrangement? Explain.

43. Don is the production manager for Corporate Manufacturing Facilities (CMF). CMF works three production shifts per day. Because Don is so integral to CMF's operations, CMF requires Don to live in housing that CMF owns so that he can be available for any emergencies that arise throughout the day. The housing is located four blocks from the CMF plant. Is Don taxed on the value of the housing? Explain.

44. Determine whether the taxpayer has received taxable income in each of the following situations. Explain why any amount(s) may be excluded:
    a. Jim is an employee of Fast Tax Prep, Inc. All employees of Fast Tax are eligible for a 30% discount on the preparation of their income tax return. Jim's tax return preparation would normally have cost $500, but he paid only $350 because of the discount.
    b. Mabel is a lawyer for a large law firm, Winken, Blinken, and Nod. Winken pays Mabel's annual licensing renewal fee of $500 and her $200 annual dues to the American Lawyers' Association. Mabel also took advantage of Winken's educational assistance plan and received payment for the $7,000 cost of taking two night school courses in consumer law.
    c. Lori Co. runs a nursery near its offices. Employees are allowed to leave their children in the nursery free of charge during working hours. Nonemployees may also use the facility at a cost of $200 per month per child. Dolph is an employee of Lori with two children. Both children stay at Lori's facility while Dolph is at work.
    d. At the sporting goods store where Melissa works, her employer allows all employees to purchase goods at a 30% discount. Melissa purchased for $700 camping and fishing supplies that retailed for $1,000. The goods had cost her employer $600.

45. Courtney is an employee of Hawkins Co. An average of three times a week she works out during her lunch hour at a health club provided by Hawkins. Discuss the taxability of Hawkins's provision of the health club in the following situations:
    a. The health club is owned by Hawkins and is located on its business premises. All employees and their dependents are allowed to use the facility. The cost of joining a comparable facility is $60 per month.
    b. The health club is located in Hawkins's office building, but is owned by Manzer Fitness World. Hawkins pays the $60 per month health club dues.
    c. Hawkins is in the health club business. The health club is used primarily by customers, although several employees, including Courtney, use the health club.

46. Dow, 42, is a manager for Winter Co. In addition to his $45,000 salary, Dow receives the following benefits from Winter during the current year:
    ■ Winter pays all its employees' health and accident insurance. Premiums paid by Winter for Dow's health insurance are $1,800.
    ■ Winter provides all employees with group term life insurance at twice their annual salary. Premiums on Dow's $90,000 of coverage are $900.
    ■ Winter has a flexible benefits plan in which employees may participate to pay any costs not reimbursed by their health insurance. Dow has $2,000 withheld from his salary under the plan. His actual unreimbursed medical costs are $2,320. Winter pays Dow the $2,000 paid into the plan during the year.
    ■ All management-level Winter employees are entitled to employer-provided parking. The cost of Dow's parking in a downtown garage is $2,400 for the year.
    ■ Winter pays Dow's $150 monthly membership fee in a health club located in the building in which Dow works. Dow uses the club during his lunch time and on weekends.
    REQUIRED: Compute Dow's gross income for the current year.

47. Jill, 38, is an employee of Primus University. Jill's annual salary is $38,000. Primus provides all employees with health and accident insurance (Jill's policy cost $1,300) and group term life insurance at twice their annual salary rounded up to the nearest $10,000 ($80,000 of coverage for Jill). In addition, Primus pays the first $1,000 of each employee's Social Security contribution. Primus has a qualified pension and a flexible benefits plan. Jill had $3,000 of her salary withheld and paid (and Primus matched the payment) into the pension plan. She also elected to have $1,000 of her salary paid into the flexible benefits plan. Because her medical costs were lower than expected, Jill got back only $900 of the $1,000 she paid into the plan. What is Jill's gross income for the current year?

48. Samantha is an employee of Strong Co. Strong provides medical insurance for all its employees. The cost of Samantha's policy for the current year is $2,600. Because Strong's medical insurance has a $300 deductible and pays only 80% of most medical expenses, it also offers employees a flexible benefits plan to pay any unreimbursed expenses. During the current year, Samantha has $100 per month paid into the flexible benefits plan. Samantha has $1,300 in medical expenses and $600 in dental expenses. The medical insurance policy pays $800 of the medical expenses. Samantha is reimbursed for the remainder of her expenses from the flexible benefits plan. Discuss the effect of Strong's provision of the medical insurance and flexible benefits plans on her gross income and the taxability of the payments that Samantha received under the plans.

49. May was injured when a forklift tipped over on her while she was moving stock in the company warehouse. Because of her injuries, she could not work for 3 weeks. Her employer paid her $400, which was half her normal wages for the 3-week period. She also received $600 in workers' compensation for the injury. May is required to include the $400 she received from her employer in her gross income but excludes the $600 workers' compensation payment. Discuss why the payments are taxed differently.

50. How much income does each taxpayer recognize in each of the following situations?
  a. Toko was injured in an automobile accident. Toko sued the driver of the other car and received $4,000 for his pain and suffering, $2,000 in lost wages while he recuperated from his injuries, and $8,000 in punitive damages.
  b. A national magazine identified Michael as an individual who consistently cheated on his taxes. As a tax preparer, Michael was incensed about the charges, sued the magazine, and won when the court ruled that the charges were false and that he was not a public figure. The court awarded Michael $10,000 for the humiliation he suffered from the libel, $80,000 for loss of his business reputation, and $100,000 in punitive damages.

51. Bill was severely injured when he was hit by a car one morning while he was out jogging. He spent 1 month in the hospital and missed 3 months of work because of the injuries he sustained in the accident. Total medical costs were $70,000. Bill received the following payments as a result of the accident:
  ■ His employer-provided accident insurance reimbursed him for $55,000 of the medical costs and provided him with $4,000 in sick pay while he was out of work.
  ■ A private medical insurance policy purchased by Bill paid him $15,000 for medical costs.
  ■ His employer gave Bill $3,000 to help him get through his rehabilitation period.
  ■ A separate disability policy that Bill had purchased paid him $6,000.
How much gross income does Bill have as a result of the payments received for the accident?

52. Horatio, Inc., owns Utah general purpose bonds with a face value of $10,000 that it purchased last year for $9,000. During the current year, Horatio receives $400 in interest on the bonds. In December, Horatio, Inc., sells the bonds for $10,200. Does Horatio have any gross income from its dealings in the bonds during the current year?

53. Determine the amount of gross income Elbert must recognize in each of the following situations:
    a. In October, Elbert sells City of Norfolk bonds with a face value of $4,000 for $6,500. Elbert had purchased the bonds 2 years ago for $3,900. Elbert had received $250 in interest on the bonds before he sold them.
    b. Elbert owns 500 shares of Tortoise, Inc., common stock for which he had paid $5,000 several years ago. Tortoise declares and distributes a 10% stock dividend during the current year. On December 31, Tortoise common stock is selling for $15 per share.
    c. In December, Elbert sells City of Quebec bonds with a face value of $7,000 for $6,800. Elbert had purchased the bonds in January for $7,100. Elbert received $1,900 in interest on the bonds before he sold them.

54. Maysa is considering making an investment in municipal bonds yielding 5%. What would the yield on a taxable bond have to be to provide a higher after-tax return than the municipal bond if Maysa is in a 28% marginal tax rate bracket?

55. Vito is having financial difficulties during the current year. Among other debts, he owes More Bank $150,000. Rather than lend Vito more money to help him out, More Bank agrees to reduce his debt to $80,000.
    a. How much gross income must Vito recognize if his assets total $250,000 and his liabilities are $200,000 before the forgiveness of debt?
    b. Assume the same facts as in part a, except that Vito's liabilities are $500,000 before the forgiveness of debt.
    c. Assume the same facts as in part a, except that Vito's total liabilities are $300,000 before the forgiveness of debt.

56. Orts Block and Tackle Shop is experiencing cash flow problems during the current year. Among other debts, Orts owes Cowdrey State Bank $80,000. After negotiations, Cowdrey agrees to reduce Orts's debt to $50,000 with a 1% increase in the interest rate on the $50,000 debt. How much income does Orts have from the debt reduction under the following circumstances?
    a. Orts is organized as a corporation. It has total assets of $180,000 and total liabilities of $200,000 before the debt reduction.
    b. Orts is a sole proprietorship owned by A.J. A.J.'s total assets are $180,000 and his total liabilities are $200,000 before the debt reduction.
    c. Assume the same facts as in part b. The Cowdrey debt was incurred to purchase a storage building with a current fair market value of $40,000. The building cost $120,000 when it was purchased in 1990 and has an adjusted basis of $90,000.

57. Helena has assets of $130,000 and liabilities of $160,000. One of Helena's debts is for $120,000. Discuss the tax consequences of the reduction of this debt in each of the following circumstances:
    a. The debt was incurred by Helena for medical school expenses. She borrowed $120,000 from her grandfather, who agreed to reduce the debt to $80,000, because Helena had done so well in school.
    b. The debt was incurred to purchase property used in Helena's business. In order to help Helena back on her feet, the bank that loaned her the money agreed to reduce the debt to $80,000.
    c. The debt was incurred to purchase equipment used in Helena's business. The debt is owed to the manufacturer of the equipment. Because the equipment did not perform as advertised by the manufacturer, the manufacturer agreed to reduce the debt to $80,000.

58. Determine the amount of income that must be recognized in each discharge of indebtedness situation that follows. Assume in all cases that the related debt was incurred before 1993.

    a. Noreen owns a building with a fair market value of $80,000 that she uses in her construction business. The building is secured by a debt of $110,000 and has an adjusted basis of $20,000. The lender reduces the debt to $85,000.

    b. Armando owns a building with a fair market value of $300,000 that he uses in his business. The building is secured by a debt of $400,000 and has an adjusted basis of $250,000. The lender reduces the debt to $340,000.

    c. Lane owns a building with a fair market value of $60,000 that she uses in her consulting business. The building has an adjusted basis of $35,000 and is secured by 2 debts: The first is a mortgage of $50,000, and the second is a mortgage of $40,000. The lender of the second mortgage agrees to reduce the mortgage to $25,000.

    d. Newton purchased a warehouse to use in his wholesaling business in 1988 at a cost of $240,000. The warehouse is currently worth $220,000 and has an adjusted basis of $210,000. Newton's business has been experiencing financial difficulties, and his bank agrees to reduce the $200,000 debt on the warehouse to $165,000 to help him out.

59. Determine the amount that should be included in the taxpayer's gross income in each of the following situations:

    a. Tim was selected as the outstanding business professor at State University and was given a cash award of $1,000.

    b. Sarah was awarded the Nobel Prize in economics. She assigned the $190,000 award to her university department to establish a scholarship fund for economics students.

    c. Salina is an apartment manager, for which she is paid $6,000 per year. The owner of the apartments offers her the option of a $300 per month living allowance or the use of one apartment rent free. Salina chooses to live in the apartment, which normally rents for $400 per month.

    d. Tom was injured in an accident at work that caused him to miss several months of work. During the time he wasn't working, he received $800 from workers' compensation and $1,300 from a disability plan paid for by his employer.

    e. Terry, an employee of Green University, has an annual salary of $45,000. Green has a qualified pension plan into which all employees contribute 5% of their annual salaries. Green matches the employee's contribution.

60. Connors Partnership owns a building that it has rented out to Corner Grocery Store for the last 10 years. Corner goes out of business and returns the property to Connors. Corner had made improvements to the store costing $30,000 during the 10-year lease period. The partnership had paid $60,000 for the building, which is now worth $200,000. Does Connors have any gross income from the ending of the lease? Discuss when Connors will recognize any income from the building.

61. Jonas owns a building that he leases to Dipper, Inc., for $5,000 per month. The owner of Dipper has been complaining about the condition of the restrooms and has proposed making improvements that will cost $24,000. Dipper's owner is willing to pay to have the improvements made if Jonas will reduce the monthly rent on the building to $4,000 for one year. What are the tax effects for Jonas of the proposal by Dipper's owner?

▲ INTEGRATIVE PROBLEMS

62. Edna, 63, is a widow and works for Rhododendron Corporation. Her annual salary at Rhododendron is $44,000. Rhododendron provides the following benefits to all employees:

    ■ Medical insurance—The cost of Edna's policy is $1,800. She incurs $950 in valid medical expenses and is reimbursed for $560 of the expenses by the company policy.

    ■ Group term life insurance—Each employee is provided with $40,000-worth of coverage under the policy.

    ■ Qualified pension plan—Rhododendron matches employee contributions up to $1,500. Edna contributes 5% of her salary to the plan.

Edna has the following other items that may affect her current-year taxes:

a. She receives $500 per month from the armed forces. The amount is paid to her because her deceased husband was in the Air Force for 25 years and it is her share of what would have been his pension. Her husband made no payments into any pension plan.

b. She receives a $200 refund of last year's state income taxes during the current year. Edna does not itemize her deductions (i.e., she takes the allowable standard deduction).

c. She has a separate medical policy she purchased to cover costs that her employer-provided policy does not cover. She pays $1,400 for the policy, which reimburses her for $350 of her medical expenses.

d. She owns 6% Puerto Rico bonds with a face value of $50,000. The bonds pay interest annually on December 20.

e. She sells stock she owned for $8,000 on July 1. She had paid $15,000 for the stock three years earlier. Edna invests the proceeds from the sale of the stock in a money-market savings account that pays 5% interest.

f. Her brother dies and leaves her the farm that had been owned by their father (her brother had inherited the farm). The farm is valued at $160,000. Edna leases the farm to a local farmer and receives $9,000 in rents during the current year.

g. On April 1, she gives $5,000 of Kao Corporation bonds she owns to her granddaughter. The bonds pay annual interest of 8% on December 31.

h. She receives a watch worth $900 from Rhododendron for her 20 years of loyal service to the company. Rhododendron does not routinely give out length-of-service awards.

i. She sells land that she had held as an investment for $23,000 on October 1. She had paid $21,000 for the land 2 years earlier. Edna invests the proceeds in State of Oregon bonds that pay 4% interest annually on December 31.

REQUIRED: Compute Edna's gross income, adjusted gross income, taxable income, and her income tax liability. Edna does not itemize her deductions and has no dependents.

63. Geraldo and Gertrude Giacamino are married and have 3 children living at home. Alice, 2, and Harry, 4, are Geraldo and Gertrude's children. Pauline, 15, is Gertrude's daughter from her first marriage. Gertrude continues to receive $100 in child support payments from her former husband. The payments will continue until Pauline is 18.

Geraldo is 45 and is employed as a senior manager with Hearty Food, Inc. (HFI). Gertrude is 38 and teaches first grade in the Pleasant City school system (Pleasant).

Geraldo earns an annual salary of $70,000 from HFI. HFI has an extensive fringe-benefits program for its employees.

HFI has a qualified pension plan that covers all its employees. Under the plan, HFI will match any contribution to the plan by up to 10% of the employee's annual salary. Geraldo makes the maximum allowable contribution of $7,000 to the plan, and it is matched by HFI.

HFI provides medical coverage to all its employees (no dependent coverage is provided) through a self-insured medical reimbursement plan. During the year, Geraldo receives $450 in reimbursements for his medical costs. He also purchases a separate insurance policy through the company to cover the medical costs of his dependent children. This policy costs him $2,300.

HFI also provides employees with group term life insurance of twice their annual salary, up to a maximum coverage of $100,000. The cost of Geraldo's group term life insurance premiums is $300.

HFI owns a child-care facility near Geraldo's office. HFI employees are entitled to use the facility free of charge during their working hours. Alice and Harry stay at the HFI child-care facility during the 9-month school year to enable Gertrude to work. HFI charges nonemployees $300 per month per child to use the facility.

HFI allows all its employees to purchase its food products at a 40% discount off retail selling price. HFI's normal retail markup is 100% of cost. Geraldo uses the discount program to purchase $600-worth of cereal that normally would have cost $1,000.

As a manager, Geraldo is also given certain other fringe benefits not available to all employees. He receives free parking in the company garage that would normally cost $175 per month. In addition, HFI pays his management association dues of $200 and pays $400 in subscriptions to various managerial journals. Because Geraldo spends a lot of time dealing with customers, the company also pays his $3,200 dues for membership in a country club.

Gertrude's salary for the 9-month school year is $24,000. Pleasant pays the premiums on a health and accident insurance policy for all teachers. The premiums on Gertrude's policy cost Pleasant $1,350. Because the policy has various deductibles and does not cover full costs, Pleasant also offers a flexible benefits plan to which employees may contribute in order to pay any medical costs that the insurance company will not reimburse. Gertrude has $1,000 withheld from her salary and paid into the plan.

Pleasant belongs to the state teachers' retirement plan. Under this plan, Pleasant pays 5% of each employee's salary into the retirement plan. Employees are not allowed to make additional contributions. The plan is a qualified plan.

Gertrude is named teacher of the year in the Pleasant school district during the current year. In addition to the plaque she receives, she is awarded $1,000 in cash and $1,000 in merchandise vouchers from local merchants. She can use the vouchers at any of the merchants' stores toward any merchandise she wishes to purchase. As of December 31, she has used $800-worth of the vouchers.

Gertrude's Uncle Ed died last year. When his estate is settled during the current year, she receives some stock valued at $12,000. Although Geraldo and Gertrude have an extensive investment portfolio, their stockbroker suggests they sell the stock when it soars in value to $18,000. They take the broker's advice and sell the stock for $18,000, although they receive only $17,400 after the broker deducts his $600 commission on the sale.

Included in their investment portfolio are various stocks and bonds as well as a rental property. They receive the following amounts (all in cash) from the stocks and bonds they own:

Albatross, Inc., common stock	$1,800
State of Hawaii bonds	600
City of Tokyo bonds	300
Puerto Rico development bonds	200

In addition to these receipts, Geraldo and Gertrude own 3,000 shares of Giacamino Girdle Co. Giacamino is organized as an S corporation and has 20,000 shares outstanding. Giacamino reports taxable income of $40,000 and pays dividends of $1 per share during the current year.

Geraldo and Gertrude purchased rental property several years ago for $60,000. During the current year, rents received are $16,000 and total allowable deductions are $25,000. In addition to the rents received, Geraldo and Gertrude collect $2,000 in security deposits from new tenants. The lease provides that the security deposits are to be returned at the end of the lease if the property is in good condition at that time. One tenant is having trouble paying his rent during the year. When the tenant is $2,000 behind in his rent payments, Geraldo and Gertrude agree to allow the tenant to paint the property in payment of his debt. The $2,000 in painting cost is included (properly) in the $25,000 in expenses. However, because Geraldo and Gertrude never receive any cash, they do not include it in the $16,000 in rents received.

Gertrude is involved in an automobile accident during the current year. She is hospitalized for several weeks, incurring total medical costs of $8,000. Her employer-provided insurance pays $6,000 of the medical costs. To pay the rest of the bill, she uses the $1,000 in her flexible benefits plan and pays the remaining $1,000 herself. Although Pleasant continues to pay her salary during the 2 months of work she misses because of the accident, her employer's plan pays her $300 in disability pay for the time she is unable to work.

REQUIRED: Calculate Geraldo and Gertrude's gross income on their 1995 joint tax return. In doing this calculation, you are to include a brief explanation of how you determined each taxable item and any items you excluded from gross income. Your solution to the problem should contain a list of each item included in gross income and its amount, with the explanations attached.

If you are using tax forms to solve this problem, you will need the following forms and schedules to complete the problem: Form 1040, Schedule A, Schedule B, Schedule D, and Schedule E. In addition, you should obtain a copy of the Form 1040 instructions as an aid in preparing the tax return.

The information you need to complete Geraldo and Gertrude's tax return appears at the end of Chapter 8. In this part, you are required only to put the information on the proper form and schedules. Do not complete page 2 of Form 1040 at this time.

Germaine, 22, is a single individual with no dependents; she recently graduated from college. She has job offers from two firms. Germaine likes both companies equally well and has decided to base her decision on which company offers the most. Details of each job offer are as follows:

    Company A—Annual salary of $30,000, employer-provided health and accident insurance (employer cost: $2,100), group term life insurance coverage at twice the annual salary (premiums for $60,000-worth of coverage are $450), employer-provided day-care facility (employer's cost per dependent is $150 per month), and company-provided parking ($900 per year).

    Company B—Annual salary of $32,000, a cafeteria plan under which employees can choose benefits of up to 10% of annual salary or take the cash equivalent. In addition, the company has a flexible benefits plan in which employees may participate by setting aside up to 10% of annual salary per year for payment of unreimbursed medical expenses.

Which do you think is the better offer for Germaine? Explain. Assume that Germaine has no other income sources and that she itemizes deductions.

▲ DISCUSSION CASE 4–1

Zane wants to invest $10,000. His options are
    a. Gibraltar Corporation bonds with an annual interest rate of 8%.
    b. State of Hawaii bonds with an annual interest rate of 5%.
    c. Series EE savings bonds; a $10,000 investment will pay $14,300 in 5 years.
Assume that Zane is a 28% marginal tax rate payer, the time value of money is 6%, and Zane intends to hold any amounts invested for 5 years. Which option will provide the greatest after-tax return? Would your answer change if Zane's marginal tax rate is 36%?

▲ TAX PLANNING CASE 4–2

You are a CPA working for a local firm and have been assigned the 1995 tax return of Bobby Crosser. In going over the data that Bobby provided to the firm, you are surprised to see that Bobby has reported no dividend income or gains from the sale of stock. You recently prepared the 1995 gift tax return of Bobby's aunt Esther. In that return, Esther had reported a gift of stock to Bobby on January 6, 1995. The stock had a fair market value of $50,000, and Esther's basis (which became Bobby's basis) in the stock was $5,000. What are your obligations under the Statements on Responsibilities in Tax Practice? In your discussion, state which standard(s) may be applicable to this situation and what might result from applying the standard(s).

▲ ETHICS DISCUSSION CASE 4–3

DEDUCTIONS

PART

III

CHAPTER 5
INTRODUCTION TO BUSINESS EXPENSES

CHAPTER 6
BUSINESS EXPENSES

CHAPTER 7
LOSSES—DEDUCTIONS AND LIMITATIONS

Introduction to Business Expenses

▲ CHAPTER LEARNING OBJECTIVES

■ Introduce the reporting of allowable deductions by individuals, corporations, and conduit entities.

■ Describe the classification of expenditures as those that are related to a taxpayer's trade or business, those for the production of income, and those for personal expenditures.

■ Discuss the criteria for distinguishing a trade or business from a production-of-income activity.

■ Describe mixed-purpose assets and mixed-use expenditures and discuss the tax treatment of such assets and expenditures.

■ Explain the ordinary, necessary, and reasonable requirements for the deduction of trade or business and production-of-income expenses.

■ Discuss the general classes of expenditures for which a deduction is not allowed.

■ Explain the general rules for deducting expenses under the cash and the accrual methods of accounting.

▲ CONCEPT REVIEW ▲

Ability to pay   A tax should be based on the amount that the taxpayer can afford to pay, relative to other taxpayers.

Accounting method   A taxpayer must adopt an accounting method that clearly reflects income.

Administrative convenience   Those items for which the cost of compliance would exceed the revenue generated are not taxed.

Annual accounting period   All entities report the results of their transactions on an annual basis (the tax year). Each tax year stands on its own, apart from other tax years.

Arm's-length transaction   A transaction in which all parties to the transaction have bargained in good faith and for their individual benefit, not for the benefit of the transaction group.

Basis   This is the amount of unrecovered investment in an asset. As amounts are expended and/or recovered relative to an asset over time, the basis is adjusted in consideration of such changes. The **adjusted basis** of an asset is the original basis, plus or minus the changes in the amount of unrecovered investment.

Business purpose   To be deductible, an expenditure or a loss must have a business or other economic purpose that exceeds any tax avoidance motive. The primary motive for the transaction must be to make a profit.

Capital recovery   No income is realized until the taxpayer receives more than the amount invested to produce the income. The amount invested in an asset represents the maximum amount recoverable.

Entity   All items of income, deduction, and so on are traced to the tax unit responsible for the item.

Legislative grace   Any tax relief provided is the result of a specific act of Congress that must be strictly applied and interpreted. All income received is taxable unless a specific provision can be found in the tax law that excludes the income from taxation. Deductions must be approached with the philosophy that nothing is deductible unless a provision in the tax law allows the deduction.

Related party   Family members and corporations that are owned by family members are considered related parties, as are certain other relationships between entities in which the power to control the substance of a transaction is evidenced through majority ownership.

Tax benefit rule   Any deduction taken in a prior year that is recovered in a subsequent year is income in the year of recovery, to the extent that a tax benefit was received from the deduction.

Wherewithal to pay   Income is recognized in the period in which the taxpayer has the means to pay the tax on the income.

Chapter 1 pointed out that deductible expenditures are grouped into three broad categories. These categories are business expenses, losses, and other itemized deductions. This chapter focuses on the general requirements for deducting business expenses. Specific business-expense deductions are the topic of Chapter 6, deductions for losses are discussed in Chapter 7, and itemized deductions that are specific to individual taxpayers are fully discussed in Chapter 8.

▲ INTRODUCTION

Tax deductions are a matter of legislative grace. As a result, two restrictions immediately apply to deductions. First, only deductions allowed by the tax law may be subtracted to compute taxable income. The deduction provisions are part of Congress's approach to implementing the ability-to-pay concept. By allowing deductions, Congress is, in effect, recognizing the inequity that could result from imposing a tax on gross income rather than taxable income. Therefore, Congress allows deductions for the costs of earning income and certain other expenditures. Second, a deduction is allowed for an item only if all the requirements for the deduction are satisfied. Because deductions are intended to provide relief from tax, the deduction rules are strictly interpreted and applied. Thus, a deduction is not allowed merely because a taxpayer thinks it is fair or equitable to use the expenditure to reduce income.

▲ **EXAMPLE 1**   Joan earns $25,000 in wages as a county property tax assessor. John owns and operates his own business selling Slippery Oil. John's Slippery Oil sales were $60,000, the cost of the oil sold was $25,000, and he had other business expenses of $10,000.

Discussion: Joan should report $25,000 in wages as gross income. Because the tax law allows a deduction for the cost of sales and business expenses, John has a gross income of $35,000 ($60,000 − $25,000) and will report $25,000 in taxable income from his business ($35,000 − $10,000). After recovering his expenses, John will pay tax on his increase in wealth according to the ability-to-pay concept. Compared with Joan's tax treatment, it would be inequitable to tax John on his gross income and deny him a deduction to recover the amounts he invested to earn a profit.

▲ **EXAMPLE 2**   Randy and Cindy are both practicing CPAs, specializing in tax. Randy has enrolled in law school so he can take tax courses. Randy has no intention of getting a law degree. Cindy has enrolled in a master's program in tax to improve her skills as a tax accountant. Eventually, Cindy hopes to earn the master's degree.

Discussion: Both Randy and Cindy have incurred expenses to improve or maintain their skills as practicing tax accountants. However, Randy cannot deduct his expenses. Educational expenses that qualify a person for a new profession (the practice of law) are not deductible. Cindy's expenses can be deducted, because they relate to her job and do not qualify her for a new profession.[1] Although treating Randy differently than Cindy seems unfair, Randy did not satisfy all the requirements of the tax law to claim an educational expense deduction.

To deduct a **business expense,** the expenditure must have a business purpose that is unrelated to its tax effect. Under the business purpose concept, there must be a business purpose for the expenditure that exceeds any tax-avoidance motive. Failure to establish a business purpose for the expense can result in the loss of the deduction. In most instances, a business purpose can be established by showing that the expense was related to a profit-motivated transaction. When the taxpayer has both business and personal reasons for an expenditure, the taxpayer risks losing the deduction. For these expenditures, the taxpayer will need to show that the business purpose was the primary or dominant motive for the transaction.

▲ **EXAMPLE 3**   Zoltan is a physician who has not seen his sister for more than 10 years, because she lives in Kenya. Zoltan would like to visit his sister and write a book about his experiences. He has never written a book. Because his trip has a business purpose—to write a book—Zoltan intends to deduct the full cost of his trip as a business deduction. Has Zoltan met the dominant motive requirement for deducting the cost of the trip?

Discussion: Because Zoltan has several motives for making the trip, he will have to prove that the dominant motive is a business purpose. Based on the facts, it would appear that Zoltan is not entitled to a deduction, because the primary purpose of his trip is a personal reason (to visit his sister). Because Zoltan has no experience in writing travel books, he would have a hard time proving that writing the book is his dominant motive.

Gross income has been defined to include only the excess of an individual's capital investment. As a result, the expenditure or consumption of capital to earn income results in a tax deduction. The capital recovery concept limits the amount of a deduction to the amount of the expenditure or the taxpayer's investment in an asset. As a result of this concept, the deduction for an item may not exceed the taxpayer's cost. For example, the payment of a $500 business expense would be limited to a $500 deduction. In this chapter, basis is used to identify the amount that can be deducted under the capital recovery concept. *Basis* is a technical term that was introduced as a construct in Chapter 2 and is discussed in detail in Chapter 10. For discussion purposes, think of basis as the cost of an asset or the dollar amount of a specific expenditure. Thus, basis represents the maximum amount of an expenditure that can be deducted as a recovery of capital.

The accounting concepts discussed in Chapter 2 influence the tax treatment of deductions. Although a deduction of basis is allowed under the capital recovery concept, the entity concept requires the taxpayer claiming the deduction to own the capital being deducted as a recovery. Thus, the entity concept prevents one taxpayer from deducting another taxpayer's expenditures.

▲ **EXAMPLE 4**   Miranda is a public accountant and is required by state law to have a license to practice public accounting. When the state license renewal fee came due, Miranda was short of money and could not renew her license. Miranda's mother paid the license renewal fee for her so she could continue working as a public accountant. Can Miranda deduct the fee as a business expense?

Discussion: The license renewal fee is Miranda's business expense, and only she can deduct the payment of the fee. Because Miranda did not pay the license renewal fee, she is not allowed a deduction for the business expense. Because the license renewal fee is not Miranda's mother's expense, her mother cannot deduct the payment of the expense. Based on these facts, neither Miranda nor her mother can deduct the payment of the license renewal fee.

Note that the bad tax result here could have been avoided if Miranda's mother had either gifted or made a valid loan to Miranda of the money necessary to pay the licensing fee and Miranda had made the payment from her own funds.

The annual accounting period concept requires the taxpayer to use an acceptable accounting method to determine the year in which a deduction should be reported. Once an accounting method is adopted, it should be used as the basis for the systematic and consistent allocation of expenses to the proper tax years. Failure to claim an expense in the correct year can result in loss of the deduction. If an expenditure, such as utilities and office supplies, benefits only one tax year, it is allowed as a deduction in the year benefited. When an expenditure provides benefits for more than one accounting period, the expenditure is usually allocated, based on the annual accounting period concept, to the proper tax years by using an acceptable accounting method. Examples of expenses that may need to be allocated are prepaid rent, prepaid interest, and prepaid insurance as well as depreciation on buildings and equipment. If the expenditure has an indefinite life, it is normally not deducted until the accounting period in which the asset is disposed of, abandoned, or proved to have lost its value. Thus, assets such as securities and land that do not have definite useful lives are not subject to amortization or depreciation for tax purposes.

As deductions are more closely examined in the rest of this chapter, the concepts discussed in Chapter 2 will be related to the specific rules and requirements for a deduction. The discussion and examples throughout this chapter consider deduction issues from the points of view of individuals, corporations, and conduit entities (partnerships and S corporations). Situations in which a tax rule applies only to individual taxpayers will be pointed out.

▲ REPORTING DEDUCTIONS

The phrases "deductions for adjusted gross income" and "deductions from adjusted gross income" identify where in the tax computation an individual taxpayer deducts an allowable expense. Because all of a corporation's expenses are related to a business purpose, it is not necessary to use these two phrases when discussing its deductions; a corporation does not have personal expenses similar to those of an individual, which are deducted from adjusted gross income. Thus, the term *adjusted gross income* is unique to the individual tax computation.

Chapter 1 introduced an income tax computational framework as an overview of the federal income tax computation. At this point, we expand the framework for computing an individual's income tax (see Exhibit 5–1) to illustrate how individuals deduct various expenses. This chapter discusses the distinctions among *trade or business*, *production of income*, and *personal expenses*. Note in Exhibit 5–1 that trade or business expenses are deducted *for* adjusted gross income, whereas production-of-income expenses are subtracted as a deduction *from* adjusted gross income.[2] Recall that amounts deducted for adjusted gross income are always deductible, but deductions from adjusted gross income are subject to various limitations.

Trade or business expenses, expenses related to the production of rent and royalty income, losses on sales of property used in a trade or business, and capital losses (limited to $3,000) are deducted from gross income to compute adjusted gross income. As a result of legislative grace, these deductions receive more favorable treatment than deductions from adjusted gross income. Unless the passive

▲ Exhibit 5–1

INDIVIDUAL INCOME TAX COMPUTATIONAL FRAMEWORK

Income "broadly defined" (includes income from all sources)
Minus: **Excluded sources of income**
Equals: **Gross income**
Minus: **Deductions for adjusted gross income**
Trade or business expenses
Rent and royalty expenses
Trade or business losses
Capital loss deduction ($3,000 maximum)
Other specifically allowable deductions
Equals: **Adjusted gross income**
Minus: **Deductions from adjusted gross income**
The greater of:
1. Standard deduction
or
2. Allowable itemized deductions:
Deductible personal expenditures
Medical expenses
Home mortgage interest/investment interest
Property taxes/state income taxes
Charitable contributions
Personal casualty losses
Other miscellaneous itemized deductions
Investment expenses for the production of income
Expenses related to tax return preparation and compliance
Unreimbursed employee business expenses
Minus: **Personal and dependency exemptions**
Equals: **Taxable income**

activity rules discussed in Chapter 7 apply, trade or business expenses and losses and rent expenses deducted for adjusted gross income are fully allowed as deductions to compute taxable income.

The allowable deduction from adjusted gross income is the greater of the taxpayer's standard deduction amount or allowable itemized deductions.[3] Itemized deductions consist of allowable personal expenditures[4] and miscellaneous itemized deductions. Most itemized deductions are subject to income limitations. For example, investment expenses are deductible as miscellaneous itemized deductions. However, miscellaneous itemized deductions must be reduced by 2 percent of adjusted gross income in calculating the amount of the total expense that can be deducted.[5] In addition, total itemized deductions are reduced for high-income taxpayers. As a result, deductions from adjusted gross income receive less favorable treatment than deductions for adjusted gross income. Except for rent and royalty expenses deducted for adjusted gross income and investment interest, all expenses for the production of income are deductible as miscellaneous itemized deductions, subject to the 2 percent of adjusted gross income limitation. The computation of allowable personal itemized deductions and the applicable limitations are discussed in Chapter 8. If the taxpayer uses the predetermined standard deduction, all tax benefits available from an itemized deduction for investment expenses are lost.

▲ **EXAMPLE 5**   Jennifer owns a dress shop. During the current year, she incurred $43,000 in valid expenses related to the dress shop. In addition, Jennifer incurred $6,000 in expenses related to production-of-income activities. If Jennifer's adjusted gross income is $83,000 without considering either of these expenses, how much expense can she deduct?

Discussion: Trade or business expenses are deductions for adjusted gross income. The $43,000 in trade or business expenses reduces her adjusted gross income to $40,000 ($83,000 − $43,000). Production-of-income expenses are deductible as miscellaneous itemized deductions, subject to the 2% of adjusted gross income limitation. Therefore, Jennifer is allowed to deduct only $5,200 [$6,000 − ($40,000 × 2%)] of the production-of-income expenses.

Note another advantage of the deductions for adjusted gross income: By reducing adjusted gross income, the amount of any deduction from adjusted gross income that is subject to a limitation increases. In this case, the $43,000 in business expenses allowed Jennifer an extra $860 ($43,000 × 2%) deduction of her production-of-income expenses. Thus, correct classification of a deduction as for adjusted gross income versus from adjusted gross income is critical in the calculation of an individual's taxable income.

Conduit Entity Reporting

Conduit entities (partnerships and S corporations) are not subject to tax. Rather, the taxable income from the conduit flows through to each owner, and each is taxed on his or her individual tax return. As discussed in Chapter 3, the conduit entity reports some items separately to the partner or shareholder, because certain income items (such as capital gains) are subject to special tax rules; they are not included in the calculation of a conduit entity's ordinary taxable income or loss.[6] Certain deductions also are subject to special tax rules—typically limitations on the amount that can be deducted by the owners—and must be reported separately. For example, investment expenses of individuals are miscellaneous itemized deductions that must be reduced by 2 percent of adjusted gross income. Therefore, as with some income items, not all deductions of a conduit are used in calculating ordinary taxable income or loss.

▲ **EXAMPLE 6**   The Hackett Group (HG), a partnership, operates a management consulting firm; it consists of three equal partners, Mark, Nancy, and Ahmed. HG's taxable income for the year is $255,000, consisting of the following:

Sales revenues	$1,500,000
Short-term capital gain	27,000
Trade and business expenses	(1,260,000)
Investment expenses	(12,000)
Taxable income	$ 255,000

How must the Hackett Group report its results to Mark, Nancy, and Ahmed for tax purposes?

Discussion: Because the Hackett Group must report each partner's share of short-term capital gain and investment expenses, the Hackett Group cannot divide the partnership's taxable income of $255,000 equally and report ordinary taxable income of $85,000 ($255,000 ÷ 3) to each partner. Rather, the Hackett Group uses only the partnership's sales revenue and business expenses to calculate the ordinary taxable income for each partner. As a result, each partner's share of the ordinary taxable income is $80,000 [($1,500,000 − $1,260,000 = $240,000) ÷ 3]. The Hackett Group must report to each partner $9,000 ($27,000 ÷ 3) of short-term capital gain and $4,000 ($12,000 ÷ 3) of investment expenses.

Because investment expenses must be reduced by 2 percent of adjusted gross income, investment expenses are not included in calculating the conduit's ordinary taxable income or loss. Otherwise, each partner would be able to deduct the full amount of the investment expenses.

▲ **EXAMPLE 7**   Assume the same facts as in example 6. Ahmed is single; his adjusted gross income for the year is $25,000, and his total itemized deductions are $12,000 (before considering the information in example 6). What is the effect on Ahmed's taxable income of stating the investment expenses separately?

Discussion: If the Hackett Group did not report both investment income and expenses separately, Ahmed's ordinary taxable income from the Hackett Group would be $85,000 ($255,000 ÷ 3). He would have an adjusted gross income of $110,000 ($25,000 + $85,000), itemized deductions of $12,000, and taxable income of $95,500 ($110,000 − $12,000 − $2,500).

Because the capital gains and investment expenses receive special tax treatment, HG must report these items separately. Ahmed's share of the ordinary income is $80,000, and his adjusted gross income is $114,000 ($25,000 + $80,000 + $9,000). The $4,000 of investment expenses is a miscellaneous itemized deduction, which is reduced by 2% of adjusted gross income.

Investment expenses	$4,000
Limitation: 2% × $114,000	(2,280)
Investment expense deduction	$1,720

Ahmed's itemized deductions total $13,720 ($12,000 + $1,720), and his taxable income is $97,780 ($114,000 − $13,720 − $2,500). Because HG reports these items separately, Ahmed's taxable income increases by $2,280 ($97,780 − $95,500).

In essence, the owner and not the conduit entity is subject to tax. The conduit is viewed as only a form of organization, the income and deductions from which flow through to each owner. This ensures that income and deductions of a conduit are treated similarly to income and deductions incurred by an individual taxpayer.

As example 7 illustrates, it is important that a conduit entity report separately any deduction that receives special tax treatment. The following is a list of commonly incurred deductions that a conduit entity must report separately:

- Charitable contributions
- Investment interest expense
- Investment expenses
- Section 179 expense
- Nondeductible expenses

Proper application of the ability-to-pay and legislative grace concepts requires the separation of expenditures that qualify for deduction from those that are not allowed by the tax law. The basic test to be applied to obtain the initial classification of expenditures is whether the expenditure is related to a profit-motivated transaction or is motivated by personal needs and wants. Thus, expenditures are initially classified as profit-motivated or personal expenditures. Figure 5–1 illustrates this classification scheme.

▲ CLASSIFICATION OF DEDUCTIONS

Profit-Motivated Expenditures

As discussed in Chapter 1, a taxpayer may legitimately plan transactions to avoid the payment of tax. Because business profits reflect tax costs and savings, the tax effect of a transaction is an important planning consideration. A legitimate business reason for entering a transaction is to save taxes. However, the tax law prohibits deductions that are motivated solely by the expected tax benefits (savings). To be deductible, the business purpose concept requires an expenditure to have a bonafide business reason other than tax avoidance. If the sole purpose of a transaction is tax savings, it will not be allowed as a deduction.

The courts maintain that the presence of a business purpose does not always require that a transaction be recognized. Where objective evidence indicates no potential for economic profit apart from tax savings, a transaction can be disregarded.[7] Thus, to be deductible, the dominant motive for incurring a business expense must be to earn a profit that is independent of any tax savings. Therefore,

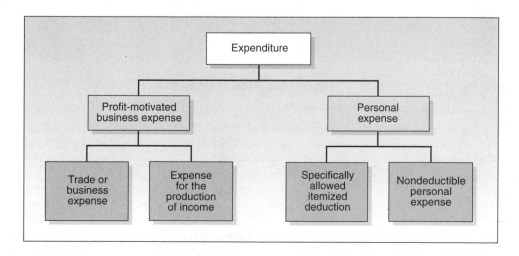

▲ **Figure 5–1**

CLASSIFICATION OF DEDUCTIONS OF AN INDIVIDUAL

only expenses that satisfy the requirement that profit be the **dominant motive** are classified as business expenses.

> ▲ **EXAMPLE 8**   Harry's son Junior wants to open a motorcycle dealership. Because Junior is short of funds, Harry purchases a building for the dealership and leases it to Junior. No lease is signed, but Harry tells Junior not to worry about paying rent until the dealership begins to show a profit. In addition, Harry agrees not to sell the building without Junior's approval. Is Harry's dominant motive in acquiring the building to obtain a profit?
>
> *Discussion:*   On the facts presented, Harry's dominant motive in acquiring the building is to help his son get his business established. Because there is no formal rental agreement and Harry will not sell the building without Junior's approval, the purchase of the building and the payment of costs related to the building are in the nature of a gift. Harry is not attempting to profit from either rental payments or potential appreciation in the value of the business. Therefore, any expenditures Harry makes regarding the building would not be classified as business expenses. As personal expenses, only those personal expenses specifically allowed by the tax law (interest, property taxes) would be deductible.

Recall from Chapter 2 that the business purpose concept means that the taxpayer's dominant motive for an expenditure is to earn an economic benefit (profit) before considering the effects of tax savings. Thus, profit-motivated expenses, or expenses related to a business purpose, are deductible as business expenses. Throughout the remainder of this text, reference to a *business expense* means that the expenditure satisfies the dominant profit-motive requirement.

Based on the legislative grace concept, business expenses are grouped into two main categories:

- Trade or business expenses
- Expenses for the production of income

Both classifications apply to individuals and certain conduit entities (partnerships, S corporations, etc.). However, production-of-income expenses do not apply to corporations. A corporation's expenses are always classified as trade or business expenses, regardless of the underlying business purpose. The deductions allowed under these two provisions of the tax law are the types of expenses that you would expect to find on a typical income statement. For example, on an income statement you would expect to find employee wages, depreciation expense, advertising, and similar items subtracted from income to determine net income. Thus, you are already familiar with several types of expenses that are allowed as business deductions.

Trade or Business or Production-of-Income Expenses?

Because business expenses are classified either as related to a trade or business or for the production of income, it is necessary to look at these two classifications more closely. Although many of the same kinds of expenses can be deducted in these two categories, the tax result can be significantly different. As explained later, classification of an activity as either a trade or business or for the production of income depends on the facts related to the particular activity. No single definition applies to all situations. Because both types of activities must be profit motivated, a trade or business will most likely be identified by the extent of the taxpayer's involvement and whether the intent is to earn a living from the activity.

Trade or Business Expenses.   If a taxpayer's activities qualify as a trade or business, the related expenses are fully deductible. As you can see from the following excerpt from the tax law, *trade or business expenses* is broadly defined:

SEC. 162. TRADE OR BUSINESS EXPENSES.

(A) IN GENERAL—There shall be allowed as a deduction all the ordinary and necessary expenses paid or incurred during the taxable year in carrying on any trade or business, including—

(1) a reasonable allowance for salaries or other compensation for personal services actually rendered;

(2) traveling expenses (including amounts expended for meals and lodging other than amounts that are lavish or extravagant under the circumstances) while away from home in the pursuit of a trade or business; and

(3) rentals or other payments required to be made as a condition to the continued use or possession, for purposes of the trade or business, of property to which the taxpayer has not taken or is not taking title or in which he has no equity.

A taxpayer may deduct "all the ordinary and necessary expenses" of operating a "trade or business." But what is a trade or business? The Internal Revenue Code contains at least 50 references to a trade or business without defining the meaning of the phrase. The Treasury regulations are similarly silent on the definition of a trade or business. Therefore, the task has been left to the courts to resolve. One interpretation observed for many years was that taxpayers who held themselves out as engaged in the selling of goods or services were engaged in a trade or business. Although noting that a person selling goods and services would usually be engaged in a trade or business, in 1987 the Supreme Court rejected these activities as the single appropriate test for a trade or business. Instead, the Court took a broader view of what constituted a trade or business.

The Court has stated that to be engaged in a trade or business a taxpayer must meet the following requirements:

- Profit motivation—The primary purpose for engaging in the activity must be to earn income or a profit.

- Continuous and regular activity—There must be continuity and regularity in the taxpayer's involvement in the activity.

- Livelihood, not a hobby—The activity must not be sporadic, a hobby, or an amusement diversion.[8]

The Court went on to say that whether an activity meets these tests must be determined by examining the facts in each case. In this regard, the Court noted that taxpayers meeting the prior "holding out as a seller of goods and services" test would normally meet the requirements for being engaged in a trade or business.

As a general rule, an employee is usually engaged in the trade or business of rendering services to the employer. The most common problem encountered in delineating a trade or business activity from a production-of-income activity involves dealings in securities. A person who transacts in securities may be an active investor, an active trader, or a dealer in securities. Unlike active traders and dealers, active investors are not considered to be in a trade or business.

An **active investor** is a person who continuously, regularly, and extensively manages her or his own portfolio with a view toward long-term appreciation in the portfolio's value and not short-term profit. Unlike a trader, an active investor purchases an investment with the intent to hold it for the long term and is less influenced by daily changes in market prices. An active investor's income is earned from interest, dividends, and gains from long-term holdings of securities. An active investor is never deemed to be engaged in a trade or business. Accordingly, the investor's activities are related to the production of income, and the investment expenses are deductible only as miscellaneous itemized deductions.

An **active trader** earns a livelihood buying and selling securities for personal profit. The active trader neither buys and sells for customers nor provides services to others that warrant fees or commissions. The main source of an active trader's income is from selling securities for more than they cost in order to make a profit. The securities are typically held for a short time before they are sold. The active trader does not intend to hold investments for a long time to collect income from interest, dividends, and long-term gains from appreciation of these investments but tries to capture the short-term swings in the market. Thus, an active trader may be distinguished from the active investor by the nature of the investing activities and the source of income. If the trader's activities are frequent and substantial, the trader will be deemed to be engaged in a trade or business. As such, the active trader's expenses will be deductible for adjusted gross income.

Distinguishing a trader from an active investor is often quite difficult. The determination of whether a taxpayer should be classified as a trader or an active investor is best left to a tax expert.

A **securities dealer** purchases a security expecting to realize a profit from selling it to a customer for a fee or commission. Dealers do not normally look to an increase in market prices to provide a profit. The dealer acts as an agent who performs the services of a wholesaler or retailer in bringing together a buyer and a seller. Dealers have customers with whom they deal in order to earn a profit. Dealers are deemed to be engaged in a trade or business.

Expenses for the Production of Income.   If the taxpayer's business activity fails to qualify as a trade or business, expenses related to the production of income may still be deductible under Section 212 of the Internal Revenue Code. Although the formal tax term for these deductions is *nonbusiness expenses*, we will refer to these items as *investment expenses*, consistent with the terminology used by most taxpayers. The tax law provides a broad definition of **production-of-income expenses** that an individual taxpayer can deduct:

> SEC. 212. EXPENSES FOR THE PRODUCTION OF INCOME.
> In the case of an individual there shall be allowed as a deduction all the ordinary and necessary expenses paid or incurred during the taxable year—
> (1) for the production or collection of income;
> (2) for the management, conservation, or maintenance of property held for the production of income, or
> (3) in connection with the determination, collection, or refund of any tax.

The objectives of Section 212 are to tax the net profits of income-motivated transactions and to allow individuals a deduction for costs related to compliance with the tax law. However, expenses deducted under this provision receive less favorable treatment than trade or business expenses. Generally, expenses related to earning rent and royalty income are treated the same (as deductions for adjusted gross income), whether they are considered to be for the production of income or trade or business expenses. However, as shown in Exhibit 5–1, other investment and tax-related expenses allowed by Section 212 are deducted from adjusted gross income as "other miscellaneous itemized deductions." In addition, total itemized deductions are often subject to special adjustments (discussed in Chapter 8) that reduce the amount allowed as a deduction for computing taxable income.

▲ **EXAMPLE 9**   Grady owns a large portfolio of stocks, bonds, and other securities. What is the treatment of Grady's securities activities in each of the following cases?

Case A

Grady spends all his time managing his portfolio. He continuously trades securities to obtain a profit from short-term price increases. Grady rarely holds a security for the dividend or interest income it may produce or for long-term appreciation in value. Grady has no other job and receives the bulk of his income from his securities dealings.

Case B

Grady is employed as a chemist for Dough Co. He spends an average of five hours per week studying investment materials and making investment decisions. Grady primarily invests in securities for their dividend and interest income and long-term appreciation potential. Because his portfolio is quite extensive, more than half of his income comes from his security investments.

Discussion: In case A, Grady's activities constitute a trade or business. His primary motive is profit, he engages in the activity on a continual and regular basis, and his securities activities are his livelihood. Grady's business expenses would be deductible for adjusted gross income. In addition, gains and losses from his securities dealings would be considered gains and losses from a trade or business.

In case B, Grady's security dealings are a production-of-income activity. He receives a substantial portion of his income from his securities, but it is not his livelihood, nor does he engage in the activity with the continuity and regularity of a trade or business. Therefore, Grady's expenses are deductible as miscellaneous itemized deductions. In addition, gains and losses Grady incurs from selling the securities are capital gains and losses.

To be deductible, investment expenses must bear a reasonable and proximate (close) relationship to the earning of taxable income. That is, the expenses must have a business purpose. Deductible investment expenses may relate to income earned in a prior year, the current year, or to be earned in a future year. In addition, the expenses may relate to a single transaction, such as the sale of a security, as well as to recurring transactions, such as the collection of interest or dividends. For example, the cost of a safe deposit box used to store stocks and bonds is an investment expense. The securities stored in the box may have paid interest and dividends in a prior year but not the current year. On the other hand, they may be paying income in the current year but may not have paid interest and dividends in prior years. Alternatively, they may never have paid interest or dividends, but they are being held for sale when their market value increases. Regardless of which situation applies, the safe deposit box rent is deductible. Other deductible expenses related to investing might include employee wages, depreciation, advertising, advisory fees, office rent, and subscriptions to financial publications.

Rental Activity

Depending on the extent of the taxpayer's activities related to renting out real estate, the activity could be deemed either a trade or business or an investment activity. For many years, the mere rental of a single piece of improved real estate was considered a trade or business, whereas the rental of unimproved real estate was subject to an "all the facts and circumstances" test to determine the classification of the rental activity.[9] Improved real estate is land that has a building or other capital improvement built on it. Unimproved real estate is raw land without a building or other structure on it. In recent years, several courts have begun to apply a facts-and-circumstances test to both improved and unimproved real estate to determine whether rental property is a trade or business or investment asset. The courts have looked to the scope of the rental activities and the extent of the taxpayer's involvement with the rental operations to classify the property.

For example, the U.S. Tax Court considered whether a rental activity was a trade or business for purposes of the home office deduction.[10] The court indicated that, as a matter of law, a rental activity is not automatically a trade or business. Classification as a trade or business depends on the facts related to the taxpayer's activities. In examining the facts, the Tax Court looked at the scope of ownership and management activities in classifying a rental activity as a trade or business instead of an investment activity. The IRS has stated that rental property must produce income from an active trade or business, as opposed to passive income that would be earned on a portfolio investment (stocks and bonds), to qualify as property used in a trade or business.

▲ **EXAMPLE 10**   Frank agreed to lease land located in downtown Chicago to Sleepytime Motels for 99 years. Under the lease, Sleepytime had the right to construct a motel on the land. Sleepytime is responsible for all expenses, claims, and liabilities related to the property. In the event of default on the lease, Frank has the right to assume ownership of the building and possession of the property. Is Frank's rental activity a trade or business or a production-of-income activity?

Discussion: Because Frank is not actively involved in the management of the property, the income earned is similar to the income that would be earned by an investor in stocks and bonds. Thus, the lease described would not constitute a trade or business. Frank's rental activity would be considered a production-of-income activity.

▲ **EXAMPLE 11**   Yolanda owns two rental properties. She obtains tenants for the properties, makes repairs when necessary, provides maintenance of the properties, pays expenses related to the properties, and is subject to claims and liabilities arising from the rental properties. Is Yolanda's rental activity a trade or business or a production-of-income activity?

Discussion: Because Yolanda actively manages the two properties, pays expenses related to the properties, and is liable for claims on the properties, she would be deemed to be engaged in a trade or business.

Note in Exhibit 5–1 that rental expenses are deductible for adjusted gross income. This is true whether the rental activity is classified as a trade or business or for the production of income. Therefore, the proper classification of rental deductions is not an issue in preparing a taxpayer's return. However, when the taxpayer decides to sell the property, the classification becomes important. Disposal of rental property at a gain results in similar tax treatment whether the property is classified as a trade or business or an investment asset. However, if the rental property is disposed of at a loss, the full amount of the loss can be deducted in the year of the sale only if the property is used in a trade or business (Exhibit 5–1). Investment property sold at a loss is classified as a capital loss. Although net capital losses are also deducted for adjusted gross income, a capital loss may be limited to a $3,000 deduction each year until it is fully used. Because of the limitation on capital losses, classification of rental real estate as an investment asset is usually less desirable than classification as a trade or business asset when the property is sold at a loss.

▲ **EXAMPLE 12**   Frank sells the property in example 10 at a $10,000 loss during 1995. How much of the loss can Frank deduct?

Discussion: Because Frank's rental activity is a production-of-income activity, the $10,000 is a capital loss. The $10,000 loss would be included in the 1995 capital gain-and-loss netting. If Frank had no other capital gains and losses during 1995, he could deduct only $3,000 of the loss in 1995, with the remaining $7,000 of loss carried forward to 1996.

▲ **EXAMPLE 13**   Assume that Yolanda sells one of her rental properties in example 11 at a $10,000 loss during 1995. How much of the loss can Yolanda deduct?

Discussion: Because Yolanda's rental activities constitute a trade or business, the $10,000 loss on the sale of the rental property is deducted in full in 1995 as a trade or business loss.

The trade or business versus investment characterization of rental real estate is also important if the taxpayer wants to claim deductions or credits, such as home office expenses, that are available only to a trade or business activity.

Personal Expenditures

An individual's personal expenditures are also grouped into two categories. The two categories are allowable personal itemized deductions and nondeductible personal expenses. In contrast to expenditures for a business purpose in which all ordinary and necessary expenses are deductible, the tax law severely limits deductions for personal expenditures. As shown in Exhibit 5–1, those personal expenses that are allowed are deductible from adjusted gross income. In addition, most personal itemized deductions are subject to a limit on deduction based on the taxpayer's adjusted gross income. A major problem in determining an individual's personal itemized deductions is that many assets and expenses are used for both business and personal purposes. Proper accounting for such assets and expenses requires segregation of the business portion from the personal portion.

Mixed Business and Personal Expenditures

These categories of expenditures, *mixed-use assets* and *mixed-use expenditures*, present special problems for individual taxpayers. A person's expenses related to mixed-use assets and mixed-use expenditures must be analyzed and allocated between profit-motivated and personal expenditures. To the extent an expense is related to a profit-motivated transaction, it is treated as a business expense. Unless the personal expenditure qualifies as an itemized deduction, it is not deductible.

Mixed-Use Assets.   A **mixed-use asset** is an asset that is used both to earn income and for personal purposes. For tax purposes, the single asset is effectively treated as two separate assets. One is a business asset, and the other is a personal use asset. For example, a taxpayer may own one car that he uses to travel for his business and to provide local transportation for his family. To deny a deduction for the business use of the car would violate both the ability-to-pay and capital recovery concepts. Because the income earned using the car is taxable, a deduction is allowed for the expense related to the business use of the car. The cost of using the car to provide local transportation for the family is a personal expense that is not deductible. Thus, an expense that is related to using a mixed-use asset must be reasonably allocated between business and personal use. The portion of the expense reasonably allocated to business use is treated the same as other expenses that are related to the profit-motivated activity. An expense allocated to personal use cannot be deducted unless it qualifies as a specifically allowed itemized deduction.

▲ **EXAMPLE 14**   Aaron purchases a computer in 1994 at a cost of $8,000. Aaron uses the computer in his dry-cleaning business and for personal purposes after work and on weekends. During 1994, Aaron's records indicate that 75% of the computer's use is for business purposes and 25% for personal purposes. How should Aaron treat the computer for tax purposes?

Discussion: Aaron must treat the computer as 2 separate assets for tax purposes. For purposes of computing depreciation on the computer, only $6,000 ($8,000 × 75%) of the cost can be depreciated for tax purposes. The remaining $2,000 of cost is considered a personal use asset. Depreciation is not allowed on personal use assets.

▲ **EXAMPLE 15**   Aaron sells the computer in 1996 for $4,000. His business use remains at 75% for 1995 and 1996. Aaron properly deducts $2,400 in depreciation on the computer for 1994 through 1996. What is Aaron's taxable gain or loss on the sale of the computer?

Discussion: Aaron must treat the sale of the computer as the sale of 2 assets—one a business asset and one a personal asset. The $4,000 sales price and the $8,000 purchase price must be allocated between business and personal use:

		Business	Personal
Selling price—$4,000 × 75%		$3,000	
$4,000 × 25%			$1,000
Less: Adjusted basis			
Original cost—$8,000 × 75%	$6,000		
$8,000 × 25%			(2,000)
Less: Depreciation	(2,400)	(3,600)	
Loss on sale		$ 600	$1,000

The $600 loss on the business portion of the computer is deductible as a business loss. However, the $1,000 loss on the personal use portion is a nondeductible personal use loss.

Mixed-Use Expenditures.

Mixed-use expenditures are also subject to special treatment. **Mixed-use expenditures** are expenses that are incurred for both profit and personal reasons. As with mixed-use assets, these expenditures must be allocated between business and personal use and deducted according to the rules for each use. In addition, certain types of mixed-use expenditures (e.g., hobby and vacation home expenses, which are discussed in Chapter 6), are subject to special rules designed to prevent taxpayer abuse by disallowing all or part of an otherwise deductible expenditure.

▲ **EXAMPLE 16**   Pam traveled to San Diego for 4 days primarily for business reasons. Her air fare cost $800, and she incurred expenses of $200 a day for lodging and incidentals. Because Pam had never been to San Diego, she stayed 2 extra days to visit the zoo and to tour the city. How much of her costs can be deducted as a business expense?

Discussion: Pam has incurred mixed-use expenditures. The expense relates to a business trip and a personal vacation. Because the primary motive (as evidenced by spending more days on business than for personal purposes) for making the trip was to conduct business, Pam can deduct the full $800 air fare. She can also deduct $200 for each day she was in San Diego to conduct business. Pam cannot deduct any part of the $200 per day for lodging and incidentals for the 2 extra days she stayed for personal reasons.

▲ TESTS FOR DEDUCTIBILITY

In classifying expenditures, only expenses that have a business purpose are treated as deductible trade or business and investment expenses. In addition to having a business purpose, these expenses must also be

- Ordinary
- Necessary
- Reasonable in amount

Note that all three requirements must be met in order to deduct a trade or business or an investment expense. Deductible trade or business and investment expenses may *not* be any of the following:

- A personal expense
- A capital expenditure
- A payment that frustrates public policy
- An expense related to tax-exempt income
- Another person's expense

The discussion that follows examines each requirement for determining deductible business and investment expenses.

Ordinary, Necessary, and Reasonable in Amount

Trade or business and investment-related activities are allowed a deduction for the ordinary and necessary expenses of earning income. In addition, the tax law provides that a trade or business can deduct reasonable salaries. According to the IRS and the courts, an expense must be reasonable in amount to be ordinary and necessary.[11] Thus, the portion of an expense that is not reasonable in amount will not be deductible because it is not ordinary or necessary. Because of their importance in identifying deductible business expenses, these terms need further consideration.

Ordinary Expense.   An expenditure must qualify as an ordinary expense to be deductible. The term *ordinary* is generally interpreted to have two meanings. First, the expense must be of a kind commonly incurred in the particular income-earning activity.[12] Thus, the expense may be said to be customary or usual in the activity. An **ordinary expense** is one that is normal, common, and accepted under the circumstances of the business community. In addition, although the expense must be common to the income-earning activity, it does not have to be a regularly recurring item for the taxpayer.

▲ **EXAMPLE 17**   Kara owned and operated a pet shop. One day, a customer was bitten by a snake. Although the accident was the customer's fault, he filed a law suit against Kara for $25,000. After Kara paid her lawyer $2,500 to defend her, the customer dropped the suit. Are the legal fees an ordinary expense for Kara?

Discussion: Lawsuits by customers are a common occurrence in today's business environment. The cost of defending the business against the disgruntled customer is a normal cost of doing business, although it is not a recurring expense. The legal fees would satisfy the ordinary test.

▲ **EXAMPLE 18**   The Russo Co., which raises hogs, entered into a contract with the local feed mill to buy hog feed. Under the terms of the agreement, Russo agreed to purchase a quantity of grain and pay for the grain in advance. The mill agreed to deliver the feed as needed and to charge the deliveries against Russo's advance payment at the lower of the market price on delivery or a maximum price agreed to in the contract. Is the advance payment of the hog feed an ordinary expense?

Discussion: The payment for the grain qualifies as an ordinary expense. The advance purchase of the grain for feeding livestock is the normal way farmers conduct their business. By ensuring that the grain is available, Russo can better plan the scope of its farm operations for the coming months.

As these examples illustrate, an ordinary expense may or may not be a frequently occurring item. Also, the determination of what is usual or customary depends on the nature of the taxpayer's business. A typical expense for a pet shop (bird seed) is not a typical expense for an auto mechanic (repair parts).

The second meaning of *ordinary* is that the expenditure is an expense that is assignable to the current accounting period. A capital expenditure that provides future benefits cannot be deducted now.[13] Capital expenditures that benefit more than one tax year should be allocated by means of a depreciation, depletion, or amortization deduction to the accounting periods receiving benefit from the use of the asset.

▲ **EXAMPLE 19**   Gustav Brothers, a partnership, buys a $20,000 machine in the current year to use in its business. The machine has a 7-year tax life. When can the partnership deduct the cost of the machine?

Discussion: The machine is to be used to earn income during several tax years. As a result, the cost of the machine must be capitalized and allocated to the years benefited by the use of the machine. The deductions allowed for depreciation are discussed in Chapter 11.

Necessary Expense.   An expense must also be necessary to be deductible. The courts have defined a **necessary expense** as one that is "appropriate and helpful" to the taxpayer's income activity.[14] An expense will be considered necessary if a reasonable and prudent businessperson would incur the expense in a similar situation. It is important to note that the term *necessary* does not mean that the expense must be essential to the continued existence of the income activity in order to be deductible. In most cases, the courts have tended to accept the taxpayer's judgment of the business necessity of the expenditure rather than attempt to determine the commercial value of the expenditure.

▲ **EXAMPLE 20**   A tax lawyer purchased a large red, white, and blue flag with the numerals 1040 for his yacht. While using his yacht, many people inquired about the flag, and the tax attorney obtained a few customers as a result of such contact. Can the lawyer deduct the cost of operating his yacht as a promotional expense?

Discussion: On similar facts, the Tax Court determined that operating the yacht was not the ordinary method of promoting the taxpayer's business. Further, the court determined that the expenses of the yacht were so personal in nature that it could not be necessary in the common sense of the word.

▲ **EXAMPLE 21**   Buster, Inc., is a women's clothing store in Fashion City. One day a year, the company pays $500 to publish a full-page advertisement in the town newspaper to announce its annual clothing sale. Is the cost of the advertisement deductible?

Discussion: The $500 paid for the sale advertisement is deductible. The expense satisfies both the ordinary and necessary tests. It is customary for clothing retailers to advertise their merchandise. In addition, the advertisement is helpful to the business, because it both promotes the store to the public and attracts the attention of the company's customers and provides them with an incentive to shop at the store—to take advantage of the sale prices.

Reasonable in Amount.   An expense must also be reasonable in amount to be deductible. An expense does not satisfy the ordinary and necessary tests unless it is reasonable in amount. The reasonableness test most often becomes an issue in transactions involving related parties. When unrelated parties are dealing at arm's length in their own best interests, the result of the negotiations will normally be a fair market value. However, related parties have incentives to shift income by charging prices higher or lower than what would be paid in an arm's-length transaction, so these costs would not constitute **reasonable expenses.**

▲ **EXAMPLE 22**   Tara operates a shoe store in a building she rents from her father for $1,000 per month. Comparable store space is readily available for rent at $400 per month. Is the rental payment reasonable?

Discussion: Tara will be allowed a $400 rent expense deduction unless she can establish that the location or other unique features of her father's building justify a higher rent than other, comparable store space. Unless Tara can prove otherwise, the $600 excess payment will be considered a nondeductible payment to her father (a gift).

▲ **EXAMPLE 23**   Roy pays Sally $100 per week to clean his medical office. When Sally became ill, he hired his daughter, Janice, to fill in and keep the office tidy. Roy paid Janice $300 a week. How much of the $300 payment is reasonable?

Discussion: Of the $300 per week paid Janice, he will be allowed to deduct only $100, because that was the amount he was paying Sally. Unless Roy can prove otherwise, Janice's $300 weekly salary will be considered excessive, because he would normally pay $100 a week for the same services.

NOTE: In each of these examples, the apparently unreasonable compensation was paid to a related party. It is unlikely that the taxpayers in these examples would have paid the same amounts had the transactions been with an unrelated party.

Not a Personal Expense

The tax law specifically disallows a deduction for personal, living, and family expenses.[15] Because deductions are a matter of legislative grace, this rule eliminates deductions for expenditures that do not have a business purpose, such as

- Premiums the insured taxpayer pays on life insurance.
- Insurance premiums paid on the taxpayer's home and personal property.
- Expenses of maintaining a home such as rent, utilities, insurance, and maintenance.
- Losses from disposing of property held for personal, living, or family purposes.
- The cost of transportation, meals, or lodging unless they are related to a trade or business, the production of income, charitable contributions, or medical expenses; the personal cost of commuting to work and back is not deductible.

- Legal fees and costs related to obtaining a divorce; the portion of the attorney's fee paid to obtain alimony or other taxable income is allowed as a deduction for the production of income.
- The costs of obtaining an education to meet the minimum requirements of the taxpayer's trade or business or that are part of a program that would qualify the taxpayer to enter a new business or profession.

Frequently, an expense will be incurred for both business and personal reasons. Does the business purpose automatically qualify the expense for deduction? According to the IRS and the courts, the answer is no. To be deductible, the expense must bear a proximate relationship to the income-producing activity.[16] In addition, the primary or dominant motivation for incurring the expense must be the business purpose. A significant business motivation is not enough.

▲ **EXAMPLE 24**   Atman and Sarita are good friends. Atman also supplies Sarita with artwork that she sells to customers in her interior decorating business. Atman took Sarita to dinner at the Greyhouse. During the meal, they discussed business, and Sarita agreed to buy several pieces of art. Atman paid for the meal. Is the cost of the meal a business expense or a personal expense?

Discussion: If Atman took Sarita to dinner just to spend time with a friend, the fact that the conversation drifted to business does not result in a business deduction for the meal. Because the dominant motive for the expense is personal, the expense is not deductible.

If Atman took Sarita to dinner so he would be able to discuss his artwork and to solicit an order for paintings and the event centered around a business discussion, Atman could deduct the cost of the meal as a business expense, because the dominant motive was a business purpose.

▲ **EXAMPLE 25**   Bud and Gloria operate a hot tub manufacturing business. In June, they attended a three-day trade show in Paris and obtained a large number of orders for their hot tubs. In June, they also sent their 13-year-old son Dave to Cannes for three weeks to visit a friend who is a lawyer. The lawyer's son lived with Bud and Gloria while in the United States as an exchange student. The lawyer also represents their biggest customer in France. The lawyer's son and Dave have developed a friendship over the years. Is the cost of the trips deductible as a business expense, or is it a personal expense?

Discussion: The cost of Bud's and Gloria's attending the trade show is a deductible business expense because the primary motive for the trip was a business purpose. Dave's trip is primarily personal and not deductible. The motivation for Dave's trip was to create goodwill with the lawyer who is associated with a customer. Dave's trip is unrelated to the active conduct of the hot tub business.

Not a Capital Expenditure

A capital expenditure that results in an asset that benefits future accounting periods is not allowed as a current deduction, because the useful life extends beyond the end of the tax year.[17] Capital expenditures include the cost of acquiring land, buildings, machinery and equipment, furniture and fixtures, the cost of perfecting or defending title to property, and purchased goodwill. Amounts paid for freight and installation charges related to getting an asset to the taxpayer's location and set up are included in the asset's basis. If the taxpayer constructs an asset for his or her own business, the property's basis includes both the direct and indirect costs of production. If an asset has a useful life that extends substantially beyond the end of the tax year of the expenditure, its immediate deduction is generally not allowed.

▲ **EXAMPLE 26**   Paula bought Colleen's advertising agency. As part of the purchase price, Paula paid Colleen $12,000 not to open another advertising agency in the area for 3 years. Can Paula deduct the $12,000 as a current business expense?

Discussion: The $12,000 payment (known as *a covenant not to compete*) will benefit Paula's business for 3 years by not having Colleen as a competitor during that period. Thus, the benefit of the payment extends substantially beyond the end of the tax year and must be capitalized and amortized as an intangible asset.

The capital recovery and the accounting period concepts require deduction of an asset's basis through depreciation, amortization, depletion, or as a reduction in the amount realized on the asset's disposition. For example, assets with a limited life, such as buildings and equipment, are subject to a depreciation expense deduction. The cost of assets with an indefinite useful life, such as land, are permanently capitalized until the asset's disposition. Based on the administrative convenience concept, tools that wear out and are thrown away within one year can be deducted in the year of purchase. Contrary to the general rule, by legislative grace Congress permits taxpayers to take a current deduction for certain long-lived assets. For example, a taxpayer can elect to expense certain

- Research and experimentation expenditures
- Soil and water conservation expenditures
- Certain depreciable business assets
- Expenditures by farmers for fertilizer
- Several other specific capital expenditures

The commission paid on the acquisition of a security is not a current deduction. When a commission is paid on the purchase of a security, it is considered part of the cost of buying the asset and is added to the security's basis. When the security is sold, the basis is deducted from the sale price as a capital recovery. The commission paid on the sale of a security is a reduction in the amount realized on the sale.

▲ **EXAMPLE 27**   Connie purchased 100 shares of Calvinator Corporation stock for $100 per share. She also paid a commission on the purchase of $400. What is the basis of the 100 shares of stock?

Discussion: The basis of the stock is the cost of obtaining the stock. Because the commission is part of the cost of acquiring the stock, it is added to basis; commissions are not current period expenses. Therefore, the cost of the 100 shares of stock is $10,400 [(100 × $100) + $400].

▲ **EXAMPLE 28**   Connie sold the 100 shares of stock purchased in example 27 for $130 per share. She paid a commission of $600 on the sale. What is Connie's gain (loss) on the sale of the stock?

Discussion: Connie has a gain of $2,000 on the sale. The $600 commission is a reduction of the amount realized on the sale; it is not a current period expense:

Selling price (100 × $130)	$13,000
Less: Commissions	(600)
Amount realized from sale	$12,400
Less: Basis of shares sold	(10,400)
Gain on sale	$ 2,000

Repair-and-Maintenance Expense.   The difference between a capital expenditure that results in an asset and a **repair-and-maintenance expense** is important. Repair-and-maintenance expenses are allowed as a deduction in the current accounting period.[18] Repairs include repainting an office, fixing a leaking water or gas line, patching a roof, and replacing a broken glass in a window. These expenses generally include the costs of keeping business assets in normal operating condition. Unlike improvements and replacements, repairs do not appreciably extend an asset's useful life or materially add to its value. **Improvements,** such as rewiring or putting a new roof on a building, should be capitalized, because they either extend useful life or add to the value of the property. A **replacement,** such as a major overhaul of a machine, that extends the life of an asset should also be capitalized. In addition, expenditures made as part of a plan to recondition, improve, or alter an asset (called *betterments*) should be capitalized as assets, although individual expenditures considered separately might qualify as repairs.[19] The costs of improvements, replacements, and betterments should be deducted in the accounting periods benefited by their use, based on an acceptable depreciation or amortization method.

Start-up Costs.   Capital expenditures can also include start-up costs. **Start-up costs** are related to investigating and creating a new active trade or business. The start-up costs to be capitalized are the expenses incurred before the new business begins its activities. Start-up costs could include

- Surveys and analyses of markets, facilities, and labor force
- Travel to develop the business and locate potential customers and suppliers
- Advertising the new business
- Salaries to train employees
- Salaries for executives and consultants
- Various other expenses such as legal and accounting fees

The items included as capitalized start-up costs must be similar to expenses that would be deductible in expanding an existing business.

If the taxpayer begins the new business, she or he can elect to amortize the start-up costs over a period of 60 months or longer.[20] The amortization deduction is allowed starting in the month the new business begins its operations. If the taxpayer does not elect to amortize the start-up costs, the costs become locked in and can be deducted only upon disposition of the business. If the taxpayer does not enter the new business, expenses related to investigating the new business are not deductible.[21] The transaction is given this treatment because the taxpayer's motivation is deemed to be primarily personal before a new business is begun. A taxpayer's efforts to investigate a business do not establish a business purpose for the expenditures.

It is important to note that a taxpayer operating an existing trade or business can claim a current deduction for the cost of investigating, expanding, or establishing new locations for the same line of business. The investigation costs are considered an ordinary and necessary expense of the existing trade or business and therefore fully deductible when incurred. However, an existing business entering an unrelated trade or business is subject to the same capitalization rules as a new business.[22] If the unrelated business is not acquired, the investigation expenses become nondeductible.

▲ **EXAMPLE 29** Jason has operated Main Street Cafe for 15 years. He would like to branch out by opening another cafe in a nearby city. Can Jason deduct the costs of investigating the feasibility of opening the second cafe?

Discussion: Whether Jason decides to expand his business and open a second cafe or not, he can deduct the costs of investigating a location for a second cafe as a current deduction. Because the expenses are related to opening a business that is related to Jason's existing business, they are allowed as a current deduction, no matter what he decides.

▲ **EXAMPLE 30** What would happen if Jason, in example 29, investigated opening a retail store selling speed boats?

Discussion: The retail speed boat store would be a new business, because it is unrelated to his cafe business. If Jason decided not to enter the retail boat business, he could not deduct any investigation expenses. The expenses would be considered nondeductible personal expenses. If Jason acquires the retail store, he would have to capitalize the investigation expenses and amortize them over 60 months, starting with the month the new business started.

The costs of organizing a corporation or partnership must also be capitalized. Organization costs are those costs incurred to organize a corporation or a partnership. Such costs include legal, accounting, filing, and other fees and costs incidental to the start-up of a corporation or a partnership. They are similar to start-up costs in that they are incurred before the entity is actually legally organized. As such, they are subject to the same election, to amortize the expenditures over a period of 60 months or more, as for start-up costs.[23]

Not Frustrate Public Policy

In a long series of cases before 1970, the courts disallowed deductions (usually for fines and penalties) for expenditures that the courts thought were frustrating public policy by encouraging unlawful conduct.[24] The courts' rationale in these cases was that it was neither ordinary nor necessary to violate the law. In 1969, Congress preempted the court battles by amending Section 162 to disallow certain categories of payments. The following payments are explicitly stated in the tax law as nondeductible expenditures:

- Direct or indirect illegal bribes or kickbacks to government officials and employees, including payments to federal, state, local, and foreign government officials and employees as well as officials and employees of a government agency

- Direct or indirect payments to any person of an amount that constitute an illegal bribe, kickback, or other illegal payment under federal or state law (if the state law is generally enforced)

- Bribes, kickbacks, or rebates by a provider of services, supplier, physician, or other persons who furnish items or services under Medicare or Medicaid

- Fines, penalties, or similar payments to a governmental unit for the violation of any law

- Certain damage payments for violation of the antitrust laws

▲ **EXAMPLE 31** Rapid Trucking Co. incurred several weight overload fines. Although Rapid took reasonable precautions to avoid violating the overall weight limit, loads that shifted during transit resulted in violations of the axle-weight limit. Can Rapid deduct the overload fines?

Discussion: Even if Rapid Trucking Co. had exercised all due care and incurred the overweight fines without willful intent, the fines would not be allowed as a deduction. A deduction for fines is specifically disallowed as being in violation of public policy.

▲ **EXAMPLE 32** Chitsa is a tax return preparer. She forgot to sign tax returns she prepared for her clients. As a result, she was fined $50 for each unsigned return. Can Chitsa deduct the fines as a cost of doing business?

Discussion: The tax law requires a return preparer to sign each return prepared for a fee. A $50 penalty is assessed for each return not properly signed. The penalties paid by Chitsa are not deductible as an expense related to her tax return preparation business.

Expenses of an Illegal Business.

Although the tax law specifically denies a deduction for the listed expenditures on the basis that they are illegal payments, a taxpayer can deduct the legal ordinary and necessary expenses related to carrying on an illegal trade or business.[25]

▲ **EXAMPLE 33** Bert is engaged in the business of illegally trafficking in liquor, gambling, and betting on horse races. The business is operated out of the Overflow Club. Under state law, the activities are illegal. What expenses may Bert deduct against his illegal income?

Discussion: Bert's income from the illegal activities is taxable under the all-inclusive income concept. The payment of fines for breaking the law and bribes paid to protect the business from raids and arrests by state and county law officers are not deductible. However, legitimate expenses incurred in the illegitimate business are deductible. Among the allowable expenses would be rent, utilities, and employee wages.

A special provision in the tax law denies all deductions other than cost of goods sold for individuals engaged in the illegal trafficking of controlled substances (drugs).[26]

Lobbying Expenses and Other Political Activities.

Relying on the ordinary and necessary requirement for deducting business expenses, in 1918 the Treasury Department promulgated regulations that denied deductions for expenditures for the promotion or defeat of legislation, and political contributions. With minor changes in language, these restrictions have been retained. The denial of such deductions has been upheld by the courts on the grounds that money was an "insidious influence" on politics.

Contributions to political campaigns and expenditures to influence public opinion about legislation, a referendum, or how to vote in an election are not deductible. This denial of deductions extends to advertising in a political party's convention program, admission to political fund-raising dinners, and events such as an inaugural ball, parades, and concerts.

▲ **EXAMPLE 34** The accounting firm of Williams, Daniels, and Thomas contributed $100 to a political campaign fund. The objective of the group managing the fund is to defeat a senator who has proposed legislation that would be unfavorable to CPAs and to support candidates who favor CPAs' positions. Can the firm deduct the $100 payment?

Discussion: The firm's political contribution is not allowed as a deduction because the fund supports the election of a candidate and attempts to influence public opinion concerning the suitability of the senator to hold office.

LOBBYING EXPENSES.   Before passage of the Omnibus Budget Reconciliation Act (OBRA) of 1993, costs incurred for lobbying in favor of or against legislation of direct interest to the taxpayer's trade or business were deductible. Under this exception to the general rule disallowing political expenditures, the taxpayer was allowed to deduct the cost of traveling, preparing testimony, and communicating the taxpayer's view directly to legislators or the legislative body. The taxpayer was also permitted to deduct membership dues paid to lobbying organizations. For tax years after 1993, OBRA disallows a deduction for expenses incurred in connection with influencing federal or state legislation or for expenses associated with attempting to influence officials in the federal executive branch. As a result, **lobbying expenses,** including dues to lobbying organizations, are no longer deductible.[27] The new rules do not apply to attempts to influence a local legislative body (i.e., town council) or to the cost associated with monitoring federal or state legislation, unless the taxpayer then attempts to influence the same or similar legislation. In addition, under the administrative convenience concept, the new law allows taxpayers who incur a *de minimis* amount of in-house lobbying expenses (less than $2,000 during the year) to deduct these expenses. In-house expenditures are expenditures for lobbying (e.g., costs of labor and materials) but do not include payments to professional lobbyists, dues, or other similar payments that are allocable to lobbying. If a taxpayer's total in-house lobbying expenditures exceed $2,000, no deduction is allowed for any of the in-house expenditures.

▲ **EXAMPLE 35**   Kathleen, a Realtor, testified before a state legislative committee, giving her thoughts on the effect of the new building code requirements on housing starts. She incurred $2,500 in costs to prepare her testimony and to travel to and stay in the state capital. Are these expenses deductible?

Discussion: Because the purpose of the expenses was to influence the legislative process, these expenses are not deductible. They are not deductible under the de minimis rule because the total expenditure exceeds $2,000. However, if Kathleen had gone to the legislative meetings only to listen and to monitor the legislation—as opposed to presenting her views—her expenses would have been deductible.

Not Related to Tax-Exempt Income

Expenses incurred to earn tax-exempt income are not allowed as a deduction.[28] Allowing the deduction of these expenses would violate the ability-to-pay concept by giving the taxpayer the double benefit of excluding income while deducting the related expenses. Frequently, taxpayers have to allocate investment expenses to both taxable and tax-exempt income. When making the allocation, expenses directly related to a class of income are allocated to that income. Expenses indirectly related to more than one class of income are allocated among the various classes of income by using a reasonable accounting method. One reasonable method of allocating indirect expenses is by total investment income.

▲ **EXAMPLE 36**   Clemons incurred $5,000 in investment expenses related to earning $3,000 in interest on taxable bonds and $3,600 in interest on tax-exempt bonds. The expenses are not directly allocable to either class of income. How much of the $5,000 in investment expenses can Clemons deduct as a production-of-income expense?

Discussion: Clemons can deduct only the portion of the expenses that is incurred to produce taxable income. The portion attributable to the production of tax-exempt income is not deductible. The investment expenses are allocated to the classes of interest income as follows:

Bonds	Total Investment Income	% of Total Income	Investment Expenses
Taxable interest income	$3,000	45.5%	$2,273
Tax-exempt interest income	3,600	54.5	2,727
Totals	$6,600	100.0%	$5,000

Clemons is allowed a deduction for the expenses related to the taxable bonds ($2,273). The investment expenses related to tax-exempt bonds ($2,727) are not deductible.

Expenditure Must Be for Taxpayer's Benefit

To be deductible, an expenditure must be for the taxpayer's benefit or be a payment of the taxpayer's obligation. A payment of another person's obligation does not result in a tax deduction for either person. The person making the payment cannot deduct an expense that is not related to her or his business, because the payment lacks a business purpose.[29] The person for whom the debt is paid is not entitled to another entity's deduction for a capital recovery.

▲ EXAMPLE 37   Marty's mother, Mary, owed $5,000 in back property taxes. To help Mary out of financial difficulty, Marty paid the property taxes. Can either Marty or Mary take a deduction for the property taxes paid by Marty?

Discussion: Although property taxes are allowed as a personal itemized deduction, Marty may not claim a deduction for payment of his mother's obligation. The property taxes were not Marty's obligation, and Marty did not benefit from the use of the property subject to the taxes. Mary may not deduct the payment of taxes, because she did not pay the expense.

In order to make sure that a deduction is allowed for the taxes, Marty could have made a gift of the $5,000 to Mary and had her pay the taxes directly.

An exception to the disallowance of the payment of another's expenses is made in the case of medical expenses of a dependent. All medical expenses paid on behalf of a taxpayer's dependent are deductible by the taxpayer, subject to the limitations on medical expense deductions.

▲ TIMING OF DEDUCTIONS— EFFECT OF ACCOUNTING METHOD

The annual accounting period concept requires taxpayers to determine the expenses that can be deducted for each tax year. To assign expenses to the correct year, the tax law requires the taxpayer to adopt an accounting method that clearly reflects income. *Accounting method* refers to the overall method used to compute income and deductions belonging to the tax year. *Accounting method* also refers to the method used to compute the amount of particular income or deduction items. For example, the taxpayer may determine net income for a business using either the cash or the accrual method. In addition, to calculate the deduction for automobile expenses, the taxpayer must elect to use either the actual cost method or the standard rate method (discussed in Chapter 6).

If the taxpayer adopts a method of accounting that does not fairly reflect income (such as accrual method for expense and the cash method for income), the IRS can designate the method to be used by the taxpayer.[30] The accounting method adopted by the taxpayer is important, because it controls the timing of a deduction. Deduction of an expense in the wrong accounting period is not allowed.

▲ **EXAMPLE 38**   Craig pays $100 for supplies on December 28, 1995. His taxable income for 1995 is the lowest it has ever been, and he does not need more deductions for the year. Although he uses the cash method of accounting and normally expenses supplies when he buys them, he decides to save the $100 deduction until 1996. He reasons that his actions are proper, because he has not used the supplies. When should Craig deduct the cost of the supplies?

Discussion: Given his accounting method, Craig must deduct the expenses in 1995. He must use a method of accounting that fairly reflects income and apply that method on a consistent basis. As a cash basis taxpayer, Craig must deduct the $100 supplies expense in 1995. Under the cash method, he cannot take the deduction in 1996.

Cash Method

A cash basis taxpayer may claim a deduction in the year an expense is paid. The basic question to be answered then is when does payment occur? If a check is honored when it is taken to the bank for deposit, an expense is generally considered paid on the date the taxpayer gives or mails the check to the creditor. If the check is not honored when presented for payment, the timing of the deduction is not clear. Depending on the facts that caused the check to be dishonored, the deduction could be delayed until the check is made good. If the check was intended as payment of the debt but was not honored because of clerical errors, the deduction should be allowed when the check was mailed if it is promptly paid. If the taxpayer did not have the funds to pay the check and intended for the check to be a promise to pay in the future (i.e., a note), the deduction should be allowed in the year the check (note) is paid.

▲ **EXAMPLE 39**   On December 31, 1995, Elvira, a cash basis taxpayer, mails a $500 check to her attorney to pay for legal fees related to her business. The attorney receives the check on January 2 and deposits it in her account. When can Elvira deduct the legal fees?

Discussion: If the check is honored by the bank when it is presented for payment, Elvira can claim the deduction when she mailed it—in 1995—although the check was not cashed until 1996.

If the check bounces because Elvira does not have sufficient funds for the check to clear, the deduction is not allowed until sufficient funds are deposited and the check clears or Elvira makes some other form of payment to the lawyer.

When a property or service is used to pay an expense, payment occurs when the taxpayer gives the property or renders the service to the creditor. If property or services are used to pay an expense, the amount deductible is generally the fair market value of the property or services given the creditor. However, a cash basis taxpayer will have to recognize the fair market value of services used to pay an expense as income and then deduct the expense incurred in providing the service. When the fair market value of an asset is more or less than its basis, the transfer of property will result in a realized gain or loss.

▲ **EXAMPLE 40**   Sandra has worked out an agreement with a local radio station for advertising. The radio station will run 30-second commercials in exchange for interior decorating services offered by her business. During the current year, she provides enough interior decorating services to compensate the radio station for $2,500-worth of advertising. Her expenses related to performing the services total $1,200. How should Sandra treat this arrangement?

Discussion: Sandra should deduct $2,500 in advertising expense and report $2,500 in service sales related to the advertising contract. Her $1,200 in expenses related to doing the work for the radio station are deductible as normal business expenses.

Payment of an expense by charging it to a credit card is treated as payment on the date the transaction is charged to the card.[31] It does not matter when the taxpayer pays the credit card company. If a taxpayer gives his or her own note payable to a creditor, or the creditor charges an item on an open account, the expense is not considered paid until the note or open account is paid off. On the other hand, a taxpayer may go to the bank and borrow money, give the bank a note for the loan, and then use the money to pay expenses. Expenses paid with borrowed money are allowed as a deduction regardless of when the loan is repaid.

▲ **EXAMPLE 41** Laval owes $3,000 in expenses that are tax deductible. However, he does not have the cash to write a check. How can Laval obtain a current deduction for the expenses?

Discussion: If Laval charges the expenses to a credit card, he is deemed to have paid the expense on the date of the charge and can take a deduction on the charge date. He can pay the credit card balance when he has the money.

If the expenses are not payable by credit card, Laval could borrow the money from a friend or a bank and give them his note. He could use the cash to pay the expense and claim a deduction on the payment date. He could repay the note when he has the funds.

If Laval pays the expense by giving a note directly to the creditor, the expense is not deductible until the note is paid.

A cash basis taxpayer may deduct prepaid expenses in the year paid if the prepayment does not create an asset that extends substantially beyond the end of the year of payment. Thus, the late 1995 purchase of office supplies to be used in January 1996 can be deducted when the supplier is paid in 1995. However, the IRS has said that if $1,000 in business insurance is prepaid for one year on July 1, 1995, the expense must be allocated by charging $500 to 1995 and $500 to 1996. The courts differ with the IRS on this issue. The courts have held that a prepayment of an expense that will be used up before the end of the tax year following the year of prepayment can be deducted when paid.[32] That is, such prepayments are deemed not to extend substantially beyond the end of the tax year. This is referred to as the **one-year rule for prepaid expenses.** In order to qualify a prepaid expense under the one-year rule, the taxpayer must show that the payment is required by the creditor and that the payment does not distort income.

▲ **EXAMPLE 42** Woody rents his office building. According to his 15-year lease, he is required to pay the $12,000 rent in advance on August 1 for the period September 1 through August 31. Woody has complied with the lease terms for the last 3 years. Can Woody deduct the $12,000 in the year it is paid?

Discussion: Woody can deduct the $12,000 annual rent when paid. Because the terms of the lease require the prepayment, the deduction will not distort income, and because it is used up before the end of the tax year following the year of prepayment, he will not need to amortize the expense. Note that a prepayment that extended beyond 1 year (e.g., a 2-year rent prepayment) would have to be allocated to the periods benefited by the expense.

Prepaid taxes are deductible in the year paid, even if the prepayment results in a refund in a later year. Under the tax benefit rule, the tax refund is reported as income.

▲ **EXAMPLE 43**   Plain County assesses property taxes annually on December 1. The taxes are not due and payable until March 1. Hortense always pays her property taxes before December 31. When can Hortense deduct the tax payments?

Discussion: Although Hortense is not under a legal obligation to pay the taxes until March 1, the taxes are deductible when paid in December under the one-year rule.

▲ **EXAMPLE 44**   Charles has $2,200 in state income taxes withheld from his paycheck during 1995. How much of the $2,200 can Charles deduct in 1995?

Discussion: State income taxes are deductible as a personal itemized deduction. Assuming that Charles itemizes his deductions on his 1995 tax return, he can deduct the $2,200 in state income taxes paid during 1995.

▲ **EXAMPLE 45**   Assume that after deducting the $2,200 in state income taxes Charles files his state tax return and receives a refund of $300. How should Charles treat the $300 refund?

Discussion: Under the tax benefit rule, the $300 refund is a recovery of an expense deducted in a prior year. Therefore, Charles must include the $300 in his gross income in the year of receipt, 1996. NOTE: The $300 is not a reduction of 1996 state taxes paid. Also, if Charles does not itemize his deductions in 1995, the refund in 1996 is not included in his gross income, because he receives no tax benefit from the state income tax deduction.

Prepaid interest is not generally deductible under the one-year rule. The tax law effectively requires all interest to be accounted for with the accrual method.[33] In essence, prepaid interest is payment for the use of money over time. As a result, it is allocated to the periods in which the money is used. The only exception to this rule is the payment of "points" on a loan used to purchase or construct a principal residence. The treatment of points is discussed further in Chapter 8.

▲ **EXAMPLE 46**   On April 1, 1995, Tasi borrows $10,000 from his bank. The $10,000, 10%-interest, 1-year note is due on March 31, 1996. In order to increase his expenses for 1995, Tasi prepays the $1,000 in interest on the note on December 31, 1995. How much of the $1,000 of prepaid interest is deductible in 1995?

Discussion: Because interest expense is a charge for the use of money over a period of time, Tasi must allocate the prepaid interest to the time period in which the money is used. Tasi may deduct only the interest related to the period of April 1 through December 31, 1995, $750 [$1,000 × (9 ÷ 12)] in 1995. The remaining $250 in prepaid interest is not allowed as a deduction until it accrues in 1996.

Accrual Method

An accrual basis taxpayer may deduct expenses in the year in which two tests are met. The first test is called the *all-events test*. The **all-events test** is met when all the events have occurred that determine that a liability exists and the amount of the liability can be determined with reasonable accuracy.

▲ **EXAMPLE 47**   Hunter manufactures and sells electronic components for radar. The electronic components are fully warranted against defects for a period of 3 years from the date of sale. Based on experience, Hunter knows that 5% of the components will be returned under the terms of the warranty. Hunter estimates that warranty costs related to 1995 sales at $15,000. Does Hunter satisfy the all-events test with regard to the $15,000 of estimated warranty expense?

Discussion: Although Hunter can reasonably anticipate $15,000 in warranty costs for 1995, the liability does not satisfy the all-events test. Because the actual payee and the nature of the claim are unknown, the amount of the warranty expense must be estimated. Thus, the warranty liability is not fixed, and it is not determinable with reasonable accuracy. None of the estimated warranty expenses is allowed as a tax deduction until the parts are actually returned and the warranty obligation becomes certain. NOTE: This treatment differs from financial accounting. In financial accounting, reasonable estimates of expenses are sufficient to fix the liability for the expense. Tax accounting differs in the requirement that the payee be known before an amount is considered fixed.[34]

The second test requires economic performance to have occurred with regard to the liability. Economic performance occurs when services or property are provided to the taxpayer or when the taxpayer uses property. Table 5–1 summarizes when economic performance is considered to have occurred for several commonly accrued expenses. For example, interest accrues with the passage of time, and compensation of employees accrues as workers perform services. Only when the all-events test and the **economic performance test** have been met can an expense be accrued and deducted for tax purposes.

▲ **EXAMPLE 48**   Assume in example 47 that in 1996 customers return defective components sold in 1994 and 1995. It costs Hunter $4,000 to replace the defective parts. When can Hunter deduct the $4,000?

Discussion: When the defective components are returned and they are replaced or the sale price is refunded, Hunter has satisfied the all-events test and economic performance has occurred. Hunter may deduct the $4,000 in warranty expenses in 1996.

The purpose of the economic performance test is to disallow a current deduction for costs that will not have to be paid in the near future. This contrasts with financial accounting for such costs, where an accrual is necessary in order to properly match expenses to the revenues being generated. In working with the income tax accrual method, you should keep in mind that matching expenses to

▲ **Table 5–1**

SUMMARY OF ECONOMIC PERFORMANCE TESTS

Source of Expense	When Economic Performance Occurs
Taxpayer is to receive property or services from others.	As taxpayer receives property or services.
Taxpayer is to use property owned by others.	As property is used by taxpayer.
Taxpayer is to provide property or services to others.	As taxpayer provides property or services to others.
Taxpayer owes interest expense.	With passage of time, as taxpayer uses money borrowed.
Taxpayer owes compensation to employees.	As employees render services.
Taxpayer owes vacation pay to employees.	When paid by taxpayer, or when accrued if paid within $2^{1}/_{2}$ months after close of year.
Payments required under ■ Workers' compensation laws. ■ Payment of liability for tort.	As payments are made by taxpayer.

revenues is not a general criterion that must always be satisfied. Rather, income tax accounting is designed to effect the ability-to-pay and wherewithal-to-pay concepts that assess the tax according to the amount available in the current period to pay taxes.

▲ **EXAMPLE 49**   Big Oil Co. enters into an offshore oil- and gas-drilling lease in 1995. In 1996, Big installs a platform and commences drilling. The terms of the lease obligate Big to remove its offshore platform and well fixtures upon abandonment of the well or termination of the lease. Based on past experience, Big estimates that the well will be productive for 10 years, at which time it will cost $2,000,000 to remove the platform and fixtures. When can Big deduct the cost of removing the platform and fixtures for financial accounting purposes? for income tax purposes?

Discussion: Proper matching of expenses to revenues for financial accounting purposes requires Big to accrue a portion of the estimated cost of removing the platform and fixtures over the life of the well. Therefore, Big would expense $200,000 ($2,000,000 ÷ 10 years) per year beginning in 1996. For income tax purposes, the cost of removing the platform and fixtures is not deductible until economic performance of the liability occurs. Thus, Big will not be able to deduct any of the costs until it begins removal and incurs costs related to the removal.

▲ **EXAMPLE 50**   Janson Corporation runs charter aircraft services. In 1995, Janson enters into a lease agreement with Dana Airlines to lease one of its aircraft for the next 4 years. The lease obligates Janson to pay Dana a base rental of $500,000 per year. In addition, Janson must pay $25 to a repair escrow account for each hour flown. The amounts in the escrow account are to be used by Dana to make necessary repairs to the aircraft. At the end of the lease, any amount remaining in the escrow account is to be returned to Janson. In 1995, the aircraft flies 1,000 hours, and Janson pays $25,000 into the escrow account. Repairs to the plane in 1996 cost $20,000. In 1997, $20,000 is released from the escrow account to pay Dana for the repairs. When can Janson deduct the costs associated with the lease?

Discussion: Janson can deduct the $500,000 rental payment each year, because both the all-events and economic performance tests are met as Janson uses the plane. However, the $25,000 paid into the escrow account for repairs is not deductible until the aircraft is repaired in 1996. That is, economic performance occurs as the repair service is rendered to Janson. Note that under financial accounting rules the amounts paid into the escrow fund would be deducted as they are paid as a cost of using the plane that year.

An exception to the economic performance test permits a current deduction for recurring items even if economic performance has not yet occurred. To use the exception, all of the following tests must be met:

■ The all-events test is met without regard to economic performance.

■ Economic performance will occur within the shorter of

a. $8^{1}/_{2}$ months after the close of the year, or

b.   A reasonable time after the close of the year

■ The item is recurring in nature and the taxpayer consistently treats similar items as incurred in the year the all-events test is met; and

■ The expense either is

a.   Not material, or

b. The accrual of the expense results in a better matching of income and expense than accruing the expense in the year in which economic performance occurs.[35]

▲ **EXAMPLE 51**   Robin enters into a 1-year maintenance contract on July 1, 1995, that costs $1,200. For financial reporting, the expenses are prorated, $600 to 1995 and $600 to 1996. When can Robin deduct the $1,200 cost of the maintenance contract?

Discussion: Under the materiality exception, Robin should deduct $600 in 1995 and $600 in 1996 for both financial and tax reporting. However, the IRS cautions that an expense that is immaterial for financial reporting might be considered material for tax reporting.

▲ **EXAMPLE 52**   If, in example 51, Robin deducts the $1,200 in maintenance contract expenses in 1995 for financial reporting, when should the expenses be deducted for tax reporting?

Discussion: If the contract expenses are material for tax reporting, Robin should deduct $600 in 1995 and $600 in 1996. If the expenses are immaterial for tax reporting, Robin should deduct the contract expenses for tax in the same year they are deducted for financial reporting. Thus, Robin could deduct the $1,200 in 1995 under the materiality exception for tax reporting.

▲ **EXAMPLE 53**   Claudio begins carrying a new line of clothing in his men's shop in 1995. He pays $5,000 for advertising the introduction of the new line in 1995. Claudio does not expect to have to run the advertising campaign in the future. When can he deduct the cost of the advertising?

Discussion: Under the matching exception, Claudio should deduct $5,000 for advertising in 1995. According to the IRS, expenses such as advertising, which cannot be practically associated with income of a particular period, should be assigned to the period in which the costs are incurred. The matching requirement is satisfied if the taxpayer reports the advertising expense in the same accounting period for both financial and tax reporting.

▲ **EXAMPLE 54**   Claudio has a commission agreement with his sales force. Under the agreement, he is to pay his salespeople a percentage of their net sales for 1995. Because of accounting requirements, it is necessary to pay the salespeople their commissions in February 1996. When can Claudio deduct the commissions?

Discussion: Based on the matching exception, Claudio can deduct the accrued commissions in 1995. Although economic performance (payment of the commissions) does not occur until 1996, deduction in 1995 results in better matching of sales income and commission expense.

Financial and Taxable Income Differences

Financial accounting rules place a strong emphasis on the matching of expenses to the income generated during the period. In addition, conservatism dictates that expenses and losses be recognized for financial accounting purposes before they are actually incurred. As a result, financial accounting promotes the use of reasonable estimates of the expenses incurred to earn income. However, tax accounting rules emphasize objectivity in measuring taxable income to be sure the proper tax is collected each year. The tax law's objectivity is essential to protecting revenue collection. Because of the time value of money, deduction of an expense too early would reduce the time value of tax collections. Deducting an expense in the wrong year to receive the benefit of a higher marginal tax rate will also reduce tax collections. Thus, the timing of deductions is a critical issue.

The all-events and economic performance tests create temporary differences between financial (book) and taxable income. For example, the tax law generally requires the use of the specific charge-off method (discussed in Chapter 6) for computing a bad debt deduction. Financial accounting requires the use of the allowance method, which uses a reasonable estimate of the current year's bad debt deduction to be charged against income.

▲ **EXAMPLE 55**   For financial reporting, Press Corporation estimates its bad debt expense to be 2% of credit sales. For 1995, Press records $500,000 in credit sales and $10,000 (2% × $500,000) in bad debt expense. However, a review of individual accounts receivable indicates that on the specific charge-off method, actual bad debts for 1995 total $6,000. How much can Press deduct for bad debts for tax purposes?

Discussion: Although the allowance method is used to estimate bad debt expense for financial reporting, the specific charge-off method must be used for tax reporting. As a result, Press should deduct $10,000 in bad debt expense for financial income reporting and $6,000 in bad debt expense for tax income. The difference in the book and tax deductions results in a $4,000 temporary difference.

For financial accounting, vacation pay accrues as it is earned by the employees. The economic performance requirement allows vacation pay as a deduction when paid or when accrued if payment occurs within 2½ months after the close of the year. Similar rules apply to allowances for warranties. Warranty repair allowances are estimated and deducted as sales are made for financial accounting, but tax accounting allows a deduction only when the taxpayer performs warranty services.

Other tax laws, which are discussed in this and later chapters in the text, also create differences between book and taxable income. These differences are temporary differences in some instances and permanent differences in others. For example, capital expenditures benefiting future tax years are not currently deductible. However, the tax law makes several exceptions to this requirement to promote economic and social objectives. Chapter 11 discusses a special provision that allows a business to expense $17,500 of the cost of new equipment in the year it is purchased. For a small business, these expenditures could be a significant drain on working capital. Allowing an immediate tax deduction for the expenditure takes into account two concepts: The immediate tax reduction recognizes that an investment in capital expenditures may reduce the taxpayer's wherewithal to pay, and the election to expense assets adds administrative convenience by eliminating the need to make annual depreciation calculations and keep detailed records for small investments in business assets.

Other temporary differences are caused by the tax law calculation of depreciation. For example, current tax depreciation rules ignore an asset's salvage value and compute depreciation over a predefined statutory life instead of the asset's useful life. These tax rules have the effect of allowing deductions for tax purposes before they are allowed for book income. Because the capital recovery concept limits the total depreciation deduction to the investment in the asset for both book and tax purposes, the difference is in the timing of deductions.

The tax laws also create permanent differences between book and taxable income. Provisions that disallow 50 percent of the cost of business meals and entertainment, limit the deduction of business gifts to $25 per donee, deny a deduction for excessive compensation paid to employees, and the federal income tax expense are examples of expenses that do not reduce taxable income but are deducted for financial reporting. As a result, these expenses create permanent differences between book and taxable income. On the other hand, the tax law allows deductions that are not recognized as expenses for financial reporting.

As discussed in Chapter 1, the personal and dependency exemptions and the standard deduction are tax accounting constructs. These constructs make the tax rate structure more progressive and enhance administrative convenience, which makes the tax law easier to enforce. The use of exemptions and standard deductions is foreign to financial reporting. Further, the tax law allows a percentage depletion deduction for certain natural resources. Percentage depletion is a tax deduction based on a percentage of income from the mineral source. The deduction is allowed even if the taxpayer has fully recovered the capital invested in the asset. This deduction violates both the capital recovery concept and financial reporting's cost depletion rules. However, Congress, in its exercise of legislative grace, has decided that it is desirable to violate the concept to provide tax incentives to promote the economic objective of developing natural resources. In doing so, the tax law has again introduced permanent differences between book and taxable income.

▲ SUMMARY

Tax deductions are a matter of legislative grace. Therefore, expenses incurred in a trade or business or for the production of income that have a business purpose are allowed as deductions. Personal expenditures are not deductible unless they are specifically allowed itemized deductions. A conduit entity is not taxed. Rather, deductions flow through to each owner and are treated similarly to deductions incurred by an individual taxpayer. Mixed-use expenditures and expenses related to using mixed-use assets must be analyzed to determine the business deductions allowed for such expenditures.

An activity will generally be considered a trade or business if it is profit motivated and the taxpayer is regularly and continuously involved in the activity to earn a livelihood. A profit-motivated activity that does not satisfy the continuous and regular involvement or the livelihood requirement will usually be considered an income-producing activity. Trade or business expenses receive preferential treatment compared to expenses for the production of income in the individual income tax calculation. Trade or business expenses and losses, rent and royalty expenses, and capital losses (subject to the $3,000 annual limitation) of individuals are deducted for adjusted gross income. As a result, they are fully deductible unless the passive activity loss limitations apply. Expenses for the production of income are generally deductions from adjusted gross income (itemized deductions). Because they are treated as miscellaneous itemized deductions, expenses for the production of income will generally be subject to an income limitation.

To be deductible, a business expense must be ordinary, necessary, and reasonable in amount. A deductible expense may not be

- A personal living expense
- A capital expenditure
- An expenditure that frustrates a public policy
- Related to earning tax-exempt income
- An expenditure for another person's benefit

The year in which a deduction is taken is determined by the taxpayer's accounting method. A cash basis taxpayer may deduct expenses when paid. An accrual basis taxpayer may deduct expenses when the all-events test is met and economic performance has occurred. Both cash and accrual basis taxpayers generally must allocate prepaid expenses and capital expenditures to the accounting period benefiting from the use of the asset. Temporary and permanent differences between financial reporting income and taxable income arise from the tax law's emphasis on the accounting period concept and objectivity in measuring and reporting allowable deductions.

▲ KEY TERMS

active investor (p. 187)
active trader (p. 188)
all-events test (p. 205)
business expense (p. 180)
dominant motive (p. 186)
economic performance test
 (p. 206)
improvements (p. 198)
lobbying expense (p. 201)

mixed-use asset (p. 191)
mixed-use expenditure (p. 192)
necessary expense (p. 194)
one-year rule for prepaid
 expenses (p. 204)
ordinary expense (p. 193)
production-of-income expense
 (p. 188)

reasonable expense (p. 195)
repair-and-maintenance expense
 (p. 198)
replacement (p. 198)
securities dealer (p. 188)
start-up costs (p. 198)

▲ PRIMARY TAX LAW SOURCES

[1] Reg. Sec. 1.162-5—Allows the deduction of education expenses that maintain or improve skills required in the taxpayer's employment or that meet the express requirements of the taxpayer's employer or applicable laws in order to retain employment.

[2] Sec. 62—Defines *adjusted gross income* for individual taxpayers and specifies the deductions allowed as deductions for adjusted gross income.

[3] Sec. 63—Defines *taxable income*; allows individual taxpayers to deduct the greater of their allowable itemized deductions or the standard deduction. Standard deduction amounts are specified and are required to be adjusted annually for inflation.

[4] Sec. 211—Generally allows specific personal expenditures as itemized deductions of individuals.

[5] Reg. Sec. 1.212-1—Requires investment-related expenses of individuals to be deducted as miscellaneous itemized deductions, subject to the 2% of adjusted gross income reduction rule.

[6] Sec. 703(a)—Requires that the taxable income of a partnership be computed in a manner similar to an individual's. However, certain deductions are not allowed, and the items listed in Sec. 702(a)(1) through 702(a)(7) must be reported sepa-

rately. Likewise, Sec. 1363(b) requires that the taxable income of an S corporation be computed in a manner similar to an individual's. Also, certain deductions are not allowed [Sec. 703(a)], and the items listed in Sec. 1366(a) must be reported separately.

[7] Knetsch v. U.S., 348 F.2d 932 (Cl. Ct. 1965)—Disallowed deductions from an investment in which the sole anticipated gain was the tax savings from the investment.

[8] Comm. v. Groetzinger, 480 U.S. 23 (1987)—Provides the current criteria for determining what constitutes a trade or business.

[9] Hazard v. Comm., 7 T.C. 372 (1946)—Held that the rental of a single parcel of improved property constituted a trade or business.

[10] Curphrey v. Comm., 73 T.C. 766 (1980)—Held that the ownership and rental of real property does not automatically constitute a trade or business, that the ultimate determination is based on the facts and circumstances of each taxpayer, and that the scope of ownership and management activities is an important consideration.

[11] Comm. v. Lincoln Electric Co., 176 F.2d 815 (6th Cir. 1949)—Held that the reasonableness of a payment is an element to

consider in determining whether the payment is ordinary and necessary.

[12] Deputy v. DuPont, 308 U.S. 488 (1940)—Held that an ordinary expense is one that is normal, usual, or customary in the particular business of the taxpayer.

[13] Comm. v. Tellier, 383 U.S. 687 (1966)—Held that the term *ordinary* distinguishes those expenditures that are currently deductible from those that are capital in nature.

[14] Welch v. Helvering, 290 U.S. 111 (1933)—Defines what constitutes an ordinary and necessary expense.

[15] Sec. 262—Provides the general rule for the disallowance of deductions for personal expenditures by individuals.

[16] U.S. v. Gilmore, 372 U.S. 39 (1963)—Held that the origin of an expense determines its deductibility.

[17] Sec. 263—Provides the general rule that disallows current period deductions for capital expenditures.

[18] Reg. Sec. 1.162-4—Allows the deduction as an ordinary and necessary business expense of incidental repairs that do not add to the value of the property or that do not appreciably prolong the life of the property.

[19] Reg. Sec. 1.263(a)-1—Defines the characteristics of a capital expenditure.

[20] Sec. 195—Provides the rules for amortization of start-up costs of a new business.

[21] Rev. Rul. 72-254—States that the expenses related to a general search for a new business are not deductible.

[22] The Colorado Springs National Bank v. U.S., 505 F.2d 1185 (10th Cir. 1974)—Held that the deductibility of the costs of investigating a new business depends on whether the business being investigated is in the same or a similar line of business in which the taxpayer is already engaged.

[23] Sec. 248—Allows a corporation to amortize over 60 months the costs of organizing the corporation. For partnerships, similar rules are found in Sec. 709.

[24] Hoover Motor Express Co. Inc. v. U.S., 356 U.S. 38 (1958)—Held that payments contrary to public policy are not ordinary and necessary.

[25] Max Cohen v. Comm., 176 F.2d 394 (10th Cir. 1949)—Held that expenses related to an illegal business are deductible as ordinary and necessary business expenses.

[26] Sec. 280E—Specifically disallows the deduction of business expenses of drug dealers (cost of goods sold is not a business expense).

[27] Sec. 162(e)—Disallows the deduction for certain lobbying and political expenditures.

[28] Sec. 265—Disallows the deduction of expenditures related to the production of tax-exempt income.

[29] Reg. Sec. 1.162-1—Disallows deductions for expenses that are not related to a taxpayer's own trade or business or production-of-income activities.

[30] Sec. 446—Provides the general rules for methods of accounting, including what constitutes a permissible method.

[31] Rev. Rul. 73-39—States that an expense of a cash basis taxpayer is deductible in the year in which it is charged to a credit card, not the year in which the credit card payment is made.

[32] Martin J. Zaninovich v. Comm., 616 F.2d 429 (9th Cir. 1980)—Allowed the deduction of prepaid expenses by a cash basis taxpayer when the expense would expire before the end of the tax year following the year of the payment and the payment was required. This is the one-year rule for prepaid expenses by cash basis taxpayers.

[33] Sec. 461—Provides the general rules for determining the year in which a deduction may be taken, provides the criteria for the all-events and economic performance tests, disallows the current deduction of prepaid interest.

[34] Hughes Properties Inc. v. U.S., 106 S. Ct. 2092 (1986)—Held that a liability must be fixed and determinable in that the payee is known before an expense can be accrued.

[35] Reg. Sec. 1.461-4—Explains the economic performance test and the application of the exception for recurring items.

1. All allowable deductions of individual taxpayers are classified as either for adjusted gross income or from adjusted gross income. Why are deductions for adjusted gross income usually more advantageous than deductions from adjusted gross income?

2. Why does the computation of adjusted gross income apply only to individual taxpayers and not to other tax entities such as corporations?

3. What is the fundamental requirement that must be satisfied in order to deduct a business expense?

4. What are the two primary categories of business expense? Why is it necessary to classify business expenses in these two categories?

5. Why must a conduit entity report certain deductions separately?

6. What is the effect on a partner's individual tax return if a partnership does not report separately the partner's pro rata share of investment expenses and instead includes these expenses in determining the partnership's ordinary taxable income?

7. The rules for deducting business expenses assure that virtually all expenses related to a trade or business or a production-of-income activity are deductible at some time during the life of the activity. However, few personal expenditures are deductible. Why is there such a difference in treatment of the expenses?

8. Discuss how well the rules for deducting expenses implement the ability-to-pay concept.

9. How are mixed-use expenditures and expenses related to mixed-use assets treated for tax reporting?

10. What is a trade or business?

11. What is an activity for the production of income?

12. Why is it important to distinguish a trade or business activity from a production-of-income activity?

13. Sam owns a 30-unit apartment complex. How would you decide whether the apartment complex represents a trade or business or an investing activity for Sam? What difference would the classification make for tax reporting?

14. What requirements must be met in order to deduct a trade or business expense? an expense related to the production of income?

15. When are capital expenditures deductible?

16. How do you distinguish a currently deductible expenditure from a capital expenditure? Give examples of each type of expenditure.

17. Why are start-up costs related to the investigation of a business opportunity treated differently depending on the current trade or business of the taxpayer?

18. Explain the rationale for not allowing a deduction for political and lobbying expenditures.

19. Explain why the income tax concepts support a deduction for some expenses of an illegal business.

20. Why are expenses related to the production of tax-exempt income not deductible?

21. What is/are the criterion (criteria) for the deduction of an expense by a cash basis taxpayer?

22. What constitutes the payment of an expense by a cash basis taxpayer?

23. What are the criteria for the current deduction of a prepaid expense by a cash basis taxpayer?

24. What tests must be met in order for an accrual basis taxpayer to deduct an expense?

25. What is the general purpose of the economic performance test?

▲ PROBLEMS

26. Alexandra is a veterinarian who is an employee of Fast Vet Services. Susan is a self-employed veterinarian. During the current year, Alexandra and Susan have the same amounts of income and deductions. Why might a deductible expense paid by Susan have an effect on her taxable income different from the payment of the same expense by Alexandra?

27. Discuss how an individual would deduct each of the following expenditures. If more than one treatment is possible, discuss the circumstances under which each type of deduction would be obtained:
    a. Amos purchased 500 shares of Lietzke stock for $50 per share. Amos also paid $1,200 in commissions on the purchase. *Cap*
    b. Dandy owns an optical store. She paid $2,000 in medical insurance premiums on her employees and $1,400 on a medical policy covering her and her family.
    c. Oscar is a finance professor at State University. He purchased professional journals costing $400 that he uses to keep current on the latest developments in finance.
    d. Gerry is a nurse. He paid $350 for nursing uniforms.
    e. Edgar owns a rental property. His rental income for the year was $13,000, and his allowable expenses were $9,000.

28. Determine how each of the following expenses would be deducted for tax purposes. If the expense is not deductible, explain why not.
    a. Chander paid $500 in interest on a loan he used to purchase equipment he used in his retail business.
    b. Peter paid $500 in interest on a loan he used to purchase 1,000 shares of Pickled Pepper stock.
    c. Portia paid $500 in interest on a loan she used to purchase her personal automobile.
    d. Jordan's primary source of income is from his wholesale warehousing business. During the current year, he paid $8,000 in state income taxes.
    e. Alphonse is a professional golfer who likes to race cars in his spare time. He spent $60,000 on various expenses related to racing cars during the current year.
    f. Barry is an insurance agent. He bought a golf cart and had his insurance company logo put on the golf cart to attract customers while he played golf.

29. Andy, Azim, and Ashwin operate the Triple-A Steak House, a popular restaurant and bar. The three, who have been friends since childhood, are equal partners in the establishment. For the year, Triple-A reported the following:

Sales revenues	$800,000
Short-term capital gains	12,000
Short-term capital losses	(5,000)
Trade and business expenses	(480,000)
Investment expenses	(3,000)
Taxable income	$324,000

    How must the Triple-A Steak House report its results to each of the partners for tax purposes?

30. Louise receives a $15,000 annual fee for serving as trustee of her mother's trust. Being a trustee is a new experience for her. She estimates that it takes her 30 hours a week to stay abreast of the bookkeeping, correspondence, and trust management functions. The trust's assets are primarily stocks, bonds, money market funds, land rentals, and oil royalties. Because Louise is independently wealthy, she would not have consented to serve as trustee for anyone other than her mother. Louise said she is lucky she didn't have a regular job—she would be unable to keep up. She intends to continue serving as trustee as long as her mother lives. Is Louise engaged in the trade or business of being a trustee? Explain why or why not.

31. Jefferson is a director of First Bank. The bank pays him a $250 director's fee and reimburses him for travel expenses for each director's meeting he attends. The directors usually meet once a week. He has not missed a meeting during the last 10 years. In fact, he visits the bank twice a week just to visit with the officers and employees to

find out what is happening in the bank and community. Jefferson is a professor of finance at the university. Is Jefferson engaged in the trade or business of being a bank director? Explain why or why not.

32. Marilyn began performing as a professional entertainer when she was 4. She has performed with several well-known entertainers. During 1994, she performs a total of about 3 weeks. In 1995, she works full time for nearly the entire year at a clerical job. During 1995, she withdraws from the entertainers' union and does not have either a manager or agent. She auditions for several jobs and rehearsed with one group but cannot find work as an entertainer. She incurs expenses for theater and movie tickets, hair styling, makeup, wigs, costumes, and other expenses common to entertainers. Is Marilyn engaged in the trade or business of being a professional entertainer? Explain why or why not.

33. Max owns an office building that he rents for $750 a month. Under the terms of the lease, the tenant is responsible for paying all property taxes and costs related to the building's operation and maintenance. The only cost to Max in relation to the lease is an annual legal fee for renewing the lease. Is Max engaged in the trade or business of renting real estate? How would you classify his deduction for the attorney's fee?

34. Don was a senior vice president of a bank until its officials found he had embezzled more than $1,000,000. Don had set up fictitious checking accounts and deposited the funds into the accounts. He then created fictitious loans to himself. The embezzled money was used for personal purposes and to keep the fictitious loan payments current. Thus, he created fictitious loans to make payments on prior fictitious loans. Don worked hard to keep the loans current so he would not be detected. Because of a tax audit, he is seeking your advice. If his embezzlement activity is a trade or business, he claims he should be able to deduct as an ordinary and necessary expense the payments on the loans to keep his actions secret. What advice would you give Don concerning his business and deductions? Explain.

35. Angela owns a duplex. She rents out one unit and lives in the other unit. During the current year, she paid $8,000 in interest on the loan she used to buy the duplex, $1,200 in property taxes on the duplex, and $2,000 in dues to the duplex association that maintains the grounds and the swimming pool. How much of each expenditure can she deduct, and how would she deduct it?

36. In 1995, RayeAnn acquired a car for $12,000. She uses the car in her advertising business and for personal purposes. Her records indicate the car is used 65% for business and that her total annual operating expenses, including depreciation, were $2,900.
   a. How should RayeAnn treat the operating costs of the car for tax purposes?
   b. In 1998, RayeAnn sells the car for $6,000. Her business use for 1996 through 1998 remained at 65%, and she properly deducted $4,680 in depreciation. What is her taxable gain or loss from the sale of the car?

37. Harry and Sydney each inherited 50% of the stock in their father's corporation when he died. Harry had been working for their father and wanted to retain control of the business. Sydney was not really interested in the family business and wanted to sell her stock to outsiders. In order to retain control of the corporation, Harry made Sydney a vice president of the corporation with an annual salary of $200,000. The only requirements of the position were that Sydney not sell her stock and that she allow Harry to run the business. Can the corporation deduct the $200,000 salary it pays to Sydney?

38. Discuss whether the following expenditures meet the ordinary, necessary, and reasonable requirements:

  a. Sadie owns 5 shares of Megaconglomerate stock. She spent $4,000 to attend the annual shareholders' meeting.

  b. Sam runs a successful medical practice. Because he has a substantial investment portfolio, he spent $3,000 to attend a seminar on investing strategies.

  c. Alana is a self-employed tax attorney. She spent $5,000 to attend the American Institute of Certified Public Accountants' annual conference on income tax developments.

  d. Kevin owns a large ranching operation. Kevin is deeply religious and feels it is important that his employees have access to religious counseling. He hired an ordained minister to live on the ranch and be available to counsel his employees on any religious problems they might have.

39. Big Star Auto regularly advertises on local television. The owner of Big Star pays her 6-year-old grandson $250 for each television commercial in which he appears for Big Star. During the current year, the grandson appeared in 100 commercials. Big Star wants to deduct the full $25,000 as a business expense. The grandson will report the $25,000 as income. Can Big Star Auto deduct the advertising fee paid to the owner's grandson? Explain.

40. Tom made the following business expenditures:

  a. Blacktopped a gravel parking lot—$2,500.

  b. Air compressor on business's central air-conditioning system failed and had to be replaced—$850.

  c. Installed a fire and security alarm system in the office building—$3,000.

  d. Painted the interior and exterior of the office and factory building—$8,500.

  e. Put new tires on 3 delivery trucks—$1,900.

What is the proper tax treatment for Tom's expenditures?

41. Leonard owns an apartment complex. During the current year, he paid $14,000 to have all the apartments painted and recarpeted. Gena purchased an apartment complex during the current year. Before she could rent out the apartments, she paid $14,000 to have the apartments painted and recarpeted. Discuss the tax treatment of the $14,000 expenditures by Leonard and Gena.

42. In auditing the Philbin Corporation's repair expense account, Sara found a $28,000 entry. Because the amount was so large, she obtained the supporting documentation. The invoice listed the Fradin Roofing Co. as providing the service. The description of the work performed by the company was not attached to the invoice. However, a notation on the check listed "office roof." What factors does Sara need to consider in determining whether the Philbin Corporation can deduct the expense?

43. Elmo was laid off from his job during the current year. He decided to start his own business and spent $5,000 investigating various types of businesses and their potential locations. In August, he opened up a bicycle repair shop. Discuss the proper treatment of the $5,000 he spent before starting the business.

What would be the proper treatment of the expenses for Elmo's investigation if he decided not to open a new business?

44. Two brothers spent $4,500 on travel, surveys, and financial forecasts to investigate the possibility of opening a bagel shop in the city. Because their suburban bagel shop has been so successful, the brothers would like to expand their operations. What is the proper treatment of their expenditures if

  a. They open a bagel shop in the city?

  b. They decide not to open a bagel shop in the city?

  c. Answer a and b assuming they are investigating opening a computer store in the city and they operate a bagel shop in the suburbs.

45. What is the proper tax treatment for each of the following expenses?
    a. All apartment house construction in Sandy Beach must comply with local and state building codes. To ensure that these codes are observed, Rex, a city building inspector, regularly visits construction sites. Shoddy Construction deposited $20,000 in a fund to provide a scholarship for Rex's son to attend college. The payment was in appreciation for Rex's help in getting around a building code violation.
    b. Rachel operates a pharmacy. She pays a 10% commission on all Medicare and Medicaid business and a 5% commission on all other business sent her way by the Last Stop Nursing Home.
    c. Kelly is a registered nurse. She receives a $1,750 per month salary working for a local clinic. Because Kelly was five minutes late to work two days in a row, the clinic fined her $25. Thus, her salary for the current month is $1,725.

46. Are the following payments deductible?
    a. A contribution to a fund to finance Honest Abe's campaign for mayor.
    b. A contribution to the Hardcore Gamblers' Association to fund efforts to persuade the public to vote in favor of parimutuel betting on licensed turtle races.
    c. Joyce, who is in the import-export business, sends an employee to Washington, D.C., to monitor current legislation. The expenses for the one-week trip are $1,500.
    d. Assume the same facts as in part c, except that the expenses total $2,200.
    e. Ruth, a small business owner, incurred $1,800 in travel, lodging, and meal expenses to testify in Washington, D.C., on the effect on small business of health-care reform.

47. Marcus is the vice president of human resources for Griffin Industries. He spent one week testifying before Congress about the effect of health-care legislation on small business. The cost of his trip was $2,750. Can Griffin Industries deduct the cost of Marcus's trip?

48. For the current year, Rufus paid an adviser $1,500 to help him manage his investments. The adviser's fee is not directly related to any particular investment owned by Rufus. Rufus owns $50,000-worth of City of Chicago bonds that pay him $4,000 in interest and $25,000-worth of Ford Motor Co. bonds that pay him $2,500 in interest each year. What is the proper tax treatment for the investment advice?

49. Tracy and Brenda are equal partners in Crescent Home Furniture, which is organized as an S corporation. For the year, the company reported sales revenue of $205,000 and business expenses of $135,000. Crescent also earned $8,000 in taxable interest and dividend income and $2,500 in tax-exempt interest on its investments. The investment portfolio consists of $32,000 in tax-exempt securities and $48,000 in taxable securities. Not included in the business expenses is a $1,500 fee Crescent paid for investment advice. How must Crescent Home Furniture report its results to Tracy and Brenda for tax purposes?

50. Determine the current tax deduction allowed in each of the following situations:
    a. Doug, John's son, bought a new car that is titled in Doug's name. John paid for Doug's auto license tag. The tag cost $280: $18 for registration plus $262 in property taxes based on the value of the auto. Doug qualifies as John's dependent for tax purposes. Doug uses the auto for personal transportation.
    b. Elvis owns Ace Auto Repair. Elvis's head mechanic was arrested for drunken driving. Because Elvis needed the mechanic back at work as soon as possible, Elvis paid the $500 bail to get the mechanic out of jail. To keep him out of jail, he paid $450 in attorney's fees and the $500 fine the court imposed on the mechanic.

51. Chin borrowed $40,000 on a 2-year loan from State Bank to purchase business equipment. Under the terms of the loan, State Bank deducted the $8,000 in interest on the loan and gave Chin the $32,000 net proceeds. Chin will repay State Bank $40,000 in 2 years. When can Chin deduct the $8,000 in interest if he is a cash basis taxpayer? Would your answer be different if Chin were an accrual basis taxpayer?

52. Pope Corporation pays $50,000 per year for hurricane insurance. Reorder Corporation has determined that it suffers only $150,000 in hurricane damage every 5 years. Reorder self-insures for hurricanes by depositing $30,000 each year in a hurricane damage fund. Discuss the deductibility of the hurricane insurance payments by Pope and Reorder.

53. Appliance Sales Corporation sells all types of appliances. In addition, it offers purchasers of its appliances the option of purchasing repair contracts. During the current year, Appliance estimates that repairs totaling $13,000 will be made under the contracts sold during the current year. Actual repair costs were $8,000 related to last year's contracts and $600 on contracts sold during the contract year. How much repair cost can Appliance deduct during the current year?

54. Gonzo Co. is an accrual basis taxpayer. Gonzo provides medical insurance for its employees through a self-insured reimbursement plan. Gonzo pays $100 per month per employee into the plan fund. The fund is then used to reimburse employees' medical expenses. During the current year, Gonzo paid $12,000 into the fund and paid medical reimbursement claims totaling $10,600. How much can Gonzo deduct for the provision of employee medical coverage? Discuss.

55. Damon's Lawn and Garden Supply, an accrual basis taxpayer, is the exclusive dealer for Tru-Cut lawn mowers. In 1995, Damon's enters into an agreement by which it will pay the Dash Corporation, the manufacturer of Tru-Cut, an additional $15 per lawn mower. In exchange, the Dash Corporation agrees to provide advertising and promotion to Damon's for a 2-year period. Damon's purchased and paid for 200 lawn mowers in 1995 and 350 lawn mowers in 1996. The Dash Corporation paid $3,750 for advertising and promotion in 1995 and $4,500 in 1996. How much of the amount paid to the Dash Corporation for advertising and promotion can Damon's deduct in 1995? in 1996?

56. Joy incurred the following expenses in her business. When can she deduct the expenses if she uses the accrual method of accounting? the cash method?
    a. Joy rents an office building for $1,000 a month. Because of a cash-flow problem, she is unable to pay the rent for November and December 1995. On January 5, 1996, Joy pays the $3,000 rent due for November, December, and January.
    b. Joy borrows $100,000 on a 1-year note on October 1, 1995. To get the loan, she has to prepay $12,000 in interest.
    c. Joy owes employees accrued wages totaling $40,000 as of December 31, 1995. The accrued wages are paid in the regular payroll on January 5, 1996.
    d. Joy purchases $1,000-worth of supplies from a local vender. The supplies are delivered on January 29, 1995. The supplies are fully used up on December 30, 1995. Because of unusual circumstances, a bill for the supplies arrives from the vendor on January 10, 1996, and is promptly paid.
    e. While at a trade convention, Joy purchases some pens and paperweights to send out as gifts to her clients. She charges the $800 cost to her credit card in December 1995. She pays the credit card bill in January 1996.

57. The Parr Corporation incurred the following expenses. When can it deduct the expenses if it uses the accrual method of accounting? the cash method?
    a. The Parr Corporation mailed a check for $10,000 to the United Way on December 26, 1995. The company's canceled check shows that the United Way did not deposit the check until January 16, 1996.
    b. For 1995, the Parr Corporation estimates its warranty expense to be 2% of sales. The company's sales for 1995 were $2,400,000. The actual warranty costs paid in 1995 were $53,000.
    c. On August 1, 1995, the Parr Corporation borrows $400,000 on a 1-year note. Because the company is experiencing a cash-flow problem, the bank agrees to allow Parr to pay the interest when the note matures. In exchange, the interest rate on the note is 10%—3% above the current market rate.

    d. The Parr Corporation advertises on radio and in the newspaper. During the year, the company was billed $25,000 for advertising. The beginning balance in the advertising payable account on January 1, 1995, was $4,000 and the ending balance on December 31, 1995, was $2,500.

    e. On August 1, 1995, the Parr Corporation pays $3,000 for a 1-year fire insurance policy for the period August 1, 1995, through July 31, 1996. Parr's insurance company requires the 1-year prepayment, which the company makes every year.

58. During the year, the Li Real Estate Co. sold 225 homes, a record number. In appreciation of this accomplishment, the company gave each seller a wall clock that had a retail value of $95. What is the company's deduction for financial accounting purposes? for tax purposes?

59. Carol is a single mother who owns a wholesale auto parts distributorship. The business is organized as a sole proprietorship. Her business has advanced, and she can no longer devote the time necessary to do her own tax return. Because she always has prepared her own return, Carol is familiar with most tax rules applicable to her business and personal affairs. However, she has come to you for advice with respect to a number of items she paid during the current year. You are to determine whether she can take a deduction for the expenditures in the current year.

▲ COMPREHENSIVE
PROBLEM

    a. Carol purchased a small building on March 2 to use as a warehouse for her auto parts inventory. To purchase the building, she borrowed $100,000 on a 30-year loan and paid $20,000 in additional cash. Carol also incurred $1,600 in legal and other fees to purchase the building. The bank charged her $3,000 in points (prepaid interest) to obtain the loan. After acquiring the building, Carol spent an additional $22,000 to renovate it for use as a warehouse. The $22,000 included $8,000 for painting.

    b. Carol had her office building painted at a cost of $5,000 and paid $3,000 to have it landscaped. Carol paid for the building renovation in part a and the office building work by borrowing $40,000 on April 1 at 6% interest (see part f for details of the interest payments).

    c. On May 1, Carol prepaid a 1-year fire insurance policy on her 2 buildings. The policy cost $2,400, and the insurer required the prepayment. On July 1, Carol prepaid a $7,200, 2-year maintenance contract on the buildings.

    d. Carol started a self-insured medical reimbursement plan for her employees this year. Based on actuarial assumptions, she deposited $9,000 in a fund to pay employees' medical expenses. Actual payments from the fund totaled $8,200.

    e. Carol purchased a new automobile costing $32,000. She can document that her business use of the automobile came to 75% and that her out-of-pocket operating costs totaled $4,000.

    f. Carol paid the following interest on business-related loans:

Warehouse	$9,800
Office building	4,200
Renovation loan	1,800

    The renovation loan was for $40,000. Because she spent only $30,000 renovating the new building and painting and landscaping the old building, she used the additional $10,000 to purchase City of New Orleans bonds with a yield of 4%.

    g. Carol became active in politics and contributed $1,000 to the presidential campaign of an independent candidate. Carol made the contribution because she believed that, if elected, the candidate would institute policies beneficial to her business. The candidate lost the election and immediately started a grassroots lobbying organization. The purpose of the organization is to keep track of elected officials' campaign promises and report to the public when they vote contrary to their stated campaign promises. Carol paid $500 in dues to join the lobbying organization.

h. Carol's oldest son began college during the current year. She paid her son's tuition and living expenses, a total of $16,000, out of the company's checking account. During the summer, her son worked for the business and Carol paid him $3,300, the same amount she paid other college students working during the summer. Because she consults her son from time to time on the operation of the business, she thinks that at least some of the $16,000 should be deductible.

i. Carol has always itemized her deductions. This year, her mother and father retired and could no longer afford the mortgage interest and property taxes on their home. Rather than have them sell the house, Carol made the payments for them. They received a statement from their bank indicating that a total of $6,200 in mortgage interest and taxes were paid in the current year. Carol knows that mortgage interest and property taxes are deductible as itemized deductions and would like to add them to her personal interest and property tax payments.

j. Because of the success of her business, Carol has received many offers to invest in various business ventures. One offer was to establish a chain of nursing homes in Florida. Carol spent two weeks in Florida evaluating the prospects of the proposed venture and incurred costs of $3,500. After careful consideration, she decided the venture was too risky and decided not to expand into the health-care business.

▲ DISCUSSION CASE 5–1

JR came by the other day to talk about one of his acquaintances. It seems the fellow is engaged in criminal activities. Being good at giving advice, JR told the fellow to be sure to report all his income from his criminal activities on his tax return to keep the IRS off his back. If he fails to file properly, he risks being sent to prison for tax evasion. JR also told his friend that he could not deduct any expenses, because his activities violate both state and federal laws. JR knew a lot about the fellow's activities and how much money the guy was making. The friend had even bought a $50,000 car just like JR's. Was JR's advice good? Why? Why not?

▲ DISCUSSION CASE 5–2

Malloy Industries manufactures air conditioners. The machines used to manufacture the air conditioners usually are insulated with asbestos. Because of health risks associated with asbestos, the Occupational Safety and Health Administration (OSHA) lowered the permissible level of asbestos fibers in the air. In addition, employers who have asbestos-insulated buildings or machines are required to monitor the amount of asbestos fibers in the air to ensure that they do not exceed the permissible level. Malloy Industries, a leader in providing its employees with a safe and healthy work environment, decided to remove the asbestos insulation from its 45 machines and replace it with another insulation material. The company determined that it would be less expensive to remove the asbestos insulation from its machines than to monitor asbestos levels on a daily basis. The company has found that the replacement material is 10% less efficient than the asbestos insulation. Should Malloy Industries capitalize or deduct the expense of replacing the asbestos insulation?

Rosita's grandmother dies in November 1994 and leaves her an investment portfolio worth $180,000. In January 1995, when Rosita receives ownership of the investments, the portfolio consists of $112,000 in tax-exempt securities and $68,000 in taxable securities. Her grandmother's accountant estimated that the tax-exempt securities would earn $8,175 in interest and the taxable securities would pay $7,140 in dividends in 1995. The management expenses were estimated at $2,100. Rosita is single, has no other investments, and earns $42,000 as an engineer. She expects that her itemized deductions, not including the management expenses, will include state income taxes of $2,800, real estate taxes of $1,600, and home mortgage interest of $4,000.

> **a.** What is Rosita's projected taxable income for 1995?
>
> **b.** Assume that Rosita switches $40,000 from tax-exempt securities to taxable securities and the rate of return on both portfolios remains the same. All the other information would remain unchanged, except that state income taxes would increase by $500. What is the effect on her taxable income of changing her investment strategy?
>
> **c.** Assume that Rosita switches $40,000 from taxable securities to tax-exempt securities and the rate of return on both portfolios remains the same. All the other information would remain unchanged, except that state income taxes would decrease by $500. What is the effect on her taxable income of changing her investment strategy?

▲ **TAX PLANNING CASE 5–3**

Dan owns a successful sports bar in downtown Providence. The state is considering legislation that would restrict the sale of alcohol in restaurants and bars on Saturdays and Sundays until after 7 P.M. The association of Providence restaurant owners is thinking about hiring a lobbyist to fight the legislation. The lobbyist has told the association that the lobbying effort would cost each owner $6,000. Dan's accountant has informed him that under the new tax law, his $6,000 contribution would not be deductible for tax purposes. Dan has told his 30 employees, most of whom are students at a local college, that if the legislation passes, he will have to lay off employees. In addition, he told them that most local restaurant owners cannot afford to pay a lobbyist $6,000 to fight the legislation, because it is not tax deductible. Ann, one of Dan's employees and an accounting major, suggests that Dan pay each employee an extra $200 dollars in salary (30 × $200 = $6,000) and that they forward the payments to the lobbyist. That way, Ann reasons, the cost will be deductible as salary expense. Dan tells his accountant about Ann's idea, and his accountant thinks it is great. In fact, he is so impressed with the idea that he has offered Ann a job when she graduates next spring. Do you think Ann's idea is a legal way to deduct the lobbying expenses? What ethical standards has Dan's accountant violated? (Refer to the Statements on Responsibilities in Tax Practice.)

▲ **ETHICS DISCUSSION CASE 5–4**

Business Expenses

▲ CHAPTER LEARNING OBJECTIVES

■ Discuss the tax treatment of those business expenses that have the potential for significant abuse because of the personal nature of the expenditures: meals and entertainment, automobile expenses, travel expenses, and business gifts.

■ Consider the tax treatment of other business expenses that have specific deduction requirements: education expenses, employee compensation, related party accrued expenses, and bad debts.

■ Discuss the criteria for deducting other business expenses and indicate when such expenses may have to be capitalized rather than deducted as a current period expense: insurance, taxes, rent, and legal fees.

■ Explain the potential for abuse and the consequent tax treatment of three mixed-use expenditure situations: hobby expenses, vacation home expenses, and home office expenses.

▲ CONCEPT REVIEW ▲

Ability to pay   A tax should be based on the amount that the taxpayer can afford to pay, relative to other taxpayers.

Accounting method   A taxpayer must adopt an accounting method that clearly reflects income.

Administrative convenience   Those items for which the cost of compliance would exceed the revenue generated are not taxed.

Annual accounting period   All entities report the results of their transactions on an annual basis (the tax year). Each tax year stands on its own, apart from other tax years.

Arm's-length transaction   A transaction in which all parties to the transaction have bargained in good faith and for their individual benefit, not for the benefit of the transaction group.

Assignment of income   The tax entity that owns the income produced is responsible for the tax on the income, regardless of which entity actually receives the income.

Basis   This is the amount of unrecovered investment in an asset. As amounts are expended and/or recovered relative to an asset over time, the basis is adjusted in consideration of such changes. The **adjusted basis** of an asset is the original basis, plus or minus the changes in the amount of unrecovered investment.

Business purpose   To be deductible, an expenditure or a loss must have a business or other economic purpose that exceeds any tax avoidance motive. The primary motive for the transaction must be to make a profit.

Capital recovery   No income is realized until the taxpayer receives more than the amount invested to produce the income. The amount invested in an asset represents the maximum amount recoverable.

Entity   All items of income, deduction, and so on are traced to the tax unit responsible for the item.

Legislative grace   Any tax relief provided is the result of a specific act of Congress that must be strictly applied and interpreted. All income received is taxable unless a specific provision can be found in the tax law that excludes the income from taxation. Deductions must be approached with the philosophy that nothing is deductible unless a provision in the tax law allows the deduction.

Related party   Family members and corporations that are owned by family members are considered related parties, as are certain other relationships between entities in which the power to control the substance of a transaction is evidenced through majority ownership.

Substance-over-form doctrine   Transactions are to be taxed according to their true intention rather than some form that may have been contrived.

Tax benefit rule   Any deduction taken in a prior year that is recovered in a subsequent year is income in the year of recovery, to the extent that a tax benefit was received from the deduction.

▲ INTRODUCTION

To deduct a business expense, the expenditure must have a bonafide business purpose. This means that you initially must classify individuals' expenses as either profit motivated or personally motivated. The profit-motivated expenses are then further classified as related to either a trade or business or to the production of income. This further classification is necessary, because trade or business expenses are deducted for adjusted gross income, whereas production-of-income expenses (i.e., investment expenses) are deducted from adjusted gross income for individual taxpayers. An individual's production-of-income expenses (other than rental and royalty expenses, which are deducted for adjusted gross income) generally are treated as miscellaneous itemized deductions. Itemized deductions are limited according to an individual's adjusted gross income and are discussed in Chapter 8. Because corporations are always considered to be in a trade or business and have no personal transactions, they do not compute adjusted gross income and the classification difference is not important.

This chapter introduces and explains specific business and mixed-use expenses. Many other expenses may be deducted on a tax return. Because of space limitations, it is necessary to confine the discussion here to expenses that are common to many different types of businesses. However, the concepts discussed in Chapter 2 provide a foundation for identifying most other deductible expenses.

In addition to determining that an expense has a business purpose and is ordinary, necessary, and reasonable in amount, you may want to review the other tests discussed in Chapter 5 as you continue to read this chapter. One is that a deductible expense may not be a personal living expense. However, taxpayers often incur expenses for both profit and personal reasons. These expenses are called *mixed-use expenses*. Hobby, vacation home, and home office expenses are mixed-use expenses, which are discussed here, along with the limitations on their deduction.

▲ BUSINESS EXPENSES

The discussion that follows focuses on deductible business expenses. Most common expenditures made in a trade or business, such as utility payments, wage payments, supplies, and rental payments, are not subject to any specific rules. However, certain types of expenses have both a business and a potential personal aspect to them. This can lead to abuse by taxpayers who attempt to convert nondeductible personal expenditures into deductible business expenses. The tax law contains specific rules to follow in those areas that have the most potential for abuse. The first category of deductions to be considered is entertainment, auto, travel, gift, and education expenses. As you read about these expenses, note the special requirements for the deduction, the types of expenses that qualify, the 50-percent limitation, and the records that are required. In the discussion of employee compensation, notice the adverse effects of excessive salary payments.

In addition, various types of deductions have special rules. The tax law makes a distinction between business and nonbusiness bad debts. As a result, the treatments of business and nonbusiness bad debts are significantly different for tax purposes. The related party rules also give rise to a potential tax problem. The discussion of other business expenses points out several instances in which an expenditure either is not deductible or must be treated as a capital expenditure.

Entertainment, Auto, Travel, Gift, and Education Expenses

Entertainment, auto, travel, gift, and education expenses are particularly troublesome for many taxpayers. Although the expenses are incurred for a business purpose, they often involve an element of personal benefit or enjoyment. As a result, these deductions are subject to significant restrictions and limitations. To be deductible, the expense must satisfy specific requirements and be properly documented. Even if the expense qualifies and the taxpayer keeps good records, only the business portion of the expense is allowed as a deduction. Because these deductions are a matter of legislative grace and the taxpayer receives personal benefit from the expense, the IRS closely monitors compliance with the requirements. The tax law in this area is sometimes very detailed and quite complex. The intent of the following discussion is to familiarize you with the basic requirements for deducting these expenses.

Meals and Entertainment.   A taxpayer may deduct 50 percent of the costs of meals and entertainment incurred for a business purpose.[1] The meal or entertainment expense must be an ordinary and necessary expense of the business and not be lavish or extravagant under the circumstances. In addition, to be deductible,

meal and entertainment expenses must be either directly related to or associated with the active conduct of an activity for which the taxpayer has a business purpose.

A meal or entertainment expense is **directly related** to the active conduct of the taxpayer's business if it meets all four of the following conditions:

- There is more than a general expectation of deriving income or a business benefit from the meal or entertainment.
- A bonafide business activity takes place during the meal or entertainment.
- The principal reason for providing the meal or entertainment is to conduct business.
- The expenses are related to the taxpayer and people involved in the business activity.[2]

▲ **EXAMPLE 1**   George is a funeral director in Saline City. While attending a convention of funeral directors in Orlando, he rented a hospitality room for one evening and provided snacks and beverages. Use of the hospitality room gave him the opportunity to meet with other funeral directors and major suppliers of funeral products to discuss business. Can George deduct the cost of the hospitality room and the snacks and beverages as a business expense?

Discussion: The entertainment clearly took place in a business setting and was for a direct business purpose. George can deduct 50% of his entertainment expense related to the hospitality room.

▲ **EXAMPLE 2**   Claudia opened a new medical clinic. To publicize the clinic, she held a grand opening and invited community leaders and businesspeople to attend. At the open house, she served food and beverages. Can Claudia deduct the cost of the grand opening as a business expense?

Discussion: There is a clear business purpose for the entertainment expense. Because there was no meaningful personal or social relationship between Claudia and the people she entertained, 50% of the expense is allowed as a deduction.

If a meal or entertainment expense is not deductible under the "directly related" test, the expense may be allowed as a deduction under the "associated with" test. A meal or entertainment expense is **associated with** the active conduct of the taxpayer's business if it meets both of the following conditions:

- There is a clear business purpose for the meal or entertainment.
- The meal or entertainment directly precedes or follows a substantial and bonafide business discussion.

▲ **EXAMPLE 3**   Jane owns and operates a business that makes bridal gowns and accessories. She invited 20 of her best customers to her plant for a business meeting. The business meeting and a tour of her plant took most of the day. She had lunch for her customers catered at the plant so she could show them her new products. To conclude the day, Jane took her husband, customers, and their spouses to dinner. Is the cost of the dinner a deductible associated with entertainment expense?

Discussion: The cost of the lunches for her customers qualifies as an expense directly related to doing business. The amount spent for the dinner qualifies as an expense "associated with" business, because the dinner directly followed the substantial business discussion. The cost of the entertainment of the spouses also qualifies, because there is a clear business purpose for their presence. If they were not there, the customer might not be either. It is appropriate for Jane's husband to attend, because the customers had their spouses present. Thus, Jane can deduct 50% of the meal and entertainment expense.

The cost of a meal includes the amount spent for food, beverage, tax, and tips. Entertainment expenses include amounts spent at night clubs, theater, and sporting events. The deduction for tickets is limited to the face value of the ticket. The fee for leasing a luxury skybox at more than one sporting event is not deductible. However, the tickets for the skybox are deductible—but only an amount equal to the highest-priced nonluxury box seat for the event is deductible.

▲ **EXAMPLE 4**   Randall wanted to entertain a client after a valid business meeting by taking her to a basketball game. However, the game was sold out. He was able to locate an associate who would sell him tickets for $50 each. The face amount printed on the ticket was $15. How much of the cost can Randall deduct?

Discussion: Randall can deduct the $15 face amount of each ticket. The $35 ($50 − $15) excess purchase price is not deductible. Randall's limited deduction is $15 (2 × $15 × 50%).

▲ **EXAMPLE 5**   Marisa is a partner in an advertising firm. The firm leases an 8-seat skybox at a baseball stadium for $162,000 a season ($2,000 per game). The price includes 8 tickets to each game. After a presentation to a potential client, Marisa and 2 other partners of the firm entertained 5 representatives of the prospective client at the firm's skybox. The fair market value of the most expensive nonluxury seat at the stadium is $40. The company spent $150 on food and drinks. How much of the entertainment costs can the firm deduct?

Discussion: The cost of entertaining is deductible, because it followed a business meeting. Although no portion of the skybox fee is deductible, the firm can deduct $235 as entertainment expense. The firm can deduct $75 ($150 × 50%) for food and drinks and $160 for the tickets ([8 × $40 = $320] × 50%). NOTE: If the firm had entertained only 6 individuals (and used 6 tickets), it would be allowed to deduct the cost of all 8 tickets.

Before 1994, social, athletic, sporting, or country club dues qualified for a deduction as an entertainment expense if the facility was used more than 50 percent of the time for a business purpose. However, the Omnibus Budget Reconciliation Act of 1993 eliminated the deduction for membership dues to business, social, athletic, or luncheon clubs paid after December 31, 1993.[3] Although the dues at these facilities are not deductible, the cost of meals, assuming there is a valid business purpose, remains deductible, subject to the 50-percent limitation.

▲ **EXAMPLE 6**   Kapil is a member of the Chariho Athletic Club. He estimates that he spends 75% of his time at the club entertaining clients. For the year, he paid dues of $1,800 and incurred food and beverage charges of $2,200. Kapil can document that $1,550 of the charges were for entertaining clients and followed a bonafide business discussion. The remaining $650 in charges are personal. What amount of the expenses at the Chariho Athletic Club can Kapil deduct as an entertainment expense?

Discussion: Although 75% of Kapil's time is spent entertaining clients, no portion of the dues is deductible. Kapil can deduct $775 ($1,550 × 50%) of the food and beverage charges. The $650 in personal charges is not deductible.

As a general rule, the meal and entertainment expenses of people whose presence is necessary to conduct the business activity are deductible. The expenses of other people can be deducted if their presence serves a clear business purpose. If entertainment expenses are incurred for business and personal reasons, only the expenses that have a business purpose are deductible. Thus, expenses of social guests are nondeductible personal expenses. In addition, the tax law requires the taxpayer or an employee of the taxpayer to be present when meals and beverages are served in order for the cost to be deductible.

▲ **EXAMPLE 7**   Tom gave a party for his clients. Tom, 6 clients, and 3 social guests were present. The party cost Tom $1,000 for food, beverages, and entertainment. How much of the $1,000 can Tom deduct as a business expense?

Discussion: Because Tom was present when the food and beverages were served, the business portion of the cost is a qualified expense. The expense for Tom and his 6 clients may be deducted because the expenditure had a business purpose. The expense related to the social guests is personal and not deductible. Tom's allowable entertainment costs are $700 [(7 ÷ 10) × $1,000]. Tom's deduction is limited to $350 ($700 × 50%).

As a further limitation, reciprocal entertaining by business associates is not permitted. Reciprocal entertaining occurs when people in a group take turns entertaining each other to attempt to make the expense tax deductible. That entertainment is treated according to its social substance rather than its business form (substance-over-form doctrine).

▲ **EXAMPLE 8**   Vanessa is an audit partner in a public accounting firm. Once a month, Vanessa has dinner with two of her college roommates who are audit partners in other firms. The three alternate picking up the check. Although the conversation often begins with personal issues, inevitably the majority of the discussion is business. Joan has saved the receipts, totaling $275, from the dinners. Do the dinners qualify as valid entertainment expenses?

Discussion: The dinners fail both the directly related test (no expectation of future profits) and the associated with test (no valid business purpose). The predominant motive for the dinner is personal. Joan can deduct no portion of the $275 as entertainment expense. In essence, the three are engaging in reciprocal entertaining.

Several exceptions to the 50-percent limitation allow a business to deduct the full cost of meals and entertainment. These exceptions also are exempt from the directly related and associated with tests for the deductibility of meals and entertainment. The more common situations in which a business expense for meals and entertainment is fully deductible are

- Expenses treated as compensation to an employee and subject to income tax withholding. This arises when the employer has a nonaccountable plan for reimbursing employees' expenses. This type of plan is discussed in Chapter 8.

- Expenses incurred while performing services for another person and that other person reimburses the expenses when the taxpayer specifically accounts for them. Note that the person who reimburses the expense is subject to the 50-percent limit.

- Recreational, social, or similar expenses primarily for the benefit of employees. The value of the entertainment is not income to employees under the de minimis fringe-benefit rule discussed in Chapter 4.

- Expenses for goods, services, and facilities that are taxable income to a recipient who is not an employee because the meal or entertainment expense represents a payment of compensation for services or a prize or an award.

- Expenses for goods, services, and facilities made available to the general public.

▲ **EXAMPLE 9**   Rubin Corporation provides the food, beverages, and entertainment for a Fourth of July picnic for its employees and their families. This is an annual event that Rubin believes benefits its employees and the company. This year, the picnic cost $5,000. How much of the $5,000 in meals and entertainment cost can Rubin deduct?

Discussion: Rubin Corporation can deduct the full $5,000, because the expense was for the recreational and social benefit of its employees. The expense is not subject to the 50% limitation. The value of the party is excluded from the employees' income under the de minimis fringe-benefit rule discussed in Chapter 4.

Auto Expenses.   A taxpayer can choose one of two methods for computing a deduction for using an auto for business purposes. These methods are the standard mileage rate method and the actual cost method. Although the standard mileage rate method is the easier way to calculate the **auto expense,** it often results in a smaller deduction. On the other hand, the actual cost method may yield a larger deduction, but it requires more record keeping. The cost of commuting from home to work and back is considered a personal expense. Neither the use of a car phone to contact customers while driving to and from work nor putting advertising on the car makes commuting deductible. As Figure 6–1 illustrates, a taxpayer's mileage or cost of travel is considered business related if the travel is

- Out of town
- From the taxpayer's home to his or her temporary workplace
- From the taxpayer's regular workplace to a temporary workplace
- From the taxpayer's regular workplace (or temporary workplace) to a second job[4]

However, the mileage between the taxpayer's second job and home is considered personal. On days when a taxpayer does not work at his or her regular job, the travel to and from the second job is considered commuting.

▲ **Figure 6–1**

BUSINESS-RELATED
TRAVEL

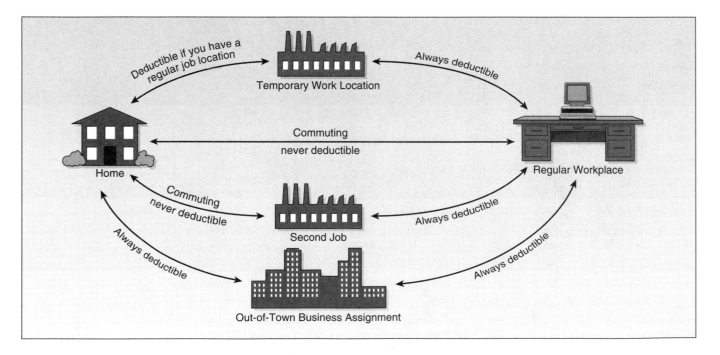

▲ **EXAMPLE 10**   On a typical day Carla drives 10 miles round trip between home and her office. In addition, she drives 75 miles to meet customers and to take care of other business needs. How many of the 85 miles she drives each day count as business-related miles?

Discussion: Carla can deduct the cost of driving the 75 business miles. The cost of transportation to work and back home is personal and not deductible.

▲ **EXAMPLE 11**   Brendan works weekdays as a nurse at a local hospital. The hospital is 14 miles from his home. He also works as a waiter at a restaurant 2 nights during the week and on weekends. The week nights he works at the restaurant, he leaves directly from the hospital. The restaurant is 6 miles from the hospital and 8 miles from his home. What portion of Brendan's travel is considered business related?

Discussion: The 14 miles (28 miles round trip) from Brendan's home to the hospital are commuting and considered personal. The 6 miles from the hospital to the restaurant are business, and the 8 miles from the restaurant to his home are personal. The mileage to and from the restaurant on the weekend is considered personal, because Brendan did not work at his regular job. NOTE: If during the week, Brendan went home before going to the restaurant, his business miles would be limited to his normal travel distance (6 miles).

Regardless of which method the taxpayer chooses, the deduction can be disallowed for failure to keep records that support the date and amount of an expense that is deducted, the mileage allocations, and the business purpose for the expense.

STANDARD MILEAGE RATE METHOD.   To use the **standard mileage rate method,** which is based on administrative convenience, a taxpayer simply deducts 30 cents (29 cents in 1994) for each business mile the car was driven.[5] The standard mileage rate is an estimate of the cost of operating a car (gas, oil, repairs, insurance, depreciation, etc.). Because these costs change over time, the standard rate is adjusted each year. In addition to the standard mileage rate, the taxpayer can deduct direct out-of-pocket expenses that are unrelated to the operating costs of the car. These include the business portion of parking, tolls, interest, and property taxes. The property taxes must be based on the car's value. Interest and property taxes are deductible only if the individual is self-employed. The standard mileage rate method is subject to several limitations and requirements that should be considered before it is used. For example, the standard mileage rate method may not be used by a business that operates more than one vehicle in the business at the same time.

▲ **EXAMPLE 12**   José purchased a new car this year and drove it 10,000 miles for business purposes and 3,000 miles for personal use. What is José's deduction for the business use of the car if he elects to use the standard mileage rate method?

Discussion: José can deduct $3,000 (10,000 × 30 cents) in auto expense based on his business mileage under the standard mileage rate method. No deduction is allowed for the personal use of the car. If he paid any parking fees or tolls out of pocket while on business, these expenses are also deductible.

ACTUAL COST METHOD.   The actual cost method is a more flexible way to compute the auto expense deduction and often results in a larger tax savings. Using the **actual cost method,** a taxpayer can deduct depreciation, gas and oil, repairs, insurance, license, and other expenses of driving the car. As with the standard mileage rate, the taxpayer can deduct the business portion of the nonoperating costs of the car. If the car is used for both business and personal purposes, the expenses must be allocated according to the miles driven for each purpose. Only mileage driven for a business purpose results in a tax deduction. If the actual cost method is used, it is important to keep mileage records to support the allocation of expenses between business and personal use. The depreciation deduction under the actual cost method is subject to significant limitations, which are discussed in Chapter 11. The actual depreciation deduction is limited to statutory caps based on when the car was acquired. For example, if a car was bought in 1995 and used 100 percent for business, the maximum depreciation deduction for 1995 is $3,060.[6] This limit changes each year of the car's depreciation life.

▲ **EXAMPLE 13**   Nancy uses her car in her business of selling real estate. In 1995, she buys a new car and drives it 18,700 miles for business and 3,800 miles for commuting to and from the office and for other personal use. Depreciation, insurance, license, gas, repairs, and other operating expenses total $6,975. She can document that she paid $125 in tolls and parking while on business, and the interest expense on her car loan is $250. What is her deduction using the standard mileage rate method and the actual cost method?

Discussion: If Nancy chooses to use the standard rate method, her car expense deduction is equal to 30 cents (the 1995 mileage rate) for each business-related mile driven plus any tolls and parking:

Standard rate deduction (18,700 miles × 30 cents) =	$5,610
Tolls and parking (100% business)	125
Interest on car loan [(18,700 ÷ 22,500 = 83%) × $250]	208
Total deduction for business use of car	$5,943

Because the tolls and parking were incurred while on business, they do not have to be allocated. The interest expense is based on the ratio of business-related miles to total miles.

Discussion: If Nancy chooses to use the actual cost method, her car expense deduction is determined by allocating the costs of operating the car between business and personal use:

Actual operating expenses	$6,975
Business use percentage (18,700 ÷ 22,500)	× 83%
Business portion of operating expenses	$5,789
Tolls and parking (100% business)	125
Interest on car loan (83% × $250)	208
Total deduction for business use of car	$6,122

Tolls and parking incurred while on business do not have to be allocated. The interest expense is allocated according to the business use percentage. If Nancy is willing to keep the records necessary to support the actual cost method, she can obtain a larger car expense deduction than under the standard mileage rate method.

Travel Expenses.   A taxpayer can deduct travel expenses incurred while pursuing a business purpose. **Travel expenses** include transportation, lodging, 50 percent of the cost of meals, and incidental expenses. Incidental expenses are items such as local transportation, telephone calls, laundry, and similar expenses that are necessary while traveling. For an expense to qualify as travel, the taxpayer must be away from her or his tax home overnight. A **tax home** is the general area in which the taxpayer conducts her or his principal business activity. To be *away* *overnight* means a period that is long enough to require the taxpayer to rest. Overnight is substantially longer than a normal workday and can be less than 24 hours. A one-day business trip usually will not satisfy the overnight test.

▲ **EXAMPLE 14** Theresa, a CPA, went to Houston for 10 days. The business purpose for making the trip was to audit a client's accounting records. The airplane ticket cost $195, the hotel cost $85 a night, and she spent $40 a day on meals and $15 a day for incidentals. She did not spend any time sightseeing or visiting friends. What is Theresa's deductible travel expense?

Discussion: All of Theresa's travel expenses are allowed as a deduction because they are related to business. However, she is still subject to the 50% limit on meals and entertainment costs. She can deduct:

Transportation	$ 195
Lodging (10 days × $85)	850
Meals [(10 days × $40) × 50%]	200
Incidentals (10 days × $15)	150
Total deductible travel expense	$1,395

If the primary purpose of the travel is personal, incidental business activity will not change the nature of the trip. The taxpayer cannot deduct any transportation costs if the purpose of the trip is primarily personal. However, lodging, 50 percent of meals, and incidental expenses directly related to conducting business while on a personal trip may be deducted. The primary purpose of the trip is determined by comparing the time devoted to business activity while on the trip to time spent on personal activities. If more than 50 percent of the total time is related to personal activities, the primary purpose will be deemed to be personal.[7]

▲ **EXAMPLE 15** Using the facts in example 14, assume that Theresa spent 6 days visiting family in Houston and 4 days auditing her client's records. What is Theresa's deductible travel expense?

Discussion: Because 60% (6 of 10 total days) of Theresa's time on the trip was related to personal activities, none of the transportation expense is deductible. She can deduct the other expenses to the extent related to business activities:

Transportation	$ -0-
Lodging (4 days × $85)	340
Meals [(4 days × $40) × 50%]	80
Incidentals (4 days × $15)	60
Total deductible travel expense	$480

If the primary reason for the trip is a business purpose (more than 50 percent of the trip is spent on business activities) and the taxpayer spends some time for personal activities, the tax result will be different. The cost of transportation is fully deductible, but a deduction for lodging, meals, and incidental expenses related to personal activities is not allowed.

▲ **EXAMPLE 16** Using the facts in example 14, assume that Theresa spent 3 days visiting family in Houston and 7 days auditing her client's records. What is Theresa's deductible travel expense?

Discussion: Because more than 50% of Theresa's time on the trip was related to business activities, she can deduct all the transportation expense. She can also deduct the other expenses to the extent they related to business activities:

Transportation	$ 195
Lodging (7 days × $85)	595
Meals [(7 days × $40) × 50%]	140
Incidentals (7 days × $15)	105
Total deductible travel expense	$1,035

Expenses incurred by a spouse or a family member who accompanies the taxpayer on the trip are not allowed as a deduction, unless there is a bonafide business purpose for the person's presence and the spouse is an employee of the taxpayer. An additional limitation is imposed on travel to attend a convention, seminar, or other meeting that qualifies as related to the production of income. Expenses for attending investment-related meetings are not deductible, unless it can be shown the meeting is related to the taxpayer's trade or business.

▲ **EXAMPLE 17**   Raul is a physician who invests in real estate partnerships. He traveled from Dallas to Tulsa to attend a seminar on tax laws affecting real estate investments. Can Raul deduct the cost of attending the seminar?

Discussion: Raul is an investor in real estate partnerships, and the travel is related to the production of income. Because the travel is not related to his medical practice (trade or business), the travel expenses are not deductible.

▲ **EXAMPLE 18**   Assume that in example 17 Raul is a tax attorney who represents clients who invest in real estate partnerships. Can Raul deduct the cost of attending the seminar?

Discussion: Because the seminar is related to his trade or business as a tax attorney, Raul may deduct the allowable costs of attending the seminar as an expense incurred in his trade or business.

▲ **EXAMPLE 19**   Yusef is a self-employed insurance agent. He and his wife Ruby traveled to Washington to attend an insurance conference. Ruby is an executive secretary for Rhody Corporation. She spent her time in Washington attending the sessions, taking notes, and setting up meetings for Yusef. Can Yusef deduct the cost of attending the seminar for both of them?

Discussion: Ruby's presence at the conference serves a useful business purpose, but because she is not Yusef's employee, the expenses related to Ruby's travel are not deductible. If the hotel rate is the same for single or double occupancy, no part of the lodging would be disallowed. But if different rates apply, Yusef can deduct only the cost of single occupancy (Yusef's). All allowable costs Yusef incurred for his attendance at the conference are deductible (subject to the 50% meal and entertainment limitation), because the seminar relates to his trade or business.

Business Gifts.   A taxpayer can deduct up to $25 per year per donee for gifts to business customers. **Business gifts** are not subject to the 50-percent limitation that applies to meals and entertainment expenses. To apply the $25 limitation, direct and indirect gifts given to a person must be counted. An indirect gift is one made to a related party, such as a taxpayer's spouse or child.

▲ **EXAMPLE 20**   Sam operates a retail store. To show his appreciation for the business of his 5 best customers, he sent candy to their spouses at their home. The candy cost Sam $45 for each box. How much of the cost of the candy can Sam deduct as a business gift?

Discussion: The gift of the candy to the spouse is an indirect gift to the customer. The $20 cost per box in excess of the annual donee limit is not deductible. Sam's deduction is limited to $125 (5 gifts at $25 each).

▲ **EXAMPLE 21**   Assume that Sam also sent each of his 5 best customers custom-made desk clocks that cost $85 each. How much of the cost of the clocks is deductible as a business gift?

Discussion: Because the annual limit of $25 per donee applies to both direct and indirect gifts, none of the cost of the clocks may be deducted as a business gift. The $25 limitation was exceeded on the gift to the spouse. Therefore, Sam is over the limit on his 5 best customers.

The amount subject to the annual limit does not include incidental expenses that do not add value to the gift, such as gift wrapping, engraving, or delivering the item to the customer. An item that could be considered either a gift or an entertainment expense is generally considered entertainment and is subject to the 50-percent limitation.

Substantiation Requirements.
Entertainment, auto, travel, and gift expenses are subject to strict documentation requirements. The tax law requires the taxpayer to keep records that will show

- The amount of the expense
- The time and place of travel or entertainment, or date and description of a gift
- The business purpose of the travel, entertainment or gift
- The business relationship to the person entertained or receiving the gift[8]

These are **substantiation requirements** and failure to keep the records necessary to meet them can result in loss of the deduction.

Education Expenses.
Because education is viewed as a personal capital expenditure, individuals are not allowed to deduct education expenses. However, the tax law does allow a taxpayer to deduct education expenses if the **education expense** meets either of the following requirements:

- The education is a requirement—either by law or the taxpayer's employer—for the taxpayer's continued employment.
- The education maintains or improves the skills required in the taxpayer's trade or business.[9]

A taxpayer who is not reimbursed for an education expense can deduct the expense as a miscellaneous itemized deduction. Remember that miscellaneous itemized deductions must be reduced by 2 percent of adjusted gross income. A taxpayer who is self-employed can deduct the cost of education expenses as an ordinary and necessary business expense. The effect is that the deduction for education expenses is *for* adjusted gross income.

▲ **EXAMPLE 22**   Juan is a lawyer for a local law firm. State law requires that he attend 40 hours of continuing education each year, at least 6 hours of which must be on ethics. Juan attended 4 seminars (8 hours each) on estate taxes and an 8-hour seminar on ethics. All tuition for the 4 seminars came to $1,200; the ethics seminar cost $250. Can Juan deduct the cost of the continuing education seminars?

Discussion: The cost of all the continuing education seminars is deductible as a miscellaneous itemized deduction. The 32 hours on estate taxes qualify, because the courses either maintain or improve his skills. The cost of the ethics seminar is deductible, because it is required by state law.

▲ **EXAMPLE 23**   Phoebe has a bachelor's degree in engineering from Local University and is employed as an engineer with Koza Construction. She is enrolled in an advanced thermal dynamics course at Local U. The cost of the course is $600. Can Phoebe deduct the cost of the course as an education expense?

Discussion: Phoebe can deduct the $600 as a miscellaneous itemized deduction. The course qualifies as a deductible education expense, because it improves her engineering skills.

Meeting one of the requirements for deducting an education expense does not guarantee that the education expense is deductible. If the education is necessary to meet the minimum educational requirements of the taxpayer's job, the cost is not deductible. Also, if the education qualifies the taxpayer for a new trade or business, the expense is not deductible.[10]

▲ **EXAMPLE 24**   Linda is a biology instructor at Wakefield College. She is considered a temporary faculty member and her contract is renewed annually. The college requires that all permanent faculty members have a graduate degree and will renew Linda's contract only if she begins work toward her master's. Linda has enrolled at Kingston University to pursue a master's degree in biology. Can Linda deduct the cost of her master's degree as an education expense?

Discussion: The cost of Linda's master's degree is not deductible. A master's in biology is the minimum requirement Linda needs to become a permanent faculty member at Wakefield College.

▲ **EXAMPLE 25**   Horace is a full-time student in computer science at State University. He works part time as a programmer for a software developer. His employer has promised him a full-time job after he graduates. Can Horace deduct the cost of his college courses as an education expense?

Discussion: The cost of Horace's college courses is not deductible. Although Horace's college courses are related to his job, he is not considered to be engaged in a trade or business, because he is working only part time. In essence, the college degree provides Horace with the qualifications needed to enter a new trade or business.

A final limitation to note here is that travel that is in itself educational is not allowed as a deduction. For example, an art teacher who travels to New York City and Washington, D.C., to tour art galleries cannot deduct the cost of the travel even though it directly relates to teaching art. In contrast, if the teacher is an expert in a particular type of art and has to travel to Paris to verify the authenticity of an art object, the cost of the trip can be deducted.

In many cases, employers reimburse employees' education expenses. As discussed in Chapter 4, an employee can exclude from income up to $5,250 of education expenses reimbursed from a qualified educational assistance plan.

Compensation of Employees

The tax law provides for the deduction of reasonable salaries, wages, bonuses, and other compensation paid to employees. Thus, employee compensation is subject to two basic tests for deductibility. First, the payments must be for services actually performed by the employee. Second, the total payment for services of the employee must be reasonable in amount.[11] The determination of whether total compensation is excessive is made for each employee. When the compensation paid to an employee is found to be excessive, only a reasonable salary deduction is allowed. Whether compensation paid an employee is reasonable is decided by considering several factors, including

- Employee's duties, responsibilities, and pay history
- Volume and complexity of the business
- Time required to do the work
- Ability and accomplishments of the employee
- General cost of living and the company pay policy
- Relationship of the compensation, the gross and net income of the business, and dividends paid to shareholders[12]

Whether the remuneration is **reasonable compensation** is usually a problem when the payment is made to a related party. Thus, reasonable compensation issues generally arise in connection with a closely held business. In addition, the business purpose of the payment may be questioned. Lack of a business purpose will result in disallowance of the total compensation paid the person.

▲ **EXAMPLE 26**   Tina is the sole shareholder of Staple Manufacturing Corporation. Tina is the president of the corporation and pays herself $200,000 a year. Her son, who is operations officer, is paid $50,000 a year. Her son seldom visits the plant, because he is a full-time student at State University. The next highest-paid employee, the general manager, is unrelated to Tina and is paid $50,000 a year. During an audit, the IRS determined that based on comparable salaries in the area, a reasonable salary for Tina should be $90,000. Based on an examination of employee records, the IRS decided that Tina's son was not an employee. The salary paid Tina's son was a sham (an assignment of income from Tina). How much of the payments to Tina and her son are deductible by Staple?

Discussion: The $110,000 ($200,000 − $90,000) excess salary paid Tina would not be a deductible expense of the corporation. The excess salary paid Tina would be taxed as a dividend payment. The salary paid to her son would be disallowed as a deduction for the corporation, because it lacks a business purpose. Under the assignment-of-income doctrine, the payment of the son's salary would be taxed as dividend income to Tina. Then, Tina would be deemed to have made a gift to her son in the amount of the salary payments. The gift received by the son is excluded from his income and is not deductible by Tina.

The tax law limits to $1,000,000 the amount a publicly traded corporation can deduct as compensation expense.[13] However, the $1,000,000 limitation applies only to a covered employee. A *covered employee* is defined as the chief executive officer (CEO) and the four officers with the highest compensations, other than the CEO, whose remuneration is required to be reported under the Securities Act of 1934. In determining a covered employee's compensation, all remuneration paid to the individual in cash or property is considered compensation. Exempted from consideration as compensation are

- Commission payments
- Qualified plan contributions (e.g., pension)
- Remuneration paid under a written binding agreement that was in effect before February 17, 1993
- Excludable employee fringe benefits (as discussed in Chapter 4)
- Performance-based compensation

For remuneration to qualify under the performance-based compensation exception, four requirements must be met. First, the payment must be made solely for the attainment of specific performance goals. The performance goal (except for stock options or stock appreciation rights) must be determined by an objective formula or standard. In essence, the formula cannot be subjective. Second, the performance goals must be established by a compensation committee consisting solely of two or more outside directors. An individual is considered an outside director if that person is not a current employee of the corporation. In addition, an individual who was previously an officer of the corporation cannot be considered an outside director. Third, the performance standards must be disclosed to and approved by the shareholders of the corporation. Fourth, the compensation committee, as described previously, must certify that the performance standards were attained before the compensation is paid.

▲ **EXAMPLE 27**   Pamela is the fourth-highest-paid officer of the Vanger Corporation. Her salary for 1995 is $750,000. She also receives a bonus of $300,000 based on the performance of Vanger Corporation's stock. The bonus paid to Pamela is based solely on the performance of the corporation's stock. The standards for the bonus have been set by the outside directors, and they have certified that the performance goal was attained. The performance standards were also approved by the stockholders. Can the Vanger Corporation deduct all her compensation ($1,050,000)?

Discussion: The corporation is entitled to a deduction for the entire $1,050,000, because the $300,000 qualifies as performance-based compensation. If one of the four requirements had not been met (e.g., the performance based standards were not approved by the shareholders), the compensation deduction would be limited to $1,000,000.

▲ **EXAMPLE 28**   Tomás is the tenth-highest-paid officer of the Mescow Corporation. His salary for 1995 is $650,000. He also receives a bonus of $400,000 based on his years of service and the performance of Mescow Corporation's stock. The standards for the bonus have been set by the outside directors, and they have certified that the requirement for earning the bonus has been attained. The performance standards have been approved by the stockholders. Can the Mescow Corporation deduct all compensation paid to Tomás ($1,050,000)?

Discussion: The corporation is entitled to a deduction for the entire $1,050,000, even though one of the four requirements (compensation is not solely based on performance) of the performance-based exception is not met. The entire compensation is deductible, because Tomás is not a covered employee. Only the CEO and the four highest-paid officers other than the CEO are covered employees.

Bad Debts

The tax law permits a capital recovery deduction for the taxpayer's basis in business and investment bad debts.[14] To be deductible, the bad debt must be related to a transaction that had a business purpose. To determine how to report the deduction, the bad debt must first be identified as a business or a nonbusiness (investment) bad debt. If the debt arose from a transaction in the taxpayer's trade or business, the bad debt is allowed as a business deduction as a **business bad debt.** Other bad debts that are not related to the taxpayer's trade or business are considered **nonbusiness bad debts.** The use of the loan proceeds by the borrower does not affect the classification as business or nonbusiness. The distinction between the two classifications is important. A business bad debt is deductible just like any other business expense. A nonbusiness bad debt cannot be deducted if the debt was voluntarily forgiven or the forgiveness of the debt was intended as a gift. In addition, nonbusiness bad debts are deducted as a short-term capital loss. The important implication of the capital loss treatment is that the deduction may be limited to $3,000 each year until the loss is fully used.

▲ **EXAMPLE 29**   Do-Rite, Inc., owes Kelly $10,000 for goods it purchased from Kelly on account. Because of financial difficulty, Do-Rite cannot repay the debt when it comes due in 1995. Kelly wants to deduct the $10,000 as a loss. How should she report the bad debt on her tax return?

Discussion: An account receivable from the sale of merchandise to Do-Rite is related to Kelly's trade or business. Therefore, Kelly can deduct the $10,000 bad debt as a 1995 business expense.

▲ **EXAMPLE 30**   Assume in example 29 that Do-Rite owes Kelly the $10,000 because the owner of Do-Rite is a friend of Kelly's and Kelly made the company a temporary loan to help it through a cash-flow shortage. Kelly does not do any business with Do-Rite. How should Kelly report the bad debt on her tax return?

Discussion: Because the loan is not related to Kelly's trade or business, the debt is a nonbusiness debt. Assuming Kelly does not have other capital gains or losses to report, she is permitted a $3,000 capital loss deduction in 1995, 1996, and 1997. The remaining $1,000 is deductible in 1998.

   If Kelly forgave the $10,000 due from Do-Rite because the company is owned by her uncle and she wanted to do him a favor, the forgiveness would very likely be considered a gift to her uncle and not allowed as a bad debt deduction.

The amount deductible as a bad debt is limited to the taxpayer's basis in the receivable. As a result, the taxpayer's accounting method is an important factor in determining the amount deductible. If the receivable represents income owed to the taxpayer, the income must have been reported as taxable income before the taxpayer has a basis for claiming a deduction. Because of the basis limitation, a cash basis taxpayer normally will not claim a bad debt expense deduction for accounts receivable. Because a cash basis taxpayer does not report income until cash is collected, there is no tax basis in the receivable to deduct. However, an accrual basis taxpayer reports taxable income as it is earned, regardless of when the cash is received, and has a tax basis for deducting an uncollectible account.

▲ **EXAMPLE 31**   Sylvia operates a successful consulting practice. During January 1995, she performs $5,000 in services for clients who still owe her as of December 31, 1996. She reviews her client files and determines that $3,000 in receivables is uncollectible. How much of a deduction is Sylvia allowed if she uses the accrual basis of accounting?

Discussion: Using the accrual method of accounting, Sylvia would report $5,000 in income from the receivables in 1995. Because the income is reported on the accrual basis as it is earned, she has a $5,000 basis for the accounts receivable. In 1996, she can take a $3,000 bad debt deduction for the uncollectible accounts. The net result is that Sylvia's taxable income from these accounts is $2,000 for the 2-year period.

▲ **EXAMPLE 32**   Assume the same facts as in example 31, except that Sylvia uses the cash basis of accounting.

Discussion: Using the cash method of accounting, Sylvia has no reported income from the receivables, because they have not been collected. Therefore, she has no basis in the receivables and is not allowed a deduction. She reports $2,000 in taxable income when she receives cash from the collectible accounts. Note that this treatment gives Sylvia the same $2,000 in income that would have been reported on the accrual basis.

The tax law permits a bad debt deduction using the **specific charge-off method.** Based on this accounting method, a business bad debt can be written off in the accounting period in which the facts known to the taxpayer indicate the account is fully or partially uncollectible.[15] If an account is partially written off in one year and later becomes fully uncollectible, the remaining balance of the account can be written off as a bad debt. A receivable may be uncollectible for several reasons. For example, the debtor may go out of business or become bankrupt, or the collateral securing the loan may be destroyed or become worthless, indicating collection of the account is unlikely. If an account is fully or partially written off and the amount of the write-off is later recovered, under the tax benefit rule the recovered amount is reported as income in the year of collection.

▲ **EXAMPLE 33**   Raquel Corporation owns and operates a furniture store. Because it has inventory, Raquel uses the accrual method of accounting. At the end of 1995, its accounts receivable total $75,000. Based on a review of the individual accounts, Raquel identifies $2,500-worth of accounts as uncollectible. For financial accounting purposes, Raquel's accountant estimates that $4,500 of its 1995 sales ultimately are uncollectible. How much can Raquel Corporation deduct on its 1995 tax return for bad debts?

Discussion: Using the specific charge-off method, Raquel Corporation may deduct only the $2,500 in bad debts identified as uncollectible. The allowance method of accounting for bad debts, which is used for financial reporting, is not generally allowed for tax purposes.

▲ **EXAMPLE 34**   Assume that in 1996, Raquel in example 33 collects $1,000 of the accounts receivable it has written off as a bad debt expense in 1995. What is the effect on Raquel's 1996 income from the collection of the bad debt?

Discussion: Based on the tax benefit rule, the recovery of the $1,000 in bad debts deducted in 1995 must be reported as income when the accounts receivable are collected in 1996.

Nonbusiness bad debts often result from loans to family and friends. To claim a bad debt deduction for these loans, the taxpayer may have to prove that the failure to collect the loan was not motivated by the intent to make a gift. Thus, the benefit of the bad debt deduction may depend on whether the taxpayer can prove that the loan was the result of a bonafide arm's-length transaction.

▲ **EXAMPLE 35**   Wenona lent her uncle $15,000 to pay hospital and medical bills. Because the loan was to her uncle, she did not intend to charge any interest on the loan nor did she require him to sign a note. Her uncle promised to pay her back as soon as possible. Wenona's uncle died without repaying her. Can Wenona deduct the loan to her uncle as a nonbusiness bad debt?

Discussion: Although her uncle defaulted on his debt, Wenona would most likely be denied a nonbusiness bad debt deduction. There is no evidence that a bonafide arm's-length loan was made to the uncle. None of the elements found in a bonafide loan is present in this situation: no note as evidence of the debt, no collateral for the loan, no provision for interest on the loan, no payment or due date, and no collection efforts on Wenona's part. Wenona would have to prove that her intent was not to make a gift to her uncle in order to get a nonbusiness bad debt deduction.

Like business bad debts, nonbusiness bad debts are accounted for using the specific charge-off method. Unlike a business bad debt, a deduction is not allowed for partial worthlessness of a nonbusiness bad debt. The nonbusiness bad debt can be deducted only when the taxpayer finally settles the loan for less than its basis.[16]

▲ **EXAMPLE 36**   Karen owes Maria $5,000. The loan is related to Maria's business. In 1995, Karen files for bankruptcy. Maria talks to Karen's lawyers and determines that only 40% of the debt is collectible. In 1996, Maria receives $1,500 from the bankruptcy proceeding in full payment of the debt. How much of the bad debt can Maria deduct in 1995 and 1996?

Discussion: Because the debt is a business bad debt, a deduction is allowed for partial worthlessness. Maria can deduct $3,000 ($5,000 × 60%), the amount estimated as uncollectible, in 1995. When the debt is finally settled in 1996, Maria can deduct the remaining $500 ($2,000 − $1,500) of the debt that she will not collect.

   Note that if Maria had received $2,800 from the bankruptcy proceeding, she would have had gross income of $800 ($2,800 − $2,000) under the tax benefit rule.

▲ **EXAMPLE 37**   Assume that the loan in example 36 was a bonafide nonbusiness bad debt. How much of the bad debt can Maria deduct in 1995 and 1996?

Discussion: A deduction is not allowed for the partial worthlessness of a nonbusiness bad debt. Maria must wait until 1996 when she knows the amount of the bad debt in order to take a deduction. At that time, Maria has a short-term capital loss of $3,500 ($5,000 − $1,500). If Maria has no other capital gains and losses in 1996, she may deduct only $3,000 of the short-term capital loss in 1996, with the remainder carried forward to 1997.

Table 6–1 summarizes the rules for deductibility of bad debts.

Related Party Accrued Expenses

The tax law limits the timing of the deduction of accrued expenses payable to a related cash basis taxpayer. Related parties are members of an individual's family and business entities in which the person directly or constructively owns more than a 50-percent interest. The arm's-length transaction and business purpose concepts require that related party transactions be scrutinized closely to discourage

▲ **Table 6–1**

BAD DEBT DEDUCTIONS

	Business Bad Debts	**Nonbusiness Bad Debts**
What is deductible?	Any debt related to the taxpayer's trade or business.	Any bonafide debt that is not related to the taxpayer's trade or business.
Amount of deduction	Bad debt deductions are limited to the taxpayer's basis in the debt.	Bad debt deductions are limited to the taxpayer's basis in the debt.
When is it deductible?	Deductible in the year of partial or total worthlessness.	Deductible when the exact amount of the worthlessness becomes known.
How is it deductible?	Ordinary business expense.	Short-term capital loss.

unwarranted tax avoidance. The ownership of a controlling interest in a business entity permits the taxpayer to exert significant control over the timing of transactions between the business and the taxpayer. The objective of the related party limitations is to defer accrued expenses from transactions that lack economic substance. For example, an accrual basis corporation and a cash basis related party could time a transaction to permit a deduction for the corporation in one year with the income reported by the related party in a later year. Thus, the taxpayers would receive benefit from the interest-free use of the deferred tax payment (the benefit is the interest related to the present value of the deferred tax).

▲ **EXAMPLE 38**   Kool Corporation, an accrual basis taxpayer, accrues a $10,000 bonus payable to Ivan for its year ending December 31, 1995. Kool pays the bonus to Ivan on February 29, 1996. Ivan owns 90% of Kool Corporation. Ivan reports his income on the cash basis. What tax savings might Ivan realize from the accrual?

Discussion: Assuming a 31% marginal tax rate and an 8% interest rate (the present value factor for one year would be 0.926), Ivan could save $229 by structuring the transaction to accelerate the deduction while deferring the income. The tax savings are solely the result of the timing of the transaction [($10,000 × 31%) − ($10,000 × 31% × 0.926)]. However, the related party rules discussed next prevent this result.

The related party rules prevent the abuse in example 38 by requiring an accrual basis taxpayer to use a cash method of accounting for expenses that are paid to a cash basis related party. If an accrual basis taxpayer accrues an expense payable to a cash basis related party, the expense is not deductible until it is paid in cash and included in the related cash basis taxpayer's gross income.[17] Thus, the tax law requires a matching of the deduction with the related reporting of income to avoid potential tax avoidance. If both parties are accrual basis taxpayers, the problem does not arise. The accrual accounting method would result in the transaction being recognized by the related parties at the same date.

▲ **EXAMPLE 39**   What is the proper treatment of the bonus in example 38?

Discussion: Kool Corporation may not deduct the accrued bonus for tax purposes until the cash is paid to Ivan and included in his taxable income. Thus, Ivan reports the $10,000 bonus as income in 1996 when it is received, and Kool Corporation deducts the expense in 1996. The related party rules require both parties to recognize the transaction on the same date.

If Ivan and Kool Corporation are both accrual basis taxpayers, they would both accrue the transaction for the year ended December 31, 1995, regardless of when the cash was paid. Ivan would report income, and Kool would claim a deduction for the expense in 1995.

Other Business Expenses

Rent paid for the use of business property, business insurance, payroll taxes on employee compensation paid by the employer, property taxes on business property, interest on business indebtedness, utilities, dues to professional and business organizations, subscriptions to trade publications, supplies, and similar expenses incurred for a business purpose are allowed as a deduction. As you read the discussion of the deductions for insurance, taxes, rent, and legal fees, pay close attention to the situations in which the expenditure is either disallowed as a deduction or required to be capitalized as an asset.

Insurance Expense.   Premiums paid for insurance to protect a taxpayer's business from loss, called *insurance expense,* are deductible. The types of insurance premiums that qualify for deduction include the following:

- Fire, theft, and other casualty insurance, and liability insurance.
- Employees' group medical and group term life insurance, and workers' compensation insurance.
- Employee performance and fidelity bonds to protect against losses caused by employees.
- Business interruption and overhead insurance to reimburse the business for lost profits and overhead from casualty or other unexpected event. However, premiums on an individual's disability income policy cannot be deducted.

▲ **EXAMPLE 40**   On July 1, 1995, Sook pays a $6,000 premium for a 3-year fire and casualty insurance policy on his business buildings and equipment. How much of the premium can Sook deduct in 1995?

Discussion: Payment of the premium in advance results in a prepaid expense that benefits tax years 1995, 1996, 1997, and 1998. Regardless of Sook's accounting method, the $6,000 basis in the policy must be allocated to the periods benefited by the prepaid expense. The allocation results in a $1,000 insurance expense deduction for 1995 [$6,000 × (6 ÷ 36 months)].

Except for qualified group term life insurance, life insurance premiums generally are not deductible. To qualify for deduction, life insurance premiums must be viewed as additional compensation to the insured person. If the payer of the insurance premiums benefits directly or indirectly when the policy pays off on the insured's death, the premium cannot be deducted.[18] Thus, insurance premiums on the life of the owner of a business, an officer of a corporation, an employee, or other person who has a financial interest in the taxpayer's business are not deductible unless they are treated as payment of compensation to the insured person. In addition, an entity other than the payer of the life insurance premiums must be the beneficiary of the policy in order for the premium to be deductible.

▲ **EXAMPLE 41**   Radon Corporation pays a $5,000 premium on a whole life insurance policy on the life of Luke. Luke is a key employee in the company. If Luke died, the company would suffer a tremendous loss. If the corporation is the beneficiary of the policy, how much of the premium can Radon deduct?

Discussion: Because Radon benefits directly or indirectly from the policy proceeds when Luke dies, the premium is not deductible. But recall from Chapter 4 that life insurance proceeds received upon the death of the insured are excluded from gross income.

▲ **EXAMPLE 42**   Assume that Luke, in example 41, is unrelated to Radon Corporation and its owners. Also, Luke's wife is the beneficiary of the life insurance policy. How much of the insurance premium can Radon deduct?

Discussion: Because Radon is not a direct or indirect beneficiary of the policy, the $5,000 premium is allowed as a deduction for additional compensation paid to Luke. Luke will have to report the $5,000 premium paid by the corporation as income. His wife can exclude the proceeds of the policy from her income when Luke dies.

Taxes.   A taxpayer is allowed a deduction for the payment of certain taxes incurred in a trade or business.[19] Some taxes are not allowed as a deduction, and others must be added to the basis of property owned by the taxpayer. Common types of deductible taxes include the following:

- State, local, and foreign real estate taxes
- State and local ad valorem personal property taxes (an ad valorem tax is based on the property's value)
- State, local, and foreign income taxes
- Payroll taxes imposed on an employer (including the employer's share of the Social Security tax and unemployment taxes)
- Sales taxes, excise taxes, fuel taxes, franchise taxes, and other miscellaneous taxes[20]

Federal income tax and gift and estate taxes are not allowed as deductions in computing federal taxable income.[21] In addition, the taxes listed are deductible *only* when they are incurred in a trade or business. The itemized deduction allowed for taxes (discussed in Chapter 8) is far more restrictive than the deductions allowed for businesses.

▲ **EXAMPLE 43**   Leslie Corporation pays the following taxes during the current year:

Federal income tax	$50,000
State and local income taxes	15,000
State and local real estate and personal property tax	2,000
State and local sales taxes	7,000

What is Leslie's deduction for taxes paid?

Discussion: Except for the federal income tax, Leslie may deduct all the taxes listed. Leslie's deduction for taxes paid is $24,000. The $50,000 federal income tax is never allowed as a deduction.

Sales taxes are deductible if they are paid for supplies and other items that are not capital expenditures. If the sales tax is related to the purchase of a long-lived asset, the tax must be added to the asset's basis. The sales tax is then deducted as a capital recovery through depreciation of the asset's basis.

▲ **EXAMPLE 44**   Leslie Corporation purchased a new microcomputer for use in its office. The microcomputer cost $8,000 and is subject to a 10% sales tax. What is Leslie's deduction for the $800 in sales tax paid on the microcomputer?

Discussion: Because the sales tax is related to the purchase of a depreciable asset, the $800 in tax is not currently deductible. The sales tax is added to the microcomputer's basis as part of the cost of acquiring the asset. A deduction is allowed for depreciation of the microcomputer's $8,800 tax basis.

If real estate is purchased or sold during the year, real estate taxes must be allocated between the buyer and the seller. The tax is allocated according to the number of days each owned the property during the period of time to which the tax relates (the property tax year).[22]

▲ **EXAMPLE 45**   Leslie Corporation sells land and a building on October 1, 1995. The property tax for the 1995 property tax year (a calendar year) is $3,600. Leslie pays its share of the property tax on the date the sale closes. What is Leslie's 1995 deduction for real estate taxes on the land and building?

Discussion: Leslie may deduct the property taxes for the period it owned the land and building. Leslie's deduction would be $2,700—the taxes related to the period January 1 through September 30, 1995 [$3,600 × (9 ÷ 12)]. The buyer should deduct the property tax for the remainder of the property tax calendar year because that entity was the owner of the property.

▲ **EXAMPLE 46** Assume that in example 45, the sales price of the building is $86,000. As part of the sales agreement, the buyer agrees to pay Leslie's share of the property taxes for 1995. Is Leslie allowed a deduction for property taxes on the building in 1995?

Discussion: The payment of another's expense in a business setting is considered income for the entity for which the expense is being paid. Therefore, the payment of Leslie's $2,700 share of the property taxes must be included as part of the sales price of the building. Leslie is deemed to have received $88,700 for the building and to have paid $2,700 in property taxes. Each party to a real estate transaction must always recognize its share of the property taxes, regardless of which party actually pays the tax.

When real estate taxes are related to **assessments for local benefits,** such as sidewalks, streets, sewers, and other improvements, the tax payment is not deductible. The tax imposed for local benefits is deemed to increase the value of the taxpayer's property and is considered a capital expenditure. As a result, the tax is added to the improved asset's basis. However, under the capital recovery concept, the taxpayer will recover the tax through depreciation, amortization, or upon its disposition.

▲ **EXAMPLE 47** The town of Guthrie imposes a special real estate tax assessment to put in new streets. Leslie Corporation has to pay $15,000 as its share of the new streets in front of its warehouse. What is Leslie's deduction for the $15,000 special property tax assessment it pays in 1995?

Discussion: The special assessment for installing streets is deemed to increase the value of Leslie's property. As a result, the special assessment is added to Leslie's basis in the land. Thus, the $15,000 tax payment is not currently deductible. When Leslie disposes of the property, the capital recovery concept permits the capitalized tax to be deducted against the amount received on the sale of the property.

Rental Payments. A deduction is allowed for the payment of rents in exchange for the use of business property. However, if the taxpayer acquires an equity interest in the rented property, the rent payments are treated as being made for the purchase of an asset. This is an application of the substance-over-form doctrine, which requires transactions to be treated according to their economic substance. Whether a payment should be deducted as rent or capitalized as the purchase of an asset depends on the intent of the parties.[23] Several factors must be considered in deciding whether a rent payment is in fact a payment toward the purchase of an asset. These include whether

- The rental agreement applies part of each payment toward the purchase of an equity interest in the asset.

- The taxpayer will be given title to the asset after making all the required rent payments.

- The taxpayer has an option to buy the asset at a nominal price at the end of the lease.[24]

▲ **EXAMPLE 48**   On July 1, 1995, Miller Corporation enters into a 5-year lease for a telephone system. Under the terms of the lease, Miller is to pay $100 per month in rent. Miller has the option of renewing the lease for 2 years for $50 a month when the original lease expires. At the end of the renewal period, the phone system will be removed, and the lease cannot be renewed. What is Miller's rent deduction for the phone lease for 1995?

Discussion: The terms of the lease indicate that Miller does not obtain an equity interest in the phone system. No part of the rental payment goes toward an equity interest in the system, nor is there any provision for ownership to be transferred at the end of the lease. Therefore, the $100 monthly rent payment is a current deduction. For 1995, Miller can deduct $600 for the 6 months' rent paid.

▲ **EXAMPLE 49**   Assume in example 48 that Miller could purchase the phone system on July 1, 1995, for $4,500 or rent it for $100 a month for 5 years. If Miller decides to rent, it can purchase the phone system for $100 at the end of the lease. What is Miller's deduction for the phone lease for 1995 if Miller decides to lease the phone system?

Discussion: Under the terms of the lease, Miller will pay more in rent ($6,000) than the asset would cost to purchase. The agreement is in the form of an installment purchase of an asset ($4,500 purchase price + $1,500 in interest). This conclusion is also supported by the fact that Miller can purchase the system for a nominal price at the end of the lease. Based on these facts, Miller should treat the rent payment as an installment purchase of an asset. Miller would be entitled to deduct imputed interest expense ($1,500 over the term of the lease) on the contract. In addition, Miller could depreciate its basis ($4,500) in the phone system.

Legal Fees.   Legal expenses are allowed as a deduction if they have a business purpose. To determine whether **legal fees** are deductible, look to the origin of the expense. If the legal fee originates in a profit-motivated activity or qualifies as a specifically allowed itemized deduction, it is deductible. If the expense originates from a personal transaction, such as a divorce or the preparation of a will, the expense is not deductible.

▲ **EXAMPLE 50**   Salvadore is being sued by a client who fell in his store and hurt himself. Salvadore has spent $5,000 in legal fees to defend his business against his customer's claims. Can Salvadore deduct the legal fees?

Discussion: The legal fees originated in Salvadore's business. Because the fees are an ordinary and necessary expense of doing business, Salvadore may deduct the $5,000 in legal expenses.

▲ **EXAMPLE 51**   Elissa, Salvadore's wife, has filed for divorce and has asked for a large property settlement. The only way Salvadore can pay Elissa the amount she is seeking is to sell his business. Salvadore has paid $6,000 in legal fees related to the divorce. Can he deduct his legal fees?

Discussion: Salvadore may not deduct the personal legal fees. The legal expenses did not arise from the conduct of his business. The fact that he may have to sell his business merely reflects the results of the legal claim that arose from a personal relationship.[25]

▲ **EXAMPLE 52**   Salvadore has been having a bad year. In August, he received a letter from the IRS stating that he owed an additional $34,000 in income taxes. Salvadore paid his attorney $12,000 to settle the case with the IRS. Can he deduct the attorney's fees?

Discussion: Salvadore will be able to deduct the attorney's fees, because they were incurred in relation to the collection of a tax. The tax law allows the deduction of any costs related to the collection of the tax. To the extent the amount in dispute relates to his business, he may deduct the attorney's fees as an ordinary and necessary business expense. However, any portion that relates to other types of income or deductions is only allowed as a miscellaneous itemized deduction.

In addition to the disallowance of personal legal fees, certain legal fees may have to be capitalized as part of an asset's basis. For example, legal fees related to establishing ownership of property, defending title to property, or otherwise related to the acquisition or improvement of an asset are not deductible. These costs must be added to the affected asset's basis. However, the taxpayer can deduct legal fees paid to protect an existing business, its reputation, and goodwill.

▲ LIMITED MIXED-USE EXPENSES

As indicated in Chapter 5, mixed-use expenses and expenses related to using mixed-use assets must be analyzed and allocated between business and personal expenses. The discussion that follows examines the three areas that Congress has determined have the greatest potential for abuse: hobby, vacation home, and home office expenses. The common thread among all three activities is that they are entered into by individuals who have an incentive to attempt to convert personal expenditures within the activity to deductible business expenses. Thus, detailed rules have been written to prevent this from happening. The legislative grace, ability-to-pay, business purpose, and capital recovery concepts all apply to these deductions and indicate that these expenses should be allowed to the extent they were incurred to earn income. As these topics are discussed, note the similarities in the calculation of the deductions and how the income from the mixed activity provides a limit on the amount deductible. The common denominator among all three mixed-use activities is that business expenses in excess of income earned in a hobby, vacation home, or home office activity are not deductible, because they lack a business purpose.

Hobby Expenses

A taxpayer may engage in an income-earning activity primarily for personal reasons that prevents its qualification as a trade or business or an investment activity. The activity may be carried on mainly for recreation and personal enjoyment, with profitability a secondary concern. In tax law jargon, this type of activity is referred to as a **hobby,** because it lacks a business purpose. However, the legislative grace, ability-to-pay, and capital recovery concepts all indicate that hobby income should be taxed only to the extent it exceeds the related expenses.

The hobby rules apply when a taxpayer has income and expenses in an activity without a predominant profit motive. The tax law considers nine factors in determining whether an activity that earns income is profit motivated and should be treated as a business or is subject to the hobby rules. These factors are

- Whether the taxpayer carries on the activity in a businesslike manner
- Expertise of the taxpayer or the taxpayer's reliance on advice of experts
- Time and effort the taxpayer spends to carry on the activity
- Expectation that the assets used in the activity will appreciate in value

- Taxpayer's success in similar activities
- Taxpayer's history of income or losses in the activity
- Amount of occasional profits, if any
- Taxpayer's financial status
- Elements of personal pleasure or recreation in the activity[26]

The courts consider and weigh all these factors in determining whether a taxpayer's activity constitutes a hobby. An activity's classification as a hobby is based on all the facts and circumstances presented by the taxpayer. Thus, the classification is subjective and is not determined by a single factor or by the presence of more factors indicating a hobby than a profit objective. The courts also will consider other factors relevant to the taxpayer's situation that may indicate a profit motive. In many situations, the determination of whether an activity is a hobby is best left to a tax expert.

A taxpayer's deductible hobby expenses cannot exceed the gross income from the hobby.[27] The expenses in excess of income are referred to as **hobby losses**. Hobby losses are not deductible. Hobby deductions must be computed in a specific order. First the deductions are grouped into three classes:

1. Expenses that could be deducted as either business expenses or itemized deductions (e.g., home mortgage interest and property taxes)

2. Expenses related to the hobby that would be deductible if the hobby had qualified as a business (e.g., supplies, utilities, repairs, auto expenses)

3. Depreciation on assets used to carry on the hobby activity

Category 1 expenses are deducted from hobby income first. If any income remains, category 2 expenses are deducted. Category 3 can then be deducted to the extent that any income remains after deducting categories 1 and 2. In addition, hobby expenses must be reported as miscellaneous itemized deductions. Recall that miscellaneous itemized deductions (discussed in depth in Chapter 8) are subject to a 2 percent of adjusted gross income limitation. Because hobby expenses are classified as miscellaneous itemized deductions, a taxpayer might not be allowed a deduction for part or all of the hobby expenses. Thus, the benefit of hobby deductions is limited in two ways: The expenses are allowed only to the extent of hobby income, and the actual amount deductible is limited as an itemized deduction. If a taxpayer uses the standard deduction instead of listing the actual itemized deductions, all benefit from the hobby deduction is lost.

▲ **EXAMPLE 53**   Barclay is a physician. As a hobby, Barclay operates a farm where she raises exotic animals. During the year, Barclay had gross income of $18,000 from the farm and paid the following expenses:

Property taxes on the farm	$ 6,000
Labor, feed, and veterinary costs	10,000
Depreciation on farm building and equipment	4,000

How much of the $20,000 that Barclay incurred as expenses can be deducted?

Discussion: Barclay's deductions are limited to the $18,000 from the farm for the year. Her deductible expenses are determined as follows:

Gross income	$18,000
Less: Category 1 expenses that would be allowed as either personal or business deductions (e.g., itemized property tax).	(6,000)
Balance of income	$12,000
Less: Category 2 expenses of operating the farm that would be deductible in a trade or business (e.g., labor, feed, vet).	(10,000)
Balance of income	$ 2,000
Less: Depreciation expense. The $4,000 expense for this category cannot exceed the balance of income before the deduction.	(2,000)
Balance of income	$ -0-

Barclay should report $18,000 in gross income and $18,000 in miscellaneous itemized deductions. The $2,000 in depreciation deductions in excess of income cannot be deducted as a hobby expense. The $2,000 in excess expenses is referred to as the *nondeductible hobby loss.*

Discussion: On the surface, it appears that Barclay's hobby has no effect on her income. However, the $18,000 in hobby expenses is subject to the 2% of adjusted gross income limitation for miscellaneous itemized deductions. For example, if Barclay's adjusted gross income were $100,000 and she had no other miscellaneous itemized deductions, her deduction for hobby expenses would be limited to $16,000:

Total allowable hobby expenses	$18,000
Less: 2% of AGI ($100,000 × 2%)	(2,000)
Actual hobby expense deduction	$16,000

Therefore, although hobby expenses technically are limited to hobby income, the net effect is that Barclay reports $2,000 in income ($18,000 − $16,000) from the hobby.

Vacation Home Expenses

A **vacation home** can be a house, apartment, condominium, mobile home, boat, or similar property. A taxpayer who owns a vacation home that is used for family vacations and then rented to unrelated people during the remainder of the year is subject to special rules. The deductibility of vacation home rental expenses depends on the rental income and the extent of the taxpayer's personal use of the home.

Table 6–2 summarizes the treatment of vacation home expenses.[28] As the table shows, if the taxpayer rents out the vacation home for a minimal period during the year (14 days or fewer), the dwelling is not considered to have been used for a business purpose and is treated as a personal residence. For administrative convenience, the rental income is not reported and rent expenses are not deducted. As discussed in Chapter 8, home mortgage interest and property taxes on the property can be deducted as a personal itemized deduction.

▲ **EXAMPLE 54**   Amber owns a summer cabin that she and her family use for personal purposes from May through August of each year. In August, Expando Corporation pays Amber $1,000 to rent her cabin for 5 days. Amber's expenses related to the cabin include $5,000 in taxes and interest and $2,000 in utilities and maintenance for the year. What is the proper treatment of the summer cabin income and expense?

▲ **Table 6–2**

SUMMARY OF VACATION
HOME USE TESTS

Rent Period	Personal Use Period	Tax Result
14 days or fewer	Remainder of year.	A personal residence. Do not report income and do not deduct rent expenses.
More than 14 days	More than 14 days, or more than 10% of the number of days rented at a fair rental price, whichever is longer.	A vacation home. Report rental income and allocate rental expenses using specified priority. Expenses are limited to gross rent income. A loss cannot be deducted.
More than 14 days	14 days or fewer, or 10% or less of the number of days rented at a fair rental price, whichever is longer.	A rental property. Report like any other rental property. Expenses must be allocated between rental and personal use.

Discussion: Because the cabin was rented for 14 days or fewer, Amber does not have to report the $1,000 received from Expando Corporation as rental income. The cabin is considered a personal residence, and Amber may not deduct any rental expense related to the rental use of the vacation home by Expando. Amber can deduct the property taxes and interest as personal itemized deductions.

If the home is rented for more than 14 days and used for personal use for a minimal length of time (the greater of 14 days or 10 percent of the days rented), the property is treated the same as investment rental property. Expenses allocable to personal use of the dwelling are not deductible. Expenses related to rental use that have a business purpose are deducted just as they would be for any other profit-motivated transaction.

As the second row of Table 6–2 shows, using the vacation home for more than 14 days as rental property and using it for more than 14 days as a personal vacation home limits the deduction for expenses to the amount of the rental income. Expenses that have a business purpose are deducted in the same order as for hobby expenses. But unlike a hobby loss, vacation home expenses in excess of current income can be carried forward indefinitely for use in a later year in which there is enough rent income to offset them.

The allocation of vacation home expenses between personal use and rental use is a controversial issue. The IRS requires that the taxpayer allocate vacation home expenses between personal and rental by using the ratio of personal days to total days of use (sum of personal days and rental days).[29] However, the courts have allowed interest expense and real estate taxes to be allocated over 365 days instead of the actual number of days the home was used for personal and rental use.[30] The court's allocation of interest expense and property tax seems more reasonable than the IRS's method, because these expenses are more closely related to a period of time than to actual use. In addition, this method allocates less interest and property taxes to the rental property, leaving more to deduct as a personal itemized deduction. This generally results in the allowance of a greater overall deduction on the vacation home. Other expenses, such as utilities and maintenance, are more closely related to use and should be allocated to actual days of use. The courts' allocation of interest and taxes, which generally results in a larger deduction for the taxpayer, continues to be opposed by the IRS. Therefore, the method of allocating vacation home expenses should be chosen after consulting with a tax expert.

▲ **EXAMPLE 55** Latoya owns a cabin that she uses for 20 days for her family's vacation during the current year. The cabin is rented to others for 40 days, for which she receives gross rental income of $5,500. Her total expenses of maintaining the cabin are

Interest and property taxes	$6,000
Utilities, insurance, and repairs	1,500
Depreciation expense	4,500

What are Latoya's allowable deductions on the cabin?

Discussion: Because Latoya used the property for personal use for more than 14 days, the total deductions allocable to the rental are limited to rent income. The first step is to allocate the expenses to rental use and personal use. Latoya has the option of using the IRS method of allocating all expenses based on the total days of use, which yields the following allocation:

	Total Cost	Rent Use Ratio	Amount Allocated to Rental Use	Amount Allocated to Personal Use
Interest and property taxes	$6,000	40/60	$4,000	$2,000
Utilities, insurance, repairs	1,500	40/60	1,000	500
Depreciation expense	4,500	40/60	3,000	1,500

Latoya's deductions for the rental are limited to the $5,500 in gross rental income. Further, the $5,500 in deductions must be taken from the expenses in the same order as deductions for hobby expenses:

Gross rental income	$5,500
Less: Deductions that are allowable as either itemized deductions or as rental expenses (interest and property taxes).	(4,000)
Balance of income	$1,500
Less: Deductions that are allowable only as a rental expense (utilities, insurance, repairs).	(1,000)
Balance of income	$ 500
Less: Depreciation. Limited to the balance of income after other expenses.	(500)
Balance of income	$ -0-

The $2,500 ($3,000 − $500) in depreciation that was disallowed because of the income limitation is carried into future years for deduction if there is enough rental income to absorb the expense. In addition, Latoya can deduct the $2,000 of personal interest and property taxes as a personal itemized deduction. Assuming that Latoya itemizes deductions, the net effect of the cabin on her income is a reduction of $2,000 because of the deductions for personal itemized interest and property taxes.

Latoya may elect to allocate interest and property taxes according to the number of days in the year, rather than days of total use, per the court's method. All other expenses would still be allocated according to days of total use. This would result in a larger total deduction by allocating less interest and property taxes against the rental income and more to Latoya's itemized deductions. The allocation of the $6,000 in interest and property taxes under this allocation choice would be

	Total Cost	Rent Use Ratio	Amount Allocated to Rental Use	Amount Allocated to Personal Use
Interest and property taxes	$6,000	40/365	$660	$5,340

Latoya's allowable rental deductions are still limited to the $5,500 in gross rental income:

Gross rental income	$5,500
Less: Interest and property taxes	(660)
Balance of income	$4,840
Less: Utilities, insurance, repairs	(1,000)
Balance of income	$3,840
Less: Depreciation	(3,000)
Net rental income	$ 840

Although Latoya has $840 in net rental income under this allocation method, her itemized deduction for interest and property taxes increases to $5,340. Assuming that Latoya itemizes deductions, the effect of using the court's allocation method for interest and taxes is to reduce her taxable income by $4,500 ($5,340 − $840). This compares with the $2,000 reduction in taxable income using the IRS allocation method.

Home Office Expenses

A taxpayer who operates a trade or business from home can claim a deduction for expenses related to its business use. Expenses such as mortgage interest, real property taxes, insurance, utilities, repairs, and depreciation can be allocated on a reasonable basis to the area of the home used for a business purpose. This deduction is commonly referred to as the **home office deduction.** To claim a deduction, strict tests must be satisfied.

A specific part of the home must be used exclusively for carrying on a trade or business. A taxpayer who does not have another business location can deduct the cost of using an area in the home for storing inventory on a regular basis. If a room is used for a trade or business and is also used for investing or personal activities, the exclusive use test is not met and no deduction for home office expenses is allowed.

The home office area must also be regularly used as the principal place to conduct a trade or business belonging to the taxpayer or as a place to meet or deal with patients, clients, or customers in the normal course of the trade or business.[31] If the portion of the home used for business is a separate structure, the taxpayer needs only to show that it was used in connection with a trade or business. If these tests are met, the taxpayer can deduct expenses related to using part of the home for business.

Employees who use an office in their home to conduct business for their employer must meet an additional test. Employee use must be "for the convenience of the employer" and "required as a condition of employment" before any deductions for a home office may be taken.[32] Because most employee use of a home office is for the convenience of the employee (i.e., people work at home because they want to, not because they are required to), most typical employee situations will not result in a deduction for home office expenses.

▲ **EXAMPLE 56**   Reginald is an engineer for Arclight Petroleum Co. Rather than work late at the office, Reginald often takes home Arclight work, which he works on in an office in his home. Reginald prefers to bring work home so that he can have dinner with his family and not have to return to his office late at night or on weekends. Can Reginald deduct any of the costs of maintaining the home office?

Discussion: Because Reginald's use of the office is related to his employment with Arclight, he must prove that the use of the home office is for Arclight's convenience and that it is required as a condition of his employment. Under the facts as given, Reginald's use is for his convenience, not Arclight's. Thus, the deduction would not be allowed. In addition, it is doubtful that Arclight requires Reginald to maintain an office in his home in order to maintain employment, which is also required for deductibility.

Expenses of maintaining the home are allocated between the home office and the areas used as a residence. The expenses may be allocated on the basis of the number of rooms or on the basis of square footage of floor space in the home. The method chosen should reasonably reflect the area used as an office. The home office deduction follows the same computational pattern as the hobby and vacation home deductions discussed earlier. However, the income limitation is based on income earned from the home office activity after deducting all other business expenses that are unrelated to the use of the home office. If the home office deductions exceed the income limitation, the excess may be carried forward and used to reduce income in a later year.

▲ **EXAMPLE 57**   Kendall uses 1 room in her home as the primary location for her business. Her home has 6 rooms and is 2,500 square feet. The office area is 300 square feet or 12% of the total area. For the current year, she had $15,000 in mortgage interest and real estate taxes and $8,000 in insurance, repairs, and maintenance related to her home. Kendall determined that depreciation on the house for the current year would be $4,000. Kendall had $21,000 in income and $17,800 in other business expenses. What is Kendall's allowable home office deduction for the current year?

Discussion: Kendall's home office deduction cannot exceed her income from the home office activity after deducting all other business expenses that are unrelated to the home office. Thus, her maximum home office deduction is $3,200 ($21,000 − $17,800). The amounts that Kendall can deduct for her home office are

Income limitation on home office expenses ($21,000 − $17,800)	$3,200
1. Deduct expenses otherwise allowed as a deduction under other tax rules:	
Interest and taxes ($15,000 × 12%)	(1,800)
Balance of income	$1,400
2. Deduct office expenses not otherwise allowed as a deduction:	
Insurance, repairs, and other expenses ($8,000 × 12%)	(960)
Balance of income	$ 440
3. Deduct depreciation on office portion of residence:	

Current-year depreciation	$4,000	
Business percentage	× .12	
Depreciation on office	$ 480	
Deduction limited to balance of income		(440)
Balance of income		$ -0-

The $40 ($480 − $440) in depreciation that was not allowed as a deduction in the current year because of the income limitation can be carried forward to next year.

You must be cognitive of two important points concerning the operation of a business from home. First, the expenses of operating the business that are not related to the home office are allowed as a deduction, even if the home office expense is disallowed because of the income limitation. Second, in order to deduct telephone expenses relating to a home office, the taxpayer must have a separate phone line for the business. If the taxpayer has only one phone, the basic phone charge cannot be deducted; only long distance business-related phone calls are allowed as a deduction.

▲ **EXAMPLE 58**   Alvin operates his business from home. His sales for the year totaled $50,000. He incurred $55,000 in travel expense, employee wages, depreciation on equipment, and other expenses unrelated to his home office. The residence expenses allocated to the home office using the approach illustrated totaled $2,000. What are Alvin's allowable deductions?

Discussion: Alvin's deductible loss from his business before considering a home office deduction is $5,000 ($50,000 − $55,000). He cannot deduct any of his home office expense in the current year because of the income limitations. However, the $2,000 in home office expenses can be carried to next year and deducted if he has enough income.

▲ SUMMARY

Meal and entertainment expenses are allowed as business deductions if the expenses are ordinary, necessary, reasonable in amount, and directly related to or associated with the active conduct of the taxpayer's business activity. However, only 50 percent of the meal and entertainment expenses is normally deductible. Auto expense deductions can be based on the actual cost of using a car for business or by using a standard mileage rate method. Regardless of which method is used, the taxpayer must keep detailed records documenting the business use of the car. If the primary reason for making an out-of-town trip is a business purpose, the travel expenses for transportation, 50 percent of meals, lodging, and incidental expenses can be deducted. When time on the trip is devoted to vacation or personal activities, the amount of the deduction may be limited. A deduction is allowed for up to $25 per donee each year for business gifts. Proper documentation is necessary to be sure that an entertainment, auto, travel, or gift expense will be allowed as a deduction.

Education expenses can be deducted if the expense either is required by the employer as a condition of employment or maintains or improves the skills required in the taxpayer's trade or business. The tax law allows a deduction for reasonable compensation to employees. Unless certain exceptions are met, the deduction for compensation paid to a covered employee of a publicly traded corporation is limited to $1,000,000. Covered employees are the CEO and the next four highest-paid officers of the corporation.

Business and nonbusiness bad debts are deductible only if there is a valid business purpose. Nonbusiness bad debts that are in fact gifts are not deductible. The bad debt deduction is determined using the specific charge-off method. Accrued expenses owed to a related cash basis taxpayer are not allowed as a deduction until the item is paid and included in the cash basis taxpayer's income. Deductions for insurance, taxes, rent, and legal fees are subject to special rules that limit the deduction or, in some instances, require capitalization of the expenditure as an asset.

The deduction for hobby, vacation home, and home office expenses is limited to the amount of income earned from the activity. If these mixed-use expenses exceed the related income, the excess expenses are not allowed as a deduction from other sources of income such as wages, dividends, and interest. Taxpayers claiming deductions for a hobby, vacation home, or home office must observe strict requirements to be able to deduct the expenses.

▲ KEY TERMS

actual cost method (p. 229)
assessment for local benefits
   (p. 243)
associated with (p. 225)
auto expense (p. 228)
business bad debt (p. 236)
business gift (p. 232)
directly related (p. 225)
education expense (p. 233)

hobby (p. 245)
hobby loss (p. 246)
home office deduction (p. 250)
legal fees (p. 244)
meal and entertainment expense
   (p. 225)
nonbusiness bad debt (p. 236)
reasonable compensation (p. 235)
specific charge-off method (p. 238)

standard mileage rate method
   (p. 229)
substantiation requirements
   (p. 233)
tax home (p. 230)
travel expenses (p. 230)
vacation home (p. 247)

▲ PRIMARY TAX LAW SOURCES

[1] Sec. 274—Provides the limitations on deductions for meals and entertainment, and business gifts; requires that deductions for such items be substantiated by adequate records.

[2] Reg. Sec. 1.274-2—Explains the general rules for meal and entertainment deductions; defines expenditures *directly related* and *associated with* business for purposes of determining the deductibility of entertainment costs.

[3] Sec. 274(a)(3)—Disallows deductions for club dues organized for business, pleasure, recreation, or social purposes.

[4] Rev. Rul. 94-47—Further explains Rev. Rul. 90-23, which provides examples of allowable deductions for a taxpayer's daily transportation expenses.

[5] Rev. Proc. 94-73—Sets the 1995 standard mileage rate for determining automobile expenses at 30 cents per mile.

[6] Rev. Proc. 95-9—Provides the maximum yearly depreciation deductions on automobiles purchased in 1995.

[7] Reg. Sec. 1.162-2—Allows deduction for travel expenses; provides treatment of business travel mixed with personal activities.

[8] Reg. Sec. 1.274-5T—Provides the substantiation rules that must be followed in deducting meals, entertainment, and travel expenses.

[9] Reg. Sec. 1.162-5(a)—Sets forth the types of educational expenses that are deductible.

[10] Reg. Sec. 1.162-5(b)—Sets forth the types of educational expenses that are not deductible.

[11] Reg. Sec. 1.162-7—Sets forth guidelines for deductions of compensation paid for personal services.

[12] Internal Revenue Service Manual 4233, Sec. 232—Provides the factors that the IRS considers in determining whether compensation is reasonable.

[13] Sec. 162(m)—Sets forth the rules for deducting compensation in excess of $1,000,000.

[14] Sec. 166—Specifies the allowable deductions for bad debts.

[15] Reg. Sec. 1.166-3—Allows a deduction for partial worthlessness of a business bad debt.

[16] Reg. Sec. 1.166-5—Defines *nonbusiness bad debt* and specifies the treatment as a short-term capital loss in the year the debt becomes worthless.

[17] Sec. 267—Defines *related parties* and disallows accrual of deductions to a cash basis related party.

[18] Sec. 264—Disallows a deduction for life insurance premiums paid on any employee when the taxpayer making the payments is the beneficiary of the policy.

[19] Sec. 164—Specifies the allowable deductions for taxes.

[20] Reg. Sec. 1.164-1—Specifies the types of taxes that are deductible as trade or business expenses.

[21] Reg. Sec. 1.164-2—Denies deductions for certain types of taxes.

[22] Reg. Sec. 1.164-6—Requires the apportionment of the deduction for real property taxes between the buyer and the seller of real property based on the number of days each party owned the property during the year.

[23] Oesterrich v. Comm., 226 F.2d 798 (9th Cir. 1958)—Held that in determining whether a lease is a valid lease or an installment sale, the intent of the parties as determined by the terms of the lease agreement is controlling.

[24] Rev. Proc. 75-21—States the criteria used to determine whether a lease is a valid lease or an installment sale of property.

[25] U.S. v. Gilmore 83 S.Ct. 623 (1963)—Held that the deductibility of legal expenses depends on whether the claim arises in connection with the taxpayer's business activities. The consequences of the transaction, in this case the sale of the business, are not a factor.

[26] Reg. Sec. 1.183-2—Sets forth the criteria for determining when an activity constitutes a hobby.

[27] Sec. 183—Limits the deductions allowed for hobbies.

[28] Sec. 280A—Limits the allowable deductions on home offices and vacation homes; defines requirements for home office expense deduction and what constitutes a vacation home.

[29] Prop: Reg. Sec. 1.280A-3—Requires that all expenses related to a vacation home be allocated between rental use and personal use on the basis of the number of days of total use of the vacation home.

[30] Bolton v. Comm., 694 F.2d 596 (9th Cir. 1982)—Affirmed the Tax Court's holding that the proper allocation of interest and taxes on a vacation home is based on the number of days in the year, rather than the number of days of total use.

[31] Comm. v. Soliman, 113 S. Ct. 701 (1993)—Held that for purposes of determining what constitutes a principal place of business for purposes of the home office deduction, the home office must be the focal point of the taxpayer's business.

[32] Sec. 280A—See footnote 28.

▲ DISCUSSION QUESTIONS

1. Most expenditures that have a business purpose and meet the ordinary, necessary, and reasonable requirements are deductible. However, specific rules must be adhered to in determining the deductibility of many expenses that meet this test. Why are these specific rules necessary?

2. What requirements must be met in order for meal and entertainment expenses to be deductible?

3. How does an entertainment expense directly related to business differ from an entertainment expense associated with business?

4. What problems does the taxpayer who uses an automobile for both business and personal purposes encounter? What option(s) does the taxpayer have regarding the automobile expense deduction?

5. What records are necessary to properly document travel, entertainment, and gift expenses?

6. Under what circumstances are business gifts deductible?

7. When are educational expenses deductible? not deductible?

8. Is it possible that an education expense incurred by one taxpayer is deductible, whereas the same expense incurred by another taxpayer is not deductible? Explain.

9. Is all compensation paid to an employee deductible? Discuss the circumstances in which employee compensation cannot be deducted.

10. Explain the difference in the tax treatment of business and nonbusiness bad debts.

11. What accounting method must be used to account for bad debts that result from the sale of merchandise or the provision of services?

12. Explain how the tax benefit rule may apply to bad debt deductions.

13. Are all reasonable compensation payments made to a related party deductible? When are the payments deductible?

14. What requirements must be met in order to deduct life insurance premiums paid on an employee's policy?

15. Are sales taxes deductible? Explain.

16. Discuss the factors that must be considered when determining whether to deduct or capitalize rental payments.

17. Are all legal fees paid by a taxpayer deductible? Explain.

18. Explain the rationale for the treatment of deductions related to hobbies, vacation homes, and home offices.

19. What is/are the requirement(s) for determining whether a residence used for personal purposes is a vacation home or a true rental property?

20. Under what circumstances can a taxpayer deduct the costs of a home office?

21. How is the income limitation for home offices different from that for hobbies and vacation homes?

22. Discuss the reporting of deductions related to a hobby versus deductions related to a vacation home or a home office. State any potential negative tax effects from the reporting requirements.

23. After a business meeting, Tray took his client to dinner. Dinner cost $65, including $5 in sales tax and a $10 tip. The cab fare to and from the restaurant cost another $25. How much may Tray deduct as an entertainment expense?

▲ **PROBLEMS**

24. Marjorie is an accountant and Alana is an attorney. They have been business acquaintances for about 10 years. They meet every Friday at 6 P.M. at a local tavern to socialize. As always happens with attorneys and accountants, they discuss what is happening in their offices. They take turns paying the bar tab, which averages $30 for each meeting. Because Marjorie has kept the receipts for the nights she paid, she would like to claim a deduction for her $600 in expenses. How much may Marjorie deduct as an entertainment expense?

25. Malina is a manager for Mail Order Co. While on a business trip to Chicago, she entertained several sales representatives of a client of Mail Order Co. The total cost of the entertainment expense was $750. When she returned home, Malina gave Mail Order Co. receipts and other information to specifically account for the entertainment expense. Mail Order reimbursed Malina for the $750 she spent on entertainment. How much can Malina deduct? what about Mail Order?

26. For each of the following situations, explain whether a deduction should be allowed for entertainment expenses:

a. Gayle, a dentist, invited 50 of her best patients to her daughter's wedding reception. The cost of the reception related to the presence of her patients was $5,000.

b. Stan is one of 5 shift supervisors responsible for 100 employees at Label House, Inc. Stan regularly meets with the other shift supervisors at the plant. In addition, Stan makes it a practice to go to lunch at least once a week with each of the other 4 shift supervisors in order to network. During the current year, Stan paid $1,500 for his and the other supervisors' lunches. Stan's job description does not require him to entertain the other supervisors.

c. Jan is a real estate broker who holds an open house for a different client each Sunday afternoon. During the open house, Jan provides cookies and soft drinks for whoever visits the house. Jan pays $2,000 for open house entertainment.

d. Felicia is vice president of sales for Drivitt, Inc. She invited the company's major clients and some of her coworkers from Drivitt to her annual Super Bowl party. Most guests attended with their spouses. The party was held in a separate room at a local sports bar and cost her $1,500.

27. Enrique owns a real estate business in Hugoville. He is an avid football fan and rents a skybox at County Stadium to see the Hugoville Hurricanes. The cost of the skybox for 8 games is $40,000, including 10 tickets to each game. The most expensive nonluxury box seat is $75. After closing a real estate deal, Enrique invites 9 business associates to watch the Monday night game in his skybox. Food and drinks cost $430. What amount can Enrique deduct as entertainment expense?

28. Julianita is a sales representative for a food distributor and spends only 1 day of the week in the office. Her office is 15 miles from home. She also has a part-time job as a bartender. Typically, she works 2 nights during the week and 1 night on the weekend. The restaurant where she works is 8 miles from her office and 12 miles from her home.

a. What portion(s) of Julianita's travel is considered business?

b. During the year, Julianita kept the following record of her travel:

	Miles	
Home to office	750	commuting
Office to home	375	"
Office to restaurant	200	Travel
Restaurant to home	1,800	commuting
Home to restaurant	600	Commuting
Home to clients to home	8,500	Travel
Clients to restaurant	1,875	Travel

If she uses the standard mileage rate, what amount can she deduct as a business expense?

29. Cassandra owns her own business and drives her van 20,000 miles a year for business and 5,000 miles a year for commuting and personal use. Cassandra purchases a new van in 1995 and wants to claim the largest tax deduction possible for business use. Cassandra's total auto expenses for 1995 are as follows:

Gas, oil, and maintenance	$3,000
Insurance	800
Interest on car loan	1,700
Depreciation	3,060
License	540
Parking fees and tolls	250

Determine Cassandra's 1995 deduction for business use of the van.

30. Mario owns his own business and drives his car 12,000 miles a year for business and 3,000 miles a year for commuting and personal use. He wants to claim the largest tax deduction possible for business use of his car. His total auto expenses for 1995 are as follows:

Gas, oil, and maintenance	$ 920
Insurance	275
Interest on car loan	100
Depreciation	3,060
License	150
Parking fees and tolls	25

Determine Mario's 1995 deduction for business use of his car.

31. Juanita traveled to San Francisco for 5 days. The following facts are related to the trip:

Round trip airfare	$650
Hotel daily rate for single or double occupancy	100
Meals—$55 per day	55
Incidentals—$15 per day	15

   a. If she spent 4 days on business and 1 day sightseeing, what amount may she deduct as travel expense?

   b. If she spent 2 days on business and 3 days sightseeing, what amount may she deduct as travel expense?

   c. Juanita spent 3 days on business and 2 days sightseeing; her husband Jorge accompanied her on the trip. Jorge went sightseeing every day and attended business receptions with Juanita at night. Assume that Jorge's expenses are identical to Juanita's. What amount may Juanita and Jorge deduct as travel expense?

32. Olga has to travel to Philadelphia for 2 days on business. Olga enjoys history and is planning to visit the Liberty Bell and other historic sites in the city. If time permits, she would like to make a side trip to nearby Gettysburg. A friend of Olga's told her, "The best part of traveling on business is that once the business is over, you can sightsee all you want and the cost is tax deductible." Olga, who is self-employed, has scheduled her trip for the Labor Day weekend so that she can spend 3 days sightseeing. Is the advice Olga's friend gave her correct? Why or why not?

33. Karl, a dentist, owns three rental properties. In January, he attended a 3-day conference in Phoenix entitled, "How to Build a Real Estate Empire with DEPCO Property." The following facts are related to the trip:

Airfare	$450
Hotel daily rate	95
Meals—$45 per day	45
Incidentals—$20 per day	20
Entertainment	140

   What amount may he deduct as travel expense?

34. Floyd owns an antique shop. During the year, Floyd and his wife Amanda, who works as a real estate broker, attended a 2-day antique show in Boston. The following facts are related to the trip:

Train per person	$ 95
Hotel daily rate—double occupancy*	105
Meals—$40 per day per person	40
Incidentals—$18 per day per person	18

*The hotel rate for double occupancy is $20 more than the single occupancy rate.

What amount can Floyd and Amanda deduct as travel expense? Explain.

35. Bob has 6 employees in his men's clothing store. Every year at Christmas, he gives the employees a party. At the party, he gives each employee a cash gift based on the number of years the employee has worked at the store. This year, the party cost $480, and the gifts totaled $1,500. How much can Bob deduct as entertainment and gift expense?

36. Cameron is a salesperson for Local Feed Co. During the current year, Cameron gave Hank, his biggest customer, a gold watch for Christmas. The watch cost $700. Cameron gave Hank the watch because he wanted to maintain a good relationship with him. How much of the $700 is deductible by Cameron? What are the tax effects for Hank?

37. For each of the following situations determine whether the expenses are deductible as an education expense:
    a. Dorothy owns a real estate business. She is enrolled in a 1-year weekend MBA program that meets in a city three hours away. She takes a train to and from the city. A one-year weekend pass for the train is $800. The fee for the MBA program, including lodging, meals, books, and tuition, is $25,000.
    b. Forest is employed as a production manager for a printing company. He is enrolled in a night course ($350) at the local college. The course is not required by his employer but does improve his job skills. *from*
    c. Elise is a recent graduate of law school and has been hired by a local firm. The firm expects Elise to pass the bar exam on her first try. To help her prepare for the bar exam, she is taking a law review course that costs $1,500. *NO – New Career.*
    d. Simon is the managing partner of an accounting firm and is required to attend 30 hours of continuing education every year. State law requires that 5 hours be in ethics training. The cost of the 5-hour ethics course is $400; the remaining 25 hours of continuing education cost $1,800.
    e. Assume the same facts as in part d, except that state law does not require 5 hours of continuing education in ethics.

38. Pat is a professor of German. During the summer, she spent two months in Germany studying local culture and perfecting her German. The cost of the summer included $2,000 for airfare, $4,000 for lodging, $1,800 for meals, and $900 for incidental expenses. How much of the travel costs can Pat deduct? Explain.

39. For each of the following situations, determine the amount that is deductible as compensation expense:
    a. Molly is the leading salesperson and third-highest-paid employee of Riveredge Corporation. She is not an officer of the company. Riveredge is a publicly traded corporation and during the year paid Molly a salary of $100,000, a bonus of $200,000, and sales commissions of $800,000. The company has no formal performance-based compensation agreement.
    b. Alejandro is the eighth-highest-paid officer of the publicly traded Mermer Corporation. The company paid him a salary of $450,000, a bonus of $500,000, and made mortgage payments of $60,000 on his behalf. The bonus he received is based on the stock price of the company and subjective evaluations from his peers. The performance goals were established by the compensation committee and were approved by the shareholders of the corporation. Before the company paid the bonus, the compensation committee certified that Alejandro had attained the performance goals.
    c. Assume the same facts as in part b, except that Alejandro is the chief executive officer of Mermer Corporation.
    d. Cory is the fourth-highest-paid officer of the closely held Mast Corporation, which has assets of $20,000,000. The company paid Cory a salary of $600,000 and a bonus of $450,000. The payments are typical of a company in the industry with comparable assets.
    e. Evita is the eighth-highest-paid officer of the Acworth Co. Her salary for the year is $675,000, and she receives a bonus during the year of $500,000. The bonus is based on a complex set of formulas that factor in stock price, peer evaluations, subordi-

nates' evaluations, and number of years with the company. The plan has been in effect since January 1, 1992.

f. Assume the same facts as in part e, except that Evita is the second-highest-paid officer.

40. Yolanda is the third-highest-paid officer of the Dewit Corporation. Her salary is $675,000. She also receives a bonus of $420,000 based on the performance of Dewit Corporation's stock. The bonus paid to Yolanda is based solely on the performance of the corporation's stock. The standards for the bonus have been set by the outside directors and have been approved by the stockholders. Before the company paid the bonus, the outside board of directors failed to certify that the performance standards had been attained. Can the Dewit Corporation deduct her entire compensation ($1,095,000)?

41. Howard loaned $4,000 to Bud 2 years ago. The terms of the loan called for Bud to pay annual interest at 10%, with the principal amount due in 4 years. Until this year, Bud had been making the required interest payments. When he didn't receive this year's payment, Howard called Bud and found out that Bud had filed for bankruptcy. Bud's accountant estimated that only 30% of his debts would be paid after the bankruptcy proceeding. No payments were received. In the next year, Howard received $1,000 in full satisfaction of the debt under the bankruptcy proceeding. What deductions are allowed to Howard, assuming that the debt was
   a. Related to Howard's business?
   b. Unrelated to Howard's business?
   c. How would your answer to parts a and b change if Howard received $1,700 in satisfaction of the debt in the next year?

42. In 1995, Grace, Inc., has total sales of $200,000. Based on total sales, the corporation estimates that its bad debts for the year are 2% of sales. As a result, the corporation deducts $4,000 in bad debts for financial accounting purposes. At the end of 1995, the controller reviews the accounts receivable ledger to identify uncollectible accounts. She determines that $1,500 in accounts receivable cannot be collected. In addition, the accountant's analysis shows that the corporation has recovered $500 in accounts receivable written off as a bad debt for tax purposes in 1994. How should this information be reported for tax purposes?

43. UCI's financial accounting records show the following transactions in the allowance for bad debts account:

Date	Description	Debits	Credits
1/01/95	Beginning balance		30,000
7/08/95	Recovery of accounts receivable written off as uncollectible in 1994		1,000
12/31/95	Accounts specifically identified as uncollectible and written off	5,000	
12/31/95	1995 addition to account based on 1995 credit sales	___	8,000
12/31/95	Ending balance		34,000

   a. If UCI's bad debts arise from the sale of merchandise, how should the transactions in the allowance for bad debts account be reported for tax purposes?
   b. If UCI uses the cash method of accounting and the bad debts expense arose from the sale of architectural services, how would your answer to the first part change?

44. Susan loaned $2,000 to her minister a year ago. The loan is not evidenced by a note and does not bear interest. The minister has moved out of town without paying her back. She doesn't want to embarrass him by asking him to repay the loan. She would rather deduct the bad debt. How much can Susan deduct for the bad debt? Explain.

45. In addition to being an employee of Rock Hard Roofing Material, Lou owns 10% of the company's common stock. Rock Hard falls on hard times in 1994. To forestall bankruptcy, Rock Hard's employees and shareholders loan the company $1,000,000. Lou's share of the total loan is $50,000—$25,000 related to her position as an employee and $25,000 related to her ownership of stock. In early 1995, creditors force Rock Hard into bankruptcy. Lou loses her entire $50,000.
   a. Is Lou's loss related to a trade or business or an investment?
   b. Can Lou deduct her loss as a bad debt expense?

46. Lonnie owns 100% of Quality Co.'s common stock. Lonnie, the president of Quality, is a cash basis taxpayer. Quality is short of cash as of December 31, 1995, the close of its tax year. As a result, it is necessary to accrue a $50,000 bonus payable to Lonnie. As soon as the cash becomes available on January 15, 1996, Quality pays Lonnie the bonus in cash. When is the bonus deductible for the accrual basis corporation? How would your answer change if Lonnie is an accrual basis taxpayer?

47. KOM pays the following insurance premiums during 1995:

Auto accident and liability insurance:

Paid 1/1/95 Coverage period 1/1/95–12/31/95	$1,000

Fire, storm, and other casualty insurance:

Paid 3/1/95 Coverage period 3/1/95–2/29/96	$3,000

Business liability insurance:

Paid 1/1/95 Coverage period 1/1/95–12/31/97	$6,000

   a. If KOM uses the accrual method of accounting, what is the amount of the 1995 insurance expense deduction?
   b. If KOM uses the cash method of accounting, what is the amount of the 1995 insurance expense deduction?

48. For each of the following situations, state whether the expense related to the transaction can be deducted as an insurance expense:
   a. Baker Co. pays the insurance premium to provide each of its employees with a $50,000 whole life insurance policy. Baker and the insurance company consider the employee the owner of the policy. As owner of the policy, the covered employee designates the beneficiary of the life insurance proceeds in the event of the employee's death. The cost for each employee's policy is $2,000 per year.
   b. Baker Co. has a nondiscriminatory self-insured medical reimbursement plan for the benefit of its employees. Once a month, Baker transfers $1,000 in cash from its general bank account to a special medical reimbursement checking account. The transfer is based on the premium an insurance company would demand to provide the same benefits to the employees.
   c. The employees of Baker Co. handle large sums of cash that are received in the mail. To protect against loss, Baker pays a $500 annual insurance premium for an employees' fidelity bond.
   d. Baker Co. is owned by Ross. Baker pays a $1,500 annual premium for a sickness and disability income continuation insurance policy on Ross. The purpose of the policy is to provide Ross with $3,500 per month of income if he is unable to work for Baker because he is sick or disabled.

49. Indicate whether the following taxes are allowed as a current deduction for taxes paid by a business:
   a. Sales tax on the purchase of a desk
   b. State and local income, real estate, and personal property taxes
   c. Federal income, estate, and gift taxes
   d. An employer's payment to the IRS of federal income and Social Security taxes withheld from an employee's wages

50. Martin receives the following tax bills, related to a rental dwelling, from the county treasurer:

    Special assessment for installing sidewalks and streets $15,000

    Real property tax on dwelling for the 1/1–12/31/1995
        property tax year, due on 12/1/95 $ 800

    On April 1, 1995, Martin sells the dwelling for $50,000. Martin's basis in the dwelling at the date of sale is $25,000. Martin's basis in the dwelling does not reflect the property tax bills. As part of the sale contract, the buyer agrees to pay the real property taxes when they come due on December 1, 1995, but Martin has to pay the special assessment before the sale closes. What is the proper tax treatment of the tax payments?

51. Can Joe Corporation deduct the following expenses related to its business?
    a. Rent paid for the use of a postage machine. The lease is a month-to-month lease that requires a $50 monthly payment. The machine was rented for the entire year.
    b. Rent paid for the use of a truck. The lease is for 3 years and requires a $7,000 yearly rental payment. At the end of the lease, Joe Corporation can purchase the truck for $100. The truck was rented for the entire year.
    c. Legal fee paid ($500) to defend title to a vacant lot Joe is holding for construction of a storage building for use in its business.
    d. Legal fee paid ($2,500) to defend against damages suffered by a customer who was injured when he fell in the company's store.

52. As a hobby, Jane creates and sells oil paintings. During the current year, her sales total $5,000. How is the tax treatment of her hobby different from the treatment of a trade or business, if
    a. Her business expenses total $3,000?
    b. Her business expenses total $7,000?
    c. Assume that Jane itemizes her deductions and that she has an adjusted gross income of $25,000 before considering the effect of the hobby. Discuss the actual amount of the deduction Jane would receive in parts a and b.

53. Candy raises canaries as a hobby. Candy uses one room in her home, the bird room, for the birds. Because the birds are loose and fly around the bird room, the room cannot be used for family activities. During the year, her gross sales were $700. However, she had to give $85 back to a customer whose bird died within 30 days of purchase. She incurred the following expenses:

Bird seed	$125
Supplies	100
Fertilized eggs	90
Depreciation on bird room	175
Interest and property tax allocated to bird room	160
Loss on birds that died before they were sold (retail sales price)	45
State license for business	10

    What is the proper tax treatment of these items for Candy's Canary Co.? How would your answer change if her gross sales are $1,200?

54. Miko owns a single-family rental dwelling that he rents out for $500 a month for the entire year. Miko lives 5 miles from the rental house and makes 2 trips each month to inspect the house and to collect rent. In connection with the rental property, he incurs the following expenses for the current year:

Advertising in local newspaper		$ 25
Repairs and maintenance		
Replace dishwasher	$350	
Clean carpets	100	
Remove dead tree	300	
Spray for roaches	120	870
Mortgage interest		3,000
Taxes		500
Depreciation		1,500
Business gift (fruit basket & wine		
given to tenant)		75

A tenant moves into the house January 2. Because the tenant goes to the same church as Miko and is having financial difficulty, Miko pays the cost of renting a moving truck ($300) and hires 2 people ($150) to help the tenant move. How should Miko report the income and deductions on his income tax return?

55. Hamid owns and lives in a duplex. He rents the other unit to an unrelated married couple for $800 per month. During the current year, he incurred the following expenses related to the duplex:

Mortgage interest		$9,000
Property taxes		1,200
Utilities		1,900
Repairs		
Fix plumbing in Hamid's unit	$300	
Shampoo carpet in both units	150	
Fix dishwasher in rental unit	200	650
Homeowner's association fee		300
Insurance		900
Special property tax assessment to		
pave sidewalks		2,000
Depreciation (both units)		4,200

How should Hamid treat the expenditures related to the duplex? Explain.

56. Lee and Sally own a winter retreat in Harlingen, Texas, that qualifies as their second home. This year they spent 30 days in their cabin. Because of its ideal location, it is easy to rent at $90 a day and was rented for 90 days this year. The total upkeep costs of the cabin for the year were as follows:

Home mortgage interest	$8,200
Real and personal property taxes	800
Insurance	600
Utilities	700
Repairs and maintenance	1,500
Depreciation	2,000

a. What is the propert treatment of this information on Lee and Sally's tax return, using the court's allocation method?

b. What is the proper treatment of this information on Lee and Sally's tax return, using the IRS allocation method?

57. Mel and Helen own a beachfront home in Narragansett, R.I. During the year, they rented the house for 5 weeks (35 days) at $1,200 per week and used the house for personal purposes 65 days. The costs of maintaining the house for the year were

Home mortgage interest	$6,600 ✓ 14
Real property taxes	4,500 ✓ 14
Insurance	650
Utilities	1,000
Repairs and maintenance	480
Depreciation (unallocated)	3,500

a. What is the proper tax treatment of this information on their tax return?

b. What is the proper tax treatment if Helen and Mel rented the house for only 2 weeks (14 days)?

58. Teresa owns a condominium in Florida. During the current year, she incurred the following expenses related to the property:

Mortgage interest	$11,000
Property taxes	1,000
Utilities	900
Maintenance fees	1,300
Repairs	800
Depreciation	6,000

Assuming that Teresa wants to take the largest deductions allowable on the condominium, determine the amount of her deductions in each of the following cases:

Case	Rental Income	Rental Days	Personal Use Days
A	$13,000	365	0
B	4,000	60	10
C	4,000	60	20
D	500	10	40
E	11,000	280	20

59. Ray, 83, is a used car dealer. He lives in a rural community and operates the business out of his home. One room in his 6-room home is used exclusively for his business office. He parks the cars in his front yard, and when customers come along, they sit on the front porch and negotiate a sale price. The income statement for Ray's auto business is as follows:

Sales		$95,000
Cost of cars sold		66,500
Gross profit		$28,500
Interest expense on cars	$3,300	
Property tax on cars	500	
Gas, oil, repairs	1,000	
Loan fees	2,850	
Depreciation on equipment	1,200	(8,850)
Net profit		$19,650

If Ray's home were rental property, the annual depreciation would be $1,900. The utilities and upkeep on the home cost Ray $5,600 for the year. Ray's mortgage interest for the year is $2,100. When asked about the loan fees, Ray bitterly responded that Jim, the bank loan officer, charged him 10% of his gross profit on cars financed through the bank. Ray said, "The money is under the table, and if I don't shell out the cash, Jim won't loan the money to my customers to buy my cars. Everybody goes to Jim—he's got the cash."

What is the proper treatment of this information on Ray's tax return?

60. Hromas uses a separate room in his personal residence as an office. The room is 400 square feet of the total 2,000 square feet in the house. During the current year, Hromas incurred the following household expenses:

Mortgage interest		$10,000
Property taxes		800
Insurance		600
Utilities		
Gas and electric	$1,800	
Cable TV	190	
Phone ($10 per month for an extra		
outlet in the office)	385	2,375
House cleaning		1,040
Long-distance phone calls (business related)		460
Depreciation (unallocated)		$4,500

How much of a deduction is Hromas allowed for the costs of the office in each of the following situations?

a. Hromas is an independent salesperson who uses the room exclusively to call customers who buy goods from him. During the current year, his sales totaled $83,000, cost of goods sold was $33,000, and he incurred other valid business expenses unrelated to the office of $25,000.

b. Hromas is an employee of Ace Computer Co. He uses the office primarily when he has to bring work home at nights and on weekends. He occasionally uses the office to pay personal bills and to study the stock market so he can make personal investments. His salary at Ace is $80,000 per year. He is not paid extra for the time he spends working at home.

61. Charlotte owns a custom publishing business. She uses 600 square feet of her home (2,100 square feet) as an office and for storage. All of her business has come from telemarketing (telephone sales), direct mailings, or referrals. In her first year of operation, she had revenues of $46,000, cost of goods sold of $25,000, and other business expenses of $16,000. The total expenses related to her home are

Home mortgage interest	$6,200
Real property taxes	1,800
Insurance	350
Utilities	900
Repairs and maintenance	550
House cleaning	800
Depreciation (unallocated)	4,000

a. What amount can Charlotte deduct for her home office?

b. Would your answer in part a change if Charlotte solicited her business through direct contact (door to door)? Explain.

▲ INTEGRATIVE PROBLEM

62. Rufus and Rhonda are a married couple with 2 dependent children. Rufus, 46, is an executive with Plowshare Corporation. Rhonda, 39, is a self-employed attorney.

Rufus receives an annual salary of $60,000. He participates in Plowshare's qualified pension plan by contributing 5% of his annual salary, which is matched by Plowshare. Rufus also receives group term life insurance at 1.5 times his annual salary. The cost to Plowshare of the coverage is $1,900. All employees are covered by a medical insurance policy (cost of Rufus's policy is $1,800). Rufus also participates in the company's flexible benefits plan by paying $150 per month into the plan. During the year, Rufus submits claims totaling $1,950 to the plan and is reimbursed for the $1,800 he paid into the plan. An additional benefit that only top level executives such as Rufus enjoy is the payment of $3,600 in country club dues by Plowshare. Although Rufus occasionally entertains clients at the club, his primary use of the facility is personal.

Rhonda bills clients a total of $130,000 for services rendered during the current year. She receives $10,000 in payments from billings in prior years and $75,000 from current-year billings. Rhonda pays the following expenses related to her legal practice:

Office rent		$13,000
Secretary's salary		$14,000
Withholdings from secretary's salary		
Federal income taxes	$1,900	
State income taxes	400	
Social Security taxes	1,071	3,371
Matching Social Security tax payment		1,071
Entertainment costs		7,400
Seminar costs		1,230
Insurance on building—one year		
prepaid on August 1		1,200
Supplies		3,200
Bar association dues		800
State licensing fee		500
Automobile costs		4,500
Business gifts		600
Salary paid to Rhonda		50,000
Salary paid to Rhonda's son		2,000

In addition to these out-of-pocket costs, Rhonda determines that $8,000 in accounts receivable from previous years' billings are uncollectible.

The entertainment costs consist of the following:

Dues to social club	$1,800
Meals while discussing	
cases with clients	2,200
Open house	3,400

Rhonda has records that show that she uses the club 80% of the time for entertainment directly related to business entertainment, 10% for entertainment associated with her business, and 10% for personal purposes. The open house costs consist of $2,800 for food and $600 for a jazz combo at a reception she hosted for clients when she moved into her new offices this year.

Rhonda uses her automobile extensively in her business. She keeps a log to record business miles and related costs. Her records show that she drove 8,000 business miles and 4,000 personal miles during the current year. In past years, she had always kept track of her business miles but failed to keep an accurate record of her actual costs. Accordingly, her records indicate that she has never depreciated any of the $28,000 cost of the automobile she purchased 2 years ago—she has used the standard mileage rate method.

Every year, Rhonda gives her top 10 clients a gift to thank them for their support of her practice. This year, she gave each client a sterling silver key chain engraved with the client's name. The cost of each key chain was $55 with an additional $5 for the engraving.

The seminar costs relate to a 3-day meeting in New York on a legal topic involving her biggest client. Because of a special airline promotion, she takes along her 16-year-old son for free. However, she has to pay $180 per night for her hotel room instead of the $150 per night single rate. A summary of the seminar costs is as follows:

Airfare	$390
Lodging (3 nights @ $180 each)	540
Meals (including $80 for her son)	220
Taxi to and from the airport	80

Rhonda pays the $2,000 salary to her son for cleaning up after the open house reception. Although she could hire a service to do the job for $500, her son needs the money to buy a used motorcycle.

Rufus is hit by a car one morning while he is out jogging. The driver of the car is at fault, and his insurance company pays Rufus $12,000 for his pain and suffering and $9,000 of his $14,000 medical expenses. The remaining medical expenses are paid by Plowshare's medical insurance policy. Rufus also receives $2,000 in disability pay from the Plowshare policy for the time he misses from work recovering from the injury.

Rufus and Rhonda have the following investment-related items during the current year:

Interest on savings account	$1,150
Interest on Puerto Rico development bonds	5,500
Cash dividends on stock	3,300
Stock dividend shares	
(200 shares received when the market value of the stock was $45 per share)	9,000

Early in the year, Rhonda inherits 900 shares of stock from her grandmother. The total value of the shares is $27,000. Later in the year, the stock value begins to fall rapidly, and she sells the shares at a $7,000 loss.

Rufus and Rhonda own a cabin in the mountains. They use the cabin on weekends and for short holidays and rent it out whenever they can. During the current year, they use the cabin 25 days and rent it out 75 days. Details on the cabin income and expenses are as follows:

Rental income	$ 6,400
Mortgage interest	16,200
Property taxes	1,800
Utilities and maintenance	840
Depreciation (unallocated)	8,200

In addition, Rufus and Rhonda have $18,000 in other allowable itemized deductions.

REQUIRED: Based on the information provided, calculate Rufus and Rhonda's taxable income and their tax liability. For purposes of this problem, assume that Rufus and Rhonda are cash basis taxpayers and want to be as aggressive as possible in taking their allowable deductions. You are not required to calculate the self-employment tax on Rhonda's law practice income.

If you are using tax forms to solve this problem, you will need the following forms and schedules to complete the problem: Form 1040, Schedule A, Schedule B, Schedule C, Schedule D, and Schedule E. In addition, you should obtain a copy of the Form 1040 instructions as an aid in preparing the tax return.

▲ DISCUSSION CASE 6–1

Recently, President Bill Clinton and Hillary Rodham Clinton have faced questions about their personal finances. The president also has faced accusations concerning marital indiscretions. In response, the Clintons have incurred a substantial amount of legal expenses. The Clintons fear that the legal expenses from these allegations, as well as any future charges, could bankrupt them. Therefore, they have established the Presidential Legal Trust Fund. The Clintons established the trust with $2,000 and have asked the American people for contributions. Because the trust does not qualify as a charitable organization, contributions to the fund are not tax deductible. However, many tax specialists have suggested that the contributions to the Presidential Legal Trust Fund constitute taxable income for the Clintons. If the income is taxable to the Clintons, they will face an enormous tax liability unless their legal expenses are deductible. Using the concepts discussed in Chapters 5 and 6, determine whether the Clintons' legal expenses are deductible.

IRS vs. *Valerie* / me

During the current year, Benjamin and Valerie Jones were notified that their 1994 tax return was being audited. The IRS commissioner has disallowed all the losses attributable to Valerie's cattle breeding and showing.

Valerie was raised on a small ranch where her family raised commercial cattle. When she was 18, she left the family ranch to attend college, where she obtained an accounting degree. Valerie is now employed as a full-time accountant by Veltkamp, Stannebein, & Bateson, a local accounting firm, and receives an annual salary of $45,000. Ben, a full-time househusband, takes care of their children, Kody and Jaycee.

In 1990, Valerie purchased 10 impregnated purebred Maine Anjou heifers, an exotic breed of cattle from France, for a total price of $16,375. Valerie entered into a contract with a local farmer to obtain pasture land for her herd. The contract requires a payment of $20 a month from April through October for each cow and calf. In the winter months, November through March, the cost of feeding each cow and calf is $1.50 per day. In February 1992, Valerie purchased a replacement bull with an exceptional pedigree for $7,500 to improve the quality of her calves.

She sells any inferior animals to the meat market, keeps her best heifers for breeding, and shows her best bull calves in livestock shows. The livestock shows provide her with the opportunity to show and sell her exotic cattle. Until 1994, Valerie had been responsible for getting the animals ready to show, which requires approximately 4 hours per day from November through January. Unfortunately, Valerie was injured while working with one of her bulls and was forced to pay someone to finish breaking and showing the bulls. During the summer months, Valerie pays someone to watch the cattle so she can spend time with her family.

In 1990 and 1991, Valerie realized losses in the amounts of $4,125 and $1,894, respectively. In 1992 and 1993, Valerie realized gains of $3,000 and $750, respectively. For 1994, Valerie realized an operating loss of $1,200 and a casualty loss of $7,500, because her new bull was struck by lightning and killed. Valerie has maintained adequate records for all tax years since she began the cattle venture.

Is Valerie involved in a legitimate business, or is she merely pursuing a hobby?

▲ **DISCUSSION CASE 6–2**

project
10/6

- reasonable possibil

Kern and Mary's son lives in Japan and was just married. Several years ago, Kern wrote a best-selling legal text. They decided to take a trip around the world and to write a travel book, *Mary's Diary*, describing the reactions of an average American woman to places and events during the trip. They entered this venture in good faith with the intent to make a profit. Their trip lasted 3 months. While in Japan, they spent 4 days visiting their son and met his new wife and her family. They worked diligently on the book during the entire trip. When they returned home, they devoted 3 months to preparing the manuscript for publication. They want to deduct the travel and manuscript preparation costs as a business expense. What advice would you give them? Explain.

▲ **DISCUSSION CASE 6–3**

The Saffron Corporation is planning to adopt a new compensation package for its top 24 managers. The plan would provide each executive with a base salary of $500,000 and a compensation supplement based on rank and years of service. The maximum amount of supplemental compensation an individual can receive is $700,000.

The company will also institute a bonus system based on financial performance measures, internal performance measures, and individual reviews conducted by the compensation committee. The committee will solicit information from other senior members of management and from employees in the individual's department. The financial and internal measures used to determine the bonus will vary according to the executive's responsibilities. For example, a financial measure used to evaluate the vice president of manufacturing might be the ratio of cost of goods sold to sales, whereas an internal measure might be the percentage of defective units to total units produced. The compensation committee is to consist of the chief executive officer, the chief financial officer, Saffron's general counsel,

▲ **TAX PLANNING CASE 6–4**

and four outside directors. The company's public accounting firm would certify that the performance measures have been attained.

Margaret and José are two managers who would be affected by the new plan. Margaret is Saffron's director of marketing and José is the director of human resources. Margaret is an officer of the company and its third-highest-paid employee. Based on projections, her compensation would be $1,200,000 under the plan: the $500,000 base salary, a supplement salary of $575,000, imputed interest of $15,000 on a company loan to her, and a $110,000 bonus. José is not an officer but is the company's tenth-highest-paid employee. His projected compensation of $1,050,000 would consist of the $500,000 base salary, a supplemental salary of $460,000, and a $90,000 bonus.

The chairman of the board of directors would like to know the tax consequences of the proposed plan for Saffron Corporation. Using Margaret's and José's anticipated compensation under the plan, determine the deductibility of the compensation payments. If any of the amounts to be paid to Margaret or José are not fully deductible by Saffron, suggest alternative compensation schemes that would be deductible and would maintain the target level of compensation.

▲ ETHICS DISCUSSION CASE 6–5

Tom is a CPA for a large regional firm. In preparing the tax return for Espresso Industries, Tom noticed that the firm had an unusually high amount of travel, meals, and entertainment expenses. Therefore, he decided to examine the supporting documentation. In doing so, Tom noticed that the business purpose for many of the meals was not provided. When Tom questioned Frank, the company controller, Frank assured him that all the meal and entertainment expenses were legitimate. After further examination, Tom found that for every business day in June, July, and August, four of the corporation's senior officers had been reimbursed for their lunch and dinner costs. Tom confronted Frank and the assistant controller, Doug, with this information. He informed Frank that his firm would not prepare the return unless the meals and entertainment that did not have a business purpose were omitted. Frank, angered by Tom's decision, told Tom to prepare the return and said that he would take it from there. The following Saturday, Tom was playing golf with Doug and asked him what Frank had meant by his remarks. Doug told Tom that Frank would simply replace Tom's number with one that includes the entire meals and entertainment expense. Can Tom prepare the tax return, knowing that the company will change the meals and entertainment expense? If he does prepare the return, what ethical standards (refer to Statements on Responsibilities in Tax Practice), if any, has Tom violated? Assume that Tom prepares the return. If asked, should he prepare next year's return?

Losses—Deductions and Limitations

▲ CHAPTER LEARNING OBJECTIVES

- ■ Explain the difference between an annual loss and a transaction loss.
- ■ Introduce the relief provisions available to taxpayers who incur net operating losses.
- ■ Discuss the general operation of a tax shelter.
- ■ Introduce the at-risk rules and explain how they limit annual loss deductions.
- ■ Discuss passive losses and explain the limitations on the deductibility of losses incurred in passive activities.
- ■ Discuss the general treatments of transaction losses incurred in a trade or business, a production-of-income activity, and personal use losses.
- ■ Explain the tax rules applicable to business casualty and theft losses.
- ■ Describe the limitations on the deductions allowed for capital losses.
- ■ Explain the tax rules applicable to personal casualty losses.

▲ CONCEPT REVIEW ▲

Ability to pay   A tax should be based on the amount that the taxpayer can afford to pay, relative to other taxpayers.

Administrative convenience   Those items for which the cost of compliance would exceed the revenue generated are not taxed.

Annual accounting period   All tax entities must report the results of their operations on an annual basis (the tax year). Each year stands on its own, apart from other tax years.

Basis   This is the amount of unrecovered investment in an asset. As amounts are expended and/or recovered relative to an asset over time, the basis is adjusted in consideration of such changes. The **adjusted basis** of an asset is the original basis, plus or minus the changes in the amount of unrecovered investment.

Business purpose   To be deductible, an expenditure or a loss must have a business or other economic purpose that exceeds any tax avoidance motive. The primary motive for the transaction must be to make a profit.

Capital recovery   No income is realized until the taxpayer receives more than the amount invested to pro-duce the income. The amount invested in an asset represents the maximum amount recoverable.

Entity   All items of income, deduction, and so on are traced to the tax unit responsible for the item.

Legislative grace   Any tax relief provided is the result of a specific act of Congress that must be strictly applied and interpreted. All income received is taxable unless a specific provision can be found in the tax law that excludes the income from taxation. Deductions must be approached with the philosophy that nothing is deductible unless a provision in the tax law allows the deduction.

Realization   No income (or loss) is recognized until it has been realized. A realization involves a change in the form and/or the substance of a taxpayer's property rights that results from an arm's-length transaction.

Related party   Family members and corporations that are owned by family members are considered related parties, as are certain other relationships between entities in which the power to control the substance of a transaction is evidenced through majority ownership.

▲ INTRODUCTION

The tax law allows the deduction of certain types of losses in the calculation of taxable income. The deductibility of losses is a matter of legislative grace and is based on the ability-to-pay concept. The reasoning behind deductions and losses is similar. In fact, many classification rules for deductions also apply to losses.

How are losses different from deductions? Deductions are the current expenditures (and amortization of capital expenditures) made for the production of current period income. Losses can result when an entity's deductions for the period exceed the income generated (i.e., a negative income for the period). This type of loss is referred to as an *annual loss*, or *activity loss*.

▲ **EXAMPLE 1**   Emma owns a restaurant. During the current year, she had gross income of $74,000 and allowable deductions related to the business of $90,000. What is Emma's income from the restaurant?

Discussion: Emma has suffered a business loss of $16,000 ($74,000 − $90,000). This loss is an annual loss created by an excess of allowable deductions over income.

Note that Emma can have more than one annual loss if she engages in multiple activities. Remember that the results of each entity must be kept separate and apart from all other entities for recording and reporting purposes. In this case, Emma would combine the allowable loss from her restaurant business with her income and deductions from her other activities on her individual tax return.

In contrast to an annual loss, a loss can also occur as a result of the disposition of an asset. An asset that is disposed of at less than its basis creates a loss that represents the taxpayer's unrecovered capital investment. This type of loss is referred to as a **transaction loss.**

▲ **EXAMPLE 2**   Alfred purchases 50 shares of Inventor, Inc., common stock for $5,000 in 1994. Alfred sells the 50 shares for $4,400 in 1995. What are the tax effects for Alfred of his investment in the Inventor, Inc., stock?

Discussion: Alfred has a loss of $600 ($4,400 − $5,000) on the sale of the stock in 1995. The loss represents Alfred's basis in the stock that was not recovered when he disposed of the stock.

Figure 7–1 outlines the general scheme for the treatment of losses. The first requirement is that a realization of the loss must have occurred. The realized loss may be either an annual loss or a transaction loss.

Under the business purpose concept, only losses that are the result of a profit-motivated transaction or venture are deductible. Thus, annual loss deductions are allowed only for activities that constitute a trade or business. Note in Figure 7–1 that an annual loss incurred in a passive activity is not generally allowed as a deduction. Thus, it is important to distinguish those activities that constitute a trade or business from those that are passive.

The tax treatment of transaction losses depends on the source of the loss. As a result, transaction losses are classified as related to a trade or business, an income-producing activity, or a personal use. Once a loss has been properly categorized, the rules for deductibility are applied by category, as with deductions. Figure 7–1 shows the general difference in treatments among the three categories of transaction losses. That is, all losses incurred in a trade or business are fully deductible. Losses incurred in an income-producing activity are subject to the capital loss limitations. Losses on personal use of property are generally disallowed. Thus, the general approach to the treatment of transaction losses is similar to the approach to deductions discussed in Chapter 5.

The purpose of this chapter is to discuss the tax treatment(s) of the most common types of losses. As with most areas of the tax law, there are exceptions

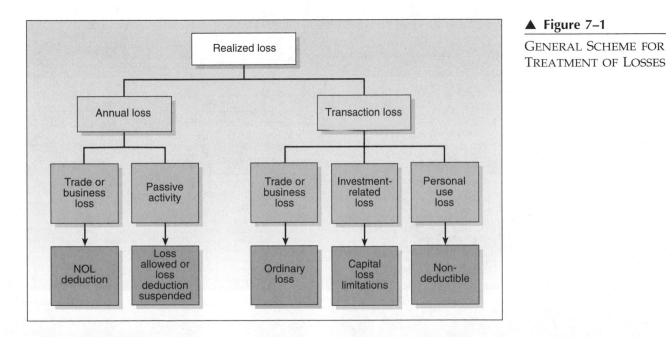

▲ **Figure 7–1**

GENERAL SCHEME FOR TREATMENT OF LOSSES

to the general treatment of losses, which are outlined in Figure 7–1. The more important of these exceptions are discussed later in the chapter.

▲ ANNUAL LOSSES

Annual losses result from an excess of deductions over income. The only deductions allowed for annual losses are for those incurred in a trade or business. Taxpayers who have annual activities with a significant personal use element (hobbies, vacation homes, home office) are not allowed to deduct expenses in excess of income. As a result, the two primary types of annual losses are net operating losses (NOL) and passive activity losses. Figure 7–2 outlines the treatment of annual losses. When an annual loss is realized, the key question is whether the taxpayer materially participates in the operation of the business. If the taxpayer does not materially participate in the business, the passive activity loss rules apply. If the taxpayer does materially participate in the business reporting the loss, a net operating loss deduction is usually allowed. However, if the entity that owns the activity is a conduit entity, the loss flows through to the owner(s) of the entity, and the material participation test is repeated with regard to each owner's share of the loss.

▲ **Figure 7–2**

TREATMENT OF
ANNUAL LOSSES

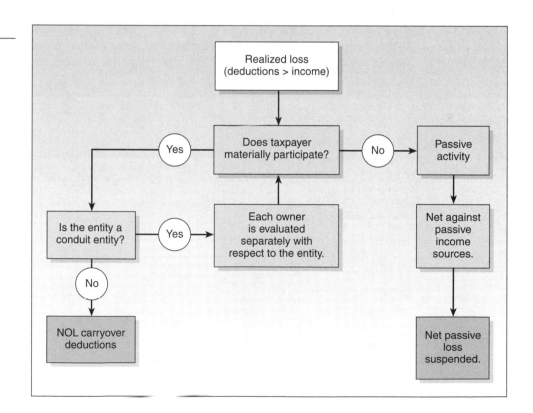

A **net operating loss (NOL)** is an annual loss incurred in a trade or business in which the taxpayer materially participates. It results from an excess of allowable deductions over income for the accounting period.

▲ **NET OPERATING LOSSES**

▲ **EXAMPLE 3** Pete is the sole proprietor of Pete's Pizza Parlor. During the current year, the pizza parlor had income of $80,000 and deductions of $100,000, resulting in a net operating loss of $20,000. What is the treatment of the loss?

Discussion: Although not a true conduit entity, the loss from the Pizza Parlor flows through to the owner, Pete, and is reported on his return. Pete is allowed to deduct the $20,000 loss from the pizza parlor against his other sources of income.

What happens when a taxable entity has an NOL? Because a taxable entity (i.e., individuals and corporations) pays tax on the income it generates, it would pay no tax for the year in which an NOL occurs. Taxable entities are not allowed to pass the loss through to their owners for deduction. With no relief from this situation, taxable entities are at a distinct disadvantage.

▲ **EXAMPLE 4** Consider the following taxable incomes (losses) for taxpayers Alicia (A) and Bernie (B), both of whom are taxable entities, for a 4-year period. The marginal tax rate for both Alicia and Bernie is 25% throughout the 4 years.

	Year 1	Year 2	Year 3	Year 4	Total
Taxpayer A	$30,000	$30,000	$30,000	$ 30,000	$120,000
Tax rate	× 25%	× 25%	× 25%	× 25%	
Tax paid	$ 7,500	$ 7,500	$ 7,500	$ 7,500	$ 30,000
Taxpayer B	$50,000	$50,000	$50,000	$(30,000)	$120,000
Tax rate	× 25%	× 25%	× 25%		
Tax paid	$12,500	$12,500	$12,500	-0-	$ 37,500
Difference in total tax paid					$ 7,500

Discussion: Although both taxpayers have the same total income over the 4-year period and the same marginal tax rate, Bernie pays $7,500 more in total tax because of the loss he suffers in year 4.

As example 4 demonstrates, the annual accounting period creates an inequity among taxpayers who suffer NOLs. If some other reporting period (i.e., every two years, every four years) had been chosen for the tax system instead of the annual accounting period, the inequity in example 4 would not have resulted.

In order to provide relief for taxpayers suffering NOLs, a carryover system allows losses incurred in one year to be deducted against income in other years. A **carryback** means that the loss may be used to reduce income in prior years. Because tax has already been paid on the prior year's income, a carryback results in a prompt refund of taxes paid. A **carryforward** means that the loss is used to offset income in future periods. In contrast to a carryback, a carryforward does not provide immediate tax savings; rather it reduces taxes to be paid on future income. An NOL may be carried back for three years. If there is not sufficient taxable income in the three-year carryback period to fully absorb the NOL, any remaining loss may be carried forward for 15 years.[1]

▲ **EXAMPLE 5** How should Bernie, in example 4, treat the $30,000 loss in year 4?

Discussion: Bernie is allowed to carry the $30,000 loss in year 4 back to year 1 and use it to offset income. This results in a refund of tax of $7,500.

	Year 1	Year 2	Year 3	Year 4	Total
Income	$50,000	$50,000	$50,000	$(30,000)	$120,000
Less: NOL	(30,000)				
Income after NOL	$20,000				
Tax rate	× 25%				
Tax after NOL	$ 5,000				
Tax paid	$12,500				
Refund due	$ 7,500				
Net tax paid after NOL	$ 5,000	$12,500	$12,500	-0-	$ 30,000

The effect of the carryback of the NOL is to equalize the taxes paid by Alicia and Bernie. After the carryback, Alicia and Bernie pay the same total tax over the 4-year period.

The carryback rules require the taxpayer to apply the loss to the earliest of the three carryback years first. If the earliest year does not have sufficient income to entirely absorb the loss, any remaining loss is carried to the second-earliest year in the carryback period. You must use the loss against all of the carryback year's income before anything can be carried forward. Thus, you cannot select one high marginal tax rate year and carry the loss back to that specific year.

▲ **EXAMPLE 6**   Assume that Bernie in example 4 had an NOL of $80,000 in year 4. What is the treatment of the NOL?

Discussion: Bernie must carry the loss back and apply it against year 1's income first. Only $50,000 of the $80,000 loss is required to eliminate the taxable income in year 1, leaving $30,000 to apply against year 2's income. Bernie receives a refund of $20,000 of the taxes paid in years 1 and 2:

	Year 1	Year 2	Year 3	Year 4
Income	$50,000	$50,000	$50,000	$(80,000)
Less: NOL	(50,000)	(30,000)		
Income after NOL	$ -0-	$20,000		
Tax rate		× 25%		
Tax after NOL	$ -0-	$ 5,000		
Tax paid	12,500	12,500		
Refund due	$12,500	$ 7,500		

A taxpayer may elect not to carry the loss back and instead carry the loss forward for 15 years. This may be advantageous when the prior three years' incomes were taxed at low marginal tax rates and the taxpayer anticipates higher marginal tax rates in the near future. In order to determine whether this option is optimal, the relative tax savings under each option and the effect of the time value of money (delaying receipt of tax savings on the carryforward) must be calculated.

▲ **EXAMPLE 7**   Assume that in example 6 Bernie anticipated a year 5 income of $200,000, which would put him in a 39% tax rate bracket. If the time value of money is 10%, should he elect to forgo the carryback and carry the NOL forward for deduction in year 5?

Discussion: The present values of the 2 options must be compared. The present value of the 3-year carryback is the $20,000 refund of taxes calculated in example 6. The carryforward option reduces year 5's taxes by $31,200 ($80,000 × 39%). Because that savings is 1 year in the future, the $31,200 must be discounted to the present in order to compare it with the $20,000. At a 10% time value of money, the $31,200 of year 5 taxes has a present value of $28,361 ($31,200 × .909). In this case, the marginal tax rate savings is greater than the time value of money factor, and the taxpayer is better off electing to carry the NOL forward.

Several additional problems need to be considered in regard to NOLs. First, what happens when losses from a conduit entity cause an individual taxpayer to have a negative taxable income? The tax return of an individual contains a mixture of business-related and specifically allowed personal itemized deductions and exemptions. Because an NOL can be caused only by a business loss, the fact of a negative individual taxable income does not necessarily mean that the taxpayer has an NOL from a trade or business for the year. In order to determine whether an individual does have an NOL, a complex set of adjustments is made to the negative taxable income figure. The complexity of these adjustments is beyond the scope of this textbook and is omitted from the discussion.

Related to the treatment of NOLs by individuals is a special treatment afforded to personal casualty and theft losses (discussed later in this chapter). Solely for purposes of the NOL computation of an individual, a personal casualty loss is considered a business-related loss. As a result, a personal casualty loss can create an NOL that can be carried back to prior years. This provision is designed to provide relief to individuals who suffer catastrophic personal casualty losses. Although this further complicates the calculation of an individual's NOL, the importance of the provision is that individuals who suffer large casualty losses may be entitled to additional relief (in addition to the casualty loss deduction) through the NOL provisions.

The last important aspect of NOLs is the deductibility of purchased NOL deductions. At one time, one corporation could acquire another corporation with an NOL carryforward and use the NOL to reduce the tax on its income. This created a market for corporations with unused NOLs because of the tax deductions that could be obtained from the acquisition. In many instances, the tax loss was the corporation's most valuable asset, and other firms would buy the tax loss corporation solely to obtain the tax benefits of the unused NOL. Congress responded to this selling of tax losses by enacting a provision that limits the benefits of an acquired NOL. These limitations apply when there has been a change of greater than 50 percent in the ownership of the acquired corporation. Although the mechanics of these provisions are beyond the scope of this book, it is important to be aware that you cannot always use purchased NOLs to reduce a corporation's taxable income.

▲ TAX-SHELTER LOSSES: AN OVERVIEW

In its broadest application, the term **tax shelter** refers to any investment activity that is designed to minimize the effect of the income tax on wealth accumulation. Under this definition, an investment in tax-exempt municipal bonds would be viewed as a tax shelter. However, in tax practice, the term is generally applied to investments that produce significant tax losses as a result of the allowable deductions associated with the investment. These losses are then used to offset taxable income from other income sources. The losses from the investment "shelter" a portion (or all) of the other sources of income from taxation. The taxpayer investing in such a shelter will have to pay a tax on the investment when it is sold. However, the deduction of losses from the shelter in tax years prior to the payment of tax on the gain presents a time value of money savings opportunity.

A taxpayer is allowed to take advantage of the provisions for deductions and losses to legitimately reduce taxable income (i.e., tax avoidance is legal). In the late 1960s and early 1970s, many high-income taxpayers made substantial investments in tax shelters to reduce their income from other sources. In a typical tax shelter, the taxpayer would invest an amount in the activity. In return, the taxpayer would be allowed to deduct a share of the losses generated by the activity on her or his individual return, reducing the tax paid on other forms of income such as salaries and investment income. The amount of the deduction provided by a tax shelter could vary from three to ten times the amount invested. For a $10,000 investment, the taxpayer could take loss deductions totaling $30,000 to $100,000. During this period, the highest marginal tax rate was 50 percent. Thus, a high marginal rate taxpayer making a $10,000 investment could be guaranteed a tax savings from the investment ranging from $15,000 to $50,000. Because of this return from saving taxes, taxpayers often made investments in tax shelters that had little or no hope of long-term economic success. The tax savings provided a high enough return that success of the venture was unimportant. Many tax shelters were activities that were not economically viable investments in the absence of the tax deductions.

In 1976, Congress reacted to this perceived abuse of tax shelters with several measures, including limitations on investment interest deductions (discussed in Chapter 8) and a set of at-risk rules to limit the amount of loss deductible. However, these limitations met with limited success, because promoters of tax shelters and their clever tax advisers found ways to work around them. As a result, offerings of publicly registered tax shelters doubled in the early 1980s.

In 1986, Congress took additional action against tax shelters by severely limiting the deductions on tax shelters through enactment of the passive activity loss rules. The basic passive loss rule disallows the deduction of current period passive losses against active and portfolio income sources (salaries, trade or business income, interest, dividends). These rules are in some cases unduly complex and in other cases have hindered investment in legitimate economic investments.

In the sections that follow, the at-risk rules, which limit the amount of any deductible loss to the amount that the taxpayer has at risk in the activity, are discussed first. Then the basic operation of the passive loss rules is presented and discussed to provide an understanding of how these important limitations on losses affect investments made by taxpayers.

Before proceeding, a few basic aspects of tax shelters should be clarified. First, many tax advantages that allow such activities to generate losses are the result of a conscious effort by Congress to attract investment capital to activities with a high national priority and/or a high degree of risk. The basic intent of the generous tax laws is to provide incentive to taxpayers to engage in activities that they ordinarily would reject because of either low returns or high risk.

A limited partnership has many tax and nontax advantages that make it a preferred vehicle for tax shelters. The flow-through of the income and deductions of a partnership to the owners allows investment by many individuals who have no actual involvement in the tax shelter's business activities. In addition, it is often possible to make special allocations of income and expense items, which allow the partnership to confer many of the special tax deductions on the tax shelter's investors. A partnership also can be structured to accept investors as limited partners, so that their maximum loss from the activity is the amount of their investment in the property. Finally, a partner's tax basis in the investment includes the partner's share of its outstanding liabilities. This can significantly increase the amount of loss that can be deducted by the partners under the at-risk rules.

The At-Risk Rules

Congress enacted the at-risk rules to disallow the deduction of artificial losses generated by tax-shelter investments. The intention of the **at-risk rules** is to limit loss deductions by individuals and closely held corporations on business and investment-related activities to the amount of the taxpayer's actual economic investment. This is done by limiting the current year's loss deduction to the amount that the taxpayer has at risk in the activity.[2] The computation of the amount at risk is presented in Exhibit 7–1.

A brief review of Exhibit 7–1 clarifies what it means to "be at risk." From the computation, the at-risk amount is equal to cash or other assets that have been contributed to the activity. In addition, any debts of the activity for which the taxpayer would be responsible if the activity could not pay them are also considered to be at risk. Thus, the amount at risk in an activity is the maximum amount of personal funds (assets) that could be lost if the activity failed.

▲ **EXAMPLE 8**   Jolene purchased a business for $200,000 by investing $20,000 of her own funds and borrowing $180,000 from State Bank. Jolene is personally liable for repayment of the loan to State Bank. What is Jolene's at-risk amount in the business?

Discussion: Jolene is at risk for $200,000. If the business is not successful, she stands to lose the $20,000 in cash she invested in the business and she would be liable for payment of the $180,000 loan. Thus, she can lose a maximum of $200,000 from her investment in the business.

The amount at risk is also adjusted for the taxpayer's share of the income (loss) from the activity and reduced by withdrawals from the activity. That is, when an activity has income that is taxed to the taxpayer, the income becomes subject to loss. Similarly, losses from the activity that are deducted by the taxpayer reduce the amount that the taxpayer has to lose. Any amounts that are withdrawn from the activity by the taxpayer are no longer subject to loss and reduce the amount at risk in the activity.

▲ **EXAMPLE 9**   During the first year that Jolene operated the business she purchased in example 8, she suffered a loss of $70,000. She also withdrew $40,000 from the business for her personal use. What is Jolene's at-risk amount in the business at the end of the first year of operation?

Discussion: Jolene has a sufficient amount at risk to enable her to deduct the loss from the business. Therefore, she *must* reduce her amount at risk by the $70,000 loss.

Items That Increase Amount at Risk:	
Cash invested by the taxpayer in the activity	$XXX
Adjusted basis of property contributed to the activity	XXX
Amounts borrowed for use in the activity for which the taxpayer is personally liable	XXX
Amounts borrowed for use in the activity for which the taxpayer has pledged property not used in the activity as security	XXX
The taxpayer's share of any income produced by the activity	XXX
Items That Decrease Amount at Risk:	
The taxpayer's share of any loss produced by the activity	(XXX)
Withdrawals of assets from the activity	(XXX)
Equals: The amount at risk in the activity	$XXX

▲ **Exhibit 7–1**

COMPUTATION OF
AMOUNT AT RISK

In addition, the $40,000 withdrawn from the business is no longer at risk. Thus, her amount at risk has declined to $90,000 ($200,000 − $70,000 − $40,000) at the end of the first year of operation.

In many cases, a taxpayer's amount at risk in an activity is the same as the taxpayer's adjusted basis. A main difference between a taxpayer's adjusted basis in an activity and the amount at risk in an activity occurs when basis is financed by nonrecourse debt. A **nonrecourse debt** is a liability that is secured only by the underlying property; the borrower is not personally liable for the debt.

▲ **EXAMPLE 10**   Assume that Jolene purchases $40,000-worth of equipment by borrowing from Local Bank. Local Bank made the loan with the equipment as the security for the debt. Jolene is not personally liable for the debt. How are Jolene's basis and at-risk amount affected by the purchase of the equipment?

Discussion: Jolene obtains a basis of $40,000 in the equipment. However, because she is not personally liable for the debt incurred to finance the purchase, she is not at risk with respect to the debt. That is, if her business fails, she will not be personally liable for repayment of the debt. Therefore, her at-risk amount does not increase.

A major exception to the at-risk rules is made for nonrecourse financing of real estate operations. Before 1987, the at-risk rules did not apply to real estate projects. In 1986, the at-risk rules were extended to real estate operations to a limited extent. After 1987, nonrecourse financing of real estate is considered as at risk only if the financing is made on reasonably commercial terms. In most cases, this allows shelter activities to acquire real estate with nonrecourse financing, which is considered at risk by the investors in the shelter.

▲ **EXAMPLE 11**   Assume that in example 10 Jolene had purchased a building for $40,000 with nonrecourse financing. Would the $40,000 be at risk?

Discussion: As long as the financing is made on reasonably commercial terms, the nonrecourse financing of real estate is considered at risk. Therefore, Jolene's at-risk amount will increase by the $40,000 in nonrecourse debt used to acquire the building.

▲ **EXAMPLE 12**   Ruben invested $10,000 in the Gold Partnership and received a 10% interest in the partnership. Gold used $50,000 in cash paid in by investors to purchase an apartment building that cost $1,000,000. The remaining $950,000 of the cost of the building was financed by a nonrecourse loan from State Insurance Co. The loan was made on terms comparable to other real estate loans in the area. What is Ruben's at-risk amount in the Gold Partnership?

Discussion: Ruben's at-risk amount includes the $10,000 cash contribution and his share of the nonrecourse loan. His $95,000 share of the nonrecourse loan ($950,000 × 10%) is considered at risk, because the loan was used to purchase real estate and was made on reasonably commercial terms. Thus, Ruben's at-risk amount is $105,000 ($10,000 cash investment + $95,000 share of real estate debt).

Under the at-risk rules, taxpayers cannot deduct any losses in excess of the amount they have at risk in the activity. Any current period losses that are not deductible because they exceed the taxpayer's at-risk amount are carried forward to the next year and are deductible when the taxpayer has enough at risk to allow the deduction.[3]

▲ **EXAMPLE 13**   Return to the facts of example 12. Assume that the Gold Partnership had a loss of $800,000 in the first year of operation and a loss of $600,000 in the second year. How much of the loss can Ruben deduct in each of the first 2 years?

Discussion: Ruben's share of the year 1 loss is $80,000. Because his at-risk amount is $105,000, he can deduct the full $80,000. This will reduce his at-risk amount in the partnership to $25,000 ($105,000 − $80,000). His share of the year 2 loss is $60,000. However, he can deduct only the $25,000 he has at risk. The remaining $35,000 of the loss is carried forward to succeeding years until he has enough at risk to deduct the loss.

Although the loss is deductible per the at-risk rules, the passive activity rules still apply. That is, if Ruben's investment in the partnership is considered a passive activity, the $80,000 and $25,000 in losses allowed by the at-risk rules still are subject to restrictions under the passive loss rules.

Passive Activity Losses

Although the at-risk rules provide some measure of protection against the deduction of artificial losses created by tax shelters, Congress felt that the rules still allowed too much room for abuse and promoted investment in ventures based on the tax characteristics of the investment rather than their economic potential. In 1986, Congress enacted the **passive activity loss (PAL) rules,** effective for tax years after 1986. The basic intent of these rules is to disallow the deduction of losses from passive activities against other forms of income. Thus, passive activity losses cannot generally be used to shelter other sources of income. Even the basic operation of the passive loss rules can be extremely complex. The complexity of the rules increases as a taxpayer engages in more and more passive activities.

Passive Activity Definition.   A **passive activity** is defined as the conduct of any trade or business in which the taxpayer does not materially participate.[4] In general, to be a **material participant,** the taxpayer must be involved in the operations of the activity on a regular, continuous, and substantial basis. The purpose of the material participation standard is to limit the passive loss deductions of those taxpayers investing in tax shelters who do not participate in the operation of the business in any meaningful way. However, the definition provided by Congress caused severe problems. Consider the following:

▲ **EXAMPLE 14**   Patricia worked for 20 years to build up her business. During the last 10 years, she reorganized the business and took on 2 partners to help her manage it. Patricia retired this year and no longer is involved in the day-to-day operations of the business. In retirement, she will attend 1 or 2 meetings a year to discuss general strategy with her partners. She still maintains a 1/3 interest in the partnership. Is Patricia's partnership interest a passive activity?

Discussion: Patricia no longer participates in the operation of the business in a material, substantial, and continuous manner. Therefore, under the general definition of *material participation,* her partnership interest would be considered passive.

It is doubtful that Congress intended to subject the partnership interest in example 14 to the passive loss rules. In response to numerous other instances of perceived inequities in the definition of material participation, the IRS provided seven separate tests under which a taxpayer would be considered a material participant in an activity.[5] The basic test for **material participation** is that the individual (including the individual's spouse) participates in the activity for more than 500 hours per year. The remaining six tests are based on lower levels of participation, combined with other factors about the operation of the business, that would indicate material participation and special rules to take care of situations such as that in example 14. Because the majority of taxpayers would qualify under the 500-hour standard, this book does not discuss the remaining six tests in detail.

The determination of material participation under these tests is best left to a tax professional.

Before passage of the Omnibus Budget Reconciliation Act of 1993, Congress defined two particular types of activities as always being passive and two types of activities as never being passive. Rental activities and limited partnership interests were always passive. Working interests in oil and gas deposits and certain low-income housing projects were and still are active and not subject to the passive loss rules.

However, beginning in 1994, taxpayers who are involved in real property as a trade or business are permitted, if they meet certain criteria, to treat rental real estate as an active activity. The criteria for and the definition of a *real property trade or business* are discussed later in the chapter. The new law has no effect on the treatment of limited partnerships—they still are always considered a passive activity.

RENTAL ACTIVITIES.   For purposes of the passive loss rules, a rental activity is always considered a passive activity, except for certain qualifying taxpayers. A **rental activity** is defined as one in which the payment received is primarily for the use of tangible property. Rentals that include significant services are not rental activities for the passive loss rules. The IRS has provided guidelines for determining when the provision of personal services is significant and does not constitute a rental activity for passive loss purposes.[6] Some of the more common forms of this type of rental include

Hotel rooms	Hospital rooms
Car rentals	Videocassette rentals
Clothing rentals	Golf course fees
Tool rentals	Automobiles rented by dealers
Cable television rentals	while repair work is done

Although this list is not all inclusive, it illustrates the basic intent—to exclude rental activities that also provide significant services from the passive loss rules. As long as the owner(s) of such activities meet the material participation standard, the activity is not considered passive. That is, even if the activity is not considered a rental activity, each owner of the activity still must meet the material participation standard in order for the activity to be considered active.

▲ **EXAMPLE 15**   Toby is the owner of a miniature golf course. Toby and his wife Eve are actively involved in the management of the business. Each devotes an average of 40 hours per week to working at the miniature golf course and performing other business functions (record keeping, bank deposits, etc.). Is the miniature golf course a passive activity for Toby and Eve?

Discussion: The activity is not a rental activity, because it provides significant personal services. Toby and Eve participate in the operation of the activity more than 500 hours per year, making them material participants in the activity. Therefore, the activity is not a passive activity.

Note that although the activity in example 15 is not a rental activity for purposes of the passive loss rules, Toby and Eve still must meet the material participation standard in order for their business to escape classification as a passive activity.

▲ **EXAMPLE 16**   Assume that in example 15 the miniature golf course is organized as a partnership. Upon forming the business, Toby and Eve did not have the necessary capital. They got their friend Alan to invest $20,000 in the business for a 1/3 interest in the partnership. Toby and Eve run the business. Alan does not have any responsibilities for operating the business. He merely receives his annual share of the partnership's income. Is the miniature golf course a passive activity for Alan?

Discussion: Although the activity is not considered a rental activity, Alan does not materially participate in the activity. Therefore, Alan's partnership interest is considered a passive activity.

Note that the activity remains an active business interest for Toby and Eve. That is, each taxpayer involved in the activity is evaluated separately. This is a result of the entity concept.

Given all the exceptions, what is a rental activity for purposes of the passive loss rules? The more common forms of passive activity rentals involve the rental of real property. This would include apartment buildings, rental houses, office building rentals, warehouse rentals, factory rentals, and so on. That is, these activities are all rentals of real property that include no significant provision of personal services.

▲ **EXAMPLE 17**   Both Alf and Bart are lawyers. The two decide to purchase an apartment building in 1994 at a cost of $600,000. They each provide half of the $60,000 down payment. Both are busy practicing law, so they hire Chester to manage the building. Chester has full control over all management decisions (getting tenants, collecting rent, taking care of repairs). Alf and Bart agree to split the profits evenly after paying Chester's salary of $50,000. Is the building a passive activity for Alf and Bart?

Discussion: The apartment building is a rental activity for passive loss purposes. It is a rental of tangible property with no significant services provided. Thus, it is a passive activity. This is true for both Alf and Bart.

LIMITED PARTNERSHIP INTERESTS.   A limited partnership interest is generally considered passive. In a **limited partnership,** one general partner organizes the partnership and is usually responsible for the day-to-day operation of its business. Limited partners are investors who purchase their interest to provide capital for the partnership. Limited partners generally have no responsibilities for operating the partnership. They merely invest money and receive their share of partnership income (loss). The limited partnership is the most popular tax-shelter vehicle. As a conduit entity, investors in a limited partnership are able to obtain a share of the losses of the tax shelter without any involvement in its operation. Because Congress has specified that limited partnership interests are passive, the degree of participation by a limited partner or the type of activity does not change the passive activity classification. To determine whether the general partner's interest is passive or active, evaluate the general partner's participation by using the rules for all taxpayers.

▲ **EXAMPLE 18**   Jonah purchased a limited partnership interest for $40,000. Monica is the general partner, oversees the operation of the partnership, and is responsible for its day-to-day operations. Is the activity passive for Jonah? for Monica?

Discussion: Because Jonah is a limited partner, the activity is passive for him. Monica is a general partner and must be evaluated according to the rules for all taxpayers to determine whether the activity is passive for her. She would appear to meet the material participation standard, making her interest active and not subject to the passive loss rules.

WORKING INTEREST IN OIL AND GAS.   **A working interest in an oil and gas deposit** is always considered an active business for purposes of the passive activity rules. A working interest is an outright ownership interest held by the operator of the property. As such, a working interest has unlimited liability for all debts of the operation and is responsible for the costs of operating the property. Royalty interests in the property held by individuals who are not active in its operation are not considered working interests. However, royalty interests in an oil and gas operation would not be passive. They are considered portfolio income, because they share only revenue from the deposit, not expenses from the operation of the oil and gas deposit.

▲ **EXAMPLE 19**   Whitney is the sole proprietor of an oil and gas drilling company. Brooke owns the mineral rights to some land on which Whitney would like to drill for oil. They enter into an agreement whereby Whitney can drill on Brooke's land; Whitney pays Brooke $2,000 for the right to drill and 1/12 of the value of any oil and gas produced from the well. Whitney is responsible for the payment of all expenses of the operation and retains the remaining value of the oil and gas produced. Is this a passive activity for either Whitney or Brooke?

Discussion: Because Whitney is the operator of the oil and gas deposit, her interest is a working interest and is always active. Although Brooke is not at all involved in the operation of the deposit, her royalty interest would not be passive, because she does not share expenses of the operation. The royalties she receives would be portfolio income.

LOW-INCOME HOUSING PROJECTS.   Most low-income housing projects have been classified as active interests. Although such projects usually constitute rental activities (and thus are passive), Congress has exempted investment in these projects from the passive loss rules to encourage the building of low-income housing (a social goal). This allows investors to seek shelter from taxes in low-income housing projects.

Types of Income.   Under the passive activity loss rules, all income must be classified as active, passive, or portfolio income. Active and passive income result from activities considered trades or businesses. Portfolio income is income from investments. The first step is to segregate portfolio income from active (i.e., activity-based) income.

PORTFOLIO INCOME.   **Portfolio income** consists of unearned income from dividends, interest, royalties, annuities, and other assets held as investments. Portfolio income also includes income from the sale of the asset creating the portfolio income. The main characteristic of portfolio income is that such investments almost always produce positive income while the investment is held. In portfolio activities, the investor only receives income from the activity and does not share in the expenses related to the activity. Any losses on portfolio investments typically occur at the point of sale.

ACTIVE INCOME.   **Active income** is income from a trade or business in which the taxpayer materially participates. This category includes wages and salaries as well as income from a trade or business in which the taxpayer materially participates. Working interests in oil and gas deposits and certain low-income housing projects are always considered active income. As with portfolio income, this category typically produces income. However, such activities may produce losses that are not subject to the passive loss rules (the NOL rules would apply).

▲ **EXAMPLE 20**   Hai is the sole proprietor of Sno-Cone Flavors, a distributor of snow cone–making accessories. Hai has only 1 employee and works full time operating the business. During the current year, the business suffered a loss of $11,000. Is this a passive activity for Hai?

Discussion: Because Hai is a material participant in the business, it is classified as an active interest. Although the business produces a loss, the loss is not subject to the passive loss rules. The loss from the sole proprietorship flows through to Hai's individual return where it is deductible against Hai's other active and portfolio income.

▲ **EXAMPLE 21**   Willa is a mechanic at Merchant Marine Co. where she receives a salary of $30,000 per year. At nights and on weekends, Willa does repair work from her garage. For the current year, Willa's repair business showed a loss of $2,500. Are these passive activities for Willa?

Discussion: Willa's job at Merchant Marine produces active income. Assuming the repair work business is not a hobby, it also is considered active. Thus, Willa can deduct the loss from the repair work business on her individual return, reducing the tax she would have paid on her salary income.

PASSIVE INCOME.   As previously defined, *passive income* is income from a trade or business in which the taxpayer does not materially participate. Rental activities are usually passive, and limited partnership interests are always passive activities. Passive activities may produce either income or loss, but most passive activities are loss activities.

Taxpayers Subject to the Limits.   All noncorporate taxable entities (individuals, estates, trusts) are subject to the passive loss rules. Conduit entities are not directly affected by these limits, because their results are passed through and taxed to the owners. Note that in Figure 7–2 a conduit entity is usually a material participant in the operation of the business. However, the loss from the conduit flows through to the owners of the entity. Each owner must then determine whether he or she materially participates in the operation of the business in order to determine whether an NOL deduction is allowed or if his or her interest in the business is a passive activity. Thus, conduit entities must report the results of their operations to owners so that the owners may apply the applicable rules for the deduction of losses.

▲ **EXAMPLE 22**   Harnads Department Store is organized as an S corporation and is owned equally by Able, Baker, and Charlene. During the current year, Harnads had a loss from operations. How does the loss affect Harnads, Able, Baker, and Charlene?

Discussion: Harnads is a conduit entity, and the loss is passed through to Able, Baker, and Charlene. Able, Baker, and Charlene each must determine whether his or her participation in the operation of Harnads is material. If any (or all) of them do materially participate, they may deduct their share of the Harnads loss on their individual tax returns. Any who do not materially participate in the operation of Harnads are subject to the passive activity loss rules.

Two classes of corporate taxpayers are not subject to the passive loss limitations:

1. Publicly held corporations.
2. Closely held corporations, which are allowed to offset net passive losses against active income of the business. However, they cannot use passive losses to offset portfolio income.

For passive loss purposes, a corporation is a **closely held corporation** if five or fewer shareholders own 50 percent or more of the stock in the corporation during the last half of the tax year. This exception for closely held corporations provides owners of small businesses with an opportunity to avoid the passive limits by incorporating their businesses. This tax-planning mechanism is discussed and illustrated in Chapter 9.

General Rule for Passive Activities.   The purpose of the passive activity rules is to deny current loss deductions for tax-shelter activities. The general rule for implementing this intent is that passive losses may only be deducted to the extent of passive income. Under the general rule, passive losses cannot be deducted against income from portfolio or active income.

▲ **EXAMPLE 23**   Harriet has a taxable income of $100,000 in 1995 from portfolio and active income sources. In addition, she owns 2 passive activities. Passive activity 1 (PA1) has a net loss of $20,000 and passive activity 2 (PA2) has a net income of $2,000 in 1995. What is the effect of the 2 passive activities on Harriet's 1995 income?

Discussion: The $2,000 of income from PA2 is included in gross income. Under the passive activity loss rules, only $2,000 of the loss from PA1 is deductible in 1995. The net $18,000 ($20,000 − $2,000) passive loss in 1995 is not deductible against Harriet's $100,000 of taxable income from portfolio and active income sources. In essence, passive losses are only deductible up to the amount of passive income.

Any passive activity loss that is not deductible in the current year is a **suspended loss.** A suspended loss is not permanently disallowed. Suspended losses are carried forward and may be deducted against passive income in subsequent years.

▲ **EXAMPLE 24**   Assume that Harriet, in example 23, purchases passive activity 3 (PA3) in 1996. The results of the 3 passive activities in 1996 are as follows:

PA1	($10,000)
PA2	3,000
PA3	12,000

What is the effect of the passive activities on Harriet's 1996 taxable income?

Discussion: Harriet's net passive loss of $18,000 from 1995 is suspended and carried forward for deduction against 1996 passive income sources:

	1995	1996
PA1	$(20,000)	$(10,000)
PA2	2,000	3,000
PA3		12,000
1995 suspended loss	$(18,000) ⟶	(18,000)
1996 suspended loss		$(13,000)

As you can see, the suspension and carryforward of the 1995 net passive loss result in Harriet's being able to deduct $5,000 of the 1995 suspended loss against 1996 passive income. The $15,000 in income from PA2 and PA3 is included in Harriet's gross income. However, it would be offset by the $15,000 loss from PA1, leaving her 1996 taxable income unchanged. The $13,000 net passive loss is carried forward to 1997.

Dispositions of Passive Activities.   When a taxpayer disposes of a passive activity in a taxable transaction, any suspended loss in the activity must be accounted for. Deductions of suspended losses are allowed when passive activities are sold and when they are disposed of because the taxpayer has died.[7] However, disposition of a passive activity by gift does not result in a deduction. In each disposition case, you must calculate the amount of suspended passive loss attributable to the activity being sold in order to determine the proper deduction. In the previous examples, this was not a problem, because the taxpayer had only one activity with a loss. Thus, all suspended loss was attributable to the one activity. However, if the taxpayer owns more than one passive activity that creates losses, the total suspended loss for the period must be allocated among the loss activities in order to keep track of the amount of suspended loss attributable to each activity. The allocation of suspended losses is made on the basis of the relative loss of each activity; each loss activity is deemed to contribute proportionately to the total amount of suspended loss.

▲ **EXAMPLE 25**   Continuing with Harriet's passive activities from example 24, assume that the 3 passive activities have the following results for 1997:

PA1	$(4,000)
PA2	2,000
PA3	(1,000)
1997 suspended loss	$(3,000)

How much of the $3,000 suspended loss is attributed to PA1? PA3?

Discussion: The $3,000 in suspended loss is allocated proportionately to the 2 loss activities based on their relative loss. That is, the 2 activities produce a total loss of $5,000 during the period. Therefore, PA1 is responsible for 4/5 ($4,000 of the total $5,000 loss), and PA3 is responsible for 1/5 ($1,000 of the total $5,000 loss). Based on this, $2,400 (4/5 × $3,000) of the suspended loss is attributed to PA1, and $600 (1/5 × $3,000) is attributed to PA3. At this point, the total suspended passive loss on PA1 is $15,400 ($13,000 from 1996 + $2,400 from 1997). PA3 has a total suspended loss of $600.

DISPOSITION BY SALE.   When an entire interest in a passive activity is sold in a taxable transaction, any suspended loss on the activity is deductible in the year of sale against portfolio and active income.

▲ **EXAMPLE 26**   Return to example 25. Assume that Harriet sells PA1 on January 2, 1998, for $42,000. Her basis in PA1 is $36,000. What is the effect of the sale of PA1 on Harriet's 1998 taxable income?

Discussion: Harriet's gain of $6,000 ($42,000 − $36,000) on the sale of PA1 is included in her gross income for 1998. The suspended loss of $15,400 is deductible against active and portfolio income sources. Thus, the net effect of the sale is a reduction in her taxable income of $9,400 ($6,000 − $15,400).

From example 26, you can see that the passive activity loss rules do not permanently disallow deductions of losses. Rather, they operate as a deferral mechanism. During the period in which the passive activity is held, the entire economic loss is deductible. To see this, look at Harriet's actual losses from PA1 versus her actual loss deductions:

	1995	1996	1997	1998	Total
Actual loss	$(20,000)	$(10,000)	$(4,000)		$(34,000)
Amount deducted	$ (2,000)	$(15,000)	$(1,600)	$(15,400)	$(34,000)

One final note of caution on dispositions by sale: The gain or loss on the sale of the activity generally is a capital gain or a capital loss. Recall from Chapter 3 that gains and losses from the sale of capital assets are treated differently than other types of gains and losses. Briefly, net capital gains are taxed at a maximum rate of 28 percent, and net capital losses are limited to a deduction of $3,000 per year. Thus, in example 26, the $6,000 capital gain Harriet had on the sale of PA1 would be subject to a maximum tax rate of 28 percent.

▲ **EXAMPLE 27**   Assume the same facts as in example 26, except that Harriet sells PA1 for only $30,000, resulting in a loss of $6,000. What is the effect on Harriet's taxable income?

Discussion: Harriet still is allowed the full deduction of the $15,400 suspended loss. However, the $6,000 loss on the sale of PA1 is a capital loss and subject to the limitations on capital losses. If this is Harriet's only capital asset sale during 1998, she is allowed to deduct only $3,000 of the capital loss in 1998, with the remaining loss carried forward to 1999.

DISPOSITION UPON DEATH.   When a taxpayer dies while holding passive activities, the passive activities become part of the estate and subject to the estate tax. For estate tax purposes, all assets are valued at the fair market value at the date of death. Heirs who receive property from an estate take as their basis the fair market value of the property at the date of death (the estate tax valuation). The result of this valuation process is that any unrealized gain on an asset is not subject to an income tax.

▲ **EXAMPLE 28**   Felipe died and left a piece of land to his son. Felipe had paid $12,000 for the land, which was worth $23,000 at the date of his death. Upon receiving the land, Felipe's son immediately sold it for $23,000. What are the income tax consequences of the sale of the land?

Discussion: The land is valued at $23,000 for estate tax purposes. The $23,000 estate tax valuation becomes the son's basis in the land. Therefore, the son has neither gain nor loss on the sale of the land. The $9,000 in unrealized gain on the land was not subject to the income tax, because the fair market value of the land was assigned for estate tax purposes, with a corresponding increase in basis to fair market value for the son.

Because the unrealized gains on property passing through an estate escape taxation, the passive loss rules limit the amount of the deduction for suspended losses on property held at death to the amount of the suspended loss in excess of any unrealized gain on the activity. The effect of this provision is to provide the same net loss deduction the decedent taxpayer would have received had that person sold the property.

▲ **EXAMPLE 29**   Assume the same facts as in example 26, except that Harriet dies on January 2, 1998. PA1 has a fair market value of $42,000 and an adjusted basis of $36,000 as of that date. The suspended loss at that date is $15,400. How much of the suspended loss can be deducted on Harriet's 1998 income tax return?

Discussion: If Harriet had sold PA1, she would have had a gain of $6,000 on the sale, and the $15,400 in suspended loss would have been deductible. This results in a net deduction of $9,400. Because she died, the $6,000 in gain is never subject to income tax. Therefore, the suspended loss deduction is limited to the $9,400 by which she would have been able to reduce her income had the property been sold. That is, $9,400 is the amount of suspended loss in excess of the unrealized gain on PA1.

If a passive activity with a suspended loss has a basis greater than its fair market value (i.e., a loss property) at death, no deduction of the suspended loss is allowed. This is the unfortunate result of the statutory language that allows deductions only for the excess of suspended losses over unrealized gains. Under the legislative grace concept, the interpretation of the language is that because the statute is silent as to unrealized losses, no suspended loss deductions are allowed.

▲ **EXAMPLE 30**   Assume the same facts as in example 26, except that Harriet dies on January 2, 1998. PA1 has a fair market value of $30,000 and an adjusted basis of $36,000 as of that date. The suspended loss at that date is $15,400. How much of the suspended loss can be deducted on Harriet's 1998 income tax return?

Discussion: Because PA1 has an unrealized loss of $6,000 as of the date of death, there is no excess of suspended loss over unrealized gain. Therefore, no suspended loss deduction is allowed on Harriet's 1998 income tax return.

DISPOSITION BY GIFT.   When a taxpayer makes a gift of property to another taxpayer, there is no income tax effect for either party. The donor does not have to recognize an unrealized gain on the property, and the donee does not have income from the receipt of the gift. The donor's basis becomes the donee's basis. This is called a *carryover basis* and is necessary to ensure that any unrealized gains on the gift property do not go untaxed.

▲ **EXAMPLE 31**   John owned property with a basis of $3,000 and a fair market value of $10,000. John gave the property to his daughter Nancy as a gift. Nancy immediately sold the property for $10,000. What are the tax effects of the gift and subsequent sale?

Discussion: The receipt of the gift is not a taxable event for either John or Nancy. Nancy takes John's basis in the property. Her gain on the sale is $7,000 ($10,000 − $3,000). This treatment ensures that unrealized gains on gift property do not escape income taxation.

Because making a gift is not a taxable event for the donor, the person who receives a gift cannot take a deduction for a suspended loss. Instead, the suspended loss is added to the basis of the donee. The effect of this treatment is to recognize that the donor does not realize (or recognize) a gain on the disposition of a gift property. Because the donor does not recognize the gain, the donor cannot take an offsetting suspended loss deduction. It is carried through to the donee and remains unrealized until the donee disposes of the property.

▲ **EXAMPLE 32**   Assume that in example 31 the property John gave to Nancy was a passive activity that had a suspended loss of $20,000 at the date of the gift. What is the tax effect of the gift for John and Nancy?

Discussion: The gift has no tax effect for either party. Because John has given the unrealized gain to Nancy (i.e., John will never be taxed on the gain), he is not allowed any deductions for the suspended loss. The suspended loss becomes part of Nancy's basis in the asset, $23,000 ($3,000 + $20,000).

This treatment prevents a taxpayer from passing suspended losses to a related taxpayer who could benefit from the suspended passive losses. Nancy is not allowed to deduct John's suspended loss against any passive income she may have. Because the suspended loss is added to the basis of the donee, the only way Nancy can benefit from the suspended loss is by selling the passive activity.

Exceptions for Rental Real Estate.   The Omnibus Budget Reconciliation Act of 1993 permits a taxpayer to treat rental real estate in which the taxpayer materially participates as an active activity and to use any losses to offset active and portfolio income. Before the new law was adopted, rental real estate was always considered passive and only taxpayers who met certain tests were permitted to use losses from rental real estate activities to offset active and portfolio income. The new law creates two exceptions, the material participation exception and the active participation exception, that permit a taxpayer to use losses from rental property to offset active and portfolio income (see Figure 7–3).

For tax years after 1993, a taxpayer qualifies under the **material participation exception** if

- More than 50 percent of the taxpayer's total personal services (work) are in real property trades or businesses in which the taxpayer materially participates.
- The taxpayer performs more than 750 hours a year of service in real property trades or businesses in which the taxpayer materially participates.
- The taxpayer materially participates in the rental activity.[8]

▲ **Figure 7–3**

DETERMINING WHETHER
RENTAL PROPERTY IS
ACTIVE OR PASSIVE

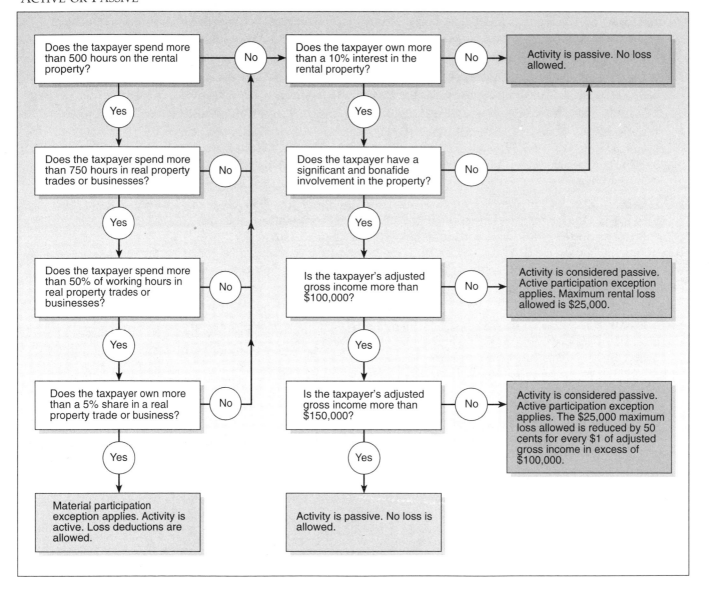

As discussed earlier in this chapter, to materially participate in an activity, the taxpayer generally must spend more than 500 hours a year working in that activity. A **real property trade or business** is any real property development, redevelopment, construction, acquisition, conversion, rental operation, management, leasing, or brokerage trade or business. In addition, an individual who is an employee of a business engaged in a real property trade or business qualifies for this exception only if the employee has an ownership interest in the business that is greater than 5 percent.

▲ **EXAMPLE 33**   Return to the facts of example 17. In 1995, Bart decides to quit practicing law and take Chester's place as the manager of the building. Bart devotes all his personal services, 2,000 hours, to managing the apartments (getting tenants, collecting rent, taking care of repairs, etc.). Alf continues to work as a lawyer. Is the apartment building a passive activity for either of them?

Discussion: In 1994, the rental activity was passive for both Alf and Bart. Under the material participation exception for rental real estate, Bart can treat the rental property as an active activity in 1995. More than 50% of his personal services are devoted to working in a real property trade or business in which he materially participates, the time he devotes to the real property trade or business is more than 750 hours, and he materially participates in the rental activity (spends more than 500 hours working in the activity). The rental property remains passive for Alf, because he fails to meet any of the tests. In fact, Alf does not even materially participate in the rental activity. NOTE: Each individual in the activity is evaluated separately, and the individual must meet all three tests to qualify a rental as an active activity.

▲ **EXAMPLE 34**   Assume the same facts as example 33, except that Alf is a real estate broker employed by a corporation in which he owns a 20% interest. He spends 1,800 hours a year as a broker and 200 hours a year helping Bart to manage the apartment building.

Discussion: Again, Bart is permitted to treat the rental activity as active only if he meets the tests described earlier. Although Alf spends more than 50% of his working hours (1,800 hours ÷ 2,000 hours) in a real property trade or business in which he materially participates and the number of hours he spends in that activity is greater than 750, he fails to materially participate in the rental real estate activity. NOTE: If Alf had spent more than 500 hours helping Bart to manage the apartment complex, he would have been able to treat the rental activity as active.

▲ **EXAMPLE 35**   Assume the same facts as example 33, except that Alf spends 525 hours as a real estate broker in a business in which he owns a 10% interest, 550 hours helping Bart to manage the apartments, and 1,200 hours practicing law.

Discussion: Although Bart continues to be entitled to consider the rental as an active activity, Alf must treat the rental property as a passive activity. Alf passes the 750-hour requirement, because he spends 1,075 hours working in a real property trade or business in which he materially participates and he materially participates in the rental activity. However, he spends less than 50% of his personal service (1,075 hours ÷ 2,275 hours) in real property trades or businesses. NOTE: If Alf spends only 1,000 hours practicing law, he passes the 50% test (1,075 hours ÷ 2,075) and thus may treat the rental activity as active.

For taxpayers who own rental real estate but who do not meet the material participation test, the tax law allows active participants in rental real estate to deduct losses as great as $25,000 per year against portfolio and active sources of income (see Figure 7–3). An **active participant** must own at least a 10-percent interest in the activity and have significant and bonafide involvement in it. *Significant and bonafide involvement* is a less stringent standard than the material participation standard discussed earlier. It requires that the individual be involved in some significant aspect of the rental (i.e., arranging financing, collecting rents, arranging for repairs and maintenance, keeping the activities records, etc.). In most cases, taxpayers eligible for this exception easily meet the significant involvement standard.

This exception, known as the **active participation exception,** is geared to individuals of more moderate means, because the $25,000 annual deduction amount is phased out when the individual's adjusted gross income exceeds $100,000. For every dollar of adjusted gross income in excess of $100,000, the taxpayer loses 50 cents of the $25,000 deduction. Thus, when adjusted gross income reaches $150,000 [($150,000 − $100,000) × $0.50 = $25,000], the deduction is no longer available.

▲ **EXAMPLE 36**   Rory is a mechanic who owns an apartment building that had a net rental loss of $20,000 during the current year. Rory's adjusted gross income is $120,000. If Rory owns no other passive activities, how much of the rental loss can he deduct?

Discussion: Because the property is rental real estate, it always is considered a passive activity unless one of the rental real estate exceptions applies. Rory owns 100% of the property, and it is assumed that he is involved in the rental in some significant way. The special deduction for rental real estate is $25,000. However, because Rory's adjusted gross income is in excess of $100,000, he must reduce the allowable deduction by $10,000 [($120,000 − $100,000) × $0.50] to $15,000. Rory can deduct $15,000 of the rental loss against his $120,000 of adjusted gross income. The remaining $5,000 is suspended and treated like any other passive loss.

The special exception is for $25,000 in losses incurred within a single tax year. Any amounts not deductible in one year are suspended as passive losses and can only be deducted in subsequent years against passive income. They cannot be deducted under the next year's $25,000 rental real estate limit.

▲ **EXAMPLE 37**   Return to example 36. Assume that in the following year, Rory's rental property has a $20,000 loss and that his adjusted gross income is $90,000. How much of a rental real estate loss deduction is Rory allowed?

Discussion: Because his adjusted gross income is less than $100,000, there is no phaseout on the $25,000 rental real estate deduction. However, Rory's current loss is only $20,000. Therefore, he is able to deduct only $20,000 under the $25,000 special annual deduction. The $5,000 in suspended loss from the prior year is carried forward and treated as any other passive loss would be treated—it can only be deducted against passive income. Rory cannot deduct the disallowed loss from the prior year against the current year's rental real estate allowance. The special deduction is allowed only on the current year's rental real estate losses.

▲ TRANSACTION LOSSES

A transaction loss results from a single disposition of property. Most transaction losses are the result of selling a property at less than its basis (i.e., incomplete capital recovery). However, other forms of disposition, such as exchanges of assets and involuntary conversions (casualties and thefts), may also produce losses.

The allowance of deductions for losses follows the same line of reasoning as for the allowance of deductions. That is, the loss must be categorized according to the activity producing the loss:

1. Trade or business losses

2. Investment-related losses

3. Personal use losses

Once categorized, the rules for deductibility of losses within each category are applied to determine the amount of deductible loss. These treatments are depicted in Figure 7–4. In general, transaction losses must have a business purpose to be deductible. Casualty losses and theft losses are the only loss deductions allowed for personal use losses.[9] If the loss is incurred in a trade or business, the taxpayer generally is allowed to take a **trade or business loss.** However, losses on sales to related parties are never allowed, regardless of their relation to a trade or business or investment activity. **Investment-related losses** involve dispositions of capital assets. Net capital loss deductions are limited for both individuals and corporations. The most important aspects of each of the three categories of transaction losses are discussed in turn.

Trade or Business Losses

In general, all transaction losses incurred in a trade or business are deductible. With one major exception, these losses are treated as ordinary losses in the period they are incurred and are deducted without limit against the income from the trade or business.[10] For an individual, a trade or business loss is deductible as a deduction for adjusted gross income.[11] An exception to this rule is for losses on exchanges of business property that must be deferred to a future period. This exception is covered in Chapter 13. The calculation of a transaction loss is straightforward—a loss results when the asset's basis is greater than the amount realized from the disposition.[12] One area that needs extra attention is the determination of the amount of loss from casualties and thefts.

Business Casualty and Theft Losses. **A casualty** is the result of some sudden, unexpected, and/or unusual event.[13] In addition to being sudden and unexpected, actual physical damage to property must occur in order to have a **casualty loss.**[14] If there is no physical damage to property, but the property declines in value because of a sudden and unexpected event, the loss in value is not considered a casualty. The most common types of casualties include damage from fire, storms, earthquakes, and accidents. Losses that occur gradually over time do not constitute casualties. Examples of losses that are not casualties would include damage from termites, losses from insects or disease, and loss in value of land because of wind erosion.[15]

A **theft** is similar to a casualty in that it must be sudden and unexpected. A theft may occur as a result of a robbery, larceny, or an embezzlement.[16] Misplacing or losing items does not constitute a theft. The damage caused by a theft is that the entire property is lost. As such, **theft losses** are treated in the same manner as casualty losses.

When a casualty occurs, one of two things can happen. The property may be fully destroyed and have no value, or it may be partially destroyed and have some remaining value. The calculation of the amount of loss depends on whether the property was fully or partially destroyed in the casualty.[17] A theft is treated as property fully destroyed (all value lost).

BUSINESS PROPERTY FULLY DESTROYED.   When a business property is fully destroyed (or stolen), the taxpayer's entire investment in the property has been

▲ **Figure 7–4**

TREATMENT OF
TRANSACTION LOSSES

lost. The capital recovery concept allows a taxpayer to fully recover the investment in business property. The measure of a taxpayer's investment in a property is its basis. Therefore, the measure of a **business casualty loss** for fully destroyed business property is the property's basis.

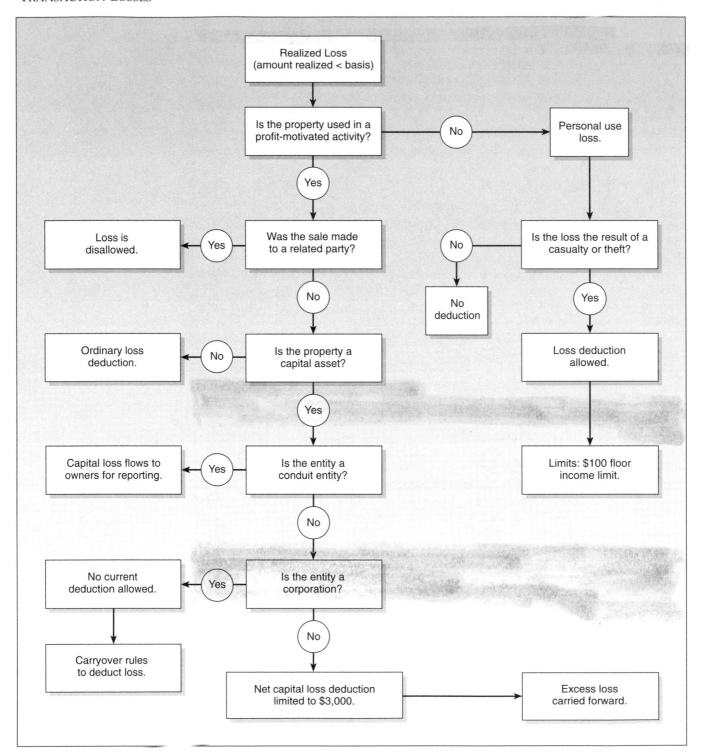

▲ **EXAMPLE 38**   A driver for Portable Phone Providers (PPP) was involved in an accident that totally destroyed one of the company's vans. The van had been purchased for $26,000, and depreciation taken to date on the van was $8,000. What is the measure of the loss on the van?

Discussion: Because the van was totally destroyed in the accident, the measure of the loss is the unrecovered investment in the van, its basis. Although the van cost $26,000, the company has recovered $8,000 of the cost through depreciation deductions. The unrecovered portion, $18,000 ($26,000 − $8,000) is the amount of the investment lost.

Most business assets are covered by insurance. Any amounts received from insurance on property subject to a casualty are a capital recovery. Thus, the amount of the loss must be reduced by any insurance proceeds received from the casualty.

▲ **EXAMPLE 39**   Assume that in example 38 PPP's van was covered by insurance and that PPP received $15,000 from the insurance company for the accident. What is PPP's casualty loss?

Discussion: PPP's loss is $3,000. Of the $18,000 of basis that was unrecovered at the date of the casualty, $15,000 was recovered from the insurance company. NOTE: When insurance proceeds are received, the loss is calculated as the difference between the amount realized (insurance proceeds) and the basis. Thus, the calculation of a casualty loss for business property fully destroyed is identical to the calculation of a loss from the sale of a property.

At this point, we should note that all casualties do not result in losses. That is, if the insurance proceeds received from a casualty exceed the adjusted basis of the property, the result of the casualty would be a **casualty gain.**

▲ **EXAMPLE 40**   Assume that in example 39 PPP received $20,000 for the destruction of its van. What is PPP's casualty gain (loss)?

Discussion: PPP has a gain of $2,000 ($20,000 − $18,000) from the casualty. PPP has recovered more than its remaining investment in the van. Therefore, under the capital recovery concept, PPP has a gain from the receipt of insurance proceeds in excess of adjusted basis.

Gains from business casualties are subject to a special election under which a casualty gain may be deferred. Because the focus of this chapter is on losses, the discussion of this election is deferred until Chapter 13.

BUSINESS PROPERTY PARTIALLY DESTROYED.   When a casualty occurs and property is not totally destroyed, an estimate of the amount lost because of the casualty must be made. The amount of the real loss from a partial destruction is the decrease in the taxpayer's wealth resulting from the casualty. This can be measured by the decline in the market value of the property that results from the casualty. The decline in the value of the property is

The fair market value of the property *before* the casualty

Less: The fair market value of the property *after* the casualty

Equals: The decline in value because of the casualty

In most cases, this is an adequate measurement of the loss the taxpayer has incurred as a result of the casualty. However, under the capital recovery concept, the maximum amount that can be recovered on any property is the amount invested in the property—its basis. Thus, a loss deduction because of a casualty can never exceed the property's basis. This leads to the following rule for measuring a loss on partially destroyed business property:

The measure of the loss is equal to the lesser of

- The decline in the value of the property

    or

- The adjusted basis of the property

The purpose of this measurement rule is to ensure that the amount of the loss deducted does not exceed the amount of unrecovered investment in the property.

▲ **EXAMPLE 41**   This year, a hurricane damaged a warehouse used by Sugar Exporters, Inc., (SEI) in its exporting operation. SEI had paid $200,000 for the warehouse and had taken $80,000 in depreciation before the hurricane. Appraisals indicated that the warehouse was worth $300,000 before the hurricane. In its damaged state, the warehouse could be sold for only $100,000. What is the amount of loss SEI suffered on the warehouse because of the hurricane?

Discussion: The value of the warehouse declined $200,000 ($300,000 − $100,000) because of the hurricane damage. However, SEI's unrecovered investment in the warehouse is $120,000 ($200,000 − $80,000).

SEI's loss is the lesser of the decline in value because of the hurricane, $200,000, or its basis in the warehouse, $120,000. In this case, the maximum amount that SEI can recover through a loss deduction is the $120,000 basis.

As with fully destroyed business property, the calculated loss must be reduced by any insurance proceeds received because of the casualty.

▲ **EXAMPLE 42**   Assume that in example 41 SEI's warehouse was covered by insurance. SEI received $100,000 from the insurance company for the hurricane damage. What is SEI's casualty loss?

Discussion: The $120,000 loss must be reduced by the $100,000 of insurance proceeds. SEI's deductible loss is $20,000 ($120,000 − $100,000).

In many instances, the measurement of the decline in the value of a property that results from a casualty poses formidable problems. That is, by definition a casualty is the result of a sudden and unexpected event. This makes it unlikely that the taxpayer had the foresight to have the property appraised shortly before the casualty. After a property has been damaged, assessing its true condition before being damaged is often difficult. Thus, the estimate of the decline in value of the property because of the casualty is difficult to obtain. For this reason, the IRS allows the taxpayer to use the cost of repairing the property to estimate the decline in value of the property.

▲ **EXAMPLE 43**   Mammoth Co. operates ski resorts throughout the western United States. In February, an avalanche at one of its resorts damaged a ski lift. The lift had cost $450,000, and Mammoth had taken depreciation of $200,000 before the casualty. It cost $160,000 to have the lift repaired. What is the amount of Mammoth's loss because of the avalanche?

Discussion: Because of the difficulty of determining the value of the ski lift before the casualty (and after the casualty), the cost of repairing the lift can be used to estimate the decline in value because of the damage. This is a partial destruction of business property, and the amount of the loss is measured by the lesser of the decline in value, $160,000, or the basis of the ski lift, $250,000 ($450,000 − $200,000). In this case, the $160,000 cost of repairing the lift is lower than the basis and is used to measure the loss. Any insurance proceeds Mammoth received would reduce the amount of the loss that is deductible.

Investment-Related Losses

Losses on transactions related to investment activities are generally allowed as deductions. However, in contrast to trade or business losses, which are always deductible in full, the amount of the current period deduction for an investment-related loss may be limited. This occurs because investment-related assets are capital assets. A *capital asset* is defined as any asset that is not a receivable, an inventory item, depreciable or real property used in a trade or business, or certain intangible assets such as copyrights.[18] Note that the items that are not capital assets are primarily assets used in a trade or business. Thus, assets that are not used in a trade or business are capital assets. This would include both investment assets and personal use assets. There are limits on the amount of loss from the sale of capital assets that is deductible in any one tax year. In addition, the tax law provides several other significant provisions related to losses on the sale of capital assets.

Capital Losses.   When a taxpayer suffers losses on the disposition of capital assets, the tax law provides a procedure for netting these losses against any gains from capital asset dispositions during the year. As discussed in Chapter 3, the purpose of this netting procedure is to produce a single position for net capital asset transactions for the entire year. The net transaction position can be either a gain or a loss. An overview of the netting procedure was presented in Chapter 3. More specific details of the treatment of capital gains and losses are covered in Chapter 12. At this juncture, the critical aspect is the treatment of net capital losses. A net capital loss occurs when a taxpayer's total capital losses exceed the taxpayer's total capital gains for a tax year. The treatment of a net capital loss for an individual is different than the treatment for a corporation.[19]

NET CAPITAL LOSSES OF INDIVIDUALS.   An individual taxpayer is limited to a deduction of $3,000 in net capital losses per year. The capital loss deduction is a deduction for adjusted gross income. Any loss in excess of $3,000 is carried forward and netted against capital gains in subsequent years. Thus, the capital loss limitation is a deferral-of-loss-recognition provision, not a total loss disallowance provision.

▲ **EXAMPLE 44**   Mona has the following total capital gains and losses for 1995 and 1996. What is Mona's deductible capital loss in 1995 and 1996?

	1995	1996
Capital gains	$12,000	$17,000
Capital losses	(20,000)	(16,000)

Discussion: Mona has a net capital loss of $8,000 in 1995. Because of the capital loss limitations, Mona can deduct only $3,000 of this loss in 1995. The remaining $5,000 of 1995 loss is carried forward to 1996 and included in the 1996 netting:

	1995	1996
Capital gains	$12,000	$17,000
Capital losses	(20,000)	(16,000)
Net 1995 capital loss	$(8,000)	
1995 capital loss deduction	3,000	
1995 capital loss carryforward	$(5,000) ⟶	(5,000)
Net 1996 capital loss		$(4,000)
1996 capital loss deduction		3,000
1996 capital loss carryforward		$(1,000)

As you can see, the carryforward of the $5,000 capital loss from 1995 to 1996 creates a net capital loss of $4,000 in 1996. Without the carryforward, Mona would have had a $1,000 ($17,000 - $16,000) net capital gain in 1996. However, when the $5,000 of 1995 loss is carried forward and included in the 1996 netting, the result is a $4,000 loss. Per the capital loss limitations, $3,000 of the net capital loss is deductible in 1996. The remaining $1,000 of net capital loss must be carried forward and included in Mona's 1997 capital gain-and-loss netting.

NET CAPITAL LOSSES OF CORPORATIONS.   In contrast to individuals, corporations are not allowed to deduct net capital losses against noncapital gain income. Corporations can use capital losses only to offset capital gains. When a corporation incurs a net capital loss for a tax year, it is allowed to carry the net capital loss back and use it to offset any net capital gains on which it paid tax in the preceding three years. Any net capital loss that is not used in the three-year carryback period may be carried forward to offset capital gains for five years.

▲ EXAMPLE 45   El Fredo Corporation has the following net capital gains and losses for 1994 through 1997:

1994	1995	1996	1997
$8,000	$5,000	$7,000	$(35,000)

Assuming that El Fredo is in a 34% marginal tax rate bracket during each of these years, what is the effect of the $35,000 capital loss in 1997?

Discussion: El Fredo cannot deduct any of the $35,000 capital loss against its 1997 income. It must carry the loss back 3 years and use the loss to reduce any capital gains during that period. For El Fredo, the loss would first be applied against the $8,000 in 1994 capital gain, resulting in a $2,720 (34% × $8,000) refund of the tax paid in 1994. Applying the remaining loss against the $5,000 and $7,000 of net capital gains in 1995 and 1996, respectively, would result in refunds of $1,700 and $2,380. The 3-year carryback would use up $20,000 of the $35,000 in 1997 net capital loss. The remaining $15,000 in loss would be carried forward and used to reduce capital gains in the next 5 years.

Specially Treated Investment Losses.   Three provisions related to losses on investment assets deserve mention. Each of these provisions provides special treatment in certain transaction loss situations.

LOSSES ON SMALL BUSINESS STOCK.   In order to encourage individuals to invest in new companies, the tax law provides an exception to the $3,000 annual loss limitation on losses incurred on qualifying **small business stock.** This provision allows an individual taxpayer to deduct up to $50,000 in losses on small business stock per year. The limit is raised to $100,000 for a married couple filing a joint return.[20] Any losses on small business stock in excess of $50,000 ($100,000 for married couples) are subject to the regular capital gain-and-loss netting procedure.

▲ **EXAMPLE 46**   Linda is a single taxpayer whose only capital asset transaction for 1995 is a $70,000 capital loss on the sale of qualifying small business stock. How much of the $70,000 loss can Linda deduct in 1995?

Discussion: Linda is allowed to deduct $50,000 of the loss under the special exception for losses on small business stock. The remaining $20,000 of the loss is a capital loss subject to the annual $3,000 limitation. Thus, she can deduct an additional $3,000. This gives Linda a total loss deduction of $53,000 in 1995. The remaining $17,000 in loss must be carried forward to 1996 and deducted under the regular capital gain-and-loss netting procedure. NOTE: If Linda had been married in 1995, she and her husband could have deducted the entire $70,000 loss in 1995.

It should be stressed that the special deduction applies to losses incurred during a given tax year. Losses in excess of the allowable $50,000 ($100,000) deduction that are carried forward as a capital loss are subject to the capital loss limitation in later years, not the small business stock limitation.[21]

▲ **EXAMPLE 47**   Assume that in example 46 Linda has one capital asset transaction in 1996 that results in a $5,000 capital gain. What is Linda's 1996 capital loss deduction?

Discussion: The $17,000 in net capital loss carries forward from 1995 to be netted against the $5,000 in capital gain in 1996, resulting in a net capital loss for 1996 of $12,000. Linda cannot use the small business stock deduction on this loss, because it occurs in 1995. Therefore, only $3,000 of the $12,000 loss can be deducted in 1996. The $9,000 remaining loss must be carried forward to 1997 and included in Linda's 1997 capital gain-and-loss netting.

To qualify as small business stock, the stock must be purchased directly from the corporation at original issue. That is, the stock cannot be acquired from another individual or other taxable entity. The corporation itself must satisfy several other requirements, the most important of which is that the contributed capital of the corporation at the time the stock is issued must be less than $1 million.

LOSSES ON RELATED PARTY SALES.   In order to receive its intended income tax effect, a transaction must be entered into at arm's length. The tax law recognizes that related party transactions often lack the necessary bargaining to characterize the transactions as arm's length. The objective of the related party rules is to defer or disallow losses on transactions that are not made at arm's length. The primary provision regarding losses is that a loss on the sale of property to a related party is disallowed as a deduction.[22]

▲ **EXAMPLE 48**   Rasheed sold 500 shares of ABC Corporation stock to his sister Tawana for $5,000. Rasheed had paid $7,500 for the stock. Can Rasheed deduct the $2,500 loss on the sale of the stock to his sister?

Discussion: Rasheed cannot deduct the loss on the sale of the stock, because Tawana is a related party. Losses on sales of property to related parties are disallowed.

If the property subject to the related party sale disallowance is later sold to an unrelated party at a gain, the gain realized on the sale may be reduced by the amount of loss previously disallowed.[23]

▲ **EXAMPLE 49**   Assume that in example 48 Tawana later sells the shares of ABC stock to an unrelated party for $9,000. How much gain does Tawana have to recognize from the sale?

Discussion: Tawana's basis is the $5,000 she paid for the stock, giving her a gain on the sale of $4,000 ($9,000 − $5,000). Tawana is allowed to reduce her $4,000 gain by Rasheed's $2,500 disallowed loss. She has to recognize only a $1,500 ($4,000 − $2,500) gain on the sale.

The gain on a subsequent sale to an unrelated party may only be reduced to zero (no gain or loss recognized). A loss cannot be created on a subsequent sale by using the previously disallowed loss.

▲ **EXAMPLE 50**   Assume that in example 49 Tawana sold the stock to an unrelated party for $6,000. How much gain does Tawana have to recognize on the sale?

Discussion: Tawana realizes a gain of $1,000 ($6,000 − $5,000) on the sale. She may use Rasheed's $2,500 disallowed loss to reduce gain on the subsequent sale but only to zero. In this case, Tawana does not recognize any gain on the sale of the stock. However, note that the remaining $1,500 of Rasheed's previously disallowed loss is permanently lost in this case.

If the subsequent sale to an unrelated party results in a loss, the disallowed loss may not be used to increase the loss on the subsequent sale.

▲ **EXAMPLE 51**   Assume that in example 49 Tawana sells the stock to an unrelated party for $3,000. How much loss does Tawana recognize on the sale?

Discussion: The loss on the sale is $2,000 ($3,000 - $5,000). Tawana is not allowed to use Rasheed's $2,500 disallowed loss to increase the loss on the sale. Tawana is allowed to recognize only the actual $2,000 loss.

The related party disallowance rule also applies to the sale to a related party of property used in a trade or business.

▲ **EXAMPLE 52**   Catherine, the CEO of the Adtech Corporation, owns 60% of the Adtech Corporation. She sells land with a basis of $35,000 to Adtech for $31,000. Can Catherine deduct the $4,000 loss?

Discussion: Catherine cannot deduct any of the loss on the sale of the land. Because Catherine owns more than 50% of Adtech, she and Adtech are related parties. The disallowed loss of $4,000 can be used only to reduce any gain Adtech might have when it sells the land.

In summary, when property is sold at a loss to a related party, no loss is allowed. However, if the property is later sold to an unrelated party at a gain, the disallowed loss can be used to reduce the gain but not below zero (i.e., no loss allowed). Also, if the property is subsequently sold to an unrelated party at a loss, no portion of the disallowed loss from the related party sale is deductible.

The related party rules apply *only* to losses on sales to related parties. No comparable provisions restrict the reporting of gains on sales to related parties. Gains on sales to related parties are treated as any other type of gain would be treated.

WASH SALES.   A **wash sale** occurs when a security (stocks, bonds, options) is sold at a loss, and during the 30-day period before or after the loss sale date, the seller purchases substantially identical securities to replace the securities sold.[24] In a wash sale, a taxpayer's economic position with respect to the shares replaced remains unchanged. A wash sale loss lacks economic substance—in essence it is an artificial loss created for tax purposes without any change in the taxpayer's underlying economic position. The wash sale provisions recognize the substance of the transaction rather than its form (substance-over-form doctrine) by disallowing recognition of all losses on wash sales. The disallowed loss is added to the basis of the replacement shares.[25]

▲ **EXAMPLE 53**   Moses owned 400 shares of Nick Nack Corporation stock that he had purchased for $20,000 several years ago. In December of the current year, Moses sold the 400 shares for $12,000. One week later, he purchased an additional 400 shares of Nick Nack stock for $12,000. What are the tax consequences of the sale of the Nick Nack stock?

Discussion: The $8,000 loss on the sale of the 400 shares of stock is a wash sale, because Moses repurchased substantially identical shares within 30 days of the sale of the shares at a loss. The $8,000 loss is disallowed. However, the disallowance is not permanent—Moses adds the $8,000 loss to the basis of the replacement shares, giving him a basis of $20,000 in the replacement shares. Moses will be able to recover the $8,000 of disallowed loss when he disposes of the stock in a transaction that does not constitute a wash sale.

The wash sale provisions do not apply to dispositions at a gain, to securities that are sold at a loss but not replaced, or to dealers in securities.

▲ **EXAMPLE 54**   Assume that in example 53 Moses repurchased only 300 shares of the Nick Nack stock for $9,000 after the $12,000 sale. What are the tax consequences of the sale of the 400 shares of stock?

Discussion: In this case, only the 300 shares of stock that are replaced are a wash sale. The loss on the 100 shares that were not replaced, $2,000 [(100 ÷ 400) × $8,000], is recognized. The $6,000 loss on the replaced shares is subject to the wash sale disallowance and is not deductible. The basis of the 300 replacement shares is $15,000 ($9,000 + $6,000).

▲ **EXAMPLE 55**   Assume that in example 53 Moses repurchased 600 shares of the Nick Nack stock for $18,000. What are the tax consequences of the sale of the Nick Nack stock?

Discussion: The $8,000 loss on the sale of the 400 shares of stock is a wash sale, because Moses repurchased substantially identical shares within 30 days of the sale of the shares at a loss. The $8,000 loss is disallowed. However, the disallowance is not permanent—Moses adds the $8,000 loss to the basis of the replacement shares, giving him a basis of $20,000 in the 400 replacement shares. The other 200 shares that he purchased have a basis of $6,000 ($18,000 ÷ 600 = $30 × 200 = $6,000).

Personal Use Losses.   Losses on the sale or other disposition of personal use assets are generally disallowed—losses on the sale of personal use items such as autos, jewelry, furniture, and clothing have no tax effect. The only personal use loss that the tax law allows as a deduction is for losses from casualty or theft. And, under the legislative grace concept, Congress has placed several restrictions on the amount of a personal use casualty loss that may be deducted. One such restriction is that **personal casualty losses** and theft losses are only deductible as personal itemized deductions. Thus, a taxpayer must itemize in order to deduct a personal casualty or theft loss. In addition, a per occurrence and an annual limitation are imposed on personal casualty and theft losses.

MEASURING THE PERSONAL CASUALTY LOSS.   In contrast to business casualty losses, which have a measurement rule for fully destroyed property (basis) and a separate rule for partially destroyed property (the lesser of the decline in value or the basis), personal casualty and theft losses are always measured as the lesser of

- The decline in the value of the property

    or

- The basis of the property

The effect of this measurement rule is to disallow losses in the value of property before the casualty that were attributable to everyday wear and tear from personal use. This is consistent with the general rule that losses from personal use are not deductible.

> ▲ **EXAMPLE 56**   Naomee was involved in an auto accident that totally destroyed her personal automobile. Naomee had purchased the auto several years ago for $30,000. A used car dealer told her that a comparable car could be bought today for $10,000. What is the amount of Naomee's loss on the casualty?
>
> *Discussion:*   The measure of the amount of loss is the lesser of the decline in value because of the casualty, $10,000, or the basis, $30,000. Thus, the amount of Naomee's loss is $10,000.
>
>   Note that the $20,000 loss in value from what Naomee paid for the auto, $30,000, and what the auto was worth before the accident, $10,000, is not a loss attributable to the casualty. The $20,000 loss in value occurred during Naomee's personal use of the auto and was not from the casualty. Thus, the loss in value from personal use is not deductible.
>
> *Discussion:*   If Naomee had used her car exclusively in a trade or business, the amount of loss would have been her $30,000 basis. The treatment is different because of the business purpose of the automobile. All expenses and losses incurred in a trade or business are deductible. Personal expenses and losses are generally not deductible.

LIMITATIONS ON PERSONAL CASUALTY LOSSES.   As with any casualty loss, the amount of loss must be reduced by any insurance proceeds received. In addition, you must file a claim for any insurance due in order to claim a deduction. Personal use casualty losses are also reduced by a $100 **statutory floor** per occurrence. The $100 statutory floor reduction is an element of administrative convenience. Because including $100 losses on individual returns adds cost and complexity to the tax system, the $100 floor eliminates the deduction of small personal casualty losses.

> ▲ **EXAMPLE 57**   Assume that in example 56 Naomee received $8,000 for her accident from her insurance company. What is Naomee's casualty loss?
>
> *Discussion:*   The $10,000 loss must be reduced by the $8,000 insurance reimbursement and the $100 statutory floor. This results in a $1,900 ($10,000 − $8,000 − $100) loss on the casualty.

The $100 statutory floor is a per occurrence limitation that is applied to each casualty or theft that occurs during the year. In addition, the tax law imposes an **annual personal casualty loss limitation** on the total of all casualty and theft losses. Total personal casualty and theft losses for the year are deductible only to the extent that they exceed 10 percent of the taxpayer's adjusted gross income.

▲ **EXAMPLE 58**   Assume that in example 57 Naomee had an adjusted gross income of $15,000 in the year she sustained the loss on her personal automobile. What is Naomee's allowable itemized deduction for the casualty?

Discussion: The $1,900 loss on the automobile would be combined with any other casualty or theft losses occurring during the year. The total personal casualty and theft loss for the year is reduced by 10% of the taxpayer's adjusted gross income. In this case, Naomee's deductible loss would be $400 [$1,900 − ($15,000 × 10%)].

 Note that Naomee's loss will reduce her taxable income only if she has deductions sufficient to allow her to itemize her allowable personal deductions. If Naomee does not itemize and uses the standard deduction, she receives no tax benefit from the casualty. The 10% annual limitation also serves to eliminate many otherwise allowable personal casualty losses. For example, if Naomee's adjusted gross income had been greater than $19,000, the 10% annual limitation would have left her with no allowable casualty loss deduction.

▲ **EXAMPLE 59**   Assume that in addition to the automobile casualty in example 58 Naomee had a gold ring stolen from her house during the same year. The ring had cost Naomee $1,300 and was worth $2,400 before it was stolen. Naomee's insurance reimbursed her $800 for the theft. What is Noamee's deductible personal casualty loss?

Discussion: The measure of loss on the ring is its $1,300 basis (because it is less than the $2,400 in value lost), which must be reduced by the insurance proceeds and the $100 statutory floor, resulting in a loss of $400 ($1,300 − $800 − $100). The losses on the automobile and the ring are combined for purposes of the annual 10% of adjusted gross income limitation. The total casualty and theft loss for the year, $2,300 ($400 + $1,900), is reduced by the $1,500 ($15,000 × 10%) annual limitation, resulting in a deductible loss of $800.

▲ SUMMARY

Losses result from either an excess of deductions over income for an entire tax year (annual loss) or an excess of basis over the amount realized from a disposition of property (transaction loss). Annual losses from a trade or business in which a taxpayer materially participates are carried back 3 years and forward 15 years to offset income in the carryover period. Such losses are deductible only to the extent that the taxpayer is at risk in the activity.

If the taxpayer does not materially participate in the operation of the trade or business generating the loss, the deduction of the loss is subject to the passive loss rules. These rules generally disallow the deduction of a net passive loss against active and portfolio income. Any loss not currently deductible is suspended and carried forward for deduction against future passive income. The material participation and active participation exceptions permit an individual to use losses from rental real estate to offset active and portfolio income. If an individual meets the material participation test, the loss from the rental property is fully deductible against active and portfolio income. If an individual meets the active participation test, the individual is allowed to deduct against active and portfolio income up to $25,000 of loss per year incurred in the rental real estate activity. When a passive activity is disposed of, any suspended loss on the activity is deductible against active and portfolio income.

The treatment of transaction losses follows the general pattern for all deductions. Losses are classified either as personal or as related to a profit-motivated transaction or venture. The only personal use losses that are deductible are casualty and theft losses. Personal casualty and theft losses are subject to a $100 per

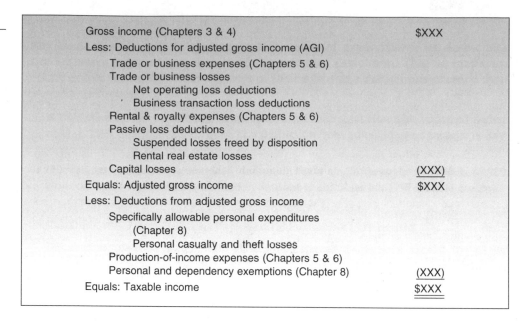

Gross income (Chapters 3 & 4)	$XXX
Less: Deductions for adjusted gross income (AGI)	
Trade or business expenses (Chapters 5 & 6)	
Trade or business losses	
Net operating loss deductions	
Business transaction loss deductions	
Rental & royalty expenses (Chapters 5 & 6)	
Passive loss deductions	
Suspended losses freed by disposition	
Rental real estate losses	
Capital losses	(XXX)
Equals: Adjusted gross income	$XXX
Less: Deductions from adjusted gross income	
Specifically allowable personal expenditures	
(Chapter 8)	
Personal casualty and theft losses	
Production-of-income expenses (Chapters 5 & 6)	
Personal and dependency exemptions (Chapter 8)	(XXX)
Equals: Taxable income	$XXX

occurrence statutory floor limitation, and all casualty and theft losses for the year are further limited to the amount of loss in excess of 10 percent of the taxpayer's adjusted gross income.

Transaction losses that are related to a trade or business are deductible in full. Investment-related losses are subject to the capital gain-and-loss netting procedure. Net capital loss deductions of individuals are limited to $3,000 per year, with any excess capital loss carried forward for use in subsequent years. Corporations incurring net capital losses are not allowed to deduct capital losses against other forms of income. Net capital losses may be carried back three years and forward five years and used to reduce the tax on any net capital gains in the carryover years.

Several types of transaction losses are subject to special rules. Up to $50,000 ($100,000 married) in losses on qualified small business stock may be deducted as an ordinary loss. Losses on sales to related parties are specifically disallowed. If a security is sold at a loss and replaced within 30 days of the sale, the wash sale rules disallow the loss.

A summary of the reporting of losses discussed in this chapter for individuals is presented in Exhibit 7–2.

▲ KEY TERMS

active income (p. 282)
active participant (p. 290)
active participation exception
  (p. 290)
annual personal casualty loss
  limitation (p. 300)
at-risk rules (p. 277)
business casualty loss (p. 292)
carryback (p. 273)
carryforward (p. 273)

casualty (p. 291)
casualty gain (p. 293)
casualty loss (p. 291)
closely held corporation (p. 284)
investment-related loss (p. 291)
limited partnership (p. 281)
material participant (p. 279)
material participation (p. 279)
material participation exception
  (p. 288)

net operating loss (p. 273)
nonrecourse debt (p. 278)
passive activity (p. 279)
passive activity loss rules (p. 279)
personal casualty loss (p. 299)
portfolio income (p. 282)
real property trade or business
  (p. 289)
rental activity (p. 280)
small business stock (p. 296)

statutory floor (p. 300)
suspended loss (p. 284)
tax shelter (p. 275)
theft (p. 291)

theft loss (p. 291)
trade or business loss (p. 291)
transaction loss (p. 271)
wash sale (p. 298)

working interest in oil and gas
deposit (p. 282)

▲ PRIMARY TAX LAW SOURCES

[1] Sec. 172—Defines a *net operating loss* and provides the rules for deducting net operating losses through a 3-year carryback and a 15-year carryforward.

[2] Sec. 465—Defines the amount at risk in an activity and limits loss deductions to the amount the taxpayer has at risk in the activity.

[3] Prop. Reg. Sec. 1.465-41—Provides examples of the application of the at-risk rules.

[4] Sec. 469—Defines *passive activities* and provides the rules for deducting passive activity losses.

[5] Reg. Sec. 1.469-5T—Provides the tests for material participation in an activity.

[6] Reg. Sec. 1.469-1T—States that suspended passive losses are carried forward to the following year, where they are treated as if they were incurred in that year; provides rules for distinguishing rental activities for purposes of the passive loss rules.

[7] Reg. Sec. 1.469-2T—Provides rules for deducting suspended losses on passive activities when the activity is disposed of in a taxable transaction.

[8] Sec. 469(c)(7)—Provides the rules for the material participation exception for rental real estate.

[9] Sec. 165—Specifies the allowable deductions for losses; limits the deductions of losses by individuals to those incurred in a trade or business, in a transaction entered into for profit, and losses resulting from storms, fires, shipwrecks, and other casualties.

[10] Sec. 65—Defines an *ordinary loss* as any loss that does not result from the sale or exchange of a capital asset.

[11] Sec. 62—Defines *adjusted gross income* for individual taxpayers and specifies the deductions allowed for adjusted gross income; allowable loss deductions include losses incurred in a trade or business, net operating losses, and capital losses.

[12] Sec. 1001—Prescribes the calculation of gains and losses on dispositions of property; defines *amount realized* for purposes of determining gain or loss on dispositions.

[13] Matheson v. Comm., 54 F.2d 537 (2d Cir. 1931)—Held that a casualty is the result of some sudden, unexpected, or unusual event.

[14] Pulvers v. Comm., 407 F.2d 838 (9th Cir. 1969)—Held that for a casualty loss to be deductible, a casualty must damage a property; mere declines in value are not deductible.

[15] Rev. Rul. 63-232—States that the loss resulting from termite damage is not a casualty loss.

[16] Reg. Sec. 1.165-8—States that a theft includes larceny, embezzlement, and robbery.

[17] Reg. Sec. 1.165-7—Provides the rules for calculating casualty losses.

[18] Sec. 1221—Defines *capital assets*.

[19] Sec. 1211—Sets forth the limit on deductions of capital losses of corporations and individuals.

[20] Sec. 1244—Defines qualified *small business stock* and allows deductions for losses of up to $50,000 ($100,000 for married, filing jointly) per year on such stock.

[21] Reg. Sec. 1.1244(b)-1—Provides the limits on the deductibility of losses on small business stock; clarifies that any loss that is carried forward to a subsequent year is not eligible for that year's special loss deduction.

[22] Sec. 267—Defines *related parties* and disallows losses on sales to related parties.

[23] Reg. Sec. 1.267(d)-1—Provides the rules for deducting disallowed losses on related party sales on subsequent sales to unrelated parties.

[24] Sec. 1091—Defines a *wash sale* and disallows current deductions for wash sale losses.

[25] Reg. Sec. 1.1091-1—States that the loss on a wash sale is disallowed on shares of stock that are actually replaced; provides basis adjustment rules for wash sale shares.

▲ DISCUSSION QUESTIONS

1. How are deductions and losses different? How are they similar? Explain.

2. Discuss the basic differences between annual losses and transaction losses.

3. What relief is provided to a business that suffers a net operating loss?

4. What is the net operating loss carryback and carryforward period? Does a taxpayer have a choice of the years to which a net operating loss can be carried? Explain.

5. What are the characteristics of a *tax shelter*, as the term is commonly used by tax practitioners?

6. What is the amount at risk in an activity? What purpose does the amount at risk serve in regard to losses?

7. How is a taxpayer's amount at risk in an activity different from the taxpayer's basis in the same activity?

8. What is a nonrecourse debt? How is financing using nonrecourse debt different from financing using recourse debt?

9. What is the purpose of the passive loss rules?

10. Are the passive loss rules disallowance-of-loss provisions or are they loss deferral provisions? Explain.

11. When a passive loss cannot be deducted in the current year, is the deduction lost forever? Describe the general circumstances under which the loss might be deducted in the future.

12. For purposes of the passive loss rules, what is a closely held corporation? How is the tax treatment of passive losses incurred by a closely held corporation different from the tax treatment of passive losses incurred by
   a. Individuals?
   b. Corporations?

13. When a business sustains a loss from a casualty, one of two measurement rules is used to determine the amount of the loss. Why is the use of two different measurement rules necessary for determining a business casualty loss?

14. What are the limitations on the deductibility of capital losses by individuals? How do the limitations compare with those for corporations?

15. Most sales of securities at a loss result in capital losses. Under what circumstances would a loss on the sale of a security be treated as an ordinary loss?

16. Explain the rationale for allowing taxpayers to use the ordinary loss treatment for qualified small business stock when it is sold at a loss.

17. What is the purpose of the related party rules as they apply to sales of property?

18. Losses incurred on the sale of business assets are generally deductible in full in the year the loss is realized. Describe a situation in which a realized loss on the sale of a business asset is not deductible in the current year, and explain why it would not be deductible.

19. What is a wash sale? How is the treatment of a wash sale different from the treatment of other sales of securities?

20. How are the rules for deducting personal casualty and theft losses different from the rules for business casualty and theft losses? Explain the difference in treatments and the rationale for the difference.

21. Effren Corporation suffers an operating loss of $80,000 during 1996. Effren was incorporated in 1994 and had an operating loss of $20,000 in 1994 and an operating income of $50,000 in 1995. What is the treatment of the 1996 loss if

    a. Effren is a corporation?

    b. Effren is an S corporation?

22. Habiby, Inc., has the following income and expenses for 1993 through 1997. What is the amount of tax that Habiby should pay each year? Use the corporate tax rate schedules in Appendix A to compute the tax liability.

	1993	1994	1995	1996	1997
Income	$280,000	$300,000	$310,000	$ 290,000	$320,000
Expenses	(180,000)	(200,000)	(235,000)	(600,000)	(220,000)
Income	$100,000	$100,000	$ 75,000	$(310,000)	$100,000

23. Post Haste corporation suffers a net operating loss of $60,000 in 1995. Post Haste was incorporated in 1993. Post Haste has a net operating loss of $25,000 in 1993 and taxable income of $40,000 in 1994. The financial vice president of Post Haste expects 1996 to be a banner year, with a taxable income of approximately $200,000. How should Post Haste treat the $60,000 loss in 1995 if it normally earns 6% on its investments?

24. Marlene opened a hair salon this year. She invested $10,000 of her own money and borrowed $60,000 from her bank to finance the purchase of the assets necessary to run the business. With the $60,000, she purchased a building for $40,000 and equipment costing $20,000. What is Marlene's amount at risk in the hair salon if the $60,000 debt was secured by

    a. The business assets purchased, and Marlene is personally liable if the business assets are insufficient to satisfy the debt?

    b. The business assets purchased, and Marlene is not personally liable for payment of the debt if the business assets are insufficient to satisfy the debt?

25. Wayne owns 20% of Label Maker Corporation. Label Maker is organized as an S corporation. During 1995, Label Maker has a loss of $200,000. At the beginning of 1995, Wayne's at-risk amount in Label Maker is $15,000.

    a. Assuming that Wayne's investment in Label Maker is not a passive activity, what is Wayne's deductible loss in 1995?

    b. In 1996, Label Maker has a taxable income of $40,000. What is the effect on Wayne's 1996 income?

26. A taxpayer had the following income (losses) for the current year:

Active Income	Portfolio Income	Passive Income
$20,000	$30,000	$(40,000)

What is the taxpayers taxable income (loss) if

    a. The taxpayer is a publicly held corporation?

    b. The taxpayer is a closely held corporation?

    c. The taxpayer is an individual and the passive income was not from a rental activity?

    d. The taxpayer is an individual and the passive income was the result of a rental activity for which the taxpayer fails to meet the material participation test but meets the active participation test?

    e. The taxpayer is an individual and the passive income was the result of a rental activity for which the taxpayer meets the material participation test?

27. Which of the following would be a passive activity? Explain.
    a. Irving owns a 1/3 interest in a partnership. The main asset of the partnership is a working interest in an oil and gas deposit. Irving's only involvement in the business is that of providing capital to finance the operation of the partnership.
    b. Muriel rents skates at the boardwalk of Atlantic City. She has no employees and runs the entire business herself.
    c. Jack owns 20% of a building that was built as low-income housing. Jack's only involvement in the activity is to provide part of the initial capital to fund the project. He has no involvement in renting the housing units.
    d. Frida owns a 15-unit apartment building. She spends 800 hours a year—all of her working hours—managing the apartment building.
    e. Assume the same facts as in part d, except that Frida spends only 600 hours a year managing the apartment building.

28. Which of the following are passive activities?
    a. Marvin owns a 1/5 share in a limited partnership. The limited partnership's sole asset is a resort hotel.
    b. Marcie owns a working interest in an oil and gas deposit. Her only involvement in the business is providing capital to finance the operation.
    c. Neil owns an 18-hole semiprivate golf course. He is a certified professional golfer and serves as the club pro. He provides lessons and is involved in the daily management of the business.
    d. Assume the same facts as in part c, except that Neil plays on the professional tour. When on break from the tour, he mingles with the members and conducts golf clinics. The club is managed by his brother and sister.
    e. Laura owns a commercial office building. She spends more than 500 hours a year managing the building. She also spends 1,700 hours working in her own real estate development firm.
    f. Assume the same facts as e, except that Laura hired a full-time manager for the commercial office building. She spends only 75 hours meeting with the manager and reviewing the operations.

29. Sidney and Gertrude own 40% of Bearcave Bookstore, an S corporation. The remaining 60% is owned by their son Boris. Sidney and Gertrude do not participate in operating or managing the store, and they invested $20,000 in the business when it opened in 1992. The bookstore reported the following net income (loss) for the years 1992 through 1995:

1992	1993	1994	1995
$(28,000)	$(16,000)	$(10,000)	$8,000

    a. How much do Sidney and Gertrude have at risk in Bearcave at the end of each year (1992–1995)?
    b. What amount can they recognize as income or loss from Bearcave for each year (1992–1995)?
    c. Assume that Sidney and Gertrude do materially participate in Bearcave for each year (1992–1995). What amount can they recognize as income or loss from Bearcave for each year (1992–1995)?

30. Janet has a taxable income of $45,000 from her salary and investment assets. She also owns 3 passive activities that have the following income (loss) for the year:

Passive activity 1	$ 10,000
Passive activity 2	$(20,000)
Passive activity 3	$(30,000)

    a. What is the effect of the passive activities on Janet's income? Explain.
    b. How much suspended loss does Janet have in each passive activity?

31. Return to the facts of problem 30. In the next year, Janet has a taxable income from her salary and investment activities of $50,000. The results for her 3 passive activities are

Passive activity 1	$ 25,000
Passive activity 2	$(10,000)
Passive activity 3	$(10,000)

    a. What is the effect of the passive activities on Janet's income? Explain.
    b. How much suspended loss does Janet have in each passive activity?

32. Mason owns a passive activity that generates a passive loss of $14,000 in 1994 and $12,000 in 1995. In 1995, Mason purchases a second passive activity that has passive income of $6,000 in 1995 and $10,000 in 1996. Discuss the effect of Mason's passive activity investments on his taxable income in 1994, 1995, and 1996. Assume that neither passive activity involves rental real estate.

33. Return to the facts of problem 32. At the end of 1996, Mason sells for $16,000 the passive activity that generated the losses. What is the effect on Mason's taxable income if his basis in the activity sold is
    a. $1,000?
    b. $28,000?

34. Jeremy owns a passive activity that has a basis of $44,000 and a suspended loss of $23,000. Jeremy's taxable income from active and portfolio income is $65,000.
    a. What is the effect on Jeremy's taxable income if he sells the passive activity for $53,000?
    b. What is the effect on Jeremy's taxable income if he sells the passive activity for $30,000?

35. Return to the facts of problem 34. Assume that Jeremy died when the passive activity had a fair market value of $53,000. What is the effect on Jeremy's taxable income for the year he died?

36. Return to the facts of problem 34. Assume that Jeremy died when the passive activity had a fair market value of $30,000. What is the effect on Jeremy's taxable income for the year he died?

37. Return to the facts of problem 34. Assume that Jeremy gave the property to his son Felipe when the property had a fair market value of $53,000. What is the effect of the gift on Jeremy's taxable income? Felipe's taxable income?

38. Ann and Joyce each own a 50% interest in a 25-unit apartment complex. Joyce devotes 800 hours a year to managing the apartment complex and spends 1,250 hours as a self-employed photographer. Ann spends 1,500 hours a year as a real estate broker in a business in which she has a 15% ownership interest. She spends 600 hours a year helping Joyce to manage the apartment complex. In 1995, the apartment complex generates a total loss of $30,000. Joyce's adjusted gross income for 1995 is $110,000, and Ann's is $120,000. How much of the loss can Joyce deduct on her tax return? How much of the loss can Ann deduct?

39. Paul is a 50% owner of 8 rental houses. He spends 600 hours a year managing the properties. In addition, he owns a 15% interest in a construction business to which he devotes 1,800 hours a year. The rental units generate a loss of $40,000, and Paul's adjusted gross income for 1995, before considering the rental properties, is $120,000.
    a. How much of the loss can Paul deduct in 1995?
    b. Assume that Paul's ownership in the construction business is only 2%. How much of the loss can he deduct?
    c. Assume that Paul spends only 400 hours a year managing the rental properties. How much of the loss can he deduct?

40. Mort is the sole owner of rental real estate that produces a net loss of $20,000 in 1994 and $18,000 in 1995 and income of $4,000 in 1996. His adjusted gross income, before considering the rental property for the years 1994 through 1996, is $130,000, $94,000 and $155,000, respectively.
    a. What is Mort's adjusted gross income for 1994, 1995, and 1996, if he meets the material participation test?
    b. What is Mort's adjusted gross income for 1994, 1995, and 1996, if he is only an active participant in the rental activity?

41. Ivan and Olga own a duplex. They collect the rents and make repairs to the property when necessary. That is, they are only active participants in the rental property. During the current year, the duplex had gross rents of $26,000 and total allowable deductions of $40,000. What is the effect of the duplex rental on their taxable income if their adjusted gross income is
    a. $45,000?   c. $110,000?
    b. $180,000?   d. $140,000?

42. Jacqueline is a 75% owner of a rental property and has a significant role in the management of the property. During the current year, the property had a rental loss of $18,000. What is the effect of the rental property on her taxable income, if her adjusted gross income is
    a. $60,000?   c. $170,000?
    b. $135,000?   d. $115,000?

43. ABC Co. owns a chain of furniture stores. How much loss can ABC Co. deduct in each of the following cases? Explain.
    a. ABC closes a store in a depressed part of the county. Rather than move furniture to other stores, ABC sells furniture that had cost $450,000 for $300,000.
    b. A fire severely damages one store. The cost of repairing the fire damage is $280,000. ABC's basis in the store building is $600,000. ABC's insurance company reimburses ABC $250,000 for the fire damage.
    c. ABC decides to begin replacing some of its older delivery vans. It sells for $3,000 one van that had a basis of $4,500.
    d. ABC discovers that one of its buildings is infested with termites. The building is old and has been fully depreciated for tax purposes. The cost of getting rid of the termites is $17,000, none of which is covered by insurance.
    e. Someone breaks into one store by destroying the security system. Cash of $7,000 is missing from a safe. In addition, televisions that had cost $18,000 and were marked to sell for $32,000 are gone. The security system had a basis of $8,000. Because the system was outdated, a security expert estimates it was worth only $2,000 at the time it was destroyed.

44. The Goodson Co. is a chain of retail electronics stores. How much of a loss can Goodson deduct in each of the following cases? Explain.
    a. A mouse gnawed a hole in the wood of a 35-inch console television. The television normally sells for $2,050. The cost of the set is $1,780, and Goodson sold the damaged set for $1,500.
    b. The company replaced its inventory system. The old system cost $45,000 and had a basis of $16,000. The company sold the old system for $7,500. The new system cost $75,000.
    c. A flood damaged one of Goodson's retail stores. The building suffered extensive water damage. The basis of the building is $60,000, and the cost of repairing the damage is $72,000. The insurance company reimbursed Goodson $50,000.
    d. The owner of Goodson sold a complete home entertainment center (e.g., projection TV, VCR, stereo system) to his sister for $7,000. The usual sales price is $8,500. The cost of the system is $6,300.
    e. Assume the same facts as in part d, except that the owner sold the home entertainment center to his sister for $5,500.

   f. The owner of Goodson finds that the controller has embezzled $10,000 from the company. Before the owner can confront the controller, the controller leaves town and cannot be found.

   g. Upon arriving at the company's headquarters, the vice president of sales finds that someone has broken in and stolen 3 computers. The damage to the outside door is extensive. The cost of repairing the door is $1,500, and the cost of replacing the 3 computers is $9,500. The original cost of the computers totals $10,500. Goodson's basis in the computers is $5,000. The thieves also stole $350 from the petty cash fund.

45. Gordon is the sole proprietor of Fashion Flowers & Florals (FFF). During the current year, one of FFF's delivery vans was involved in an automobile accident. The van had a basis of $7,500. What is FFF's allowable casualty loss deduction under each of the following situations?

   a. A comparable van sells for $5,000. FFF's van was totally destroyed in the accident. FFF's insurance paid $4,200 on the casualty.

   b. A comparable van sells for $10,000. FFF's van was totally destroyed in the accident. FFF's insurance paid $8,000 on the casualty.

46. Assume the same facts in problem 45. What is FFF's allowable casualty loss deduction under each of the following situations?

   a. A comparable van sells for $5,000. After the accident, the insurance adjuster estimated the van was worth $2,000. The insurance company paid FFF $1,500 on the casualty.

   b. A comparable van sells for $10,000. After the accident, the insurance adjuster estimated the value of the van at $2,000. The insurance company paid FFF $1,500 on the casualty.

47. Fogerty's Fresh Farm Produce was burglarized during the current year. In addition to taking $460 in cash from the safe, the burglars took 40 cases of beer that had cost $1,800 and had a retail value of $3,900. In entering the store, the burglars broke a glass door and damaged the security system. It cost $230 to replace the door and $600 to repair the security system. The security system had been completely depreciated for tax purposes. What is the company's deductible loss from the burglary if its insurance company paid out $2,400 on the insurance claim?

48. Wilbur owns a 25% interest in the Talking Horse Corporation, which is organized as an S corporation. His basis in the property is $18,000, and he does not materially participate in the business. For the year, Talking Horse reported an operating loss of $30,000 and a capital loss of $5,000. Wilbur's adjusted gross income is $65,000. Explain what effect these losses would have on Wilbur's adjusted gross income. If Wilbur materially participates in Talking Horse, explain what effect these losses would have on Wilbur's adjusted gross income.

49. During 1995, Yoko has total capital gains of $3,500 and total capital losses of $13,000. What is the effect of the capital gains and losses on Yoko's 1995 taxable income? Explain.

   a. Assume that in 1996 Yoko has total capital gains of $8,000 and total capital losses of $4,000. What is the effect of the capital gains and losses on Yoko's taxable income in 1996? Explain.

   b. How would your answer change if Yoko's total capital losses are $9,500 in 1996?

50. Goldie sells 400 shares of Bear Corporation stock for $3,000 on December 14, 1995. Goldie paid $28,000 for the stock in February 1992. Assuming that Goldie has no other capital asset transactions in 1995, what is the effect of the sale on her 1995 income?

   a. Assume that Goldie has no capital asset transactions in 1996. What is the effect of the Bear Corporation stock sale on her 1996 income?

   b. On July 2, 1997, Goldie sells 100 shares of Panda common stock for $18,000. Goldie purchased the stock on September 4, 1995, for $7,000. What is the effect of the sale on Goldie's 1997 income?

51. Labrador Corporation has total capital gains of $18,000 and total capital losses of $35,000 in 1995. Randy owns 25% of Labrador's outstanding stock. What is the effect on Labrador's and Randy's 1995 taxable incomes if
    a. Labrador is a corporation? Explain how Labrador and Randy would treat the capital gains and losses.
    b. Labrador is a subchapter S corporation? Explain how Labrador and Randy would treat the capital gains and losses.

52. Bongo Corporation is incorporated in 1993. It has no capital asset transactions in 1993. From 1994 through 1997, Bongo has the following capital gains and losses:

	1994	1995	1996	1997
Capital gains	$10,000	$5,000	$12,000	$40,000
Capital losses	(2,000)	(6,000)	(50,000)	(20,000)

Assuming that Bongo's marginal tax rate during each of these years is 34%, what is the effect of Bongo's capital gains and losses on the amount of tax due each year?

53. Ellen, a single individual, sold some stock she owned in ABC Co. at a loss of $70,000. Assuming that Ellen had no other dispositions of capital assets during the year, how much of the loss can she deduct?
    a. How would your answer change if the stock was qualified small business stock?
    b. Assume the same facts as in part a, except that Ellen is married.

54. Rick, a single taxpayer, owned 30,000 shares of qualifying small business stock that he had purchased for $300,000. During the current year, he sold 10,000 of the shares for $25,000. What are the tax effects for Rick from selling the shares?
    a. Assume that Rick also sold other capital assets at a gain of $12,000. What are the tax effects of Rick's capital asset transactions?
    b. Assume the same facts as in part a. In the year after selling the 10,000 shares of qualified small business stock, Rick had total capital gains of $16,000 and total capital losses of $12,000. What are the effects of Rick's capital asset transactions on his taxable income?

55. Evita sold 2 pieces of land during the current year. She had used the first piece as a parking lot for her pet store (she owns the store as a sole proprietor). The land cost Evita $40,000, and she sold the land for $30,000. The second piece was a building lot she had purchased as a speculative investment. Evita paid $40,000 for the lot and sold it for $30,000. Assuming that Evita had no other dispositions during the year, what is her deductible loss from the 2 sales?

56. Elliot sold some stock he had purchased for $6,000 to his sister for $4,000. Several years later, his sister sold the stock for $7,000. What is the effect of the sales on Elliot and his sister?
    a. Assume that the subsequent sale by his sister was for $5,000.
    b. Assume that the subsequent sale by his sister was for $2,000.

57. Howard Co. is 100% owned by Rona. During the current year, Howard sold some land to Rona for $50,000 that had cost Howard $80,000 and that had a fair market value of $100,000. What are the tax effects of the sale for Howard Co. and Rona?

58. Darlene owns 500 shares of Sandmayor, Inc., common stock that she purchased several years ago for $20,000. During the current year, the Sandmayor stock declines in value. Darlene decides to sell the stock to realize the tax loss. On December 17, she sells the 500 shares for $12,000. Her investment adviser tells her she thinks the Sandmayor stock probably will begin to increase in value next year. On this advice, Darlene purchases 600 shares of Sandmayor common stock on January 10 of the next year for $15,000. The adviser turns out to be right—Darlene sells the 600 shares in May for $22,000. What are the effects of the sales on Darlene's taxable income in each year? Explain.

59. Ed owned 1,000 shares of Northern Co. for which he had paid $12,000 several years ago. On November 24, he purchased an additional 600 shares for $4,800. Ed sold the original 1,000 shares for $9,000 on December 14. What are the effects of the December 14 sale? Explain.

60. James owns a ski cabin in Colorado that he uses solely for family vacations. When James and his family arrived at the cabin for their regular August vacation, they discovered that the cabin had been broken into sometime in the last year. Several items were stolen, and some furniture was damaged. Here are the details of the items stolen and damaged:

	Cost	Value Before	Value After	Insurance Proceeds
Fishing equipment	$ 800	$ 250	-0-	$ 100
Stereo	$1,200	$1,600	-0-	$1,300
Furniture	$4,000	$2,000	$500	$1,000

In addition, it cost $400 to replace a window. The insurance company would not cover the cost of replacing the window, even though it was obvious that breaking it was how the thieves had gained entry. To guard against future break-ins, James had special locks installed on the windows at a cost of $900.

What is the amount of James's casualty (theft) loss before considering any annual limitations that may apply?

61. Kevin is the sole proprietor of Murph's Golf Shop. During the current year, a hurricane hit the beach near Kevin's shop. His business building, which had a basis of $75,000, was damaged. In addition, his personal automobile for which he had paid $28,000 was damaged. Fair market values (FMV) before and after the hurricane were

Case A	FMV Before	FMV After
Building	$150,000	$100,000
Automobile	7,000	2,000

Case B		
Building	$150,000	-0-
Automobile	7,000	-0-

a. What is Kevin's gross loss in each of the above cases?
b. Assume that in case A, Kevin received $40,000 from his insurance company for the building and $2,000 for his automobile. What is his allowable loss?
c. Assume that the insurance proceeds were $150,000 and $2,000 in case B. What is the tax effect for Kevin of the casualty?

62. Jamila was involved in an auto accident during the current year that totally destroyed her car. Jamila had purchased the car 2 years ago for $28,000. Jamila had used the car in her business 75% of the time over the past 2 years. She had properly deducted $4,000 in depreciation for the business use of the car. The insurance company paid her $16,000, the fair market value of the car before it was destroyed. Assuming that Jamila had an adjusted gross income of $45,000 during the current year before considering the effect of the auto accident, what is the effect of the accident on her taxable income?

63. Andy sold the following assets during the year.

	Gain (Loss)
Personal automobile	$(15,000)
ABC stock	8,000
Personal furniture	1,000
BCCI bonds	(14,000)

What is Andy's deductible loss? Explain.

64. Calzone Trucking Co. is a corporation that is 100% owned by Fred Calzone. Before he incorporated in 1993, Fred had operated the business as a sole proprietorship. The taxable income (loss) of Calzone for 1993 through 1995 is as follows:

	1993	1994	1995
Taxable income (loss)	$27,000	$(65,000)	$16,000

The 1995 taxable income includes a net long-term capital gain of $9,000. Calzone Trucking's 1996 operating income is $47,000 before considering the following transactions:

a. A hail storm caused part of the roof of the truck barn to collapse. A truck inside the barn sustained damage from the falling debris. The truck barn had a fair market value of $76,000 before the damage and an adjusted basis of $37,000. Repairs to the roof cost $8,200, of which $6,500 was reimbursed by insurance. The truck, which had an adjusted basis of $49,000, was worth $63,000 before the damage and had a fair market value after the damage of $46,000. Calzone Trucking's insurance company paid $13,600 for the damages.

b. Another truck was totally destroyed when its brakes failed and plunged off a cliff. Fortunately, the driver was able to jump from the truck and escaped unharmed. The truck, which had an adjusted basis of $29,000, was worth $44,000 before the accident. Calzone received $23,800 from its insurance company for the destruction of the truck. In addition, the company was cited for failure to properly maintain the truck and paid a $7,500 fine to the state trucking commission.

c. Calzone sold equipment that had become obsolete for $11,000. The equipment had cost $36,000, and depreciation of $17,000 had been taken on the equipment before the sale.

d. Calzone sold stock it owned in 2 other companies. Retro Corporation stock, which had cost $32,500, sold for $46,500. Shares of Tread Corporation stock with a cost of $73,000 sold for $31,000. Both stocks had been purchased in 1992.

e. Fred's son wanted to start a delivery business. To help his son out, Fred sold him one of Calzone's used trucks for $10,000. The truck had a fair market value of $22,000 and an adjusted basis of $15,000 at the date of the sale.

REQUIRED: Calculate Calzone Trucking's 1996 taxable income. Indicate the amount and the effect of any carryforwards or carrybacks on Calzone Trucking's current, past, or future income.

The enactment of the passive loss rules has generally diminished the attractiveness of tax shelters as investments. However, rental real estate continues to provide a viable tax shelter for certain taxpayers. Explain why this is true.

The Wakefield Savings and Loan is located in a two-story building in downtown Wakefield. The building has a basement in which the heating system for the bank is located. The bank also uses the basement to store records and photocopying equipment. Last fall, the Saugutuxet River overflowed and flooded the basement. The flood destroyed all the bank's records and damaged all the equipment. The building suffered no serious structural damage.

This is the second time in ten years that the basement has flooded. The state and county conducted a flood control study after the first flood but adopted no formal flood control plans. Fearful of another flood, the bank now stores all its records on the first and second floors.

The bank has claimed a casualty loss for the damaged records, equipment, and the decline in the market value of the building. The bank contends that because the basement of the building can no longer be used for storage, it is entitled to a casualty loss equal to the difference between the fair market value of the building before the casualty and the fair market value after the casualty. Is Wakefield Savings and loan entitled to a casualty loss for the decline in the value of the building? Would your answer change if the bank expanded the first floor and used the new space as a storage facility?

▲ DISCUSSION CASE 7–2

Jay is single and works as a salesman. In 1995, he was selected the company's outstanding salesperson. In recognition of this honor, he received a $75,000 bonus. The bonus put him in the 36% tax bracket. Jay owns 2,400 shares of stock in Amtrav Corporation, which qualifies as small business stock. His broker has advised him to sell most, if not all, of his Amtrav stock. If he sells all his shares in the current year, he will recognize a $25 per share loss on the stock. Unfortunately, even if he sells all his stock, he will remain in the 36% tax bracket. He expects his marginal tax rate will drop to 28% next year, but it will be 31% and 36%, respectively, for the years after that. He does not anticipate any other capital gains or losses during the next 3 years. If Jay's goal is to minimize his taxes, develop a strategy for how many shares and in what year(s) Jay should sell his Amtrav stock. Assume that if he does not sell all his stock in the current year, his loss per share will remain constant and that the time value of money is 8%.

▲ TAX PLANNING CASE 7–3

Anthony owns a 1992 Luxuro automobile that has a fair market value of $18,000. His son James, who is 19, borrows the car without his father's knowledge and totals it in 1994. James has been involved in 2 car accidents, and his father is afraid that James will not be able to get insurance. Therefore, Anthony decides not to file an insurance claim and deducts the loss on his 1994 tax return. In 1995, Anthony decides to have his friend Brigid, a local CPA, prepare his tax return. In preparing his 1995 return, Brigid reviews Anthony's 1994 return and finds that Anthony took a casualty loss on the Luxuro. Aware that Anthony has insurance, she is perplexed as to why Anthony deducted the loss. Anthony tells her of his son's fearsome driving record and his worry that his son could not get insurance. What are Brigid's responsibilities (refer to the Statements on Responsibilities in Tax Practice), if any, concerning Anthony's 1994 tax return? What effect does the issue have on Brigid's preparation of Anthony's 1995 return?

▲ ETHICS DISCUSSION CASE 7–4

INCOME TAX ENTITIES

CHAPTER 8
TAXATION OF INDIVIDUALS

CHAPTER 9
OTHER TAX ENTITIES

Taxation of Individuals

▲ CHAPTER LEARNING OBJECTIVES

■ Explain the requirements for exemption deductions for dependents.

■ Introduce the filing status of individual taxpayers and discuss the effect of filing status on the income tax paid by individuals.

■ Discuss the components of the individual income tax calculation.

■ Indicate the expenditures that are allowed as deductions for adjusted gross income and discuss those that present particular problems for individual taxpayers.

■ Introduce the deductions from adjusted gross income for specifically allowed personal expenditures, and explain the requirements for deduction and the applicable limitations.

■ Introduce the special provisions for the calculation of the tax of a dependent.

■ Provide a comprehensive example of an individual tax calculation.

▲ CONCEPT REVIEW ▲

Ability to pay   A tax should be based on the amount that a taxpayer can afford to pay, relative to other taxpayers.

Administrative convenience   Those items for which the cost of compliance would exceed the revenue generated are not taxed.

Annual accounting period   All entities must report the results of their operations on an annual basis (the tax year). Each tax year stands on its own, apart from other tax years.

Business purpose   To be deductible, an expenditure or a loss must have a business or other economic purpose that exceeds any tax avoidance motive. The primary motive for the transaction must be to make a profit.

Entity   All transactions must be traced to a single tax entity for recording and reporting by that entity.

Legislative grace   Any tax relief provided is the result of a specific act of Congress that must be strictly applied and interpreted. All income received is taxable unless a specific provision can be found in the tax law that excludes the income from taxation. Deductions must be approached with the philosophy that nothing is deductible unless a provision in the tax law allows the deduction.

Pay as you go   A tax should be collected as close as possible to the time in which the income is earned.

Tax benefit rule   Any deduction taken in a prior year that is recovered in a subsequent year is income in the year of recovery, to the extent that a tax benefit was received from the deduction.

▲ INTRODUCTION

Individuals are by far the biggest single group of taxpaying entities. During 1992, individuals filed more than 56 percent of all returns received by the IRS. These returns accounted for more than 60 percent of all income tax collected during 1992. Individuals are unique. Unlike corporations, which are formed to conduct a business, individuals engage in both business and personal transactions. As a result of this split for individuals, calculating the tax base of an individual requires consideration of deductions for both business-related expenditures and specifically allowable personal expenditures.

Individuals are taxable entities. Because all individuals who meet certain income requirements must file an annual tax return, they must adopt an accounting period. Although individuals may adopt a fiscal year if they keep a complete set of accounting records, most use a calendar year for convenience. Individuals must also choose an accounting method for reporting their various business and personal activities. Although individuals may use any method of accounting that clearly reflects their income (i.e., cash, accrual, hybrid), unless the individual sells inventories—which require use of the accrual (hybrid) method—most individuals choose the simpler cash method.

This chapter discusses the unique features of calculating the tax base for individual taxpayers. Exhibit 8–1 presents the format for calculating an individual's taxable income, which generally is equal to gross income minus allowable deductions. Because deductions in general are allowed only under the business purpose concept, most personal expenditures by individuals are not deductible. A characteristic unique to individuals is that some minimal amount of personal expenditure is necessary to exist, money that is not available for paying taxes. Congress has recognized this characteristic by allowing some deductions for personal expenditures.

A review of Exhibit 8–1 reveals that the basic taxable income calculation involves splitting deductions into two distinct classes—deductions for adjusted

INDIVIDUAL INCOME TAX
CALCULATION

Gross income (all income received less exclusions)	$XXX
Less: Deductions *for* adjusted gross income	(XXX)
Equals: Adjusted gross income (AGI)	$XXX
Less: Deductions *from* adjusted gross income	
The greater of	
1. Itemized deductions	
OR	
2. Applicable standard deduction	(XXX)
Less: Personal and dependency exemptions	(XXX)
Equals: Taxable income	$XXX
Calculation of tax due (refund)	
Tax on taxable income (from rate schedule/table)	$XXX
Add: Additional taxes	XXX
Less: Tax credits	(XXX)
Equals: Net tax	$XXX
Less: Amounts withheld for payment of tax	(XXX)
Estimated tax payments	(XXX)
Equals: Tax due (refund of tax paid)	$XXX

gross income and deductions from gross income. This split creates an intermediate income figure called *adjusted gross income* (AGI). The basic difference between the two classes of deductions is that for-AGI deductions are closely related to the earning of income and most from-AGI deductions are personal expenditures. Adjusted gross income is important in determining the amount of allowable from-AGI deductions, because Congress has created limits that tie some allowable personal deductions to the adjusted gross income of the taxpayer. Individuals also receive personal exemption deductions for themselves and dependency exemption deductions for others who qualify as their dependents.

The remainder of the chapter discusses the basic allowable deductions for and from adjusted gross income of individuals, the dependency exemption deduction requirements, and limitations of deductions placed on high-income taxpayers and children younger than 14. The chapter concludes with a brief discussion of calculating the tax and filing the return. Exemptions and filing status of the taxpayer are discussed first, because they affect many of the topics discussed throughout the chapter.

▲ PERSONAL AND DEPENDENCY EXEMPTIONS

In general, each individual taxpayer filing a tax return is allowed a personal exemption deduction of $2,500 in 1995 ($2,450 in 1994).[1] This is an amount that Congress has allowed all taxpayers in order to recognize such basic personal living costs as food and clothing, which are not otherwise allowed as a deduction. Like the standard deduction, the personal exemption amount is raised each year to account for inflation.

In addition to the personal exemption deduction, individuals are allowed a dependency exemption deduction for each qualifying dependent.

▲ **EXAMPLE 1** Nelson and Alice are a married couple filing a joint return for 1995. They have 2 dependent sons, Peter and Rick. What is their total deduction in 1995 for personal and dependency exemptions?

Discussion: Nelson and Alice each are allowed a personal dependency deduction and a total of 2 dependency exemptions for Peter and Rick. Their total exemption deduction for 1995 is $10,000 (4 × $2,500). NOTE: The exemption for a spouse on a joint return is always considered a personal exemption. A spouse on a joint return is never considered a dependent; spouses are always considered taxpayers.

Dependency Requirements

In order to qualify as a **dependent,** an individual must meet five tests.[2] These tests are the gross income test; the support test; the relationship, or member of the household, test; the citizen or residency test; and the joint return test.

Gross Income Test. The **gross income test** states that to be a dependent an individual's gross income (as defined for tax return purposes) must be less than the dependency exemption amount ($2,500 in 1995). Note that excludable forms of income do not count in determining gross income for purposes of this test.

▲ **EXAMPLE 2** Jerry's mother Jolene lived with him throughout all of 1995. Her only sources of income were $300 from a savings account, $3,500 in interest from tax-exempt municipal bonds, and $2,600 in Social Security benefits. Does Jolene pass the gross income test for dependency?

Discussion: Although Jolene's economic income is $6,400, her gross income for tax purposes is only $300. Because this is less than the $2,500 exemption amount, she passes the gross income test. NOTE: Although Jolene has passed the gross income test, she also must satisfy the other 4 requirements before Jerry can claim her as a dependent.

Two exceptions to the gross income test are provided for children of the taxpayer. The gross income test is waived for any child of the taxpayer who is either (a) younger than 19 at the end of the tax year, or (b) a full-time student younger than 24 at the end of the tax year.[3]

▲ **EXAMPLE 3** Refer to example 1. Assume that Rick is 17 and earns $3,500 per year bagging groceries after school. Peter is 25, a college student, and made $4,800 working during the summer. Do Rick and Peter pass the gross income test for dependency?

Discussion: Rick passes the gross income test, because he is a child of the taxpayer and is younger than 19. Peter does not pass the test, even though he is a full-time college student, because he is older than 24 and has gross income in excess of $2,500. NOTE: Peter does not qualify as a dependent, because he failed the gross income test. Although Rick has passed the test, he also must satisfy the other 4 tests before he can qualify as a dependent.

Support Test. The **support test** requires that the taxpayer claiming the dependency exemption provide more than half the support of the dependent. Support is not necessarily related to the income of the dependent. This test simply requires a tallying up of amounts spent on support and determining whether the taxpayer seeking the dependency exemption has provided more than half of the entire amount spent on support.

▲ **EXAMPLE 4** Refer to example 2. Assume that Jolene spent all of her $6,400 in income to support herself. Jerry spent an additional $4,500 to support Jolene. Does Jolene meet the support test?

Discussion: Jerry did not provide more than half of Jolene's total support of $10,900 ($6,400 + $4,500) in 1995. Therefore, Jolene does not meet the support test and does not qualify as a dependent. NOTE: The fact that $6,100 of the income was not taxable has no bearing on the support test.

▲ **EXAMPLE 5**   Assume that in example 4 Jolene spent only $3,000 of the income she received in 1995 on her own support. She put the remaining $3,400 in a savings account. Does Jolene pass the support test?

Discussion: Jerry has provided more than half of Jolene's total support of $7,500 in 1995. Therefore, Jolene does pass the support test.

Two additional support situations are worth noting. First, in the case of two or more individuals who collectively provide more than 50 percent of the support of an individual who meets all the other tests for dependency, any member of the support group who contributes more than 10 percent of the total support may claim the dependency exemption through a multiple support agreement.[4] All members of the support group must agree in writing (the **multiple support agreement**) which person in the group is entitled to receive the exemption.

▲ **EXAMPLE 6**   Suzanne, Latifa, and Ben each provide 1/3 of the support of their brother Ozzie during 1995. Assuming that Ozzie meets all other dependency tests, who may take the dependency exemption for Ozzie in 1995?

Discussion: Although none of his siblings has individually provided more than half of Ozzie's support, as a group they have met the support test. By executing a multiple support agreement, the 3 can decide who will take the dependency exemption. NOTE: Only 1 member of the group may take the dependency exemption each year. It cannot be split among the group.

The second support situation deals with support of children of divorced parents. In this case, the custodial parent is entitled to the dependency exemption, regardless of actual support provided. In order for the noncustodial parent to obtain the dependency exemption, the custodial parent must agree in writing to give up the right to claim the exemption.

▲ **EXAMPLE 7**   Donna and Doug were divorced last year. Donna has custody of their dependent son. Doug paid $3,800 in child support payments during the current year. The cost of supporting the son during the year was $5,000. Who is entitled to the dependency exemption for the son?

Discussion: Because Donna is the custodial parent, she is entitled to the dependency exemption, regardless of the amount of support Doug paid during the year. The only way that Doug can take a dependency exemption for their son is if Donna agrees in writing that Doug can take the exemption deduction. The written agreement must be attached to Doug's return.

Relationship or Member of Household Test.   Under the **relationship, or member of household, test** a dependent must either be a relative of the taxpayer or a member of the taxpayer's household for the entire year. *Relatives* are defined as ancestors (grandfather), lineal descendants (granddaughter, son), and blood relationships such as aunt, nephew, or niece. Once a relative relationship is established, it does not change with divorce or death of a spouse. Thus, a wife's nephew continues to qualify as a relative even if the wife dies or the husband and wife divorce. Note that individuals who are not relatives meet this test if they are members of the taxpayer's household for the entire tax year.

Citizen or Residency Test.   Under the **citizen or residency test,** a dependent must be either (a) a citizen of the United States, or (b) a resident of the United

States, Canada, or Mexico. Alien children adopted by U.S. citizens and living with them in a foreign country qualify under this test.

Joint Return Test.   Dependents who are married may not file joint returns with their spouses for the exemption year in question. An exception to this test, which is known as the **joint return test,** is provided for married dependents who are not required to file a tax return (see the section on filing requirements) <u>but file a return solely for the purpose of obtaining a refund</u>.

▲ FILING STATUS

A basic concept of the income tax system is that taxpayers pay tax according to their ability to pay. The measure of ability to pay is straightforward for an entity such as a corporation—gross income minus business-related deductions provides a reasonable measure of a corporate entity's ability to pay tax. Although this same measure may be appropriate for measuring the ability to pay tax on an individual's business income, it does not take into account a basic fact of life—individuals must incur some minimum level of personal expenditure just to stay alive. The income tax law takes this into account by allowing exemptions and setting tax rates. For example, by imposing a higher marginal tax rate at a lower level of income for an unmarried person than for a married couple, the unmarried person pays a higher average tax rate. Based on ability to pay, a single person with a taxable income of $30,000 can afford to pay more tax than a married couple with the same $30,000 in taxable income. The tax law recognizes this difference in ability to pay by basing exemptions, standard deductions, and average tax rates on the taxpayer's **filing status.**

Individuals are classified in two groups—married and unmarried. Married taxpayers may either commingle all their income and deductions and file one return (joint return), or they may each file a separate return. Unmarried taxpayers may be classified as single or, if they qualify, as a head of household. This results in four filing statuses:

- Married, filing jointly (including a surviving spouse)
- Married, filing separately
- Single
- Head of household

Married, Filing Jointly

To qualify for the status of **married, filing jointly,** the taxpayers must be legally married as of the last day of the tax year.[5] If a spouse dies during the year, filing status is determined as of the date of death of the spouse if the survivor did not remarry during the year. Taxpayers who are divorced during the year or who are legally separated at the end of the year are not considered married for tax purposes. As originally conceived, the joint return filing status was designed to divide the combined income of a married couple in half and tax each half at the same rate as a single individual. The income-splitting benefit of a joint return has eroded through the years as Congress has made changes in the basic rate schedules. However, a married couple filing jointly may still pay less tax than a single individual at the same level of income. For example, an examination of the 1995 tax rate schedules in Appendix A shows that a single individual begins paying a 28-percent marginal tax rate at $23,350, whereas a married couple does not enter the

28-percent rate bracket until their taxable income reaches $39,000. Thus, at incomes greater than $23,350, married couples filing jointly pay less total tax than a single taxpayer with the same taxable income. The effect is to assess a lower average tax rate on the joint return.

In 1954, Congress recognized that the death of a spouse usually works a hardship on the survivor when a dependent child is still living in the home. In recognition of this hardship, a **surviving spouse** who has at least one dependent child or stepchild living at home may use the joint return tax rates to compute the tax for two tax years after the year in which the spouse died. In the year of death, the surviving spouse also files a joint return.

▲ **EXAMPLE 8**   Juan and Bonita are married and have 2 dependent children living at home. In 1995, Juan is killed in an avalanche while skiing. What is their filing status for 1995? How will Bonita file for subsequent years?

Discussion: In the year of Juan's death, Bonita files a joint return. In 1996 and 1997, Bonita files as a surviving spouse and uses the joint return tax rates if at least 1 of her 2 children remains a dependent and continues to live at home. If Bonita were to remarry, she would file either a joint return with her new spouse or file separately as a married taxpayer.

Married, Filing Separately

Although married taxpayers may file separate returns, there are very limited circumstances in which it is to a couple's advantage to choose this status. An examination of the tax rate schedules in Appendix A shows that married couples filing separately pay higher marginal tax rates at lower income levels than any other filing status category. As a result, the **married, filing separately,** status has the highest average tax rate of any income level greater than $19,500 in 1995. In addition, Congress has carefully crafted most other tax relief provisions to take away any advantage this filing status might offer. Its primary use is in situations of marital or financial disagreement in which the husband and wife cannot agree to file together and are not divorced or legally separated by year end.

Single

A **single** taxpayer is a person who is not married on the last day of the tax year and who does not have any dependents to support. Although single individuals pay more than a married couple filing jointly on the same taxable income, their taxes are less than those paid by a married couple filing separately. Some solace for the single taxpayer can be found in the so-called marriage penalty tax imposed on married taxpayers who have roughly equal incomes. This marriage penalty results from a married couple paying a higher tax on a joint return than each would have paid had they remained single.

▲ **EXAMPLE 9**   Harold and Sadie are a married couple with a taxable income of $60,000. If they had filed as single individuals, Harold's taxable income would have been $28,000 and Sadie's taxable income would have been $32,000. What is their "marriage penalty tax" for 1995?

Discussion: The marriage penalty is the difference in the tax that a married couple pays on their joint income versus what they would have paid had they been single taxpayers. For Harold and Sadie, the marriage tax is $1,000, calculated as follows:

Using 1995 Tax Rate Schedules

Tax on $60,000 for a Married Couple Filing a Joint Return

$[\$5,850 + 28\% \times (\$60,000 - \$39,000)] =$ $11,730

Tax on $28,000 for a Single Individual

$[\$3,503 + 28\% \times (\$28,000 - \$23,350)] =$ $4,805

Tax on $32,000 for a Single Individual

$[\$3,503 + 28\% \times (\$32,000 - \$23,350)] =$ 5,925   10,730

Marriage penalty tax $ 1,000

Head of Household

The head of household filing status recognizes that some single taxpayers share a characteristic of married taxpayers—the burden of extra living costs to support a relative. In order to qualify as a **head of household,** the unmarried taxpayer must pay more than half the cost of maintaining a home that is the principal residence for more than half the year for

- A qualified dependent, including children, parents, and other relatives; the taxpayer's parents do not have to live in the taxpayer's home if they meet the dependency tests

    or

- An unmarried child or other direct lineal descendent (i.e., grandchild) who does not qualify as a dependent[6]

▲ **EXAMPLE 10**   Larry is legally divorced. His 4-year-old son lives with him for the entire year. Larry is entitled to a dependency deduction for his son. What is Larry's filing status?

Discussion: Because Larry is unmarried and maintains a household for a dependent child for more than half the year, he is entitled to file as a head of household.

▲ **EXAMPLE 11**   Assume that in example 10 Larry's son is unmarried, 26, and does not qualify as a dependent. If the son lives in Larry's home for the entire year, what is Larry's filing status?

Discussion: Although the son is not Larry's dependent, he is an unmarried child and lives in Larry's home for more than half the year. Therefore, Larry may file as a head of household, provided that he pays more than half the cost of maintaining the home. NOTE: If Larry's son were married, the son would have to qualify as Larry's dependent for Larry to claim head of household status.

A related relief provision allows an abandoned spouse to file as a head of household. A married person is treated as an **abandoned spouse** if a dependent child lives in the taxpayer's home for more than half the year and the taxpayer's spouse does not live in the home at any time during the last half of the year.[7] The benefit provided by this provision is that a married taxpayer is considered unmarried for the entire year.

▲ **EXAMPLE 12**   Loretta and Bob married in 1987. They have one child, Bobby, who is 7. During the current year, Loretta learned that Bob was having an affair with his secretary, Ellen. Bob and Ellen left the state together on March 3. Loretta is unaware of Bob's whereabouts, and no formal divorce proceedings have been initiated. What is Loretta's filing status for the current year?

Discussion: Because Loretta has a dependent child living with her and her husband has not lived in the home during the last 6 months of the tax year, Loretta is considered unmarried for the entire year. Therefore, she may file as a head of household.

Note that if formal divorce proceedings had begun and Loretta and Bob were legally separated, Loretta would have been considered unmarried under the general rules and she would have qualified as a head of household. The primary use of the abandoned spouse provision is in cases in which one spouse has left the household and no formal divorce proceedings have begun as of the end of the tax year.

▲ DEDUCTIONS FOR ADJUSTED GROSS INCOME

This category of deductions generally consists of those expenditures that have a business purpose as well as certain expenditures that Congress has specifically allowed in the calculation of adjusted gross income. The allowable deductions in this category are listed in Exhibit 8–2.[8]

It should be noted that expenditures in this category of deductions are *always* allowed as deductions. That is, after determining the allowable amount of each deduction, that amount is not subject to any income-level limitations and is always deductible. This is not always the case for deductions from adjusted gross income.

For reporting purposes, trade or business expenses, rent and royalty expenses, and reimbursed employee business expenses are subtracted directly from the related items of gross income. That is, the expenses are netted against their related gross income and reported as a net figure in the income tax calculation.

▲ **EXAMPLE 13**   Teresa is the sole proprietor of a carpet-cleaning business. During the current year, Teresa had gross income from the business of $93,000 and allowable expenses of $36,000. How should this information be reported on her return?

Discussion: The allowable trade or business expenses are netted separately against the gross income, resulting in trade or business income of $57,000. In calculating taxable income, the $57,000 in trade or business income is reported as gross income.

▲ **EXAMPLE 14**   Assume the same facts as in example 13, except that Teresa's allowable trade or business expenses totaled $101,000.

▲ Exhibit 8–2

LIST OF DEDUCTIONS ALLOWED FOR ADJUSTED GROSS INCOME

Trade or business expenses (losses)
Reimbursed employee business expenses
Capital loss deduction
Rental and royalty expenses
Alimony paid
Deduction for contributions to a retirement plan (other than an employer-provided plan)
Moving expenses
Net operating loss deduction
50% of the self-employment tax paid on business income
25% of a self-employed person's medical insurance premiums
Interest reported as income that has been repaid as a result of cashing in a certificate of deposit before its due date (early withdrawal penalty)
Certain deductions of life tenants and income beneficiaries of property
Certain required repayments of supplemental unemployment insurance benefits
Reforestation expenses
Certain portion of lump-sum distributions from pension plans subject to the special averaging convention

Discussion: In this case, the netting of expenses against income results in a loss of $8,000 ($93,000 − $101,000). Because it is a loss from a trade or business, it is deductible for adjusted gross income. Thus, the net figure of $8,000 is shown as a deduction for adjusted gross income.

The remaining items discussed in this section of the chapter appear as separate deductions on the tax return. Previous chapters discussed several of these deductions (e.g., trade or business expenses, rental and royalty expenses, capital losses). The deduction for alimony paid recognizes that the receiver of the alimony must recognize the income on his or her return and is allowed to avoid double taxation of the income.

Reimbursed Employee Business Expenses

It has long been held that an employee is engaged in a trade or business. However, not all employee business expenses are deductible for AGI as trade or business expenses. That is, the tax law allows a deduction for adjusted gross income only for those employee business expenses that are reimbursed by the employer, known as *reimbursed employee business expenses.*[9] Unreimbursed employee business expenses are included in miscellaneous itemized deductions, which are subject to a limitation of 2 percent of adjusted gross income (discussed later). Therefore, it is important to properly account for employee business expenses on the tax return. Unfortunately, Congress further complicated this distinction in 1988 when it restricted the deduction for adjusted gross income to those situations in which employees were reimbursed for their expenses under an accountable plan. Employees who receive reimbursements from a nonaccountable plan may deduct their expenses only as miscellaneous itemized deductions.[10]

Accountable Reimbursement Plans.   An **employer reimbursement plan** is an **accountable plan** if employees are required to make an adequate accounting of their expenses with their employer and to return excess reimbursements to the employer. An adequate accounting requires that the employee give the employer adequate documentation to support the expenditure being reimbursed as a valid business expense. This would include details as to time, place, and amount of the expense as well as the business purpose for the expense. Plans that reimburse employees by preset amounts for meals, lodging, and/or mileage (called *per-diem payments*) are considered accountable plans, provided that the employee is required to establish the business purpose for the payment and the per-diem amount does not exceed that paid by the federal government.

The treatment of reimbursements and expenses by the employee under an accountable plan depends upon the amount of reimbursement in relation to the actual expense. There are three scenarios:

- Reimbursement equals actual expenses (any excess reimbursement is returned to the employer). In this case, the effect on the employee's income is a net change of zero. That is, the employee is neither in receipt of income from a reimbursement in excess of actual costs nor is the employee in a net deduction situation. No income is included in the employee's gross income, and no deductions, either for or from adjusted gross income, are allowed.

- Reimbursement is less than actual expenses. The employee may be in a net deduction situation. The reimbursement must be included in the employee's gross income. The portion of the expenses reimbursed is deductible for adjusted gross income, thus canceling out the inclusion of the reimbursement in gross income. Actual expenses in excess of the reimbursement are deductible as miscellaneous itemized deductions, subject to the 2-percent adjusted gross income limitation. Further, any deduction taken for meals or entertainment costs is subject to the 50-percent limitation on meals and entertainment (see Chapter 6) before applying the overall 2% limitation.

- Reimbursement is greater than actual expenses (i.e., excess reimbursement is not returned to the employer). In this case, the employee has net income, because the reimbursement is greater than actual expenses. The excess reimbursement is included in the employee's gross income.

Nonaccountable Reimbursement Plans.   If an employer reimbursement plan is a **nonaccountable plan,** the employee must include the reimbursement (if any) in gross income. No deductions for adjusted gross income are allowed. The employee can take deductions for expenses only as itemized deductions. As a matter of administrative convenience, employees (but not self-employed individuals) may choose to take deductions for meals and automobile mileage using the allowable federal per-diem rates rather than using actual costs. Any deduction for meals or entertainment is subject to the 50-percent limit on meals and entertainment before applying the overall 2-percent of adjusted gross income limitation.

For your reference, a summary of the reporting of reimbursements under the two types of plans is presented in Exhibit 8–3.

▲ **EXAMPLE 15**   Santamaria Co. requires its employees to adequately account for all reimbursed business expenses. Sarah, an account executive, submitted for reimbursement the following valid business expenses:

Transportation costs	$ 600
Meals	400
Lodging costs	800
Entertainment	200
Total costs	$2,000

What are the tax consequences if Santamaria reimburses Sarah the $2,000?

Discussion: Because there has been an adequate accounting, Sarah has no tax effects. None of the reimbursement is included in her gross income, and she is allowed no deductions for the expenses. NOTE: In this case, the employer is the taxpayer who effectively gets the deduction for the business expenses. Therefore, the employer is subject to the 50% limitation on meals and entertainment. The actual deduction for the employer is only $1,700 [$600 + $200 ($400 × 50%) + 800 + $100 ($200 × 50%)].

▲ **EXAMPLE 16**   What are the tax consequences if Santamaria reimburses Sarah for $1,500 instead of $2,000?

Discussion: In this case, Sarah is in a net deduction situation. The amount of the reimbursement, $1,500, is included in her gross income, and $1,500 of the expenses is deducted for AGI. The remaining $500 in unreimbursed expenses is deductible from AGI as a miscellaneous itemized deduction. Because Sarah is getting an actual deduction for meals and entertainment in this case, the 50% limit applies. Therefore, the individual costs must be allocated between for- and from-AGI, using the reimbursement ratio. The reimbursement ratio is the reimbursement divided by the total costs and equals 75% ($1,500 ÷ $2,000) in this case. The remaining 25% of each expense is unreimbursed. The allocation of deductions between for- and from-adjusted gross income is

	75% for AGI	25% from AGI	100% Total
Transportation costs	$ 450	$150	$ 600
Meals	300	100	400
Lodging	600	200	800
Entertainment	150	50	200
Total cost allocated	$1,500	$500	$2,000

Of the $500 in from-AGI expenses, only $50 ($100 × 50%) of the meals and $25 ($50 × 50%) of the entertainment costs are deductible, resulting in a total itemized deduction of $425 ($150 + $50 + $200 + $25). The $425 is combined with other allowable miscellaneous itemized deductions and subjected to the 2% of adjusted gross income limitation.

▲ **EXAMPLE 17**   Assume that Santamaria reimburses Sarah in the amount of $2,200 for the $2,000 in actual expenses. Although the Santamaria's plan requires employees to return excess reimbursements, Sarah does not return the excess.

Discussion: In this case, because the plan is an accountable plan, Sarah is deemed to have made an adequate accounting of the $2,000 in actual expenses. The excess reimbursement, $200, must be included in her gross income.

Note that Santamaria will deduct the same amount that was allowed in example 15. The employer may deduct the $200 excess reimbursement as wages paid to Sarah.

▲ **Exhibit 8–3**

TREATMENT OF EMPLOYEE BUSINESS EXPENSES

Type of Plan	Gross Income Effect	Deduction For AGI	Deduction From AGI
Accountable Plans			
Reimbursement = Actual expenses	None	None	None
Reimbursement < Actual expenses	Full amount of reimbursement is included in gross income.	Reimbursed expenses; no 50% rule for meals and entertainment.	Unreimbursed expenses as miscellaneous itemized; 50% rule applies for meals and entertainment. Two percent overall limit for miscellaneous deductions applies.
Reimbursement > Actual expenses	Excess reimbursement is included in gross income.	None	None
Nonaccountable Plans			
Reimbursement received	Full amount of reimbursement is included in gross income.	None	All employee business expenses are deductible as miscellaneous itemized deductions; 50% rule applies for meals and entertainment. Two percent overall limit for miscellaneous deductions applies.
No reimbursement	None	None	Same as for reimbursement received

▲ **EXAMPLE 18**   Assume the same facts as in example 15, except that Sarah either does not have to make an adequate accounting or does not have to return any excess reimbursement. That is, Santamaria's plan is a nonaccountable plan.

Discussion: In all of these examples, 15 to 17, the reporting is the same if the plan is nonaccountable. The reimbursement must be included in Sarah's gross income, and Sarah is allowed to deduct only actual costs as miscellaneous itemized deductions, subject to the 50% limitation on meals and entertainment. In each of these instances, Sarah is allowed a miscellaneous itemized deduction of $1,700 (the calculation follows). This is combined with her other miscellaneous itemized deductions and subjected to the 2% adjusted gross income limitation for miscellaneous itemized deductions.

Transportation costs	$ 600
Meals ($400 × 50%)	200
Lodging	800
Entertainment ($200 × 50%)	100
Total miscellaneous deduction	$1,700

Deductions for Self-Employed Taxpayers

The deductions for adjusted gross income that self-employed taxpayers are allowed to take for health insurance premiums and self-employment taxes are designed to provide some measure of equity in the treatment of employees and self-employed individuals. Recall that health insurance premiums paid by an employer for an employee are excluded from the employee's gross income. Because self-employed individuals are not employees, they cannot take advantage of this fringe benefit. In order to partially equalize the treatment of employees and self-employed individuals, the tax law allows self-employed individuals to deduct 25 percent of the cost of their health insurance premiums as a deduction for adjusted gross income.[11] The remaining premium cost is considered a personal medical expense that is deductible from adjusted gross income. If the self-employed taxpayer or spouse is eligible to be covered by employer-provided medical insurance, the deduction for adjusted gross income is not allowed.

▲ **EXAMPLE 19**   Rory is the sole proprietor of Rory's Western Wear. During the current year, Rory paid $1,800 for his own health insurance. How should Rory deduct the $1,800 health insurance cost?

Discussion: Because Rory is self-employed, he can deduct $450 ($1,800 × 25%) of the health insurance premiums as a deduction for adjusted gross income. The remaining $1,350 of the health insurance premium's cost is a personal medical expense that is combined with his other allowable medical expenses. Personal medical expenses (discussed later) are allowed as a personal itemized deduction.

If Rory's wife Eleanor is covered by medical insurance provided by her employer, the entire $1,800 can be deducted only as an itemized medical expense.

The second deduction for adjusted gross income that self-employed taxpayers may take is for one-half of the self-employment tax paid. The self-employment tax is the method through which self-employed individuals contribute to the Social Security system. The self-employment tax rate for 1995 is 15.3 percent of self-employment income. This is equal to the rate paid by employees (7.65 percent), which is matched by employers. The employer's payment into the employee's Social Security account is not taxed to the employee. The deduction of one-half of the self-employment tax equalizes the treatment for employees and self-employed individuals. In determining self-employment income, the net earnings from self-employment are reduced by one-half of the self-employment tax paid.[12] The effect of this provision is that only 92.35 percent [100% − (50% × 15.3%)] of the net earnings from self-employment is subject to the self-employment tax.

▲ **EXAMPLE 20**   Ramona is the sole proprietor of Rangoon Foods. During 1995, Rangoon had a taxable income of $80,000. Assuming that Ramona had no other sources of self-employment income, what is Ramona's 1995 self-employment income subject to the self-employment tax?

Discussion: Only 92.35% of the net earnings from self-employment is subject to the self-employment tax. Thus, Ramona's self-employment income is $73,880 ($80,000 × 92.35%).

The amount of income subject to the self-employment tax is the lesser of the ceiling amount or 92.35 percent of self-employment earnings. The 15.3 percent self-employment tax rate consists of two components, Old Age, Survivors, and Disability Insurance (OASDI) and Medicare Health Insurance (MHI). For 1995, the OASDI component is levied at 12.4 percent on the first $61,200 of self-employment income, and the MHI component is levied at 2.9 percent of total self-employment income. In effect, the rate is 15.3 percent on the first $61,200 of self-employment income and 2.9 percent on income in excess of $61,200.

▲ **EXAMPLE 21**   In example 20, what are Ramona's 1995 self-employment tax and her deduction for self-employment taxes paid?

Discussion: Ramona's self-employment tax is $9,732.

Tax on $61,200 in Income	
$61,200 × 15.3%	$9,364
Tax on Income in Excess of $61,200	
$73,880 − $61,200 = $12,680 × 2.9%	368
Self-Employment Tax	$9,732

Ramona is allowed to deduct 1/2 of the self-employment tax, $4,866, as a deduction for adjusted gross income.

Retirement Plan Contribution Deductions

Employees who participate in qualified employer pension plans are allowed to defer recognition of income paid into and earnings on assets in such plans until they are withdrawn from the plan. Recall from Chapter 4 that employees' payments into a qualified employer-sponsored pension plan are excluded from the employee's gross income. Taxpayers who do not have access to an employer-sponsored pension plan have several options under which they can accumulate assets for retirement in a tax-deferred manner. These retirement plans are different from employer-provided plans in that the taxpayer makes contributions to the plan and takes deductions for adjusted gross income for the amounts contributed. As with employer-sponsored plans, earnings on amounts paid into these plans are deferred until they are withdrawn. The effect of this arrangement is to reduce adjusted gross income (and ultimately taxable income) by the amount contributed to the plan, providing the same tax relief as an employer-sponsored plan. Self-employed taxpayers are allowed to establish their own separate retirement savings plan (referred to as a *Keogh*, or *H.R. 10, Plan*). One type of plan in which all individuals may participate is an individual retirement account.

Individual Retirement Accounts.   All taxpayers are allowed to contribute as much as $2,000 per year of their earned income to an **individual retirement account (IRA).** Taxpayers who have no earned income are not eligible to establish IRA accounts. If a husband and wife both have earned sources of income, each may contribute the $2,000 maximum amount to separate IRA accounts. An IRA can also be established for a nonworking spouse. However, the total amount paid into the two IRAs, if one spouse does not work, cannot exceed $2,250 and no one account can receive more than $2,000.

▲ **EXAMPLE 22**   Irving and Gloria are married, and each has earned income. Irving makes $16,000 per year, and Gloria earns $28,000 per year. What is the maximum amount they can contribute to their individual retirement accounts?

Discussion: Because both Irving and Gloria have earned income, each may contribute the $2,000 maximum to his or her own account, a total of $4,000 between them.

▲ **EXAMPLE 23**   Assume that in example 22 only Gloria works and Irving stays home with the children. What is the maximum amount they can contribute to their individual retirement accounts?

Discussion: Irving is a nonworking spouse. Irving and Gloria can contribute a maximum total of $2,250 to their 2 accounts. They may divide the $2,250 between the 2 accounts in any manner they choose as long as no single account receives more than $2,000. They can divide the contributions equally between the 2 accounts, or 1 account could receive the maximum $2,000 while the other's account receives $250.

If neither spouse is covered by an employer-sponsored retirement plan, all allowable contributions made to their IRAs are deductible for adjusted gross income. The effect of the deduction is to reduce the taxpayer's earned income by the amount paid in to the IRA.

▲ **EXAMPLE 24**   Return to example 22. Neither Irving nor Gloria is covered by an employer-sponsored pension plan. If they each contribute the maximum allowable amount to their IRAs, what is their deduction for adjusted gross income?

Discussion: Because neither Irving nor Gloria is covered by an employer-sponsored plan, they may each contribute $2,000 to their plans and deduct $2,000 for adjusted gross income. This would give them a total deduction of $4,000 for adjusted gross income. Note that the effect of the deduction is to reduce their individual earned incomes by the $2,000 contribution. Irving is taxed on only $14,000 ($16,000 − $2,000) of his earned income, and Gloria is taxed on only $26,000 ($28,000 − $2,000) of her earned income. This gives them the same tax treatment as employees who contribute to employer-sponsored pension plans and receive an exclusion for the amounts they pay in to the plan.

Unmarried taxpayers who participate in an employer-sponsored plan must reduce the amount of their IRA deductions proportionately when their adjusted gross income reaches $25,000. The entire deduction must be reduced to zero when adjusted gross income reaches $35,000. If at least one spouse is covered by an employer-sponsored plan, the amount of the IRA deduction for a married couple must be reduced when adjusted gross income reaches $40,000 and is reduced to zero when adjusted gross income reaches $50,000.[13] Thus, in both cases the allowable deduction is reduced over a $10,000 range of adjusted gross income. When adjusted gross income exceeds the top end of the range, no deduction is allowed.

▲ **EXAMPLE 25** Assume the same facts as in example 24, except that Gloria participates in an employer-sponsored retirement plan. Irving and Gloria continue to make the maximum contribution to their IRAs, and they have an adjusted gross income of $46,000. What is their allowable deduction for the $4,000 they contribute to their IRAs?

Discussion: Because 1 spouse participates in an employer-sponsored retirement plan, Irving and Gloria must reduce their $4,000 IRA deduction proportionately when their adjusted gross income exceeds $40,000. The entire deduction must be reduced to zero when adjusted gross income reaches $50,000. This gives a $10,000 range of adjusted gross income over which the $4,000 deduction is reduced. A general formula for calculating the percentage reduction for a married couple is

$$\frac{\text{Adjusted gross income} - \$40,000}{\$10,000}$$

Irving and Gloria's reduction:

$$\text{Percentage reduction in IRA deduction} = \frac{\$46,000 - \$40,000}{\$10,000}$$

$$= \frac{\$6,000}{\$10,000} = 60\%$$

Based on the reduction percentage, Irving and Gloria must reduce the amount of their IRA deduction to $1,600 [$4,000 − ($4,000 × 60%)].

Irving and Gloria may still contribute the $4,000 maximum to their IRA accounts. It is only the amount of the allowable deduction that must be reduced when 1 taxpayer is covered by a separate pension plan, not the allowable contribution amount. The tax benefit of making nondeductible contributions is that the earnings on the contributions are allowed to accumulate tax free until they are withdrawn. John and Gloria do not have to make the maximum contribution to get the $1,600 deduction. They may choose to contribute only the deductible amount, or they may contribute some amount less than the $4,000 maximum.

▲ **EXAMPLE 26** Assume the same facts as in example 25, except that Irving and Gloria's adjusted gross income is $38,000. What is the amount of their IRA deduction?

Discussion: Although Gloria participates in an employer-sponsored plan, their adjusted gross income is below the level at which the IRA deduction is reduced. Therefore, they are allowed to deduct their entire $4,000 contribution.

▲ **EXAMPLE 27** Assume the same facts as in example 25, except that Irving and Gloria's adjusted gross income is $56,000. What is the amount of their IRA deduction?

Discussion: Their adjusted gross income is beyond the IRA deduction phase-out level, and they are not allowed a deduction for their contribution.

Moving Expenses

Moving expenses are deductible if they meet two tests.[14] The *distance test* requires that the commuting distance from the old residence to the new job be 50 miles farther than the commuting distance was to the old job. This requirement effectively eliminates the deduction for moves within the same general area and for job changes in the same general area. The *time test* requires the taxpayer to be employed at the new location for 39 weeks in the 12-month period following the move. Self-employed individuals must work in the new location for 78 weeks during the succeeding 2-year period. The time requirements are waived for death, disability, or discharge or transfer that is not the fault of the employee.

Before passage of the Omnibus Budget Reconciliation Act of 1993, expenses associated with moving were only deductible from adjusted gross income as itemized deductions. Taxpayers were permitted a deduction, subject to some limitations, for five different types of expenses: (1) the cost of moving household goods and personal effects to the new residence, (2) the transportation cost and the cost of lodging and meals (subject to the meal limitation) for moving the taxpayer and family from the old residence to the new residence, (3) the cost of premove house-hunting trips, including travel to the new location, lodging, and meal expense (subject to the meal limitation), (4) the cost of temporary living expenses, such as lodging and meals (subject to the meal limitation) in the new location, and (5) expenses associated with buying a new residence or selling the old residence.

For tax years after 1993, moving expenses are allowed as a deduction for adjusted gross income. However, the new law severely curtails the type of expenses the taxpayer is allowed to deduct. Under the new law, a taxpayer is permitted to deduct only (1) the cost of moving household goods and personal effects to the new residence, and (2) the transportation and lodging costs of moving the taxpayer and family from the old residence to the new residence. No deduction is permitted for meals incurred in transporting the taxpayer and family from the old residence to the new residence. If the taxpayer drives from the old residence to the new residence, mileage is allowed at 9 cents per mile. There is no limit on the amount of moving expenses that are deductible so long as the expenses incurred are not lavish or unreasonable. For example, the cost of refitting drapes in the new residence and taking a vacation during the move are not part of the reasonable cost of a move and are disallowed.

▲ **EXAMPLE 28**   Millie takes a job in New City during 1995. New City is 750 miles from Old City, where Millie had been working. She expects to meet the 39-week test. Millie incurs $2,900 in costs for moving her household goods and personal effects. In addition, she incurs $400 in lodging expenses, $100 in meal expenses, and pays $20 in tolls en route to New City. Before moving to New City, she flies to New City to find an apartment. The cost of the flight is $350, and she incurs lodging costs of $200 and meal expenses of $75. How much of these costs can Millie deduct as moving expenses?

Discussion: Millie's moving expense deduction is $3,388. She is allowed to deduct the cost of transporting her household goods and personal effects ($2,900). In addition, Millie is allowed to deduct a total of $488 [lodging of $400, tolls of $20, and $68 in mileage (750 miles @ 9 cents per mile)] traveling to New City. The meal expenses and the costs associated with finding an apartment are not deductible.

▲ DEDUCTIONS FROM ADJUSTED GROSS INCOME

This class of deductions consists of expenditures that Congress has allowed for certain costs that individuals incur and that reduce the amount available to pay taxes. There is a minimum deduction allowable to all taxpayers called the *standard deduction*. As a matter of legislative grace and under the administrative convenience concept, taxpayers who incur minimum levels of the allowable itemized deductions may choose to use the minimum deduction instead of incurring the cost necessary to substantiate itemized deductions.

Standard Deduction

The amount of the standard deduction is based on the filing status of the taxpayer. The deduction is based on a statutorily determined amount for each category of filing status. Because costs are affected by inflation, the standard deduction amounts are adjusted upward each year for inflation.[15] Standard deduction amounts for 1994 and 1995 are provided in Table 8–1.

Filing Status	1994	1995
Single taxpayers	$3,800	$3,900
Married taxpayers, filing jointly	6,350	6,550
Married taxpayers, filing separately	3,175	3,275
Head of household	5,600	5,750
Surviving spouse	6,350	6,550

▲ **Table 8–1**

STANDARD DEDUCTION
AMOUNTS—1994 & 1995

In addition to the regular standard deductions allowed all taxpayers, taxpayers who are either blind (as defined by the tax law)[16] or who have attained age 65 by the end of the tax year are allowed additional standard deductions. Single taxpayers are allowed an additional standard deduction of $950 in 1995 (no change from 1994) for each condition. Married taxpayers and a surviving spouse are allowed an additional $750 in 1995 (no change from 1994) for each condition.

▲ **EXAMPLE 29**   Malcolm, a single taxpayer, is 62 and legally blind. What is Malcolm's 1995 standard deduction?

Discussion: Malcolm's standard deduction is equal to the sum of the $3,900 standard deduction for a single taxpayer and an additional standard deduction of $950 for his blindness, a total of $4,850.

If Malcolm is 65 as of December 31, 1995, he is entitled to an additional $950 standard deduction for age, bringing his total standard deduction to $5,800. This is the maximum standard deduction allowed a single taxpayer.

▲ **EXAMPLE 30**   Carl and Wenona file a joint tax return for 1995. Carl is 67, and Wenona is 59. In addition, Wenona is legally blind. What is the amount of Carl and Wenona's 1995 standard deduction?

Discussion: Carl and Wenona's standard deduction is equal to the sum of the married, filing jointly, standard deduction, $6,550, and 2 additional standard deductions of $750 each (total $1,500) for Carl's age and Wenona's blindness, a total of $8,050.

Note that the additional standard deductions allowed for age and blindness are added to the general standard deduction amount for comparison with the taxpayer's itemized deductions. The additional standard deduction amounts are not added to the taxpayer's itemized deductions.

▲ **EXAMPLE 31**   Return to the facts of example 30. If Carl and Wenona's allowable itemized deductions total $6,000, what is their deduction from adjusted gross income for 1995?

Discussion: Carl and Wenona deduct the greater of their itemized deductions ($6,000) or their allowable standard deduction ($8,050). In this case, the $8,050 standard deduction is greater, and they will not itemize on their return.

▲ **EXAMPLE 32**   Assume that in example 31 Carl and Wenona's allowable itemized deductions total $11,000. What is their deduction from adjusted gross income in 1995?

Discussion: Carl and Wenona deduct the greater of their itemized deductions ($11,000) or their allowable standard deduction ($8,050). In this case, Carl and Wenona should choose to itemize their deductions to get the $11,000 deduction. NOTE: The $1,500 additional standard deduction Carl and Wenona receive for age and blindness is not added to the itemized deduction amount. In effect, taxpayers with such conditions who itemize their deductions do not receive any additional benefit because of their condition.

Itemized Deductions

Individuals are allowed to deduct certain personal expenditures as deductions from adjusted gross income in lieu of the standard deduction. That is, taxpayers itemize deductions only when the sum of their allowable deductions exceeds their standard deduction.

> ▲ **EXAMPLE 33**   Raymond is a single individual with total allowable itemized deductions in 1995 of $2,500. How much of a deduction from adjusted gross income is Raymond allowed on his 1995 return?
>
> *Discussion:*   Because the standard deduction for a single taxpayer in 1995 is $3,900, Raymond uses the standard deduction amount to calculate his 1995 taxable income.
>
> ▲ **EXAMPLE 34**   Assume that Raymond's total allowable itemized deductions are $7,200 in 1995. How much can Raymond deduct on his 1995 return?
>
> *Discussion:*   Because Raymond's allowable itemized deductions exceed the $3,900 standard deduction, he deducts the $7,200 in itemized deductions in calculating his 1995 taxable income.

In allowing certain personal expenditures to be deducted, Congress has exercised its power under the legislative grace concept to restrict the amount of deductible expenditures. These restrictions limit deductions to amounts exceeding a stated percentage of the taxpayer's adjusted gross income. Only amounts in excess of the limit are deductible. Restricting these deductions provides an element of administrative convenience. That is, with these limitations, many taxpayers will not have sufficient amounts of deductions to itemize, choosing instead to use the standard deduction amount. The use of the standard deduction lowers compliance costs, both for the taxpayer, who does not have to keep records of small amounts of expenses, and the government, which does not have to audit the standard deduction. This chapter discusses in turn each general category of itemized deductions and any applicable limitations. Table 8–2 provides a summary of the categories of allowable itemized deductions and their limitations.

Medical Expenses.   Individuals are allowed a deduction for their unreimbursed medical costs as well as those of their spouse and any dependents. An individual does not have to meet the gross income test or the joint return test to qualify for medical expense purposes.[17] A person who meets the support, relative, and residency tests is considered a dependent for purposes of the medical expense deduction. This treatment recognizes situations in which taxpayers are expending significant amounts on behalf of relatives who, because they earn too much money or are married, are not technically dependents. In addition, note that the medical expense area is the only context in which you are allowed a deduction for the payment of expenses of another taxpayer.

Medical expenses are defined as those expenditures incurred for "diagnosis, cure, mitigation, treatment, or prevention of disease," as well as those that are incurred because of problems "affecting any structure or function of the body."[18] This definition encompasses the majority of costs we usually think of as medical expenses—doctor bills, dentistry, optometry, surgery, medicine and drugs, hospital charges, and so on. Deductions for medicines and drugs are limited to prescription drugs and insulin. In addition to these typical costs, taxpayers can deduct the cost of health and accident insurance premiums and transportation costs of 9 cents per mile for travel to and from the place of medical care.[19] Exhibit 8–4 lists deductible and nondeductible medical costs.

Unreimbursed medical costs are deductible only to the extent that they exceed 7.5 percent of adjusted gross income. That is, medical costs below the 7.5-percent limit are effectively disallowed.[20] This limitation severely restricts the benefit of

Type of Expense	Allowable Expenses	Limitations
Medical expenses	Unreimbursed medical expenses—doctors, dentists, optometrists, eyeglasses, hearing aids, medical insurance premiums, travel to medical care	Only prescription medicine and drugs and insulin allowed as medical expenses Total medical expenses limited to the excess of 7.5% of adjusted gross income
Taxes	State and local income taxes, property taxes	Property taxes must be ad valorem
Interest	Qualified home mortgage interest	Interest on up to $1,000,000 in acquisition debt on taxpayer's principal residence and 1 other residence Interest on up to $100,000 in home equity loan interest
	Investment interest	Investment interest deduction cannot exceed net investment income
Charitable contributions	Cash and property contributed to qualifying educational, religious, charitable, scientific, or literary organizations	Total deduction cannot exceed 50% of adjusted gross income Contributions of long-term capital gain property deducted at fair market value cannot exceed 30% of adjusted gross income
Casualty and theft losses	Losses on personal use property from casualty or theft	Amount of loss is the lesser of the decline in value of the property or its adjusted basis $100 statutory floor per occurrence 10% of adjusted gross income limitation for all casualties and thefts
Miscellaneous	Gambling losses, disabled work-related expenses, unrecovered annuity investment	Fully deductible
	Unreimbursed employee business expenses, investment expenses (other than interest), hobby deductions, costs related to tax returns	2% of adjusted gross income limitation

▲ **Table 8–2**

SUMMARY OF ALLOWABLE ITEMIZED DEDUCTIONS

▲ **Exhibit 8–4**

EXAMPLES OF MEDICAL
EXPENSES

Deductible Items	Nondeductible Items
The cost of all medical drugs, special foods, and drinks your doctor prescribes for treatment of an illness; pills or other birth control items your doctor prescribes; vitamins, iron, etc. your doctor prescribes; insulin.	Toothpaste Cosmetics Vitamins for general health Veterinarian's fees
Payments to or for a doctor, surgeon, dentist, osteopath, ophthalmologist, optometrist, psychiatrist, psychologist, hospital care, therapy, lab fees, diagnostic tests, X-ray examination or treatment, nursing care.	Illegal operations or drugs Cosmetic surgery Funeral or burial expenses
Special items or equipment such as false teeth, eyeglasses, hearing aids, crutches, prescribed elastic hose, artificial limbs, guide dogs for the blind or deaf, motorized wheelchair, hand controls on a car, special telephone for the deaf.	Maternity clothing Diaper service
Transportation to get medical care—to and from doctor, dentist, hospital, etc.	Life insurance premiums Loss-of-earnings insurance premiums
Health and accident insurance premiums, supplementary Medicare premiums.	Premiums of automobile insurance Basic Medicare premiums

the medical expense deduction for taxpayers with high incomes and/or those covered by medical insurance. Although low-income taxpayers are more likely to have medical expenses that exceed the 7.5% limitation, most low-income taxpayers use the standard deduction and therefore receive no benefit for the medical expenses incurred.

▲ **EXAMPLE 35**   Ari is a single individual with an adjusted gross income of $40,000. During the current year, he incurred several medical expenses. What is his allowable deduction for the following expenses?

Doctors	$2,500
Dentist	250
Optometrist	150
Prescription drugs	375
Aspirin, cold pills	45
Contact lenses	200
Crutch rental for broken leg	80
Health insurance premiums	1,300
Transportation—100 miles to and from doctors, dentists, etc.	9
Reimbursements for medical care	⟨$2,800⟩

Discussion: All of these are allowable medical expenses, with the exception of the $45 for aspirin and cold pills, which are not prescription drugs. In addition, Ari is allowed a deduction of 9 cents per mile for the 100 miles of transportation costs. His total allowable medical expenses before reimbursement are $4,864 ($2,500 + $250 + $150 + $375 + $200 + $80 + $1,300 + $9). Unreimbursed medical expenses are $2,064 ($4,864 − $2,800). This is subject to the 7.5% of AGI limitation, which is $3,000 (7.5% × $40,000). Therefore, Ari is not entitled to a medical expense deduction because his unreimbursed expenses do not exceed the AGI limitation.

Taxes. Deductions are allowed for amounts paid for state and local income taxes, real estate taxes, and other personal property taxes.[21] Because most individuals are cash basis taxpayers, the deduction allowed is for **taxes** paid during the year, not the ultimate total of the tax imposed. Thus, taxpayers who itemize deductions normally have an adjustment for state and local taxes paid in the year following the deduction. If the taxpayer obtains a state or local tax refund, the tax benefit rule requires that person to include the refund in the subsequent year's taxable income. Similarly, if the taxpayer pays additional taxes, these are added to the tax paid for the subsequent year to determine that year's deduction.

▲ **EXAMPLE 36**   Alana's withholding for state income taxes totals $2,400 during 1995. Alana is single, and her itemized deductions—including state income taxes—total $10,000. In filing her state income tax return, Alana receives a refund of $200. What is the proper treatment of the refund?

Discussion: Because Alana's 1995 deduction is recovered through the $200 refund in 1996, the $200 is included in her 1996 gross income. NOTE: The tax benefit rule applies only to taxpayers who itemize deductions. A taxpayer who elects to use the standard deduction has not claimed a deduction for taxes paid. Therefore, a taxpayer who uses the standard deduction and receives a refund of state income taxes has no income to recognize.

▲ **EXAMPLE 37**   Assume the same facts as example 36, except that her total itemized deductions, including state income taxes, are $4,000 ($2,400 in state taxes + $1,600 in other itemized deductions). What is the proper tax treatment of the refund?

Discussion: Alana must include $100 of the refund as income. The actual amount of her state itemized deductions should have been $2,200 ($2,400 claimed minus the $200 refund). If Alana had deducted the actual amount of taxes ($2,200) in preparing her return, she would have had $3,800 in itemized deductions. Because the $3,800 is less than the standard deduction of $3,900, she would have prepared her return using the standard deduction. Under the tax benefit rule, the $100 benefit she derived by claiming $4,000 of itemized deductions, instead of the standard deduction of $3,900, must be included on her 1996 income tax return.

▲ **EXAMPLE 38**   Assume the same facts as in example 36, except that Alana owes an additional $300 in state income taxes when she files her 1995 state income tax return. How should Alana treat the $300 paid with the state return?

Discussion: Alana pays the $300 in additional state taxes in 1996. Because she is a cash basis taxpayer, the $300 in tax paid in 1996 should be deducted as state income taxes paid in 1996.

In order to be deductible, personal property taxes must be ad valorem, that is, based on the value of the property being taxed.

▲ **EXAMPLE 39**   State A charges a vehicle licensing fee that is based on the type of vehicle and its weight. State B's vehicle licensing fee is $25 plus 1% percent of the fair market value of the vehicle. Is either fee deductible as a tax?

Discussion: State A's fee is not based on the value of the vehicle and is not a deductible personal property tax. State B's fee is partially based on the value of the vehicle. Therefore, the fee in excess of the $25 fixed charge is deductible as a personal property tax.

An individual cannot use any of the following in calculating itemized tax deductions: federal taxes, including income and Social Security taxes; water use and sewer taxes; excise taxes on alcohol, tobacco, or firearms; gasoline taxes; utility taxes; assessments for local benefits such as sidewalks; and sales taxes.[22] Note that assessments for local benefits are not considered taxes and would be added to the basis of the property. It should be stressed that although these taxes are not deductible by individuals as itemized deductions, they may be deductible or capitalized as part of the cost when incurred in a trade or business (Chapter 6).

Interest Expense. Itemized deductions for interest payments have been severely restricted in recent years. Personal interest (credit cards, auto loans, student loans) is specifically disallowed. The only interest deductible as an itemized deduction is qualified home mortgage interest and investment interest.[23] Each type of interest is subject to several restrictions.

HOME MORTGAGE INTEREST. Only interest on debt that is secured by the taxpayer's principal residence and one other residence is deductible as **qualified home mortgage interest**.[24] The second residence either must qualify as a vacation home (see Chapter 6 for vacation home requirements) if it is rented out during the year or not be rented at all during the year in order to qualify as a second residence. If a second home is considered rental property (i.e., a rental loss is allowed), the portion of the interest expense attributable to the personal use of the home is considered personal interest and is not deductible. A *residence* includes a house, cooperative apartments, condominiums, and mobile homes and boats that have living accommodations (living quarters, cooking facilities, etc.).

Qualified home mortgage interest includes both acquisition debt and home equity debt. **Acquisition debt** is any debt incurred to acquire, construct, or substantially improve a qualified residence of the taxpayer. **Home equity debt** is any debt that is secured by a personal residence that is not acquisition debt. However, there is a cap on the level of indebtedness for each type of qualified home mortgage interest:

- Interest paid on acquisition debt of $1 million or less is deductible. Interest on debt in excess of $1 million is considered personal interest and is not deductible. Acquisition debt includes the cost of acquiring, constructing, or substantially improving a qualified residence.

- Interest paid on home equity debt of $100,000 or less is also deductible. However, total debt (acquisition plus home equity) cannot exceed the fair market value of the property. Home equity debt is any debt, other than acquisition debt, which is secured by the residence. The proceeds of home equity debt can be used for any purpose.

Points are prepaid interest amounts that must be paid in order to acquire financing. They are expressed as a percentage of the value of the loan and paid at loan acquisition. As such, they represent prepaid interest, which usually is capitalized and amortized over the term of the loan. A special provision in the tax law allows points paid to acquire an initial mortgage on a taxpayer's principal residence to be deducted in the year the points are paid.[25] However, points paid to refinance an existing mortgage must be capitalized and amortized as interest expense over the term of the loan. Loan origination fees that replace charges for services in obtaining the loan are not deductible as points. Prepayment penalties for the early payment of a mortgage are also deductible as qualified home mortgage interest.

▲ **EXAMPLE 40**   Anita purchases a new home in 1995, borrowing $80,000 from Local Bank to finance the purchase. Anita also pays $1,600 in points and $1,000 in loan origination fees. Interest paid on the $80,000 mortgage in 1995 totals $8,400. What is Anita's allowable 1995 interest deduction?

Discussion: Assuming that the $80,000 debt is secured by the property, Anita can deduct the $8,400 in mortgage interest and the $1,600 in points paid to obtain the mortgage—$10,000 in all. The loan origination fees are not deductible interest.

▲ **EXAMPLE 41**   Zane's home is worth $250,000. He purchased the home 20 years ago using a $100,000 mortgage. During the current year, Zane paid $5,400 in interest on the original mortgage, which has a balance of $45,000. Zane also borrowed $110,000 on a home equity loan and used the proceeds to pay off personal debts, buy a new sports car, and take a trip around the world. Zane paid $11,000 in interest (i.e., a 10% interest rate) on the home equity loan. How much is Zane's allowable interest deduction?

Discussion: The $5,400 paid on the original mortgage is qualified home mortgage interest. Although the total debt ($100,000 + $110,000) is less than the fair market value of the home, only $100,000 of the home equity is considered qualified debt. The deduction for the home equity loan would be $10,000 (10% × $100,000), for a total allowable interest deduction of $15,400. The excess home equity debt ($10,000) is considered personal debt, and the $1,000 in interest is nondeductible. NOTE: The $100,000 home equity loan is considered qualified debt, regardless of the use of the proceeds. In this case, even though Zane used the proceeds for purely personal purposes, the interest is deductible.

INVESTMENT INTEREST.   Interest paid on debt used to purchase portfolio investments is deductible. Thus, interest paid on an investment in a passive activity is not included in the investment interest deduction. Expenses related to passive activities are subject to the passive activity rules and are not included in the investment interest calculation. In addition, as stated in Chapter 5, interest paid to produce tax-exempt income is not deductible and therefore is not part of the investment interest deduction.

The deduction for **investment interest** is limited to the net investment income of the taxpayer for the year. Any interest not currently deductible because of this limitation may be carried forward indefinitely and applied to future years. **Net investment income** is defined as investment income less investment expenses (other than interest). *Investment income* consists of gross income from property held for investment purposes (i.e., not a passive activity), gains (losses) from the disposition of such properties, and portfolio income (as defined for passive loss rules). For tax years beginning after 1992, net long-term capital gains, which are taxed at the maximum 28% long-term capital gain rate, are not included in the investment income calculation. *Investment expenses* include all ordinary and necessary expenses directly connected to the production of the investment income.

▲ **EXAMPLE 42**   Kareem pays interest related to his investment activities totaling $40,000 in 1995. His investment income is $30,000, and investment expenses are $6,000. What is his 1995 investment interest deduction?

Discussion: The deduction is limited to $24,000 ($30,000 − $6,000), Kareem's net investment income. The $16,000 in disallowed interest is carried forward to 1996 for deduction against 1996 net investment income.

▲ **EXAMPLE 43**   Assume that in 1996, Kareem pays $36,000 in investment interest and has investment income of $44,000 and $5,000 in investment expenses. What is Kareem's 1996 investment interest deduction?

Discussion: Kareem's net investment income is $39,000 ($44,000 − $5,000). He is allowed to deduct the $36,000 in current-year interest and $3,000 of the previously disallowed interest. His carryover of disallowed investment interest to 1997 is $13,000 ($16,000 − $3,000).

Charitable Contributions.   Individuals are allowed to deduct contributions to organizations that are organized for religious, charitable, educational, scientific, or literary purposes.[26] Deductions are also allowed for contributions to organizations that work to prevent cruelty to animals or children and for contributions to government units. The top panel of Exhibit 8–5 contains examples of organizations that do and those that do not qualify as **charitable organizations.**

Most charitable contributions are made in cash and do not present valuation problems. However, when a taxpayer contributes property to a charitable organization, the type of property determines the amount of the contribution.[27] As indicated in the lower panel of Exhibit 8–5, property of a type that would produce ordinary income or short-term capital gain if it were sold is limited to the lesser of (1) the fair market value of the property on the date of the contribution, or (2) the adjusted basis of the property. This limitation makes it an unwise tax-planning strategy to donate ordinary income property that has a fair market value that is less than the adjusted basis (i.e., loss property).

▲ **EXAMPLE 44**   Tomas owns 2 properties that are ordinary income properties. Both properties have a fair market value of $10,000. Property A has an adjusted basis of $6,000, and property B has an adjusted basis of $25,000. Which property would be the better to contribute to his alma mater?

Discussion: If Tomas contributes property A, his deduction is only $6,000 (fair market value is greater than adjusted basis). A contribution of property B results in a deduction of $10,000 (fair market value is less than adjusted basis). However, if Tomas contributes property B, he loses the $15,000 ($10,000 − $25,000) in unrealized loss on the property. By contributing property A, his deduction is lower, but he avoids tax on the $4,000 ($10,000 − $6,000) in unrealized gain on the property.

If Tomas wished to contribute property B, it would be better to sell the property, realize the ordinary loss of $15,000, and contribute the $10,000 in cash from the sale. The charitable contribution deduction would still be $10,000, and Tomas would have an ordinary loss deduction of $15,000 on the sale. Note that one big advantage of gifting property A is the avoidance of tax on the $4,000 in unrealized gain on property A.

Taxpayers can deduct the fair market value of contributions of property that would result in a long-term capital gain if the property were sold. However, the taxpayer may elect to reduce the amount of the contribution to the adjusted basis of the property in order to use a higher contribution ceiling, as discussed next.

▲ **EXAMPLE 45**   Assume that in example 44 both of Tomas's properties were long-term capital gain properties. Which of the 2 is the better to contribute?

Discussion: Deductions for contributions of long-term capital gain property are allowed for the fair market value of the property. In this case, both properties would result in a deduction of $10,000. However, Tomas would be better off if he contributes property A and avoids the tax on the $4,000 in unrealized gain on the property.

		▲ Exhibit 8–5

SUMMARY OF
CHARITABLE
CONTRIBUTION RULES

Examples of Qualified Charities:

Churches, mosques, synagogues
Salvation Army, Red Cross, CARE, Goodwill,
    United Way, Boy Scouts, Girl Scouts,
    Boys/Girls Club of America
Fraternal orders (if gift used for charitable
    purpose)
Nonprofit schools and hospitals
Veterans' groups
Certain cultural groups
Federal, state, and local governments

Examples of Nonqualifying Organizations:

Chambers of Commerce and other business
    leagues or organizations
Civic leagues
Communist organizations
International organizations
Social clubs
Country clubs

Examples of Allowable Contribution Items:

Cash
Clothing
Furniture
Fixtures
Inventory
Real property
Stocks, bonds
Paintings, works of art
Jewelry
Automobiles
Appliances
Out-of-pocket costs for performing charitable
    work—special uniforms, mileage, etc.

Items That Are Not Deductible:

Political contributions
Raffle, bingo, or lottery tickets
Tuition to a private school
The value of a person's time
Value of blood donated to a blood bank or
    Red Cross
Gifts to individuals

Type of Property:	Amount of Contribution:	Maximum Deduction (Limit):
Cash	Amount contributed	50% of adjusted gross income
Ordinary income or Short-term capital gain property	The lesser of 1. the fair market value at the time of the contribution	50% of adjusted gross income
	or	
	2. the adjusted basis of the property	50% of adjusted gross income
Long-term capital gain property	Fair market value at the date of contribution	30% of adjusted gross income
	An election can be made to reduce the amount of the contribution to the adjusted basis of the property.	50% of adjusted gross income

There are three major limitations on the deductible amount of charitable contributions. The overall amount of the charitable contribution deduction cannot exceed 50 percent of the taxpayer's adjusted gross income. Contributions of capital gain property that are deducted at fair market value cannot exceed 30 percent of adjusted gross income. But a taxpayer who is willing to give up the deduction related to the property's appreciation (i.e., use the adjusted basis as the deductible amount) is not subject to the 30-percent limit. In addition, contributions to certain nonoperating private foundations are subject to rather complex limitations that are beyond the scope of this discussion. Any contributions in excess of the limitations are carried forward for deduction for five years.

▲ **EXAMPLE 46**   Antonia owns stock for which she paid $20,000 several years ago; she would like to donate the stock to the Girl Scouts. The stock is worth $25,000, and Antonia's adjusted gross income is $40,000. Assuming that she has made no other charitable contributions, what is her allowable deduction?

Discussion: Because the sale of the stock would produce a long-term capital gain if Antonia sold the stock, she is allowed to use the $25,000 fair market value as the amount of her contribution. However, deductions for contributions of property that are measured at fair market value are limited to 30% of adjusted gross income. In this case, Antonia's current deduction would be limited to $12,000 (30% × $40,000), with the $13,000 remainder carried forward for deduction in the subsequent 5 years.

Antonia has the option of measuring the amount of her contribution at her adjusted basis in the stock, $20,000. Property measured at the adjusted basis is subject to the general 50% of adjusted gross income limit for charitable contributions. By valuing her contribution at $20,000 (her basis), she could deduct the entire $20,000 in the current year. However, she would have no remaining deduction carryforward under this election.

Miscellaneous Itemized Deductions.   This category of deductions, **miscellaneous itemized deductions,** includes amounts expended for unreimbursed employee business expenses, investment expenses (other than investment interest), hobby-related deductions, and gambling losses to the extent of gambling winnings. In addition to the limitations imposed on specific types of deductions in this category (i.e., meals and entertainment), some expenditures are fully deductible, whereas others are subject to an annual limitation of 2 percent of adjusted gross income.[28]

FULLY DEDUCTIBLE EXPENDITURES.   Gambling losses (not to exceed the amount of gambling winnings), impairment-related work expenses of a disabled person, and the unrecovered investment in an annuity contract when the annuity ceases because of death (discussed in Chapter 3) are deductible without regard to the annual limitation imposed on other types of miscellaneous expenses. Thus, it is important to segregate these expenditures from other allowable miscellaneous deductions.

PARTIALLY DEDUCTIBLE EXPENDITURES.   Unreimbursed employee business expenses, investment expenses (other than investment interest), fees for tax advice and preparation, and hobby-related deductions are deductible only to the extent that the total expenditures in this category exceed 2 percent of the taxpayer's adjusted gross income. Examples of expenditures that qualify in this category are provided in Exhibit 8–6.

▲ **EXAMPLE 47**   Odakota has an adjusted gross income of $30,000 in the current year. Odakota incurred $800 in employment-related expenses that were not reimbursed by his employer and $200 for tax return preparation. What is Odakota's allowable miscellaneous itemized deduction?

Discussion: Of the $1,000 total allowable expenditures, only the amount in excess of $600 ($30,000 × 2%)—$400—is deductible.

The 2-percent limitation is an annual limitation that is imposed after any specific limitations imposed on each category of expenditure. For example, unreimbursed employee meals and entertainment are subject to the 50 percent limitation on meals and entertainment before the 2-percent annual limitation is applied. In addition, hobby expenses are limited to hobby income before application of the 2-percent annual limitation.[29]

Fully Deductible Miscellaneous Expenditures:

Gambling losses (to extent of gambling winnings)
Impairment-related work expenses of a disabled person
Unrecovered investment in annuity contracts because of death

Partially Deductible Expenditures:

Employee Business Expenses

Certain employment agency fees
Certain employment-related education
Dues to professional organizations
Subscriptions to professional journals
Small tools and supplies
Uniforms not adaptable to general use
Union dues and expenses

Investment Expenses

Legal and accounting fees
Safe deposit box rental
Investment counsel fees
Clerical help and office rent in caring for
  investments
Fees paid in connection with property held
  for the production of income

Other Allowable Expenses

Hobby-related deductions
Fees for tax advice
Fees for tax preparation

Nondeductible Expenditures:

Burial or funeral expenses
Fees and licenses, such as marriage
  licenses and dog tags
Fines and penalties
Home repairs
Home insurance
Rent on a personal residence

▲ **EXAMPLE 48**   Lois paints in her spare time. During the current year, she sold some paintings at a local arts and crafts fair for $300. Her costs for painting supplies and transportation to and from the fair were $800. If Lois had an adjusted gross income of $25,000 (including the hobby income) and had no other miscellaneous itemized deductions, what is the effect of the hobby on her taxable income?

Discussion: Because her painting is considered a hobby, Lois must include the $300 in her gross income, and her allowable hobby deductions are limited to the $300 in income. The actual amount of the hobby expense deduction is subject to the 2% annual limitation. Because her allowable hobby deductions are less than $500 ($25,000 × 2%), none of her hobby costs is deductible. This results in her hobby increasing her taxable income by $300.

In regard to the limitation on investment interest discussed earlier, investment expenses are determined after applying the 2-percent annual limitation. However, any other miscellaneous itemized deductions are applied against the 2-percent limitation before investment expenses are reduced for purposes of the investment interest limitation.[30]

▲ **EXAMPLE 49**   Kareem, in example 42, pays interest related to his investment activities totaling $40,000 in 1995. His investment income is $30,000, and investment expenses are $6,000. Kareem has an adjusted gross income of $50,000 and no other allowable miscellaneous itemized deductions. What is his 1995 investment interest deduction?

Discussion: The investment interest deduction is limited to Kareem's net investment income. For purposes of this calculation, investment expenses are those allowable after applying the 2% annual miscellaneous itemized deduction limitation. Thus, Kareem's investment expense deduction is only $5,000 [$6,000 − ($50,000 × 2%)], and net investment income is $25,000 ($30,000 − $5,000). His allowable investment interest deduction is $25,000.

In comparing the results in this example to those in example 42, Kareem's investment interest deduction has increased by $1,000. This is because the 2% limitation reduces his deductible investment expenses to $5,000. Because Kareem receives no benefit for $1,000 of his investment expenses, they are not used in determining his net investment income.

▲ **EXAMPLE 50**   Assume that in example 49 Kareem also has $600 in allowable unreimbursed employee business expenses. What is his 1995 investment interest deduction?

Discussion: In determining the amount of investment expenses lost because of the 2% annual limitation, other deductions subject to the limitation must be taken against the limit first. In this case, the $600 in employee expenses is applied first against the $1,000 limit, leaving only $400 of the investment expenses subject to the limitation. This leaves Kareem with $5,600 ($6,000 − $400) in investment expenses and a net investment income of $24,400. Thus, only $24,400 of the investment interest is deductible. NOTE: The investment interest deduction of $24,400 is $600 less than the $25,000 in example 49 but $400 more than would be permitted (see example 42) if this provision did not exist.

▲ ITEMIZED DEDUCTIONS AND EXEMPTIONS— REDUCTIONS BY HIGH-INCOME TAXPAYERS

The tax law requires that high-income taxpayers must reduce the amount of their allowable itemized deductions and personal and dependency exemption amounts. In general, taxpayers with adjusted gross incomes in excess of $114,700 in 1995 ($111,800 in 1994) must reduce their otherwise allowable itemized deductions by 3 percent of adjusted gross income in excess of $114,700 ($111,800 in 1994). In making this reduction to account for the **itemized deduction phase-out,** allowable deductions for medical expenses, investment interest, gambling losses, and casualty and theft losses are not subject to reduction. In addition, deductions subject to the 3-percent reduction rule may not be reduced by more than 80 percent of the otherwise allowable amount.[31]

▲ **EXAMPLE 51**   Charles and Aretha are a married couple filing a joint return in 1995. They have adjusted gross income of $250,000 and total itemized deductions of $22,000. Included in the $22,000 is $5,000 in allowable medical expenses and $7,000 in investment interest. How much of the $22,000 in itemized deductions may Charles and Aretha actually deduct on their return?

Discussion: The $12,000 in medical and investment interest expenses is not subject to the reduction rule. The remaining $10,000 is subject to reduction, but the reduction may not exceed $8,000 ($10,000 × 80%). The basic reduction is for 3% of AGI in excess of $114,700. This equals $4,059 [3% × ($250,000 − $114,700)]. Because the basic reduction is less than the $8,000 maximum reduction, total itemized deductions are reduced by $4,059. This leaves them with deductible itemized deductions of $17,941 ($22,000 − $4,059).

Note that if Charles and Aretha's AGI is $400,000, the 3% reduction rule would be $8,559 [3% × ($400,000 − $114,700)]. Because this is in excess of the $8,000 maximum reduction, they would reduce their total itemized deductions by the $8,000 maximum, resulting in a deduction of $14,000 ($22,000 − $8,000).

High-income taxpayers also must reduce their exemption deductions. The basic reduction is 2 percent of the allowable exemption amount for each $2,500 (or portion thereof) in adjusted gross income in excess of the threshold amount and is known as the **exemption deduction phase-out.** The threshold amount varies by filing status, as shown in Table 8–3.

Note that in Table 8–3 the third column shows the AGI level at which the phase-out ends. This means that taxpayers with AGIs in excess of these amounts are not be entitled to a deduction for personal and dependency exemptions.

▲ **EXAMPLE 52**   Martina is a single taxpayer with adjusted gross income of $130,000 in 1995. What is her allowable personal exemption amount?

Discussion: Because Martina's adjusted gross income is in excess of $114,700, she must reduce her $2,500 personal exemption by 2% for each $2,500 increment (or portion thereof) of adjusted gross income in excess of $114,700. Thus, the first step is to calculate the number of $2,500 increments:

$$\$130,000 \ - \ \$114,700 \ = \ \$15,300 \text{ in excess of } \$114,700$$

$$\$15,300 \ \div \ \$2,500 \ = \ 6.12 \text{ increments} \ = \ 7 \text{ phase-out increments}$$

$$\text{Percentage of exemption lost} \ = \ 7 \times 2\% \ = \ 14\%$$

Because of the phase-out, Martina loses 14% of her exemption, leaving her 86% (100% − 14%) of her $2,500 exemption as her actual deduction, $2,150 ($2,500 × 86%).

▲ **EXAMPLE 53**   Bill and Catherine are a married couple, have 2 dependents, and file a joint return for 1995. Bill and Catherine's adjusted gross income is $320,000. What is their allowable exemption deduction?

Discussion: Bill and Catherine's adjusted gross income is greater than the top of the phase-out range for a married couple filing jointly ($294,550). Therefore, their exemption deductions are fully phased out, and they are not entitled to deductions for exemptions.

Two aspects to note in calculating the exemption phase-out are that the total exemption amount—not each individual exemption—is subject to the phase-out. Therefore, high-income taxpayers with larger numbers of exemptions lose more than taxpayers with the equivalent income but fewer exemptions. Second, each portion of a $2,500 increment results in a 2-percent reduction. Thus, in example 52, Martina lost a full 2 percent for the 0.12 increment. A rule of thumb to follow in doing this calculation is to always round up.

1995		
Filing Status	**Threshold Amount**	**Phase-Out Ends**
Single	$114,700	$237,200
Head of household	$143,350	$265,850
Married, filing jointly	$172,050	$294,550
Married, filing separately	$ 86,025	$147,275
Surviving spouse	$172,050	$294,550
1994		
Filing Status	**Threshold Amount**	**Phase-Out Ends**
Single	$111,800	$234,300
Head of household	$139,750	$262,250
Married, filing jointly	$167,700	$290,200
Married, filing separately	$ 83,850	$145,100
Surviving spouse	$167,700	$290,200

▲ **Table 8–3**

THRESHOLD AGI FOR EXEMPTION PHASE-OUT: 1995, 1994

▲ EXEMPTION AND STANDARD DEDUCTION RESTRICTIONS ON DEPENDENTS

The tax law provides several restrictions on the use of exemptions and standard deductions by dependents. Any individual who can be claimed as a dependent of another is not allowed a personal exemption in the calculation of his or her own taxable income. Note that this requirement is not negotiable: If the dependency tests are met, no personal exemption deduction is allowed.

▲ **EXAMPLE 54**   Andreas, 20, is a full-time college student at City Tech. He earns $4,200 during 1995 that he uses to pay for living expenses. His father gives him an additional $9,600 to pay for college-related costs and additional living expenses. How much is Andreas's 1995 personal exemption?

Discussion: Because Andreas meets all the tests for dependency, his father receives a dependency exemption for Andreas. Andreas is not allowed a personal exemption, because he qualifies as a dependent of his father.

The second restriction on a dependent is the amount of the allowable standard deduction. A dependent's standard deduction is the greater of

- $650 ($600 in 1994)

    or

- The dependent's earned income or the standard deduction amount for a single individual, whichever results in a smaller deduction

The intent of this provision is to deny the benefit of a full standard deduction to a dependent who has large amounts of unearned income. This takes away some of the incentive for high marginal tax rate taxpayers to shift significant amounts of unearned income to lower marginal tax rate dependents. However, dependents with earned sources of income are still allowed to use the standard deduction to reduce the tax on earned income.

▲ **EXAMPLE 55**   Return to the facts of example 54. What is Andreas's standard deduction amount for 1995?

Discussion: Because Andreas has earned income of $4,200, he is allowed a standard deduction of the full $3,900 single standard deduction. Assuming that Andreas has no deductions for AGI, his taxable income for 1995 is $300 ($4,200 − $3,900).

▲ **EXAMPLE 56**   Amy is a dependent of her parents; she earns $2,200 from a summer job and receives $1,200 in interest in 1995 from a savings account established by her grandfather. What is Amy's standard deduction?

Discussion: Because Amy is a dependent, her standard deduction is the greater of $650 or her earned income, $2,200. Her standard deduction is limited to the $2,200 in earned income. NOTE: Assuming that Amy has no deductions for AGI, her taxable income is $1,200. Thus, she has not been able to shield any of her unearned income through use of a personal exemption deduction or the standard deduction.

▲ CALCULATING TAX LIABILITY

After determining the taxpayer's taxable income, the tax is computed using the appropriate rate schedule for the taxpayer's filing status. Individuals with taxable incomes of less than $100,000 generally use the tax tables provided by the IRS. A 1994 tax table and tax rate schedules for 1994 and 1995 can be found in Appendix A.

The next step in completing the tax liability calculation is to add any additional taxes due with the return and deduct any allowable tax credits to arrive at the net tax liability for the year (see Exhibit 8–1). Several other taxes are paid with an individual's income tax return. These taxes include the self-employment tax, the alternative minimum tax (see Chapter 14), recapture taxes, and the Social Security tax on unreported tip income. The net tax liability is then compared to amounts withheld from the taxpayer's salary and payments of estimated taxes to determine the amount of tax due (or the refund to be received) with the return.[32] If the amount of tax due is greater than $500 and more than 10 percent of the tax liability, the taxpayer may be penalized for the underpayment of estimated taxes.[33]

Tax on Unearned Income of a Minor Child

In 1986, Congress complicated the tax calculation for a minor child with significant amounts of unearned income (interest, dividends, royalties, etc.). The provision enacted is designed to eliminate the tax rate advantage that could have been gained under prior law by shifting unearned forms of income from the parents to a minor child. The basic thrust of the law is to tax the **net unearned income** of a child who has not attained the age of 14 **(minor child)** at the parent's marginal tax rate (the **kiddie tax**).[34] Although not specifically stated, this treatment is an extension of the assignment-of-income doctrine for investment income. That is, the substance of giving minor children investment property is to make an assignment of the parents' unearned income to the children in an attempt to lower taxes. For purposes of this calculation,

> Net unearned income = Unearned income
>
> Less: $650
>
> Less: The greater of $650 or the costs of
> producing the unearned income

Note that under this definition, any unearned income in excess of $1,300 ($650 + $650) is taxed at the parents' marginal tax rate. The remaining taxable income of the child is taxed at the child's marginal tax rate. This treatment has the effect of disallowing the assignment of unearned income in excess of $1,300 to a minor child.

▲ **EXAMPLE 57**   Dan and Madeline are a married couple with a taxable income of $55,000 in 1995. Their daughter, Dawn, 10, has interest income of $850 and dividend income of $950 in 1995. What is Dawn's 1995 tax liability?

Discussion: Because Dawn is younger than 14 and has unearned income in excess of $1,300, the tax on unearned income of a minor child applies.

Calculation of Dawn's Taxable Income	
Gross income ($850 + $950)	$1,800
Less: Standard deduction	(650)
Exemption	-0-
Taxable income	$1,150
Net Unearned Income Taxed at Parents' Rate	
$1,800 − $650 − $650 =	500
Remainder taxed at Dawn's rate	$ 650
Tax Calculation	
Tax on $500 at parents' marginal tax rate ($500 × 28%)	$ 140
Tax on $650 at Dawn's rate ($650 × 15%)	98
Total tax due	$ 238

In most cases, parents whose children are subject to this special tax may calculate the tax and report it on their own return rather having the child file a separate return.

▲ FILING REQUIREMENTS

Whether an individual is required to file a return depends on the taxpayer's gross income. General **filing requirements** for individuals are that they must file a return when their gross income exceeds the sum of (1) their standard deduction amount (including the additional amount for age but not for blindness), and (2) their allowable personal (not dependency) exemptions. There are three major exceptions to this general rule:

- Individuals with net earnings from self-employment in excess of $400 must file a return, regardless of their gross income level.
- Married taxpayers filing separate returns are required to file if their gross income exceeds $2,500, the personal exemption amount.
- Dependents with unearned income greater than $650 must file a return.[35]

> ▲ **EXAMPLE 58**   Matthew, who is a single taxpayer, is 66 and legally blind. In 1995, he receives $5,000 in Social Security and $7,600 in dividends. Is he required to file a tax return for 1995?
>
> *Discussion:*   Matthew must file a 1995 return, because his $7,600 gross income (the Social Security is not taxable in this case) is greater than the $7,350 filing requirement for a single taxpayer who is 65 or older. Note that the $950 additional standard deduction for blindness is not included in the filing requirement levels. As a result, Matthew must file a return, even though he will not have taxable income ($7,600 − $3,900 − $950 − $950 − $2,500 < 0).

Of course, taxpayers with gross income less than the required filing level will want to file when they are entitled to a refund of taxes. The filing levels for various taxpayers are given in Table 8–4.

▲ SUMMARY

Calculating taxable income for an individual is complex because of several factors. First, unlike other income tax entities, individuals engage in both business and personal transactions. Congress has allowed individuals to take certain deductions for personal expenditures and has allowed for some element of convenience

▲ Table 8–4

1994 & 1995 FILING REQUIREMENTS

Filing Status	1994 Gross Income	1995 Gross Income
Single	$ 6,250	$ 6,400
Single—age 65 or older	7,200	7,350
Married, filing jointly	11,250	11,550
Married, filing jointly—one spouse 65 or older	12,000	12,300
Married, filing jointly—both 65 or older	12,750	13,050
Surviving spouse	8,800	9,050
Surviving spouse—age 65 or older	9,550	9,800
Married, filing separately	2,450	2,500
Head of household	8,050	8,250
Dependent with unearned income	600	650

through use of the standard deduction. This causes a split of an individual's deductions into those for adjusted gross income and those from adjusted gross income. In addition, Congress has chosen to limit the availability and the amount of certain deductions to dependents and high-income taxpayers. To aid you in your study, the appendix to this chapter contains a comprehensive example of the tax calculation for an individual taxpayer. You should review the example to get a feel for how an individual's tax return calculation is put together.

▲ KEY TERMS

abandoned spouse (p. 323)
accountable plan (p. 325)
acquisition debt (p. 338)
charitable organization (p. 340)
citizen or residency test (p. 320)
dependent (p. 319)
employer reimbursement plan (p. 325)
exemption deduction phase-out (p. 345)
filing requirements (p. 348)
filing status (p. 321)
gross income test (p. 319)
head of household (p. 323)
home equity debt (p. 338)

individual retirement account (IRA) (p. 330)
investment interest (p. 339)
itemized deduction phase-out (p. 344)
joint return test (p. 321)
kiddie tax (p. 347)
married, filing jointly (p. 321)
married, filing separately (p. 322)
medical expenses (p. 334)
minor child (p. 347)
miscellaneous itemized deductions (p. 342)
moving expenses (p. 331)

multiple support agreement (p. 320)
net investment income (p. 339)
net unearned income (p. 347)
nonaccountable plan (p. 326)
points (p. 338)
qualified home mortgage interest (p. 338)
relationship or member of household test (p. 320)
single (p. 322)
support test (p. 319)
surviving spouse (p. 322)
taxes (p. 337)

▲ PRIMARY TAX LAW SOURCES

[1] Sec. 151—Allows a personal exemption deduction; requires the deduction to be adjusted annually for inflation; disallows a personal exemption deduction for a dependent.

[2] Sec. 152—Allows dependency exemption deductions; defines *dependent* and specifies the tests for dependency; requires the deduction to be adjusted annually for inflation.

[3] Reg. Sec. 1.151-3—Defines *child, student,* and *educational institution* for purposes of determining dependency exemptions.

[4] Reg. Sec. 1.152-3—Explains the rules for claiming dependency exemptions under multiple support agreements.

[5] Sec. 6013—Allows a married couple to file a joint return; specifies that marital status is determined on the last day of the tax year or at date of death of spouse.

[6] Sec. 2—Defines *surviving spouse* and *head of household*; allows an abandoned spouse to file as a head of household.

[7] Sec. 7703—Defines *abandoned spouse.*

[8] Sec. 62—Defines *adjusted gross income* for individual taxpayers and specifies the deductions allowed as deductions for adjusted gross income.

[9] Reg. Sec. 1.62-2—Provides the rules for reimbursements of employee business expenses.

[10] IRS Announcement 90-7—Provides an overview of the rules for reporting employee business expense reimbursements.

[11] Sec. 162(l)—Allows a self-employed individual to deduct for adjusted gross income 25% of the medical insurance premiums paid during the year. NOTE: This provision expired on December 31, 1993. However, the last time this provision expired, it was reinstated retroactively. As this book went to press, Congress was expected to introduce legislation that would allow self-employed individuals a 25% deduction for medical insurance premiums paid in 1994.

[12] Sec. 1402—Defines *self-employment income* and provides for the tax to be paid on base amounts as specified in the Social

Security Act for each tax year; allows the reduction of self-employment income by one-half of the Social Security tax paid.

[13] Sec. 219—Allows a deduction for contributions to an individual retirement account; prescribes the maximum amounts deductible and limitations on deductions for active participants in other pension plans.

[14] Sec. 217—Allows a deduction for moving expenses and specifies the allowable expenses.

[15] Sec. 63—Defines *taxable income*; allows individual taxpayers to deduct the greater of their allowable itemized deductions or the standard deduction; specifies standard deduction amounts and requires their annual adjustment for inflation.

[16] Reg. Sec. 1.151-1—Defines *blindness* for purposes of additional standard deduction amount; provides examples of items that constitute support for purposes of the dependency exemption.

[17] Reg. Sec. 1.213-1—States that a medical dependent does not have to pass the gross income and joint return tests.

[18] Sec. 213—Allows the deduction of medical expenses as an itemized deduction for individual taxpayers; defines *medical expenses* and prescribes limitations on the amount of the deduction.

[19] Rev. Proc. 94-73—Provides the standard mileage rates for use of an automobile for medical and charitable purposes.

[20] Sec. 213—See footnote 18.

[21] Sec. 164—Specifies the allowable deductions for taxes.

[22] Reg. Sec. 1.164-2—Lists taxes that individuals cannot deduct as itemized deductions.

[23] Sec. 163—Specifies the allowable deductions for interest; disallows personal interest other than qualified home mortgage interest and investment interest.

[24] Reg. Sec. 1.163-10T—Provides the rules for determining the deduction for qualified residence interest.

[25] Sec. 461—Allows a current deduction for points paid to acquire a home mortgage.

[26] Sec. 170—Allows a deduction for contributions to qualifying charities.

[27] Reg. Sec. 1.170A-1—Provides general rules for determining amounts of charitable contributions; disallows a deduction for the contribution of time or services to a qualifying organization.

[28] Sec. 67—Defines *allowable miscellaneous itemized deductions*; provides for 2% of adjustment gross income limitation on miscellaneous itemized deductions; exempts certain miscellaneous itemized deductions from the 2% of adjusted gross income limit.

[29] Reg. Sec. 1.67-1T—Provides that any specific limitations on miscellaneous itemized deductions are to be applied before considering the 2% of adjusted gross income limitation.

[30] H.R. REP. NO. 841, 99th Cong., 2d Sess. (1986)—States that investment expenses are determined after applying the 2% of adjusted gross income limitation and that any other miscellaneous itemized deductions are applied against the 2% limit before any investment expenses are reduced.

[31] Sec. 68—Requires phase-out of itemized deductions by high-income taxpayers; specifies when deductions are phased out and requires the adjustment of the phase-out level annually for inflation.

[32] Sec. 31—Provides that amounts withheld as tax from salaries and wages are allowed as credits against that year's tax liability.

[33] Sec. 6654—Provides that all individuals must pay estimated taxes when their tax liability is expected to be greater than $500; imposes a penalty for not paying the proper amount of estimated tax.

[34] Sec. 1—Imposes a tax on the taxable income of different classes of individual taxpayers; specifies that the tax on the unearned income of a child younger than 14 (minor child) is taxed at the higher of the child's or the parents' marginal tax rate.

[35] Sec. 6012—Provides the general requirements for filing an income tax return.

1. What is the difference between a personal exemption and a dependency exemption? Are all taxpayers allowed a personal exemption?

2. What are the five tests that must be met in order to claim a dependency exemption? Briefly explain each test.

3. Which parent is entitled to claim the dependency exemption for a child when the parents are divorced? Can the other parent ever claim the dependency exemption?

4. What is a multiple support agreement? When is a multiple support agreement necessary?

5. Why is a taxpayer's filing status important?

6. What is a surviving spouse? Explain the tax benefit available to a surviving spouse.

7. Under what circumstances can a married person file as a head of household?

8. What is (are) the main difference(s) between deductions for AGI and deductions from AGI?

9. Why are deductions for adjusted gross income "better" than deductions from adjusted gross income?

10. What is an accountable employee expense reimbursement plan? What is the significance of such a plan?

11. Why are self-employed taxpayers allowed to deduct a portion of their medical insurance premiums and self-employment tax for adjusted gross income?

12. Are all taxpayers allowed a deduction for an individual retirement account contribution? Explain.

13. What general requirements must be met in order to obtain a deduction for moving expenses?

14. What expenses associated with moving are allowed as a deduction?

15. What is the standard deduction? Explain its relationship to a taxpayer's itemized deductions.

16. One general requirement for deduction is that the expense be the taxpayer's, not that of another. Is this always true? Explain.

17. Explain the limitations placed on deductions for medical expenses.

18. What is an ad valorem tax? What is the significance of an ad valorem tax?

19. Which types of interest are deductible as itemized deductions? What (if any) limitations are imposed on the deduction?

20. In what year(s) are points paid to acquire a loan deductible? Explain.

21. Why is interest paid on a loan used to purchase municipal bonds not deductible?

22. What limits are placed on deductions for charitable contributions?

23. Explain how the deduction allowed for a charitable contribution of ordinary income property is different than the deduction for donation of long-term capital gain property.

24. What limitations are placed on miscellaneous itemized deductions?

25. What is the purpose of the itemized deduction and exemption deduction phase-outs? Which itemized deductions are not subject to the phase-out?

26. Explain the operation of the itemized deduction phase-out. What stops a taxpayer from losing all itemized deductions under the phase-out?

27. What is the standard deduction amount for a dependent? Under what conditions can a dependent claim the same standard deduction as a single individual who is not a dependent?

28. Why did Congress enact the "kiddie tax"?

29. What determines who must file a tax return?

▲ PROBLEMS

30. Determine whether each of the following individuals can be claimed as a dependent in the current year. Assume that any tests not mentioned have been satisfied.
   a. Nico is 20 and a full-time college student who received a scholarship for $10,000 (tuition, books, and fees totaled $11,000). His father gave him an additional $8,000 to pay for room and board and other living expenses.
   b. Lawrence paid $6,000 of his mother's living expenses. His mother received $2,000 in Social Security benefits and $3,000 from a qualified employer retirement program, all of which was spent on her support.
   c. Megan's father had no sources of income. During the year, Megan paid all of her father's support, including the cost of his returning to his native Ireland and establishing residence there.
   d. Tawana and Ralph are both college students. They are married and had income during the year totaling $4,000. Tawana and Ralph filed a joint return to receive a refund of the taxes withheld on the $4,000. Her parents gave them an additional $9,000 to help them through college.
   e. Assume the same facts as in part d, except that Tawana and Ralph had $8,000 in income.

31. Determine whether each of the following individuals can be claimed as a dependent in the current year. Assume that any tests not mentioned have been satisfied.
   a. Marvin's father, Bert, lives with him. Bert's only income is $5,200 in Social Security. Bert gives Marvin $2,000 per year to help him pay the household bills. Marvin pays all other costs of maintaining the household. During the current year, Marvin spent $10,000 in addition to the $2,000 his father gave him for food, rent, and other household costs.
   b. Darren and Darla were divorced during the current year. Darla has custody of their 3-year-old son. Darren pays Darla $300 per month in child support. Darla pays the other $100 per month it costs to support their son.
   c. Carlos is 25 and a college student. Carlos lives with his parents, who also give him $500 per month toward his college expenses. Carlos earns the other $5,000 he needs to cover his expenses with a part-time job at a convenience store.
   d. Andrew's mother, Julia, lives in a nursing home. Julia's $6,700 in Social Security is paid to the state, which pays the entire $22,000 cost of her nursing home. Andrew gives Julia $300 per month to pay other incidental costs not covered by the state.

32. Determine the filing status in each of the following situations:
   a. Angela was single for most of the year. She married Tim on December 30.
   b. Earl was divorced during the current year. Their son lives with Earl's former spouse. Earl lives alone.
   c. Rita is married to Bob, and they have 2 children, ages 2 and 4, at home. Bob and Rita had a fight in March; Bob left and never returned. Rita has no idea where Bob might be.
   d. Joe is single. Joe provides all the support for his parents, who live in a nursing home. Joe's parents' only source of income is Social Security.
   e. Sam's wife died in February of last year. Their children are all of legal age and none lives in the household. Sam has not remarried.
   f. Would your answer to part e change if Sam had a dependent son or daughter who still lived in the home?

33. What is the filing status of each of the following taxpayers?
   a. Tom was married to JoAnne until they separated on November 15. On December 27, a formal separation agreement was filed in court.
   b. Wanda is single. She provides a household for her 22-year-old son who works as a lifeguard at the local swimming pool. Her son earned $8,700 from his job this year.

c. Randy is single. He gave his parents $10,000 to help them pay the cost of living in a retirement home in Florida. The cost of the retirement home is $15,000 per year. Randy's parents receive $6,000 per year in Social Security and $8,000 per year in taxable dividends.

d. Andrea is married to Hal. They have 2 children who live at home. Hal became despondent over his job situation and left the country in April. Andrea has not heard from Hal since he left and doesn't know where he is.

34. During the current year, Carson paid $1,500 in child support and $2,000 in alimony to his ex-wife. What is Carson's allowable deduction, and how should it be deducted on his tax return?

35. Mona works for Leonardo Corporation as a sales representative. Leonardo gives her a travel allowance of $300 per month. During the current year, she spent the following amounts on valid travel expenses:

Transportation	$1,700
Meals	800
Lodging	1,300
Entertainment	1,000

How should Mona treat the $300 per month travel allowance and the travel costs she incurred if

a. Leonardo's reimbursement plan is an accountable plan?

b. Leonardo's reimbursement plan is a nonaccountable plan?

36. Alvin is an employee of York Co. During the year, Alvin incurred the following employment-related expenses:

Travel	$3,000
Meals	2,000
Lodging	4,000
Entertainment	1,000

a. How should Alvin treat these expenses if York Co. has an accountable employee business expense reimbursement plan and Alvin is reimbursed

  1. $10,000?

  2. $8,500?

  3. $11,000?

b. How would your answer to part a change if York's reimbursement plan was nonaccountable?

c. How would your answer to part a change if Alvin is self-employed (i.e., he receives no reimbursements)?

37. Harold works for the Zanten Corporation. Ken is self-employed. Zanten pays all of Harold's medical insurance premiums, whereas Ken purchases medical insurance from his insurance agent. Explain how the payment for Ken's and Harold's medical insurance are treated for tax purposes. Does this treatment meet Adam Smith's equality criterion?

38. Evelyn is a self-employed engineer. During 1995, Evelyn's income from her engineering business was $40,000. Evelyn paid $3,200 for her medical insurance policy.

a. How should the medical insurance policy payment be reflected on Evelyn's 1995 tax return?

b. What is Evelyn's 1995 self-employment tax deduction?

39. Mae is single and earns a salary of $32,000. Mae also owns a house that she rents. During 1995, Mae receives $12,000 in rental income from the house. Her allowable expenses related to the rental property total $16,000. Assuming that Mae has no other sources of income and does not itemize her deductions, what is her 1995 taxable income?

40. Ferris and Jody are married and file a joint return. During the current year, Ferris had a salary of $32,000. Neither Ferris nor Jody is covered by an employer-sponsored pension plan. Determine the maximum IRA contribution and deduction amounts in each of the following cases:

a. Jody earns $18,000, and their adjusted gross income is $47,000.
b. Jody does not work, and their adjusted gross income is $33,000.
c. Jody earns $40,000, and their adjusted gross income is $66,000.
d. Jody earns $12,000, and their adjusted gross income is $39,000.

41. Assume the same facts as in problem 40, except that Ferris is covered by an employer-sponsored pension plan.

42. Myron graduated from college this year and landed a job with Hobo Corporation. Myron incurred the following expenses related to the move:

Meals during the move	$350
Trailer rental	800
Lodging during the move	400
House-hunting trip	
Lodging	200
Meals	100
Transportation	450
Temporary living costs	
Lodging	900
Meals	400
Incidentals	100

Myron drove his own car and pulled the trailer containing his belongings to the new location, a distance of 1,500 miles. Myron took the house-hunting trip after he secured the job. Although Myron found an apartment to rent during the trip, it was not available until 3 weeks after he was to start work, so Myron stayed in a hotel until he could move into his new apartment. Myron was required to pay a $1,000 security deposit on the new apartment. What is Myron's allowable moving expense deduction?

43. Nina graduated from college in the current year and took a job in another state. She spent $1,100 moving her household goods. Because the moving company would not be responsible for her pet boa constrictor, Nina had to pay another company $500 to deliver the snake to her new residence. In traveling to the new job location, Nina spent $300 on lodging and $200 on meals. She drove her automobile 1,800 miles to get to the new job location.

After securing the job, Nina made a trip to look for an apartment to rent. She incurred the following costs on the trip:

Airfare	$350
Meals	80
Lodging	130

She paid a real estate management company a $300 fee for finding her an apartment and a damage deposit of $200, as well as the last month's rent of $850. However, the apartment was not available until 15 days after she started her new job. She lived in a hotel during this time and paid $970 for the hotel and $250 for meals.

Upon moving into the apartment, Nina bought new furniture costing $3,300 and draperies costing $1,100. What is Nina's allowable moving expense deduction?

44. Determine the maximum deduction from AGI in the current year for each of the following taxpayers:

a. Pedro and Juanita are married. They have total itemized deductions of $3,600.
b. Avery is single and legally blind. His itemized deductions total $6,500.
c. Janet is divorced. Her 25-year-old son lives with her while attending college. Her total itemized deductions are $4,100.

d. Bruce is single. Bruce provides all the support for his parents who live in a nursing home. Bruce's parents' only source of income is Social Security. Bruce's itemized deductions total $8,000.

45. Alicia is 27 and has never been married. For 1995, her gross income totals $32,000, she has $800 in allowable for-AGI deductions and total itemized deductions of $4,700.
   a. What is Alicia's 1995 taxable income?
   b. What is Alicia's 1995 income tax?
   c. If Alicia has $4,000 withheld from her paycheck during 1995, is she entitled to a refund or does she owe additional taxes?

46. Arthur and Cora are married and have 3 dependent children. For 1995, they have a gross income of $72,000. Their allowable deductions for adjusted gross income total $3,200, and they have total allowable itemized deductions of $13,000.
   a. What is Arthur and Cora's 1995 taxable income?
   b. What is Arthur and Cora's 1995 income tax?

47. Jasper and June incurred the following medical expenses during the current year:

Medical insurance premiums	$3,500
Prescription drugs	800
Hearing aid	1,600
Root canal	950
Weight loss program *maybe*	2,400

If Jasper and June were reimbursed for $1,650 of these costs, what is their allowable medical expense deduction if
   a. Their adjusted gross income is $35,000?
   b. Their adjusted gross income is $90,000?

48. Lian was injured in an automobile accident this year. She was hospitalized for 4 weeks and missed 3 months of work after getting out of the hospital. The costs related to her accident were

Hospitalization	$22,000
Prescription drugs	2,000
Doctor's fees	8,000
Wheelchair rental	400
Visits by home nursing service	1,600

Lian's employer-provided insurance policy paid $23,000 of the costs. She also received $4,000 in disability pay from her employer while she was absent from work. By the end of the year, Lian was able to pay only $6,000 of the costs that weren't covered by her medical insurance. What is Lian's allowed itemized deduction for medical expenses if her adjusted gross income was $30,000 before considering any of this information?

49. Jim resides in Minnesota and owns some business interests in Hawaii. During 1995, he pays the following taxes:

Minnesota state income tax withheld	$3,900 *yes*
Hawaii estimated tax payments	1,300 *yes*
Utility and telephone taxes	275
Additional Minnesota tax for 1993 because of an error	120 *yes*
Interest and penalties on 1993 error	23
Sales tax paid on new automobile	760

Jim itemized his deductions on his 1994 tax return. He received a $218 refund of Minnesota taxes and paid an additional $745 in Hawaii taxes on his 1994 state income tax returns. What is Jim's allowable deduction for 1995 taxes paid?

50. Herbert buys a lot on March 1, 1995, for $13,000; he plans to build a new home on it. As part of the sales agreement, Herbert agrees to pay the entire $230 in property taxes on the property for the year. How much of the $230 can Herbert deduct? What is Herbert's basis in the lot?

51. Troy's 1993 tax return was audited. The auditor determined that Troy inadvertently understated his ending inventory in calculating his business income. The error created an additional tax liability of $5,000. The IRS charged interest on the additional tax liability of $600. Explain whether the interest on the additional tax liability is deductible.

52. Robin purchased a new home costing $80,000 in the current year. She paid $8,000 down and borrowed the remaining $72,000 by securing a mortgage on the home. She also paid $2,330 in closing costs, which included $1,440 in points to obtain the mortgage. She paid $3,888 in interest on the mortgage during the year. What is Robin's allowable itemized deduction for interest paid?

53. Buford owed $90,000 on the mortgage on his residence. Because the interest rate on the mortgage was high relative to current interest rates, Buford refinanced the mortgage at a lower rate. He paid $1,800 in points to refinance the loan for 20 years. The refinancing took place on July 1. How much of the $1,800 in points is deductible in the current year?

54. Keith bought his home several years ago for $110,000. He paid $10,000 down on the purchase and borrowed the remaining $100,000. When the home was worth $140,000 and the balance on his mortgage was $70,000, Keith borrowed $50,000 using a home equity loan. Keith used the proceeds of the loan to pay off some gambling debts. During the year, Keith paid $6,800 in interest on the original home mortgage and $3,000 in interest on the home equity loan. What is Keith's allowable itemized deduction for interest paid?

55. Astrid originally borrowed $850,000 to acquire her home. When the balance on the original mortgage was $700,000, she purchased a ski chalet by borrowing $400,000, which was secured by a mortgage on the chalet. Astrid paid $85,000 in interest on her home mortgage and $20,000 in interest on the chalet's mortgage. What is Astrid's allowable itemized deduction for interest paid?

56. Barbara had the following items of investment income during 1995:

Interest on savings account	$1,100
Cash stock dividends	1,800
Municipal bond interest	3,000
Net long-term capital gain from sale of stock	4,100

Barbara's only other source of income was her $56,000 salary. Barbara paid $11,000 in interest on a loan she used to purchase the stocks and bonds that produced the income listed. Assuming that she has no other deductions for adjusted gross income, what is Barbara's allowable deduction for investment interest paid?

57. Liang paid $16,000 in interest on debt that was used to purchase portfolio investments. He received $4,000 in dividends on stock, $2,500 in royalties, and $1,800 in interest on municipal bonds during the year. His investment-related expenses totaled $500. Liang's adjusted gross income was $80,000.

   a. Assuming that Liang had no other qualifying miscellaneous itemized deductions during the year and that none of the debt was used to acquire the municipal bonds, how much of the $16,000 in interest paid can he deduct?

   b. What would Liang's deduction be if he also had $1,200 in qualifying miscellaneous itemized deductions (employee business expenses)?

   c. Assume that in part b the qualifying expenses totaled $3,000.

58. Jana gave property worth $22,000 to her alma mater during the current year. She had purchased the property several years ago for $16,000.
  a. What is Jana's maximum deduction if the property is ordinary income property?
  b. What is Jana's maximum deduction if the property is capital gain property?
  c. How would your answer change if Jana's adjusted gross income was $30,000?

59. Lauren owns stock for which she paid $18,000 several years ago. She is considering donating the stock to the United Way. The fair market value of the stock is $38,000. Her adjusted gross income is $40,000. Lauren has $4,000-worth of other itemized deductions. Lauren expects that her adjusted gross income and itemized deductions will remain constant over the next 5 years. Assume a present value factor of 9%. Should she deduct the fair market value of the stock or elect to reduce the amount of her contribution to the adjusted basis of the property? Explain.

60. Determine the allowable charitable contribution in each of the following situations.
  a. Brett played in a charity golf tournament. The fee for the tournament was $1,000. The value of the greens fees, meals, and incidentals that Brett received was $100.
  b. Adrian purchased a statue at a church auction for $800. The fair market value of the statue was $50.
  c. James is a CPA. As a volunteer, he does the books for the local chapter of the United Way. James estimates that his normal fee for the work would be $450.

61. Constance incurs $6,000 in valid employment-related expenses during the current year. Her employer reimburses her for only $4,000 of the expenses. She also incurs $900 in other allowable miscellaneous expenses. Constance's adjusted gross income is $26,000 without considering the effect of these expenses and the reimbursement. What is Constance's allowable deduction if
  a. Her employer's reimbursement plan is an accountable plan?
  b. Her employer's reimbursement plan is a nonaccountable plan?

62. Cody is a financial analyst for Woolwood, Inc. His adjusted gross income for the current year was $65,000. Cody incurred the following out-of-pocket expenses during the current year:

Dues to financial analysts' association	$ 250
Subscriptions to professional journals	480
Parking at work	600
Entertaining underwriters	300 50%
Business suits	1,000
Tax return preparation fee	600
Legal fees paid for his divorce	2,000
Safe deposit box rental	120

What is Cody's allowable itemized deduction?

63. In his spare time, Don makes wooden boats as a hobby. In the current year, Don sells 1 boat to a friend for $400. Don estimates that it cost him $300 to make the boat and that he incurred another $200 in costs related to his boat hobby. How should Don treat the sale of the boat and the related expenses? Assume that Don's adjusted gross income is $30,000 and that he has no other qualifying miscellaneous itemized deductions.

64. Lee is a college professor with an adjusted gross income of $30,000. Lee had a lot of bad luck this year. First, a tornado blew off the roof of his house, causing $3,200 in damage. His insurance company would reimburse him only $800 for the roof damage. Later in the year, he was out at a local pub one night when his $500 car stereo was stolen. His insurance company would not pay anything for the stereo, because it was only worth $220 at the time and Lee's policy does not cover losses of less than $300. What is Lee's allowable casualty and theft loss for the year?

65. Michael owns a hair salon. During the current year, a tornado severely damaged the hair salon and destroyed his personal automobile, which was parked outside. It cost Michael $13,000 to make the necessary repairs to the hair salon. He had paid $27,000 for the automobile, which was worth $19,000 before the tornado. Michael's business insurance reimbursed him for $9,000 of the salon repair costs. His automobile insurance company paid only $15,000 for the automobile destruction. If Michael's adjusted gross income was $30,000 before considering the effects of the tornado, what is his deductible loss from the tornado?

66. Orley is a single individual with no dependents who had an adjusted gross income of $142,000 in 1995. Orley's itemized deductions totaled $16,000, which included $2,000 in deductible medical costs and $5,000 in investment interest.
  a. What is Orley's 1995 taxable income?
  b. Assume that Orley's adjusted gross income was $450,000. What is his 1995 taxable income?

67. Hal and Laura are married and have 3 dependent children. What is their total allowable exemption deduction in 1995 if
  a. Their adjusted gross income is $80,000?
  b. Their adjusted gross income is $223,000?
  c. Their adjusted gross income is $400,000?

68. Determine the taxable income of each of the following dependents in 1995:
  a. Louis is 11 and receives $850 in interest income.
  b. Jackson is 16. He earns $1,500 from his newspaper route and receives $300 in dividends on GCM stock.
  c. Loretta is 18. She earns $4,000 as a lifeguard during the summer. In addition, Loretta won a rescue contest and received a municipal bond worth $1,000. During the year, the bond paid $20 in interest.
  d. Eva is 8. Her income consists of municipal bond interest of $600, stock dividends of $1,400, and interest credited to her savings account of $350.
  e. Elaine is a college student. Her only income consists of $2,500 from her part-time job delivering pizzas. Her itemized deductions total $235.
  f. Greg is 2. Greg has certificates of deposit given to him by his grandparents that paid $1,900 in interest.

69. For each of the dependents in problem 68 calculate the income tax on their taxable income. In each case, assume that their parents' taxable income was $60,000.

70. Calculate the tax in 1994 and 1995 for each of the situations that follow. Use the tax tables where appropriate.
  a. Mark is single with no dependents and has a taxable income of $38,500.
  b. Harry and Linda are married and have a taxable income of $38,500.
  c. Apara is single. His unmarried son lives with him throughout the year. Apara pays all costs of maintaining the household. Apara's taxable income is $80,000.
  d. Randy and Raina are married. Because of marital discord they are not living together at the end of the year, although they are not legally separated or divorced. Randy's taxable income is $22,000, and Raina's taxable income is $48,000.

71. For each of the taxpayers in problem 70, calculate the tax or refund due in 1995, given the following additional information:
  a. Mark has $8,330 withheld from his salary during the year.
  b. Harry has $4,000 withheld from his salary. Linda makes estimated tax payments totaling $2,200.
  c. Apara's withholding totals $18,800. He is also entitled to a $350 tax credit.
  d. Randy makes estimated tax payments of $6,000, and Raina has $8,500 in tax withheld from her salary.

72. Determine whether each of the following taxpayers must file a return in 1995:
  a. Jamie is a dependent who has wages of $1,800.
  b. Joel is a dependent who had interest income of $900.

c. Martin is self-employed. His gross business receipts are $11,000, and business expenses are $12,000. His only other income is $1,400 in dividends from some stock he owns.

d. Valerie is 68 and unmarried. Her income consists of $4,500 in Social Security benefits and $3,700 she receives from a qualified employer-provided pension plan.

e. Raul and Yvonne are married and have 2 dependent children. Their only income is Raul's $11,000 salary.

73. Stanley and Ethel (both are 48) are married and have 2 children. Their 15-year-old daughter Denise lives at home and earns $3,000 per year working nights and weekends at a local pizza parlor. Their son Roger is 22, a college student, and works during the summer at a youth camp and during the school year as a referee for intramural sports. In 1995, Roger's total earnings are $5,500, all of which he spends on his support. Stanley pays Roger's tuition, fees, and books, a total cost of $8,000.

     Stanley is the district manager for Madison Assurance Co. Ethel is a teacher at the local junior high school. Their income from their jobs is as follows:

▲ **INTEGRATIVE PROBLEMS**

	Salary	Federal Tax Withheld	State Tax Withheld
Stanley	$80,000	$10,000	$4,800
Ethel	30,000	3,200	1,500

     Madison Assurance Co. has a cafeteria benefits plan that allows employees to select benefits of up to 10% of their annual salary or receive the cash equivalent of the allowable benefits. Stanley selected medical insurance, $50,000 in group term life insurance, and company-provided parking. The total cost to Madison of these benefits is $6,800. Stanley takes the remaining benefits to which he is entitled in cash.

     The school district in which Ethel works provides all employees with medical insurance and group term life insurance equal to 150% of the employee's annual salary. The district also has a qualified noncontributory pension plan to which the district contributes 3% of each employee's annual salary (employees are not allowed to make contributions to the plan).

     In addition to the insurance coverage provided by their employers, Stanley and Ethel purchase a separate medical insurance policy and a disability policy to cover themselves and their children. They also purchase an additional $100,000 in whole life insurance on each other. See the checkbook analysis that follows for the cost of these policies.

     Stanley's job requires him to travel to the offices in his region to consult with his managers and their clients. Madison has an accountable reimbursement plan from which Stanley receives $16,000 for the following expenses:

Transportation	$4,000
Lodging	7,000
Meals	3,000
Entertainment	6,000

     Each week, Stanley purchases a $5 lottery ticket at the convenience store next to his office. In June, Stanley finally hits it big with a $10,000 jackpot. In August, he receives a check for $7,000, which reflects $2,000 withheld for federal income taxes and $1,000 withheld for payment of state income taxes.

     Stanley continues to pay $300 in alimony each month to his former wife. He tells you that next year the payments will decline to $100 per month when his twin daughters reach age 18. By written agreement, his former spouse has given up the dependency exemption for 1 of the daughters to Stanley.

     During the year, Stanley and Ethel receive the following portfolio income:

Interest on savings account	$2,300
Cash dividends on stock	1,500
Interest on Local City bonds	4,000
Interest on Singapore city bonds	1,000

Stanley owns 10,000 shares of Logger Well Drilling common stock for which he paid $30,000. Early in 1995, Logger appears to be on the verge of a banner year. Ethel's father asks Stanley to sell him some of the stock, and Stanley agrees to sell him 2,000 shares at the current market value of $4.50 per share. Later in the year, Logger is indicted on charges of selling equipment illegally to an underdeveloped country, and the stock crashes. Stanley manages to sell his remaining shares through his broker for $2 per share before the stock totally bottoms out.

Stanley and Ethel own a duplex that they rent out during the year. Information pertaining to the rental is as follows:

Rental income	$12,000
Interest on duplex mortgage	9,000
Property taxes, maintenance, repairs	5,000
Allowable depreciation	8,000

One night, while returning from Fathers' Day at Roger's college, Stanley falls asleep at the wheel and crashes his car into a ditch. Stanley had paid $33,000 for the car, which is worth $18,000 at the time of the accident. The car is a total wreck and Stanley's insurance company reimburses him $14,000. Stanley suffers several major injuries in the accident, requiring hospitalization. He incurs $8,000 in medical expenses. His employer-provided policy reimburses him for $4,800 of the costs, and his privately purchased policy gives him $3,200 for medical costs. In addition, his employer's policy pays him $3,000 for the time he misses from work, and his private policy pays him $1,300 for lost work time.

Stanley and Ethel have always itemized their deductions. They paid their tax return preparer $400 to prepare their 1994 return. They feel it is money well spent, because they receive (in 1995) a $980 federal tax refund and a $200 state tax refund of their 1994 taxes.

An analysis of their checkbook reveals the following payments in 1995:

Automobile insurance	$ 800
Homeowners insurance	1,100
Medical insurance	1,700
Life insurance	600
Disability insurance	240
Dentist	450
Optometrist	300
Veterinarian	80
Cold pills, cough medicine, etc.	65
Health club dues	240
Chamber of Commerce contribution	1,000
Contribution to candidate for governor	500
United Way	200
License fee on automobiles (based on weight)	640

During 1995, Stanley and Ethel take out a $20,000 home equity loan that they use to pay off some personal debts and to take a vacation. Interest paid on this loan totals $1,500 during 1995. Stanley and Ethel purchased their current home by paying down $15,000 and signing a $185,000 mortgage note, secured by the home. The home is worth $280,000, and the balance on the original mortgage is $146,000. Interest paid on the home mortgage totals $19,000 during 1995. They also pay $385 in interest on their personal credit cards and $1,150 in property taxes on their home during 1995.

REQUIRED: Compute Stanley and Ethel's taxable income for 1995, the tax on this income, and the amount of any refund or additional tax due. You should provide a summary schedule of these calculations (in proper form) with a supplemental discussion of the treatment of each item given in the facts—even if an item does not affect their taxable income calculation, you should discuss why it doesn't enter into the computation. See the appendix to this chapter for an example of the presentation required.

If you are using tax forms to solve this problem, you will need the following forms and schedules: Form 1040, Schedule A, Schedule B, Schedule D, Schedule E, Form 2106, and

Form 4684. In addition, you should obtain a copy of the Form 1040 instructions to help you prepare the tax return.

74. In integrative problem 63 in Chapter 4, you were asked to calculate Geraldo and Gertrude's gross income for 1995. In this second phase, the additional information necessary for you to calculate their taxable income, income tax liability, and additional tax (or refund) due for 1995 is provided. PLEASE NOTE: The gross income items from problem 63 still apply. However, some additional items may affect the amount of gross income that Geraldo and Gertrude must report. That is, several items included in the gross income from integrative problem 63 are either not reported as gross income or need to be combined with the additional information in this problem to determine the correct treatment. Therefore, you should make the appropriate adjustments to the gross income in integrative problem 63, and begin your tax calculation under a heading of "Gross Income from Problem 63, As Adjusted."

From this point on, any items of gross income from the information in this problem should be added to determine the gross income for tax purposes. *You do not need to list all the individual gross income items from integrative problem 63 in your solution.* However, you should explain the adjustments you made to the phase 1 gross income figure as part of your discussion of the solution.

Additional Information for Geraldo and Gertrude.   Geraldo and Gertrude have the following amounts withheld from their paychecks for the payment of state income taxes, federal income taxes, and Social Security taxes during 1995.

State income taxes	$ 8,000
Federal income taxes	12,000
Social Security taxes	6,000

In addition to the amounts withheld from their salaries, they also make estimated federal tax payments of $3,500 and an additional estimated payment on their state income tax of $1,000. Geraldo feels these amounts are just about right, based on their 1994 taxes. They received a refund of $1,300 on their 1994 federal income tax return, so Geraldo has reduced his 1995 estimated federal payments from what was paid in during 1994. Conversely, they ended up owing the state an additional tax due of $500 for 1994. Therefore, Geraldo decided to pay in the $1,000 in estimated state tax payments this year so they wouldn't get caught short again.

Geraldo enjoys woodworking in his spare time. In addition to home improvement projects, Geraldo specializes in making flying wooden birds. The birds are somewhat of a novelty item, and Geraldo sells a few of them locally. He also attends a national and a regional woodworker fair every year to show off his birds. At the fairs, he gets a booth and sells his birds. During 1995, Geraldo's sales total $2,500. He estimates that it cost him $1,800 in supplies to make the birds he sold. It cost him an additional $1,500 to attend the 2 regional woodworker fairs (he can document the costs, which include $300 in meals). Geraldo considers his 1995 results about average.

Gertrude has a side job selling plastic household items. During the school year, she puts on 3 or 4 houseware parties each month to sell her products. When school is out, the number of parties typically doubles. In addition to giving the parties, she has a list of repeat customers who call her up and order products when they need them. Her business has grown so much that she was able to buy herself a new car in 1995. She uses the car for hauling products to the parties and for seeing to other business-related tasks in addition to commuting to her Local School job and running personal errands. Gertrude is a meticulous record keeper and has documentation for the following costs related to the new automobile:

Number of business related miles	6,000
Number of personal miles	8,000
Number of commuting miles	4,000
Gasoline	$1,500
Maintenance	120
Insurance	300
Excise tax on purchases	240

For purposes of this problem, assume that the allowable 1995 tax depreciation based on Gertrude's total cost of $24,000 is $3,060. She would like to take the maximum allowable deduction on the automobile.

Details of the Income and Expense from Gertrude's Houseware Business

Total sales	$22,000
Inventory—beginning of 1995	4,000
Inventory—end of 1995	6,000
Purchases of inventory	14,000
Promotional gifts	400
Office supplies	300
Annual houseware convention cost	1,600

The promotional gifts are plastic flapjack flippers with Gertrude's business card imprinted on them; she gives them to everyone who attends one of her parties. The flippers cost Gertrude $1 each.

Gertrude does not use a specific room of the house to conduct her business, nor does she have a separate business telephone line. She estimates that 20% of the use of the home phone is for her business. Monthly telephone service costs $15. She paid $200 for an advertisement in the local phone book. She also made $350-worth of business-related long-distance telephone calls. Gertrude stores her inventory in a neighbor's old garage. She pays the neighbor $25 per month for the use of the garage.

A freak rainstorm in April causes their neighbor's garage roof to leak. Inventory that had cost $600 and retailed for $1,100 is totally ruined by the flooding caused by the leaking roof. Neither the neighbor's nor Gertrude's insurance covers any of the loss. Another $900-worth of inventory that would have retailed for $1,900 is slightly discolored from the flooding. Although Gertrude probably could sell the damaged goods for $1,200, she does not want to take a chance on spoiling her reputation and gives the damaged items to the Local School cafeteria. Gertude deleted the $1,500 cost ($600 + $900) of the items damaged when she assembled the inventory-and-purchasing figures listed previously.

The annual convention cost relates to Gertrude's attending the company's annual meeting at which new products are introduced. Geraldo accompanies her on the trip. Although Gertrude attends meetings and receptions during the entire trip, Geraldo spends his days playing golf and sightseeing. He attends a few of the business receptions with Gertrude in the evening. A breakdown of the $1,600 in costs:

Airfare ($450 each)	$900
Hotel (same price single or double occupancy)	300
Meals (for both Geraldo and Gertrude)	250
Geraldo's greens fees	150

Geraldo is not reimbursed for employee business expenses that he incurs in his job at HFI. He can document that he spent $600 on meals and $800 in golfing fees related to the entertainment of HFI customers at the country club. (HFI paid his dues of $3,200.) The only other expense Geraldo incurs is the $700 cost of taking a night course in total quality management at the local college. Geraldo takes the class because he thinks it will help him understand the changes that are taking place in his work environment.

Local School does not provide Gertrude with everything she needs to do an adequate job in the classroom. During 1995, she purchases equipment and supplies for use in the classroom that cost $250.

The accident in which Gertrude is injured also totals the family station wagon. Geraldo and Gertrude paid $18,000 for the wagon 4 years ago. Their insurance company reimburses them $1,400 for the wagon, although a comparable station wagon is selling for $3,000 at a local dealer.

Other costs incurred	
Home mortgage interest	$7,000
Home equity loan interest	1,000
Points paid to refinance home mortgage	900
Closing costs to refinance	678
Credit card interest	330
Cash contribution to church	500
Purchase of Girl Scout cookies	40
Cash contribution to Humane Society	80
Church raffle tickets	30
Property taxes on home	450
Vehicle licensing fees (not including Gertrude's new car)	240
Doctors' fees	700
Dental costs	1,300
Prescription medicine and drugs	600
Vitamins, aspirin, cold pills, etc.	420
Optometrist fees	160
Eyeglasses	120
Contact lenses	400
Health club dues	480
Skinny-Quick diet drink	350
Home owner's insurance	700
Automobile insurance (not including Gertrude's new car)	550

Geraldo and Gertrude bought their home 10 years ago for $96,000. Their home is worth $140,000. In order to take advantage of low interest rates during 1995, they refinance their $85,000 mortgage balance on July 1, 1995, over a 15-year period. They pay $900 in points and $678 in other closing costs (legal fees, abstracting, etc.) to get the refinancing. In February, they obtain a $20,000 home equity loan and use the proceeds to pay off credit card debt and the balances on their automobile loans.

The vehicle licensing fees were paid on the 2 automobiles Geraldo and Gertrude use solely for personal use. It cost $20 per car for the actual licensing fee; the additional fee is based on the value of the car.

The medical costs listed are in addition to Geraldo's medical costs (which are reimbursed by HFI) and the costs Gertrude incurs in her automobile accident. Of the medical costs listed, $560 is reimbursed by insurance. Gertrude and Geraldo are on a health kick this year. They join a health club to work out on a regular basis, and both go on the Skinny-Quick diet plan to lose a few pounds.

In going through their records, they discover 2 investment-related items not listed in integrative problem 63 that they think might affect their taxes. In early January, Geraldo sold 100 shares of Perpetrator, Inc., common stock to his brother for $5,000. Geraldo purchased the stock in 1989 for $8,000.

The second investment-related item is a $20,000 loan that Geraldo made in 1991 to one of HFI's former employees. The employee needed the money to start a new business, and Geraldo felt at the time that the loan was a good investment. However, in 1994 the business began to falter, and the employee ended up filing for bankruptcy. Geraldo had held out hope that he would get some of his money back from the bankruptcy proceeding, because he had adequately documented the fact of the loan. However, in 1995 the employee is convicted of embezzlement and sentenced to 20 years in jail. Because the employee is in jail, Geraldo is convinced that he won't get any of the $20,000 loan back.

REQUIRED: Based on the information here and in integrative problem 63 in Chapter 4, calculate Geraldo and Gertrude's 1995 taxable income, the tax liability on the taxable income, and the amount of any tax or refund due. You should present the calculation in good form and provide a discussion of each item affecting their taxable income, as well as any items that are omitted. See the appendix to this chapter for an example of the presentation required.

If you are using tax forms to solve this problem, you will need the following additional forms and schedules to complete the problem: Form 2106, Form 4562, Form 4684, Schedule C, and Schedule SE. In addition, you should obtain a copy of the Form 1040 instructions to help you prepare the tax return.

▲ DISCUSSION CASE 8–1

Congress is working toward establishing a national health-care system. At the same time, the tax law permits unreimbursed medical expenses to be deducted only if they exceed 7.5% of the taxpayer's adjusted gross income. Why does Congress, apparently intent on providing an equitable national health-care plan, place a stringent limitation on the deduction of medical expenses? Who benefits the most from this limitation?

▲ DISCUSSION CASE 8–2

Chapter 8 discusses expenditures that are deductible either for adjusted gross income (e.g., alimony) or from adjusted gross income (e.g., medical expenses) and explains the advantage of having an expenditure classified as a deduction for adjusted gross income. Select an example of each type of deduction (i.e., for and from) and present an argument as to why that deduction is incorrectly classified. That is, why the expenditure that is a deduction for adjusted gross income should be reclassified as a deduction from adjusted gross income, and why the expenditure that is a deduction from adjusted gross income should be reclassified as a deduction for adjusted gross income.

▲ TAX PLANNING CASE 8–3

Janek and Maliati are married and have 2 children. In addition to their principal residence, they own a vacation home in New Hampshire. The couple usually rents the house for 180 days during the year and uses it for personal purposes 15 days. Both Janek and Maliati are professors at Warren College. They anticipate that their adjusted gross income for the year, before considering the rental property, will be $135,000. Information concerning the rental property is as follows:

Rental income	$10,000
Management fee	1,450
Interest	6,000
Taxes	3,200
Utilities	1,400
Repairs	750
Depreciation (unallocated)	6,000

Next week, both Janek and Maliati need to tell the chairs of their respective departments whether they are going to teach during summer school. Each course pays $5,000, and each would teach 1 course. Their children want the family to spend an extra week (7 days) at their summer home. Janek and Maliati expect their itemized deductions to be

Medical expenses	$2,000
Real estate taxes (principal residence)	3,500
State income taxes	1,800
Interest (principal residence)	4,800
Home equity loan	1,600
Charitable contributions	2,200
Miscellaneous deductions	3,200

Janek is concerned that the family's decisions could have a dramatic effect on their tax liability. You are a graduate accounting student who is taking one of Janek's courses. He asks you to determine the tax consequences if

a. Neither he nor Maliati teaches summer school, and the family spends an extra week in New Hampshire.
b. Both he and Maliati teach summer school, but the family does not spend an extra week in New Hampshire.
c. Both he and Maliati teach summer school, and the family spends an extra week in New Hampshire.

Specifically, Janek would like you to determine the increase or decrease in their tax liability for each scenario. He also would like you to explain the cause(s) of any changes in their tax liability for each scenario.

Tom, an executive for a large corporation, enjoys the challenge of preparing his tax return. Tom is aggressive in preparing his return and searches through all the available publications in an effort to reduce his tax liability. In all the years Tom has completed his return, he has never been audited. However, in preparing his 1994 tax return, Tom misinterpreted a complex change in the law and is being audited. Aware that he probably should have an expert represent him before the IRS, Tom has hired Josephine, a local CPA. During the audit process, Josephine finds expenses that Tom had failed to deduct. However, the IRS also disallowed some of Tom's other deductions. During a meeting, Josephine and the IRS agent agree on Tom's revised taxable income. When Josephine receives the auditor's change letter, she checks the agent's calculation and finds that the agent has miscalculated the new tax liability by $750 in Tom's favor. In fact, Tom will now receive a refund. What are Josephine's responsibilities (refer to Statements on Responsibilities in Tax Practice), if any, concerning the audited return?

▲ ETHICS DISCUSSION CASE 8–4

Appendix to Chapter 8

Comprehensive Tax Return Illustration

Pierre and Charlotte are married and have 2 children, ages 14 and 17. Pierre, 47, is employed as a salesman for Old Line Boot Co. Charlotte, 49, runs a candle shop in a local mall. She is the sole owner of the candle shop; the business is not incorporated. Details regarding Pierre's employment with Old Line:

1995 commissions earned	$55,000
Federal income taxes withheld	6,000
State income taxes withheld	4,000

Employee Benefits Received

Health and accident insurance	$1,500
Group term life insurance ($100,000)	400
Subscriptions to trade journals	300
Contribution to qualified retirement plan	2,500

Old Line's qualified retirement program matches employee contributions to the plan of 5%, up to $50,000 in current-year compensation. Pierre contributes the maximum in 1995 (and Old Line matches the contribution). In addition to the benefits listed, Old Line has a flexible benefits program into which an employee may contribute as much as $4,000 per year to pay medical expenses, dependent insurance, and child-care costs not covered by Old Line's medical policy. Pierre elects to pay $3,000 into the plan. The first $3,000 in unreimbursed medical expenses is paid from the plan.

Old Line does not reimburse employees for business expenses. Instead, Old Line gives Pierre $150 per month for travel and other employment-related expenses. Pierre is not required to account for his expenses with Old Line. Pierre incurs the following employment-related expenditures:

Lodging	$800
Meals	300
Entertainment	600

In addition to these expenses, Pierre can document that he uses his personal automobile for business a total of 12,000 miles during 1995. However, he does not keep very good records of his actual expenses. He thinks he spends in the neighborhood of $1,500 for gas, oil, and repairs on the automobile for the year. Allocable depreciation on his automobile would be $1,000.

Charlotte has gross sales of $110,000 in her candle shop business for the year. She lists the following expenses:

Rent on business property	$12,000
Supplies purchased	800
Interest on debt to finance candle inventory	4,050
Utilities	2,500
Employee salaries	28,000
Candle purchases	60,000

| Cost of special promotional candles | 450 |
| Employees' medical insurance premiums | 1,400 |

Charlotte's inventory of candles on January 1 is $40,000. By December 31, it is $65,000. The promotional candles are imprinted with the shop's logo, and Charlotte has them passed out at a university football game.

Because she is not covered by Pierre's medical policy, Charlotte purchases her own policy at a cost of $1,600. In addition, Charlotte makes a $3,000 qualified contribution to her self-employed retirement plan during 1995.

In order to stay abreast of the latest developments in candle-making, Charlotte attends the annual candlemakers exhibition in Chicago. She spends 3 days attending the convention. At night, she visits friends and relatives living in the area. Her costs of the trip were

Airfare	$350
Lodging	600
Meals	180
Car rental, gasoline, etc.	160

In addition to these costs, she takes her biggest supplier out to dinner and a basketball game one night. At dinner, Charlotte tries to convince the supplier to offer her speedier delivery and better credit terms. The dinner costs Charlotte $200. Because of the popularity of the local basketball team, Charlotte has to purchase the 2 tickets from a scalper for $100 apiece (the face value of the tickets is $50 apiece).

Charlotte makes estimated tax payments to the federal government of $3,200 and $1,900 to the state. In addition, she pays her share of Social Security taxes on the salaries of her employees, $2,100, and state unemployment compensation taxes of $280.

Pierre and Charlotte pay $9,000 in mortgage interest, $850 in property taxes, and $1,300 in insurance on their home mortgage. Pierre and Charlotte regularly attend church and estimate that they put about $10 per week into the collection plate. In addition, they give clothing for which they had paid $800 to the Salvation Army. The Salvation Army estimates the value of the clothes at $160. Pierre and Charlotte also purchase $40-worth of Girl Scout cookies and a $100 raffle ticket for a new car given away by a local charity.

They had the following medical expenses during the year:

Dependent medical insurance premiums	$1,400
Doctor's fees	800
Dental costs	1,100
Eyeglasses for the boys	450
Surgery on son's broken leg	1,800
Hospital costs for surgery	3,800
Prescription drugs	385

Of these costs, Pierre's medical insurance pays $2,000, Charlotte's insurance covers $300, and they use the $3,000 put into Pierre's flexible benefits plan to pay other costs.

Pierre was divorced several years ago. He pays $6,000 in alimony to his former spouse and $3,000 in child support during 1995.

Pierre and Charlotte also receive $420 in interest on their personal savings account and $260 in dividends on some stock they own.

What are Pierre and Charlotte's taxable income, the tax on the taxable income, and their tax or refund due for the year?

Solution.   The first step in calculating the taxable income is to determine the taxpayers' gross income. Pierre's gross income from Old Line is

Commissions received		$55,000
Travel advance—$150 × 12		1,800
Reductions in taxable salary		
Retirement plan contributions	$2,500	
Salary reduction plan	3,000	(5,500)
Taxable employee benefits		
Group term life premiums—50 × $3.48		174
Total gross income from Old Line		$51,474

The medical insurance premiums and the trade journal subscriptions paid by Old Line are excludable employee fringe benefits. The premiums on the first $50,000 of group term life insurance are excludable, but premiums on Pierre's coverage in excess of $50,000 are taxable, per the IRS table (see Table 4–1, Chapter 4). NOTE: The $51,474 in gross income calculated here is reported to Pierre by Old Line on Pierre's annual statement of wages, Form W-2. Because Old Line does not have an accountable plan, Pierre must include the travel advance in his gross income. Pierre's employee business expenses are allowed as miscellaneous itemized deductions, because the plan is nonaccountable.

Calculating Charlotte's gross income is more complex, because she is in a trade or business. As such, she is allowed to deduct all ordinary and necessary business expenses for adjusted gross income on her individual income tax return. As a matter of form, the income (loss) from a trade or business is calculated separately, and the net figure reported as gross income. In addition, because Charlotte has inventories, she must report sales and cost of goods sold using the accrual basis. It is assumed in this example that Charlotte and Pierre elect to use the hybrid method, which accounts for all other income and expenses on the cash basis.

Charlotte's Business Income		
Sales		$110,000
Cost of goods sold:		
Beginning inventory	$ 40,000	
Purchases	60,000	
Goods available for sale	$100,000	
Less: Ending inventory	65,000	
Cost of goods sold		35,000
Gross profit		$ 75,000
Business expenses:		
Rent on business property	$12,000	
Supplies	800	
Business interest	4,050	
Utilities	2,500	
Employee salaries	28,000	
Social Security taxes on salaries	2,100	
State unemployment taxes	280	
Promotional candles	450	
Employees' medical insurance	1,400	
Travel	1,350	
Total deductible expenses		52,930
Net business income		$ 22,070

Charlotte is not allowed to deduct the insurance premiums she pays on her own medical insurance, because she is not an employee. The $3,000 contribution to her retirement plan is not a trade or business expense and may be deducted only as a separate deduction for adjusted gross income. The allowable travel deduction is figured as follows:

Airfare	$ 350
Lodging	600
Meals—$180 × 50%	90
Car rental	160
Entertainment—$300 × 50%	150
Total travel deduction	$1,350

All of Charlotte's days in Chicago constituted business days, and she is allowed to deduct all her costs. The entertainment cost is deductible, because the meal was directly related to her business (a valid business discussion was held), and the basketball game was associated with the business discussion at the meal. However, the deduction for tickets is limited to the face value of the tickets ($100 in this case).

Because Charlotte is self-employed, she will have to pay the 15.3% self-employment tax on her business income. The amount of her business income subject to tax is $20,382 ($22,070 × 92.35%). The tax amounts to $3,118 ($20,382 × 15.3%) and is added to the federal income tax and paid with the income tax return. Charlotte is allowed to deduct 50% of the tax, $1,559, as a deduction for adjusted gross income. Self-employed individuals are also allowed a for-adjusted gross income deduction of 25% of the cost of their medical insurance. However, this deduction is not allowed if the individual's spouse is covered by another plan or if the individual is eligible for coverage by the spouse's plan. In this case, Charlotte must treat her medical insurance as an itemized deduction.

In addition to the self-employment tax deduction and retirement plan contribution deduction, Pierre and Charlotte are allowed a deduction for adjusted gross income for the $6,000 in alimony paid. The child support payment is nondeductible. This leaves them with an adjusted gross income of $63,665: gross income of $74,224 ($51,474 + $22,070 + $420 + $260) and deductions for adjusted gross income of $10,559 ($6,000 + $1,559 + $3,000).

Pierre and Charlotte are allowed deductions from adjusted gross income for medical expenses, home mortgage interest, taxes, charitable contributions, and for Pierre's employee business expenses (miscellaneous itemized deductions). All the medical costs are allowable medical expenses, a total of $11,335. This is reduced by the $5,300 in reimbursements and 7.5% of adjusted gross income, for an actual deduction of $1,260.

Medical insurance premiums

Dependents	$ 1,400
Charlotte	1,600
Doctors	800
Dental	1,100
Eyeglasses	450
Surgery	1,800
Hospital	3,800
Prescription drugs	385
Total allowable medical	$11,335
Less: Reimbursements	
Pierre's insurance	(2,000)
Salary reduction plan	(3,000)
Charlotte's insurance	(300)
Unreimbursed medical expenses	$ 6,035
Less: $63,665 × 7.5%	4,775
Deductible medical expenses	$ 1,260

The home mortgage interest of $9,000 is deductible, as is the $850 in property taxes paid on their home. The insurance on the home is a personal living expense and therefore not deductible. They are also entitled to a deduction of $5,900 ($4,000 + $1,900) for state income taxes paid. Their charitable contribution deduction is $680—$10 per week for 52 weeks of cash contributions to their church, a total of $520, and $160 for the clothing contribution (ordinary income property is valued at the lower of fair market value or adjusted basis). The Girl Scout cookies and the raffle ticket are not deductible charitable contributions.

Because Old Line's employee reimbursement plan is nonaccountable, Pierre must deduct his employee business expenses as miscellaneous itemized deductions. His total allowable deductions total $4,850, which is reduced by 2% of adjusted gross income for an allowable deduction of $3,577. In taking this deduction, Pierre is subject to the 50% limitation on meals and entertainment. In addition, because he has not kept adequate records of his automobile expenses, he must use the standard mileage method (30 cents per mile).

Lodging	$ 800
Meals—$300 × 50%	150
Entertainment—$600 × 50%	300
Automobile costs—12,000 × 0.30	3,600
Total	$4,850
Less: $63,665 × 2%	(1,273)
Deductible expenses	$3,577

Pierre and Charlotte's itemized deductions total $21,267, and they are entitled to 4 exemption deductions, a total of $10,000 ($2,500 × 4). This gives them a taxable income of $32,398 ($63,665 − $21,267 − $10,000). The tax on $32,398 for a married couple, filing jointly, in 1995 is $4,860 ($32,398 × 15%). Charlotte's self-employment tax of $3,118 is added to the $4,860, for a net tax of $7,978. Pierre and Charlotte had $9,200 ($6,000 + $3,200) in tax withheld and paid, for a refund due of $1,222 ($7,978 − $9,200). Pierre and Charlotte's income tax calculation is shown here:

Pierre and Charlotte, 1995 Income Tax Calculation

Gross income

Pierre's salary		$51,474	
Charlotte's business income		22,070	
Interest income		420	
Dividend income		260	$74,224

Deductions for adjusted gross income

Alimony paid		$ 6,000	
Charlotte's self-employment tax		1,559	
Charlotte's retirement plan contribution		3,000	10,559

Adjusted gross income $63,665

Deductions from adjusted gross income

Medical expenses	$11,335		
Less: Reimbursements	(5,300)		
Unreimbursed medical	$6,035		
Less: $63,665 × 7.5%	(4,775)	$1,260	
Home mortgage interest		9,000	
Taxes			
Property taxes	$ 850		
State income taxes			
Pierre	4,000		
Charlotte	1,900	6,750	
Charitable contributions			
Cash payments	$ 520		
Clothing donated	160	680	
Miscellaneous itemized deductions			
Employee business expenses	$ 4,850		
Less: $63,665 × 2%	(1,273)	3,577	(21,267)
Personal and dependency exemptions ($2,500 × 4)			(10,000)

Taxable income $32,398

Calculation of tax due/refund

Tax on $32,398 × 15%	$ 4,860
Self-employment tax—$20,382 × 15.3%	3,118
Net tax	$ 7,978
Amounts withheld and paid in—$6,000 + $3,200	(9,200)
Refund of taxes withheld and paid in	$ 1,222

Other Tax Entities

▲ CHAPTER LEARNING OBJECTIVES

■ Highlight the tax and nontax advantages of a corporation.

■ Elaborate on the special rules for corporations, such as the dividends received deduction, passive activity losses, capital loss limitations, and charitable contributions limitations.

■ Discuss the treatment of distributions to shareholders.

■ Elaborate on the tax definitions of *trust* and *estate*.

■ Explain the income taxation of fiduciaries.

■ Highlight the tax and nontax advantages of a conduit entity.

■ Explain the calculation of basis in a partnership and an S corporation.

■ Discuss the legal characteristics of a partnership.

■ Elaborate on the treatment of distributions made by the partnership.

■ Discuss the requirements necessary to obtain S corporation status.

■ Discuss income-splitting opportunities using multiple entities.

▲ CONCEPT REVIEW ▲

Accounting method A taxpayer must adopt an accounting method that clearly reflects income.

Annual accounting period All entities must report the results of their operations on an annual basis (the tax year). Each tax year stands on its own, apart from other tax years.

Basis This is the amount of unrecovered investment in an asset. As amounts are expended and/or recovered relative to an asset over time, the basis is adjusted in consideration of such changes. The **adjusted basis** of an asset is the original basis, plus or minus the changes in the amount of unrecovered investment.

Business purpose To be deductible, an expenditure or a loss must have a business or other economic purpose that exceeds any tax avoidance motive. The primary motive for the transaction must be to make a profit.

Capital recovery No income is realized until the taxpayer receives more than the amount invested to produce the income. The amount invested in an asset represents the maximum amount recoverable.

Conduit entity An entity for which the tax attributes flow through to its owners for tax purposes.

Entity All items of income, deductions, and so on are traced to the tax unit responsible for the item.

Legislative grace Any tax relief provided is the result of a specific act of Congress that must be strictly applied and interpreted. All income received is taxable unless a specific provision can be found in the tax law that excludes the income from taxation. Deductions must be approached with the philosophy that nothing is deductible unless a provision in the tax law allows the deduction.

Realization No income (or loss) is recognized until it has been realized. A realization involves a change in the form and/or the substance of a taxpayer's property rights that results from an arm's-length transaction.

Related party Family members and corporations that are owned by family members are considered related parties, as are certain other relationships between entities in which the power to control the substance of a transaction is evidenced through majority ownership.

Substance-over-form doctrine Transactions are to be taxed according to their true intention rather than some form that may have been contrived.

▲ INTRODUCTION

Although individuals are the biggest group of taxpaying entities (discussed in Chapter 8) and generally the most commonly referred to in an entry-level tax course, many different legal, natural, economic, social, and cultural entities exist. Not all entities are taxpayers. Because of legislative grace, only three types of entities are taxable. Individuals, corporations, and fiduciaries (trusts and estates) are taxed on their income. All other entities are either exempt or are considered conduit entities. Whether an entity is taxable, tax exempt, or a conduit can depend on practical considerations or the theoretical foundations of the entities. For example, a university is an entity comprised of students, faculty, and staff personnel. It would be practically impossible for a taxing agency to assess or collect tax on all types of income earned only within the boundaries and population of the university (e.g., old tax exams traded for a history term paper). Also, that type of taxation would constitute a form of double taxation if the U.S. government also taxed the individual citizens of the university on their income.

One example of a tax conduit entity is the partnership. The partnership form of business theoretically was created primarily as an aggregation of owners, not as a separate entity. The income of the entity flows through to the individual owners in relation to their ownership shares.[1] This conduit entity pays no income tax.[2] The owners (partners) report the income on their personal tax returns. Other conduit entities are S corporations, limited liability entities, and sole proprietorships. (As discussed in Chapter 2, sole proprietorships are not pure conduits.)

This chapter presents a discussion of the role of taxable (corporations and fiduciaries) and conduit entities (partnerships and S corporations) within the U.S. income tax system and describes the calculation of the tax bases for the various taxable entities. It also discusses components of the tax base and calculations that are unique to various entities. Finally, it presents planning opportunities and other uses of various entities.

▲ CORPORATIONS

A **corporation** is an artificial entity created under the auspices of state law. As a separate legal entity, a corporation can enter into contracts in its name, own property, be sued, and must pay income tax based on its taxable income.

Attaining corporate status is fairly simple. Articles of incorporation are drafted and filed with the appropriate state agency (e.g., the Division of Corporations and Commercial Code of the state of Utah). Then the state grants a charter, and the corporation issues stock to shareholders. Once the corporation is formed and operating, it must hold stockholder meetings and record the minutes. Also, it must maintain stock transfer records and file annual reports with the appropriate state agency. It must follow a myriad of formal rules. All these requirements are costly, both in terms of time and actual money paid. For example, legal fees, charter and franchise fees, underwriter fees, and other organizational costs can be extensive.

Adhering to all the rules required by the state of incorporation provides the entity with a separate legal identity that has the nontax attributes of limited liability, unlimited life, and free transferability of ownership. These nontax factors generally are the impetus for operating a business in the corporate form.

When individuals are trying to choose the type of entity appropriate for their businesses, the single characteristic that is generally most important is limited liability. That is, an owner's liability extends only to the amount invested in the entity. Business creditors may not look beyond the assets of the entity to satisfy debts. Accordingly, owners with extensive assets in addition to their business investment generally choose the corporate entity form.

The limited liability attribute can be misleading for small business owners. That is, most shareholders of closely held corporations are required to personally guarantee loans to the corporation. Bankers and other creditors want assurance that the corporate debts are secured. Therefore, shareholders of closely held corporations often have only partial limited liability.

The need to raise relatively large sums of money also is a factor in choosing a corporate form. The characteristics of free transferability of ownership, continuity of life, limited liability, and centralized management are suitable for raising large amounts of money from many sources. For example, **free transferability of ownership** means that a corporate shareholder may sell or buy shares at any time without restriction. This characteristic led to the creation of major stock exchanges such as the American Stock Exchange and the New York Stock Exchange. **Continuity of life** and **centralized management** ensure that the business will continue to exist, regardless of which shareholders trade their stock and/or which managers come and go. **Limited liability** means that investors are not risking more of their personal assets than the amount they paid for the stock.

Corporate entities must pay tax on their taxable income.[3] Therefore, some entities that resemble corporations may try to avoid corporate status solely to avoid corporate taxation. Attempting to avoid corporate status for tax purposes raises a problem with the IRS.[4] The service may characterize an unincorporated entity as a corporation for tax purposes because of the actual corporate attributes of the entity. That is, the IRS may invoke the doctrine of substance over form, disregard the unincorporated nature of the entity, and assess corporate income tax.[5] Conversely, the IRS could ignore the form of an incorporated entity if it does not meet the actual attributes of a corporation.[6] Then the income becomes taxable directly to the shareholders as a conduit, because the entity is noncorporate.

▲ **EXAMPLE 1**   Allen and Brenda form Allbre Corporation under the laws of the state of Alaska. The corporation is used merely to hold most of Allen's and Brenda's personal assets, which they legally transferred to the corporation. The shareholders have no business purpose for the corporation. It was created to protect their personal assets from creditors of other risky, exploratory activities. Will Allbre Corporation hold up to IRS scrutiny as a corporation?

Discussion: For tax purposes, the entity will probably not be considered separate from the owners. Allbre has no business objective. For tax purposes, a corporation must have a reason to carry on a business and, accordingly, report the gains therefrom.[7]

In addition to having a business purpose, a corporation must, under tax law, have associates (i.e., owners), limited liability, continuity of life, centralized management, and free transferability of interests.[8] An unincorporated entity that has no more than two of four characteristics (associates and business purpose do not count in this assessment) will not be classified as a corporation for tax purposes.[9] (Associates and business purpose are considered common to both corporate and noncorporate business organizations).

▲ **EXAMPLE 2**   Colin and Dora are partners in the Coldo Partnership. Their partnership agreement provides that the partnership terminates upon the withdrawal of either partner, that a partner may not freely transfer his or her ownership interest in the partnership without the consent of the other partner, that both partners may participate in management activities, and that both partners are jointly and individually liable for the partnership debts. Could the IRS assert that the Coldo Partnership is a corporation for tax purposes?

Discussion: None of the determining corporate characteristics is present. Although the partnership has associates and a business purpose, these are not determinative. A majority (at least 3 of 4) of the other characteristics would cause a problem for Colin and Dora. In this case, Coldo does not have limited liability, continuity of life, centralized management, or free transferability of interest.

Income Tax Considerations

Although nontax factors generally outweigh tax considerations when choosing a business entity, tax issues do need to be addressed. For example, deciding whether a business should be a sole proprietorship or a corporation often begins with a comparison of the tax rates for these two entities.

Tax Rate Differentials.   Sole proprietorships operate as conduits that tax the individual owner on the income of the business. Therefore, tax rate tables for individuals are compared to corporate tax rates. Individuals are subject to four tax rate schedules.[10] Each schedule is for a different individual taxpaying entity and is based on filing status (i.e., married people who file a joint return or surviving spouses, heads of households, single people, and married people who file separate returns). The schedules for all taxable entities appear in Appendix A. Each individual schedule has a five-step progression for taxing taxable income.

The initial rate is 15 percent, followed by a second step rate of 28 percent; the third step rate is 31 percent, followed by a 36 percent rate; the top rate for all remaining taxable income is 39.6 percent. The amounts of taxable income at which the tax rates change from 15 percent to 28 percent and from 28 percent to 31 percent are different for each of the four individual tax rate schedules.

The **corporate tax rate** schedule for corporate taxpayers appears in Table 9–1. (Because corporations do not marry, there is no need for different rate schedules based on filing status. Also, the corporate income tax rate schedule is not subject to inflation indexing as individual taxpayer rate schedules are.) The corporate schedule includes four progressive rates:

- The rate is 15 percent for the first $50,000 of taxable income.
- The rate is 25 percent for the next $25,000 of taxable income.
- The rate is 34 percent for taxable income up to $10,000,000.
- The rate for all additional taxable income is 35 percent.

However, Congress felt that the benefits of the lower (15 percent and 25 percent) brackets should be available only to corporations with low amounts of income. Accordingly, a 5 percent surtax is levied on corporate taxpayers with income greater than $100,000 and less than $335,000. Therefore, a fifth marginal tax rate of 39 percent exists for income between $100,000 and $335,000. The effect of this surtax is to tax corporations with incomes greater than $335,000 and less than $10,000,000 at a flat rate of 34 percent. The Omnibus Budget Reconciliation Act of 1993 added a 35 percent rate for taxable income greater than $10,000,000. As with the 15 and 25 percent rates, the benefit of the 34 percent rate is phased out with a 3 percent surtax on taxable income in excess of $15,000,000. This adds a sixth marginal tax rate of 38 percent for income between $15,000,000 and $18,333,333. The effect is to tax corporations with incomes greater than $18,333,333 at a flat rate of 35 percent.

The top 1995 individual income tax rate of 39.6 percent allows business owners to use a corporation to shelter income taxes when taxable income exceeds $256,500. Also, as Figure 9–1 shows, a corporation is taxed at a lower rate than are married individuals filing jointly for taxable incomes between $39,000 and $75,000. Therefore, under the right circumstances, business owners can lower their income tax liabilities by incorporating. However, if the corporation distributes dividends to the individual owner-shareholder, the individual incurs additional income taxes. This situation is a classic case of double taxation, which may mitigate the tax advantage of incorporating. Double taxation occurs when dividends of a corporation (which are paid out of earnings that have previously been taxed) are taxed again to the shareholders receiving the dividends.

▲ Table 9–1

CORPORATE INCOME TAX RATE SCHEDULE

Taxable Income	Tax Rate
Not over $50,000	15%
Over $50,000 but not over $75,000	25%
Over $75,000 but not over $100,000	34%
Over $100,000 but not over $335,000	39%
Over $335,000 but not over $10,000,000	34%
Over $10,000,000 but not over $15,000,000	35%
Over $15,000,000 but not over $18,333,333	38%
Over $18,333,333	35%

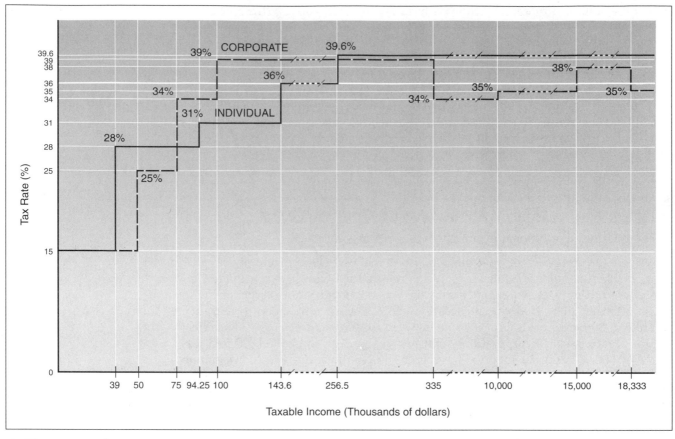

▲ Figure 9–1

COMPARISON OF TAX
RATES (1995), CORPORATE
VERSUS INDIVIDUAL
(MARRIED)

▲ EXAMPLE 3   Ellen, a married individual, owns and operates a convenience store as a sole proprietorship. The net income from the convenience store consistently has been $50,000 a year. What would be the difference in tax dollars if the store is operated as a corporation rather than a sole proprietorship?

Discussion: Corporate taxes would be $7,500 ($50,000 × 15%). Because Ellen is married, her filing status is married, filing jointly, giving her a tax bill of $8,930 [$5,850 + ($12,000 × 28%)] in 1995, if she operates the store as a proprietorship. Accordingly, she saves $1,430 ($8,930 − $7,500) in taxes by incorporating. (This result assumes that after-tax corporate earnings are not distributed to the stockholder.)

▲ EXAMPLE 4   Assume the same facts as in example 3, except that the corporate entity distributes a $20,000 cash dividend to Ellen. Now, what would be the difference in tax dollars if the store is operated as a corporation rather than a sole proprietorship?

Discussion: The corporate tax remains $7,500 (dividends are not deductions that reduce taxable income). However, Ellen has additional taxable income of $20,000 from the dividend she received. Her tax liability increases by $5,600 ($20,000 × 28%). Therefore, the total tax liability for Ellen and her corporation is $13,100 ($7,500 + $5,600). Because of the dividend, she owes $4,170 ($13,100 − $8,930) more in income tax than she would as a sole proprietor. NOTE: Instead of paying the $20,000 to Ellen as a dividend, her corporation could pay her the $20,000 as salary. Thus, the corporation's taxable income is reduced by $20,000, which saves corporate income taxes of $3,000 ($20,000 × 15%). This tax saving does not fully offset the $5,600 in additional income taxes owed by Ellen upon receipt of the $20,000 salary.

▲ **EXAMPLE 5**   Assume the same facts as in example 3, except the convenience store nets $200,000 annually. What would be the difference in tax dollars if the store is operated as a corporation rather than a sole proprietorship?

Discussion: Corporate taxes are $61,250 [($50,000 × 15%) + ($25,000 × 25%) + ($25,000 × 34%) + ($100,000 × 39%)]. The tax on $200,000 for a married couple filing jointly in 1995 is $56,923 [$36,618.50 + (36% × $56,400)], which is what Ellen would owe in tax from her business if she operated it as a proprietorship. Accordingly, she saves $4,327 ($61,250 − $56,923) by remaining with the sole proprietorship. This result assumes no dividends are distributed by the corporation to the shareholder. NOTE: The results of examples 3 and 5 are different because the store is making significantly different amounts of money—the marginal tax rate for corporations (34% plus the 5% surtax) is higher than the marginal tax rate for individuals (36%) at a $200,000 taxable income level. See Figure 9–1. Also, although the lowest marginal tax rate is the same for both entities (15%), the corporate tax rate schedule changes brackets at a higher amount of taxable income than does the tax rate schedule for individuals—$50,000 for corporations versus $39,000 for married individuals filing jointly.

Personal Service Corporations.   This type of corporation is denied the benefit of the graduated corporate tax rates.

Personal service corporations are regular corporations in which

- The performance of personal services is the principal activity.
- The services are performed by owner-employees.
- The owner-employees together own more than 10 percent of the stock.[11]

Taxable income of a **personal service corporation (PSC)** is subject to a flat rate of 35 percent. The flat tax rate encourages owner-employees of PSCs to take corporate earnings out of the corporation as salary. Taxable incomes of individuals up to $143,600 are taxed at rates lower than 35 percent.

▲ **EXAMPLE 6**   A chiropractic clinic is formed as a corporation by four chiropractors who own all the stock in the corporation. During the current year, the clinic's gross profit before the chiropractors are paid is $500,000. They agree each will take a salary of $120,000. What are the tax effects to the corporation and the chiropractors?

Discussion: The clinic's taxable income becomes $20,000 ($500,000 − $480,000). The tax liability for the personal service corporation is $7,000 (35% × $20,000) because of the 35% flat tax rate. However, the chiropractors will not incur a marginal rate higher than 31% of their salaries. In fact, the marginal rate could be lower for individual chiropractors, depending on the number of exemptions, amount of itemized deductions, and amount of deductions for adjusted gross income that they can claim.

Owner-Employee Status.   Another consideration in choosing the corporate form of doing business is the effect of a stockholder who also serves as a corporate employee. This consideration is especially important for the owner(s) of closely held corporations. These owners generally participate in the day-to-day activities of the business and have owner-employee status. Accordingly, they receive salaries and employee fringe benefits. From the corporate entity viewpoint, salaries and fringe benefits are deductible expenses that reduce taxable income.

The entity concept drives the ability of owners to be corporate employees for income tax purposes. Corporations are deemed separate entities, taxable on their own income. Accordingly, corporate owners (shareholders) can be employees of their corporation(s).

Attempts to reduce corporate taxable income through the use of the owner-employee status can have pitfalls. Chapter 5 describes some of them. The substance-over-form doctrine, dealing with the issues of lack of business purpose, unreasonableness of salary, and discriminatory fringe benefits, is the usual focus of IRS scrutiny. Closely held businesses are often objects of concern on these issues. Yet, benefits do accrue to owner-employees taking advantage of the corporate form of business.

FRINGE BENEFITS.   Recall from the discussion in Chapter 4 that employers receive significant tax advantages by paying certain expenses of their employees. Legislative grace excludes from taxation the following employee benefits:

- Employer-provided term life insurance up to $50,000 coverage
- Employer-sponsored accident and health-care plans
- Employer-provided educational assistance
- No additional cost services
- Qualified employee discounts
- Working-condition fringes
- De minimis fringes

The cost of these types of fringe benefits is deductible by a corporate employer. Thus, the benefits provide an owner-employee with a dual advantage. The value of the benefits is generally excludable from taxation for the owner-employee who receives them, and the corporation receives a tax deduction. These advantages are especially useful for the shareholder of a closely held corporation who is also an employee of the corporation.[12]

Caution must be exercised with fringe-benefit exclusions. The exclusion provisions are available only for employees. Owners (partners) of partnerships and sole proprietors are not considered employees. Therefore, they must include these types of benefits in their gross income, whereas their employees receive them tax free. Because of related party concerns about owner-employees and the legislative grace afforded fringe benefits, Congress has established a set of nondiscriminatory rules. That is, historically some employers have provided tax-free fringe benefits to only a few highly compensated employees or to corporate officers. Therefore, most types of fringe benefits must be offered at least equally to nonshareholder employees in order to retain the exclusion status for the recipients.

CHILDREN AS EMPLOYEES.   Another tax-planning strategy for reducing corporate taxable income is the valid employment of an owner-employee's children in the business. This strategy allows the corporation to deduct the wages or salaries as expenses, lowering taxable income, and it may permit the child to receive income tax free. That is, the child can earn as much as $3,900 in 1995 with no income tax liability because of the standard deduction amount for single individuals. Therefore, employing children in an incorporated business can allow a transfer of cash from parents to children free of income tax.

▲ **EXAMPLE 7**   Darianne is 12 and is paid $5 per hour by Momndad Corporation. Darianne's parents are the only stockholders of the corporation. How many hours could she work during 1995 and pay no income tax on her wages?

Discussion: Darianne could work 780 hours ($3,900 ÷ $5) during 1995 without paying income tax. Further, if Darianne contributes $2,000 to an IRA, she could earn as much as $5,900 by working 1,180 hours. This approach permits the corporation to take $2,000 more in business wage expense deduction.

Negative aspects of using children as employees include the incidence of payroll taxes and the possibility of the IRS's asserting that this related party transaction fails the test for reasonable amount of compensation.

UNREASONABLE COMPENSATION.   As discussed in Chapter 5, an expense must be reasonable in amount to be deductible. Related parties often face scrutiny of their transactions for reasonableness. Therefore, wages paid to children who are employees of their parents' corporation must be comparable to wages paid to any other employee for comparable services.

▲ **EXAMPLE 8**   Gregory Corporation has a single shareholder, Greg G. Gregory. The corporation hires Greg's 3 teenage children to answer telephone calls, take messages, prepare invoice forms, and do light cleanup. They are paid $4.25 per hour. Will the employment of the children pass IRS scrutiny?

Discussion: Because the children are actually working and the children's wages are not excessive (i.e. $4.25 per hour is the minimum wage), the IRS would find their compensation reasonable.

EMPLOYMENT TAXES.   Businesses are liable for the payment of Social Security (FICA) and federal and state unemployment compensation (FUTA and SUTA) taxes, referred to collectively as **employment taxes.** Therefore, additional business expenses are based on the 7.65-percent employer rate for FICA and the applicable rates for unemployment taxes, which may be as much as 6.2 percent. Accordingly, as much as 13.85 percent of the children's wages may be additional payroll-tax expense. If the business is organized by the parents as a sole proprietorship, they are not required to pay Social Security or other employment tax on their minor children's earnings.

DOUBLE TAXATION.   Obtaining cash distributions is generally the ultimate objective of corporate owners. In addition to salaries, cash is distributed to shareholders via dividends. Salaries are deductible expenses; dividend payments are not. Dividends are payments of already taxed earnings of corporations. When shareholders receive the dividends, the dividends are taxed again. This **double taxation** arises because the corporation is recognized as a separate taxpaying entity. It receives privileges afforded a legal person, and benefits accrue to its owners (e.g., limited liability, free transferability of interests, and continuity of life).

Special Rules for Corporations

Calculating a corporation's taxable income is basically the same as calculating taxable income for individual taxpayers. However, several notable exceptions are unique to the corporate computation. The dividends-received deduction, passive loss limitation, capital loss limitation, charitable contributions, and organizational costs are special treatment items.

Dividends-Received Deduction.   Double taxation occurs when corporate after-tax profits are distributed as dividends to shareholders. The corporation is not allowed a tax deduction for dividends paid, and the individual shareholders include the dividends in their gross income. Accordingly, if one corporation is a shareholder in another corporation, triple taxation results. To rectify this problem, legislative grace provides a deduction for dividends received by shareholders.

The **dividends-received deduction (DRD)** generally provides only partial relief of the triple taxation problem. However, the actual amount of the DRD depends on the percentage of ownership held by the recipient shareholder in the distributing corporation.[13] Generally, the DRD is 70 percent of the dividends received from U.S. taxable corporations. Table 9–2 presents the three different deduction rates and the related ownership percentages for dividend recipients.

The 70-percent and 80-percent DRDs are subject to certain limitations:

- The taxable income limitation creates a ceiling (maximum value) for the DRD. It is limited to 70 percent or 80 percent, respectively, of taxable income computed without the deductions for dividends received, any net operating loss (NOL) carryovers, and capital loss carrybacks to the current year.

- The taxable income limitation is disregarded if a loss (NOL) results after deducting the DRD using the general rules.

▲ **EXAMPLE 9**   Hershal Corporation has the following income and expense items for the current tax year:

Dividend income received from less than 20%-owned domestic corporations	$100,000
Net income from operations	30,000

What is the amount of Hershal's DRD?

Discussion: Because Hershal owns less than 20% of the distributing corporations, the 70% deduction percentage applies. Under the general rule, the DRD is $70,000 (70% × $100,000 dividends). The taxable income limitation is $91,000 (70% × $130,000 taxable income before DRD). Because $70,000 is less than $91,000, Hershal Corporation may take the full 70% DRD.

▲ **EXAMPLE 10**   Walker Corporation suffers a $20,000 net loss from operations for the current year and receives $180,000 in dividend income from corporations in which it owns 50% of the stock, resulting in a taxable income before the DRD of $160,000. What are the amounts of the DRD and the actual taxable income calculated for tax purposes?

Discussion: The DRD under the general rule is $144,000 (80% × $180,000). The taxable income limitation is $128,000 (80% × $160,000 in taxable income calculated without the DRD). Also, a loss does not result after deducting the DRD calculated under the general rule, so the taxable income limitation applies:

Net loss from operations	$ (20,000)
Dividend income	180,000
General rule DRD ($180,000 × 80%)	(144,000)
Taxable income calculated under the general rule	$ 16,000

▲ **Table 9–2**

DIVIDENDS-RECEIVED
DEDUCTION RATES

% Ownership	Deduction Percentage
< 20%	70%
20%–80%	80%
80% or more	100%

Therefore, the DRD is limited to $128,000 (80% × $160,000), and the actual amount of taxable income for the current year is $32,000 ($160,000 − $128,000). NOTE: The taxable income limitation does not apply if, after taking into account the full DRD, the corporation has an NOL for the tax year.

▲ **EXAMPLE 11**   Cunningham Corporation incurs a net loss from operations of $70,000 for the current year. Cash dividends received from 30%-owned domestic corporations are $200,000, resulting in taxable income before the DRD of $130,000. What are the amounts of the DRD and the actual taxable income calculated for the current tax year?

Discussion: The DRD under the general rule is $160,000 ($200,000 × 80%). The taxable income limitation is $104,000 ($130,000 × 80%). The taxable income limitation does not apply in this case, because an NOL would result after the DRD, computed under the general rule, is subtracted from the operating loss and the dividend income:

Net loss from operations	$(70,000)
Dividend income	200,000
General rule DRD	(160,000)
NOL calculated under the general rule	$(30,000)

Therefore, the full $160,000 DRD is allowed.

As this example demonstrates, legislative grace permits income (dividends) to cause a net operating loss by applying the dividends-received deduction. Cunningham Corporation reports an NOL of $30,000 by deducting the full $160,000 DRD. If the taxable income limitation were in effect, Cunningham would report a taxable income of $26,000 ($130,000 − $104,000).

The dividends-received deduction provides small business owners who incorporate with an opportunity to partially shield from federal taxation the dividends they obtain from their invested capital.

▲ **EXAMPLE 12**   Conchita, a single taxpayer, operates Kapow Co., a garlic-packaging business, as a sole proprietorship. During the current year, the business income was $100,000. Conchita annually invests any excess cash in common stock of Tortilla's, Inc., a U.S. corporation. Tortilla paid Kapow $20,000 in dividends as of the end of the current year. What are the tax effects of the dividend income?

Discussion: Because the business operates as a sole proprietorship, the dividends are taxed at Conchita's marginal tax rate, 31%. Therefore, Conchita pays additional income tax of $6,200 ($20,000 × 31%), leaving her with after-tax dividend income of $13,800 ($20,000 − $6,200).

If Conchita incorporates her business, she can partially shield the dividend income from taxation because of the dividends-received deduction. Assuming Kapow Co., Inc., purchases the Tortilla's, Inc., stock, 70% of the dividends received by Kapow are deductible in determining corporate taxable income. Accordingly, only $6,000 [$20,000 − ($20,000 × 70%)] in dividend income is included in Kapow's taxable income. The $6,000 in added income results in increased taxes of $2,040 ($6,000 × 34%). Therefore, the after-tax dividend income is $17,960 ($20,000 − $2,040). A tax savings of $4,160 ($17,960 − $13,800) results when the corporate form of business is used.

Passive Activity Losses.   Generally, regular corporate taxpayers are not subject to the passive loss limitations discussed in Chapter 7.[14] Exceptions to this general rule concern personal service corporations (PSCs) and closely held regular corporations that are not PSCs.

PSCs are not permitted to use passive activity losses to reduce any of their income from personal services or income generated from their portfolio investments.

▲ **EXAMPLE 13**   A dental clinic is formed as a corporation by dentists who own all the stock in the corporation. The corporation acquires an interest in an oil exploration and drilling limited partnership. The partnership incurs operating losses that are passive. Can these losses be deducted in the current year?

Discussion: Because the dental clinic is a PSC (all owner-employees are providing the dental services), the passive activity losses (from the limited partnership) are suspended and cannot be used to offset the service income or any portfolio income of the corporation.

As demonstrated in example 13, architects, doctors, dentists, accountants, lawyers, and others whose primary income comes from providing services cannot avoid the passive activity loss limitations by incorporating. However, a closely held corporation that is not a personal service corporation can use the provision that permits use of passive activity losses to offset the corporation's active income—but not its portfolio income. Congress has effectively prevented shareholders from sheltering any portfolio income by transferring passive investments to their closely held corporations. However, closely held nonservice corporations are permitted to offset active income with passive activity losses.

▲ **EXAMPLE 14**   Kyle owns 55% of Boots, Inc. This entity is a rattlesnake-breeding ranch and boot factory formed as a corporation. During the current annual accounting period, Boots, Inc., has an operating income of $20,000, dividend income from investments in stock of other corporations of $3,000, interest income from savings and loan CDs of $2,000, and a loss from an investment in a limited partnership of $24,000. How much of the passive activity loss can be used to offset other income?

Discussion: Boots, Inc., is a closely held nonservice corporation, because Kyle owns more than 50% of the stock and the principal source of income is not from services. Accordingly, any corporate passive activity losses may be used to offset active income but may not be used to offset portfolio income. Therefore, the $24,000 passive activity loss may offset the $20,000 in operating (active) income. The $4,000 of loss remaining may not be used to offset the dividend or interest income. The $4,000 loss is carried over to the subsequent year to offset any passive or active income of that year.

An individual who owns a business operated as a sole proprietorship and also has passive activity losses cannot offset the operating (active) income with passive losses. Yet, if the individual incorporates the business and transfers the business assets and the passive activity investment assets to the corporation, the passive activity loss can shield the active income.

Capital Loss Limitations.   Corporations, in contrast to individuals, are not permitted to deduct net capital losses against other income (see Chapter 7 for this discussion). Corporations can use capital losses only to offset capital gains. When a corporation incurs a net capital loss for a tax year, it is allowed to carry the net capital loss back and use it to offset any net capital gains on which it paid tax in the previous three years. Any unused capital loss from the three-year carryback period may be carried forward to offset future capital gains for five years.[15] When carried back or forward, both short-term and long-term capital losses are treated as short-term capital losses.

▲ **EXAMPLE 15**   Gonzo, Inc., has the following income, gains, and losses for 1994 through 1997:

	1994	1995	1996	1997
Ordinary income	$50,000	$45,000	$40,000	$ 20,000
Net long-term capital gain (loss)	10,000	5,000	4,000	(30,000)
Total income	$60,000	$50,000	$44,000	$(10,000)

What is the effect of the net capital loss in 1997?

Discussion: Gonzo, Inc., cannot deduct any of the net capital loss to shield its 1997 ordinary income. Therefore, its taxable income is $20,000. The net capital loss is carried back to 1994 (3 years) and reduces the $10,000 in 1994 net capital gain to zero. Because Gonzo's 1994 marginal tax rate is a flat 25% for the taxable income from $50,000 to $60,000, Gonzo can file for a refund of $2,500 ($10,000 × 25%) for 1994. The new 1994 taxable income is $50,000. The $20,000 balance of the unused net capital loss is carried back to 1995 to offset that $5,000 net capital gain. Because Gonzo's total 1995 income decreases by $5,000 ($50,000 − $45,000) and the corporate rate is a flat 15% up to $50,000, Gonzo is due a refund of $750 ($5,000 × 15%) for 1995. Then, the unused net capital loss balance is carried to 1996, reducing the $4,000 net capital gain to zero and resulting in a tax refund of $600 ($4,000 × 15%) at a marginal rate of 15% for 1996. The 3-year carryback uses $19,000 ($10,000 + $5,000 + $4,000) of 1997's $30,000 net long-term capital loss. The remaining $11,000 ($30,000 − $19,000) of loss is carried forward as a short-term loss to reduce future capital gains over the next 5 years. The total refund Gonzo receives because of the carrybacks is $3,850 ($2,500 + $750 + $600).

Charitable Contribution Limitations.

Like individuals, corporations face certain limitations on the deductibility of **charitable contributions.** Generally, the rules governing charitable contributions made by corporations are the same as those pertaining to contributions made by individuals.[16] However, there are certain differences. For example, annual corporate charitable deductions are limited to 10 percent of taxable income (computed without regard to the charitable contribution deduction, NOL carrybacks, capital loss carrybacks, or the dividends-received deduction). Current-year contributions must be deducted against the limit before any carryover contributions may be deducted.

▲ **EXAMPLE 16**   King Corporation has the following items on its books for the current tax year:

Net income from operations	$125,000
Dividends received (70% rules)	10,000
Charitable contributions made in current year	15,000
Charitable contribution carryover from the previous year	3,000

What is the maximum amount of charitable contribution deduction allowed for the current year?

Discussion: The contribution deduction is limited to $13,500. For purposes of the 10% limitation only, King Corporation's taxable income is computed as follows:

Net income from operations	$125,000
Dividend income	10,000
Taxable income without the dividends-received deduction and the charitable contribution deduction	$135,000
Charitable contribution limit	× 10%
Maximum amount of charitable deduction	$ 13,500

Taxable income for the current year is $114,500.

Net income from operations	$125,000
Dividend income	10,000
	$135,000
Less:	
Charitable contributions	(13,500)
Dividends-received deduction (70% × $10,000)	(7,000)
Corporate taxable income	$114,500

NOTE: The current year's excess charitable contribution of $1,500 ($15,000 − $13,500) is carried over to the next tax year. It is subject to that year's limitation rules. The deductions of carryovers of excess charitable contributions are limited to 5 years subsequent to the year of the contribution. Any excess contribution not deducted after 5 years is lost forever.

Another difference between charitable contributions made by individuals and contributions by corporations affects accrual basis corporations. Generally, deductions are permitted only for actual contributions given during a tax year. However, accrual basis corporations may elect to deduct a pledge made during a given year so long as the actual contribution is made by the fifteenth day of the third month after the close of the year of the pledge.

A third difference between individual contributors and corporate contributors concerns donated inventory items. Generally, the value of **donated inventory** is the adjusted basis of the inventory. However, an exception is provided for a corporate taxpayer that donates inventory for either of two types of uses:

- Items given solely for the care of the ill, needy, or infants
- Items donated to a university or qualified research organization to be used for research, experimentation, or research training in the biological or physical sciences

The amount of deduction under this exception is the inventory's fair market value, less 50 percent of the income that would be recognized if the inventory were sold at its fair market value. However, there is a ceiling, or maximum amount of deduction, which is twice the basis of the donated inventory items.[17]

▲ **EXAMPLE 17**   Tech Corporation contributes some of its scientific software to the Department of Biophysics Research at Northwest University during the current year. As of the date of the contribution, the inventory had a fair market value of $50,000. Tech's basis in the software is $20,000. What is the amount of the charitable contribution deduction?

Discussion: The transaction qualifies under the exception for certain corporate inventory. Software given to a university for research or research training is qualified inventory. The amount of Tech's contribution is $35,000 [$50,000 − (50% × $30,000)].

▲ **EXAMPLE 18**   Assume the same facts as in example 17, except that the basis of the inventory is $10,000. What is the amount of the charitable contribution in this case?

Discussion: The amount of Tech's contribution (before any limitations) is $30,000 [$50,000 − (50% × $40,000)]. However, the actual amount of the contribution deduction is limited to $20,000 (2 x $10,000), the ceiling of twice the basis of the inventory.

Organizational Costs.   Because a corporation is a legal entity formed under state law, creating it requires various expenditures. Most expenses benefit future periods of the corporation's life. Specifically, **organizational costs** provide benefits over the life of the entity. Therefore, the corporation generally cannot deduct such expenditures until the corporation liquidates. Assets with an indefinite life may not be amortized for tax purposes. However, a corporation may elect to amortize qualified organizational expenses over a period of 60 months or more.[18] If the election to amortize these expenses is not made on the tax return for the first taxable year, the costs are not deductible until the corporation ceases business and liquidates. Organizational expenditures may include the following:

- Legal services incident to organization, such as drafting the corporate charter, bylaws, minutes of organizational meetings, terms of original stock certificates
- Necessary accounting services
- Expenses of temporary directors and of organizational meetings of directors or shareholders
- Fees paid to the state of incorporation[19]

Expenses that are not considered organizational expenditures include those incurred for the issue, or sales, of shares of corporate stock (e.g., commissions, printing costs). These costs are considered selling expenses and, accordingly, reduce stockholders' equity.

▲ **EXAMPLE 19**   NewCor, Inc., a calendar-year corporation, was formed during the current year and began business operations on October 1. NewCor, Inc., paid $4,200 to attorneys, accountants, and state regulatory agencies to organize the corporation. Can NewCor deduct any of the $4,200?

Discussion: If NewCor, Inc., files an election to amortize its organizational costs over 60 months, it may deduct $210 during the current year:

$$\$4,200 \div 60 \text{ months} = \$70 \text{ per month}$$
$$\$70 \times 3 \text{ months} = \$210$$

Calculation of Taxable Income

A corporation's taxable income calculation is similar to the computation of taxable income for an individual taxpayer. However, there are several important differences. Some differences involve the special items discussed earlier (the dividends-received deduction, the passive loss treatment, the capital loss limitation, the charitable contribution limitations, and organizational cost deductions). Other differences involve personal consumption-type expenses and exemptions that are allowed only to individuals. Corporations may not deduct personal use expenditures, nor is there a corporate standard deduction. Also, corporations are not permitted personal and dependency exemption deductions. Accordingly, there is no such thing as adjusted gross income for corporate taxpayers. The tax formula for corporations essentially involves a computation that is simpler than that for an individual. See Exhibit 9–1 for the formula for corporate taxpayers and Table 9–1 for corporate tax rates.

▲ **EXAMPLE 20**   Elway Corporation had the following items of income for its calendar year 1995:

Operating income	$250,000
Dividend income (5%-owned corporations)	20,000
Long-term capital gains	8,000
Long-term capital losses	(6,000)
Short-term capital gains	3,000
Capital loss carryover from 1994	(9,000)
Charitable cash contributions	50,000

What is the amount of the corporation's 1995 taxable income?

Discussion: The taxable income is $229,000. Netting the current year's capital gains and capital losses with the 1994 carryover results in a net short-term capital loss of $4,000 ($8,000 − $6,000 + $3,000 − $9,000). Because corporations can use capital losses only to reduce capital gains, Elway derives no benefit from the net capital loss in 1995. The net capital loss can be carried forward to offset future capital gains. The charitable contributions are subject to the taxable income limitation [$50,000 > (10% × $270,000 = $27,000)].

Operating income		$250,000
Dividend income		20,000
Gross income		$270,000
Less: Special deductions		
Dividends received		
(70% × $20,000)	$14,000	
Charitable contributions		
(10% × $270,000)	27,000	$ 41,000
Taxable income		$229,000

NOTE: The $23,000 ($50,000 − $27,000) excess charitable contribution may be carried over to 1996.

Accounting Periods and Methods

A regular corporation generally has the same choices for its annual accounting period as individuals—calendar years or fiscal years. Compared to other entity forms (partnerships, S corporations), the selection of an annual accounting period is not restricted.[20] A new corporation may select its annual accounting period without prior approval of the IRS.

▲ **Exhibit 9–1**

CORPORATE INCOME TAX FORMULA

Gross income (all income less exclusions)		$ XXX
Less: Trade or business expenses		(XXX)
Less: Special deductions		
Dividends received	$XXX	
Passive losses	XXX	
Charitable contributions	XXX	
Organizational costs	XXX	(XXX)
Taxable income		$ XXX

▲ **EXAMPLE 21**   GnuCor, Inc., was incorporated during 1995. The corporate board of directors selected a fiscal year end of January 31. Is this action in compliance with the annual accounting period concept?

Discussion: Because GnuCor, Inc., is newly formed, no prior IRS approval is necessary. Therefore, the fiscal year will be recognized. Also, the corporation will have a different tax period than its individual shareholders. NOTE: If GnuCor, Inc., decides to change its fiscal year, IRS approval is necessary.

The selection of an accounting method is more restrictive for corporations than individuals. Regular corporations are generally denied the use of the cash method for tax purposes (unless the entity's average annual gross receipts are $5 million or less). Personal service corporations and S corporations may choose either the cash or accrual method.[21] Also, as discussed in Chapter 3, both individual and corporate taxpayers that have inventories must use the accrual method to account for sales and costs of goods sold inventories.

Distributions to Shareholders

Cash or other property distributed to a shareholder is generally taxable to the shareholder.[22] Also, the distributing corporation may not deduct the amount of dividends distributed for tax purposes (called **corporate distributions**). These rules originate from the tax definition of a **dividend**: a distribution by a corporation out of either its current or accumulated earnings and profits. **Earnings and profits (E&P)** generally represent undistributed, previously taxed corporate profits. Current earnings and profits are considered to be distributed first, followed by accumulated earnings and profits, if necessary.[23]

▲ **EXAMPLE 22**   Disco Corporation distributes a total of $100,000 to its shareholders during 1995. Accumulated earnings and profits are a deficit of $350,000 as of January 1, 1995. Current earnings and profits for 1995 are $300,000. How is the $100,000 distribution treated by the shareholder recipients?

Discussion: The amount of current earnings and profits is sufficient to classify the $100,000 as dividend income to the shareholders. A year-end deficit in accumulated earnings and profits of Disco Corporation will not change the outcome, because dividends are assumed to be paid out of the current year's E&P first.

If a corporate distribution exceeds both the current and accumulated earnings and profits, the capital recovery concept dictates that the distribution is tax free to shareholders. Therefore, the basis in the stock held by shareholders is reduced by the amount of the tax-free return of capital. If a shareholder receives a distribution in excess of the basis of the stock (excess capital recovery), the shareholder recognizes a capital gain.

▲ **EXAMPLE 23**   ABC Corporation distributes $200,000 in cash ($2 per share) when its current and cumulative earnings and profits are $50,000. What is the effect of the distribution on Jerry, who owns 500 shares of ABC stock for which she paid $10,000?

Discussion: The first 25% ($50,000 ÷ $200,000) of the distribution is a taxable dividend for Jerry of $250 [25% × ($2 × 500 shares)]. The remainder of Jerry's $1,000 distribution is deemed a recovery of capital to the extent of her basis in the shares of stock. Because Jerry's basis is $10,000, the remaining $750 of the dividend ($1,000 − $250) reduces the basis of her stock to $9,250 ($10,000 − $750). NOTE: If Jerry's basis had been less than $750, the distribution in excess of the basis causes recognition of a capital gain. The stock's basis then becomes zero.

The term *earnings and profits* is not technically defined in the tax law. Yet, it is designed to be a measure of a corporation's economic ability to pay dividends without impairing capital. Earnings and profits are conceptually analogous to the financial accounting term *retained earnings*, although several differences exist. Even without a technical definition, it is possible to determine earnings and profits by examining various transactions noted in tax law that affect them.[24] A detailed discussion of earnings and profits and their related transactions is beyond the scope of this text.

Multiple Corporations

The choice of the corporate form for doing business can offer many benefits. One benefit that has been effectively eliminated—because it was abused—is the use of multiple corporations to split income. That is, under prior law, tax planners made use of the entity concept that recognizes the corporate taxpayer as a single tax-paying unit. By carefully planning the income of each corporation (eg., keeping each corporation's income at or below $50,000), all income of the taxpayer was taxed at the lowest marginal rate. Because lawmakers deemed that the use of multiple corporations lacked sound business purpose (tax saving was the dominant objective), corporate members of a controlled group (discussed later) must share the tax benefits of lower tax rates.

> ▲ **EXAMPLE 24**   Emanuel is the sole shareholder of a corporate business that earns $100,000 in taxable income annually. Therefore, the corporate tax liability is $22,250 [(15% × $50,000) + (25% × $25,000) + (34% × $25,000)]. Emanuel decided he could reduce his total corporate tax liability by splitting his business operations into 2 separate corporate entities reporting $50,000 in taxable income each. Therefore, the total tax liability of 2 corporations would be $15,000 ($50,000 × 15% × 2). This plan apparently saves $7,250. Will the plan pass IRS scrutiny?
>
> *Discussion:* No. Emanuel's 2 corporations are members of a controlled group. Accordingly, each rate bracket must be shared by the 2 corporations. That is, the income of the 2 corporations is combined for purposes of computing the tax liability. The total tax liability becomes $22,250; the amount of tax is the same as if only 1 corporation had reported all the income.

Controlled Groups.   A **controlled group** is a group of two or more corporations that are owned directly or indirectly by the same shareholder(s).[25] The group of corporations may include a parent-subsidiary relationship, a brother-sister relationship, or a combination of these two types. If a parent or subsidiary group owns 80 percent or more of the stock of another corporation, the other corporation is included in the **parent-subsidiary relationship** (controlled group).

> ▲ **EXAMPLE 25**   Elvira Corporation owns 80% of Keith Corporation's stock and 45% of Mark Corporation's stock. Keith Corporation owns 35% of Mark Corporation's stock. Does a controlled group exist?
>
> *Discussion:* Yes. Elvira, Keith, and Mark are members of the same parent-subsidiary controlled group. Elvira directly owns 80% of Keith Corporation's stock. Therefore, Elvira is the group's parent corporation. Also, Mark's stock is controlled by the 80% ownership group of Elvira (45%) and Keith corporations (35%). See Figure 9–2.

Another type of controlled group is a group of two or more corporations defined by two tests. Passing both tests, not just one, creates a **brother-sister re-**

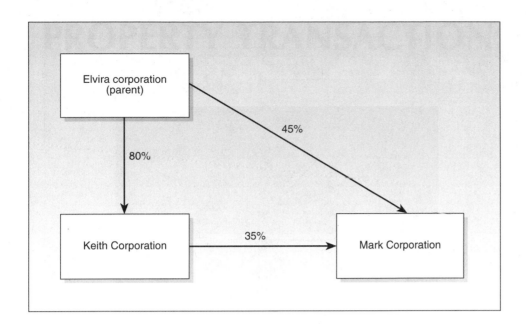

▲ **Figure 9–2**

PARENT–SUBSIDIARY
CONTROLLED GROUP
(EXAMPLE 25)

lationship. The first test (the 80-percent test) requires that five or fewer persons own 80 percent or more of the stock of each corporation in the group. The second test (the 50-percent test) requires that five or fewer persons own more than 50 percent of the stock of each corporation in the group (considering only the identical stock ownership that each person has with respect to each corporation). A shareholder's identical ownership is the percentage of stock held in common by the shareholder in each of the corporations. That percentage is equal to the smallest percentage of stock of any single corporation that the shareholder owns. For example, a person owning 20 percent of Rocket Corporation and 45 percent of Fueler Corporation has an identical ownership of 20 percent in the two corporations.

▲ **EXAMPLE 26**   DeWayne and Latifa own stock in Fritzy Corporation and Kragen Corporation:

	Stock Ownership Percentage		
Shareholder	Fritzy Corp.	Kragen Corp.	Identical Ownership
DeWayne	40%	55%	40%
Latifa	60%	45%	45%
Totals	100%	100%	85%

Are Fritzy and Kragen a brother-sister controlled group?

Discussion: Because 5 or fewer people (DeWayne and Latifa) own at least 80% of each corporation's stock (they together own 100% of each) and DeWayne and Latifa own more than 50% of each corporation's stock (they have an identical ownership of 85%), both the 80% test and the 50% test are satisfied. Accordingly, Fritzy and Kragen are a brother-sister controlled group. See Figure 9–3.

▲ Figure 9–3

BROTHER–SISTER
CONTROLLED GROUP
(EXAMPLE 26)

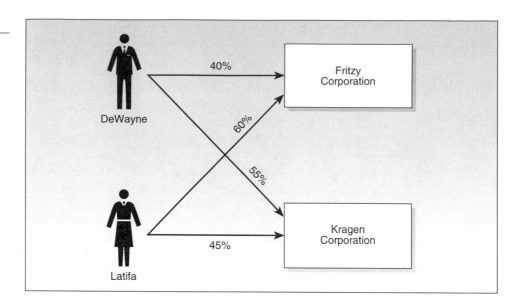

▲ Figure 9–3

BROTHER–SISTER
CONTROLLED GROUP
(EXAMPLE 26)

▲ FIDUCIARIES

A person who occupies a position of special confidence, especially a trustee, guardian, receiver, conservator, executor, or administrator, is considered a **fiduciary.** Such people have legal title to property, which they hold for the benefit of others, subject to strict duties under state law. Many, but not all, fiduciaries are required to file income tax returns on behalf of the entity (e.g., trust or estate) for which they are responsible.

Estates

An **estate** is created upon the death of an individual. Generally, the estate is merely a temporary, transitional entity. It holds the deceased person's property until the property is distributed to its beneficiaries. After all the property is transferred from the estate, its purpose has ended and it ceases to exist. During the estate's life, the property held by the executor may earn income. That income is taxed to the estate, and taxes are paid from estate assets. The taxable income of the estate is taxed using the fiduciary tax rates (see Table 9–3).

Trusts

A **trust** is a legal entity created when a person transfers ownership of property to a **trustee** to be held for the benefit of another person. Occasionally, a will directs

▲ Table 9–3

FIDUCIARY TAX RATES
(ESTATES AND TRUSTS)
(1995)

If Taxable Income Is		The Tax Is	Of the
Over—	But Not Over—		Amount Over—
$ -0-	$1,550	................15 %	$ -0-
1,550	3,700	$ 232.50 + 28 %	1,550
3,700	5,600	834.50 + 31 %	3,700
5,600	7,650	1,423.50 + 36 %	5,600
7,650	....	2,161.50 + 39.6%	7,650

NOTE: Net long-term capital gain income is taxed at a maximum 28% rate.

the creation of a trust. This **testamentary trust** is funded by assets formerly held by the estate. The person who transfers the corpus, or trust assets, to the trustee is called the **grantor.** The directions given the trustee by the grantor are included in the trust instrument, or indenture. Often the trustee is a bank's trust department, another competent professional (e.g., an attorney or an accountant), or a trusted family member.

The trustee's primary purpose is to preserve the trust assets for the benefit of the beneficiaries. The trustee generally invests the corpus to earn the return desired by the grantor. If the grantor wants a beneficiary to receive an annual income distribution, the trustee must use her or his best judgment to bring the greatest return on investment without greatly risking the corpus. If the trustee is required to distribute all annual income to the trust beneficiaries, the trust is called a **simple trust.** All other trusts are called **complex trusts.** In addition, there is generally a **remainderman** who is the beneficiary and will receive the balance of the trust assets when the trust is terminated. The grantor may designate almost any mixture of trust income and/or corpus to be distributed to beneficiaries.

For a trust to be recognized as a taxable entity, no more than 5 percent of its assets may revert to the grantor or spouse (a **reversionary interest**) upon termination (if the trust was created or had additional assets transferred to it after March 1, 1986). If a trust does not meet this requirement, trust income is taxed to the grantor.[26] This type of trust is known as a **grantor trust.**

▲ **EXAMPLE 27**   During 1994, Halah contributed common stock worth $200,000 to a simple trust managed by the trustee of the Second National Bank and Trust. Halah designated her teenage daughter Nadia as the beneficiary of the trust income. The trust instrument requires that the trust principal be returned to Halah upon Nadia's 24th birthday. In the current year, the Halah Trust earned $23,000 in dividend income. All $23,000 was distributed to Nadia. Who is responsible for reporting the $23,000 in dividend income?

Discussion: Because more than 5% of the trust assets revert to her at termination, Halah retains a reversionary interest in the trust assets. Therefore, Halah must include the $23,000 in her current gross income.

▲ **EXAMPLE 28**   Assume that Halah, in example 27, created the trust with her daughter Nadia as income beneficiary and the American Red Cross as the beneficiary of the trust principal upon Nadia's 24th birthday. During the current year, the Halah Trust earned $23,000 in dividend income, and all of it was distributed to Halah. Who is responsible for recognizing the $23,000 in income?

Discussion: Because Halah does not hold a reversionary interest in the trust assets (all assets go to the Red Cross at termination), the income beneficiary, Nadia, is taxed on the $23,000. The income retains the characteristics of dividends for Nadia.

Income Taxation of Fiduciaries

The general rules of individual income taxation govern fiduciary income taxation.[27] As with corporate taxation, a thorough understanding of taxation of individuals precedes the study of income taxation of fiduciaries—only a few tax rules are different for fiduciaries. The principal difference in the calculation of taxable income is the deduction for distributions to beneficiaries.

Most of the gross income received by a fiduciary consists of interest, dividends, royalties, and rents (i.e., forms of investment income). Therefore, the fiduciary's deductible expenses are those directly connected to the production of investment income, such as management or asset maintenance fees. The treatment of any tax-exempt income (e.g., municipal bond interest) is similar to its treatment for individuals. As with individuals, any allocable related expenses of tax-exempt income are not deductible by the fiduciary.

Unlike corporations, fiduciaries and beneficiaries are not subjected to double taxation on the income earned by an estate or trust. The fiduciary entity receives a deduction for income distributed to beneficiaries.[28] Then, beneficiaries report the amount of their receipts as income on their individual returns, much as owners of conduit entities do. Therefore, income is taxed just once. Either the fiduciary or the beneficiary pays the income tax. If not all of the current income is distributed, both fiduciary and beneficiary will pay some tax.

▲ **EXAMPLE 29**   During the current year, the Carson P. Taylor Trust earns interest income of $20,000. Patricia Taylor, the beneficiary, receives a $9,000 distribution from the trust. What are the tax effects of these events?

Discussion: Patricia reports $9,000 on her individual income tax return. The trust is taxed on its undistributed earnings, $11,000, less an allowable exemption of $100 (explained shortly).

Trusts that distribute income to beneficiaries follow the general distribution rules for conduit entities. That is, the income received by the beneficiary retains the same character it had when earned by the trust.

▲ **EXAMPLE 30**   The Barber Trust received $8,000 in dividends, $4,000 in corporate bond interest, $2,000 in capital gain income, and $6,000 in municipal bond tax-exempt interest. The trust distributes all its receipts to beneficiaries. What is the character of the receipts in the hands of the beneficiaries?

Discussion: Beneficiaries are deemed to have obtained the same $8,000 in dividends, $4,000 in interest, $2,000 in capital gains, and $6,000 in tax-exempt income as were earned by the trust. Therefore, the beneficiaries are not taxed on their share of the tax-exempt income. In addition, their share of the capital gain income will become part of their personal capital gain-and-loss netting.

Charitable Contributions.   Congress encourages fiduciaries to make donations to qualified charitable organizations by allowing unlimited charitable deductions, which is not true for individuals or corporations. Also, the annual accounting period concept is partially disregarded as a matter of legislative grace. A fiduciary may elect to deduct a contribution in one year but not actually make the payment until near the close of the following tax year.

One limitation on the generous deduction rules for charitable contributions involves tax-exempt income. If the fiduciary distributes to charitable organizations funds that are the result of tax-exempt income, that distribution does not qualify for a deduction against fiduciary taxable income.

▲ **EXAMPLE 31**   The Lawrence Trust receives $10,000 in tax-exempt interest and $30,000 in taxable dividends during the current tax year. Also, the trust gives $12,000 to the United Way. How much may the trust deduct as a charitable contribution for the current year?

Discussion: Twenty-five percent ($10,000 ÷ $40,000) of the year's income is tax exempt. Therefore, 25% of the charitable contribution is nondeductible. Only $9,000 (75% × $12,000) is deductible by the trust.

Estates	$600
Simple trusts	$300
Other trusts	$100

Accounting Periods.   Because the taxation of trust distributions could be deferred by choosing a fiscal year, Congress requires trusts to use a calendar year as their tax year.[29] Estates, however, are free to choose a tax year. Congress probably deemed death too high a price to pay for gaining favorable tax treatment for a beneficiary.

Exemption Amounts.   Fiduciaries, unlike individuals, are not allowed a standard deduction amount. This provision is consistent with the purpose of the standard deduction for individuals. Because fiduciaries (i.e., trusts or estates) do not have personal itemized deductions, there is no need for relief under the administrative convenience concept.

A fiduciary, like an individual taxpayer and unlike a corporation, may claim an exemption deduction.[30] The amount of the statutory exemption depends on the type of fiduciary (see Exhibit 9–2). Unlike the personal exemption amount for individuals, the exemption for fiduciaries is not indexed for inflation.

Income Tax Calculation

The fiduciary income tax formula is not much different from the corporate income tax formula. Fiduciaries deduct their expenses and specially allowed deductions (exemptions, beneficiary distributions, charitable contributions) from fiduciary income.

▲ **EXAMPLE 32**   During 1995, the Armstrong Trust receives $25,000 in dividend income from corporate stock and has a $15,000 long-term capital gain from the sale of stock. The trust expenses total $10,000. The trust agreement states that all net capital gains are characterized and accumulated as trust corpus. All ordinary income must be distributed annually. What are the amounts of the trust's taxable income and its income tax liability?

Discussion: The trust is a complex trust, because all income is not distributed to the beneficiaries. The $10,000 in trust expenses, the $25,000 in dividend income distributed to the beneficiaries, and the $100 trust exemption are deducted from the $40,000 in trust income, resulting in a taxable income of $4,900.

Armstrong Trust 1995	
Gross income ($25,000 + $15,000)	$40,000
Less: Expenses	(10,000)
Less: Income distributed to beneficiaries	(25,000)
Less: Exemption	(100)
Taxable income	$ 4,900

The income tax liability is determined by using the fiduciary rate schedule in Table 9–3:

$$[\$834.50 + 31\% (\$4,900 - \$3,700)] = \$1,207$$

▲ **EXAMPLE 33**   The Sadler Trust received $10,000 in dividend income, $5,000 in tax-exempt income, and $12,000 in long-term capital gains from the sale of corporate stock.

Trust expenses not related to the tax-exempt income total $1,000. All trust income (after expenses) must be distributed annually. What is the trust's taxable income?

Discussion: Because all net trust income is distributed to the beneficiaries, the Sadler Trust is a simple trust. The amount distributed to beneficiaries is $26,000 ($10,000 + $12,000 + $5,000 − $1,000), resulting in a deduction of $21,000 ($26,000 − $5,000 in tax-exempt income) for the trust. The trust's taxable income is zero:

Sadler Trust	
Gross income ($10,000 + $12,000)	$22,000
Less: Expenses	(1,000)
Less: Income distributed to beneficiaries	(21,000)
Taxable income	$ -0-

Because all the income was distributed to beneficiaries, the trust has no taxable income and, accordingly, no tax liability. Therefore, the exemption amount is not needed. (Trusts cannot have net operating losses, because they are not a trade or business.) NOTE: The beneficiaries will include the dividend income, the tax-exempt income, and the long-term capital gains in their income per the categories from the trust.

▲ CONDUIT ENTITIES

Every entity is classified as either a taxable or a conduit entity. Tax conduits are characterized by the flow-through of their tax attributes directly to the owners of the entity.[31,32] The incidence of taxation of a conduit entity's income rests with the entity's owners.

Trusts, as discussed in the previous section, are either taxable or conduit entities. The characterization depends on whether trust income is distributed to beneficiaries. The other types of tax conduits do not rely on distributions for characterization. Partnerships, S corporations, and sole proprietorships are required by tax law to allocate their income, gains, losses, deductions, and credits to owners, regardless of any distributions. This flow-through effect could force owners to recognize income without the benefit of the wherewithal to pay.

Accounting Periods

All entities must follow the annual accounting period concept. That is, the results of operations are reported annually, and each tax year stands apart from other tax years. Although conduits do not pay income tax, they are not immune from reporting their financial results to the government as other entities do.

Although conduits are required to report annually, partnerships and S corporations have restrictions on their selection of fiscal years.[33,34] Generally, most partnerships, S corporations, and conduit trusts must use a calendar year for tax purposes. The intent of this requirement is to reduce the ability to defer taxes when fiscal year conduit entities pass income through to owners.

▲ EXAMPLE 34   Henry and Laurel are equal partners in HL Partnership. Both partners are calendar-year taxpayers. The partnership chose a March 31 fiscal year end. For the year April 1, 1995, through March 31, 1996, HL Partnership reports $1,000,000 in net operating income. In what tax year will the individual partners report their respective shares of partnership income if the partnership tax year is valid?

Discussion: The initial result is that each partner reports $500,000 on her or his 1996 individual income tax return, due by April 15, 1997. This result defers reporting the income earned by HL for more than 13 months. However, this result is no longer valid.

The partnership is required to have the same tax year as the partners' (calendar year). Therefore, HL must adopt a calendar year, and Henry and Laurel must report the $500,000 on their 1995 tax returns.

A partnership or S corporation may select a tax year other than the prescribed calendar year, with certain restrictions. These conduit entities may elect a fiscal year that results in a tax deferral of three months or less. For example, a partnership with calendar-year partners may select a September 30 (or October 31 or November 30) fiscal year end. However, the entity must make annual required payments on April 15 of the following year. The required payments are to offset the tax deferral advantage that calendar-year owners receive if their conduit entity uses a fiscal year.

The amount of the required payment is calculated as the previous year's taxable income multiplied by the maximum tax rate for individuals plus 1 percent and then by the deferral ratio. The deferral ratio equals the number of deferral months divided by 12 months.

▲ **EXAMPLE 35**   Big Orange Partnership elects a fiscal year end of September 30. For the tax year of October 1, 1995, through September 30, 1996, Big Orange's taxable income is $400,000. What is the amount of the required payment due for the privilege of selecting a 3-month deferral because of the fiscal year?

Discussion: The required payment is $37,000 [$400,000 × 37% (top individual rate + 1%) × 3/12 (the deferral ratio)]. The payment is due by April 15, 1997.

The required payment is effectively a deposit that approximates the value of the fiscal year deferral, resulting in no real tax advantage. Therefore, conduit entities must have good reasons other than tax deferral to elect fiscal years. Accordingly, businesses that have a natural business year other than the calendar year—and can establish that fact to the satisfaction of the IRS—do not have to make required payments (see Chapter 14).

Accounting Methods

A conduit entity can elect to use the cash, accrual, or hybrid method, following the basic rules for these methods. Also, special methods, such as those for installment sales or long-term construction contracts, must be used if the requirements for using the methods are met. Any of these elections or methods are determined at the entity level. Therefore, the conduit construct governs—owners report the items of income, deductions, gains, losses, and credits following the method(s) of determination for the entities. For example, a partnership electing the accrual method for income recognition forces its partners to report income of the partnership on the accrual method, even if the partners use the cash method.[35]

The characterization of income and deduction items occurs at the entity level. The items flowing through to owners cannot be reclassified by the owners. Also, because many items such as capital gains and losses, charitable contributions, rental income and expense, and certain other items are subject to special tax treatments, these items are reported separately. Therefore, any limitations (e.g., capital loss limitations) are applied at the owner level.

Basis in Partnerships and S Corporations

Basis in a partnership or S corporation may be the most critical attribute for owners. Basis establishes the amount of unrecovered investment in the conduit entity.

Not only does basis establish the realized gain or loss on disposition of the investment through application of the capital recovery concept, it determines the taxability of distributions from the conduit entity to owners. Also, the amount of unrecovered basis determines whether an owner may recognize losses flowing from the conduit entity to the owner.

Basis is dynamic. Throughout the life of the investment, basis is adjusted to reflect the tax results of many entity transactions. Although S corporations and partnerships have a few different adjustments to their owners' bases, the primary adjustments are the same.

Basis is established when an investor purchases an ownership interest (e.g., shares of corporate stock or a partnership interest) in an entity. The cost of the investment is the initial basis amount.[36] (Exhibit 9–3 provides a general formula for determining the basis in an investment.)

Instead of contributing cash to an entity, investors may contribute real or personal property. The tax results do not change for a contribution of property. The tax law permits a tax-free transaction when property is contributed in exchange for an ownership interest.[37] Therefore, the basis in the contributed property is substituted for the basis in the ownership interest.[38]

After the initial basis amount is determined, periodic increases and decreases occur. When a conduit entity reports net operating income or gains, those items flow through to owners who must recognize them on their personal tax returns. Because they are taxed to the owners, these items are added to the basis amount. They represent additional investments in the entity similar to an actual additional contribution to the entity of cash or other property.

▲ **EXAMPLE 36**   Lanier contributes land with a basis of $10,000 and a fair market value of $35,000 to the LMN Partnership for a 30% interest in the business. At the close of the year, LMN reports operating income of $50,000. No cash or property was distributed by LMN to Lanier during the year. What is Lanier's share of the income, and how does it affect the basis of her partnership interest?

Discussion: Lanier's share of the partnership income is $15,000 (30% × $50,000). Lanier reports the $15,000 on her personal income tax return. The basis of her partnership interest increases by the amount of the income recognized. Her initial basis, the $10,000 adjusted basis of the property contributed, plus income recognized, $15,000, equals an adjusted basis of $25,000 at the end of the year. NOTE: Lanier is required to include the partnership income in her gross income. Yet, Lanier received no cash or other property. The entity's assets increase because the operating earned income remains with the partnership. Lanier's share of the increase in partnership assets is analogous to an additional contribution of property to the partnership by the partner. Therefore, the basis in the ownership interest increases to reflect the partner's share of the additional assets of the partnership.

▲ Exhibit 9–3

GENERAL BASIS FORMULA FOR AN INTEREST IN PARTNERSHIPS OR S CORPORATIONS

Initial investment or contribution	$ XXX
Add: Additional forms of investment	
Share of entity income	XXX
Contribution of assets	XXX
Deduct: Returns of capital investment	
Share of entity losses	(XXX)
Withdrawals or dividends received	(XXX)
Adjusted basis in investment	$ XXX

Not only will entity income and contributions to conduit entities affect an investor's basis amount but so will entity losses and withdrawals from conduit entities. Losses flow through to owners and are recognizable by them on their personal income tax returns. However, following the capital recovery concept, losses are recognized only to the extent a basis amount exists.

▲ **EXAMPLE 37**   Widdell has an initial basis of $5,000 in his 10% interest in the WW Partnership. WW Partnership reports a net operating loss of $60,000 for the current year. What amount can Widdell recognize for the current year?

Discussion: Widdell's share of the partnership loss is $6,000 (10% × $60,000). However, the amount of loss recognition is limited to the amount of basis. Therefore, Widdell is allowed to deduct only $5,000 of the loss. Widdell's total capital is recovered via the loss. NOTE: Widdell's remaining basis is zero, and the additional $1,000 loss is suspended until the basis amount again becomes positive—through future partnership income or additional capital contributions by Widdell.

Distribution of capital from conduit entities to owners is a true capital recovery. Withdrawals by partners and dividends to S corporation shareholders are nontaxable reductions of each owner's basis. However, if the withdrawal or dividend exceeds the amount of an owner's basis, the excess amount is a taxable capital gain.

▲ **EXAMPLE 38**   Edna and Lucille have been equal partners in the KAK Partnership for several years. At the close of the current year, Edna's basis in her ownership interest is $10,000, and Lucille's basis is $4,000. At that time, the partnership distributes cash in the amount of $5,000 to each partner. What are the tax and basis effects of these withdrawals?

Discussion: Edna receives her $5,000 tax free; it is merely a recovery of capital. Her basis is reduced to $5,000 ($10,000 − $5,000). Lucille receives $4,000 tax free as a recovery of capital. However, the excess $1,000 capital recovery is recognized as a capital gain. Lucille's basis amount is now zero.

	Edna	Lucille
Initial basis	$10,000	$4,000
Cash withdrawal	(5,000)	(5,000)
Remaining basis	$ 5,000	$ -0-
Taxable gain	$ -0-	$1,000

Basis computations are discussed further in the subsections about partnerships and S corporations. Each entity has basis adjustments that are unique.

Sole Proprietorships

The most common business form in the United States is the sole proprietorship. Individuals need do nothing formally to establish a sole proprietorship. This ease of formation results because the business is not separate from the individual owner from a tax perspective. Sometimes, the separation issue becomes blurred because of financial accounting rules that require proprietors to exclude reporting of nonbusiness items (e.g., personal expenses or nonbusiness income) from proprietorship financial reports. Schedule C of Form 1040 is the vehicle for reporting the items of proprietorship income, expenses, and credits. This reporting mechanism has the appearance of separating the proprietor from the proprietor's business. Yet, this reporting procedure reinforces the conduit nature of the sole proprietorship. The net operating income flows directly to the individual proprietor's Form 1040 as an item of gross income.

Because sole proprietorships are not separate taxable entities, owner-employee salaries and owner-employee fringe benefits are not deductible by sole proprietorships. Proprietors may take cash withdrawals from their businesses, but these payments are not going from one taxable entity to another. The only entity involved is the individual. Proprietorship cash draws are analogous to taking money from one pocket and putting it into another pocket in the same pair of pants. Partnerships also have these characteristics.

Sole proprietors cannot be employees of their businesses, because individuals cannot hire themselves. Therefore, salaries or fringe benefits such as group term life insurance are not available to proprietors. The business is not allowed a deduction for these items, and fringe-benefit recipients are not permitted exclusions for those benefits. Of course, wages and fringe-benefit payments on behalf of employees are deductible as proprietorship expenses.

As discussed in the first section of this chapter, a sole proprietor's child is not subject to Social Security taxes when validly employed in the parent's business. Sole proprietors can obtain multiple benefits by employing their children. Wages are deductible expenses of the business, and the parent-proprietor also saves 7.65 percent (employer's share of Social Security) of the child's wages. This procedure allows the parent-proprietor to put cash into the hands of children with positive results. Depending on the amount of the child's earned income, it is possible for the child to escape income taxation and Social Security taxation entirely (see examples 7 and 8).

Although a proprietor's child may escape payment of Social Security tax, the proprietor generally cannot. Self-employed individuals pay a tax on any self-employment income of $400 or more. As discussed in Chapter 8, self-employment income in 1995 is subject to a tax of 15.3% on the first $61,200 of self-employment income and 2.9% on the excess. A self-employed individual may deduct half of all self-employment taxes paid as a for-AGI deduction.

▲ **EXAMPLE 39** Fletcher is a self-employed consultant with business net income of $50,000. How much self-employment tax is due?

Discussion: As discussed in Chapter 8, only 92.35% of self-employed income is subject to tax because of the deduction allowed for self-employment taxes paid. Fletcher's self-employment tax is $7,065 ($50,000 × 92.35% × 15.3%).

▲ **EXAMPLE 40** How much of an income tax deduction is Fletcher, in example 39, allowed?

Discussion: Fletcher's income tax deduction is one-half of the total of self-employment taxes paid, $3,533 ($7,065 × 50%).

Partnerships

Although **partnerships** are considered conduits for the purpose of income taxation, they are treated as separate entities under local law. Therefore, partnerships can transact business and own property in their own names, separate from the partners. These common legal characteristics are similar to those for other business forms, such as corporations. Although partnerships are deemed aggregations of the partners' interests for income tax purposes, on occasion the characteristics become blurred. This section also introduces two new business forms, limited liability companies and limited liability partnerships, referred to collectively as *limited liability entities.*

Legal Characteristics.

Both corporations and partnerships are generally established with a business purpose and have two or more owners (associates). Therefore, the courts and Treasury regulations have settled on the absence of the four corporate characteristics to establish the existence of a partnership for tax purposes (see the discussion in the first section of this chapter). A general partnership is characterized as follows for tax purposes:

- A partner's liability is not limited.
- The life of the partnership depends on the life of the partner(s).
- All partners share in the partnership management.
- Partnership interests are not freely transferable.[39]

Certain types of partnerships can take on the corporate characteristic of limited liability in order to make capital acquisition easier. These limited partnerships have at least one partner whose liability is limited to the amount of his or her investment in the partnership. This attribute provides a measure of safety for the limited partners' personal assets. The limited partnership form of business has been a popular medium for investors in risky activities, such as mining or oil and gas exploration.

To obtain the limited liability attribute, limited partners give up any right to participate in the management of the business. Management is left to at least one general partner, whose liability is not limited and who is responsible for the ongoing activities of the business.

Partners Are Not Employees.

The theoretical construct of the conduit entity provides that an employer/employee relationship cannot exist between a partnership and its partners. Remember that a partnership is generally considered a loose aggregation of owners (or owners' interests). Therefore, although **partners** receive compensatory payments for providing services to the business organization, they are not employees for purposes of payroll taxes and related withholding. Also, partners, like sole proprietors, are not allowed excludable employee benefits, such as group term life insurance, accident or health insurance, employer-provided meals and lodging, or death benefits. One exception to the lack of an employer/employee relationship concerns retirement plans. Under certain conditions, partners who also work for the partnership may participate in retirement plans of the organization. (The details of the restrictions placed on participating owners are beyond the scope of this text.)

Compensation to a partner may be classified in either of two ways. First, a partnership may offer a partner a guaranteed payment, determined without regard to the partnership's income. A **guaranteed payment** is a payment that must be made to a partner without regard to the profits of the partnership. This type of compensation is included as ordinary income to the partner and is a deductible compensation expense for the partnership.

> ▲ **EXAMPLE 41**   Bowlen Partnership pays Helena (a 20% owner) $5,000 monthly for managing the day-to-day affairs of the business. The partnership earned $200,000 during the current year without considering the $60,000 compensation paid to Helena. What are the tax effects for Helena and for the partnership of the $60,000 payment?

Discussion: Because the $60,000 was paid to Helena regardless of the partnership earnings (determined without regard to the amount of partnership earnings), it is a guaranteed payment. Therefore, Helena includes the $60,000 in her gross income and her self-employment income. The partnership may deduct the $60,000 as a compensation expense. Accordingly, the partnership's reported ordinary income is $140,000 ($200,000 − $60,000), and Helena's partnership share is $28,000 (20% × $140,000).

    Helena's total ordinary income includes both the cash compensation classified as a guaranteed payment ($60,000) and her share of the partnership's ordinary income ($28,000). Therefore, Helena recognizes $88,000 in gross income and computes the applicable self-employment tax on these earnings—although she received payments of only $60,000.

If a partner receives compensatory payments based in any way on the partnership's gross or net income, the payments are classified as the partner's share of partnership profits. The partnership records the payments as nondeductible withdrawals, and the partner recognizes the income in the year of receipt.

   ▲ **EXAMPLE 42**   Preehya receives compensation set at 10% of the ABX Partnership's monthly net income, so long as there is income. Otherwise, no compensatory payment is made for that month. Are these payments considered guaranteed payments or Preehya's share of partnership profits?

Discussion: Because any compensation received is based on partnership income, these payments are treated as the partner's share of partnership profits and not as a guaranteed payment.

Basis of Partnership Interest.
Often, the primary motivation for an owner to invest in a partnership form of business is to obtain the flow-through tax effect of losses and/or other deductions. These losses are used to reduce the individual taxpayer's taxable income. Therefore, it is imperative that an owner have adequate basis. The basis amount establishes the maximum amount that a partner can deduct against other income in a given year. That is, the capital recovery concept dictates that losses may be used only to recover the amount of capital invested in the partnership and no more. A partner's basis may never go below zero.

   ▲ **EXAMPLE 43**   José contributes undeveloped land with a basis of $10,000 and fair market value of $50,000 to the JKL Partnership for a 20% interest. The partnership reports an annual operating loss of $40,000 for the current year. What is José's share of the partnership loss, and how does it affect his basis?

Discussion: José's share of partnership loss is $8,000 (20% × $40,000). José recognizes this amount on his personal tax return. After the loss, José's basis is $2,000 ($10,000 initial basis − $8,000 loss flow-through).

   ▲ **EXAMPLE 44**   Assume that the JKL Partnership, in example 43, reported a loss of $60,000. How would this result affect José?

Discussion: José's share of partnership loss is $12,000 (20% × $60,000). José's personal loss deduction is limited by the amount of his basis in his partnership interest. Therefore, José is limited to a loss deduction of $10,000 for the current year. His remaining basis amount is zero, and the additional $2,000 loss flow-through recognition is suspended until his basis increases enough to absorb it.

PARTNERSHIP DEBT.   Recall that basis begins with a person's contribution of assets or services in exchange for a capital interest. However, the use of the partnership form adds a unique complexity to basis calculations. Basis is increased by a partner's share of partnership liabilities, or **partnership debt.** Partnership debt assumed by a partner and the partner's share of partnership debt are deemed to be additional cash contributions by the partner to the partnership.[40] Likewise, basis is decreased by any partner's debt that is assumed by the partnership and by any decreases in the partner's share of partnership liabilities. Decreases in debt are deemed cash distributions to partners.[41] These allocations of debt have resulted in partnerships becoming the entity of choice for highly leveraged business ventures (e.g., real estate and natural resource exploration).

▲ **FXAMPLE 45**   Lou and Bud form the QED Partnership to develop and manage real estate. Each partner contributes $100,000 to the partnership. The partnership borrows a total of $1,000,000 from Texas Southwest Savings, Building, and Loan Association. What are the partners' bases amounts?

Discussion: Each partner adds the amount of his cash contribution ($100,000) to his share (50%) of the total partnership liability of $1,000,000. Each partner's basis is $600,000 [$100,000 + (50% × $1,000,000)].

▲ **EXAMPLE 46**   Tinker, Everett, and Cheryl form the Diamond Partnership by contributing the following:

Tinker: $100,000 cash for a 50% partnership interest.

Everett: $50,000 cash for a 25% partnership interest.

Cheryl: Real estate valued at $78,000 but encumbered by a mortgage of $28,000 that is assumed by the partnership. Cheryl's basis in the property is $32,000. She receives a 25% partnership interest.

What is the amount of each partner's basis in his or her partnership interest?

Discussion: Tinker and Everett add their respective shares of debt assumed by the partnership to their cash contributions to arrive at their bases in their partnership interests ($114,000 and $57,000, respectively). Cheryl adds her share of partnership debt (25%) to the basis of the property contributed to the partnership ($32,000) and subtracts the amount of debt relief ($28,000) that results from the partnership's assuming the mortgage on the contributed real estate. Therefore, Cheryl's basis in her partnership interest is $11,000 ($32,000 + $7,000 − $28,000).

	Tinker	Everett	Cheryl
Basis of property or cash contributed	$100,000	$50,000	$32,000
Plus: Debt assumed by the partnership			
(50%)	14,000		
(25%)		7,000	7,000
Less: Debt relief			(28,000)
Basis of interest	$114,000	$57,000	$11,000

Partnership Distributions.   A partner's receipt of a cash or property distribution from a partnership is generally tax free and referred to as a **partnership distribution.**[42] This result is consistent with the capital recovery concept. That is, no gain is recognized until after the basis in the capital investment is recovered. Any excess of cash (or the basis of property) over the basis in a partner's interest is a recognizable gain for the recipient partner.[43]

▲ **EXAMPLE 47**   Sophia receives a partnership distribution of $10,000 cash from ECM Partnership. Sophia's basis in her partnership interest is $2,000 before the distribution. What is the effect of the distribution on Sophia?

Discussion: Sophia receives $2,000 as a tax-free recovery of capital. Sophia's basis reduces to zero. She recognizes $8,000 as a capital gain for the excess recovery of her investment in the partnership.

Initial basis	$2,000
Recovery of capital	(2,000)
Remaining basis	$ -0-
Excess distribution, capital gain recognized	
($10,000 − $2,000)	$8,000

Partnership Terminations.   State laws vary on the situations that terminate a partnership. However, tax law provides two conditions that cause a partnership to terminate for tax purposes, regardless of state law provisions. Either of the following situations causes termination:

- If no partner continues to operate the business through the partnership, the partnership terminates.

- If at least 50 percent of the total interest in both partnership capital and profits is sold or exchanged within any 12-month period, a termination occurs.[44]

Terminations close the partnership tax year and force partners to include their shares of partnership income (or losses) for the short, closed year in their personal returns. This situation could cause partners to include more than 12 months of income on their personal returns for the termination year. Also, when a termination occurs, a liquidating distribution of partnership property is deemed to have been made. Partners are required to recognize gains or losses on these distributions, even if no property is actually distributed.

Limited Liability Companies (LLCs).   The limited liability company is a relatively new and unique form of business organization created under state laws. The **limited liability company (LLC)** combines the corporate characteristic of limited liability with the conduit tax treatment of partnerships. Whereas corporations are created by filing articles of incorporation, LLCs file articles of organization. The entity must have two or more members, have an objective to carry on a business, and establish a specific method for dividing the profits and losses from the business.

An unincorporated organization such as an LLC is not subject to corporate taxation, unless it has more corporate characteristics than noncorporate characteristics. As presented earlier in this chapter, the corporate characteristics on which the determination turns are

1.   Limited liability of the owners
2.   Free transferability of interests
3.   Continuity of life
4.   Centralization of management

That is, the test for conduit tax treatment hinges on whether the LLC has no more than one of the last three corporate characteristics in the list (items 2 through 4). If an LLC has at least two of the characteristics of items 2 through 4, it is taxed as a corporation, not as a conduit entity. So long as the entity possesses only one of the other three corporate characteristics, partnership tax treatment prevails.

The key planning feature of LLCs is limited liability. Owners have no personal liability for debts of the business. This feature provides a defense against astronomical lawsuits and exposure to unlimited personal liability.

Limited Liability Partnerships (LLPs).   Another new form of organization growing in popularity is the limited liability partnership. The **limited liability partnership (LLP)** is simply a general partnership with the added characteristic of limited liability for owners. States allowing this type of entity are responding to concerns about the traditional concepts of partner liability—general partners are unconditionally liable for partnership debts. Accordingly, an LLP permits the usual partnership conduit tax treatment but limits the liabilities of its owners (partners). Thus, an organization that seeks conduit tax treatment and limited personal liability for all owners has two options that provide virtually the same tax treatment—LLPs and LLCs. So nontax factors determine whether the entity should be an LLC or LLP.

Generally, it takes more effort (and cost) to operate as an LLC. Forming a board of directors, appointing operating officers, modifying membership agreements, registering with state regulatory agencies, paying franchise taxes or fees, and such are common requirements for LLCs but not for LLPs. The ease of converting to LLP status seems to favor that form. Also, some states' laws require the business organizations of such professionals as accountants and lawyers to use the partnership form. The LLP appears to be the logical choice for these service-related businesses.

During 1994, all the Big Six accounting firms converted from general partnerships to limited liability partnerships (LLPs). However, before taxpayers decide to establish an organization as an LLP or LLC, they should contact a professional tax adviser. Detailed examination of this topic is beyond the scope of this textbook.

S Corporations

Corporations, chartered under the laws of one of the 50 states, may obtain conduit entity tax status by making a valid election per Subchapter S of the Internal Revenue Code of 1986.[45] Therefore, the S corporation retains the legal characteristics of the corporate form (limited liability, free transferability of interests, continuity of life, and centralized management) while obtaining taxation characteristics similar to a partnership's.

Qualification Requirements.   S corporation status is attained when a qualified corporation elects this status. The election is effective for the current tax year if the election is filed at any time during the preceding year or on or before the fifteenth day of the third month of the current year. Therefore, a calendar-year corporate taxpayer desiring S corporation status for 1995 must file the election at any time from January 1, 1994, through March 15, 1995. The characteristics that qualify a corporation to make the election are that it

- Must be a domestic corporation
- Cannot be a member of an affiliated group of corporations (generally, an S corporation cannot own 80 percent or more of another corporation)

- May not have more than 35 shareholders (married individuals who are both shareholders are deemed to be one shareholder for S corporation status)
- Must have as its shareholders only individuals, estates, and certain trusts
- Cannot have a nonresident alien as a shareholder
- Has only one class of stock outstanding
- All shareholders consent to the election[46]

Every qualifying requirement must be met at the time of the election and at all times thereafter. The election terminates immediately when one or more of the qualifying characteristics is no longer met. As of the date of termination, the corporation becomes a taxable corporate entity.

▲ **EXAMPLE 48**   Pedry Corporation has been a qualified calendar-year S corporation since 1987. On April 1 of the current year, Hilda sells her 100 shares of Pedry stock to Holder Co., a limited partnership. Does this transaction affect the status of Pedry Corporation?

Discussion: Pedry's S corporation election terminates on April 1. Partnerships may not be shareholders in S corporations. Therefore, Pedry is an S corporation through March 31 and a taxable corporation from April 1 through December 31. NOTE: If the termination of the election is inadvertent, the S status may continue uninterrupted if the corporation corrects the disqualifying action. Therefore, if Hilda becomes aware of the results of her actions and can revoke the sale of the stock to the limited partnership, Pedry's S status will continue.

Revocation of the S Election.   An S corporation may forfeit its election voluntarily. If holders of more than 50 percent of the total shares of stock consent to revoke the S status, the revocation is effective for the current year if made on or before the fifteenth day of the third month of the year.

▲ **EXAMPLE 49**   RAD Corporation is a qualifying S corporation with 5 individual shareholders. Ralph owns 60% of the stock. Aileen, Alice, Doug, and Dorian each own 10% of the shares of stock. Ralph no longer desires S status. Therefore, on June 30 of the current year, he files an intent to terminate. Is the termination valid? If it is, when is it effective?

Discussion: The termination is valid, because Ralph owns more than 50% of the shares of RAD Corporation. The earliest effective date for the termination of S status is January 1 of the next tax year, because the termination was not made on or before the fifteenth day of March during the current year.

Once an election is terminated, the corporation may not make a new election for five years without special consent of the commissioner of the IRS.[47]

Change from C Corporation to S Corporation.   In the early years of a business operation, losses are commonplace. Therefore, S corporations usually provide greater benefits to owners than corporations because of the conduit nature of S corporations. Even if a corporation with unused NOLs makes a valid election for S status, the NOL attribute does not carry over to the S corporation. In fact, the running of the carryforward period continues during S corporation status. If the S election is never revoked, unused NOLs from regular-corporation years expire after the 15-year carryforward period.[48] However, if S status is terminated and the corporation reverts to regular corporate status, any unused unexpired NOLs may be used to offset new corporation income. Therefore, to counteract these complications, a corporation that anticipates losses in future tax years should make the S election before the loss year.

Employee Status of Stockholders.   Shareholder-employees of an electing S corporation are generally treated the same as other employees. Shareholder-employees must include salaries in their gross income. The S corporation may deduct the salary expense and the related payroll taxes. Likewise, employee fringe benefits paid by the S corporation for shareholder-employees who own no more than 2 percent of the corporate stock are deductible by the corporation. However, shareholder-employees exclude the value of the fringe benefits from their gross incomes only if the individual shareholder-employee owns 2 percent, or less, of the S corporation's stock.

Any S corporation shareholder who owns more than 2 percent of the stock is treated differently with regard to fringe benefits. The shareholder-employee is treated like a partner, and the cost of the fringe benefit is treated as a distribution of the corporation's earnings.[49] The S corporation may not deduct the cost of these fringe benefits as a business expense. Shareholder-employees owning more than 2 percent of the corporation's stock may deduct their fringe benefits on their individual tax returns if the benefits qualify as an itemized deduction.

> ▲ **EXAMPLE 50**   Golic Corporation, an electing S corporation, has a company health-care plan for all employees. Mike, an employee, owns 15% of the corporate stock, and Bob, also an employee, owns 1%. Mike's health benefits total $1,200 in the current year, and Bob's benefits total $1,800. How are the costs of these benefits treated by each shareholder-employee and by the S corporation?
>
> *Discussion:*   The $1,800 cost of Bob's benefits is a deductible business expense by the corporation and is excludable from gross income by Bob. Mike's $1,200 in benefits is not deductible by the corporation, because Mike owns more than 2% of the corporate stock. Mike recognizes the $1,200 as gross income. The $1,200 is deductible by Mike only to the extent that his medical expenses are allowable itemized deductions.

Distributions and Basis Adjustments.   Following the general rules for conduit entities, cash distributions from an S corporation to its shareholders are generally tax free and reduce the shareholders' basis in the corporate stock (see Exhibit 9–3). If distributions exceed a shareholder's basis, the excess amount is treated as a capital gain.[50] Recall that the capital recovery concept governs the treatment of distributions from conduit entities.

> ▲ **EXAMPLE 51**   Julio pays $20,000 for stock in an S corporation and receives shares equal to a 10% interest in the corporation in 1995. The S corporation reports taxable income of $150,000 in 1995. What are the tax effects of these events?
>
> *Discussion:*   Julio's initial basis in his ownership (stock) is the amount contributed, $20,000. Then, Julio's share of S corporation taxable income, $15,000 (10% × $150,000), is reported on his individual tax return. The recognition of the $15,000 allows Julio to increase the basis of his stock to $35,000 ($20,000 + $15,000). NOTE: Contrary to the wherewithal-to-pay concept, S corporation shareholders owe taxes on their shares of the corporate earnings but may receive no cash to pay the tax.
>
> ▲ **EXAMPLE 52**   Julio, in example 51, receives a cash distribution of $18,000 from the S corporation on December 31, 1995. What is the effect of this event?
>
> *Discussion:*   The $18,000 is a recovery of capital to the extent of Julio's basis. The basis amount is adjusted to reflect income flow-throughs (or gains, losses, deductions, etc.)

before recovering capital amounts.[51] Therefore, the recoverable basis is $35,000. After the tax-free receipt of the $18,000, Julio's adjusted basis is $17,000 ($35,000 − $18,000).

▲ **EXAMPLE 53**   Assume Julio receives a distribution of $40,000 instead of the $18,000 in example 52. How does that change the tax effects of the distribution?

Discussion: Applying the capital recovery concept, the first $35,000 (Julio's basis) is tax free. The excess $5,000 ($40,000 − $35,000) is a capital gain. NOTE: The results of examples 51 to 53 do not change, even if the S corporation incurs debt. Recall from the discussion of partnerships that partnership debt causes the partners' bases to increase relative to their shares of the debt. This is not the case with S corporations and their shareholders. (See examples 45 and 46. Compare them to examples 51 to 53.)

See Exhibit 9–4 for a general comparison of the characteristics of conduit entities.

▲ USES OF ENTITIES

A myriad of tax-planning opportunities exists when all the various taxable and conduit entities are considered. Recall the discussion of tax planning in Chapter 1. The primary objective of tax planning is to maximize wealth through timing of income and deductions and income splitting. However, do not lose sight of other objectives that may, or may not, have direct effects on this objective. For example, the corporate form of business offers the nontax benefit of limited liability. Often, this characteristic drives the choice of entity. However, individuals choosing the corporate form must be aware of the disadvantages (e.g., double taxation), as well as the advantages, that stem from tax rules for corporations.

Income Splitting

One basic tax-planning use of entities involves splitting income among two or more taxable entities. Income splitting can provide tax savings in a tax system like that of the United States in which progressive tax rates exist across taxable entities. That is, net tax liabilities can be reduced by shifting income to the entity with the lowest marginal tax rate. For example, if one entity has a marginal rate of 34 percent and a second entity has a marginal rate of 15 percent, every dollar of income shifted from the first entity to the second saves 19 cents in taxes. (Many of the issues surrounding income splitting are discussed in this chapter in the subsection "Income Tax Considerations" under Corporations.)

▲ **EXAMPLE 54**   Dino and Wilma operate their stone quarry and rock-polishing business as a sole proprietorship. The business generally earns $100,000 annually. The couple's 1995 joint tax liability on a taxable income of $88,450 ($100,000 − $6,550 standard deduction − $5,000 in personal exemptions) is $19,696 [$5,850 + 28% × ($88,450 − $39,000)]. Can the couple decrease their income tax liability by shifting business income to a corporate entity—by incorporating their business?

Discussion: They will see a decrease in tax liability if the shifted income is taxed at a marginal rate lower than that of individuals. Therefore, if no more than $50,000 in taxable income rests with the corporation, incorporation decreases the marginal tax rate from 28% to 15%. (See Figure 9–1 for the income levels at which rates change for corporations and individuals.)

   If Dino and Wilma incorporate their business and pay themselves a total salary of $50,000, they shift $50,000 of their individual income to the corporation. Therefore, the corporate taxable income is $50,000 ($100,000 − $50,000 salary). The corporate tax liability is $7,500 ($50,000 × 15%), disregarding the effects of payroll taxes on the taxable income. Dino and Wilma's joint taxable income is $38,450 ($50,000 − $6,550

Characteristic	Limited Liability Companies	General Partnership	S Corporation	Sole Proprietors
Limited personal liability of owners	Yes	No; yes for LLPs	Yes	No
Double taxation	No	No	No	No
Permitted type and number of owners	No restriction on type; two or more members.	No restriction on type; two or more partners.	Individuals, estates, and certain trusts; from 1 to 35 shareholers.	N/A
Permitted classes of ownership interests	Multiple classes are permitted.	Multiple classes are permitted.	Limited to one class of stock.	N/A
Continuity of existence	Usually limited by articles and LLC bylaws or regulations.	Limited	Not limited	Limited
Transferability of interests	Usually limited by articles and LLC bylaws or regulations.	May be limited by partnership agreement and/or state law.	Limited by code restrictions on type and number of owners; may be limited by shareholder agreement.	Not limited
Necessary documentation	Articles of organization; state LLC laws.	State partnership laws.	Charter/articles of incorporation; bylaws; minutes of directors' & shareholders' meetings; stock records.	Minimal
State franchise tax imposed	Yes (generally)	No	Yes	No

▲ Exhibit 9–4

COMPARISON OF
CONDUIT ENTITY
CHARACTERISTICS

standard deduction − $5,000 in personal exemptions). Their joint individual income tax liability is $5,768 ($38,450 × 15%). The total tax liability is $13,268 ($7,500 + $5,768). A tax savings of $6,428 ($19,696 − $13,268) results from incorporating the business.

▲ **EXAMPLE 55**   Cynthia is a sole proprietor, real estate property manager, and investor. She owns small rental houses and condominium units. Cynthia has her office in 1 room of her personal residence, and she properly deducts home-office and related business expenses (as discussed in Chapter 6). Her personal residence is 1 unit in the condominium complex. Is there a plan that uses an alternative entity form that may save tax dollars and increase Cynthia's net wealth?

Discussion: One alternative may be the use of the corporate form of business. That is, Cynthia incorporates her business and transfers ownership of all her real estate properties, and the accompanying mortgages, to the entity. Then, the corporation hires Cynthia to actively manage the properties. As a condition of employment, Cynthia is required to live in 1 of the properties (her former personal residence) so that she is available to tenants of the complex at all hours. Therefore, Cynthia may be able to exclude the value of her residence from her gross income (see Chapter 4). The corporation receives a deduction for insurance, utilities, and depreciation on the residence that otherwise would not be deductible for an individual. Accordingly, the total business income is reduced over what it would be under the former sole proprietorship.

A simple formula that allows individuals to select the best entity, or entities, to meet their personal objectives does not exist. Each taxpayer has a unique set of objectives, and these are intertwined with unique sets of personal and business attributes. All must be weighed and considered in developing a sound tax plan regarding the choice of entity.

S corporations and partnerships offer many similar advantages and disadvantages for investors. Primarily, the flow-through nature of their tax attributes makes these two forms of business quite popular. However, only S corporations provide limited liability to owners. Therefore, in addition to protecting the personal wealth of owners, the limited liability afforded by S corporation status makes capital acquisition easier. To obtain these S corporation benefits, owners are subject to many of the disadvantages of the corporate form in general. For example, state franchise fees, organizational costs, filing fees, and costs of record keeping can be substantial. Also, many states do not recognize the S election for state income tax purposes. (The S election is a federal tax alternative.) Therefore, a single corporation could be a conduit entity for federal income tax purposes and a taxable entity for state income tax authorities.

Partnerships and S corporations both present disadvantages for owner-employees. Although S corporations may hire and pay salaries to their shareholders who work for the organization, partnership owners cannot be employees. However, common fringe benefits paid for owners working for the business are generally not deductible by either business form.

The regular corporation provides limited liability for owners and offers the advantage of being a separate taxable entity, independent of its owners. Therefore, owners pay income tax on corporate earnings only if the corporation makes distributions to the owners (dividends). Also, owners may be employees of the corporation. Accordingly, the corporate entity may reduce corporate taxable income by deducting owner-employee salaries and fringe benefits. Of course, double taxation results when owners receive dividends.

There is no easy answer to the question of which entity to choose. Just try to weigh the objectives and the characteristics of the taxpayer with the attributes of the various entities.

▲ SUMMARY

Not all entities are taxpayers. Only individuals, corporations, and fiduciaries are taxed on their income. Partnerships, S corporations, limited liability entities, and sole proprietorships are conduit entities and are not taxed. Conduit entity income flows through to the tax returns of the owners of the entities. The owners pay the income tax.

A corporation is a taxable legal entity separate from its owners. It has the nontax attributes of limited liability, unlimited life, centralized management, and transferability of ownership. However, if three or more of these characteristics are missing from an entity, the IRS may reclassify the entity as a conduit for tax purposes.

Generally, nontax factors outweigh tax considerations in regard to choosing a business entity. However, tax rate differentials between corporations and individuals often are critical in choosing which form to do business in. For businesses with net incomes of less than $100,000, the corporate form will probably reap tax savings in comparison with the sole proprietorship. Also, owner-employee status provides tax savings for a corporate entity that provides fringe benefits and hires children as employees.

Corporate entities receive a unique dividends-received deduction. Generally, 70 percent of the dividends received from U.S. corporations is deductible from corporate income to mitigate the effects of double, or triple, taxation. Also, the passive loss limitation rules do not affect corporate taxpayers. Exceptions exist for personal service corporations and closely held corporations. Corporations generally have no restrictions concerning their choices of annual accounting periods. However, the selection of an accounting method is fairly restrictive. Only small corporations (gross receipts of $5 million or less) are permitted to use the cash method.

Corporations face certain tax disadvantages, including capital loss limitations and charitable contribution limitations. Also, corporate distributions (dividends) are not deductible, and using multiple corporations to split income is not permitted.

Fiduciary taxation is special, because the fiduciary is responsible for reporting income and paying income taxes on behalf of such entities as trusts and estates. Fiduciary income taxation rules generally follow the rules for individual taxation. However, the law provides no standard deduction amount, allows unlimited charitable contributions, and provides an exemption amount.

Conduit entities (partnerships and S corporations) are characterized by the flow of their tax attributes through to the owners of the entity. The incidence of taxation of a conduit entity's income rests with the owners. However, this flow-through effect may cause owners to pay income taxes without having the benefit of the entity's wherewithal to pay.

Conduit entities must follow the annual accounting period concept and report their financial results as other entities do. Generally, conduits use a calendar year for tax purposes. However, a partnership or S corporation may select a tax year other than a calendar year if the entity makes certain annual payments or can establish a natural business year other than a calendar year to the satisfaction of the IRS.

Basis in a partnership or S corporation establishes the amount of unrecovered investment in the entity. Basis establishes realized gain or loss upon disposition of the investment through application of the capital recovery concept, and it determines the taxability of distributions from the conduit entity to owners. Also, the amount of unrecovered basis determines whether an owner may recognize losses flowing from the conduit entity to the owner.

Basis is dynamic. It is adjusted to reflect the tax results of many entity transactions. Generally, the bases of partnerships and S corporations are adjusted similarly. However, partnerships receive a unique benefit: Basis is increased by a partner's share of partnership debt. Therefore, a partnership can obtain a greater benefit from the flow-through of losses than can similarly situated S corporation shareholders.

Sole proprietorships, partnerships, limited liability companies, limited liability partnerships, and S corporations each offer certain advantages. Sole proprietorships are the easiest to create. Partnerships are almost as easy to form and offer the special basis adjustment rules for partnership debt. Limited liability companies and limited liability partnerships are generally treated as partnerships with the added characteristic of limited liability. S corporations are merely corporations that file the federal election to be treated as a conduit entity. However, the characteristics that qualify a corporation to make the election can be difficult to achieve and maintain. Yet, the corporate characteristics of limited liability, unlimited life, and free transferability of interest remain intact with the S corporation election.

Innumerable tax-planning opportunities exist when all the various entities are considered. For example, proper use of income splitting can provide substantial tax savings. However, a simple formula that allows individuals to select the best entity, or entities, for meeting their objectives does not exist. All of the taxpayer's objectives and characteristics need to be analyzed in conjunction with the attributes of the various entities.

▲ KEY TERMS

brother-sister relationship (p. 390)
centralized management (p. 375)
charitable contribution (p. 385)
complex trust (p. 393)
continuity of life (p. 375)
controlled group (p. 390)
corporate distribution (p. 389)
corporate tax rate (p. 377)
corporation (p. 375)
dividend (p. 389)
dividends-received deduction (DRD) (p. 382)
donated inventory (p. 386)
double taxation (p. 381)
earnings and profits (p. 389)

employment taxes (p. 381)
estate (p. 392)
fiduciary (p. 392)
free transferability of ownership (p. 375)
grantor (p. 393)
grantor trust (p. 393)
guaranteed payment (p. 401)
limited liability (p. 375)
limited liability company (p. 404)
limited liability partnership (p. 405)
organizational costs (p. 387)
parent-subsidiary relationship (p. 390)

partners (p. 401)
partnership (p. 400)
partnership debt (p. 403)
partnership distribution (p. 403)
personal service corporation (PSC) (p. 379)
remainderman (p. 393)
reversionary interest (p. 393)
simple trust (p. 393)
testamentary trust (p. 393)
trust (p. 392)
trustee (p. 392)

▲ PRIMARY TAX LAW SOURCES

[1] Sec. 704—Prescribes the allocation methods for partnership items and describes the limitations on recognizing losses.

[2] Sec. 701—States that a partnership is not subject to income tax and that each partner is liable for taxes only on his or her individual share.

[3] Sec. 11—Imposes income tax on corporate entities and provides the tax rates.

[4] Rev. Proc. 89-12, 1989-1 C.B. 798.—States that where the only general partner of a limited partnership is a corporation, partners must follow certain prescribed guidelines or the IRS may assert that the partnership is an association.

[5] Morrissey v. CIR, 296 U.S. 344 (1935)—Established in a landmark case that unincorporated businesses may be treated as associations taxed as corporations.

[6] Higgins v. Smith, 308 U.S. 473 (1940)—Held that if a corporation as defined by state law has as its only purpose the reduction of its owners' taxes, if it has no real business purpose, or if it has no economic function, the IRS may assert that it is a sham corporation.

[7] Moline Properties, Inc., 319 U.S. 436 (1943)—Held that, in general, so long as a business activity is carried on, a corporation will be considered a separate taxable entity.

[8] U.S. v. Kintner, 216 F.2d 418 (9th Cir. 1954)—Discussed the characteristics of a professional association that may cause it to be classified as a corporation. This case led to the promulgation of Reg. Sec. 301.7701-2.

[9] Reg. Sec. 301.7701-2—Lists the corporate characteristics that are determinative in defining whether an entity is considered an association for tax purposes.

[10] Sec. 1—Imposes income tax on all individuals and other noncorporate entities; provides the tax rate schedules for non corporate taxpayers.

[11] Sec. 448(d)—Describes the criteria that establish a personal service corporation.

[12] Sec. 267—Describes the relationships that aid in defining closely held corporations.

[13] Sec. 243—Describes the procedures for calculating and determining the limitations on the dividends-received deduction.

[14] Sec. 469—Prescribes the treatment and definitions of *passive activity losses*.

[15] Sec. 1212—Provides the rules for the carryback and carryforward of capital losses by corporations.

[16] Sec. 170—Provides the rules for deducting charitable contributions.

[17] Sec. 170(e)(3)—Prescribes the treatment of inventory given to certain qualified charities by a corporation.

[18] Sec. 248—Permits the amortization and deduction of organizational expenses over a period of not less than 60 months at the election of the corporation.

[19] Reg. Sec. 1.248-1—Gives examples of items that are considered organizational expenditures and examples of items that are not considered organizational expenditures.

[20] Sec. 444—Restricts partnerships, S corporations, and personal service corporations to taxable years that are calendar years, natural business years, or specially electable fiscal years with a September, October, or November year end.

[21] Sec. 448—Describes the corporate exceptions for using the accrual method of accounting.

[22] Sec. 301—Provides the tax treatment of corporate dividend distributions.

[23] Sec. 316—Provides that distributions are made out of the earnings and profits of the current year first and that a distribution is a taxable dividend if paid out of the current or accumulated earnings and profits.

[24] Sec. 312—Describes the adjustments to taxable income for the determination of earnings and profits.

[25] Sec. 1563—Defines *controlled group*.

[26] Sec. 671—States that trust income and deductions are attributable to grantors.

[27] Sec. 641—States the general rules for the taxation of estates and trusts.

[28] Sec. 651—Permits a deduction for trusts distributing current income.

[29] Sec. 645—Requires that trusts use a calendar year as their tax year.

[30] Sec. 642—Provides the exemption amounts for fiduciaries.

[31] Sec. 701—Provides that partners, not partnerships, are subject to income tax.

[32] Sec. 1363—Explains that S corporations are not subject to income tax, and states that the S corporation computes its taxable income in a manner similar to that used by an individual taxpayer, except for the items that are subject to separate statement.

[33] Sec. 706—States that the taxable year adopted by a partnership must generally be the same as the taxable year used by partners who own more than 50 percent of the partnership.

[34] Sec. 1378—States that taxable years of S corporations may be only a permitted year. A permitted year is either a calendar year or a fiscal year approved by the IRS because it serves a business purpose.

[35] Sec. 703—States that elections related to the computation and reporting of partnership items are made at the partnership level and not by the individual partners.

[36] Sec. 705—Sets forth the rules for determining the basis of a partner's investment or interest in a partnership.

[37] Sec. 721—States that no gain or loss is recognized by the contributing partner or by the partnership upon the contribution of property to a partnership.

[38] Sec. 722—States that partners' bases in their interests in the partnership are the adjusted bases of the property contributed to attain the partnership interests.

[39] Sec. 761—Defines the terms *partnership*, *partner*, and *partnership agreement* for tax purposes.

[40] Sec. 752—Describes the effect of partnership debt on a partner's basis in that person's partnership interest.

[41] Reg. Sec. 1.752—Details how liabilities affect the basis of a partner's interest in a partnership.

[42] Sec. 733—Explains the effects of a distribution on the basis of a partner's interest.

[43] Sec. 731—Describes the situations in which partners recognize gain or loss on the distribution of partnership assets; provides that the partnership does not recog-

nize any gain or loss upon the distribution of assets to a partner.

[44] Sec. 708(b)—Prescribes the conditions that cause termination of a partnership.

[45] Sec. 1362—Discusses the rules for election, disqualification, and revocation of S status.

[46] Sec. 1361—Provides the qualifying characteristics of corporations making the S election.

[47] Reg. Sec. 1.1372-5—Provides that the usual five-year wait for making the S corporation election after a revocation is unnecessary under certain circumstances.

[48] Sec. 172—Prescribes the procedures for net operating loss carrybacks and carryovers.

[49] Sec. 1372—Requires that the S corporation be treated as a partnership in regard to fringe benefits.

[50] Sec. 1368—Describes the tax effects of distributions by S corporations to their shareholders.

[51] Sec. 1367—Describes the rules for adjusting the basis of a shareholder's stock in the S corporation to account for income, losses, distributions, and expenses of the corporation.

▲ DISCUSSION QUESTIONS

1. How does the doctrine of substance over form affect the determination of corporate status?

2. Will an entity incorporated under state law be considered a corporation for tax purposes until it is dissolved and liquidated? Explain.

3. Herman, an unmarried individual with two dependent children, owns and operates a used car lot as a sole proprietorship. The net income from the business is consistently near $90,000 annually. Based solely on income taxes, consider whether the corporate form of business would produce savings.

4. Refer to question 3. What other factors should Herman consider when choosing between a sole proprietorship and a corporate form of doing business?

5. How do the highest marginal tax rates for individuals compare with the highest marginal tax rates for corporations?

6. Explain the advantages to taxpayers of hiring their children to work in their business enterprises.

7. Duane, the sole stockholder in the Flying R ranch, employs his 13-year-old son at a rate of $4.50. How many hours could Duane's son work during 1995 and pay no income tax on his wages?

8. An accounting firm is formed as a corporation by accountants who own all the stock in the corporation. The corporation acquires an interest in an exotic leather-importing limited partnership. The exotic leather partnership incurs operating losses. Can these losses be deducted currently?

9. Red Corporation owns 80% of Blue Corporation's stock and 45% of Yellow Corporation's stock. Blue Corporation owns 35% of Yellow Corporation's stock. Does a controlled group exist? Explain.

10. Explain the difference between a simple trust and a complex trust.

11. Trusts may be classified as either conduit entities or taxable entities. Explain how this result can occur.

12. A partnership is treated as an aggregation of the proprietary interests of the partners. Following this approach, what is the tax effect of
   a. Contributions of appreciated property to a partnership by its partners?
   b. Distributions of assets from a partnership to partners?
   c. Realization of income by a partnership?

13. Golden Partnership realizes operating income of $45,000 and a long-term capital gain of $6,000 during the current year. Susan Gold is a 1/3 partner. The partnership made

no cash or property distributions this year. How do these events affect Susan's individual tax return for the current year?

14. How do liabilities affect the basis of a partner's interest in a partnership?

15. How can a partner deduct losses in excess of the cash or basis of property contributed to a partnership?

16. What situation may cause a partner to recognize a gain when she or he receives a distribution from the partnership?

17. Generally, each partner in a partnership is taxed as if she or he owns a portion of the underlying partnership assets and directly earns the income produced by the assets. If a partnership and its partners are cash basis taxpayers, which tax concept(s) is (are) being violated? Explain.

18. What are the major differences in the tax treatments of a partnership and a corporation?

19. Janice, Ellen, Dana, and Fred form a limited partnership with Janice as the only general partner. She will perform all management duties. Each partner owns a 1/4 interest in the limited partnership. The partnership agreement states that the 3 remaining partners must agree to any sale or transfer of the ownership interest of the fourth partner to an outsider. Which entity classification will the IRS most likely use for this business? Why?

20. Discuss the comparative advantages and disadvantages of general partnerships and limited partnerships.

21. Compare and contrast the characteristics of general partnerships, C corporations, S corporations, limited liability companies, and limited liability partnerships.

22. How are the following treated by each of the entities discussed in this chapter:
    a. Tax-exempt interest income?
    b. Cash dividend income?
    c. Net capital gains?

23. How do S corporation liabilities affect the basis of an S corporation shareholder's stock?

24. List the advantage(s) of the corporation form of organization.

25. Billy Bob is the sole shareholder of Pony Ranch Corporation and is employed by the corporation to operate the business. The corporation provides excludable meals and lodging for Billy Bob at a cost of $12,000 annually. Billy Bob's marginal tax rate is 28%; the marginal tax rate of the corporation is 34%.
    a. What are the after-tax costs of the meal and lodging benefits for the corporation?
    b. What is the actual value of the benefits if they are not excludable for Billy Bob?

▲ PROBLEMS

26. The Boo-Ball Corporation receives dividend income from Flew-Ball, a domestic corporation, in the amount of $120,000. The Boo-Ball Corporation owns 18% of Flew-Ball Corporation. Boo-Ball's net income from operations is $25,000. What is the amount of Boo-Ball's dividends-received deduction?

27. The John Corporation suffers a $22,000 net loss from operations for the current year but receives $150,000 in dividend income from corporations in which it owns 50% of the stock. What are the amounts of the dividends-received deduction and the corporation's actual taxable income for the current year?

28. The Bat-Ball Corporation incurs a net loss from operations of $62,000 for the current year. The Bat-Ball Corporation received $175,000 in cash dividends from 30%-owned domestic corporations. What are the amounts of the dividends-received deduction and the actual taxable income for the current tax year?

29. 3Bears Corporation has $50,000 in taxable income before special deductions. Taxable income includes $60,000 in dividend income received from other corporations in which 3Bears owns less than a 20% interest. What is 3Bears's taxable income?

30. Adele owns 60% of Trouble, Inc. This entity is a perfume factory formed as a regular corporation. During the current annual accounting period, Trouble, Inc., had an operating income of $18,000, dividend income from investments in stock of other corporations of $2,800, interest income from First National of $1,500, and a loss from an investment in a limited partnership of $22,000. How much of the passive activity loss can be used to offset other income?

31. Elvira owns 100% of the stock of Midnite Corporation, a manufacturer of galobnotites. During the current year, Midnite has operating income of $50,000, dividend income of $16,000 from investments in other corporations, losses from investments in limited partnerships of $46,000, and pays $20,000 in dividends.
    a. What are the amounts of taxable income and tax liability reported by Midnite for the current year?
    b. Assume Midnite Corporation is operated as an S corporation. Explain why the amount of taxable income resulting from the items reported by both Midnite Corporation and Elvira are different from your answers in part a.

32. The Baker Corporation has the following entries on its books for the current tax year:

Net income from operations	$120,000
Dividends received (70% rules)	12,000
Charitable contributions made in current year	13,000
Charitable contribution carryover from the previous year	2,500

    What is the maximum amount of charitable contribution deduction allowed for the current year? What is Baker's taxable income for the current year?

33. Fairplay Corporation has gross income of $150,000 and taxable income of $50,000. The company included no special deductions in the calculation of its taxable income. While reviewing the tax return, Fairplay's accountant found $20,000 in charitable contributions improperly classified as advertising and promotion expense. He sent the return back to the tax department for correction. What is Fairplay's corrected taxable income?

34. The New Tech Corporation contributes some of its scientific equipment inventory to the Computer Department of Great University during the current year. At the date of the contribution, the equipment has a fair market value of $32,000. New Tech's basis in the equipment is $12,000. What is the amount of the charitable contribution deduction? Would your answer change if New Tech's basis in the equipment was $6,000?

35. Big C Corporation, a calendar-year corporation, was formed during the current year and began business operations on September 1. Big C paid $8,000 to attorneys, accountants, and state regulatory agencies to organize the corporation. Big C also paid $6,000 in commissions on the sale of corporate stock. Can Big C deduct any part of the $14,000? Explain.

36. The Viking Corporation had the following items of income for its calendar year 1995:

Operating income	$350,000
Dividend income (12% owned corporations)	15,000
Long-term capital gains	9,000
Short-term capital gains	3,000
Capital loss carryover from 1994	8,000
Charitable cash contributions	12,000
Net operating loss carryover from 1994	35,000

    a. What is the amount of the corporation's 1995 taxable income and tax liability?
    b. Assume Viking is, and always has been, an S corporation wholly owned by Warren, a single taxpayer with no other income or deductions. Will either Viking Corporation or Warren realize any tax savings over the situation described in part a? Explain.

37. Charger, Inc., had the following items for 1995:

Net operating income	$ 40,000
Dividend income (50%-owned corporation)	100,000

Charitable cash contributions	20,000
Net operating loss carryover from 1994	10,000

a. What are the amounts of the corporation's 1995 taxable income and tax liability?

b. Assume Charger is, and always has been, an S corporation wholly owned by Suzanne, a married individual with no dependents and no other income or deductions. What are the tax liabilities of Charger and Suzanne?

c. Explain why the answers in parts a and b are different.

38. The Toy Corporation distributed $175,000 in cash ($1.75 per share) at a time when its accumulated earnings and profits were $40,000. What is the effect of the distribution on Bernice, who owns 500 shares of Toy stock for which she paid $8,000?

39. Dance Corporation distributes $150,000 in cash to its shareholders during 1995. Accumulated earnings and profits are $25,000 as of January 1, 1995. Current earnings and profits for 1995 are $65,000. Jack, the sole shareholder of Dance Corporation, has a basis of $30,000 in the stock. What is the tax effect of this distribution for Jack?

40. Which of the following corporations are members of a brother-sister controlled group? Explain.

I.

	Corporation	
	A	**B**
Shareholder 1	90%	10%
Shareholder 2	10%	90%

II.

	Corporation	
	A	**B**
Shareholder 1	70%	30%
Shareholder 2	30%	70%

III.

	Corporation	
	A	**B**
Shareholder 1	79%	79%
Shareholder 2	20%	1%
Shareholder 3	1%	20%

IV.

	Corporation	
	A	**B**
Shareholder 1	90%	10%
Shareholder 2	10%	-0-
Shareholder 3	-0-	90%

41. Hiram owns 90% of Little Burro Corporation. Last year, Little Burro acquired 100% of the corporate stock of one of its suppliers, Small Bean, Inc. For the current year, Little Burro's taxable income is $100,000, and Small Bean's taxable income is $75,000. Discuss the income tax consequences for Hiram and the two corporations for the current year.

42. Hobson transfers $400,000 in cash and property to a revocable grantor trust created in the current year. His daughter, Glenda, will receive the income from the trust for her life. Hobson's granddaughter, Wanda, is to receive the remainder at Glenda's death. The trust's income for the year consists of $48,000 in dividends and $9,000 in long-term capital gains. All the dividend income is distributed to Glenda. The capital gains are applied to trust principal and not distributed. Hobson's marginal tax rate is 31%. Glenda's marginal tax rate is 28%, and Wanda's marginal tax rate is 15%.

a. What is the total amount of income tax liability attributable to the trust's income for the year?

b. Explain and discuss alternative ways to structure the trust instrument.

43. Starita creates a trust and transfers property that will generate income for distribution to her minor child Terri, 12, until Terri reaches the age of 21. At that age, all trust property, including any accumulated income, is to be paid to Terri. During the current year, the trust distributes $10,000 for Terri's support and distributes and invests $6,000 in a bank CD in Terri's name. The balance of the trust income, $15,000, accumulates in the trust. Who is responsible for the tax on this year's trust income? Explain your reasoning, and discuss any other way to structure the trust instrument that may be beneficial to either Terri or Starita.

44. The Willow Trust receives $2,000 in municipal bond interest and $20,000 from U.S. government securities during the current year. The trust gives Planned Parenthood $1,000 annually. What is the amount of the charitable contribution deduction for the current year?

45. During the current year, Okner Trust receives $8,000 in dividend income from corporate stock, $2,000 in U.S. government security interest, and a $1,000 short-term capital gain. Trust administrative expenses total $500. The trust agreement states that all interest is distributed annually and all other forms of income and gains are accumulated as trust corpus. Determine the trust's taxable income and the trust's income tax liability.

46. Kyle Partnership begins operations in November 1994 and elects an October 31 fiscal year end. For the year ending October 31, 1995, the partnership has net income of $70,000. Will the elected fiscal year pass IRS scrutiny? Does the partnership have to make a deposit? If so, how much?

47. Fawn contributes undeveloped land with a basis of $15,000 and a fair market value of $90,000 to the Deer Partnership for a 25% interest in the partnership. What is Fawn's share of the partnership's operating income (loss), and how does the share affect Fawn's basis in each of the following situations?
    a. Deer Partnership reports an annual operating loss of $40,000 for the current year.
    b. Deer Partnership reports annual operating income of $25,000.
    c. Deer Partnership reports annual operating loss of $80,000.

48. Jacqui and Joanne plan to buy a bed-and-breakfast inn for $200,000. Jacqui will contribute $20,000 toward the purchase and will operate the enterprise. Joanne's primary role is that of investor. She will contribute $100,000. However, she will be an active participant because of her involvement in management decisions. They will borrow the balance of the purchase price from a local bank. Advise Jacqui and Joanne on a choice of business form. Consider that the enterprise is expected to realize operating losses of $50,000 annually for the first 3 years. During the fourth year, the inn should realize a meager profit.

49. John and Kathy form JK Partnership on January 1, 1995. John contributes $200,000 in cash for a 40% interest. Kathy contributes real estate valued at $450,000 and encumbered by a mortgage of $150,000, which is assumed by the partnership. Kathy's basis in the real estate is $100,000. She receives a 60% partnership interest. What is the amount of each partner's basis in his or her partnership interest?

50. Janice receives a partnership distribution of $31,000 in cash from AXE Partnership. Janice's basis in her partnership interest is $27,000 before the distribution. What is (are) the tax effect(s) of the distribution for Janice? What actions could Janice have taken before the distribution to change the results?

51. In January 1994, Waller pays $60,000 for 20% of the common stock of Baker, Inc., a qualified S corporation. Baker, Inc., reports a net loss from operations of $50,000 for 1994. For 1995, Baker, Inc., reports operating income of $20,000. On January 2, 1996, Baker, Inc., distributes $15,000 to Waller. What are the tax effects of these events for Waller?

52. Natrone pays $35,000 for stock in an S corporation and receives shares equal to a 20% interest in the corporation in the current year. At the same time, he pays $35,000 for a 20% interest in a general partnership. Both entities have outstanding mortgage debt of

$75,000, and both report ordinary taxable income of $10,000. What is the maximum cash distribution each entity can make this year to Natrone without causing him to recognize income? Explain your answer(s) in terms of the underlying concepts and facts that support your calculations.

53. Lyra and Misha, a married couple, are the sole shareholders of Niki, Inc. Niki owns 80% of Gladly Corporation. During the current year, Gladly distributes a $20,000 cash dividend to Niki, Inc. Niki's taxable income before dividends is $75,000. Niki distributes all after-tax income to its shareholders. This distribution is the only source of income for Lyra and Misha.
   a. Determine the amount of after-tax income Lyra and Misha realize because of their corporate ownership.
   b. How will your answer in part a change if Niki, Inc., is an S corporation? Explain.

54. Monica and Mike, a married couple, recently incorporated their drapery business. To complete the entity transformation from sole proprietorship to corporation, they transferred ownership of sewing machines, cleaning equipment, assorted fabric, and $100,000 in municipal bonds to the corporation. The municipal bonds are collateral for bank loans to the corporation for business expansion. The business is expected to generate annual operating profits of $100,000. Tax-exempt interest will be $13,000 annually.
   a. Determine the amount of after-tax earnings and profits available to distribute as cash dividends.
   b. Will electing S corporation treatment save Monica and Mike and/or their corporation any money? Explain the result(s).

55. Last year, Linoa paid $25,000 for a 10% ownership interest in FasTrack Corporation. During the current year, FasTrack defaulted on a $100,000 loan to Third Security National Bank. Discuss the monetary implications for Linoa if the bank insists she repay the $100,000 loan under each of the following situations:
   a. FasTrack is a corporation.
   b. FasTrack is an S corporation.
   c. FasTrack is a partnership, and Linoa is a general partner.
   d. FasTrack is a partnership, and Linoa is a limited partner.

56. The laws of the country of Artichoke (a newly organized eastern European country) allow a legal entity called a *sharing association*. The characteristics of this legal entity are
   a. Its objective is to carry on a business for a profit.
   b. It has two or more owners.
   c. Transferability of its ownership interests is restricted.
   d. All owners share in management activities.
   e. Determination of the entity's life is independent of its owners.
   f. Owners have limited liability.
   Determine whether U.S. tax law will treat Artichoke's sharing association as a corporation or as a partnership.

57. Natalie operates her bookkeeping service as a corporation. She is the sole shareholder and is an employee functioning as the chief operating officer of the business. The corporation employs several other individuals and offers them good fringe benefits: group term life insurance, health insurance, disability insurance, and a 12% qualified pension plan. Natalie's good friend, Ricci, operates a custom software development company. The business is an S corporation, and Ricci is the sole shareholder. She is also an employee who serves as the manager. Upon Natalie's recommendation, Ricci copied the fringe-benefit package of Natalie's corporation. Discuss the tax ramifications to Natalie and her corporation and to Ricci and her corporation. Assume both businesses are quite profitable. Make recommendations that may benefit one or both individuals.

58. Gena, the 75% owner of Enterprise Business Systems, receives the benefits of $2,400-worth of premiums for health and accident insurance annually. The business's net operating income for the year is $50,000, before considering Gena's benefit. Determine the business's net income for the year and the tax effects for Gena for each of the following entities:

a. A corporation
b. An S corporation

c. A sole proprietorship
d. A partnership

▲ DISCUSSION CASE 9–1

Four managers working for a certain Big Six accounting firm agree to join together and create their own tax-planning and management-consulting firm. Initially, Kelley, Barbara, Kuzuyo, and Leonard plan to operate their venture as a general partnership. All partners will share equally in decision making and business income and losses. The four individuals' ages range from 30 to 36. All have small children. Discuss the pros and cons of the various alternative business forms available to the individuals. Based upon known (and assumed) characteristics of the four owners, recommend the entity they should choose.

▲ DISCUSSION CASE 9–2

Astrid, a single individual, is a sales representative for several sporting goods manufacturers. She operates her enterprise as a sole proprietorship. Astrid has one employee, Melvin, who serves as office manager for the business. Gross revenues are $250,000 annually. Annual operating expenses are

Melvin's salary	$30,000
Payroll taxes & fees	3,000
Utilities	1,200
Rent	4,800
Selling expenses	8,000
Premiums paid for Melvin:	
$50,000 term life insurance policy	300
Health-care insurance policy	2,700

Astrid takes an annual draw of $3,000 to pay for insurance coverage equal to Melvin's. Astrid uses the remaining funds personally. Astrid is considering incorporating her business. Discuss the benefits that will accrue to Astrid by incorporating. Recommend any alternative courses of action.

▲ TAX PLANNING CASE 9–3

John Johnson and his wife Joanne have 2 children, Joe, 16, and Jamie, 4. John is self-employed, and Joanne works as a swimming coach for Local University. John's business is manufacturing Jaugernauts. Through the years, Johnson's Jaugernauts has been fairly successful, providing a before-tax income of approximately $100,000 per year. The business has several employees, including a secretary-receptionist, 2 sales people, 4 production workers, and 2 truck drivers.

Last year, Joanne entered a contest and won a sizable block of stock in a computer company. This stock is expected to produce approximately $10,000 per year in taxable dividends. Other than this stock, their investment assets consist mainly of savings accounts and certificates of deposits. However, in 1980 John invested in a tax shelter that provided him with tax write-offs until the Tax Reform Act of 1986 curtailed his loss deduction from the shelter (i.e., the losses are considered passive losses).

John and Joanne have come to you for advice. They would like to rearrange their business and personal affairs to obtain a better tax situation. Discuss at least 3 actions (don't feel limited if you can think of more than 3) John and Joanne could take, and indicate the advantages and disadvantages of each action. Specific numerical calculations are not required, but if you think such an example would help explain your point, please feel free to use it.

For a number of years, Nina was a mechanical engineer for a chemical company. Nina always enjoyed working around her home in her spare time, doing necessary repairs and maintenance. However, she was always frustrated by the multitude of tools she had to carry around to do her various tasks. One evening, she drew up a design for a gizmo that could do the work of 12 different common home repair tools. At first, she made a few gizmos by hand and gave them to her friends as gag gifts. Their reaction to the gizmo was so enthusiastic that Nina took out a patent on it, got a loan from her friend at Local Bank, quit her job, and began a small-scale manufacturing operation.

In setting up her business, Nina took most of her advice from her brother-in-law, an assistant district attorney. Accordingly, she organized the business as a corporation and pays salaries to herself, her husband Stan, and their 3 children (the children are 2, 9, and 13). In addition, she put her investment portfolio inside the corporation.

After the first year of business, the corporate books show a loss of $25,000 after paying salaries of $30,000 to Nina, $20,000 to Stan (Stan continues to earn $18,000 from his full-time job), and $5,000 to each of the children.

a. What tax-related mistakes has Nina made regarding the business? Be specific. Indicate any negative effects that could arise from this arrangement.

b. Is there anything Nina can do to rectify the problems you identified? Explain, and indicate how each solution you propose cures or mitigates the problem.

▲ TAX PLANNING
CASE 9–4

Assume you are a CPA and a tax specialist. Your clients include Ale and Grains, Inc., an S corporation, and Gustav and Heidi Lager, a married couple who are shareholders and the operators of Ale and Grains. The S corporation has had 35 qualified shareholders for several years. Gustav and Heidi have come to you to let you know that they have just obtained a divorce. Both individuals will continue to operate Ale and Grains for the ownership group, and neither party plans to dispose of her or his ownership interest. They know that certain rules govern the number of shareholders allowed in an S corporation, but they tell you not to be concerned—because all that will change will be their mailing addresses. They refer to the doctrine of substance over form and how it fits this situation. Write a letter to Gustav, Heidi, and the other shareholders offering your advice. Refer to the AICPA Code of Professional Conduct and the Statements on Responsibilities in Tax Practice where necessary.

▲ ETHICS
DISCUSSION
CASE 9–5

PROPERTY TRANSACTIONS

CHAPTER 10
ACQUISITIONS OF PROPERTY

CHAPTER 11
COST RECOVERY ON PROPERTY: DEPRECIATION,
DEPLETION, AND AMORTIZATION

CHAPTER 12
PROPERTY DISPOSITIONS

CHAPTER 13
NONRECOGNITION TRANSACTIONS

Acquisitions of Property

▲ CHAPTER LEARNING OBJECTIVES

■ Distinguish and define different types and classes of property.

■ Provide an overview of the property investment cycle from acquisition through disposition, and discuss the tax problems encountered throughout the cycle.

■ Explain the calculation of a property's adjusted basis.

■ Distinguish a realized from a recognized gain or loss on a disposition of property.

■ Explain how to determine the initial basis of purchased property.

■ Discuss the tax aspects of various ways to purchase the assets of a business.

■ Describe the rules for determining the initial basis of gift property, inherited property, personal use property converted to business use property, and property received from a spouse.

■ Explain the tax problems associated with determining the initial basis of securities.

▲ CONCEPT REVIEW ▲

Accounting method   A taxpayer must adopt an accounting method that clearly reflects income.

All-inclusive income   All income received is taxable unless a specific provision can be found in the tax law that either excludes the income from taxation or defers its recognition to a future tax year.

Annual accounting period   All entities must report the results of their operations on an annual basis (the tax year). Each tax year stands on its own, apart from other tax years.

Arm's-length transaction   A transaction in which all parties to the transaction have bargained in good faith and for their individual benefit, not for the benefit of the transaction group.

Basis   This is the amount of unrecovered investment in an asset. As amounts are expended and/or recovered relative to an asset over time, the basis is adjusted in consideration of such changes. The **adjusted basis** of an asset is the original basis, plus or minus the changes in the amount of unrecovered investment.

Business purpose   To be deductible, an expenditure or a loss must have a business or other economic purpose that exceeds any tax avoidance motive. The primary motive for the transaction must be to make a profit.

Capital recovery   No income is realized until the taxpayer receives more than the amount invested to produce the income. The amount invested in an asset represents the maximum amount recoverable.

Conduit entity   An entity for which the tax attributes flow through to its owners for tax purposes.

Entity   All items of income, deduction, and so on are traced to the tax unit responsible for the item.

Legislative grace   Any tax relief provided is the result of a specific act of Congress that must be strictly applied and interpreted. All income received is taxable unless a specific provision can be found in the tax law that excludes the income from taxation. Deductions must be approached with the philosophy that nothing is deductible unless a provision in the tax law allows the deduction.

Realization   No income (or loss) is recognized until it has been realized. A realization involves a change in the form and/or the substance of a taxpayer's property rights that results from an arm's-length transaction.

Related party   Family members and corporations that are owned by family members are considered related parties, as are certain other relationships between entities in which the power to control the substance of a transaction is evidenced through majority ownership.

Substance-over-form doctrine   Transactions are to be taxed according to their true intention rather than some form that may have been contrived.

▲ INTRODUCTION

Chapter 5 discussed the general criteria for deducting expenses. Expenses incurred in a trade or business, for the production of income, and certain personal expenditures are deductible when they are paid or incurred. However, expenditures incurred in these activities that provide benefits that extend significantly beyond the end of the tax year cannot be deducted as a current expense. These expenditures, which provide long-lived benefits, are called *capital expenditures*. Thus, capital expenditures result in assets that provide economic or personal benefits that extend significantly beyond the end of the accounting period in which the expenditure is made. The term **property** is used in taxation to refer to long-lived assets that are owned by a taxpayer. Throughout the remaining chapters, the terms *property* and *asset* are used interchangeably to mean anything owned or possessed by a taxpayer.

The capital recovery concept provides the foundation for the tax accounting for property. According to this concept, the amount invested in an asset is recovered tax free before the taxpayer realizes any taxable income from the property investment. The two basic methods of recovering the capital invested in an asset are by deducting a portion of the cost of the asset against income during the life of the asset (e.g., through depreciation deductions) and by offsetting the invested amount against any amounts realized from the disposition of the asset at the end of its period of use. The amount of investment in an asset is the asset's basis. An asset's basis establishes the initial amount of capital investment that can be recovered tax free as a capital recovery, it is used to determine the amount of any annual deductions allowed for depreciation, and it represents the amount of unrecovered capital for determining gain or loss upon the disposition of the asset. Therefore, determining the correct basis of property is essential in order to properly account for the tax effects of investments in property.

The next four chapters discuss the tax aspects related to the acquisition, use, and disposition of property. This chapter begins with a discussion of the different classes of property and their characteristics. An overview of the property investment cycle is discussed next; it provides the framework for the study of chapters 10 through 13. The remainder of the chapter deals with problems involved in determining the initial basis of property when it is acquired.

▲ CLASSES OF PROPERTY

For tax purposes, property is classified by both its use and its type. The use of property determines whether deductions are allowed for current-year expenditures (i.e., repairs, maintenance) relating to the property and for capital recovery deductions for depreciation, depletion, or amortization. In order to take any deductions relating to property, the property must have a business purpose: It must be used in a trade or business or held for the production of income. This is the general requirement for deductibility of expenses discussed in Chapter 5. Deductions for expenditures on property that is held for purely personal use are not generally allowed. Only those specifically allowed expenditures (discussed in Chapter 8) on **personal use property,** such as property taxes and home mortgage interest, are deductible. In addition, only casualty and theft losses on personal use property are deductible. Thus, proper classification of the use of an asset is essential to determining the effect of the property on taxable income.

> ▲ **EXAMPLE 1**   Ellen, a physician, purchased a television set for her patients to watch while they wait for their appointments. What is the proper classification of the television for Ellen?
>
> *Discussion:*   Because the television is used in relation to Ellen's business, it is classified as property used in a trade or business. Ellen may deduct any annual expenditures made relative to the television as an ordinary and necessary business expense. In addition, Ellen may deduct the appropriate amount of depreciation on the television during its tax life.
>
> ▲ **EXAMPLE 2**   When Ellen purchased the television in example 1, she purchased another television that she put in her family room at home. What is the proper classification of the second television set?
>
> *Discussion:*   The second television is used for personal purposes and therefore is a personal use asset. Ellen is not allowed any deductions for expenditures made relative to the second television, nor is she allowed to depreciate the television, because it is a personal use asset.

As these examples illustrate, the use of the property, not the type of property, is the key factor in determining deductibility. That is, any property can be used in any of the three basic categories. In addition, a single property may be used in more than one category. Such property is referred to as a **mixed-use property** (also called *mixed-use asset*). Proper accounting for mixed-use property requires a reasonable allocation of costs among the uses of the property.

▲ **EXAMPLE 3**   Don purchased a duplex at a cost of $80,000. Don resides in 1 unit and rents out the other unit. How should Don account for the duplex?

Discussion: The duplex is mixed-use property. The unit Don uses as his residence is a personal use asset and must be accounted for separately from the unit that is rented. Don will be allowed an itemized deduction only for the interest and property taxes from the personal use unit. However, on the rental unit he will be able to deduct all ordinary and necessary expenses of maintaining the unit. For example, if Don pays the utility bill of both units, only the portion that is reasonably allocable to the rental unit is deductible. In addition, Don may take the allowed depreciation deductions on the rental unit but is not allowed any depreciation deduction on the personal unit.

The type of property also affects the deductions allowed during the period the property is used. All property may be classified as tangible property or intangible property. **Tangible property** is any property that has a physical existence. That is, tangible property has form, shape, and substance. Land, buildings, machinery, equipment, automobiles, and furniture are all examples of tangible property. **Intangible property** lacks any physical characteristics and exists only because of economic rights the property possesses. Stocks, bonds, copyrights, trademarks, goodwill, and patents are examples of intangible property.

Tangible property is broken down further for tax purposes into real property and personal property. Real property consists of land and any structures permanently attached to land. A building and its structural components, such as the air-conditioning system, electrical wiring, and an elevator are considered real property. Real property is often referred to as **real estate,** and the terms are used interchangeably. Personal property is any tangible property that is not real property. Machinery, equipment, livestock, automobiles, computers, and paintings are all examples of personal property. Personal property is often referred to as **personalty,** and the terms are used interchangeably. Personal property is a *type* of property that is different from personal use property, which is a *use* of property. The type of property should not be confused with its use.

In contrast to the use of property, the type of property does not change from taxpayer to taxpayer. That is, land is always real property and a computer is always personal property, regardless of the use of the property. The type of property determines such things as the amount of allowable depreciation on the property. Personal property generally has a shorter useful life than real property, and the amount and timing of the depreciation deductions on the two properties are adjusted for the difference in useful lives. The allowable depreciation methods for different types of property are discussed in Chapter 11. Property type is also important in determining the tax effects of property dispositions. As will be discussed in Chapter 12, depreciable real property and depreciable personal property are subject to special rules that reclassify income from capital gain income to ordinary income at disposition. The type of property determines the amount of the gain that is reclassified. Table 10–1 provides a summary of the different types of property.

Generating income involves the acquisition and use of property to produce that income. That is, businesses acquire factories, equipment, supplies, and so on to produce products that are sold to generate income. Similarly, investors purchase

▲ **THE PROPERTY INVESTMENT CYCLE**

▲ **Table 10–1**

SUMMARY OF
PROPERTY TYPES

Type of Property	Property Characteristics	Examples
Personal property (Personalty)	Property that has a physical existence and that is not real estate or permanently attached to real estate. Personal property has form, shape, and substance.	Machinery, equipment, automobiles, trucks, computers, furniture, fixtures, telephone systems, works of art, livestock, video equipment.
Real property (Real estate)	Land and any structures that are permanently attached to land. Real property has form, shape, and substance.	Land and land improvements such as landscaping, shrubbery, sidewalks, parking lots, and fences; buildings, grain silos, barns, sheds, greenhouses.
Intangible property	Property that lacks a physical existence; the rights to the property exist only on paper. Intangible property does not have form, shape, or physical substance.	Patents, copyrights, trademarks, goodwill, covenants not to compete, stocks, bonds, and other securities.
Personal use property	Any property that is used by the taxpayer for purely personal purposes. Personal use property can be personal property, real property, or intangible property.	Personal residence, clothing, furniture, home computer, lawnmower, personal automobile.

stocks and bonds to produce dividend and interest income as well as appreciation in the value of the security. Individuals acquire homes, furniture, clothing, and automobiles that they use in their personal activities. Acquisition of property begins a property investment cycle that has income tax effects throughout the period in which the taxpayer uses the property.

The property investment cycle and the tax accounting related to it are illustrated in Figure 10–1. In the top panel of Figure 10–1, the investment process begins with acquisition of the property. The most common method of acquiring property is by purchase. However, property may also be acquired through other means, such as by gift or inheritance. The initial basis of the property must be determined at acquisition. The **initial basis** of an asset is generally the cost of acquiring the asset and placing it into service. When assets are acquired by means other than purchase, special rules apply for determining the initial basis to assign to the asset for tax purposes. The cost of acquiring an asset by purchase and the special rules for other methods of acquisition are discussed later in this chapter.

Adjusted Basis

Under the capital recovery concept, a taxpayer is allowed to recover the amount of capital invested in an asset tax free. Thus, basis sets the limit on the maximum amount that can be recovered tax free. As an asset is used to generate income, it may be necessary to adjust the initial basis to account for additional capital investments in the asset or for recoveries of capital investment.[1] As Figure 10–1 illustrates, these adjustments result in an amount that is referred to as the *adjusted*

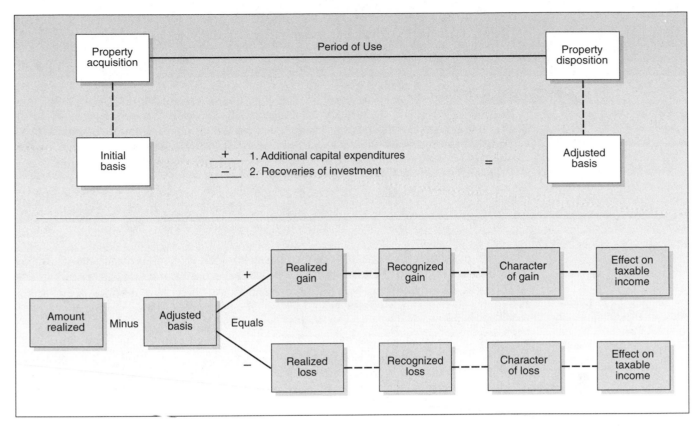

▲ **Figure 10–1**

PROPERTY INVESTMENT
CYCLE

basis. Adjusted basis is equal to the initial basis, plus or minus the cumulative effects of the adjustments. Adjusted basis roughly corresponds to the book-value concept studied in financial accounting.

At any point in time, the remaining capital investment to be recovered is represented by an asset's adjusted basis. An asset's adjusted basis may never be less than zero (a negative number). For investments such as publicly traded corporate stocks, few, if any, adjustments to the initial basis are needed. But for other types of assets, such as depreciable assets used in a business, the adjusted basis calculation is made at least annually and on the date of an asset's disposition. Exhibit 10–1 presents a general format for computing an asset's adjusted basis.

Increases in Basis.   As Exhibit 10–1 indicates, there are two broad categories of increases in basis. An asset's basis is increased by expenditures that are an additional investment in the asset. Additional investments are expenditures made on behalf of the asset that cannot be deducted as a current period expense and must be capitalized as part of its basis.[2] Additional investments would include improvements to an asset that enlarge an asset (adding a room onto a building) or extends its useful life (putting a new roof on a building). In addition, any costs of defending the ownership of the property and special assessments for such local benefits as widening the street in front of a building are capitalized as part of the cost of the property.

Basis is also increased by items that constitute taxable income but are not withdrawn from the asset for personal or other use. The taxable income of a conduit entity that is allocated to the owner of the entity is added to the basis of the investment in the entity, because the owner is taxed on the income yet does not necessarily receive income.[3,4] This category of basis addition includes the bargain element that is recognized as income in a bargain purchase of property.

Decreases in Basis.   Decreases in basis are grouped into three broad categories. The first group of decreases results from annual expense deductions that are allowed when the asset is used to earn income. The deduction of an expense is a capital recovery of an investment in an asset. The capital recovery results from reducing the taxable income for the year in which the deduction is claimed. In addition, any losses from a conduit entity that are allocated to the owner of the entity are subtracted from the basis of the investment, because the owner is entitled to the allowable loss deduction on the investment.

Basis is also reduced as a result of disposing of part of the asset. For example, a gift of half of a taxpayer's interest in an asset reduces the taxpayer's basis by half. If property is subject to a casualty, the asset's basis is reduced by the amount of loss deducted.

Special income items also reduce basis. For example, a payment received from a utility company for an easement for power lines does not constitute a realization, because the form or substance of the taxpayer's property rights does not change; such a payment is excluded from income. For tax purposes, the payment is treated as a capital recovery and a reduction in the basis of the land. Similarly, a shareholder who receives a nontaxable dividend from a corporation treats the payment as a recovery of the stock's basis. If the shareholder receives nontaxable dividends that ultimately reduce the stock's basis to zero, any additional nontaxable dividends mean the shareholder must recognize gain (from the "sale" of the asset).

▲ **EXAMPLE 4**   On July 1, 1995, Cynthia buys 500 shares of Watkins common stock at $35 per share ($17,500 total cost). On December 31, 1995, Watkins pays a $4 per share cash distribution. Watkins reports that $3 per share is taxable as a dividend and $1 per share is a nontaxable dividend. What is Cynthia's adjusted basis in the Watkins stock?

▲ **Exhibit 10–1**

COMPUTATION OF
ADJUSTED BASIS

Initial basis	$XXX
Increases in basis from	
■ Additional investments	
• Capital invested	
• Costs of protecting ownership	
• Special property tax assessments for local benefits	XXX
■ Reinvestment of income	
• Income taxed to owners of conduit entities	XXX
Decreases in basis from	
■ Annual tax deductions resulting in a reduction of tax liability	
• Depreciation, depletion, and amortization	
• Losses from conduit entities	(XXX)
■ Dispositions of all or part of interest in an asset	
• Casualty loss	
• Sale or gift of part of an asset	(XXX)
■ Capital recovery resulting from excluded income	
• Nontaxable dividends	
• Easements	(XXX)
Equals: Adjusted basis	$XXX*

*Adjusted basis cannot be less than zero.

Discussion: Cynthia's adjusted basis in the Watkins stock after she receives the dividend is $34 per share. Cynthia must reduce her $17,500 initial basis by the $500 nontaxable dividend that is excluded from gross income ($1 × 500). Thus, Cynthia's adjusted basis on December 31, 1995, for the 500 shares is $17,000. The $3 per share taxable dividend is reported as gross income and does not affect the basis of the stock.

▲ **EXAMPLE 5** James buys an office building in 1990. He pays $30,000 for the land and $170,000 for the building. Shortly after he acquires the property, the city imposes a $20,000 special property tax assessment to pave streets and install sidewalks. In addition, James pays $25,000 to remodel two rooms in the building to make them suitable for his use. When a dispute arises with a neighbor concerning property lines, James pays his attorney $2,000 to protect his interest in the land. Total depreciation deducted from 1990 through 1995 is $35,000. A fire in 1995 results in an $8,000 uninsured casualty loss to the building, which James deducts as a loss on his tax return. What is James's adjusted basis in the property on December 31, 1995?

Discussion: James's adjusted basis in the building is $152,000 and in the land is $52,000, computed as follows:

Expenditure	Building	Land
Initial basis	$170,000	$30,000
Remodel offices	25,000	
Special tax assessment for local benefits		20,000
Attorney's fee to defend title		2,000
Depreciation deducted	(35,000)	
Casualty loss from fire	(8,000)	
Adjusted basis	$152,000	$52,000

The expenditures must be identified as adjustments to either the basis of the land or the basis of the building. The $2,000 legal fee to defend title to the land increases the land's basis. The $20,000 in special tax assessments for local benefits is considered to attach to the basis of the land and also increases the land's basis. The $25,000 spent to remodel the building for his use is added to its basis. The $35,000 deduction for depreciation and the $8,000 casualty loss deduction are capital recoveries that reduce the basis of the building.

The recovery of capital investment may occur at several different times. Assets that have definite useful lives may be recovered over the period of use through depreciation, depletion, or amortization deductions. To allocate the depreciation deduction to the correct accounting period, you must use tax accounting rules to correctly measure the basis subject to depreciation. If the basis of an asset is undervalued, depreciation deductions may be permanently lost. In addition, an asset's basis must be reduced by the larger of the depreciation allowable, based on tax accounting methods for computing depreciation, or by the amount of depreciation actually deducted on the taxpayer's returns.[5] Therefore, claiming smaller deductions than those to which the taxpayer is entitled can result in lost basis and unused deductions. On the other hand, a taxpayer who claims inflated depreciation deductions may be subject to penalties. Thus, proper determination of the basis in business assets is crucial to computing annual deductions for depreciation, depletion, and amortization. The example that follows highlights the importance of properly reporting depreciation deductions. Do not be concerned with depreciation methods until Chapter 11.

▲ **EXAMPLE 6**   Kalil Corporation uses a machine in its business that cost $10,000. Using tax depreciation methods, Kalil is entitled to total allowable depreciation on the machine of $9,000. However, because of clerical errors, Kalil actually deducted a total of $6,000 in allowed depreciation on its tax returns. Kalil sells the machine on July 1 for $5,000. What are the tax effects to Kalil of the clerical errors?

Discussion: Kalil Corporation must report a gain of $4,000 from the sale of the asset [$5,000 − ($10,000 − $9,000 allowable depreciation)]. The tax law requires Kalil to reduce its basis in the machine by the larger of the depreciation that it actually deducted or the amount it should have deducted based on tax deprecation methods. As a result, Kalil has lost the benefit of $3,000 in depreciation to which it was entitled under the capital recovery concept ($9,000 allowable − $6,000 allowed). Kalil Corporation might be able to salvage some of the lost basis by filing amended tax returns to correct the error.

Basis in Conduit Entities

Partnerships and S Corporations are conduit entities. As a result, the income and deductions of these entities are passed through and included in the gross income of the owners of the entity. Ownership of an interest in a conduit entity creates an interesting tax accounting problem. Effectively, owners must determine the adjusted basis of their investment using an equity accounting method. Using the equity accounting method, the investor increases and decreases the basis of the investment for items that change the amount that may be excluded from income under the capital recovery concept. These adjustments are fully explained in Chapter 9; Exhibit 10–2 presents the effect of these adjustments on adjusted basis.

The taxpayer's adjusted basis for the investment in the conduit entity can be zero, but it may not be a negative number, as explained in Chapter 9.

▲ **EXAMPLE 7**   Tina owns a 25% interest in Quality Conduit Entity. At the beginning of the current year, Tina's adjusted basis for her investment was $75,000. For the current year, Quality reports the following pass-through tax information:

▲ **Exhibit 10–2**

CONDUIT ENTITY
BASIS COMPUTATION

Initial basis in stock (cost) or basis of investment at the beginning of the current year	**$X,XXX**
Increases in basis:	
• Additional capital invested during the year	
• Taxable and nontaxable income allocated to the owner for the current year	
• Liability adjustment	
—A partner's share of any increase in liabilities related to the partnership	XXX
Decreases in basis:	
• Cash received from the entity	
• Property received from the entity:	
—If a partnership, subtract the partnership's basis for the property	
—If an S corporation, subtract the fair market value of the property	
• Deductions, losses, and nondeductible expenses allocated to the owner for the current year	
• Liability adjustment	
—A partner's share of any decrease in liabilities related to the partnership	(XXX)
Equals: Adjusted basis in the conduit entity	$X,XXX

Ordinary income	$100,000
Capital losses	10,000
Nondeductible expenses	5,000
Charitable contributions	1,600

During the year, Quality distributes $15,000 in cash to Tina. What is Tina's basis in Quality Conduit Entity at the end of the current year?

Discussion: At the end of the year, Tina's basis in Quality is $80,850. The adjusted basis is computed as follows:

Adjusted basis at beginning of year	$75,000
Add: Share of current income	25,000
Deduct: Share of deductions and losses	
Capital losses	(2,500)
Nondeductible expenses	(1,250)
Charitable contributions	(400)
Deduct: Cash received	(15,000)
Adjusted basis at end of year	$80,850

The capital loss and charitable contribution limitations are applied on Tina's personal tax return to determine the amounts that she may deduct. Tina must reduce her basis in the Quality stock, regardless of whether she can deduct the capital loss, the charitable contributions, or the nondeductible expenses on her personal tax return. These adjustments are illustrated in Chapter 9.

If all or a portion of the taxpayer's interest in the partnership or S corporation is sold, the adjusted basis reduces the sales price as a capital recovery to compute the gain or loss on the sale. Thus, the equity accounting method requires an investor in a partnership or S corporation to continuously record adjustments to the basis of the investment.

▲ **EXAMPLE 8**   Using the adjusted basis computed in example 7, what would Tina's gain or loss be if she sells her interest at the end of the current year for $100,000? $50,000?

Discussion: If Tina sells the investment in Quality for $100,000, she would report a $19,150 gain ($100,000 − $80,850) from the sale. If she sells the investment in Quality for $50,000, Tina would report a $30,850 loss. Tina's adjusted basis in the investment in Quality is subtracted from the sales price as a capital recovery.

Property Dispositions

The amount invested in an asset that has not been recovered through deductions related to its use for a business purpose is recovered at the date of its disposition. When an asset is sold, exchanged, abandoned, or otherwise disposed of, a realization of income occurs with respect to the **property disposition.** At this point, the tax effect of the realization must be determined. This process is illustrated in the lower panel of Figure 10–1. Capital is recovered upon disposition by offsetting the adjusted basis at the date of disposition with the amount realized from the disposition.[6] The **amount realized** from a disposition is the amount received from the disposition (generally the sales price of the property), less the expenses incurred to make the disposition. Thus, if the amount realized is greater than the adjusted basis, the taxpayer has a **realized gain** on the disposition. If the amount realized is less than the adjusted basis, the taxpayer has not fully recovered the capital investment and has a **realized loss** on the disposition. Calculating the amount realized and gains and losses realized on property dispositions is discussed in detail in Chapter 12.

As a general rule, taxpayers must recognize any gain realized on a property disposition under the all-inclusive income concept. *To recognize a gain* means to include it in the current year's taxable income calculation. However, gains from certain types of asset exchanges, involuntary conversions of property, and the sale of a principal residence may not be recognized in total in the year the disposition occurs. That is, provisions in the tax law allow gains from these transactions to be fully or partially deferred for recognition in a future tax year. Similarly, not all realized losses are recognized in the current year. Losses on certain types of transactions are disallowed (e.g., personal use losses) and therefore are never deductible, whereas other realized losses are deferred for future recognition (e.g., wash sale losses). Thus, after determining the amount of realized gain or loss from a disposition of property, you must determine the amount of gain or loss to be recognized in the current year. Chapter 13 discusses the tax treatments of commonly encountered transactions that are not recognized (nonrecognition transactions) in the year of realization.

The character of the recognized gain or loss determines its ultimate effect on taxable income for the current period. Thus far, all gains and losses have been characterized as being either ordinary (no special treatment) or capital. For individuals, capital gains are subject to a maximum tax rate of 28 percent, whereas net capital loss deductions are limited to $3,000 per year. In addition to ordinary gains and capital gains, sales of certain business assets produce what are referred to as *Section 1231 gains and losses*. Net Section 1231 gains receive long-term capital gain treatment, whereas net Section 1231 losses are deductible as ordinary losses. Because of the differences in treatment for the different types of gains, it is important to properly characterize each gain or loss. Chapter 12 discusses how to characterize the different types of gains and losses and their effect on taxable income for the year.

In order to properly characterize the gain or loss from a disposition of property, the holding period must be determined. The term *holding period* means the length of time an asset is owned. An asset's holding period normally begins on the day after it is acquired and ends on the day of its disposition.[7] In determining the holding period, include the day the asset is sold and exclude the day it was bought. The holding period of an asset acquired on January 1, 1995, begins on January 2, 1995. If the asset is still held on January 3, 1996, it is held for more than one year. Another way to remember this rule is that an asset that is held for one calendar year plus one day from its acquisition date is held for more than one year.

▲ **EXAMPLE 9**   Timothy purchases stock in Real Corporation on July 1, 1995. He sells the stock on July 3, 1996. What is Timothy's holding period?

Discussion: Timothy's holding period begins on July 2, 1995, and ends on July 3, 1996. Thus, Timothy held the stock for more than one year.

In certain types of acquisition transactions, the basis of another taxpayer or another asset is carried over to the basis of the asset acquired. The term **carryover basis** refers to all or part of an asset's basis that transfers from one owner to another or from one asset to another. Transactions resulting in a carryover basis are subject to special rules for determining the holding period. These rules require an adding on (tacking on) of the holding period of the previous asset or of a previous owner. Situations that involve a carryover basis are discussed later in this chapter and in Chapter 13.

Initial basis represents the taxpayer's total investment in an asset on its acquisition date. The initial basis of a purchased asset generally is the cost of acquiring and placing the asset into service. If an asset is acquired by means other than a purchase, its initial basis may be more difficult to determine. As stated earlier, the initial basis of a property has tax effects throughout the period in which the asset is used. In order to properly account for the investment in an asset throughout its tax life, you must determine the initial basis correctly. The remainder of this chapter discusses the tax rules and problems associated with different types of property acquisitions.

▲ INITIAL BASIS

When an asset is purchased, it is necessary to determine the amount invested to establish an initial basis in a transaction. Once the total investment is determined, it must be assigned to the specific asset(s) purchased. If one asset is purchased, the assignment of the amount invested is straightforward. But in many transactions, such as the purchase of multiple assets or a business, the taxpayer must use a reasonable method to allocate a single purchase price to multiple assets. In addition, self-constructed assets require allocation of costs to the constructed asset.

▲ PURCHASE OF ASSETS

Determining the Amount Invested

In an arm's-length transaction, the amount paid for an asset is assumed to be its fair market value. But for practical business reasons (e.g., a forced sale in liquidation of a business), a taxpayer might pay more or less than the true fair market value for an asset. When an asset is purchased with cash, the initial basis of the asset is easy to identify and is the same as the amount of cash paid. Measuring the basis of an asset can become complex when other forms of value are used to pay for the asset. The initial basis (amount invested) in an asset is equal to the purchase price of the asset plus any cost incurred to get the asset ready for its intended use.[8]

The purchase price of an asset is the sum of the

- Cash paid
- Fair market value of other property given to another entity in the exchange
- Fair market value of the taxpayer's services given to another entity in the exchange
- Increases in the taxpayer's liabilities related to the purchase (i.e., increases in debts owed by the taxpayer)

The purchase of an asset by using debt financing (e.g., assuming the seller's debt on the property or obtaining a bank loan to purchase the asset) results in an initial basis equal to the total amount paid for the asset.[9] Effectively, these buyers are treated as if they borrowed money and then used the cash to pay the seller for the asset. When the taxpayer pays off the debt, the asset's basis is not changed. The repayment of the debt merely reduces the lender's claims against the taxpayer. Depending on whether the asset is a business or personal use asset, interest paid on the loan may or may not yield an interest expense deduction, as previously discussed in chapters 5 and 8. The payment of interest expense on the loan does not affect the asset's basis.

▲ **EXAMPLE 10**   Lorenzo purchased a new car by paying the dealer $2,000 cash down and signing an installment note to be paid monthly for $15,000 with interest at 13%. What is the initial basis of the car?

Discussion: Lorenzo's initial basis in the new car is $17,000. His basis includes the $2,000 cash plus the $15,000 note that increased his personal liability. The interest paid on the installment note does not affect the basis of the car. As he pays on the note each month, he reduces his indebtedness. The basis in the car is not affected by the repayment of the loan.

In addition to the purchase price of the property, any other costs incurred to get the property ready for its intended use are capitalized as part of the initial basis. Such costs would include commissions, sales tax paid on the purchase, legal fees, recording fees, accounting fees, transportation costs, installation and testing costs, licensing fees, title insurance, surveys, and any other cost that must be incurred to place the property in service.

▲ **EXAMPLE 11**   Eve Corporation purchased an apartment building by paying $10,000 cash and borrowing $130,000 on a 12%, 30-year mortgage. Eve paid legal fees of $2,000 related to the purchase. Because the apartments were in a rundown condition, Eve spent $13,000 painting the apartments and $20,000 in other repair work before it could rent out the apartments. What is Eve's initial basis in the apartment building?

Discussion: The purchase price of the building is $140,000 ($10,000 cash + $130,000 increase in liabilities). Eve Corporation will also add the $2,000 in legal fees to its basis as an acquisition cost. Painting and repair work are usually expensed as ongoing maintenance. However, in this case the painting and repair work had to be performed in order to get the apartments into condition to rent. Therefore, the costs are capitalized as a cost of getting the apartment building placed into service. The total initial basis in the apartment building is $175,000.

▲ **EXAMPLE 12**   Holly purchased a new home for $85,000. To complete the sale and obtain a mortgage to finance the purchase, Holly paid the following:

Attorney fees for title opinion	$ 150
Points paid to acquire mortgage	2,000
Title insurance	250
Survey	125
Fee to record the deed	25
Total additional costs	$2,550

What is Holly's basis in the home?

Discussion: Holly's basis in her new home is $85,550. Her basis includes the $85,000 paid the seller plus $550 in costs paid to establish her ownership of the home. The points paid to acquire the mortgage are not related to the acquisition cost of the home. They are prepaid interest charges on the mortgage that are deductible as interest in the year of acquisition (see Chapter 8).

If property taxes are owed on an asset when it is acquired and the buyer agrees to pay the taxes for the seller, the payment of the seller's taxes must be added to the asset's basis as part of the acquisition cost.[10] Thus, in the year real estate is acquired, property taxes must be allocated between the buyer and the seller. The taxes should be allocated according to the number of days each owned the property during the period covered by the tax assessment. The period covered by the assessment is called the *real property tax year*. For purposes of the allocation, the buyer's ownership period begins on the date of the sale.

▲ **EXAMPLE 13**   On March 1, 1995, Mark Corporation purchases a vacant city lot for $15,000 as an investment. The annual real estate tax on the lot is $120. The property tax year is a calendar year with the current year's tax payable on November 1, 1995.

In the contract with the seller, Mark Corporation agrees to pay the $120 in real estate tax for the current year when the payment comes due on November 1. What is Mark's basis in the lot?

Discussion: Mark's basis in the lot is increased by the $19 [(59 ÷ 365) × $120] in real estate tax that it pays on behalf of the seller. The $101 in property tax related to the part of the year that the lot is owned by Mark Corporation is deductible as a property tax. Thus, Mark's basis in the lot is $15,019.

Basis of a Bargain Purchase

In Chapter 3, we applied the all-inclusive income concept to employee and share-holder bargain purchases. This concept requires recognition of income to the extent of the difference between the fair market value of an asset and its sales price. Because the bargain element (discount) is recognized as income, a basis is established in the asset. The asset's basis is equal to the amount paid plus the income recognized from the discount. Thus, the basis of an asset acquired in a bargain purchase is its fair market value on the date purchased. Likewise, a person who provides a service in exchange for an asset must recognize the fair market value of the asset received as income from services. The initial basis of the asset is its fair market value, and the fair market value of the asset is the amount of income recognized from the services. For these kinds of asset acquisitions, the asset's basis generally is the amount paid plus imputed income recognized for tax purposes. Again, the asset's basis usually is equal to its fair market value.

▲ **EXAMPLE 14**   Jack is an employee of Charles Construction Co. Charles is a home builder that is developing a new subdivision. Charles has built 5 new houses that are priced to sell for $150,000. To get a family in the subdivision and to thank Jack for his efforts as an employee, Charles sells a house to him for $100,000. What are the tax effects of the purchase for Jack?

Discussion: Jack has a $150,000 initial basis in his new home. Because of the bargain purchase rules, Jack has to recognize $50,000 in gross income. His basis in the new home is the sum of the $100,000 purchase price plus the $50,000 in income recognized from the bargain purchase.

Purchase of Multiple Assets

When more than one asset is bought for a single price (called a **multiple asset purchase**), the cost must be allocated to the individual assets in proportion to their fair market value on the date purchased.[11] This allocation of the purchase price is necessary because one or more of the assets may be subject to depreciation or the assets may be disposed of in different accounting periods. If the taxpayer does not make a reasonable allocation of the purchase price to the individual assets purchased, the IRS may decide to reallocate the cost.

An appraisal of the individual assets usually provides a reasonable basis for allocating the purchase price. As an alternative, the buyer and seller could agree, at arm's length, on an allocation of the purchase price. Another method that is commonly used to allocate the cost of real estate is based upon the property's tax-assessed value. As noted in Chapter 1, assessed values are usually less than actual fair market values. However, the assessed value does give a reasonable measure of the relative value of the assets (by ratio). Using this method, the purchase price is allocated to land and buildings according to the relative values placed on property by the tax assessor. The reasonable allocation of the purchase price of furniture and equipment is a more complex issue and generally should be based on appraisals, not assessed values. Allocating the cost of furniture and equipment should take into account the age and condition of each item.

▲ **EXAMPLE 15**   The Kay Partnership paid $150,000 for land and a building. At the date of purchase, the property tax valuations showed that the land was assessed at $10,000 and the building at $40,000. What is the basis of the land? the building?

Discussion: The basis in the land is $30,000, and the basis of the building is $120,000. The $150,000 purchase price should be allocated on a reasonable basis to the individual assets. Based on the property tax assessments, the purchase price should be allocated as follows:

Asset	Assessed Value	Percentage of Assessed Value		Purchase Price	Cost Basis
Land	$10,000	20%	×	$150,000	$ 30,000
Building	40,000	80%	×	150,000	120,000
Totals	$50,000	100%			$150,000

Purchase of a Business

A taxpayer who is interested in acquiring the assets of a business may purchase the assets directly from the owner. A purchase of assets results in the actual transfer of ownership of the assets to the purchaser. If the assets are owned by a corporation, the taxpayer may choose to buy the corporation's stock. The purchase of the corporation's stock results in ownership of the entity. Ownership of the entity results in indirect ownership of the corporation's assets. The tax effects of the two approaches for acquiring a business are explained in the discussion that follows.

Purchase of the Assets of a Business.   The purchase of the assets of a business results in a direct transfer of ownership of the assets. The main problem encountered in a direct purchase of assets is the allocation of the purchase price to the assets acquired. A taxpayer who purchases the assets of a business usually wants to allocate as much of the purchase price as possible to assets that will be subject to depreciation, amortization, or some other form of annual capital recovery and as little as possible to those assets that are not recoverable until they are sold. When the price paid exceeds the sum of the value of the individual assets, the excess price is considered **goodwill.** Before August 10, 1993, goodwill was considered to have an indefinite life. Thus, any cost allocated to goodwill purchased before August 10, 1993, was not subject to capital recovery until the owner disposed of the business. Therefore, taxpayers preferred to allocate their investment to assets that permitted a current recovery of their investment, such as depreciable equipment. In 1993, Congress enacted new Section 197, which allows goodwill purchased after August 9, 1993, to be amortized over 15 years. (Chapter 11 discusses the effect of this new amortization rule for goodwill and other intangible assets.)

One approach to allocating the purchase price is for the buyer and seller to agree to a written allocation of the purchase price to individual assets. If the buyer and seller do not agree to an allocation, the purchase price must be allocated to all the acquired assets according to their relative fair market values. To identify the amount paid for goodwill, the purchase price is allocated to identifiable assets based on their relative market values. If the purchase price exceeds the total fair market value of the identifiable assets, the excess payment is considered goodwill.[12]

▲ **EXAMPLE 16**   Sandra Corporation purchased the following business assets from Rafael:

Identifiable Asset	Rafael's Adjusted Basis	Fair Market Value
Accounts receivable	$ 100	$ 100
Furniture and fixtures	500	800
Equipment	300	600
Building	1,400	1,000
Land	100	300
Totals	$2,400	$2,800

Sandra Corporation paid $2,100 in cash and assumed $1,000 of Rafael's liabilities. Thus, Sandra's total cost for the assets is $3,100 ($2,100 cash + $1,000 increase in liabilities). What is Sandra's basis in the assets purchased?

Discussion: Sandra Corporation should allocate the purchase price according to the relative fair market values of the acquired assets. Because the $3,100 purchase price exceeds the total fair market value of $2,800, Sandra is considered to have paid $300 for goodwill. Each identifiable asset will have a tax basis equal to its fair market value on the date acquired by Sandra. Rafael's adjusted basis for the assets does not affect Sandra's allocation of the purchase price to the assets acquired.

▲ **EXAMPLE 17**   Assume that in example 16 Sandra Corporation paid Rafael $2,100 for the assets and did not assume any of his liabilities. What is Sandra's basis in the assets purchased?

Discussion: Sandra should allocate the $2,100 purchase price to the identifiable assets acquired in proportion to their relative fair market values on the date acquired:

Identifiable Asset	FMV	% FMV	Allocated Basis
Accounts receivable	$ 100	3.6	$ 76
Furniture and fixtures	800	28.6	600
Equipment	600	21.4	449
Building	1,000	35.7	750
Land	300	10.7	225
Totals	$2,800	100.0	$2,100

Because the amount paid for the identifiable assets is less than their total fair market value, none of the purchase price is allocated to goodwill. Rafael's adjusted basis for the assets is not relevant to Sandra's allocation of the purchase price to the assets acquired.

The relative market value allocation of the purchase price results in a reasonable assignment of a cost basis to each asset purchased. The use of a relative market value allocation is important for two reasons. First, the purchase price is objectively allocated among those assets subject to depreciation and amortization and those assets for which the cost is locked in until the asset is disposed of. For example, the basis of accounts receivable is recovered as the accounts are collected. The cost of buildings, furniture, and equipment is recovered through depreciation. The land is locked in and is not recoverable until its disposition. Second, the amounts subject to capital recovery are based on current costs paid by the buyer instead of the seller's adjusted basis.

Purchase of Corporate Stock.   The purchase of a corporation's stock to gain control over its business assets has a completely different result than the direct purchase of the assets. Because the corporation is a separate and distinct tax entity, the taxpayer owns shares of stock instead of the corporation's assets. Thus, the new owner controls the assets through the ownership of the entity, rather than through direct ownership of the individual business assets. As a separate entity, the corporation retains control over the assets, and it is entitled to the tax deductions and benefits resulting from the business use of the assets. The shareholder is entitled to receive a return on the amount invested in the stock in the form of dividends. Because of the entity concept, the corporation's tax basis in its assets does not change to reflect the amount the shareholder paid to purchase stock.

▲ **EXAMPLE 18**   Assume that in example 16 Sandra Corporation purchased 100% of Rafael Corporation's stock for $3,100 to gain control over its assets. The facts related to Rafael's assets are the same as in example 16. What is the tax effect of the stock purchase for Sandra?

Discussion: Sandra Corporation owns 100% of Rafael Corporation's stock with a tax basis of $3,100. Sandra and Rafael Corporation are separate tax entities. Sandra should expect to receive dividend income from the investment in the stock. When Sandra Corporation sells the stock in the future, it may reduce the sales price by the $3,100 basis to compute the gain or loss on the disposition.

▲ **EXAMPLE 19**   What are the tax effects of Sandra's purchase for Rafael Corporation?

Discussion: Rafael Corporation's basis in its assets is not affected by the purchase of its stock by a shareholder. Rafael Corporation will continue to use its assets in its business, and it will continue to compute depreciation and other capital recovery deductions according to the corporation's basis in the assets. The corporation is indifferent about who owns its stock and does not revalue its assets when ownership shares change hands.

The purchase of a corporation's stock instead of its assets has several pitfalls. The basis of the corporation's assets is not affected by the amount paid for its stock by a shareholder. Thus, there is a potential loss of depreciation deductions based on current values of the company's assets. The corporation keeps its tax history even though its controlling shareholders (owners) may change. As a result, the corporation must continue to use accounting methods adopted by previous owners. An additional serious problem with buying a corporation is that all the tax problems created by previous owners continue and could result in unexpected liabilities for the new owner.

Constructed Assets

Taxpayers who construct property for their own use must capitalize both the direct and indirect construction costs.[13] **Direct construction costs** are those costs actually incurred to physically construct the asset. Examples of direct costs include materials, labor, supplies, architectural fees, and payments to subcontractors. **Indirect construction costs** are other general costs of the business that indirectly support the construction project. Indirect costs include interest on funds to finance the construction, taxes, general administrative costs, depreciation on equipment, and pension costs for workers on the project. Because all the indirect costs are costs that are normally expensed in the period incurred, the effect of capitalizing them as part of the asset's cost is to delay the tax deduction for the costs. The value of the time the taxpayer devotes to the construction of the asset is not included in the property's basis.

▲ **EXAMPLE 20**   Fred is constructing a building for use in his business. The land cost $20,000, direct labor costs were $40,000, and the cost of construction materials totaled $35,000. Fred paid architects, subcontractors, and permit fees totaling $85,000. The interest on his construction loan was $10,000. In addition, Fred considers his allocation of $7,000 in indirect administrative costs to the construction activity to be reasonable. The value of Fred's time related to the building's construction was $4,000. Fred's income taxes for the year were $40,000. What is Fred's basis in the building?

Discussion: Fred's cost basis in the land is $20,000 and in the building is $177,000. His cost basis in the building includes direct labor, direct materials, other costs directly related to the construction of the building, and a reasonable allocation of indirect costs. The building's cost does not include the $4,000 value of Fred's time. The income taxes are not related to the construction and are not allocated to the building. Fred's cost basis in the building is composed of the following:

Direct labor	$ 40,000
Direct materials	35,000
Other direct costs	85,000
Construction interest	10,000
Allocated indirect costs	7,000
Cost basis in building	$177,000

Note that the effect of the requirement that indirect costs be allocated to the building is to reduce the current year's deductions by the $17,000 in interest and allocated indirect costs that are not allowed as current-year deductions. These costs will have to be recovered over the life of the building through depreciation deductions.

▲ SPECIALLY VALUED PROPERTY ACQUISITIONS

Although the general rule is that the initial basis of property is its cost as measured by the amount paid by the taxpayer to acquire and place the property in service, several situations require the use of a different basis. In the transfers considered next, the property's initial basis may be its fair market value, the adjusted basis in the hands of a prior owner, or a basis determined by referring to the basis in a related asset. The discussion that follows explains special valuation rules that apply when property has been acquired by means other than an arm's-length transaction.

▲ BASIS OF PROPERTY ACQUIRED BY GIFT

In Chapter 4, a *gift* was defined as a transfer of property proceeding from a "detached and disinterested generosity . . . out of affection, respect, admiration, charity, or like impulses." [14] Thus, by definition, a transfer of property from a donor to a donee is not a profit-motivated, arm's-length transaction. Neither the donor nor the donee recognizes any income or pays income tax on the transfer of gift property. However, the donor may be subject to a gift tax imposed on the transfer, based on the fair market value of the gift. Whether the donor must pay a gift tax depends on several factors, including the fair market value of the gift, total gifts made during the year, and exclusions and credits that the donor may use to reduce or eliminate the gift tax. Although computation of the gift tax is a topic that is beyond the scope of this discussion, considering the effect of the gift tax on the basis of an asset is necessary.

The receipt of property by gift and the payment of gift tax on the transfer ultimately have an income tax effect. The donee may have to determine the property's income tax basis on the date of gift in order to compute depreciation, depletion, or amortization deductions. In addition, the property's adjusted basis must be calculated upon disposition of the property to determine the income tax effect of the disposition. Depending on the property's adjusted basis in the hands of the donor, the fair market value of the asset on the date of gift, the amount of gift tax paid, and the amount received upon disposition of the property, the appropriate basis could be any one of three different amounts.

General Rule for Gift Basis

Because there is no realization upon the transfer of property from one taxpayer to another as a gift, the general rule for gift property is that the basis of the donor carries over to the donee. This result holds as long as the fair market value of the property on the date of gift is greater than the donor's adjusted basis for the property (i.e., the property has appreciated in value). Thus, the tax law allows the transfer of unrealized gains from one taxpayer to another through the use of gifts.

> ▲ **EXAMPLE 21**   DeWayne owns stock worth $10,000 for which he paid $2,000. DeWayne is a 31% marginal tax rate payer. DeWayne's son needs $10,000 to pay for college tuition next year. DeWayne must sell the stock to come up with the cash necessary to pay his son's college expenses. DeWayne's son is a 15% marginal tax rate payer. Should DeWayne sell the stock or gift it to his son to sell?
>
> *Discussion:*   DeWayne should gift the stock and have his son sell it. If DeWayne sells the stock, the $8,000 gain will result in a tax of $2,480 ($8,000 × 31%). By gifting the stock to his son, the $8,000 gain is effectively transferred to the son through the carryover of basis. His son will pay a tax of only $1,200 ($8,000 × 15%) on the $8,000 gain. Thus, DeWayne will save $1,280 ($2,480 − $1,200) by gifting the stock to his son to sell.

In addition to the carryover of basis, any gift tax paid by the donor on the net appreciation in the value of the property is treated as a capital expenditure and is added to the donee's basis. The donee's basis in gift property received is the donor's adjusted basis plus the gift tax paid on the asset's net appreciation (i.e., the increase in the asset's value while it was owned by the donor).[15] The pattern of the values in the transaction can be represented as follows:

Date Determined	Value Pattern	Basis
At the date of gift	Fair market value of gift *is greater than* donor's adjusted basis.	Donor's adjusted basis plus gift tax on net appreciation is used to compute gain, loss, and depreciation.

The calculation to determine the donee's basis on the date of the gift is

Donor's adjusted basis on date of gift $X,XXX

Plus: Gift tax paid by donor on net appreciation

$$\frac{\text{FMV of gift} \quad \text{Less} \quad \text{Donor's adjusted basis}}{\text{FMV of gift}} \quad \times \quad \text{Gift tax paid} \quad = \quad \text{XXX}$$

Equals: Donee's basis on date of gift $X,XXX

The sum of the donor's adjusted basis on the date of gift plus the gift tax related to the net appreciation in value may not be greater than the asset's fair market value on the date of gift. The application of this formula automatically imposes the fair market value limitation.

> ▲ **EXAMPLE 22**   Elena purchases 10 acres of land in 1976 for $40,000. On January 20, 1995, Elena gives the land to her son, Demetri. Elena pays $5,000 in gift tax on the transfer based on the land's $50,000 fair market value. What is Demetri's basis in the land received from Elena?
>
> *Discussion:*   Demetri has a basis of $41,000 in the land he receives from his mother. Demetri's basis is Elena's adjusted basis of $40,000 plus the $1,000 in gift tax paid on the appreciation in the value of the asset. The gift tax on the net appreciation while the land was owned by Elena is added to Demetri's basis [$1,000 = ($10,000 appreciation ÷ $50,000 fair market value of gift) × $5,000 gift tax paid)].

Split Basis Rule for Loss Property

Although the general rule for gifts allows the transfer of unrealized gains from one taxpayer to another, the result does not hold true for loss transfers. If the fair market value of the property at the date of the gift is less than the donor's basis, a split basis rule applies. A **split basis rule for gifts** means that the property has one basis for determining gains and a separate basis for determining losses upon disposition. Thus, the basis of a gift of a loss property depends on the sale price of the asset upon its disposition. The basis for determining gains is the donor's adjusted basis.[16] The basis for determining losses and for computing depreciation is the fair market value on the date of the gift.[17] The use of the split basis rule for gifts effectively eliminates the transfer of unrealized losses from one taxpayer to another by gift. The pattern of the gift values that invoke the special rules can be represented as follows:

Date Determined	Value Pattern	Basis
	Donor's adjusted basis	Donor's adjusted basis is used to compute gain.
On the date of gift	*is greater than*	
	fair market value of gift.	Fair market value is used to compute a loss and depreciation.

If the property is sold for an amount between the basis for gain and the basis for loss, the basis is assumed to be equal to the selling price.

Whenever the fair market value is less than the donor's basis at the date of the gift, any gift tax paid by the donor is not capitalized as part of the donee's basis in the gift property, because the property has not appreciated. Remember that only gift tax paid on net appreciation can be added to the donor's basis. As a result of not adding gift tax on a loss property, the donee's basis can never be more than the donor's adjusted basis.

▲ **EXAMPLE 23** Assume that in example 22 Elena's adjusted basis is $40,000, the fair market value of the land on the date of gift is $28,000, and that Elena paid $3,000 in gift tax on the transfer based on the land's $28,000 fair market value. What is Demetri's basis in the land if Demetri sells the land for $46,000? for $24,000?

Discussion: Demetri's gain basis in the land is his mother's $40,000 adjusted basis. Because the fair market value of the property at the date of gift is less than Elena's adjusted basis, none of the gift tax can be added to basis. Demetri will report a $6,000 ($46,000 − $40,000) gain on the sale of the land.

   If Demetri sells the land for $24,000, his basis for computing a loss on the sale of the land is the $28,000 fair market value on the date of the gift. Demetri has a loss on the sale of $4,000 ($24,000 − $28,000).

Special Sales Price Basis.   At this point, the donee has a dilemma if the property is sold for less than its adjusted basis but for more than its fair market value on the date of gift. In this special situation, the donee should not report a gain or a loss. The property's basis is considered to be the same as the sales price.

▲ **EXAMPLE 24** Refer to example 23. Assume that Demetri sells the land for $33,000.

Discussion: Demetri's gain basis is Elena's $40,000 adjusted basis. However, use of his gain basis produces a loss. His loss basis is the $28,000 fair market value on the date of gift. Here, use of the loss basis produces a gain. As a result, Demetri will not report gain or loss on the sale of the land. His basis ($33,000) will be the same as the sales price ($33,000).

Holding Period

The holding period for gifts follows the general rules for determining holding period. Whenever the donor's adjusted basis is used to compute a gain or loss on the donee's disposition of property received by gift, the donee's holding period includes the period of time the property was owned by both the donor and the donee.[18] As stated earlier, whenever a carryover basis is used, the holding period of the previous owner carries over to the new owner. However, if fair market value is used as the gift's basis, the donee's holding period begins on the date of gift. When fair market value is used, there is no carryover of basis and thus no carryover of holding period.

▲ BASIS OF PROPERTY ACQUIRED BY INHERITANCE

When a person dies (decedent), a personal representative (executor) is appointed to determine the value of property owned by the person on the date of death, pay estate taxes, and distribute the remaining assets to the heirs of the estate. The property owned on the date of death is normally valued at its fair market value at the date of death,[19] or the executor may elect to use the fair market value on the alternate valuation date. The total value of the assets may be subject to a transfer tax called the *estate tax*. Whether an estate tax is paid depends on the size of the estate and the dollar amount of estate tax exemptions and credits that the estate can use to reduce the tax.

Property passing from a decedent to an heir receives a fair market value basis. The property's new basis is stepped up or stepped down from the decedent's adjusted basis to its fair market value. Because of elections available to an executor, the executor can use one of three dates to establish the fair market value of assets owned on the date of death. These dates are the date of death, an alternate valuation date, and the distribution date. Because the assets owned at the date of the decedent's death are valued per the estate tax rules, the heirs have no control over the valuation of the assets.

Primary Valuation Date

The general rule for the initial basis of inherited property is its fair market value on the date of the deceased owner's death. The date of death is called the **primary valuation date.** Absent any special elections by the executor of the estate, the date of death is used to value the assets of the estate. The adjusted basis of the decedent does not carry over to an heir. Because fair market value establishes the heirs' basis, none of the estate tax paid may be used to increase the basis of inherited property. Under the holding period rules, **inherited property** is always treated as held for more than a year, even if the decedent bought it the day before dying and the heir sold it the day after the deceased's death.

▲ **EXAMPLE 25**   Sam dies on January 1, 1995. On the date of his death, he owned 100 shares of Dandy common stock. He purchased the stock 5 years ago for $500. The stock trades for $50 per share on January 1, 1995, $75 per share on April 15, 1995, and $45 per share on July 1, 1995. The Dandy stock is inherited by Betty, Sam's daughter. What is Betty's basis in the stock?

Discussion: Betty's initial basis for the stock is its $5,000 fair market value on the day of Sam's death (100 shares × $50). If Betty sells the stock on the day after she receives it from Sam's estate, she reports it as having been held for more than one year.

Alternate Valuation Date

The executor of the estate may elect not to use the primary valuation date to value the assets of the estate. The **alternate valuation date** is six months after the date of the decedent's death.

Alternate Valuation Date
6 Months after Death

1/1/95 ———————————→ 7/1/95
Fair market   Fair market value
value at death   at alternate date

The alternate valuation date may be used only if *all three* of the following conditions are met:

■ The alternate value of the total estate is less than the value on the date of death.

■ The total estate tax based on the alternate value of the estate's assets is less than the tax due based on the date of death asset valuation.

■ The executor of the estate uses the alternative valuation date to compute the estate tax.[20]

▲ **EXAMPLE 26**   Refer to example 25. Assume that the executor elects to value Sam's estate on the alternate valuation date. The election reduces the amount of Sam's gross estate and the estate taxes. What is Betty's basis in the stock?

Discussion: Betty's basis for gain or loss on disposition of the stock is $4,500, its fair market value on July 1, 1995 (100 shares × $45). If Betty sells the stock on the day after she receives it from Sam's estate, she reports it as being held for more than one year.

Distribution Date

Although an executor may elect to use the alternate valuation date for the estate, specific assets may be distributed to beneficiaries before the end of the six-month period.

When the alternate valuation date has been elected and property is distributed before the six-month valuation date, its basis is its fair market value on the date it is distributed from the estate. The assets still held by the estate on the alternate valuation date are assigned a basis equal to their fair market value on the alternate date. Assets may not be valued at a date later than the alternate valuation date.

Alternate Valuation Date
6 Months after Death

| 1/1/95 ─────── Distribution Date ────────→ 7/1/95 |
Fair market	Fair market value of an	Fair market value
value at	asset distributed before	at alternate
death	alternate valuation date	date

▲ **EXAMPLE 27**   Refer to example 25. Assume that the executor elects the alternate valuation date. Also assume that the executor transfers the stock to Betty on April 15, 1995. The alternate valuation date election reduces the amount of Sam's gross estate and the estate taxes. What is Betty's basis in the stock?

Discussion: Betty's initial basis for gain or loss on disposition of the stock is its $7,500 fair market value on April 15, 1995 (100 shares × $75). The stock is valued in Sam's estate at $75 per share. If Betty sells the stock on the day after she receives it from Sam's estate, she reports it as being held for more than one year. Other assets still held by the estate at the end of the six-month period have a basis equal to their fair market value on the alternate valuation date.

▲ **EXAMPLE 28**   Refer to example 25. Assume that the executor elects the alternate valuation date. Also assume that the executor transfers the stock to Betty on October 15, 1995, when the shares are trading for $85. The alternate valuation date election reduces the amount of Sam's gross estate and the estate taxes. What is Betty's basis in the stock?

Discussion: Betty's basis for gain or loss on disposition of the stock is $4,500, its fair market value on July 1, 1995 (100 shares × $45). The latest that assets can be valued is the alternate valuation date. The value on the date of distribution applies only when the alternate date is elected and property is distributed before the alternate date.

Other Considerations

Any unrealized gain on property held by a decedent on the date of death escapes income taxation. On the other hand, unrealized losses at the date of death will never be allowed as an income tax deduction. If a taxpayer sells an appreciated asset and then dies before the sales proceeds are spent or given away, the gain is subject to income tax and the sales proceeds still held on the date of death are subject to the estate tax. If possible, a taxpayer should continue to own appreciated assets and let them pass through the estate to step up their basis to fair market value. When the estate or an heir sells the appreciated asset after the date of death, no income tax is paid on the appreciation in value during the time the decedent held the property. On the other hand, if a loss asset is sold before death, the loss can be deducted for income tax, whereas the fair market value of the asset (i.e., the sale proceeds) is subject to estate tax. Thus, the taxpayer can receive the benefit of a loss deduction for income tax purposes that would be lost if the property is held at death. The estate tax value would be about the same amount, because it is assessed on a stepped-down basis.

▲ **EXAMPLE 29**   Frank has a serious heart problem and is near death. He owns stock that has a cost basis of $10,000 and has a fair market value of $90,000. Should Frank sell the stock?

Discussion: If Frank sells the stock, he must report $80,000 in gain on the sale. Unless Frank can find a way to get the $90,000 in sale proceeds out of his estate, the full $90,000 may also be subject to estate tax. Thus, the appreciation on the stock is subject to both income and estate tax. By continuing to hold the stock, no income tax will be paid on the $80,000 unrealized appreciation in the value of the stock. Frank should not sell the stock.

▲ **EXAMPLE 30**   Based on the information in example 29, should Frank sell the stock if its fair market value is only $1,000?

Discussion: If the stock is worth only $1,000, Frank could sell the stock and recognize a $9,000 loss on the sale. If the sale proceeds are still held on the day he dies, only $1,000 would be included in his gross estate. Frank benefits by the amount of the income tax savings on the $9,000 tax loss if he sells the stock before he dies.

If a husband and wife own property as tenants by the entirety or as joint tenants with the right of survivorship, each is treated as owning half the property. When one dies, the survivor's basis in the property is the adjusted basis of the survivor's half-interest plus the fair market value of the other half-interest inherited from the deceased spouse.

▲ **EXAMPLE 31**   Ralph and Mae paid $50,000 for their home in 1970, which they own as tenants by the entirety. When Ralph died this year, estate tax appraisals placed the fair market value of the home at $140,000 on the date of death and $135,000 on the alternate valuation date. The executor of Ralph's estate elected the alternate valuation date. What is Mae's basis in the home?

Discussion: Mae's basis in the home is $92,500 ($25,000 + $67,500). Mae should add the cost basis of her half-interest ($25,000) to the fair market value on the valuation date used by the executor for the half-interest she inherited from Ralph ($67,500 = $1/2 \times $135,000).

When people who are not married own a joint interest in property, the survivor's basis in the property is the amount the survivor actually paid toward the purchase of the asset plus the fair market value of the inherited interest.

▲ **EXAMPLE 32**   Assume in example 31 that Ralph and Mae are brother and sister. In addition, Mae paid $10,000 for a 20% joint tenant interest in the home, which cost $50,000 in 1970. The executor of Ralph's estate elected the alternate valuation date. What is Mae's basis in the home?

Discussion: Mae's basis in the home is $118,000 ($10,000 + $108,000). Mae should add the cost basis of her 20% interest ($10,000 = 20% × $50,000) to the fair market value on the valuation date used by the executor for the 80% interest she inherited from Ralph ($108,000 = 80% × $135,000).

▲ PROPERTY ACQUIRED FROM A SPOUSE

When property is acquired from a spouse by gift or purchase, the basis of the property carries over from one person to the other. Because the transfer is to a related party, the realization concept is not applied, resulting in "giftlike" treatment. Neither spouse recognizes a gain or loss from the transaction, and the property has a carryover basis. Unlike a gift, the fair market value of the property at the time of the transfer is ignored. Thus, the spouse receiving the property assumes the adjusted basis of the spouse giving up the property for both gain and loss basis.

▲ **EXAMPLE 33**　Juan and Rosita are husband and wife. Juan owns a farm that has an adjusted basis to him of $150,000. Juan wants Rosita to own the farm as her separate asset. To accomplish the transfer of ownership, Rosita has agreed to purchase the farm from Juan for $300,000. What is Rosita's basis in the farm?

Discussion:　If Rosita buys the farm from Juan for $300,000, her basis in the farm is $150,000. The purchase price is disregarded, because the transaction is treated as a gift (substance over form controls this situation). Also, Juan will not realize a taxable gain from the sale of the farm. Juan's adjusted basis carries over and becomes Rosita's basis. If Rosita and Juan decide that a sale is not appropriate and Juan makes a gift of the farm to Rosita, her basis remains at $150,000.

▲ **EXAMPLE 34**　What is Rosita's basis in the farm in example 33 if she buys it from Juan for $100,000?

Discussion:　If Rosita buys the farm from Juan for $100,000, her basis in the farm is still $150,000. Regardless of the amount Rosita pays for the farm, the purchase price is disregarded. Juan will not realize a deductible loss from the sale of the farm. Juan's $150,000 adjusted basis becomes Rosita's basis.

The carryover basis rule also applies when property is received from a former spouse incident to a divorce.[21] Property received within one year after a marriage ends is considered incident to divorce. Later transfers are also subject to the carryover basis rule if they are related to the cessation of the marriage. Transfers made under the terms of a divorce or separation agreement within six years of the date the marriage ends are considered related to the cessation of the marriage.

▲ **EXAMPLE 35**　Kelly and Marsha divorce on June 1, 1994. Marsha owns the family home she inherited from her parents. Her basis in the home is $75,000, and its fair market value on June 1, 1994, is $100,000. Under the terms of their divorce agreement, Marsha retains possession of the family home until June 1, 1996. On that date, she is required to deed ownership of the home to Kelly. What is Kelly's basis in the home when it is transferred to him on June 1, 1996?

Discussion:　When Kelly receives ownership of the home from Marsha on June 1, 1996, the transfer is considered related to the cessation of the marriage. As a result, the transfer receives giftlike treatment, and Marsha's $75,000 basis carries over to Kelly.

Because the original basis of the spouse carries over, the holding period of the original owner carries over to the subsequent owner. The holding period for the property includes the time owned by the acquiring spouse plus the time held by the spouse giving up the property.

When property held for personal use is changed to property held for a business purpose, a split basis problem similar to the special valuation rule for gifts may develop. The split basis problem arises from the legislative grace concept's disallowance of personal deductions. Depending on the facts at the time the asset is changed to business use, the asset may have a basis equal to its adjusted basis, its fair market value, or its value on disposition. Because the asset may be subject to depreciation, depletion, or amortization while it is used in the business activity, the correct basis must be identified to compute the annual deduction.

▲ PERSONAL USE PROPERTY CONVERTED TO BUSINESS USE

General Rule for Basis

If the fair market value of personal use property is more than its adjusted basis on the date business use begins, the general basis rule applies. The asset's adjusted basis is used to compute depreciation and gain or loss on its disposition. As the asset is used in the business, its basis must be further reduced by depreciation allowed or allowable in computing taxable income.

▲ **EXAMPLE 36**   Mary purchases her home for $100,000 in 1992. The purchase price is properly allocated as $90,000 to the structure and $10,000 to the land. Because of tremendous growth in her business, she needs office space for her employees and herself. In 1995, she pays a contractor $15,000 to convert her home into suitable office space. At the date the home is changed to business property, the house is appraised at $130,000 and the land at $20,000. What is Mary's basis in the building for business purposes?

Discussion: Mary's basis in the office building is $105,000 ($90,000 + $15,000). Her business basis is her adjusted basis of $90,000 plus the $15,000 cost of improvements to prepare it for business use. The $10,000 basis of the land also carries over to the business.

The $105,000 basis also is used to compute depreciation on the building. If Mary deducts depreciation totaling $8,000 and then sells the property, her adjusted basis is $107,000 ($105,000 building less $8,000 depreciation plus $10,000 basis of the land). Her gain or loss on the sale is computed by comparing the sales price to her $107,000 adjusted basis.

Split Basis Rule

If the fair market value of personal use property is less than its adjusted basis on the date it is changed to business use, it will have one basis for gain and a different basis for loss and depreciation.[22] An expense must be incurred for a business purpose to be deductible. The legislative grace concept prohibits the deduction of personal living expenses or losses related to a personal use asset. Because the property's loss of value occurred while it was held for personal use, the lost value cannot be deducted. The **split basis rules for business property** prevent the deduction of the disallowed personal loss through depreciation or as a loss from the sale of a business asset. The following basis rules apply when the personal use asset's fair market value is less than its adjusted basis on the date it changes to business property:

- The initial basis for gain is the property's adjusted basis on the conversion date.
- The initial basis for loss and depreciation is the property's fair market value on the conversion date.
- If the property is later sold for an amount that falls between the adjusted basis for gain and the adjusted basis for loss, the adjusted basis for the sale is the sales price.

The pattern of the values involved in this situation can be diagramed as follows:

Date Determined	Value Pattern	Basis
At the date business use begins	Adjusted basis *is greater than* fair market value	Adjusted basis is used to compute a gain. Fair market value is used to compute a loss and depreciation.

If the property is sold for an amount between the basis for gain and the basis for loss, the basis is assumed to be equal to the sales price.

▲ **EXAMPLE 37**   Latoya owns a personal use asset that cost her $50,000 five years ago. During the current year, when the asset's fair market value was $30,000, she started using the asset in her business. What is Latoya's basis in the asset for business purposes?

Discussion: The nondeductible loss in value related to personal use is $20,000 ($50,000 − $30,000 fair market value). Because the fair market value is less than adjusted basis, depreciation is calculated using the $30,000 fair market value. Using the lower value avoids deduction of the loss of value attributable to personal use. The basis for determining gain is the $50,000 adjusted basis before conversion to business use.

▲ **EXAMPLE 38**   Refer to example 37. Assume that after deducting $7,000 in depreciation on the asset, Latoya sells it for $60,000. What is Latoya's gain or loss on the sale?

Discussion: In order to determine the appropriate basis, Latoya must subtract the $7,000 in depreciation from both the gain basis and the loss basis to arrive at the adjusted basis for gain and for loss. Latoya's adjusted basis on the date of sale is calculated as follows:

	Gain Basis	Loss Basis
Initial basis at date converted	$50,000	$30,000
Less: Depreciation deducted while used in business (based on FMV)	(7,000)	(7,000)
Adjusted basis at date of sale	$43,000	$23,000

The $60,000 sales price means that the asset was sold at a gain. Therefore, the $43,000 adjusted basis for computing gain is used to determine that Latoya has a $17,000 gain on the sale.

▲ **EXAMPLE 39**   Assume the same facts as in example 38, except that Latoya sells the asset for $20,000. What is Latoya's gain or loss on the sale?

Discussion: The $20,000 sales price means that the asset is sold at a loss. Therefore, the $23,000 adjusted basis for determining loss is used to determine that Latoya has realized a loss of $3,000 on the sale.

▲ **EXAMPLE 40**   Assume the same facts as in example 38, except that Latoya sells the asset for $35,000. What is Latoya's gain or loss on the sale?

Discussion: When the $35,000 sales price is compared to the $43,000 gain basis, a loss results. Similarly, comparison with the $23,000 loss basis results in a gain. Therefore, the adjusted basis is equal to the selling price, and neither gain nor loss is realized on the sale.

Example 39 illustrates that any loss related to the period of personal use is not allowed as a deduction because of the split basis rule. The use of fair market value for computing depreciation also prevents taxpayers from recovering personal use losses through depreciation deductions. Also, note that the split basis rule is similar to the gift split basis rule in that it applies when property with an unrealized loss is converted from personal use to business use. Depreciation is calculated using the fair market value.

Acquiring securities is usually straightforward. The initial basis is equal to the cost paid to acquire the security. The cost of a security includes the purchase price and any commissions paid on the purchase.[23] In certain circumstances, a taxpayer acquires securities subject to special rules or does so without paying a purchase price. These situations include the receipt of stock dividend shares, stock issued in a tax-free transfer to a controlled corporation, and shares acquired in a wash sale.

▲ **BASIS IN SECURITIES**

Stock Dividends

Most stock dividends are nontaxable dividends. When additional shares of a corporation's stock are received as a nontaxable dividend, part of the basis of the original stock must be allocated to the new stock received as a dividend.[24] Because the basis of the new shares is made by referring to the basis of the old shares, the holding period for the new shares of stock includes the holding period of the old shares. If the stock received as a dividend is the same class as the original stock, the allocation is made by using the following formula:

Basis per share = Original cost ÷ Total shares held after dividend

▲ **EXAMPLE 41**   Reginald owns 200 shares of Arko common stock for which he paid $22,000 on December 14, 1993. On July 8, 1995, Arko declares and distributes a 10% stock dividend. Reginald receives 20 additional shares of Arko common stock from the dividend. What is Reginald's basis in the 220 shares of stock he owns?

Discussion: Reginald must allocate part of the $22,000 original basis of the 200 shares to the basis of the 20 new shares. The total basis of the 220 shares remains at $22,000. However, the basis per share of the 220 shares is now $100. All 220 shares are deemed to have been held since December 15, 1993.

Basis before dividend = $22,000 ÷ 200 = $110 per share

Basis after dividend   = $22,000 ÷ 220 = $100 per share

If the dividend shares are of a different class of stock than the original stock, the original basis is allocated according to the relative fair market values of the original stock and the stock received as a dividend.[25] Fair market values are determined on the date the new shares are distributed by the corporation. If, for example, preferred stock is distributed as a dividend to common stockholders, the allocation of the original basis is made by using the following formulas:

$$\text{Basis of preferred stock} = \frac{\text{FMV of preferred stock}}{\left\{\begin{array}{c}\text{FMV of preferred stock}\\+\\\text{FMV of common stock}\end{array}\right\}} \times \begin{array}{c}\text{Original}\\\text{common stock}\\\text{basis}\end{array}$$

$$\text{Basis of common stock} = \frac{\text{FMV of common stock}}{\left\{\begin{array}{c}\text{FMV of preferred stock}\\+\\\text{FMV of common stock}\end{array}\right\}} \times \begin{array}{c}\text{Original}\\\text{common stock}\\\text{basis}\end{array}$$

▲ **EXAMPLE 42**   Mac Corporation distributed to its common shareholders 1 share of preferred stock for each share of common stock they held on the record date. The common stock had a $50 per share market value, and the preferred stock had a $20 per share market value on the stock dividend distribution date. Asha, a Mac Corporation shareholder, owned 100 shares of common stock on the record date. She had purchased the common stock on March 9, 1990, for $3,000. Asha received 100 shares of preferred stock as a dividend. What is Asha's basis in the stock?

Discussion: Asha's $3,000 basis in the common stock must be allocated between the common and preferred stock in proportion to their relative market values on the date the stock dividend is distributed. Asha's basis in the preferred stock is $857, and her basis in the common stock is $2,143. The basis of each type of stock is determined as follows:

Market value of preferred stock	= 100 × $20	=	$2,000
Market value of common stock	= 100 × $50	=	5,000
Total market value			$7,000

Allocation of $3,000 original cost:

Preferred = ($2,000 ÷ $7,000) × $3,000 = $857 or $8.57 per share
Common = ($5,000 ÷ $7,000) × $3,000 = $2,143 or $21.43 per share

The holding period for both the common and preferred stock begins on March 10, 1990, the day after Asha originally purchased the common shares.

Taxable Stock Dividends.   Whenever the shareholder has the option of receiving cash or stock as a dividend, the dividend is taxable even if the shareholder elects to receive the stock. The amount of taxable income from the dividend is the fair market value of the shares on the date of distribution. In the case of a taxable stock dividend, the shareholder has a basis equal to the amount of income recognized.[26] The inclusion of the income recognized in the basis of the shares is necessary to ensure that the income is not taxed twice. Because the basis of the dividend is made by reference to the fair market value, the holding period of the shares begins on the date of distribution.

▲ **EXAMPLE 43**   Tanya purchases 500 shares of Upubco common stock on January 18, 1993, at a total cost of $4,600. On April 12, 1995, Upubco declares a 10% stock dividend with the option to receive $8 cash in lieu of taking the dividend shares. The dividend is distributed on June 15, 1995, when the fair market value of the stock is $8 per share. What are the tax effects for Tanya if she elects to take the cash option?

Discussion: Tanya recognizes the $400 [(500 × 10%) × $8] in cash received as income when she receives the cash. The basis of her original 500 shares is unaffected by the dividend.

▲ **EXAMPLE 44**   Assume that in example 43 Tanya elects to receive the stock instead of taking the cash option. What are the tax effects for Tanya?

Discussion: Because a cash option is available, Tanya must recognize the fair market value of the stock received on the date of distribution. Her taxable income is $400 [(500 × 10%) × $8]. Her basis in the 50 dividend shares is the $400 in income recognized. The holding period for the new shares begins on June 16, 1995. The basis of the original 500 shares is unaffected by the dividend.

Transfers of Assets to a Controlled Corporation

A special tax provision permits the transfer of assets and related liabilities to a corporation in exchange for the corporation's stock in a tax-free transaction. This provision is referred to as a *Section 351 transfer*. To qualify for this special treatment, the person(s) transferring property must own 80 percent or more of the corporation's stock immediately after the exchange of the property for stock.

The transfer is not taxable, because a realization is not deemed to occur with respect to the assets transferred. Whoever transfers the assets has a continuing proprietary interest in the assets that is represented by ownership of corporation's stock. Thus, Section 351 permits a tax-free incorporation of a business by treating the transaction as a mere change in the form of the entity. As a result, the shareholder's basis in the stock received in the exchange generally is the same as the basis of the assets transferred to the corporation. The shareholder has a carryover basis in the stock. In some instances, a Section 351 transfer does require recognizing gain, which has the effect of increasing the shareholder's basis in the stock. Although this topic is best left for a corporate tax course, you should be aware of the availability of this tax-planning opportunity for incorporating a business tax free.

▲ **EXAMPLE 45**   Ted owned Ted's Store, a proprietorship. Ted's basis in the assets used in Ted's Store was $25,000. Also, Ted owed $1,000 in liabilities related to the business. Ted decided to incorporate Ted's Store in a tax-free transaction. The new corporation was named Video, Inc. Ted transferred all the proprietorship's assets and liabilities to the corporation in exchange for 100 shares of its stock. After the exchange, Ted owned 100% of Video, Inc.'s outstanding stock. What is the tax effect of the exchange?

Discussion: Ted's tax basis in the 100 shares of Video, Inc.'s stock is $24,000. The transfer of Ted's Store's assets and liabilities to the corporation is merely a change in the form of organization used to conduct the business. Ted's proprietary interest in the business assets used by Ted's Store is now represented by 100 shares of Video, Inc.'s stock instead of direct ownership of the individual assets. Ted's adjusted basis in Ted's Store's assets carries over to become the basis of the 100 shares of stock— $24,000 ($25,000 asset basis − $1,000 in liabilities assumed by Video, Inc.). Ted has a carryover basis in his Video, Inc., stock because the transaction is nontaxable.

Video, Inc.'s basis in the assets received from Ted is $25,000, and the corporation owes $1,000 in liabilities related to the assets. Because the transaction is nontaxable, Video, Inc., has a carryover basis in the assets it received from Ted in exchange for its stock. The assets are not marked up to fair market value, because the transfer is a change in the form of doing business, not a change in the ownership of the assets.

Wash Sale Stock Basis

A wash sale occurs when a security (stock, bond, option, etc.) is sold at a loss and is replaced within 30 days *before or after* the sale date with a substantially identical security.[27] Because the taxpayer's ownership interest has not changed as a result of the sale and repurchase of the stock, the transaction lacks economic substance. Thus, the form of a transaction has been used to create a paper tax loss. As a result, the substance-over-form doctrine applies to the artificial loss. The wash sale loss is not allowed as a current deduction. Deductions for wash sale losses were discussed in Chapter 7.

Because a wash sale loss cannot be used as a current deduction, the taxpayer still has an unrecovered investment in the stock sold. The capital recovery concept permits the unrecovered investment to be added to the basis of the new stock.

▲ **EXAMPLE 46**   Tracy purchases 100 shares of DHI stock for $20,000 in 1990. On December 31, 1995, Tracy sells all 100 shares for $15,000 so she can use the $5,000 capital loss to offset capital gains from other transactions. When the stock market reopens on January 4, 1996, Tracy repurchases 100 shares of DHI for $16,000. What are the tax effects for Tracy of the sale and repurchase of the DHI stock?

Discussion: Because the stock sold at a loss was replaced within 30 days of the sale date, the $5,000 wash sale loss cannot be deducted. The wash sale loss is added to Tracy's basis in the stock purchased on January 4, 1996. Tracy's basis in the DHI stock bought on January 4, 1996, is the sum of the $16,000 cost plus the $5,000 wash sale loss, a total basis of $21,000.

▲ **EXAMPLE 47**   On November 30, 1996, Tracy sells the 100 shares of DHI stock purchased on January 4, 1996, for $29,000. What is Tracy's gain on the sale?

Discussion: Tracy has a gain on the sale of $8,000 ($29,000 − $21,000). Note that the effect of adding the $5,000 in disallowed wash sale loss to the basis of the acquired shares is to decrease the gain on the subsequent sale by the $5,000 loss previously disallowed. That is, Tracy had a gain of $13,000 ($29,000 − $16,000) based on the actual purchase price of the shares. However, the wash sale loss basis adjustment brings the gain down to $8,000.

Example 47 illustrates that a loss from a wash sale is not disallowed forever. The loss is merely deferred until the taxpayer's interest in the replacement stock is disposed of in a taxable transaction. When the replacement stock is sold, the deferred loss is included in the amount subject to capital recovery. As a result, the deferred loss either decreases the gain or increases the loss that would otherwise have been recognized on the sale of the replacement stock.

Frequently, a taxpayer sells shares of stock and then repurchases either a larger or smaller number of replacement shares. If so, the wash sale rule applies on a first-in, first-out basis only to the extent the loss stock is replaced. As a result, a loss on shares of stock not replaced is deductible. Likewise, the basis of the shares of stock purchased in excess of the number of shares sold is not affected by the wash sale.

▲ **EXAMPLE 48**   Assume that in example 46 Tracy repurchases 150 shares of DHI for $24,000 on January 4, 1996. What is her basis in the replacement stock?

Discussion: The wash sale disallowance rule applies only to the shares sold at a loss that are replaced. Thus, the loss on the 100 shares sold is added to the basis of the first 100 shares repurchased during the 30 days before or after the wash sale date. The basis of the 50 shares that are not replacement stock under the wash sale rule is not affected. Tracy's basis is as follows:

Cost of 100 replacement shares	$16,000
Add: Deferred wash sale loss on 100 shares	5,000
Basis of 100 shares reacquired on 1/4/96	$21,000
Basis of extra 50 shares acquired 1/4/96	
($24,000 ÷ 150 = $160 × 50)	$ 8,000

▲ **EXAMPLE 49**   Assume that in example 46 Tracy repurchases only 50 shares of DHI for $8,000. What is her basis in the replacement stock?

Discussion: Because she repurchased only 50 of the 100 shares, the loss on the 50 shares replaced is disallowed and is added to the basis of the replacement shares. Tracy can deduct loss on the 50 shares she did not replace. Tracy's basis in the 50 replacement shares is the sum of the $8,000 replacement cost plus $2,500 [(50 ÷ 100) × $5,000] in deferred loss from the wash sale, $10,500.

▲ **SUMMARY**

An asset owned by a taxpayer may be classified according to its business, investment, personal, or mixed use. Because deductions are permitted by legislative grace, a deduction for expenses and losses related to personal and mixed-use assets may be limited. Also, assets may be classified as real property, personal property, and intangible property. Personal property, as used in this classification scheme, refers to any tangible property that is not real estate; it does not refer to property held for personal use by the taxpayer.

Amounts allowed as a capital recovery for tax purposes reduce the amount of income that must be recognized under the all-inclusive income concept. If an asset is used for a business purpose, the full amount of the investment will usually be subject to capital recovery, either as the asset is used to earn income or upon its disposition. The tax law requires that a capital recovery be reported in the proper annual accounting period based on the taxpayer's accounting method.

An asset's initial basis on the date acquired must be adjusted over time for amounts that represent additional capital investments and recoveries. The adjusted investment amount is called the asset's *adjusted basis*. Adjusted basis represents the unrecovered capital investment in an asset.

The adjusted basis of an investment in a conduit entity is determined by using an equity accounting method. Thus, increases and decreases in the owner's investment in the conduit entity are reflected in the owner's accounting records and tax returns as the changes take place.

The initial basis of a purchased asset is its cost. Cost includes the purchase price of the asset plus any other costs incurred to acquire and place the asset into service. The purchase price is the sum of any amount paid for the asset in cash, the fair market value of property or services given to the seller, and the assumption of a liability by the buyer. If the purchase price includes more than one asset, it must be reasonably allocated to the individual assets acquired. If goodwill is among the purchased assets, a portion of the purchase price must be allocated to goodwill. The basis of a self-constructed asset includes all direct and indirect costs related to construction of the asset.

When property is received as a gift, the general rule provides that the donee receives a carryover of the donor's basis. If the fair market value of the gift is greater than the donor's basis, the gift tax paid by the donor on the net appreciation in the value of the asset is added to the donee's basis. When the fair market value of the gift is less than the donor's basis (the property has an unrealized loss) the split basis rule applies. The split basis rule provides that the donee's basis for gain is the donor's basis and the basis for loss is the fair market value of the gift. If the asset is sold for a price that falls between the special gain basis and loss basis, the basis is equal to the selling price and no gain or loss results from the disposition.

Inherited property generally has a basis equal to the asset's fair market value on the date of the original owners's death. As an alternative, the executor of the estate may elect to value the estate's assets six months later, on the alternate valuation date.

The transfer of property between spouses by gift or sale does not have an income tax effect. The basis of the property remains the same in the hands of either spouse. The transfer between spouses is treated like a gift.

When property is converted from personal to business use, a split basis problem can result. The tax treatment is similar to the split basis rule for gifts. The basis for gain is the property's adjusted basis, and the basis for loss (and depreciation) is an adjusted fair market value. As with gifts, if the sales price falls between the gain basis and the loss basis, the basis is equal to the selling price.

The basis of a taxable stock dividend is the fair market value of the stock on the date it is distributed by the corporation. However, the basis of a nontaxable stock dividend is determined by allocating the taxpayer's investment in the original stock to the old shares and to the new shares received as a dividend.

Section 351 permits the tax-free incorporation of a business. The basis of the assets transferred to the corporation becomes the basis in the stock received from the corporation by the shareholders. A Section 351 transfer is merely a change in the form of the business entity, and no adjustments to the basis of the assets transferred to the corporation are made. A loss on a wash sale is added to the basis of the replacement securities.

Table 10–2 summarizes the basis rules discussed in this chapter. The table briefly states how the asset's basis is determined according to how an asset was acquired.

▲ **Table 10–2**

SUMMARY OF
BASIS RULES

How Asset Was Acquired	Basis of Asset Acquired
Purchase of a single asset	Cost—Generally, the asset's fair market value on the date purchased plus any other costs incurred to obtain the asset and place it into service.
Purchase of several assets for a single price	Cost—The single purchase price is allocated to individual assets according to their relative fair market values on the date purchased.
Purchase of the assets of a business	Cost—The single purchase price is allocated to individual assets according to their relative fair market values on the date purchased. If the purchase price exceeds the total fair market value of the identifiable assets, the excess is allocated to goodwill.
Purchase of the stock of a corporation	Cost—Purchase price plus any other costs incurred to obtain the stock, such as commissions and legal fees.
Self-constructed assets	Cost—Total direct and indirect construction costs.

(continued on next page)

How Asset Was Acquired	Basis of Asset Acquired
Gift:	
Fair market value on date of gift greater than donor's adjusted basis	Donor's adjusted basis plus gift tax on net appreciation.
Fair market value on date of gift less than donor's adjusted basis	Gain—Donor's adjusted basis (gift tax cannot be added to basis).
	Loss and depreciation—Fair market value on gift date.
	If asset is sold for an amount that is between the gain basis and the loss basis, the basis is deemed to be equal to the selling price.
Inheritance	Fair market value of the asset on the date of death or alternate valuation date.
Property acquired from a spouse by gift, purchase, or divorce settlement	Cost basis of spouse transferring property carries over to spouse receiving property.
Conversion of personal use property to business use	Gain—Adjusted basis.
	Loss and depreciation—Lesser of the adjusted basis or the fair market value when put into business use.
	If asset is sold for an amount that is between the gain basis and the loss basis, the basis is deemed to be equal to the selling price.
Conduit entity	Initial basis determined by how interest in entity was acquired; initial basis is adjusted for investments and recoveries of capital, using an equity accounting method.
Stock dividend:	
Taxable	Fair market value of stock on distribution date.
Nontaxable	A part of old stock's basis is allocated to the new stock.
Nontaxable transfers to a controlled corporation	Basis of property transferred to corporation carries over to stock received from corporation.
Wash sale stock	Cost of replacement stock plus deferred loss on wash sale.

▲ KEY TERMS

alternate valuation date (p. 445)
amount realized (p. 433)
carryover basis (p. 434)
direct construction costs (p. 440)
goodwill (p. 438)
indirect construction costs (p. 440)
inherited property (p. 445)
initial basis (p. 428)

intangible property (p. 427)
mixed-use property (p. 426)
multiple asset purchase (p. 437)
personal use property (p. 426)
personalty (p. 427)
primary valuation date (p. 445)
property (p. 425)
property disposition (p. 433)

real estate (p. 427)
realized gain (p. 433)
realized loss (p. 433)
split basis rules for business property (p. 449)
split basis rule for gifts (p. 443)
tangible property (p. 427)

▲ Primary Tax Law Sources

[1] Sec. 1016—Prescribes the adjustments that must be made to the basis of property.

[2] Reg. Sec. 1.1016-2—Gives examples of items that are added to basis as adjustments.

[3] Sec. 705—Prescribes the adjustments that must be made to a partner's basis.

[4] Sec. 1367—Prescribes the adjustments that must be made to an S corporation shareholder's basis.

[5] Reg. Sec. 1.1016-3—Requires adjustment of the basis of a depreciable asset even if depreciation was not claimed on the asset.

[6] Sec. 1001—Prescribes the computation of gain or loss on the disposition of property.

[7] Reg. Sec. 1.1223-1—Explains the rules for determining the holding period of assets in different circumstances.

[8] Sec. 1012—States that the general rule for the initial basis of a property is the property's cost.

[9] Crane v. Comm., 331 U.S. 1 (1947)—Held that mortgage debt must be included in the basis of property in order to properly reflect the economic cost of the property.

[10] Reg. Sec. 1.1001-1—Requires adjustment of the selling price (and therefore basis of the buyer) to account for property taxes paid as part of a sales agreement.

[11] Reg. Sec. 1.61-6(a)—Requires a reasonable apportionment of the cost of properties sold to the individual properties.

[12] Sec. 1060—Requires an allocation of the purchase price of the identifiable assets of a business, either by agreement with the seller or by the use of relative fair market values.

[13] Reg. Sec. 1.263A-1T—Discusses the uniform capitalization rules as they apply to property constructed by taxpayers for their own use.

[14] Comm. v. Duberstein, 363 U.S. 278 at 283 (1960)—Held that a Cadillac received by a taxpayer from a businessman to whom he occasionally gave names of potential customers was not a tax-free gift.

[15] Sec. 1015—States that the general rule for the basis of property received by gift is the donor's adjusted basis.

[16] Reg. Sec. 1.1015-1—Explains the split basis rule for gifts and gives examples of the application of the rule.

[17] Perkins v. Comm., 125 F.2d 150 (6th Cir. 1942)—Held that the basis amount for depreciation is the value of the property as of the gift transfer date when fair market value is less than the adjusted basis.

[18] Sec. 1223—Provides the rules for determining the holding period of property.

[19] Sec. 1014—States that the basis of property acquired from a decedent is its fair market value at the date of death, unless the executor elects to value the estate assets on the alternate valuation date.

[20] Sec. 2032—Provides the rules for an executor to elect to value the estate assets at the alternate valuation date.

[21] Sec. 1041—States that transfers between spouses (including transfers incident to a divorce) are treated as gifts for income-recognition and basis purposes.

[22] Reg. Sec. 1.167(g)-1—States that the basis for computing depreciation on personal use property that has been converted to business use is the lesser of the fair market value or the adjusted basis of the property at the date of the conversion.

[23] Reg. Sec. 1.263(a)—Gives examples of capital expenditures; specifically states that the commissions paid on the purchase of securities are capital expenditures.

[24] Sec. 307—Requires the allocation of the adjusted basis of securities to nontaxable dividend shares received.

[25] Reg. Sec. 1.307-1—Requires the allocation of adjusted basis using relative market values when stock of a different class is received in a nontaxable stock dividend.

[26] Sec. 301—States that the basis of stock received in a taxable stock dividend is its fair market value on the date of distribution.

[27] Sec. 1091—Defines a *wash sale* and prescribes the rules for treatment of disallowed losses on wash sales.

1. What effect does a property's use have on the cost recovery allowable on the property?

2. What is the difference between a property's use and its type?

3. Explain the difference between tangible property and intangible property.

4. How is personal property different from personal use property?

5. Explain the role an asset's initial basis plays in determining the income to be recognized upon disposal of the the asset.

6. Explain the difference between a property's initial basis and its adjusted basis.

7. Larry is interested in acquiring a business owned by Jane. If Jane's business is organized as a corporation, what options are available to Larry in acquiring the business? Explain to Larry the difference in the options.

8. What tax problems does a taxpayer encounter when purchasing more than one asset for a single price? Explain.

9. What are the tax implications of a taxpayer's self-construction of assets for use in the taxpayer's trade or business?

10. List some costs, which are normally expensed, that must be capitalized when a taxpayer self-constructs an asset for use in a trade or business.

11. Why are gifts of property not income to the person receiving the gift?

12. A person who receives property as a gift makes no investment in order to receive the property. Why is a basis assignment to the gift property necessary, even though the donee has no investment in the property?

13. What is the general rule for determining the basis of gift property?

14. Janine is planning to make a gift of 50 shares of Acran, Inc., stock to her nephew to help with his college tuition. The stock originally cost Janine $5,000, and its current value is $4,000. Explain to Janine why the gift might not be the best way to achieve her goal.

15. What is the general rule for determining when the holding period of an asset begins?

16. What type(s) of asset acquisitions do not follow the general rule for determining when the holding period of the asset begins?

17. When is the primary valuation date for valuing inherited property? Does the executor of the estate have to do anything to use the primary valuation date?

18. When is the alternate valuation date for valuing inherited property? When elected, are all assets valued on the alternate date? Explain.

19. Are commissions paid to acquire securities a deductible expense? If not, are they ever deductible?

20. What are the tax effects if a sole proprietor converts the business to a corporation?

21. For each of the following assets, determine whether the asset is personal property, real property, intangible property, or personal use property:
    a. Festus purchased a revolver to use in his job as deputy sheriff.
    b. Anthony purchased a building to use as a hair salon. He also purchased 5 hair dryers and 5 specially made salon chairs.
    c. Andrea uses a room in her home as an office for the exclusive purpose of running her mail order business.
    d. Geraldine received a new automobile from her grandfather as a high school graduation present.
    e. Agard Corporation purchased a dormitory to use as housing for employee training.
    f. Egbert invented a new light bulb that will last for 20 years. He applied for and received a patent entitling him to exclusive use of the light bulb technology.

22. For each of the following assets, determine whether the asset is personal property, real property, intangible property, or personal use property:
    a. Farmer Susan bought a tractor to use in her farm operations.
    b. Sidney bought all the assets of Harcourt's Hardcourt Club for $460,000. The total fair market value of the identifiable assets of Harcourt was $330,000.
    c. Jamie bought her father a new riding lawn mower for his birthday.
    d. Barclay bought a new riding lawn mower to use in her landscaping business.
    e. Farmer Edward installed 3 miles of fence around some land he intends to use to graze his cattle.
    f. Lanny spent $4,200 on shrubs, trees, and other landscaping of his principal residence.

23. Determine the adjusted basis of each of the following assets:
    a. Tong bought an apartment building at a cost of $140,000. The purchase price was properly allocated as $110,000 to the building and $30,000 to the land. Two years after purchasing the building, Tong installed a new roof at a cost of $3,200. Tong also paid a landscaping service $4,000 to plant some trees, shrubs, and build a new walkway. Annual property taxes and maintenance costs on the building total $6,600. Tong has owned the building for 3 years and has deducted the allowable depreciation of $4,000 per year on the building.
    b. Stephanie purchased an automobile three years ago at a cost of $24,000. Stephanie uses the automobile 75% in her business and 25% personal. Stephanie purchased a 5-year repair warranty on the automobile for $3,000. To date, she has deducted the $5,400 in allowable depreciation on the business use portion of the automobile.

24. Determine the adjusted basis of each of the following assets:
    a. André purchases a parcel of land in 1993 at a cost of $17,000. In 1995, the adjoining property owner sues André, claiming that part of André's property belongs to him under the right of adverse possession. André incurs $4,000 in legal fees in successfully defending against the lawsuit. André pays annual property taxes of $300 on the land and has paid $3,700 in interest on the loan he took out to acquire the property.
    b. René purchases 1,000 shares of Cramdem Co. common stock for $8 per share on October 13, 1994. In 1995, Cramdem pays a taxable cash dividend of 30 cents per share. René sells 300 shares on August 22, 1996, for $3 per share. On December 2, 1996, Cramdem pays a nontaxable cash dividend of 10 cents per share.
    c. Rufus owns 10 acres of land he purchased as an investment for $6,000. He spent an additional $34,000 subdividing the land into residential parcels and having utility lines run to the property. After the subdividing and utility lines had been completed, he gifted one acre of the land to his sister as a wedding present.

25. Amos and Thomas formed the Show Corporation during the current year. Amos owns 40% of Show's stock, Thomas owns 20%, and Arthur owns the remaining 40% of the stock. Amos paid $50,000 for his interest, and Thomas paid $25,000. Amos and Thomas are responsible for Show's daily operations and serve as co-chief executive officers. During the current year, Show Corporation had an operating loss of $60,000 and paid out $10,000 in dividends. What are Amos's and Thomas's adjusted bases in the Show Corporation stock if
    a. Show Corporation is organized as a corporation?
    b. Show Corporation is organized as an S corporation?

26. Return to the facts of problem 25. Assume that Show Corporation is organized as an S corporation. In its second year of operations, Show had an operating income of $40,000 and paid out $20,000 in dividends. On December 31, Amos gave a 10% interest in Show (i.e., 1/4 of his interest) to his son, Buddy. What is Amos's adjusted basis in the Show stock? What is Buddy's adjusted basis in the Show stock?

27. Paula purchases a 40% interest in Dancer Enterprises for $62,000 on January 2, 1995. Dancer is organized as a partnership and has an income of $30,000 in 1995. Dancer also distributes a total of $20,000 to the partners in 1995. What are the tax effects to Paula of her investment in Dancer? What is her adjusted basis in the partnership at the end of 1995?

28. Troy owns 600 of the 1,000 shares outstanding of Oiler Corporation. Troy's adjusted basis in the Oiler stock at the beginning of the current year is $84,000. Oiler Corporation is organized as an S corporation and reports the following results for the current year:

Operating income before special items	$59,000
Charitable contributions	6,000
Nondeductible expenses	12,000
Cash dividends paid	25,000

What is Troy's adjusted basis in the Oiler Corporation stock at the end of the current year?

29. Alberta owns 5 acres of land she purchased several years ago for $6,500. A new housing development is being built on the north side of her property. The owner of the development needs part of Alberta's land to run utility and sewer lines to the new development. The owner offers Alberta $13,000 for half of her land, but Alberta decides to wait to see if the land will appreciate further after the development is built. Alberta agrees to grant the developers an easement to run the utility and sewer lines through her property for $4,000. Does Alberta have income from the granting of the easement? Explain.

30. Leineia owns 1,000 shares of Serous Corporation common stock. She paid $26 per share several years ago. On December 31, 1995, Serous Corporation distributes a $5 per share cash dividend. Serous reports that $3 per share is taxable and $2 is a nontaxable dividend. On February 3, 1996, Leineia receives an offer for the stock of $25 per share.
    a. What are the tax effects of the December 31 distribution?
    b. What are the potential tax effects of the sale?

31. Carl Corporation acquires a business use warehouse for $200,000 on January 2, 1987. From 1987 through 1993, Carl Corporation properly deducts $5,000 in depreciation expense annually. During 1994, Carl Corporation incurs a net operating loss. Therefore, Carl deducts no depreciation after 1993. Also, Carl has a $185,000 offer from Kelsa Co. to buy the warehouse. The sale will be completed on July 1, 1995, if Carl accepts the offer. Assume Carl Corporation accepts the offer. What is the tax treatment of the sale?

32. Hannibal owns a farm. He purchases a tractor in 1991 at a cost of $25,000. Because 1991 is a bad year, he does not deduct any depreciation on the tractor in 1991. He sells the tractor in 1995 for $13,000. He takes straight-line depreciation on the tractor of $12,500 for the years 1992 to 1995. The total allowable straight-line depreciation for the tractor for 1991 to 1995 is $15,000. What is Hannibal's gain (loss) on the sale of the tractor? Explain.

33. Jolene owns a dry-cleaning business. During the current year, a rainstorm leaked through her roof and shorted out a dry-cleaning machine. The cost of repairing the machine was $300, none of which was compensated by Jolene's insurance. The adjusted basis of the machine before the casualty was $14,000. What is Jolene's adjusted basis in the machine after the casualty?

34. During the current year, Horace's personal residence was damaged by a tornado. The residence had an adjusted basis of $40,000 before the tornado. The cost of repairing the damage was $11,000. Horace's insurance company reimbursed him $8,000 for the repairs. Horace itemizes his deductions and had an adjusted gross income of $23,000 for the year. What is Horace's adjusted basis in the residence after the tornado?

35. Erin purchases 2 acres of land in 1995 by paying $4,000 in cash at closing and borrowing $40,000 to be repaid at $8,000 per year for the next 5 years with interest on the unpaid balance at 10%. In addition, Erin agrees to allow the seller to store some farm equipment on the land for 2 years (rental value of $1,000 per year). In return, the seller agrees to pay the $800 in points required to obtain the $40,000 loan. Erin also pays legal and abstracting fees of $700 on the purchase. What is Erin's initial basis in the land?

    a. In 1996, Erin pays $250 in property tax on the land. In addition, the county paves the road that runs by the land and assesses each taxpayer $1,300 for the paving. What is Erin's adjusted basis in the land at the end of 1996?

    b. In 1997, Erin sells 1 acre of the land to her brother for $18,000. What is Erin's gain (loss) on the sale of the land? What is her basis in the remaining acre of land?

36. Florian Corporation purchased a piece of land for investment purposes on May 1. Florian paid the seller $5,000 cash and agreed to pay the seller $2,000 per year for the next 5 years plus interest at 10% per year on the outstanding balance. As part of the purchase agreement, Florian agreed to pay all property taxes for the year, a total of $300. In addition, Florian paid legal fees of $350 connected with the purchase and gave the seller a car worth $2,000 (Florian's basis was $11,000). What is Florian Corporation's basis in the land?

37. Barbara wanted to go into the long-distance trucking business. She bought a used tractor-trailer for $80,000. However, the trailer wasn't suitable for Barbara's needs, so she sold it for $13,000 and purchased the trailer she needed for $26,000. What is Barbara's basis in the tractor? What is Barbara's basis in the trailer?

38. The Lester Partnership wanted to develop a shopping mall. The land it wanted for the mall was formerly a farm. The farmer wanted $260,000 for the land, $80,000 for the farm buildings, and $130,000 for the farmhouse. Although it wanted only the land, Lester agreed to the farmer's terms. Lester then paid Ace Wrecking Co. $20,000 to tear down the buildings. Lester was able to sell the scrap lumber from the buildings for $12,000. What is Lester's basis in the land?

39. Fala is the sole shareholder of Campbell Co. During the current year, Campbell sold Fala land that had a fair market value of $44,000 for $20,000. Campbell had paid $30,000 for the land. What are the tax effects of the sale for Fala and Campbell? What is Fala's basis in the land?

40. Izzy is an employee of Kosmo's Kustom Kars, Inc. The company rebuilds classic automobiles for resale. Last year, Izzy bought a rebuilt 1956 Thunderbird for $20,000 from the company. A car like Izzy's Thunderbird generally sells for $30,000. On December 20 of the current year, Izzy receives an offer of $25,000 for the car. What are the tax results if Izzy completes the sale? Should Izzy sell the car?

41. Evan purchased a condominium by paying $1,000 in cash and borrowing $77,000. He also paid $3,000 in legal fees, title search costs, and other closing fees in making the purchase. While having a drink to celebrate the closing of the purchase, the seller was distressed to learn that it was going to cost him $600 to have the furniture moved out of the condominium. The furniture was worth only $500, and the seller was going to give it to a local charity. Because Evan was going to rent out the condominium, he needed to furnish it to obtain the best rental price. Evan told the seller not to worry, he would take care of the furniture for him. The seller was so happy that he bought Evan another drink. Assuming that the assessed property tax values of the land and the building were $4,000 and $18,000, respectively, what is Evan's basis in each of the assets acquired?

42. Hester Corporation purchased a building by giving stock with a fair market value of $30,000 (original cost was $21,000) and borrowing $210,000. Hester paid closing costs of $10,000 on the purchase. What is the basis of the land and the building if the assessed property tax value of the land was $10,000 and the building's assessed property tax value was $40,000? Could any other basis be used? Explain.

43. Earl purchased all the assets and assumed the liabilities of Buddy's Market Shop. Details concerning the adjusted basis and fair market value of Buddy's assets are as follows:

Asset	Adjusted Basis	Fair Market Value
Inventory	$ 30,000	$ 40,000
Equipment	22,000	70,000
Land	10,000	15,000
Building	118,000	155,000
Liabilities	(60,000)	(60,000)

  a. If Earl paid $250,000 for Buddy's net assets, what is Earl's basis in the assets purchased?

  b. Assume that Buddy's Market Shop is a closely held corporation and that Earl paid $250,000 for all the stock. What is Earl's basis, and what is the basis of the assets of the corporation?

44. ABC Co. purchased all the assets of John's Saw Shop. Details on basis and fair market values of John's Saw Shop's assets are as follows:

Asset	Adjusted Basis	Fair Market Value
Inventory	$10,000	$12,000
Machinery & equipment	2,000	17,000
Land	13,000	11,000
Building	20,000	10,000

  a. What is ABC's basis in the assets purchased if ABC paid $40,000 for them?

  b. What is ABC's basis in the assets purchased if ABC paid $60,000 for them?

  c. What is ABC's basis if John's Saw Shop is a corporation and ABC purchased all of John's stock for $60,000?

45. Julia received 1,000 shares of Cookery Corporation stock from her grandfather as a wedding present. The shares were selling for $20 per share on the date of the gift. Grandfather had paid $4,000 for the shares 4 years earlier. Grandfather paid $2,000 in gift tax on the transfer of the shares to Julia.

  a. What is Julia's basis in the Cookery Corporation shares?

  b. Two months after her wedding, Julia wanted to take a trip to Europe. To get the money she needed for the trip, she sold 400 Cookery shares at $18 per share and paid a $400 commission on the sale. What is Julia's gain or loss on the sale of the 400 shares? What is her holding period for the shares?

46. Stockton paid $10,000 for 1,000 shares of Megacron, Inc., common stock on the day his niece Chama was born. Stockton's plan was to give the stock to Chama when she is ready to go to college. Eighteen years later, Chama is ready to leave for Eastern Private University. She needs the money for tuition. However, the market value of the stock is $6,000. Stockton's marginal tax rate is 31%. Chama's marginal tax rate is 15%.

  a. Should Stockton sell the shares and give the proceeds to Chama? Explain.

  b. What alternative course(s) of action does this situation offer?

47. For his 18th birthday, Kevin gave his son, Gabe, 5 Krugerrands. Kevin had paid $500 per Krugerrand 2 years earlier. On Gabe's birthday, Krugerrands were selling for $450. What is Gabe's basis in the Krugerrands? Explain.

  a. One month after his birthday, Gabe sold 2 of the Krugerrands for $525 each and used the money to buy a motorcycle. What is Gabe's gain or loss on the sale of the 2 Krugerrands? What is the holding period on the 2 Krugerrands he sold?

  b. Six months after Gabe's birthday, the Krugerrand market was nosediving. On the advice of his aunt, Gabe sold his 3 remaining Krugerrands for $375 each. What is Gabe's gain or loss on the sale of the 3 Krugerrands? What is the holding period on the 3 Krugerrands?

  c. Assume the same facts as in part b, except that Gabe sold the 3 Krugerrands for $475 each. What is Gabe's gain or loss on the sale of the 3 Krugerrands?

48. Florence's daughter, Eunice, needs $8,000 to start a new business. Florence has agreed to give Eunice the money she needs but will have to sell some securities she owns in order to raise that much cash. Florence has 1,400 shares of Tom Corporation common stock, which is selling for $6 per share. Florence's basis in the shares is $5 per share. Florence is in the 28% marginal tax rate bracket, and Eunice is in the 15% marginal tax rate bracket. Should Florence sell the shares and give the proceeds to her daughter? Explain.

49. Alex received an automobile from his mother as a graduation present. The auto had cost his mother $22,000 and had a fair market value of $14,000 on the date of the gift. No gift taxes were paid on the gift. Alex's first job will be as a traveling salesperson, and he will use the car in his business.
   a. What is Alex's basis for computing depreciation on the automobile? Explain.
   b. What is Alex's initial basis in the automobile? Explain.

50. Refer to problem 49. Alex used the automobile for 3 years and then sold it. During this period, he properly deducted a total of $10,000 in depreciation. What is Alex's gain (loss) on the automobile if he sold it for
   a. $3,000?
   b. $13,000?
   c. $8,000?

51. Yohanse's aunt Millie gave him a storage warehouse valued at $250,000 to use in his delivery business. The warehouse has been vacant since Millie received it through an inheritance from her grandfather several years ago. At that time, the warehouse had a value of $300,000 and a basis of $50,000.
   a. What is Yohanse's depreciable basis for the warehouse? Explain.
   b. What is Yohanse's initial basis in the warehouse? Explain.

52. Refer to problem 51. Yohanse used the warehouse for 4 years and sold it. During this period, he properly deducted a total of $25,000 in depreciation. What is Yohanse's gain (loss) on the warehouse if he sold it for
   a. $285,000?
   b. $215,000?
   c. $245,000?

53. Tommi inherits Dierhopf Corporation common stock from her uncle Norvel. Norvel's adjusted basis in the stock is $200,000, and the fair market value is $380,000. Six months after Norvel's death, the stock's value is $420,000. Nine months after his death, the stock's value is $350,000.
   a. Can the executor elect the alternate valuation date? Explain.
   b. Assume the executor transfers the stock to Tommi 9 months after the date of death. What is Tommi's basis?

54. Jesse's grandfather died on April 13, 1995. Jesse inherited the following property:

Property	Basis	FMV—April 13	FMV—Oct. 13
Land	$ 5,000	$20,000	$13,000
Stock	14,000	10,000	12,000
Watch	50	500	500

   a. What is Jesse's basis in the inherited property?
   b. What is Jesse's basis in the property if the executor of the estate elects the alternate valuation date?
   c. Assume that the executor elected the alternate valuation date and distributed title to the land to Jesse on June 23, 1995, when the fair market value of the land was $17,000. What is Jesse's basis in her inherited property?
   d. Assume that the executor elected the alternate valuation date and distributed the property to Jesse on December 2, 1995, when the fair market values were $15,000 for the land, $11,500 for the stock, and $500 for the watch. What is Jesse's basis in her inherited property?

55. Taylor died on February 19, 1995. Among the assets in Taylor's estate were 500 shares of Dane Co. preferred stock. Taylor had paid $14 per share for the stock on August 13, 1989. Market values per share for Dane preferred stock on various dates were as follows:

February 19, 1995	$12
April 1, 1995	$18
August 19, 1995	$10
November 21, 1995	$16

    Taylor's will provided that his niece Sherry was to receive the Dane shares. What is Sherry's basis in the shares in each of the following circumstances?
    a. No elections are made by the executor, and the shares are given to Sherry on April 1, 1995.
    b. The executor validly elects the alternate valuation date, and Sherry receives the shares on November 21, 1995.
    c. The executor validly elects the alternate valuation date, and Sherry receives the shares on April 1, 1995.

56. Harry and Freddi, a married couple, purchased 100 shares of Opaque Mutual Fund in 1986 for $2,400 as joint tenants with the right of survivorship. Freddi died during the current year. Fair market value of the shares is $5,000 on the date of death. Six months later the value is $5,100. What is Harry's basis in the 100 shares?

57. Loretta and Louanne paid $40,000 for a truck to use in their remodeling business. They bought it as joint tenants (50:50 ownership) with the right of survivorship. Several months after the purchase, Loretta died tragically when scaffolding on which she was working broke. Louanne was appointed executor of Loretta's estate, and she decided to liquidate the business immediately. She received an offer of $36,000 for the truck.
    a. Assume Louanne accepted the offer. What is the tax treatment of the sale?
    b. Are there any alternative courses of action that Louanne can take to positively change the tax effects? (Assume the FMV of the truck is $35,000 as of the alternate valuation date.)

58. Jessica owns a house with a basis of $90,000 and a fair market value of $150,000. On June 2, 1995, she marries Rick. As part of their prenuptial agreement, Rick is to pay Jessica $75,000 for a one-half interest in the house. What are the tax effects of the sale of the half-interest to Rick?

59. Katherine and Patrick were divorced in the current year. As part of the divorce agreement, Patrick agreed to give Katherine his interest in their residence, which was worth $100,000. Patrick and Katherine had paid $80,000 for the house 5 years ago. What are the tax consequences to Patrick and Katherine of the agreement that made Katherine sole owner of the house? Explain.

60. Alexis purchased a duplex by paying $10,000 cash and assuming the seller's $70,000 mortgage. Alexis paid legal fees of $1,000 and spent $9,000 on painting and carpeting the 2 units before renting out 1 unit and moving into the other unit (i.e., 1 unit is her personal residence). Three years later, Alexis purchased a house and moved out of the duplex unit and rented it out. She had taken $4,500 in depreciation on the rental unit and had her unit repainted at a cost of $500 before renting it out. Because of a general decline in property values, the duplex was worth only $70,000 when she moved out of it. What is her adjusted basis in the duplex?

61. Phoebe opened a bait delivery service during the current year. In starting up the business, she decided to use her personal truck as a delivery vehicle. She had paid $15,000 for the truck, which was worth $9,000 when she turned it into a delivery truck. What is her initial basis in the truck? What is her basis for depreciation on the truck? Explain.

    a. After using the truck for 2 years, Phoebe sold the truck and used the $4,600 in proceeds as a down payment on a new delivery van. Phoebe had correctly deducted $2,700 in straight-line depreciation on the truck during the 2 years of business use. What is her gain or loss on the sale of the truck?

    b. Assume the same facts as in part a, except that Phoebe sold the truck for $7,200. What is her gain or loss on the sale?

62. On January 5, 1995, Henry purchases 500 shares of Wichmann, Inc., common stock at a cost of $24,000. On April 1, Henry purchases an additional 250 shares for $9,000. On November 13, 1995, Wichmann, Inc., declares and distributes a 20% stock dividend. On December 23, 1995, Wichmann distributes a 50-cents per share cash dividend. On February 19, 1996, Henry sells 700 shares of the Wichmann, Inc., stock for $35 per share. How much income (loss) does Henry recognize in 1995 and 1996 on his Wichmann, Inc., stock?

63. On September 14, 1995, Wenona purchases 1,000 shares of Campbell Corporation common stock at a total cost of $8,000. In December 1996, Campbell pays a nontaxable stock dividend of 1 share of preferred stock for every 10 shares of common. On the date of the dividend announcement, Campbell's common stock is selling for $14 per share and its preferred stock for $20 per share. What is the basis of the preferred and common shares Wenona owns?

64. Monica owns 1,400 shares of Northeast Utilities common stock. In August of this year, when its stock was selling for $10 per share, Northeast announced a 20% stock dividend. In lieu of receiving the dividend shares, stockholders had the option of receiving $2 per share in cash. What are the tax effects to Monica if she elects to take the shares of stock instead of the cash? Explain.

65. Betty owns Betty's Car Repair Shop, a proprietorship. Betty's basis in the assets used in the business is $50,000. The fair market value of the assets is $60,000. Also, Betty owes $10,000 in liabilities related to the business. Betty has decided to incorporate the business using a tax-free transaction. She will name the new entity The Garage, Inc. Betty plans to transfer all assets and liabilities from the sole proprietorship to The Garage, Inc., in exchange for 1,000 shares of The Garage, Inc., common stock. After the exchange, Betty will own 100% of the outstanding stock of The Garage, Inc. What are the tax effects of the exchange for Betty and for The Garage, Inc.?

66. Abbie owns a fishing boat chartering business near San Diego. She owns 5 boats with appraised total value of $280,000. Abbie's adjusted basis in the boats is $50,000. She has outstanding debts relating to the business of $48,000. All the other equipment of the business is fully depreciated and has negligible fair market value. Abbie is concerned about her personal liability.

    a. What actions may Abbie take to limit her personal exposure?

    b. What is the tax treatment of her actions?

67. Eric owns 700 shares of Razor, Inc., stock for which he paid $3,150 in 1992. On December 14, 1995, Eric sells the 700 shares for $3 per share and pays a commission of $350 on the sale. On January 3, 1996, Eric purchases 400 shares of Razor, Inc., for $2 per share and pays an $80 commission on the purchase. What is Eric's recognized gain or loss on the sale of the 700 shares? What is his basis in the 400 shares purchased in 1996?

68. Steele bought 200 shares of Splendid, Inc., common stock 14 months ago for $5,000. He sells all the stock on December 20 of the current year for $9,000. On January 15 of the next year, he buys 250 shares of Splendid, Inc., stock for $10,500.

    a. Explain what Steele is trying to accomplish with these transactions. Will it pass IRS scrutiny?

    b. How will your explanation change if Steele sells the stock for $4,000 on December 20 and purchases 250 shares for $5,500 on January 15?

69. On November 14, 1995, Noel sells 2,000 shares of Marker, Inc., stock for $6,000. He had purchased the stock 2 years earlier for $10,000. Because the price of the stock continued to drop, Noel purchases additional shares of Marker stock on December 10, 1995. What are the tax effects of the sale of the stock and the basis in the new shares if Noel
  a. Repurchases 2,000 shares for $5,000?
  b. Repurchases 800 shares for $2,000?
  c. Repurchases 4,000 shares for $9,000?

70. Lance and Lola are married taxpayers with 2 dependent children. Lance works as a plumber for Fast Fix-it Co. Lola, who is self-employed, sells specialty fishing lures. During 1995, they have the following property transactions:

▲ **INTEGRATIVE PROBLEM**

  1. Lance decides to open his own plumbing company. He acquires the following assets to get the business started:
    a. Lance purchases a small office building on March 28 for $4,000 cash and borrows $36,000 with interest at 14% for 25 years. For property tax purposes, the land is assessed at $2,000 and the building at $8,000.
    b. Lance converts his personal truck into a business truck on April 1. Lance had paid $16,000 for the truck, which was worth $10,000 when it was converted to business use. Lance paid $400 to have his business logo painted on the truck.
    c. Lance purchases the following assets from Fred, a retired plumber, for $28,000 on April 5:

Asset	Fred's Basis	FMV
Plumbing equipment	$ 3,000	$ 6,000
Plumbing supplies	-0-	3,000
Plumbing inventory	12,000	16,000
Totals	$15,000	$25,000

    d. Lance's father gives him 2,000 shares of Tetra Corporation stock to help him finance the cost of starting the new business. Lance's father had paid $5 per share for the stock, which was worth $3 per share on the day Lance received the stock. Lance uses the stock as collateral for a loan he uses to pay Fred for the assets purchased in part c.
  2. Lola wins a new automobile in a bass-fishing contest. The automobile has a list price of $28,000, but a local car dealer tells her that automobile would typically sell for $24,000. Lola intends to use the automobile in her business. Lola receives the automobile on March 3. Her records for the remainder of the year show that she drives the automobile 8,000 miles for business purposes and 4,000 miles for personal use. Lola purchases an extended warranty contract on the automobile from her local car dealer. The warranty costs $600 and provides additional coverage for 5 years from the date of purchase (March 5, 1995).
  3. Lola's grandmother dies during 1995 and leaves Lola the family plate collection. The plates had been passed from generation to generation since the family first emigrated from Latvia. Lola doesn't know what the original cost of the plates was, but they were valued in her grandmother's estate at $38,000. The estate paid $8,200 in estate taxes on the plates.
  4. Lola and Lance's house is damaged by a tornado in 1995. They had paid $44,000 for the house in 1988; $4,000 of the cost was properly allocated to the land. In 1990, they added a swimming pool at a cost of $15,000. Just before the casualty, they had paid a landscape company $3,600 to rework the landscape in the yard. The value of the house before the casualty was $92,000. Repairs to the house cost $37,000, $23,000 of which was reimbursed by insurance. Lance and Lola's 1995 adjusted gross income is $46,000.

5. Lola uses a room in their home exclusively and regularly as an office for her fishing lure business. The room is 10 feet by 12 feet. According to the original purchase documents, the total square footage of their house is 1,800 square feet. Lola began using the room as an office on April 4, 1990. At that time, she purchased a desk and a filing cabinet for $800. In 1992, she traded lures that had cost her $900 (fair market value was $1,600) for a photocopier. The 1995 casualty did not affect the home office.

6. On April 16, 1990, Lola purchased an automobile to use in her fishing lures business by paying $2,000 in cash and borrowing $13,000. During 1990, she drove the automobile 4,800 total miles and documented 3,600 business miles.

7. Lance and Lola have a rental house. The house was acquired by Lola from her former husband in 1985 as part of their divorce settlement. They had paid $80,000 for the house in 1983. In 1985, it was appraised at $100,000 ($10,000 land value and $90,000 structures value). Lola lived in the house until 1986 when she married Lance. They began renting out the house in October 1986. Lola estimates that the house had increased in value to $110,000 when she began renting it out.

8. Lance and Lola own the following stocks:
   a. Corporate Capital Resources—500 shares, purchased August 1, 1993, for $35 per share. They paid $1,000 in brokerage commissions to acquire the stock. On October 4, 1994, Corporate Capital Resources distributed a 2-for-1 stock split.
   b. Lance and Lola received 1,000 shares of Meek Corporation common stock as a wedding gift from Lola's uncle. Her uncle had paid $4,000 for the stock in 1980. The fair market value of the stock on the date of the gift was $20,000. The uncle paid $500 in gift tax on the transfer.

9. Lola's father died on November 2, 1992. Lola inherited a parcel of land for which her father had paid $500 in 1971. On November 2, 1992, the land was appraised at $8,000. The executor of the estate elected to use the alternate valuation date. The value of the land on May 2, 1993, was $8,600. Lola received the land from the estate in August 1993 when it was worth $9,000.

Based on the information provided, determine the *initial basis* of each of Lance and Lola's assets. If more than 1 basis is possible, list the alternatives and explain when each basis would apply.

▲ DISCUSSION CASE 10–1

Monica is planning to start her own accounting, tax, and financial planning business. Her uncle Gus has given her file cabinets, a desk, computer equipment, and book cases that were in his den until he sold his house. Gus recently moved to a lakefront cottage and no longer needs the furniture and equipment. Gus's adjusted basis for all the items is $3,500, and the fair market value is $2,000. Monica will convert 20% of her personal residence into her office and will use it exclusively for her business. Monica's residence has a fair market value of $150,000 and an adjusted basis of $80,000 (10% is allocated to the land). What are the tax ramifications of the gifts and the conversion? What will be the depreciable basis of the property? Explain your answers in terms of the underlying concepts that govern the result.

▲ DISCUSSION CASE 10–2

Several years ago, Steve gave his nephew Rashan 600 shares of Dalmont Corporation common stock valued at $12,000 with a basis of $3,000. Steve's intent was to ensure that Rashan has money for college. Rashan is now a senior in high school, and the stock is worth $16,000. Rashan is considering selling the shares to put toward his first semester's tuition. His marginal tax rate is 15% and will remain at that rate throughout his college years because of part-time work. Steve is terminally ill and has no more than 16 months to live. He asks Rashan to give the shares of stock back to him and tells Rashan not to worry about it. Steve's will states that Rashan gets the 600 shares of Dalmont Corporation stock. Rashan is confused. He can cover his tuition, fees, and other college expenses for the first two years from savings and student loans. But he does not understand what Steve is trying to accomplish by asking for the stock. Explain all the tax ramifications to Rashan.

Lynn bought 100 shares of Filidelfia Corporation stock for $10,000 three years ago. She sells 50 shares for $4,000 on December 24 of this year. On January 17 of next year, she plans to buy 100 more shares of Filidelfia stock for $7,000. Explain the tax treatment of these transactions. Include a discussion of the underlying concepts that govern the results. What alternative actions may Lynn take to change the results?

▲ DISCUSSION
CASE 10–3

Luther, 72, is a lifelong bachelor who has been very successful in his business and investment endeavors. Luther realizes that he should begin to do some tax planning for his death. Although he intends to leave the bulk of his $200,000,000 estate to the Northern State Technical University School of Accounting, he does have a few nieces and nephews for whom he would like to provide (although not too lavishly). Listed here is a selection of assets he is thinking of giving to his nephews and nieces:

▲ TAX PLANNING
CASE 10–4

Asset	Fair Market Value	Basis	Suspended Loss
Keating S&L stock	$ 10,000	$ 200,000	
Impressionist painting	$5,000,000	-0-	
Land held as an investment	$2,000,000	$1,500,000	
Limited partnership interest	$ 100,000	$ 400,000	$1,300,000
Rental property	$4,000,000	$1,000,000	$2,500,000
General Motors stock	$2,000,000	$1,000,000	

Consider each of the following questions from Luther's point of view (what is best from the standpoint of his tax situation). Explain.

a. Which of these properties would be best to give away to his favorite nephew? Why?
b. Which of these properties would be the worst to give away? Why?
c. Which property(ies) should Luther definitely retain? Why?
d. Which property(ies) should Luther consider selling? Why?

Twenty years ago, Consuela Guererro invented and patented a high-speed burrito-stuffing machine. Through the years, Consuela has jealously guarded her invention, allowing its use in only El Consuela's, a chain of restaurants in which she owns 60% of the stock (basis = $200,000). On the advice of her accountant, the patent is owned and manufacturing of the burrito stuffer is done exclusively by Consuela's wholly owned corporation, Stuff, Inc. (Consuela's basis in the Stuff, Inc., stock is $250,000.)

▲ TAX PLANNING
CASE 10–5

Consuela has been approached by the Frijoles Co. about acquiring her burrito-stuffing operation. Specifically, Frijoles would like to acquire Stuff, Inc.'s patent and burrito-stuffer manufacturing operation. Consuela is tired after spending so many years fighting off the competition, and she has agreed to sell to Frijoles. Consuela feels that the patent and manufacturing equipment are worth at least $2,000,000, although they are carried on Stuff, Inc.'s books at their adjusted basis of $100,000. Consuela wants your advice on how best to structure her exit from the burrito-stuffing business. She intends to retain her ownership interest in El Consuela's.

a. From Consuela's point of view, should she sell the burrito-stuffer assets owned by Stuff, Inc., directly to Frijoles, or should she sell her stock in Stuff, Inc.? In your discussion, consider not only the tax aspects of the alternatives but also how each alternative could influence the proposed $2,000,000 purchase price.
b. Consider question a from Frijoles' point of view.

▲ ETHICS DISCUSSION CASE 10–6

Assume you are a CPA. A new client, Mark, a local chiropractor, has brought you the financial information for his business at the close of the past year. Previously, Mark prepared his own tax returns and had them reviewed by Blacke & Co. You find the information to be organized and fairly straightforward. Mark does bring one recent transaction to your attention. He sold an x-ray machine for $10,000 near the end of the past year. The machine had cost $25,000 three years earlier. Mark did not deduct depreciation expense in the year of acquisition. His business incurred an operating loss that year. Therefore, Mark "saved" some of his basis and did not report a loss as big as he could have. For the following year and for this year, Mark recorded depreciation of $5,000 annually. Mark tells you that he would like to "reclaim" the depreciation he did not deduct in the year of acquisition. He insists there will not be a problem, because he could have taken the depreciation 3 years ago. Also, by applying it to the adjusted basis for the sales transaction, he will not report a loss. So, the recognized loss will not be used to offset other income. Advise Mark on the propriety of this transaction. You may wish to consult the Statements on Responsibilities in Tax Practice.

Cost Recovery on Property: Depreciation, Depletion, and Amortization

▲ CHAPTER LEARNING OBJECTIVES

■ Discuss the recovery of the cost of long-lived assets and the general criteria for taking deductions for depreciation, depletion, or amortization on an investment in a long-lived asset.

■ Illustrate how the timing of the cost-recovery deduction affects the real after-tax return on an investment in property.

■ Identify the factors involved in and the general approach to calculating depreciation on assets acquired before 1981.

■ Discuss the general changes in the approach to calculating depreciation on assets acquired after 1980 under the Accelerated Cost Recovery System (ACRS).

■ Determine the amount of cost recovery allowed on certain classes of assets under the ACRS depreciation rules.

■ Explain the changes made to ACRS for property acquired after 1986 and determine the amount of cost recovery on various classes of assets under the Modified Accelerated Cost Recovery System (MACRS).

■ Discuss the limitations on depreciation deductions for listed property in general and the specific limitation on depreciation of automobiles.

■ Explain the deduction for depletion and how to calculate depletion using the cost method and the statutory percentage method.

■ Discuss the amortization deduction for intangible assets.

CHAPTER 11

▲ CONCEPT REVIEW ▲

Accounting method A taxpayer must adopt an accounting method that clearly reflects income.

Administrative convenience Those items for which the cost of compliance would exceed the revenue generated are not taxed.

Annual accounting period All entities must report the results of their operations on an annual basis (the tax year). Each tax year stands on its own, apart from other tax years.

Basis This is the amount of unrecovered investment in an asset. As amounts are expended and/or recovered relative to an asset over time, the basis is adjusted in consideration of such changes. The **adjusted basis** of an asset is the original basis, plus or minus the changes in the amount of unrecovered investment.

Business purpose To be deductible, an expenditure or a loss must have a business or other economic purpose that exceeds any tax avoidance motive. The primary motive for the transaction must be to make a profit.

Capital recovery No income is realized until the taxpayer receives more than the amount invested to produce the income. The amount invested in an asset represents the maximum amount recoverable.

Conduit entity An entity for which the tax attributes flow through to its owners for tax purposes.

Entity All items of income, deduction, and so on are traced to the tax unit responsible for the item.

Legislative grace Any tax relief provided is the result of a specific act of Congress that must be strictly applied and interpreted. All income received is taxable unless a specific provision can be found in the tax law that excludes the income from taxation. Deductions must be approached with the philosophy that nothing is deductible unless a provision in the tax law allows the deduction.

Related party Family members and corporations that are owned by family members are considered related parties, as are certain other relationships between entities in which the power to control the substance of a transaction is evidenced through majority ownership.

▲ INTRODUCTION

Based on the legislative grace concept, business expenses are classified as related either to a trade or business or to a production-of-income activity. To be deductible, an expense must have a business purpose and be related to the current tax year. If an expenditure results in a long-lived asset that benefits several annual accounting periods, its cost is generally allocated on a reasonable basis to the tax years in which it is used to produce income. According to the capital recovery concept, a taxpayer does not realize taxable income until after the capital used to produce the income is recovered. As discussed in Chapter 10, an asset's basis is the maximum amount of investment in an asset that can be subtracted from income as a capital recovery. Tax depreciation, amortization, and depletion are tax accounting methods used to periodically recover the investment in assets. These accounting methods provide a reasonable allocation of bases to the annual accounting periods benefited by the use of the assets. The discussion that follows first considers the types of property subject to depreciation, amortization, and depletion and then discusses the bases of assets subject to capital recovery. After examining these issues, which apply to all the accounting methods discussed in this chapter, the text turns to tax accounting for depreciation, amortization, and depletion.

This chapter considers several different depreciation methods. Generally, a taxpayer can choose among two or more alternative depreciation methods. The method the taxpayer chooses determines the timing and the amount of the annual depreciation deduction. The timing and the amount of the depreciation expense affect the present value of the tax savings from the deduction (the time value of money effect). As a general rule, the earlier the taxpayer can claim a depreciation deduction, the greater its present value is.

▲ **EXAMPLE 1**   Angelo has $100,000 to invest in an asset. The cost of asset A will be deductible immediately. The cost of asset B cannot be deducted until it is sold. Both assets produce the same annual revenue and cost flows and will be held for 10 years. If Angelo is in a 31% marginal tax rate bracket during the 10-year period and the cost of capital is 10%, which asset will provide the greater real after-tax return?

Discussion: The deduction for both assets provides a $31,000 ($100,000 × 31%) tax savings. However, because asset A's tax savings occur in the first year, it results in real tax savings of $31,000. The present value of the future deduction for asset B is only $11,966 [$31,000 × 0.386 (the present value of $1 at 10% for 10 years)]. As a result of deferring the capital recovery on asset B for 10 years, its present value to Angelo is decreased by $19,034 ($31,000 − $11,966), compared to the immediate tax savings resulting from asset A.

More likely, a taxpayer will be faced with a situation in which the investment can be recovered as the asset is used to earn income.

▲ **EXAMPLE 2**   Tawana purchases an apartment building for $100,000 at the beginning of 1995 for use as rental property. Assume that Tawana is in the 31% marginal tax bracket, her cost of capital is 10%, and that she sells the building at the end of 10 years for $100,000, its original cost. To determine the effect of depreciation on the transaction, ignore the cost of the land, which is not included in the $100,000 cost basis of the building. Also, assume that the maximum marginal tax rate applicable to net capital gains of 28% applies. What are the tax effects of the purchase, use, and disposition of the building?

Discussion: The $100,000 cost of the building is depreciated using the MACRS depreciation system (explained later in this chapter). The depreciation calculations and the annual tax savings at a 31% marginal tax rate discounted at 10% are as follows:

Year	MACRS Depreciation Rate	Annual Depreciation Deduction	31% Tax Rate Savings	10% PV Factor	PV of Tax Savings
1995	3.485	$ 3,485	$ 1,080	.909	$ 982
1996	3.636	3,636	1,127	.826	931
1997	3.636	3,636	1,127	.751	846
1998	3.636	3,636	1,127	.683	770
1999	3.636	3,636	1,127	.621	700
2000	3.636	3,636	1,127	.564	636
2001	3.636	3,636	1,127	.513	578
2002	3.636	3,636	1,127	.467	526
2003	3.636	3,636	1,127	.424	478
2004	3.637	3,637	1,127	.386	435
Totals		$36,210	$11,223		

Present value of tax savings on building $6,882

Sale of Building:

Sales price		$100,000
Less: Adjusted basis:		
Building—cost	$100,000	
Less: Depreciation	(36,210)	(63,790)
Gain on sale of property		$ 36,210
Tax on gain at capital gain rate (28% × $36,210)		$ 10,139
Present value factor		× .386
Present value of tax cost of gain on sale		(3,914)
Net tax savings from depreciation deduction		$2,968

The present value of Tawana's tax savings related to depreciation on the building is $6,882 (effectively a cash inflow resulting from reducing taxes that would have been paid out). When Tawana sells the building at the end of 10 years, she realizes and recognizes a $36,210 gain. The gain recognized stems from the depreciation deducted over the 10-year period in which the building was used. The gain on the sale of the building is taxed at the 28% capital gains rate for an individual. The present value of the tax to be paid on the gain from the sale of the building is $3,914 (a cash outflow). Thus, Tawana has been able to earn a $2,968 profit. The profit results from the timing differences in the present value (depreciation deductions versus gain on the sale) and from marginal tax rate differences (ordinary tax rates versus capital gains tax rate).

In example 2, notice the following points:

- The earlier the depreciation deduction is taken, the greater will be the present value of the tax savings to the taxpayer.

- A taxpayer can receive an economic benefit by accelerating the recovery of basis and deferring income related to the property. In example 2, the property is sold for its original purchase price. Yet, the effect of depreciation is to provide the taxpayer with a positive present value.

- The taxpayer benefits when deductions can be claimed at regular tax rates and any gain from the sale of the property is taxed at a lower rate. The depreciation deductions in example 2 reduce ordinary income subject to tax at 31 percent. However, the gain on the sale of the building is subject to tax at the 28-percent capital gains rate. Limitations on this effect are explained in Chapter 12.

▲ PROPERTY SUBJECT TO PERIODIC CAPITAL RECOVERY

Allocation of a long-lived asset's basis to several tax years results in periodic capital recovery deductions for depreciation, amortization, or depletion. Tangible properties with definite useful lives, such as buildings and office equipment, are subject to **depreciation.** Intangible properties with definite useful lives, such as patents, copyrights, or an agreement not to compete, are subject to **amortization.** Natural resources that waste away through use, such as oil or coal, are subject to **depletion.**[1]

Two tests must be met in order to claim an expense deduction for the periodic capital recovery of an asset's basis. A depreciable asset, an intangible asset, and a natural resource are allowed periodic capital recovery if the asset is

- Used in a trade or business or held for the production of income (i.e., there is a business purpose).
- It has a determinable (limited) useful life in the taxpayer's business use.

An asset is subject to periodic capital recovery if its useful life (value) is used up in order to earn income.[2] Because tangible property is subject to wear and tear, to decay from natural causes, to exhaustion, and to obsolescence as it is used to produce income, it has a limited life. Similarly, the life of a natural resource is generally limited by the fact that the resource is removed from its source and sold to produce income. In addition, the same forces that cause a depreciable asset to lose its value may affect a natural resource. For example, the natural resource may erode, decay, or become obsolete because of technological or environmental factors. An intangible property may have a life that is limited by law, the terms of a contract, obsolescence, or other factors.

A taxpayer may not take a deduction for the periodic capital recovery of the basis of an asset held for personal use. A taxpayer can depreciate the business basis of a mixed-use asset but not the personal use part of the asset's basis. An intangible asset used for both business and personal purposes, such as an extended (repair) warranty agreement on a car, can be amortized and deducted to the extent the asset is used for a business purpose. Table 11–1 illustrates examples of depreciable and nondepreciable assets that an individual might own.

▲ **EXAMPLE 3**   On January 1, 1995, Melody buys a new car that she plans to use 80% of the time in her business and 20% of the time for personal transportation. She also buys a 5-year extended repair warranty on her new car for $500. Can Melody deduct the cost of the extended warranty as an expense?

Discussion: The $500 paid for the extended warranty is not a current expense. The extended warranty is an intangible long-lived asset that provides benefits for 5 tax years. Because the asset provides business benefits, its cost is subject to amortization. The annual amortization is $100 ($500 ÷ 5 years). However, Melody is allowed a deduction of only $80 for the expense related to business use of the car (80% business use × $100). She cannot deduct the $20 expense related to personal use of the car.

An asset found in a typical business that is not subject to depreciation is inventory. When inventory is sold, its cost basis is subtracted from sales as a deduction for the cost of goods sold.

▲ **EXAMPLE 4**   Mitch uses the following assets in his corner grocery store:

Inventory	Store building
Shelving	Land
Black-topped parking lot	Shopping carts

Which of the assets are subject to depreciation?

Discussion: Mitch may depreciate the shelving, store building, black-topped parking lot, and the shopping carts. These assets are used to conduct the grocery business, and they have a limited useful life in Mitch's business. The land cannot be depreciated, because it has an indefinite useful life. The sale of inventory results in a deduction for the cost of goods sold.

Depreciable Asset	Nondepreciable Asset
House held for rent to others	House used as taxpayer's personal residence
Auto used for a *business purpose* (e.g., if 60% of the miles an auto is driven relates to business use, 60% of the auto is a business asset subject to depreciation)	Auto used for commuting to and from work and for other personal uses
Furniture in business office	Furniture in taxpayer's personal residence
	Land (land is never depreciable)
Microcomputer used in a business	Microcomputer used by members of the family for personal recordkeeping and educational purposes

▲ **Table 11–1**

ASSETS OWNED BY INDIVIDUALS

▲ Basis Subject to Periodic Capital Recovery

Periodic capital recovery is generally calculated using the taxpayer's initial basis in the asset. Therefore, the basis rules discussed in Chapter 10 provide the starting point for computing the capital recovery deduction. The **depreciable basis** of an asset is the amount of basis that is subject to depreciation and is the amount used to determine the annual depreciation deduction.[3] The depreciable basis does not change during an asset's tax life unless additional capital expenditures are made for the asset. The total capital recovered as an expense deduction over an asset's useful life may never be more than its depreciable basis.

▲ **EXAMPLE 5** Ralph's brother, Herman, gave him a truck that Herman had held for personal use. Herman had paid $15,000 for the truck when it was new. As of the date of the gift, the truck was worth $6,000, and the gift was not subject to gift tax. What is Ralph's initial basis in the truck?

Discussion: Ralph's basis is determined using the gift rules. Because the fair market value of the truck is less than Herman's basis, Ralph has a split basis (i.e., the gain basis is the $15,000 and the loss basis is $6,000).

▲ **EXAMPLE 6** Ralph, in example 5, immediately began using the truck 100% of the time in his repair business. What is Ralph's depreciable basis for the truck?

Discussion: Ralph's depreciable basis is $6,000. Depreciation on this gift property is calculated by using the lesser of the donor's basis or fair market value on the transfer date. Limiting the depreciable basis to $6,000 prevents a capital recovery deduction for the decrease in the truck's value related to Herman's personal use of the truck.

Absent any capital expenditures on the truck, Ralph's depreciable basis remains at $6,000 throughout the period he uses the truck. However, Ralph's adjusted basis decreases as he takes the annual depreciation deductions on the truck. Depreciable basis is used only to calculate the annual deduction on the asset.

▲ Capital Recovery from Depreciation or Cost Recovery

The depreciation rules that are in effect at the time an asset is placed into service determine the depreciation method to be used over the life of the asset. An asset is placed in service when it is set up and ready for its intended use for a business purpose. This general rule provides certainty and consistency when computing the depreciation deduction for a specific asset. However, frequent changes in the tax laws make the depreciation rules seem complex when computing depreciation for assets acquired over several years. As the time line in Figure 11–1 shows, depreciation methods have undergone three major changes since 1980. In addition, several important, but less dramatic, changes have been made in the rules in nearly every session of Congress. Taxpayers and tax advisers alike face significant difficulty in coping with the frequent changes in the depreciation rules.

Property acquired before 1981 could be depreciated according to the facts and circumstances related to the use of the asset in the taxpayer's business. Taxpayers who chose to do so could use an alternative method known as the *Class Life Asset Depreciation Range (ADR)*. Few assets acquired after 1980 are subject to depreciation using these two methods.

Beginning in 1981, a mandatory depreciation method called the **Accelerated Cost Recovery System** and referred to by the acronym **ACRS** took effect. Also, a special election to immediately expense assets replaced a more limited additional first-year depreciation deduction that was allowed before 1981. In 1986, Congress modified the ACRS rules and introduced a revised version of ACRS known as the **Modified Accelerated Cost Recovery System (MACRS).** Taxpayers must use the

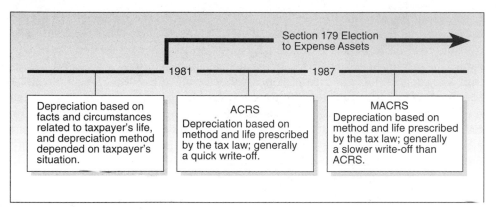

▲ Figure 11–1

MAJOR CHANGES IN
DEPRECIATION METHODS
SINCE 1980

MACRS system for assets placed in service after 1986. Each of these depreciation methods is explained here. The terminology related to depreciation has changed so frequently that it is sometimes confusing. In the discussion that follows, *depreciation* and *cost recovery* are used interchangeably to mean *depreciation* as it is generally understood.

The basic depreciation constructs, which provide the foundation from which current tax depreciation rules developed, may be familiar to you. Although few assets are still subject to this depreciation system, an understanding of depreciation is useful in learning the ACRS and MACRS cost-recovery systems.

The most commonly used depreciation method before 1981 was the facts and circumstances method. A second method, the Class Life Asset Depreciation Range (ADR), was introduced in the 1970s to promote uniformity in depreciation calculations among taxpayers.

▲ DEPRECIATION BEFORE 1981

Facts and Circumstances Method

Before 1981, financial and tax accounting for depreciation were similar. Both financial and tax depreciation were generally computed according to

- The capital investment in an asset to be recovered through depreciation
- The asset's salvage value
- The asset's useful life
- An appropriate annual depreciation method
- An appropriate method of allocating depreciation for the first and last year of an asset's life

For tax purposes, this approach to computing depreciation is known as the *facts and circumstances method*. Under the facts and circumstances method, the capital investment subject to depreciation was the asset's tax basis less its estimated salvage value. The determination of an asset's salvage value was a complex issue that was often a source of controversy with the IRS. To help lessen disputes between the IRS and taxpayers, the depreciation rules allowed taxpayers to reduce an asset's estimated salvage value by as much as 10% of its basis. If an asset's estimated salvage value did not exceed 10% of its basis, salvage value could be ignored. When using the facts and circumstances method, an important consideration was matching an asset's depreciation to the tax years benefited by its use (i.e., matching income and expense). The basis of an asset was depreciated over its useful life in the taxpayer's business and not its actual physical life. Because the useful life of an asset in the taxpayer's business was also an estimate, this was an additional source of controversy between the IRS and taxpayers.

Taxpayers had considerable freedom to choose a reasonable depreciation method. However, a requirement was that once a depreciation method was adopted for an asset, that method had to be used consistently for the life of the asset. For assets acquired before 1981, depreciation was generally computed using one of the methods typically taught in a financial accounting or finance course, such as

- Straight line (SL)
- Declining balance (150-percent DB, 175-percent DB, or 200-percent DB)
- Sum-of-years digits
- Any other reasonable method, such as units of output, machine hours, or miles a car was driven

If the declining balance method was used, the taxpayer could choose whether to switch to the straight-line method to optimize the deduction over its remaining useful life.

Because an asset may be used for less than a full 12 months, a taxpayer had to use a reasonable method to allocate depreciation to the first and last year of an asset's life. Generally, an asset was treated as placed in service on the first day of the month if it was actually placed in service on or before the fifteenth day of the month. If an asset was placed in service after the fifteenth day of the month, it was treated as placed in service on the first day of the following month. The allocation worked the same way in figuring the month of an asset's disposition. If an asset was disposed of after the fifteenth day of the month, the disposition was treated as if it had occurred on the first day of the following month. Thus, a full month's depreciation was allowed for the last month of use. Taxpayers also used several other methods to allocate depreciation to the first and last year of an asset's use. The objective was to adopt a reasonable allocation method and then apply it consistently.

▲ **EXAMPLE 7**   On April 23, 1971, Glen purchased and placed in service a machine costing $10,000. Assuming that Glen elected to use straight-line depreciation, the machine had an estimated life of 5 years and an estimated salvage value of $1,000. What would the depreciation have been in 1971?

Discussion: During 1971, Glen used the machine for 8 months. Because the machine was purchased after April 15, the machine was subject to depreciation beginning on May 1, 1971. Because salvage value of as much as 10% of cost could be ignored, the annual full-year depreciation would have been $2,000 ($10,000 ÷ 5 years). Glen could take only 8 months of depreciation in 1971, resulting in depreciation of $1,333 [(8 ÷ 12) × $2,000]. For 1972 and subsequent years, Glen could claim a full year's depreciation—$2,000. At the end of 1975, the machine had 4 months remaining in its depreciable life. For 1976, Glen should have claimed a $667 deduction for the period of January 1 through April 30, 1976 [$2,000 × (4 ÷ 12)]. The machine's 5-year useful tax life therefore affected 6 annual accounting periods.

Class Life Asset Depreciation Range (ADR)

The ADR system was introduced in 1971 as an alternative to the facts and circumstances depreciation method. An objective of ADR was to reduce disputes between the IRS and taxpayers concerning the length of an asset's useful life and the amount used as its estimated salvage value. ADR was elective, so the taxpayer could choose whether to use this method. Because of complexities related to record keeping and other factors beyond the scope of this discussion, ADR was not an overwhelming success. However, features included in ADR are helpful in understanding MACRS, used today.

One important feature of ADR was that it grouped depreciable assets into broadly defined classes. For each class, the IRS specified the average life of the assets in the class. The average life was called the *asset guideline period*. For example, office equipment used in all business activities was assigned a 10-year guideline period. Assets used in the manufacture of glass products had a 14-year guideline period. Today, MACRS uses a similar concept, except that the asset guideline period is called the asset's **class life.** A second important feature of ADR was that it required the adoption of a depreciation convention for depreciating assets in their first year of use. After 1980, both ACRS and MACRS specify the convention that applies in the first and last years an asset is used.

The Accelerated Cost Recovery System (ACRS) was introduced into the tax law by the Economic Recovery Act of 1981. ACRS applies to property placed in service after 1980 and before 1987. ACRS is an excellent example of how Congress attempts to influence the economy through tax legislation. A primary objective of the Economic Recovery Act of 1981 was to provide incentives for investment that would lead to economic expansion.[4] To accomplish its economic objectives, Congress adopted a radically new approach to accounting for depreciation. Traditional tax and financial accounting depreciation methods that were based on estimated useful lives, salvage values, and a variety of depreciation methods and assumptions were abandoned in favor of ACRS. Unlike the facts and circumstances method, ACRS does not attempt to match an asset's depreciation to the annual accounting period that benefits from its use. The primary purpose of the ACRS system was to greatly accelerate the capital recovery taxpayers received from depreciating property. In fact, ACRS and MACRS both use the term *cost recovery* instead of *depreciation* to identify the deduction.

An additional factor that influenced the switch to cost recovery from traditional depreciation methods was the continuing concern over the complexity of the tax law. Cost recovery enhanced administrative convenience by standardizing the depreciation rules, which helped reduce the continuing conflict between the IRS and taxpayers concerning an asset's estimated useful life and its salvage value. This is accomplished by having fewer and prespecified useful lives, no salvage value considered in the computation, and standard acquisition and disposition-year conventions applicable to all assets. To compute depreciation on an asset using cost recovery, you need to know

■ The asset's depreciable basis

■ The class life of the asset

■ Whether you want to use the prescribed or the alternative depreciation method

■ The first and last year convention that applies to the asset's class[5]

The Tax Reform Act of 1986 replaced ACRS with the Modified Accelerated Cost Recovery System. MACRS applies to property placed in service after 1986. By 1986, Congress was more concerned with raising revenue than stimulating the

▲ COST RECOVERY IN GENERAL

economy. The 1986 act reduced tax rates from a high of 50 percent for individuals to 28 percent and from 46 percent for corporations to 34 percent. In order to minimize the loss of revenue from tax rate reductions, it was necessary to broaden the tax base. One way Congress broadened the tax base was by specifying longer recovery periods for depreciable assets that would result in slower depreciation than allowed by ACRS. Although MACRS recovery periods are longer than those used under ACRS, most taxpayers still depreciate assets more quickly than they would have under the facts and circumstances method.

In addition to accelerating the recovery of an investment through ACRS and MACRS, Congress introduced the Section 179 election to expense depreciable assets placed in service after 1981. The Section 179 election replaces the deduction for additional first-year depreciation that was allowed before 1981. Initially, Section 179 allowed an expense deduction of as much as $5,000 in the year of acquisition on qualifying property. However, the 1986 act increased the limit to $10,000 for years after 1986. This limit has been increased to $17,500 for qualifying property placed in service after December 31, 1992. The discussion that follows considers characteristics common to both ACRS and MACRS.

Property Subject to Cost Recovery

ACRS and MACRS apply to new and used tangible depreciable property. Tangible depreciable property includes buildings, land improvements, and equipment. Tangible property can be depreciated only if it is used in a trade or business or held for the production of income and has a determinable useful life. Therefore, land, intangible assets, and personal use assets cannot be depreciated under ACRS or MACRS.

Neither ACRS nor MACRS applies to any property that the taxpayer elects to depreciate using an accounting method that is based on units of production or any basis other than years of use. A taxpayer who uses the standard mileage rate method to compute an auto expense deduction has elected a special depreciation method. The car is depreciated using a standard depreciation rate per mile (e.g., 12 cents per mile for 1995). As a result, the car is not subject to ACRS or MACRS. Therefore, a taxpayer can avoid the use of ACRS or MACRS by electing to depreciate an asset using an alternative depreciation method that is not based on years of use. To be valid, the election must be made in the first year the asset is placed in service.

Basis Subject to Cost Recovery

Depreciable basis is the asset's original basis for depreciation, less any amount deducted under the Section 179 election to expense assets. An asset's basis for depreciation does not have to be reduced by its salvage value. Using cost recovery, an asset's basis subject to capital recovery can be reduced to zero, even if the asset still has a substantial remaining useful life and salvage value. Thus, cost recovery permits full recovery of an asset's basis.

▲ **EXAMPLE 8**   In 1992, Estelle Corporation purchases office equipment costing $17,000 for use in its repair business. Because equipment is eligible to be expensed under Section 179, Estelle elects to expense $10,000 of the cost of the equipment. What is Estelle Corporation's depreciable basis in the equipment?

Discussion: Estelle's initial basis in the equipment is $17,000. The election to expense reduces the depreciable basis to $7,000 ($17,000 − $10,000). Estelle recovers its $17,000 investment in the equipment through $10,000 of expense in the year of purchase and $7,000 in depreciation charges over the tax life of the equipment.

If Estelle had purchased the equipment after 1992, say, in 1995, it could have expensed the entire $17,000 cost under Section 179. Because the corporation fully recovers its capital investment in 1995, the depreciable basis in the equipment is zero, and the corporation is allowed no further capital recovery deductions on its initial $17,000 investment.

Class Lives

Both ACRS and MACRS require that assets be categorized in classes. The class life of an asset determines its cost-recovery period. In general, assets have longer class lives under MACRS class than the same assets under ACRS. The tax law standardizes the depreciation calculation by specifying the recovery period, depreciation method, and first and last year convention for each class of assets. Thus, ACRS and MACRS eliminate several sources of potential conflict between the IRS and taxpayers concerning an asset's useful life and standardizes the calculation of the depreciation deduction.

▲ **EXAMPLE 9**   Refer to the equipment Estelle Corporation purchased in example 8. Using Table A11–1 in the appendix to Chapter 11, what is the class life of the equipment?

Discussion: According to Table A11–1, equipment has a class life of 10 years under MACRS. Estelle's $7,000 of depreciable basis must be recovered over either 7 years or 10 years. All property that is 10-year class-life property is depreciated under MACRS, using the same methods and conventions.

If Estelle Corporation had purchased the equipment in 1984, it would have been subject to the rules for ACRS. Under ACRS, equipment was depreciated over 5 years. MACRS uses longer class lives as one means of reducing the cost recovery on depreciable assets.

Depreciation Methods

Generally, ACRS and MACRS depreciation are computed using declining balance depreciation methods. However, MACRS requires the use of straight-line depreciation for real estate throughout its entire recovery period. The depreciation deduction is maximized under both ACRS and MACRS by switching to the straight-line method in the year that straight-line depreciation is equal to or greater than the declining balance depreciation. The switch is made to allow the optimal (largest) deduction and to fully depreciate the asset by the end of its ACRS or MACRS recovery period.

An election can be made to use the straight-line method instead of the declining balance method. A straight-line election under MACRS permits the taxpayer to recover the asset's basis over its regular recovery period. If the straight-line method is elected for property other than real estate, it applies to all property in the class for which the election is made that is placed into service during the year. Elections related to real estate property lives are made on a property-by-property basis.

Conventions

Under both ACRS and MACRS, the **depreciation convention** used to allocate depreciation to the first and last years is specified for each class life. The conventions used in ACRS are referred to as the *half-year, full-month,* and *mid-month conventions.* Under a **half-year convention,** one half-year of depreciation is allowed in the year of acquisition, and no depreciation is allowed in the year of disposition. The **full-month convention** bases the acquisition and disposition years' deductions on the number of months the property was in service during the year. Under this convention, all property is deemed to have been placed in service or disposed of on the first day of the month of acquisition or disposition. This results in a full month of depreciation in the month of acquisition and no depreciation for the disposition month. The **mid-month convention** also allocates according to the number of months in service, but the months of acquisition and disposition are counted only as half months. A taxpayer is never allowed a full year's depreciation in the year of acquisition or disposition under the mid-month convention.

MACRS uses the mid-year, mid-quarter, and mid-month conventions to allocate depreciation in the first and last years of an asset's life.[6] The mid-month convention is the same as used for ACRS. The **mid-year convention** assumes that all property is placed into service and disposed of in the middle of the year. Under this convention, a half-year of depreciation is allowed in both the first and last years of use. The **mid-quarter convention** assumes that all property is placed in service and disposed of in the middle of the quarter of the year of acquisition and disposition. Assets placed into service during the first quarter are depreciated from the middle of the first quarter to the end of the year, or 10.5 months ÷ 12 of a full year's depreciation.

Determining the appropriate convention to use to allocate first and last years' depreciation is one of the nuances of ACRS and MACRS. However, as will be explained later, fairly simple rules delineate which convention should be used. The important point underlying all the conventions is that the precise date of acquisition or disposition is not crucial in making the allocation, as was the case in computing depreciation under the facts and circumstances method.

IRS Percentage Tables

Once an asset's depreciable basis and class life are known and the taxpayer has decided whether to use the prescribed method or to elect the straight-line depreciation method, percentage tables published by the IRS are used to obtain a depreciation rate. The asset's depreciable basis is multiplied by the depreciation rate to determine the annual deduction. Some of the IRS's percentage tables are reproduced in the appendix to this chapter. The percentage tables are constructed to permit full capital recovery of an asset's basis over its recovery period. In addition, the percentage tables incorporate the proper first-year convention, and they make the switch from the declining balance to the straight-line method to optimize the deduction. In effect, the columns of the percentage tables are the depreciation schedule for each recovery period of an asset. The use of tables standardizes the depreciation calculation and minimizes the possibility of error in the depreciation calculation—a taxpayer does not have to perform the mechanics of declining balance depreciation to benefit from the method.

▲ SECTION 179 ELECTION TO EXPENSE ASSETS

Section 179 allows an annual current expense deduction for as much as $17,500 ($10,000 for property placed in service before 1993) of the cost of qualifying depreciable property purchased for use in a trade or business. The deduction for expensed assets is treated as a depreciation deduction. This election allows many small businesses to expense assets as they are purchased instead of depreciating them over several years. The immediate deduction promotes administrative convenience by eliminating the need for extensive depreciation schedules for very small purchases.

Qualified Taxpayers

Each year, individuals, corporations, S corporations, and partnerships may elect to deduct as an expense up to $17,500 in investment in qualified property to be used in an active trade or business.[7] A husband and wife are considered one entity for purposes of the election to expense. Although the phrase "active trade or business" is not defined in the tax law, it appears to have the same meaning as the phrase "trade or business" (Chapter 5). The elements of profit motivation, regularity and continuity of the taxpayer's involvement in the activity, and the absence of hobby, amusement, and similar motivations are important factors to consider when determining whether an activity qualifies for the Section 179 election. This interpretation is supported by the fact that the deduction is not allowed for assets purchased for use in an activity related to the production of income (an investment activity). However, the portion of a mixed-use asset that is used in a trade or business does qualify for immediate deduction under Section 179. Estates and trusts cannot use the Section 179 election to expense assets. The election is not available to these entities because they are formed to protect and conserve the entity's assets for the benefit of the beneficiaries and not to operate an active trade or business.

Qualified Property

The Section 179 expense deduction is allowed only on depreciable, tangible, personal property. Examples of eligible property include trucks, machinery, furniture, microcomputers, and store shelving. Real property, such as buildings and their structural components, do not qualify for the special election to expense. Also excluded from the deduction are land and improvements made directly to the land, such as a parking lot, sidewalks, or a swimming pool. In addition, qualifying property does not include intangible assets such as patents, copyrights, and goodwill.

▲ **EXAMPLE 10**   Kelly purchased a new microcomputer and a new telephone system and installed a new roof and air conditioning system in her office building. Which of the expenditures qualify for the election to expense?

Discussion: The microcomputer and the telephone system are depreciable, tangible, personal property and therefore qualify under Section 179. The roof and air conditioning system are an integral part of the office building. Therefore, the roof and air conditioning system are real property and do not qualify for immediate expensing.

Only qualifying property purchased from an unrelated party qualifies as Section 179 property. If an asset is acquired from a related party, the asset's cost cannot be deducted under Section 179. For purposes of this related party rule, the taxpayer's family includes a spouse, an ancestor (grandparent, parent), and lineal descendants (child, grandchild, etc.). In addition, a corporation or partnership in which the taxpayer owns more than a 50-percent interest is a related party. Therefore, an asset purchased from a brother, sister, or from an in-law is qualified Section 179 property, because it is not considered as having been acquired from a related party for purposes of Section 179.

▲ **EXAMPLE 11**   Michelle purchased an airplane from her brother to use in her business. Does the airplane qualify as Section 179 property?

Discussion: If Michelle acquires the airplane from her brother, it qualifies as Section 179 property, because her brother is not a related party under Section 179 provisions.

▲ **EXAMPLE 12**   What if Michelle acquired the airplane in example 11 from a corporation in which she owned 51% of the stock?

Discussion: If Michelle acquired the airplane from the 51%-owned corporation, it would not qualify as Section 179 property. For purposes of Section 179, ownership of more than 50% of the interest in a corporation or a partnership results in a prohibited related party purchase. Thus, the airplane does not qualify for the Section 179 expense deduction.

Limitations on Deduction

The Section 179 election to expense deduction is subject to three limitations:

- A taxpayer's annual Section 179 deduction cannot exceed $17,500 for property placed in service after December 31, 1992. Before 1993, the limit was $10,000.

- If the taxpayer's investment in Section 179 property exceeds $200,000 for the tax year, the $17,500 annual deduction is reduced by one dollar for each dollar of investment over $200,000 for the tax year. If a taxpayer purchases more than $217,500 of qualifying property, the taxpayer may not take any election to expense deduction for any of the purchases.

- The Section 179 deduction allowed for a tax year cannot exceed the taxable income from the active conduct of all of the taxpayer's trade or business activities.

Annual Deduction Limit.   The annual $17,500 deduction limit does not have to be prorated according to the length of time an asset is used during the year. Regardless of the date of acquisition, the taxpayer can deduct as an expense up to $17,500 of the total cost of assets purchased during the year. The $17,500 annual deduction limit applies to all tax entities entitled to use Section 179. Thus, the annual limit applies separately to a partnership and to its individual partners. The annual limit also applies separately to an S corporation and to its shareholders.[8] Because the partnership and S corporation are conduit entities, the Section 179 deduction is allocated proportionately to the owners of the entity. Because the Section 179 deduction flows from the entity through to its owners, a portion of the entity's total deduction is allocated to each owner, who subtracts it as an expense on the personal tax return. However, the Section 179 deduction allocated to the taxpayer from the conduit entity plus the taxpayer's Section 179 deduction from all other sources cannot exceed the $17,500 annual limit. Any excess Section 179 election resulting from allocations from several entities must be carried forward to be used in subsequent years.

▲ **EXAMPLE 13**   Roberto is a 40% shareholder and full-time employee of an S corporation. During 1995, the S corporation invested $57,500 in equipment qualifying for the Section 179 deduction. Roberto also owns a proprietorship that constructs kitchen cabinets. The cabinet business qualifies as an active business for Roberto. During 1995, Roberto purchased $11,000-worth of equipment to use in his cabinet business. What is the maximum amount of the current year's capital expenditures that Roberto can deduct as a Section 179 expense?

Discussion: Roberto's deductible Section 179 expenditures are limited to $17,500. The S corporation can elect to deduct $17,500 of its $57,500 of capital expenditures. The remaining $40,000 is subject to regular depreciation. The S corporation allocates $7,000

(40% × $17,500) of its Section 179 deduction to Roberto. Thus, Roberto's qualified Section 179 expenditures total $18,000 ($7,000 from S corporation + $11,000 from the cabinet business). However, the $17,500 annual deduction limit applies at the shareholder level as well as at the S corporation level. Therefore, Roberto may elect to deduct only $17,500 as a Section 179 expense.

A taxpayer may choose to use all, part, or none of the $17,500 deduction. By electing to expense less than the limit for a tax year, the taxpayer can avoid a Section 179 deduction carryforward resulting from either the annual limitation or the trade or business income limitation.

▲ **EXAMPLE 14**   Based on the information in example 13, how should Roberto allocate his current year's Section 179 deduction in 1995?

Discussion: Roberto should claim as a Section 179 deduction the $7,000 allocated to him from the S corporation plus $10,500 of the cost of the equipment purchased for use in the cabinet business. The remaining $500 cost of the equipment used in his cabinet business is depreciated, using regular depreciation methods.

If Roberto expenses the $11,000-worth of equipment he purchased for the cabinet business, he will lose $500 of the deduction allocated to him from the S corporation because of exceeding the $17,500 annual limitation by $500 ($11,000 + $7,000 = $18,000) this year. The $500 carries forward to be used in subsequent years. Any amounts that flow to a taxpayer from a conduit entity should always be expensed under Section 179 before any amount is elected from another trade or business of the taxpayer.

After an asset's basis is reduced by the amount expensed under Section 179, the remaining basis is subject to regular depreciation.

▲ **EXAMPLE 15**   Devra Corporation purchases a machine costing $39,000 for use in its business. Devra wants to expense $17,500 of the asset's cost under Section 179. If Devra makes the Section 179 election to expense $17,500 of the asset's cost, what is its depreciable basis in the machine?

Discussion: Devra's depreciable basis for regular depreciation is $21,500. The depreciable basis of the machine is its $39,000 cost, less the $17,500 it elects to expense under Section 179. The reduction of depreciable basis by amounts expensed under Section 179 is necessary to ensure that the total capital recovery on the machine does not exceed the $39,000 invested.

The Section 179 deduction can be allocated to reduce the basis of qualifying assets in any manner the taxpayer chooses. This allows the deduction to be allocated equally to all assets acquired during the year or to specific assets. This option is important. Two general rules apply to choosing assets to expense. First, do not use the Section 179 election to expense automobiles. As discussed later, automobiles are subject to annual depreciation deduction limits ($3,060 in 1995). For purposes of this annual limitation, the Section 179 expense is treated as a depreciation deduction. Because MACRS depreciation on most automobiles exceeds the first-year annual limitation amount, using the election to expense on an automobile does not result in additional tax savings. Second, based on time value of money concepts, taxpayers should take the depreciation deduction as early as possible. This is accomplished by expensing the assets with the longest life and depreciating assets with the shortest life using regular depreciation methods.

▲ **EXAMPLE 16**   Gwendolyn purchased equipment costing $17,500 and a micro-computer that also cost $17,500 for use in her business in 1995. Under MACRS, the equipment is 7-year property, and the microcomputer is 5-year property. How should Gwendolyn allocate her $17,500 Section 179 expense deduction?

Discussion: If Gwendolyn wants to deduct the $17,500 maximum election to expense, she should elect to expense the $17,500 cost of the equipment. The $17,500 cost of the microcomputer will be deducted over its 5-year class life, resulting in greater deductions sooner than if she elected to expense the microcomputer.

   Gwendolyn could elect to deduct less than the full $17,500 Section 179 limit. Because Section 179 is elective, Gwendolyn can decide how much to deduct and the specific assets to expense. This allows taxpayers who do not want or need the extra deductions in the current year to spread the deductions out through depreciation charges rather than expensing them currently.

Annual Investment Limit.
The $17,500 annual deduction limit is reduced dollar for dollar by the amount of the investment in qualifying property in excess of $200,000. As a result of this limitation, a taxpayer that purchases $217,500 or more of qualified property during the tax year cannot expense any amount under Section 179. Because of the $200,000 annual investment limitation, only relatively small businesses can use the election to expense.

▲ **EXAMPLE 17**   During 1995, the Allen Partnership places $204,000 of Section 179 property in service for use in its business. What is Allen's maximum Section 179 deduction?

Discussion: Allen's election to expense is reduced to $13,500 by the $200,000 annual investment limit. Because the partnership invested $4,000 more than the $200,000 annual investment limitation ($204,000 − $200,000), it must reduce the annual deduction limit dollar for dollar by the excess ($17,500 − $4,000 = $13,500). NOTE: The $4,000 lost through the annual investment limit is not carried forward to future years. It is lost forever.

Active Trade or Business Income Limit.
The Section 179 deduction is limited to the total taxable income from the taxpayer's active conduct of any trade or business during the year. Total taxable income is the amount of taxable income computed before deducting the Section 179 expense. For purposes of the income limit, the taxpayer can include salaries and wages, income from a proprietorship, and any trade or business income allocated to the taxpayer from a partnership or S corporation in which the taxpayer actively participates (i.e., passive activities do not enter into the calculation). If the taxable income from the active conduct of a trade or business is less than the allowable Section 179 deduction, any expense election that is over the limit carries forward for use in subsequent years.

▲ **EXAMPLE 18**   During 1995, Michael has a $5,000 net loss in his cabinet-making business. To supplement the family's income, Serena, Michael's wife, earns $7,000 working part time as a cashier at a local grocery store. In addition, they earn $1,000 in interest income on their savings account. Michael also purchases $8,000-worth of equipment for use in his business. For 1995, what is Serena and Michael's maximum Section 179 deduction?

Discussion: Their maximum deduction is $2,000, because Michael and Serena's taxable business income is only $2,000 ($7,000 salary − $5,000 business loss). The interest income cannot be counted, because it is from an investment. Thus, the business income limitation applies, and they can deduct only $2,000 for 1995. They can still elect to expense the full

$8,000 Michael paid for the equipment. The $6,000 that they cannot deduct in 1995 carries forward, to be deducted as a Section 179 expense in subsequent years.

Any Section 179 deduction that is elected and not used because of the taxable income limit can be carried forward and used in a later year. The deductions are carried forward and used on a first-in, first-out basis against the $17,500 annual limit after current-year deductions. All or part of the deferred deduction can be used in a year in which the investment in qualifying property is less than the annual limits. The basis of an expensed asset for regular depreciation is reduced by the amount expensed under Section 179, even though the deduction cannot be used in the current year and is carried forward.[9] As stated earlier, a taxpayer does not have to use the full $17,500 expense deduction or expense the full cost of an asset. Instead of claiming the full deduction, an election to expense an amount equal to the income limitation would avoid the carryover. This alternative is desirable if the taxpayer continuously invests in qualified property and would not expect to use the carryforward in the next tax year. The portion of an asset's basis not expensed remains subject to regular depreciation.

▲ **EXAMPLE 19** Assume that in example 18 Michael purchases $16,000-worth of equipment in 1996. During 1996, Michael has $40,000 in taxable income from his business, and Serena earns a salary of $10,000. What is their maximum Section 179 deduction in 1996?

Discussion: Michael and Serena may elect to expense up to $17,500 as a Section 179 expense, because their taxable business income exceeds $17,500. Michael's current-year purchases of qualified property are less than $17,500, so the amount they can expense depends on the amount elected in 1995. If they elected to expense only the $2,000 income limit amount, there is no deduction carryforward from 1995, and they can expense only the $16,000 in 1996 purchases. If they had elected to expense the full $8,000 purchased in 1995, they could also expense $1,500 ($17,500 limit − $16,000 current year purchases) of the 1995 carryforward. This leaves $4,500 of the 1995 carryforward for use in 1997.

In this case, if they had anticipated continuing qualifying purchases in 1996, they should have elected to expense only the $2,000 limit in 1995. This would have allowed them to depreciate the remaining $6,000-worth of equipment rather than take it slowly over what may be a longer period.

Notice the similarity to the loss limitations discussed in Chapter 7. The effect of the taxable active trade or business income limit is to prevent the Section 179 deduction from creating business losses that offset income from investment income sources.

ACRS applies to property placed in service during the period January 1, 1981, through December 31, 1986. Under ACRS, depreciation is computed by multiplying the asset's depreciable basis by a percentage obtained from an IRS table. This straightforward computation is possible because the tax law specifies the recovery period, depreciation method, and the acquisition- and disposition-year conventions to be used. Because the most common forms of personal property were fully depreciated by 1990, this discussion examines ACRS recovery periods, depreciation methods, conventions, and the straight-line election for real property. Table 11–2 provides an overview of the ACRS depreciation method.

▲ ACCELERATED COST RECOVERY SYSTEM (ACRS)

▲ **Table 11–2**

OVERVIEW OF THE
ACCELERATED COST
RECOVERY SYSTEM

ACRS Recovery Period Class	ACRS Method	ACRS Convention	Straight-Line Election Recovery Period (Alternate ACRS)
3-, 5-, 10-, 15-year personal property	150% DB	Half-year	3-yr—3, 5, 12 5-yr—5, 12, 25 10-yr—10, 25, 35 15-yr—15, 35, 45
15-year real estate (Before 3/16/84)	175% DB	Full-month	15, 35, 45
18-year real estate (After 3/15/84 and before 5/9/85)	175% DB	Before 6/23/84—Full-month After 6/22/84—Mid-month	18, 35, 45
19-year real estate (after 5/8/85 and before 1987)	175% DB	Mid-month	19, 35, 45
15-year low-income housing	200% DB	Full-month	19, 35, 45

ACRS Real Property Recovery Periods

Real property under ACRS is classified as low-income housing and other real property. Low-income housing is assigned a 15-year class life. All other real estate is classified as 15-, 18-, or 19-year class life property, depending on the date it was placed in service:

■ 15-year—Real estate placed in service after December 31, 1980, but before March 16, 1984

■ 18-year—Real estate placed in service after March 15, 1984, but before May 9, 1985

■ 19-year—Real estate placed in service after May 8, 1985, but before January 1, 1987

   This three-way classification of real property by acquisition date is a confusing aspect of real property depreciation under ACRS. The important point to remember when dealing with real property depreciation is to look up the real estate in the IRS's ACRS percentage tables (in the appendix to this chapter) according to its acquisition date to determine the property's recovery class. Because several changes have been made in the real estate depreciation rules, you should rely on the IRS tables as a guide to the proper cost-recovery deduction.

   ▲ EXAMPLE 20   On September, 9, 1985, Joe purchased an office building as a rental investment. What is the class life of the office building?

   Discussion: Because Joe acquired the office building after May 8, 1985, and before January 1, 1987, it has a 19-year class life.

   ▲ EXAMPLE 21   Sandscreen Corporation purchased an office building for use in its business on April 3, 1983. What is the class life of the office building?

   Discussion: Sandscreen acquired the office building after December 31, 1980, and before March 16, 1984, so it has a 15-year class life.

Use of ACRS Percentage Tables

The ACRS percentage table for 19-year real estate is presented in Table 11–3. In using the real estate tables, you must find the correct table for the type of real estate being depreciated (i.e., low-income housing or other) and for the correct class life for the property by looking at the date the property was placed in service. Note that the real estate table columns correspond to the month of acquisition because of the use of either the full-month or mid-month convention for real property. For real property, each month column is a depreciation schedule for real property placed in service in that month.

▲ **EXAMPLE 22**   On May 5, 1986, Sharon acquired property that cost $120,000 for use as an office for her CPA practice. The basis allocated to the building was $100,000 and the land was $20,000. How much depreciation could Sharon deduct for 1986?

Discussion: Because the building is not low-income housing, it is 19-year real property based on the May 5, 1986, acquisition date. Using the IRS percentage table in Table 11–3, Sharon would read across the row labeled *year 1* and down the column labeled *month 5*, to find 5.8% as the 1986 deduction percentage. She should deduct $5,800 for 1986 ($100,000 × 5.8%). The month-5 column becomes the depreciation schedule for the remaining life of the building.

ACRS Depreciation Methods

Under ACRS, depreciation is accelerated as a result of a short recovery period that is less than the asset's economic useful life and by using declining balance depreciation methods. The percentage tables used for real estate other than low-income housing are based on the 175-percent declining balance method. Depreciation of low-income housing is based on the 200-percent declining balance method. The real estate tables make the switch from declining balance to the straight-line method to maximize the depreciation deduction.

▲ **Table 11–3**

ACRS 19-YEAR REAL PROPERTY PERCENTAGE TABLE

If the recovery year is	And the month in the first recovery year the property is placed in service is											
	1	2	3	4	5	6	7	8	9	10	11	12
	The applicable percentage is											
1	8.8	8.1	7.3	6.5	5.8	5.0	4.2	3.5	2.7	1.9	1.1	0.4
2	8.4	8.5	8.5	8.6	8.7	8.8	8.8	8.9	9.0	9.0	9.1	9.2
3	7.6	7.7	7.7	7.8	7.9	7.9	8.0	8.1	8.1	8.2	8.3	8.3
4	6.9	7.0	7.0	7.1	7.1	7.2	7.3	7.3	7.4	7.4	7.5	7.6
5	6.3	6.3	6.4	6.4	6.5	6.5	6.6	6.6	6.7	6.8	6.8	6.9
6	5.7	5.7	5.8	5.9	5.9	5.9	6.0	6.0	6.1	6.1	6.2	6.2
7	5.2	5.2	5.3	5.3	5.3	5.4	5.4	5.5	5.5	5.6	5.6	5.6
8	4.7	4.7	4.8	4.8	4.8	4.9	4.9	5.0	5.0	5.1	5.1	5.1
9	4.2	4.3	4.3	4.4	4.4	4.5	4.5	4.5	4.5	4.6	4.6	4.7
10–19	4.2	4.2	4.2	4.2	4.2	4.2	4.2	4.2	4.2	4.2	4.2	4.2
20	0.2	0.5	0.9	1.2	1.6	1.9	2.3	2.6	3.0	3.3	3.7	4.0

ACRS Conventions

In addition to providing the calculation of the depreciation percentages, ACRS percentage tables incorporate mandatory first-year conventions for computing the deduction. The conventions used for real property are a little complex. Depending upon when the property was placed in service, either a full-month or a mid-month convention applies. Under the full-month convention, real estate is treated as if it were placed in service on the first day of the month, regardless of when it was actually placed in service during the month. No depreciation deduction is allowed in the month of disposition under the full-month convention. Under the mid-month convention, one-half month's depreciation is allowed in the month the property is placed in service, regardless of the actual day use begins. A half-month's depreciation deduction is also allowed in the month of the property's disposition. The real property conventions for ACRS are as follows:

Full Month

- 15-year real property
- 18-year property placed in service before June 23, 1984
- Low-income housing

Half Month

- 18-year property placed in service after June 22, 1984
- 19-year real estate

If real estate is disposed of during the year, the table's percentages for the year of disposition have to be adjusted to the month of disposition, using the appropriate convention.

▲ **EXAMPLE 23**   Baldwin Corporation's depreciable basis in an office building it purchased on May 31, 1986, is $100,000. If Baldwin sells the office building on February 28, 1995, how much depreciation can Baldwin deduct on the building in 1995?

Discussion: For 1995, Baldwin Corporation should deduct $525 in depreciation on the building. Because the asset was placed in service in the fifth month of Baldwin's tax year in 1986, it should use the month-5 column in the 19-year ACRS percentage table (Table 11–3) for as long as the asset is used. The year of disposition, 1995, is the 10th year the asset was used. To determine the deduction for 1995, read across the row labeled *year 10* to column 5 to find 4.2%. The deduction for 12 months in year 10 is $4,200 ($100,000 × 4.2%). Because Baldwin sold the asset in February, it must adjust the annual table deduction to claim 1.5 months (January + ½ month for February) of depreciation, using the mid-month convention. Baldwin can deduct $525 in depreciation [$4,200 × (1.5 months ÷ 12 months)] on the building in 1995.

ACRS Straight-Line Election

A taxpayer who did not want to take advantage of the accelerated deductions available under the regular ACRS method could elect to use the alternate ACRS method. The alternate ACRS method permitted recovery of an asset's depreciable basis using the straight-line method during one of three periods. ACRS real property was depreciated over its recovery period, or the taxpayer could have chosen to use the straight-line method over 35 or 45 years. If the taxpayer chose the straight-line method, the straight-line deduction had to be determined using the appropriate mid-month or full-month convention. The election to use straight-line was made on a property-by-property basis. For example, if the taxpayer placed two buildings in service in 1985, the taxpayer could have chosen straight-line cost recovery for one and depreciated the other using the regular ACRS method. An advantage of electing the straight-line option for real estate was that the election avoided depreciation recapture. Depreciation recapture occurs when real estate is disposed of at a gain. The gain is treated as ordinary income to the extent that the accelerated (e.g., declining balance) depreciation allowed as a deduction exceeds depreciation that would have been allowed using the straight-line method. Depreciation recapture is explained and illustrated in Chapter 12.

▲ **EXAMPLE 24**   Mildred purchased a building for $100,000 on May 15, 1986. She elected to use 19-year straight-line depreciation for the building. What is Mildred's depreciation deduction for the first year?

Discussion: For 1986, Mildred's depreciation deduction is $3,289. The straight-line depreciation deduction for one year is $5,263 ($100,000 ÷ 19). Based on the mid-month convention, Mildred can deduct depreciation for 7.5 months (the middle of May to the end of December) of the first year—$3,289 [5,263 × (7.5 ÷ 12)].

▲ MODIFIED ACCELERATED COST RECOVERY (MACRS)

MACRS took effect in 1987. MACRS retained the basic ACRS approach to calculating the depreciation deduction. However, several modifications to the class lives, depreciation methods, and conventions had the overall effect of spreading the cost of depreciable assets over a longer period. The first change was to lengthen the recovery period under MACRS for most assets. For example, a car was considered three-year property under ACRS, and its cost was recovered over three tax years. Under MACRS, a car is five-year property. In addition, personal property under MACRS is subject to a mid-year convention. The application of the MACRS mid-year convention for the first and last years results in the cost of five-year property being recovered over six tax years, further lengthening the recovery period. The second significant difference between the two systems is that for several classes of personal property MACRS allows 200-percent declining balance depreciation instead of the 150-percent declining balance depreciation allowed under ACRS.

A major difference between MACRS and ACRS is in the treatment of real property. Under MACRS, real property must be depreciated using the straight-line method instead of the 175-percent declining balance method allowed by ACRS. The effect of this change is to significantly reduce the present value of the tax savings from the depreciation deductions for real property.

A taxpayer can choose to use MACRS, make a straight-line election over the MACRS recovery period, or elect to use a third depreciation method known as the *Alternative Depreciation System (ADS)* on all property. Several other changes introduced by MACRS also are examined in the discussion that follows.

To compute depreciation using MACRS or ADS, you need to know the

- Property's depreciable basis
- Property's MACRS recovery period
- Depreciation method to be used
- Applicable first and last year convention

Under MACRS, an asset is assigned to a MACRS property class according to its ADR class life. Using a class life goes back to the class life ADR system that was in effect before ACRS (1981). The asset's MACRS property class determines its recovery period. Then, using specified depreciation methods and conventions, the IRS calculates the deduction for each recovery period and presents them in table form, as with ACRS. Thus, the general approach used to determine depreciation under MACRS is the same as for ACRS. This discussion explains how to calculate depreciation using MACRS. Table 11–4 provides an overview of the discussion that follows.

Each asset subject to MACRS must be placed in a MACRS class according to its ADR class life. Table A11–1 (in the appendix to this chapter) is an excerpt from IRS Revenue Procedure 87-56, which specifies the ADR class lives used to place assets in MACRS classes. An asset's MACRS class determines its recovery period. MACRS provides 3-, 5-, 7-, 10-, 15-, and 20-year recovery periods. Most personal property is in the 3-, 5-, or 7-year class. The 10-, 15-, and 20-year classes generally include land improvements and specialized types of buildings and other property. In addition, residential real estate is given a 27.5-year recovery period, whereas nonresidential real estate placed in service before May 13, 1993, is assigned a 31.5-year recovery period. The recovery period for nonresidential real estate placed in service after May 12, 1993, is increased to 39 years. Table 11–5 lists the MACRS recovery classes and examples of property assigned to each class. Revenue Procedure 87-56 gives the recovery periods for both MACRS (under the column labeled *General Depreciation System*) and ADS (the column labeled *Alternative Depreciation System*) for broad classes of assets and industry groups. If personal property is not listed in a specific asset class or identified with a specific industry in the revenue procedure, it is assigned a 7-year life for MACRS and a 12-year life for ADS.

▲ **Table 11–4**

OVERVIEW OF THE MODIFIED ACCELERATED COST RECOVERY SYSTEM

MACRS Recovery Period Class	MACRS Method	MACRS Convention	Straight-Line Election	ADS
3-, 5-, 7-, 10-year	200% DB	Half-year Mid-quarter	SL over MACRS recovery period	SL over alternate MACRS recovery period
15-, 20-year	150% DB	Half-year Mid-quarter	SL over MACRS recovery period	SL over alternate MACRS recovery period
27.5-year residential rental property	SL	Mid-month	SL over MACRS recovery period	SL over alternate MACRS recovery period (40 years)
31.5-year real estate other than residential rental property	SL	Mid-month	SL over MACRS recovery period	SL over alternate MACRS recovery period (40 years)
39-year real estate other than residential rental property	SL	Mid-month	SL over MACRS recovery period	SL over alternate MACRS recovery period (40 years)

Recovery Class	Examples of Property in Recovery Class
3 years	Tractor units for over-the-road use
	Race horses older than 2 years and any other horse older than 12 years when placed in service
	Breeding hogs
	Special tools and handling devices used in manufacture of food and beverages, and rubber, glass, and fabricated metal products
5 years	Automobiles, taxis, buses, trucks, airplanes, helicopters, trailers, and trailer-mounted containers
	Computers and peripheral equipment
	Office machinery such as typewriters, copiers, calculators
	Assets used by general construction contractors and real estate developers
	Breeding and dairy cattle
	Logging machinery and sawmill equipment
	Qualified technological equipment
	Property used in research and experimentation
	Alternative energy property (e.g., geothermal, solar energy)
7 years	Office furniture, fixtures, and equipment
	Breeding or work horses 12 years or younger when placed in service
	Machinery used in various types of manufacturing
	Assets used to provide recreational services for a fee or admission charge, such as, bowling alleys, billiard and pool establishments, theaters, concert halls, and miniature golf courses
	Assets used to provide rides, attractions, and amusement in theme and amusement parks
	Tangible personal property with no class life
10 years	Water transportation equipment, such as vessels, barges, tugboats
	Single-purpose agricultural buildings
	Fruit- or nut-bearing trees and vines
15 years	Land improvements directly to or added to the land; includes sidewalks, roads, drainage facilities, fences, landscaping shrubbery
	Service station buildings and land improvements
	Car washes and related land improvements
	Billboards
20 years	Farm buildings
	Municipal sewers
27.5 years	Residential real estate
	Apartment buildings, houses, and mobile homes for which 80% or more of the gross rental income is from dwelling units
31.5 years	Nonresidential real estate placed in service before May 13, 1993
	Office buildings, warehouses, factories, hotels, motels
39 years	Nonresidential real estate placed in service after May 12, 1993

▲ EXAMPLE 25   In 1995, Drake purchases the following assets for use in his business:

Purchase Date	Asset	Cost
1/7	Truck (light)	$ 8,000
2/11	Machinery	5,000

4/5	Microcomputer	6,000
5/11	Land	50,000
6/1	Sidewalks	10,000
8/3	Warehouse	150,000
9/4	Office furniture	25,000

What are the MACRS and ADS recovery periods for each of the assets Drake places in service during 1995?

Discussion: Using Table A11–1, the recovery periods for MACRS (General Depreciation System column) and ADS (Alternative Depreciation System column) are as follows:

| | Recovery Period | |
Asset	MACRS	ADS
Truck	5	5
Machinery	7	10
Microcomputer	5	5
Land	not depreciable	
Sidewalks	15	20
Warehouse	39	40
Office furniture	7	10

NOTE: The warehouse is 39-year property, because it was placed in service after May 12, 1993. If the warehouse had been placed in service before May 13, 1993, the recovery period would be 31.5 years.

Using MACRS Percentage Tables

The MACRS percentage table for personal property appears in Table 11–6. The deduction is calculated by multiplying the asset's depreciable basis by the appropriate percentage from the table under the asset's recovery period and the year of the useful life being calculated. Each column is a depreciation schedule for assets in that recovery period.

▲ **EXAMPLE 26**   The Kwan Partnership purchases a machine in the 7-year class on January 5, 1995, for $2,500. Assume that Kwan does not elect to expense any part of the asset's cost under Section 179. What amount may the partnership deduct as depreciation expense for each year of the asset's recovery period?

Discussion: Kwan may deduct a total of $2,500 over the machine's 7-year recovery period. Because the machine qualifies as 7-year property, it should use the 7-year column of Table 11–6. The deduction is determined each year by multiplying the $2,500 depreciable basis by the appropriate percentage for the year being calculated. This is the depreciation schedule for the asset:

Year	MACRS %	Depreciable Basis	Depreciation
1995	14.29	$2,500	$ 357
1996	24.49	2,500	612
1997	17.49	2,500	437
1998	12.49	2,500	312
1999	8.93	2,500	223
2000	8.92	2,500	223
2001	8.93	2,500	223
2002	4.46	2,500	113
Total depreciation			$2,500

▲ Table 11–6

MACRS DEPRECIATION 200% OR 150% DECLINING BALANCE, SWITCHING TO STRAIGHT-LINE (*Applicable recovery periods: 3, 5, 7, 10, 15, 20 years; applicable convention: mid-year*)

If the recovery year is	And the recovery period is					
	3 Years	5 Years	7 Years	10 Years	15 Years	20 Years
	The depreciation rate is					
1	33.33	20.00	14.29	10.00	5.00	3.750
2	44.45	32.00	24.49	18.00	9.50	7.219
3	14.81	19.20	17.49	14.40	8.55	6.677
4	7.41	11.52	12.49	11.52	7.70	6.177
5		11.52	8.93	9.22	6.93	5.713
6		5.76	8.92	7.37	6.23	5.285
7			8.93	6.55	5.90	4.888
8			4.46	6.55	5.90	4.522
9				6.56	5.91	4.462
10				6.55	5.90	4.461
11				3.28	5.91	4.462
12					5.90	4.461
13					5.91	4.462
14					5.90	4.461
15					5.91	4.462
16					2.95	4.461
17						4.462
18						4.461
19						4.462
20						4.461
21						2.231

Note that although the machine is 7-year class property, it takes 8 years to fully depreciate its cost. The mid-year convention used by MACRS assumes that assets are placed in service in the middle of the year and disposed of in the middle of the year. Thus, the first year and the eighth year are allowed only a half year of depreciation.

The MACRS percentage table for 39-year nonresidential real property appears in Table 11–7. This table is used in the same manner as the ACRS real estate table. In using the real estate tables, you must select the correct table for the type of real estate being depreciated (i.e., residential or other).

▲ **EXAMPLE 27** On February 5, 1995, Pauline acquires property that cost $120,000 for use as an office for her medical practice. The basis allocated to the building is $100,000 and the land is $20,000. What amount of depreciation on the property can Pauline deduct for 1995?

Discussion: The land is not depreciable. The $100,000 building cost is depreciated using the schedule for 39-year nonresidential real property. Using the IRS percentage table in Table 11–7, Pauline should read across the row labeled *year 1* and down the column labeled *month 2* to find the first-year percentage, 2.247%. Pauline should deduct $2,247 in depreciation on the building for 1995 ($100,000 × 2.247%). The year-2 column of the table becomes the depreciation schedule for the building for the rest of its period of use.

MACRS Depreciation Methods

MACRS depreciates property in the 3-, 5-, 7-, and 10-year classes using the 200-percent declining balance method with an optimal switch to straight-line. Assets

If the recovery year is	And the month in the first recovery year the property is placed in service is											
	1	2	3	4	5	6	7	8	9	10	11	12
	The depreciation rate is											
1	2.461	2.247	2.033	1.819	1.605	1.391	1.177	0.963	0.749	0.535	0.321	0.107
2–39	2.564	2.564	2.564	2.564	2.564	2.564	2.564	2.564	2.564	2.564	2.564	2.564
40	0.107	0.321	0.535	0.749	0.963	1.177	1.391	1.605	1.819	2.033	2.247	2.461

in the 15- and 20-year classes are depreciated using the 150-percent declining balance method. A taxpayer can elect to depreciate property in these classes on a straight-line basis over the MACRS recovery period (see Table A11–16 in the appendix to this chapter for rate schedules under this election). The straight-line election results in a slower depreciation rate than would be obtained using MACRS. An additional election permits a taxpayer to use the ADS. The ADS requires that the asset be depreciated using the straight-line method over a recovery period that is generally longer than the MACRS recovery period. This election generally results in a slower depreciation rate than that obtained using the straight-line method over the MACRS recovery period. With these elections, a taxpayer has the choice of three depreciation patterns for 3-, 5-, 7-, 10-, 15-, and 20-year MACRS property.

▲ EXAMPLE 28   Lorange Corporation purchases 5-year property costing $28,000 on March 14, 1995. What should Lorange do if it wants to recover its $28,000 cost as quickly as possible (i.e., maximize the cost recovery)?

Discussion: In order to maximize cost recovery, Lorange should elect to expense $17,500 of the cost under Section 179. This leaves a depreciable basis in the property of $10,500 ($28,000 − $17,500), which should be recovered using the regular MACRS 200% declining balance method over the 5-year recovery period. The regular MACRS method provides the fastest depreciation write-off for any property.

▲ EXAMPLE 29   Assume that in example 28 Lorange wants to recover the $28,000 cost as slowly as possible (i.e., minimize the cost recovery). Which options should Lorange elect?

Discussion: The slowest cost recovery is obtained by not using Section 179 and by electing to use straight-line depreciation over the ADS life of the property. The ADS recovery period is always greater than or equal to the MACRS recovery period. Thus, the use of the ADS life generally stretches the depreciation deductions over a longer period of time, thereby diminishing the deduction amounts for each year in the recovery period.

Lorange could also elect an intermediate recovery scheme by using the straight-line method over the MACRS life. This method depreciates the property more slowly than the 200% declining balance method but more rapidly than straight-line during the ADS life. Using the ADS life instead of the regular MACRS method has the effect of stretching out the recovery period.

MACRS Conventions

MACRS requires the use of one of three conventions: a mid-year, mid-month, and mid-quarter convention. Generally, the mid-year convention applies to all classes of property except real estate. The mid-year convention assumes that an asset is placed in service (and disposed of) in the middle of the year. As a result, it takes four tax years to fully depreciate a three-year asset, six years to depreciate a five-year asset, and so forth for the other categories of property. The mid-month convention is used for real estate and is applied in the same manner as under ACRS. All MACRS conventions apply in the year of an asset's acquisition and in the year of its disposition.

▲ **EXAMPLE 30**   Based on the information in example 25 and assuming that Drake expensed $17,500-worth of the office furniture under Section 179, what is his depreciation on the assets purchased for 1995?

Discussion: Using the MACRS percentage tables in tables 11–6 and 11–7, Drake's depreciation is calculated by multiplying the depreciable basis by the first-year percentage for the class of asset as follows:

Recovery Period	Asset	Depreciable Basis	MACRS %	Depreciation Deduction
Section 179	Deduction for furniture			$17,500
5-yr.	Truck	$ 8,000	20.0	1,600
5-yr.	Microcomputer	6,000	20.0	1,200
7-yr.	Office furniture			
	($25,000 − $17,500)	7,500	14.29	1,072
7-yr.	Machinery	5,000	14.29	715
15-yr.	Sidewalks	10,000	5.0	500
39-yr.	Warehouse	150,000	0.963	1,445

The IRS tables' first-year percentages reflect the mid-year convention for 3-, 5-, 7-, and 10-year property and the mid-month convention for real estate. The IRS tables provide the percentage for a full year of depreciation for each class of property. Therefore, the tables' percentages must be adjusted for the last year's depreciation if an asset is disposed of before the end of its recovery period.

▲ **EXAMPLE 31**   Assume that Drake sells the microcomputer in example 30 on December 14, 1997. What is the allowable 1997 depreciation deduction on the microcomputer?

Discussion: The 1997 depreciation deduction for the microcomputer is $576. From Table 11–6, the depreciation percentage for 5-year property for the third year (1997) is 19.2%. A full year's depreciation would be $1,152 ($6,000 × 19.2%). Only half of the annual depreciation is allowed in the year of disposition, given the mid-year convention—$576 ($1,152 × 1/2).

If real estate is disposed of during the year, the IRS tables' percentages have to be adjusted to the month of disposition using the mid-month convention.

▲ **EXAMPLE 32**   Tomas Corporation's depreciable basis in a store building it purchased on May 31, 1993, is $100,000. If Tomas sells the store building on March 1, 1999, what is its 1999 depreciation deduction?

Discussion: The property is 39-year nonresidential rental property that was placed into service in the fifth month of Tomas's tax year. Therefore, the MACRS percentages from Table 11–7, column 5, are the depreciation schedule for the property. The asset is used in 1999, its seventh year. To determine the deduction for 1999, Tomas should read across year 7 to column 5 to find 2.564%. The deduction for 12 months in year 7 is $2,564 ($100,000 × 2.564%). Because Tomas sold the asset in March, it has to adjust the annual table's deduction to claim 2.5 months' depreciation using the mid-month convention (January + February + 1/2 month for March). Tomas Corporation can deduct $534 in depreciation [$2,564 × (2.5 months ÷ 12 months)] in 1999.

If more than 40 percent of the depreciable basis of personal property placed in service during the tax year is acquired during the last three months of the tax year, the taxpayer must use a mid-quarter convention. The mid-quarter convention applies only to personal property placed in service during the year. Real estate is never subject to the mid-quarter convention; it is always depreciated using the mid-month convention. This convention requires the calculation of depreciation from the middle of the quarter in which an asset is placed in service through the end of the year. The first year's depreciation using the mid-quarter convention is computed by multiplying the depreciation on the asset for the full year by the applicable percentage for the quarter of acquisition:

Property Placed in Service during	Months Used	Percentage
1st quarter	10.5 ÷ 12	87.5
2nd quarter	7.5 ÷ 12	62.5
3rd quarter	4.5 ÷ 12	37.5
4th quarter	1.5 ÷ 12	12.5

Fortunately, MACRS percentage tables (appendix to this chapter, tables A11–8 through A11–11) with appropriate depreciation percentages by the quarter of acquisition are available for computing the depreciation deduction. Thus, the major problem is identifying those situations in which more than 40 percent of the personal property acquired during a year is placed in service the last three months of the year.

▲ **EXAMPLE 33**   On February 2, 1995, the Rogers Partnership purchases a microcomputer for $3,500. It purchases office furniture for $6,000 on November 15, 1995. How much depreciation may the partnership deduct for 1995?

Discussion: Because more than 40% {63% = [$6,000 ÷ ($6,000 + $3,500)]} of the depreciable basis of personal property in the 5- and 7-year classes was placed in service during the last 3 months of the year, Rogers must use the mid-quarter convention. Rogers can use the mid-quarter convention MACRS percentage tables in the appendix to this chapter. From Table A11–8, the depreciation on the microcomputer placed in service in the first quarter is $1,225 ($3,500 × 35% for 5-year property). From Table A11–11 in the appendix to this chapter, the depreciation on the office furniture placed in service in the fourth quarter is $214 ($6,000 × 3.57% for 7-year property). The partnership's 1995 depreciation deduction is $1,439 ($1,225 + $214).

The use of the mid-quarter convention generally results in a smaller depreciation charge than the mid-year convention because of the small portion of the first-year depreciation allowed on the fourth quarter purchases. Therefore, taxpayers wishing to maximize deductions should plan their personal property purchases to avoid having more than 40 percent of such purchases fall into the last three months of the tax year. In certain situations, the Section 179 election can be used to avoid the mid-quarter convention by expensing assets purchased in the fourth quarter.

▲ **EXAMPLE 34**   Ari purchases 5-year property costing $30,000 on April 4, 1995. He purchased other 5-year property costing $25,000 on November 3, 1995. What is Ari's maximum depreciation deduction for 1995?

Discussion: Ari's fourth quarter purchases are 45% [$25,000 ÷ ($30,000 + $25,000)] of his total purchases during the year. Therefore, the mid-quarter convention applies. However, the 40% rule is based on the depreciable basis placed in service during the fourth quarter. Because the Section 179 election reduces the depreciable basis of assets expensed, Ari can reduce the depreciable basis placed in service during the fourth quarter by expensing $17,500 of the $25,000-worth of property purchased on November 3. This reduces the depreciable basis of the property to $7,500 and the percentage placed in service during the fourth quarter to 20% [$7,500 ÷ ($30,000 + $7,500)]. Ari is not subject to the mid-quarter convention and uses the general mid-year convention for personal property. The overall result is to give Ari a greater depreciation deduction on the property purchases.

Alternative Depreciation System (ADS)

The election to use the ADS is made on a class-by-class, year-by-year basis for property other than real estate. For real estate, the ADS is elected on a property-by-property basis in the year of acquisition. The ADS must be used to calculate depreciation deductions for purposes of the alternative minimum tax (discussed in Chapter 14).

If a taxpayer elects to use the **Alternative Depreciation System (ADS),** the depreciation is usually computed using the straight-line method over the specified, longer alternative recovery period. Certain types of assets may be depreciated using the 150-percent declining balance method over the ADS recovery period. The deduction for the first and last years of an asset's recovery period must be calculated using the applicable mid-year, mid-quarter, or mid-month convention. An asset's life for computing the ADS deduction is determined by using the column for the Alternative Depreciation System in Table A11–1.

▲ **EXAMPLE 35**   On March 9, 1995, Antonia Corporation places in service a photocopier that cost $5,000 (5-year MACRS class) and a file cabinet that cost $500 (7-year MACRS class). Antonia does not need the accelerated depreciation deductions provided under MACRS and would like to spread the deductions on the assets out for as long as possible. What is Antonia's depreciation deduction for these 2 assets for 1995?

Discussion: Antonia's smallest total depreciation deduction for 1995 is $442 ($25 + $417). The first-year depreciation for the filing cabinet is determined by using the straight-line method with the mid-year convention for the 10-year ADS recovery period for file cabinets (Table A11–1). This results in a deduction of $25 [($500 ÷ 10) × 1/2]. The first-year depreciation for the photocopier is determined by using the straight-line method with the mid-year convention for the 6-year ADS recovery period (Table A11–1). This results in a deduction of $417 [($5,000 ÷ 6) × 1/2].

A taxpayer may elect to use the ADS for several reasons. First, the taxpayer may be experiencing a low income (or loss) period and does not need the greater MACRS deductions currently. By electing ADS, the taxpayer effectively defers the deduction to a future tax year when income is expected to be greater. A second reason for electing to use ADS is to avoid the alternative minimum tax. Taxpayers with large purchases of depreciable assets may become subject to the alternative minimum tax because of the greater MACRS depreciation deductions that are not allowed in computing the alternative minimum tax. In some cases, the taxpayer could actually pay less current tax by electing to take smaller depreciation deductions.

Limitations on Listed Property

Because taxpayers have abused the opportunity to claim depreciation deductions for mixed-use property, Congress enacted the listed property rules in 1984. The

listed property rules require taxpayers to adequately substantiate the extent of an asset's business use.[10] If listed property is not used predominately in a trade or business, the business use portion of the asset must be depreciated under the Alternative Depreciation System. Another important aspect of the listed property rules is that an annual dollar limitation is placed on the depreciation deduction for automobiles.[11]

Listed Property in General

Listed property includes the following categories:

> Passenger autos—Any four-wheeled vehicle that is manufactured for use on public highways and that weighs 6,000 pounds or less; specifically excluded are ambulances, hearses, and vehicles used in the business of transporting people for hire (e.g., taxi cabs).

> Other property used for transportation—Trucks, buses, airplanes, trains, boats, motorcycles, and any other vehicle used for transporting persons and goods; excluded are qualified nonpersonal use vehicles such as cement mixers, clearly marked police cars, combines, and several other vehicles. The exclusion is based on the fact that the nature (design) of the vehicle results in minimal personal use.

> Property of a type that is generally used for purposes of entertainment, recreation, or amusement—Photographic, phonographic, communication, and video recording equipment, but these assets are excluded if they are used either exclusively at the taxpayer's regular business establishment or in connection with the taxpayer's principal trade or business. A regular business establishment includes a qualifying home office (see Chapter 6 for home office qualifications).

> Any computer or peripheral equipment—Microcomputers, printers, modems, and other property related to the computer; these assets are excluded if they are used exclusively at a regular business establishment. A regular business establishment includes a qualifying home office.

> Any cellular telephone or similar communications equipment.

If more than 50 percent of an asset's total use for each year of its tax life is related to the taxpayer's trade or business, the asset is treated the same as any other business asset. Using the asset in an investment activity (i.e., production-of-income use) is not counted as business use to satisfy the 50-percent test. When listed property is used 50 percent or less in the taxpayer's business, the Section 179 expense election does not apply to the asset and the annual depreciation deduction must be calculated using the Alternative Depreciation System (ADS).[12]

> ▲ **EXAMPLE 36**   On May 1, Sara placed into service a computer that cost her $3,500. Sara uses the computer 60% of the time to manage her investments, 30% of the time in her consulting business, and 10% of the time for personal record keeping. Sara would like to expense $1,000 of the computer's cost under Section 179. What method must Sara use to compute her depreciation deduction?

> *Discussion:* Sara must use ADS. Because Sara's trade or business use (30%) is not more than 50% of the computer's total use, she cannot use MACRS or make a Section 179 election. She must use straight-line to depreciate the business and investment use portion (a total of 90%) over the ADS life.

▲ **EXAMPLE 37**   Assume that in example 36 Sara used the computer 60% of the time in her consulting business, 30% of the time to manage her investments, and 10% of the time for personal record keeping. How should Sara compute her depreciation deduction?

Discussion: Sara may use MACRS. Because Sara's trade or business use (60%) is more than 50% of the computer's total use, she may use MACRS and she can make a Section 179 election for the business portion of the asset. The computer is basically treated the same as other mixed-use business assets. The business and investment use portion of the asset (90%) is recovered as any other business asset would be.

	Business Use	Investment Use	Personal Use
Original basis	$2,100	$1,050	$350
Cost recovery:			
Election to expense	$2,100		
MACRS Depreciation			
(20% × $1,050)		$210	

Because Sara's business use is greater than 50%, she can elect to expense the business use portion of the computer (60% × $3,500). The investment use of the computer (30% × $3,500) can be depreciated using the regular 5-year MACRS recovery period for computers ($1,050 × 20%). The personal use portion of the computer (10% × $3,500) is not subject to cost recovery.

Limitation on Passenger Autos.

Passenger autos are subject to a limitation on the annual amount of the deductible depreciation. Based on the year an auto is placed in service, the annual depreciation deduction for a passenger automobile cannot exceed a specified amount. Any depreciation that is disallowed because of the annual limitations may be deducted when the auto's recovery period ends. Table A11–15 in the appendix to this chapter lists the auto depreciation tables and the annual auto limits that are allowed for 100-percent business use of an auto placed in service in 1994 and 1995. If an auto is used less than 100 percent for a business purpose, the annual **passenger automobile limitation** amount must be reduced by multiplying it by the business use percentage.[13] The depreciation subject to the first-year annual limitation includes any amount that is expensed using Section 179. As previously mentioned, the annual limitation on the auto depreciation deduction makes it impractical to deduct any of the cost of an auto under Section 179.

▲ **EXAMPLE 38**   In 1995, Oscar purchases a new car for $20,000. Based on his mileage records, Oscar uses the car 80% of the time for a qualified business use. What is Oscar's depreciation deduction on the car for 1995?

Discussion: Automobiles are 5-year MACRS property. The allowable depreciation on a passenger automobile is the lesser of the regular MACRS depreciation or the passenger automobile limitation. Oscar's 1995 depreciation deduction for the car is limited to $2,448. Oscar would compute his depreciation deduction for 1995 as follows:

Regular MACRS Depreciation

Initial basis	$20,000
Business use percentage	× 80%
Business depreciable basis	$16,000
MACRS table percentage	× 20%
Total regular MACRS depreciation	$ 3,200

Passenger Automobile Limitation

Annual depreciation limit for an automobile placed in service in 1995 (from Table A11–15)	$ 3,060
Oscar's business use percentage	× 80%
Oscar's maximum depreciation on the auto	$ 2,448

Although the computed depreciation deduction using MACRS is $3,200, Oscar's deduction cannot exceed the annual limitation, adjusted for the percentage of business use, $2,448. Note that the effect of the auto depreciation limit is to make the Section 179 election a poor choice for an automobile, because the 179 election is considered depreciation for purposes of applying the auto limit.

Adequate Record Keeping. Listed property is subject to special record-keeping requirements for documenting business use and amounts expended. To substantiate deductions, the taxpayer must be able to prove the

- Amount of each expenditure related to the property, such as the cost of the property, repairs, insurance, and other expenses
- Use of the asset, including documentation of the amount of business, investment, and other use of the asset
- Date of the expenditure or use of the asset
- Business purpose for the expenditure or the use of the asset

The best way to prove the required items is to keep adequate written records that show the needed information. The records should contain receipts when possible and any other documentation necessary to prove the existence of these items. The most common method of substantiation is a diary or a log book in which the taxpayer records the necessary information as the expense is incurred.

▲ DEPLETION

A taxpayer who owns an economic interest in a natural resource is entitled to a capital recovery deduction for depletion. A taxpayer has an economic interest if two basic requirements are met. First, an investment in the natural resource must be still in place. *In place* means that the mineral deposit has not been removed from its original source (e.g., is still under ground). Second, capital recovery of the taxpayer's investment depends on the amount of income from the extraction of the natural resource.[14] Minerals, oil and gas, other natural deposits, and timber are subject to depletion. Depletion is an accounting method used to recover the basis of an investment in a natural resource as it is used up to earn income. An investment in personal and real property (e.g., machinery, equipment, and buildings) related to recovering the natural resource remains subject to the depreciation rules and not depletion.

▲ **EXAMPLE 39**   DeWayne invested $90,000 in a coal mine. The $90,000 investment was allocated as follows: $25,000 as the basis in machinery and equipment, $50,000 as the basis in the coal deposit still in place below ground, and $15,000 as the basis of the residual value of the land. How should DeWayne recover his investment?

Discussion: DeWayne's $50,000 investment in the coal deposit in place is subject to depletion. The $25,000 investment in the machinery and equipment used to recover the coal is subject to depreciation. The basis of the land is not subject to depletion or depreciation. The basis of the land will be recovered at disposition.

Depletion Methods

Two methods are used to compute depletion of natural resources: the cost depletion method and the percentage (statutory) depletion method. The taxpayer is allowed to deduct the greater figure yielded by the two methods each year. Therefore, a taxpayer may use the cost method in one year and the percentage method in another year. Regardless of which depletion method is used, the deduction reduces the adjusted basis of the natural resource. A deduction for cost depletion is allowed until the depletable basis has been fully recovered. In most cases, the taxpayer may continue to use percentage (statutory) depletion after the initial basis has been fully recovered. This use of percentage depletion violates the capital recovery concept by permitting total depletion deductions over the life of the natural resource to exceed the property's depletable basis. As a result, the taxpayer's depletion deduction can exceed the cost of the depletable asset. Although this is clearly a benefit for regular tax purposes, the depletion in excess of cost is not allowed for alternative minimum tax purposes.[15] As with the use of MACRS depreciation, taking depletion deductions in excess of cost could trigger the alternative minimum tax and make the use of percentage depletion undesirable.

> ▲ **EXAMPLE 40**   Assume that the coal mine in example 39 has operated for several years and that before deducting depletion for the current year DeWayne's adjusted basis for depletion of the coal deposit is $2,000. Further, assume that DeWayne's cost depletion for the current year is $2,000 and his percentage depletion is $2,500. What is DeWayne's current depletion deduction, and how does it affect his depletable basis?
>
> *Discussion:*   DeWayne is allowed to deduct the $2,500 in percentage depletion, because it is greater than the $2,000 cost depletion. DeWayne's $2,000 adjusted basis in the coal deposit is reduced by the percentage depletion deduction to zero. At this point, DeWayne has claimed $500 more in capital recovery deductions than he had invested in the coal deposit ($2,500 deduction − $2,000 basis). Because DeWayne has fully recovered his basis, he cannot claim cost depletion in future years. However, he may continue to claim percentage depletion as long as he has gross income from the sale of the coal.

Cost Depletion

To compute **cost depletion,** you must know the basis subject to depletion, the recoverable quantity of the natural resource, and the quantity of the natural resource sold during the year. The basis of the natural resource subject to depletion is the basis that would be used to compute a gain on its sale.[16] For other assets, the basis construct has been used to describe the amount subject to capital recovery. For natural resources, *unrecovered basis* better describes the amount being recovered through depletion, because the estimate of the quantity of the resource to which the basis relates is subject to change each year. Cost depletion is calculated using a units-of-production method. The following computation is the general framework for calculating cost depletion using the units-of-production method:

$$\text{Cost Depletion} = \frac{\text{Basis of natural resource subject to capital recovery (unrecovered basis)}}{\text{Estimated number of mineral units to be recovered (e.g., tons of mineral, barrels of liquid)}} \times \begin{array}{c}\text{Number of units sold during tax year}\end{array}$$

The cost depletion computation allocates the unrecovered basis over the number of mineral units of the natural resource (useful life of the resource) to which the investment relates.

▲ **EXAMPLE 41**   In example 39, DeWayne estimates that his $50,000 investment in the coal deposit will result in 350,000 recoverable tons of coal. During 1995, DeWayne mines and sells 40,000 tons of coal. What is DeWayne's cost depletion deduction for 1995?

Discussion: DeWayne's cost depletion deduction for 1995 is $5,714 [($50,000 basis ÷ 350,000 tons of coal) × 40,000 tons sold]. DeWayne's unrecovered basis of the coal deposit after deducting $5,714 for 1995's depletion is $44,286 ($50,000 − $5,714).

Because an estimate of the remaining recoverable units at the end of each year is used to make the computation, the cost depletion per unit will probably change for each tax year. Based on the annual accounting period concept, depletion deductions for prior years are not corrected because of a change in the estimated remaining recoverable units. The adjustment related to a change in the estimate is allocated to current and future years by incorporating the new estimate in the formula.

▲ **EXAMPLE 42**   Assume that during 1996 DeWayne in example 41 sells 105,000 tons of coal. Based on mining reports, DeWayne increases his estimate of recoverable coal by 5,000 tons. What is DeWayne's cost depletion deduction for 1996?

Discussion: DeWayne's cost depletion deduction for 1996 is $14,762. DeWayne's unrecovered basis in the coal deposit after deducting $14,762 for 1996's depletion is $29,524 ($44,286 − $14,762).

  At the end of 1995, the estimated coal to be mined and sold is 310,000 tons (350,000 original estimate − 40,000 tons sold). The 5,000-ton revision in DeWayne's estimate increases the recoverable coal to 315,000 tons. The increase in the number of recoverable mineral units in 1996 affects 1996 and later years. DeWayne's 1996 cost depletion is $14,762 [($44,286 unrecovered basis ÷ 315,000 tons of coal) × 105,000 tons sold]. Based on the annual accounting period concept, the 1995 depletion deduction is not revised for the change in the estimate of recoverable mineral units in 1996.

Percentage Depletion

Percentage depletion (also called **statutory depletion**) is calculated by multiplying gross income from the sale of the natural resource by a statutory percentage.[17] The statutory percentage is the depletion rate specified by the tax law. For example, depletion (by percentage) is allowed for

Sulphur, uranium	22%
Gold, copper, silver, iron ore	15%
Asbestos, brucite, coal	10%
Gravel, peat, sand	5%

In addition, the tax law specifies a statutory depletion rate for many other natural resources, including oil and gas. The maximum allowable percentage depletion deduction for the tax year is limited to 50 percent of the taxable income from the natural resource before subtracting the depletion deduction.[18]

▲ **EXAMPLE 43**   In example 41, DeWayne sells the 40,000 tons of coal in 1995 for $1.20 per ton. After deducting operating expenses, DeWayne's taxable income from the property before deducting percentage depletion is $10,000. What is DeWayne's maximum depletion deduction for 1995?

Discussion: DeWayne's percentage depletion deduction is $4,800 (40,000 tons × $1.20 × 10% depletion rate for coal). Because 50% of the taxable income from the property, $5,000 ($10,000 × 50%), is greater than the computed percentage depletion, $4,800, the taxable income limit does not apply. However, because the cost depletion computed in example 41 is greater than the percentage depletion, DeWayne should deduct cost depletion for 1995. DeWayne's maximum 1995 depletion deduction is $5,714, using the cost depletion method. NOTE: Cost depletion is not subject to the 50% taxable income limit.

▲ **EXAMPLE 44**   In example 42, DeWayne sells the 105,000 tons of coal in 1996 for $1.50 per ton. After deducting operating expenses, DeWayne's taxable income from the property before deducting percentage depletion is $30,000. What is DeWayne's maximum depletion deduction for 1996?

Discussion: Based on the taxable income limitation, DeWayne's maximum allowable percentage depletion deduction is $15,000 ($30,000 × 50%). The tentative percentage depletion deduction is $15,750 (105,000 tons × $1.50 × 10% depletion). From example 42, cost depletion is $14,762, which is less than percentage depletion. However, the $15,000 taxable income limitation applies, because it is less than the $15,750 tentative percentage depletion deduction. Thus, the allowable percentage depletion is $15,000.

For 1996, DeWayne should deduct the $15,000 in percentage depletion because it is greater than the $14,795 in cost depletion computed in example 42. As a result, DeWayne reduces his recoverable basis in the coal deposit by the percentage depletion deduction instead of the cost depletion deduction. DeWayne's recoverable basis in the coal deposit at the end of 1996 is $29,286 ($44,286 − $15,000 percentage depletion).

▲ INTANGIBLE ASSETS

Patents, copyrights, agreements not to compete, franchises, and goodwill are all intangible assets.[19] Capital recovery of the investment in an intangible asset is allowed as an expense deduction through amortization. The basis of an intangible is allocated on a straight-line basis over its useful life. To qualify for amortization, the intangible asset must be used for a business purpose and it must have a limited useful life that can be estimated with reasonable accuracy. As a result of the limited life requirement, determining whether a specific intangible asset qualifies for amortization has required an analysis of the facts related to the taxpayer. Because goodwill does not have a useful life that can be estimated with reasonable accuracy, goodwill generally is not subject to amortization. However, in 1993 Congress enacted Section 197, which allows goodwill and other intangibles purchased after August 9, 1993, to be amortized over 15 years. In addition, a transitional relief rule allows taxpayers to elect to amortize intangibles purchased after July 25, 1991, over the 15-year period. This section is a step toward simplifying tax law and offers an element of administrative convenience to the task of determining useful lives of intangibles. Also, through legislative grace, Congress now allows the amortization of goodwill that has been purchased.

Not all intangible assets are subject to the 15-year amortization period. Generally, intangibles subject to the 15-year amortization period are those that are acquired in connection with the purchase of assets constituting a trade or business. Exhibit 11–1 provides a list of qualifying Section 197 assets.

▲ **Exhibit 11–1**

INTANGIBLE ASSETS
SUBJECT TO 15-YEAR
AMORTIZATION

- Goodwill and going concern value
- Certain types of intangible property that generally relate to work force, information base, know-how, customers, suppliers, or other similar items
- Any license, permit, or other right granted by a government unit or agency
- Any covenant not to compete (or other similar arrangement) entered into in connection with the acquisition of a trade or business (including a stock acquisition) or an interest in a trade or business
- Any franchise, trademark, or trade name

Examples of intangible assets covered by the new provisions include customer lists, subscription lists, insurance expirations, patient or client files, and lists of newspaper, magazine, radio, or television advertisers.

▲ **EXAMPLE 45**   Natasha is a partner in Future Designs. Natasha has decided to leave the partnership and move to a different state. In 1995, Future and Natasha enter an agreement not to compete. Future pays Natasha $50,000 for Natasha's agreement not to compete or interfere with Future's conduct of business within 250 miles of Future's home office for 5 years. The agreement is effective beginning September 1, 1995. What is the tax effect of the transaction for Future and for Natasha?

Discussion: Future can amortize the $50,000 investment in the agreement not to compete by using straight-line amortization over 15 years. For 1995, Future can deduct $1,111 for 4 months' amortization of the investment in the agreement [($50,000 ÷ 15) × (4 ÷ 12)]. Based on the claim-of-right doctrine, Natasha must report the entire $50,000 payment she receives in 1995 as ordinary income related to services. If the agreement had taken effect before August 9, 1993, Future could have amortized the $50,000 over the 5-year term of the agreement.

▲ **EXAMPLE 46**   Assume that in example 45 the $50,000 payment is properly characterized as goodwill related to the sale of Natasha's partnership interest to the remaining partners in Future. What is the effect of the transaction for Future and for Natasha?

Discussion: Future's $50,000 payment to Natasha is capitalized as goodwill and is subject to capital recovery over 15 years. Because Natasha has sold goodwill, she has a gain from the sale of a capital asset.

▲ **EXAMPLE 47**   On January 1, 1995, Nisalke Co. sells all assets used in its business to Layden Co. The assets consist of real estate, a customer list, goodwill, a patent, and a covenant not to compete. The values allocated to each asset are as follows:

Real estate	$10,000,000
Customer list	800,000
Goodwill	500,000
Patent	1,000,000
Covenant	900,000
Total purchase price	$13,200,000

The real estate is subject to a recovery period of 39 years. The customer list has a 6-year useful life, the covenant not to compete lasts 3 years, and the patent has 10 years remaining on its useful life. What is Layden's intangible amortization amount for 1995?

Discussion: The four intangible assets must be amortized over 15 years. Total amortization for 1995 is $213,333 ($3,200,000 ÷ 15). Although the company receives the benefit of amortizing the $500,000 of goodwill now, the other intangibles are amortized for a period longer than their useful lives. If Section 197 had not been enacted, the total amortization for 1995 would have been $533,333 [$300,000 ($900,000 ÷ 3) from the covenant; $133,333 ($800,000 ÷ 6) from the customer list; $100,000 ($1,000,000 ÷ 10) from the patent; and zero from goodwill]. Layden reports $320,000 ($533,333 − $213,333) more in taxable income for the current tax year, as a result of the 15-year amortization rule of Section 197.

Certain intangible assets, such as sports franchises, are specifically excluded from the 15-year amortization period. Prior law continues to apply to these excluded assets, which are listed in Exhibit 11–2. For example, patents and copyrights not acquired in the purchase of a trade or business are amortized over periods of 17 years and 50 years plus the author's life, respectively. These amortization periods are statutorily set useful lives.

▲ **EXAMPLE 48**   On January 4, 1995, Conroy Co. purchases from Technical Process Co., Inc., the patent to the process for extruding certain plastic forms. Conroy pays $170,000 for the newly developed patent process. The purchase does not represent an acquisition of Technical Process Co. What is the amount of patent amortization in 1995?

Discussion: Because the patent was not acquired as part of the purchase of a trade or business, the amortization period is 17 years (the legal life set by the government). Therefore, Conroy's 1995 deduction for amortization is $10,000 ($170,000 ÷ 17).

▲ SUMMARY

The deduction for depreciation demonstrates the application of many of the concepts previously discussed in this text. It is well established that an annual deduction is allowed for the recovery of capital invested in a long-lived asset that is used up to earn income. The problem over the years has been how to determine the deduction for the capital recovery. The central concern of taxpayers is to recover their investment as quickly as possible to maximize the present value of depreciation deductions. However, Congress and the IRS have generally been concerned with protecting the collection of revenue. In addition, Congress has varied the amount of allowable depreciation as a method of stimulating capital investment.

Tangible real and personal property with a limited useful life used in a trade or business or in a production-of-income activity are subject to depreciation. An asset's depreciable basis is generally determined using the basis rules discussed in Chapter 10. Assets are depreciated according to the tax law in effect at the time the asset is placed in service. Before 1981, taxpayers usually used the facts and circumstances method to compute depreciation. The facts and circumstances method was a source of continuing controversy between taxpayers and the IRS,

• Interests in notional principal contracts and other similar financial instruments
• Stock, partnership interests
• Interests in land
• Certain computer software
• Interests in films, videotapes, books, and other like property, unless acquired in an acquisition of a trade or business
• Patents and copyrights, unless acquired in an acquisition of a trade or business
• Professional sports franchises
• Certain purchased mortgage service rights
• Interests under an existing lease of tangible property

▲ **Exhibit 11–2**

INTANGIBLE ASSETS SPECIFICALLY EXCLUDED FROM 15-YEAR AMORTIZATION because the depreciation computation used a variety of estimates (e.g., estimated life and salvage value) and taxpayers had a wide variety of choices in regard to depreciation methods and acquisition- and disposition-year conventions.

ACRS was a revolutionary new approach to depreciation that was introduced in 1981. Because ACRS more precisely prescribed how depreciation was to be calculated, it eliminated several areas of controversy that existed under the old system. Under ACRS, the tax law determined the recovery period, depreciation method, salvage value (none considered), and the first- and last-year conventions for real estate and personal property. Although buildings acquired from 1981 through 1986 are still being depreciated under ACRS, most personal property assets are fully depreciated under the shorter ACRS recovery periods. The main current concern with ACRS is calculating depreciation on real property acquired during the period of 1981 through 1986.

As ACRS was being introduced, Congress added the Section 179 election to expense assets to the tax law. This election, which applies to personal property, primarily benefits small businesses. Initially, this election allowed taxpayers to expense as much as $5,000 in qualified investment in Section 179 property. The amount allowed as an expense was increased to $10,000 beginning in 1987 and to $17,500 beginning in 1993, subject to two limitations. The annual deduction under Section 179 is reduced dollar for dollar when the taxpayer places more than $200,000 in qualified property in service during the year. In addition, the annual election to expense is limited to the taxpayer's taxable active business income for the year. The Section 179 expense deduction is treated as a regular depreciation. Therefore, any amount expensed under Section 179 reduces an asset's depreciable basis.

After 1986, MACRS is used to depreciate personal property and real estate. MACRS is a modification of ACRS that generally spreads the depreciation deduction over a longer time period. To depreciate property using MACRS, you need to know

- The property's depreciable basis
- The MACRS recovery period
- Whether regular MACRS or straight-line is to be used
- The applicable convention

Given this information, depreciation is calculated by multiplying the asset's depreciable basis by a prescribed percentage obtained from an IRS table. If an asset is disposed of before the end of its recovery period, the table percentages have to be adjusted according to the applicable convention in order to claim depreciation for the fractional part of the last year in which the asset was used. Instead of using the declining balance method prescribed by MACRS, a taxpayer may elect to use the straight-line method with the same first- and last-year's conventions as under regular MACRS. Listed property is subject to special record-keeping requirements and limitations. The depreciation deduction for automobiles is subject to an annual limit based on the year of acquisition and use.

A deduction for depletion is allowed when a taxpayer has an economic interest in a mineral in place and the investment must be recovered from income received from its removal and sale. The depletion deduction is determined by using the cost or percentage depletion method. A straight-line amortization deduction is allowed for intangible assets that have a useful life that can be estimated with reasonable accuracy. To lessen the difficulty of estimating useful lives, Congress enacted Section 197 in 1993. This provision allows certain purchased intangibles, including goodwill, to be amortized over 15 years.

▲ KEY TERMS

Accelerated Cost Recovery System (ACRS) (p. 476)
Alternative Depreciation System (ADS) (p. 499)
amortization (p. 474)
class life (p. 479)
cost depletion (p. 503)
depletion (p. 474)
depreciable basis (p. 476)

depreciation (p. 474)
depreciation convention (p. 481)
full-month convention (p. 482)
half-year convention (p. 482)
listed property (p. 500)
listed property rules (p. 500)
mid-month convention (p. 482)
mid-quarter convention (p. 482)
mid-year convention (p. 482)

Modified Accelerated Cost Recovery System (MACRS) (p. 476)
passenger automobile limitation (p. 501)
percentage depletion (statutory depletion) (p. 504)
Section 179 (p. 482)

▲ PRIMARY TAX LAW SOURCES

[1] Reg. Sec. 1.167(a)-2—Specifies the requirements that must be met in order to depreciate a property.

[2] U.S. v. Ludley, 274 U.S. 295 (1927)—Stated the original depreciation theory: By using up a depreciable asset, a gradual sale is made of the asset.

[3] Prop. Reg. Sec. 1.168-2—Requires the use of the property's unadjusted basis in order to compute depreciation under the cost-recovery system.

[4] S. REP. NO. 144, 97th Cong., 1st Sess., 47 (1981)—States congressional motives in enacting ACRS—that Congress felt that the old depreciation rules were unnecessarily complicated and did not provide "the investment stimulus necessary that is essential for economic expansion."

[5] Sec. 168—Prescribes the calculations necessary for determining depreciation using cost recovery (ACRS and MACRS).

[6] Reg. Sec. 1.168(d)-1—Explains and gives examples of MACRS conventions.

[7] Reg. Sec. 1.179-3—Provides definitions related to the Section 179 election to expense deduction.

[8] Reg. Sec. 1.179-2—Discusses dollar limitations on the Section 179 expense deduction and the application of the limitations to partnerships (and their partners) and S corporations (and their shareholders).

[9] Reg. Sec. 1.179-1—Requires the reduction of the unadjusted basis of an asset for any amounts expensed under Section 179.

[10] Reg. Sec. 1.274-5T—Explains the sub-stantiation requirements for various types of listed property.

[11] Sec. 280F—Defines *listed property* and provides limits on the deduction of depreciation when listed property is used 50 percent or less in a taxpayer's trade or business.

[12] Reg. Sec. 1.280F-3T—Explains the calculation of depreciation deductions on listed property when the trade or business use of the property is 50 percent or less.

[13] Reg. Sec. 1.280F-2T—Explains the limitations on depreciation deductions for passenger automobiles.

[14] Sec. 611—Specifies the requirements for a depletion deduction for natural resources.

[15] Sec. 57—States that the percentage depletion deduction in excess of the cost of the property is an addition to a taxpayer's alternative minimum taxable income.

[16] Sec. 612—Requires the use of basis for computing gain in the cost depletion calculation.

[17] Sec. 613—Specifies the calculation of percentage depletion and provides statutory rates for various types of depletable property.

[18] Reg. Sec. 1.613-2—Provides examples of the 50 percent of taxable income limit on percentage depletion deductions.

[19] Reg. Sec. 1.167-3—Defines intangible assets for which a periodic expense deduction (through amortization) may be taken; specifically disallows any periodic deductions for goodwill.

▲ DISCUSSION QUESTIONS

1. How does the allowable capital recovery period affect the potential return on the investment in an asset?

2. Which two tests must be met in order to claim a periodic recovery deduction on a capital expenditure?

3. What types of capital expenditures are not deductible over time (i.e., their cost is recovered upon disposition of the asset)?

4. What is the depreciable basis of an asset? What role does depreciable basis play in determining the annual cost recovery on a depreciable asset?

5. How is facts and circumstances depreciation different from ACRS and MACRS cost recovery?

6. What was the purpose of changing from the facts and circumstances depreciation method to the ACRS method?

7. In general, which types of property may be expensed under Section 179, and what is the current maximum limit on the deduction?

8. What limitations are placed on the maximum amount to be expensed under Section 179?

9. Is the Section 179 election to expense an incentive to all businesses to invest in qualifying property?

10. What types of property are still subject to depreciation using ACRS?

11. How is MACRS different from ACRS?

12. In general, taxpayers want to depreciate property as rapidly as possible. Under what circumstances might a taxpayer not want to use accelerated depreciation? How can this be done under MACRS?

13. What is the purpose of the acquisition- and disposition-year convention?

14. What acquisition- and disposition-year conventions are used in MACRS and to what types of property does each of the conventions apply?

15. Why is the calculation of depreciation using MACRS generally considered easier and more efficient than the calculation using the facts and circumstances method?

16. What is the Alternate Depreciation System? How is it different from a straight-line election under MACRS?

17. Why might a taxpayer elect to depreciate assets using the Alternative Depreciation System (ADS)?

18. Why are restrictions placed on the cost recovery of listed property?

19. When a taxpayer purchases an automobile for use in trade or business, what limits are placed on the cost recovery on the automobile?

20. Which types of property are allowed a deduction for depletion?

21. How is cost depletion different from percentage depletion?

22. Which income tax concepts might taxpayers who take depletion deductions be violating?

23. How are the costs of intangible assets recovered?

▲ PROBLEMS

24. Peter Corporation purchased the following assets during 1995. Identify which assets are not subject to cost recovery using depreciation, and state why that is so.
    a. Land
    b. Copyright
    c. Building
    d. Goodwill
    e. Inventory for sale in its store

    f. 500 shares of Excellent common stock *- dis/*

    g. A house to be rented out *- life,*

    h. Equipment for use in its business *- life*

    i. An interest in an oil well *- lil*

    j. A car that will be used 60% for business and 40% for personal use *oil - lels*

25. For each of the following expenditures incurred during the current year, indicate whether it should be treated as a repair expense or capitalized and depreciated using MACRS:

    a. Replacement of the roof on an apartment building *- Capitalize*

    b. Replacement of the condenser in a central air conditioning unit *-*

    c. Replacement of the tires on a delivery truck *- mat*

    d. Addition of 10 tons of gravel to parking lot to restore surface *-*

    e. Repainting of the interior and exterior of an apartment building *-*

26. Which of the following assets are subject to cost recovery using either ACRS or MACRS?

    a. A warehouse purchased in 1980

    b. A store building purchased in 1992

    c. An automobile purchased in 1990 for which the taxpayer elected to use the standard mileage allowance method to determine the allowable auto expense deduction

    d. A stamping machine purchased in 1991 that the taxpayer elects to depreciate based on hours of use

27. In each of the following situations, determine the depreciable basis of the asset:

    a. Rudy inherited his father's pickup truck. The truck was immediately <u>placed in service</u> in Rudy's delivery business. The fair market value of the truck at the date of Rudy's father's death was $8,000, and the value on the alternate valuation date was $7,500. The executor of the estate did not make any special elections. The truck originally cost Rudy's father $15,000.

    b. Maline purchased an office building to use as the main office of her mail order business. She paid the seller $25,000 in cash. In addition, she gave the seller her personal note for $100,000, plus 10 acres of real estate. At the date of the transaction, the real estate, which cost $10,000, was worth $25,000. Property tax records showed the land was assessed at $10,000 and the building was assessed at $40,000.

    c. Steve owned a computer that he bought for $3,500. The computer was used for personal family activities. When he started his business, Steve took the computer to his new office. The computer was worth $1,000 when he began using it in his business.

    d. Martha's aunt Mabel gave her a used table, which had been stored in Mabel's garage, to use in the conference room in Martha's office. Mabel had paid $1,500 for the table several years ago, and it was worth only $500 at the date of the gift. Mabel did not pay any gift tax on the transfer.

28. A taxpayer purchased $20,000-worth of property that qualified for the Section 179 deduction during the current year. The taxpayer would like to deduct the greatest depreciation expense possible (including the Section 179 deduction) on the property. For each of the following entities, indicate how the depreciation expense should be determined:

    a. An individual   d. A partnership

    b. A corporation   e. A trust or an estate

    c. An S corporation

29. Firefly, Inc., acquires business equipment in July 1995 for $211,000.

    a. What is Firefly's maximum Section 179 deduction for 1995?

    b. What happens to any portion of the annual limit not deducted in 1995? Explain.

    c. What is the depreciable basis of the equipment?

30. In 1995, Theo purchases $14,000 of Section 179 property for use in his delivery business. During 1995, Theo has $9,000 in taxable income from his business.
  a. What is Theo's maximum Section 179 deduction in 1995?
  b. Theo's business taxable income for 1996 is $4,000. He purchased $1,000 of new Section 179 property in 1996. What is Theo's maximum Section 179 deduction in 1996?

31. Rufus operates Freedonia Co. as a sole proprietorship. In 1995, he purchases $205,000-worth of equipment. Rufus's taxable income from the business is $4,000.
  a. What is Rufus's maximum Section 179 deduction in 1995?
  b. What is the depreciable basis of the equipment?

32. Brad is a shareholder and full-time employee of an S corporation. During 1995, Brad earns a $30,000 salary from the S corporation and is allocated $32,000 as his share of its net operating loss. In addition, Brad owns a limited partnership interest from which he earns $12,000 during 1995. Kanika, Brad's wife, operates a small business as a proprietorship. During 1995, Kanika purchases $20,000-worth of equipment for use in her business, which had a taxable income of $13,000 before the Section 179 deduction.
  a. What is Brad and Kanika's maximum Section 179 deduction for 1995?
  b. Assume that Brad is allocated $5,000 in Section 179 expense from the S corporation for 1996 and Kanika purchases an additional $14,000-worth of equipment for use in her business. Also, assume that their taxable active business income is $75,000 for 1996. What is Brad and Kanika's maximum Section 179 deduction for 1996?

33. Jennifer owns a $1/4$ interest in the Thomas Partnership. Jennifer also owns and operates an architectural consulting business. During the current year, the partnership purchases $36,000-worth of property qualifying under Section 179 and elects to expense $17,500. Jennifer purchases $20,000-worth of qualifying Section 179 property for use in her architectural consulting business. What should Jennifer do to maximize her cost recovery? Explain.

34. Arnold purchased an apartment building at a cost of $120,000. Arnold properly allocated $20,000 of the cost to the land and $100,000 to the building. Assuming that Arnold would like to deduct the maximum depreciation on the building, what is Arnold's first-year depreciation on the building if he purchased the building on
  a. June 30, 1982?
  b. June 30, 1984?
  c. June 30, 1986?

35. Refer to problem 34. Arnold sells the apartment building on October 14, 1997. What is Arnold's 1997 depreciation deduction if he purchased the building on
  a. June 30, 1982?
  b. June 30, 1984?
  c. June 30, 1986?

36. Nova Corporation purchases an office building for use in its business on November 30, 1985. The building costs $175,000, $25,000 of which is allocated to the cost of the land. Nova sells the building on March 3, 1995.
  a. What is the depreciation on the office building for 1985, 1986, and 1995, assuming that Nova wants to depreciate the building as quickly as possible?
  b. What is the depreciation on the office building for 1985, 1986, and 1995, assuming that Nova elects to depreciate the building straight-line over the class life of the building?

37. Determine the MACRS class life and recovery period of each of the following assets:
  a. Tugboat
  b. Microcomputer
  c. Taxi cab
  d. Breeding hogs
  e. Breeding cattle
  f. Greenhouse
  g. Office furniture
  h. Land improvements

38. Leon bought machinery (7-year MACRS property) on March 15, 1995, at a cost of $45,000. What is Leon's 1995 cost-recovery deduction if

    a. He wants the maximum deduction allowable?

    b. He wants the minimum deduction allowable?

    c. How would your answer to part a change if Leon also purchased equipment costing $80,000 (7-year MACRS property) and a fleet of heavy-duty trucks (5-year MACRS property) costing $140,000?

39. Rograin Corporation purchased turning lathes costing $140,000 and a computer system costing $63,000 during the current year. The lathes are 7-year MACRS property, and the computer system is 5-year MACRS property.

    a. What is Rograin's maximum Section 179 deduction?

    b. Assuming that Rograin deducted the maximum Section 179 expense, what are the depreciable bases of the lathes and the computer system?

40. In 1995, Rose purchases office furniture (7-year MACRS property) costing $30,000 for use in her consulting business. What is her maximum 1995 cost-recovery deduction on the furniture if her business income before any special elections is

    a. $40,000?

    b. $4,000?

    c. Assume the same facts as in part b. In 1996, Rose purchases a computer workstation (5-year MACRS property) costing $6,000. What is Rose's maximum 1996 cost-recovery deduction if her business income before any special elections is $28,000 in that year?

41. Kringle Co. purchased 7-year MACRS property costing $14,000 in 1995. Kringle's 1995 business income before any cost-recovery deductions is $6,000. What is Kringle's maximum 1995 cost-recovery deduction on the property? Assume that Kringle plans to purchase more than $20,000-worth of personal property during the next 5 years.

42. On May 1, 1995, Tara purchases a machine costing $25,000 (7-year MACRS property) for use in her machine shop. According to the manufacturer, the machine has an estimated useful life of 100,000 machine hours and no salvage value. Based on Tara's experience, she will probably use the machine for about 5 years at the rate of 20,000 machine hours per year. If Tara uses the machine for 18,000 hours in 1995, what is the greatest depreciation deduction that she may claim?

43. Baker, Inc., purchases office furniture (7-year MACRS property) costing $35,000 and a computer system (5-year MACRS property) costing $35,000 in 1995. What is Baker's maximum cost-recovery deduction in 1995? (HINT: Maximize the Section 179 election effect.)

44. Chen Corporation purchased the following business assets during the current year:

Asset Purchased	Cost	Class Life
Office furniture	$12,000	7
Microcomputer	$ 8,000	5
Delivery truck	$33,000	5

What is Chen's maximum current-year cost-recovery deduction on the assets purchased? (HINT: Maximize the Section 179 election effect.)

45. During 1995, Schottenheim Corporation buys 7 personal computers (PCs) and a small mainframe computer to use in its general sales offices. Schottenheim bought 4 PCs for $9,000 on March 29, 3 PCs for $8,000 on September 26, and the small mainframe for $28,000 on October 5. The corporation makes no other capital expenditures this year.

    a. What issues should the corporation consider when determining its 1995 cost-recovery deductions on the computers?

    b. The corporation has a contractual agreement to resell the small mainframe to the original vendor for $15,000 on March 1, 1998. How will the 1995 decisions affect the 1998 calculations if Schottenheim decides to sell that computer?

46. Harold purchases the following business assets on the dates indicated:

Asset	Date Purchased	Cost	Class Life
Photocopy equipment	2/14/95	$ 5,000	5
Dump truck	7/16/95	$25,000	5
Bus	11/24/95	$25,000	5

  a. What is Harold's 1995 cost-recovery deduction if he does not elect to expense any of the assets under Section 179?
  b. Determine the gain (loss) if Harold sells the bus for $15,000 on July 1, 1997.
  c. What could Harold do to maximize his 1995 deduction?

47. The Gladys Corporation buys equipment (7-year MACRS property) costing $50,000 on April 12, 1995. In 1998, new and improved models of the equipment make it obsolete, and Gladys sells the old equipment for $18,000 on December 27, 1998.
  a. What is Gladys Corporation's gain (loss) on the sale, assuming that Gladys takes the maximum cost-recovery deduction allowable on the equipment?
  b. What is Gladys Corporation's gain (loss) on the equipment, assuming that Gladys takes the minimum cost-recovery deduction allowable on the equipment?

48. Joan is interested in buying a special diagnostic machine for use in her medical practice. The machine will cost her $10,000, and it will have a $2,000 salvage value at the end of its 8-year life. Joan would like to know the actual cost of the machine after considering the effect of the present value of tax savings from depreciation. If Joan buys the machine, she will place it in service on April 1, 1995. Based on the following assumptions, what is Joan's after-tax cost? Assume that Joan is in the 28% marginal tax rate bracket and that the time value of money is worth 10%.
  a. Joan will depreciate the machine over 5 years using MACRS.
  b. Joan will depreciate the machine using the straight-line method over the 7-year ADS life.
  c. Joan will deduct the $10,000 investment as an expense in 1995.

49. Guadalupe purchases an office building to use in her business at a cost of $120,000. Guadalupe properly allocates $20,000 of the cost to the land and $100,000 to the building. Assuming that Guadalupe would like to deduct the maximum depreciation on the building, what is her first-year depreciation on the building if she purchased the building on
  a. June 30, 1992?
  b. June 30, 1994?

50. Refer to problem 49. Guadalupe sells the building on October 14, 1999. What is Guadalupe's 1999 depreciation deduction if she purchased the building on
  a. June 30, 1992?
  b. June 30, 1994?

51. Anton purchases a building on May 4, 1993, at a cost of $240,000. The land is properly allocated $40,000 of the cost. Anton sells the building on October 18, 1997, for $240,000. What is Anton's gain (loss) on the sale if he uses the regular MACRS system and the building is
  a. An apartment building?
  b. An office building?
  c. How would your answer(s) to parts a and b change if Anton makes a straight-line election on the building?
  d. How would your answers to parts a and b change if the building was purchased on May 4, 1995, and sold on October 18, 1999?

52. On October 1, 1995, Barbara pays $135,000 for a store building. She moves into the building and begins business on November 1. She properly allocates $125,000 of her cost to the building and $10,000 to the land. On November 21, 1995, she installs $25,000-worth of new display shelving. Barbara wants to claim the maximum allowable depreciation on the property she purchased. On January 2, 1999, Barbara sells the land and building for $145,000 and the display shelving for $15,000.

a. What is Barbara's maximum depreciation deduction for 1995?

b. What is Barbara's maximum depreciation deduction for 1999?

c. What is Barbara's gain or loss on the sale of the land and building?

d. What is Barbara's gain or loss on the sale of the shelving?

53. Leroy purchases a microcomputer and a desk for use in his home office. The microcomputer costs $6,000, and the desk costs $2,000. During the first year, Leroy uses the computer and his desk 40% of the time in his consulting business and 20% of the time managing his investments. The remaining 40% of the use is for personal activities. What is Leroy's maximum cost-recovery deduction on the microcomputer and the desk?

Assume that Leroy uses the microcomputer and the desk 70% of the time in his consulting business, 20% for managing his investments, and 10% for personal use purposes. What is his maximum first-year cost-recovery deduction?

54. Madina, a single individual, is a self-employed engineering consultant. In 1995, she bought a new automobile and personal computer. She paid $15,500 for the automobile on February 3. It is used 45% of the time for business. Madina paid $2,000 for the computer on October 22 and uses it 85% for business. Madina would like to know the amount of her maximum deduction for cost recovery in 1995. However, she is not sure she needs the maximum deduction amount, because her 1995 gross income from consulting is only $24,000. Make a recommendation to Madina about her 1995 cost-recovery deductions.

55. On June 1, 1995, Kay buys a new car for $22,000. Kay drives her car 20,000 miles while on business, 2,000 miles for personal activities, and 500 miles in commuting to and from work. What is Kay's maximum depreciation deduction on the car for 1995?

56. On July 4, 1995, Lawrence invests $100,000 in a mineral property. He estimates that he will recover 800,000 units of the mineral from the deposit. During 1995, Lawrence recovers and sells 50,000 units of the mineral for $1.50 per unit.

a. What are Lawrence's cost depletion deduction for 1995 and his adjusted basis for the mineral deposit after deducting depletion?

b. If the percentage depletion rate for the mineral is 10%, what are his depletion deduction for 1995 and his adjusted basis for the mineral deposit after deducting depletion?

c. If the statutory percentage depletion rate for the mineral is 10% and Lawrence's income from the mineral before the depletion deduction is $7,000, what are his depletion deduction for 1995 and his adjusted basis for the mineral deposit after deducting depletion?

57. Isidro purchases an interest in an oil-producing property for $50,000 on November 3, 1995. His geologist estimates 10,000 barrels of oil are recoverable. The entity sells 1,000 barrels for $20,000 during November and December 1995. Assume the percentage depletion rate for oil is 15%. Operating expenses related to the revenues are $3,000.

a. Advise Isidro on the amount of depletion he should deduct in 1995.

b. At the end of 1996, the geologist estimates the remaining number of recoverable barrels is 15,000. Isidro has an offer of $190,000 for his investment. In 1996, the entity sold only 2,000 barrels of oil. Gross revenues were $50,000 and operating expenses total $4,000. If Isidro sells the property, what is the amount of his realized gain?

58. On June 2, 1995, Lokar Corporation receives the patent on an internally developed extrusion process. Total costs associated with that patent are $68,000. Also, Lokar purchases substantially all of the assets of Barrios Corporation for $750,000 on September 8, 1995. The values of the assets as listed in the purchase agreement are as follows:

Inventory	$250,000
Manufacturing equipment	300,000
Patent on compression process	105,000
Goodwill	95,000

Assume negotiations are not completed. The purchase agreement can be modified to reflect a reallocation of the purchase price to the individual assets. Advise Lokar on an optimum way to allocate the price. Determine the maximum 1995 cost-recovery deductions for the developed and purchased assets. Explain your reasoning.

59. On April 18, 1995, Petros buys all the assets of Brigid's Bra Shop for $265,000. Included in the purchase price is a payment of $20,000 to Brigid not to open a competing bra shop in the state for a period of 5 years. Information on Brigid's assets at the date of sale is as follows:

Asset	Adjusted Basis	Fair Market Value
Inventory	$ 8,500	$ 10,000
Store equipment	3,500	15,000
Building	80,000	130,000
Patent	500	30,000

The patent is on a special bra that Brigid developed and patented 5 years ago. Petros would like to know the maximum amount of the deduction he will be allowed on the purchase of Brigid's assets for 1995.

▲ INTEGRATIVE PROBLEMS

60. In problem 70 of Chapter 10, you were asked to determine the initial basis of Lance and Lola's business, investment, and personal use assets. In this problem, you are to determine the adjusted basis of the assets as of December 31, 1995. You should disclose all calculations made to arrive at the December 31, 1995, basis values. For depreciable assets and amortizable assets, present the basis in the following form:

Asset: _____

Date acquired: _____

Initial basis: _____

Depreciation/Amortization life: _____

Depreciation/Amortization deducted to December 31, 1995: _____
  (per the schedule here)

Basis at December 31, 1995: _____

Depreciation/Amortization Schedule:

Year	Depreciable Basis	Depreciation Percentage	Depreciation

Additional Information

Lola's 1990 automobile: Although Lola keeps mileage records, her cost records are not good enough to use the actual cost method. Therefore, she deducts the standard mileage rate each year. For 1990 through 1994, Lola drives her old car 90,000 miles in all; 72,000 miles are business miles. (Assume that the depreciation portion of the standard mileage rate is 11 cents per mile for all years involved.)

Assume that Lola and Lance have always deducted the maximum depreciation allowable. However, in 1995, because their income is less as a result of the opening of Lance's new business, they do not wish to expense any eligible amounts.

61. Gloria has worked for several years in a friend's pottery shop. In 1990, she decides to open her own business. In August 1990, she leases a building and spends $3,000 installing shelving, counters, and display cabinets. Another pottery in a nearby town is going out of business, and Gloria buys the following assets for $8,000:

Asset	Fair Market Value
Inventory	$6,000
Pottery wheels	$2,400
Kiln	$1,200

In addition, Gloria purchases a computer system at a cost of $10,000.

Although business is slow at first, it begins to pick up during 1992. On March 14, 1993, she negotiates the purchase of the building she had been leasing for $75,000. The 1992 property tax statement had assessed the land at $2,000 and the building at $30,000.

During 1995, Gloria learns that her previous employer's wife has been transferred and he needs to sell his pottery. Because Gloria's business has been steadily improving, she decides to expand by buying out the business. On July 3, she purchases her former employer's business by investing $20,000 of her own cash and borrowing $120,000 from Local Bank. In the transaction, she receives the following assets:

Asset	Adjusted Basis	Fair Market Value
Land	$ 5,000	$10,000
Building	18,000	80,000
Inventory	11,000	15,000
Equipment	1,500	5,000

As part of her expansion, Gloria decides to begin providing delivery service for customers who place large orders. In August, she converts a van she had purchased for personal use in 1991 for $24,000 into a business van by paying $1,000 to have the shop's logo painted on the van. At the time of conversion, comparable vans are selling for $9,000.

REQUIRED: Determine Gloria's maximum 1995 cost-recovery deduction on her business assets. Assume that she has always taken the maximum allowable cost-recovery deduction on her business assets but has never had enough business income to elect to expense assets under Section 179. In 1995, Gloria estimates that her net business income before any cost-recovery deductions will be at least $32,000, and she would like to take the maximum allowable deduction in 1995.

▲ DISCUSSION CASE 11–1

Bonnie and Rick, a married couple, purchase a 2-bedroom condominium in Park City, Utah, on October 4 of the current year. The total purchase price is $118,000, including complete furnishings. Park County's tax assessor appraises the structure at $100,000 and the land and common area at $10,000. Furnishings (acquired 5 years ago by the previous owner) include:

1 sofa sleeper	8 place settings of silverware
1 end table	12 water glasses
2 lamps	1 set of pots and pans
2 color TVs	6 coffee mugs
1 set fireplace tools	1 queen-sized bed
1 dining table	1 king-sized bed
7 chairs	2 dressers
12 dinner plates	2 nightstands
1 refrigerator	2 table lamps
1 microwave oven	6 towels
1 coffee maker	4 sets of bed linens

Bonnie and Rick immediately place the property in service as a rental. They want to know their options in regard to deductions related to the rental property. Explain.

▲ DISCUSSION CASE 11–2

Fiona is a professional bass violinist with the St. Paul Symphony Orchestra. In February of the current year, she purchases at auction for $200,000 an eighteenth-century bass violin built by the renowned Asa Santavar. Fiona is thrilled by her acquisition. The violin is a treasured artwork and a quality investment. Also, it is an asset she will use almost daily in her profession. May Fiona deduct part of her expenditure this year? Explain.

▲ TAX PLANNING CASE 11–3

You are the resident tax expert for Wetzel's Pretzels, an international producer of junk food. The controller has come to you with the company's capital expenditures budget for next year. The budget shows that Wetzel's Pretzels plans to spend $1,000,000 next year on personal property. The largest single item in the budget is the purchase of new, high-tech pretzel twisters costing $450,000. The pretzel twisters are on order, but because of high demand for the technology, Wetzel's Pretzels will not receive the new twisters until November. The remaining $550,000 is for company automobiles, delivery trucks, personal computers, and office furniture. These items will be purchased throughout the year as needed.

The controller asks your advice on the tax aspects of these purchases. She is particularly interested in making sure that Wetzel's Pretzels is able to deduct the maximum amount regarding these purchases in the year of purchase.

How would you advise the controller? That is, are there any tax problems associated with these purchases? If so, suggest one or more ways in which Wetzel's can take advantage of the situation.

Maura is negotiating with Nagama Corporation, a seaweed food-supplement processor, to purchase all its assets. Maura and Nagama have generally agreed that the purchase price is $500,000. However, Maura is not sure how to classify the difference between the identifiable asset values and the total sales price in the sales agreement. The sale will close sometime between December 15 of the current year and January 10 of next year. An independent appraiser determined the values of the assets as follows:

	Adjusted Basis	FMV
Inventory of seaweed products	$10,000	$ 40,000
Machinery/equipment—5-year property	20,000	40,000
Machinery/equipment—7-year property	60,000	70,000
Patent on seaweed production process	-0-	150,000

Maura has served as director of marketing for Nagama for 16 years. Harry Nagama, the corporation's president, founder, and developer of the production process, tells Maura he will agree to a sales contract structured however she would like. Discuss Maura's options for classifying the difference between the identifiable assets and the purchase price. What are the cost-recovery amounts related to the purchased assets in the year of acquisition?

Steem Advertising Corporation acquires 10 notebook-style personal computers in 1994 for its account executives to use. Steem pays $40,000 for the computers and bundled software. You are the newly hired CPA, and you expect to advise Steem on tax issues regarding tax years 1995 and 1996. Upon examining the firm's records for 1994, you find that each computer was expensed and deducted in 1994. Later, when examining one of the computers, you notice it has several games loaded in the hard drive. Also, you find several items of personal correspondence saved in a subdirectory of the word-processing software package. What should you do? What are your obligations under the Statements on Responsibilities in Tax Practice?

Appendix to Chapter 11

MACRS Class Lives
ACRS Real Property Depreciation Schedules
MACRS Depreciation Schedules

Section 1. Purpose

▲ Rev. Proc.
87-56

The purpose of this revenue procedure is to set forth the class lives of property that are necessary to compute the depreciation allowances available under section 168 of the Internal Revenue Code, as amended by section 201(a) of the Tax Reform Act of 1986 (Act), 1986-3 (Vol. 1) C.B. 38. Rev. Proc. 87-57, page 17, this Bulletin, describes the applicable depreciation methods, applicable recovery periods, and applicable conventions that must be used in computing depreciation allowances under section 168.

Section 2. General Rules of Application

.01 In general. This revenue procedure specifies class lives and recovery periods for property subject to depreciation under the general depreciation system provided in section 168(a) of the Code or the alternative depreciation system provided in section 168(g).

.02 Definition of Class Life. Except with respect to certain assigned property described in section 3 of this revenue procedure, for purposes of both the general depreciation system and the alternative depreciation system, the term "class life" means the class life that would be applicable for any property as of January 1, 1986, under section 167(m) of the Code (determined without regard to paragraph 4 thereof and determined as if the taxpayer had made an election under section 167(m)). The class life that would be applicable for any property as of January 1, 1986, under section 167(m), is the asset guideline period (midpoint class life) for the asset guideline class in which such property is classified under Rev. Proc. 83-35, 1983-1 C.B. 745. However, for purposes of the alternative depreciation system, section 168(g)(3)(B) assigns a class life to certain property that is taken into account under section 168 rather than the class life that would be applicable as of January 1, 1986. The class life of property that is either determined as of January 1, 1986, under Rev. Proc. 83-35 or assigned under section 168(g)(3)(B) may be modified by the Secretary pursuant to authority granted under section 168(i)(1). See section 4 of this revenue procedure.

.03 Rev. Proc. 83-35. Rev. Proc. 83-35 sets out the asset guideline classes, asset guideline periods and ranges, and annual asset guideline repair allowance percentages for the Class Life Asset Depreciation Range System. The asset guideline periods (midpoint class lives) set out in Rev. Proc. 83-35 are also used in defining the classes of recovery property under the Accelerated Cost Recovery System (that is, section 168 of the Code as in effect prior to amendment by section 201 of the .Act). Rev. Proc. 83-35 remains effective for property subject to depreciation under those systems. Rev. Proc. 83-35 does not apply to property subject to depreciation under section 168, other than as a basis for determining the class lives of such property under section 2.02 of this revenue procedure.

.04 Property with No Class Life.   Property that is neither described in an asset guideline class listed in section 5 of this revenue procedure nor assigned a class life under section 168(g)(3)(B) of the Code is treated as property having no class life for purposes of section 168 unless and until a class life is prescribed by the Secretary pursuant to the authority granted under section 168(i)(1). See section 4 of this revenue procedure. The general and alternative depreciation systems contain separate rules for classifying property that does not have a class life.

Section 5. Tables of Class Lives and Recovery Periods

.01   Except for property described in section 5.02, below, the class lives (if any) and recovery periods for property subject to depreciation under section 168 of the Code appear in the tables below. These tables are based on the definition of class life in section 2.02 of this revenue procedure and the assigned items described in section 3 of this revenue procedure.

.02   For purposes of depreciation under the general depreciation system, residential rental property has a recovery period of 27.5 years and nonresidential real property has a recovery period of 31.5 years. For purposes of the alternative depreciation system, residential rental and nonresidential real property each has a recovery period of 40 years.

.04   In addition to specifying class lives for each asset guideline class, the tables list certain property for which a recovery period is assigned, notwithstanding such property's class life (if any). See section 3 of this revenue procedure. The listed assigned property classes (denoted A-E) generally do not correspond to asset guideline classes for which class lives are specified in the tables. The class life (if any) of an item of assigned property described in classes A-E is determined by reference to the asset guideline class (if any) containing such item of property. If an item of assigned property described in classes A-E is not contained in any asset guideline class, such item of property has no class life.

Examples.   Qualified technological equipment as defined in section 168(i)(2) (class B) is assigned a recovery period of 5 years for both the general and alternative depreciation systems, notwithstanding such property's class life (if any). Property which is a computer or peripheral equipment, high technology telephone station equipment installed on the customer's premises or high technology medical equipment within the meaning of section 168(i)(2), may be described in asset guideline class 00.12 (class life 6 years), 48.13 (class life 10 years) or 57.0 (class life 9 years), respectively. Property used in connection with research and experimentation referred to in section 168(e)(3)(B) (class C) is assigned a recovery period of 5 years for the general depreciation system, notwithstanding its class life (if any). Such property's recovery period for the alternative depreciation system is based on its class life (if any). An item of property used in connection with research and experimentation has a class life if such property is contained in an asset guideline class.

.05   The following special rules are incorporated from Rev. Proc. 83-35, sections 2.02(iii) and (iv):

1 Asset guideline class 00.3, "Land Improvements," includes "other tangible property" that qualifies under section 1.48-1(d) of the Income Tax Regulations. However, a structure that is essentially an item of machinery or equipment or a structure that houses property used as an integral part of an activity specified in section 48(a)(1)(B)(i) of the Code, if the use of the structure is so closely related to the use of the property that the structure clearly can be expected to be replaced when the property it initially houses is replaced, is included in the asset guideline class appropriate to the equipment to which it is related.

▲ Table A11-1

IRS TABLE OF MACRS CLASSES (*Partial Table*)

Asset Class	Description of Assets Included	Class Life (in years)	Recovery Periods (in years)	
			General Depreciation System	Alternative Depreciation System
Specific Depreciable Assets Used in All Business Activities, Except as Noted:				
00.11	Office Furniture, Fixtures, and Equipment: Includes furniture and fixtures that are not a structural component of a building. Includes such assets as desks, files, safes, and communications equipment. Does not include communications equipment that is included in other classes	10	7	10
00.12	Information Systems: Includes computers and their peripheral equipment used in administering normal business transactions and the maintenance of business records, their retrieval and analysis. Information systems are defined as: 1) Computers: A computer is a programmable electronically activated device capable of accepting information, applying prescribed processes to the information, and supplying the results of these processes with or without human intervention. It usually consists of a central processing unit containing extensive storage, logic, arithmetic, and control capabilities. Excluded from this category are adding machines, electronic desk calculators, etc., and other equipment described in class 00.13. 2) Peripheral equipment consists of the auxiliary machines which are designed to be placed under control of the central processing unit. Nonlimiting examples are: Card readers, card punches, magnetic tape feeds, high speed printers, optical character readers, tape cassettes, mass storage units, paper tape equipment, keypunches, data entry devices, teleprinters, terminals, tape drives, disc drives, disc files, disc packs, visual image projector tubes, card sorters, plotters, and collators. Peripheral equipment may be used on-line or off-line. Does not include equipment that is an integral part of other capital equipment that is included in other classes of economic activity, i.e., computers used primarily for process or production control, switching, channeling, and automating distributive trades and services such as point of sale (POS) computer systems. Also, does not include equipment of a kind used primarily for amusement or entertainment of the user	6	5*	5*

*Property described in asset class 00.12 which is qualified technological equipment as defined in section 168(i)(2) is assigned a recovery period of 5 years notwithstanding its class life. See section 3 of the revenue procedure.

▲ **Table A11–1**
(continued)

IRS TABLE OF MACRS CLASSES *(Partial Table)*

Asset Class	Description of Assets Included	Class Life (in years)	Recovery Periods (in years) General Depreciation System	Recovery Periods (in years) Alternative Depreciation System
Specific Depreciable Assets Used in All Business Activities, Except as Noted:				
00.13	Data Handling Equipment, except Computers: Includes only typewriters, calculators, adding and accounting machines, copiers, and duplicating equipment	6	5	6
00.21	Airplanes (airframes and engines), except those used in commercial or contract carrying of passengers or freight, and all helicopters (airframes and engines)	6	5	6
00.22	Automobiles, Taxis	3	5	5
00.23	Buses	9	5	9
00.241	Light General Purpose Trucks: Includes trucks for use over the road (actual unloaded weight less than 13,000 pounds)	4	5	5
00.242	Heavy General Purpose Trucks: Includes heavy general purpose trucks, concrete ready mix-truckers, and ore trucks, for use over the road (actual unloaded weight 13,000 pounds or more)	6	5	6
00.25	Railroad Cars and Locomotives, except those owned by railroad transportation companies	15	7	15
00.26	Tractor Units For Use Over-The-Road	4	3	4
00.27	Trailers and Trailer-Mounted Containers	6	5	6
00.28	Vessels, Barges, Tugs, and Similar Water Transportation Equipment, except those used in marine construction	18	10	18
00.3	Land Improvements: Includes improvements directly to or added to land, whether such improvements are section 1245 property or section 1250 property, provided such improvements are depreciable. Examples of such assets might include sidewalks, roads, canals, waterways, drainage facilities, sewers (not including municipal sewers in Class 51), wharves and docks, bridges, fences, landscaping, shubbery, or radio and television transmitting towers. Does not include land improvements that are explicitly included in any other class, and buildings and structural components as defined in section 1.48-1(e) of the regulations. Excludes public utility initial clearing and grading land improvements as specified in Rev. Rul. 72-403, 1972-2 C.B. 102	20	15	20

(continued on next page)

▲ **Table A11–1**
(continued)

IRS TABLE OF MACRS CLASSES *(Partial Table)*

Asset Class	Description of Assets Included	Class Life (in years)	Recovery Periods (in years) General Depreciation System	Recovery Periods (in years) Alternative Depreciation System
Specific Depreciable Assets Used in All Business Activities, Except as Noted:				
00.4	Industrial Steam and Electric Generation and/or Distribution Systems: Includes assets, whether such assets are section 1245 property or 1250 property, providing such assets are depreciable, used in the production and/or distribution of electricity with rated total capacity in excess of 500 Kilowatts and/or assets used in the production and/or distribution of steam with rated total capacity in excess of 12,500 pounds per hour for use by the taxpayer in its industrial manufacturing process or plant activity and not ordinarily available for sale to others. Does not include buildings and structural components as defined in section 1.48-1(e) of the regulations. Assets used to generate and/or distribute electricity or steam of the type described above but of lesser rated capacity are not included, but are included in the appropriate manufacturing equipment classes elsewhere specified. Also includes electric generating and steam distribution assets, which may utilize steam produced by a waste reduction and resource recovery plant, used by the taxpayer in its industrial manufacturing process or plant activity. Steam and chemical recovery boiler systems used for the recovery and regeneration of chemicals used in manufacturing, with rated capacity in excess of that described above, with specifically related distribution and return systems are not included but are included in appropriate manufacturing equipment classes elsewhere specified. An example of an excluded steam and chemical recovery boiler system is that used in the pulp and paper manufacturing industry	22	15	22
Depreciable Assets Used in the Following Activities:				
01.1	Agriculture: Includes machinery and equipment, grain bins, and fences but no other land improvements, that are used in the production of crops or plants, vines, and trees; livestock; the operation of farm dairies, nurseries, greenhouses, sod farms, mushroom cellars, cranberry bogs, apiaries, and fur farms; the performance of agriculture, animal husbandry, and horticultural services	10	7	10
01.11	Cotton Ginning Assets	12	7	12
01.21	Cattle, Breeding or Dairy	7	5	7
01.22	Horses, Breeding or Work	10	7	10

▲ Table A11–1
(continued)

IRS TABLE OF MACRS CLASSES (Partial Table)

Asset Class	Description of Assets Included	Class Life (in years)	Recovery Periods (in years)	
			General Depreciation System	Alternative Depreciation System
Depreciable Assets Used in the Following Activities:				
01.221	Any horse that is not a race horse and that is more than 12 years old at the time it is placed in service	10	3	10
01.222	Any race horse that is more than 2 years old at the time it is placed in service	*	3	12
01.23	Hogs, Breeding	3	3	3
01.24	Sheep and Goats, Breeding	5	5	5
01.3	Farm buildings except structures included in Class 01.4	25	20	25
01.4	Single purpose agricultural or horticultural structures (within the meaning of section 48(p) of the Code)	15	7	15
10.0	Mining: Includes assets used in the mining and quarrying of metallic and nonmetallic minerals (including sand, gravel, stone, and clay) and the milling, beneficiation and other primary preparation of such materials	10	7	10
13.1	Drilling of Oil and Gas Wells: Includes assets used in the drilling of onshore oil and gas wells and the provision of geophysical and other exploration services; and the provision of such oil and gas field services as chemical treatment, plugging and abandoning of wells and cementing or perforating well casings. Does not include assets used in the performance of any of these activities and services by integrated petroleum and natural gas producers for their own account	6	5	6
15.0	Construction: Includes assets used in construction by general building, special trade, heavy and marine construction contractors, operative and investment builders, real estate subdividers and developers, and others except railroads	6	5	6
20.1	Manufacture of Grain and Grain Mill Products: Includes assets used in the production of flours, cereals, livestock feeds, and other grain and grain mill products	17	10	17
57.0	Distributive Trades and Services: Includes assets used in wholesale and retail trade, and personal and professional services. Includes section 1245 assets used in marketing petroleum and petroleum products	9	5	+9

(continued on next page)

*Property described in asset class 00.12 which is qualified technological equipment as defined in section 168(i)(2) is assigned a recovery period of 5 years notwithstanding its class life. See section 3 of the revenue procedure.
+Any high technology medical equipment as defined in section 168(i)(2)(C) which is described in asset guideline class 57.0 is assigned a 5-year recovery period for the alternative depreciation system.

▲ Table A11–1
(continued)

IRS TABLE OF MACRS CLASSES (Partial Table)

Asset Class	Description of Assets Included	Class Life (in years)	Recovery Periods (in years)	
			General Depreciation System	Alternative Depreciation System
Depreciable Assets Used in the Following Activities:				
57.1	Distributive Trades and Services-Billboard, Service Station Buildings and Petroleum Marketing Land Improvements: Includes section 1250 assets, including service station buildings and depreciable land improvements, whether section 1245 property or section 1250 property, used in the marketing of petroleum and petroleum products, but not including any of these facilities related to petroleum and natural gas trunk pipelines. Includes car wash buildings and related land improvements. Includes billboards, whether such assets are section 1245 property or section 1250 property. Excludes all other land improvements, buildings and structural components as defined in section 1.48-1(e) of the regulations	20	15	20
79.0	Recreation: Includes assets used in the provision of entertainment services on payment of a fee or admission charge, as in the operation of bowling alleys, billiard and pool establishments, theaters, concert halls, and miniature golf courses. Does not include amusement and theme parks and assets which consist primarily of specialized land improvements or structures, such as golf courses, sports stadia, race tracks, ski slopes, and buildings which house the assets used in entertainment services	10	7	10
80.0	Theme and Amusement Parks: Includes assets used in the provision of rides, attractions, and amusements in activities defined as theme and amusement parks, and includes appurtenances associated with a ride, attraction, amusement or theme setting within the park such as ticket booths, facades, shop interiors, and props, special purpose structures, and buildings other than warehouses, administration buildings, hotels, and motels. Includes all land improvements for or in support of park activities, (e.g., parking lots, sidewalks, waterways, bridges, fences, landscaping, etc.) and support functions (e.g., food and beverage retailing, souvenir vending and other nonlodging accommodations) if owned by the park and provided exclusively for the benefit of park patrons. Theme and amusement parks are defined as combinations of amusements, rides, and attractions which are permanently situated on park land and open to the			

▲ **Table A11–1**
(continued)

IRS TABLE OF MACRS CLASSES *(Partial Table)*

Asset Class	Description of Assets Included	Class Life (in years)	Recovery Periods (in years)	
			General Depreciation System	Alternative Depreciation System
Depreciable Assets Used in the Following Activities:				
80.0 *(cont.)*	public for the price of admission. This guideline class is a composite of all assets used in this industry except transportation equipment (general purpose trucks, cars, airplanes, etc., which are included in asset guideline classes with the prefix 00.2), assets used in the provision of administrative services (asset classes with the prefix 00.1), and warehouses, administration buildings, hotels and motels	12.5	7	12.5
Certain Property for Which Recovery Periods Assigned:				
	A. Personal Property With No Class Life		7	12
	Section 1245 Real Property With No Class Life		7	40
	B. Qualified Technological Equipment, as defined in section 168(i)(2).	+ +	5	5
	C. Property Used in Connection with Research and Experimentation referred to in section 168(e)(3)(B)	+ +	5	class life if no class life—12
	D. Alternative Energy Property described in sections 48(l)(3)(viii) or (iv), or section 48(l)(4) of the Code.	+ +	5	class life if no class life—12
	E. Biomass property described in section 48(l)(15) and is a qualifying small production facility within the meaning of section 3(17)(c) of the Federal Power Act, (16 U.S.C. 796(17)(C)), as in effect on September 1, 1986	+ +	5	class life if no class life—12

+ +The class life (if any) of property described in classes B, C, D, or E is determined by reference to the asset guideline classes in this revenue procedure. If an item of property described in paragraphs B, C, D, or E is not described in any asset guideline class, such item of property has no class life.

▲ Table A11–2

ACRS COST-RECOVERY TABLE FOR 15-YEAR REAL PROPERTY—EXCEPT LOW-INCOME HOUSING *(Assuming full-month convention; property placed in service after December 31, 1980 but before March 16, 1984)*

If the recovery year is	The applicable percentage is (Use the column for the month in the first year the property is placed in service)											
	1	2	3	4	5	6	7	8	9	10	11	12
1	12	11	10	9	8	7	6	5	4	3	2	1
2	10	10	11	11	11	11	11	11	11	11	11	12
3	9	9	9	9	10	10	10	10	10	10	10	10
4	8	8	8	8	8	8	9	9	9	9	9	9
5	7	7	7	7	7	7	8	8	8	8	8	8
6	6	6	6	6	7	7	7	7	7	7	7	7
7	6	6	6	6	6	6	6	6	6	6	6	6
8	6	6	6	6	6	6	5	6	6	6	6	6
9	6	6	6	6	5	6	5	5	5	6	6	6
10	5	6	5	6	5	5	5	5	5	5	6	5
11	5	5	5	5	5	5	5	5	5	5	5	5
12	5	5	5	5	5	5	5	5	5	5	5	5
13	5	5	5	5	5	5	5	5	5	5	5	5
14	5	5	5	5	5	5	5	5	5	5	5	5
15	5	5	5	5	5	5	5	5	5	5	5	5
16	—	—	1	1	2	2	3	3	4	4	4	5

▲ Table A11–3

ACRS TABLE FOR LOW-INCOME HOUSING

If the recovery year is	The applicable percentage is (Use the column for the month in the first year the property is placed in service)											
	1	2	3	4	5	6	7	8	9	10	11	12
1	13	12	11	10	9	8	7	6	4	3	2	1
2	12	12	12	12	12	12	12	13	13	13	13	13
3	10	10	10	10	11	11	11	11	11	11	11	11
4	9	9	9	9	9	9	9	9	10	10	10	10
5	8	8	8	8	8	8	8	8	8	8	8	9
6	7	7	7	7	7	7	7	7	7	7	7	7
7	6	6	6	6	6	6	6	6	6	6	6	6
8	5	5	5	5	5	5	5	5	5	5	6	6
9	5	5	5	5	5	5	5	5	5	5	5	5
10	5	5	5	5	5	5	5	5	5	5	5	5
11	4	5	5	5	5	5	5	5	5	5	5	5
12	4	4	4	5	4	5	5	5	5	5	5	5
13	4	4	4	4	4	4	5	4	5	5	5	5
14	4	4	4	4	4	4	4	4	4	5	4	4
15	4	4	4	4	4	4	4	4	4	4	4	4
16	—	—	1	1	2	2	2	3	3	3	4	4

If the recovery year is	And the month in the first recovery year the property is placed in service is										
	1	**2**	**3**	**4**	**5**	**6**	**7**	**8**	**9**	**10–11**	**12**
	The applicable percentage is										
1	10	9	8	7	6	6	5	4	3	2	1
2	9	9	9	9	9	9	9	9	9	10	10
3	8	8	8	8	8	8	8	8	9	9	9
4	7	7	7	7	7	7	8	8	8	8	8
5	6	7	7	7	7	7	7	7	7	7	7
6	6	6	6	6	6	6	6	6	6	6	6
7	5	5	5	5	6	6	6	6	6	6	6
8	5	5	5	5	5	5	5	5	5	5	5
9	5	5	5	5	5	5	5	5	5	5	5
10	5	5	5	5	5	5	5	5	5	5	5
11	5	5	5	5	5	5	5	5	5	5	5
12	5	5	5	5	5	5	5	5	5	5	5
13	4	4	4	5	5	4	4	5	4	4	4
14	4	4	4	4	4	4	4	4	4	4	4
15	4	4	4	4	4	4	4	4	4	4	4
16	4	4	4	4	4	4	4	4	4	4	4
17	4	4	4	4	4	4	4	4	4	4	4
18	4	4	4	4	4	4	4	4	4	4	4
19			1	1	1	2	2	2	3	3	4

▲ **Table A11–4**

ACRS COST-RECOVERY TABLE FOR 18-YEAR REAL PROPERTY (18-YEAR 175% DECLINING BALANCE) *(Assuming full-month convention; property placed in service after March 15, 1984, but before June 23, 1984)*

If the recovery year is	And the month in the first recovery year the property is placed in service is											
	1	**2**	**3**	**4**	**5**	**6**	**7**	**8**	**9**	**10**	**11**	**12**
	The applicable percentage is											
1	9	9	8	7	6	5	4	4	3	2	1	0.4
2	9	9	9	9	9	9	9	9	9	10	10	10.0
3	8	8	8	8	8	8	8	8	9	9	9	9.0
4	7	7	7	7	7	8	8	8	8	8	8	8.0
5	7	7	7	7	7	7	7	7	7	7	7	7.0
6	6	6	6	6	6	6	6	6	6	6	6	6.0
7	5	5	5	5	6	6	6	6	6	6	6	6.0
8	5	5	5	5	5	5	5	5	5	5	5	5.0
9	5	5	5	5	5	5	5	5	5	5	5	5.0
10	5	5	5	5	5	5	5	5	5	5	5	5.0
11	5	5	5	5	5	5	5	5	5	5	5	5.0
12	5	5	5	5	5	5	5	5	5	5	5	5.0
13	4	4	4	5	4	4	5	4	4	4	5	5.0
14	4	4	4	4	4	4	4	4	4	4	4	4.0
15	4	4	4	4	4	4	4	4	4	4	4	4.0
16	4	4	4	4	4	4	4	4	4	4	4	4.0
17	4	4	4	4	4	4	4	4	4	4	4	4.0
18	4	3	4	4	4	4	4	4	4	4	4	4.0
19		1	1	1	2	2	2	3	3	3	3	3.6

▲ **Table A11–5**

ACRS COST-RECOVERY TABLE FOR 18-YEAR REAL PROPERTY (18-YEAR 175% DECLINING BALANCE) *(Assuming mid-month convention; property placed in service after June 22, 1984, and before May 9, 1985)*

▲ **Table A11–6**

ACRS Cost-Recovery Table for 19-year Real Property (19-Year 175% Declining Balance)
(Assuming mid-month convention; property placed in service after May 8, 1985)

If the recovery year is	And the month in the first recovery year the property is placed in service is											
	1	2	3	4	5	6	7	8	9	10	11	12
	The applicable percentage is											
1	8.8	8.1	7.3	6.5	5.8	5.0	4.2	3.5	2.7	1.9	1.1	0.4
2	8.4	8.5	8.5	8.6	8.7	8.8	8.8	8.9	9.0	9.0	9.1	9.2
3	7.6	7.7	7.7	7.8	7.9	7.9	8.0	8.1	8.1	8.2	8.3	8.3
4	6.9	7.0	7.0	7.1	7.1	7.2	7.3	7.3	7.4	7.4	7.5	7.6
5	6.3	6.3	6.4	6.4	6.5	6.5	6.6	6.6	6.7	6.8	6.8	6.9
6	5.7	5.7	5.8	5.9	5.9	5.9	6.0	6.0	6.1	6.1	6.2	6.2
7	5.2	5.2	5.3	5.3	5.3	5.4	5.4	5.5	5.5	5.6	5.6	5.6
8	4.7	4.7	4.8	4.8	4.8	4.9	4.9	5.0	5.0	5.1	5.1	5.1
9	4.2	4.3	4.3	4.4	4.4	4.5	4.5	4.5	4.5	4.6	4.6	4.7
10	4.2	4.2	4.2	4.2	4.2	4.2	4.2	4.2	4.2	4.2	4.2	4.2
11	4.2	4.2	4.2	4.2	4.2	4.2	4.2	4.2	4.2	4.2	4.2	4.2
12	4.2	4.2	4.2	4.2	4.2	4.2	4.2	4.2	4.2	4.2	4.2	4.2
13	4.2	4.2	4.2	4.2	4.2	4.2	4.2	4.2	4.2	4.2	4.2	4.2
14	4.2	4.2	4.2	4.2	4.2	4.2	4.2	4.2	4.2	4.2	4.2	4.2
15	4.2	4.2	4.2	4.2	4.2	4.2	4.2	4.2	4.2	4.2	4.2	4.2
16	4.2	4.2	4.2	4.2	4.2	4.2	4.2	4.2	4.2	4.2	4.2	4.2
17	4.2	4.2	4.2	4.2	4.2	4.2	4.2	4.2	4.2	4.2	4.2	4.2
18	4.2	4.2	4.2	4.2	4.2	4.2	4.2	4.2	4.2	4.2	4.2	4.2
19	4.2	4.2	4.2	4.2	4.2	4.2	4.2	4.2	4.2	4.2	4.2	4.2
20	0.2	0.5	0.9	1.2	1.6	1.9	2.3	2.6	3.0	3.3	3.7	4.0

▲ **Table A11–7**

MACRS Depreciation for 200% or 150% Declining Balance, Switching to Straight-Line
(Applicable recovery periods: 3, 5, 7, 10, 15, 20 years; applicable convention: mid-year)

If the recovery year is	And the recovery period is					
	3 Years	5 Years	7 Years	10 Years	15 Years	20 Years
	The depreciation rate is					
1	33.33	20.00	14.29	10.00	5.00	3.750
2	44.45	32.00	24.49	18.00	9.50	7.219
3	14.81	19.20	17.49	14.40	8.55	6.677
4	7.41	11.52	12.49	11.52	7.70	6.177
5		11.52	8.93	9.22	6.93	5.713
6		5.76	8.92	7.37	6.23	5.285
7			8.93	6.55	5.90	4.888
8			4.46	6.55	5.90	4.522
9				6.56	5.91	4.462
10				6.55	5.90	4.461
11				3.28	5.91	4.462
12					5.90	4.461
13					5.91	4.462
14					5.90	4.461
15					5.91	4.462
16					2.95	4.461
17						4.462
18						4.461
19						4.462
20						4.461
21						2.231

If the recovery year is	And the recovery period is					
	3 Years	5 Years	7 Years	10 Years	15 Years	20 Years
	The depreciation rate is					
1	58.33	35.00	25.00	17.50	8.75	6.563
2	27.78	26.00	21.43	16.50	9.13	7.000
3	12.35	15.60	15.31	13.20	8.21	6.482
4	1.54	11.01	10.93	10.56	7.39	5.996
5		11.01	8.75	8.45	6.65	5.546
6		1.38	8.74	6.76	5.99	5.130
7			8.75	6.55	5.90	4.746
8			1.09	6.55	5.91	4.459
9				6.56	5.90	4.459
10				6.55	5.91	4.459
11				0.82	5.90	4.459
12					5.91	4.460
13					5.90	4.459
14					5.91	4.460
15					5.90	4.459
16					0.74	4.460
17						4.459
18						4.460
19						4.459
20						4.460
21						0.557

▲ **Table A11–8**

MACRS DEPRECIATION FOR 200% OR 150% DECLINING BALANCE, SWITCHING TO STRAIGHT-LINE *(Applicable recovery periods: 3, 5, 7, 10, 15, 20 years; applicable convention: mid-quarter; property placed in service in first quarter)*

If the recovery year is	And the recovery period is					
	3 Years	5 Years	7 Years	10 Years	15 Years	20 Years
	The depreciation rate is					
1	41.67	25.00	17.85	12.50	6.25	4.688
2	38.89	30.00	23.47	17.50	9.38	7.148
3	14.14	18.00	16.76	14.00	8.44	6.612
4	5.30	11.37	11.97	11.20	7.59	6.116
5		11.37	8.87	8.96	6.83	5.658
6		4.26	8.87	7.17	6.15	5.233
7			8.87	6.55	5.91	4.841
8			3.33	6.55	59.0	4.478
9				6.56	5.91	4.463
10				6.55	5.90	4.463
11				2.46	5.91	4.463
12					5.90	4.463
13					5.91	4.463
14					5.90	4.463
15					5.91	4.462
16					2.21	4.463
17						4.462
18						4.463
19						4.462
20						4.463
21						1.673

▲ **Table A11–9**

MACRS DEPRECIATION FOR 200% OR 150% DECLINING BALANCE, SWITCHING TO STRAIGHT-LINE *Applicable recovery periods: 3, 5, 7, 10, 15, 20 years; applicable convention: mid-quarter; property placed in service in second quarter)*

▲ Table A11–10

MACRS DEPRECIATION FOR 200% OR 150% DECLINING BALANCE, SWITCHING TO STRAIGHT-LINE (*Applicable recovery periods: 3, 5, 7, 10, 15, 20 years; applicable convention: mid-quarter; property placed in service in third quarter*)

If the recovery year is	And the recovery period is					
	3 Years	5 Years	7 Years	10 Years	15 Years	20 Years
	The depreciation rate is					
1	25.00	15.00	10.71	7.50	3.75	2.813
2	50.00	34.00	25.51	18.50	9.63	7.289
3	16.67	20.40	18.22	14.80	8.66	6.742
4	8.33	12.24	13.02	11.84	7.80	6.237
5		11.30	9.30	9.47	7.02	5.769
6		7.06	8.85	7.58	6.31	5.336
7			8.86	6.55	5.90	4.936
8			5.53	6.55	5.90	4.566
9				6.56	5.91	4.460
10				6.55	5.90	4.460
11				4.10	5.91	4.460
12					5.90	4.460
13					5.91	4.461
14					5.90	4.460
15					5.91	4.461
16					3.69	4.460
17						4.461
18						4.460
19						4.461
20						4.460
21						2.788

▲ Table A11–11

MACRS DEPRECIATION FOR 200% OR 150% DECLINING BALANCE, SWITCHING TO STRAIGHT-LINE (*Applicable recovery periods: 3, 5, 7, 10, 15, 20 years; applicable convention: mid-quarter; property placed in service in fourth quarter*)

If the recovery year is	And the recovery period is					
	3 Years	5 Years	7 Years	10 Years	15 Years	20 Years
	The depreciation rate is					
1	8.33	5.00	3.57	2.50	1.25	0.938
2	61.11	38.00	27.55	19.50	9.88	7.430
3	20.37	22.80	19.68	15.60	8.89	6.872
4	10.19	13.68	14.06	12.48	8.00	6.357
5		10.94	10.04	9.98	7.20	5.880
6		9.58	8.73	7.99	6.48	5.439
7			8.73	6.55	5.90	5.031
8			7.64	6.55	5.90	4.654
9				6.56	5.90	4.458
10				6.55	5.91	4.458
11				5.74	5.90	4.458
12					5.91	4.458
13					5.90	4.458
14					5.91	4.458
15					5.90	4.458
16					5.17	4.458
17						4.458
18						4.459
19						4.458
20						4.459
21						3.901

If the recovery year is	And the month in the first recovery year the property is placed in service is											
	1	2	3	4	5	6	7	8	9	10	11	12
	The depreciation rate is											
1	3.485	3.182	2.879	2.576	2.273	1.970	1.667	1.364	1.061	0.758	0.455	0.152
2	3.636	3.636	3.636	3.636	3.636	3.636	3.636	3.636	3.636	3.636	3.636	3.636
3	3.636	3.636	3.636	3.636	3.636	3.636	3.636	3.636	3.636	3.636	3.636	3.636
4	3.636	3.636	3.636	3.636	3.636	3.636	3.636	3.636	3.636	3.636	3.636	3.636
5	3.636	3.636	3.636	3.636	3.636	3.636	3.636	3.636	3.636	3.636	3.636	3.636
6	3.636	3.636	3.636	3.636	3.636	3.636	3.636	3.636	3.636	3.636	3.636	3.636
7	3.636	3.636	3.636	3.636	3.636	3.636	3.636	3.636	3.636	3.636	3.636	3.636
8	3.636	3.636	3.636	3.636	3.636	3.636	3.636	3.636	3.636	3.636	3.636	3.636
9	3.636	3.636	3.636	3.636	3.636	3.636	3.636	3.636	3.636	3.636	3.636	3.636
10	3.637	3.637	3.637	3.637	3.637	3.637	3.636	3.636	3.636	3.636	3.636	3.636
11	3.636	3.636	3.636	3.636	3.636	3.636	3.637	3.637	3.637	3.637	3.637	3.637
12	3.637	3.637	3.637	3.637	3.637	3.637	3.636	3.636	3.636	3.636	3.636	3.636
13	3.636	3.636	3.636	3.636	3.636	3.636	3.637	3.637	3.637	3.637	3.637	3.637
14	3.637	3.637	3.637	3.637	3.637	3.637	3.636	3.636	3.636	3.636	3.636	3.636
15	3.636	3.636	3.636	3.636	3.636	3.636	3.637	3.637	3.637	3.637	3.637	3.637
16	3.637	3.637	3.637	3.637	3.637	3.637	3.636	3.636	3.636	3.636	3.636	3.636
17	3.636	3.636	3.636	3.636	3.636	3.636	3.637	3.637	3.637	3.637	3.637	3.637
18	3.637	3.637	3.637	3.637	3.637	3.637	3.636	3.636	3.636	3.636	3.636	3.636
19	3.636	3.636	3.636	3.636	3.636	3.636	3.637	3.637	3.637	3.637	3.637	3.637
20	3.637	3.637	3.637	3.637	3.637	3.637	3.636	3.636	3.636	3.636	3.636	3.636
21	3.636	3.636	3.636	3.636	3.636	3.636	3.637	3.637	3.637	3.637	3.637	3.637
22	3.637	3.637	3.637	3.637	3.637	3.637	3.636	3.636	3.636	3.636	3.636	3.636
23	3.636	3.636	3.636	3.636	3.636	3.636	3.637	3.637	3.637	3.637	3.637	3.637
24	3.637	3.637	3.637	3.637	3.637	3.637	3.636	3.636	3.636	3.636	3.636	3.636
25	3.636	3.636	3.636	3.636	3.636	3.636	3.637	3.637	3.637	3.637	3.637	3.637
26	3.637	3.637	3.637	3.637	3.637	3.637	3.636	3.636	3.636	3.636	3.636	3.636
27	3.636	3.636	3.636	3.636	3.636	3.636	3.637	3.637	3.637	3.637	3.637	3.637
28	1.970	2.273	2.576	2.879	3.182	3.485	3.636	3.636	3.636	3.636	3.636	3.636
29	0.000	0.000	0.000	0.000	0.000	0.000	0.152	0.455	0.758	1.061	1.364	1.667

▲ **Table A11–12**

MACRS DEPRECIATION FOR RESIDENTIAL RENTAL PROPERTY
(Applicable recovery period: 27.5 years; Applicable convention: mid-month)

▲ Table A11–13

MACRS Depreciation for Nonresidential Real Property
(Applicable recovery period: 31.5 years; applicable convention: mid-month; property placed in service before May 13, 1993)

If the recovery year is	And the month in the first recovery year the property is placed in service is											
	1	2	3	4	5	6	7	8	9	10	11	12
	The depreciation rate is											
1	3.042	2.778	2.513	2.249	1.984	1.720	1.455	1.190	0.926	0.661	0.397	0.132
2	3.175	3.175	3.175	3.175	3.175	3.175	3.175	3.175	3.175	3.175	3.175	3.175
3	3.175	3.175	3.175	3.175	3.175	3.175	3.175	3.175	3.175	3.175	3.175	3.175
4	3.175	3.175	3.175	3.175	3.175	3.175	3.175	3.175	3.175	3.175	3.175	3.175
5	3.175	3.175	3.175	3.175	3.175	3.175	3.175	3.175	3.175	3.175	3.175	3.175
6	3.175	3.175	3.175	3.175	3.175	3.175	3.175	3.175	3.175	3.175	3.175	3.175
7	3.175	3.175	3.175	3.175	3.175	3.175	3.175	3.175	3.175	3.175	3.175	3.175
8	3.175	3.174	3.175	3.174	3.175	3.174	3.175	3.175	3.175	3.175	3.175	3.175
9	3.174	3.175	3.174	3.175	3.174	3.175	3.174	3.175	3.174	3.175	3.174	3.175
10	3.175	3.174	3.175	3.174	3.175	3.174	3.175	3.174	3.175	3.174	3.175	3.174
11	3.174	3.175	3.174	3.175	3.174	3.175	3.174	3.175	3.174	3.175	3.174	3.175
12	3.175	3.174	3.175	3.174	3.175	3.174	3.175	3.174	3.175	3.174	3.175	3.174
13	3.174	3.175	3.174	3.175	3.174	3.175	3.174	3.175	3.174	3.175	3.174	3.175
14	3.175	3.174	3.175	3.174	3.175	3.174	3.175	3.174	3.175	3.174	3.175	3.174
15	3.174	3.175	3.174	3.175	3.174	3.175	3.174	3.175	3.174	3.175	3.174	3.175
16	3.175	3.174	3.175	3.174	3.175	3.174	3.175	3.174	3.175	3.174	3.175	3.174
17	3.174	3.175	3.174	3.175	3.174	3.175	3.174	3.175	3.174	3.175	3.174	3.175
18	3.175	3.174	3.175	3.174	3.175	3.174	3.175	3.174	3.175	3.174	3.175	3.174
19	3.174	3.175	3.174	3.175	3.174	3.175	3.174	3.175	3.174	3.175	3.174	3.175
20	3.175	3.174	3.175	3.174	3.175	3.174	3.175	3.174	3.175	3.174	3.175	3.174
21	3.174	3.175	3.174	3.175	3.174	3.175	3.174	3.175	3.174	3.175	3.174	3.175
22	3.175	3.174	3.175	3.174	3.175	3.174	3.175	3.174	3.175	3.174	3.175	3.174
23	3.174	3.175	3.174	3.175	3.174	3.175	3.174	3.175	3.174	3.175	3.174	3.175
24	3.175	3.174	3.175	3.174	3.175	3.174	3.175	3.174	3.175	3.174	3.175	3.174
25	3.174	3.175	3.174	3.175	3.174	3.175	3.174	3.175	3.174	3.175	3.174	3.175
26	3.175	3.174	3.175	3.174	3.175	3.174	3.175	3.174	3.175	3.174	3.175	3.174
27	3.174	3.175	3.174	3.175	3.174	3.175	3.174	3.175	3.174	3.175	3.174	3.175
28	3.175	3.174	3.175	3.174	3.175	3.174	3.175	3.174	3.175	3.174	3.175	3.174
29	3.174	3.175	3.174	3.175	3.174	3.175	3.174	3.175	3.174	3.175	3.174	3.175
30	3.175	3.174	3.175	3.174	3.175	3.174	3.175	3.174	3.175	3.174	3.175	3.174
31	3.174	3.175	3.174	3.175	3.174	3.175	3.174	3.175	3.174	3.175	3.174	3.175
32	1.720	1.984	2.249	2.513	2.778	3.042	3.175	3.174	3.175	3.174	3.175	3.174
33	0.000	0.000	0.000	0.000	0.000	0.000	0.132	0.397	0.661	0.926	1.190	1.455

▲ Table A11–14

MACRS Depreciation for Nonresidential Real Property
(Applicable recovery period: 39 years; applicable convention: mid-month; property placed in service after May 12, 1993)

If the recovery year is	And the month in the first recovery year the property is placed in service is											
	1	2	3	4	5	6	7	8	9	10	11	12
	The depreciation rate is											
1	2.461	2.247	2.033	1.819	1.605	1.391	1.177	0.963	0.749	0.535	0.321	0.107
2–39	2.564	2.564	2.564	2.564	2.564	2.564	2.564	2.564	2.564	2.564	2.564	2.564
40	0.107	0.321	0.535	0.749	0.963	1.177	1.391	1.605	1.819	2.033	2.247	2.461

Recovery Year	Mid-Year Convention	Mid-Quarter Convention Car Placed in Service in				Maximum Depreciation Limit*	
		1st Quarter	2nd Quarter	3rd Quarter	4th Quarter	1994	1995
1	20.00%	35.00%	25.00%	15.00%	5.00%	$2,960	$3,060
2	32.00%	26.00%	30.00%	34.00%	38.00%	$4,700	$4,900
3	19.20%	15.60%	18.00%	20.40%	22.80%	$2,850	$2,950
4	11.52%	11.01%	11.37%	12.24%	13.68%	$1,675	$1,775
5	11.52%	11.01%	11.37%	11.30%	10.94%	$1,675	$1,775
6	5.76%	1.38%	4.26%	7.06%	9.58%	$1,675	$1,775

*These amounts must be reduced if business use is less than 100%. The depreciation deduction for an automobile cannot exceed the amounts in the last column (adjusted for business use).

▲ Table A11–15

MACRS Depreciation for a Car Placed in Service in 1994 and 1995, 200% Declining Balance Method

If the recovery year is	And the recovery period is					
	3 Years	5 Years	7 Years	10 Years	15 Years	20 Years
	The depreciation rate is					
1	16.67	10.00	7.14	5.00	3.33	2.50
2	40.00	20.00	14.29	10.00	6.67	5.00
3	40.00	20.00	14.29	10.00	6.67	5.00
4	16.67	20.00	14.29	10.00	6.67	5.00
5		20.00	14.29	10.00	6.67	5.00
6		10.00	14.29	10.00	6.67	5.00
7			14.29	10.00	6.67	5.00
8			7.14	10.00	6.67	5.00
9				10.00	6.67	5.00
10				10.00	6.67	5.00
11				5.00	6.67	5.00
12					6.67	5.00
13					6.67	5.00
14					6.67	5.00
15					6.67	5.00
16					3.33	5.00
17						5.00
18						5.00
19						5.00
20						5.00
21						2.50

▲ Table A11–16

MACRS Depreciation for Optional Straight-Line (*Applicable recovery periods: 3, 5, 7, 10, 15, 20 years; applicable convention: mid-year*)

Property Dispositions

▲ CHAPTER LEARNING OBJECTIVES

- ■ Explain the calculation of realized gain or loss from the sale or other disposition of property.

- ■ Discuss what constitutes the amount realized from a disposition of property.

- ■ Differentiate a realized gain or loss from a property disposition and the amount of gain or loss that is recognized in the tax year of the disposition.

- ■ Describe capital assets and the year-end netting procedure used to determine the effect of capital asset transactions on taxable income.

- ■ Present year-end tax-planning strategies to take advantage of the capital asset netting procedure.

- ■ Describe Section 1231 assets and the year-end netting procedure used to determine the effect of Section 1231 transactions on taxable income.

- ■ Explain the reclassification of gain on the sale of depreciable assets as ordinary income under the depreciation recapture provisions.

- ■ Identify Section 1245 and Section 1250 assets and the depreciation recapture rule applicable to each type.

- ■ Provide a framework for analyzing the effect of a variety of different asset dispositions on taxable income for the year.

▲ CONCEPT REVIEW ▲

All-inclusive income   All income received is taxable unless a specific provision can be found in the tax law that either excludes the income from taxation or defers its recognition to a future tax year.

Annual accounting period   All entities must report the results of their operations on an annual basis (the tax year). Each tax year stands on its own, apart from other tax years.

Arm's-length transaction   A transaction in which all parties to the transaction have bargained in good faith and for their individual benefit, not for the benefit of the transaction group.

Basis   This is the amount of unrecovered investment in an asset. As amounts are expended and/or recovered relative to an asset over time, the basis is adjusted in consideration of such changes. The **adjusted basis** of an asset is the original basis, plus or minus the changes in the amount of unrecovered investment.

Business purpose   To be deductible, an expenditure or a loss must have a business or other economic purpose

that exceeds any tax avoidance motive. The primary motive for the transaction must be to make a profit.

Capital recovery   No income is realized until the taxpayer receives more than the amount invested to produce the income. The amount invested in an asset represents the maximum amount recoverable.

Legislative grace   Any tax relief provided is the result of a specific act of Congress that must be strictly applied and interpreted. All income received is taxable unless a specific provision can be found in the tax law that excludes the income from taxation. Deductions must be approached with the philosophy that nothing is deductible unless a provision in the tax law allows the deduction.

Realization   No income (or loss) is recognized until it has been realized. A realization involves a change in the form and/or the substance of a taxpayer's property rights that results from an arm's-length transaction.

Wherewithal to pay   Income is recognized in the period in which the taxpayer has the means to pay the tax on the income.

A taxpayer realizes gain or loss on property when the form or substance of the property or its underlying property rights change as a result of an arm's-length transaction. Realization of gain or loss typically occurs upon disposition of property in a transaction with another entity. The most common way to dispose of an asset is by sale. However, property is also disposed of through exchanges, casualties and thefts, and abandonments or retirements.

▲ INTRODUCTION

Figure 12–1 presents an overview of the steps involved in analyzing a disposition of property. The first step is to calculate the amount realized from the disposition. Under the capital recovery concept, taxpayers do not recognize gain until they have recovered all capital invested in the property. The amount of unrecovered investment in the property is measured by the property's basis. As Chapter 10 explained, many properties are subject to adjustments to account for additional investment and deductions for cost recoveries throughout their lives. These adjustments give the property an adjusted basis at the date of disposition.

The second step is to calculate the gain or loss realized on the disposition. The gain or loss realized on a disposition is the difference between the amount realized from the disposition of the property and the adjusted basis of the property.

A gain on the disposition of a property represents an amount realized in excess of the unrecovered investment in the property. A gain is taxable under the all-inclusive income concept. On the other hand, a loss on a disposition represents a loss of capital invested in the property. As Figure 12–1 shows, some realized gains and losses are not recognized for tax purposes. Realized gains from certain types of transactions (like-kind exchanges, casualties and thefts, sales of personal residences) have been granted tax relief. Because these sale-and-replacement

▲ **Figure 12–1**

PROPERTY DISPOSITION
PROCEDURE

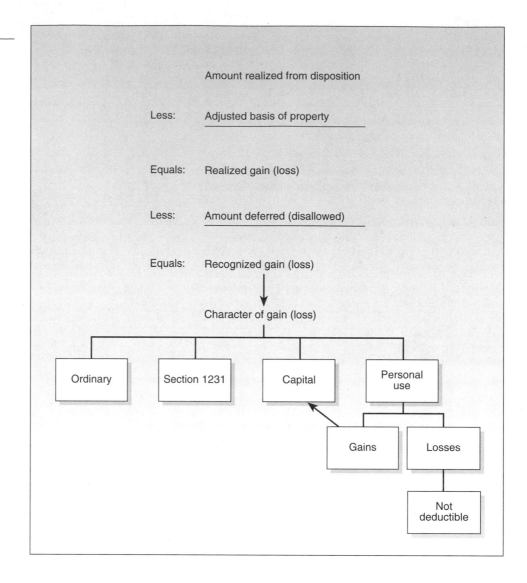

transactions require the reinvestment of the amount realized from the disposition, the taxpayer lacks the necessary wherewithal to pay. As a result, gains from these transactions are deferred for recognition in a future accounting period. Because these deferrals are a matter of legislative grace, few transactions qualify for this special relief. (The most common nontaxable transactions and their unique characteristics are discussed in Chapter 13.) Deductions for losses on dispositions are also subject to the legislative grace concept. Therefore, certain types of realized losses are deferred (e.g., like-kind exchanges, wash sales), whereas others are specifically disallowed (e.g., losses on sales of personal use property). Thus, the third step in the analysis of the disposition of property is to determine the amount of gain or loss that is to be recognized in the current tax year. A **recognized gain** or **a recognized loss** is one that is included in the calculation of the current year's taxable income.

▲ **EXAMPLE 1**   Ramona sold 600 shares of Barcelona stock to her father, Hermano, for $9,000. The stock had cost Ramona $15,000. One year later, Hermano sold the 600 shares for $12,000. What are Ramona's and Hermano's realized and recognized gains or losses on the sales of the Barcelona stock?

Discussion: Ramona has realized a loss of $6,000 ($9,000 − $15,000) on the sale of the stock. However, the loss is disallowed, because the sale is to a related party. Thus, Ramona has a nondeductible loss from the sale of the stock.

Her father realized a gain of $3,000 ($12,000 − $9,000) on his sale of the stock. However, under the related party rules, Hermano can use Ramona's disallowed loss to reduce his gain to zero (as discussed in Chapter 7, the disallowed loss cannot be used to create a loss on the second sale). Hermano has realized a gain on the sale of the stock, but it is not recognized because of the related party rules.

▲ **EXAMPLE 2** Michael exchanged a computer used in his dental practice with an adjusted basis of $600 for a new computer. The new computer cost $3,000, but Michael was given a trade-in value of $1,000 for his old computer and had to pay only $2,000 out of pocket for the new computer. Has Michael realized a gain from the exchange of his computer? If so, is the gain recognized in the current period?

Discussion: The exchange of the computers is a disposition of the old computer. Michael has realized a gain of $400 ($1,000 trade-in value − $600 adjusted basis) on the exchange. The substance of the transaction is a sale of his old computer for $1,000 and the purchase of the new computer for $3,000.

In this case, Michael would not recognize any gain on the exchange in the current period. This is an exchange of business property for like-kind business property that can be deferred under the wherewithal-to-pay concept. Although Michael has realized a gain on the transaction, the net effect is that he pays out $2,000 in cash to effect the exchange. Michael has no assets remaining after the exchange with which to pay the tax on the realized gain. The definition of like-kind property and other rules regarding exchanges are discussed in Chapter 13.

After calculating the amount of gain or loss to be recognized, you must determine the character of the gain or loss. The tax law provides different treatments for gains and losses from different categories of property. As Figure 12–1 shows, all recognized gains and losses are categorized as one of the following:

1. Ordinary gains and losses
2. Capital gains and losses
3. Section 1231 gains and losses
4. Personal use gains and losses

Different procedures and rules apply to each category of gains and losses in determining the effect of the gains and losses on current taxable income. Exhibit 12–1 contains a representative list of assets in each of the four categories.

This chapter presents and discusses the basic treatments of dispositions of property. The first topic is how the amount of realized gain or loss is determined, followed by how to characterize recognized gains and losses as ordinary, capital, or Section 1231. The final, and perhaps the most complex, topic is reclassifying gains from the sale of depreciable property as ordinary income under the depreciation recapture rules. Detailed discussion of determining gains and losses deferred under the wherewithal-to-pay concept appears in Chapter 13.

Whenever a property disposition occurs, the taxpayer must calculate the realized gain or loss. Realized gain or loss is equal to the difference between the amount realized and the adjusted basis of the property.[1] The rules for determining a

▲ REALIZED GAIN OR LOSS

Ordinary Income Assets	Capital Assets
Inventories, receivables	Stocks, bonds, options
Gains from depreciation	Rental property (if not considered a trade or
Losses on small business stock	business)
Depreciable property held ≤ 1 year	Investments in conduit entities
Sales of copyrights, artistic compositions, etc., by the person creating the property	Investments in passive activities
	Personal use property sold at a gain (but not at a loss)
Section 1231 Assets	**Personal Use Assets**
To qualify, the property must be used in a trade or business and held for more than 1 year	Residence, automobile, clothing, furniture, etc.
Land, buildings, equipment, machinery, automobiles, computers, furniture, etc.	Any asset used for personal purposes (e.g., a computer used at home solely for personal purposes)
Unharvested crops, timber, coal, domestic iron ore	
Livestock used for draft, breeding, dairy, or sporting purposes	

property's basis and the common adjustments to basis were discussed in Chapters 10 and 11. Thus, the primary focus of this section is on determining the amount realized from a disposition of property.

Amount Realized

The amount realized from a disposition must be calculated in order to determine whether the taxpayer has realized a gain or a loss. The amount realized is the gross sales price less all expenses incurred to complete the sale (selling expenses). The **gross sales price** is the price agreed upon by the seller and the buyer. In an arm's-length transaction, the gross sales price is equal to the fair market value of the property. Selling expenses include commissions, legal fees, title costs, advertising, and any other costs incurred to complete the disposition transaction. When the property sold has an objectively determined market value, this is a straightforward computation.

▲ **EXAMPLE 3** Alvah sold 200 shares of Brett Co. stock for $25 per share. He paid $300 in commissions to his stockbroker for making the sale. Alvah had purchased the stock for $18 per share plus a $200 commission. What is Alvah's realized gain on the sale of the stock?

Discussion: The realized gain on the sale is $900, determined as follows:

Amount realized from sale ($5,000 − $300)	$4,700
Adjusted basis of shares sold ($3,600 + $200)	(3,800)
Realized gain on sale	$ 900

Note the effect of the commissions Alvah paid on the gain from the sale. Commissions paid to buy or sell property are never deducted as current expenses. When Alvah bought the stock, the $200 in commissions became part of the stock's basis (i.e., he had to pay the commissions in order to acquire the stock). When Alvah sold the stock, the commissions reduced the amount realized from the sale (i.e., they are a selling expense). On both sides of the transaction, the effect of the commissions is to reduce the amount of gain that Alvah realized from the stock investment.

The gross sales price of a property that does not have an objectively deter-mined market value is any value received from the buyer less any value given back to the buyer. More formally, the gross selling price includes

Amounts received by the seller from the buyer

- Cash
- Fair market value of property received
- Fair market value of services received
- Amount of the seller's expenses paid by the buyer
- Amount of the seller's debt assumed by the buyer

LESS:
Amounts given by seller to the buyer

- Amount of the buyer's expenses paid by the seller
- Amount of the buyer's debt assumed by the seller

As you can see, the gross selling price is not always obvious. The terms of the sales agreement must be carefully analyzed in order to determine how much the buyer actually paid the seller for the property. In analyzing more complex situa-tions, keep in mind that what you are determining is what the buyer actually paid the seller for the property.

▲ **EXAMPLE 4**   Arnold had a tractor that Jack wanted to buy. Jack had $300 in cash. Arnold agreed to sell Jack the tractor for the $300 in cash if Jack would agree to mow Arnold's field for 1 year. Arnold usually pays a neighbor $1,000 per year to mow the field. What is the gross selling price of the tractor?

Discussion: The gross selling price is equal to the $300 in cash plus the $1,000 value of the mowing services Jack agreed to provide as part of the sale. Thus, Arnold sold the tractor to Jack for $1,300.

▲ **EXAMPLE 5**   On April 1, Blake Corporation sold Zeke some land that it had bought for $8,000. Under the terms of the sale, Zeke was to pay Blake $13,000 in cash. In addition, Zeke also had to pay property taxes of $1,000 on the land for the entire year. Blake incurred commissions and legal fees of $1,600 related to the sale. What are the gross selling price, the amount realized, and Blake Corporation's gain (loss) on the sale of the land to Zeke?

Discussion: From Chapter 3, the payment of another's expenses in a business setting constitutes income to the person whose expenses are being paid. Therefore, the pay-ment of Blake Corporation's share of the property taxes by Zeke is part of the sales price of the property. The gross selling price is equal to the $13,000 cash payment plus the $250 payment of Blake's property tax obligation ($1,000 × 3/12 for January, Feb-ruary, and March). Blake's amount realized is $11,650 ($13,250 − $1,600), resulting in a gain of $3,650 ($11,650 - $8,000) on the sale of the land.

Effect of Debt Assumptions

A buyer's assumption of the seller's debt increases the gross sales price.[2] Con-versely, any debt of the buyer assumed by the seller in the transaction re-duces the gross sales price. To understand why the assumption of debt by the buyer constitutes a realization of income for the seller, consider the following examples:

▲ **EXAMPLE 6**   The Lydia Partnership owns some land that has a fair market value of $70,000 on which it owes a debt of $40,000. The partnership sold the land to Kerry for $70,000 in cash (no debt assumption was part of the sales agreement). What is the gross selling price of the land? How much cash does the partnership have after the sale of the land?

Discussion: The gross selling price is the $70,000 in cash that Kerry paid to the Lydia Partnership. After receiving the $70,000, the partnership will have to pay off the $40,000 debt on the land, and it will have only $30,000 in cash remaining.

▲ **EXAMPLE 7**   Assume in example 6 that Kerry agreed to assume Lydia's debt on the land as part of the sales agreement. How much cash will Kerry pay to the partnership to purchase the land?

Discussion: Because the agreed-upon fair market value of the land is $70,000, Kerry will pay Lydia Partnership only $30,000 in cash if she assumes the $40,000 debt on the land. From Lydia's point of view, the transaction is equivalent to the transaction in example 6: In either case, the partnership receives $30,000 in cash from the sale after subtracting the debt on the property.

As these examples demonstrate, assuming another's debt is the same as paying cash to the debtor, who then uses it to pay off the debt. Therefore, any debt of the seller that is assumed by the buyer is always included in the amount realized by the seller.

In exchanges of property, parties often trade the debts they have on their properties. Trading debt along with the property often eliminates the need for the parties to obtain additional financing for the transaction.

▲ **EXAMPLE 8**   Doris and Cory each own land that they would like to trade. Details of the fair market values and the debts of each are as follows:

	Doris	Cory
Fair market value	$15,000	$25,000
Mortgage debt on land	(5,000)	(20,000)
Equity in land	$10,000	$ 5,000

Doris and Cory agree to exchange their land and assume each other's debt, with any difference paid in cash. Who will have to pay cash, and how much will that person have to pay?

Discussion: Cory will have to pay Doris $5,000. Although Cory's land is worth $10,000 more than Doris's land, Doris's land has a net of mortgage cash value of $10,000 ($15,000 − $5,000). Therefore, in a sale of her land with an assumption of her mortgage, she would expect to receive $10,000 in cash. On the other hand, Cory's net of mortgage cash value is only $5,000 ($25,000 − $20,000). Therefore, if Cory sold the land with the assumption of his mortgage, he would expect to receive $5,000. Because they are exchanging their land and their mortgages, they are really exchanging net mortgage value. Thus, Cory must pay Doris $5,000 to effect the exchange.

▲ **EXAMPLE 9**   What are the gross selling prices of Doris's and Cory's properties from the exchange in example 8?

Discussion: The gross selling prices realized by Doris and Cory will be the fair market values of their properties.

Doris realizes a gross selling price equal to $15,000:

Cash received from Cory	$ 5,000
Fair market value of land received	25,000
Mortgage assumed by Cory	5,000
Less: Assumption of Cory's mortgage	(20,000)
Gross selling price	$15,000

Cory realizes a gross selling price equal to $25,000:

Fair market value of land received	$15,000
Mortgage assumed by Doris	20,000
Less: Assumption of Doris's mortgage	(5,000)
Less: Cash paid to Doris	(5,000)
Gross selling price	$25,000

After determining the amount of realized gain or loss to be recognized in the current period, you must classify the recognized gain or loss according to the character of the asset creating the gain or loss. Characterizing gains and losses from property dispositions follows the general classification scheme outlined for deductions and losses in chapters 5 through 7. In general, gains and losses on the sale of property used in a trade or business are considered ordinary gains and losses. However, gains on the sale of certain types of business assets, referred to as *Section 1231 property*, can be treated as capital gains under certain circumstances. This treatment is different from gains and losses from production-of-income activities, which are always considered capital gains and losses. Gains from the sale of personal use assets are capital gains, whereas losses on dispositions of personal use assets (other than casualty and theft losses) are specifically disallowed. Each asset type and the treatment of its gains and losses are discussed in turn.

▲ CHARACTER OF GAIN OR LOSS

Capital gains and losses result from the disposition of capital assets. Historically, net capital gains have received preferential treatment over other types of income, whereas deductions for capital losses have been limited. The various preferences and limitations applicable to capital gains have varied throughout the years, depending on the economic and political climate. In more recent times (i.e., before 1987), 60 percent of an individual's net long-term capital gains was allowed as a deduction for adjusted gross income. Thus, only 40 percent of a net long-term capital gain was subject to tax. During this period, the top marginal tax rate was 50 percent. This meant that the actual maximum marginal tax rate on a long-term capital gain was only 20 percent (40% × 50%). For a taxpayer in the 50-percent marginal tax rate bracket, classifying a gain as a capital gain produced significant tax savings.

The basic economic rationale for extending favorable treatment to long-term gains on capital assets is that such gains result from holding the property for a long time. During this holding period, inflation acts to reduce the purchasing power of the gains realized. The reduction of the gain subject to tax is often justified as necessary to offset the inflationary effects, which have less impact on assets held for a short time. Although this is true for assets held for lengthy

▲ CAPITAL GAINS AND LOSSES

periods, it is not necessarily true for the one-year holding period that qualifies a disposition for long-term capital gain treatment. A better justification for a differential rate of tax for long-term capital gains is that it provides incentives for investors to provide capital to companies on a more permanent basis, thereby expanding the amount of capital available to companies and lowering the cost of capital.

Whatever the rationale for extending preferential treatment to long-term capital gains, capital gains have been an important part of the tax law almost from its inception. Although much of the benefit of capital gains was removed in 1986 by the elimination of the 60-percent capital gains deduction, all the mechanisms for calculating net capital gains and losses for the year are still part of the tax law. More important, the limits on deductibility of net capital losses (discussed in Chapter 7) remained in effect after the 1986 repeal of the capital gains deduction.

Capital Asset Definition

A *capital asset* is defined as any asset that is not

1. An inventory item
2. A receivable
3. Real or depreciable property used in a trade or business
4. A copyright, literary, musical, or artistic composition, letter or memorandum, or similar property held by the person creating the property or held by a person who received the property as a gift from its creator
5. Certain U.S. government publications[3]

A cursory examination of the list of properties that are not capital assets reveals that most trade or business assets are not capital assets. The first three categories excluded from capital asset status form the asset core of any business.

The fourth category consists of assets that are essentially inventories for their creators and are thus excluded from capital asset status. For example, an artist is in the trade or business of creating paintings. Artists who sell their paintings are like merchants who sell inventory. The exclusion of such property for anyone who receives it as a gift from its creator is intended to stop the conversion of ordinary income to capital gain income through gifts of the property. However, note that not all sales of paintings would constitute inventory sales. For example, a collector of art may purchase a painting for long-term appreciation. For the collector, the painting is a capital asset that creates a capital gain or loss upon disposition.

The last category of assets was added to the list of noncapital assets to stop former presidents of the United States from obtaining large charitable contribution deductions for giving their papers to nonprofit organizations after they left office. As such, it is not of concern to most taxpayers.

Long-Term versus Short-Term Classification

Preferential treatment for capital gains has always been limited to net long-term capital gains. Therefore, all capital gains and losses must be classified as either short or long term. In order to be a long-term gain or loss, the property must be held for more than one year. Gains and losses from property held exactly one year or less are short-term gains and losses.[4]

The holding period of an asset is generally the length of time the taxpayer actually owns the property. However, situations arise that do not fit this rule and that are inequitable if the law were strictly applied.

▲ **EXAMPLE 10**   Heidi received 100 shares of stock from her uncle Guiseppi as a graduation present. Guiseppi had paid $600 for the shares 5 years earlier. On the date of the gift, the shares were worth $2,000. One month after receiving the shares, Heidi sold them for $2,100, net of commissions. What is Heidi's gain on the sale of the stock? Is the gain short-term or long-term?

Discussion: Heidi's gain on the sale is $1,500 ($2,100 − $600). Because the fair market value of the shares on the date of the gift was greater than her uncle's basis, Heidi's basis is equal to her uncle's basis. Although Heidi has personally held the stock for only 1 month, the gain on the stock is the result of holding the shares for more than 5 years. Therefore, the gain on the sale of the stock is a long-term capital gain.

Example 10 illustrates a basic rule for determining the holding period of a property: Whenever a taxpayer's basis is determined, either in whole or in part, by reference to another asset's basis, the holding period of the other asset is included in the taxpayer's holding period. Under this rule, the prior holding period of any property with a carryover basis (see Chapter 10) is added to the current holding period. However, if the taxpayer's basis is made by reference to a market value at the date of acquisition, the holding period begins at the date of acquisition. The primary exception to the market value rule is for inherited property, which is always considered long term.[5]

▲ **EXAMPLE 11**   Rolf received a gift of stock from his mother, Sheila, as a graduation present. Sheila had paid $500 for the stock 5 years earlier. On the date of the gift, the stock was worth $400. Six months later, Rolf sold the stock for $350. What is Rolf's gain (loss) on the sale of the stock? Is the gain (loss) short term or long term?

Discussion: Because the fair market value of the stock at the date of the gift was less than Sheila's basis, the split basis rule for gifts applies. Rolf's basis for computing losses is equal to the fair market value of the stock on the date of the gift. Rolf has a loss of $50 ($350 − $400) on the sale. The loss is a short-term capital loss, because he held the stock for only 6 months. Rolf does not get his mother's holding period, because Rolf's basis is the fair market value at the date of acquisition.

▲ **EXAMPLE 12**   Assume the same facts as in example 11, except that Rolf sold the stock 6 months later for $600. What is Rolf's gain (loss) on the sale? Is the gain (loss) short term or long term?

Discussion: Under the split basis rule for gifts, Rolf's basis for determining gain is his mother's basis. Rolf has a gain of $100 ($600 − $500) on the sale of the stock. Because Rolf's basis is Sheila's basis, he receives his mother's holding period. Thus, Rolf has a $100 long-term capital gain on the sale.

Capital Gain-and-Loss Netting Procedure

Exhibit 12–2 presents the procedure for determining the net capital gain or loss for a tax year.[6] The first step in the process is to identify all gains and losses from the sale of capital assets during the year. The gains and losses are then separated into short-term and long-term gains and losses per the holding period of the property sold.

The second step is to combine all the capital gains and losses for the year into a single position. That is, the taxpayer has either gained in total from capital asset dispositions during the year or has lost in total during the year. This is accomplished by first netting together all short-term gains and losses to produce a single net short-term gain or loss amount for the year. The long-term gains and losses are also netted together to produce a net long-term gain or loss amount for the

▲ **Exhibit 12–2**

CAPITAL GAIN-AND-LOSS
NETTING PROCEDURE

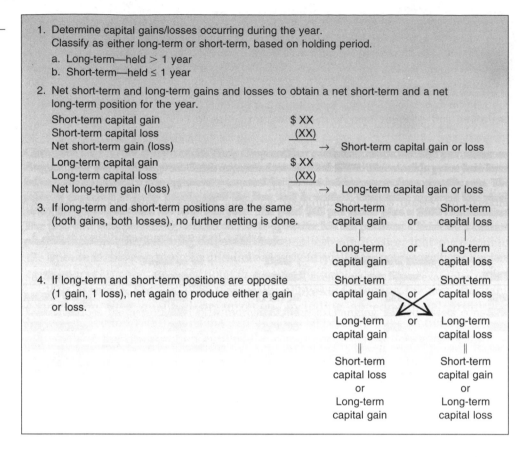

1. Determine capital gains/losses occurring during the year.
   Classify as either long-term or short-term, based on holding period.
   a. Long-term—held > 1 year
   b. Short-term—held ≤ 1 year

2. Net short-term and long-term gains and losses to obtain a net short-term and a net long-term position for the year.

Short-term capital gain	$ XX
Short-term capital loss	(XX)
Net short-term gain (loss)	→ Short-term capital gain or loss
Long-term capital gain	$ XX
Long-term capital loss	(XX)
Net long-term gain (loss)	→ Long-term capital gain or loss

3. If long-term and short-term positions are the same (both gains, both losses), no further netting is done.

   Short-term capital gain **or** Short-term capital loss
   |
   Long-term capital gain **or** Long-term capital loss

4. If long-term and short-term positions are opposite (1 gain, 1 loss), net again to produce either a gain or loss.

   Short-term capital gain **or** Short-term capital loss
   Long-term capital gain **or** Long-term capital loss
   ‖ ‖
   Short-term capital loss **or** Short-term capital gain
   or **or**
   Long-term capital gain Long-term capital loss

year. If the result of these two nettings is the same—both are losses or both are gains—no further netting is required; a single position of gain or loss has been achieved. However, if the results of the first netting are opposite—one is a gain and one is a loss—a second netting is necessary to obtain a single position for the year, either a gain or a loss. In doing the capital gain-and-loss nettings, keep in mind that the ultimate goal of the netting is to reduce all capital gains and losses for the year to a single net position—the taxpayer has either gained or lost on the whole for the year and that is the position that ultimately affects the taxpayer's taxable income.

▲ **EXAMPLE 13**   Johanna had the following capital gains and losses for the current tax year:

Short-term capital gains	$ 5,000
Long-term capital gains	4,000
Short-term capital losses	(6,000)
Long-term capital losses	(12,000)

What is Johanna's net capital gain (loss) position for the year?

Discussion: Johanna has a net short-term capital loss of $1,000 and a net long-term capital loss of $8,000 for the year:

Short-term capital gains	$5,000	
Short-term capital losses	(6,000)	
Net short-term capital loss		$(1,000)

Long-term capital gains	$ 4,000	
Long-term capital losses	(12,000)	
Net long-term capital loss		$(8,000)

Because the short- and long-term positions are both losses, no further netting is necessary. Johanna's capital asset transactions for the year have produced a loss.

▲ **EXAMPLE 14**   Assume the same facts as in example 13, except that Johanna's long-term capital gains for the year totaled $20,000 instead of $4,000. What is Johanna's net capital gain (loss) position for the year?

Discussion: Johanna has a net long-term capital gain of $7,000 for the year:

Short-term capital gains	$5,000	
Short-term capital losses	(6,000)	
Net short-term capital loss		$(1,000)
Long-term capital gains	$20,000	
Long-term capital losses	(12,000)	
Net long-term capital gain		8,000
Net long-term capital gain		$ 7,000

Because the short-term position was a $1,000 loss and the long-term position was an $8,000 gain, the short-term and long-term positions are netted again to produce a single position for the year, which is a $7,000 long-term capital gain.

The tax law prescribes the treatment of the gain or loss after the position for the year has been determined. Table 12–1 summarizes these treatments for individuals and corporations.

Capital Gain/Loss Position	Individual Treatment	Corporate Treatment
Net short-term capital gain	Ordinary income.	Ordinary income.
Net short-term capital loss	Deductible loss for AGI; limited to $3,000 per year with indefinite carryforward of excess loss to future years' netting.	No current deduction; may carry back 3 years and forward 5 years to offset capital gains.
Net long-term capital gain	Taxed at a maximum rate of 28%.	Ordinary income.
Net long-term capital loss	Deductible loss for AGI; limited to $3,000 per year with indefinite carryforward of excess loss to future years' netting. Any short-term losses are applied against the $3,000 limit before long-term capital losses are deducted.	No current deduction; may carry back 3 years and forward 5 years to offset capital gains.

▲ **Table 12–1**

TREATMENT OF CAPITAL GAINS AND LOSSES

A review of Table 12–1 reveals that under current tax law only net long-term capital gains are accorded tax relief. Net long-term capital gains of individuals are subject to a maximum tax rate of 28 percent.[7] Under the current tax rate structure, only individuals in the 31-percent marginal tax brackets and higher receive any capital gains tax relief.

▲ **EXAMPLE 15**   Return to the facts of example 14. Johanna had a net long-term capital gain of $7,000 for the current year. Assuming that she is a single individual whose taxable income from all other sources was $100,000 during the current year, what amount of tax relief does Johanna receive on her $7,000 net long-term capital gain?

Discussion: Johanna's taxable income for the year is $107,000. From the tax rate schedules in Appendix A, Johanna is in the 31% marginal tax rate bracket. Therefore, the tax on her $7,000 net long-term capital gain is limited to a maximum rate of 28%. This yields a tax of $1,960 ($7,000 × 28%) on the capital gain versus a tax of $2,170 ($7,000 × 31%) at Johanna's marginal tax rate. Her tax savings from the net long-term capital gain is $210 [$7,000 × (31% − 28%)].

▲ **EXAMPLE 16**   Assume, in example 15, that Johanna's taxable income from other sources was only $30,000 during the current year. What amount of tax relief does Johanna receive on her $7,000 net long-term capital gain?

Discussion: Johanna's taxable income for the year is $37,000. From the tax rate schedules in Appendix A, Johanna is in the 28% marginal tax rate bracket. Because the maximum tax rate on long-term capital gains of 28% is equal to her marginal tax rate, Johanna receives no tax relief on her $7,000 net long-term capital gain.

Note also that short-term capital gains of individuals and all net capital gains of corporations are treated as ordinary income. They receive no special tax relief under current law. It would seem, then, that these capital gains and losses have no tax significance. Although this is true whenever an individual or a corporation has a net capital gain position for the year, the primary benefit of these gains is through the capital gain-and-loss netting procedure. That is, these gains can be used to offset and reduce capital losses occurring during the year. As shown in Table 12–1 (and covered in Chapter 7), capital loss deductions for both individuals and corporations are limited. Therefore, a tax benefit does result to the extent that a net short-term gain is used to offset a capital loss in the netting procedure.

The loss treatments in Table 12–1 are the same treatments studied in Chapter 7. The one refinement presented in this chapter is the ranking of the loss deductions for individuals. Individuals are allowed to deduct as much as $3,000 per year in net capital losses. When an individual has both a net short-term capital loss and a net long-term capital loss during the same year, the short-term losses are applied against the $3,000 limit first. Although this ranking has no effect under current law, it is an outgrowth of treatments of capital losses before 1987. Under prior law, each dollar of net long-term capital losses yielded only 50 cents of deductible loss. This means that a $2,000 net long-term capital loss yielded only a $1,000 deduction under prior law. Taking the fully deductible short-term losses first against the $3,000 limit was beneficial to the taxpayer under prior law. Under current law, both long-term and short-term capital losses are deductible dollar for dollar. However, the tax law still requires that short-term losses be deducted first.

▲ **EXAMPLE 17**   Return to the facts of example 13 in which Johanna had a net short-term capital loss of $1,000 and a net long-term capital loss of $8,000 during the current year. How much of the losses can Johanna deduct in the current year, and how much is carried forward to subsequent years?

Discussion: Johanna is allowed to deduct a maximum of $3,000 in capital losses per year with any excess loss carried forward to subsequent years. Johanna's total capital loss for the year is $9,000. Her $3,000 deduction is composed of the $1,000 short-term capital loss and $2,000 of the long-term capital loss. The remaining $6,000 of the net long-term capital loss is carried forward and used in the next year's netting as a $6,000 long-term capital loss carryforward.

Capital Gain Exclusion on Qualified Small Business Stock.

To stimulate investment in certain small businesses, the Omnibus Budget Reconciliation Act of 1993 added Section 1202 to the Code. The incentive provided by Section 1202 allows 50 percent of the gains (not reduced by any capital losses) from qualified small business stock that is held for more than five years to be excluded from taxation. The effect of the provision is to limit the marginal tax rate on such gains to a maximum of 14 percent (50% $\times$ 28% maximum capital gains rate). The maximum gain that can be excluded in a year is limited to the greater of 10 times the investor's basis in the stock or $10 million for each qualified small business. One-half of the exclusion amount is treated as a tax preference under the individual alternative minimum tax provisions (discussed in Chapter 14).

▲ **EXAMPLE 18**   Isabel purchased 1,000 shares of qualified small business stock on November 19, 1995. On December 20, 2000, Isabel sells the 1,000 shares at a gain of $120,000. What is the effect of the sale of the stock on Isabel's tax liability, assuming that she had no other capital asset transactions in the year 2000 and is in the 36% marginal tax bracket?

Discussion: Because the stock is qualified small business stock that Isabel held for more than 5 years, she excludes 50% of the gain, $60,000, from her capital gain income. Because she has no other capital gains and losses during the year 2000, her net capital gain position is a net long-term capital gain of $60,000 ($120,000 gain $-$ $60,000 exclusion). The gain is taxed at the 28% maximum capital gains tax rate, resulting in a tax liability of $16,800 ($60,000 $\times$ 28%). Note that tax on the gain is 14% of the total gain ($16,800 $\div$ $120,000 = 14%).

▲ **EXAMPLE 19**   Assume the same facts as in example 18, except that Isabel has a net capital loss of $20,000 from her other capital asset transactions in the year 2000. What is the effect of the sale of the stock on Isabel's tax liability in the year 2000?

Discussion: The 50% exclusion is taken before the capital gain-and-loss netting. Therefore, Isabel is entitled to an exclusion of $60,000. The $60,000 long-term capital gain that remains after the exclusion is netted against the $20,000 capital loss, resulting in a net long-term capital gain of $40,000. Isabel's tax on the $40,000 net long-term capital gain is $11,200 ($40,000 $\times$ 28%).

Qualifying small business stock is stock originally issued after August 10, 1993, by a corporation that did not have gross assets in excess of $50 million after August 10, 1993, and before the stock issuance. The stock must be purchased at its original issue directly from the corporation or through its underwriter. That is, the stock cannot be acquired from another individual or entity. The small business issuing the stock must generally be an active corporation that uses substantially all its assets (at least 80 percent of the value) in the active conduct of a trade or business during the five-year holding period. Generally, only stock in manufacturing, retailing, and wholesaling businesses qualify for the exclusion. Banking, leasing, real estate, farming, mineral extraction, and hotels, motels, restaurants, or similar businesses are specifically denied treatment as qualified small business stock. In addition, the stock of certain service corporations does not qualify.

Non-qualifying service corporations include those in the fields of health, law, engineering, accounting, architecture, performing arts, athletics, and financial and brokerage services.

Only noncorporate investors are eligible to claim the exclusion. Conduit entities, such as partnerships and S corporations, may hold qualified small business stock and may be able to pass the gain through to a partner or shareholder eligible for the exclusion.

▲ **EXAMPLE 20**   GARS Partnership was organized by 4 equal owners: 3 individuals (Garth, Adam, and Rachelle) and Solide Corporation. GARS Partnership purchased 10,000 shares of Mystuk Corporation stock directly from the corporation for $100,000 at its original issue on December 11, 1995. Mystuk is a pharmaceutical manufacturing enterprise, the gross assets of which have never exceeded $35 million. GARS held the stock until December 30, 2000, when it was sold for $220,000. What are the tax implications of the sale for GARS Partnership and the partners?

Discussion: Mystuk Corporation stock qualifies as small business stock. Its gross assets did not exceed $50 million after August 10, 1993, and before the stock was issued. Mystuk is an active manufacturer, and the original issue of the stock was after August 10, 1993. GARS realized a $120,000 gain ($220,000 − $100,000) on the stock sale. Because GARS is a conduit entity, the gain passes through to the partners. Each partner is allocated 25%, or $30,000, of the gain. Garth, Adam, and Rachelle can exclude $15,000 (50% × $30,000) of their individual shares of the gain. However, Solide Corporation must recognize all $30,000 of its share of the partnership's realized gain. Corporations are not allowed the benefits of the 50% exclusion.

Capital Gains and Losses—Planning Strategies

Before the end of any tax year, taxpayers should analyze their net capital gain or loss position for the year and determine whether there are any actions they might take to use the capital gain-and-loss netting procedures to their advantage. In this regard, the taxpayer may be in either a net capital gain position or a net capital loss position before the end of the year.

Net Capital Gain Position.   A taxpayer with a net capital gain position will have to pay tax on the net capital gains for the year. Therefore, the taxpayer should consider reducing the net capital gain by selling capital assets on which there is an unrealized loss. To obtain the maximum tax benefit, the taxpayer should take losses that cancel out the net capital gain to date. In addition, individuals can take $3,000 in losses over and above the net capital gain to take advantage of the net capital loss deduction provisions.

▲ **EXAMPLE 21**   Before the end of the current year, Ramsey has a net long-term capital gain of $20,000 on all capital asset transactions occurring throughout the year. What is Ramsey's optimal year-end tax-planning strategy for capital gains and losses?

Discussion: Any capital losses Ramsey realizes before the end of the year will reduce the $20,000 net long-term capital gain. Optimally, Ramsey will sell capital assets with unrealized losses to produce additional capital losses of $23,000. This will change his capital gain/loss position to a net loss of $3,000 ($20,000 − $23,000) for the year. He will then be able to deduct the entire $3,000 of net capital loss.

STRATEGY PITFALL: If Ramsey sells stock to create the $23,000 loss, he will not be able to repurchase any shares of the same company for 30 days. If he repurchases shares in the same company within 30 days, the wash sale rules disallow the loss on the shares replaced. Therefore, this strategy is contingent upon the taxpayer's either not desiring to remain a shareholder in the loss shares or being willing to wait more than 30 days to replace the shares.

Net Capital Loss Position.   A taxpayer with a net capital loss position before the end of the year should act to avoid the limitations on capital loss deductions. For individuals, the optimal action is to take unrealized capital gains to reduce the net capital loss for the year to the $3,000 maximum deduction amount.

▲ **EXAMPLE 22**   Golda has a net capital loss of $15,000 before the end of the current tax year. What is Golda's optimal year-end tax-planning strategy for capital gains and capital losses?

Discussion: Because Golda can deduct only $3,000 of her $15,000 net capital loss, Golda should sell capital assets with unrealized gains to produce a capital gain of $12,000. The effect of the strategy is to fully use the net capital loss within the current period by offsetting the loss with a capital gain.

Note that if Golda sells securities to produce the desired capital gain, nothing prevents her from repurchasing the shares, because there is no gain equivalent to the rules that disallow wash sale losses.

Example 22 illustrates the previously mentioned benefit of capital gains under current tax law—the ability to deduct capital gains against capital losses that would otherwise be nondeductible in the current period. Taxpayers in net capital loss situations may take capital gains that are essentially tax free in the current period and take advantage of the capital gain-and-loss netting procedure.

Short Sales.   Another tax-planning strategy available to taxpayers is a short sale against the box. This technique allows taxpayers to lock in gains on securities in the current period and defer recognition of the gain to the next period. The strategy provides a mechanism for deferring a gain to a period with lower marginal tax rates and takes advantage of the time value of money savings on the deferral of a gain.

A **short sale against the box** is a short sale of stock that the taxpayer already owns. Selling short is a technique for investing in a security that is expected to decline in value. Figure 12–2 illustrates the short-sale process.

In the first step of a true **short sale,** short sellers sell a security that they do not own and receive the net selling price from the buyer. Because short sellers do not actually own the securities, they borrow them from their brokers, who give the actual shares of stock to the buyers. At a later date, the short seller purchases the shares previously sold on the open market and gives them back to the broker to repay the shares borrowed at the initial short-sale date. This is called *closing the short sale.* The short seller's profit or loss is the difference between what the shares were sold for in the first step minus the price that the short seller paid to buy the shares back in the second step. Short sellers are betting that the shares sold short will decline in value and they will be able to buy them back for less than they were initially sold.

The potential deferral mechanism of the short sale is that the gain or loss on the short sale cannot be determined until the buy-back price is known at the closing of the short sale (i.e., step 2 is completed). Thus, shares sold short in December and repurchased in January do not produce a recognized gain or loss until January.[8]

▲ **EXAMPLE 23**   Galen sold short 100 shares of Harvest Co. common stock on December 22 for $25 per share. He paid a commission on the short sale of $2 per share. By

▲ **Figure 12–2**

SHORT SALES

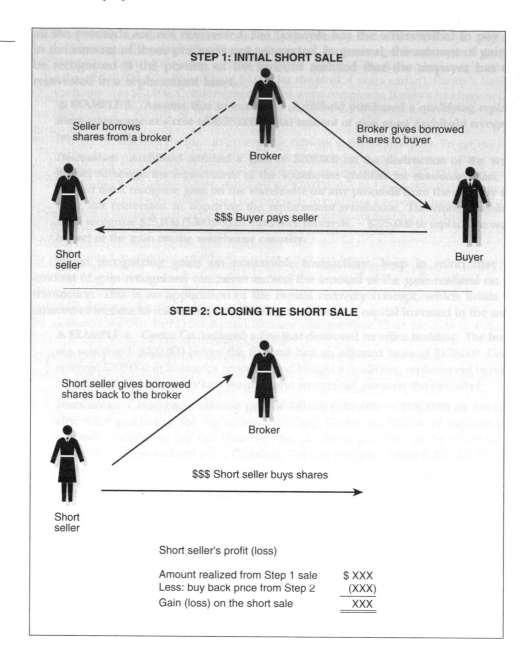

STEP 1: INITIAL SHORT SALE

Seller borrows
shares from a broker

Broker

Broker gives borrowed
shares to buyer

$$$ Buyer pays seller

Short
seller

Buyer

STEP 2: CLOSING THE SHORT SALE

Short seller gives borrowed
shares back to the broker

Broker

$$$ Short seller buys shares

Short
seller

Short seller's profit (loss)

Amount realized from Step 1 sale	$ XXX
Less: buy back price from Step 2	(XXX)
Gain (loss) on the short sale	XXX

January 5 of the next year, Harvest Co. stock had declined in value to $13 per share. Galen purchased the 100 shares sold short for $13 per share and paid $1 per share in commissions on the purchase. Galen gave the 100 shares to his broker to close the December 22 short sale. What is Galen's gain (loss) on the short-sale, and when is it recognized for tax purposes?

Discussion: Galen realized $2,300 [100 × ($25 − $2)] from the short sale, and he has a basis in the shares purchased to close the short sale of $1,400 [100 × ($13 + $1)]. Galen has realized a gain of $900 ($2,300 − $1,400) on the short sale that will not be recognized for tax purposes until January when the short sale is closed.

▲ **EXAMPLE 24**   Assume the same facts as in example 23, except that the value of the Harvest Co. stock increased and Galen had to repurchase the shares for $35 per share and he paid a $3 per-share commission on the purchase. What is Galen's gain (loss) on the short sale, and when is it recognized for tax purposes?

Discussion: In this case, Galen's basis in the repurchased shares is $3,800 [100 × ($35 + $3)]. Galen has realized a loss of $1,500 ($2,300 − $3,800) on the short sale that is recognized for tax purposes in January.

In a short sale against the box, a short sale is made of shares that the taxpayer already owns. That is, the taxpayer executes step 1 of the short-sale process. Shares are sold, and borrowed shares are given to the buyer. The short sale is then closed by giving the shares already owned (rather than buying them on the market) to the broker in the next tax year. This allows the taxpayer to lock in a gain on the shares owned in the current tax year while deferring recognition of the gain until the next tax year.

▲ **EXAMPLE 25**   Priscilla owns 500 shares of Rocker common stock that she acquired early this year at a cost of $20 per share. The stock has increased in value this year and is worth $45 per share in December. Priscilla is afraid that the stock will soon decline in value and would like to take her profit. The problem is that she is already in the 31% marginal tax rate bracket this year and would like to take the gain next year when she anticipates being in a lower tax bracket. What options are available to Priscilla? What are the consequences of these options?

Discussion: Priscilla has 3 options. She can sell the stock in the current year and pay tax on the gain at her 31% marginal tax rate (because Priscilla has held the stock less than 1 year, it will be taxed as ordinary income). Her second option is to wait and sell the stock next year and pay tax in the next year. The risk of this option is that the stock will decline in value before she sells and she will lose some of her profit.

The third option is to sell the 500 shares short at the current market value and complete the short sale next year by giving the 500 shares she owns to the broker. Ignoring transaction costs, this option would allow her to realize the $22,500 (500 × $45) of current market value and defer recognition of her $12,500 [$22,500 − (500 × $20)] gain on the short sale until the next year, when the short sale is completed.

Note the difference in the basic short sale and the short sale against the box: In a true short sale, the profit (loss) on the shares sold short is not known until the short sale is closed by purchasing the shares. In a short sale against the box, the profit is known when the initial short sale is made, because the short seller knows the basis of the shares that will be used to complete the short sale. This technique allows taxpayers to lock in gains on stocks near the end of the year and defer recognition of the gains until the next tax year.

Worthless Securities.   When a security becomes worthless, a technical disposition does not take place. However, the tax law recognizes the loss of investment suffered by the taxpayer in such situations; taxpayers with **worthless securities** are deemed to have realized the loss on the last day of the tax year in which the security is determined to be worthless. The realized loss is equal to the basis of the worthless security. The last day of the tax year is the date of realization in determining the holding period of the security for classification of the loss as short or long term.[9]

▲ **EXAMPLE 26**   Zev owns 500 shares of Newstart Co. that he purchased on November 4, 1995, for $20,000. In April 1996, Newstart declares bankruptcy, and Zev is unable to sell his shares. The bankruptcy court liquidates the company, and the shareholders receive no cash for their stock. How should Zev treat the loss on his Newstart stock?

Discussion: The Newstart stock is deemed to be worthless on December 31, 1996, which is when Zev realizes the loss of his $20,000 basis. The loss is a long-term capital loss, because Zev has held the stock for more than one year (November 4, 1995, to December 31, 1996). NOTE: If the stock in Newstart was qualified small business stock, Zev could deduct the loss as an ordinary loss (see Chapter 7).

Basis of Securities Sold.   When taxpayers sell only some of the securities they hold, the shares being sold must be identified if the securities were purchased at different times and at different prices. Because securities are generic, it is often difficult to precisely identify specific shares as from a specific purchase. The tax law provides that, in the absence of a specific identification of the shares sold, the shares are sold in a first-in, first-out order (FIFO).[10]

▲ **EXAMPLE 27**   DeWitt sold 400 shares of Rubble, Inc., common stock for $8,000 and paid a $500 commission on the sale. DeWitt had purchased his Rubble shares as follows:

Purchase Date	Number of Shares	Total Cost
February 1994	200	$3,000
November 1994	300	$3,000

What is DeWitt's gain or loss on the sale of the 400 shares?

Discussion: DeWitt's amount realized on the sale of the 400 shares is $7,500 ($8,000 − $500). Because he purchased the 500 shares at two different times and at different prices, he must either specifically identify the shares sold or determine the basis of the 400 shares in first-in, first-out order. Assuming that DeWitt cannot specifically identify the 400 shares, his basis would be $5,000:

Basis of 200 shares from February purchase	$3,000
Basis of 200 shares from November purchase	
$3,000 ÷ 300 = $10 per share × 200 shares	2,000
Basis of 400 shares	$5,000

DeWitt would realize a gain of $2,500 ($7,500 − $5,000) on the sale of the shares.

The first-in, first-out rule for the sale of securities can be overridden by directing in writing that certain lots of securities are to be sold. Thus, a taxpayer who has purchased shares at different times and at different prices can determine the amount of gain or loss to be recognized on a particular sale of shares.

▲ **EXAMPLE 28**   Cathi owns 600 shares of Wetzel's Pretzels common stock. Cathi purchased the 600 shares as follows:

Purchase Date	Number of Shares	Total Cost
October 1991	200	$ 6,000
May 1992	200	$ 9,000
December 1993	200	$14,000

Before December 28, 1995, Cathi has a net capital gain of $7,000. On December 28, 1995, Wetzel's Pretzel's stock is trading for $60 per share. If Cathi wants to sell some Wetzel's Pretzel stock to decrease her 1995 taxable income, what should she do?

Discussion: The optimal strategy in a net capital gain situation is to take capital losses to reduce capital gain income. In this case, Cathi should direct her broker, in writing, to sell the 200 shares purchased in December 1993. Ignoring sales commissions, the sale would result in a $2,000 [(200 × $60) − $14,000] capital loss, reducing her net capital gain to $5,000.

If Cathi does not specify in writing the precise shares to be sold, the October 1991 shares would be sold under the FIFO rule, resulting in a $6,000 ($12,000 − $6,000) capital gain. However, by specifying that the loss shares be sold, Cathi can control whether she has a gain or a loss on the sale.

▲ SECTION 1231 GAINS AND LOSSES

The discussion of capital assets noted that most business assets do not receive capital gain (loss) treatment. Therefore, dispositions of assets used in a trade or business would generally produce ordinary gains and losses. However, Congress has provided capital gain relief for certain long-lived business assets. The rationale for this treatment is that long-lived assets sold at a gain have characteristics common to capital assets and deserve the same treatment in order to negate inflationary gains and to promote capital investment in long-lived business assets. The assets accorded this special relief are referred to as *Section 1231 property*. The basic intention of Section 1231 is to provide long-term capital gain status to net **Section 1231 gains** for a tax year while preserving the ordinary loss deduction for years in which a business has net **Section 1231 losses.** Therefore, this provision provides the best of both worlds—preferential capital gain treatment for net gains and ordinary loss deductions for net losses.

Definition of Section 1231 Property

Assets eligible for the preferential treatment under Section 1231 include

1. Property used in a trade or business that is held for more than one year and that is depreciable property or real property

2. Timber, coal, and domestic iron ore

3. Cattle and horses held for draft, breeding, dairy and sporting purposes that are held for 24 months or more

4. Other livestock held for draft, breeding, dairy, and sporting purposes that are held for 12 months or more

5. Unharvested crops

The assets qualifying for Section 1231 treatment must be held for more than one year, consistent with the holding period requirement for long-term capital gains. Assets that are held for less than a year are never given Section 1231 treatment and always produce ordinary income. The first category affects most businesses, because the category includes all fixed assets of a business. Note that **Section 1231 property** is property that is used primarily to operate the business. Property such as inventory that is sold to produce the income of the business generally is not Section 1231 property. However, the last three categories are inventory-type items for which Congress has applied the legislative grace concept in order to grant the special treatment provided by Section 1231.

Section 1231 Netting Procedure

As with capital gains and losses, the tax treatments accorded Section 1231 property apply to the net gain or loss on all Section 1231 transactions occurring during a tax year. The netting procedure involves two separate nettings of transactions occurring during the current tax year and a separate netting of any net Section 1231 gains in the current year against net 1231 loss deductions taken during the previous five years. Figure 12–3 outlines the netting procedure.[11]

The first step in the **Section 1231 netting procedure** is to net together all casualty (theft) gains and losses on Section 1231 property to produce a single net casualty gain or loss for the year. If the result of the first netting is a loss, all casualty gains and losses for the year are considered ordinary losses. This results in a net ordinary casualty loss deduction for the year. If the result of the first netting is a gain, the net casualty gain is carried into the second netting. The purpose of this separate netting of casualty and theft losses is to provide the maximum benefit possible for casualty and theft losses—ordinary loss deductions for net casualty losses and capital gain treatment of net casualty gains.

In the second netting, all other Section 1231 gains and losses occurring during the year are netted together with any net casualty gain from the first netting. As in the first netting, if the result of the second netting is a loss, all gains and losses for the year are considered ordinary. This results in a net ordinary loss deduction for Section 1231 transactions for the year.

▲ **Figure 12–3**

SECTION 1231 NETTING

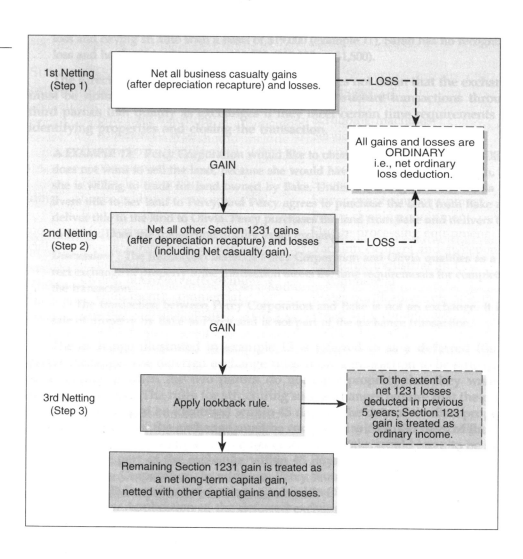

▲ **EXAMPLE 29**   After summarizing the results of all its transactions for the year, Bemigi Corporation had the following gains and losses from Section 1231 property:

Casualty gains	$23,000
Casualty losses	(5,000)
Section 1231 gains	35,000
Section 1231 losses	(60,000)

What is the effect of the Section 1231 transactions on Bemigi's taxable income for the current year?

Discussion: In order to determine the tax effect, Bemigi must go through the Section 1231 netting procedure:

Step 1: Net all casualty gains and losses

Casualty gains	$23,000
Casualty losses	(5,000)
Net casualty gain	$18,000

Because this netting results in a gain, the net gain is carried to the second netting.

Step 2: Net all other 1231 gains and losses with the net casualty gain

Net casualty gain	$ 18,000
Section 1231 gains	35,000
Section 1231 losses	(60,000)
Net Section 1231 loss	$ (7,000)

Because the Section 1231 netting produced a loss, all Section 1231 gains and losses for the year are considered ordinary losses. The result is that the Section 1231 transactions reduce Bemigi's taxable income by $7,000. This is a favorable result, because there are no restrictions on the deductibility of an ordinary loss.

When the result of the second netting is a gain, another netting must take place. This netting is required by the **lookback recapture rule,** which effectively nets the current-year net Section 1231 gain against any Section 1231 ordinary loss deductions taken in the previous five years. Any current-year net Section 1231 gain in excess of Section 1231 ordinary losses deducted in the previous five years is treated as a long-term capital gain. After applying the lookback rule's netting, the Section 1231 gain is added to other long-term capital gains and combined with other capital gains and losses in the capital gain-and-loss netting.

▲ **EXAMPLE 30**   Assume that Bemigi Corporation had the following Section 1231 gains and losses in the next year (according to the results in example 29). What is the tax treatment of the Section 1231 gains and losses if Bemigi's only Section 1231 transactions during the previous 5 years were those that produced the $7,000 Section 1231 loss in example 29?

Casualty loss	$(8,000)
Section 1231 gains	33,000
Section 1231 losses	(6,000)

Discussion: The Section 1231 netting procedure results in the following:

Step 1: The casualty loss is an ordinary loss. It is not carried to the second netting.

Step 2: Net together the other Section 1231 gains and losses.

Section 1231 gains	$33,000
Section 1231 losses	(6,000)
Net Section 1231 gain	$27,000

Step 3: Because the second netting produced a net Section 1231 gain for the year, ordinary loss deductions taken under Section 1231 during the previous 5 years must be recaptured as ordinary income before any long-term capital gain treatment is allowed.

Net Section 1231 gain	$27,000
Section 1231 loss deduction from last year	(7,000)
Long-term capital gain	$20,000

The results of the Section 1231 netting are summarized as follows:

Ordinary casualty loss deduction	$(8,000)
Ordinary income under lookback rule	7,000
Long-term capital gain	20,000

The ordinary income from the lookback recapture rule and the ordinary loss from the casualty are combined (added or subtracted) in the calculation of Bemigi's taxable income. The $20,000 long-term capital gain is combined with any other capital gains and losses in the capital gain-and-loss netting procedure to determine its effect on taxable income.

Once ordinary Section 1231 loss deductions have been recaptured as ordinary income, they do not have to be recaptured again. The intent of the lookback rule is to net together ordinary loss deductions against net Section 1231 gains to equalize the characterization of gains and losses over the five-year lookback period. Once an ordinary loss deduction of one year has been offset by Section 1231 gain of a later year, there is no need for further recapture.

▲ **EXAMPLE 31**   Assume that in the year after that described in example 30, Bemigi Corporation had the following Section 1231 gains and losses:

Section 1231 gains	$40,000
Section 1231 losses	(12,000)

What is the effect of the Section 1231 gains and losses on Bemigi's taxable income?

Discussion: Bemigi has a net Section 1231 gain of $28,000 ($40,000 − $12,000) for the year. Because Bemigi recaptured all of its Section 1231 ordinary loss deductions last year, the entire $28,000 gain is a long-term capital gain. The $28,000 long-term capital gain is combined with other capital gains and capital losses in the capital gain-and-loss netting procedure.

Given that the current treatment of long-term capital gains is not of great benefit to many taxpayers (see Table 12–1), why is the Section 1231 capital gain relief important? As with any net capital gain, one benefit under current law is the reduction of otherwise currently nondeductible capital losses. Without the Section 1231 provisions, many taxpayers would pay tax on their gains from selling business assets while realizing little or no current relief from net capital losses.

▲ **EXAMPLE 32**   Assume that in example 30, which produced a net long-term capital gain of $20,000 from the Section 1231 netting, Bemigi also had the following capital gains and losses for the year. What is the treatment of the capital gains and losses?

Short-term capital gains	$13,000
Long-term capital losses	(30,000)

Discussion: The capital gain-and-loss netting procedure produces a net short-term capital gain of $3,000:

Short-term capital gain		$13,000
Long-term capital gain from Section 1231	$20,000	
Long-term capital loss	(30,000)	
Net long-term capital loss		(10,000)
Net short-term capital gain		$ 3,000

Note that without the long-term capital gain from the Section 1231 netting, Bemigi would have had a long-term capital loss of $17,000 ($13,000 − $30,000) for the year. As a corporation, Bemigi would not be allowed to deduct any of the capital loss in the current year. The capital loss would be carried back 3 years and used to offset net capital gains. If Bemigi had no capital gains in the carryback period, it could carry the capital loss forward for 5 years. However, because the Section 1231 netting produced a capital gain, Bemigi has effectively deducted the $17,000 loss in the current year.

Dispositions of Rental Activities

Guidelines for determining whether a rental activity is a trade or business were discussed in Chapter 5. We noted that because rental expenses are deductions for adjusted gross income, classification of a rental activity as a trade or business or a production-of-income activity does not affect the current deductibility of the rental expenses. However, the importance of the classification is in the treatment of the gain or loss from the disposition of the rental property. If the rental property is held for the production of income, any gain or loss on its disposition is a capital gain or loss. On the other hand, if the rental activity constitutes a trade or business, any gain or loss on the property is a Section 1231 gain or loss. Because the capital gain and Section 1231 netting procedures both treat net gains as capital gains, the main difference in treatments is for rental property sold at a loss.

▲ **EXAMPLE 33**   Teresa owns a rental property that has an adjusted basis of $120,000. During the current year, she sold the property for $100,000. Assuming that she had no other property transactions during the year, how much of the loss is deductible if the rental activity is considered a trade or business for Teresa? a production-of-income activity for Teresa?

Discussion: Teresa has realized a loss of $20,000 on the sale of the rental property. If the rental activity is a trade or business, the loss is a Section 1231 loss that is deductible in full as an ordinary loss. (With no other transactions during the year, the result of the 1231 netting procedure would be a $20,000 loss.)

If the rental activity is a production-of-income activity, the loss is a capital loss. Because she has no other property transactions during the current year, Teresa has a net capital loss of $20,000. Her current capital loss deduction is limited to $3,000.

In extending capital gain relief on assets held for more than one year through the capital gain and Section 1231 provisions, Congress was concerned that only gains derived from appreciation in the value of the property were granted tax relief. In many instances, the entire gain on the disposition of a property is derived from appreciation.

▲ DEPRECIATION RECAPTURE

▲ **EXAMPLE 34**   Raquel purchases 300 shares of Houston Co. stock on September 4, 1992, at a cost of $4,500. On April 5, 1995, Raquel sells the 300 shares of stock for $8,500. Is Raquel's $4,000 gain on the sale derived from appreciation in the value of the stock?

Discussion: Raquel's $4,000 gain is totally derived from appreciation in the price of the Houston Co. stock. Because Raquel is not allowed to recover any of her $4,500 investment in the stock until the stock is sold, any gain on the sale of the stock is attributable solely to price appreciation.

We can conclude from example 34 that when the investment in the asset is recovered only at disposition, any gain on the sale is derived from price appreciation. However, through depreciation deductions, taxable entities recover capital investments in many assets while the asset is used to produce income. As an asset is depreciated, the basis in the asset is reduced. When the asset is disposed of, the gain or loss is measured as the difference between the amount realized and the adjusted basis of the asset. As a result, some—and perhaps all—of the gain on the sale of a depreciable asset derives from depreciation previously deducted on the asset.

▲ **EXAMPLE 35**   In 1993, Latifa Corporation purchases a computer to be used solely in its trade or business at a cost of $15,000. Latifa elects to use straight-line depreciation on the computer. In 1995, when the adjusted basis of the computer is $9,000, the corporation sells the computer for $10,000. How much of Latifa's $1,000 gain on the sale derives from the depreciation it took on the computer?

Discussion: The entire $1,000 gain is attributable to depreciation. That is, the computer has not appreciated in value from its original acquisition cost. It has actually lost $5,000 in value since Latifa purchased it. Only because Latifa took $6,000 in depreciation on the computer (reducing its basis) did the corporation have a gain.

Example 35 illustrates the basic rationale for disallowing long-term capital gain treatment for gains from depreciation deductions. Although the computer has lost $5,000 in value, the $6,000 in depreciation taken on the computer has resulted in a gain of $1,000 on the sale of the computer. This gain is created by the depreciation that was deducted as an ordinary expense for the business, reducing the tax on ordinary income. Allowing long-term capital gain treatment on the sale of the computer would allow an ordinary deduction to create a capital gain on the disposition. As previously discussed, one purpose of the preferential treatment for capital gains and Section 1231 property is that the gains have been artificially increased by inflation. However, with depreciable assets, a portion of the gain is created through ordinary deductions. The purpose of the depreciation recapture rules is to reclassify gains from depreciation as ordinary income.

Recapture can be seen as giving back the ordinary deduction that created the gain. Only the gain remaining in excess of the recaptured amount is accorded capital gain or Section 1231 treatment. Thus, **depreciation recapture** is the reclassification as ordinary income of all or part of a gain on the disposition of a capital asset or a Section 1231 asset. The recaptured amount does not receive preferential treatment in the calculation of taxable income.

There are two primary recapture provisions, referred to as *Section 1245 recapture* and *Section 1250 recapture.* All depreciable assets must be classified as either a Section 1245 property or a Section 1250 property and the appropriate recapture rule applied when the asset is disposed of at a gain. In studying these provisions, keep in mind that the intent of the two provisions is to reclassify gains from depreciation as ordinary income. Depreciation deductions do not create losses. Therefore, the depreciation recapture provisions do not apply to depreciable assets sold at a loss.

Section 1245 Recapture Rule

Section 1245 property is subject to a full recapture of all depreciation taken as ordinary income.[12] The practical effect of this provision is to deny capital gain or Section 1231 treatment on any Section 1245 property that is disposed of at less than its original cost.

▲ **EXAMPLE 36**   Reactor Tractor Co. purchases machinery in 1993 at a cost of $40,000. In 1995, when the adjusted basis of the machinery is $15,000, Reactor sells the machinery for $26,000. The machinery is Section 1245 property. What is the character of the $11,000 gain on the sale of the machinery?

Discussion: Machinery used in a trade or business is a Section 1231 property. However, Reactor is required to recapture as ordinary income any gain on the sale that derives from depreciation before any of the gain is considered Section 1231 gain. In this case, the $11,000 gain is totally derived from the $25,000 ($40,000 − $15,000) in depreciation taken on the machinery. Therefore, all gain on the sale is ordinary income. None of the gain is eligible for treatment under the Section 1231 netting procedure.

▲ **EXAMPLE 37**   Assume the same facts as in example 36, except that the machinery is sold for $47,000, resulting in a gain on the sale of $32,000. What is the character of the $32,000 gain on the sale of the machinery?

Discussion: Of the total gain on the sale, $25,000 derives from the reduction in basis for depreciation and is recaptured as ordinary income. The remaining $7,000 of gain derives from price appreciation in the machinery and is characterized as gain from the sale of a Section 1231 asset.

Amount realized	$47,000
Adjusted basis ($40,000 − $25,000)	(15,000)
Gain on sale	$32,000
Gain from depreciation—ordinary income	(25,000)
Gain from price appreciation—Section 1231 gain	$ 7,000

These two examples illustrate a basic result of the **Section 1245 recapture rule:** No capital gain or Section 1231 treatment results from the sale of a Section 1245 property unless it is sold for more than its original cost. Note that the $7,000 in Section 1231 gain in example 37 is the appreciation in price from the $40,000 original cost to the $47,000 selling price. This result always holds for a Section 1245 property.

Section 1250 Recapture Rule

The recapture rule for gains on the sale of Section 1250 assets is more generous than under Section 1245. Under the **Section 1250 recapture rule,** only gains that are attributable to excess depreciation are recaptured as ordinary income. *Excess depreciation* is defined as the total depreciation taken to date, less the allowable straight-line depreciation on the asset.[13] Note that if a Section 1250 asset has been depreciated using the straight-line method, no recapture of depreciation occurs, because no excess depreciation has been deducted on the asset.

▲ **EXAMPLE 38**   Ragwood Co. purchased a factory building in 1980 at a cost of $800,000. The factory building is sold in 1995 for $700,000. The maximum allowable depreciation on the building as of the date of sale was $600,000. Straight-line depreciation for the same period would have been $400,000. The building is a Section 1250 property. What is the character of the gain on the sale of the building if Ragwood took the maximum allowable depreciation deduction on the building?

Discussion: The gain on the sale of the building is $500,000. The factory building is a Section 1231 property. However, before any of the gain is Section 1231 gain, the excess depreciation of $200,000 must be recaptured as ordinary income. This leaves $300,000 of Section 1231 gain:

Amount realized on sale	$ 700,000
Adjusted basis ($800,000 − $600,000)	(200,000)
Gain on sale	$ 500,000
Depreciation recapture—ordinary income	
($600,000 − $400,000)	(200,000)
Section 1231 gain	$ 300,000

▲ **EXAMPLE 39**   Assume that in example 38 Ragwood had deducted straight-line depreciation during the time it held the factory building. What is the character of the gain on the sale of the building?

Discussion: Using straight-line depreciation, the gain on the sale of the building would have been $300,000 [$700,000 − ($800,000 − $400,000)]. Because Ragwood used the straight-line method to depreciate the building, there is no excess depreciation to recapture. Thus, the entire $300,000 gain is Section 1231 gain.

A comparison of these examples reveals the basic result of the Section 1250 recapture rule: The Section 1231 gain (or capital gain) is always equal to the gain that would have occurred had straight-line depreciation been used. The gain remaining after depreciation recapture on a Section 1250 property is equal to the sum of the straight-line depreciation plus any price appreciation in the property. Note that this recapture result is more generous than that under Section 1245, which allows only true price appreciation to result in Section 1231 or capital gain.

▲ **EXAMPLE 40**   A depreciable asset used in a trade or business that was purchased for $80,000 was sold for $95,000. Actual depreciation deducted on the asset totaled $35,000. Allowable straight-line depreciation for the same period would have been $20,000. What is the character of the gain if the asset is a Section 1245 property? a Section 1250 property?

Discussion: The gain on the sale of the asset is $50,000 [$95,000 − ($80,000 − $35,000)]. The character of the gain under Section 1245 and Section 1250 is calculated as follows:

	Section 1245	Section 1250
Gain on Sale	$ 50,000	$ 50,000
Depreciation recapture—ordinary income		
Section 1245—all depreciation	(35,000)	
Section 1250—excess depreciation		
($35,000 − $20,000)		(15,000)
Section 1231 gain	$ 15,000	$ 35,000

Under Section 1245, the Section 1231 gain is equal to the price appreciation in the asset ($95,000 − $80,000). Under Section 1250, the Section 1231 gain is equal to the sum of the $15,000 price appreciation and the $20,000 straight-line depreciation deduction that is not recaptured under Section 1250.

The depreciation recapture rules apply to all depreciable assets.[14] There are no exceptions in the tax law that override the depreciation recapture rules. Whenever a gain is recognized on a depreciable asset, the applicable recapture rule must be applied to determine the character of the gain. In applying the recapture rules, any amounts expensed under Section 179 are considered depreciation. As a final reminder, the depreciation recapture rules apply only to gains caused by depreciation; losses are not subject to recapture.

Installment Sales of Depreciable Assets.   In an installment sale, gain is recognized proportionately in the years in which the taxable entity receives the sales proceeds (see Chapter 3). A special provision overrides the general installment sales recognition rules when a depreciable asset is sold in an installment sale. This provision requires all income characterized as ordinary income because of depreciation recapture to be recognized in the year of the sale.[15] Only the capital gain or Section 1231 gain on an installment sale is recognized using the installment sales method.

▲ **EXAMPLE 41**   Joe sold an apartment building he had purchased in 1985 as an investment. Joe had paid $190,000 for the building and had taken depreciation of $90,000 on the building up to the date of sale. Straight-line depreciation on the building would have been $50,000. The terms of the sale required the buyer to pay Joe $20,000 at closing and $50,000 per year for the next 4 years, with interest on the unpaid balance at 8%. The apartment building is Section 1250 property. How much gain must Joe recognize on the sale of the building in the year of sale, and what is the character of the gain to be recognized?

Discussion: The sale of the apartment building is an installment sale. Joe must use the installment sales method to recognize income from the sale, unless he elects to recognize the entire gain of $120,000 in the year of sale. Joe's realized gain and the character of the gain are calculated as follows:

Amount realized [$20,000 + ($50,000 × 4)]	$220,000
Adjusted basis ($190,000 − $90,000)	(100,000)
Realized gain on sale	$120,000
Section 1250 recapture—ordinary income	
Excess depreciation ($90,000 − $50,000)	(40,000)
Long-term capital gain	$ 80,000

Because the apartment building is depreciable property, the $40,000 in ordinary income from the recapture of depreciation must be recognized in the year of sale. Only the $80,000 long-term capital gain is recognized using the installment sales method. Joe would recognize $7,273 in long-term capital gain in the year of sale using the installment sales method:

$$\text{Gain recognized} = \frac{\text{Capital gain}}{\text{Contract price}} \times \text{Cash received}$$

$$\text{Gain recognized} = \frac{\$80,000}{\$220,000} \times \$20,000 = \$7,273$$

As each $50,000 installment payment is received, Joe will recognize $18,182 in long-term capital gain:

$$\text{Gain recognized} = \frac{\$80,000}{\$220,000} \times \$50,000 = \$18,182$$

Over the 5-year period of the installment sale, Joe's recognized gain and its character are as follows:

Character of Gain	Year 1	Year 2	Year 3	Year 4	Year 5	Total Gain
Ordinary	$40,000					$ 40,000
Capital	$ 7,273	$18,182	$18,182	$18,182	$18,181	$ 80,000
Total gain recognized						$120,000

Section 1245 and Section 1250 Properties

In order to apply the proper recapture rule, you must determine the type of depreciable property. Depreciable assets fall into two basic categories: tangible personal property and real property (see Chapter 11). Historically, the distinction between **Section 1245 property** and **Section 1250 property** was between these two basic classes of property. All depreciable tangible personal property was Section 1245 property, and all depreciable real property was Section 1250 property. Note that assets that are not depreciable because (1) they have indefinite lives (e.g., land) or (2) they are capital assets or Section 1231 assets that are not depreciable, are not subject to depreciation recapture. In 1981, the ACRS depreciation system drastically increased the allowable depreciation deductions on real property by allowing accelerated depreciation over a 15-year life. In allowing this rapid acceleration of depreciation on real property, Congress took back some of the benefit by reclassifying most real property as Section 1245 property using the accelerated ACRS method.

Table 12–2 compares the asset classifications for assets purchased before 1981 and those purchased after 1981. The key difference in classification of assets ac-

▲ **Table 12–2**

SECTION 1245 AND 1250 PROPERTIES

	Section 1245	Section 1250

Assets acquired before 1981	Depreciable personal property:
	  Autos, trucks, equipment
	  Machinery, computers
	  Greenhouses, grain silos
	  Patents, copyrights
	  Leaseholds
	  Livestock
		Depreciable real property:
		  Office buildings
		  Apartment buildings
		  Warehouses
		  Factory buildings
		  Low-income housing

Assets acquired 1981–1986	Depreciable personal property Depreciable real property that does not qualify as Section 1250 property	Residential rental property Low-income housing Any real property that has been depreciated using the straight-line method Real property used predominantly outside the U.S.

Assets acquired after 1986	Depreciable personal property:
	  Autos, trucks, equipment
	  Machinery, computers
	  Greenhouses, grain silos
	  Patents, copyrights
	  Leaseholds
	  Livestock
		Depreciable real property:
		  Office buildings
		  Apartment buildings
		  Warehouses
		  Factory buildings
		  Low-income housing

quired from 1981 through 1986 is for real property. Note that only four types of real property purchased from 1981 through 1986 qualify for the more generous Section 1250 treatment:

- Residential rental property
- Low-income housing
- Any real property that is depreciated using the straight-line method
- Real property used predominantly outside the United States

The third general category causes most of the confusion. For example, a factory building purchased in 1977 (before 1981) is always a Section 1250 property, regardless of the depreciation method used. The same factory building purchased in 1983 would be a Section 1245 property if the regular ACRS (accelerated) method was used. However, if the owner of the factory building had elected to use the straight-line method, the building would be a Section 1250 property. On the other hand, an apartment building is always considered Section 1250 property, regardless of when it is purchased or which depreciation method is used.

You should note, in the last row of Table 12–2, that any real property purchased after 1986 is Section 1250 property. This result occurs because all real property purchased after 1986 is subject to the MACRS depreciation system. Under MACRS, all real property is depreciated using the straight-line method. Thus, all real property purchased after 1986 is once again Section 1250 property, and the original distinction between Section 1245 and Section 1250 properties is restored. The practical effect of this reclassification and the use of straight-line depreciation for real property under MACRS is that there is no excess depreciation to recapture on real property purchased after 1986.

▲ SUMMARY

Whenever property is disposed of, the realized gain or loss from the disposition must be calculated. Dispositions of property occur as a result of sales, exchanges, casualties and thefts, and abandonments and retirements. The realized gain or loss is equal to the amount realized, less the adjusted basis of the property. The amount realized from a disposition is the gross selling price, less the costs incurred in making the disposition. The gross selling price is equal to the net value received by the taxpayer for the property.

All realized gains and losses are not recognized in the period in which they are realized. Gains from certain types of transactions (discussed in Chapter 13) are deferred for future recognition. Losses from other types of transactions (wash sales, related party sales) are also deferred. Losses on the sale of personal use assets are never deductible. Thus, after the realized gain or loss on a disposition has been calculated, the amount that must be recognized in the current period must be determined.

Recognized gains and losses are then categorized according to the use of the property creating the gain or loss. All property can be categorized as ordinary income property, capital gain property, Section 1231 property, or personal use property. Once categorized, gains and losses are treated according to the rules for the particular category of property.

Ordinary gains and losses receive no special treatment in the calculation of taxable income. Losses on the sale of personal use property are not deductible, whereas gains on personal use property are subject to tax as capital gains. Thus, the primary distinction as to the effect on income involves ordinary income property, capital gain property, and Section 1231 property.

Before any gain on the sale of a depreciable asset is characterized as a capital gain or a Section 1231 gain, the appropriate depreciation recapture rule must be applied. Thus, gains on disposition of depreciable capital assets and Section 1231 property will produce ordinary income to the extent permitted under the depreciation recapture rules. This requires that the appropriate depreciation recapture be calculated before proceeding with the capital asset and Section 1231 netting. In addition, because the ultimate result of the Section 1231 netting is to tax net Section 1231 gains as long-term capital gains, the Section 1231 netting must be performed before the capital gain-and-loss netting. The year-end process for property dispositions is charted in Exhibit 12–3.

Section 1231 netting is done after applying the applicable depreciation recapture rules. If the netting results in a loss, all Section 1231 gains and losses for the year are considered ordinary gains and losses. If the Section 1231 netting results in a gain, the resulting gain is treated as a long-term capital gain that is combined with other capital gains and losses in the capital gain-and-loss netting procedure.

The goal of the capital gain-and-loss netting procedure is to reduce all gains and losses for the year to a net position that is either a gain or a loss. This is accomplished by determining a net short-term gain or loss for the year and a net long-term gain or loss for the year. If the short-term and long-term positions are the same, no further netting is required. If the two positions are opposite, a second netting of the short-term and long-term positions is required to reduce the transactions to one net position for the year, either a gain or a loss.

The preferential treatment for net capital gains is that net long-term capital gains of individuals are limited to a maximum tax rate of 28 percent. Net capital loss deductions are limited. For individuals, only $3,000 in net capital losses is deductible, with any remaining loss carried forward indefinitely. Corporations can

▲ **Exhibit 12–3**

SUMMARY OF THE
PROPERTY DISPOSITION
PROCESS

1. Determine the amount of realized and recognized gain or loss from each property disposition occurring during the year.
2. Classify all recognized gains and losses as
   a. Ordinary income property
   b. Capital gain property
   c. Section 1231 property
   d. Personal use property
3. All depreciable property sold at a gain is classified as either Section 1245 or Section 1250 property, and the appropriate depreciation recapture rule is applied. Any gain remaining is either a capital gain or a section 1231 gain, according to the classification made in step 2. *Depreciable property sold at a loss is not subject to recapture.*
4. Perform the Section 1231 netting procedure. If the netting results in a loss, the loss is ordinary. If the netting process results in a gain, the net Section 1231 gain is a long-term capital gain.
5. Perform the capital gain-and-loss netting procedure. Include in the netting any long-term capital gain from the Section 1231 netting.
6. Apply the treatment rules for capital gains and losses to the results of the capital gain-and-loss netting.
   a. Net long-term capital gains of individuals are subject to a maximum tax rate on the gain of 28%.
   b. Deductions for net long-term capital losses are limited:
      1. Individuals can deduct only $3,000 in net capital losses per year.
      2. Corporations can deduct net capital losses only against capital gains. This is done by allowing a three-year carryback and five-year carryforward for deduction of a current-year net capital loss.

deduct capital losses only against capital gains. Thus, a current-year capital loss can be deducted only against capital gains from the previous three years (carryback period) and in the succeeding five years (carryforward period).

Because of the different treatments accorded various types of gains and losses, the proper characterization of gains and losses on dispositions is crucial to the proper calculation of taxable income.

▲ KEY TERMS

depreciation recapture (p. 562)
gross sales price (p. 542)
lookback recapture rule (p. 559)
recognized gain (p. 540)
recognized loss (p. 540)
Section 1231 gain (p. 557)
Section 1231 loss (p. 557)

Section 1231 netting procedure (p. 558)
Section 1231 property (p. 557)
Section 1245 property (p. 566)
Section 1245 recapture rule (p. 563)

Section 1250 property (p. 566)
Section 1250 recapture rule (p. 563)
short sale (p. 553)
short sale against the box (p. 553)
worthless security (p. 555)

▲ PRIMARY TAX LAW SOURCES

[1] Sec. 1001—Defines gain or loss on the sale or other disposition of property.

[2] Reg. Sec. 1.001-2—Discusses the effect of discharges of liabilities on the amount realized from the sale or other disposition of property.

[3] Sec. 1221—Defines *capital assets.*

[4] Sec. 1222—Defines *holding periods for short-term and long-term capital gains and losses.*

[5] Sec. 1223—Provides rules for determining the holding period of property in different circumstances.

[6] Reg. Sec. 1.1222-1—Defines the *capital gain-and-loss netting procedure.*

[7] Sec. 1—Limits the tax on net long-term capital gains of individuals to a maximum of 28 percent.

[8] Sec. 1233—Defines a *short sale* and provides the tax rules for short sales.

[9] Sec. 165—Treats losses from worthless securities as occurring on the last day of the tax year in which the security becomes worthless.

[10] Reg. Sec. 1.1012-1—Provides rules for identifying securities sold, including what constitutes specific identification of a security sold.

[11] Reg. Sec. 1.1231-1—Explains the Section 1231 netting procedure and gives examples of its application.

[12] Reg. Sec. 1.1245-1—Explains the general operation of Section 1245 and gives examples of the application of Section 1245 in various situations.

[13] Reg. Sec. 1.1250-2—Defines *excess depreciation* and gives examples of the calculation of excess depreciation for purposes of recapture under Section 1250.

[14] Reg. Sec. 1.1245-6—States that all other nonrecognition provisions of the tax law are overridden by Section 1245. A similar provision is found in Section 1.1250-1 of the Treasury regulations relating to Section 1250 recapture.

[15] Sec. 453—Requires amounts recaptured under Section 1245 or Section 1250 to be recognized in the year of disposition when property is sold on an installment basis.

▲ DISCUSSION QUESTIONS

1. Whenever a disposition of property occurs, a gain or loss on the disposition has been realized. However, not all gains and losses realized in the current period are recognized for tax purposes. What is the difference between a realized gain (loss) and a recognized gain (loss)?

2. In determining the amount of a realized gain or loss to be recognized in the current year, certain types of gains and losses are deferred, whereas others are disallowed. What is the difference between deferring a gain or loss realized in the current period and disallowing the recognition of a current period loss? Give at least one example of each that has been studied to date in this course.

3. What effect does the assumption of a seller's debt have on the amount realized from the disposition of the property?

4. Are brokerage commissions paid on the sale of stock a current period expense? Explain.

5. In a transaction in which the seller of property agrees to take other property from the buyer as part of the sales price, why is the buyer's adjusted basis unimportant in determining the amount realized by the seller?

6. Why is a distinction made between long-term capital gain (loss) property and short-term capital gain (loss) property?

7. What is (are) the current tax advantage(s) of selling an asset at a long-term capital gain?

8. What is the purpose of the capital gain-and-loss netting procedure?

9. Evaluate the following statement:

    Corporations can never deduct net capital losses.

10. Under what conditions may a taxpayer exclude a portion of a realized capital gain?

11. What basic tax-planning strategy should a taxpayer with a large net capital gain for the year pursue before the end of the year?

12. What is a short sale against the box? When should it be used?

13. When is a security deemed worthless for tax purposes?

14. How should taxpayers determine the basis of securities sold when their portfolios contain several purchases of the same stock at different prices? Explain.

15. When does a taxpayer realize a loss on a worthless security? What is the amount of realized loss? What rules govern the recognition of a loss on a worthless security? Explain.

16. What is a Section 1231 property?

17. What is the tax advantage of selling a Section 1231 property at a gain?

18. One primary problem in properly accounting for property dispositions is differentiating capital assets and Section 1231 property. Why is it important to correctly identify as either a capital asset or a Section 1231 property an asset that has been disposed of? Explain.

19. Explain the lookback rule as it applies to the Section 1231 netting procedure.

20. Why is it important to determine whether a rental property constitutes a trade or business or an investment activity for the taxpayer owning the property?

21. The chapter noted that all depreciable property is subject to the depreciation recapture rules. What is the intent of the depreciation recapture rules?

22. How are the recapture provisions for Section 1245 and Section 1250 property different?

23. Is an installment sale of a depreciable property treated the same as an installment sale of property that is not subject to depreciation?

24. Are buildings always Section 1250 property? If not, explain the circumstances under which a building would not be Section 1250 property.

25. Some tax theorists have noted that in the majority of cases a sale of a depreciable asset will not be accorded capital gain treatment. What would prompt tax theorists to make this statement?

26. Determine the amount realized in each of the following property dispositions:
    a. Herbert sold some land he owned to Elroy in exchange for $5,500 in cash and 2 breeding hogs (adjusted basis of $500) worth $1,800. In closing the sale, Herbert incurred legal fees of $400 and title search costs of $100.
    b. Saada Corporation sold a building it owned to Paris. Paris will finance the purchase by obtaining a $100,000 loan and will pay an additional $25,000 in cash. As part of the sales agreement, Saada agreed to pay the $2,000 in points that Paris had to pay to obtain the loan. The corporation incurred commission costs of $6,000 and $2,000 in various legal fees in making the sale.
    c. Andrew and Sandra agreed to exchange land that each owned. Andrew's land was worth $22,000, and Sandra's land was worth $28,000. Therefore, in the exchange of the land, Andrew had to pay Sandra $6,000.
    d. Artworld, Inc., sold its building to Paula for $80,000 in cash. As part of the sales agreement, Paula agreed to assume Artworld's $30,000 mortgage on the property.

27. Determine the amount realized in each of the following property dispositions:
    a. Umberto wanted to buy Kevin's truck. Because Umberto had no cash and could not obtain a loan to finance the purchase, Kevin agreed to let Umberto pay him $200 a month for 6 months. In addition, Umberto agreed to put a new roof on Kevin's house as part of the truck purchase. Umberto estimated that his cost of reroofing the house would be $600, although he would have charged Kevin $2,000 if Kevin were a paying customer.
    b. During the current year, a tornado totally destroyed a warehouse that Ajax, Inc., used in its manufacturing operation. The warehouse had a fair market value of $195,000. Ajax's insurance company paid $170,000 on the destruction of the warehouse. The president of Ajax was upset that the insurance company did not pay full fair market value, because Ajax had paid annual insurance premiums of $10,000 for the last 10 years on the warehouse.
    c. Paloma Pitchfork Co. sold an apartment complex it owned to Greedy Investors, Inc. The terms of the sale called for Greedy to pay $100,000 cash, assume Paloma's $400,000 mortgage debt on the property, and give Paloma 10,000 shares of Horticulture, Inc., common stock. Greedy had paid $5 per share for the Horticulture stock, which is currently trading for $20 per share.
    d. Melinda and Nancy agreed to exchange apartment buildings and the related mortgage debt on each building. Melinda's apartment building was worth $250,000 and was encumbered by a mortgage of $100,000. Nancy's building was worth $300,000 and had a $200,000 mortgage. In addition to exchanging the properties and the underlying debt, Nancy paid Melinda $50,000 cash to complete the exchange.

28. Determine the amount of gain or loss realized and the amount of gain or loss to be recognized in each of the following dispositions:
    a. On October 1, the Rufus Partnership sold land to Gerald for which it had paid $20,000. Gerald agreed to pay Rufus $18,000 and to assume Rufus's $13,000 mortgage on the land. In addition, Gerald agreed to pay the $1,200 in property taxes on the land for the entire year.
    b. Carrie sold to her brother Dolph for $5,000 stock that had cost her $8,000. Several years later, Dolph sold the stock for $11,000.
    c. Jill wanted to refurnish her new home. As part of her refurnishing plan, she sold all her old living room furniture for $1,300; it had cost her $3,500. She used the $1,300 as a down payment on new furniture costing $5,600.
    d. Upon obtaining a job in New City, Gary sold his house for $120,000. Gary paid selling expenses of $7,600 on the sale. Gary had paid $50,000 for the house and had added a den at a cost of $22,000 and a new swimming pool costing $16,000 during the time he held the house.

29. Determine the amount of gain or loss realized and the amount of gain or loss to be recognized in each of the following dispositions:

   a. Jorge owned 800 shares of Archer Co. stock. Jorge had purchased 300 of the shares at a cost of $9,000 and 500 of the shares at a cost of $10,000. During the current year, Jorge instructed his broker to sell 400 of the shares when the market value of the shares hit $24. Jorge paid a $600 commission on the sale.

   b. Alana owned 300 shares of Courtney common stock that had cost her $6,000. On February 1, she sold the 300 shares for $4,200 and paid a $300 commission on the sale. On February 19, Alana purchased 500 shares of Courtney common stock for $5,300 plus a $400 commission on the purchase.

   c. Janet went down to the local flea market one Saturday morning and purchased a painting for $20. Although she didn't really want the painting, she felt that the frame alone was worth $20. When she returned home, she took the old painting out of the frame and found another painting hidden in the back. She took the new painting to a local art dealer who told her the painting was almost certainly a Pistachio and worth at least $20,000. Janet decided that she would wait a couple of years, get another expert's opinion, and see if she could sell the painting for more than $20,000.

   d. Enrique owned some land that he was holding as an investment. A local developer wanted to build a new housing project on the north side of his land. The local utility company wanted to run utility lines along the east side of Enrique's land. Enrique had paid $8,000 for the land but did not want to sell the land yet, because he thought the new housing project would greatly enhance its value. Enrique agreed to accept $2,000 from the utility company for an easement to run its lines along the edge of his property. Enrique estimates that the lines will use up about 1/50 of his land.

30. During 1995, James sold some land he had purchased in 1992 as an investment. In 1992, he had paid $4,000 in cash and borrowed $22,000 to purchase the land. He had paid legal fees of $440 and commissions of $560 on the purchase. He sold the land on October 1, 1995, to DeWayne, who gave James 200 shares of Aardvark common stock with a fair market value of $9,600 (DeWayne had paid $3,700 for the stock) and assumed James's debt on the land, which was $20,800 at the time of sale. James paid legal fees of $400 and $1,800 of commissions on the sale. DeWayne paid legal fees of $575 and commissions of $980 related to the purchase. In addition, DeWayne agreed to pay the property taxes of $800 on the land for the entire year.

   a. What is James's gain (loss) on the sale of the land?
   b. What is DeWayne's basis in the land?

31. Guerda owned 1,000 shares of Ditchdirt common stock. During the current year, she sold 350 shares of the stock for $12 per share and paid a commission of $250 on the sale. Guerda had purchased the 1,000 shares as follows:

Purchase Date	# of Shares	Purchase Price	Commissions Paid
1/14/92	100	$ 850	$ 50
6/13/92	150	$1,100	$100
10/30/92	400	$3,600	$400
2/22/93	250	$3,200	$300
11/29/93	100	$1,150	$150

What is Guerda's gain or loss on the sale of the stock?

32. Return to the facts of problem 31. Assume that Guerda later sold an additional 400 shares of the Ditchdirt stock for $18 per share, paying a commission of $500 on the sale. What is Guerda's gain or loss on the sale of the stock?

33. Return to the facts of problem 31. Assume that Guerda sold the remaining 250 shares of Ditchdirt stock for $12 per share and paid a commission of $200 on the sale. What is Guerda's gain or loss on the sale?

34. Classify each of the following assets as ordinary income property, capital asset property, Section 1231 property, or personal use property. If more than one classification is possible, explain the circumstances that would determine the proper classification of the property.

   a. Sarah is a sculptor. During the current year, she gave one of her statues to her niece as a gift.

   b. Petros sells facsimiles of Greek artifacts in a store he owns. Because of a cash-flow problem during the current year, he sold some accounts receivable to a discounter for 75% of face value.

   c. Lana is a college professor. She owns an apartment building and rents apartments out to students.

   d. Ryan uses his automobile 75% of the time in his job as a real estate salesperson. The remaining use of the automobile is for personal purposes.

   e. Fred owns a used car business. During the current year, he purchased a piece of land across the street from his used car business. Fred intends to expand his business and feels that he will ultimately need the space for the extra inventory he wants to purchase over the next few years.

   f. Althea got a tip from a friend that a new golf course was going to be developed south of town. Because she thought the surrounding land was sure to appreciate in value after the golf course was built, Althea purchased several plots of land near where her friend told her the golf course was to be built.

35. Classify each of the following assets as ordinary income property, capital asset property, Section 1231 property, or personal use property. If more than one classification is possible, explain the circumstances that would determine the proper classification of the property.

   a. Letters written by then-Vice President Harry Truman to Helena Desponsa on the day Franklin Delano Roosevelt died. Desponsa still holds the letters.

   b. Ritva is a home-building contractor. She built her own principal residence.

   c. Domingos, a real estate broker, owns undeveloped land as an investment.

   d. Chas Automotive Plaza, Inc., owns cars held for resale to customers.

   e. Arcie, Inc., bought a utility van from Chas Automotive Plaza to use in its concrete installation business.

   f. Anne Marie Arcie, the president of Arcie, Inc., bought a car to use for commuting to the corporate offices from her home.

36. Spencer purchases 100 shares of Reality Virtual Corporation common stock for $1,200 on July 30, 1995. He sells 75 shares of this stock for $525 on December 27, 1995. On January 12, 1996, Spencer purchases 300 shares of Reality Virtual stock; the price is $2 per share.

   a. What are the tax effects of these transactions?

   b. What is the adjusted basis of Spencer's stock on April 15, 1996, when the FMV of the stock is $9 per share?

37. Mort begins investing in stocks in 1995. Listed here are Mort's stock transactions for 1995 and 1996. Determine Mort's gain or loss on his stock transactions for 1995 and 1996. In addition, for each sale of stock, determine whether the gain or loss is short term or long term.

Stock	Transaction Date	Transaction	Price Per Share	Commissions Paid
Pepper Farm	5/24/95	Purchased 50 shares	$ 8	$ 50
Acala Steel	10/5/95	Purchased 200 shares	$14	$200
Horton, Inc.	12/10/95	Purchased 300 shares	$ 3	$100
Acala Steel	12/28/95	Sold 50 shares	$18	$ 70
Horton, Inc.	2/4/96	Purchased 200 shares	$ 2	$ 30
Pepper Farm	2/15/96	Sold 25 shares	$12	$ 25
Horton, Inc.	3/1/96	Sold 100 shares	$ 2	$ 20
Pepper Farm	8/13/96	Sold 25 shares	$13	$ 35
Angor Mills	11/11/96	Purchased 800 shares	$ 6	$400
Angor Mills	12/4/96	Sold 300 shares	$ 9	$250
Horton, Inc.	12/19/96	Sold 400 shares	$ 7	$250

38. Rudy had the following capital gains and losses for the current year. What is the effect of the capital asset transactions on Rudy's taxable income? Explain, and show any calculations.

Short-term capital loss	$13,500
Long-term capital gain	$ 9,600
Long-term capital loss	$ 2,300

39. The Judith Corporation had the following gains and losses from sales of capital assets during the current year. What is the effect of the capital asset transactions on Judith's taxable income? Explain, and show any calculations.

Short-term capital gain	$1,400
Short-term capital loss	$2,900
Long-term capital loss	$6,200

40. Tate had the following gains and losses from sales of capital assets during the current year. What is the effect of the capital asset transactions on Tate's taxable income? Explain, and show any calculations.

Short-term capital gain	$ 1,700
Long-term capital gain	$14,200
Long-term capital loss	$ 3,400

41. Troy had the following gains and losses from sales of capital assets during the current year. What is the effect of the capital asset transactions on Troy's taxable income? Explain, and show any calculations.

Short-term capital gain	$8,600
Short-term capital loss	$ 300
Long-term capital gain	$4,700
Long-term capital loss	$6,600

42. For each of the following capital asset dispositions, determine whether the taxpayer has realized a gain or loss on the disposition and whether that gain or loss is short term or long term:

a. Ari received some stock from his grandfather Stephan for Christmas. Stephan had paid $4,300 for the stock 3 years earlier. The stock had a fair market value of $7,000 on December 24. Ari sold the stock on December 28 for $7,100 and paid a commission of $500 on the sale.

b. Joan owns 600 shares of Archibald common stock that she had purchased in 1993 for $7,920. On July 1, 1995, Archibald declares and distributes a 10% stock dividend. Joan sells the 660 shares of Archibald stock on November 14, 1995, for $13,400 and pays a $700 commission on the sale.

    c. On April 1, 1995, LeRoy sells to his son for $3,000 shares of stock for which he had paid $8,000 two years earlier. His son sells the shares for $11,000 on June 14, 1995.

    d. Lee owns 800 shares of Bolstead, Inc., stock that she had purchased for $20,000 on October 11, 1994. On July 5, 1995, Lee sells 400 shares of Bolstead stock for $7,000. On July 27, 1995, Lee purchases an additional 600 shares of Bolstead stock for $6,000. On December 3, 1995, Lee sells the remaining 1,000 shares of Bolstead stock for $12,000.

43. For each of the following capital asset dispositions, determine whether the taxpayer has realized a gain or loss and whether that gain or loss is short term or long term:

    a. Larry's aunt June dies on May 4, 1995. As part of her will, Larry receives some land that June had purchased in 1978 for $2,000. On May 4, 1995, the land is worth $40,000. Larry receives title to the land on October 15, 1995, and sells it on November 27, 1995, for $40,000. Larry pays $3,000 in commissions and other selling expenses in making the sale.

    b. Sterling receives 4,000 shares of Suburb Corporation stock as a birthday present from his mother-in-law on May 6, 1995. His mother-in-law had paid $18,000 for the stock 8 years earlier. On May 6, 1995, the stock has a fair market value of $4,000. On June 18, 1995, Sterling sells 1,000 shares of the stock for $800.

    c. Assume the same facts as in part b. Suburb Corporation becomes the target of a takeover attempt in July, and its stock soars. Sterling sells the remaining 3,000 shares for $19,000 on August 6, 1995.

    d. Bert owns 1,000 shares of Crooner Capital Corporation common stock for which he paid $8,000 in 1990. On March 13, 1995, Crooner declares a dividend of 1 share of preferred stock for each 10 shares of common stock owned. On the date the preferred shares are distributed, Crooner common shares are selling for $7 per share, and its preferred shares are selling for $10 per share. On November 14, 1995, Bert sells the 100 preferred shares for $1,100.

44. In 1995, Harry sells the automobile he has used in his job as a salesman for $3,000. The automobile cost $14,000 four years earlier. Harry used the automobile 80% of the time in his job and 20% of the time for personal purposes. At the date of sale, Harry had taken $8,000 in depreciation on the automobile. What is Harry's realized gain or loss on the sale of the automobile? How much of the gain (loss) is recognized for tax purposes? Explain, and show how you determined the gain or loss on the sale.

45. Yorgi purchases qualified small business stock in Gnu Co., Inc., on January 17, 1995, for $100,000. Yorgi sells the shares of stock for $500,000 on December 30, 2001. The stock retains its qualified small business status through the date of the sale.

    a. Determine the amount of realized and recognized gain on the sale.

    b. What is Yorgi's effective tax rate on this transaction? (Assume Yorgi's marginal tax rate is 31% in the year 2001.)

46. Neila holds an extensive portfolio of securities. She sells 500 shares of Bolero Corporation stock for $10,000 and pays $500 in sales commissions on September 23 of the current year. Neila acquired the stock for $4,500 plus $450 in commissions in 1992. Offer Neila an optimal year-end tax-planning strategy for her capital gains and losses.

47. Jeremy owns 2,000 shares of Quilliam Quantum common stock that he acquired several years ago for $25 per share. For the current year, Jeremy's net capital gain position is a long-term capital gain. Jeremy also has a nonbusiness bad debt outstanding that he believes will result in a $33,000 loss next year when bankruptcy proceedings for the debtor are concluded. In late December of the current year, Quilliam common stock is selling for $40 per share. Jeremy does not want to take the gain on the stock this year in anticipation of the large loss on the nonbusiness bad debt next year. However, he is concerned that the Quilliam stock may decline in value before the end of the current year. What options are available to Jeremy? Explain, and show any calculations related to the options.

48. On December 12, 1995, Ben sells short 400 shares of Westie Corporation stock at $10 per share. He buys 500 shares of Westie stock on January 8, 1996, at $13 per share. On January 15, 1996, Ben closes the short sale by delivering 400 of the shares purchased on January 8.

   a. What is Ben's gain or loss on the short sale, and when is it recognized?

   b. Assume that the facts remain the same, except that Ben's January 8 purchase is at $9 per share. Explain how your answers in part a will change.

49. Opal's neighbor, Jilian, persuades her to invest in Schaake Corporation, a new venture, on March 4, 1995. Opal pays $20,000 for 2,000 shares of common stock. On February 6, 1996, Schaake Corporation declares bankruptcy and closes its doors forever. The venture failed. Opal never receives a return on her investment or a reimbursement of her original investment. What are the tax consequences to Opal?

50. Fred's Foam Foundations (FFF) is a sole proprietorship that Fred started in 1991. Before 1995, FFF had not disposed of any property it owned. During 1995, FFF has the following gains and losses:

Casualty loss on foam truck	$3,200
Section 1231 gains	$6,300
Section 1231 losses	$1,200

What is the effect of these transactions on Fred's 1995 taxable income? Explain, and show the calculations.

51. Refer to the facts in problem 50. In 1996, FFF has the following gains and losses:

Casualty gain on building	$ 7,300
Section 1231 gains	$ 2,000
Section 1231 losses	$14,100

What is the effect of these transactions on Fred's 1996 taxable income? Explain, and show the required calculations.

52. Rhinelander Corporation has the following net Section 1231 gains and losses for 1991 through 1995:

1991	$ 13,000
1992	$(7,000)
1993	$(18,000)
1994	$ 16,000
1995	$ 3,000

   a. What is the proper characterization of the net Section 1231 gains and losses for 1991–1995 for Rhinelander Corporation?

   b. Assume that in 1996 Rhinelander has a net Section 1231 gain of $14,000. What is the proper characterization of the $14,000 gain?

53. Tawana purchases some rental property in 1995 at a cost of $200,000. In 1997, Tawana is experiencing cash-flow problems and wants to sell the rental property. The adjusted basis of the rental property is $185,000.

   a. What are the tax consequences to Tawana if she can sell the rental property for $220,000? If there is any uncertainty in the tax consequences, explain why there is an uncertainty and what the resolution of the uncertainty will have on the ultimate tax consequences of the sale.

   b. What are the tax consequences for Tawana if she can sell the rental property for $150,000? If there is any uncertainty in the tax consequences, explain why there is an uncertainty and what the resolution of the uncertainty will have on the ultimate tax consequences of the sale.

54. The Gladys Corporation buys equipment (7-year MACRS property) costing $50,000 on April 12, 1995. In 1998, new and improved models of the equipment make it obsolete, and Gladys sells the old equipment for $18,000 on December 27, 1998.

a. What is the character of Gladys Corporation's gain (loss) on the sale, assuming that Gladys took the maximum cost-recovery deductions allowable on the equipment?

b. What is the character of Gladys Corporation's gain (loss) on the equipment, assuming that Gladys took the minimum cost-recovery deduction allowable on the equipment?

NOTE: The depreciation calculations for this problem were done for problem 47, Chapter 11.

55. Alex purchases a building in 1985 at a cost of $400,000. ACRS depreciation on the building totals $290,000, whereas straight-line depreciation would be $210,000 for the same period. Alex sells the building in 1995 for $500,000.

a. What is Alex's gain on sale if he deducts the ACRS depreciation on the building?

b. If the building is an office building that Alex rents to various businesses, what is the character of the gain? Assume that Alex holds the building as an investment.

c. How would your answer to part b change if the building were an office building Alex uses in his consulting business?

d. How would your answer to part b change if the building were an apartment building held as an investment?

56. Alex purchases a building in 1985 at a cost of $400,000. ACRS depreciation on the building totals $290,000, whereas straight-line depreciation would be $210,000 for the same period. Alex sells the building in 1995 for $500,000.

a. What is Alex's gain on sale if he deducts the straight-line depreciation on the building?

b. If the building is an office building that Alex rents to various businesses, what is the character of the gain? Assume that Alex holds the building as an investment.

c. How would your answer to part b change if the building were an office building Alex uses in his consulting business?

d. How would your answer to part b change if the building were an apartment building held as an investment?

57. Alex purchases an apartment building in 1985 at a cost of $400,000. ACRS depreciation on the building totals $290,000, whereas straight-line depreciation would be $210,000 for the same period. Alex sells the building in 1995 for $500,000. The sales agreement calls for the buyer to pay Alex $100,000 in 1995 and $50,000 per year for the next 8 years, with interest on the unpaid balance at 9%. If Alex used the ACRS method to depreciate the building, how much gain would he have to recognize in 1995 and what would be the character of the gain?

58. Anton purchases a building on May 4, 1993, at a cost of $240,000. The land is properly allocated $40,000 of the cost. Anton sells the building on October 18, 1997, for $240,000. What is Anton's gain (loss) on the sale if he uses the regular MACRS system and the building is

a. An apartment building?

b. An office building?

NOTE: The depreciation calculations for this problem were done for problem 51, Chapter 11.

59. In problem 70 in Chapter 10 and problem 60 in Chapter 11, you determined the initial basis and the adjusted basis of Lance and Lola's assets as of December 31, 1995. During 1996, Lance and Lola have the following transactions related to the assets:

a. Lola has stopped using for business purposes the automobile she acquired in 1990 after winning the automobile in 1995. She tried to sell the car but had little luck until November 1995, when she agreed to sell it for $4,000. However, the buyer did not have the cash, and the actual sale did not occur until February 1996.

b. In June, one of Lance's employees drops a torch while working in the shop and starts a fire. The cost of repairing the damage is $25,000. Lance's insurance policy reimburses him $19,000 for the fire damage.

▲ **INTEGRATIVE PROBLEM**

c. The real estate market begins to deteriorate in 1996. Lance and Lola decide to sell their rental house before it loses any more value. They sell the house for $95,000 on June 4, 1996. They paid $250 to advertise the property for sale. In addition, they paid $5,000 in brokerage commissions and $475 in legal fees on the sale. Because their renters had a one-year rental agreement, Lance and Lola had to pay the renters $700 to vacate the lease.

d. The land that Lance inherited is next to a new housing development. The developer needs to run the utility lines through Lance's property and attempts to buy the land from Lance. Lance does not want to sell the land, because he and Lola intend to build their dream home on the property one day. The developer agrees to pay Lance $1,000 for an easement to run the utility lines along one side of Lance's property.

e. While assessing the damage caused by the fire, the contractor Lance had hired to do the repairs finds an antique cash register that had been sealed behind a wall. Lance sells the cash register to a local dealer for $2,200.

f. To help pay for the uninsured portion of the fire damage, Lance sells his plumbing equipment for $7,000. He uses $5,000 of the proceeds to purchase some older plumbing equipment.

g. Lance raises the additional cash he needs to complete the building repairs by selling 1,000 shares of Tetra Corporation stock for $1.50 per share (brokerage commissions paid are $100). He also sells 300 shares of Corporate Capital Resources stock for $14 per share (brokerage commissions are $250).

h. Lola decides to upgrade her home office by adding a new deluxe computer workstation. Because the workstation has a built-in desk and filing cabinet, she no longer needs her old desk and filing cabinet. She gives the old desk and filing cabinet to the housekeeper. The housekeeper agrees to clean the house for 10 weeks in exchange for the desk and filing cabinet. The housekeeper normally charges $30 per week.

i. In December, Lance and Lola's stockbroker advises them that bad news about the Meek Corporation is likely to be forthcoming and probably will cause the stock's value to decline. Because of their current income situation, the broker advises Lance and Lola to sell the stock short to protect their gain. On December 17, they sell the 1,000 shares of Meek stock short for $23 per share. Brokerage commissions on the short sale are $1,400. They close the short sale on January 27, 1997, by delivering the 1,000 shares to the broker.

j. In addition to these transactions, Lance tells you that a company in which he and Lola had invested went bankrupt in 1994. They had purchased the stock from Lance's brother for $37,500 in 1990. The company was dissolved in 1994, and the shareholders received nothing from the bankruptcy proceeding. Lance and Lola had no other capital asset transactions in 1994 and 1995.

REQUIRED: For each of these transactions, determine the realized and recognized gain or loss and the character of the gain or loss. Do the appropriate year-end netting procedures, and determine the effect of the transactions on Lance and Lola's 1996 adjusted gross income. Assume that Lance and Lola's adjusted gross income before considering these transactions was $47,000.

▲ COMPREHENSIVE PROBLEMS

60. Duke Plumbing and Wallpaper Co. has been in business since 1979. During the current year, it had the following property transactions:

a. A warehouse purchased in 1985 for $200,000 was sold for $190,000. Depreciation taken on the building to date of sale totaled $160,000 (straight-line depreciation would have been $133,000).

b. Wallpaper that had a cost of $75,000 became obsolete when a new type of wallpaper was developed. Duke was unable to sell the wallpaper and ended up throwing it in the trash.

c. Two of Duke's service trucks collided in the parking lot, destroying both trucks. The older truck had cost $18,000 and had an adjusted basis of $4,000. The fair market value of the older truck was $9,000, which was reimbursed by Duke's insurance company. The newer truck had been purchased 3 months earlier for $22,000. The newer truck had a fair market value of $17,000, which was reimbursed by Duke's insurance company.

d. Plumbing equipment purchased in January for $6,000 was sold in November for $3,500. The equipment was advertised as being the easiest equipment of its kind to use in installing new plumbing fixtures. However, it was so complicated to operate that none of Duke's employees could figure out how to use it, and Duke decided it was easier to do it the old-fashioned way.

e. Duke's computer system became obsolete and was sold for $1,300. Duke had paid $12,000 for the system 4 years earlier and had taken $9,000 in depreciation on the system as of the date of sale.

f. Because the 2 service trucks that were destroyed (in part c) had to be replaced, Duke decided to sell its other service truck and buy 3 new trucks. The third service truck had cost $19,000 two years earlier and had an adjusted basis of $13,000. Duke received $15,000 from the sale of the truck.

g. An antique plumbing plunger for which Duke had paid $5,000 and was fully depreciated was sold for $8,600.

h. Duke decided not to replace the warehouse it sold in part a. The office building it had erected in 1989 at a cost of $140,000 to service the warehouse was no longer of any use and was sold for $158,000. The office building had an adjusted basis of $122,000.

REQUIRED: For each of these transactions, determine the gain or loss that must be recognized on the transaction and the character of the gain or loss. Determine the effect of all the transactions on Duke's taxable income for the year.

61. Barney is a farmer who had the following transactions during 1995:

A barn that had cost $34,000 in 1990 with an adjusted basis of $19,000 was destroyed by a tornado. Barney's insurance paid him $23,000 for the casualty.

Barney's prize bull, for which he had paid $17,000 and which had an adjusted basis of $9,000, was in the barn when the tornado hit. Although the bull was not killed, he was injured severely enough that he could no longer breed. The bull was worth only $300 after the casualty (at stud he was valued at more than $20,000), but he had been such a favorite of Barney's that Barney kept him and put him out to pasture. Barney's insurance company refused to pay anything for the bull's injuries.

Breeding cattle that had cost $17,500 in 1993 with an adjusted basis of $6,720 were sold for $21,000.

A tractor that had cost $18,000 and had an adjusted basis of $8,500 was sold for $4,200.

Stock in Old Mill Co. that Barney had purchased on November 13, 1994, for $32,000 became worthless when Old Mill went out of business on April 1, 1995.

A horse Barney had purchased in February for $8,000 as a gift for his daughter came up lame and had to be sold for $1,000.

Barney sold 80 acres of farmland for $39,000. Barney had received the land as a gift from his uncle when he first went into farming. Barney's uncle had paid $2,000 for the land, which was worth $5,000 at the time of the gift.

What is the effect of these transactions on Barney's taxable income for 1995? In solving this problem, first determine the amount and character of gain (loss) on each of the transactions. Then, perform the appropriate netting procedures. Your answer should be a summary of the gains (losses) as they would appear on Barney's tax return.

As a gift for her granddaughter Ella's 13th birthday, Melanie purchases 500 shares of Soft'n Sales Corporation stock on July 10, 1995. Melanie buys the stock directly from the underwriter for a total of $20,000. Soft'n Sales has just gone public, and Melanie believes the stock will be a good investment for Ella's college education. Melanie tells Ella that she will receive control of the stock on her 18th birthday so long as Ella maintains an A average in high school.

Soft'n Sales is a software development enterprise in San Diego. It just introduced a new database program that is currently number one in sales. In about 10 months it will

▲ DISCUSSION CASE 12–1

introduce a new spreadsheet program that integrates with the database program. Other new products are in developmental stages. At the date of the public offering, Soft'n Sales's gross assets total $10 million. These assets include mostly intangibles, equipment, and raw materials for product development. The company owns no real estate and holds no investment securities. All capital is reinvested within the enterprise.

The year 2000 arrives. Explain Melanie's options for transferring the stock to Ella to use for college expenses. What are the tax implications of each option?

▲ DISCUSSION CASE 12–2

Christoffe sold 1,000 shares of HoTech Corporation preferred stock for $37 per share on August 3 of the current year. Sales commissions totaled $300. The stock's price has been falling since HoTech's management was sued for patent infringement four months ago. The price is expected to keep falling until the law suit is settled. Christoffe received the stock as a Christmas gift from his wife last year. She paid $48 per share plus a $400 commission. The year-end is approaching, and he wants to optimize his tax position. Christoffe's current portfolio contains the following corporate stock:

Stock	Number of Shares	Date Acquired	Adjusted Basis per Share	FMV
MURF Corp.	1,000	1/12/90	$11	$28
Tellics, Inc.	2,000	10/2/91	$15	$29
HIGG Corp.	200	12/9/93	$41	$90

Make recommendations to Christoffe.

▲ TAX PLANNING CASE 12–3

At the beginning of 1995, Heather owned the following stocks:

Stock	Date Purchased	# of Shares	Per Share Price	Commissions
Clutch common	11/30/94	250	$40	$ 500
Pauley preferred	4/13/94	100	$10	$ 100
Leines common	10/14/92	1,000	$35	$2,000

In addition to these stocks, Heather had received 400 shares of Poor Boy preferred stock from her grandfather as a gift on December 25, 1994. The shares were selling for $25 per share on December 24, 1994. No gift tax was paid on the transfer of the stock. Her grandfather had purchased the shares for $5 per share in 1972.

During 1995, Heather had the following stock transactions:

Stock	Transaction	Date	Sales Price	Commissions Paid
Poor Boy	Sold 100 shares	3/12	$ 2,200	$200
Leines	Sold 400 shares	6/8	$ 5,300	$300
Clutch	Sold 200 shares	10/18	$ 4,700	$270
Ragtop common	Purchased 2,000	12/18	$20,000	$600
Leines	Purchased 200	12/25	$ 3,550	$450

a. What is Heather's net capital gain (loss) for 1995?

b. On December 28, 1995, Heather's stocks have the following fair market values:

Pauley	$13 per share
Clutch	$28 per share
Leines	$23 per share
Poor Boy	$37 per share
Ragtop	$ 4 per share

Assuming that the commission paid on any sale is equal to 5% of the selling price, what action(s) would you recommend to Heather to minimize her 1995 tax? Discuss the potential tax effects of selling each of the stocks Heather owns at the end of the year.

c. Assume that in addition to the stock sales, Heather sold some land she had inherited from her father. Her father had paid $5,000 for the land in 1982. Her father died on April 14, 1991, when the land was worth $12,000. Heather sold the land on May 21, 1995, for $50,000. Legal fees and commissions of $5,500 were paid on the sale. What is Heather's net capital gain (loss) for 1995?

d. Given the fair market values, what action would you recommend Heather take to minimize her 1995 tax? Explain.

Rosie has owned a successful luncheonette for several years. Tired of the long hours and eager to try another way of life, Rosie has decided to buy a fishing boat and start a charter service near Key West. The only obstacle is the sale of the following assets of the luncheonette to fund her fishing boat endeavor:

▲ TAX PLANNING CASE 12–4

Asset	Date Acquired	Adjusted Basis	Original Cost
Building	1/12/83	$ 5,000 ($6,600 if SL depreciation used)	$50,000
Land	1/12/83	$10,000	$10,000
Equipment	2/9/92	$ 7,800	$25,000
Supplies	Current year	$ 5,000	$ 5,000

Hank, Rosie's part-time cook, has offered her $175,000 for the luncheonette, which Rosie believes is a fair price. However, she is concerned about the tax consequences of the sale. For example, she wonders how to allocate the sales price among the assets to receive the most advantageous tax results. Make reasonable recommendations to Rosie, and explain the tax effects of structuring the sale according to your recommendations.

You are a CPA who works for a local accounting firm. While having lunch at Willie's Diner last Thursday, you overheard Beth Murray describe how Bart (her spouse) was able to get a $2,000 business loss, free car maintenance for 2 years, and $4,000 cash to spend on their vacation in exchange for an old truck. You didn't think too much about the conversation until you returned to your office. While you were at lunch, Bart Murray dropped off the tax information for his business, Bart's Mobile Glass Service, for the past year. Your curiosity gets the best of you. You open the packet of information and immediately look for the truck sale information. The only documentation you find is a hand-written memo stating, "1990 Dodge truck sold for $4,000 and loss on sale = $2,000." The memo is initialed by Bart Murray. Attached to the memo is a photocopy of a check from Haroldene Harvey's Auto Castle, Inc., for $4,000. Haroldene Harvey is also your client. You know that Haroldene and Bart are neighbors and good friends. Your review of Bart Murray's asset and depreciation schedules confirms that the truck had an adjusted basis of $6,000 as of the sale date. What are your obligations under the Statements on Responsibilities in Tax Practice (Appendix D)? Discuss what you should do in this situation.

▲ ETHICS DISCUSSION CASE 12–5

CHAPTER 13

Nonrecognition Transactions

▲ CHAPTER LEARNING OBJECTIVES

■ Introduce three commonly encountered classes of property transactions for which the nonrecognition (deferral) of gains is allowed.

■ Discuss the rationale for nonrecognition (deferral) of gain on the three classes of property transactions.

■ Explain the common characteristics of the three classes of nonrecognition transactions and how the characteristics affect the nonrecognition of gain calculations and adjustments.

■ Describe the basic nonrecognition rules for like-kind exchanges of property and the calculation of the basis of property received in a like-kind exchange.

■ Identify properties that qualify as like-kind for the deferral of gains and losses on exchanges.

■ Explain the effects of "boot" paid and received in like-kind exchanges.

■ Describe involuntary conversions of property and how gains (but not losses) may be deferred when a qualified replacement property is purchased.

■ Discuss what constitutes a qualified replacement property for property that is involuntarily converted.

■ Describe the provisions for deferring gain (but not loss) on the sale and timely replacement of a taxpayer's principal residence.

■ Explain when a taxpayer may elect to exclude up to $125,000 of gain on the sale of a principal residence.

▲ CONCEPT REVIEW ▲

All-inclusive income   All income received is taxable unless a specific provision can be found in the tax law that either excludes the income from taxation or defers its recognition to a future tax year.

Annual accounting period   All entities must report the results of their operations on an annual basis (the tax year). Each tax year stands on its own, apart from other tax years.

Basis   This is the amount of unrecovered investment in an asset. As amounts are expended and/or recovered relative to an asset over time, the basis is adjusted in consideration of such changes. The **adjusted basis** of an asset is the original basis, plus or minus the changes in the amount of unrecovered investment.

Legislative grace   Any tax relief provided is the result of a specific act of Congress that must be strictly applied and interpreted. All income received is taxable unless a specific provision can be found in the tax law that excludes the income from taxation. Deductions must be ap-

proached with the philosophy that nothing is deductible unless a provision in the tax law allows the deduction.

Realization   No income (or loss) is recognized until it has been realized. A realization involves a change in the form and/or the substance of a taxpayer's property rights that results from an arm's-length transaction.

Related party   Family members and corporations that are owned by family members are considered related parties, as are certain other relationships between entities in which the power to control the substance of a transaction is evidenced through majority ownership.

Substance over form   Transactions are to be taxed according to their true intention rather than some form that may have been contrived.

Wherewithal to pay   Income is recognized in the period in which the taxpayer has the means to pay the tax on the income.

Chapter 12 noted that a gain or a loss realized on a disposition of property may not be recognized in the year the transaction takes place. Earlier discussions of nonrecognition focused on realized losses that are permanently disallowed (e.g., personal use losses) and those that are deferred (e.g., wash sales) for recognition. In addition, gains on certain types of dispositions are not recognized in the period in which they are realized.

▲ INTRODUCTION

Under the all-inclusive income concept, any gain realized on a disposition of property is taxable (i.e., recognized in the period of realization). However, Congress has granted tax relief to certain types of transactions. These transactions are referred to as **nonrecognition transactions.** It should be noted that, with one exception, these transactions are not nontaxable in the sense that tax will never be paid on the realized gain. Rather, recognition of these gains is deferred until a future period. One exception to the deferral-of-gain treatment is a special provision that allows taxpayers who have attained age 55 to exclude up to $125,000 in gain on the sale of their principal residence.

The purpose of this chapter is to discuss commonly encountered nonrecognition transactions. Three common classes of nonrecognition transactions are

- Exchanges of like-kind property
- Involuntary conversions of property
- Sale of a principal residence

Although each type of nonrecognition transaction is distinct, the underlying rationale for deferral of gains from each class is the same. In addition, these transactions share characteristics and mechanisms for deferring gains and losses upon their disposition.

▲ RATIONALE FOR NONRECOGNITION

There are two interrelated reasons that the three classes of transactions have been granted tax relief. First, in each transaction, the initial realization is considered part of a continuing investment process. That is, although one asset has been disposed of, another asset with similar characteristics has taken its place. Under the substance-over-form doctrine, the new property acquired in the transaction is viewed as a continuation of the original investment. This view represents a refinement of the realization concept, which postpones recognition of appreciation in value until the taxpayer disposes of a property. In effect, the nonrecognition provisions mandate deferral of the tax consequences if a disposition and its timely replacement provide the taxpayer with a continuing interest in a similar property.

> ▲ **EXAMPLE 1**   Archibald, Inc.'s warehouse was destroyed by a fire. The warehouse had an adjusted basis of $100,000 and a fair market value before the fire of $325,000. Archibald received $300,000 from its insurance company for the loss of the warehouse. Archibald used the $300,000 to purchase another warehouse costing $400,000. What is Archibald's realized gain (loss) on the casualty?
>
> *Discussion:*   Archibald has realized a gain of $200,000 ($300,000 − $100,000) on the casualty. The loss on business property fully destroyed is the adjusted basis of the property, $100,000. However, the receipt of the $300,000 in insurance proceeds results in a gain of $200,000 on the casualty.
>
>   A casualty loss on business property is an involuntary conversion. Because the warehouse is critical to Archibald's business, it was replaced. Thus, the new warehouse is a continuation of the investment in the original warehouse, and Archibald may defer the gain on the involuntary conversion. In effect, the tax law views the destruction of the warehouse and its replacement as not constituting a realization of the appreciation in the value of the warehouse.

The second rationale for not recognizing these transactions is that the taxpayer lacks the wherewithal to pay the tax on the realized gain, because the amount realized on the transaction is reinvested in the replacement asset. A primary requirement for total deferral of gain in all three classes of transactions is that any amounts realized from the disposition must be fully reinvested in a replacement asset.

> ▲ **EXAMPLE 2**   In example 1, does Archibald have the wherewithal to pay tax on the $200,000 realized gain on the warehouse?
>
> *Discussion:*   In acquiring the replacement warehouse, Archibald reinvested the entire $300,000 it received from its insurance company. It does not have any cash remaining to pay the tax on the $200,000 gain. Archibald does not have the wherewithal to pay tax on the gain, because all the insurance proceeds were used to replace the warehouse.

▲ COMMONALITIES OF NONRECOGNITION TRANSACTIONS

The continuity of investment criteria and lack of wherewithal to pay for the three classes of nontaxable transactions provide five distinctive commonalities in the tax treatment of these transactions. Figure 13–1 illustrates these factors. First, the wherewithal-to-pay concept provides the rationale for deferring gain. Thus, all three nonrecognition transactions provide for the deferral of realized gains. Deferring gains is mandatory for like-kind exchanges and the sale of a principal residence. However, deferring gains from involuntary conversions is usually elective. On the loss side, deferring realized losses on like-kind exchanges is mandatory. Losses on involuntary conversions are never deferred and are recognized in

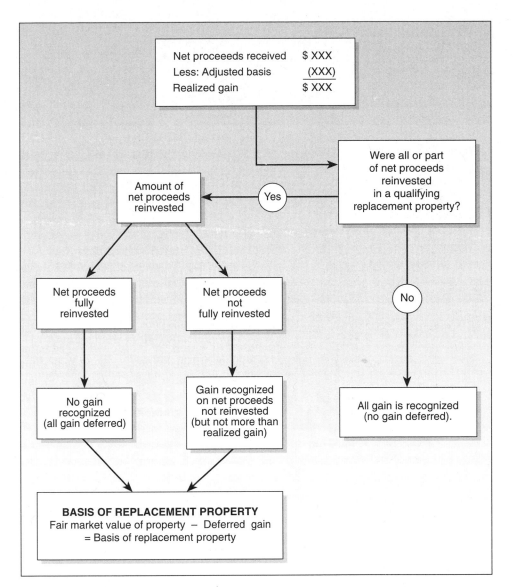

▲ **Figure 13–1**

COMMONALITIES OF
NONRECOGNITION
TRANSACTIONS

the period of realization. A loss on the sale of a principal residence is a personal use loss that is never deductible and therefore not deferrable.

Second, classification of a nonrecognition transaction as a continuation of an investment requires a replacement asset. Each type of nonrecognition transaction requires the purchase of a qualified replacement asset within a specified time period. The time allowed for the qualified replacement varies with each type of nonrecognition transaction. As you can see in Figure 13–1, the transaction is taxable and treated as any other disposition of property if a qualified replacement property is not purchased within the allowable time period.

The third factor common to these transactions also is a result of the wherewithal-to-pay concept. Although the transactions qualify for nonrecognition, gains on all the transactions must be recognized when the taxpayer has the wherewithal to pay the tax on some portion of the realized gain. As depicted in Figure 13–1, no gain is recognized so long as the entire proceeds received in the nonrecognition transaction are reinvested in a qualified replacement asset. However, if all the proceeds are not reinvested, the taxpayer has the wherewithal to pay tax in the amount of those proceeds not reinvested. In general, the amount of gain to be recognized is the portion of the amount realized that the taxpayer has not reinvested in a replacement asset.

▲ **EXAMPLE 3**   Assume that in example 1 Archibald purchased a qualifying replacement warehouse at a cost of $275,000. What amount of gain must Archibald recognize on the casualty?

Discussion: Archibald realized a gain of $200,000 on the destruction of the warehouse. Although the replacement of the warehouse qualifies for nonrecognition, Archibald must recognize gain on the warehouse for any proceeds from the casualty that were not reinvested in acquiring the replacement warehouse. Therefore, Archibald must recognize $25,000 ($300,000 in insurance proceeds − $275,000 to replace the warehouse) of the gain on the warehouse casualty.

When recognizing gains on nontaxable transactions, keep in mind that the amount of gain recognized can never exceed the amount of the gain realized on the transaction. This is an application of the capital recovery concept, which limits the amount of income to the amount realized in excess of the capital invested in the asset.

▲ **EXAMPLE 4**   Gecko Co. suffered a fire that destroyed its office building. The building was worth $200,000 before the fire and had an adjusted basis of $170,000. Gecko received $200,000 in insurance proceeds and bought a qualifying replacement building for $150,000. What are Gecko's realized and recognized gains on the casualty?

Discussion: Gecko has a realized gain of $30,000 ($200,000 − $170,000) on the casualty. After purchasing the replacement building, Gecko has $50,000 of the insurance proceeds available to pay tax. However, the maximum gain that can be recognized is the amount of the realized gain. Therefore, Gecko's recognized gain is $30,000 (no gain is deferred).

The fourth common attribute is the mechanism used to defer gains and losses from the transaction. Recall that a *deferral* means that a realized gain (or loss) is not recognized in the current period but will be recognized in some future period. The mechanism for effecting the deferral is through an adjustment of the replacement asset's basis.[1] A general formula for adjusting the basis of the replacement asset is

Basis of replacement asset = Fair market value of replacement

Less:	Gain deferred
or	
Plus:	Loss deferred (exchanges only)
Equals:	Basis of replacement asset

The rationale for adjusting the basis of the replacement asset lies in the capital recovery concept. In a gain deferral situation, the realized gain on the transaction is an excess capital recovery that is not being taxed in the period of realization. Moreover, without the basis adjustment, the deferred gain would never be recognized. As a continuation of investment, the amount of capital recovery allowed on the replacement asset must be reduced by the amount of any gain deferred. In subsequent periods, the amount of capital recovery taken on the replacement asset through depreciation and at disposition of the replacement asset will be reduced by the amount of the gain deferred. While the replacement asset is being used, taxable income will increase by the amount of the gain deferred in calculating the replacement asset's basis.

▲ **EXAMPLE 5**   Jordan owns land with a fair market value of $10,000. Jordan had purchased the land as an investment in 1991 for $6,000. In 1995, he trades the land in a qualifying like-kind exchange for another parcel of land that is worth $10,000. What are Jordan's realized and recognized gains on the like-kind exchange and the basis in the new parcel of land?

Discussion: Jordan has realized a gain of $4,000 on the exchange of the land. However, all of it is deferred, because Jordan has no wherewithal to pay the tax on the $4,000 gain. The basis of the new parcel of land is $6,000:

Amount realized (fair market value of land received)	$10,000
Adjusted basis of land exchanged	(6,000)
Realized gain on exchange	$ 4,000
Recognized gain on exchange	-0-
Deferred gain on exchange	$ 4,000

Basis of new parcel = $10,000 − $4,000 = $6,000

By reducing the basis in the second parcel, Jordan will not be able to recover the deferred gain tax free when he disposes of the second parcel in a taxable transaction. When Jordan disposes of the second parcel in a taxable transaction, his realized gain will be a combination of the $4,000 in gain deferred on the exchange and any subsequent gain (loss) in value of the second parcel.

▲ **EXAMPLE 6**   In 1996, Jordan sells the second parcel of land for $13,000. What are his realized and recognized gains on the sale?

Discussion: Jordan has realized a gain of $7,000 ($13,000 − $6,000) on the sale of the land. The sale of the land is a taxable transaction, and he must recognize the entire $7,000 gain.

The $7,000 recognized gain is composed of 2 separate gains on the individual parcels. The first parcel yielded a $4,000 gain, which was not recognized on the exchange for the second parcel. The second parcel was worth $10,000 when Jordan received it in the exchange. It appreciated in value by $3,000 while Jordan held it. Thus, Jordan's $7,000 gain is the result of a $4,000 gain on his initial land investment and a $3,000 gain on the subsequent investment acquired in the like-kind exchange. Over the 2-year period, the same amount of gain is recognized for the exchange deferral as would have been recognized if no deferral had been allowed on the exchange:

	Gain Recognized		
	1995	**1996**	**Total**
No gain deferral allowed	$4,000	$3,000	$7,000
With exchange deferral	-0-	$7,000	$7,000

Note in examples 5 and 6 that Jordan's basis in the new parcel of land is equal to his basis in the parcel of land exchanged (carryover basis). This reflects the fact that Jordan made no additional investment to obtain the second parcel of land. The amount of his investment has not changed in continuing his investment in land, resulting in a carryover of his initial $6,000 investment to the investment in the second parcel. However, the general basis adjustment takes into account any additional investment made to acquire the replacement asset.

▲ **EXAMPLE 7**   Assume that in example 5 Jordan exchanges his land for another parcel of land that is worth $12,000. Because his land is worth only $10,000, Jordan has to pay $2,000 to make the exchange. What are Jordan's realized and recognized gains on the exchange and his basis in the new parcel of land?

Discussion: Jordan realizes a gain of $4,000 on the exchange of the land. However, all gain from the like-kind exchange is deferred, because Jordan has no wherewithal to pay the tax on the $4,000 gain. The basis of the new parcel of land is $8,000:

Amount realized ($12,000 − $2,000)	$10,000
Adjusted basis	(6,000)
Realized gain on exchange	$ 4,000
Recognized gain on exchange	-0-
Deferred gain on exchange	$ 4,000

Basis of new parcel = $12,000 − $4,000 = $8,000

The $8,000 basis in the second parcel of land is the $6,000 invested in the first parcel (which remains unrealized) and the additional $2,000 Jordan paid to acquire the second parcel.

▲ **EXAMPLE 8**   Assume that in example 5 Jordan exchanges his land for another parcel of land that is worth $7,000. Because his land is worth $10,000, Jordan receives $3,000 in the exchange. What are Jordan's realized and recognized gains on the exchange and his basis in the new parcel of land?

Discussion: Jordan has realized a $4,000 gain on the exchange. However, Jordan has $3,000 in cash after the exchange that is available to pay tax. Therefore, he must recognize $3,000 of the $4,000 gain, leaving only $1,000 of the gain to be deferred. His basis in the new land is $6,000:

Amount realized ($7,000 + $3,000)	$10,000
Adjusted basis	(6,000)
Realized gain on exchange	$ 4,000
Recognized gain on exchange (cash received)	3,000
Deferred gain on exchange	$ 1,000

Basis of new parcel = $7,000 − $1,000 = $6,000

The final commonality is the carryover of the tax attributes of the first asset to the replacement asset to reflect the replacement asset's status as a continuation of the investment in the first asset. These attributes include the holding period of the first asset and any unrecognized depreciation recapture on the first asset.[2,3] These carryovers are essential to give full effect to the second asset as the continuation of the investment in the first asset.

▲ **EXAMPLE 9**   Kolby Co. purchases machinery in 1993 at a cost of $30,000. In 1995, Kolby exchanges the machinery for other machinery with a fair market value of $20,000. MACRS depreciation on the machinery was $18,500. The exchange qualifies as a like-kind exchange. What are Kolby's realized gain, recognized gain, and basis in the new machinery?

Discussion: Kolby has a realized gain of $8,500 on the exchange. Because Kolby has no wherewithal to pay after the exchange, the entire gain is deferred. The basis of the new machinery is $11,500:

Amount realized (FMV of new machinery)	$20,000
Adjusted basis ($30,000 − $18,500)	(11,500)
Realized gain on exchange	$ 8,500
Recognized gain on exchange	-0-
Deferred gain on exchange	$ 8,500

Basis of new machinery = $20,000 − $8,500 = $11,500

▲ **EXAMPLE 10** Assume that Kolby immediately sells the machinery received in the exchange in example 9 for $20,000. What are the amount of recognized gain on the sale and the character of the gain on the sale?

Discussion: Kolby's realized and recognized gain on the sale is $8,500 ($20,000 − $11,500). Machinery used in a trade or business is Section 1231 property. However, because the machinery is depreciable property, it is subject to the depreciation recapture rules under Section 1245 (see Chapter 12).

Although Kolby has taken no depreciation on the machinery sold, the tax attributes of the initial machinery attach to the machinery sold. As a continuation of the original investment in the machinery, the machinery sold is considered to have been held since 1993 when the initial purchase took place. In addition, characterization of any gain on a taxable disposition of the machinery must view the $18,500 in depreciation taken on the initial machinery as having been taken on the machinery sold. Thus, the entire $8,500 in gain is recaptured as ordinary income under Section 1245.

Carrying over the depreciation recapture for nonrecognition transactions gives the gain from disposition of the replacement the attributes of the original asset. This effectively eliminates the use of nonrecognition transactions to avoid the depreciation recapture rules.

A realized gain or loss is never recognized on an exchange of business or investment property for other like-kind property for business or investment use. Realized gain or loss on a transaction that qualifies as an exchange of like-kind property for other like-kind property must always be deferred.[4] However, gains on like-kind exchanges must be recognized when the taxpayer has the wherewithal to pay the tax after the exchange is completed. The wherewithal to pay is evidenced by the receipt of other nonqualifying property with the like-kind property (in tax jargon, other nonqualifying property is called **boot,** so named because, along with the like-kind property, one party has received nonqualified property "to boot"). Thus, gains are recognized to the extent that boot is received in the exchange. However, realized losses on like-kind exchanges are never recognized, even when boot is received in the deal.

▲ LIKE-KIND EXCHANGES

Exchange Requirement

To qualify for nonrecognition, a direct exchange of like-kind property must occur. Thus, a sale of property and a purchase of like-kind property from another would not be considered an exchange, unless the two transactions were interdependent. If the sale and purchase transactions are interdependent, the transactions are treated as an exchange under the substance-over-form doctrine.

▲ **EXAMPLE 11** Sarah sold her business car to Karen for $3,000. The auto had an adjusted basis of $4,500 at the date of sale. Sarah used the $3,000 as a down payment on a new business car she purchased from Acne Auto Sales for $19,000. What are the tax effects for Sarah of the sale and purchase of the autos?

Discussion: Because the 2 transactions are not interdependent, an exchange of like-kind property has not occurred. Sarah realizes and recognizes a loss on the sale of her business car of $1,500 ($3,000 − $4,500). Her basis in the new car for business is the $19,000 purchase price.

Classifying the transaction in example 11 as a sale has important tax implications. As a sale, Sarah can deduct the loss she realizes on the transaction.

However, if the transaction had been characterized as an exchange, Sarah would not be allowed to recognize the loss. Nonrecognition of gains and losses on exchanges of like-kind property is mandatory. Thus, a taxpayer wishing to recognize a loss on the disposition of an asset that is to be replaced must be careful not to make the sale and purchase transactions interdependent. Sale and repurchase from a dealer in property usually collapse under IRS scrutiny and are treated as an exchange of property.

▲ **EXAMPLE 12**   Assume that in example 11 Sarah sold her old auto to Acne Auto Sales for $3,000. She deposited the check in the bank and wrote a separate check to Acne Auto Sales for $19,000 to purchase the new auto. What are the tax effects for Sarah of the sale and purchase of the autos?

Discussion: Because the sale and purchase transactions were made with the same dealer in property, the IRS would collapse the 2 transactions and treat them as a direct exchange of property. That is, although the form of the transaction is a sale and a purchase, the substance of the transaction is an exchange of autos between Sarah and Acne Auto Sales.

Because the transaction is an exchange of like-kind business property for like-kind business property, Sarah is not allowed to recognize the $1,500 loss on the exchange. The loss is added to the basis of the new auto. Thus, instead of recognizing a $1,500 loss and having an auto with a basis of $19,000 (example 11), Sarah has no recognized loss and her basis in the auto is $20,500 ($19,000 + $1,500).

The direct exchange of property requirement does not mean that the exchange must be simultaneous. Taxpayers are allowed to structure transactions through third parties that qualify as exchanges if they meet certain time requirements for identifying properties and closing the transaction.

▲ **EXAMPLE 13**   Percy Corporation would like to obtain land owned by Olivia. Olivia does not want to sell the land, because she would have to recognize a large gain, but she is willing to trade for land owned by Bake. Under a binding contract, Olivia delivers title to her land to Percy, and Percy agrees to purchase the land from Bake and deliver title to the land to Olivia. Percy purchases the land from Bake and delivers title to Olivia. Does the transaction qualify as an exchange?

Discussion: The transaction between Percy Corporation and Olivia qualifies as a direct exchange of property if the transaction meets the time requirements for completing the transaction.

The transaction between Percy Corporation and Bake is not an exchange. It is a sale of property by Bake to Percy and is not part of the exchange transaction.

The exchange illustrated in example 13 is referred to as a **deferred (third-party) exchange.** The deferred exchange rules allow a transaction to be structured as an exchange when the two parties do not have property that they want to exchange directly.[5] The rules for structuring such exchanges require that the property to be exchanged be identified within 45 days of the date of the first property transfer. In addition, the exchange must be completed within 180 days of the first property transfer. In example 13, the land owned by Bake would have to be identified as being part of the exchange within 45 days of the transfer of land from Olivia to Percy Corporation. In addition, Percy would have 180 days to purchase the land from Bake and transfer title to the land to Olivia to qualify the transaction as an exchange. Application of the deferred exchange rules can be quite complex in practice and is generally beyond the scope of this text. However, you should know that exchanges can still be made when one party does not own the property the other party desires to receive in the exchange.

Like-Kind Property Requirements

The **like-kind exchange rules** require that the property being transferred in an exchange be used either in a trade or business or held as an investment. This excludes personal use property (residences, personal automobiles, etc.) from the nonrecognition rules for like-kind exchanges. In addition, stock-in-trade (inventories); other property held primarily for sale; stocks, bonds, notes, other securities; partnership interests; and intangible assets are specifically excluded from the exchange nonrecognition rules. Exchanges of these assets generally result in recognized gains and losses.

The property received in the exchange must be like-kind property and be held for business or investment use. This is interpreted as meaning that the property is of like kind in the taxpayer's hands, not the prior owner's. Thus, a taxpayer can make a like-kind exchange with a dealer in property, even though the dealer does not hold the property for business or investment use. In addition, the requirement that both the property exchanged and the property received be held for business or investment use is interpreted as meaning that business use property can be exchanged for property to be held as an investment and vice versa, so long as the two properties are of like kind.

> ▲ **EXAMPLE 14**   Ace Trucking Co. owned a parcel of land it had acquired several years earlier as an investment. Ace needed more land for parking its trucking fleet, so it exchanged the investment land for a parcel of land adjacent to its truck barn. Is the exchange of land eligible for treatment as a like-kind exchange?
>
> *Discussion:*   Exchanging land held for investment purposes for land to be used in a trade or business is a like-kind exchange. Investment property can be exchanged for business use property so long as both properties are of like kind. In this case, the two parcels of land are of like kind.

Central to the exchange nonrecognition provisions is that the properties exchanged are like kind. The Treasury regulations on like-kind exchanges give the following interpretation of what constitutes **like-kind property:**

> The words "like kind" have reference to the nature or character of the property and not to its grade or quality. One kind or class of property may not be exchanged for property of a different kind or class. The fact that any real estate involved is improved or unimproved is not material, for that fact relates only to the grade or quality of the property and not to its kind or class.[6]

According to the IRS interpretation, *like-kind property* means that the properties exchanged must be of the same class of property. Only two classes of property are eligible for exchange treatment—tangible personal property and real property. The exchange requirement allows any real property to be exchanged for any other real property in a like-kind exchange. For example, unimproved land exchanged for an office building is a like-kind exchange, because both properties are real property.

Until July 1, 1992, any personal property could be exchanged for any other personal property and receive like-kind exchange treatment. To qualify as like-kind property, personal property exchanges after July 1, 1992, must be of like class.[7] *Like class* is defined as being within the same general asset class as defined for cost-recovery purposes (see Table A11–1 in the appendix to Chapter 11). The **general asset classes** are as follows:

00.11	Office furniture, fixtures, and equipment
00.12	Information systems (computers and peripheral equipment)
00.13	Data-handling equipment, except computers
00.21	Airplanes (airframes and engines), except those used in commercial or contract-carrying of passengers or freight, and all helicopters
00.22	Automobiles, taxis
00.23	Buses
00.241	Light general purpose trucks
00.242	Heavy general purpose trucks
00.25	Railroad cars and locomotives, except those owned by railroad transportation companies
00.26	Tractor units for use over the road
00.27	Trailers and trailer-mounted containers
00.28	Vessels, barges, tugs, and similar water-transportation equipment, except those used in marine construction
00.4	Industrial steam and electrical generation and/or distribution systems

▲ **EXAMPLE 15**   Peter Peppers, Inc., exchanged an automobile for a delivery van. Are the two properties of like kind?

Discussion: Exchanging an automobile used in a trade or business for a delivery van to be used in a trade or business is not a like-kind exchange, because the properties are not of like class. Automobiles are in class 00.22, whereas a delivery van would be in class 00.241 (light general purpose trucks).

▲ **EXAMPLE 16**   Sherry exchanged a computer she used in her trade or business for a laser printer. Are the two properties of like kind?

Discussion: The properties are like-kind properties. Both fall into asset class 00.12, computers and peripheral equipment.

▲ **EXAMPLE 17**   Clemons exchanged a parcel of land he held as an investment for an office building to be used in his business. Are the two properties of like kind?

Discussion: An exchange of real property for other real property is a like-kind exchange. It does not matter that the land is unimproved property and the building is improved property. Clemons's exchange is a like-kind exchange.

If both properties being exchanged do not fall within one of the general asset classes, the properties are like kind if they fall within the same product class. **Product class** is defined as the four-digit product class of the *Standard Industrial Classification Manual* **(SIC Codes).**[8] Two sample classes are shown in Exhibit 13–1. Additional selected SIC product classes appear in the appendix to this chapter. An asset cannot have both an asset class and a product class for purposes of determining like-kind exchange treatment. Therefore, if one asset being exchanged is in a general asset class and the other asset is not, the two properties are not like kind (even if both are in the same product class).

▲ **EXAMPLE 18**   Andrea exchanged an automobile used in her trade or business for a motor home to be used in her trade or business. Are the two properties of like kind?

Discussion: Automobiles are in general asset class 00.22. Mobile homes are not included in any general asset class but are in Product Class 3711 (Exhibit 13–1). Because the automobile is in a general asset class and the mobile home is not, the properties

▲ **Exhibit 13–1**

Sample SIC Product Class Codes

3711 Motor Vehicles and Passenger Car Bodies

Ambulances	Chassis, motor vehicle	Patrol wagons
Amphibian motor vehicles, except tanks	Fire department vehicles	Personnel carriers, for highway use
Assembling complete automobiles	Flushers, street	Road oilers
Automobiles	Hearses	Snowplows
Bodies, passenger automobile	Mobile lounges	Station wagons
Brooms, powered	Motor buses, except trackless trolley	Street sprinklers and sweepers
Car bodies	Motor homes, self-contained	Taxicabs
Cars, armored	Motor trucks, except off-highway	Tractors, truck: for highway use
Cars, electric: for highway use	Motor vehicles, including amphibian	Universal carriers, military

3531 Construction Machinery and Equipment

Aerial work platforms	Dredging machinery	Rock crushing machinery, portable
Aggregate spreaders	Excavators: e.g., cable, clamshell, crane,	Rollers, road
Asphalt plants	derrick, dragline, power shovel	Rollers, sheepsfoot and vibratory
Automobile wrecker hoists	Extractors, piling	Sand mixers
Backfillers, self-propelled	Finishers and spreaders, construction	Scarifiers, road
Backhoes	Finishers, concrete and bituminous	Scrapers, construction
Ballast distributors	Grader attachments, elevating	Screeds and screeding machines
Batching plants, bituminous	Graders, road (construction machinery)	Screeners, portable
Batching plants, for aggregate concrete	Grapples: rock, wood, etc.	Ship cranes and derricks
Blades for graders, scrapers, dozers,	Grinders, stone: portable	Shovel loaders
and snowplows	Hammer mills (rock and ore crushing	Shovels, power
Breakers, paving	machines), portable	Silos, cement (batch plant)
Buckets, excavating: clamshell, concrete,	Hammers, pile driving	Slag mixers
dragline, drag scraper, shovel	Line markers, self-propelled	Snowplow attachments
Bulldozers, construction	Locomotive cranes	Soil compactors: vibratory
Cabs, construction machinery	Log splitters	Spreaders and finishers, construction
Capstans, ship	Logging equipment	Subgraders, construction equipment
Carriers, crane	Mixers: e.g., concrete, ore, sand, slag,	Subsoiler attachments, tractor-mounted
Chip spreaders, self-propelled	plaster, mortar, bituminous	Surfacers, concrete grinding
Chippers, commercial: brush, limb,	Mortar mixers	Tampers, powered
and log	Mud jacks	Tamping equipment, rail
Concrete buggies, powered	Pavers	Teeth, bucket and scarifier
Concrete plants	Pile-driving equipment	Tractors, construction
Concrete grouting equipment	Planers, bituminous	Tractors, crawler
Concrete gunning equipment	Plaster mixers	Tractors, track-laying
Construction machinery, except mining	Plows, construction: excavating and	Trenching machines
Cranes, construction	grading	Trucks, off-highway
Cranes, except industrial plant	Post hole diggers, powered	Vibrators for concrete construction
Crushers, mineral: portable	Power cranes, draglines, and shovels	Wellpoint systems
Derricks, except oil and gas field	Pulverizers, stone: portable	Winches, all types
Distributors (construction machinery)	Railway track equipment: e.g., rail-layers,	Work platforms, elevated
Ditchers, ladder	ballast distributors	
Dozers, tractor mounted: material moving	Rakes, land clearing: mechanical	
Draglines, powered	Road construction and maintenance	
Drags, road (construction and road	machinery	
maintenance equipment)		

Source: U.S. Office of Management and Budget, *Standard Industrial Classification Manual*, Washington, D.C.: Executive Office of the President, 1987.

are not like kind. Note that this result holds even though automobiles are included in Product Class 3711.

▲ **EXAMPLE 19** Franny's Firewood, Inc., exchanged a log splitter for a mechanical rake. Are the two properties of like kind?

Discussion: Neither the log splitter nor the rake falls within a general asset class. Both assets are in Product Class 3531. Therefore, the log splitter and the rake are like-kind properties.

▲ **EXAMPLE 20**   Assume that in example 19 Franny's had exchanged the log splitter for a snowplow. Are the two properties of like kind?

Discussion: Neither the log splitter nor the snowplow falls within a general asset class. The log splitter is in Product Class 3531, and the snowplow is in Product Class 3711. Because the two assets are not in the same product class, they are not like-kind properties.

The following is a list of exchanges that never qualify for like-kind exchange treatment:

- Exchanges involving personal use property
- Exchanges of stocks, bonds, and inventories
- Exchanges of intangible property
- Exchanges of tangible personal property for real property
- Exchanges of livestock of a different sex
- Exchanges of partnership interests

Effect of Boot

When properties of different values are exchanged, the party with the lower-valued property must equalize the transaction by transferring cash, securities, or other property not of like kind (boot). Boot does not taint the like-kind nature of the exchange. However, any gain or loss realized on the transfer of the nonqualifying property must be recognized.

▲ **EXAMPLE 21**   Geraldine traded in her old cash register, which was worth $10,000, for a new cash register with a fair market value of $25,000. In obtaining the new cash register, Geraldine gave the dealer $5,000 in cash and stock with a fair market value of $10,000. Geraldine had adjusted bases of $7,000 in the old cash register and $4,000 in the stock. What are the tax consequences of the exchange?

Discussion: The exchange of the cash registers is a like-kind exchange for Geraldine. Her realized gain on the exchange is $3,000, none of which is recognized. Her basis in the new cash register is $22,000:

Amount realized (trade-in value)	$10,000
Adjusted basis	(7,000)
Realized gain	$ 3,000
Recognized gain (no boot received)	-0-
Deferred gain	$ 3,000

Basis in new cash register = $25,000 − $3,000 = $22,000

Although the exchange of the cash registers is tax free, stock is not like-kind property, and its disposition as part of the exchange transaction is a taxable transaction. Geraldine has a gain, realized and recognized, of $6,000 ($10,000 − $4,000) on the transfer of the stock.

Receipt of Boot.   The receiver of boot in a like-kind exchange has the wherewithal to pay tax on the exchange to the extent of the boot received. Therefore, a gain on a like-kind exchange is recognized to the extent of any boot received (but never more than the realized gain on the exchange). Losses on like-kind exchanges are never recognized, even when boot is received. The most common form of boot payment is cash. However, anything of value can be used to equalize the exchange. Therefore, receipts of other assets, services, and assumptions of debt constitute boot.[9]

▲ **EXAMPLE 22**   Endorra Corporation owns a building with a fair market value of $70,000 and an adjusted basis of $40,000. The corporation exchanges the building for land with a fair market value of $45,000 and receives $25,000 in cash. Both properties are investment properties for Endorra. What are Endorra Corporation's realized gain, recognized gain, and basis in the land?

Discussion: The exchange of a building for land is a like-kind exchange. Endorra Corporation realizes a gain of $30,000 on the building. Because it is in receipt of $25,000 in cash boot, the corporation must recognize $25,000 of the gain. Endorra's basis in the land is $40,000:

Amount realized ($45,000 + $25,000)	$70,000
Adjusted basis	(40,000)
Realized gain	$30,000
Recognized gain (cash boot received)	(25,000)
Deferred gain	$ 5,000

Basis in land = $45,000 − $5,000 = $40,000

▲ **EXAMPLE 23**   Assume that Endorra had a $10,000 mortgage on the building. As part of the exchange, the owner of the land agrees to assume the $10,000 mortgage and pay the corporation $15,000 in cash. What are Endorra's realized gain, recognized gain, and basis in the land?

Discussion: Endorra realizes a gain of $30,000 on the building. The corporation is in receipt of $25,000 in boot from the $10,000 mortgage assumption and the $15,000 in cash. Therefore, it must recognize a gain of $25,000. Endorra Corporation's basis in the land is $40,000:

Amount realized ($45,000 + $10,000 + $15,000)	$70,000
Adjusted basis	(40,000)
Realized gain	$30,000
Recognized gain (liability assumed + cash received)	(25,000)
Deferred gain	$ 5,000

Basis in land = $45,000 − $5,000 = $40,000

Example 23 illustrates that the assumption of a liability is considered boot received and therefore subject to current taxation. This occurs because a buyer who assumes a mortgage in essence gives cash to the seller, which the seller uses to pay off the existing mortgage. In example 23, the owner of the land could have paid Endorra $25,000 in cash to effect the exchange. Endorra would then have used $10,000 of the cash to pay off its mortgage, leaving the corporation with $15,000 in cash. This treatment of debt assumptions makes the taxation of exchanges neutral with respect to debt. That is, the same result is obtained regardless of whether the property being exchanged includes the assumption of debt on the property. However, if a mortgage is assumed and boot is paid in the transaction, the boot paid is offset by the boot received in the mortgage assumption.[10]

▲ **EXAMPLE 24**   Assume that in example 22 Endorra's mortgage on the building is $30,000. In order to make the exchange for the land, the corporation has to pay $5,000. What are Endorra's realized gain, recognized gain, and basis in the land?

Discussion: Endorra realizes a gain of $30,000 on the building. The corporation is in receipt of mortgage boot of $30,000, but it is allowed to offset the mortgage boot with the $5,000 cash boot it paid to make the exchange. Thus, Endorra recognizes a gain of $25,000 on the exchange. The corporation's basis in the land is $40,000:

Amount realized ($45,000 + $30,000 − $5,000)	$70,000
Adjusted basis	(40,000)
Realized gain	$30,000
Recognized gain (liability assumed − cash boot paid)	(25,000)
Deferred gain	$ 5,000

$$\text{Basis in land} = \$45,000 - \$5,000 = \$40,000$$

Note that the amount by which the cash boot offsets the mortgage is equal to the amount by which Endorra could have reduced its mortgage ($25,000) and then traded the mortgaged building for the land in an even exchange.

The tax law does not allow the receiver of money or other boot property to use liabilities assumed in the exchange to offset the boot received.

▲ **EXAMPLE 25**   Raul owned land with a fair market value of $30,000 and an adjusted basis of $8,000. Raul traded the land for another parcel of land with a fair market value of $35,000 and encumbered by a $10,000 mortgage. In the exchange, Raul assumed the $10,000 mortgage and received $5,000 in cash. What are Raul's realized gain, recognized gain, and his basis in the land acquired in the exchange?

Discussion: Raul has realized a gain of $22,000 on the exchange of the land. Raul must recognize a gain equal to the $5,000 in cash boot. He cannot offset the $5,000 cash boot with the $10,000 he paid in mortgage boot. His basis in the new land is $18,000:

Amount realized ($35,000 + $5,000 − $10,000)	$30,000
Adjusted basis	(8,000)
Realized gain	$22,000
Recognized gain (cash boot received)	(5,000)
Deferred gain	$17,000

$$\text{Basis in land} = \$35,000 - \$17,000 = \$18,000$$

The $18,000 basis in the land consists of the $8,000 basis in the original parcel of land, plus the extra $10,000 in debt Raul took on in the exchange.

When both properties being exchanged are encumbered by mortgages and the mortgages on the properties are exchanged, the mortgages are netted out. Only the party that has the larger mortgage is considered to have received mortgage boot. The party with the smaller mortgage is a net payer of mortgage boot and does not recognize gain from the net mortgage boot paid.

▲ **EXAMPLE 26**   Tara owns an office building, and the Barney Partnership owns an apartment building. Each property is encumbered by a mortgage. They agree to exchange their properties and their mortgages, with any difference to be paid in cash. The fair market values (FMV), mortgages, and adjusted bases for each property are listed here. Who must pay the cash to make the exchange, and how much must that taxpayer pay? What are the tax effects of the exchange for Tara and the Barney Partnership?

	Tara's Office Building	Barney's Apartment Building
FMV	$220,000	$250,000
Mortgage	$ 80,000	$150,000
Adjusted basis	$100,000	$175,000

Discussion: The partnership must pay Tara $40,000 to make the exchange. Tara's property has a net of mortgage value of $140,000 ($220,000 − $80,000), and Barney's net of mortgage value is $100,000 ($250,000 − $150,000). Therefore, the partnership must pay the $40,000 difference in the net value being exchanged.

Tara realizes a gain of $120,000 on her office building. She will have to recognize the $40,000 in cash boot she receives, but she is not allowed to offset the $40,000 with the $70,000 ($80,000 − $150,000) of net mortgage boot she pays on the exchange. Her basis in the apartment building is $170,000:

Amount realized ($250,000 + $40,000 + $80,000 − $150,000)	$220,000
Adjusted basis	(100,000)
Realized gain	$120,000
Recognized gain (cash boot received)	(40,000)
Deferred gain	$ 80,000

Basis in apartments = $250,000 − $80,000 = $170,000

Tara's basis in the apartment building is her $100,000 basis in the office building plus the additional $70,000 ($150,000 − $80,000) of debt she takes on in the exchange.

Barney realizes a gain of $75,000 on its apartment building. The partnership is in receipt of net mortgage boot of $70,000 ($150,000 − $80,000). However, it is allowed to use the $40,000 cash boot paid to Tara to offset the mortgage boot paid to Tara. Therefore, the partnership will recognize a gain of only $30,000. Barney's basis in the office building is $175,000:

Amount realized ($220,000 + $150,000 − $80,000 − $40,000)		$250,000
Adjusted basis		(175,000)
Realized gain		$ 75,000
Recognized gain - net mortgage boot:		
Barney's mortgage assumed by Tara	$150,000	
Tara's mortgage assumed by Barney	(80,000)	
Net mortgage boot received	$ 70,000	
Less: Cash boot paid	(40,000)	
Net boot received		(30,000)
Deferred gain		$ 45,000

Basis in office building = $220,000 − $45,000 = $175,000

The recognition of gains on like-kind exchanges to the extent of any boot received is based on the wherewithal-to-pay concept. However, this concept is not applicable to losses—losses do not require that resources be available for payment of tax on the transaction. Therefore, losses on like-kind exchanges are never recognized, even when boot is received in the exchange.

▲ **EXAMPLE 27**   Genevieve exchanged an apartment building held as an investment for a parcel of land. The apartment building had a fair market value of $43,000 and an adjusted basis of $65,000. Because the land was worth only $30,000, Genevieve received $13,000 in cash in the exchange. What are Genevieve's realized and recognized gain (loss) on the exchange and her basis in the land?

Discussion: Genevieve has a realized loss of $22,000 on the exchange. Losses on like-kind exchanges are never recognized. Her basis in the land is $52,000:

Amount realized ($30,000 + $13,000)	$ 43,000
Adjusted basis	(65,000)
Realized loss	$(22,000)
Recognized loss	-0-
Deferred loss	$(22,000)

Basis in land = $30,000 + $22,000 = $52,000

Note that in this case, Genevieve's basis in the land is not equal to the basis she had in the building, because she has recovered $13,000 of her investment with no tax consequences. Thus, her unrecovered investment is $52,000 ($65,000 − $13,000).

Related Party Exchanges

Tax law subjects transactions involving related parties to careful scrutiny. Many transactions between related parties are either disallowed or subject to special limitations. Like-kind exchange treatment is allowed for qualifying exchanges between related parties. However, for related party exchanges occurring after July 10, 1989, each party to the exchange must hold the property received in the exchange for two years to continue its qualification as a like-kind exchange. If either party disposes of the property received in the exchange sooner than two years, both parties must immediately recognize the tax effects of the initial exchange. Note that the recognition takes places in the year of the disposition. The year in which the original exchange occurred is not amended under the annual accounting period concept.

▲ **EXAMPLE 28**   Fred owns land with a fair market value of $85,000 and an adjusted basis of $5,000. Dan wants to buy the land from Fred. Nance Corporation, which is wholly owned by Fred, owns an apartment building with a fair market value of $85,000 and an adjusted basis of $70,000. In December 1995, Fred exchanges his land for Nance Corporation's apartment building. What are the tax consequences to Fred and Nance Corporation?

Discussion: An exchange of land for an apartment building is a like-kind exchange. The fact that Fred and Nance are related parties will not affect the nonrecognition of the exchange transaction in 1995. Fred has a realized gain of $80,000 ($85,000 − $5,000), none of which is recognized in 1995. Fred's basis in the apartments is $5,000. Nance has a realized gain of $15,000 ($85,000 − $70,000), none of which is recognized in 1995. Nance's basis in the land is $70,000. So long as both Fred and Nance hold the properties for two full years from the date of the exchange, no gains will be recognized from the exchange.

▲ **EXAMPLE 29**   In January 1996, Nance Corporation sells the land acquired from Fred to Dan for $85,000. What are the tax consequences to Fred and Nance Corporation of the sale to Dan?

Discussion: Because Nance sold the land acquired from Fred without holding it for two full years, the original exchange no longer qualifies as a like-kind exchange. Fred must recognize his $80,000 in realized gain on the land in 1996. This gives him a basis in the apartment buildings of $85,000. Nance must recognize the $15,000 gain realized on the apartment building in 1996, leaving Nance with a basis of $85,000 in the land. The sale of the land to Dan results in no realization of gain ($85,000 − $85,000).

Carryover of Tax Attributes

When property is exchanged in a qualifying like-kind exchange, the tax attributes of the asset carry over and are attributed to the new asset acquired in the exchange. As a continuation of investment, the holding period of the new asset includes the period during which the initial asset was held. More important, if the asset being exchanged is a depreciable asset, the recapture potential of the first asset carries to the second asset. The recapture potential of an asset is the maximum amount of recapture on the asset at the time of the exchange. For a Section 1245 asset, the recapture potential is equal to the depreciation taken on the asset as of the date it is exchanged. The recapture potential of a Section 1250 asset is the excess depreciation taken on the asset as of the date of the exchange.

▲ **EXAMPLE 30**   Kelly purchased a machine used in her business that had a fair market value of $16,000 by trading in an old machine and giving $9,000. Kelly had paid $14,000 for the old machine, which had an adjusted basis of $3,000 at the date of the trade. What are the tax effects for Kelly of the exchange?

Discussion: Kelly has realized a gain of $4,000 on the old machine. Kelly will not have to recognize any of the gain, because she did not receive any boot in the exchange. Her basis in the new machine is $12,000:

Amount realized ($16,000 − $9,000)	$7,000
Adjusted basis ($14,000 − $11,000)	(3,000)
Realized gain	$4,000
Recognized gain	-0-
Deferred gain	$4,000

Basis in new machine = $16,000 − $4,000 = $12,000

In addition, the $11,000 in depreciation taken on the old machine is attributed to the new machine as the carryover of the recapture potential. That is, the first $11,000 of any gain on a taxable disposition of the second machine will be ordinary income from the recapture of the depreciation deductions taken on the old machine. In addition, any depreciation deductions on the new machine will also be subject to recapture.

▲ **EXAMPLE 31**   Three years after acquiring the new machine in example 30, Kelly sold the machine for $14,000. Depreciation taken on the machine was $6,200. What is the character of the gain on the sale of the machine?

Discussion: Kelly must recognize a gain of $8,200 [$14,000 − ($12,000 − $6,200)] on the sale of the machine. Machinery used in a trade or business is a Section 1245 asset. Kelly must recognize any gain on the sale of the asset as ordinary income to the extent of the depreciation taken on the machine. Although Kelly has deducted only $6,200 in depreciation on the machine sold, the $11,000 in depreciation taken on the previous machine is attributed to the new machine. Therefore, Kelly is considered to have deducted $17,200 in depreciation on the machine she sold for purposes of applying the depreciation recapture rules, and her $8,200 gain on the sale is ordinary income.

▲ INVOLUNTARY CONVERSIONS

An **involuntary conversion** occurs whenever a gain or loss is realized from a transaction that occurs against the taxpayer's will. That is, an involuntary conversion is a disposition of property that is beyond the control of the taxpayer. Involuntary conversions result when property is destroyed or damaged in a casualty or theft, when a government unit condemns property under its power of eminent domain, or when a foreign government seizes or nationalizes property. Property that is sold under a threat or imminence of a condemnation or seizure is considered an involuntary conversion. In addition, the selling of livestock because of disease or drought is treated as an involuntary conversion.

Treatment of Involuntary Conversion Gains and Losses

The key to understanding the tax treatment of involuntary conversions is that the disposition of the property was not within the taxpayer's control. Although the taxpayer may have been fully insured and realized a gain on the conversion, replacement of the income-producing capacity of an asset involuntarily converted may take months or years. This puts the business at a distinct disadvantage. Because of the detrimental nature of involuntary conversions, the tax law provides the maximum relief possible.

To provide tax relief, losses on involuntary conversions of business or investment property are always recognized in full. Personal casualty and theft losses are deductible, subject to the event and adjusted gross income limitations discussed in Chapter 7. However, a condemnation loss on a personal use asset is not deductible.

When an involuntary conversion results in a gain, taxpayers may elect to defer the gain if they purchase qualified replacement property. Under the wherewithal-to-pay concept, any involuntary conversion proceeds that are not reinvested in a qualified replacement property must be recognized.[11] However, the amount of gain recognized can never exceed the gain realized on the involuntary conversion.

▲ **EXAMPLE 32**   Bolder Co.'s truck storage shed was destroyed by an avalanche. The shed had cost $160,000 and had an adjusted basis of $70,000 when it was destroyed. The shed was worth $200,000, and Bolder received $180,000 from its insurance company for the casualty. What is the minimum amount of gain Bolder must recognize in each of the following cases? What is the basis of the replacement shed in each case?

Case A

Bolder purchased a qualified replacement shed for $230,000.

Discussion: Bolder has realized a gain of $110,000 on the casualty. Because Bolder used all the insurance proceeds to replace the shed, Bolder has no wherewithal to pay tax on the gain. None of the gain must be recognized. Bolder's basis in the new shed is $120,000:

Amount realized (insurance proceeds)		$180,000
Adjusted basis		(70,000)
Realized gain		$110,000
Recognized gain:		
Insurance proceeds received	$180,000	
Amount reinvested in new shed	230,000	
Insurance proceeds remaining		
after replacement		-0-
Deferred gain		$110,000

$$\text{Basis of new shed} = \$230,000 - \$110,000 = \$120,000$$

Note that the basis of the new shed ($120,000) is equal to the $70,000 basis of the old shed plus the additional $50,000 ($230,000 − $180,000) of out-of-pocket cost of purchasing the replacement shed.

Case B

Bolder purchased a qualified replacement shed costing $150,000.

Discussion: After replacing the shed, Bolder has $30,000 of the insurance proceeds remaining. Bolder must recognize $30,000 of the $110,000 gain on the shed. Bolder's basis in the new shed is $70,000:

Realized gain		$110,000
Recognized gain:		
Insurance proceeds received	$180,000	
Amount reinvested in new shed	(150,000)	
Insurance proceeds remaining		
after replacement		(30,000)
Deferred gain		$ 80,000

Basis of new shed = $150,000 − $80,000 = $70,000

In an involuntary conversion, the taxpayer typically receives insurance proceeds or a cash payment for the property from the government condemning or seizing the property. In the rare case of a direct conversion to another piece of property (no cash payment received), no gain on the conversion is recognized. The basis of the property converted is carried over to the basis of the property received.[12] If the direct conversion results in a loss, the loss on the conversion is recognized.

The deferral of gain realized on an involuntary conversion is not mandatory. A taxpayer may choose to recognize the entire gain on an involuntary conversion. A gain deferral provides a time value of money savings on the income tax deferred and is usually the preferred alternative. However, situations do arise in which a gain on an involuntary conversion can be recognized without paying additional tax. For example, a taxpayer with a large net capital loss that could not otherwise be deducted in the current year may elect to recognize gain if the property involuntarily converted produces either a capital gain or a Section 1231 gain (which is treated as a long-term capital gain). In such cases, the recognized gain is offset by the capital loss, with no additional tax required of the taxpayer. Because the gain is fully recognized, the basis of the replacement property is not reduced, resulting in larger deductions on the property in future tax years.

▲ **EXAMPLE 33**   A rental property Cecilia held as an investment is destroyed by a flood in 1995. Cecilia had purchased the property in 1990, and it had an adjusted basis of $95,000 when it was destroyed. Cecilia receives $115,000 in insurance proceeds, which she uses to buy a qualifying rental property costing $140,000. Cecilia has a net capital loss of $33,000 from her other capital asset transactions during 1995. What are the tax consequences if Cecilia recognizes the $20,000 gain on the involuntary conversion in 1995?

Discussion: The $20,000 realized gain ($115,000 − $95,000) is a capital gain. Because the property was depreciated using the MACRS system, there is no excess depreciation to recapture if the gain is recognized. The entire gain would be a long-term capital gain that would be netted against the $33,000 net capital loss. Cecilia would then have a net capital loss of $13,000. If Cecilia elects to recognize the gain, she pays no additional tax in 1995. In addition, her basis in the replacement property would be $140,000, versus a basis of $120,000 if she elects to defer the gain. The election to recognize the gain does not increase her 1995 tax liability and she may deduct the additional $20,000 of basis in the new property through depreciation over the life of the new property.

As example 33 illustrates, cases in which an election to recognize a gain on an involuntary conversion can prove beneficial. However, don't forget that the depreciation recapture rules may reclassify most, if not all, of the gain as ordinary income. Under such circumstances, recognition of the gain may not provide the desired offset of the net capital loss. The important point is that by making the deferral of a gain on an involuntary conversion elective rather than mandatory (as in like-kind exchanges), the taxpayer is given maximum flexibility in obtaining the optimal tax result for the particular situation. Combined with the recognition of losses on involuntary conversions, the tax law provides taxpayers who suffer an involuntary conversion the maximum tax relief possible in all situations.

Qualified Replacement Property

Taxpayers may defer gains on involuntary conversions only if they purchase qualified replacement property within two years of the close of the tax year in which the involuntary conversion occurred; this time limit is referred to as the involuntary conversion replacement period. Qualified replacement property must be "property similar or related in service or use."[13] This requirement is referred to as the *functional use test*. The functional use test requires that the replacement property perform the same function or have the same use to the taxpayer as the property involuntarily converted. The functional use test is applicable to all business and investment property—other than a condemnation of real property—that is subject to an involuntary conversion. The replacement requirement for condemned business or investment real property is that the taxpayer must purchase like-kind property.[14] As discussed earlier, *like kind* means that the taxpayer can purchase any other type of real property. Thus, the replacement requirements for condemnations of real property are more generous than for other types of conversions.

> ▲ **EXAMPLE 34**   One of Sno-Cone, Inc.'s ice-making factories was destroyed by a fire. Sno-Cone used the insurance proceeds from the fire to purchase another ice-making factory. Is the new ice-making factory a qualified replacement property?
>
> *Discussion:* Sno-Cone must replace the factory with property that has the same functional use. Because the new ice-making facility performs the same function as the factory involuntarily converted, it is a qualified replacement property.
>
> ▲ **EXAMPLE 35**   Assume that Sno-Cone did not need to purchase another ice-making facility to maintain its production capacity and used the insurance proceeds to purchase a lollipop factory. Is the lollipop factory a qualified replacement property?
>
> *Discussion:* The lollipop factory does not perform the same function in Sno-Cone, Inc.'s business as the ice-making factory. It is not a qualified replacement property.
>
> ▲ **EXAMPLE 36**   Assume the same facts as in example 35, except that the ice-making factory was condemned and bought by the local government. Is the purchase of the lollipop factory a qualified replacement property?
>
> *Discussion:* Sno-Cone must replace the condemned business real property with like-kind property. Because a lollipop factory is real property, it is like-kind property that is a qualified replacement property for condemned real property.

In general, qualified replacement property must be purchased within two years after the close of the tax year in which the involuntary conversion occurred. If a property is sold under a threat of condemnation, the replacement period begins at the date of the threat of condemnation. In addition, the replacement period for condemned business or investment real property is extended to three years.

A realized loss on the sale or exchange of a taxpayer's personal residence is not deductible because of the restrictions on loss deductions for personal use assets. On the other hand, a realized gain from the sale or exchange of a personal residence is taxable under the all-inclusive income concept. However, taxpayers who purchase a qualified replacement residence must defer the gain they realize. As with all nonrecognition transactions, any proceeds from the sale of a principal residence that are not reinvested in acquiring the replacement residence must be recognized and are subject to tax under the wherewithal-to-pay concept.

▲ SALE OF A PRINCIPAL RESIDENCE

Principal Residence

To be eligible for gain deferral, both the old and the new residences must be used as the principal residence of the taxpayer. A **principal residence** is where the taxpayer lives most of the time. A taxpayer can have only one principal residence at a time. A principal residence can be a house, mobile home, cooperative apartment, condominium, or a houseboat, provided it is where the taxpayer lives. Ordinarily, it is not difficult to determine whether the old and new properties constitute the taxpayer's residences. However, the distinction is crucial, because the deferral provisions do not apply to the sale of a vacation home, even if the proceeds are used to purchase a home that is occupied year-round. Similarly, gain on the sale of a principal residence cannot be deferred if the proceeds are invested in a vacation home.

> ▲ **EXAMPLE 37** Althea owned a ski cabin that she held as a rental property. Althea lived in an apartment that she rented from an unrelated party. Althea sold the ski cabin at a gain and used the proceeds to purchase a house, which she moved into and used as her residence. Can the gain on the sale of the rental property be deferred?
>
> *Discussion:* Althea is taxed on the gain realized from the sale of the ski cabin. Both the residence sold and the residence purchased must be Althea's principal residence. She had held the ski property for investment; it was not where Althea lived during the year.

If the old residence ceases to be the taxpayer's principal residence before the sale takes place, the nonrecognition provisions do not apply. Abandonment or conversion of the old residence to a rental property before sale would disqualify the property from the nonrecognition provisions. However, temporarily renting out a residence while it is being advertised for sale will not normally change the status of a principal residence. In determining whether a residence is a principal residence, the tax law looks at "all the facts and circumstances" about the residence, including "the good faith of the taxpayer." [15]

> ▲ **EXAMPLE 38** The Smith family owned and lived in a house in St. Louis for many years. In February 1995, Francine Smith is transferred by her company to Mississippi. The Smiths move to Mississippi the next month. Because they are unable to sell their house before they move, they rent the house out on a month-to-month rental contract to help pay the cost of maintaining both the St. Louis property and a new home in Mississippi until the St. Louis house can be sold. Is the St. Louis house a principal residence?
>
> *Discussion:* All the facts and circumstances indicate that renting the St. Louis house was not an attempt to convert the house to a rental property. Rather, the month-to-month rental of the property to defray the costs of holding two residences would indicate a continuing desire to sell the property, not an intent to convert it to rental property.

Replacement Period

To qualify for nonrecognition, the old residence must be replaced by a new residence within a period that begins two years before the sale of the old residence and ends two years after the sale of the old residence; this period is referred to as the *principal residence replacement period.* Allowing the two-year replacement period before and after the sale of the old residence recognizes the realities of the marketplace: Many people must move before they are able to sell their old residence.

▲ **EXAMPLE 39**   Assume that in example 38 the Smith family purchases a new residence in Mississippi in June 1995. The St. Louis house is sold in November 1995. Does the Mississippi residence meet the two-year replacement period requirement?

Discussion: The Mississippi residence was purchased within two years of the sale of the St. Louis residence. The replacement period requirements are satisfied.

   Once the replacement is made in June 1995, the Smiths have until June 1997 to sell the St. Louis home. If the St. Louis home is not sold by then, they cannot defer any gain on the sale of the St. Louis residence.

In addition to acquiring the property during the two-year period, the taxpayer must occupy and use the new residence as a principal residence during that period. The occupancy and use requirements have been strictly interpreted by the courts to mean actual physical occupancy and actual use of the property as a principal residence.

▲ **EXAMPLE 40**   In 1969, President Richard Nixon purchased the "San Clemente White House" as a replacement for his New York City residence. He used the San Clemente property on weekends and holidays with the intent of living there full time after his presidential term ended. Does the San Clemente property qualify as a replacement principal residence for the New York City residence sold in 1969?

Discussion: Congress's Joint Committee on Internal Revenue Taxation determined that the use of a house on weekends with an intent to occupy after leaving the White House did not meet the actual occupancy and use test. It was determined that there were no statutory exceptions that would allow a taxpayer not to physically occupy and use the property as a principal residence during the two-year replacement period. Although Nixon occupied San Clemente as his principal residence sooner than he had initially anticipated, he did not do so within two years of the sale of his New York City residence, and his gain deferral was denied.[16]

To discourage use of the nonrecognition provisions as a deferral technique in a rising real estate market, the tax law does not allow deferral on subsequent sales for a two-year period. Therefore, a taxpayer who buys more than one principal residence during the two-year period following the sale of an old residence must use the last residence purchased as the replacement residence for calculating the deferral of gain on the sale of the old residence. Gains on other sales during the two-year period are recognized.

▲ **EXAMPLE 41**   Joe Bob sells his principal residence on March 14, 1995. He purchases a qualified replacement residence on July 4, 1995. On January 6, 1996, he sells the second residence and uses the proceeds to purchase another principal residence on April 28, 1996. Can Joe Bob defer the gain from the sale of both residences?

Discussion: Because Joe Bob sold the first replacement residence sooner than two years from the sale of his first principal residence, he cannot defer the gain on its sale. He defers the gain on the March 14, 1995, sale, using the residence purchased on April 28, 1996, to calculate the gain deferral.

The two-year resale rule would work a hardship on an employee who is transferred and therefore has no control over the timing of the sales and purchases. The provision is waived for any sale that is caused by a change in the location of employment. To qualify as a change in location, the move must meet the distance and time tests for deducting moving expenses.

▲ **EXAMPLE 42**   Assume that in example 41 Joe Bob sells his residence on January 6, 1996, because he is being transferred to another state by his employer. Can Joe Bob defer the gain from the sale of both residences?

Discussion: Because a change in the location of his employment necessitates the sale of the first replacement residence, Joe Bob can defer the gain on the sale of both residences.

Deferral of Gain

As with all nonrecognition provisions, a gain on the sale of a principal residence is not recognized if the taxpayer does not have the wherewithal to pay the tax on the gain after purchasing the replacement property. So long as the proceeds received from the sale of the residence are fully reinvested in the new residence, no gain on sale is recognized. However, realized gains are recognized to the extent that proceeds from the sale are not reinvested.

The amount that must be reinvested in the new residence is the adjusted sales price of the old residence. The **adjusted sales price** is equal to the amount realized on the sale, less fixing-up expenses. Fixing-up expenses are noncapital expenditures that prepare the residence for sale, are incurred within 90 days before the sale, and paid within 30 days after the sale. The reduction of the amount realized from the sale by the fixing-up expenses reflects the fact that such costs are nondeductible, because they are related to a personal use asset, yet the amount expended on such costs is not available for reinvestment by the taxpayer. Exhibit 13–2 presents the framework for calculating the amount of deferred gain on the sale of a principal residence.

▲ **EXAMPLE 43**   Walter sold his principal residence for $113,000. Walter paid selling expenses of $9,000 and incurred $4,000 in fixing-up expenses to prepare the residence for sale. Walter's adjusted basis in the residence was $84,000. What are Walter's

Amount realized on sale (selling price less selling expenses)		$XXX
Less: Adjusted basis		(XXX)
Realized gain on sale		$XXX
Calculation of Deferred Gain		
Amount realized	$XXX	
Less: Fixing-up expenses	(XXX)	
Adjusted sales price	$XXX	
Cost of new residence	(XXX)	
Recognized gain—Excess (if any) of adjusted sales price over cost of new residence		(XXX)
Deferred gain		$XXX
Calculation of Basis of New Residence		
Cost of new residence		$XXX
Less: Deferred gain		(XXX)
Basis of replacement residence		$XXX

▲ **Exhibit 13–2**

SALE OF PRINCIPAL RESIDENCE GAIN DEFERRAL CALCULATION

recognized gain and his basis in the new residence in each of the qualified replacement cases that follow?

	Case A	Case B	Case C
Replacement residence cost	$126,000	$95,000	$75,000

Discussion: In each case, Walter has realized a gain of $20,000. Walter's adjusted sales price, which he must reinvest, is $100,000:

Amount realized ($113,000 − $9,000)	$104,000
Adjusted basis	(84,000)
Realized gain on sale	$ 20,000

Adjusted sales price = $104,000 − $4,000 = $100,000

	Case A	Case B	Case C
Realized gain on sale	$ 20,000	$ 20,000	$ 20,000
Recognized Gain			
Adjusted sales price	$100,000	$100,000	$100,000
Cost of new residence	126,000	95,000	75,000
Excess—Recognized gain	-0-	$ 5,000	$ 20,000
Deferred Gain	$ 20,000	$ 15,000	$ -0-
Basis of New Residence			
Cost of new residence	$126,000	$ 95,000	$ 75,000
Less: Deferred gain	(20,000)	(15,000)	-0-
Basis	$106,000	$ 80,000	$ 75,000

In case A, the entire adjusted sales price has been reinvested in acquiring the new $126,000 residence, and none of the $20,000 gain is recognized. In case B, $5,000 of the adjusted sales price was not reinvested and is taxed under the wherewithal-to-pay concept. In case C, $25,000 of the adjusted sales price was not reinvested. However, the amount of recognized gain cannot exceed the gain realized on the sale. The full $20,000 in realized gain is recognized in case C.

The provisions for deferring gain on the sale of a principal residence also require deferral of gain when a new principal residence is acquired by exchange. In addition, a gain resulting from the condemnation of a principal residence may be deferred by using either the rules for involuntary conversions or the sale of principal residence provisions. Under no circumstances may a loss from the sale, exchange, or condemnation of a principal residence be deferred. These are personal use losses that are not deductible and therefore not deferrable. The only loss on a principal residence that is deductible is a casualty loss, which is deductible under the personal casualty loss rules.

▲ **EXAMPLE 44**   Courtney sold her principal residence for $63,000, paying selling expenses of $2,000. Fixing-up expenses were $500. Courtney's adjusted basis in the residence was $76,000. Courtney purchased another principal residence for $82,000. What are the tax effects of the sale and purchase of the principal residences for Courtney?

Discussion: Courtney has realized a loss of $15,000 [($63,000 − $2,000) − $76,000] on the sale of her residence. A loss on the sale of a principal residence is a personal use loss, which is not deductible. The basis in the new residence is her $82,000 cost. The $15,000 loss is not deferred into the basis of the new residence.

For many taxpayers, the principal residence represents the largest single investment asset they own. Older taxpayers who have owned the same residence for many years often have very large gains when they sell the property. Much of this gain comes from inflation in property values and corresponding deflation in the purchasing power of the dollar during the long period the property was held. To afford older citizens some tax relief when they realize these big gains and either do not replace the property or purchase a much smaller property, Congress has provided a one-time exclusion of up to $125,000 in gain on the sale of a principal residence.[17] An *exclusion from income* means that the income will never be subject to tax. Thus, an election to exclude gain does not require that a replacement residence be purchased.

▲ **SALE OF A PRINCIPAL RESIDENCE— TAXPAYERS OLDER THAN 55**

Gain Exclusion Requirements

To be eligible to elect the exclusion of gain, the taxpayer must meet the following requirements:

- The taxpayer or the taxpayer's spouse must have attained age 55 before the closing date of the sale.

- The taxpayer or the taxpayer's spouse may not have previously made an election to exclude gain on the sale of a principal residence.

- The residence must have been owned and used as the principal residence of the taxpayer or the taxpayer's spouse during three of the previous five years. For purposes of the three-year residence test, up to two years of living in a nursing facility while taxpayers are incapable of caring for themselves can be counted in the three-year period.

One-Time Exclusion of Gain

The election to exclude gain is available only once during the lifetime of a taxpayer. The $125,000 exclusion is the maximum amount that can be excluded when making the one-time election to exclude. You are not allowed to exclude a series of gains up to a total gain of $125,000. Taxpayers who are eligible for exclusion and who buy a replacement residence should try to defer the gain under the sale of principal residence rules to avoid wasting their one-time election. However, taxpayers who purchase a much smaller residence, and therefore can defer little or none of the gain, probably should use the gain exclusion to take advantage of the time value of money savings on the excluded gain.

> ▲ **EXAMPLE 45**   Horatio and Maude are both older than 55. They sold their principal residence for $175,000 and moved in with their son and his family. Selling expenses were $9,000. Their adjusted basis in the residence was $28,000. What is their recognized gain on the sale of the residence?
>
> *Discussion:*   Horatio and Maude realized a gain of $138,000 on the sale. Because at least 1 of them is older than 55, they may elect to exclude up to $125,000 of the gain. The election to exclude leaves them with a recognized gain of $13,000:

Amount realized on sale ($175,000 − $9,000)	$166,000
Adjusted basis	(28,000)
Realized gain	$138,000
Less: Maximum $125,000 gain exclusion	(125,000)
Recognized gain	$ 13,000

▲ **EXAMPLE 46**   Assume the same facts as in example 45, except that Horatio and Maude purchased a new principal residence costing $180,000. Should they use their election to exclude gain on the sale?

Discussion: Because Horatio and Maude purchased a new principal residence, they must use the deferral rules for sale of a principal residence if they do not elect to take their $125,000 gain exclusion. In this case, they have reinvested the entire adjusted sales price in the new residence and can defer the entire gain. Thus, they should not elect to use their one-time gain exclusion:

Realized gain		$138,000
Recognized gain		
Adjusted sales price	$166,000	
Cost of new residence	180,000	
Recognized gain (no excess)		-0-
Deferred gain		$138,000

Basis in new residence = $180,000 − $138,000 = $42,000

The limit of one election to exclude for the taxpayer or the taxpayer's spouse precludes using the election when one spouse has used the election before marrying the current spouse.[18]

▲ **EXAMPLE 47**   Lee and Kathleen married in 1990. In 1995, they sell their principal residence at a gain of $80,000 and do not buy another principal residence. Lee is 53, and Kathleen is 59. In 1987, while Kathleen was married to Gary (who was 56 at the time), Gary and Kathleen elected to exclude the gain on the sale of their principal residence. Can Lee and Kathleen exclude the $80,000 gain on the sale of their principal residence?

Discussion: Because Kathleen previously used the one-time election to exclude gain (while she was married to Gary), Lee and Kathleen are not eligible to exclude the $80,000 gain. This result holds, even though Lee has never used the election. If one spouse "spends" the election to exclude gain in a previous marriage (or while single), the election is no longer available in a subsequent marriage.

Interaction of Deferral and Exclusion Provisions

If an eligible taxpayer has a gain in excess of $125,000 and makes a qualified replacement, the election to exclude and the deferral of gain on sale of a principal residence may both be used to minimize current gain recognition. Using both provisions is necessary only when the gain on sale cannot be fully deferred through use of the deferral provisions. This is often the case when an eligible taxpayer buys less expensive housing when purchasing a new residence. When both provisions are being used, the $125,000 excludable gain cannot be taxed and therefore does not have to be invested in a replacement residence. Thus, the adjusted sales price for calculating the gain deferral is reduced by the $125,000 in excluded gain.

▲ **EXAMPLE 48**   Hal and Renee are both older than 55. During the current year, they sold their house for $265,000. Selling expenses were $18,000, and they incurred $4,000 in fixing-up expenses. The adjusted basis of the house was $67,000. They purchased a $90,000 condominium to use as their residence. What are the amount of gain they must recognize on the sale and the basis in the condominium?

Discussion: Hal and Renee have realized a gain of $180,000 on the sale of the house. They may elect to exclude $125,000 of the gain. Because they bought a new residence, they must use the sale of principal residence deferral rules on the remaining $55,000 of gain. This results in a recognized gain of $28,000 and a basis in the condominium of $63,000:

Amount realized ($265,000 − $18,000)	$247,000
Adjusted basis	(67,000)
Realized gain	$180,000
Excluded gain	(125,000)
Gain remaining for deferral	$ 55,000

Gain Deferral

Adjusted Sales Price

Amount realized from sale	$247,000	
Less: Fixing-up expenses	(4,000)	
Less: Excluded gain	(125,000)	
Adjusted sales price	$118,000	
Cost of condominium	(90,000)	
Recognized gain		(28,000)
Deferred gain		$ 27,000

Basis in condominium = $90,000 − $27,000 = $63,000

The key factor in applying the exclusion and deferral provisions to the same transaction is that the $125,000 is never subject to tax. Thus, it does not have to be reinvested, and the adjusted sales price is reduced to determine the amount of gain recognized on the purchase of the new residence. This subtraction occurs because adjusted sales price represents the wherewithal to pay.

▲ SUMMARY

The all-inclusive income concept requires that all gains are subject to tax when they are realized in an arm's-length transaction. However, Congress has provided current period tax relief for gains from like-kind exchanges, involuntary conversions, and the sale of a principal residence. Although each nonrecognition transaction has unique characteristics, the three classes of transactions have five distinctive commonalities. First, the rationale for nonrecognition of these transactions comes from the wherewithal-to-pay concept. Because this concept is a basis for not recognizing gains, all the transactions allow for the deferral of gains. The deferral is mandatory for like-kind exchanges and the sale of a principal residence. Gains on involuntary conversions are deferred at the election of the taxpayer. Losses on like-kind exchanges must be deferred. Involuntary conversion losses are deducted in the period of realization. Realized losses on a principal residence cannot be deducted or deferred.

Each nonrecognition transaction is viewed as the continuation of an ongoing investment in the asset disposed of in the transaction. Therefore, each nonrecognition transaction requires the acquisition of a qualified replacement property within a prescribed period in order for gain to be deferred.

Gains are fully deferred when the entire proceeds of the realization are reinvested in a replacement property. However, any amount realized on a nonrecognition disposition that is not reinvested in a qualifying replacement property is subject to tax under the wherewithal-to-pay concept. The amount of gain to be recognized cannot exceed the gain realized on the transaction.

The deferral of gains (and losses on like-kind exchanges) is effected through an adjustment of the basis of the replacement property. The basis of the replacement property is reduced for any gain deferred on the nonrecognition transaction. Losses on like-kind exchanges are deferred by increasing the basis of the replacement property.

As a continuation of the original investment in the property on which gain has been realized, the tax attributes of the original property attach to the replacement property. Under this attribution, the holding period of the replacement property includes the holding period of the original property. In addition, any depreciation recapture potential on the original property is attributed to the replacement. The recapture potential of a property is the maximum amount of depreciation recapture on the property as of the date of disposition.

▲ **Table 13-1**

CHARACTERISTICS OF NONRECOGNITION TRANSACTIONS

Characteristic	Like-Kind Exchanges	Involuntary Conversions	Sale of Principal Residence	
			Deferral	Exclusion
Property eligible for nonrecognition	Business or investment property other than inventories, securities, intangible assets, and partnership interests.	Property used in a trade or business or held for investment.	Principal residence of the taxpayer.	Principal residence of the taxpayer.
Replacement property requirement	Like-kind business or investment property. Like-kind property is property of the same general class.	Property must have the same functional use to the taxpayer as the property converted. Condemned real property must be replaced with like-kind property.	Principal residence of the taxpayer.	No property purchase required.
Replacement period	Property to be received in the exchange must be identified within 45 days and transaction completed within 180 days of first transfer of property.	Two years from the end of the tax year of the conversion. Taxpayer has 3 years to replace condemned real property.	Replacement period begins 2 years before sale and ends 2 years after sale.	No property purchase required.
Realized gains	Deferral of gains is mandatory. Gains are recognized to the extent of boot received in the exchange.	Deferral of gains is elective. If deferral is elected, any proceeds not reinvested must be recognized.	Deferral of gains is mandatory. Any part of the adjusted sales price that is not reinvested must be recognized.	Taxpayers who are at least 55 may elect to exclude up to $125,000 in gain.
Realized losses	Deferral of losses is mandatory.	Losses are recognized.	Losses are not deductible or deferred.	Losses are not deductible or deferred.
Basis of replacement property	Gains: reduce by deferred gain. Losses: increase by deferred loss.	Reduce basis by deferred gain.	Reduce basis by deferred gain.	None. Property purchase not required.

A special provision allows taxpayers who are at least 55 years old as of the date of sale of a principal residence to exclude a maximum of $125,000 in gain. The exclusion is a once-in-a-lifetime election and cannot be used if the taxpayer or the taxpayer's spouse has previously elected to exclude gain on the sale of a principal residence. If an election to exclude is made and the taxpayer also acquires a qualified replacement residence, the taxpayer must use the sale of principal residence deferral rules to defer any gain on sale in excess of the $125,000 exclusion.

Table 13–1 compares and summarizes the characteristics and requirements for nonrecognition in each of the nonrecognition transactions.

▲ KEY TERMS

adjusted sales price (p. 605)	involuntary conversion (p. 599)	principal residence (p. 603)
boot (p. 589)	like-kind exchange rules (p. 591)	product class (p. 592)
deferred (third-party) exchange (p. 590)	like-kind property (p. 591)	SIC Codes (p. 592)
general asset class (p. 592)	nonrecognition transaction (p. 583)	

▲ PRIMARY TAX LAW SOURCES

[1] Reg. Sec. 1.1031(c)-1—Requires adjustment of the basis of property acquired in a nontaxable exchange. Similar provisions are found in Reg. Sec. 1.1033(b)-1 for involuntarily converted property and Reg. Sec. 1.1034-1 for replacement of a principal residence.

[2] Sec. 1223—The general rule for holding period requires a carryover of holding period when a carryover basis is used.

[3] Reg. Sec. 1.1250-3—Requires the carryover of excess depreciation on any Section 1250 property acquired in a tax-free transaction. Reg. Sec. 1.1245-4 contains a similar provision applicable to Section 1245 property.

[4] Sec. 1031—Provides rules for like-kind exchanges of property.

[5] Reg. Sec. 1.1031(k)-1—Provides the rules for deferred exchanges and gives examples of qualifying exchanges.

[6] Reg. Sec. 1.1031(a)-1—Gives the general definition of *like-kind property* for purposes of Section 1031.

[7] Reg. Sec. 1.1031(a)-2—Expands on the definition of *like-kind property* as it applies to personal property.

[8] U.S. Office of Management and Budget, *Standard Industrial Classification Manual* (Washington, D.C.: Executive Office of the President, 1987).

[9] Reg. Sec. 1.1031(b)-1—Discusses the treatment of boot in like-kind exchanges.

[10] Reg. Sec. 1.1031(d)-2—Provides rules for treatment of mortgage assumptions in like-kind exchanges.

[11] Sec. 1033—Provides rules for deferring gains on involuntary conversions.

[12] Reg. Sec. 1.1033(a)-2—Provides the rules for direct conversions of property.

[13] Sec. 1033—See footnote 11.

[14] Reg. Sec. 1.1033(g)-1—Allows condemned real property used in a trade or business or for the production of income to be replaced with like-kind property.

[15] Reg. Sec. 1034-1—Discusses what constitutes a taxpayer's principal residence for purposes of Section 1034.

[16] JOINT COMM. ON INTERNAL REVENUE TAXATION, EXAMINATION OF PRESIDENT NIXON'S TAX RETURNS FOR 1969 THROUGH 1972, H.R. REP. NO. 966, 93d Cong., 2d Sess. 117–118 (1974).

[17] Sec. 121—Allows taxpayers who have attained age 55 to exclude up to $125,000 in gain on the sale of a principal residence.

[18] Reg. Sec. 1.121-2—Discusses limitations on the exclusion of gain from the sale of a principal residence.

▲ DISCUSSION QUESTIONS

1. How does the wherewithal-to-pay concept affect the recognition of gains on asset dispositions? What else is necessary for nonrecognition of a gain upon disposition of an asset?

2. How is the tax treatment of a deferred gain similar to and different from the treatment of an excluded gain?

3. When a gain on a property disposition is deferred, the basis of the replacement property is reduced by the amount of gain deferred. Which concept supports this treatment? Explain.

4. When a gain on a depreciable property is deferred through a nonrecognition transaction, the tax attributes of the first property carry over to the second property. Why is this important, particularly with respect to like-kind exchanges of property?

5. What is boot? How does boot affect the recognition of gains (losses) on like-kind exchanges?

6. What constitutes an exchange of assets?

7. Does an exchange have to occur simultaneously to qualify for nonrecognition? Explain.

8. Define *like-kind property* as it applies to like-kind exchanges, and give examples of like-kind properties and properties that are not of like kind.

9. Why does the assumption of a mortgage when exchanging related assets constitute boot?

10. Discuss the restrictions placed on like-kind exchanges between related parties. Include the reasoning behind the restriction in your discussion.

11. What is the recapture potential of an asset?

12. The rules for gain/loss recognition on involuntary conversions are more liberal than those for exchanges. What features of an involuntary conversion contribute to the difference in treatments for the two types of transactions?

13. How long does a taxpayer who suffers an involuntary conversion of an asset have to replace the asset to qualify for nonrecognition? Explain.

14. What is a principal residence of a taxpayer?

15. Losses on exchanges must be deferred. A loss on an involuntary conversion is never deferred. In contrast, a loss on the sale of a principal residence is never recognized. Explain why losses on the sale of a principal residence are treated differently than losses on exchanges and involuntary conversions.

16. How long does a taxpayer have to replace a principal residence? Why is the replacement period different from that for an involuntary conversion replacement?

17. In general, taxpayers cannot defer gain on more than one sale of principal residence every two years. Explain the rationale for this restriction and the circumstances under which the two-year period provision is waived.

18. How much must be reinvested in a replacement residence to completely defer any gain on the sale of a principal residence?

19. What are the requirements for excluding gain on the sale of a principal residence?

▲ PROBLEMS

20. Which of the following exchanges of property are like-kind exchanges?
    a. Waldo traded in his business auto for a computer to use in his business.
    b. Germaine exchanged an interest in a condominium she used as a principal residence for a tract of undeveloped land.
    c. Jorge traded his racehorse for a mare to use for breeding.
    d. Arnold traded stock in Palmtree Co. for stock in Webster Co.
    e. Lorraine traded 5 Reggie Jackson baseball cards for 1 Robin Ventura baseball card.

21. Which of the following exchanges of property are like-kind exchanges?
    a. Horace traded his personal residence for another personal residence.
    b. Lian traded an apartment building she rented out for a warehouse to use in her business.
    c. Arthur owns a hardware store. He traded some roofing materials for a cash register.
    d. Wenona traded in an automobile she used 75% of the time for business purposes. She expects to use the new automobile for business purposes about 75% of the time.
    e. Ace Construction Co. traded a used dump truck for a crane.

22. Murray Corporation exchanged land with a fair market value of $23,000 and an adjusted basis of $16,000 for an automobile. Does Murray have a recognized gain on the exchange? Explain.

    Assume that Murray Corporation exchanged the land for another parcel of land worth $30,000. How much boot must be paid to make the exchange, and who must pay the boot? Does Murray have a recognized gain on the exchange?

23. Jalapeno Co. traded in its old delivery van for a new delivery van. The old van had cost $22,000 and had an adjusted basis of $9,000. Jalapeno was given a $7,500 trade-in allowance on the new van and paid the remaining $18,500 of the $26,000 purchase price in cash.
    a. What is Jalapeno's realized gain (loss) on the exchange?
    b. How much of the realized gain (loss) is recognized on the exchange?
    c. How much of the realized gain (loss) is deferred?
    d. What is the basis of the new delivery van?

24. Pauline's Pastry Shop decided to remodel its offices this year. As part of the remodeling, Pauline's traded furniture with a cost of $6,200 that had been expensed in the year of purchase (Section 179 expense election) for new furniture costing $17,000. Pauline's received a $3,000 credit for the old furniture and borrowed the remaining $14,000.
    a. What is Pauline's realized gain (loss) on the old furniture?
    b. How much of the realized gain (loss) is recognized on the exchange?
    c. How much of the realized gain (loss) is deferred?
    d. What is the basis of the new furniture?

25. Beaver Corporation owns a parcel of land with a fair market value (FMV) of $95,000 and a basis of $40,000. Beaver exchanges the land for a building with a FMV of $65,000. The corporation also receives $30,000 in cash. Both properties are investment properties for Beaver.
    a. What is Beaver's amount realized on the exchange?
    b. What is Beaver's realized gain (loss) on the exchange?
    c. How much of the realized gain (loss) must Beaver recognize?
    d. What is the character of the recognized gain (loss)?
    e. What is Beaver's basis in the building it acquired?

26. Armando owns a pizza parlor. Because his business was declining, he traded his old pizza oven in on a smaller oven that was worth $24,000. The old oven had cost $32,000 and had an adjusted basis of $17,000. Because Armando's oven was worth $26,000, he agreed to take the $2,000 difference in olive oil and pepperoni.
    a. What is Armando's realized gain (loss) on the old oven?
    b. How much of the realized gain (loss) is recognized on the exchange?
    c. What is the character of the recognized gain (loss)?
    d. How much of the realized gain (loss) is deferred?
    e. What is the basis of the new oven?

27. Reginald exchanged an apartment building he held as an investment for an office building to use in his tuxedo rental business. The apartment building was worth $130,000 and had a $20,000 mortgage. The office building was worth $110,000. The owner of the office building agreed to assume Reginald's $20,000 mortgage to equalize the exchange. The apartments had cost $200,000 and had an adjusted basis of $160,000.

    a. What is Reginald's realized gain (loss) on the apartment building?

    b. How much of the realized gain (loss) is recognized on the exchange?

    c. What is the character of the recognized gain (loss)?

    d. How much of the realized gain (loss) is deferred?

    e. What is the basis of the office building acquired in the exchange?

28. Fremont Corporation and Hawkins Corporation exchanged equipment. The particulars regarding each company's equipment are as follows:

	Fremont	Hawkins
Fair market value	$39,000	$48,000
Adjusted basis	18,000	54,000
Cash paid	9,000	

What are Fremont's and Hawkins's realized and recognized gains (losses) on the exchange and the bases in the equipment they acquire in the exchange?

29. Shirley has an old tractor that has an adjusted basis of $3,000 and a fair market value of $1,000. Shirley wants to trade the tractor in on a new tractor that costs $28,000. How would you advise Shirley to structure the transaction to obtain the best tax result?

30. Elrod traded an apartment building he owned for a piece of undeveloped land. The land had a fair market value of $40,000. The owner of the land assumed Elrod's $25,000 mortgage on the apartment building in the exchange. Elrod had purchased the apartment building in 1989 for $75,000, and it had an adjusted basis of $50,000 when it was traded. What are Elrod's realized and recognized gains (losses) on the exchange and his basis in the land he received in the exchange?

31. Olga traded in a computer she had used in her trade or business for a new computer. The old computer had cost Olga $7,000 and had an adjusted basis of $1,400. The computer dealer gave Olga a $3,000 trade-in allowance on the old computer, and Olga paid the remaining $6,500 price of the new computer in cash. What are Olga's realized and recognized gains on the trade-in of her old computer? What is the basis of the new computer?

32. Return to the facts of problem 31. Two years after acquiring the new computer, Olga sold it for $8,200. The adjusted basis of the computer was $6,400. What is the character of the recognized gain on the sale of the computer?

33. Evelyn's Excavating Service traded an excavator for a new backhoe. The excavator had a fair market value of $37,000 and an adjusted basis of $24,000. The backhoe was worth $34,000. The owner of the backhoe agreed to assume Evelyn's $8,000 loan on the excavator, and Evelyn's paid $5,000 in cash in the exchange. What are Evelyn's realized and recognized gains (losses) on the exchange and Evelyn's basis in the backhoe?

    The owner of the backhoe, Susan, had an adjusted basis in the backhoe of $18,000. How much of the realized gain must Susan recognize on the exchange? What is the basis in the excavator?

34. Oscar and Harriet agreed to exchange apartment buildings and the mortgages on the buildings, with any difference to be paid in cash. Particulars of their respective buildings are as follows:

	Oscar	Harriet
Fair market value	$78,000	$96,000
Mortgage	53,000	76,000
Adjusted basis	47,000	72,000

    a. How much cash must be paid, and who must pay the cash to equalize the exchange?
    b. What are Oscar's realized and recognized gains on the exchange and his basis in the apartment building acquired in the exchange?
    c. What are Harriet's realized and recognized gains on the exchange and her basis in the apartment building acquired in the exchange?

35. On July 8, 1995, Cynthia and her daughter Constance agree to exchange land they held for investment. Both tracts of land are worth $18,000. Cynthia had acquired her land 4 years earlier at a cost of $9,000. Constance had paid $16,000 for her land investment the previous year. What are the tax effects for Cynthia and Constance of the exchange?
    On February 15, 1997, Constance sells the land acquired in the exchange for $21,000. What are the tax effects of the sale? Explain.

36. Which of the following are qualified replacement properties for properties involuntarily converted? Explain.
    a. The proceeds from a warehouse destroyed by a fire were used to purchase a manufacturing plant. The warehouse and the manufacturing plant are both used in the taxpayer's manufacturing business.
    b. Assume the same facts as in part a, except that the warehouse was held as an investment and rented out to businesses. The manufacturing plant will also be rented out to a manufacturing business.
    c. An office building used in a trade or business was condemned. The proceeds from the condemnation were used to buy an apartment complex that will be used as an investment activity.
    d. The insurance proceeds from the destruction of a construction crane were used to buy a fleet of fork lifts. The crane and the fork lifts are used in the taxpayer's construction business.
    e. An antique vase was stolen from the lobby of a business. The insurance proceeds were used to buy a painting, which was hung in the same lobby.

37. Which of the following are qualified replacement properties for properties involuntarily converted? Explain.
    a. The city of Marble River announces plans to condemn Heima's rental apartment complex on July 2, 1995. On August 7, 1995, Heima purchases a warehouse to use as a rental. The city pays Heima $890,000 on November 1, 1995, as the condemnation proceedings come to a close.
    b. The city of Marble River also announces plans to condemn Heima's principal residence on July 2, 1995. He receives a check for $150,000 on the November 1, 1995, condemnation closing date. On March 29, 1997, Heima purchases a new residence.
    c. Lila uses the insurance proceeds from the destruction of her commercial fishing boat by Hurricane Fredd to buy new fishing equipment and nets for her other fishing boat.
    d. Milo uses the insurance proceeds from a fire that totally destroyed his warehouse near the pier to buy 100% of the common stock of Storage Space Corporation, a company that owns and operates 3 warehouse facilities.

38. A fire in the factory of Franny's Famous Frankfurters destroyed several stuffing machines. The machines had an adjusted basis of $133,000 and a fair market value of $160,000. Franny's insurance company reimbursed Franny's $120,000 for the destruction of the machines. Franny's used the insurance proceeds to buy some secondhand stuffers costing $100,000. What are Franny's realized and recognized gains (losses) on the fire and the basis in the replacement stuffers?

39. Grant Industries' warehouse is condemned by the city on August 18, 1995. Because of widespread publicity leading up to the condemnation, Grant anticipates the condemnation and purchases a replacement warehouse on April 15, 1995, for $670,000. The city pays Grant $430,000 for the condemned property, which had an adjusted basis to Grant of $220,000.

a. What is Grant's realized gain (loss) on the condemnation?

b. What is the minimum amount of gain Grant must recognize on the condemnation?

c. If Grant elects to recognize the minimum amount of gain on the condemnation, what is the basis in the new warehouse?

40. Refer to the facts of problem 39. Under what circumstances might Grant elect to recognize the entire gain on the condemnation? Explain.

41. One of Reddy's Fancy Dog Food factories was destroyed by a tornado. The factory had an adjusted basis of $450,000. Reddy's received $600,000 from its insurance company to cover the loss. What is the minimum amount of gain that must be recognized in each of the following situations and the basis of any property purchased with the insurance proceeds?

a. Reddy's decided that the lost production could be made up by its other factories and used the proceeds to pay a cash dividend to its shareholders.

b. Reddy's purchased another factory for $650,000.

c. Reddy's purchased another factory for $500,000.

d. Reddy's purchased another factory for $400,000.

42. A fire totally destroys a manufacturing plant owned by Ansel Corporation in 1995. The plant, located in Louisiana, had been used for more than 30 years and was fully depreciated at the date of the fire. Ansel's insurance pays $370,000 for the destruction. In analyzing qualified replacement properties, Ansel is able to buy a qualified replacement manufacturing plant for $300,000 in Oklahoma. What is the minimum amount of gain Ansel must recognize on the insurance proceeds? What is the basis of the Oklahoma manufacturing plant?

43. MacKenzie owns a boat rental business. During the current year, a tidal wave swept through the harbor where MacKenzie kept her boats anchored. Four boats were totally destroyed by the tidal wave, but the rest of the rental fleet escaped serious damage. MacKenzie replaced the 4 boats within 6 months of the tidal wave. Details on each boat destroyed and the cost of its replacement are as follows:

Boat	Insurance Proceeds	Adjusted Basis	Replacement Cost
Sailboat	$ 46,000	$21,000	$ 42,000
Yacht	$124,000	$88,000	$140,000
Speedboat	$ 67,000	$78,000	$ 80,000
Fishing boat	$123,000	$96,000	$ 92,000

a. What is the realized gain (loss) on each of the boats?

b. What is the minimum amount of gain or loss that must be recognized on each of the boats?

c. Assuming that MacKenzie elects to recognize the minimum amount of gain or loss on each boat, what is the basis of each replacement boat?

44. Alley's automobile dealership, which had an adjusted basis of $120,000, is destroyed by a hurricane in 1995. Alley's receives $210,000 from its insurance company to cover the loss. Alley's has begun to rebuild the dealership at an estimated cost of $250,000. Assume that the rebuilding costs at least $250,000.
   a. What is the minimum gain Alley's must recognize on the hurricane damage?
   b. Alley's is organized as a corporation. Because of the slump in the automobile industry, Alley's has net operating losses totaling $400,000 that it is carrying forward from the previous 5 years. Alley's expects to have another operating loss in 1995. In light of the circumstances, what would you advise Alley's? Why?

45. Aretha sold her house for $135,000. Aretha paid commissions of $9,000 and incurred $2,500 in valid fixing-up expenses readying the house for sale. Aretha had purchased the house for $68,000 and made capital improvements costing $14,000 on the house before the sale date. How much gain must Aretha recognize in each of the following cases?
   a. Aretha moved to Brazil and did not buy another residence, preferring to move from town to town and live with the locals in each town.
   b. Aretha bought a new residence costing $180,000. What is Aretha's basis in the new residence?
   c. Aretha bought a new residence costing $117,000. What is Aretha's basis in the new residence?
   d. Aretha bought a condominium for $83,000 that she used as her residence. What is Aretha's basis in the condominium?

46. In each of the following principal residence sale and replacements, determine the amount of realized gain (loss), the recognized gain (loss), and the basis of the replacement property:

Case	Selling Price	Selling Expenses	Fixing-up Expenses	Adjusted Basis	New Residence Cost
A	$ 40,000	$ 2,200	$ 300	$ 43,000	$ 50,000
B	170,000	15,000	1,300	62,000	190,000
C	95,000	6,000	1,000	45,000	76,000
D	220,000	19,000	3,000	185,000	138,000
E	80,000	4,000	500	27,000	-0-

47. In each of the following cases, determine the amount of realized gain (loss), the recognized gain (loss), and the basis of any property acquired:
   a. Cheryl sold her house for $73,000. She paid $4,000 in commissions on the sale and had $1,000 of valid fixing-up expenses. Cheryl had paid $83,000 for the house 4 years earlier. She bought another house costing $78,000.
   b. Alexandra was transferred to San Diego by her employer. She sold the house she had lived in for 1 year for $62,000 and paid selling expenses of $3,000. The house had cost Alexandra $55,000. Alexandra used the proceeds of the sale to purchase a sailboat for $57,000. The sailboat was fully equipped, and Alexandra lived in the sailboat after moving to San Diego.
   c. Oswald sold his principal residence for $320,000 and paid selling expenses of $20,000 on the sale. Oswald had purchased the house for $80,000. Oswald used the proceeds from the sale to purchase a cooperative apartment to live in and a cabin at the lake that he used on weekends. The apartment cost $200,000, and the cabin cost $180,000.
   d. Ushi is transferred by her employer to North Carolina in March 1995. Ushi is unable to sell her home in Texas (which had a basis of $113,000) before moving to North Carolina. She rents out the Texas house on a 6-month rental contract, figuring that she can sell it within that period. In July 1995, she purchases a new residence in North Carolina at a cost of $137,000. The Texas property has not sold at the end of the 6-month lease, and she continues to rent it out on a month-to-month basis. The Texas house finally sells in November 1996 for $132,000. Ushi pays $10,000 in expenses relating to the sale.

48. After trying to sell his house for several years, Randy traded the house for a condominium owned by Dorr Real Estate. As part of the exchange, Randy agreed to give Dorr Real Estate 400 shares of Peat Pollyperk common stock that had a fair market value of $10,000 (Randy had paid $3,000 for the stock 4 years earlier). Randy's basis in the house was $72,000. Condominiums in the same complex as Randy's had been selling for $90,000. What are the tax effects of the trade for Randy? Explain. What are the tax effects of the trade for Dorr Real Estate? Explain.

49. The city of Stillcreek decided to expand the runway at the local airport. To get the land for the expansion, it condemned the property it needed and paid the owners the current appraised value. Buster's house was condemned, and he was paid $85,000 for his property. Buster had purchased the property for $70,000 and had made $30,000 in improvements to the property. Buster used the proceeds to purchase a new residence for $60,000.
   a. What is Buster's realized gain (loss) on the condemnation of his residence?
   b. How much of the realized gain (loss) must Buster recognize?
   c. What is the basis of the new residence?

50. Manuel and Rita sold their home for $196,000, incurring selling expenses of $13,000. They had purchased the residence for $16,000 and had made capital improvements totaling $20,000 during the 20 years they lived in the house. They moved to Texas and purchased a mobile home for $62,000.
   a. Assuming that both Manuel and Rita are younger than 55 at the date of the sale, what are the tax consequences of the sale?
   b. How would your answer to part a change if Manuel is 62 and Rita is 49?

51. Joe was divorced from Estelle several years ago. As part of the divorce agreement, Joe received the house that he and Estelle had purchased for $22,000 in the early years of their marriage. Joe retired this year and wants to sell his house and buy a cabin in Colorado to live out his golden years. A real estate appraiser told Joe that his house would probably sell for $300,000, net of commissions and other closing costs. Joe has his eye on a cabin in his favorite area of Colorado that is listed for sale at $138,000. Joe would like some advice on the tax consequences of the sale of his house and the purchase of the cabin. What would you tell him?

▲ COMPREHENSIVE PROBLEM

52. Five years ago, Ace owned 2 fine racehorses—OntheInside and AtthePost. These horses were born and raised on Ace's horse farm. Thus, his $2,000 tax basis for each horse was quite low compared with their market value. Because of his compulsive gambling, Ace was forced to trade the horses for more conservative business property.

In the trade, Ace received $150,000-worth of heavy equipment for use in his new earth-moving business. Shortly after the trade, Ace decided the business was too dirty for him. Thus, Ace traded the heavy equipment on which he had deducted $10,000 in depreciation for 4 single-family homes to be held for rental purposes.

The homes, with a combined value of $350,000, were taken subject to a $200,000 mortgage. After paying off the mortgage and deducting $15,000 in depreciation on the homes, Ace traded them for a 25-unit apartment building worth $750,000.

When the building burned down the day after the trade, the insurance company paid Ace $740,000. Ace used $5,000 of the proceeds to buy back OntheInside and AtthePost, because he loved the old hay burners. He used the remaining $735,000 to buy a farm to go back into the horse-breeding business.
   a. How much gain did Ace realize and how much must he recognize when he traded the horses for the equipment? What is his basis in the equipment?
   b. How much gain did Ace realize and how much must he recognize when he traded the equipment for the 4 single-family homes? What is his basis in the houses?
   c. How much gain did Ace realize and how much must he recognize when he traded the 4 single-family homes for the apartment building? What is his basis in the apartment building?

    d. How much gain did Ace realize and how much must he recognize when the apartment building was involuntary converted and was replaced with the farm land and racehorses?

    e. What are the bases in the farm land and horses?

Glenda, 34 and single, has lived for 5 years in a house with an adjusted basis of $85,000. In May 1995, she decides to move so that her daughter can attend school in a different school district. She lists her house with a Realtor for $140,000. In July 1995, Glenda purchases a new residence for $200,000 and moves in.

    Six months later, she lowers the asking price for the old house to $120,000. Six months after that, Glenda drops the price to $105,000. Finally, after living in the new house for 20 months and becoming frustrated that her old house has not sold, Glenda considers moving back to her former residence. Her Realtor tells her the new house will sell fairly easily. Advise Glenda on the tax consequences of her choices.

▲ **DISCUSSION CASE 13–1**

In October 1995, fire completely destroys the principal residence of Olaf, who is 66, single, and lives in Bemidji, Minnesota. Olaf owned the home for 16 years; his adjusted basis is $58,000. Olaf receives insurance proceeds of $200,000.

    Olaf plans to move to Scottsdale, Arizona, no later than 1998 to be near his daughter. That is the year she is scheduled to finish her five-year tour of duty with the U.S. Foreign Service and is planning to return to her home in Scottsdale. Olaf also owns a condominium at Hilton Head, South Carolina. He paid $120,000 for the apartment in February 1994. Olaf has never used the one-time election to exclude gain on the sale of a personal residence. Advise Olaf on his options and their tax consequences.

▲ **DISCUSSION CASE 13–2**

In 1991, Joe and Jill sold their principal residence for $250,000. Their adjusted basis in the property was $136,000. Because both were older than 55 at the date of the sale, they elected to exclude $125,000 from their realized gain. To complete the sale, Joe and Jill had to take back a second mortgage for $20,000. The buyers borrowed $205,000 from a local bank and put down $25,000 in cash.

    In 1995, Joe and Jill are notified that the buyers have defaulted on the second mortgage and filed for bankruptcy. A large manufacturing plant near the house has closed, and the housing market is overstocked; the value of the house has dropped significantly—below the amount remaining on the bank's mortgage. Joe and Jill want to deduct the loss on the second mortgage. The IRS Hot Line adviser tells them the loss is not recognizable, because they have no basis in the mortgage debt. Joe and Jill never reported as income the payments they received on the second mortgage. Advise Joe and Jill on the deductibility of the defaulted mortgage.

▲ **DISCUSSION CASE 13–3**

Outdoor Amusements Center is a sole proprietorship owned by Adrian. The center's facilities include a go-cart track, miniature golf course, and 10 trampolines. In July, a tornado destroyed all the trampolines. Miraculously, the go-cart and miniature golf facilities sustained no significant damage in the tornado.

    Adrian had bought the trampolines two years earlier for $35,000. The trampolines were insured, and Adrian received a check for $35,000 from her insurance company in early August. By early September, all the trampolines had been replaced at a cost of $40,000.

a. Does Adrian have to recognize any gain because of the tornado damage to the trampolines? Explain. NOTE: The trampolines are 7-year MACRS property. Adrian has always deducted the maximum depreciation possible on the trampolines.

b. Adrian owns some stock in GoGoKarts, Inc. She paid $20,000 for the stock several years earlier. Because of the sluggishness of the economy and a recent rise in oil prices, the

▲ **TAX PLANNING CASE 13–4**

stock is worth only $5,000. Her broker has recommended that she sell the stock and realize the tax savings from the loss. However, Adrian is hesitant to sell, because she believes that GoGoKarts will eventually rebound. She would like to know the tax advantages she would realize in the current year from such a sale and how the trampoline casualty could affect those advantages. Assuming that she has no other gains from property transactions during the year, should she sell the stock? Explain your reasoning.

▲ TAX PLANNING CASE 13–5

Thelma owns and operates a fishing boat charter service on Santa Catalina Island. While vacationing in the northeastern part of the United States, Thelma met Doug and his sister Lara, owners of DL Enterprises. DL owns two fishing boat charter services. One is in Portsmouth, New Hampshire, and one is in Newport, Oregon. Doug would like to relocate one of the businesses to a warmer climate. So, Thelma, Doug, and Lara decide to trade businesses. Thelma will relocate to Newport, and Doug will move to Santa Catalina. Lara will remain in Portsmouth and operate that business. Doug insists that Thelma sign a covenant not to compete for 5 years. The following are the assets involved in the exchange:

	FMV	
	Thelma	Doug/Lara
Boats	$500,000	$550,000
Equipment	60,000	20,000
Covenant not to compete	40,000	

Also, Doug and Lara pay Thelma $30,000 in cash. Thelma's adjusted bases are $325,000 for the boats and $70,000 for the equipment. Advise Thelma on the income tax consequences of the proposed exchange. Discuss any reasonable alternatives that may produce better results for Thelma.

▲ ETHICS DISCUSSION CASE 13–6

You are a staff accountant in the tax department of Coopers & Marwick, CPAs. While discussing some tax-planning matters with one of your office's biggest (in total billings) and best clients, McDonald Krump, you learn that he sold his personal residence in 1994. He replaced the residence (estate) shortly thereafter. During your conversations, Krump mentioned he "took a bath" on the sale of the former residence but will eventually recoup his loss through use of tax deferral provisions. Because you are an expert on real estate matters, your curiosity is getting the best of you in regard to Krump's sale and subsequent purchase. Therefore, after hours you snoop through copies of Krump's 1994 tax returns and working papers. You find the following in regard to the sale of his residence:

Amount realized	$2,200,000
Adjused basis	2,600,000
Loss realized	$ (400,000)
Cost of replacement	$3,300,000
Plus deferred loss	400,000
Basis of replacement residence	$3,700,000

The working papers were approved and initialed by Jacob Deerborn, the senior tax partner in your office. Deerborn also signed the form as the "paid preparer" representing your firm. Coincidently, Deerborn, Krump, and your father belong to the same country club and play at least one round of golf together weekly. What are your obligations under the Statements on Responsibilities in Tax Practice? Discuss your obligations.

Appendix to Chapter 13

Selected SIC Product Classes

3711 Motor Vehicles and Passenger Car Bodies

Ambulances
Amphibian motor vehicles, except tanks
Assembling complete automobiles
Automobiles
Bodies, passenger automobile
Brooms, powered
Car bodies
Cars, armored
Cars, electric: for highway use
Chassis, motor vehicle
Fire department vehicles
Flushers, street
Hearses
Mobile lounges
Motor buses, except trackless trolley
Motor homes, self-contained
Motor trucks, except off-highway
Motor vehicles, including amphibian
Patrol wagons
Personnel carriers, for highway use
Road oilers
Snowplows
Station wagons
Street sprinklers and sweepers
Taxicabs
Tractors, truck: for highway use
Universal carriers, military

3531 Construction Machinery and Equipment

Aerial work platforms
Aggregate spreaders
Asphalt plants
Automobile wrecker hoists
Backfillers, self-propelled
Backhoes
Ballast distributors
Batching plants, bituminous
Batching plants, for aggregate concrete
Blades for graders, scrapers, dozers, and snowplows
Breakers, paving
Buckets, excavating: clamshell, concrete, dragline, drag scraper, shovel
Bulldozers, construction
Cabs, construction machinery
Capstans, ship
Carriers, crane
Chip spreaders, self-propelled
Chippers, commercial: brush, limb, and log
Concrete buggies, powered
Concrete grouting equipment
Concrete gunning equipment
Concrete plants
Construction machinery, except mining
Cranes, construction
Cranes, except industrial plant
Crushers, mineral: portable
Derricks, except oil and gas field
Distributors (construction machinery)
Ditchers, ladder
Dozers, tractor mounted: material moving
Draglines, powered
Drags, road (construction and road maintenance equipment)
Dredging machinery
Excavators: e.g., cable, clamshell, crane, derrick, dragline, power shovel
Extractors, piling
Finishers and spreaders, construction
Finishers, concrete and bituminous
Grader attachments, elevating
Graders, road (construction machinery)
Grapples: rock, wood, etc.
Grinders, stone: portable
Hammer mills (rock and ore crushing machines), portable
Hammers, pile driving
Line markers, self-propelled
Locomotive cranes
Log splitters
Logging equipment
Mixers: e.g., concrete, ore, sand, slag, plaster, mortar, bituminous
Mortar mixers
Mud jacks
Pavers
Pile-driving equipment
Planers, bituminous
Plaster mixers
Plows, construction: excavating and grading
Post hole diggers, powered
Power cranes, draglines, and shovels
Pulverizers, stone: portable
Railway track equipment: e.g.,

rail layers, ballast distributors
Rakes, land clearing: mechanical
Road construction and
  maintenance machinery
Rock crushing machinery,
  portable
Rollers, road
Rollers, sheepsfoot and vibratory
Sand mixers
Scarifiers, road
Scrapers, construction
Screeds and screeding machines
Screeners, portable
Ship cranes and derricks

Shovel loaders
Shovels, power
Silos, cement (batch plant)
Slag mixers
Snowplow attachments
Soil compactors: vibratory
Spreaders and finishers,
  construction
Subgraders, construction
  equipment
Subsoiler attachments, tractor-
  mounted
Surfacers, concrete grinding

Tampers, powered
Tamping equipment, rail
Teeth, bucket and scarifier
Tractors, construction
Tractors, crawler
Tractors, tracklaying
Trenching machines
Trucks, off-highway
Vibrators for concrete
  construction
Wellpoint systems
Winches, all types
Work platforms, elevated

2451 Mobile Homes

Buildings, mobile: commercial
  use
Mobile buildings for commercial
  use (e.g., offices, banks)

Mobile classrooms
Mobile dwellings
Mobile homes, except recreational

3589 Service Industry Machinery, Not Elsewhere Classified

Cafeteria food warming
  equipment
Carpet sweepers, except
  household electric vacuum
  sweepers
Carwashing machinery, including
  coin-operated
Cookers, steam: restaurant type
Cooking equipment, commercial
Corn popping machines,
  commercial
Dirt sweeping units, industrial
Dishwashing machines,
  commercial
Floor sanding, washing, and

polishing machines:
  commercial type
Food warming equipment,
  commercial
Fryers, commercial
Garbage disposers, commercial
Janitors' carts
Mop wringers
Ovens, cafeteria food warming:
  portable
Ovens, microwave (cooking
  equipment): commercial
Pressure cookers, steam:
  commercial
Sanding machines, floor

Scrubbing machines
Servicing machines, coin-
  operated: except drycleaning
  and laundry
Sewage treatment equipment
Sewer processing equipment
Sewer cleaning equipment, power
Sludge processing equipment
Vacuum cleaners and sweepers,
  electric industrial and
  commercial
Water purification equipment
Water type conditioners
Water filters and softeners
Water treatment equipment

3546 Power-Driven Handtools

Buffing machines, hand: electric
Cartridge-activated hand power
  tools
Caulking hammers
Chain saws, portable
Chipping hammers, electric
Drills, hand: electric
Flexible shaft metalworking
  machines, portable

Grinders, pneumatic and electric:
  portable (metalworking
  machinery)
Grinders, snagging
Guns, pneumatic: chip removal
Hammers: portable electric and
  pneumatic: e.g., chipping,
  riveting, caulking
Handtools, power-driven:

woodworking or metalworking
Masonry and concrete drilling
  tools, power: portable
Powder-actuated hand tools
Riveting hammers
Sanders, hand: electric
Saws, portable hand held: power-
  driven—woodworking or
  metalworking.

3537 Industrial Trucks, Tractors, Trailers, and Stackers

Adapters for multiweapon rack loading on aircraft
Aircraft engine cradles
Aircraft loading hoists
Boat cradles
Bomb lifts
Bomb trucks
Cabs for industrial trucks and tractors
Cars, industrial: except automotive cars and trucks and mining cars
Containers, air cargo: metal
Cranes, mobile industrial truck
Die and strip handlers
Docks, loading: portable,
Dollie (hand or power trucks), industrial: except mining
Drum cradles

Engine stands and racks, metal
Forklift trucks
Hoists, aircraft loading
Hoppers, end dump
Hospital dollies
Industrial truck cranes
Industrial trucks and tractors
Laundry containers on wheels
Lift trucks, industrial: fork, platform, straddle, etc.
Mobile straddle carriers
Pallet assemblies for landing mats
Pallet loaders and unloaders
Palletizers and depalletizers
Pallets, metal
Platforms, cargo: metal
Ramps, aircraft—loading
Ramps, loading: portable, adjustable, and hydraulic

Skid boxes, metal
Skids, metal
Stackers, power (industrial truck stackers)
Stacking carts
Stacking machines, automatic
Stands, ground servicing aircraft
Straddle carriers, mobile
Tables, lift: hydraulic
Tractors, industrial: for use in plants, depots, docks, and terminals
Truck trailers for use in plants, depots, docks, and terminals
Trucks, industrial (except mining): for freight, baggage, etc.
Tunnell kiln cars

3523 Farm Machinery and Equipment

Agricultural implements and machinery
Ammonia applicators and attachments (agricultural machinery)
Bale throwers
Balers, farm: e.g., hay, straw, cotton
Barn cleaners
Barn stanchions and standards
Blowers and cutters, ensilage
Blowers, forage
Brooders
Cabs, agricultural machinery
Calf savers (farm equipment)
Cattle feeding, handling, and watering equipment
Cattle oilers (farm equipment)
Chicken brooders
Cleaning machines for fruits, grains, and vegetables: farm
Combines (harvester-threshers)
Conveyors, farm (agricultural machinery)
Corn pickers and shellers, farm
Corrals, portable
Cotton picker and stripper harvesting machinery

Cream separators, farm
Crop driers, farm
Crushers, feed (agricultural machinery)
Cultivators, agricultural field and row crop
Cutters, ensilage
Dairy equipment, farm
Drags (agricultural equipment)
Driers: grain, hay, and seed (agricultural implements)
Dusters, mechanical: agricultural
Elevators, farm
Farm machinery and equipment
Feed grinders, crushers, and mixers (agricultural machinery)
Feeders, chicken
Fertilizing machinery, farm
Field type rotary tillers (agricultural machinery)
Fruit, vegetables, berry, and grape harvesting machines
Gates, holding (farm equipment)
Grading, cleaning, and sorting machines: fruit, grain, and vegetable
Grain drills, including legume

planters (agricultural machinery)
Grain stackers
Greens mowing equipment
Grounds mowing equipment
Hair clippers for animal use, hand and electric
Hammer and roughage mills (agricultural machinery)
Harrows: disc, spring, and tine
Harvesting machines
Haying machines: mowers, rakes, loaders, stackers, balers, presses
Hog feeding, handling, and watering equipment
Hulling machinery, agricultural
Incubators, except laboratory and infant
Irrigation equipment, self-propelled
Land rollers and levelers (agricultural machinery)
Listers
Loaders, farm type (general utility)
Milking machines
Mowers and mower-conditioners, hay

Peanut combines, diggers, packers, and threshers (agricultural equipment)
Planting machines, agricultural
Plows, agricultural: disc, moldboard, chisel, etc.
Potato diggers, harvesters, and planters
Poultry brooders, feeders, and waterers
Poultry vision control devices
Presses and balers, farm: hay, cotton,
Rakes, hay
Rotary hoes
Roughage mills

Seeders (agricultural machinery)
Separators, grain and berry: farm
Shears, sheep: power
Shellers, nut
Shredders (agricultural machinery)
Silo fillers (agricultural machinery)
Soil pulverizers and packers (agricultural machinery)
Sorting machines for agricultural products
Sprayers, hand: agricultural
Spraying machines (agricultural machinery)

Spreaders, fertilizer
Tractors, wheel: farm type
Trailers and wagons, farm
Transplanters
Turf equipment, commercial
Vine pullers
Volume guns (irrigation equipment)
Water troughs
Weeding machines, farm
Windmills for pumping water (agricultural machinery)
Tobacco curers
Windrowers (agricultural machinery)

3553 Woodworking Machinery

Bandsaws, woodworking
Box making machines for wooden boxes
Cabinet makers' machinery
Furniture makers' machinery (woodworking)
Jointers (woodworking machines)
Lathes, wood turning: including accessories
Mortisers (woodworking machines)
Pattern makers' machinery (woodworking)

Planers, woodworking
Planing mill machinery
Presses, woodworking: particleboard, hardboard, medium density fiberboard (MDF), and plywood
Sanding machines, except portable floor sanders (woodworking machinery)
Sawmill machines
Saws, power: bench and table (woodworking machinery), except portable

Scarifing machines (woodworking machinery)
Shapers, woodworking machinery
Surfacers (woodworking machines)
Tenoners (woodworking machines)
Veneer mill machines
Venetian blind machines (woodworking machinery)
Woodworking machines

TAX CONSIDERATIONS

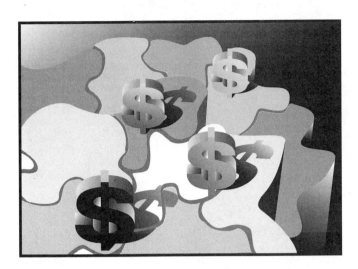

CHAPTER 14
OTHER FACTORS AFFECTING TAX LIABILITY

CHAPTER 15
TAX RESEARCH

Other Factors Affecting Tax Liability

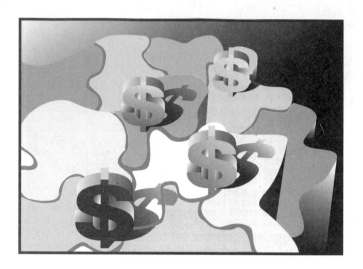

▲ CHAPTER LEARNING OBJECTIVES

■ Discuss taxpayer's selection of an accounting period and the restrictions on accounting periods imposed on partnerships and S corporations.

■ Explain the restrictions placed on the use of the cash method of accounting.

■ Expand on the tax treatment of long-term contracts to include the lookback method computation that must be done at the completion of the contract and the exemption from the percentage-of-completed-contract method of accounting for long-term contracts.

■ Explain basic tax accounting for inventories, including using the lower of cost-or-market method of valuation and the election to use the last in, first out inventory flow assumption.

■ Discuss the use of tax credits to achieve various policy goals.

■ Provide an overview of the tax credits available to businesses and the income tax rules applicable to several of the most commonly encountered business tax credits.

■ Discuss the use of tax credits for individuals and explain the provisions of the individual tax credits.

■ Present an overview of the alternative minimum tax system and its purpose in the income tax system.

■ Discuss the general computation of the alternative minimum tax and provide an overview of the income tax items that affect the calculation of the tax.

▲ **CONCEPT REVIEW** ▲

Ability to pay   A tax should be based on the amount that the taxpayer can afford to pay, relative to other taxpayers.

Accounting method   A taxpayer must adopt an accounting method that clearly reflects income.

Administrative convenience   Those items for which the cost of compliance would exceed the revenue generated are not taxed.

Annual accounting period   All entities must report the results of their operations on an annual basis (the tax year). Each tax year stands on its own, apart from other tax years.

Conduit entity   An entity for which the tax attributes flow through to its owners for tax purposes.

Entity   All items of income, deductions, and so on are traced to the tax unit responsible for the item.

Legislative grace   Any tax relief provided is the result of a specific act of Congress that must be strictly applied and interpreted. All income received is taxable unless a specific provision can be found in the tax law that excludes the income from taxation. Deductions must be approached with the philosophy that nothing is deductible unless a provision in the tax law allows the deduction.

In addition to the income and deduction items discussed throughout the text, other factors affect the determination of a taxpayer's tax liability. The selection of a tax entity's annual accounting period and its accounting method can have a significant effect on the amount and timing of the entity's taxable income. Special methods of accounting for the treatment of individual items, such as long-term contracts and inventories, have similar income effects. Tax credits, which are given for engaging in certain specified types of transactions and activities, may significantly reduce a taxpayer's liability. Finally, all taxpayers must pay a defined minimum amount of tax on their income. This minimum amount is called the *alternative minimum tax.*

This chapter discusses each of these additional factors that could affect the tax liability. The purpose of the chapter is not to provide an in-depth discussion of all the other relevant factors in calculating the tax liability. Rather, it is designed to acquaint the reader with various aspects that have the greatest potential for affecting the tax liability.

▲ **INTRODUCTION**

The annual accounting period concept requires all tax entities to report the results of their operations on an annual basis. The period for which an entity reports is referred to as the *taxable year*. A taxable year may be either a calendar year (ending on December 31) or a fiscal year.[1] A *fiscal year* is defined as

1. A period of 12 months ending on the last day of any month other than December.
    or
2. A 52- to 53-week taxable year. The 52- to 53-week fiscal year ends on the same day of the same week each year. The year must end either the last time a particular day occurs during the month (e.g., the last Wednesday in October) or the day that occurs closest to the end of a particular month (e.g., the Friday closest to March 31, even if that Friday happens to be April 2).

▲ **ACCOUNTING PERIODS**

The primary rationale for allowing taxpayers to select fiscal taxable years is to make the closing of the books and preparation of the tax return of the taxpayer easier and more cost efficient. That is, many businesses have both peak and slow periods. By allowing them the flexibility to close their books and prepare their returns after the end of peak seasons, businesses are able to comply with the tax law in a more timely and efficient manner. In addition, the fiscal year provision gives the government an element of administrative convenience. By spreading the filing of returns out over other periods, the government is able to process and audit returns with fewer personnel than would be required if all tax entities filed their returns on the basis of a calendar year.

▲ **EXAMPLE 1**   Rondo Corporation manufactures toys. Its peak sales season revolves around Christmas sales. Rondo's production facilities operate at full capacity from April through June to satisfy Christmas sales demand. The production facilities are shut down in July and August each year for maintenance. From September through March, the production facilities operate at 30% to 60% of capacity, depending on demand.

Discussion: By selecting a fiscal year ending July 31 or August 31, Rondo can more efficiently close its books and prepare its tax returns. During this time, there is no production to account for and the record-keeping staff has more time to make the entries necessary to close the books and compile the information necessary to prepare its tax return.

▲ **EXAMPLE 2**   Roland, a CPA, is busy preparing tax returns from December through April. From May through the middle of November, Roland and his staff have several not-for-profit audits that keep them busy. From November 15 through December 15, business is slack. Can Roland elect a fiscal year ending November 15 to report his income?

Discussion: A fiscal year must end either on the last day of any month other than December or on the same day of the same week each year. Thus, Roland could not elect a fiscal year ending November 15. Roland does have several options for meeting his needs. First, he could elect a fiscal year ending on November 30. This would allow him some slack time to close his books and prepare his tax return. A second option would be to elect a 52- to 53-week year. Under this option, he could elect to close his books on the last Friday of November. This would be past his busy season and allow him a few more days to close his books and prepare his return than the November 30 fiscal year.

A taxable entity establishes a taxable year by keeping its books on the basis of that year and filing its first tax return based on that taxable year.[2] This requires the entity to formally close its books on that date and file a timely tax return for the selected tax year. If the entity does not close its books on that date or if it does not keep formal books, it must use a calendar year. In addition, if the entity closes its books on a date that does not qualify as a fiscal year (e.g., November 15), it must use a calendar year for tax purposes. Because of the record-keeping requirement, most individuals (who do not keep formal books) use calendar years.

▲ **EXAMPLE 3**   Maldonado Corporation begins operations during 1995. It would like to use a fiscal year ending on July 31 to report its income. What must Maldonado do to establish a July 31 fiscal year?

Discussion: To establish a July 31 fiscal year, Maldonado must keep its books on the basis of a July 31 fiscal year and file its first tax return on that basis. This requires Maldonado to close its books on July 31, 1995, and file its first tax return on the 1995 results up to July 31.

Under the entity concept, each tax entity is responsible for reporting its own results to the government. This concept is extended to the selection of the taxable year by not allowing the books of one entity to establish the taxable year of another entity.

▲ **EXAMPLE 4**   Fred and Dalena are equal partners in Golf Millionaires, Inc. The partnership keeps its books on the basis of a fiscal year ending March 31 and reports its results to the government on that basis. Fred and Dalena receive the bulk of their income from Golf Millionaires and therefore do not keep separate books. Can Fred and Dalena elect to use a March 31 fiscal year?

Discussion: Fred and Dalena may not use the books of their partnership to establish their individual tax years. Under the entity concept, each tax entity is considered separate and apart from other entities. Because Fred and Dalena do not keep individual books, they must use a calendar year to report their income. NOTE: As discussed later, Golf Millionaires may not be eligible to use a March 31 fiscal year.

Taxpayers are generally free to choose which accounting period they will use as their taxable year. However, the tax law limits the choices of several types of entities.

Limitations on Choice of Taxable Year

Without any restrictions on the selection of a taxable year, owners of conduit entities could obtain a tax deferral benefit by having the entity select a taxable year different from that of the owners'.

▲ **EXAMPLE 5**   Return to the facts of example 4. If Golf Millionaires is allowed to use a March 31 fiscal year while its 2 owners use a calendar year, Fred and Dalena will effectively be allowed a 9-month deferral on the reporting of their income from Golf Millionaires. This happens because income from a conduit entity is deemed to be earned on the last day of the entity's tax year. Because Fred and Dalena would receive their income from Golf Millionaires on March 31, they would not report it on their individual returns until December 31, resulting in a 9-month deferral of income.

Because of this potential deferral, in 1986 Congress enacted a set of rules that limits the choice of taxable years for partnerships and S corporations. In addition, trusts are required to use a calendar year.

Partnership Limitations.   The selection of a partnership tax year is done on a hierarchical basis that attempts to match the tax years of the partnership to the partners'.[3] First, the partnership must use the same tax year as that used by those partners having a majority interest (more than 50 percent), called the **majority-interest tax year,** in partnership profits and capital.

▲ **EXAMPLE 6**   Carla, Ted, and Don are partners in the CTD Partnership. Carla owns 60% of CTD. Ted and Don each own 20% of CTD. Carla, Ted, and Don all use calendar years. What taxable year must CTD use?

Discussion: Because more than 50% of the partnership interests use a calendar year, CTD must also use a calendar year. Note that the effect of this rule is to have the partnership's year-end match the year-ends of the majority of the partners'.

▲ **EXAMPLE 7**   Assume that in example 6 Carla established a January 31 fiscal year. What taxable year must CTD use?

Discussion: Because Carla owns more than 50% of CTD, CTD must use the same fiscal year as Carla, January 31. As in example 6, the effect of this rule is to match 60% of the partnership's profits to Carla's taxable year, with only 40% subject to deferral.

If the majority-interest partners do not have the same tax year, the partnership must use the tax year of its principal partners, referred to as the **principal partner tax year.** A principal partner is a partner with at least a 5-percent interest.[4]

▲ **EXAMPLE 8**   Conrad Limited Partnership is owned by 20 limited partners each of which has a 4% interest in the partnership profits and capital. Hal is the general partner and owns 10% of the partnership. The remaining 10% is owned by Morgan Corporation. Both Hal and Morgan have fiscal years that end on July 31. The tax years of the 20 limited partners are diverse; there is no majority-interest tax year. What tax year must Conrad Limited use?

Discussion: Because there is no majority-interest tax year, the partnership must use the tax year of the principal partners. In this case, none of the limited partners qualifies as principal partner, because each owns less than a 5% interest in the partnership. Hal and Morgan Corporation are the only principal partners. Because the 2 principal partners have the same tax year, the partnership must use that tax year—a fiscal year ending July 31.

When the principal partners do not have the same tax year, the partnership must use the tax year that results in the least aggregate deferral of income of the partners.[5] Because the purpose of the partnership limitations is to effect the least amount of deferral, under this rule a partnership will always use the tax year of at least one of the partners (i.e., at least one partner gets no deferral). The deferral of each partner for each tax year possible is determined by the number of months that fall between the end of the partnership's tax year and the end of the partner's tax year. The aggregate deferral is determined by adding the products of the number of months of deferral for each partner multiplied by each partner's ownership interest. The tax year that produces the shortest deferral is the **least aggregate deferral tax year.**

▲ **EXAMPLE 9**   Tiger and Tetra are equal partners in Tetra Tigers Tinkers (TTT). Tiger uses the calendar year. Tetra has a fiscal year ending November 30. What tax year must TTT use?

Discussion: Because TTT can meet neither the majority-interest rule nor the principal partner rule, it must determine its taxable year by using the least aggregate deferral method. The 2 options are the fiscal years of the 2 partners, December 31 and November 30. The aggregate deferral is counted as the number of months from the end of the partnership year multiplied by the ownership percentage for each partner. These are then added to obtain the total deferral:

Using December 31 Year-End

Tiger (0 months × 50%)	-0-
Tetra (11 months × 50%)	5.5
Total deferral	5.5

Using November 30 Year-End

Tiger (1 month × 50%)	0.5
Tetra (0 months × 50%)	-0-
Total deferral	0.5

The use of a November 30 year-end by TTT will result in the least aggregate deferral of income to the partners.

A partnership can use a taxable year other than that prescribed by the hierarchical rules if it can establish to the IRS's satisfaction that a valid business purpose exists for having a different tax year.[6] To establish a **business purpose tax year,** the partnership must obtain permission from the IRS to use the particular tax year. To obtain IRS approval, the partnership must establish that the year selected does not create for either the partnership or its partners significant deferral of income or shifting of deductions. The type of business purpose tax year granted most frequently is the natural business year. The natural business year test (discussed in the next section) also applies to S corporations.

S Corporation Limitations.   In general, an S corporation must use a calendar year.[7] However, it can choose an alternate year under the ownership tax year or the natural business year exceptions. An **ownership tax year** is the tax year of more than 50 percent of the owners of the corporation.[8] Thus, the ownership tax year is similar in concept to the majority-interest tax year of a partnership.

▲ **EXAMPLE 10**   Ragweed Corporation is an S corporation that is equally owned by Arthur, Bake, and Charlene. Arthur uses a calendar year. Bake and Charlene use a fiscal year ending March 31. What is the ownership tax year?

Discussion: Bake and Charlene have the same tax year and own more than 50% of the corporation. Therefore, the ownership tax year is Bake and Charlene's tax year—the fiscal year ending March 31. Ragweed can use either a calendar year or a fiscal year ending March 31.

A **natural business year** is defined as "the annual accounting period encompassing all related income and expenses."[9] In order to establish a natural business year, an S corporation (or a partnership) must have peak and off-peak business periods. The natural business year is the end of the peak business period. The natural business year recognizes that the income and expenses of some businesses are reflected more accurately when the books are closed at the end of the peak season. In addition, businesses with peak and off-peak periods can more easily and efficiently close their books and prepare their tax returns at the end of their busiest seasons.

▲ **EXAMPLE 11**   Atkins Department Store is an S corporation. The bulk of Atkins's business occurs during the Christmas season and through January, dealing with returns and exchanges of merchandise. During the rest of the year, business is relatively slow. What is Atkins's natural business year?

Discussion: Based on the facts presented, Atkins's peak season ends by the end of January. Therefore, Atkins's natural business year would be a fiscal year ending January 31. This tax year would allow Atkins to close its books and prepare its returns at the beginning of its off-peak season. Note also that by closing the books on January 31, returns and exchanges from the busiest sales period will be reflected in the income for that tax year, providing a more accurate reflection of annual income.

A mechanical test is used to determine a natural business year.[10] Under this test, an annual accounting period qualifies as a natural business year if the gross receipts from sales or services for the final two months of the current year and each of the two preceding years equal or exceed 25 percent of the gross receipts for the entire 12-month period.

▲ **EXAMPLE 12**   Rocco's Rebels is a manufacturer of toys. Rocco's heaviest sales period occurs during August and September when retailers are stocking their shelves for Christmas. Gross sales for August and September and the 12-month periods ending on September 30 of the current year and each of the 2 preceding years are as follows:

	Aug. & Sept.	12-Month Period
Current year	$35,000	$125,000
Preceding year 1	$31,250	$120,000
Preceding year 2	$25,000	$100,000

Does September 30 qualify as a natural business year under the gross receipts test?

Discussion: In order to qualify under the gross receipts test, the gross receipts for the last 2 months of the fiscal year (August and September) must equal or exceed 25% of the current year's and the 2 preceding years'. Here is the calculation of the gross receipts percentage for the 3 applicable periods:

$$\text{Current year} \qquad \$35,000 \div \$125,000 = 28\%$$

$$\text{Preceding year 1} \qquad \$31,250 \div \$120,000 = 26\%$$

$$\text{Preceding year 2} \qquad \$25,000 \div \$100,000 = 25\%$$

Because the gross receipts for August and September for the current and 2 preceding years equal or exceed 25% in each of those years, September 30 qualifies as a natural business year.

▲ ACCOUNTING METHODS

Taxpayers are required to maintain the accounting records necessary to enable them to file their annual tax returns. In order to properly characterize income and deduction items, taxpayers must select an accounting method. An *accounting method* is defined as the method or system by which taxpayers determine the amount of their income, gains, losses, deductions, and credits, as well as the proper time to recognize these items. As such, the tax law recognizes two distinct types of accounting methods: (1) **overall accounting methods,** which refer to the general accounting method adopted by taxpayers in keeping their books, and (2) **individual accounting treatments,** which are the individual treatments of specific items when the tax law provides the taxpayer with options for the treatment of an item. The three acceptable overall methods are the cash method, the accrual method, and the hybrid method. Depreciation methods, accounting for inventories, installment sales accounting, and accounting for long-term contracts are all examples of individual accounting treatments.

In selecting an overall method of accounting, taxpayers are required to use for taxable income computation the method of accounting that they regularly use for their books. The method must be used consistently from period to period and must clearly reflect the income of the taxpayer. The commissioner of the Internal Revenue Service has the authority to reject the use of any method that does not clearly reflect the income of the taxpayer.[11] Once adopted, an accounting method must be used consistently from one tax period to the next. Taxpayers wishing to change their methods of accounting must generally obtain prior approval from the IRS. When such consent is granted, the taxpayer must make transitional adjustments to income for the change as prescribed in the tax law.[12] The purpose of the transitional adjustments is to prevent the taxpayer from getting a tax advantage (e.g., getting a double deduction or never having to recognize an item of income because of differences in the two methods) by changing accounting method. In general, the required adjustments spread the effect of making the change in method out over several tax years.

We have already discussed the general operation of the overall accounting methods and applications of the methods to income and deductions. This text also has covered operation of the MACRS depreciation system and its options, as well as the general calculations required in accounting for installment sales and long-term contracts. The sections that follow present and discuss restrictions on the use of the cash method by certain taxpayers and additional information on how to account for long-term contracts. This chapter also introduces and discusses the general rules applicable to accounting for inventories.

Restrictions on Use of the Cash Method

As with accounting periods, taxpayers generally have a significant degree of latitude in selecting their accounting method. However, certain provisions restrict the choice for certain types of taxpayers. For example, the basic requirement that a taxpayer keep books on the basis of the method selected limits most individuals to using the cash method; most people do not keep the records necessary to compute taxable income on the accrual basis. Another basic restriction imposed on taxpayers who have inventories of goods is that they must use the accrual basis to account for sales and cost of goods sold. This requires taxpayers with inventories to select either the accrual or hybrid method to compute their taxable income. In addition, three types of entities must use the accrual method:

- Corporations
- Partnerships that have at least one partner that is a regular corporation
- Any tax shelter activity[13]

For purposes of these restrictions, any method that accounts for some but not all items on the cash basis (i.e., the hybrid method) is considered a cash method. Therefore, these three types of entities cannot use the hybrid method of accounting. The restriction on corporations is designed to prevent a corporation from manipulating its cash receipt-and-disbursement policies to obtain a tax advantage. The partnership restriction is a logical extension of the corporate restriction to prevent using a partnership to defer taxes through the cash method. Similarly, tax shelter activities (as defined in the tax law) are not allowed to use the cash method to increase losses by manipulating income and expense items.[14]

The restrictions on corporations and partnerships are somewhat mitigated by two exceptions. First, corporations and partnerships in which a corporation is a partner may still elect to use the cash method (if they are otherwise eligible to do so) if its average annual gross receipts for the previous three years are $5 million or less. This provision makes the exception somewhat useless for corporations. That is, corporations eligible to use the cash method cannot have inventories. In order to have sales in excess of $5 million, it is likely that the corporation would be engaged in the sale of inventories and be required to use the accrual method under the general rule for inventories. Because it is rare (perhaps impossible) for a large number of corporations that do not have inventories to have sales in excess of $5 million, the exception that provides the choice of methods is negated.

▲ **EXAMPLE 13**   For 3 years, Jackamani Corporation has had average annual sales of $3,600,000. What accounting methods may Jackamani select if Jackamani is in the financial consulting business and does not have inventories?

Discussion: Because Jackamani's average annual gross receipts for the previous 3 years are less than $5,000,000, Jackamani is exempted from the restriction on accounting methods that applies to corporations. In addition, because Jackamani does not have inventories, it is not required to use the accrual method. Therefore, Jackamani can use either the cash method or the accrual method.

▲ **EXAMPLE 14**   Assume the same facts as in example 13, except that Jackamani is a manufacturer of tack for racehorses.

Discussion: Although Jackamani meets the $5,000,000 average annual sales exception, it must use the accrual method because it has inventories. NOTE: Jackamani may also elect to use the hybrid method and use the accrual method only to account for sales and cost of goods sold.

▲ **EXAMPLE 15**   Assume the same facts as in example 13, except that Jackamani has average annual gross sales of $7,000,000. In addition, Jackamani is an S corporation. What accounting methods may Jackamani select?

Discussion: Because Jackamani is an S corporation, the corporation exception does not apply. In addition, Jackamani does not have inventories and therefore may elect to use either the cash method or the accrual method.

A second exception allows a corporation or a partnership with a corporate partner that is engaged in farming to use the cash method, regardless of the amount of its gross receipts. However, if the corporation is also engaged in a separate nonfarming business, it must account for that portion of its business by using the accrual method, unless one of the other exceptions applies. A farming business includes the raising and/or harvesting of crops and livestock, the operation of a nursery or sod farm, and the raising and harvesting of trees bearing fruit, nuts, or other crops, or ornamental trees. A farming business does not include the processing of commodities or products beyond the activities normally incident to the growing, raising, or harvesting of the products.[15]

▲ **EXAMPLE 16**   Kumquat Korporation (KK) owns a large grove of kumquat trees. When the kumquats are ready for harvest, the corporation picks, washes, inspects, and packages the kumquats for distribution. Can KK use the cash method of accounting?

Discussion: Picking, washing, inspecting, and packaging the kumquats all are activities incidental to the raising of the fruit. Therefore, KK may use the cash method to account for its activities.

▲ **EXAMPLE 17**   Assume the same facts as in example 16, except that KK also uses some kumquats to make preserves, which it sells to fruit wholesalers. Can KK use the cash method of accounting?

Discussion: The preserve-making operation is not incident to the raising of the fruit. Because it involves inventories, KK must use the accrual method to account for the preserve-making operation. However, KK can still elect to account for its farming operation using the cash method.

Long-Term Construction Contracts

Taxpayers are generally required to account for long-term construction contracts using the percentage-of-completed-contract method.[16] A long-term construction contract is any contract for the manufacture, building, installation, or construction of property that is not completed within the tax year in which the contract is entered into. Under the percentage-of-completed-contract method, income from long-term contracts is recognized during each period according to the degree of completion of the project during that period. The degree of completion must be based on estimated costs rather than the degree of the project's physical completion. The formula for determining each year's gross income recognition is

$$\text{Contract price} \times \frac{\text{Actual costs incurred during the year}}{\text{Total estimated contract costs}} = \text{Gross income}$$

The purpose of requiring the percentage of completed contract method is to ensure that the accounting by taxpayers entering into long-term contracts clearly reflects income. Before 1986, taxpayers had the option of recognizing income under the completed contract method. Under this method, all income and related costs were deferred until the tax year in which the project was completed. As Exhibit 14–1 illustrates, using this method could result in significant time value of money savings. In Exhibit 14–1, note that although Ace Construction Co. recognizes the same amount of income and pays the same amount of tax on the contract over the two-year period, deferring the payment of $113,750 in taxes from 1995 to 1996 under the completed contract method results in a time value of money savings of $10,351 when discounted at 10%. Although this does not appear to be large in relation to the size of this particular contract, when projects are spread out over periods of three to five years, the savings can be significant.

The Lookback Method. Because the percentage-of-completed-contract method uses the taxpayer's estimated total contract costs to determine each period's income recognition, the taxpayer could underpay the tax due each period by inflating the estimated contract costs. To remove the incentive to overestimate

▲ **Exhibit 14–1**

COMPARISON OF PERCENTAGE-OF-COMPLETED-CONTRACT AND COMPLETED CONTRACT METHODS

Basic Facts: Early in 1995, Ace Construction Co. enters into a contract to build a bridge for Logan County. The contract price is $2,500,000. Ace estimates its total costs of constructing the bridge to be $2,000,000. In 1995, Ace incurs $1,300,000 in costs. The bridge is completed in 1996 with Ace incurring additional costs of $700,000. Ace is in the 35% marginal tax rate bracket.

Recognition of Gross Profit from Contract

		Percentage-of-Completed-Contract Method	Completed Contract Method
1995	$2,500,000 $\times \dfrac{\$1,300,000}{\$2,000,000} - \$1,300,000$	$325,000	$ -0-
1996	$2,500,000 $\times \dfrac{\$\ 700,000}{\$2,000,000} - \$700,000$	$175,000	
	$2,500,000 - ($1,300,000 + $700,000)		$500,000
Total income recognized		$500,000	$500,000

Income Taxes Paid

		Percentage-of-Completed-Contract Method	Completed Contract Method
1995	$325,000 $\times$ 35%	$113,750	$ -0-
1996	$175,000 $\times$ 35%	61,250	
	$500,000 $\times$ 35%		175,000
Total taxes paid		$175,000	$175,000

Time Value of Money Savings at 10%

$113,750 - ($113,750 $\times$ 0.909) = $10,351

costs, upon completion of the contract the taxpayer must use the **lookback method** to determine whether each year's taxes have been under- or overpaid according to the actual total costs of the contract. If the taxpayer has underpaid (i.e., costs were overestimated), the taxpayer must pay interest on the income deferred by the underpayment. Conversely, if an overpayment has been made, the taxpayer receives interest on the overpayment.

The purpose of the lookback method is to compensate for any deferral or acceleration of income that results from using estimated costs rather than actual costs in applying the percentage-of-completed-contract method. This is accomplished by charging the taxpayer interest on any underpayment or paying the taxpayer interest on any overpayment of tax because of differences in actual and estimated costs. Thus, any time value of money savings that a taxpayer could obtain by underestimating costs during the life of the contract is offset by the interest charge on the resulting underpayment.

Calculating the interest due (receivable) under the lookback method has three basic steps:

1. At the completion of a contract, recalculate the tax due for each year of the contract using the actual contract costs.

2. Compute the difference between the actual amount paid for each period and the amounts calculated in step 1.

3. Calculate the interest charge for each amount calculated in step 2 from the end of the period being calculated to the end of the period of completion, using the applicable federal interest rate. The amount of interest payable (due) is equal to the sum of the individual period interest charges.[17]

▲ **EXAMPLE 18**   Assume the same facts as in Exhibit 14–1, except that the costs incurred in 1996 to complete the contract were only $500,000. The actual total cost of the project was only $1,800,000 (not the $2,000,000 originally estimated). In 1995, Ace would compute the income to be recognized using the estimated $2,000,000 cost, recognize gross profit of $325,000 on the contract, and pay a tax of $113,750 on the income reported. How much interest must Ace pay in 1996 under the lookback method if the interest rate is 6%?

Discussion: Under the lookback method, Ace must recompute the 1995 tax using the $1,800,000 in actual costs. This results in a gross profit of $505,556 and a tax based on actual costs of $176,945:

Step 1—Recalculate 1995 Gross Profit

$$\$2,500,000 \times \frac{\$1,300,000}{\$1,800,000} - \$1,300,000 = \$505,556$$

Step 2—Tax on Recomputed Gross Profit

$$\$505,556 \times 35\% = \$176,945$$

The third step requires Ace to pay interest at 6% on the $63,195 ($176,945 − $113,750) underpayment of tax that resulted from the use of the $2,000,000 estimate in 1995. This results in an interest payment of $3,792 ($63,195 × 6%).

If a taxpayer underestimates the total contract costs, the gross profit recognized in the years before completion will be overstated, and an overpayment of tax will occur. In this case, the taxpayer is entitled to a refund of interest on the overpaid tax. It should also be noted that the lookback method is a hypothetical calculation of the tax that would have been paid during the period of the contract, not an actual recalculation in the sense that the taxpayer must file an amended return for each year. Under the annual accounting period concept, each tax year is deemed to stand on its own, apart from other tax years. Thus, the interest paid (due) under the lookback method is reported in the period in which the contract is completed.

The lookback method is generally applicable to all contracts that must be accounted for with the percentage-of-completed-contract method. However, two exceptions to the use of the lookback method apply to small contracts. The lookback method does not apply to

1. Home construction contracts

   or

2. Any contract completed within two years of the commencement of the contract, the gross contract price of which does not exceed

   a. $1 million

      or

   b. 1 percent of the average annual gross receipts for the three tax years preceding the tax year of completion

The intention of these exceptions is to exclude those contracts from the lookback method for which only a small amount of interest would be payable (due). In addition, exempting small contracts from the lookback rule adds an element of administrative convenience for both taxpayers and the government in the calculation of the amounts payable (due) under the method.

Taxpayers Exempt from Percentage-of-Completed-Contract Method. Three categories of contracts are exempted from using the percentage-of-completed-contract method. Contracts that can be accounted for using the completed contract method must meet one of the following tests:

- Home construction contract—Eighty percent or more of the estimated cost of the contract must be attributable either to a dwelling unit or to improvements to real property related to a dwelling unit and located on the same site as a dwelling unit.

- Two-year test—Any contract that, at the time of commencement of the contract, is estimated to be completed within two years.

- Gross receipts test—Any contract entered into by a taxpayer whose average annual gross receipts for the preceding three tax years are less than $10 million.

As with the exceptions to the lookback rule, the intent of these exceptions is to allow taxpayers who would not obtain a significant deferral from using the percentage-of-completed-contract method to use the administratively simple completed contract method.

Accounting for Inventories

When inventories are an income-producing factor, the entity must use the accrual method to account for cost of goods sold.[18] Inventories include goods held for resale, as well as inventories of raw materials and supplies that will become part of the merchandise produced by a manufacturer. The inventory method selected by a taxpayer must conform to the best accounting practices in the taxpayer's trade or business, and it must clearly reflect income. The best accounting practices in a trade or business are synonymous with generally accepted accounting practices. In most cases, tax accounting and financial accounting for inventories are similar. However, the commissioner of the IRS has the authority to determine whether an inventory method clearly reflects income, and conflicts often arise.

▲ **EXAMPLE 19**   Thor Corporation is a manufacturer of power tools. During the current year, it wrote down the cost of obsolete parts. The parts were kept on hand, and the selling price of the parts was not reduced. The practice is generally acceptable in Thor's trade or business. Can Thor write down the parts for tax purposes?

Discussion: The tax law allows obsolete or slow-moving inventory to be written down only if the selling price of the inventory is reduced. Although Thor's write-down conformed to generally accepted accounting principles, the commissioner of the IRS determined that the write-down did not clearly reflect income, because Thor did not reduce the selling price of the obsolete parts. The Supreme Court ruled in favor of the commissioner, and Thor was not allowed to write down the obsolete parts for tax purposes.[19]

Example 19 illustrates that generally accepted accounting principles may be used in accounting for inventory only when the tax law does not specify the treatment or when the tax law allows alternative treatments.

Exhibit 14–2 provides the formula for calculating costs of goods sold. As you can see, the taxpayer must determine inventories at the beginning and end of the year and must record purchases of goods during the year. A manufacturer must also keep inventories of raw materials, supplies, and work in process to determine the cost of goods manufactured during the tax year. Taxpayers have several options in determining the cost of inventory items. Inventories may be valued either at cost or at the lower of cost-or-market value. In order to determine the cost of items on hand at the end of the period, an inventory flow assumption must be adopted. Taxpayers are generally required to use the first-in, first-out (FIFO) assumption, although they could elect to use either the average cost method or last-in, first-out (LIFO) inventory valuation.

Determining Inventory Cost.   The cost of inventories and purchases must be determined. In the case of purchased inventory, cost is equal to the invoice price of the merchandise, less trade discounts, plus freight, and other transportation costs. Manufacturers must use the **full absorption costing method** to determine inventory cost. Under this method, all direct costs (direct materials and direct labor), as well as overhead costs, must be included in the cost of goods manufactured.

As of 1986, manufacturers and certain retailers and wholesalers are required to determine the cost of their inventories using the uniform capitalization rules.[20] Retailers and wholesalers with average annual gross revenue of less than $10

▲ **Exhibit 14–2**

COST-OF-GOODS-SOLD CALCULATION

Acne Retailers sells widgets that it purchases from various manufacturers. At the beginning of 1995, Acne has $22,000-worth of widgets on hand. During the year, Acne purchases widgets costing $94,000. At the end of 1995, Acne has $17,000-worth of widgets in its inventory. What is Acne's 1995 cost of goods sold?

Beginning inventory	$ 22,000
Add: Purchases of inventory	94,000
Goods available for sale	$116,000
Less: Ending inventory	(17,000)
Equals: Cost of goods sold	$ 99,000

million are exempt from these rules. In addition, farmers and ranchers who elect to use the cash method are not required to maintain inventories and thus are exempt.

The **uniform capitalization (unicap) rules** require a "reasonable allocation" of all direct and indirect costs to the cost of inventory. Indirect costs include all costs other than selling and general and administrative costs that are not related to production (e.g., general accounting salaries). Thus, many costs that are normally expensed for financial accounting purposes, such as storage costs, purchasing agents' salaries, and general and administrative costs that benefit production, must be allocated to the cost of inventory. Exhibit 14–3 provides a list of costs that must be capitalized under the unicap rules.

The imposition of the unicap rules has created an administrative nightmare for businesses. Because these rules do not conform to generally accepted accounting principles, firms are forced to keep two sets of inventory records to comply with the rules. In addition, the unicap rules further complicate the calculation of deferred taxes for financial accounting purposes. These are significant costs, which raises the question of whether the additional tax revenue generated under the unicap rules significantly exceeds the cost of implementing the rules.

LOWER OF COST-OR-MARKET VALUATION.   Taxpayers may elect to use the lower of cost-or-market valuation to determine inventory values.[21] *Cost* refers to the amount determined under the cost method using the unicap rules. *Market for purchased merchandise* means the bid price for the particular inventory item in the volume in which it is normally purchased by the taxpayer. For manufactured goods, market is the total reproduction cost at current bid prices.

The **lower of cost-or-market method** requires a comparison of cost and market for each inventory item. Comparison of the total cost and total market value of nonsimiliar inventory items is not permitted.

▲ **EXAMPLE 20**   Ward Manufacturing produces 4 different products. The cost and market value at the end of Ward's tax year for each of the products is provided. What is Ward's inventory value if it elects to use the lower of cost-or-market method?

Product	Cost	Market
A	$14,000	$15,000
B	8,000	3,000
C	23,000	21,000
D	12,000	5,000

Cost	Treatment
Direct materials	Capitalize
Direct labor	Capitalize
Indirect materials (consumed in production operation)	Capitalize
Indirect labor (worked in production process, but not directly on product)	Capitalize
Storage, handling, and insurance on materials or merchandise	Capitalize
Fringe benefits for direct and indirect labor	Capitalize
Pension costs for direct and indirect labor	Capitalize
Depreciation on production facilities	Capitalize
Property taxes, insurance, maintenance, etc. on production facilities	Capitalize
Interest paid related to production facilities	Capitalize
Mixed service costs (personnel costs, data processing, purchasing)	Allocated

▲ **Exhibit 14–3**

TREATMENT OF COSTS UNDER UNIFORM CAPITALIZATION RULES

Discussion: Ward must take the lower of cost or market for each of the 4 individual inventory items. The lower value for each inventory item is added to obtain the total inventory value. This results in a total inventory value of $43,000. Ward cannot compare the total cost of the 4 products with the total market value to compute the lower of cost or market.

Product	Cost	Market	Lower of Cost-or-Market Value
A	$14,000	$15,000	$14,000
B	8,000	3,000	3,000
C	23,000	21,000	21,000
D	12,000	5,000	5,000
Total	$57,000	$44,000	$43,000

Inventory Flow Assumptions. Merchandise that can be readily identified with specific invoices or production records is valued by reference to the invoice or production records. This type of valuation is referred to as the *specific identification method* and is used by dealers in large or unique items (e.g., automobile and heavy equipment dealers, antique store owners). However, such specific identification procedures are not economically feasible for businesses that have many units of a particular product that are not easily identifiable with specific invoices or production records. In such cases, an inventory flow assumption must be made. An inventory flow assumption prescribes the order in which goods in inventory are assumed to be sold. The FIFO method is generally required for tax purposes. However, taxpayers may elect to use either the average cost method or the LIFO method. The application of these flow assumptions follows those used in financial accounting.

▲ **EXAMPLE 21** Maynard Corporation's inventory records for the current year for its designer hairbrushes disclose the following:

Date	Units Purchased	Cost per Unit	Total Cost
Beginning Inventory	200	$3	$ 600
February 13	400	$5	$2,000
July 24	600	$6	$3,600
November 18	300	$7	$2,100
Totals	1,500		$8,300

A physical count of the hairbrushes at the end of the year shows that Maynard has 250 on hand. What is Maynard's ending inventory value using the average cost, FIFO, and LIFO methods?

Discussion: Maynard's ending inventory value under each assumption is calculated as follows:

Average Cost Method:

Average cost per unit = Total cost ÷ Total units available

      = $8,300 ÷ 1,500 = $ 5.53 per unit

Multiplied by ending inventory units   × 250

Equals ending inventory value $1,383

FIFO Method

Under the FIFO method, the first units in inventory are assumed to be sold first. The 250 units on hand at the end of the year are the last 250 units purchased. The 300 units purchased on November 18 cost $7 per unit. Under a FIFO flow assumption, the ending inventory value would be $1,750 (250 × $7).

LIFO Method

The LIFO method assumes that the last units purchased are the first units sold. The 250 units on hand at the end of the year are the first 250 units purchased. The ending inventory under LIFO is composed of the 200 units of beginning inventory and 50 of the units purchased on February 13. This gives an inventory value of $850:

Beginning inventory (200 × $3)	$600
February 13 purchase (50 × $5)	250
LIFO inventory cost	$850

Taxpayers have considerable leeway in selecting which inventory flow assumption to use for tax purposes. However, in order to use the average cost method, the taxpayer must be able to show that it is applicable to all goods in its inventory, not to just one particular line of inventory. This requires the taxpayer to use average cost on all inventory items, not just a select few. Because the LIFO flow assumption usually results in a larger cost of goods sold (with less taxable income) than the other methods, it is subject to several limitations.

Electing LIFO.   A taxpayer wishing to switch to LIFO must file an application with the IRS for the tax year in which the change is to be made. The LIFO application must specify the precise inventories of the taxpayer to which the method is to be applied.[22] Approval is automatic. However, once elected, a taxpayer cannot switch to another inventory method without the written consent of the commissioner of the IRS.

LIFO is deemed to be a cost-based method of inventory valuation. Taxpayers cannot use the lower of cost-or-market valuation method in tandem with a LIFO assumption. If a taxpayer who has been using the lower of cost-or-market method makes a LIFO election, any previous write-downs to the beginning inventory (the previous year's ending inventory) for the year of change must be added to income to restore the inventory to a cost basis.

▲ **EXAMPLE 22**   Roger Corporation elects to use the LIFO inventory method beginning in 1995. Roger's ending inventory for 1994 is valued at $23,000 using the lower of cost-or-market method. The cost of the 1994 ending inventory is $26,000. What is the effect of the change to LIFO on Roger's 1995 taxable income?

Discussion: Because LIFO is a cost-based method, Roger must restore the $3,000 ($26,000 − $23,000) lower of cost-or-market write-down to the 1995 beginning inventory. If this higher inventory figure had been used to compute 1994 cost of goods, cost of goods sold would have been $3,000 less, and taxable income would have increased by the $3,000 write-down. Therefore, in converting the 1995 beginning inventory to a cost basis, Roger must add the $3,000 1994 write-down to its 1995 income.

A final requirement for the use of LIFO for tax purposes is that the taxpayer must also use it for financial reporting purposes. This is known as the *financial conformity rule.*[23] This rule prevents taxpayers from using the LIFO advantage for tax purposes while reporting higher income for financial reporting by using another inventory flow assumption.

▲ INCOME TAX CREDITS

A tax credit is a direct reduction in the tax liability of the taxpayer receiving the credit. As such, tax credits are not part of the tax base used to compute the tax liability. Because they are not part of the base and reduce the tax liability dollar for dollar, tax credits are neutral with respect to the marginal tax rate of the taxpayer. That is, in contrast to tax deductions, a $100 tax credit is worth a $100 reduction in taxes to taxpayers in the 15- and 31-percent marginal tax rate brackets.

Most tax credits are nonrefundable—if the amount of the credit exceeds the tax liability, the taxpayer is not entitled to a refund of the excess. Although most business tax credits are nonrefundable, they generally provide that any amount of credit not used in the current year may be carried forward and used in future years; these are known as **nonrefundable tax credits.** Tax credits available only to individuals are not allowed this carryforward, although the earned income credit is refundable. A **refundable tax credit** means that the taxpayer is entitled to a refund of the excess credit. This is a form of negative income tax—the taxpayer not only pays no tax but receives a payment from the government that is based on the income of the taxpayer.

The neutrality of tax credits with respect to marginal tax rates allows Congress to target specific activities with the certainty that taxpayers engaging in the activity will receive the expected tax relief. Tax credits are used to

- Encourage investment in specific types of assets or engage in specific activities
- Provide equitable treatment among taxpayers
- Provide tax relief for low-income, elderly, and disabled taxpayers

As you can see, certain credits are used to encourage investment by businesses, whereas others are geared specifically to tax relief for individuals. The discussion that follows delineates those tax credits available to businesses and those targeted specifically for individuals.

Business Tax Credits

There are numerous tax credits for engaging in certain types of business activities. Congress enacted each credit for a specific purpose. Table 14–1 provides a list of business tax credits and a summary of their individual purposes. The list is quite extensive; this chaper discusses some of the more important ones.

Investment Tax Credit.   Congress has used the **investment tax credit (ITC)** since 1962 to stimulate the economy by allowing a credit for a percentage of the cost of qualifying property (generally, only personal property has been allowed the ITC). Congress has turned the ITC on and off many times since the first credit was enacted. In 1986, Congress repealed the ITC, and it is not in force today. However, history suggests that Congress will not hesitate to reinstate the credit if it feels it is necessary to get the economy moving. Because the ITC is a nonrefundable credit, some businesses may have unused ITCs that they continue to carry over and use.

Foreign Tax Credit.   Taxpayers may claim a tax credit for foreign taxes paid on foreign source income.[24] Alternatively, the taxpayer may elect to deduct the foreign taxes paid in computing taxable income.[25] In most cases, the value of the credit exceeds the value of the deduction, and taxpayers find it advantageous to use the tax credit. The purpose of the **foreign tax credit** is to alleviate the effects of double taxation on businesses that pay taxes to another country on the income

Business Tax Credit	Purpose of Credit
Investment tax credit (currently repealed)	To encourage new investment in equipment, which is a stimulant to the economy and increases employment
Foreign tax credit	To provide relief from double taxation of foreign source income
Research & experimental credit	To encourage research in new technology, which will strengthen the country's technological base
Targeted jobs credit	To encourage employers to hire unemployed workers from disadvantaged groups
Rehabilitation tax credit	To encourage the rehabilitation of older buildings and structures to preserve them for future generations
Business energy credits	To encourage energy conservation and promote the use of alternative fuels
Low-income housing credit	To encourage construction of low-income housing
Disabled access credit	To encourage small businesses to provide access for disabled people
Alcohol fuels credit	To encourage the use of fuels with an alcohol base
Oil recovery credit	To encourage domestic production of oil through use of tertiary recovery methods
Reforestation credit	To provide relief to commercial timber products businesses for replanting and seeding trees

earned in that country. The maximum tax credit allowed is the tax that is assessed by the United States on the foreign source income.[26] That is, taxpayers may use the foreign tax credit only to offset taxes that would have been paid to the United States on the foreign source income:

$$\text{Limit} = \frac{\text{Foreign source taxable income}}{\text{Worldwide taxable income}} \times \frac{\text{U.S. income tax}}{\text{before tax credits}}$$

Note that the formula sets a maximum allowable credit. If the actual foreign taxes paid are less than the limit, the actual foreign tax is the amount of the allowable credit. When the foreign taxes paid exceed the limit, the unused portion can be carried back two years and forward for five years, subject to each year's individual foreign tax credit limit.

▲ **EXAMPLE 23**   Geraldo Corporation engages in operations in several foreign countries as well as in the United States. During the current year, Geraldo's worldwide taxable income was $800,000. Geraldo's foreign source income was $200,000, on which it paid total foreign taxes of $30,000. What is Geraldo's allowable foreign tax credit?

Discussion: The foreign tax credit on Geraldo's foreign source income is limited to the lesser of the actual taxes paid or the limit calculated by the formula. Geraldo's U.S. tax on $800,000 in taxable income is $272,000 ($800,000 × 34%). This produces a limit of $68,000:

$$\text{Limit} = \frac{\$200,000}{\$800,000} \times \$272,000 = \$68,000$$

Because the actual taxes paid are less than the limit, Geraldo's foreign tax credit is the $30,000 in actual foreign taxes paid.

▲ **EXAMPLE 24**   Assume the same facts as in example 23, except that Geraldo paid $85,000 in foreign taxes. What is Geraldo's foreign tax credit?

Discussion: Geraldo's foreign tax credit is limited to the $68,000 calculated in example 23. The $17,000 ($85,000 − $68,000) excess may be carried back 2 years and used to offset tax paid, subject to each year's foreign tax credit limit. If the entire credit is not used in the carryback period, any unused portion may be carried forward for 5 years and used, subject to each year's individual limit on foreign taxes paid.

Research and Experimental Credit.

The purpose of the **research and experimental (R&E) tax credit** is to encourage research and development of new technologies and processes. Two separate credits are allowed. The first credit is for incremental research expenditures. The incremental credit is equal to 20 percent of the qualified research expenditures in the current year in excess of the base amount.[27]

Qualified expenditures must be technical in nature, intended to be useful in the development of a new or improved business component of the taxpayer, or be elements of a process of experimentation for a functional purpose. Obviously, this characterization of qualified expenditures leads to numerous interpretations that are beyond the scope of this text.[28] The basic point is that the credit is meant to encourage expenditures on new technology and for experimentation leading to new technology, not for fine-tuning existing processes or custom orders of a particular product.

The base amount for computing the credit is equal to the product of (1) the fixed base percentage, which is the ratio of the taxpayer's total qualified research expenses for the base period of 1984 to 1988 to its total gross receipts for the same period (limited to a maximum of 16 percent), and (2) the taxpayer's average annual gross receipts for the four previous years. The minimum base amount may not be less than 50 percent of the current year's expenditures.[29]

▲ **EXAMPLE 25**   Creator Corporation spent $400,000 on qualified research activities during the current year. Its fixed base percentage is 13%, and average annual gross receipts for the previous 4 years were $1,300,000. What is Creator's base amount for computing the incremental research credit?

Discussion: The base amount is the fixed base percentage multiplied by the average annual gross receipts for the 4 previous years. Creator's base amount for the current year is $169,000 ($1,300,000 × 13%) per this calculation. However, the minimum base amount is 50% of current-year expenditures, $200,000 ($400,000 × 50%). Therefore, for purposes of computing the incremental research credit, Creator's base amount is $200,000, the minimum amount allowable.

▲ **EXAMPLE 26**   Refer to example 25. What is Creator's current-year incremental research expenditure credit?

Discussion: The incremental research expenditure credit is equal to 20% of the excess of the current year's expenditures, minus the base amount. Creator's credit is $40,000 [20% × ($400,000 − $200,000)].

The deduction for research and experimental expenditures must be reduced by the amount of the credit.

▲ **EXAMPLE 27**   Refer to examples 25 and 26. What is Creator Corporation's allowable deduction for research and experimentation expenditures?

Discussion: The $400,000 in qualified expenditures must be reduced by the $40,000 tax credit. Therefore, Creator can deduct only $360,000 of the qualified expenditures in calculating its taxable income.

The second component of the R&E credit is the basic research credit. This credit is equal to 20 percent of qualified expenditures for research that is intended to advance scientific knowledge without a specific commercial objective. In order to qualify, two conditions must be met: The payments must be made in cash under a written agreement, and the research must be performed or controlled by a university, college, or other nonprofit scientific research organization. Amounts expended for the basic research credit cannot be used in the calculation of the incremental research credit.

Rehabilitation Tax Credit.

Although the investment tax credit provided incentive for investing in personal property (e.g., machinery and equipment), the credit was not available for the purchase of real property. Congress felt that some incentive was needed for rejuvenating inner cities and historic structures; it created two types of **rehabilitation tax credits:** a 10-percent older buildings credit and a 20-percent historic structures credit.[30] The older buildings credit applies to structures placed in service before 1936. To qualify for the historic structures credit, a building must be certified as historic by the Department of the Treasury and must be located in a registered historic district or listed on the National Register of Historic Places. Both tax credits can be taken on a building that qualifies for both credits. To avoid a double tax benefit, the basis of the building or structure must be reduced by the amount of credit taken.

In order to qualify for the 10-percent older buildings credit, the rehabilitation expenditures must be incurred to improve or rehabilitate property that is used in the taxpayer's trade or business or that is held for investment purposes. The credit for historic structures is not as restrictive—residential real estate can qualify for the historic structures credit but not for the older buildings credit. The structure must also be "substantially rehabilitated." A *substantial rehabilitation* means that the rehabilitation expenditures exceed the greater of the property's adjusted basis or $5,000. In addition, at least 75 percent of the external walls (including at least 50-percent use as external walls) and at least 75 percent of the internal structural framework must remain in place.

▲ **EXAMPLE 28**   Eskimo Joe's purchased a building in downtown Stillwater at a cost of $20,000. The building was originally placed in service in 1928. Joe's spent $50,000 to rehabilitate the building for use as a restaurant. The external walls remained in place, and only minor modifications were made to the existing internal structural framework. Do the expenditures qualify for the rehabilitation expenditure credit?

Discussion: The expenditures qualify for the 10% rehabilitation credit because the building is used in Eskimo Joe's trade or business, the property was originally placed in service before 1936, the $50,000 of rehabilitation expenditures exceed Eskimo Joe's $20,000 basis [the greater of Eskimo Joe's adjusted basis ($20,000) in the property or $5,000)], and the 75% tests for external walls and internal structural framework are met. Eskimo Joe's tax credit is $5,000 ($50,000 × 10%). Joe's adjusted basis in the building is $65,000 ($20,000 + $50,000 − $5,000).

▲ **EXAMPLE 29**   Assume the same facts as in example 28, except that the building has been certified by the Department of Treasury as a historic structure and is listed on the National Register of Historic Places. What would be the total amount of rehabilitation credits Eskimo Joe's could take on the building?

Discussion: Because the rehabilitation expenditures qualify for both the 10-percent older buildings credit and the 20-percent historic structures credit, Eskimo Joe's tax credit is $15,000 (30% × $50,000). Joe's adjusted basis in the building would be $55,000 ($20,000 + $50,000 − $15,000).

In order to retain the full benefit of the tax credit, the property must be held five full years. If a rehabilitated structure is sold before the end of the five-year period, the credit is recaptured (added to the tax liability) in proportion to the number of years (or portions thereof) the actual holding period fell short of the five-year required holding period.

▲ **EXAMPLE 30**   Assume that the building in example 28 is rehabilitated on June 4, 1995. Eskimo Joe's takes the proper credit on its 1995 tax return. On February 4, 1998, Eskimo Joe's sells the building. How much of the $5,000 rehabilitation tax credit must be recaptured in 1998?

Discussion: Eskimo Joe's has not held the building 5 full years. Eskimo Joe's must recapture the credit attributable to the portion of the 5-year holding period requirement it did not meet. In this case, the building was held for 2 years and 8 months. Therefore, Eskimo Joe's held the property for only 2 full years, leaving 3 years (2 full years plus a portion of a third) subject to recapture. Eskimo Joe's must recapture $3,000 ($5,000 × 3/5) of the credit by adding it to its 1998 tax liability.

Individual Tax Credits

In contrast to business tax credits, which are designed mainly to provide an incentive for businesses to invest in certain activities, the tax credits available for individuals are generally intended to provide tax relief to certain classes of taxpayers. Congress has favored the use of credits (rather than deductions) in these situations, because the amount of the relief is equal for taxpayers in different marginal tax brackets. In addition, because the credits are targeted for low-income taxpayers, many of whom do not itemize deductions, the use of a credit assures that these taxpayers get the intended relief. One of the credits, the earned income credit, is refundable. This allows the taxpayer to receive a refund of tax in excess of any amounts paid during the year. In effect, this feature allows the government to provide a cash subsidy to taxpayers (an effect not possible with deductions).

Table 14–2 lists the tax credits available only to individual taxpayers and the purpose of each credit. Note the brevity of the list, compared with that for busi-

▲ **Table 14–2**

INDIVIDUAL TAX CREDITS & THEIR PURPOSE

Individual Tax Credit	Purpose of Credit
Earned income credit	To provide tax relief to low-income taxpayers
Child and dependent care credit	To provide tax relief to taxpayers who incur child and dependent care expenses so that they can be employed
Tax credit for the elderly and the disabled	To provide extra tax relief to low-income taxpayers who either are elderly or retired because of a permanent and total disability
Residential mortgage interest credit (currently expired)	To increase home ownership in areas that are experiencing prolonged economic depression

nesses. One characteristic of the individual credits is that they begin to phase out (i.e., are reduced) when some measure of the taxpayer's income (e.g., earned income or adjusted gross income) reaches a predetermined level. The use of a phase-out rule gives a larger credit to lower-income taxpayers and either reduces or eliminates the credit for those with higher incomes. The earned income credit and the credit for child and dependent care illustrate the operation of individual tax credits.

Earned Income Credit.   The **earned income credit (EIC)** provides tax relief to low-income taxpayers. Unlike the other individual tax credits, the EIC is refundable. That is, even if the taxpayer has no tax liability, the taxpayer can receive a refund equal to the amount of the credit. Because the amount of credit is dependent on the taxpayer's earned income and phases out after the taxpayer's income reaches a predetermined level, married taxpayers are required to file a joint return in order to take the EIC. This prevents taxpayers from filing separate returns and obtaining a credit based only on each spouse's income. By filing a separate return, the couple would be able to receive a higher credit or in some cases qualify for the credit when their combined income would exceed the maximum allowable earned income (EI).

Before 1994, a taxpayer was eligible for the earned income credit only if at least one qualifying child was living in the taxpayer's home. In essence, a qualifying child had to be younger than 19 (24, if a full-time student), be the child, stepchild, foster child or a descendent of the taxpayer, and reside for more than half the year with the taxpayer. For tax years after 1993, the eligibility requirements for the earned income credit have changed substantially. To be eligible for the earned income credit, the taxpayer no longer needs to have a qualifying child living in the home, although taxpayers still are categorized according to the number of children at home. Instead, the taxpayer must meet all of the following requirements:

1. The taxpayer's principal place of abode for more than one-half of the year must be in the United States.

2. The taxpayer or the taxpayer's spouse must be older than 25 but not older than 65.

3. The taxpayer or taxpayer's spouse cannot be a dependent of another taxpayer.[31]

The general formula for calculating the earned income credit is the lesser of the following:

1. Maximum credit allowed = Earned income (EI) up to maximum allowable for the category × Credit percentage for the category.
    or

2. Maximum credit allowed − [(Greater of AGI or EI − EI/AGI phase-out income level) × Phase-out percentage for the category].

Applying the phase-out rate to the greater of the taxpayer's earned income or adjusted gross income yields two results. First, the EIC does not begin to phase out until adjusted gross income (or earned income, if greater) reaches $11,280 ($5,130 for taxpayers with no children). Second, the EIC is phased out completely when adjusted gross income (or earned income, if greater) reaches $26,663 ($9,230 for taxpayers with no children and $24,387 for taxpayers with one child) in 1995.

The 1995 credit percentages appear in the third column of Table 14–3. Multiplying the maximum earned income level in column 2 by the credit percentage

Category	Maximum Earned Income	Credit Percentage	EI/AGI Phase-out Income Level	Phase-Out Percentage	Maximum EI/AGI Income	Maximum Credit Allowed
No children	$4,100	7.65%	$ 5,130	7.65%	$ 9,230	$ 314
One child	$6,160	34.00%	$11,280	15.98%	$24,387	$2,094
More than 2 children	$8,640	36.00%	$11,280	20.22%	$26,663	$3,110

in column 3 yields the maximum credit allowed, set forth in the last column. For a taxpayer with no children, the maximum credit is $314 ($4,100 × 7.65%); for a taxpayer with one child the maximum credit is $2,094 ($6,160 × 34%); for a taxpayer with two or more children, the maximum credit is $3,110 ($8,640 × 36%). The earned income levels in Table 14–3 are indexed for inflation and increase each year. Note that if the taxpayer's income equals the maximum earned income in column 2 ($4,100 for a taxpayer with no children), the taxpayer owes no tax for the year and is due a refund of the full amount of the credit, $314.

▲ **EXAMPLE 31**   Bo and April are married and have 1 dependent child who lives in their home during the entire tax year. Bo and April have earned income of $13,000 in 1995. They have no other sources of income or deductions. What are Bo and April's income tax liability and their basic EIC for 1995?

Discussion: Bo and April's taxable income is zero, and they have no tax liability:

Gross income = Earned income = Adjusted gross income	$13,000
Less:	
Standard deduction	(6,550)
Less:	
Personal and dependency exemptions ($2,500 × 3)	(7,500)
Taxable income	$ -0-

Bo and April's Basic EIC is $1,819:

The lesser of
1. $6,160 × 34% = $2,094
    or
2. $2,094 − [($13,000 − $11,280) × 15.98% = $1,819

Although Bo and April owe no tax, they are entitled to a refund of the $1,819 EIC and any amounts withheld from their income during the year.

Because the credit is refundable, taxpayers who expect to receive the credit can fill out a form and get an advance from their employer based on an estimate of the amount of their credit. Any EIC advanced is reported as a reduction of the EIC on the taxpayer's return. The advanced EIC is limited to 60 percent of the maximum credit available for taxpayers with one child.

Child and Dependent Care Credit.   Taxpayers who pay someone to care for their child and/or other dependent so the taxpayers can work are eligible for a credit based on the amount of their expenses and their earned income level; it is known as the **child and dependent care credit.** This credit is designed to encourage taxpayers who work and have children to provide them with adequate care while they are at work. It also provides tax relief to lower-income working families who have children at home. The child and dependent care credit is a nonrefundable credit.

To qualify for the credit, two conditions must be met:

1. The taxpayer must incur employment-related expenses.

2. The expenses must be for the care of qualified individuals.

An employment-related expense is one that must be paid to enable the taxpayer to work and must be paid for either household services or for the care of a qualified individual. Generally, the expenses must be incurred within the taxpayer's home, although out-of-the-home expenses for dependents younger than 13 and for a disabled dependent or spouse (if the disabled person spends at least eight hours per day in the home) also qualify. The exception for the disabled encourages individuals to keep disabled dependents or a spouse in the home rather than institutionalize them.[32]

A qualifying individual includes any dependent younger than 13 or a dependent or a spouse of the taxpayer who is physically or mentally incapacitated.

▲ **EXAMPLE 32**   Aria is a CPA, and her husband is an auto mechanic. They employ a housekeeper who cleans the house and cooks and takes care of their 6-year-old son. Are Aria and her husband entitled to a credit for child and dependent care?

Discussion: The expenditures for the housekeeper are eligible for the credit. They allow Aria and her husband to be employed, are spent for household services, and their 6-year-old son is a qualifying individual (he is younger than 13).

▲ **EXAMPLE 33**   Assume the same facts as in example 32. Because her husband's shop is open 7 days a week, he doesn't have time to take care of their yard. They hired a lawn service to fertilize and mow the lawn. Does the cost of the lawn service qualify for the child and dependent care credit?

Discussion: The child and lawn care services do allow Aria and her husband to be employed. However, the lawn care services are not paid for either household services or for the care of a qualifying dependent. Therefore, they are not eligible costs for the credit. However, the housekeeper costs are still eligible for the credit.

▲ **EXAMPLE 34**   Julie's husband Paul was injured in an accident at work several years ago and is confined to a wheelchair. Because he is unable to take care of himself, Julie leaves Paul at a day-care center while she works. Is Julie eligible for the child and dependent care credit?

Discussion: Because her husband is disabled, Julie may leave him outside the home. She is eligible for the credit so long as Paul spends at least 8 hours per day at home.

The amount of the credit is generally 30 percent of the qualified expenditures incurred, limited to $2,400 ($4,800 with two or more qualifying individuals). The 30-percent rate is reduced by 1 percent for each $2,000 (or portion thereof) of the taxpayer's adjusted gross income in excess of $10,000. The maximum reduction is limited to 10 percent, leaving a minimum allowable credit of 20 percent. The 20-percent minimum credit limit is reached when the taxpayer's adjusted gross income exceeds $28,000.[33]

▲ **EXAMPLE 35**   Jorge is a single parent with 2 dependent children living with him. During 1995, Jorge has an adjusted gross income of $23,000 and pays $3,000 in qualified child-care expenses. Assuming that both children are younger than 13, what is Jorge's child and dependent care credit?

Discussion: Because his AGI is in excess of $10,000, Jorge must reduce the 30% general credit rate by 1% for each $2,000 (or portion thereof) of AGI in excess of $10,000. Jorge's credit is $690:

Amount of qualified child care expenses				$3,000
Basic credit rate		30%		
Reduction for excess AGI:				
Jorge's AGI	$23,000			
Less:	(10,000)			
Excess AGI	$13,000			
Divided by number of $2,000	÷ 2,000			
increments (rounded up)	7			
Reduction % per increment	× 1%	7%	× 23%	
Child care credit				$ 690

The expenditures qualifying for the credit cannot exceed the earned income of the taxpayer. For married taxpayers, the lower earned income of the two is used for the purpose of the limit. The purpose of the limit on expenditures is consistent with the purpose of the credit—to allow the taxpayer to be gainfully employed. If the expense of child care is in excess of the income earned by working, the employment does not provide a net gain to the household income.

▲ **EXAMPLE 36** Doug and Dorothy are married and have 2 dependent children younger than 13. Dorothy is an airline pilot who earns $150,000 per year. Doug is interested in art and is employed part time at an art gallery. Doug earned $3,000 at the art gallery. Qualified child-care expenses were $8,000. What is Doug and Dorothy's child and dependent care credit?

Discussion: Qualifying child-care expenditures are limited to the earned income of the lesser-paid spouse. In this case, Doug's earned income ($3,000) is less than the amount expended for child care ($8,000). Only the $3,000 is eligible for the credit. Because their AGI is in excess of $28,000, they are allowed the minimum 20% credit. This results in a child and dependent care credit of $600 ($3,000 × 20%).

▲ THE ALTERNATIVE MINIMUM TAX

In exercising its power of legislative grace, Congress in many instances has chosen to use the tax system to encourage taxpayers to engage in various transactions it deems socially or economically desirable. This text has discussed many provisions that provide tax relief on transactions that depart from the treatment prescribed by the general concepts of taxation. As the number of such relief provisions proliferated through the years, Congress became increasingly aware that many taxpayers were carefully planning their affairs to take maximum advantage of these provisions. The result of this planning documented in various reports by the Treasury Department and academic studies showed that a large number of corporations and individuals with quite large economic incomes were paying little or no taxes.

Because Congress was hesitant to single out any one incentive by repealing its relief provisions, the politicians decided to impose an additional tax on those taxpayers who take too much advantage of a specified set of tax incentives. The set of tax incentives that became subject to this new tax is called *tax preference items*. Tax preference items are provisions in the tax law that treat certain items of income or deduction preferentially as compared with other items. In addition, in order to be considered a tax preference item, Congress must specify the item as such (i.e., all items that depart from the general concepts of taxation are not tax preference items).

In 1969, Congress enacted the first tax on preference items. This initial tax was called the *add-on minimum tax,* because the tax on preference items was paid in addition to the regular income tax liability. So as not to totally discourage taxpayers from engaging in tax preference activities, the first tax was 10 percent of tax preference items in excess of $30,000 (i.e., the first $30,000 of tax preference items was exempt from the tax). With minor adjustments, this system remained in effect until 1978. However, studies indicated that the tax was not very successful in its goal of assuring that all taxpayers paid their fair share of taxes. A new system of taxing preference items was initiated in 1978 called the **alternative minimum tax (AMT).** As its name implies, this tax is an alternative calculation of the tax liability that results in the minimum amount of tax that the taxpayer must pay. In effect, the AMT is a separate, parallel tax system. Within this system, many preference items allowed in the calculation of the regular tax liability are either not allowed or the amount of tax relief provided is greatly diminished.

There are two aspects of the AMT system that need to be pointed out before we discuss the mechanics of the system. First, using a parallel system of tax rules requires all but the smallest taxpaying units to keep a separate set of accounting records to compute the tax. Second, changes in the system in 1986, 1989, and 1993 have greatly increased the number of taxpayers who are subject to the tax. For example, the top **alternative minimum tax rate** paid by individual taxpayers has been increased to 28 percent, compared with a top marginal regular tax rate of 39.6 percent. The narrow spread between the two rates has subjected individual taxpayers with fairly minimal amounts of preference items to the tax. Thus, it has become an increasingly important aspect of individual taxation in recent years. The system is extremely complex. The discussion that follows provides an overview of the system and the effects it can have on taxpayers.

Basic AMT Computation

As a separate tax system, the AMT is calculated by applying a tax rate to a tax base.[34] The tax base is called **alternative minimum taxable income (AMTI).** Exhibit 14–4 provides the general calculation of the AMT. The starting point for the calculation of AMTI is regular taxable income, the taxable income as computed under the general tax system that has been discussed throughout the text. As shown in Exhibit 14–4, AMTI is determined by making two separate categories of

Regular taxable income	$XXX
Add (Subtract): Adjustments	XXX
Add: Preferences	XXX
Add (Subtract): Net operating loss adjustment	(XXX)
Equals: Tentative alternative minimum taxable income	$XXX
Subtract: Applicable exemption amount	(XXX)
Equals: Alternative minimum taxable income	$XXX
Times: Tax rate (20% for corporations, 26% and 28% for individuals)	× XX%
Equals: Tentative minimum tax before foreign tax credit	$XXX
Subtract: AMT foreign tax credit	(XXX)
Equals: Tentative minimum tax	$XXX
Subtract: Regular tax liability	(XXX)
Equals: Alternative minimum tax (if positive)	$XXX

▲ **Exhibit 14–4**

BASIC AMT CALCULATION

modifications to the regular taxable income. The first modification is for adjustments and the second is for preferences. *Adjustments* are generally made to items that are treated differently in the current period but that will reverse themselves in future periods. As such, adjustments may be either positive or negative (generally positive in the first period and negative in future periods as the difference in treatment reverses itself). The net operating loss adjustment has been singled out in the computation, because it must be made after considering all other adjustments and preferences. *Preferences* are items that are never allowed for AMT purposes. Because they are never allowed, they do not reverse over time and thus are always positive adjustments in calculating AMTI.

As with the first add-on minimum tax, the AMT recognizes that there should be some allowable level of preference items through the use of exemption amounts. However, these exemption amounts are phased out at varying levels of tentative AMTI, resulting in reduced (possibly no) exemption amounts for taxpayers with large amounts of tax preference items. Subtraction of the applicable exemption amount yields the tax base, AMTI. The tentative tax is calculated by applying a flat rate to AMTI. Corporate taxpayers pay an AMT rate of 20%. All other taxpayers, individuals and fiduciaries, are subject to an AMT rate of 26 percent on the first $175,000 of AMTI and 28 percent on AMTI in excess of $175,000. Multiplication of the AMTI by the AMT rate yields the tentative minimum tax amount before foreign tax credits. Foreign tax credits are the only tax credits allowed against the AMT liability. Subtraction of the allowable foreign tax credit provides what is referred to as the *tentative minimum tax liability*. It is tentative because it must be compared with the regular tax liability to determine whether the AMT is applicable. Because the AMT is the minimum amount of tax that the taxpayer must pay, if the regular tax liability is greater than the tentative minimum tax, the AMT is not applicable and the taxpayer pays the regular tax liability. On the other hand, if the tentative minimum tax is greater than the regular tax, the taxpayer is subject to the AMT. Although the full amount of the tentative AMT is paid, the tax law views the taxpayer as paying the tax in two separate components—the regular tax liability and the additional tax imposed because of the AMT. Thus, as a definition, the AMT is equal to the tentative minimum tax in excess of the regular tax liability.

▲ **EXAMPLE 37**   Nigel Corporation's regular tax liability during the current year is $650,000. Nigel's tentative alternative minimum tax is $800,000. How much AMT must Nigel pay, and what is Nigel's total tax liability?

Discussion: Because Nigel's tentative minimum tax is greater than its regular tax liability, it is subject to the AMT and must pay the $800,000 tax calculated using the AMT rules. Nigel is deemed to pay $650,000 in regular tax liability and an AMT of $150,000 ($800,000 − $650,000).

▲ **EXAMPLE 38**   Assume the same facts as in example 37, except that Nigel's regular tax liability is $900,000. How much AMT must Nigel pay, and what is Nigel's total tax liability?

Discussion: Because Nigel's regular tax liability exceeds the tentative minimum tax, Nigel must pay the $900,000 regular tax liability. No AMT is due (AMT cannot be negative). Note that the purpose of the AMT is to ensure that taxpayers pay a certain minimum amount of tax. When the regular tax liability exceeds this minimum amount, the regular tax liability is the amount that must be paid.

The remainder of the chapter discusses the individual components of the AMT calculation. Because of the great technical complexity of many of the adjustments and preferences, this book makes no attempt to present every detail of every item that affects the AMT. The purpose of the discussion is to provide a basic understanding of the approach the AMT uses to tax those taxpayers whose use of tax incentives is excessive (as defined by the AMT).

AMT Adjustments.   The purpose of the AMT adjustments is to account for the effect of items that must be determined using either alternative calculations or alternative accounting methods for AMT purposes. Many of these adjustments are extremely technical. Further complicating the AMT calculation is that not all adjustments apply to all types of taxpayers. Table 14–4 provides a brief description of the AMT adjustments by type of taxpayer affected.[35]

▲ **Table 14–4**

AMT ADJUSTMENT ITEMS

Adjustment Item	Brief General Description
Applicable to All Taxpayers	
Depreciation on property placed in service after 12/31/86	AMT depreciation calculated using ADS system (longer life and straight-line method).
Mining exploration & development costs	Must be amortized over 10 years for AMT purposes.
Long-term contracts	Taxpayers using completed contract method must use percentage-of-completed-contract method for AMT purposes.
Amortization of pollution control facilities	Must be amortized over a longer period for AMT.
Gains deferred on installment sales	Gains may not be deferred on installment sales for AMT purposes.
Gain/loss on properties subject to AMT rules that affect basis	Any AMT adjustments that affect the basis of property must be reflected in the gain/loss on the property when it is disposed of.
Net operating loss deduction	NOL is recalculated using AMT rules for income and deductions. NOL deduction is limited to 90% of AMTI (after all other adjustments and preferences).
Applicable to Individuals and Fiduciaries	
Limitation on deductions from AGI	Most deductions from AGI disallowed or reduced; no personal exemption or standard deduction.
Exercise of incentive stock options	Excess of fair market value over option price at date of exercise is included in AMTI.
Research and development expenditures	Amounts expensed in excess of 10-year amortization are added back.
Certain tax shelter farming activities	Losses not deductible against current period passive losses; can only deduct against future period income from farming activities.
Applicable to Corporate Taxpayers	
Adjusted current earnings	Three-fourths of the excess of adjusted current earnings (a measure based on financial accounting income) over AMTI before the ACE adjustment.

In general, the use of the AMT calculation or method results in either acceleration of income items or deferral of deduction items. The net effect of either is a higher taxable income in the initial period(s) of difference. However, most **alternative minimum tax adjustment** items are not disallowed for AMT purposes; they are merely spread out (in the case of deductions) or accelerated (in the case of income items), with the difference in the two calculations being temporary, not permanent. That is, the initial differences reverse themselves over time and therefore have the opposite effect on AMTI. Thus, adjustments can be either positive or negative in the calculation of AMTI. This effect is best illustrated by the depreciation adjustment, which applies to property placed in service after December 31, 1986 (i.e., property subject to the MACRS depreciation system). The AMT requires depreciation to be computed using the alternative depreciation system (discussed in Chapter 11). The ADS system uses the straight-line method and longer depreciation lives than MACRS. The use of ADS in calculating depreciation causes AMT depreciation to be lower initially. However, in later years, the ADS depreciation will exceed the MACRS depreciation, and the effect of the adjustment will reverse itself in the AMTI calculation.

▲ **EXAMPLE 39**   Ortno Corporation purchases depreciable property costing $45,000 in 1995. The property is 3-year MACRS property and has an ADS life of 5 years. What is Ortno's AMT adjustment for each of the applicable years? Assume that Ortno uses straight-line depreciation on the property for regular tax purposes.

Discussion: Ortno must add the excess of MACRS depreciation over the allowable ADS depreciation for AMT purposes. When depreciation under ADS exceeds MACRS, the difference is subtracted in computing AMTI. The adjustments for the 5-year ADS life are as follows:

Year	MACRS Depreciation	ADS Depreciation	AMT Adjustment
1995	$ 7,500	$ 4,500	$ 3,000
1996	$15,000	$ 9,000	$ 6,000
1997	$15,000	$ 9,000	$ 6,000
1998	$ 7,500	$ 9,000	$(1,500)
1999	$ -0-	$ 9,000	$(9,000)
2000	$ -0-	$ 4,500	$(4,500)
Total	$45,000	$45,000	$ -0-

Note that over the 5-year ADS life, the difference between the MACRS and ADS depreciation deduction reverses itself. This is reflected in the AMT adjustment by reducing AMTI when the ADS depreciation exceeds MACRS depreciation. Thus, over the 5-year ADS life, the effect of the depreciation difference is zero.

The use of different calculation methods for AMT purposes requires the taxpayer to keep a separate set of accounting records to verify the AMT calculations. This is especially important when the calculation difference affects the basis of an asset. That is, because the methods compute adjustments to basis differently under the AMT, the asset has a different basis for AMT purposes than for regular tax purposes. When the asset is sold or otherwise disposed of, the gain or loss for regular tax purposes is different than for the AMT. This requires another adjustment to AMTI in order to reflect the difference.

▲ **EXAMPLE 40**   Refer to the property purchased by Ortno Corporation in example 39. Assume that Ortno sells the property in 1999 for $15,000. What is the effect of the sale on Ortno's AMTI (i.e., what adjustment must be made)?

Discussion: Because the allowable depreciation is different under the 2 systems, the basis of the property at the date of sale is also different. For regular tax purposes, the property is fully depreciated (zero basis), resulting in a gain of $15,000 on the sale. The AMT basis of the property is $9,000 [$45,000 − $36,000 (4.5 years of depreciation)], which results in an AMT gain of $6,000. The $9,000 ($15,000 − $6,000) difference in the gains is subtracted in the AMTI calculation as an adjustment. The $9,000 adjustment is the amount of gain that is included in regular taxable income that should not be included in AMTI because of the reduced depreciation deductions for AMT purposes.

The primary adjustments that are required of individual taxpayers are for deductions from adjusted gross income that are either modified or not allowed for AMT purposes. The only itemized deductions allowed from AGI for AMT purposes are

1. Medical expenses in excess of 10% of AGI (i.e., not 7.5%)

2. Charitable contributions

3. Casualty and theft losses

4. Qualified housing interest

5. Investment interest

6. Miscellaneous itemized deductions not subject to the 2 percent of AGI reduction (gambling losses and premature cessation of annuities)

Therefore, individuals must add back excess medical expenses, taxes, interest other than qualified housing and investment interest, miscellaneous itemized deductions subject to the 2-percent limitation, and personal and dependency exemption amounts deducted in arriving at taxable income. In addition, the standard deduction is not allowed and is added back by taxpayers who do not itemize. However, the 3 percent of AGI phase-out rule for itemized deductions is not applicable for AMT purposes. Therefore, the amount of any itemized deduction reduction from the phase-out rule is subtracted in the AMTI calculation.

Qualified housing interest for AMT purposes is more restrictive than the itemized deduction allowed for qualified residence interest. Interest on a qualified residence is allowed for AMT purposes only if the loan was used to acquire, construct, or substantially improve the residence. Thus, under the AMT, home equity loan interest is deductible only if the proceeds of the loan were used to improve the residence.

▲ **EXAMPLE 41**   George and Cassandra purchased a home in 1987 at a cost of $100,000. They initially borrowed $85,000 to purchase the home. In 1995, when the home was worth $125,000, they took out a home equity loan for $40,000 that they used to purchase a personal automobile. How much of the loan interest related to their residence is deductible for regular tax and for AMT purposes?

Discussion: Interest on both loans is deductible for regular tax purposes. The home equity loan only has to be secured by the principle residence and be less than $100,000 to qualify for deduction. However, the interest paid on the home equity loan is not deductible for AMT purposes, because it was not used to improve the residence. Therefore, the home equity loan interest will be added as an adjustment in the calculation of AMTI.

Two factors cause the calculation of investment interest to be redone for AMT purposes. First, any interest earned on tax-exempt securities is excluded for regular tax purposes. However, certain private activity bond interest is subject to the AMT through its inclusion as a preference item (see the discussion of preferences).

Therefore, investment income must be increased by any such interest earned by the taxpayer for AMT purposes. Second, recall from Chapter 8 that in the definition of net investment income, investment expenses are those expenses that remain after applying the 2-percent miscellaneous itemized deduction limit. In determining investment expenses for regular tax purposes, any other miscellaneous itemized deductions are taken against the 2-percent limit first. For AMT purposes, none of the other miscellaneous deductions is allowed, necessitating a recalculation of investment expenses.

▲ EXAMPLE 42   Vanessa has total taxable investment income of $14,000 in the current year. Vanessa also received $2,000 in private activity bond interest that is exempt from regular tax. Vanessa's investment expenses were $3,000, and she paid interest related to the investments of $15,000. Vanessa's AGI is $40,000, and she had other miscellaneous itemized deductions totaling $1,600. What is Vanessa's allowable investment interest deduction for regular tax and AMT purposes?

Discussion: Vanessa's investment interest deduction is limited to her net investment income (investment income − investment expenses). For regular tax purposes, her investment interest deduction is $11,000:

Investment income		$14,000
Less: Investment expenses		
Miscellaneous itemized deduction limit—		
2% × $40,000 =	$ 800	
Other miscellaneous itemized deductions	1,600	
Amount of limit applied to investment expenses	$ -0-	
Deductible investment expenses		(3,000)
Net investment income		$11,000

For AMT purposes, the $2,000 in private activity bond interest is taxable. Therefore, Vanessa's AMT investment income is increased to $16,000. The other miscellaneous itemized deductions are not allowed for AMT, and the $800 limit is applied to Vanessa's investment expenses, lowering them to $2,200. This results in an investment interest deduction for AMT purposes of $13,800:

Investment income ($14,000 + $2,000)		$16,000
Less: Investment expenses		
Miscellaneous itemized deduction limit	$ 800	
Investment expenses	3,000	
Deductible investment expenses		(2,200)
Net investment income		$13,800

The additional $2,800 ($13,800 − $11,000) of investment interest allowed as an AMT deduction is shown as a subtraction adjustment in the calculation of AMTI.

The final adjustment is the **AMT net operating loss deduction.** For AMT purposes, the NOL deduction must be recomputed using the AMT rules for income and deductions.

▲ EXAMPLE 43   Worth Corporation suffers a net operating loss of $90,000 in 1995. In calculating the loss, Worth has total net positive adjustments and credits of $20,000. What is Worth's AMT net operating loss?

Discussion: For AMT purposes, the NOL must be calculated using the adjustment and preference items. Therefore, the NOL is reduced by the $20,000 in positive adjustments and preferences to $70,000. Worth can carry the NOL back to 1992 and obtain a refund of taxes. The $90,000 loss is used against 1992's regular taxable income, and the $70,000 is used in 1992's AMT calculation in determining the amount of the refund.

A further limitation on the AMT net operating loss deduction is that it cannot exceed 90 percent of alternative minimum taxable income, computed after all other adjustments and preferences.

▲ **EXAMPLE 44**   Assume the same facts as in example 43. In 1992, Worth had a taxable income of $40,000, and its AMTI before the NOL carryback was $60,000. How much of the 1995 NOL can Worth deduct against its 1992 income for regular tax and AMT purposes?

Discussion: The $90,000 regular NOL can be fully used against the 1992 regular taxable income, reducing it to zero. The AMT net operating loss is limited to $54,000 (90% × $60,000 AMTI) in the calculation of AMTI.

Note that the different NOL rules for the 2 systems create a disparity in the amount of NOL carryforward. For regular tax purposes, Worth has an NOL carryforward to 1993 of $50,000 ($90,000 − $40,000), whereas the AMT carryforward is only $16,000 ($70,000 − $54,000). As with most of the other adjustments, this creates a separate and parallel set of carryforwards.

AMT Preferences.   Preferences are different from adjustments in two distinct ways. First, **alternative minimum tax preferences** apply to all taxpayers. There are no specific preferences for corporate and noncorporate taxpayers, as is the case with adjustments. Second, preferences are always added in the computation of AMTI. Although the preference items reflect differences in how the two systems treat such items (as is the case with adjustments), preference items either do not reverse or Congress has determined that the taxpayer should not have the benefit of any reversal. Because preference reversals are not allowed, there is no correlative adjustment to the basis of the property for AMT purposes, as is the case with adjustments. The list of preference items is much shorter than the number of adjustment items. Table 14–5 lists the preference items and provides a brief description of the AMT treatment of the item.[36]

The preference item that can have the greatest effect on individual taxpayers is the private activity bond interest tax preference. Interest paid on debt by state and local governments is excluded from gross income to enable municipalities to

▲ **Table 14–5**

AMT PREFERENCE ITEMS

Preference Item	Brief General Description
Percentage depletion in excess of basis	Percentage depletion deductions in excess of the basis of the property are disallowed.
Intangible drilling costs on oil & gas properties	Limited to 65% of the net income from each property.
Tax-exempt interest from private activity bonds	Interest is taxable for AMT purposes.
Excess depreciation on property placed in service before 1/1/1987	Depreciation in excess of straight-line is not allowed for AMT purposes.
Reserves for bad debts of financial institutions	Financial institutions must use the specific write-off method for bad debts.

raise capital at lower rates than comparable taxable debt instruments. Many municipalities have used this exclusion to float bond issues for private activities, such as the construction of industrial facilities. To attract new jobs to the community, these facilities are then leased to private businesses. The indirect effect of such arrangements is to give the private business financing at a lower rate than it could obtain by financing its own facilities. Congress reacted to this perceived inequity by disallowing the exclusion of interest on private activity bonds for AMT purposes. A **private activity bond** is one in which the proceeds are used by anyone other than a government unit. Examples of private activity bonds include industrial development bonds, mortgage subsidy bonds, and student loan bonds. Fortunately, the issuers of the bonds have the obligation to disclose to purchasers whether the bond is a private activity bond or a wholly exempt bond. However, taxpayers who purchase private activity bonds have the responsibility for properly reporting the interest earned on their returns.

AMT Exemptions. After making all the required adjustments and adding the preference items to taxable income, the result is the tentative alternative minimum taxable income. In determining the AMTI tax base, an exemption amount is allowed as a reduction of the tentative AMTI. The exemption amount is designed to eliminate taxpayers with relatively moderate amounts of taxable income who do not have significant amounts of adjustments and/or preferences from the AMT. The exemption amount starts at a tentative amount based on the type of taxpayer and is then reduced by 25 percent of every dollar by which the tentative AMTI exceeds a specified level for each type of taxpayer. Table 14–6 provides the exemption amounts and their phase-out ranges by type of taxpayer. Note that the effect of the phase-out is to deny exemption amounts to taxpayers whose AMTI exceeds the amounts in the last column of the table.

The practical effect of the exemption is that average individual taxpayers may ignore the AMT with little risk of it applying to them. However, corporations and individuals with more substantial incomes need to be aware of what could happen when they engage in transactions that result in AMT adjustments and preferences. Because of the complexity of the AMT calculation, the aid of a tax specialist is virtually a necessity for high-income individuals.

AMT Tax Credits. In general, the only tax credit allowed against the tentative AMT is the foreign tax credit.[37] As a result, all other tax credits (e.g., child-care credit) are lost when the AMT applies. Although the foreign tax credit is allowed

▲ Table 14–6

AMT EXEMPTION
AMOUNTS AND
PHASE-OUTS

Type of Entity	Filing Status	Initial Exemption	Phase-Out begins at AMTI of	No exemption if AMTI exceeds
Corporation	N.A.	$40,000	$150,000	$310,000
Fiduciary	N.A.	$22,500	$ 75,000	$165,000
Individual	Single and head of household	$33,750	$112,500	$247,500
Individual	Married couple filing jointly	$45,000	$150,000	$330,000
Individual	Married couple filing separately	$22,500	$ 75,000	$165,000

for AMT purposes, it is limited to 90 percent of the tentative AMT. The purpose of this limit is to prevent a taxpayer with substantial foreign source income from using the credit to completely avoid paying U.S. tax.

THE AMT CREDIT AGAINST THE REGULAR TAX.   Most adjustments made in calculating AMTI are merely timing differences. The AMT calculation for these items accelerates income for AMT purposes so that it is reported earlier than it would be for regular tax purposes. This creates a form of double jeopardy when a taxpayer is subject to the AMT in earlier years and the regular tax in later years when the timing difference reverses. That is, the accelerated income is taxed first under the AMT and again later, when the timing difference reverses for regular tax purposes.

▲ **EXAMPLE 45**   Perry Corporation uses the completed contract method to account for its home construction contracts. During the current year, Perry entered into a contract to build a home and expected $200,000 in profit. The home is 40% complete at the end of the current year and is completed in the subsequent year. Assuming that Perry has no other taxable income in each of the 2 years, what is Perry's tax liability in each year?

Discussion: Under the completed contract method, no income is recognized until the year in which the contract is completed. Therefore, Perry will have no regular taxable income in the first year and will report $200,000 in taxable income in the second year. For AMT purposes, the completed contract method is not allowed. Perry must make an adjustment in calculating AMTI to account for the profit it would have recognized using the percentage-of-completed-contract method. This will result in Perry's paying an AMT of $8,000 in the first year.

Regular taxable income	$ -0-
Add: Adjustment for completed contract method	
Amount recognized under percentage	
of completion method ($200,000 × 40%)	80,000
Less: AMT exemption	(40,000)
Equals: AMTI	$40,000
Times: Corporate AMT rate	× 20%
Equals: Tentative minimum tax	$ 8,000
Less: Regular tax liability	-0-
Equals: AMT	$ 8,000

In the second year, the entire $200,000 will be reported for regular tax purposes. The regular tax on $200,000 for a corporation is $61,250. In calculating the AMT, Perry has a negative adjustment of $80,000 [$200,000 reported for regular tax − $120,000 ($200,000 × 60%) reported using the percentage-of-completed-contract method]. The net result is that no AMT is due in the second year, and Perry pays the $61,250 in regular tax:

Regular taxable income	$200,000
Less: Adjustment for completed contract method	(80,000)
Less: AMT exemption	(40,000)
Equals: AMTI	$ 80,000
Times: Corporate AMT rate	× 20%
Equals: Tentative minimum tax	$ 16,000
Less: Regular tax liability	(61,250)
Equals: AMT	-0-

The result of the reversal of income recognition on the contract is to tax the $80,000 recognized for AMT purposes in the first year under the AMT and to tax the same $80,000 again in the second year when the regular tax applies.

To avoid double taxation of reversal items, Congress enacted a minimum tax credit that can only be used to reduce the regular tax liability in later years when the regular tax exceeds the alternative minimum tax. The **AMT minimum tax credit** is calculated each year in which the AMT applies. The amount of the credit is the difference between the actual AMT for the year and a recomputed AMT. The recomputed AMT is the AMT that would have been paid if the reversal adjustments did not enter into the AMTI calculation. That is, the AMT is recalculated using only preference items and those adjustments that do not reverse. The credit is carried forward and used to reduce the regular tax liability in those years in which the regular tax is greater than the AMT. The credit may be used only to reduce the regular tax to the tentative AMT amount.[38]

▲ **EXAMPLE 46**   Assume the same facts as in example 45. What is Perry's minimum tax credit in the first year and its tax liability in the second year?

Discussion: The minimum tax credit is the difference between the AMT as computed, $8,000, and the AMT recomputed without the timing differences. In this case, without the $80,000 adjustment in the first year, Perry's AMT would have been zero and no AMT would have been paid. Thus, the minimum tax credit to carry forward to year 2 is $8,000 ($8,000 − $0). In the second year, the regular tax and the AMT would have been calculated as in example 45, resulting in a regular tax liability of $61,250. Perry is allowed to reduce the $61,250 by the $8,000 minimum tax credit from the first year, resulting in a net tax due of $53,250.

Tax Planning and the AMT.   Given the narrowness of the gap between the 28-percent top AMT individual rate and the 39.6-percent maximum tax rate that applies to high-income individuals, it is easy to trigger the AMT. Thus, it is important for tax-planning purposes to consider AMT implications along with the regular tax. Although the overall goal of tax planning remains the maximization of wealth via the minimization of taxes, it should be recognized that too small a reduction in the regular tax may trigger the AMT. When an individual expects the AMT to apply, a strategy opposite to that for regular tax purposes is often appropriate. A rule of thumb to follow for regular tax-planning purposes is to defer income and accelerate deductions. Because the AMT tax rate for individuals is lower than that for the regular tax, a taxpayer subject to the AMT would generally be better off to accelerate income into the AMT year and defer deductions to a regular tax year.

▲ **EXAMPLE 47**   Eve is a financial consultant with several large clients. Her contract with her large clients allows her to bill them for services monthly or quarterly, at her option. In reviewing her current-year tax situation, Eve has determined that she will be subject to the alternative minimum tax at the 26 percent rate. Because of several reversing adjustments, Eve does not think that she will be subject to the AMT next year, but she will be in the 31% marginal tax rate bracket. If Eve submits monthly bills for November to her large clients, she estimates that she will receive $40,000 before the end of the year. What is Eve's tax savings on the $40,000 of income if she submits the monthly bills?

Discussion: Because Eve is subject to the AMT, she will pay $10,400 ($40,000 × 26%) in tax. Delaying the billing to next year will result in a tax of $12,400 ($40,000 × 31%). Billing this year saves $2,000 ($12,400 − $10,400) in taxes. However, because she will have to pay the tax a year earlier, Eve should also consider the time value of money effect. Assuming a 10% time value of money, the present value of paying the tax next year is \$11,272 (\$12,400 $\times$ 0.909 PV factor). Eve's real tax savings by billing in the current year is \$872 (\$11,272 $-$ \$10,400).

Although the planning result in example 47 is a straightforward application of the basic strategy, the complexity of the AMT calculation makes it difficult to apply the basic strategy in most situations. For example, should a taxpayer eligible to use the completed contract method of accounting for long-term contracts elect to use the percentage-of-completed-contract method to avoid paying the AMT? General answers to such questions do not usually hold up. The only reliable way for taxpayers to make such decisions is through the use of long-term planning projections that show the effect of all alternative courses of action possible. In order to make such long-term projections, taxpayers need to be aware of the adjustments and preferences that can trigger the AMT and consider them when evaluating investment opportunities.

▲ KEY TERMS

alternative minimum tax (AMT) (p. 651)
alternative minimum tax adjustment (p. 654)
alternative minimum tax preference (p. 657)
alternative minimum tax rate (p. 651)
alternative minimum taxable income (AMTI) (p. 651)
AMT minimum tax credit (p. 660)
AMT net operating loss deduction (p. 656)
business purpose tax year (p. 631)
child and dependent care credit (p. 648)

earned income credit (EIC) (p. 647)
foreign tax credit (p. 642)
full absorption costing method (p. 638)
individual accounting treatments (p. 632)
investment tax credit (ITC) (p. 642)
least aggregate deferral tax year (p. 630)
lower of cost-or-market method (p. 639)
lookback method (p. 636)

majority-interest tax year (p. 629)
natural business year (p. 631)
nonrefundable tax credit (p. 642)
overall accounting methods (p. 632)
ownership tax year (p. 631)
principal partner tax year (p. 630)
private activity bond (p. 658)
refundable tax credit (p. 642)
rehabilitation tax credit (p. 645)
research and experimental (R&E) credit (p. 644)
uniform capitalization (unicap) rules (p. 639)

[1] Sec. 441—Allows taxpayers to use either a calendar year or a fiscal year to compute taxable income. Defines *fiscal year.*

[2] Reg. Sec. 1.441-1T—Explains how to establish a tax year.

[3] Sec. 706—Provides the rules for selecting a partnership tax year.

[4] Reg. Sec. 1.706-1—Defines a *principal partner* for purposes of selecting a partnership tax year and illustrates the principal partner tax year.

[5] Reg. Sec. 1.706-1T—Explains the computation of the least aggregate deferral tax year for a partnership.

[6] Rev. Rul. 87-57—Explains the factors necessary for a partnership to establish a business purpose tax year.

[7] Sec. 1378—Defines the tax years that can be used by an S corporation.

[8] Rev. Proc. 87-32—Explains the ownership tax year test and how to adopt an ownership tax year.

[9] Reg. Sec. 1.706-1—Defines *natural business year.*

[10] Rev. Proc. 87-32—Provides examples of the test for a natural business year.

[11] Sec. 446—Defines the general rules for methods of accounting and provides the

▲ PRIMARY TAX LAW SOURCES

authority for the IRS to change a taxpayer's method of accounting.

[12] Sec. 481—Prescribes the adjustments necessary when a taxpayer makes a change in an accounting method.

[13] Sec. 448—Requires corporations, partnerships with a corporate partner, and tax shelter activities to use the accrual method.

[14] Reg. Sec. 1.448-1T—Defines *tax shelter activity*.

[15] Reg. Sec. 1.448-1T—Defines *farming business* and gives examples of the exception that allows a farming business to use the cash method.

[16] Sec. 460—Requires the use of the percentage-of-completed-contract method for long-term construction contracts.

[17] Reg. Sec. 1.460-6—Illustrates the application of the lookback method.

[18] Sec. 471—Requires the use of the accrual method to calculate cost of goods sold when inventories are an income-producing factor.

[19] Thor Power Tool Co. v. Comm., 439 U.S. 522 (1979)—Held that the clear reflection of income is a more important factor than industry practice in determining the appropriateness of an accounting method.

[20] Reg. Sec. 1.263A-1T—Prescribes the application of the unicap rules as they apply to inventories.

[21] Reg. Sec. 1.471-4—Discusses the rules and definitions applicable to the use of lower of cost-or-market valuation.

[22] Reg. Sec. 1.472-3—Prescribes the procedures necessary to make a LIFO election.

[23] Reg. Sec. 1.472-2—Discusses the financial conformity rule and gives examples of its application.

[24] Sec. 27—Allows the foreign tax credit.

[25] Sec. 911—Provides for the exclusion of as much as $70,000 in foreign earned income in lieu of the foreign tax credit.

[26] Sec. 901—Specifies the calculation of and the limitations on the foreign tax credit.

[27] Sec. 41—Allows a tax credit for increasing research activities.

[28] Reg. Sec. 1.41-2—Defines *qualified research expenses*.

[29] Omnibus Budget Reconciliation Act of 1989. Pub. L. No. 101-239, 103 Stat. 2106.

[30] Sec. 47—Allows a tax credit for qualified rehabilitation expenditures.

[31] Sec. 32—Allows the earned income credit and prescribes the limitations on the amount of the credit.

[32] Reg. Sec. 1.44A-1—Discusses the general requirements and defines the terms applicable to the child and dependent care credit.

[33] Sec. 21—Allows a tax credit for child and dependent care expenses and prescribes the limits on the amount of the credit.

[34] Sec. 55—Requires the calculation of the alternative minimum tax and defines its calculation.

[35] Sec. 56—Prescribes the adjustment items that must be taken into account in calculating the alternative minimum tax.

[36] Sec. 57—Prescribes the preference items that must be added in calculating the alternative minimum taxable income.

[37] Sec. 59—Allows a credit for foreign tax paid (subject to limitations) against the tentative alternative minimum tax.

[38] Sec. 53—Allows the AMT credit against the regular tax and defines the calculation of the credit.

▲ DISCUSSION QUESTIONS

1. What is the difference between a calendar year and a fiscal year?

2. Under what circumstances might a taxpayer find the use of a fiscal year advantageous?

3. How does a taxpayer select a taxable year?

4. Why do most individuals use calendar years rather than fiscal years?

5. Why are restrictions placed on the selection of a tax year by partnerships and S corporations?

6. What is the difference between an overall method of accounting and an individual accounting treatment?

7. What are the general requirements a taxpayer must meet in selecting an accounting method?

8. Which types of tax entities generally cannot elect to use the cash method of accounting?

9. Explain the two exceptions under which an entity that is generally not allowed to use the cash method of accounting still may elect to use the cash method.

10. What is the general accounting requirement for taxpayers who have long-term construction contracts?

11. What is the purpose of the lookback method of accounting for long-term construction contracts?

12. Do all taxpayers with long-term construction contracts have to use the percentage-of-completed-contract method of accounting? Explain.

13. What is the "cost" of inventory?

14. Briefly explain the uniform capitalization rules as they apply to inventories.

15. Do the uniform capitalization rules promote or hinder administrative convenience? Explain.

16. What restrictions are placed on taxpayers who elect to value their inventories at the lower of cost-or-market value?

17. What must a taxpayer do to make an election to use LIFO?

18. Why are tax credits rather than a deduction used to provide tax relief?

19. What is the difference between a refundable tax credit and a nonrefundable tax credit?

20. Why are tax credits often used? Give examples of tax credits that meet the purposes indicated.

21. What is the purpose of the foreign tax credit?

22. Are all foreign taxes paid automatically eligible for the foreign tax credit? (What limitations, if any, are imposed?)

23. What is the purpose of the research and experimental tax credit?

24. What types of expenditures qualify for the rehabilitation expenditure tax credit?

25. What restrictions are placed on the rehabilitation expenditures tax credit?

26. How are business tax credits different from individual tax credits?

27. What are the general criteria for eligibility for the earned income credit?

28. What are the general criteria for eligibility for the child and dependent care credit?

29. What are *qualifying dependents* for purposes of the child and dependent care credit?

30. Does the child care credit help promote a progressive tax rate structure? Explain.

31. What is the purpose of the alternative minimum tax?

32. Why is the alternative minimum tax a more important planning consideration now than it was before 1986?

33. What is the tax base for the alternative minimum tax? Explain the general computation of the base.

34. What is the basic difference between an AMT adjustment and a preference?

35. Why is MACRS depreciation on real property not included as an AMT adjustment? Explain.

36. Why can AMT adjustments be negative?

37. What is the AMT exemption amount? Is it available for all taxpayers?

38. What tax credits are allowed for AMT purposes? Are there any limits on the amount of credit that can be used for AMT purposes?

39. What is the purpose of the AMT credit against the regular tax?

▲ **PROBLEMS**

40. What tax year must be used by each of the following taxpayers? Explain.
    a. Rodney works for Big Co. His only other source of income is from interest and dividends. Although Rodney usually itemizes his deductions, he does not keep any formal books or records, relying instead on wage statements and other documents in preparing his return.
    b. John and Gloria own Spoke and Pedal Cyclery as equal partners. John and Gloria both use calendar years to report their income.
    c. Fax, Inc., is an S corporation wholly owned by Helena. Helena uses a calendar year to report her income.
    d. Assume the same facts as in part c, except that Fax, Inc., is a corporation.
    e. Bloodworth Trust holds assets for the benefit of Albert's children. The children use fiscal years ending June 30 to report their income.

41. Determine the tax year that must be used by each of the following partnerships. Explain.
    a. MNO Partnership is owned equally by Jane, Larry, and Ruby. Jane and Larry use a fiscal year ending on October 31, and Ruby uses a calendar year.
    b. Terry is the general partner of the LBO Partnership. Terry owns 25% of the partnership. The remaining 75% is owned by limited partners, none of whom owns more than a 3% interest.
    c. Kurt and Connie own the Alfa Partnership. Kurt owns 60% of Alfa and has a fiscal year ending June 30. Connie owns the remaining 40% of Alfa and reports her income using a calendar year.

42. Determine the tax year(s) that can be used by each of the following S corporations. Explain.
    a. Red, Ed, and Ling are equal owners of RET Corporation. Red and Ed use a calendar year. Ling uses a fiscal year ending July 31.
    b. Assume the same facts as in part a, except that Red and Ed each own a 15% interest in RET and Ling owns the remaining 70%.
    c. Assume the same facts as in part a. RET's business is seasonal, with March and April the heaviest revenue months. Revenues for the current and 2 previous years were as follows:

	March & April	12-Month Period
Current year	$40,000	$140,000
1st preceding year	$35,000	$130,000
2nd preceding year	$30,000	$120,000

    d. Assume the same facts as in part c, except that revenues for the second preceding year totaled $150,000.

43. Which accounting method must each of the following taxpayers use? Explain.
    a. Rodney works for Big Co. His only other source of income is from interest and dividends. Although Rodney usually itemizes his deductions, he does not keep any formal books or records, relying instead on wage statements and other documents in preparing his return.
    b. Fax, Inc., is an S corporation wholly owned by Helena. Helena uses a calendar year to report her income.
    c. Assume the same facts as in part b, expect that Fax, Inc., is a corporation. Fax, Inc.'s annual revenues have never exceeded $250,000 in any year.

   d. Assume the same facts as in part c, except that Fax, Inc.'s annual revenues usually are between $8,000,000 and $9,000,000.
   e. Spoke and Pedal Cyclery is organized as a partnership. Spoke and Pedal is owned by John and Gloria as equal partners.

44. Which accounting method must each of the following taxpayers use? Explain.

   a. Earlene is the sole proprietor of The Sports Store. The Sports Store sells athletic equipment and clothing. Earlene keeps adequate records of the store's operation but does not keep formal records of her other individual income and expense items.
   b. Archer Partnership is owned equally by Adolph and the Blake Corporation. Adolph reports his income on the cash basis, whereas Blake uses the accrual method of accounting.
   c. Wheaton Corporation is owned by Carol and her family. The corporation raises grain that it harvests and sells to wholesalers.
   d. Assume the same facts as in part c, except that some grain is sold at the bakery that Wheaton owns. The bakery processes the grain into various products that it sells to wholesalers.

45. WCM is a construction company that is solely owned by Bill. WCM is primarily engaged in the construction of single-family dwellings and small business offices. During the current year, WCM entered into 2 contracts. One contract is for building a house. The second contract is for construction of a small shopping mall. Information regarding the 2 contracts is as follows:

		Current Year	Second Year	Third Year
Home Contract				
Contract price	$150,000			
Total estimated costs	$100,000			
Costs incurred		$10,000	$ 90,000	
Shopping Mall				
Contract price	$500,000			
Total estimated costs	$300,000			
Costs incurred		$50,000	$200,000	$75,000

   a. Determine the gross profit to be recognized for each year of each contract, assuming that WCM uses
   - The completed contract method of accounting
   - The percentage-of-completed-contract method
   b. Under what conditions can WCM use the completed contract method?

46. Bridge & Ball Works builds highways, bridges, and other major construction projects. Because of its size it is required to use the percentage-of-completed-contract method to account for its construction contracts. Determine the amount of gross profit to be recognized in each year and any other additions or subtractions to income from the following contract:

Contract price	$2,000,000
Total estimated costs	(1,500,000)
Estimated gross profit	$ 500,000

Actual Costs Incurred	
Year 1	$ 400,000
Year 2	700,000
Year 3	100,000
Total actual costs	$1,200,000

47. BGL is a construction firm specializing in building hotels and office complexes. BGL is required to use the percentage-of-completion-method to account for its construction contracts. Determine the amount of gross profit that GBL must recognize in each year and any other additions or subtractions to income from the following contract:

Contract price	$2,800,000
Total estimated costs	1,950,000
Estimated gross profit	$ 850,000

Actual Costs Incurred

Year 1	$ 600,000
Year 2	$ 850,000
Year 3	$ 650,000
Total actual costs	$2,100,000

48. Artho Corporation sells 3 different products. Information on the ending inventory of each product is as follows:

	Total Cost	Total Market Value
Item #1	$ 3,000	$ 2,000
Item #2	$10,000	$18,000
Item #3	$33,000	$30,000

What are all the ending inventory values possible for Artho? Explain Artho's options in this regard.

49. The Aeroflight Co. sells 4 different golf balls. Information on the ending inventory of each golf ball is as follows:

Type of Golf Ball	Total Cost	Total Market Value
HT 90	$4,750	$ 4,200
LT 90	$5,600	$ 6,400
HT 100	$7,350	$ 7,000
LT 100	$8,400	$10,000

What are all the ending inventory values possible for Aeroflight? Explain Aeroflight's options in this regard.

50. Provided here is information regarding the purchase and sale (in chronological order) of an inventory item during the current year:

	Number of Units	Cost per Unit
Beginning inventory	400	$11
Purchase	500	$12
Sale	700	
Purchase	800	$13
Sale	600	
Purchase	300	$12
Sale	500	

Determine the ending inventory value for each of the following inventory flow assumptions:

a. FIFO   **b.** LIFO   **c.** Average cost

 51. Groff Corporation has been valuing its inventory using the lower of cost-or-market method for many years. During the current year, Groff elects to switch to the LIFO inventory valuation method. At the beginning of the year, product A had a cost of $24,000 and a market value of $18,000. What adjustment must Groff make to the beginning inventory value to enable it to use LIFO? Explain.

52. Flagler Corporation paid $42,000 in foreign taxes on $400,000 of foreign source income during the current year. Flagler's total taxable income was $1,000,000. What is Flagler's foreign tax credit?

    Assume that Flagler paid $200,000 on its foreign source income. What is Flagler's foreign tax credit?

53. Clinton Corporation spent $800,000 on qualified research activities during the current year. Clinton's fixed base percentage is 10%, and its annual average gross receipts for the 4 preceding years were $2,000,000. What is Clinton's allowable incremental research and experimentation tax credit?

    Assume that Clinton's annual average gross receipts for the preceding 4 years were $10,000,000. What is Clinton's allowable incremental research tax credit?

54. Lavinia owns an advertising agency. In February 1995, Lavinia purchases for $40,000 a building that was originally placed in service in 1930. Lavinia spends $60,000 rehabilitating the building for use as her advertising agency office. The rehabilitation is completed in November 1995.

    a. What criteria must Lavinia meet to qualify for the older buildings rehabilitation tax credit?

    b. Assuming that Lavinia meets all qualifying criteria, what are the amounts for Lavinia's older buildings credit and the basis of the building?

    c. What criteria must Lavinia meet to qualify for the historic structures credit?

    d. Assume the criteria in part c were met and that the building qualifies for both credits. What is the total of the rehabilitation credits for 1995? What is the basis of the building?

55. Return to the facts of problem 54, and assume that Lavinia sells the building in April 1998.

    a. How much of the older buildings tax credit must Lavinia recapture?

    b. Assuming the building qualified for both credits, how much of the historic structures credit must Lavinia recapture?

56. Determine the total allowable 1995 earned income credit in each of the following situations:

    a. Judy is single and earned $6,000 in salary for the year. In addition, she received $2,000 in unemployment compensation during the year.

    b. Monica is a single parent with 1 dependent child. Monica earned $9,000 from her job as a taxicab driver. She also received $3,000 in child support from her ex-husband.

    c. Paul and Yvonne are married and have 3 dependent children. Their earned income is $18,000, and they received $2,000 in interest income from their savings account.

    d. Hattie is married to Herbert, and they have 2 dependent children. During February, Herbert left and hasn't been seen or heard from since. Hattie earned $13,000 from her job. During January and February, Herbert earned $4,000, but Hattie has no idea how much he earned for the entire year.

57. Determine the amount of the child and dependent care credit to which each of the following taxpayers is entitled:
   a. Michael and Gladys are married and have a 7-year-old child. Their adjusted gross income is $44,000, and they paid $2,300 in qualified child-care expenses during the year. Michael earned $12,000 and Gladys earned $30,000 from their jobs.
   b. Jill is a single parent with an 11-year-old daughter. Jill's adjusted gross income was $26,500, and she paid $1,800 in qualified child-care expenses.
   c. Cory is a single parent who earned $9,000 and received other nontaxable government assistance totaling $4,300 during the year. She paid $1,200 in qualified child-care expenses during the year.
   d. Roosevelt and Myrtle are married and have 2 children. Roosevelt earns $94,000, and Myrtle has a part-time job from which she earned $3,200 during the year. They paid $6,000 in qualified child-care expenses during the year.
   e. Randy is single and earns $80,000 per year. He maintains a home for his father, who has been confined to a wheelchair since he had a stroke several years ago. Randy's father receives $8,000 in Social Security but has no other income. Because his father requires constant attention, Randy hires a helper to take care of his father while he is at work. Randy paid the helper $16,000 during the current year.

58. Determine the total amount of tax due and the amount of the alternative minimum tax in each of the following situations:
   a. Wilbur Corporation's regular tax liability is $220,000, and its tentative minimum tax is $300,000.
   b. Gene's regular tax liability is $8,000, and her tentative minimum tax is $3,000.

59. Stan purchases machinery costing $36,000 for use in his business in 1995. The machinery is 7-year MACRS property and has an ADS life of 12 years. Prepare a depreciation schedule using the regular MACRS method and the ADS depreciation. Indicate how much of an adjustment Stan must make in computing his alternative minimum tax each year.

60. Assume that in problem 59, Stan sells the machinery in the year 2001 for $20,000. Determine the effect of the sale on Stan's regular taxable income and his alternative minimum taxable income for the year 2001.

61. Alice and Frank had the following items on their current-year tax return:

Adjusted gross income			$32,000
Less: Deductions for adjusted gross income			
Medical expenses	$3,000		
Less: 7.5% × $32,000	(2,400)	$ 600	
Home mortgage interest		4,500	
Home equity loan interest		800	
State income taxes		1,900	
Property taxes		700	
Charitable contributions (cash)		200	
Miscellaneous itemized deductions	$ 940		
Less: 2% × $32,000	(640)	300	(9,000)
Less: Exemptions (2 × $2,500)			(5,000)

Determine the amount of the adjustments that Alice and Frank will have to make in computing their alternative minimum tax.

62. Joan and Matthew are married with 2 children and reported the following items on their current-year tax return:

Adjusted gross income			$135,000
Less: Deductions for adjusted gross income			
Medical expenses	$12,000		
Less: 7.5% × $135,000	(10,125)	$ 1,875	
Home mortgage interest		13,500	
Home equity loan (for college education)		9,000	
State income taxes		11,000	
Property taxes		6,500	
Charitable contributions		7,000	
Miscellaneous itemized deductions	$ 3,000		
Less: 2% × $135,000	(2,700)	300	(49,175)
Less: Exemptions (4 × $2,500)			(10,000)

Determine Joan and Matthew's regular tax liability and, if applicable, the amount of their alternative minimum tax. Explain the adjustments they will have to make in computing their tentative alternative minimum tax.

63. Pauline is considering investing in bonds. Her broker has given her several options to consider. The first option is to invest in city bonds with an interest rate of 6%. The second option involves the purchase of private activity bonds (subject to the AMT) that yield 7.5% interest. A third option is the purchase of High-Flier Utility bonds yielding 9% interest. Assuming that Pauline's regular marginal tax rate is 28%, which investment would you recommend? In your answer, consider all circumstances that could affect the after-tax return on the bond investments.

64. Determine the AMT exemption amount for each of the following taxpayers:
   a. Nominal Corporation has an alternative minimum taxable income of $100,000.
   b. Janine is a single individual with an alternative minimum taxable income of $120,000.
   c. Jagged Corporation has an alternative minimum taxable income of $200,000.
   d. Peter and Wendy have an alternative minimum taxable income of $120,000.
   e. Popup Corporation has an alternative minimum taxable income of $900,000.

▲ DISCUSSION CASE 14–1

Harry and Matilda are married and have the following tax return data for 1995:

Income		
Salaries		$ 90,000
Cash dividends		2,000
Tax-exempt bond interest		13,000
Total income		$105,000
Exclusions		
Tax-exempt bond interest		(13,000)
Gross income		$ 92,000
Deductions for adjusted gross income		
Loss on rental property	$ 8,000	
NOL carryforward	35,000	(43,000)
Adjusted gross income		$ 49,000
Deductions from adjusted gross income (after limitations)		
Medical expenses	$ 2,000	
Taxes	16,000	
Home mortgage interest	12,000	
Home equity loan interest	5,000	
Charitable contributions	8,000	
Misc. itemized deductions	3,000	(46,000)
Personal and dependency exemptions		(10,000)
Taxable income		$ (7,000)

Do Harry and Matilda owe any income tax for 1995? Explain why they might owe tax in 1995, and discuss the items on their tax return that could cause them to pay income tax in 1995. Be sure to adequately explain each item. Calculations are not required.

▲ DISCUSSION CASE 14–2

Alex and Jeff have differing views on the current tax system. Alex believes that any tax system that has two tax structures, a regular tax and an alternative minimum tax, is inefficient and inequitable. In fact, the system violates all canons of taxation espoused by Adam Smith. Jeff, however, feels that Congress should use the tax code as a vehicle for encouraging taxpayers to engage in various social and economic transactions. Therefore, he argues that the alternative minimum tax is necessary to ensure that each taxpayer pays some amount of tax. With whom do you agree? Why?

▲ TAX PLANNING CASE 14–3

Reg and Rhonda are married and have 2 children, ages 5 and 3. Rhonda has not worked since the birth of their first child. Now that the children are older, she would like to return to work and has a job offer that would pay her $22,000 per year. In order for her to take the job, the children will have to be put into a day-care center. The day-care center will cost $400 per month. Given the high cost of the day-care center, Reg and Rhonda are wondering whether it is worth it for Rhonda to take the job. They project their current-year taxable income (without considering Rhonda's job) as $40,000. If Rhonda accepts the job, how much additional cash will she receive from the job after considering the day-care cost and any tax effects? What other factors should Rhonda consider in deciding whether to accept the job?

Nina is the auditor for Geiger Construction, a local builder. Geiger recently completed the renovation of a historic building in downtown Kingston. The building, which consists of 5 separate shops, is owned by the Restoring Historic Kingston Partnership (RHKP). Nina is also the tax accountant for Merlin, one of the limited partners in RHKP. In preparing Merlin's 1995 tax return, the partner information return from RHKP (which Nina did not prepare) indicates that Merlin is entitled to both an older buildings credit and a historic structures credit. Nina properly deducts both credits. Later that year, Nina is conducting the audit of Geiger Construction, and she compliments the owner on the wonderful job the company did in restoring the building while meeting the requirements necessary for the building to qualify for the historic rehabilitation credits. Marshall, the owner of Geiger Construction, informs Nina that because of an unforeseen structural problem, the company was not able to meet the historic rehabilitation requirements. The company could preserve only 50%, not the required 75%, of the external walls. What is Nina's obligation (refer to Statements on Responsibilities in Tax Practice), if any, with respect to Merlin's filed tax return? Does she have any obligation to Merlin's other partners? to the preparer of the partnership return?

▲ **ETHICS DISCUSSION CASE 14–4**

Tax Research

▲ CHAPTER LEARNING OBJECTIVES

- ■ Explain the difference between primary and secondary tax authorities.

- ■ Identify the different types of legislative, administrative, and judicial primary authorities.

- ■ Describe the hierarchy or different levels of importance attributable to each of the primary authorities.

- ■ Prepare citations to each of the primary authorities.

- ■ Identify and describe the purpose of the different types of secondary authorities.

- ■ Understand the difference between tax planning and tax compliance.

- ■ Describe the basic steps involved in tax research.

- ■ Apply the tax research process to a comprehensive problem.

- ■ Describe the basic methods used by the IRS to select tax returns that will be examined.

- ■ Explain the different types of examinations and ways in which the IRS attempts to settle disputes with taxpayers administratively. '

Tax research is the process by which the tax consequences of a completed or proposed transaction are determined. The tax treatment of any transaction must be based on some supporting authority. Indeed, all the rules in this text originated in some supporting authoritative pronouncement. Tax research is simply the means by which these authoritative pronouncements are located, evaluated, and applied to a specific set of facts.

All tax authorities fall into one of two classes: primary and secondary. **Primary authorities** relate to the three principal functions of government: legislative/ executive, administrative, and judicial. The legislative authorities include the Constitution, tax treaties, the law as enacted by Congress (i.e., Internal Revenue Code), and the meaning of the law as described by the various congressional committee reports that accompany enactment of the law.

The tax law as enacted by Congress contains general language, so interpretations are necessary. The administrative authorities are the official interpretations of the law prepared by the Department of the Treasury and the Internal Revenue Service. These sources consist of regulations, revenue rulings, revenue procedures, and some other miscellaneous pronouncements. Whenever the IRS and a taxpayer disagree about the interpretation and application of a specific Code provision, the courts may be called upon to decide the matter. Decisions by the various trial and appellate courts are the judicial authorities. All legislative, administrative, and judicial primary authorities are commonly referred to as the *tax law*. Figure 15–1 summarizes these primary sources of authority.

Secondary authorities serve primarily as tools for locating the relevant primary authorities. They also provide information that leads to better understanding, interpretation, and application of the primary authorities. Secondary authorities include all other statements, pronouncements, explanations, or interpretations of the law that are not primary; they consist chiefly of tax services, citators, computer software systems that research tax databases, and tax journals and newsletters.

This chapter first examines more closely the different types of primary and secondary authorities and the hierarchy, or different levels of importance, attributable to each type. This is followed by a step-by-step discussion of how these authorities are used to determine the tax consequences related to a specific set of facts. The chapter concludes with an overview of the audit-and-appeals process as prescribed by the Internal Revenue Service.

▲ INTRODUCTION

▲ PRIMARY SOURCES OF FEDERAL INCOME TAX LAW

Legislative Sources

The legislative primary authorities consist of the U.S. Constitution, new tax laws enacted by Congress and incorporated in the Internal Revenue Code, reports issued by congressional committees as new laws are enacted, and treaties with other countries, which are negotiated by the president with the advice and consent of the Senate. Collectively, these authorities are sometimes referred to as *statutory authorities*. They are generally accorded a higher level of authority than other administrative or judicial primary authorities.

The U.S. Constitution.   The authority for the imposition of the federal income tax is found in Article I, Section 7, of the U.S. Constitution. It grants Congress the authority to impose taxes to pay debts and provide for the common defense and general welfare of the United States. It also requires that all tax legislation originate in the House of Representatives. Early attempts at an income tax were

▲ Figure 15–1

PRIMARY SOURCES OF
TAX LAW AUTHORITY

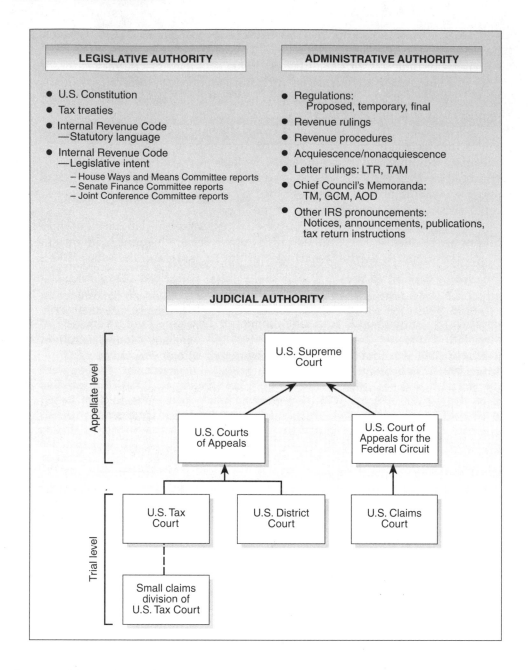

frustrated by additional requirements in Article I that direct taxes be apportioned among the states in proportion to the Census. As a result, most early attempts to raise revenue for the federal government were in the form of an excise tax. A tax based on income became an integral source of federal revenue with ratification of the Sixteenth Amendment to the Constitution in 1913. The Sixteenth Amendment permits a tax on income, from whatever source derived, without apportionment among the states and without regard to the Census.

Although the constitutional authority for an income tax is clear, tax protesters frequently have challenged it on the ground that it violates other constitutional rights. For example, protesters have claimed that their right to due process is violated, that they have religious or conscientious objections to defense expenditures, and that the filing of tax returns violates their protection from self-incrimination. Tax protesters' activities include filing incomplete tax returns, modifying return forms in such a way that they cannot be processed by the IRS, or claiming deductions for items clearly not allowed. The various methods are intended to hinder the administration of the tax law or frustrate the collection of the tax due. Tax protesters have not been successful in the courts and are subject to substantial penalties for their protest activities and for failure to file a proper return and pay the tax due.

Internal Revenue Code of 1986.   The most important source of current federal income tax law is the Internal Revenue Code of 1986, as amended (the Code, or I.R.C.). What is commonly referred to as the *Internal Revenue Code*, or simply *the Code*, is actually Title 26 of the *United States Code*. The *U.S. Code* is a consolidated and coordinated compilation of all laws enacted by Congress. All laws dealing with the same subject are brought together under one title. Other titles of the *U.S. Code* include Title 10, dealing with armed forces, and Title 28, dealing with the judiciary and judicial procedure.

Whenever Congress enacts a new tax law, the amendments are integrated into the I.R.C. The Code has been amended almost annually since it was comprehensively overhauled in 1986. The Code was comprehensively reorganized and amended in 1954, and from that time until 1986 it was referred to as the *Internal Revenue Code of 1954.*

STRUCTURE.   The Code has many different subdivisions, each with a different designation. For example, there are subtitles, chapters, subchapters, parts, and subparts. The contents of the Code can be broadly defined by examining the names of its nine subtitles, which appear in Exhibit 15–1.

Each subtitle is further subdivided into chapters. Exhibit 15–2 shows that Subtitle A, which deals with income taxes, has chapters numbered 1 through 6 and that one chapter has been repealed. Each chapter may again be subdivided into numerous subchapters. Exhibit 15–3 lists some of the more common subchapters of Chapter 1, which deals with normal taxes and surtaxes. Each subchapter may also be subdivided into parts and subparts.

The basic reference to a particular part of the Code is typically by section number. Reference to larger divisions, such as subtitles and chapters, is generally omitted. The section numbers run consecutively from 1 to 9602, although many numbers in the sequence are missing to allow for further expansion of the tax law. Each section of the Code may be further subdivided into subsections, paragraphs, subparagraphs, and clauses. Exhibit 15–4 provides a comprehensive

Subtitle	Name	Beginning Code Section Number
A	Income Taxes	Sec. 1
B	Estate and Gift Taxes	Sec. 2001
C	Employment Taxes	Sec. 3101
D	Miscellaneous Excise Taxes	Sec. 4001
E	Alcohol, Tobacco, and Certain Other Excise Taxes	Sec. 5001
F	Procedure and Administration	Sec. 6001
G	The Joint Committee on Taxation	Sec. 8001
H	Financing of Presidential Election Campaigns	Sec. 9001
I	Trust Fund Code	Sec. 9501

▲ **Exhibit 15–1**

SUBTITLES OF THE INTERNAL REVENUE CODE

▲ **Exhibit 15–2**

Chapter	Name	Beginning Code Section Number
1	Normal Taxes and Surtaxes	Sec. 1
2	Tax on Self-Employment Income	Sec. 1401
3	Withholding of Tax on Nonresident Aliens and Foreign Corporations	Sec. 1441
4	[Repealed]	
5	Tax on Transfers To Avoid Income Tax	Sec. 1491
6	Consolidated Returns	Sec. 1501

example of the arrangement for Section 170(b)(1)(A) dealing with percentage limitations on charitable contributions.

Some words of caution about reading the Code are warranted. You must always read the entire section, not just the smallest subdivision that may contain the apparent answer to a tax question. Frequently, other divisions of the section contain special rules or definitions that could be applicable.

For example, Section 170(a) generally allows a deduction for any charitable contribution to a qualified organization, including an educational institution. However, Section 170(l) limits the deduction to 80 percent of the amount otherwise allowable if the contribution entitles the donor to purchase tickets for seating at an athletic event in an athletic stadium of the educational institution (so-called donor seating).

Similarly, you must review other sections within the subpart, part, or other larger division that contains the particular section for similar limitations or cross-references to other parts of the Code that may be relevant. Section 168, for example, provides the general rules for computing the accelerated cost-recovery deduction for depreciable property, including automobiles. It is located in Part VI, entitled "Itemized Deductions for Individuals and Corporations," of Subchapter A. Section 280F, however, which is located in Part IX, entitled "Items Not Deductible," limits the depreciation deduction in cases in which expensive cars are purchased or they are not used at least 50 percent of the time in a trade or business.

Occasionally, the Code will specify that certain conditions must be met before the ultimate treatment can be determined. Under these circumstances, it is im-

▲ **Exhibit 15–3**

Subchapter	Name	Beginning Code Section Number
A	Determination of Tax Liability	Sec. 1
B	Computation of Taxable Income	Sec. 61
C	Corporate Distributions and Adjustments	Sec. 301
D	Deferred Compensation	Sec. 401
E	Accounting Periods and Methods of Accounting	Sec. 441
I	Natural Resources	Sec. 611
J	Estates, Trusts, Beneficiaries, and Decedents	Sec. 641
K	Partners and Partnerships	Sec. 701
N	Tax Based on Income from Sources within or without the United States	Sec. 861
O	Gain or Loss on Disposition of Property	Sec. 1001
P	Capital Gain or Loss	Sec. 1201
S	Tax Treatment of S Corporations and Their Shareholders	Sec. 1361

Title 26:	Internal Revenue Code
Subtitle A:	Income Tax
Chapter 1:	Normal Taxes and Surtaxes
Subchapter B:	Computation of Taxable Income
Part VI:	Itemized Deductions for Individuals and Corporations
Section:	Sec. 170 CHARITABLE, ETC., CONTRIBUTIONS AND GIFTS
Subsection:	(a) ALLOWANCE OF DEDUCTION
Paragraph:	(1) GENERAL RULE—There shall be allowed as a deduction any charitable contribution. . . . only if verified under regulations prescribed by the Secretary.
	. . . .
Subsection:	(b) PERCENTAGE LIMITATIONS
Paragraph:	(1) INDIVIDUALS—In the case of an individual, the deduction provided in subsection (a) shall be limited as provided in the succeeding subparagraphs.
Subparagraph:	(A) GENERAL RULE—Any charitable contribution to a [church] . . . shall be allowed to the extent that the aggregate of such contributions does not exceed 50 percent of the taxpayer's contribution base for the taxable year.
	. . . .

portant to understand, for example, whether conditions 1, 2, *and* 3 must be satisfied or whether condition 1, 2, *or* 3 will satisfy. Obviously, the ultimate treatment can be drastically different, depending on which of the interpretations is applicable.

THE LEGISLATIVE PROCESS.   Figure 15–2 presents a diagram of the process by which amendments to the Code are enacted. Typically, amendments to the Code are initiated by the president or a member of Congress as a *bill*. In accordance with the constitutional requirements, the bill is introduced in the House of Representatives, where it is referred to the Ways and Means Committee, which has jurisdiction over all tax matters. After hearings and deliberations, a bill approved by the committee is sent back to the full House. Under what is referred to as the *closed rule*, the House can only approve or disapprove the bill as written by the Ways and Means Committee. Bills approved by the House are sent to the Senate.

The bill follows a similar path in the Senate. It is first referred to the Finance Committee, which has jurisdiction over all tax matters in the Senate. The Senate Finance Committee may accept the bill as approved by the House, make some amendments to it, or make so many amendments that the resulting bill is really a substitute. After the committee approves the bill, it is referred to the full Senate. In contrast with the House's closed rule procedure, any senator may propose changes to the bill when it is being considered by the full Senate. Usually, the versions passed by the House and Senate are not the same, and any differences are resolved by a joint conference committee. Members of the joint conference committee are the most senior, or ranking, members of the House Ways and Means Committee and the Senate Finance Committee.

After the conference committee negotiates a resolution of the differences in the House and Senate versions of a bill, it is sent back to both the House and the Senate, where it can only be approved or disapproved. If the bill is passed by both the House and Senate, it is sent to the president. The president may approve

▲ **Figure 15–2**
THE LEGISLATIVE PROCESS FOR A TAX LAW

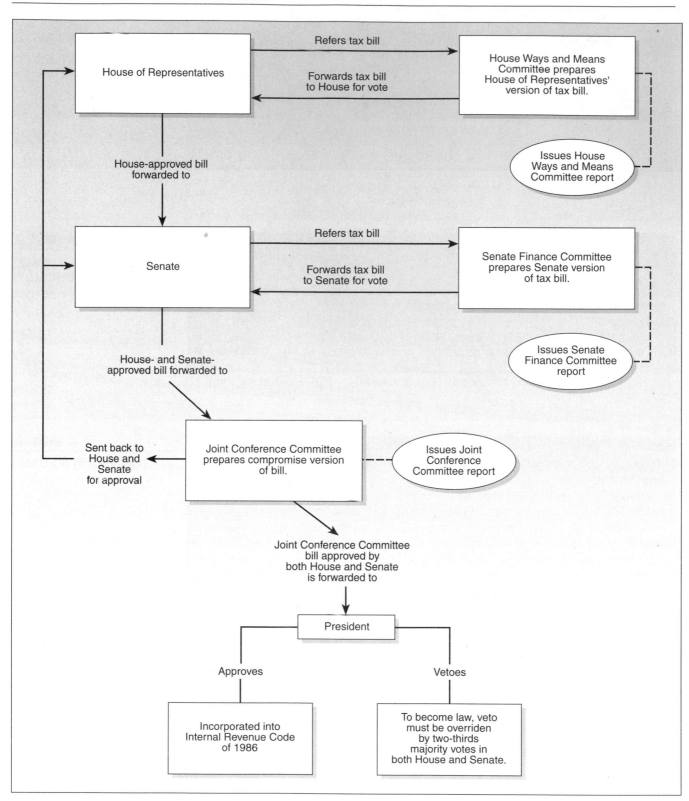

the bill by signing it, or the president may veto it. A veto can be overridden by a two-thirds majority of both the House and Senate.

Several documents that accompany a bill through the legislative process provide insight into Congress's intent in enacting the new legislation. As each committee approves a bill, it writes a report that describes why the change in the law was considered necessary, explains each change, and often provides examples of how a particular rule is to be applied. Accordingly, the House Ways and Means Committee report, Senate Finance Committee report, and Joint Conference Committee report provide information that helps the IRS, taxpayers, and the courts understand and interpret the bill as it was approved at each stage of the process.

After a bill is enacted, the Joint Committee on Taxation prepares a general explanation of the bill as approved by the president. This report is commonly referred to as the *blue book* because of the color of its binding. The Joint Committee on Taxation should not be confused with the Joint Conference Committee. The Joint Conference Committee is an integral part of the legislative process that develops a new bill.[1] The Joint Committee on Taxation's primary responsibility is to oversee the operation and administration of the tax system as a whole. It is not directly involved in the legislative process of enacting a new bill.

Tax Treaties.   Although the Code is the primary source of tax law in the United States, Congress also enters into tax treaties with various countries. Tax treaties are separate laws that define how citizens of the two countries are to be taxed on income derived from working or investing in the other country. As such, they are important for individuals and corporations that do business in foreign countries. At times, the provisions of a tax treaty may override provisions of the Code.[2] Because of their variety and complexity, details of specific tax treaties are beyond the scope of this text.

Administrative Sources

The agency within the administrative branch of government with overall responsibility for the administration of the Internal Revenue Code is the Treasury Department.[3] This responsibility is fulfilled by the Internal Revenue Service, a branch of the Treasury Department that is directly responsible for interpreting, administering, and enforcing the tax laws. The official in charge of the IRS is called the *commissioner* and is given general legal assistance by the Office of the Chief Counsel.[4]

The Treasury Department provides overall interpretive guidance by issuing Treasury regulations. In fulfilling its function, the IRS issues revenue rulings, revenue procedures, and a variety of other pronouncements.[5] It is important to keep in mind that regulations, rulings, and other pronouncements have different levels of authority, or weight. This is analogous to saying that a Supreme Court decision is more important than a decision of some lower court. These varying levels of authority play an important role in the tax research process described later in the chapter.

Treasury Regulations.   A Treasury regulation is the Treasury Department's official explanation of a related provision in the Internal Revenue Code. Regulations are the only administrative interpretations that require an intensive review and public comment process before they can be issued in final form. Regulations may be classified as interpretative or legislative. An **interpretative regulation** is issued under the general authority of the Treasury Department to provide official interpretations of I.R.C. provisions. A **legislative regulation** is issued when Congress specifically delegates the authority to the Treasury Department to write the specific rules for a designated Code section. For example, Section 469(l) specifically requires the Treasury Department to prescribe such regulations as may be necessary or appropriate to carry out all the provisions of Section 469. Because of this specific delegation of authority to Treasury by Congress, legislative regulations have a higher level of authority than interpretative regulations.

A regulation may be issued in a proposed, temporary, or final form. **Proposed regulations** are issued to let the public know what the IRS believes is the proper interpretation of a related Code provision and to provide an opportunity for the public to comment before they are issued in final form. Proposed regulations are not binding on taxpayers or the IRS until they are issued as **final regulations.** **Temporary regulations** are issued to provide taxpayers with guidance until a final regulation is issued. Section 7805(e), added in 1988, requires all temporary regulations to also be issued as proposed regulations and specifies that the regulation will expire if it is not amended or issued as a final regulation within three years. A regulation issued in its final form represents the Treasury Department's official interpretation and may be different from the position taken in a proposed or temporary regulation.

Revenue Rulings and Procedures.

Although regulations provide valuable interpretative information, they include only statements of general principles and cannot address every situation that could arise under a given Code section. **Revenue rulings** are interpretations by the IRS of the Code and regulations as they apply to specific factual situations. They represent official policy of the IRS and are binding on the IRS until they are revoked, amended, or otherwise changed. They do not, however, carry the same force and effect as a regulation and will be held invalid by a court if they are found to conflict with the intent of the regulation or I.R.C. provision to which they relate.

Revenue procedures are issued to explain internal IRS administrative practices and procedures. For example, a revenue procedure may explain the means by which employers may submit withholding information on computer tapes instead of paper documents. Familiarity with these pronouncements facilitates the processing of the taxpayer's returns and assures compliance with other administrative matters when dealing with the IRS.

The IRS issues hundreds of revenue rulings and procedures every year. Because of the great volume, they are not subject to as extensive a review process as regulations. Because of the lower level of review, revenue rulings and revenue procedures are given less weight than regulations as an authoritative source of the tax law.

Acquiescence and Nonacquiescence.

Whenever the IRS loses in a U.S. Tax Court proceeding, it will notify taxpayers as to whether it agrees or disagrees with the decision by issuing an **acquiescence** or **nonacquiescence.** These will not be issued if the IRS loses in any other court or for memorandum decisions of the U.S. Tax Court. (Other forums for resolving disputes between the IRS and taxpayers and the distinction between regular and memorandum decisions by the tax court are more fully discussed later in the chapter.)

It is important to understand that issuance of an acquiescence or nonacquiescence by the IRS is equivalent to a revenue ruling. Recall that a revenue ruling is the IRS's interpretation and application of the law to a specific factual situation.

When the tax court interprets and applies the law to a specific factual situation, the IRS can in essence make a ruling by signifying that it agrees (or disagrees) with the decision. Like a revenue ruling, an acquiescence or nonacquiescence is binding on the IRS in other, similar, factual situations unless it is later withdrawn.

Other Pronouncements.   The IRS issues various other interpretive pronouncements to aid taxpayers in complying with the tax law. A **private letter ruling (LTR)** is issued by the National Office of the IRS in response to specific questions raised by taxpayers and typically deals with prospective transactions. By issuing revenue procedures, the IRS restricts the areas in which it will issue private letter rulings. An LTR applies only to the taxpayer requesting the ruling and does not bind the IRS to take the same position when dealing with a different taxpayer. If the IRS believes that the transaction represented in an LTR may be of importance to taxpayers in general, it may issue a revenue ruling.

A **technical advice memorandum (TAM)** may be thought of as an LTR for a completed transaction.[6] A TAM originates as a request for assistance by a local office of the IRS and typically arises as part of an ongoing audit. Like the LTR, the TAM is issued by the National Office of the IRS and is not binding on the IRS. LTRs and TAMs are generically referred to as **letter rulings,** and although they are not officially published by the government, they are unofficially made available to the public by many private publishers such as Commerce Clearing House and Research Institute of America. Although they are accorded a lower level of authority, letter rulings are a useful source in determining the current position of the IRS on an issue.

Chief counsel's memoranda are issued by the Office of Chief Counsel of the IRS and include technical memoranda, general counsel's memoranda, and actions on decisions. These documents originate in the process of preparing other authoritative pronouncements and are frequently relied on by IRS personnel in disputes with taxpayers. **Technical memoranda (TM)** are used to explain Treasury regulations. Over the last few years, the use of TM has decreased and been replaced with what is referred to as the *preamble* to Treasury regulations. **General counsel's memoranda (GCM)** explain the authority and reasoning used to prepare revenue rulings, private letter rulings, and technical advice memoranda. **Actions on decisions (AOD)** explain whether the Chief Counsel's Office believes that an adverse court decision should be appealed. If the unfavorable decision is rendered by the tax court, the AOD may suggest that an acquiescence or nonacquiescence be issued. Like letter rulings, these documents are not binding on the service and are not officially published by the government. Nevertheless, they are helpful in understanding the position of the IRS and are made unofficially available by private publishers.

The IRS does publish a variety of other items that are designed to help taxpayers comply with the tax law. These include notices, announcements, IRS publications, and tax return instructions. Caution is warranted, however, because these items are sometimes incomplete and misleading. And, although they are published by the IRS, the taxpayer may not rely on them as an authoritative source for a position taken on a tax return.

Judicial Sources

If a taxpayer and the IRS disagree on the interpretation and application of the Code, the matter may have to be resolved in court. Court decisions are official interpretations and applications of the Code by the judicial branch of government and therefore represent the third source of primary authority. All litigation must start in a trial court. It is the trial court's responsibility to determine the facts and then interpret and apply the law. Whenever the taxpayer or the IRS loses at the trial level, either party may appeal the decision to a higher court. No appellate court, including the Supreme Court, holds another trial (lawyers' arguments must be based on the record of the original trial). These courts' primary responsibility is to determine whether the law was correctly applied to the facts. Only rarely will an appellate court disturb the findings of fact by the trial court. Losses at the first appellate level may be further appealed to the Supreme Court, decisions of which are final and binding on all lower courts.

Trial Courts.   Taxpayers may choose one of three different courts in which to initiate litigation: U.S. District Court, U.S. Claims Court, and U.S. Tax Court. These courts of original jurisdiction are referred to as the **trial courts.** Taxpayers willing to pay the tax in dispute and then sue for a refund have the option of taking their case to a U.S. District Court or the U.S. Claims Court. Each **U.S. District Court** hears cases on legal issues involving the entire *United States Code,* of which the Internal Revenue Code is but one small part. Therefeore, district court judges must be generalists in matters of federal law and are not specialists in federal tax law. District courts are located throughout the country—each is assigned to serve a specific geographic area. In order to have a jury trial, taxpayers must file in district court. The **U.S. Claims Court** hears cases concerning any monetary claim against the federal government. Because income tax refunds are only one type of claim that can be filed against the federal government, claims court judges are not specialists in federal tax law. Unlike the district courts, the claims court does not allow jury trials.

As an alternative, taxpayers may choose not to pay the additional tax and then file a petition in **U.S. Tax Court** for relief. There are two distinct advantages in choosing the tax court. First, as indicated, the case can be taken to the tax court without first paying the tax. This is why the tax court is often referred to as the "poor person's court." Second, the tax court offers an opportunity for the issues to be decided by a court that specializes in tax matters.

The tax court has traditionally issued two types of decisions: regular and memorandum. **Tax Court regular decisions** are those that are presumed to have value as precedents or involve issues that have not previously been considered. All other decisions are **Tax Court memorandum decisions.** Regular decisions are generally regarded as stronger authorities than memorandum decisions. Although the distinction has become somewhat blurred over the years, recall that the IRS will issue an acquiescence or nonacquiescence only for regular decisions.

In cases in which the amount of tax in dispute is less than $10,000, a taxpayer may elect to use the small claims division of the tax court. The purpose of the small claims division is to allow taxpayers to obtain a ruling on their case with a minimal amount of formality, delay, and expense. Caution is warranted, however, because small claims cases cannot be appealed, the decisions are not published, and the decisions cannot be used as precedents in other courts.

Both the tax court and the claims court are referred to as *national courts* because they hear cases from taxpayers living anywhere in the United States. A district court can hear cases only from taxpayers who live within the specific geographical area over which the court presides.[7] Taxpayers must consider these jurisdictional differences, whether to pay first, whether the technical expertise of the tax court is desirable, the advantages of a jury, and prior decisions on similar issues when selecting a trial court.

Appellate Courts.   Decisions of the district courts and tax court are appealed to one of 12 regional **U.S. Courts of Appeals** (previously the U.S. Circuit Courts of Appeals and occasionally still referred to as such). Each circuit court has a specific geographical area over which it has sole jurisdiction. Decisions of the U.S. Claims Court must be appealed to the **U.S. Court of Appeals for the Federal Circuit** in Washington, D.C. Decisions by all appellate courts have precedence over trial court decisions. For example, if a circuit court has previously ruled on an issue, all the district courts within that circuit must follow that decision in any future cases.

The tax court will also follow the holdings of a circuit court but only for taxpayers residing within the specific geographical jurisdiction of the appellate court. Outside that circuit, the tax court may hold differently on exactly the same facts and issues. This so-called *Golsen* rule has been justified by the tax court on the ground that it is a trial court with national jurisdiction. The claims court is bound to follow only decisions of the U.S. Court of Appeals for the Federal Circuit.

Although trial courts are bound only by the decisions of their own circuit court, they frequently look to other circuit court decisions as well as decisions of other trial courts in forming their own opinions. Similarly, each circuit court does not need to follow prior decisions of other circuit courts but does look to these decisions for guidance.

Supreme Court.   All decisions of appellate courts may be further appealed to the **U.S. Supreme Court.** Unlike the circuit courts, which must rule on every case that is appealed from the trial courts, the Supreme Court does not have to accept every case that is appealed from the circuit courts. The Supreme Court decides which cases it wants to review by granting a writ of certiorari. Granting the writ of certiorari simply means that at least four of the nine justices on the Court feel the case is important enough for them to review it. Conversely, denying a writ of certiorari means only that the Court does not think the case is important enough for it to review at that time. It does not reverse or in any other way directly affect the decision of the lower court. Review will, however, strengthen the authority or importance of the case in the hierarchy of primary authorities. The Court limits its review of tax cases to those of major importance or to those in which the decisions of the circuit courts conflict.

If the Supreme Court agrees to review a decision, its interpretation and application of the law are the final authority, and all lower courts, taxpayers, and the IRS must follow its decision. If Congress is unhappy with the Court's interpretation and application of the law, its only recourse is to follow the legislative process described earlier and amend the Code.

Citations to Primary Authorities

Whenever a reference is made to any primary authority, it is important to include a citation indicating where the full text of the document may be found. This is an especially crucial part of the tax research process described later in this chapter. Although it is beyond the scope of this text to discuss citation formats in any great depth, a brief review is necessary. Exhibit 15–5 illustrates citations to most of the primary authorities previously discussed and provides the basis for the discussion that follows.

Committee Reports.   All reports issued by the House Ways and Means Committee, the Senate Finance Committee, and the Joint Conference Committee are

▲ **Exhibit 15–5**

CITATIONS TO PRIMARY
AUTHORITIES

Primary Authority	Citation
Committee report	HOUSE COMMITTEE ON WAYS AND MEANS, H.REP.NO. 432, 98th Cong., 2d Sess. (March 5, 1984).
Internal Revenue Code	Sec. 469(e)(1)(A).
Treasury regulation—final	Reg. Sec. 1.269-1(a)(3).
Treasury regulation—proposed	Prop. Reg. Sec. 1.704-3(c).
Treasury regulation—temporary	Temp. Reg. Sec. 1.441-1T(a)(2).
Revenue ruling—permanent	Rev. Rul. 54-56, 1954-2 C.B. 108.
Revenue ruling—temporary	Rev. Rul. 84-101, I.R.B. No. 28, 5.
Revenue procedure—permament	Rev. Proc. 88-12, 1988-1 C.B. 17.
Revenue procedure—temporary	Rev. Proc. 93-15, I.R.B. 3, 12.
Private letter ruling	LTR 8450056 (PLR).
U.S. Tax Court—regular decision	J.B. Linderman, 60 T.C. 609 (1973).
U.S. Tax Court—memorandum decision	Thomas E. Lesslie, 36 TCM 495 (1977), TC Memo ¶77, 111.
Acquiescence	Phillip G. Larson, 66 T.C. 159 (1976), *acq.* 1979–1 C.B. 1.
U.S. District Court	Arnold v. U.S., 289 F. Supp. 206, 68-2 USTC ¶9590, 22 A.F.T.R.2d 5661 (D.Ct. N.Y., 1968).
U.S. Claims Court	Zuchman v. U.S., 524 F.2d 729, 75-2 USTC ¶9778, 36 A.F.T.R.2d 75-6193 (Cl.Ct., 1975).
U.S. Courts of Appeals	Comm. v. Percy W. Phillips, 275 F.2d 33, 60-1 USTC ¶9294, 5 A.F.T.R.2d 855 (4th Cir. 1960).
U.S. Supreme Court	Commissioner v. Duberstein, 80 S. Ct. 1190, 60-2 USTC ¶9515, 5 A.F.T.R.2d 1626 (1960).

cited in the same general manner. The example in Exhibit 15–5 is for a House Ways and Means Committee report and tells the reader that it is the 432nd report issued by the House of Representatives during the second session of the 98th Congress and was issued on March 5, 1984. The name of the committee frequently is omitted from the citation. This generally occurs when reference to the committee that issued the report is made in a related text discussion.

Code and Regulations.　References to the Code have been introduced previously. Spelling out *Internal Revenue Code* or inserting *I.R.C.* is usually omitted in practice, because it is understood that the reference is to the Internal Revenue Code of 1986, as amended. The last group of numbers in any Code citation should reflect the smallest subdivision of a section that relates to the tax issue under consideration.

Treasury regulations follow a similar citation pattern, but they are preceded by a number that specifies the general area of tax to which the regulation relates. Most regulations start with *1*, signifying that they deal with income taxes. Other common numbers are *20*, relating to estate taxes; *25*, involving gift taxes; and *301* or *601*, dealing with administrative rules. The first numbers after the period state the related Code section. The Code section number is followed by a hyphen and the number of the regulation. Several different regulations may be issued under the same Code section. The last group of numbers gives the smallest subdivision of the regulation that is appropriate. Proposed and temporary regulations follow the same format, except that they are preceded by *Prop.* or *Temp.* In addition— and only for temporary regulations—a *T* follows the regulation number. Again, spelling out *Treasury* or inserting *Treas.* is usually omitted in practice; common practice is to abbreviate *Section* as *Sec.*, instead of using the symbol for *section*, §.

Other IRS Pronouncements.   All other pronouncements of the IRS are initially published weekly by the U.S. Government Printing Office in the *Internal Revenue Bulletin* **(I.R.B.).** Semiannually, the last six months of the I.R.B. are reorganized and published in a permanent document called the *Cumulative Bulletin* **(C.B.).** Citations to most IRS documents should be to the C.B. Whenever the latest C.B. does not include the referenced document, a temporary citation is made to the I.R.B.

As Exhibit 15–5 illustrates, revenue rulings and procedures are cited similarly. The numbers following *Rev. Rul.* provide the reader with the following information: the ruling was the 56th ruling issued in 1954 and can be found on page 108 of the second volume of the 1954 *Cumulative Bulletin*. The temporary citation yields this information: The ruling is the 101st ruling issued in 1984 and can be found on page 5 of the 28th weekly issue of the *Internal Revenue Bulletin*. Revenue procedures read the same way.

Letter rulings, including private letter rulings and technical advice memoranda, are given an official seven-digit number. The first two digits provide the year the ruling was issued, the next two indicate the week, and the final three digits are the number assigned to that ruling for that week. The citation in Exhibit 15–5 tells the reader that the ruling was issued in 1984, during the 50th week and was the 56th ruling issued that week. Sometimes, the citation includes a designation after the number that tells the reader which type of letter ruling is being cited [i.e., either a private letter ruling (PLR) or a technical advice memorandum (TAM)].

Court Decisions.   All judicial citations follow the same format: case name, volume number of the reporter in which the case is published, name of the reporter, and the page of the reporter on which the case begins. Sometimes, the year of the decision or the name of the court is added in parentheses at the end. A **reporter** is a series of books published by the federal government or by a private publishing company that provides the full text of court decisions. The two biggest private publishers of reporters are the Research Institute of America (RIA, formerly Prentice-Hall) and Commerce Clearing House (CCH). Complete citations typically include one citation to a government reporter and at least one additional citation to a CCH or RIA reporter. Different reporters are cited for each court that renders a decision.

TAX COURT.   Regular decisions of U.S. Tax Court are published by the Government Printing Office (GPO) in a reporter called *Reports of the United States Tax Court* **(T.C.).** CCH and RIA also publish regular tax court decisions in separate special decision reporters. Both are called *Tax Court Reporter*. However, common tax practice is to cite only T.C., the official GPO reporter. The citation for the *Linderman* case in Exhibit 15–5 provides the information that the case can be found on page 609 of volume 60 of *Reports of the United States Tax Court* and that it was decided in 1973.

Memorandum decisions of U.S. Tax Court are not published in any government reporter. They are, however, published by both RIA and CCH under the title *Tax Court Memorandum Decisions.* Common practice is to cite RIA's reporter as *TC Memo* and CCH's as *TCM.* As Exhibit 15–5 illustrates, citations for both services follow exactly the same format. For example, the *Lesslie* case can be found on page 495 of volume 36 of *Tax Court Memorandum Decisions* (TCM) and in the 1977 volume of TC Memo, at paragraph 77,111. A complete citation would include citations to both reporters.

Whenever the IRS issues an acquiescence (*acq.*) or nonacquiescence (*nonacq.*) to an unfavorable regular decision of U.S. Tax Court, it should be included in the citation, as it is for the *Larson* case in Exhibit 15–5. This informs the reader that the acquiescence can be found on page 1 of volume 1 of the 1979 *Cumulative Bulletin*.

ALL OTHER COURTS EXCEPT THE U.S. SUPREME COURT.   The U.S. government does not officially publish the decisions of the district courts, claims court, or the appellate courts in any reporter. West Publishing Co., however, is treated as the official publisher, and any citation to decisions from these courts should include a citation to one of its reporters. This includes the **Federal Supplement (F. Supp.)** for all district court cases and the **Federal Reporter, 2d series (F.2d)** for claims court and appellate court cases.

These decisions are also reported by RIA in *American Federal Tax Reports* (A.F.T.R. and A.F.T.R.2d) and by Commerce Clearing House in *U.S. Tax Cases* (USTC). The CCH and RIA reporters include only tax cases, whereas the West reporters include all cases decided by the respective courts. A complete citation should cite all three reporters. For example, the citation for the *Arnold* case in Exhibit 15–5 provides the following information: The case can be found on page 206 of volume 289 of the *Federal Supplement*; it is a case decided by the U.S. District Court for New York in 1968; it can also be found at paragraph 9590 of volume 68-2 of *U.S. Tax Cases* and on page 5661 of volume 22 of *American Federal Tax Reports*, second series. Decisions of the appellate courts and the claims court are cited the same way.

SUPREME COURT.   Decisions of the United States Supreme Court are officially printed by the government in the **United States Reports (U.S.)** reporter. Because of their importance, these decision are also published by West Publishing in **Supreme Court Reports (S. Ct.)** and are included in the A.F.T.R. and *U.S. Tax Cases* series. A complete citation should include reference to either the S. Ct. or U.S. reporters and both the A.F.T.R. and USTC reporters. The *Duberstein* case in Exhibit 15–5 is an example of a citation that provides references to all three sources.

▲ SECONDARY SOURCES OF FEDERAL INCOME TAX LAW

Answers to federal tax questions must be based on the primary authorities. However, as we have discussed, the number of these authorities is vast, they are constantly changing, and they are not indexed or coordinated in any logical fashion. The most important role of secondary authorities is to provide help in locating the legislative, administrative, or judicial primary authorities that provide the answers about the tax consequences related to a specific factual situation. Tax services, including computerized versions, and citators are two types of secondary authorities that are used for this purpose. Secondary authorities, including textbooks, journals, and editorial comments in tax services, may also be used to help understand and interpret the law. These are unofficial interpretations only and have no legal authority.

Tax Services

Tax services, one type of secondary authority, principally are tools for locating the primary authorities related to various factual circumstances. They generally consist of a multivolume set of loose-leaf binders that are constantly updated. Tax services fall into two major categories, based on the amount of editorial discussion provided by the publisher. The first category consists of those services with limited editorial discussion and numerous brief interpretations and citations to the primary authorities (other than the Code and regulations, which are provided in full text). These abridged interpretations, or annotations, are indexed according to the Code section to which they relate. They consist chiefly of brief interpretations of revenue rulings and procedures, court cases, letter rulings, and other miscellaneous pronouncements. The researcher must know the Code section that relates to the tax question or may use a topical index to find the appropriate section. Services in this category include *Standard Federal Tax Reporter (CCH)* and *United States Tax Reporter (RIA)*. It is important to remember that the researcher using these services should not rely on the synopses given in the annotations, because they represent only the editors' interpretation of the related authority. The researcher should always read the full text of the appropriate primary authority before reaching any conclusions.

The second category of tax services contains extensive editorial discussion and interpretation of the law, with citations to the primary authorities provided in the footnotes. These services also provide full text of the Code and regulations but are arranged by topical headings determined by the editor. An index is useful for locating the relevant part of the service that discusses the related Code, regulations, and other primary authorities. Services in this category include the Research Institute of America's *Federal Tax Coordinator 2d*, the Bureau of National Affairs's *Tax Management Portfolios*, and *Mertens Law of Federal Income Taxation*, published by Callaghan and Co. The researcher should always read the entire text of the authority cited in the footnotes to be sure that the analysis and interpretation provided in the editorial discussion are proper.

Both categories of tax services should always be checked for current developments, which usually appear in a separate volume. In addition, the publishers of most services provide paperback versions of the Code and regulations, which are convenient and may provide answers to some basic questions. Abridged paperback versions of most tax services, called *tax guides*, are also available from the publishers. Because their coverage is limited, these should be used only for orientation purposes and not for research.

Citators

Citators are used primarily to determine the history of a judicial decision and how that decision has been criticized, approved, or otherwise commented upon in other court decisions. This type of information also is available for revenue rulings, revenue procedures, and certain other administrative pronouncements. Citators are a valuable tool in the "validation" step of tax research, described later in this chapter. Citators refer to the case being evaluated as the **cited case,** and any cases discussing that case are called the **citing cases.** Cited cases are listed alphabetically, followed by the citing cases and rulings.

The history of a cited case refers to all other decisions by higher or lower courts in the same case. For example, if the cited case has been appealed to a higher court, the citator provides the name of the appellate court and whether it affirmed, reversed, or modified the decision of the cited case. Similarly, if the cited case is an appellate court decision, the citator provides the name of the trial court and states whether the cited case affirmed, reversed, or otherwise modified the decision of the lower court. For revenue rulings, citators provide historical citations to related rulings that revoke, modify, or supersede the cited ruling and to any earlier rulings affected by the cited ruling. Citators further provide *citing references*, which provide other rulings or court cases that have discussed the cited ruling.

The citator also gives information about how the decision of the cited case has been interpreted by other courts. These courts can, in their decisions, agree or disagree with the cited case, differentiate the facts or law in their case from the cited case, or may simply refer to the cited case without comment. Some citators use abbreviations to indicate which of these reasons are specified by the citing court. These notations are most useful when the citing cases are numerous.

The citators most frequently used are Research Institute of America's *Federal Tax Citator*, which comes as a multivolume set separate from its tax service, and Commerce Clearing House's two-volume set, which is included in its tax service. As a final step, the researcher using these citators must always check their supplements or current development sections.

Tax Periodicals

Numerous publications, law school journals, and newsletters dealing with tax matters also serve as secondary authorities and sources of tax information. These are especially valuable for planning and notification of new developments. Examples of these sources include *Journal of Taxation, TAXES—The Tax Magazine, Tax Advisor, Estate Planning, University of Virginia Law Review, Tax Notes,* and *Daily Tax Report.* Some tax services, or a separate service such as *Federal Tax Articles* (published by Commerce Clearing House), provide topical indexes to articles in these and other publications.

Computer-Assisted Tax Research

One additional and important secondary source of tax information is referred to as **computer-assisted tax research (CATR).** The researcher can use a computer to gain access to a large tax database containing the full text of virtually all primary and secondary authorities. The researcher uses key words that appear in the document to find a specific authority. The system can also search the database for particular words that must be absent from the document, before or after a specified date, or within so many words of a specified term. Numerous other search terms and strategies are available.

The major CATR systems are LEXIS and WESTLAW and have several useful features. To be complete, tax libraries must keep on hand printed versions of tax services, reporters, cumulative bulletins, newsletters, and the like. Most libraries will not have all the authorities, because they are expensive, require a considerable amount of storage space, and involve staff time to keep them current. In contrast, a CATR system is complete, and all the researcher needs is a terminal with a modem, keyboard, screen, and printer. Cost is a bit more controversial. Some argue that CATR technology is still too expensive to be cost effective. After all, the client ultimately bears the cost of these systems. Others, however, contend that when convenience, completeness, and timeliness are factored in, a CATR system is less expensive than maintaining a traditional tax library.

A recent expansion of the CATR concept is the use of CD-ROM technology, which puts tax databases on compact disks. Instead of using the telephone to access an external database, the researcher has at hand virtually every primary and secondary authority, stored on only a few compact disks. The CDs and a CD reader are acquired for a one-time, up-front cost. The CD-ROM systems eliminate the cost of telephone and search time on an external database, learning time for new staffers to become proficient, and other costs typically associated with on-line CATR systems. In other words, the variable cost of the traditional CATR system is converted to the more fixed cost of the CATR CD-ROM system. The biggest disadvantage of these systems is the difficulty of keeping the material current. Some systems give their purchasers access to an on-line system for up-to-the-minute research, replace the CDs periodically with those that contain more current material, and/or send users monthly floppy disks that contain current information.

Tax research is simply the process by which the answers to tax questions are determined. From an initial set of facts, the researcher identifies the tax issues to be resolved. The researcher must locate the governing Code section and any administrative or judicial interpretations and evaluate and apply them to the facts. The researcher must draw conclusions and communicate the results and recommendations to the interested parties.

Tax Compliance versus Tax Planning

Tax research usually becomes important for either a transaction that has already been completed or for one that is being contemplated. Finding the answer to a completed transaction is commonly referred to as *compliance work* and typically arises during the preparation of a tax return. Determining the tax consequence of transactions that have not yet been completed is called *tax planning*. In planning situations, tax research is undertaken in order to find the "best" way to accomplish a desired result. Frequently, the best method depends on both tax and nontax considerations.

> ▲ **EXAMPLE 1**   Edna, a client, tells you she would like to give her son some apartment buildings that she owns. She wants to know the best way to transfer this property to him.
>
> *Discussion:*   The alternatives might include a sale, a gift, or transferring the property to a trust, with Edna's son as beneficiary. Each method has different tax consequences. You also know that Edna does not really trust her son and is quite worried that he will simply take all the profits and let the building deteriorate. This nontax factor may lead you to conclude that the "best" method would be to set up a trust, even if the tax consequences are not the most favorable.

Whether tax research is for compliance or planning, it is important to use a systematic procedure for your research. The basic steps involved in this process are

1. Establish the facts and determine the issues.
2. Locate the relevant authorities.
3. Assess the importance of the authorities.
4. Reach conclusions, make recommendations, and communicate the results.

Step 1: Establish the Facts and Determine the Issues

All tax research begins with determining the facts. The facts help define the initial tax issues and the apparently applicable Code provisions and any administrative or judicial interpretations. Reviewing these authorities most likely leads to the need for more information. Such additional information may yield citations of other applicable authorities, which again may require the researcher to track down further factual information. Following the trail of facts and authorities is an inherent part of the tax research process.

> ▲ **EXAMPLE 2**   Let us return to your client, Edna. Assume she sold the property to her son and that the sale resulted in a loss. Is the loss deductible?

Discussion: The applicable statutory provision is Sec. 267 of the Code. Sec. 267(a)(1) disallows losses between persons specified in Sec. 267(b), which includes members of family, as defined in Sec. 267(c)(4). Sec. 267(c)(4) specifies that members of a family include the taxpayer's brothers and sisters, spouse, ancestors, and lineal descendants. Your initial conclusion is that the loss will be disallowed as a deduction. But further discussion with the taxpayer yields the information that the son is really a stepson who was never legally adopted. This additional fact changes your conclusion. Under the authority of Reg. Sec. 1.267(c)-1(a)(4), only legally adopted lineal descendants are members of the family. Edna may take the loss as a deduction.

Facts relevant to a tax situation include the taxpayer's method of accounting, the marital status of the taxpayer, whether the parties to a transaction are related, the domicile and citizenship of the taxpayer, and whether the taxpayer is a partner or S corporation shareholder. When the taxpayer is a corporation, relevant tax facts include whether it is an S or C corporation, whether it is tax exempt, and whether it is a financial institution, insurance company, or personal holding company. In some cases, the facts are well established, and the only issue is how the tax law is interpreted and how that interpretation applies to the facts. These are generally referred to as *questions of law*, in contrast to questions of fact.

Step 2: Locate the Relevant Authorities

Secondary authorities are most useful for locating the applicable primary authorities. Usually, this means research begins with the index to one of the tax services. The index provides a reference to the part of the service that contains the full text of the relevant Code section and regulations, as well as annotations of court decisions and administrative pronouncements. Remember that any editorial commentary included in the tax services is secondary authority only. All conclusions and recommendations must be based on primary authorities. Further, conclusions should never be based on the annotations provided by the editorial staff of the publishers of the tax services. You must examine and evaluate the full text of the court case, revenue ruling, or other primary authority, as indicated in step 3.

Step 3: Assess the Importance of the Authorities

Once you have located the apparently applicable authorities, you must evaluate them to determine whether they actually are applicable to the facts and issues and to assess their importance. Determining whether the authority is relevant to the tax issues under consideration is accomplished by reading the full text of the document. Determining the importance, or relative weight, of the authorities is more difficult. In many cases, the Code and regulations do not provide a conclusive answer to the issues involved in a specific set of facts. You may have to rely on other administrative or judicial authorities, and these are frequently in conflict. To determine the inherent strength or weakness of these authorities, you need a general understanding of the hierarchy of the authorities and how to use a citator.

Code and Regulations. Sometimes, simply reading the applicable Code section yields the answer to a tax question. More often, however, the statutory language is ambiguous or does not directly address the issues identified. Under these circumstances, the secondary authorities—especially the citators and annotations in the tax services—are useful for finding other primary authorities that may be helpful in evaluating and applying the statute. In relatively rare circumstances, you will find no other regulations, IRS pronouncements, or court decisions that conclusively deal with the issue. When this occurs, you must examine the legislative history of the provision, as provided by the committee reports, for congressional intent. One other point bears repeating. Compliance work frequently requires determining the answer to a transaction that occurred some years earlier. Accordingly, it is important to be sure that the version of the Code or Treasury regulation you are using applies to the period in which the transaction occurred.

The Code is generally considered the highest authority, because it is the law as enacted by Congress. If the issue deals with international tax matters, treaties as enacted by Congress may supersede provisions in the Code. The courts can invalidate a section of the Code or a treaty only if it violates the U.S. Constitution.

Treasury regulations, representing the official interpretation of the law by the Treasury Department, are often referred to as having *the force and effect of the law.* The courts can invalidate them only by determining that they are inconsistent with the statute to which they relate. In assessing the importance of Treasury regulations, it is important to remember that there are different types of regulations. Temporary regulations are accorded the same weight as final regulations. Proposed regulations carry no authority, because they are only indications of what the Treasury Department may decide. They are not binding on either the taxpayer or the IRS. Recall that there also are interpretive and legislative regulations. Legislative regulations, by their very nature, are accorded more authority than interpretive regulations.

Pronouncements. Revenue rulings, issued by the IRS, represent agency policy and are binding on the IRS and its personnel until they are revoked, modified, superseded, or withdrawn. Although they are accorded considerable importance, they do not have the force and effect of a Treasury regulation, primarily because they are subjected to only a limited review before they are issued. The courts frequently find that a ruling is inconsistent with the Code section or regulation it is interpreting. It is important to use a citator to determine not only the current status of the ruling but also *how* the ruling has been evaluated by the courts. Because an acquiescence or nonacquiescence by the IRS to an adverse tax court decision is tantamount to a revenue ruling, acquiescenses and nonacquiescenses are accorded the same weight as revenue rulings. This procedure should be followed in assessing the importance of any other IRS pronouncement.

Court Decisions. Numerous factors affect the strength of a court decision. One factor is whether the decision was issued by a trial or appellate court. A decision by the U.S. Court of Appeals for the Third Circuit would be more authoritative than a trial court decision. An opinion by the Supreme Court would be the highest authority.

Another important factor is whether the decision was issued by the tax court or some other trial court. Recall that the tax court is generally considered to have more technical expertise than other trial courts.

▲ **EXAMPLE 3** On a very technical question, your research turns up an applicable tax court decision that provides favorable support for the position your client wants to take. You also find a district court decision on substantially identical facts but with opposite results.

Discussion: If the two cases are identical in all other respects, the tax court decision is the higher authority. Similarly, a regular decision of the U.S. Tax Court generally carries more weight than a memorandum decision.

Other factors to be considered in determining the level of authority of a court decision include whether the decision is unanimous or split and the jurisdictional issues regarding the taxpayer's residence, discussed earlier. All the factors can be determined by actually reading the case.

The most important factor determining the relative importance or weight accorded a court decision is how other courts have viewed the decision. Using a citator is crucial for determining how the opinion stacks up with other decisions on the same issue. A strong decision would be one with a long history of favorable evaluation by other courts.

Step 4: Reach Conclusions, Make Recommendations, and Communicate the Results

The final research step is both objective and subjective. You must reach objective conclusions about each primary authority and how it applies to the facts and issues under consideration. In reporting to the client, you must include all your conclusions, whether they result in a favorable outcome for the taxpayer or not. These objective conclusions state what you believe is the current state of the law.

From these conclusions, you must subjectively determine which of the often-conflicting interpretations is the correct one to recommend. Your recommendation should include a research memorandum that encompasses a statement of the relevant facts, the tax issues considered, the conclusions and recommendations reached for each issue, and the authorities, reasoning, and analysis used to arrive at each conclusion and recommendation. Always provide citations to supporting primary authorities.

The research memorandum provides the basis for a separate letter to the taxpayer, which, although containing basically the same information, is less detailed. The importance of the research memorandum and letter cannot be over emphasized. All your research will be wasted if you do not communicate the results effectively.

▲ COMPREHENSIVE RESEARCH EXAMPLE

Step 1: Establish the Facts and Determine the Issues

Sam, a surgeon, and his wife Sara own and rent out a vacation home. During the year, they use the home 20 days and rent it for 40 days. Rental income for the year was $4,000. Total expenses are as follows:

Interest and taxes	$4,200
Utilities and maintenance	1,500
Depreciation	6,000

Sam has asked for assistance in determining the tax treatment of these expenditures.

Step 2: Locate the Relevant Authorities

Using the index to any of the tax services leads to Sec. 280A, "Disallowance Of Certain Expenses in Connection with Business Use of Home, Rental of Vacation Homes, Etc." A review of the editorial discussion and annotations indicates that Prop. Reg. Sec. 1.280A-3 and *Bolton v. Commissioner*, 694 F.2d 556, 51 A.F.T.R.2d 83-305, 83-20 USTC ¶9699 (9th Cir. 1982), affirming 77 T.C. 104 (1981), may also be applicable.

Step 3: Assess the Importance of the Authorities

Completion of this step requires review of each authority identified to determine its applicability. Always examine the relevant Code section first. If questions remain unanswered, you must look to the administrative and judicial interpretations to see if they provide definitive answers or at least some direction.

The Code.   Exhibit 15–6 provides the relevant portions of Sec. 280A. The general rule of Sec. 280A(a) limits a taxpayer's business deductions for expenses incurred for a dwelling unit if that unit was used as a personal residence during the taxable year. Under Sec. 280A(d)(1), the general rule of Sec. 280A(a) applies if the taxpayer's personal use of the dwelling unit exceeds the greater of 14 days or 10 percent of the number of days the unit is rented. Because Sam and Sara's personal use of

▲ **Exhibit 15–6**

CODE SECTION 280A

Sec. 280A Disallowance of **Certain Expenses** in Connection with Business Use of Home, Rental of Vacation Homes, etc.

(a) **General rule.** Except as otherwise provided in this section, in the case of a taxpayer who is an individual or an S corporation, no deduction otherwise allowable under this chapter shall be allowed with respect to the use of a dwelling unit which is used by the taxpayer during the taxable years as a residence.

(b) **Exception for interest, taxes, casualty losses, etc.** Subsection (a) shall not apply to any deduction allowable to the taxpayer without regard to its connection with his trade or business (or with his income-producing activity).

(c) **Exceptions for certain business or rental use; limitation on deductions for such use.**

. . . .

   (3) **Rental use.** Subsection (a) shall not apply to any item which is attributable to the rental of the dwelling unit or portion thereof (determined after the application of subsection (e)).

. . . .

   (5) **Limitation on deductions.** In the case of a use described in paragraph (1), (2), or (4), and in the case of a use described in paragraph (3) where the dwelling unit is used by the taxpayer during the taxable year as a residence, the deductions allowed under this chapter for the taxable year by reason of being attributed to such use shall not exceed the excess of—

   (A) the gross income derived from such use for the taxable year, over

   (B) the sum of—

      (i) the deductions allocable to such use which are allowable under this chapter for the taxable year whether or not such unit (or portion thereof) was so used, and

      (ii) the deductions allocable to the trade or business (or rental activity) in which such use occurs (but which are not allocable to such use) for such taxable year. . . .

(e) **Expenses attributable to rental.**

   (1) **In general.** In any case where a taxpayer who is an individual or an S corporation uses a dwelling unit for personal purposes on any day during the taxable year (whether or not he is treated under this section as using such unit as a residence), the amount deductible under this chapter with respect to expenses attributable to the rental of the unit (or portion thereof) for the taxable year shall not exceed an amount which bears the same relationship to such expenses as the number of days during each year that the unit (or portion thereof) is rented at a fair rental bears to the total number of days during such year that the unit (or portion thereof) is used.

   (2) **Exception for deductions otherwise allowable.** This subsection shall not apply with respect to deduction which would be allowable under this chapter for the taxable year whether or not such unit (or portion thereof) was rented.

the vacation home exceeds both 14 days and 10 percent of the rental days, the general limitation applies.

Sec. 280A(b) provides that nonbusiness expenditures otherwise deductible (e.g., taxes, interest, and casualty losses) are not subject to the general limitation in Sec. 280A(a). Sec. 280A(c)(3) provides another exception to the general limitation by allowing a deduction for "any item attributable to rental of the unit" (e.g., utilities, maintenance, and depreciation). The latter so-called maintenance expenditures, however, must first be allocated to the rental use under the rules of Sec. 280A(e) and then are limited under the rules of Sec. 280A(c)(5).

Sec. 280A(e) requires that the maintenance expenditures attributable to the rental use be allocated using the following formula:

$$\frac{\text{Number of days in the tax year the unit is rented}}{\text{Total number of days in the tax year the unit is used}}$$

All maintenance expenditures are multiplied by this ratio to arrive at a tentative deduction figure. Applying the formula to the facts for Sam and Sara results in the following calculation:

$$\frac{40 \text{ (days rented)}}{60 \text{ (days used)}} = 66.67\% \times \$7,500 = \$5,000$$

In other words, of the total maintenance expenditures of $7,500, the maximum amount allocable to the rental activity that may be deducted is $5,000.

Sec. 280A(c)(5) may further limit deductions for maintenance expenditures. It provides that all expenses (interest, taxes, casualty losses, and maintenance expenditures) allocable to the rental activity cannot exceed the gross rental income. Further, it requires that deductions allowed (e.g., interest, taxes, and casualty losses), whether the unit was used as a rental or not, be allocated to the rental activity and to the amount otherwise allowable as itemized deductions. Any maintenance expenditures are then allowable to the extent that gross rental income exceeds the interest, taxes, and casualty losses allocable to the rental use. Although Sec. 280A(e) does provide the rules for allocating the maintenance expenditures, it provides no guidance for allocating the interest, taxes, and casualty losses. As the editorial commentary in the tax service noted, this has been an area of dispute, with the proposed regulations suggesting one method and the court in *Bolton* suggesting another allocation method.

Regulations. Prop. Reg. Sec. 1.280A-3(c)(1) requires that interest and taxes be allocated in the same fashion as maintenance expenditures under Sec. 280A(e). For Sam and Sara, a tentative conclusion is that the allocation used should be 40:60 (as suggested in the proposed regulation), which would yield the following calculations:

	Total	Rental Use	Itemized Deduction	Not Deductible
Gross rental income	$4,000	$4,000	—	—
Interest & taxes	(4,200)	(2,800)	$1,400	
Excess		$1,200		
Maintenance	(7,500)	(1,200)		$6,300
Total		$ -0-	$1,400	$6,300

Court Decision.   In *Bolton*, the U.S. Court of Appeals for the Ninth Circuit affirmed a decision of the U.S. Tax Court, which held that the interpretation provided in the proposed regulation was inconsistent with the statute, its history, and the legislative purpose behind Sec. 280A. The courts held that interest and taxes, unlike maintenance expenditures, are expenses that continue or accrue on a daily basis throughout the year. Accordingly, they should be allocated according to a ratio of days rented to total days in the year.

For Sam and Sara, a tentative conclusion using an allocation of 40:60 for the maintenance expenditures and 40:365 for interest and taxes, as suggested in *Bolton*, would be as follows:

	Total	Rental Use	Itemized Deduction	Not Deductible
Gross rental income	$4,000	$4,000	—	—
Interest & taxes	(4,200)	(460)	$3,740	
Excess		$3,540		
Maintenance	(7,500)	(3,540)		$3,960
Total		$ -0-	$3,740	$3,960

It should be noted that the proposed regulations were initially issued on August 7, 1980, and amended on July 21, 1983. The ninth circuit's decision in *Bolton* was rendered on December 2, 1982, which was before the last revision to the proposed regulations. The citator provides the information that the IRS has not issued an acquiescence or nonacquiescence to the unfavorable tax court decision, that the ninth circuit's decision has been cited in numerous tax court regular and memorandum decisions, and that its decision has been followed by the tenth circuit in *Edith McKinney v. Comm.*, 732 F.2d 416, 52 A.F.T.R.2d 83-6281, 83-2 USTC ¶9655 (10th Cir. 1983).

Step 4: Reach Conclusions, Make Recommendations, and Communicate the Results

The conclusion reached by the court in *Bolton* is much more favorable for Sara and Sam than the position taken by the proposed regulations. The tax court's allocation formula results in a smaller allocation of interest and taxes to the rental unit, an increase in itemized deductions, and a decrease in taxable income for the current year.

A recommendation to Sara and Sam to follow the allocation formula in *Bolton* should be accompanied by some words of caution. The proposed regulations, which were struck down, have not been amended to reflect the tax court and ninth circuit decisions. The failure to amend the proposed regulations could be a signal that the IRS will continue to litigate similar cases in hopes of receiving a favorable decision in another circuit. You should prepare a research memorandum and letter to Sara and Sam that reflects these findings and conclusions.

The federal income tax system is based on self-assessment, which requires taxpayers to report and pay their taxes correctly. IRS examinations, or audits, can vary from a letter that requests supporting information by mail to a full-scale, continuous examination of large corporations in which teams of IRS agents work at each taxpayer's office. Taxpayers who do not agree to changes suggested by

▲ **THE AUDIT AND APPEAL PROCESS WITHIN THE IRS**

the IRS during an audit can appeal the matter to a higher administrative level within the IRS. Generally, taxpayers cannot be charged with any additional taxes, interest, or penalties without first being formally notified. Whenever settlement cannot be reached with the IRS, the taxpayer can initiate litigation in one of the trial courts described previously.

Tax Return Selection Processes

The IRS cannot possibly examine every return that is filed. It does examine as many returns as possible, given its staffing and facility levels. Currently, this amounts to about only 2 percent of all returns filed. The IRS uses five general methods to verify that taxpayers are properly self-assessing their taxes. One of the most important is a computerized return selection program called the *Discriminant Function System* **(DIF).** Through mathematical analysis of historical data, this program selects those returns with the highest probability of containing errors. Selected returns are typically examined only for specific items such as charitable contributions or employee business expenses. A related program is the *Taxpayer Compliance Measurement Program* **(TCMP).** Returns are randomly selected from different income levels, and every item on the return is comprehensively audited. The results are used to set the parameters for the *DIF* computer selection program.

Virtually all returns are checked for mathematical, tax calculation, and clerical errors during the initial processing of the returns. If an error is discovered under this **document perfection program,** the IRS recalculates the amount of tax due and sends an explanation to the taxpayer. Another program of increasing importance is called the **information-matching program.** Information returns from banks, employers, and others on forms such as the W-2 for wages and withholding and the 1099 for miscellaneous income are matched to the taxpayer's return. For any omitted or incorrect items, the IRS recomputes the tax and sends an explanation to the taxpayer. Finally, a number of **special audit programs** are designed by the IRS and combine computer and manual selection based on various standards that are changed periodically. Some of the standards used include the size of the refund, the amount of adjusted gross income reported, the amount or type of deduction claimed, and so on.

Types of Examinations

There are three basic types of IRS examinations. **Correspondence examinations** are those that can be routinely handled by mail. Most originate at the IRS service centers and involve routine requests for supporting documents such as canceled checks or some other written instruments. A written reply to the questions raised, along with copies of supporting documents, usually completes the examination.

Office examinations are conducted at the local district office of the IRS and usually involve middle-income, nonbusiness returns and small sole proprietorships. The taxpayer is notified by letter of the date and time of the exam, as well as the items for which proof is requested. Most taxpayers appear for themselves, although some may be represented by their return preparers or other tax advisers. The audit is relatively informal, and the IRS agent has considerable discretion in resolving factual questions such as substantiation of travel expenses. For questions of law, however, the agent must follow IRS policy as expressed in Treasury regulations, revenue rulings and procedures, and the like, even if the taxpayer has court decisions that indicate otherwise.

Field examinations are conducted at the taxpayer's place of business and can involve any item on the income tax return as well as any items on the payroll and excise tax returns. These examinations are handled by more experienced IRS agents, and almost all taxpayers are represented by their tax advisers. As with office examinations, IRS agents must follow their own rulings on matters of law and are accorded a great deal of latitude in settling matters of fact.

Settlement Procedures

After the examination, the agent prepares a report, known as the **revenue agent's report (RAR),** describing how each issue was settled and the amount of any additional tax or refund due the taxpayer. The agent also prepares a **waiver of restrictions on assessment (Form 870),** which states that the taxpayer waives any restrictions against assessment and collection of the tax by the IRS. Both items are mailed to the taxpayer in a letter commonly called the **30-day letter,** along with an IRS publication describing the taxpayer's appeal rights.

A signed Form 870 means that the taxpayer agrees to the proposed changes, but it is not binding on either the taxpayer or the IRS. The taxpayer merely agrees to pay the additional tax due while reserving the right to file for a refund in a subsequent court action. Generally, the IRS rejects a settlement reached by its agents only if there is fraud or a misrepresentation of a material fact.

Administrative Appeals

A taxpayer who does not agree with the agent's report may request a meeting with agents from the **IRS Appeals Division** within 30 days of the date of the letter. If the additional tax due exceeds $2,500, the taxpayer must include a written response to the agent's findings; the taxpayer's response is called a **protest letter.** When the amount is less than $2,500 or is the result of a correspondence or office examination, no written protest is required.

The administrative appeal process allows taxpayers one additional opportunity to reach a settlement before resorting to the courts. The appeals division has the authority to consider the **hazards of litigation.** For example, when the facts or the law are uncertain, or both, the appeals division may settle issues it does not want to litigate, even if the IRS position has some merit. After what may be lengthy negotiations, taxpayers who finally reach an agreement with the IRS, or who simply don't want to pursue the matter, sign the Form 870 (or Form 870-AD, if the IRS has conceded some issues) and pay the full amount of the deficiency plus any penalties and interest.

Taxpayers unable to reach an agreement in the appeals division, or who have bypassed the appeals division by failing to respond to the 30-day letter, are sent a **statutory notice of deficiency.** This letter is the official notification by the IRS that it intends to assess or charge the taxpayer for some additional taxes and is commonly referred to as a **90-day letter.**

Taxpayers who are not interested in going to court can simply wait 90 days to have the deficiency formally assessed and then pay any additional amounts due. Taxpayers who want to litigate in district court or the claims court first must pay the amounts due and file for a refund in the court of their choice. Taxpayers who do not want to pay first must file a petition with the U.S. Tax Court within 90 days of the date of the letter. The decision to take an unresolved issue to court involves a number of additional factors and typically is made only with the advice of legal counsel specializing in tax litigation.

▲ SUMMARY

Tax research is the process by which the primary tax law authorities are located, evaluated, and applied to a specific factual situation. The different types of primary authorities are related to the three principal functions of government: legislative, administrative, and judicial. Legislative authorities include the Constitution, treaties, the Internal Revenue Code of 1986, and the committee reports issued by Congress as new tax laws are enacted. Administrative authorities consist of Treasury regulations, revenue rulings, revenue procedures, and other miscellaneous pronouncements issued by the Internal Revenue Service. Judicial authorities include decisions by the various trial and appellate courts in tax-related matters.

Secondary authorities are all other publications that are helpful in locating, evaluating, and applying the primary authorities to the specific factual situation under consideration. They consist primarily of tax services, citators, and computer software systems that research tax databases, tax journals, and tax newsletters.

A systematic procedure must be followed in order to locate, evaluate, and apply the primary authorities to a specific factual situation. The steps involved in this process are to establish the facts and identify the issues, locate the relevant authorities, evaluate and apply the authorities to the facts, reach conclusions and make recommendations, and communicate the results to interested parties.

This chapter also reviewed the audit and appeal process within the Internal Revenue Service. Among the procedures used by the IRS to select returns for examination are the *Taxpayer Compliance Measurement Program*, the document perfection program, the information-matching program, and a number of special audit programs. Selected returns are subject to correspondence, office, or field examinations. An appeal process is available within the IRS if the taxpayer disagrees with the results of the examination. Taxpayers unable to reach an agreement with the IRS through the appeals process may proceed to court for ultimate resolution of the tax issues.

▲ KEY TERMS

30-day letter (p. 697)

90-day letter (p. 697)

acquiescence (p. 680)

action on decision (AOD) (p. 681)

chief counsel's memorandum (p. 681)

citator (p. 687)

cited case (p. 687)

citing case (p. 687)

computer-assisted tax research (CATR) (p. 688)

correspondence examination (p. 696)

Cumulative Bulletin (C.B.) (p. 685)

Discriminant Function System (DIF) (p. 696)

document perfection program (p. 696)

Federal Reporter, 2d series (F.2d) (p. 686)

Federal Supplement, (F. Supp.) (p. 686)

Federal Tax Citator (p. 688)

field examination (p. 697)

final regulation (p. 680)

general counsel's memorandum (GCM) (p. 681)

hazards of litigation (p. 697)

information-matching program (p. 696)

Internal Revenue Bulletin (I.R.B.) (p. 683)

interpretive regulation (p. 679)

IRS Appeals Division (p. 697)

legislative regulation (p. 680)

letter ruling (p. 681)

nonacquiescence (p. 680)

office examination (p. 696)

primary authorities (p. 673)

private letter ruling (LTR) (p. 681)

proposed regulation (p. 680)

protest letter (p. 697)

reporter (p. 685)

Reports of the United States Tax Court (T.C.) (p. 685)

revenue agent's report (RAR) (p. 697)

revenue procedure (p. 680)

revenue ruling (p. 680)
secondary authorities (p. 673)
special audit program (p. 696)
statutory notice of deficiency
 (p. 697)
Supreme Court Reports (S. Ct.)
 (p. 686)
Tax Court memorandum decision
 (p. 682)
Tax Court Memorandum Decisions
 (TCM) (p. 685)

Tax Court regular decision
 (p. 682)
tax service (p. 686)
*Taxpayer Compliance Measurement
 Program* (TCMP) (p. 696)
technical advice memorandum
 (TAM) (p. 681)
technical memorandum (TM)
 (p. 681)
temporary regulation (p. 680)
trial court (p. 682)

United States Reports (U.S.) (p. 686)
U.S. Claims Court (p. 682)
U.S. Courts of Appeals (p. 683)
U.S. Court of Appeals for the
 Federal Circuit (p. 683)
U.S. District Court (p. 682)
U.S. Supreme Court (p. 683)
U.S. Tax Court (p. 682)
waiver of restrictions on
 assessment (Form 870) (p. 697)

▲ PRIMARY TAX LAW SOURCES

[1] See Secs. 8001–8023 for information on the organization, membership, powers, and other matters relating to the Joint Committee on Taxation.

[2] Sec. 894—Requires application of the Internal Revenue Code to give due regard to any treaty obligations of the United States.

[3] Sec. 7801—Specifies the powers and the duties of the secretary of the Treasury.

[4] Sec. 7802—Establishes the position of commissioner of the Internal Revenue Service, whose duties are to be prescribed by the secretary of the Treasury.

[5] Sec. 7805—Authorizes the secretary of the Treasury to issue the rules and regulations necessary for the enforcement of the income tax law.

[6] The abbreviations given here are those commonly used in citing various tax materials. However, some of these abbreviations are different from those specified by *The Bluebook, A Uniform System of Citation* (the lawyer's bible) and do not appear in the list of abbreviations used by the *Cumulative Bulletin*, to which the *Bluebook* defers on tax matters. Thus, tax researchers occasionally may encounter cites to Tech. Adv. Mem. instead of TAM, to Tech. Mem. instead of TM, and to PLR instead of LTR.

[7] See Secs. 7401–7434 for organization, jurisdiction, and other procedural matters relating to the Tax Court. Similar matters for district court cases involving tax-related issues are covered in Sections 7401–7434.

▲ DISCUSSION QUESTIONS

1. Differentiate primary tax law authorities and secondary tax law authorities.

2. Briefly describe the three categories of primary authorities and the different types of authorities within each category.

3. Name the different types of secondary authorities.

4. On what grounds have tax protesters challenged the income tax?

5. The Internal Revenue Code is just one part of the *U.S. Code*. Explain.

6. Name the different subdivisions of the Internal Revenue Code.

7. What would be the general nature of Sec. 612? Sec. 6601?

8. How many chapters are there within Subtitle A?

9. What are some of the things to look out for when reading the Code?

10. Give examples of how the Code is sometimes used to achieve economic and social objectives.

11. Briefly describe the process by which a new tax law is passed.

12. What are the three reports that are issued as part of the legislative process?

13. How are the Joint Conference Committee and the Joint Committee on Taxation different?

14. What is a Treasury regulation? Are they binding on the courts?

15. Differentiate an interpretive regulation and a legislative regulation.

16. Differentiate a proposed regulation and a temporary regulation.

17. What are revenue rulings? revenue procedures?

18. How are a revenue ruling and a Treasury regulation different? a revenue ruling and a private letter ruling?

19. What does it mean when the IRS issues an acquiescence or nonacquiescence?

20. What is the difference between a revenue ruling and a case in which the IRS has issued an acquiescence?

21. Name the other types of pronouncements issued by the IRS, and briefly describe their content.

22. What are the three trial courts? Which is most important?

23. What is meant by the *Golsen* rule?

24. Do district courts have to follow the decisions of all circuit courts?

25. What does it mean when the Supreme Court issues a writ of certiorari?

26. Assume that the Supreme Court interprets a certain Code section in a manner that members of Congress believe is contrary to what they meant when they originally enacted that part of the Code. What (if anything) can Congress do?

27. Interpret the following citations:
    a. SENATE FINANCE COMMITTEE, S. REP. NO. 2, 97th Cong., 2d Sess. (April 15, 1982).
    b. LTR 8101067.
    c. Rev. Proc. 78-172, 1978-2 C.B. 22.
    d. Lacy v. Comm., 344 F.2d 123, 89-1 USTC ¶1221, 43 A.F.T.R. 89-2233 (9th Cir. 1989).

28. Provide the correct citations for the following:
    a. The fifteenth revenue procedure issued in 1993 and found on page 12 of the third *Internal Revenue Bulletin* issued in 1993.
    b. Subsection (a) of the first temporary income tax regulation interpreting Section 63.
    c. An acquiescence issued by the IRS on page 1 of volume 1 of the 1992 *Cumulative Bulletin* related to *Chasteen v. Comm.*, which was reported on page 132 of volume 77 of *Reports of the United States Tax Court* in 1991.

29. Why is it that some court decisions will have two or three different citations?

30. Describe the two major categories of tax services.

31. When can a researcher rely on an editorial opinion expressed in the tax services?

32. Differentiate a cited case and a citing case.

33. What is meant by the history of a cited case?

34. Assume that you have found an excellent article in *Tax Notes* that provides a favorable interpretation of Sec. 469. Can you rely on that article as authority for your position? In general, what role do tax periodicals and newsletters play in tax research?

35. What are some of the advantages and disadvantages of CATR?

36. Briefly describe the steps involved in tax research.

37. Briefly describe the different types of programs used by the IRS to select a return for audit.

38. What are the three different types of IRS examinations?

39. What is included in the 30-day letter, and what options does the taxpayer have after receiving one?

40. What does the 90-day letter represent, and what are the choices the taxpayer has after receiving one?

Income Problems

41. Gary is an internal auditor for Bodine Information Systems (BIF). In 1992, BIF opened a large production plant in Las Vegas, Nevada. Subsequently, Gary has had to spend several months each year at the Las Vegas facility. Gary has always fancied himself a proficient blackjack player. During his trips to Las Vegas, he stays at a hotel on the Strip and spends a considerable amount of his off-duty time gambling.

In February 1993, Gary applies for (and receives) a $20,000 line of credit at the hotel to be used for gambling. The line of credit allows him to receive gambling chips in exchange for signing markers. The markers are negotiable drafts payable to the hotel and drawn on Gary's personal bank account. The hotel's practice is to hold the markers for 60 days, at which time Gary pays them with a personal check.

By the beginning of 1994, Gary is gambling heavily at the hotel. He requests and receives an increase in his credit limit to $100,000. Gary continues to lose heavily, and through some accounting oversights by the hotel, his debt has risen to $325,000 by October 1994. The checks that Gary writes to cover the markers are returned for insufficient funds, and the hotel immediately cuts off his credit. The hotel subsequently files suit in state court, seeking repayment of the $325,000 owed on the markers.

In early 1995, Gary negotiates a settlement with the hotel whereby he will settle the debt for 4 monthly payments of $25,000 ($100,000). Gary pays the $100,000 per the terms of the agreement. He seeks your advice as to the tax consequences of the settlement with the hotel. That is, does he have to include in his gross income the amount of the debt he didn't have to repay?

42. Adrian is a salesperson who represents several different wholesale companies. On January 2, 1995, she receives by mail a commission check from Ace Distributors in the amount of $10,000 and dated December 30, 1994. Adrian is concerned about the year in which the $10,000 is taxable. Although the check is dated 1994, she contends that it would have been unreasonable for her to drive the 50 miles to the Ace offices on a Saturday (December 30, 1994, is a Saturday) to collect the check. Further, Adrian maintains that even if she had made the trip on Saturday to collect the check, by the time she returned home, her bank would have closed and she could not have received credit for the check until Monday. Adrian would like you to determine whether she should include the $10,000 on her 1994 or 1995 tax return.

43. Your client, Bonita, a successful California insurance broker, receives $500,000 in settlement of her defamation suit against XYZ Credit Reporting Co. and wants to know if any of it is taxable. She explains that a few years earlier she had applied to the Mutual General Life Insurance Co. for an agency license. Mutual General requested a credit report. XYZ supplied Mutual General with a report that was false and defamatory and that ruined her personal and business reputation. The case was settled for a lump sum of $500,000. The settlement agreement made no distinction between damages awarded for injury to her personal reputation and those for loss of future income. It just referred to her ruined career, humiliation, and mental anguish.

Read and analyze the following authorities, and determine how much, if any, of the $500,000 settlement payment must be included in Bonita's gross income.

Sec. 104.
Roemer v. Comm., 716 F.2d 693 (9th Cir. 1983).
Threlkeld v. Comm., 848 F.2d 81 (6th Cir. 1988).
Keller v. Comm., 62 TCM 401 (1991).
Rev. Rul. 85-143.

44. Hawaii law requires the state to deposit a portion of its annual pineapple income in the Hawaiian Long-lasting Fund. All income from the fund is deposited in the state's general fund. The fund's general manager is permitted to use the funds to buy only certain income-producing assets, such as government and corporate obligations, preferred and common stock of U.S. corporations, and equity interests in partnerships and other entities that invest in real estate. Each year, a portion of the fund's income is transferred to a dividend fund that distributes the dividends to native Hawaiians.

At issue is whether such payments constitute income to native Hawaiians and, if so, what type of income is being received—is any income generated from the distributions either investment income or passive activity income?

45. After Maria and Tatsuo are divorced, their 2 minor children continue to live with Maria. Pursuant to their divorce decree, Tatsuo pays Maria $1,000 per month in child support and $1,800 per month in alimony. The divorce decree specifies that, in the event of a court-ordered increase in child support, the alimony payment amount will decrease by the amount of the child support increase. That is, Tatsuo's total monthly payment cannot exceed $2,800. Read the following authorities and determine how much gross income Maria has from the payments received from Tatsuo:

> Sec. 71.
> Temp. Reg. Sec. 1.71–1T.
> Madeline Davis Heller, 68 TCM 838 (1994).

46. Lorissa owes Waterbury State Bank $200,000. During the current year, she is unable to make the required payments on the loan and negotiates the following terms to extinguish the debt. Lorissa transfers to Waterbury ownership of investment property with a value of $90,000 and a basis of $55,000, common stock with a value of $50,000 and a basis of $70,000. Lorissa also pays Waterbury $5,000 cash and Waterbury forgives the remaining amount of debt. Before the agreement, Lorissa's assets are $290,000 and her liabilities are $440,000.

Read and analyze the following authorities and determine how much gross income Lorissa has from the extinguishment of the debt:

> Sec. 108.
> Reg. Sec. 1.61–12.
> Reg. Sec. 1.1001–2.
> Julian S. Danenberg, 73 T.C. 370 (1979).
> James J. Gehl, 102 T.C. 74 (1994).

Deduction Problems

47. Mason is the owner of Brickman, Inc., which specializes in laying brick patios, terraces, and walkways. In 1995, Mason bids on a contract with State University to build several large terraces as well as the walkways adjoining the terraces. Although he is the low bidder, Mason is approached by Don, purchasing agent for State University, who lets Mason know that in order to secure the contract, Mason must make a cash payment to a firm that is building a swimming pool for Don. Mason makes the required payment and secures the contract. Later, Don demands, and Mason makes, a payment to a rancher for the purchase of a horse for Don's children. The payments made by Mason are not illegal under state law. Mason seeks your advice as to the deductibility of these payments.

Read and analyze the following authorities, and determine whether Mason can deduct the payments he made to Don:

> Sec. 162.
> Raymond Bertolini Trucking v. Comm., 736 F.2d 1120 (6th Cir. 1984).
> Car-Ron Asphalt Paving Co. Inc. v. Comm., 758 F.2d 1132 (6th Cir. 1985).

48. Jefferson is a grade school teacher whose annual income from teaching is $20,000. Jefferson has always enjoyed bowling, and in 1994 his local pro urges him to turn professional. He subsequently begins working for his pro as an unpaid assistant and enters an apprenticeship program with the Professional Bowlers' Association of America (PBA). As an apprentice, he accumulates credits toward becoming a member of the PBA by taking approved classes, working as an assistant pro, and playing in pro tournaments. Jefferson expects to be approved as a full member of the PBA next year.

Although Jefferson continues to teach full time, he goes to the bowling alley each day after school and practices after fulfilling his duties as an unpaid assistant. During the summer months, he spends 12 to 15 hours each day at the bowling alley. In addition, he participates in as many PBA tournaments as he can work into his schedule.

Jefferson has come to you for advice on the deductibility of the expenses he has incurred in his bowling career. Since deciding to turn pro, he has won money in tournaments every year. However, his expenses have exceeded his earnings by $5,000 to $10,000 per year.

49. Seaweed Salvagers is a corporation engaged in the production of various foodstuffs from seaweed. Seaweed's primary salvaging plant is located in California. Because the salvaging technology hasn't changed through the years, Seaweed's primary salvaging equipment was purchased in the early 1970s. At that time, the primary insulation material used in the machines was asbestos. In 1986, the Occupational Safety and Health Administration lowered the standard for concentrations of allowable airborne asbestos fibers in the workplace. In addition, California requires employers to monitor airborne concentration levels to ensure that they do not exceed permissible exposure levels.

To comply with these requirements and to provide its workers with a safe workplace, Seaweed institutes an asbestos abatement program. After careful study, Seaweed determines that the major asbestos problem occurs during ordinary repairs and maintenance of the equipment. Initially, Seaweed institutes a program of continuous monitoring and encapsulation during repair and maintenance periods. However, Seaweed finds that this is inadequate because (a) it did not ensure that all parts of the plant are in compliance, (b) repairs and maintenance costs are increasing dramatically, and (c) the extra down time during maintenance and repairs causes production to drop to a level that is financially unprofitable.

During the current year, Seaweed begins removing the asbestos insulation from the machinery and replacing it with an alternative, environmentally friendly insulation material. The new insulation material is about 15% less efficient than the asbestos material and results in no energy or other cost savings. The cost of replacing the insulation in 1 machine is about $13,000. The annual repair and maintenance cost of 1 machine averages $45,000. Each machine has an estimated fair market value of $600,000.

Seaweed believes that it should be able to expense the cost of removing the asbestos insulation and replacing it with the alternative insulation. Read and analyze the following authorities, and determine whether Seaweed can deduct the asbestos removal costs:

Sec. 263.
Reg. Sec. 1.162-4.
Reg. Sec. 1.263(a)-1.
Indopco Inc. v. Comm., 112 S. Ct. 1038 (1992).
LTR 9240004.
Rev. Rul. 94-38.

50. Hanna and Helmut, a married couple, have the following items of income during 1995:

Salaries (earned equally)	$28,000
Taxable interest	13,000
Tax-exempt interest	3,000
Social Security benefits	8,000

Hanna is covered by her employer's retirement plan; Helmut is not covered by any type of pension plan. Hanna and Helmut would like to make the maximum deductible contribution to their individual retirement account (IRA).

Hanna and Helmut seek your advice in determining their maximum IRA contribution deduction in 1995 as well as their 1995 adjusted gross income. Read and analyze the following authorities to determine Hanna and Helmut's maximum IRA contribution deduction and their adjusted gross income for 1995:

Sec. 219.
Sec. 86.
Announcement 88-38.

51. Don and Rosetta purchase a new residence on February 19, 1992, for $100,000. Because they are unable to obtain conventional financing, they negotiate the following terms with the seller. They put down $5,000, and the seller agrees to finance the remaining $95,000 with an interest-only note for 3 years. The note carries an interest rate of 10% (simple interest, payable annually on February 19) and requires payment of the principal amount on or before February 19, 1995. On January 15, 1995, Don and Rosetta obtain a 30-year mortgage from First International Savings and Loan and pay the $95,000 balance due on the original note. As part of the refinancing, Don and Rosetta pay points (from their own funds) totaling $2,850. The payment of points is customary where Don and Rosetta live, and the amount is in line with what other lenders are charging. Don and Rosetta would like to know the proper tax treatment of the refinancing points they paid.

Don and Rosetta seek your advice in determining the deduction for the points they paid to acquire the mortgage from First International Savings and Loan. Read and analyze the following authorities to determine the deduction for the points in 1995:

Sec. 163.
Sec. 461.
James Richard Huntsman, 91 T.C. 917 (1988).
Huntsman v. Comm., 905 F.2d 1182 (1990).

52. Larry is a professional gambler, specializing in dog racing. He spends 50 to 60 hours per week studying racing forms and placing bets at the track. During the current year, Larry has winnings of $240,000 on $380,000 of bets placed. Larry has no other business income. His wife Jane is employed as a university professor and earns $55,000 annually. They also have $15,000 in income from various investments. Because Larry devotes all of his time to his dog-racing activities, he feels that he should be able to deduct the loss he incurred in his "business" against their other income.

Read and analyze the following authorities to determine the deduction Larry is allowed for his dog-racing losses:

Sec. 162.
Sec. 165.
Commissioner v. Groetzinger, 480 U.S. 23 (1987).
Pete C. Valenti, 68 TCM 730 (1994).

Loss Problems

53. Sterling is a college professor with an extensive stock portfolio. Last year, Sterling met Wheeler, a stockbroker with the firm of Ransom, LaForge, and Adkins. In order to get Sterling's business, Wheeler offered to use his investment expertise on Sterling's behalf, for which he would receive 1/4 of any profits and would also assume 1/4 of any losses if Sterling would give Wheeler $300,000 to invest. Sterling accepted Wheeler's offer. During 1994, Wheeler makes a net profit of $120,000 on trades with Sterling's money. On January 31, 1995, Sterling pays Wheeler $30,000 per their agreement. In addition, Sterling pays normal brokerage commissions on the purchases and sales that Wheeler executes in making the $120,000 net profit on the $300,000 investment. The commissions are properly included in the calculation of the net profit. Sterling would like to know the proper tax treatment of the $30,000 payment he made to Wheeler.

54. Kimberly is a developer of apartment complexes. In 1993, Kimberly forms Deckside Apartments, a partnership, and initiates development of the Deckside Apartment complex. The Staten Investment Fund agrees to provide financing for the development at an annual interest rate of 10%, secured by a mortgage on the property. However, state law limits the annual interest rate for noncorporate borrowers to 8%. To avoid this state usury law, Kimberly incorporates Hump Day, Inc., under state law. Kimberly is the only shareholder of Hump Day, Inc. The next day, Deckside Apartments and Hump Day, Inc., enter into a written agreement under which the corporation holds title to the apartments solely for the purpose of obtaining financing. Hump Day cannot convey, assign, or encumber the property without the permission of Deckside, has no obligation to maintain the property, assumes no liability regarding the financing, and is held harmless from any liability it might sustain as the agent for Deckside.

Staten Investment Fund agrees to provide the financing to Hump Day, Inc., as the corporate nominee of Deckside, provided that Kimberly personally guarantees the note. Upon completion of the apartments, Kimberly, through Hump Day, Inc., obtains the permanent financing from Staten and pays off the short-term construction loans that she had obtained for the construction of the apartments. An apartment manager is hired to oversee the operation of the apartments. All rents collected are deposited to and expenses paid from an account opened by the partnership.

During 1995, the apartments generate substantial operating losses. Kimberly seeks your advice as to the proper treatment of these losses.

55. Fingeland's Forest Choppers is a corporation engaged in the production of timber and lumber. In 1993, Fingeland's reforests a clear-cut area by planting nursery-grown seedlings. In 1994, a severe drought kills 80% of the seedlings, forcing Fingeland's to replant the entire area in 1995. The loss is not covered by insurance. Fingeland's had capitalized the cost of preparing the site for reforestation and the seedling planting costs in a deferred reforestation account in 1993.

Fingeland's would like to know whether it can deduct as a casualty loss the costs it incurred to replant the clear-cut area in 1995.

Read and analyze the following authorities, and determine whether Fingeland's can deduct the costs as a casualty loss, and if so, in what year the loss is deductible:

Sec. 165.
Sec. 611.
Reg. Sec. 1.611-3.
Rev. Rul. 81-2.
Rev. Rul. 87-59.
Rev. Rul. 90-61.

56. Mae and Vernon are equal owners of Denson, Inc., an S corporation. Denson owns 5,000 shares of stock in Cowboy Country. Denson paid $300,000 for the Cowboy Country stock, which is qualified small business stock. During the current year, Denson sells 4,000 shares of Cowboy Country for $100,000. Denson's accountant is preparing the current-year tax return and is unsure of the reporting of the stock sale to Mae and Vernon.

Read and analyze the following authorities and determine how the sale of the stock should be reported to Mae and Vernon:

> Sec. 1244.
> Sec. 1363.
> Reg. Sec. 1.1244(a)-1.
> Virgil D. Rath, 101 T.C. 196 (1994).

Property Problems

57. Dagwood has come to you with a pressing problem. In November 1987, he purchased an office building that he had rented out to various businesses. On May 2, 1995, a fire swept through the building, totally destroying it. To make matters worse, his lifelong accountant was trapped in the building and perished in the fire (along with all of Dagwood's income tax records). The following is all of the information Dagwood has available about the building.

Dagwood is sure that he purchased the building in November 1987, because he has a property tax statement indicating that the land was revalued at $30,000 and the building at $300,000 for property tax purposes at that time. The date is further supported by a canceled check dated November 28, 1987, for $550,000, payable to the company from which he had purchased the property. Although he doesn't have the tax records to support any deductions on the property, he's confident that his former accountant took the maximum deductions allowable on the property as it had always produced a loss for income tax purposes.

He recently received a check for $400,000 from his insurance company for the destruction of the building. In the interim, Dagwood has been obtaining estimates of the cost of putting another office building on the property. However, his analysis of the construction costs, combined with the potential rental income generated by the building, indicates that putting another office building on the property would not be profitable in either the short or the long term. He has received an offer to sell the land for $84,000. If he does sell the land, he is considering purchasing an upscale apartment building in another part of town.

Before he proceeds with the sale of the land and the purchase of the apartment building, he needs to know the tax effects of the fire and the sale of the land. Dagwood is afraid that he may have a big tax bill to pay and won't be able to afford the apartment building after he settles up with the IRS.

Read and analyze the following authorities and determine how much gain or loss, if any, Dagwood will have to recognize from the fire if he purchases the apartment building:

> Sec. 1033.
> Rev. Rul. 64-237.
> Rev. Rul. 59-361.
> Henry G. Masser, 30 T.C. 741 (1958).

58. On November 3, 1993, Jim and Pam sell their principal residence for $150,000, incurring selling expenses of $10,000. They had purchased the residence in 1988 at a cost of $90,000 and had made no significant improvements to it before the sale. In filing their 1993 return, they properly defer recognition of the gain on the sale, as they anticipate purchasing a new principal residence of equal or greater value within 2 years.

In 1994, before they purchase a new home, Jim and Pam divorce. In February 1995, Jim purchases a personal residence for $80,000. Pam does not purchase a new residence before November 3, 1995.

Read and analyze the following authorities, and determine how much gain, if any, Jim must report on the sale of the residence:

Sec. 1034.
Reg. Sec. 1.1034-1.
Rev. Rul. 74-250.
Rev. Rul. 80-5.

59. Martha, 65, sells her residence on March 15, 1995, for $165,000 net of commissions and other selling costs. She purchased the residence on July 20, 1992, for $105,000. Before the purchase, Martha sold her previous home on April 5, 1992, for $95,000. Martha had paid $80,000 for the residence and had made $10,000 in capital improvements before the sale. Martha moves to a retirement community and therefore does not plan to purchase another residence.

Martha asks you to prepare her 1995 tax return. In going over her previous year returns, you find that the accountant who prepared her 1992 tax return had elected to exclude the $5,000 gain on the 1992 sale rather than defer the gain. When you ask Martha about this, she is confused. She tells you that she knows that if you sell one house for $95,000 and purchase another house for $105,000, none of the gain is taxable. Because no gain was shown on the 1992 return, she signed it without reviewing the details.

Read the following authorities, and determine how much gain Martha will have to report on the 1995 sale:

Sec. 121.
Sec. 1034.
Sec. 6511.
Reg. Sec. 1.121-4.
Reg. Sec. 1.1034-1.
Mary K. Robarts, 103 T.C. 72 (1994).

Accounting Methods/Procedure Problems

60. The Kona Rural Electric Co-op (KREC) is an accrual basis public utility. All new customers are required to pay a deposit equal to 3 times the customer's estimated monthly bill or $100, whichever is greater. The purpose of the deposit is to ensure that timely payment is made on accounts. The funds so received are not segregated from other KREC funds and are used in the ordinary course of business. Interest at the rate of 5% is paid annually on the deposits. Customers may elect to receive a check for the interest or may accept the payment as a credit on their monthly bill.

KREC's policy is to refund the deposit when a customer discontinues service or when the customer has made timely monthly payments for 8 consecutive months or for 9 of 12 consecutive months. When deposits are refunded, interest is paid on the deposit through the date of the refund. KREC's experience with the deposit requirement is that 80% of all deposits are returned within 1 year of receipt. Approximately 5% of all deposits are ultimately used to satisfy delinquent customer accounts.

KREC would like to know whether the deposits should be included in income when they are received or deferred until they are used to satisfy customer accounts.

61. Wildcat Enterprises (WCE) is a client involved in the transportation of African lions from Zambia to the United States. In 1992, the cost of the lions increases substantially because of unrest within the local government and wildlife conservationists' concerns. As a result, WCE's inventories and receivables are substantially higher than in prior years. WCE has always used the cash method to report its income.

During the 1995 audit of WCE's 1993 return, the IRS agent determines that the cash method does not properly reflect income. Accordingly, the agent recomputes taxable income using the accrual method and assesses a deficiency of $750,000. In addition, the agent disallows a deduction for some personal use of the company airplane and assesses an additional deficiency of $500.

After much discussion, the agent agrees that the use of the wrong accounting method does not constitute negligence. However, she does determine that the improper deduction related to the airplane is due to negligence and adds a 5% negligence penalty of $37,525 (i.e., she assesses the penalty based on the total deficiency of $750,500).

WCE has come to you for advice. WCE believes that it should not be assessed the negligence penalty on the total underpayment, because only $500 of the deficiency is due to negligence. Read and analyze the following authorities, and determine whether WCE should be assessed the negligence penalty on the total underpayment or just on the $500 that was due to negligence:

Sec. 6662.
Asphalt Products Co. Inc. v. Comm., 482 U.S. 117 (1987).

62. Tomiko owns the copyright to several classic Motown songs. In 1993, he became aware that Tinseltown Records was selling several of his songs without his permission. He sues Tinseltown seeking $1,000,000 in damages. In 1995, the court awards Tomiko $500,000 in compensatory damages, $50,000 in prejudgment interest, postjudgment interest to the date of payment, and court costs. Tinseltown is aware that Tomiko is likely to appeal the judgment and offers to settle for $600,000 with no payment of postjudgment interest or court costs. On the advice of his attorney, Tomiko rejects the settlement offer.

On December 29, 1995, Tomiko receives a check for $600,000 from Tinseltown. An accompanying letter notes that the payment is in full settlement of the order of the court. Tomiko believes that if he cashes the check, he will forfeit his right to appeal the judgment, the postjudgment interest, and court costs. Accordingly, he immediately returns the check to Tinseltown via overnight mail, stating in a letter that his appeal rights are not exhausted and he is returning the check until such time as the issue is settled. Tinseltown remails the check on December 31, 1995. Included with the check is a letter advising Tomiko that Tinseltown intends to deduct the $600,000 in 1995 and that the funds are available for his unrestricted use. On January 15, 1996, Tomiko files an appeal seeking an increase in the damage award. The next day, he deposits Tinseltown's check into his business account. On June 5, 1996, the appeals court rejects Tomiko's appeal for higher damages. Tomiko is a cash basis taxpayer. In what year should he include the $600,000 in income?

Read the following authorities, and determine the proper year for Tomiko to include the $600,000 in income:

Sec. 451.
Reg. Sec. 1.451-2.
Walter I. Bones, 4 T.C. 415 (1944).
Fromson v. Comm., 74 A.F.T.R.2d, 5642 (1994), 94-2 USTC ¶50, 425.

TAX RATE SCHEDULES AND TAX TABLES

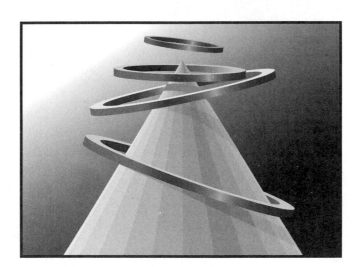

- 1995 Individual Tax Rate Schedules
- 1994 Individual Tax Rate Schedules
- Corporate Tax Rate Schedule
- 1995 Estate and Trust Tax Rate Schedule
- 1994 Estate and Trust Tax Rate Schedule
- 1994 Individual Tax Table

▲ 1995 INDIVIDUAL TAX RATE SCHEDULES

▲ Table A–1

SINGLE TAXPAYERS

If Taxable Income Is Over	But Not Over	The Tax Is	of the Amount Over
$ 0	23,350	................15%	$ 0
23,350	56,550	$ 3,502.50 + 28%	23,350
56,550	117,950	12,798.50 + 31%	56,550
117,950	256,500	31,832.50 + 36%	117,950
256,500	....	81,710.50 + 39.6%	256,500

▲ Table A–2

MARRIED TAXPAYERS
FILING JOINTLY
AND SURVIVING SPOUSE

If Taxable Income Is Over	But Not Over	The Tax Is	of the Amount Over
$ 0	39,000	................15%	$ 0
39,000	94,250	$ 5,850.00 + 28%	39,000
94,250	143,600	21,320.00 + 31%	94,250
143,600	256,500	36,618.50 + 36%	143,600
256,500	....	77,262.50 + 39.6%	256,500

▲ Table A–3

HEAD OF HOUSEHOLD

If Taxable Income Is Over	But Not Over	The Tax Is	of the Amount Over
$ 0	31,250	................15%	$ 0
31,250	80,750	$ 4,687.50 + 28%	31,250
80,750	130,800	18,547.50 + 31%	80,750
130,800	256,500	34,063.00 + 36%	130,800
256,500	....	79,315.00 + 39.6%	256,500

▲ Table A–4

MARRIED TAXPAYERS
FILING SEPARATELY

If Taxable Income Is Over	But Not Over	The Tax Is	of the Amount Over
$ 0	19,500	................15%	$ 0
19,500	47,125	$ 2,925.00 + 28%	19,500
47,125	71,800	10,660.00 + 31%	47,125
71,800	128,250	18,309.25 + 36%	71,800
128,250	....	38,631.25 + 39.6%	128,250

▲ 1994 INDIVIDUAL TAX RATE SCHEDULES

If Taxable Income Is Over	But Not Over	The Tax Is	of the Amount Over
$ 0	22,750	................15%	$ 0
22,750	55,100	$ 3,412.50 + 28%	22,750
55,100	115,000	12,470.50 + 31%	55,100
115,000	250,000	31,039.50 + 36%	115,000
250,000	....	79,639.50 + 39.6%	250,000

▲ Table A–5

SINGLE TAXPAYERS

If Taxable Income Is Over	But Not Over	The Tax Is	of the Amount Over
$ 0	38,000	................15%	$ 0
38,000	91,850	$ 5,700.00 + 28%	38,000
91,850	140,000	20,778.00 + 31%	91,850
140,000	250,000	35,704.50 + 36%	140,000
250,000	....	75,304.50 + 39.6%	250,000

▲ Table A–6

MARRIED TAXPAYERS
FILING JOINTLY
AND SURVIVING SPOUSE

If Taxable Income Is Over	But Not Over	The Tax Is	of the Amount Over
$ 0	30,500	................15%	$ 0
30,500	78,700	$ 4,575.00 + 28%	30,500
78,700	127,500	18,071.00 + 31%	78,700
127,500	250,000	33,199.00 + 36%	127,500
250,000	....	77,299.00 + 39.6%	250,000

▲ Table A–7

HEAD OF HOUSEHOLD

If Taxable Income Is Over	But Not Over	The Tax Is	of the Amount Over
$ 0	19,000	................15%	$ 0
19,000	45,925	$ 2,850.00 + 28%	19,000
45,925	70,000	10,389.00 + 31%	45,925
70,000	125,000	17,852.25 + 36%	70,000
125,000	....	37,652.25 + 39.6%	125,000

▲ Table A–8

MARRIED TAXPAYERS
FILING SEPARATELY

▲ CORPORATE TAX RATE SCHEDULE

▲ Table A–9

If Taxable Income Is Over	But Not Over	The Tax Is	of the Amount Over
$ 0	50,000	...............15%	$ 0
50,000	75,000	$ 7,500 + 25%	50,000
75,000	100,000	13,750 + 34%	75,000
100,000	335,000	22,250 + 39%	100,000
335,000	10,000,000	113,900 + 34%	335,000
10,000,000	15,000,000	3,400,000 + 35%	10,000,000
15,000,000	18,333,333	5,150,000 + 38%	15,000,000
18,333,333	....	6,416,667 + 35%	18,333,333

▲ 1995 ESTATE AND TRUST TAX RATE SCHEDULE

▲ Table A–10

If Taxable Income Is Over	But Not Over	The Tax Is	of the Amount Over
$ 0	1,550	..............15%	$ 0
1,550	3,700	$ 232.50 + 28%	1,550
3,700	5,600	834.50 + 31%	3,700
5,600	7,650	1,423.50 + 36%	5,600
7,650	....	2,161.50 + 39.6%	7,650

▲ 1994 ESTATE AND TRUST TAX RATE SCHEDULE

▲ Table A–11

If Taxable Income Is Over	But Not Over	The Tax Is	of the Amount Over
$ 0	1,500	..............15%	$ 0
1,500	3,600	$ 225.00 + 28%	1,500
3,600	5,500	813.00 + 31%	3,600
5,500	7,500	1,402.00 + 36%	5,500
7,500	....	2,122.00 + 39.6%	7,500

▲ 1994 INDIVIDUAL TAX TABLES

1994 Tax Table

Use if your taxable income is less than $100,000. If $100,000 or more, use the Tax Rate Schedules.

Example. Mr. and Mrs. Brown are filing a joint return. Their taxable income on line 37 of Form 1040 is $25,300. First, they find the $25,300–25,350 income line. Next, they find the column for married filing jointly and read down the column. The amount shown where the income line and filing status column meet is $3,799. This is the tax amount they must enter on line 38 of their Form 1040.

Sample Table

At least	But less than	Single	Married filing jointly *	Married separately	Head of a household
			Your tax is—		
25,200	25,250	4,106	3,784	4,593	3,784
25,250	25,300	4,120	3,791	4,607	3,791
25,300	25,350	4,134	(3,799)	4,621	3,799
25,350	25,400	4,148	3,806	4,635	3,806

If line 37 (taxable income) is— / **And you are—**

At least	But less than	Single	Married filing jointly *	Married filing separately	Head of a household
			Your tax is—		
0	5	0	0	0	0
5	15	2	2	2	2
15	25	3	3	3	3
25	50	6	6	6	6
50	75	9	9	9	9
75	100	13	13	13	13
100	125	17	17	17	17
125	150	21	21	21	21
150	175	24	24	24	24
175	200	28	28	28	28
200	225	32	32	32	32
225	250	36	36	36	36
250	275	39	39	39	39
275	300	43	43	43	43
300	325	47	47	47	47
325	350	51	51	51	51
350	375	54	54	54	54
375	400	58	58	58	58
400	425	62	62	62	62
425	450	66	66	66	66
450	475	69	69	69	69
475	500	73	73	73	73
500	525	77	77	77	77
525	550	81	81	81	81
550	575	84	84	84	84
575	600	88	88	88	88
600	625	92	92	92	92
625	650	96	96	96	96
650	675	99	99	99	99
675	700	103	103	103	103
700	725	107	107	107	107
725	750	111	111	111	111
750	775	114	114	114	114
775	800	118	118	118	118
800	825	122	122	122	122
825	850	126	126	126	126
850	875	129	129	129	129
875	900	133	133	133	133
900	925	137	137	137	137
925	950	141	141	141	141
950	975	144	144	144	144
975	1,000	148	148	148	148

1,000

At least	But less than	Single	Married filing jointly *	Married filing separately	Head of a household
1,000	1,025	152	152	152	152
1,025	1,050	156	156	156	156
1,050	1,075	159	159	159	159
1,075	1,100	163	163	163	163
1,100	1,125	167	167	167	167
1,125	1,150	171	171	171	171
1,150	1,175	174	174	174	174
1,175	1,200	178	178	178	178
1,200	1,225	182	182	182	182
1,225	1,250	186	186	186	186
1,250	1,275	189	189	189	189
1,275	1,300	193	193	193	193

If line 37 (taxable income) is— / **And you are—**

At least	But less than	Single	Married filing jointly *	Married filing separately	Head of a household
			Your tax is—		
1,300	1,325	197	197	197	197
1,325	1,350	201	201	201	201
1,350	1,375	204	204	204	204
1,375	1,400	208	208	208	208
1,400	1,425	212	212	212	212
1,425	1,450	216	216	216	216
1,450	1,475	219	219	219	219
1,475	1,500	223	223	223	223
1,500	1,525	227	227	227	227
1,525	1,550	231	231	231	231
1,550	1,575	234	234	234	234
1,575	1,600	238	238	238	238
1,600	1,625	242	242	242	242
1,625	1,650	246	246	246	246
1,650	1,675	249	249	249	249
1,675	1,700	253	253	253	253
1,700	1,725	257	257	257	257
1,725	1,750	261	261	261	261
1,750	1,775	264	264	264	264
1,775	1,800	268	268	268	268
1,800	1,825	272	272	272	272
1,825	1,850	276	276	276	276
1,850	1,875	279	279	279	279
1,875	1,900	283	283	283	283
1,900	1,925	287	287	287	287
1,925	1,950	291	291	291	291
1,950	1,975	294	294	294	294
1,975	2,000	298	298	298	298

2,000

At least	But less than	Single	Married filing jointly *	Married filing separately	Head of a household
2,000	2,025	302	302	302	302
2,025	2,050	306	306	306	306
2,050	2,075	309	309	309	309
2,075	2,100	313	313	313	313
2,100	2,125	317	317	317	317
2,125	2,150	321	321	321	321
2,150	2,175	324	324	324	324
2,175	2,200	328	328	328	328
2,200	2,225	332	332	332	332
2,225	2,250	336	336	336	336
2,250	2,275	339	339	339	339
2,275	2,300	343	343	343	343
2,300	2,325	347	347	347	347
2,325	2,350	351	351	351	351
2,350	2,375	354	354	354	354
2,375	2,400	358	358	358	358
2,400	2,425	362	362	362	362
2,425	2,450	366	366	366	366
2,450	2,475	369	369	369	369
2,475	2,500	373	373	373	373
2,500	2,525	377	377	377	377
2,525	2,550	381	381	381	381
2,550	2,575	384	384	384	384
2,575	2,600	388	388	388	388
2,600	2,625	392	392	392	392
2,625	2,650	396	396	396	396
2,650	2,675	399	399	399	399
2,675	2,700	403	403	403	403

If line 37 (taxable income) is— / **And you are—**

At least	But less than	Single	Married filing jointly *	Married filing separately	Head of a household
			Your tax is—		
2,700	2,725	407	407	407	407
2,725	2,750	411	411	411	411
2,750	2,775	414	414	414	414
2,775	2,800	418	418	418	418
2,800	2,825	422	422	422	422
2,825	2,850	426	426	426	426
2,850	2,875	429	429	429	429
2,875	2,900	433	433	433	433
2,900	2,925	437	437	437	437
2,925	2,950	441	441	441	441
2,950	2,975	444	444	444	444
2,975	3,000	448	448	448	448

3,000

At least	But less than	Single	Married filing jointly *	Married filing separately	Head of a household
3,000	3,050	454	454	454	454
3,050	3,100	461	461	461	461
3,100	3,150	469	469	469	469
3,150	3,200	476	476	476	476
3,200	3,250	484	484	484	484
3,250	3,300	491	491	491	491
3,300	3,350	499	499	499	499
3,350	3,400	506	506	506	506
3,400	3,450	514	514	514	514
3,450	3,500	521	521	521	521
3,500	3,550	529	529	529	529
3,550	3,600	536	536	536	536
3,600	3,650	544	544	544	544
3,650	3,700	551	551	551	551
3,700	3,750	559	559	559	559
3,750	3,800	566	566	566	566
3,800	3,850	574	574	574	574
3,850	3,900	581	581	581	581
3,900	3,950	589	589	589	589
3,950	4,000	596	596	596	596

4,000

At least	But less than	Single	Married filing jointly *	Married filing separately	Head of a household
4,000	4,050	604	604	604	604
4,050	4,100	611	611	611	611
4,100	4,150	619	619	619	619
4,150	4,200	626	626	626	626
4,200	4,250	634	634	634	634
4,250	4,300	641	641	641	641
4,300	4,350	649	649	649	649
4,350	4,400	656	656	656	656
4,400	4,450	664	664	664	664
4,450	4,500	671	671	671	671
4,500	4,550	679	679	679	679
4,550	4,600	686	686	686	686
4,600	4,650	694	694	694	694
4,650	4,700	701	701	701	701
4,700	4,750	709	709	709	709
4,750	4,800	716	716	716	716
4,800	4,850	724	724	724	724
4,850	4,900	731	731	731	731
4,900	4,950	739	739	739	739
4,950	5,000	746	746	746	746

Continued on next page

* This column must also be used by a qualifying widow(er).

1994 Tax Table—Continued

5,000 / 6,000 / 7,000

If line 37 (taxable income) is— At least	But less than	Single	Married filing jointly *	Married filing separately	Head of a household
5,000					
5,000	5,050	754	754	754	754
5,050	5,100	761	761	761	761
5,100	5,150	769	769	769	769
5,150	5,200	776	776	776	776
5,200	5,250	784	784	784	784
5,250	5,300	791	791	791	791
5,300	5,350	799	799	799	799
5,350	5,400	806	806	806	806
5,400	5,450	814	814	814	814
5,450	5,500	821	821	821	821
5,500	5,550	829	829	829	829
5,550	5,600	836	836	836	836
5,600	5,650	844	844	844	844
5,650	5,700	851	851	851	851
5,700	5,750	859	859	859	859
5,750	5,800	866	866	866	866
5,800	5,850	874	874	874	874
5,850	5,900	881	881	881	881
5,900	5,950	889	889	889	889
5,950	6,000	896	896	896	896
6,000					
6,000	6,050	904	904	904	904
6,050	6,100	911	911	911	911
6,100	6,150	919	919	919	919
6,150	6,200	926	926	926	926
6,200	6,250	934	934	934	934
6,250	6,300	941	941	941	941
6,300	6,350	949	949	949	949
6,350	6,400	956	956	956	956
6,400	6,450	964	964	964	964
6,450	6,500	971	971	971	971
6,500	6,550	979	979	979	979
6,550	6,600	986	986	986	986
6,600	6,650	994	994	994	994
6,650	6,700	1,001	1,001	1,001	1,001
6,700	6,750	1,009	1,009	1,009	1,009
6,750	6,800	1,016	1,016	1,016	1,016
6,800	6,850	1,024	1,024	1,024	1,024
6,850	6,900	1,031	1,031	1,031	1,031
6,900	6,950	1,039	1,039	1,039	1,039
6,950	7,000	1,046	1,046	1,046	1,046
7,000					
7,000	7,050	1,054	1,054	1,054	1,054
7,050	7,100	1,061	1,061	1,061	1,061
7,100	7,150	1,069	1,069	1,069	1,069
7,150	7,200	1,076	1,076	1,076	1,076
7,200	7,250	1,084	1,084	1,084	1,084
7,250	7,300	1,091	1,091	1,091	1,091
7,300	7,350	1,099	1,099	1,099	1,099
7,350	7,400	1,106	1,106	1,106	1,106
7,400	7,450	1,114	1,114	1,114	1,114
7,450	7,500	1,121	1,121	1,121	1,121
7,500	7,550	1,129	1,129	1,129	1,129
7,550	7,600	1,136	1,136	1,136	1,136
7,600	7,650	1,144	1,144	1,144	1,144
7,650	7,700	1,151	1,151	1,151	1,151
7,700	7,750	1,159	1,159	1,159	1,159
7,750	7,800	1,166	1,166	1,166	1,166
7,800	7,850	1,174	1,174	1,174	1,174
7,850	7,900	1,181	1,181	1,181	1,181
7,900	7,950	1,189	1,189	1,189	1,189
7,950	8,000	1,196	1,196	1,196	1,196

8,000 / 9,000 / 10,000

If line 37 (taxable income) is— At least	But less than	Single	Married filing jointly *	Married filing separately	Head of a household
8,000					
8,000	8,050	1,204	1,204	1,204	1,204
8,050	8,100	1,211	1,211	1,211	1,211
8,100	8,150	1,219	1,219	1,219	1,219
8,150	8,200	1,226	1,226	1,226	1,226
8,200	8,250	1,234	1,234	1,234	1,234
8,250	8,300	1,241	1,241	1,241	1,241
8,300	8,350	1,249	1,249	1,249	1,249
8,350	8,400	1,256	1,256	1,256	1,256
8,400	8,450	1,264	1,264	1,264	1,264
8,450	8,500	1,271	1,271	1,271	1,271
8,500	8,550	1,279	1,279	1,279	1,279
8,550	8,600	1,286	1,286	1,286	1,286
8,600	8,650	1,294	1,294	1,294	1,294
8,650	8,700	1,301	1,301	1,301	1,301
8,700	8,750	1,309	1,309	1,309	1,309
8,750	8,800	1,316	1,316	1,316	1,316
8,800	8,850	1,324	1,324	1,324	1,324
8,850	8,900	1,331	1,331	1,331	1,331
8,900	8,950	1,339	1,339	1,339	1,339
8,950	9,000	1,346	1,346	1,346	1,346
9,000					
9,000	9,050	1,354	1,354	1,354	1,354
9,050	9,100	1,361	1,361	1,361	1,361
9,100	9,150	1,369	1,369	1,369	1,369
9,150	9,200	1,376	1,376	1,376	1,376
9,200	9,250	1,384	1,384	1,384	1,384
9,250	9,300	1,391	1,391	1,391	1,391
9,300	9,350	1,399	1,399	1,399	1,399
9,350	9,400	1,406	1,406	1,406	1,406
9,400	9,450	1,414	1,414	1,414	1,414
9,450	9,500	1,421	1,421	1,421	1,421
9,500	9,550	1,429	1,429	1,429	1,429
9,550	9,600	1,436	1,436	1,436	1,436
9,600	9,650	1,444	1,444	1,444	1,444
9,650	9,700	1,451	1,451	1,451	1,451
9,700	9,750	1,459	1,459	1,459	1,459
9,750	9,800	1,466	1,466	1,466	1,466
9,800	9,850	1,474	1,474	1,474	1,474
9,850	9,900	1,481	1,481	1,481	1,481
9,900	9,950	1,489	1,489	1,489	1,489
9,950	10,000	1,496	1,496	1,496	1,496
10,000					
10,000	10,050	1,504	1,504	1,504	1,504
10,050	10,100	1,511	1,511	1,511	1,511
10,100	10,150	1,519	1,519	1,519	1,519
10,150	10,200	1,526	1,526	1,526	1,526
10,200	10,250	1,534	1,534	1,534	1,534
10,250	10,300	1,541	1,541	1,541	1,541
10,300	10,350	1,549	1,549	1,549	1,549
10,350	10,400	1,556	1,556	1,556	1,556
10,400	10,450	1,564	1,564	1,564	1,564
10,450	10,500	1,571	1,571	1,571	1,571
10,500	10,550	1,579	1,579	1,579	1,579
10,550	10,600	1,586	1,586	1,586	1,586
10,600	10,650	1,594	1,594	1,594	1,594
10,650	10,700	1,601	1,601	1,601	1,601
10,700	10,750	1,609	1,609	1,609	1,609
10,750	10,800	1,616	1,616	1,616	1,616
10,800	10,850	1,624	1,624	1,624	1,624
10,850	10,900	1,631	1,631	1,631	1,631
10,900	10,950	1,639	1,639	1,639	1,639
10,950	11,000	1,646	1,646	1,646	1,646

11,000 / 12,000 / 13,000

If line 37 (taxable income) is— At least	But less than	Single	Married filing jointly *	Married filing separately	Head of a household
11,000					
11,000	11,050	1,654	1,654	1,654	1,654
11,050	11,100	1,661	1,661	1,661	1,661
11,100	11,150	1,669	1,669	1,669	1,669
11,150	11,200	1,676	1,676	1,676	1,676
11,200	11,250	1,684	1,684	1,684	1,684
11,250	11,300	1,691	1,691	1,691	1,691
11,300	11,350	1,699	1,699	1,699	1,699
11,350	11,400	1,706	1,706	1,706	1,706
11,400	11,450	1,714	1,714	1,714	1,714
11,450	11,500	1,721	1,721	1,721	1,721
11,500	11,550	1,729	1,729	1,729	1,729
11,550	11,600	1,736	1,736	1,736	1,736
11,600	11,650	1,744	1,744	1,744	1,744
11,650	11,700	1,751	1,751	1,751	1,751
11,700	11,750	1,759	1,759	1,759	1,759
11,750	11,800	1,766	1,766	1,766	1,766
11,800	11,850	1,774	1,774	1,774	1,774
11,850	11,900	1,781	1,781	1,781	1,781
11,900	11,950	1,789	1,789	1,789	1,789
11,950	12,000	1,796	1,796	1,796	1,796
12,000					
12,000	12,050	1,804	1,804	1,804	1,804
12,050	12,100	1,811	1,811	1,811	1,811
12,100	12,150	1,819	1,819	1,819	1,819
12,150	12,200	1,826	1,826	1,826	1,826
12,200	12,250	1,834	1,834	1,834	1,834
12,250	12,300	1,841	1,841	1,841	1,841
12,300	12,350	1,849	1,849	1,849	1,849
12,350	12,400	1,856	1,856	1,856	1,856
12,400	12,450	1,864	1,864	1,864	1,864
12,450	12,500	1,871	1,871	1,871	1,871
12,500	12,550	1,879	1,879	1,879	1,879
12,550	12,600	1,886	1,886	1,886	1,886
12,600	12,650	1,894	1,894	1,894	1,894
12,650	12,700	1,901	1,901	1,901	1,901
12,700	12,750	1,909	1,909	1,909	1,909
12,750	12,800	1,916	1,916	1,916	1,916
12,800	12,850	1,924	1,924	1,924	1,924
12,850	12,900	1,931	1,931	1,931	1,931
12,900	12,950	1,939	1,939	1,939	1,939
12,950	13,000	1,946	1,946	1,946	1,946
13,000					
13,000	13,050	1,954	1,954	1,954	1,954
13,050	13,100	1,961	1,961	1,961	1,961
13,100	13,150	1,969	1,969	1,969	1,969
13,150	13,200	1,976	1,976	1,976	1,976
13,200	13,250	1,984	1,984	1,984	1,984
13,250	13,300	1,991	1,991	1,991	1,991
13,300	13,350	1,999	1,999	1,999	1,999
13,350	13,400	2,006	2,006	2,006	2,006
13,400	13,450	2,014	2,014	2,014	2,014
13,450	13,500	2,021	2,021	2,021	2,021
13,500	13,550	2,029	2,029	2,029	2,029
13,550	13,600	2,036	2,036	2,036	2,036
13,600	13,650	2,044	2,044	2,044	2,044
13,650	13,700	2,051	2,051	2,051	2,051
13,700	13,750	2,059	2,059	2,059	2,059
13,750	13,800	2,066	2,066	2,066	2,066
13,800	13,850	2,074	2,074	2,074	2,074
13,850	13,900	2,081	2,081	2,081	2,081
13,900	13,950	2,089	2,089	2,089	2,089
13,950	14,000	2,096	2,096	2,096	2,096

* This column must also be used by a qualifying widow(er).

Continued on next page

1994 Tax Table—Continued

If line 37 (taxable income) is— At least	But less than	Single	Married filing jointly *	Married filing separately	Head of a household
14,000					
14,000	14,050	2,104	2,104	2,104	2,104
14,050	14,100	2,111	2,111	2,111	2,111
14,100	14,150	2,119	2,119	2,119	2,119
14,150	14,200	2,126	2,126	2,126	2,126
14,200	14,250	2,134	2,134	2,134	2,134
14,250	14,300	2,141	2,141	2,141	2,141
14,300	14,350	2,149	2,149	2,149	2,149
14,350	14,400	2,156	2,156	2,156	2,156
14,400	14,450	2,164	2,164	2,164	2,164
14,450	14,500	2,171	2,171	2,171	2,171
14,500	14,550	2,179	2,179	2,179	2,179
14,550	14,600	2,186	2,186	2,186	2,186
14,600	14,650	2,194	2,194	2,194	2,194
14,650	14,700	2,201	2,201	2,201	2,201
14,700	14,750	2,209	2,209	2,209	2,209
14,750	14,800	2,216	2,216	2,216	2,216
14,800	14,850	2,224	2,224	2,224	2,224
14,850	14,900	2,231	2,231	2,231	2,231
14,900	14,950	2,239	2,239	2,239	2,239
14,950	15,000	2,246	2,246	2,246	2,246
15,000					
15,000	15,050	2,254	2,254	2,254	2,254
15,050	15,100	2,261	2,261	2,261	2,261
15,100	15,150	2,269	2,269	2,269	2,269
15,150	15,200	2,276	2,276	2,276	2,276
15,200	15,250	2,284	2,284	2,284	2,284
15,250	15,300	2,291	2,291	2,291	2,291
15,300	15,350	2,299	2,299	2,299	2,299
15,350	15,400	2,306	2,306	2,306	2,306
15,400	15,450	2,314	2,314	2,314	2,314
15,450	15,500	2,321	2,321	2,321	2,321
15,500	15,550	2,329	2,329	2,329	2,329
15,550	15,600	2,336	2,336	2,336	2,336
15,600	15,650	2,344	2,344	2,344	2,344
15,650	15,700	2,351	2,351	2,351	2,351
15,700	15,750	2,359	2,359	2,359	2,359
15,750	15,800	2,366	2,366	2,366	2,366
15,800	15,850	2,374	2,374	2,374	2,374
15,850	15,900	2,381	2,381	2,381	2,381
15,900	15,950	2,389	2,389	2,389	2,389
15,950	16,000	2,396	2,396	2,396	2,396
16,000					
16,000	16,050	2,404	2,404	2,404	2,404
16,050	16,100	2,411	2,411	2,411	2,411
16,100	16,150	2,419	2,419	2,419	2,419
16,150	16,200	2,426	2,426	2,426	2,426
16,200	16,250	2,434	2,434	2,434	2,434
16,250	16,300	2,441	2,441	2,441	2,441
16,300	16,350	2,449	2,449	2,449	2,449
16,350	16,400	2,456	2,456	2,456	2,456
16,400	16,450	2,464	2,464	2,464	2,464
16,450	16,500	2,471	2,471	2,471	2,471
16,500	16,550	2,479	2,479	2,479	2,479
16,550	16,600	2,486	2,486	2,486	2,486
16,600	16,650	2,494	2,494	2,494	2,494
16,650	16,700	2,501	2,501	2,501	2,501
16,700	16,750	2,509	2,509	2,509	2,509
16,750	16,800	2,516	2,516	2,516	2,516
16,800	16,850	2,524	2,524	2,524	2,524
16,850	16,900	2,531	2,531	2,531	2,531
16,900	16,950	2,539	2,539	2,539	2,539
16,950	17,000	2,546	2,546	2,546	2,546

If line 37 (taxable income) is— At least	But less than	Single	Married filing jointly *	Married filing separately	Head of a household
17,000					
17,000	17,050	2,554	2,554	2,554	2,554
17,050	17,100	2,561	2,561	2,561	2,561
17,100	17,150	2,569	2,569	2,569	2,569
17,150	17,200	2,576	2,576	2,576	2,576
17,200	17,250	2,584	2,584	2,584	2,584
17,250	17,300	2,591	2,591	2,591	2,591
17,300	17,350	2,599	2,599	2,599	2,599
17,350	17,400	2,606	2,606	2,606	2,606
17,400	17,450	2,614	2,614	2,614	2,614
17,450	17,500	2,621	2,621	2,621	2,621
17,500	17,550	2,629	2,629	2,629	2,629
17,550	17,600	2,636	2,636	2,636	2,636
17,600	17,650	2,644	2,644	2,644	2,644
17,650	17,700	2,651	2,651	2,651	2,651
17,700	17,750	2,659	2,659	2,659	2,659
17,750	17,800	2,666	2,666	2,666	2,666
17,800	17,850	2,674	2,674	2,674	2,674
17,850	17,900	2,681	2,681	2,681	2,681
17,900	17,950	2,689	2,689	2,689	2,689
17,950	18,000	2,696	2,696	2,696	2,696
18,000					
18,000	18,050	2,704	2,704	2,704	2,704
18,050	18,100	2,711	2,711	2,711	2,711
18,100	18,150	2,719	2,719	2,719	2,719
18,150	18,200	2,726	2,726	2,726	2,726
18,200	18,250	2,734	2,734	2,734	2,734
18,250	18,300	2,741	2,741	2,741	2,741
18,300	18,350	2,749	2,749	2,749	2,749
18,350	18,400	2,756	2,756	2,756	2,756
18,400	18,450	2,764	2,764	2,764	2,764
18,450	18,500	2,771	2,771	2,771	2,771
18,500	18,550	2,779	2,779	2,779	2,779
18,550	18,600	2,786	2,786	2,786	2,786
18,600	18,650	2,794	2,794	2,794	2,794
18,650	18,700	2,801	2,801	2,801	2,801
18,700	18,750	2,809	2,809	2,809	2,809
18,750	18,800	2,816	2,816	2,816	2,816
18,800	18,850	2,824	2,824	2,824	2,824
18,850	18,900	2,831	2,831	2,831	2,831
18,900	18,950	2,839	2,839	2,839	2,839
18,950	19,000	2,846	2,846	2,846	2,846
19,000					
19,000	19,050	2,854	2,854	2,857	2,854
19,050	19,100	2,861	2,861	2,871	2,861
19,100	19,150	2,869	2,869	2,885	2,869
19,150	19,200	2,876	2,876	2,899	2,876
19,200	19,250	2,884	2,884	2,913	2,884
19,250	19,300	2,891	2,891	2,927	2,891
19,300	19,350	2,899	2,899	2,941	2,899
19,350	19,400	2,906	2,906	2,955	2,906
19,400	19,450	2,914	2,914	2,969	2,914
19,450	19,500	2,921	2,921	2,983	2,921
19,500	19,550	2,929	2,929	2,997	2,929
19,550	19,600	2,936	2,936	3,011	2,936
19,600	19,650	2,944	2,944	3,025	2,944
19,650	19,700	2,951	2,951	3,039	2,951
19,700	19,750	2,959	2,959	3,053	2,959
19,750	19,800	2,966	2,966	3,067	2,966
19,800	19,850	2,974	2,974	3,081	2,974
19,850	19,900	2,981	2,981	3,095	2,981
19,900	19,950	2,989	2,989	3,109	2,989
19,950	20,000	2,996	2,996	3,123	2,996

If line 37 (taxable income) is— At least	But less than	Single	Married filing jointly *	Married filing separately	Head of a household
20,000					
20,000	20,050	3,004	3,004	3,137	3,004
20,050	20,100	3,011	3,011	3,151	3,011
20,100	20,150	3,019	3,019	3,165	3,019
20,150	20,200	3,026	3,026	3,179	3,026
20,200	20,250	3,034	3,034	3,193	3,034
20,250	20,300	3,041	3,041	3,207	3,041
20,300	20,350	3,049	3,049	3,221	3,049
20,350	20,400	3,056	3,056	3,235	3,056
20,400	20,450	3,064	3,064	3,249	3,064
20,450	20,500	3,071	3,071	3,263	3,071
20,500	20,550	3,079	3,079	3,277	3,079
20,550	20,600	3,086	3,086	3,291	3,086
20,600	20,650	3,094	3,094	3,305	3,094
20,650	20,700	3,101	3,101	3,319	3,101
20,700	20,750	3,109	3,109	3,333	3,109
20,750	20,800	3,116	3,116	3,347	3,116
20,800	20,850	3,124	3,124	3,361	3,124
20,850	20,900	3,131	3,131	3,375	3,131
20,900	20,950	3,139	3,139	3,389	3,139
20,950	21,000	3,146	3,146	3,403	3,146
21,000					
21,000	21,050	3,154	3,154	3,417	3,154
21,050	21,100	3,161	3,161	3,431	3,161
21,100	21,150	3,169	3,169	3,445	3,169
21,150	21,200	3,176	3,176	3,459	3,176
21,200	21,250	3,184	3,184	3,473	3,184
21,250	21,300	3,191	3,191	3,487	3,191
21,300	21,350	3,199	3,199	3,501	3,199
21,350	21,400	3,206	3,206	3,515	3,206
21,400	21,450	3,214	3,214	3,529	3,214
21,450	21,500	3,221	3,221	3,543	3,221
21,500	21,550	3,229	3,229	3,557	3,229
21,550	21,600	3,236	3,236	3,571	3,236
21,600	21,650	3,244	3,244	3,585	3,244
21,650	21,700	3,251	3,251	3,599	3,251
21,700	21,750	3,259	3,259	3,613	3,259
21,750	21,800	3,266	3,266	3,627	3,266
21,800	21,850	3,274	3,274	3,641	3,274
21,850	21,900	3,281	3,281	3,655	3,281
21,900	21,950	3,289	3,289	3,669	3,289
21,950	22,000	3,296	3,296	3,683	3,296
22,000					
22,000	22,050	3,304	3,304	3,697	3,304
22,050	22,100	3,311	3,311	3,711	3,311
22,100	22,150	3,319	3,319	3,725	3,319
22,150	22,200	3,326	3,326	3,739	3,326
22,200	22,250	3,334	3,334	3,753	3,334
22,250	22,300	3,341	3,341	3,767	3,341
22,300	22,350	3,349	3,349	3,781	3,349
22,350	22,400	3,356	3,356	3,795	3,356
22,400	22,450	3,364	3,364	3,809	3,364
22,450	22,500	3,371	3,371	3,823	3,371
22,500	22,550	3,379	3,379	3,837	3,379
22,550	22,600	3,386	3,386	3,851	3,386
22,600	22,650	3,394	3,394	3,865	3,394
22,650	22,700	3,401	3,401	3,879	3,401
22,700	22,750	3,409	3,409	3,893	3,409
22,750	22,800	3,420	3,416	3,907	3,416
22,800	22,850	3,434	3,424	3,921	3,424
22,850	22,900	3,448	3,431	3,935	3,431
22,900	22,950	3,462	3,439	3,949	3,439
22,950	23,000	3,476	3,446	3,963	3,446

* This column must also be used by a qualifying widow(er).

Continued on next page

1994 Tax Table—Continued

23,000

At least	But less than	Single	Married filing jointly *	Married filing separately	Head of a household
23,000	23,050	3,490	3,454	3,977	3,454
23,050	23,100	3,504	3,461	3,991	3,461
23,100	23,150	3,518	3,469	4,005	3,469
23,150	23,200	3,532	3,476	4,019	3,476
23,200	23,250	3,546	3,484	4,033	3,484
23,250	23,300	3,560	3,491	4,047	3,491
23,300	23,350	3,574	3,499	4,061	3,499
23,350	23,400	3,588	3,506	4,075	3,506
23,400	23,450	3,602	3,514	4,089	3,514
23,450	23,500	3,616	3,521	4,103	3,521
23,500	23,550	3,630	3,529	4,117	3,529
23,550	23,600	3,644	3,536	4,131	3,536
23,600	23,650	3,658	3,544	4,145	3,544
23,650	23,700	3,672	3,551	4,159	3,551
23,700	23,750	3,686	3,559	4,173	3,559
23,750	23,800	3,700	3,566	4,187	3,566
23,800	23,850	3,714	3,574	4,201	3,574
23,850	23,900	3,728	3,581	4,215	3,581
23,900	23,950	3,742	3,589	4,229	3,589
23,950	24,000	3,756	3,596	4,243	3,596

24,000

At least	But less than	Single	Married filing jointly *	Married filing separately	Head of a household
24,000	24,050	3,770	3,604	4,257	3,604
24,050	24,100	3,784	3,611	4,271	3,611
24,100	24,150	3,798	3,619	4,285	3,619
24,150	24,200	3,812	3,626	4,299	3,626
24,200	24,250	3,826	3,634	4,313	3,634
24,250	24,300	3,840	3,641	4,327	3,641
24,300	24,350	3,854	3,649	4,341	3,649
24,350	24,400	3,868	3,656	4,355	3,656
24,400	24,450	3,882	3,664	4,369	3,664
24,450	24,500	3,896	3,671	4,383	3,671
24,500	24,550	3,910	3,679	4,397	3,679
24,550	24,600	3,924	3,686	4,411	3,686
24,600	24,650	3,938	3,694	4,425	3,694
24,650	24,700	3,952	3,701	4,439	3,701
24,700	24,750	3,966	3,709	4,453	3,709
24,750	24,800	3,980	3,716	4,467	3,716
24,800	24,850	3,994	3,724	4,481	3,724
24,850	24,900	4,008	3,731	4,495	3,731
24,900	24,950	4,022	3,739	4,509	3,739
24,950	25,000	4,036	3,746	4,523	3,746

25,000

At least	But less than	Single	Married filing jointly *	Married filing separately	Head of a household
25,000	25,050	4,050	3,754	4,537	3,754
25,050	25,100	4,064	3,761	4,551	3,761
25,100	25,150	4,078	3,769	4,565	3,769
25,150	25,200	4,092	3,776	4,579	3,776
25,200	25,250	4,106	3,784	4,593	3,784
25,250	25,300	4,120	3,791	4,607	3,791
25,300	25,350	4,134	3,799	4,621	3,799
25,350	25,400	4,148	3,806	4,635	3,806
25,400	25,450	4,162	3,814	4,649	3,814
25,450	25,500	4,176	3,821	4,663	3,821
25,500	25,550	4,190	3,829	4,677	3,829
25,550	25,600	4,204	3,836	4,691	3,836
25,600	25,650	4,218	3,844	4,705	3,844
25,650	25,700	4,232	3,851	4,719	3,851
25,700	25,750	4,246	3,859	4,733	3,859
25,750	25,800	4,260	3,866	4,747	3,866
25,800	25,850	4,274	3,874	4,761	3,874
25,850	25,900	4,288	3,881	4,775	3,881
25,900	25,950	4,302	3,889	4,789	3,889
25,950	26,000	4,316	3,896	4,803	3,896

26,000

At least	But less than	Single	Married filing jointly *	Married filing separately	Head of a household
26,000	26,050	4,330	3,904	4,817	3,904
26,050	26,100	4,344	3,911	4,831	3,911
26,100	26,150	4,358	3,919	4,845	3,919
26,150	26,200	4,372	3,926	4,859	3,926
26,200	26,250	4,386	3,934	4,873	3,934
26,250	26,300	4,400	3,941	4,887	3,941
26,300	26,350	4,414	3,949	4,901	3,949
26,350	26,400	4,428	3,956	4,915	3,956
26,400	26,450	4,442	3,964	4,929	3,964
26,450	26,500	4,456	3,971	4,943	3,971
26,500	26,550	4,470	3,979	4,957	3,979
26,550	26,600	4,484	3,986	4,971	3,986
26,600	26,650	4,498	3,994	4,985	3,994
26,650	26,700	4,512	4,001	4,999	4,001
26,700	26,750	4,526	4,009	5,013	4,009
26,750	26,800	4,540	4,016	5,027	4,016
26,800	26,850	4,554	4,024	5,041	4,024
26,850	26,900	4,568	4,031	5,055	4,031
26,900	26,950	4,582	4,039	5,069	4,039
26,950	27,000	4,596	4,046	5,083	4,046

27,000

At least	But less than	Single	Married filing jointly *	Married filing separately	Head of a household
27,000	27,050	4,610	4,054	5,097	4,054
27,050	27,100	4,624	4,061	5,111	4,061
27,100	27,150	4,638	4,069	5,125	4,069
27,150	27,200	4,652	4,076	5,139	4,076
27,200	27,250	4,666	4,084	5,153	4,084
27,250	27,300	4,680	4,091	5,167	4,091
27,300	27,350	4,694	4,099	5,181	4,099
27,350	27,400	4,708	4,106	5,195	4,106
27,400	27,450	4,722	4,114	5,209	4,114
27,450	27,500	4,736	4,121	5,223	4,121
27,500	27,550	4,750	4,129	5,237	4,129
27,550	27,600	4,764	4,136	5,251	4,136
27,600	27,650	4,778	4,144	5,265	4,144
27,650	27,700	4,792	4,151	5,279	4,151
27,700	27,750	4,806	4,159	5,293	4,159
27,750	27,800	4,820	4,166	5,307	4,166
27,800	27,850	4,834	4,174	5,321	4,174
27,850	27,900	4,848	4,181	5,335	4,181
27,900	27,950	4,862	4,189	5,349	4,189
27,950	28,000	4,876	4,196	5,363	4,196

28,000

At least	But less than	Single	Married filing jointly *	Married filing separately	Head of a household
28,000	28,050	4,890	4,204	5,377	4,204
28,050	28,100	4,904	4,211	5,391	4,211
28,100	28,150	4,918	4,219	5,405	4,219
28,150	28,200	4,932	4,226	5,419	4,226
28,200	28,250	4,946	4,234	5,433	4,234
28,250	28,300	4,960	4,241	5,447	4,241
28,300	28,350	4,974	4,249	5,461	4,249
28,350	28,400	4,988	4,256	5,475	4,256
28,400	28,450	5,002	4,264	5,489	4,264
28,450	28,500	5,016	4,271	5,503	4,271
28,500	28,550	5,030	4,279	5,517	4,279
28,550	28,600	5,044	4,286	5,531	4,286
28,600	28,650	5,058	4,294	5,545	4,294
28,650	28,700	5,072	4,301	5,559	4,301
28,700	28,750	5,086	4,309	5,573	4,309
28,750	28,800	5,100	4,316	5,587	4,316
28,800	28,850	5,114	4,324	5,601	4,324
28,850	28,900	5,128	4,331	5,615	4,331
28,900	28,950	5,142	4,339	5,629	4,339
28,950	29,000	5,156	4,346	5,643	4,346

29,000

At least	But less than	Single	Married filing jointly *	Married filing separately	Head of a household
29,000	29,050	5,170	4,354	5,657	4,354
29,050	29,100	5,184	4,361	5,671	4,361
29,100	29,150	5,198	4,369	5,685	4,369
29,150	29,200	5,212	4,376	5,699	4,376
29,200	29,250	5,226	4,384	5,713	4,384
29,250	29,300	5,240	4,391	5,727	4,391
29,300	29,350	5,254	4,399	5,741	4,399
29,350	29,400	5,268	4,406	5,755	4,406
29,400	29,450	5,282	4,414	5,769	4,414
29,450	29,500	5,296	4,421	5,783	4,421
29,500	29,550	5,310	4,429	5,797	4,429
29,550	29,600	5,324	4,436	5,811	4,436
29,600	29,650	5,338	4,444	5,825	4,444
29,650	29,700	5,352	4,451	5,839	4,451
29,700	29,750	5,366	4,459	5,853	4,459
29,750	29,800	5,380	4,466	5,867	4,466
29,800	29,850	5,394	4,474	5,881	4,474
29,850	29,900	5,408	4,481	5,895	4,481
29,900	29,950	5,422	4,489	5,909	4,489
29,950	30,000	5,436	4,496	5,923	4,496

30,000

At least	But less than	Single	Married filing jointly *	Married filing separately	Head of a household
30,000	30,050	5,450	4,504	5,937	4,504
30,050	30,100	5,464	4,511	5,951	4,511
30,100	30,150	5,478	4,519	5,965	4,519
30,150	30,200	5,492	4,526	5,979	4,526
30,200	30,250	5,506	4,534	5,993	4,534
30,250	30,300	5,520	4,541	6,007	4,541
30,300	30,350	5,534	4,549	6,021	4,549
30,350	30,400	5,548	4,556	6,035	4,556
30,400	30,450	5,562	4,564	6,049	4,564
30,450	30,500	5,576	4,571	6,063	4,571
30,500	30,550	5,590	4,579	6,077	4,582
30,550	30,600	5,604	4,586	6,091	4,596
30,600	30,650	5,618	4,594	6,105	4,610
30,650	30,700	5,632	4,601	6,119	4,624
30,700	30,750	5,646	4,609	6,133	4,638
30,750	30,800	5,660	4,616	6,147	4,652
30,800	30,850	5,674	4,624	6,161	4,666
30,850	30,900	5,688	4,631	6,175	4,680
30,900	30,950	5,702	4,639	6,189	4,694
30,950	31,000	5,716	4,646	6,203	4,708

31,000

At least	But less than	Single	Married filing jointly *	Married filing separately	Head of a household
31,000	31,050	5,730	4,654	6,217	4,722
31,050	31,100	5,744	4,661	6,231	4,736
31,100	31,150	5,758	4,669	6,245	4,750
31,150	31,200	5,772	4,676	6,259	4,764
31,200	31,250	5,786	4,684	6,273	4,778
31,250	31,300	5,800	4,691	6,287	4,792
31,300	31,350	5,814	4,699	6,301	4,806
31,350	31,400	5,828	4,706	6,315	4,820
31,400	31,450	5,842	4,714	6,329	4,834
31,450	31,500	5,856	4,721	6,343	4,848
31,500	31,550	5,870	4,729	6,357	4,862
31,550	31,600	5,884	4,736	6,371	4,876
31,600	31,650	5,898	4,744	6,385	4,890
31,650	31,700	5,912	4,751	6,399	4,904
31,700	31,750	5,926	4,759	6,413	4,918
31,750	31,800	5,940	4,766	6,427	4,932
31,800	31,850	5,954	4,774	6,441	4,946
31,850	31,900	5,968	4,781	6,455	4,960
31,900	31,950	5,982	4,789	6,469	4,974
31,950	32,000	5,996	4,796	6,483	4,988

* This column must also be used by a qualifying widow(er).

Continued on next page

1994 Tax Table—Continued

If line 37 (taxable income) is—		And you are—			
At least	But less than	Single	Married filing jointly *	Married filing separately	Head of a household
		Your tax is—			
32,000					
32,000	32,050	6,010	4,804	6,497	5,002
32,050	32,100	6,024	4,811	6,511	5,016
32,100	32,150	6,038	4,819	6,525	5,030
32,150	32,200	6,052	4,826	6,539	5,044
32,200	32,250	6,066	4,834	6,553	5,058
32,250	32,300	6,080	4,841	6,567	5,072
32,300	32,350	6,094	4,849	6,581	5,086
32,350	32,400	6,108	4,856	6,595	5,100
32,400	32,450	6,122	4,864	6,609	5,114
32,450	32,500	6,136	4,871	6,623	5,128
32,500	32,550	6,150	4,879	6,637	5,142
32,550	32,600	6,164	4,886	6,651	5,156
32,600	32,650	6,178	4,894	6,665	5,170
32,650	32,700	6,192	4,901	6,679	5,184
32,700	32,750	6,206	4,909	6,693	5,198
32,750	32,800	6,220	4,916	6,707	5,212
32,800	32,850	6,234	4,924	6,721	5,226
32,850	32,900	6,248	4,931	6,735	5,240
32,900	32,950	6,262	4,939	6,749	5,254
32,950	33,000	6,276	4,946	6,763	5,268
33,000					
33,000	33,050	6,290	4,954	6,777	5,282
33,050	33,100	6,304	4,961	6,791	5,296
33,100	33,150	6,318	4,969	6,805	5,310
33,150	33,200	6,332	4,976	6,819	5,324
33,200	33,250	6,346	4,984	6,833	5,338
33,250	33,300	6,360	4,991	6,847	5,352
33,300	33,350	6,374	4,999	6,861	5,366
33,350	33,400	6,388	5,006	6,875	5,380
33,400	33,450	6,402	5,014	6,889	5,394
33,450	33,500	6,416	5,021	6,903	5,408
33,500	33,550	6,430	5,029	6,917	5,422
33,550	33,600	6,444	5,036	6,931	5,436
33,600	33,650	6,458	5,044	6,945	5,450
33,650	33,700	6,472	5,051	6,959	5,464
33,700	33,750	6,486	5,059	6,973	5,478
33,750	33,800	6,500	5,066	6,987	5,492
33,800	33,850	6,514	5,074	7,001	5,506
33,850	33,900	6,528	5,081	7,015	5,520
33,900	33,950	6,542	5,089	7,029	5,534
33,950	34,000	6,556	5,096	7,043	5,548
34,000					
34,000	34,050	6,570	5,104	7,057	5,562
34,050	34,100	6,584	5,111	7,071	5,576
34,100	34,150	6,598	5,119	7,085	5,590
34,150	34,200	6,612	5,126	7,099	5,604
34,200	34,250	6,626	5,134	7,113	5,618
34,250	34,300	6,640	5,141	7,127	5,632
34,300	34,350	6,654	5,149	7,141	5,646
34,350	34,400	6,668	5,156	7,155	5,660
34,400	34,450	6,682	5,164	7,169	5,674
34,450	34,500	6,696	5,171	7,183	5,688
34,500	34,550	6,710	5,179	7,197	5,702
34,550	34,600	6,724	5,186	7,211	5,716
34,600	34,650	6,738	5,194	7,225	5,730
34,650	34,700	6,752	5,201	7,239	5,744
34,700	34,750	6,766	5,209	7,253	5,758
34,750	34,800	6,780	5,216	7,267	5,772
34,800	34,850	6,794	5,224	7,281	5,786
34,850	34,900	6,808	5,231	7,295	5,800
34,900	34,950	6,822	5,239	7,309	5,814
34,950	35,000	6,836	5,246	7,323	5,828

If line 37 (taxable income) is—		And you are—			
At least	But less than	Single	Married filing jointly *	Married filing separately	Head of a household
		Your tax is—			
35,000					
35,000	35,050	6,850	5,254	7,337	5,842
35,050	35,100	6,864	5,261	7,351	5,856
35,100	35,150	6,878	5,269	7,365	5,870
35,150	35,200	6,892	5,276	7,379	5,884
35,200	35,250	6,906	5,284	7,393	5,898
35,250	35,300	6,920	5,291	7,407	5,912
35,300	35,350	6,934	5,299	7,421	5,926
35,350	35,400	6,948	5,306	7,435	5,940
35,400	35,450	6,962	5,314	7,449	5,954
35,450	35,500	6,976	5,321	7,463	5,968
35,500	35,550	6,990	5,329	7,477	5,982
35,550	35,600	7,004	5,336	7,491	5,996
35,600	35,650	7,018	5,344	7,505	6,010
35,650	35,700	7,032	5,351	7,519	6,024
35,700	35,750	7,046	5,359	7,533	6,038
35,750	35,800	7,060	5,366	7,547	6,052
35,800	35,850	7,074	5,374	7,561	6,066
35,850	35,900	7,088	5,381	7,575	6,080
35,900	35,950	7,102	5,389	7,589	6,094
35,950	36,000	7,116	5,396	7,603	6,108
36,000					
36,000	36,050	7,130	5,404	7,617	6,122
36,050	36,100	7,144	5,411	7,631	6,136
36,100	36,150	7,158	5,419	7,645	6,150
36,150	36,200	7,172	5,426	7,659	6,164
36,200	36,250	7,186	5,434	7,673	6,178
36,250	36,300	7,200	5,441	7,687	6,192
36,300	36,350	7,214	5,449	7,701	6,206
36,350	36,400	7,228	5,456	7,715	6,220
36,400	36,450	7,242	5,464	7,729	6,234
36,450	36,500	7,256	5,471	7,743	6,248
36,500	36,550	7,270	5,479	7,757	6,262
36,550	36,600	7,284	5,486	7,771	6,276
36,600	36,650	7,298	5,494	7,785	6,290
36,650	36,700	7,312	5,501	7,799	6,304
36,700	36,750	7,326	5,509	7,813	6,318
36,750	36,800	7,340	5,516	7,827	6,332
36,800	36,850	7,354	5,524	7,841	6,346
36,850	36,900	7,368	5,531	7,855	6,360
36,900	36,950	7,382	5,539	7,869	6,374
36,950	37,000	7,396	5,546	7,883	6,388
37,000					
37,000	37,050	7,410	5,554	7,897	6,402
37,050	37,100	7,424	5,561	7,911	6,416
37,100	37,150	7,438	5,569	7,925	6,430
37,150	37,200	7,452	5,576	7,939	6,444
37,200	37,250	7,466	5,584	7,953	6,458
37,250	37,300	7,480	5,591	7,967	6,472
37,300	37,350	7,494	5,599	7,981	6,486
37,350	37,400	7,508	5,606	7,995	6,500
37,400	37,450	7,522	5,614	8,009	6,514
37,450	37,500	7,536	5,621	8,023	6,528
37,500	37,550	7,550	5,629	8,037	6,542
37,550	37,600	7,564	5,636	8,051	6,556
37,600	37,650	7,578	5,644	8,065	6,570
37,650	37,700	7,592	5,651	8,079	6,584
37,700	37,750	7,606	5,659	8,093	6,598
37,750	37,800	7,620	5,666	8,107	6,612
37,800	37,850	7,634	5,674	8,121	6,626
37,850	37,900	7,648	5,681	8,135	6,640
37,900	37,950	7,662	5,689	8,149	6,654
37,950	38,000	7,676	5,696	8,163	6,668

If line 37 (taxable income) is—		And you are—			
At least	But less than	Single	Married filing jointly *	Married filing separately	Head of a household
		Your tax is—			
38,000					
38,000	38,050	7,690	5,707	8,177	6,682
38,050	38,100	7,704	5,721	8,191	6,696
38,100	38,150	7,718	5,735	8,205	6,710
38,150	38,200	7,732	5,749	8,219	6,724
38,200	38,250	7,746	5,763	8,233	6,738
38,250	38,300	7,760	5,777	8,247	6,752
38,300	38,350	7,774	5,791	8,261	6,766
38,350	38,400	7,788	5,805	8,275	6,780
38,400	38,450	7,802	5,819	8,289	6,794
38,450	38,500	7,816	5,833	8,303	6,808
38,500	38,550	7,830	5,847	8,317	6,822
38,550	38,600	7,844	5,861	8,331	6,836
38,600	38,650	7,858	5,875	8,345	6,850
38,650	38,700	7,872	5,889	8,359	6,864
38,700	38,750	7,886	5,903	8,373	6,878
38,750	38,800	7,900	5,917	8,387	6,892
38,800	38,850	7,914	5,931	8,401	6,906
38,850	38,900	7,928	5,945	8,415	6,920
38,900	38,950	7,942	5,959	8,429	6,934
38,950	39,000	7,956	5,973	8,443	6,948
39,000					
39,000	39,050	7,970	5,987	8,457	6,962
39,050	39,100	7,984	6,001	8,471	6,976
39,100	39,150	7,998	6,015	8,485	6,990
39,150	39,200	8,012	6,029	8,499	7,004
39,200	39,250	8,026	6,043	8,513	7,018
39,250	39,300	8,040	6,057	8,527	7,032
39,300	39,350	8,054	6,071	8,541	7,046
39,350	39,400	8,068	6,085	8,555	7,060
39,400	39,450	8,082	6,099	8,569	7,074
39,450	39,500	8,096	6,113	8,583	7,088
39,500	39,550	8,110	6,127	8,597	7,102
39,550	39,600	8,124	6,141	8,611	7,116
39,600	39,650	8,138	6,155	8,625	7,130
39,650	39,700	8,152	6,169	8,639	7,144
39,700	39,750	8,166	6,183	8,653	7,158
39,750	39,800	8,180	6,197	8,667	7,172
39,800	39,850	8,194	6,211	8,681	7,186
39,850	39,900	8,208	6,225	8,695	7,200
39,900	39,950	8,222	6,239	8,709	7,214
39,950	40,000	8,236	6,253	8,723	7,228
40,000					
40,000	40,050	8,250	6,267	8,737	7,242
40,050	40,100	8,264	6,281	8,751	7,256
40,100	40,150	8,278	6,295	8,765	7,270
40,150	40,200	8,292	6,309	8,779	7,284
40,200	40,250	8,306	6,323	8,793	7,298
40,250	40,300	8,320	6,337	8,807	7,312
40,300	40,350	8,334	6,351	8,821	7,326
40,350	40,400	8,348	6,365	8,835	7,340
40,400	40,450	8,362	6,379	8,849	7,354
40,450	40,500	8,376	6,393	8,863	7,368
40,500	40,550	8,390	6,407	8,877	7,382
40,550	40,600	8,404	6,421	8,891	7,396
40,600	40,650	8,418	6,435	8,905	7,410
40,650	40,700	8,432	6,449	8,919	7,424
40,700	40,750	8,446	6,463	8,933	7,438
40,750	40,800	8,460	6,477	8,947	7,452
40,800	40,850	8,474	6,491	8,961	7,466
40,850	40,900	8,488	6,505	8,975	7,480
40,900	40,950	8,502	6,519	8,989	7,494
40,950	41,000	8,516	6,533	9,003	7,508

* This column must also be used by a qualifying widow(er).

Continued on next page

1994 Tax Table—Continued

41,000

If line 37 (taxable income) is— At least	But less than	Single	Married filing jointly *	Married filing separately	Head of a household
41,000	41,050	8,530	6,547	9,017	7,522
41,050	41,100	8,544	6,561	9,031	7,536
41,100	41,150	8,558	6,575	9,045	7,550
41,150	41,200	8,572	6,589	9,059	7,564
41,200	41,250	8,586	6,603	9,073	7,578
41,250	41,300	8,600	6,617	9,087	7,592
41,300	41,350	8,614	6,631	9,101	7,606
41,350	41,400	8,628	6,645	9,115	7,620
41,400	41,450	8,642	6,659	9,129	7,634
41,450	41,500	8,656	6,673	9,143	7,648
41,500	41,550	8,670	6,687	9,157	7,662
41,550	41,600	8,684	6,701	9,171	7,676
41,600	41,650	8,698	6,715	9,185	7,690
41,650	41,700	8,712	6,729	9,199	7,704
41,700	41,750	8,726	6,743	9,213	7,718
41,750	41,800	8,740	6,757	9,227	7,732
41,800	41,850	8,754	6,771	9,241	7,746
41,850	41,900	8,768	6,785	9,255	7,760
41,900	41,950	8,782	6,799	9,269	7,774
41,950	42,000	8,796	6,813	9,283	7,788

42,000

At least	But less than	Single	Married filing jointly *	Married filing separately	Head of a household
42,000	42,050	8,810	6,827	9,297	7,802
42,050	42,100	8,824	6,841	9,311	7,816
42,100	42,150	8,838	6,855	9,325	7,830
42,150	42,200	8,852	6,869	9,339	7,844
42,200	42,250	8,866	6,883	9,353	7,858
42,250	42,300	8,880	6,897	9,367	7,872
42,300	42,350	8,894	6,911	9,381	7,886
42,350	42,400	8,908	6,925	9,395	7,900
42,400	42,450	8,922	6,939	9,409	7,914
42,450	42,500	8,936	6,953	9,423	7,928
42,500	42,550	8,950	6,967	9,437	7,942
42,550	42,600	8,964	6,981	9,451	7,956
42,600	42,650	8,978	6,995	9,465	7,970
42,650	42,700	8,992	7,009	9,479	7,984
42,700	42,750	9,006	7,023	9,493	7,998
42,750	42,800	9,020	7,037	9,507	8,012
42,800	42,850	9,034	7,051	9,521	8,026
42,850	42,900	9,048	7,065	9,535	8,040
42,900	42,950	9,062	7,079	9,549	8,054
42,950	43,000	9,076	7,093	9,563	8,068

43,000

At least	But less than	Single	Married filing jointly *	Married filing separately	Head of a household
43,000	43,050	9,090	7,107	9,577	8,082
43,050	43,100	9,104	7,121	9,591	8,096
43,100	43,150	9,118	7,135	9,605	8,110
43,150	43,200	9,132	7,149	9,619	8,124
43,200	43,250	9,146	7,163	9,633	8,138
43,250	43,300	9,160	7,177	9,647	8,152
43,300	43,350	9,174	7,191	9,661	8,166
43,350	43,400	9,188	7,205	9,675	8,180
43,400	43,450	9,202	7,219	9,689	8,194
43,450	43,500	9,216	7,233	9,703	8,208
43,500	43,550	9,230	7,247	9,717	8,222
43,550	43,600	9,244	7,261	9,731	8,236
43,600	43,650	9,258	7,275	9,745	8,250
43,650	43,700	9,272	7,289	9,759	8,264
43,700	43,750	9,286	7,303	9,773	8,278
43,750	43,800	9,300	7,317	9,787	8,292
43,800	43,850	9,314	7,331	9,801	8,306
43,850	43,900	9,328	7,345	9,815	8,320
43,900	43,950	9,342	7,359	9,829	8,334
43,950	44,000	9,356	7,373	9,843	8,348

44,000

At least	But less than	Single	Married filing jointly *	Married filing separately	Head of a household
44,000	44,050	9,370	7,387	9,857	8,362
44,050	44,100	9,384	7,401	9,871	8,376
44,100	44,150	9,398	7,415	9,885	8,390
44,150	44,200	9,412	7,429	9,899	8,404
44,200	44,250	9,426	7,443	9,913	8,418
44,250	44,300	9,440	7,457	9,927	8,432
44,300	44,350	9,454	7,471	9,941	8,446
44,350	44,400	9,468	7,485	9,955	8,460
44,400	44,450	9,482	7,499	9,969	8,474
44,450	44,500	9,496	7,513	9,983	8,488
44,500	44,550	9,510	7,527	9,997	8,502
44,550	44,600	9,524	7,541	10,011	8,516
44,600	44,650	9,538	7,555	10,025	8,530
44,650	44,700	9,552	7,569	10,039	8,544
44,700	44,750	9,566	7,583	10,053	8,558
44,750	44,800	9,580	7,597	10,067	8,572
44,800	44,850	9,594	7,611	10,081	8,586
44,850	44,900	9,608	7,625	10,095	8,600
44,900	44,950	9,622	7,639	10,109	8,614
44,950	45,000	9,636	7,653	10,123	8,628

45,000

At least	But less than	Single	Married filing jointly *	Married filing separately	Head of a household
45,000	45,050	9,650	7,667	10,137	8,642
45,050	45,100	9,664	7,681	10,151	8,656
45,100	45,150	9,678	7,695	10,165	8,670
45,150	45,200	9,692	7,709	10,179	8,684
45,200	45,250	9,706	7,723	10,193	8,698
45,250	45,300	9,720	7,737	10,207	8,712
45,300	45,350	9,734	7,751	10,221	8,726
45,350	45,400	9,748	7,765	10,235	8,740
45,400	45,450	9,762	7,779	10,249	8,754
45,450	45,500	9,776	7,793	10,263	8,768
45,500	45,550	9,790	7,807	10,277	8,782
45,550	45,600	9,804	7,821	10,291	8,796
45,600	45,650	9,818	7,835	10,305	8,810
45,650	45,700	9,832	7,849	10,319	8,824
45,700	45,750	9,846	7,863	10,333	8,838
45,750	45,800	9,860	7,877	10,347	8,852
45,800	45,850	9,874	7,891	10,361	8,866
45,850	45,900	9,888	7,905	10,375	8,880
45,900	45,950	9,902	7,919	10,389	8,894
45,950	46,000	9,916	7,933	10,405	8,908

46,000

At least	But less than	Single	Married filing jointly *	Married filing separately	Head of a household
46,000	46,050	9,930	7,947	10,420	8,922
46,050	46,100	9,944	7,961	10,436	8,936
46,100	46,150	9,958	7,975	10,451	8,950
46,150	46,200	9,972	7,989	10,467	8,964
46,200	46,250	9,986	8,003	10,482	8,978
46,250	46,300	10,000	8,017	10,498	8,992
46,300	46,350	10,014	8,031	10,513	9,006
46,350	46,400	10,028	8,045	10,529	9,020
46,400	46,450	10,042	8,059	10,544	9,034
46,450	46,500	10,056	8,073	10,560	9,048
46,500	46,550	10,070	8,087	10,575	9,062
46,550	46,600	10,084	8,101	10,591	9,076
46,600	46,650	10,098	8,115	10,606	9,090
46,650	46,700	10,112	8,129	10,622	9,104
46,700	46,750	10,126	8,143	10,637	9,118
46,750	46,800	10,140	8,157	10,653	9,132
46,800	46,850	10,154	8,171	10,668	9,146
46,850	46,900	10,168	8,185	10,684	9,160
46,900	46,950	10,182	8,199	10,699	9,174
46,950	47,000	10,196	8,213	10,715	9,188

47,000

At least	But less than	Single	Married filing jointly *	Married filing separately	Head of a household
47,000	47,050	10,210	8,227	10,730	9,202
47,050	47,100	10,224	8,241	10,746	9,216
47,100	47,150	10,238	8,255	10,761	9,230
47,150	47,200	10,252	8,269	10,777	9,244
47,200	47,250	10,266	8,283	10,792	9,258
47,250	47,300	10,280	8,297	10,808	9,272
47,300	47,350	10,294	8,311	10,823	9,286
47,350	47,400	10,308	8,325	10,839	9,300
47,400	47,450	10,322	8,339	10,854	9,314
47,450	47,500	10,336	8,353	10,870	9,328
47,500	47,550	10,350	8,367	10,885	9,342
47,550	47,600	10,364	8,381	10,901	9,356
47,600	47,650	10,378	8,395	10,916	9,370
47,650	47,700	10,392	8,409	10,932	9,384
47,700	47,750	10,406	8,423	10,947	9,398
47,750	47,800	10,420	8,437	10,963	9,412
47,800	47,850	10,434	8,451	10,978	9,426
47,850	47,900	10,448	8,465	10,994	9,440
47,900	47,950	10,462	8,479	11,009	9,454
47,950	48,000	10,476	8,493	11,025	9,468

48,000

At least	But less than	Single	Married filing jointly *	Married filing separately	Head of a household
48,000	48,050	10,490	8,507	11,040	9,482
48,050	48,100	10,504	8,521	11,056	9,496
48,100	48,150	10,518	8,535	11,071	9,510
48,150	48,200	10,532	8,549	11,087	9,524
48,200	48,250	10,546	8,563	11,102	9,538
48,250	48,300	10,560	8,577	11,118	9,552
48,300	48,350	10,574	8,591	11,133	9,566
48,350	48,400	10,588	8,605	11,149	9,580
48,400	48,450	10,602	8,619	11,164	9,594
48,450	48,500	10,616	8,633	11,180	9,608
48,500	48,550	10,630	8,647	11,195	9,622
48,550	48,600	10,644	8,661	11,211	9,636
48,600	48,650	10,658	8,675	11,226	9,650
48,650	48,700	10,672	8,689	11,242	9,664
48,700	48,750	10,686	8,703	11,257	9,678
48,750	48,800	10,700	8,717	11,273	9,692
48,800	48,850	10,714	8,731	11,288	9,706
48,850	48,900	10,728	8,745	11,304	9,720
48,900	48,950	10,742	8,759	11,319	9,734
48,950	49,000	10,756	8,773	11,335	9,748

49,000

At least	But less than	Single	Married filing jointly *	Married filing separately	Head of a household
49,000	49,050	10,770	8,787	11,350	9,762
49,050	49,100	10,784	8,801	11,366	9,776
49,100	49,150	10,798	8,815	11,381	9,790
49,150	49,200	10,812	8,829	11,397	9,804
49,200	49,250	10,826	8,843	11,412	9,818
49,250	49,300	10,840	8,857	11,428	9,832
49,300	49,350	10,854	8,871	11,443	9,846
49,350	49,400	10,868	8,885	11,459	9,860
49,400	49,450	10,882	8,899	11,474	9,874
49,450	49,500	10,896	8,913	11,490	9,888
49,500	49,550	10,910	8,927	11,505	9,902
49,550	49,600	10,924	8,941	11,521	9,916
49,600	49,650	10,938	8,955	11,536	9,930
49,650	49,700	10,952	8,969	11,552	9,944
49,700	49,750	10,966	8,983	11,567	9,958
49,750	49,800	10,980	8,997	11,583	9,972
49,800	49,850	10,994	9,011	11,598	9,986
49,850	49,900	11,008	9,025	11,614	10,000
49,900	49,950	11,022	9,039	11,629	10,014
49,950	50,000	11,036	9,053	11,645	10,028

* This column must also be used by a qualifying widow(er).

Continued on next page

1994 Tax Table—Continued

If line 37 (taxable income) is—		And you are—			
At least	But less than	Single	Married filing jointly *	Married filing separately	Head of a household
		Your tax is—			

50,000

At least	But less than	Single	Married filing jointly *	Married filing separately	Head of a household
50,000	50,050	11,050	9,067	11,660	10,042
50,050	50,100	11,064	9,081	11,676	10,056
50,100	50,150	11,078	9,095	11,691	10,070
50,150	50,200	11,092	9,109	11,707	10,084
50,200	50,250	11,106	9,123	11,722	10,098
50,250	50,300	11,120	9,137	11,738	10,112
50,300	50,350	11,134	9,151	11,753	10,126
50,350	50,400	11,148	9,165	11,769	10,140
50,400	50,450	11,162	9,179	11,784	10,154
50,450	50,500	11,176	9,193	11,800	10,168
50,500	50,550	11,190	9,207	11,815	10,182
50,550	50,600	11,204	9,221	11,831	10,196
50,600	50,650	11,218	9,235	11,846	10,210
50,650	50,700	11,232	9,249	11,862	10,224
50,700	50,750	11,246	9,263	11,877	10,238
50,750	50,800	11,260	9,277	11,893	10,252
50,800	50,850	11,274	9,291	11,908	10,266
50,850	50,900	11,288	9,305	11,924	10,280
50,900	50,950	11,302	9,319	11,939	10,294
50,950	51,000	11,316	9,333	11,955	10,308

51,000

At least	But less than	Single	Married filing jointly *	Married filing separately	Head of a household
51,000	51,050	11,330	9,347	11,970	10,322
51,050	51,100	11,344	9,361	11,986	10,336
51,100	51,150	11,358	9,375	12,001	10,350
51,150	51,200	11,372	9,389	12,017	10,364
51,200	51,250	11,386	9,403	12,032	10,378
51,250	51,300	11,400	9,417	12,048	10,392
51,300	51,350	11,414	9,431	12,063	10,406
51,350	51,400	11,428	9,445	12,079	10,420
51,400	51,450	11,442	9,459	12,094	10,434
51,450	51,500	11,456	9,473	12,110	10,448
51,500	51,550	11,470	9,487	12,125	10,462
51,550	51,600	11,484	9,501	12,141	10,476
51,600	51,650	11,498	9,515	12,156	10,490
51,650	51,700	11,512	9,529	12,172	10,504
51,700	51,750	11,526	9,543	12,187	10,518
51,750	51,800	11,540	9,557	12,203	10,532
51,800	51,850	11,554	9,571	12,218	10,546
51,850	51,900	11,568	9,585	12,234	10,560
51,900	51,950	11,582	9,599	12,249	10,574
51,950	52,000	11,596	9,613	12,265	10,588

52,000

At least	But less than	Single	Married filing jointly *	Married filing separately	Head of a household
52,000	52,050	11,610	9,627	12,280	10,602
52,050	52,100	11,624	9,641	12,296	10,616
52,100	52,150	11,638	9,655	12,311	10,630
52,150	52,200	11,652	9,669	12,327	10,644
52,200	52,250	11,666	9,683	12,342	10,658
52,250	52,300	11,680	9,697	12,358	10,672
52,300	52,350	11,694	9,711	12,373	10,686
52,350	52,400	11,708	9,725	12,389	10,700
52,400	52,450	11,722	9,739	12,404	10,714
52,450	52,500	11,736	9,753	12,420	10,728
52,500	52,550	11,750	9,767	12,435	10,742
52,550	52,600	11,764	9,781	12,451	10,756
52,600	52,650	11,778	9,795	12,466	10,770
52,650	52,700	11,792	9,809	12,482	10,784
52,700	52,750	11,806	9,823	12,497	10,798
52,750	52,800	11,820	9,837	12,513	10,812
52,800	52,850	11,834	9,851	12,528	10,826
52,850	52,900	11,848	9,865	12,544	10,840
52,900	52,950	11,862	9,879	12,559	10,854
52,950	53,000	11,876	9,893	12,575	10,868

53,000

At least	But less than	Single	Married filing jointly *	Married filing separately	Head of a household
53,000	53,050	11,890	9,907	12,590	10,882
53,050	53,100	11,904	9,921	12,606	10,896
53,100	53,150	11,918	9,935	12,621	10,910
53,150	53,200	11,932	9,949	12,637	10,924
53,200	53,250	11,946	9,963	12,652	10,938
53,250	53,300	11,960	9,977	12,668	10,952
53,300	53,350	11,974	9,991	12,683	10,966
53,350	53,400	11,988	10,005	12,699	10,980
53,400	53,450	12,002	10,019	12,714	10,994
53,450	53,500	12,016	10,033	12,730	11,008
53,500	53,550	12,030	10,047	12,745	11,022
53,550	53,600	12,044	10,061	12,761	11,036
53,600	53,650	12,058	10,075	12,776	11,050
53,650	53,700	12,072	10,089	12,792	11,064
53,700	53,750	12,086	10,103	12,807	11,078
53,750	53,800	12,100	10,117	12,823	11,092
53,800	53,850	12,114	10,131	12,838	11,106
53,850	53,900	12,128	10,145	12,854	11,120
53,900	53,950	12,142	10,159	12,869	11,134
53,950	54,000	12,156	10,173	12,885	11,148

54,000

At least	But less than	Single	Married filing jointly *	Married filing separately	Head of a household
54,000	54,050	12,170	10,187	12,900	11,162
54,050	54,100	12,184	10,201	12,916	11,176
54,100	54,150	12,198	10,215	12,931	11,190
54,150	54,200	12,212	10,229	12,947	11,204
54,200	54,250	12,226	10,243	12,962	11,218
54,250	54,300	12,240	10,257	12,978	11,232
54,300	54,350	12,254	10,271	12,993	11,246
54,350	54,400	12,268	10,285	13,009	11,260
54,400	54,450	12,282	10,299	13,024	11,274
54,450	54,500	12,296	10,313	13,040	11,288
54,500	54,550	12,310	10,327	13,055	11,302
54,550	54,600	12,324	10,341	13,071	11,316
54,600	54,650	12,338	10,355	13,086	11,330
54,650	54,700	12,352	10,369	13,102	11,344
54,700	54,750	12,366	10,383	13,117	11,358
54,750	54,800	12,380	10,397	13,133	11,372
54,800	54,850	12,394	10,411	13,148	11,386
54,850	54,900	12,408	10,425	13,164	11,400
54,900	54,950	12,422	10,439	13,179	11,414
54,950	55,000	12,436	10,453	13,195	11,428

55,000

At least	But less than	Single	Married filing jointly *	Married filing separately	Head of a household
55,000	55,050	12,450	10,467	13,210	11,442
55,050	55,100	12,464	10,481	13,226	11,456
55,100	55,150	12,478	10,495	13,241	11,470
55,150	55,200	12,494	10,509	13,257	11,484
55,200	55,250	12,509	10,523	13,272	11,498
55,250	55,300	12,525	10,537	13,288	11,512
55,300	55,350	12,540	10,551	13,303	11,526
55,350	55,400	12,556	10,565	13,319	11,540
55,400	55,450	12,571	10,579	13,334	11,554
55,450	55,500	12,587	10,593	13,350	11,568
55,500	55,550	12,602	10,607	13,365	11,582
55,550	55,600	12,618	10,621	13,381	11,596
55,600	55,650	12,633	10,635	13,396	11,610
55,650	55,700	12,649	10,649	13,412	11,624
55,700	55,750	12,664	10,663	13,427	11,638
55,750	55,800	12,680	10,677	13,443	11,652
55,800	55,850	12,695	10,691	13,458	11,666
55,850	55,900	12,711	10,705	13,474	11,680
55,900	55,950	12,726	10,719	13,489	11,694
55,950	56,000	12,742	10,733	13,505	11,708

56,000

At least	But less than	Single	Married filing jointly *	Married filing separately	Head of a household
56,000	56,050	12,757	10,747	13,520	11,722
56,050	56,100	12,773	10,761	13,536	11,736
56,100	56,150	12,788	10,775	13,551	11,750
56,150	56,200	12,804	10,789	13,567	11,764
56,200	56,250	12,819	10,803	13,582	11,778
56,250	56,300	12,835	10,817	13,598	11,792
56,300	56,350	12,850	10,831	13,613	11,806
56,350	56,400	12,866	10,845	13,629	11,820
56,400	56,450	12,881	10,859	13,644	11,834
56,450	56,500	12,897	10,873	13,660	11,848
56,500	56,550	12,912	10,887	13,675	11,862
56,550	56,600	12,928	10,901	13,691	11,876
56,600	56,650	12,943	10,915	13,706	11,890
56,650	56,700	12,959	10,929	13,722	11,904
56,700	56,750	12,974	10,943	13,737	11,918
56,750	56,800	12,990	10,957	13,753	11,932
56,800	56,850	13,005	10,971	13,768	11,946
56,850	56,900	13,021	10,985	13,784	11,960
56,900	56,950	13,036	10,999	13,799	11,974
56,950	57,000	13,052	11,013	13,815	11,988

57,000

At least	But less than	Single	Married filing jointly *	Married filing separately	Head of a household
57,000	57,050	13,067	11,027	13,830	12,002
57,050	57,100	13,083	11,041	13,846	12,016
57,100	57,150	13,098	11,055	13,861	12,030
57,150	57,200	13,114	11,069	13,877	12,044
57,200	57,250	13,129	11,083	13,892	12,058
57,250	57,300	13,145	11,097	13,908	12,072
57,300	57,350	13,160	11,111	13,923	12,086
57,350	57,400	13,176	11,125	13,939	12,100
57,400	57,450	13,191	11,139	13,954	12,114
57,450	57,500	13,207	11,153	13,970	12,128
57,500	57,550	13,222	11,167	13,985	12,142
57,550	57,600	13,238	11,181	14,001	12,156
57,600	57,650	13,253	11,195	14,016	12,170
57,650	57,700	13,269	11,209	14,032	12,184
57,700	57,750	13,284	11,223	14,047	12,198
57,750	57,800	13,300	11,237	14,063	12,212
57,800	57,850	13,315	11,251	14,078	12,226
57,850	57,900	13,331	11,265	14,094	12,240
57,900	57,950	13,346	11,279	14,109	12,254
57,950	58,000	13,362	11,293	14,125	12,268

58,000

At least	But less than	Single	Married filing jointly *	Married filing separately	Head of a household
58,000	58,050	13,377	11,307	14,140	12,282
58,050	58,100	13,393	11,321	14,156	12,296
58,100	58,150	13,408	11,335	14,171	12,310
58,150	58,200	13,424	11,349	14,187	12,324
58,200	58,250	13,439	11,363	14,202	12,338
58,250	58,300	13,455	11,377	14,218	12,352
58,300	58,350	13,470	11,391	14,233	12,366
58,350	58,400	13,486	11,405	14,249	12,380
58,400	58,450	13,501	11,419	14,264	12,394
58,450	58,500	13,517	11,433	14,280	12,408
58,500	58,550	13,532	11,447	14,295	12,422
58,550	58,600	13,548	11,461	14,311	12,436
58,600	58,650	13,563	11,475	14,326	12,450
58,650	58,700	13,579	11,489	14,342	12,464
58,700	58,750	13,594	11,503	14,357	12,478
58,750	58,800	13,610	11,517	14,373	12,492
58,800	58,850	13,625	11,531	14,388	12,506
58,850	58,900	13,641	11,545	14,404	12,520
58,900	58,950	13,656	11,559	14,419	12,534
58,950	59,000	13,672	11,573	14,435	12,548

* This column must also be used by a qualifying widow(er).

Continued on next page

1994 Tax Table—_Continued_

If line 37 (taxable income) is— / And you are—

At least	But less than	Single	Married filing jointly *	Married filing separately	Head of a household

Your tax is—

59,000

At least	But less than	Single	Married filing jointly	Married filing separately	Head of a household
59,000	59,050	13,687	11,587	14,450	12,562
59,050	59,100	13,703	11,601	14,466	12,576
59,100	59,150	13,718	11,615	14,481	12,590
59,150	59,200	13,734	11,629	14,497	12,604
59,200	59,250	13,749	11,643	14,512	12,618
59,250	59,300	13,765	11,657	14,528	12,632
59,300	59,350	13,780	11,671	14,543	12,646
59,350	59,400	13,796	11,685	14,559	12,660
59,400	59,450	13,811	11,699	14,574	12,674
59,450	59,500	13,827	11,713	14,590	12,688
59,500	59,550	13,842	11,727	14,605	12,702
59,550	59,600	13,858	11,741	14,621	12,716
59,600	59,650	13,873	11,755	14,636	12,730
59,650	59,700	13,889	11,769	14,652	12,744
59,700	59,750	13,904	11,783	14,667	12,758
59,750	59,800	13,920	11,797	14,683	12,772
59,800	59,850	13,935	11,811	14,698	12,786
59,850	59,900	13,951	11,825	14,714	12,800
59,900	59,950	13,966	11,839	14,729	12,814
59,950	60,000	13,982	11,853	14,745	12,828

60,000

At least	But less than	Single	Married filing jointly	Married filing separately	Head of a household
60,000	60,050	13,997	11,867	14,760	12,842
60,050	60,100	14,013	11,881	14,776	12,856
60,100	60,150	14,028	11,895	14,791	12,870
60,150	60,200	14,044	11,909	14,807	12,884
60,200	60,250	14,059	11,923	14,822	12,898
60,250	60,300	14,075	11,937	14,838	12,912
60,300	60,350	14,090	11,951	14,853	12,926
60,350	60,400	14,106	11,965	14,869	12,940
60,400	60,450	14,121	11,979	14,884	12,954
60,450	60,500	14,137	11,993	14,900	12,968
60,500	60,550	14,152	12,007	14,915	12,982
60,550	60,600	14,168	12,021	14,931	12,996
60,600	60,650	14,183	12,035	14,946	13,010
60,650	60,700	14,199	12,049	14,962	13,024
60,700	60,750	14,214	12,063	14,977	13,038
60,750	60,800	14,230	12,077	14,993	13,052
60,800	60,850	14,245	12,091	15,008	13,066
60,850	60,900	14,261	12,105	15,024	13,080
60,900	60,950	14,276	12,119	15,039	13,094
60,950	61,000	14,292	12,133	15,055	13,108

61,000

At least	But less than	Single	Married filing jointly	Married filing separately	Head of a household
61,000	61,050	14,307	12,147	15,070	13,122
61,050	61,100	14,323	12,161	15,086	13,136
61,100	61,150	14,338	12,175	15,101	13,150
61,150	61,200	14,354	12,189	15,117	13,164
61,200	61,250	14,369	12,203	15,132	13,178
61,250	61,300	14,385	12,217	15,148	13,192
61,300	61,350	14,400	12,231	15,163	13,206
61,350	61,400	14,416	12,245	15,179	13,220
61,400	61,450	14,431	12,259	15,194	13,234
61,450	61,500	14,447	12,273	15,210	13,248
61,500	61,550	14,462	12,287	15,225	13,262
61,550	61,600	14,478	12,301	15,241	13,276
61,600	61,650	14,493	12,315	15,256	13,290
61,650	61,700	14,509	12,329	15,272	13,304
61,700	61,750	14,524	12,343	15,287	13,318
61,750	61,800	14,540	12,357	15,303	13,332
61,800	61,850	14,555	12,371	15,318	13,346
61,850	61,900	14,571	12,385	15,334	13,360
61,900	61,950	14,586	12,399	15,349	13,374
61,950	62,000	14,602	12,413	15,365	13,388

62,000

At least	But less than	Single	Married filing jointly	Married filing separately	Head of a household
62,000	62,050	14,617	12,427	15,380	13,402
62,050	62,100	14,633	12,441	15,396	13,416
62,100	62,150	14,648	12,455	15,411	13,430
62,150	62,200	14,664	12,469	15,427	13,444
62,200	62,250	14,679	12,483	15,442	13,458
62,250	62,300	14,695	12,497	15,458	13,472
62,300	62,350	14,710	12,511	15,473	13,486
62,350	62,400	14,726	12,525	15,489	13,500
62,400	62,450	14,741	12,539	15,504	13,514
62,450	62,500	14,757	12,553	15,520	13,528
62,500	62,550	14,772	12,567	15,535	13,542
62,550	62,600	14,788	12,581	15,551	13,556
62,600	62,650	14,803	12,595	15,566	13,570
62,650	62,700	14,819	12,609	15,582	13,584
62,700	62,750	14,834	12,623	15,597	13,598
62,750	62,800	14,850	12,637	15,613	13,612
62,800	62,850	14,865	12,651	15,628	13,626
62,850	62,900	14,881	12,665	15,644	13,640
62,900	62,950	14,896	12,679	15,659	13,654
62,950	63,000	14,912	12,693	15,675	13,668

63,000

At least	But less than	Single	Married filing jointly	Married filing separately	Head of a household
63,000	63,050	14,927	12,707	15,690	13,682
63,050	63,100	14,943	12,721	15,706	13,696
63,100	63,150	14,958	12,735	15,721	13,710
63,150	63,200	14,974	12,749	15,737	13,724
63,200	63,250	14,989	12,763	15,752	13,738
63,250	63,300	15,005	12,777	15,768	13,752
63,300	63,350	15,020	12,791	15,783	13,766
63,350	63,400	15,036	12,805	15,799	13,780
63,400	63,450	15,051	12,819	15,814	13,794
63,450	63,500	15,067	12,833	15,830	13,808
63,500	63,550	15,082	12,847	15,845	13,822
63,550	63,600	15,098	12,861	15,861	13,836
63,600	63,650	15,113	12,875	15,876	13,850
63,650	63,700	15,129	12,889	15,892	13,864
63,700	63,750	15,144	12,903	15,907	13,878
63,750	63,800	15,160	12,917	15,923	13,892
63,800	63,850	15,175	12,931	15,938	13,906
63,850	63,900	15,191	12,945	15,954	13,920
63,900	63,950	15,206	12,959	15,969	13,934
63,950	64,000	15,222	12,973	15,985	13,948

64,000

At least	But less than	Single	Married filing jointly	Married filing separately	Head of a household
64,000	64,050	15,237	12,987	16,000	13,962
64,050	64,100	15,253	13,001	16,016	13,976
64,100	64,150	15,268	13,015	16,031	13,990
64,150	64,200	15,284	13,029	16,047	14,004
64,200	64,250	15,299	13,043	16,062	14,018
64,250	64,300	15,315	13,057	16,078	14,032
64,300	64,350	15,330	13,071	16,093	14,046
64,350	64,400	15,346	13,085	16,109	14,060
64,400	64,450	15,361	13,099	16,124	14,074
64,450	64,500	15,377	13,113	16,140	14,088
64,500	64,550	15,392	13,127	16,155	14,102
64,550	64,600	15,408	13,141	16,171	14,116
64,600	64,650	15,423	13,155	16,186	14,130
64,650	64,700	15,439	13,169	16,202	14,144
64,700	64,750	15,454	13,183	16,217	14,158
64,750	64,800	15,470	13,197	16,233	14,172
64,800	64,850	15,485	13,211	16,248	14,186
64,850	64,900	15,501	13,225	16,264	14,200
64,900	64,950	15,516	13,239	16,279	14,214
64,950	65,000	15,532	13,253	16,295	14,228

65,000

At least	But less than	Single	Married filing jointly	Married filing separately	Head of a household
65,000	65,050	15,547	13,267	16,310	14,242
65,050	65,100	15,563	13,281	16,326	14,256
65,100	65,150	15,578	13,295	16,341	14,270
65,150	65,200	15,594	13,309	16,357	14,284
65,200	65,250	15,609	13,323	16,372	14,298
65,250	65,300	15,625	13,337	16,388	14,312
65,300	65,350	15,640	13,351	16,403	14,326
65,350	65,400	15,656	13,365	16,419	14,340
65,400	65,450	15,671	13,379	16,434	14,354
65,450	65,500	15,687	13,393	16,450	14,368
65,500	65,550	15,702	13,407	16,465	14,382
65,550	65,600	15,718	13,421	16,481	14,396
65,600	65,650	15,733	13,435	16,496	14,410
65,650	65,700	15,749	13,449	16,512	14,424
65,700	65,750	15,764	13,463	16,527	14,438
65,750	65,800	15,780	13,477	16,543	14,452
65,800	65,850	15,795	13,491	16,558	14,466
65,850	65,900	15,811	13,505	16,574	14,480
65,900	65,950	15,826	13,519	16,589	14,494
65,950	66,000	15,842	13,533	16,605	14,508

66,000

At least	But less than	Single	Married filing jointly	Married filing separately	Head of a household
66,000	66,050	15,857	13,547	16,620	14,522
66,050	66,100	15,873	13,561	16,636	14,536
66,100	66,150	15,888	13,575	16,651	14,550
66,150	66,200	15,904	13,589	16,667	14,564
66,200	66,250	15,919	13,603	16,682	14,578
66,250	66,300	15,935	13,617	16,698	14,592
66,300	66,350	15,950	13,631	16,713	14,606
66,350	66,400	15,966	13,645	16,729	14,620
66,400	66,450	15,981	13,659	16,744	14,634
66,450	66,500	15,997	13,673	16,760	14,648
66,500	66,550	16,012	13,687	16,775	14,662
66,550	66,600	16,028	13,701	16,791	14,676
66,600	66,650	16,043	13,715	16,806	14,690
66,650	66,700	16,059	13,729	16,822	14,704
66,700	66,750	16,074	13,743	16,837	14,718
66,750	66,800	16,090	13,757	16,853	14,732
66,800	66,850	16,105	13,771	16,868	14,746
66,850	66,900	16,121	13,785	16,884	14,760
66,900	66,950	16,136	13,799	16,899	14,774
66,950	67,000	16,152	13,813	16,915	14,788

67,000

At least	But less than	Single	Married filing jointly	Married filing separately	Head of a household
67,000	67,050	16,167	13,827	16,930	14,802
67,050	67,100	16,183	13,841	16,946	14,816
67,100	67,150	16,198	13,855	16,961	14,830
67,150	67,200	16,214	13,869	16,977	14,844
67,200	67,250	16,229	13,883	16,992	14,858
67,250	67,300	16,245	13,897	17,008	14,872
67,300	67,350	16,260	13,911	17,023	14,886
67,350	67,400	16,276	13,925	17,039	14,900
67,400	67,450	16,291	13,939	17,054	14,914
67,450	67,500	16,307	13,953	17,070	14,928
67,500	67,550	16,322	13,967	17,085	14,942
67,550	67,600	16,338	13,981	17,101	14,956
67,600	67,650	16,353	13,995	17,116	14,970
67,650	67,700	16,369	14,009	17,132	14,984
67,700	67,750	16,384	14,023	17,147	14,998
67,750	67,800	16,400	14,037	17,163	15,012
67,800	67,850	16,415	14,051	17,178	15,026
67,850	67,900	16,431	14,065	17,194	15,040
67,900	67,950	16,446	14,079	17,209	15,054
67,950	68,000	16,462	14,093	17,225	15,068

* This column must also be used by a qualifying widow(er).

Continued on next page

1994 Tax Table—_Continued_

If line 37 (taxable income) is—		And you are—			
At least	But less than	Single	Married filing jointly*	Married filing separately	Head of a household
		Your tax is—			

68,000

At least	But less than	Single	MFJ*	MFS	HoH
68,000	68,050	16,477	14,107	17,240	15,082
68,050	68,100	16,493	14,121	17,256	15,096
68,100	68,150	16,508	14,135	17,271	15,110
68,150	68,200	16,524	14,149	17,287	15,124
68,200	68,250	16,539	14,163	17,302	15,138
68,250	68,300	16,555	14,177	17,318	15,152
68,300	68,350	16,570	14,191	17,333	15,166
68,350	68,400	16,586	14,205	17,349	15,180
68,400	68,450	16,601	14,219	17,364	15,194
68,450	68,500	16,617	14,233	17,380	15,208
68,500	68,550	16,632	14,247	17,395	15,222
68,550	68,600	16,648	14,261	17,411	15,236
68,600	68,650	16,663	14,275	17,426	15,250
68,650	68,700	16,679	14,289	17,442	15,264
68,700	68,750	16,694	14,303	17,457	15,278
68,750	68,800	16,710	14,317	17,473	15,292
68,800	68,850	16,725	14,331	17,488	15,306
68,850	68,900	16,741	14,345	17,504	15,320
68,900	68,950	16,756	14,359	17,519	15,334
68,950	69,000	16,772	14,373	17,535	15,348

69,000

At least	But less than	Single	MFJ*	MFS	HoH
69,000	69,050	16,787	14,387	17,550	15,362
69,050	69,100	16,803	14,401	17,566	15,376
69,100	69,150	16,818	14,415	17,581	15,390
69,150	69,200	16,834	14,429	17,597	15,404
69,200	69,250	16,849	14,443	17,612	15,418
69,250	69,300	16,865	14,457	17,628	15,432
69,300	69,350	16,880	14,471	17,643	15,446
69,350	69,400	16,896	14,485	17,659	15,460
69,400	69,450	16,911	14,499	17,674	15,474
69,450	69,500	16,927	14,513	17,690	15,488
69,500	69,550	16,942	14,527	17,705	15,502
69,550	69,600	16,958	14,541	17,721	15,516
69,600	69,650	16,973	14,555	17,736	15,530
69,650	69,700	16,989	14,569	17,752	15,544
69,700	69,750	17,004	14,583	17,767	15,558
69,750	69,800	17,020	14,597	17,783	15,572
69,800	69,850	17,035	14,611	17,798	15,586
69,850	69,900	17,051	14,625	17,814	15,600
69,900	69,950	17,066	14,639	17,829	15,614
69,950	70,000	17,082	14,653	17,845	15,628

70,000

At least	But less than	Single	MFJ*	MFS	HoH
70,000	70,050	17,097	14,667	17,861	15,642
70,050	70,100	17,113	14,681	17,879	15,656
70,100	70,150	17,128	14,695	17,897	15,670
70,150	70,200	17,144	14,709	17,915	15,684
70,200	70,250	17,159	14,723	17,933	15,698
70,250	70,300	17,175	14,737	17,951	15,712
70,300	70,350	17,190	14,751	17,969	15,726
70,350	70,400	17,206	14,765	17,987	15,740
70,400	70,450	17,221	14,779	18,005	15,754
70,450	70,500	17,237	14,793	18,023	15,768
70,500	70,550	17,252	14,807	18,041	15,782
70,550	70,600	17,268	14,821	18,059	15,796
70,600	70,650	17,283	14,835	18,077	15,810
70,650	70,700	17,299	14,849	18,095	15,824
70,700	70,750	17,314	14,863	18,113	15,838
70,750	70,800	17,330	14,877	18,131	15,852
70,800	70,850	17,345	14,891	18,149	15,866
70,850	70,900	17,361	14,905	18,167	15,880
70,900	70,950	17,376	14,919	18,185	15,894
70,950	71,000	17,392	14,933	18,203	15,908

71,000

At least	But less than	Single	MFJ*	MFS	HoH
71,000	71,050	17,407	14,947	18,221	15,922
71,050	71,100	17,423	14,961	18,239	15,936
71,100	71,150	17,438	14,975	18,257	15,950
71,150	71,200	17,454	14,989	18,275	15,964
71,200	71,250	17,469	15,003	18,293	15,978
71,250	71,300	17,485	15,017	18,311	15,992
71,300	71,350	17,500	15,031	18,329	16,006
71,350	71,400	17,516	15,045	18,347	16,020
71,400	71,450	17,531	15,059	18,365	16,034
71,450	71,500	17,547	15,073	18,383	16,048
71,500	71,550	17,562	15,087	18,401	16,062
71,550	71,600	17,578	15,101	18,419	16,076
71,600	71,650	17,593	15,115	18,437	16,090
71,650	71,700	17,609	15,129	18,455	16,104
71,700	71,750	17,624	15,143	18,473	16,118
71,750	71,800	17,640	15,157	18,491	16,132
71,800	71,850	17,655	15,171	18,509	16,146
71,850	71,900	17,671	15,185	18,527	16,160
71,900	71,950	17,686	15,199	18,545	16,174
71,950	72,000	17,702	15,213	18,563	16,188

72,000

At least	But less than	Single	MFJ*	MFS	HoH
72,000	72,050	17,717	15,227	18,581	16,202
72,050	72,100	17,733	15,241	18,599	16,216
72,100	72,150	17,748	15,255	18,617	16,230
72,150	72,200	17,764	15,269	18,635	16,244
72,200	72,250	17,779	15,283	18,653	16,258
72,250	72,300	17,795	15,297	18,671	16,272
72,300	72,350	17,810	15,311	18,689	16,286
72,350	72,400	17,826	15,325	18,707	16,300
72,400	72,450	17,841	15,339	18,725	16,314
72,450	72,500	17,857	15,353	18,743	16,328
72,500	72,550	17,872	15,367	18,761	16,342
72,550	72,600	17,888	15,381	18,779	16,356
72,600	72,650	17,903	15,395	18,797	16,370
72,650	72,700	17,919	15,409	18,815	16,384
72,700	72,750	17,934	15,423	18,833	16,398
72,750	72,800	17,950	15,437	18,851	16,412
72,800	72,850	17,965	15,451	18,869	16,426
72,850	72,900	17,981	15,465	18,887	16,440
72,900	72,950	17,996	15,479	18,905	16,454
72,950	73,000	18,012	15,493	18,923	16,468

73,000

At least	But less than	Single	MFJ*	MFS	HoH
73,000	73,050	18,027	15,507	18,941	16,482
73,050	73,100	18,043	15,521	18,959	16,496
73,100	73,150	18,058	15,535	18,977	16,510
73,150	73,200	18,074	15,549	18,995	16,524
73,200	73,250	18,089	15,563	19,013	16,538
73,250	73,300	18,105	15,577	19,031	16,552
73,300	73,350	18,120	15,591	19,049	16,566
73,350	73,400	18,136	15,605	19,067	16,580
73,400	73,450	18,151	15,619	19,085	16,594
73,450	73,500	18,167	15,633	19,103	16,608
73,500	73,550	18,182	15,647	19,121	16,622
73,550	73,600	18,198	15,661	19,139	16,636
73,600	73,650	18,213	15,675	19,157	16,650
73,650	73,700	18,229	15,689	19,175	16,664
73,700	73,750	18,244	15,703	19,193	16,678
73,750	73,800	18,260	15,717	19,211	16,692
73,800	73,850	18,275	15,731	19,229	16,706
73,850	73,900	18,291	15,745	19,247	16,720
73,900	73,950	18,306	15,759	19,265	16,734
73,950	74,000	18,322	15,773	19,283	16,748

74,000

At least	But less than	Single	MFJ*	MFS	HoH
74,000	74,050	18,337	15,787	19,301	16,762
74,050	74,100	18,353	15,801	19,319	16,776
74,100	74,150	18,368	15,815	19,337	16,790
74,150	74,200	18,384	15,829	19,355	16,804
74,200	74,250	18,399	15,843	19,373	16,818
74,250	74,300	18,415	15,857	19,391	16,832
74,300	74,350	18,430	15,871	19,409	16,846
74,350	74,400	18,446	15,885	19,427	16,860
74,400	74,450	18,461	15,899	19,445	16,874
74,450	74,500	18,477	15,913	19,463	16,888
74,500	74,550	18,492	15,927	19,481	16,902
74,550	74,600	18,508	15,941	19,499	16,916
74,600	74,650	18,523	15,955	19,517	16,930
74,650	74,700	18,539	15,969	19,535	16,944
74,700	74,750	18,554	15,983	19,553	16,958
74,750	74,800	18,570	15,997	19,571	16,972
74,800	74,850	18,585	16,011	19,589	16,986
74,850	74,900	18,601	16,025	19,607	17,000
74,900	74,950	18,616	16,039	19,625	17,014
74,950	75,000	18,632	16,053	19,643	17,028

75,000

At least	But less than	Single	MFJ*	MFS	HoH
75,000	75,050	18,647	16,067	19,661	17,042
75,050	75,100	18,663	16,081	19,679	17,056
75,100	75,150	18,678	16,095	19,697	17,070
75,150	75,200	18,694	16,109	19,715	17,084
75,200	75,250	18,709	16,123	19,733	17,098
75,250	75,300	18,725	16,137	19,751	17,112
75,300	75,350	18,740	16,151	19,769	17,126
75,350	75,400	18,756	16,165	19,787	17,140
75,400	75,450	18,771	16,179	19,805	17,154
75,450	75,500	18,787	16,193	19,823	17,168
75,500	75,550	18,802	16,207	19,841	17,182
75,550	75,600	18,818	16,221	19,859	17,196
75,600	75,650	18,833	16,235	19,877	17,210
75,650	75,700	18,849	16,249	19,895	17,224
75,700	75,750	18,864	16,263	19,913	17,238
75,750	75,800	18,880	16,277	19,931	17,252
75,800	75,850	18,895	16,291	19,949	17,266
75,850	75,900	18,911	16,305	19,967	17,280
75,900	75,950	18,926	16,319	19,985	17,294
75,950	76,000	18,942	16,333	20,003	17,308

76,000

At least	But less than	Single	MFJ*	MFS	HoH
76,000	76,050	18,957	16,347	20,021	17,322
76,050	76,100	18,973	16,361	20,039	17,336
76,100	76,150	18,988	16,375	20,057	17,350
76,150	76,200	19,004	16,389	20,075	17,364
76,200	76,250	19,019	16,403	20,093	17,378
76,250	76,300	19,035	16,417	20,111	17,392
76,300	76,350	19,050	16,431	20,129	17,406
76,350	76,400	19,066	16,445	20,147	17,420
76,400	76,450	19,081	16,459	20,165	17,434
76,450	76,500	19,097	16,473	20,183	17,448
76,500	76,550	19,112	16,487	20,201	17,462
76,550	76,600	19,128	16,501	20,219	17,476
76,600	76,650	19,143	16,515	20,237	17,490
76,650	76,700	19,159	16,529	20,255	17,504
76,700	76,750	19,174	16,543	20,273	17,518
76,750	76,800	19,190	16,557	20,291	17,532
76,800	76,850	19,205	16,571	20,309	17,546
76,850	76,900	19,221	16,585	20,327	17,560
76,900	76,950	19,236	16,599	20,345	17,574
76,950	77,000	19,252	16,613	20,363	17,588

* This column must also be used by a qualifying widow(er).

Continued on next page

1994 Tax Table—*Continued*

If line 37 (taxable income) is—		And you are—				If line 37 (taxable income) is—		And you are—				If line 37 (taxable income) is—		And you are—			
At least	But less than	Single	Married filing jointly *	Married filing separately	Head of a household	At least	But less than	Single	Married filing jointly *	Married filing separately	Head of a household	At least	But less than	Single	Married filing jointly *	Married filing separately	Head of a household
		Your tax is—						Your tax is—						Your tax is—			
77,000						**80,000**						**83,000**					
77,000	77,050	19,267	16,627	20,381	17,602	80,000	80,050	20,197	17,467	21,461	18,482	83,000	83,050	21,127	18,307	22,541	19,412
77,050	77,100	19,283	16,641	20,399	17,616	80,050	80,100	20,213	17,481	21,479	18,497	83,050	83,100	21,143	18,321	22,559	19,427
77,100	77,150	19,298	16,655	20,417	17,630	80,100	80,150	20,228	17,495	21,497	18,513	83,100	83,150	21,158	18,335	22,577	19,443
77,150	77,200	19,314	16,669	20,435	17,644	80,150	80,200	20,244	17,509	21,515	18,528	83,150	83,200	21,174	18,349	22,595	19,458
77,200	77,250	19,329	16,683	20,453	17,658	80,200	80,250	20,259	17,523	21,533	18,544	83,200	83,250	21,189	18,363	22,613	19,474
77,250	77,300	19,345	16,697	20,471	17,672	80,250	80,300	20,275	17,537	21,551	18,559	83,250	83,300	21,205	18,377	22,631	19,489
77,300	77,350	19,360	16,711	20,489	17,686	80,300	80,350	20,290	17,551	21,569	18,575	83,300	83,350	21,220	18,391	22,649	19,505
77,350	77,400	19,376	16,725	20,507	17,700	80,350	80,400	20,306	17,565	21,587	18,590	83,350	83,400	21,236	18,405	22,667	19,520
77,400	77,450	19,391	16,739	20,525	17,714	80,400	80,450	20,321	17,579	21,605	18,606	83,400	83,450	21,251	18,419	22,685	19,536
77,450	77,500	19,407	16,753	20,543	17,728	80,450	80,500	20,337	17,593	21,623	18,621	83,450	83,500	21,267	18,433	22,703	19,551
77,500	77,550	19,422	16,767	20,561	17,742	80,500	80,550	20,352	17,607	21,641	18,637	83,500	83,550	21,282	18,447	22,721	19,567
77,550	77,600	19,438	16,781	20,579	17,756	80,550	80,600	20,368	17,621	21,659	18,652	83,550	83,600	21,298	18,461	22,739	19,582
77,600	77,650	19,453	16,795	20,597	17,770	80,600	80,650	20,383	17,635	21,677	18,668	83,600	83,650	21,313	18,475	22,757	19,598
77,650	77,700	19,469	16,809	20,615	17,784	80,650	80,700	20,399	17,649	21,695	18,683	83,650	83,700	21,329	18,489	22,775	19,613
77,700	77,750	19,484	16,823	20,633	17,798	80,700	80,750	20,414	17,663	21,713	18,699	83,700	83,750	21,344	18,503	22,793	19,629
77,750	77,800	19,500	16,837	20,651	17,812	80,750	80,800	20,430	17,677	21,731	18,714	83,750	83,800	21,360	18,517	22,811	19,644
77,800	77,850	19,515	16,851	20,669	17,826	80,800	80,850	20,445	17,691	21,749	18,730	83,800	83,850	21,375	18,531	22,829	19,660
77,850	77,900	19,531	16,865	20,687	17,840	80,850	80,900	20,461	17,705	21,767	18,745	83,850	83,900	21,391	18,545	22,847	19,675
77,900	77,950	19,546	16,879	20,705	17,854	80,900	80,950	20,476	17,719	21,785	18,761	83,900	83,950	21,406	18,559	22,865	19,691
77,950	78,000	19,562	16,893	20,723	17,868	80,950	81,000	20,492	17,733	21,803	18,776	83,950	84,000	21,422	18,573	22,883	19,706
78,000						**81,000**						**84,000**					
78,000	78,050	19,577	16,907	20,741	17,882	81,000	81,050	20,507	17,747	21,821	18,792	84,000	84,050	21,437	18,587	22,901	19,722
78,050	78,100	19,593	16,921	20,759	17,896	81,050	81,100	20,523	17,761	21,839	18,807	84,050	84,100	21,453	18,601	22,919	19,737
78,100	78,150	19,608	16,935	20,777	17,910	81,100	81,150	20,538	17,775	21,857	18,823	84,100	84,150	21,468	18,615	22,937	19,753
78,150	78,200	19,624	16,949	20,795	17,924	81,150	81,200	20,554	17,789	21,875	18,838	84,150	84,200	21,484	18,629	22,955	19,768
78,200	78,250	19,639	16,963	20,813	17,938	81,200	81,250	20,569	17,803	21,893	18,854	84,200	84,250	21,499	18,643	22,973	19,784
78,250	78,300	19,655	16,977	20,831	17,952	81,250	81,300	20,585	17,817	21,911	18,869	84,250	84,300	21,515	18,657	22,991	19,799
78,300	78,350	19,670	16,991	20,849	17,966	81,300	81,350	20,600	17,831	21,929	18,885	84,300	84,350	21,530	18,671	23,009	19,815
78,350	78,400	19,686	17,005	20,867	17,980	81,350	81,400	20,616	17,845	21,947	18,900	84,350	84,400	21,546	18,685	23,027	19,830
78,400	78,450	19,701	17,019	20,885	17,994	81,400	81,450	20,631	17,859	21,965	18,916	84,400	84,450	21,561	18,699	23,045	19,846
78,450	78,500	19,717	17,033	20,903	18,008	81,450	81,500	20,647	17,873	21,983	18,931	84,450	84,500	21,577	18,713	23,063	19,861
78,500	78,550	19,732	17,047	20,921	18,022	81,500	81,550	20,662	17,887	22,001	18,947	84,500	84,550	21,592	18,727	23,081	19,877
78,550	78,600	19,748	17,061	20,939	18,036	81,550	81,600	20,678	17,901	22,019	18,962	84,550	84,600	21,608	18,741	23,099	19,892
78,600	78,650	19,763	17,075	20,957	18,050	81,600	81,650	20,693	17,915	22,037	18,978	84,600	84,650	21,623	18,755	23,117	19,908
78,650	78,700	19,779	17,089	20,975	18,064	81,650	81,700	20,709	17,929	22,055	18,993	84,650	84,700	21,639	18,769	23,135	19,923
78,700	78,750	19,794	17,103	20,993	18,079	81,700	81,750	20,724	17,943	22,073	19,009	84,700	84,750	21,654	18,783	23,153	19,939
78,750	78,800	19,810	17,117	21,011	18,094	81,750	81,800	20,740	17,957	22,091	19,024	84,750	84,800	21,670	18,797	23,171	19,954
78,800	78,850	19,825	17,131	21,029	18,110	81,800	81,850	20,755	17,971	22,109	19,040	84,800	84,850	21,685	18,811	23,189	19,970
78,850	78,900	19,841	17,145	21,047	18,125	81,850	81,900	20,771	17,985	22,127	19,055	84,850	84,900	21,701	18,825	23,207	19,985
78,900	78,950	19,856	17,159	21,065	18,141	81,900	81,950	20,786	17,999	22,145	19,071	84,900	84,950	21,716	18,839	23,225	20,001
78,950	79,000	19,872	17,173	21,083	18,156	81,950	82,000	20,802	18,013	22,163	19,086	84,950	85,000	21,732	18,853	23,243	20,016
79,000						**82,000**						**85,000**					
79,000	79,050	19,887	17,187	21,101	18,172	82,000	82,050	20,817	18,027	22,181	19,102	85,000	85,050	21,747	18,867	23,261	20,032
79,050	79,100	19,903	17,201	21,119	18,187	82,050	82,100	20,833	18,041	22,199	19,117	85,050	85,100	21,763	18,881	23,279	20,047
79,100	79,150	19,918	17,215	21,137	18,203	82,100	82,150	20,848	18,055	22,217	19,133	85,100	85,150	21,778	18,895	23,297	20,063
79,150	79,200	19,934	17,229	21,155	18,218	82,150	82,200	20,864	18,069	22,235	19,148	85,150	85,200	21,794	18,909	23,315	20,078
79,200	79,250	19,949	17,243	21,173	18,234	82,200	82,250	20,879	18,083	22,253	19,164	85,200	85,250	21,809	18,923	23,333	20,094
79,250	79,300	19,965	17,257	21,191	18,249	82,250	82,300	20,895	18,097	22,271	19,179	85,250	85,300	21,825	18,937	23,351	20,109
79,300	79,350	19,980	17,271	21,209	18,265	82,300	82,350	20,910	18,111	22,289	19,195	85,300	85,350	21,840	18,951	23,369	20,125
79,350	79,400	19,996	17,285	21,227	18,280	82,350	82,400	20,926	18,125	22,307	19,210	85,350	85,400	21,856	18,965	23,387	20,140
79,400	79,450	20,011	17,299	21,245	18,296	82,400	82,450	20,941	18,139	22,325	19,226	85,400	85,450	21,871	18,979	23,405	20,156
79,450	79,500	20,027	17,313	21,263	18,311	82,450	82,500	20,957	18,153	22,343	19,241	85,450	85,500	21,887	18,993	23,423	20,171
79,500	79,550	20,042	17,327	21,281	18,327	82,500	82,550	20,972	18,167	22,361	19,257	85,500	85,550	21,902	19,007	23,441	20,187
79,550	79,600	20,058	17,341	21,299	18,342	82,550	82,600	20,988	18,181	22,379	19,272	85,550	85,600	21,918	19,021	23,459	20,202
79,600	79,650	20,073	17,355	21,317	18,358	82,600	82,650	21,003	18,195	22,397	19,288	85,600	85,650	21,933	19,035	23,477	20,218
79,650	79,700	20,089	17,369	21,335	18,373	82,650	82,700	21,019	18,209	22,415	19,303	85,650	85,700	21,949	19,049	23,495	20,233
79,700	79,750	20,104	17,383	21,353	18,389	82,700	82,750	21,034	18,223	22,433	19,319	85,700	85,750	21,964	19,063	23,513	20,249
79,750	79,800	20,120	17,397	21,371	18,404	82,750	82,800	21,050	18,237	22,451	19,334	85,750	85,800	21,980	19,077	23,531	20,264
79,800	79,850	20,135	17,411	21,389	18,420	82,800	82,850	21,065	18,251	22,469	19,350	85,800	85,850	21,995	19,091	23,549	20,280
79,850	79,900	20,151	17,425	21,407	18,435	82,850	82,900	21,081	18,265	22,487	19,365	85,850	85,900	22,011	19,105	23,567	20,295
79,900	79,950	20,166	17,439	21,425	18,451	82,900	82,950	21,096	18,279	22,505	19,381	85,900	85,950	22,026	19,119	23,585	20,311
79,950	80,000	20,182	17,453	21,443	18,466	82,950	83,000	21,112	18,293	22,523	19,396	85,950	86,000	22,042	19,133	23,603	20,326

* This column must also be used by a qualifying widow(er).

Continued on next page

1994 Tax Table—Continued

If line 37 (taxable income) is—		And you are—			
At least	But less than	Single	Married filing jointly *	Married filing separately	Head of a household
			Your tax is—		

86,000

At least	But less than	Single	Married filing jointly	Married filing separately	Head of a household
86,000	86,050	22,057	19,147	23,621	20,342
86,050	86,100	22,073	19,161	23,639	20,357
86,100	86,150	22,088	19,175	23,657	20,373
86,150	86,200	22,104	19,189	23,675	20,388
86,200	86,250	22,119	19,203	23,693	20,404
86,250	86,300	22,135	19,217	23,711	20,419
86,300	86,350	22,150	19,231	23,729	20,435
86,350	86,400	22,166	19,245	23,747	20,450
86,400	86,450	22,181	19,259	23,765	20,466
86,450	86,500	22,197	19,273	23,783	20,481
86,500	86,550	22,212	19,287	23,801	20,497
86,550	86,600	22,228	19,301	23,819	20,512
86,600	86,650	22,243	19,315	23,837	20,528
86,650	86,700	22,259	19,329	23,855	20,543
86,700	86,750	22,274	19,343	23,873	20,559
86,750	86,800	22,290	19,357	23,891	20,574
86,800	86,850	22,305	19,371	23,909	20,590
86,850	86,900	22,321	19,385	23,927	20,605
86,900	86,950	22,336	19,399	23,945	20,621
86,950	87,000	22,352	19,413	23,963	20,636

87,000

At least	But less than	Single	Married filing jointly	Married filing separately	Head of a household
87,000	87,050	22,367	19,427	23,981	20,652
87,050	87,100	22,383	19,441	23,999	20,667
87,100	87,150	22,398	19,455	24,017	20,683
87,150	87,200	22,414	19,469	24,035	20,698
87,200	87,250	22,429	19,483	24,053	20,714
87,250	87,300	22,445	19,497	24,071	20,729
87,300	87,350	22,460	19,511	24,089	20,745
87,350	87,400	22,476	19,525	24,107	20,760
87,400	87,450	22,491	19,539	24,125	20,776
87,450	87,500	22,507	19,553	24,143	20,791
87,500	87,550	22,522	19,567	24,161	20,807
87,550	87,600	22,538	19,581	24,179	20,822
87,600	87,650	22,553	19,595	24,197	20,838
87,650	87,700	22,569	19,609	24,215	20,853
87,700	87,750	22,584	19,623	24,233	20,869
87,750	87,800	22,600	19,637	24,251	20,884
87,800	87,850	22,615	19,651	24,269	20,900
87,850	87,900	22,631	19,665	24,287	20,915
87,900	87,950	22,646	19,679	24,305	20,931
87,950	88,000	22,662	19,693	24,323	20,946

88,000

At least	But less than	Single	Married filing jointly	Married filing separately	Head of a household
88,000	88,050	22,677	19,707	24,341	20,962
88,050	88,100	22,693	19,721	24,359	20,977
88,100	88,150	22,708	19,735	24,377	20,993
88,150	88,200	22,724	19,749	24,395	21,008
88,200	88,250	22,739	19,763	24,413	21,024
88,250	88,300	22,755	19,777	24,431	21,039
88,300	88,350	22,770	19,791	24,449	21,055
88,350	88,400	22,786	19,805	24,467	21,070
88,400	88,450	22,801	19,819	24,485	21,086
88,450	88,500	22,817	19,833	24,503	21,101
88,500	88,550	22,832	19,847	24,521	21,117
88,550	88,600	22,848	19,861	24,539	21,132
88,600	88,650	22,863	19,875	24,557	21,148
88,650	88,700	22,879	19,889	24,575	21,163
88,700	88,750	22,894	19,903	24,593	21,179
88,750	88,800	22,910	19,917	24,611	21,194
88,800	88,850	22,925	19,931	24,629	21,210
88,850	88,900	22,941	19,945	24,647	21,225
88,900	88,950	22,956	19,959	24,665	21,241
88,950	89,000	22,972	19,973	24,683	21,256

89,000

At least	But less than	Single	Married filing jointly	Married filing separately	Head of a household
89,000	89,050	22,987	19,987	24,701	21,272
89,050	89,100	23,003	20,001	24,719	21,287
89,100	89,150	23,018	20,015	24,737	21,303
89,150	89,200	23,034	20,029	24,755	21,318
89,200	89,250	23,049	20,043	24,773	21,334
89,250	89,300	23,065	20,057	24,791	21,349
89,300	89,350	23,080	20,071	24,809	21,365
89,350	89,400	23,096	20,085	24,827	21,380
89,400	89,450	23,111	20,099	24,845	21,396
89,450	89,500	23,127	20,113	24,863	21,411
89,500	89,550	23,142	20,127	24,881	21,427
89,550	89,600	23,158	20,141	24,899	21,442
89,600	89,650	23,173	20,155	24,917	21,458
89,650	89,700	23,189	20,169	24,935	21,473
89,700	89,750	23,204	20,183	24,953	21,489
89,750	89,800	23,220	20,197	24,971	21,504
89,800	89,850	23,235	20,211	24,989	21,520
89,850	89,900	23,251	20,225	25,007	21,535
89,900	89,950	23,266	20,239	25,025	21,551
89,950	90,000	23,282	20,253	25,043	21,566

90,000

At least	But less than	Single	Married filing jointly	Married filing separately	Head of a household
90,000	90,050	23,297	20,267	25,061	21,582
90,050	90,100	23,313	20,281	25,079	21,597
90,100	90,150	23,328	20,295	25,097	21,613
90,150	90,200	23,344	20,309	25,115	21,628
90,200	90,250	23,359	20,323	25,133	21,644
90,250	90,300	23,375	20,337	25,151	21,659
90,300	90,350	23,390	20,351	25,169	21,675
90,350	90,400	23,406	20,365	25,187	21,690
90,400	90,450	23,421	20,379	25,205	21,706
90,450	90,500	23,437	20,393	25,223	21,721
90,500	90,550	23,452	20,407	25,241	21,737
90,550	90,600	23,468	20,421	25,259	21,752
90,600	90,650	23,483	20,435	25,277	21,768
90,650	90,700	23,499	20,449	25,295	21,783
90,700	90,750	23,514	20,463	25,313	21,799
90,750	90,800	23,530	20,477	25,331	21,814
90,800	90,850	23,545	20,491	25,349	21,830
90,850	90,900	23,561	20,505	25,367	21,845
90,900	90,950	23,576	20,519	25,385	21,861
90,950	91,000	23,592	20,533	25,403	21,876

91,000

At least	But less than	Single	Married filing jointly	Married filing separately	Head of a household
91,000	91,050	23,607	20,547	25,421	21,892
91,050	91,100	23,623	20,561	25,439	21,907
91,100	91,150	23,638	20,575	25,457	21,923
91,150	91,200	23,654	20,589	25,475	21,938
91,200	91,250	23,669	20,603	25,493	21,954
91,250	91,300	23,685	20,617	25,511	21,969
91,300	91,350	23,700	20,631	25,529	21,985
91,350	91,400	23,716	20,645	25,547	22,000
91,400	91,450	23,731	20,659	25,565	22,016
91,450	91,500	23,747	20,673	25,583	22,031
91,500	91,550	23,762	20,687	25,601	22,047
91,550	91,600	23,778	20,701	25,619	22,062
91,600	91,650	23,793	20,715	25,637	22,078
91,650	91,700	23,809	20,729	25,655	22,093
91,700	91,750	23,824	20,743	25,673	22,109
91,750	91,800	23,840	20,757	25,691	22,124
91,800	91,850	23,855	20,771	25,709	22,140
91,850	91,900	23,871	20,786	25,727	22,155
91,900	91,950	23,886	20,801	25,745	22,171
91,950	92,000	23,902	20,817	25,763	22,186

92,000

At least	But less than	Single	Married filing jointly	Married filing separately	Head of a household
92,000	92,050	23,917	20,832	25,781	22,202
92,050	92,100	23,933	20,848	25,799	22,217
92,100	92,150	23,948	20,863	25,817	22,233
92,150	92,200	23,964	20,879	25,835	22,248
92,200	92,250	23,979	20,894	25,853	22,264
92,250	92,300	23,995	20,910	25,871	22,279
92,300	92,350	24,010	20,925	25,889	22,295
92,350	92,400	24,026	20,941	25,907	22,310
92,400	92,450	24,041	20,956	25,925	22,326
92,450	92,500	24,057	20,972	25,943	22,341
92,500	92,550	24,072	20,987	25,961	22,357
92,550	92,600	24,088	21,003	25,979	22,372
92,600	92,650	24,103	21,018	25,997	22,388
92,650	92,700	24,119	21,034	26,015	22,403
92,700	92,750	24,134	21,049	26,033	22,419
92,750	92,800	24,150	21,065	26,051	22,434
92,800	92,850	24,165	21,080	26,069	22,450
92,850	92,900	24,181	21,096	26,087	22,465
92,900	92,950	24,196	21,111	26,105	22,481
92,950	93,000	24,212	21,127	26,123	22,496

93,000

At least	But less than	Single	Married filing jointly	Married filing separately	Head of a household
93,000	93,050	24,227	21,142	26,141	22,512
93,050	93,100	24,243	21,158	26,159	22,527
93,100	93,150	24,258	21,173	26,177	22,543
93,150	93,200	24,274	21,189	26,195	22,558
93,200	93,250	24,289	21,204	26,213	22,574
93,250	93,300	24,305	21,220	26,231	22,589
93,300	93,350	24,320	21,235	26,249	22,605
93,350	93,400	24,336	21,251	26,267	22,620
93,400	93,450	24,351	21,266	26,285	22,636
93,450	93,500	24,367	21,282	26,303	22,651
93,500	93,550	24,382	21,297	26,321	22,667
93,550	93,600	24,398	21,313	26,339	22,682
93,600	93,650	24,413	21,328	26,357	22,698
93,650	93,700	24,429	21,344	26,375	22,713
93,700	93,750	24,444	21,359	26,393	22,729
93,750	93,800	24,460	21,375	26,411	22,744
93,800	93,850	24,475	21,390	26,429	22,760
93,850	93,900	24,491	21,406	26,447	22,775
93,900	93,950	24,506	21,421	26,465	22,791
93,950	94,000	24,522	21,437	26,483	22,806

94,000

At least	But less than	Single	Married filing jointly	Married filing separately	Head of a household
94,000	94,050	24,537	21,452	26,501	22,822
94,050	94,100	24,553	21,468	26,519	22,837
94,100	94,150	24,568	21,483	26,537	22,853
94,150	94,200	24,584	21,499	26,555	22,868
94,200	94,250	24,599	21,514	26,573	22,884
94,250	94,300	24,615	21,530	26,591	22,899
94,300	94,350	24,630	21,545	26,609	22,915
94,350	94,400	24,646	21,561	26,627	22,930
94,400	94,450	24,661	21,576	26,645	22,946
94,450	94,500	24,677	21,592	26,663	22,961
94,500	94,550	24,692	21,607	26,681	22,977
94,550	94,600	24,708	21,623	26,699	22,992
94,600	94,650	24,723	21,638	26,717	23,008
94,650	94,700	24,739	21,654	26,735	23,023
94,700	94,750	24,754	21,669	26,753	23,039
94,750	94,800	24,770	21,685	26,771	23,054
94,800	94,850	24,785	21,700	26,789	23,070
94,850	94,900	24,801	21,716	26,807	23,085
94,900	94,950	24,816	21,731	26,825	23,101
94,950	95,000	24,832	21,747	26,843	23,116

* This column must also be used by a qualifying widow(er).

Continued on next page

1994 Tax Table—*Continued*

If line 37 (taxable income) is—		And you are—				If line 37 (taxable income) is—		And you are—			
At least	But less than	Single	Married filing jointly *	Married filing sepa-rately	Head of a house-hold	At least	But less than	Single	Married filing jointly *	Married filing sepa-rately	Head of a house-hold
		Your tax is—						Your tax is—			

95,000

95,000	95,050	24,847	21,762	26,861	23,132	98,000	98,050	25,777	22,692	27,941	24,062
95,050	95,100	24,863	21,778	26,879	23,147	98,050	98,100	25,793	22,708	27,959	24,077
95,100	95,150	24,878	21,793	26,897	23,163	98,100	98,150	25,808	22,723	27,977	24,093
95,150	95,200	24,894	21,809	26,915	23,178	98,150	98,200	25,824	22,739	27,995	24,108
95,200	95,250	24,909	21,824	26,933	23,194	98,200	98,250	25,839	22,754	28,013	24,124
95,250	95,300	24,925	21,840	26,951	23,209	98,250	98,300	25,855	22,770	28,031	24,139
95,300	95,350	24,940	21,855	26,969	23,225	98,300	98,350	25,870	22,785	28,049	24,155
95,350	95,400	24,956	21,871	26,987	23,240	98,350	98,400	25,886	22,801	28,067	24,170
95,400	95,450	24,971	21,886	27,005	23,256	98,400	98,450	25,901	22,816	28,085	24,186
95,450	95,500	24,987	21,902	27,023	23,271	98,450	98,500	25,917	22,832	28,103	24,201
95,500	95,550	25,002	21,917	27,041	23,287	98,500	98,550	25,932	22,847	28,121	24,217
95,550	95,600	25,018	21,933	27,059	23,302	98,550	98,600	25,948	22,863	28,139	24,232
95,600	95,650	25,033	21,948	27,077	23,318	98,600	98,650	25,963	22,878	28,157	24,248
95,650	95,700	25,049	21,964	27,095	23,333	98,650	98,700	25,979	22,894	28,175	24,263
95,700	95,750	25,064	21,979	27,113	23,349	98,700	98,750	25,994	22,909	28,193	24,279
95,750	95,800	25,080	21,995	27,131	23,364	98,750	98,800	26,010	22,925	28,211	24,294
95,800	95,850	25,095	22,010	27,149	23,380	98,800	98,850	26,025	22,940	28,229	24,310
95,850	95,900	25,111	22,026	27,167	23,395	98,850	98,900	26,041	22,956	28,247	24,325
95,900	95,950	25,126	22,041	27,185	23,411	98,900	98,950	26,056	22,971	28,265	24,341
95,950	96,000	25,142	22,057	27,203	23,426	98,950	99,000	26,072	22,987	28,283	24,356

96,000

96,000	96,050	25,157	22,072	27,221	23,442	99,000	99,050	26,087	23,002	28,301	24,372
96,050	96,100	25,173	22,088	27,239	23,457	99,050	99,100	26,103	23,018	28,319	24,387
96,100	96,150	25,188	22,103	27,257	23,473	99,100	99,150	26,118	23,033	28,337	24,403
96,150	96,200	25,204	22,119	27,275	23,488	99,150	99,200	26,134	23,049	28,355	24,418
96,200	96,250	25,219	22,134	27,293	23,504	99,200	99,250	26,149	23,064	28,373	24,434
96,250	96,300	25,235	22,150	27,311	23,519	99,250	99,300	26,165	23,080	28,391	24,449
96,300	96,350	25,250	22,165	27,329	23,535	99,300	99,350	26,180	23,095	28,409	24,465
96,350	96,400	25,266	22,181	27,347	23,550	99,350	99,400	26,196	23,111	28,427	24,480
96,400	96,450	25,281	22,196	27,365	23,566	99,400	99,450	26,211	23,126	28,445	24,496
96,450	96,500	25,297	22,212	27,383	23,581	99,450	99,500	26,227	23,142	28,463	24,511
96,500	96,550	25,312	22,227	27,401	23,597	99,500	99,550	26,242	23,157	28,481	24,527
96,550	96,600	25,328	22,243	27,419	23,612	99,550	99,600	26,258	23,173	28,499	24,542
96,600	96,650	25,343	22,258	27,437	23,628	99,600	99,650	26,273	23,188	28,517	24,558
96,650	96,700	25,359	22,274	27,455	23,643	99,650	99,700	26,289	23,204	28,535	24,573
96,700	96,750	25,374	22,289	27,473	23,659	99,700	99,750	26,304	23,219	28,553	24,589
96,750	96,800	25,390	22,305	27,491	23,674	99,750	99,800	26,320	23,235	28,571	24,604
96,800	96,850	25,405	22,320	27,509	23,690	99,800	99,850	26,335	23,250	28,589	24,620
96,850	96,900	25,421	22,336	27,527	23,705	99,850	99,900	26,351	23,266	28,607	24,635
96,900	96,950	25,436	22,351	27,545	23,721	99,900	99,950	26,366	23,281	28,625	24,651
96,950	97,000	25,452	22,367	27,563	23,736	99,950	100,000	26,382	23,297	28,643	24,666

97,000

97,000	97,050	25,467	22,382	27,581	23,752
97,050	97,100	25,483	22,398	27,599	23,767
97,100	97,150	25,498	22,413	27,617	23,783
97,150	97,200	25,514	22,429	27,635	23,798
97,200	97,250	25,529	22,444	27,653	23,814
97,250	97,300	25,545	22,460	27,671	23,829
97,300	97,350	25,560	22,475	27,689	23,845
97,350	97,400	25,576	22,491	27,707	23,860
97,400	97,450	25,591	22,506	27,725	23,876
97,450	97,500	25,607	22,522	27,743	23,891
97,500	97,550	25,622	22,537	27,761	23,907
97,550	97,600	25,638	22,553	27,779	23,922
97,600	97,650	25,653	22,568	27,797	23,938
97,650	97,700	25,669	22,584	27,815	23,953
97,700	97,750	25,684	22,599	27,833	23,969
97,750	97,800	25,700	22,615	27,851	23,984
97,800	97,850	25,715	22,630	27,869	24,000
97,850	97,900	25,731	22,646	27,887	24,015
97,900	97,950	25,746	22,661	27,905	24,031
97,950	98,000	25,762	22,677	27,923	24,046

$100,000 or over — use the Tax Rate Schedules on page 58

* This column must also be used by a qualifying widow(er).

TAX RETURN PROBLEM

▲ INTRODUCTION

This tax return problem represents an ongoing accumulation of tax return preparation material for the Schnappauf family. The information is presented in three phases, which correspond to the three major components of computing income tax—gross income, deductions and losses, and property transactions. If your instructor assigns these problems at the end of each major segment (i.e., Chapter 4, Chapter 8, and Chapter 13), you should complete the appropriate portions of the forms indicated. If you are not using a tax software package, you should not complete the second page of Form 1040 until you have completed Chapter 13.

Completing the tax return problem will help you understand the reporting procedures for the information in each major segment of the text. In addition, it will aid you in reviewing the major topics discussed in the book; it serves as an overview of the course.

▲ THE SCHNAPPAUF FAMILY

Bill and Joyce Schnappauf are married and live in Wakefield, Rhode Island. Bill is 37 and Joyce is 35. The Schnappaufs have three children, Will, 6, Danny, 4, and Tommy, 1. In March 1994, Bill was promoted from district sales manager to regional sales manager. The new job requires that Bill spend more time at the company's regional sales office in Quincy, Massachusetts. Before the promotion, he spent two days a month at the Quincy office and most of the month meeting with sales personnel in their territories. The Schnappaufs, both life-long residents of Rhode Island, decided to stay in Rhode Island but move closer to Bill's office. In February 1995, the Schnappaufs provided you with the following basic information for preparing their 1994 federal income tax return:

1. The Schnappaufs use the cash method of accounting and file their return on a calendar-year basis.

2. Unless otherwise stated, assume that the Schnappaufs want to minimize the current year's tax liability. That is, they would like to defer income when possible and take the largest deductions possible, a practice they have followed in the past.

3. Joyce's Social Security number is 371-42-5207.

4. Bill's Social Security number is 150-52-0546.

5. Will's Social Security number is 372-46-2611.

6. Danny's Social Security number is 377-42-3411.

7. Tommy's Social Security number is 375-49-6511.

8. They do not have any foreign bank accounts or foreign trusts.

9. The Schnappaufs' original Rhode Island address was 27 Northup Street, Wakefield, Rhode Island (02879); their new Rhode Island address is 3242 Heights Drive, Barrington, Rhode Island (02806). The address on the 1040 form should be the Barrington address.

10. The Schnappaufs do not wish to contribute to the presidential election campaign.

▲ PHASE I— CHAPTERS 1–4

The first phase of the tax return problem is designed to introduce you to some of the tax forms and the supporting documentation (forms W-2, 1099-INT, etc.) needed to complete a basic tax return. The first four chapters focus on the income aspects of individual taxation. Accordingly, this phase of the tax return focuses on the basic concepts of income.

Bill Schnappauf is employed by USC Equipment Corporation, a Rhode Island firm that manufactures and distributes gaming equipment. Until his promotion, Bill was the Rhode Island, Massachusetts, and Connecticut district sales manager and worked out of the company's Quincy office. Joyce Schnappauf is self-employed as an author and illustrator of children's books.

1. Bill's W-2 is provided (Exhibit B–1). The W-2 reflects his salary of $82,000 and bonus of $55,000 for 1994.

2. During the year, the Schnappaufs received five 1099-INTs for interest (see exhibits B–2 to B–6) and five 1099-DIVs (see exhibits B–7 to B–11) for dividends.

3. Joyce and her brother Bob are co-owners of and active participants in a furniture-restoration business. Joyce owns 30% and Bob owns 70% of the business. This business was formed as an S corporation in 1990. During 1994, the company paid $1,700 in dividends. Joyce's basis in the S corporation is $8,700.

4. The Schnappaufs received their 1993 federal income tax refund of $621 on May 12, 1994.

5. On May 15, 1994, they received an income tax refund from the state of Rhode Island, and the state mailed the Schnappaufs a Form 1099-G in January 1995 (see Exhibit B–12). In 1993, their total itemized deductions were $38,500.

6. During 1994, Joyce was the lucky ninety-third caller to a local radio station and won a complete stereo system. Despite her repeated calls to the radio station, she has not received a Form 1099-MISC. The manufacturer's suggested price for a similar stereo system is $1,100. However, Joyce has a catalog from Supersonic Electronics that advertises the system for $980.

7. The Schnappaufs received a Form W-2G in January 1995 (see Exhibit B–13) related to their winnings during a trip to the Yardly Casino in Connecticut.

8. On June 26, 1994, Bill received a check for $8,300 from the United Insurance Co. Bill was unaware of it, but he was the designated beneficiary of an insurance policy on the life of his father. The policy had a maturity value of $8,100, and the statement enclosed by the company showed that his father had paid premiums on the policy of $3,700. Of the amount Bill received, $200 was designated as interest accrued since the day his father died.

9. To complete phase I, you will need Form 1040, Schedule B, and Schedule D.

INSTRUCTIONS: If you are using tax software to prepare the tax return, and/or are not completing phases II or III of the problem, ignore the instructions that follow.

If you are preparing the return manually, you cannot complete some of the forms (e.g., Form 1040) used in phase I until you receive additional information, provided in phase II or phase III. Therefore, as a general rule, you should only post the information to the appropriate form and not compute totals for that form. The following specific instructions will assist you in preparing Part I of the return.

a. The only form that can be totaled is Schedule B.

b. Only post the appropriate information to Schedule D. Do not total any column. More information is provided in phases II and III of the tax return problem.

c. Do not calculate total income or adjusted gross income on page 1 of Form 1040.

d. Post the appropriate information on page 2 of Form 1040, but do not total this page, compute the federal tax liability, or determine the refund or balance due.

▲ PHASE II— CHAPTERS 5–8

In the continuing saga of a year in the life of the Schnappauf family, this is the second phase of the tax return problem that you began at the end of Chapter 4. This phase of the tax return incorporates material from chapters 5, 6, 7, and 8 by providing you with information concerning the Schnappaufs' deductions for 1994.

In March 1994, Bill was named regional sales manager for USC Equipment. On September 16, 1994, the Schnappaufs sold their Wakefield home and moved to Barrington, Rhode Island. They closed on their Barrington home on September 19, 1994. The Schnappaufs provided you with the following information for preparing their 1994 tax return:

1. Joyce writes children's books for a variety of publishers. As a freelance writer, Joyce incurs costs associated with preparing a manuscript for which she does not yet have a contract. During the year, Joyce made 4 business trips, each 3 days long, to meet with various publishers. For shorter trips that are closer to home, she drives over and back the same day. The information on Joyce's business is listed next. The Schnappaufs' homes in both Wakefield and Barrington have 3 telephones but only 1 telephone line (number).

Royalties (see exhibits B–14 to B–16)	
Office supplies	$1,800
Airfare (4 trips)	4,000
Lodging (12 nights)	1,500
Meals (12 days)	850
Telephone (monthly fee—Wakefield and Barrington)	230
Long-distance business-related telephone calls	450
Business-related postage	1,100
Printing/copying	600
Legal fees	500
Interest on auto	1,035

2. On January 2, 1994, Joyce purchased a new car to be used in her business. The car, a Roadster, cost $15,500; Joyce paid $5,500 in cash and financed the balance through Roadster Motor Credit. She used the car 35% of the time for business in 1994. She drove the car a total of 13,000 miles during 1994. The total expenses for the 13,000 miles driven were as follows: car repairs and maintenance expenses, $125; insurance, $540; and gas, $945. The correct depreciation expense for 1994 is $543 (i.e., $15,500 × 35% × 10%).

3. In both Wakefield and Barrington, Joyce worked out of her home. In Wakefield, her home office was located in an area of the family room. Her home office occupied 150 square feet, and the total square footage of the house was 2,500. However, in the Barrington house, Joyce's home offce is located in a room that is used exclusively for her work. The room is 420 square feet, and the total square footage of the house is 3,500. The Wakefield home cost $60,000 when purchased on July 7, 1985. The local practice is to allocate 10% of the purchase price to land. The Barrington house cost $275,000, and the local practice is to allocate 15% of the price of the house to land. Joyce started her business on January 1, 1989. The depreciation percentage for the Wakefield house is 0.03175 and for the Barrington house is 0.00749. The fair market value (FMV) of the Wakefield house on January 1, 1989, was $108,000. The total household expenses for 1994 are as follows:

	Wakefield	Barrington
Heat	$1,500	$600
Insurance	380	125
Electricity	800	230
Repairs	800	-0-

4. Bill and Joyce each contributed $2,000 to their respective IRA accounts for 1994. Bill participated in USC's pension plan; Joyce's retirement vehicle is her IRA account.

5. On June 15, 1994, the Schnappaufs' 1993 station wagon was totaled in Hurricane Ann. They had purchased the car in November 1993 for $27,300. The Schnappaufs received a check for $24,300 from Zippy Insurance Co. that represented the fair market value of the car minus a $500 deductible. On July 6, 1994, the Schnappaufs replaced the car totaled in the hurricane with a new 1994 station wagon. The new car cost $28,500, and the Schnappaufs received a rebate check from the car's manufacturer for $1,500.

6. The hurricane also damaged part of the Schnappaufs' Wakefield house. A tree fell and created a hole in the roof above the kitchen. Water damaged the kitchen, causing the brand new dishwasher to short out; it had to be replaced. In addition, the linoleum floor needed to be replaced. The cost of fixing the hole in the roof was $1,000; because the Schnappaufs carried replacement-value insurance, they received $750 ($1,000 minus $250 deductible) to fix the roof. The information concerning the property is as follows:

Property	Original Cost	FMV Before	FMV After	Reimbursement
Dishwasher	$ 550	$ 550	-0-	$ 525
Floor	$1,400	$1,100	-0-	$1,500

7. In 1994, the Schnappaufs incurred the following medical expenses (before considering the $625 reimbursement they received):

Medical premiums	$1,440
Doctors	1,500
Chiropractor	300
Dentist	840
Vet fees (family dog Sandy)	175
Prescription drugs	225
Over-the-counter drugs (aspirin, cough syrup)	325

In addition, Bill purchased an Exsoaligner machine for $850. The machine was recommended by the chiropractor to help strengthen Bill's back muscles.

8. On July 1, 1992, Bill loaned $15,000 to his uncle George. George used the money in his business. The loan agreement required George to pay Bill interest at 8% per year with the interest due on December 31 of each year. The loan is due in 5 annual installments of $3,000 each, beginning on July 1, 1994. On April 8, 1994, Bill received a letter notifying him that George had filed for bankruptcy. Bill was unaware of George's financial problems, because George had paid interest on the loan in 1992 and 1993. The bankruptcy letter indicates that creditors should expect to receive 20 cents for each dollar owed them. On

January 8, 1995, Bill receives $2,500 from the bankruptcy court in full settlement of the loan.

9. The Schnappaufs paid the following property taxes:

Wakefield house	$1,750
Barrington house	1,400
Bill's car (ad valorem)	225
Joyce's car (ad valorem)	325

10. During 1994, the Schnappaufs, as listed here, received three 1098s for the cost of interest on bank loans; they also had interest on their personal credit cards:

Jefferson Trust 1098 (see Exhibit B–17) (Wakefield house—#4786102)
Jefferson Trust 1098 (see Exhibit B–18) (Home equity—#4786102H)
Narragansett Bay Bank 1098 (see Exhibit B–19) (Barrington house—#5731025)

Dempsey's Department Store revolving account	$125
Brooks' Bargain Basement revolving account	85
Jefferson Trust bank card	340

11. Bill and Joyce made charitable contributions of cash in 1994 to the Wakefield United Fund Campaign ($1,750), Christ the King Church in Kingston, Rhode Island ($4,300), and St. Paul's Church in Barrington ($1,800). They also donated some property to the Salvation Army on July 15, 1994.

Property	FMV	Original Cost	Date Acquired
Antique table	$275	$125	1/4/87
Dishwasher	$135	375	5/6/86
Sofa bed	$185	625	12/14/85
Man's suits (2)	$130	225	11/19/90

The Schnappaufs have received the proper acknowledgments in writing from each of the charities.

12. The Schnappaufs incurred the following expenses:

Type	Amount
1993 tax preparation fee (paid in 1994)	$775
Safety deposit box	75
Investment journals	285
Investment advice	540
Publications (related to Bill's business)	220

13. The Schnappaufs hired a local moving company to move to Barrington. Because the closing of the Wakefield house was 3 days before the closing on the Barrington house, the Schnappaufs had to stay in a hotel. The costs incurred in the move were as follows:

Transportation of goods	$1,800
Transportation of family	10
Lodging (3 nights @ $85 per night)	255
Meals (3 days)	225
Total	$2,290

14. Other information:
    a. The name of Joyce's business is Queensbridge Books, and her employer I.D. # is 05-3456345.

b. The Barrington house is 47 miles from the Wakefield house. Bill's Quincy office is 52 miles from the Barrington house. The Wakefield house was 82 miles from the Quincy office. NOTE: Before and after the promotion, Bill's regular workplace was the Quincy office.

c. The Salvation Army's address is 15 High Street, Wakefield, R.I. 02879.

d. To complete phase II, you will need the following additional forms: Schedule A, Schedule C, Schedule SE, and forms 3903, 4562, 4684, 8283, 8606, and 8829.

INSTRUCTIONS: If you are using tax software to prepare the tax return, and/or are not completing phase III of the problem, ignore the instructions that follow.

As in phase I, there are forms in phase II that cannot be completed without additional information, provided in phase III. The following instructions will aid you in doing this phase of the return:

a. The only forms that can be completed at the end of phase II are forms 3903, 8606, and 8283.

b. Do not calculate total income or adjusted gross income on page 1 of Form 1040.

c. Post the appropriate information on page 2 of Form 1040, but do not total this page, compute the federal tax liability, or determine the refund or balance due.

d. Do not calculate the Schnappaufs' total itemized deductions on Schedule A.

e. Do not total Joyce's expenses on Schedule C.

f. Do not compute Joyce's self-employment tax (i.e., Schedule SE).

g. Do not complete the summary section of Form 4562.

h. Complete Form 4684 only to the point at which adjusted gross income is requested.

i. On Form 8829, complete Part I, post the appropriate indirect expenses, and calculate the allowable depreciation. Do not calculate the allowable home office deduction.

This is the third and final phase of the Schnappauf family's tax return. This phase incorporates the material in chapters 9 to 13 and requires you to analyze the various types of property transactions discussed in those chapters.

▲ **PHASE III— CHAPTERS 9–13**

1. On February 11, 1994, Bill inherited his parents' summer home. The house, located in Lake Tahoe, Nevada, had a fair market value of $185,000 at the date of his father's death. His parents had purchased the house in 1955 for $9,500 and made $27,500-worth of capital improvements to the house. Approximately 20% of the total value of property is attributable to the land. Because Bill and Joyce ultimately would like to use the property as a vacation home or perhaps move to that area in the future, they decided to rent the property. Bill actively participates in the management of the property. The property was first advertised for rent on March 1, 1994, but was not rented until April 15, 1994.

Bill provided the following income and expense information for the Lake Tahoe rental property for 1994:

Rents	$8,700
Repairs	1,500
Management fee	3,000
Advertising expense	500
Property taxes	2,600
Insurance	800

In addition, Bill bought a new stove for $750 and a new refrigerator for $950.

2. On December 5, 1985, Bill and Joyce acquired a duplex for $50,000. They paid $5,000 down and financed the balance with Waterford Savings Bank. The property is located in a town adjacent to Wakefield, and Bill spent about 200 hours managing the property. During 1994, the Schnappaufs had the following income and expenses relating to the duplex. The property was rented continuously since December 15, 1985, and—with the exception of the first year—has never shown a loss. As with the Wakefield personal residence, the value of the land is 10% of the purchase price.

Income	$7,950
Repairs	635
Property tax (through 6/30/94)	1,100
Interest	3,600
Insurance	420

3. When the Schnappaufs decided to move closer to Bill's office, they decided to sell the duplex so that they could afford to buy a larger and more expensive home. On August 10, 1994, they sold the duplex for $85,000 (see exhibits B–20 and B–21).

4. During 1994, the Schnappaufs had several sales of marketable securities. Bill's college roommate is a broker with Pebble Beach Investors and manages their portfolio. The selling price listed is net of brokerage commissions. In other words, it represents the amount the Schnappaufs actually received.

Asset	Date Acquired	Date Sold	Selling Price	Basis
150 shares Lion Corp.	5/12/79	7/15/94	$ 3,700	*
300 shares Kangaroo Corp.	7/30/84	10/25/94	12,800	**
50 shares Baja Inc.	4/10/94	10/23/94	1,020	$ 640
25 shares Karen Corp.	4/28/94	8/4/94	375	725
60 shares Robins Indus.	9/11/94	10/27/94	4,275	5,400
300 shares Paper Prod. Inc.	1/7/91	5/20/94	$ 2,760	3,450

*When Joyce graduated from college on May 12, 1979, her father gave her 150 shares of Lion Corporation. Her father had acquired the stock on October 27, 1971, for $1,300. At the date of the gift, the fair market value of the stock was $1,800. In January 1988, Lion Corporation split 2 for 1.
**The Schnappaufs acquired 500 shares of preferred stock in Kangaroo Corporation for $7,810. Shortly after the purchase, they received a nontaxable 10% stock dividend.

5. On May 12, 1994, Joyce purchased a computer system for $3,500 (including monitor and keyboard). She also bought $850-worth of software, a laser printer ($1,100), and a fax machine ($1,450). All the computer equipment is used exclusively in her business.

6. On June 12, 1994, she sold her old computer system for $1,200. She had acquired the system on February 18, 1991, for $5,000. When the Schnappaufs prepared their 1991 tax return, they elected to expense the computer using Section 179. In addition, Joyce sold the software for $350. The original cost of the software, all acquired in 1991, was $920. All the computer equipment was used exclusively in her business.

7. On January 9, 1994, Joyce sold her old car for $5,200. She had purchased the car on August 31, 1991, for $11,500. Throughout 1991, 1992, and 1993, Joyce used the car 40% of time for business. During the life of the car, she used

actual costs instead of the mileage rate. NOTE: The car was not used for business or personal use during 1994.

8. The Schnappaufs sold their Wakefield home on September 16, 1994 (see Exhibit B–22). They paid $8,200 in commissions on the sale of the house and incurred no fix-up costs. They closed on their Barrington house on September 19, 1994.

9. Bob, Joyce's brother and a CPA, prepared the subchapter S tax return for the furniture-restoration business for the year 1994 and sent Joyce her Schedule K-1 (see Exhibit B–23). Joyce's basis in the stock of the business is $8,700.

10. Because Bill and Joyce anticipated a significant tax liability from the sale of their duplex and securities during 1994, they made an estimated federal tax payment on January 12, 1995, of $19,500.

11. Other information:
    a. The rental property in Lake Tahoe is located at 110 Paraiso Drive, Lake Tahoe (88197).
    b. The duplex is located at 20 French Street, Kingston, Rhode Island (02881).

INSTRUCTIONS: To complete phase III, you need the following additional forms: Schedule E, Form 2119, two copies of Form 4562, and forms 4797 and 8582. You now have all the information necessary to complete the schedules that you did not finish in phases I and II.

▲ **Exhibit B–1**

a Control number 437689		OMB No. 1545-0008	This information is being furnished to the Internal Revenue Service. If you are required to file a tax return, a negligence penalty or other sanction may be imposed on you if this income is taxable and you fail to report it.	
b Employer's identification number 05-7652473			**1** Wages, tips, other compensation $137,042.24	**2** Federal income tax withheld $28,641.00
c Employer's name, address, and ZIP code USC Equipment Corp. 18 Perry Road Warwick, RI 02887			**3** Social security wages $ 60,600.00	**4** Social security tax withheld $ 3,757.20
			5 Medicare wages and tips $137,042.24	**6** Medicare tax withheld $ 1,987.11
			7 Social security tips	**8** Allocated tips
d Employee's social security number 150-52-0546			**9** Advance EIC payment	**10** Dependent care benefits
e Employee's name, address, and ZIP code Bill Schnappauf 3242 Heights Drive Barrington, RI 02806			**11** Nonqualified plans	**12** Benefits included in box 1
			13 See Instrs. for box 13 C – $42.24	**14** Other

15 Statutory employee ☐	Deceased ☐	Pension plan ☑	Legal rep. ☐	942 emp. ☐	Subtotal ☐	Deferred compensation ☐

16 State	Employer's state I.D. No.	17 State wages, tips, etc.	18 State income tax	19 Locality name	20 Local wages, tips, etc.	21 Local income tax
RI	05-R7652473	$137,042.24	$7,257.00			

Department of the Treasury–Internal Revenue Service

Form W-2 Wage and Tax Statement 1994

Copy C For **EMPLOYEE'S RECORDS** (See Notice on back.)

Notice to Employee:

Refund.– Even if you do not have to file a tax return, you should file to get a refund if box 2 shows Federal income tax withheld, or if you can take the earned income credit.

Earned Income Credit.– You must file a tax return if any amount is shown in box 9.

For 1994, if you earn less than $9,000 and you have no children, if you earn less than $23,755 and you have one qualifying child, or if you earn less than $25,296 and you have more than one qualifying child, you may qualify for the earned income credit. Any EIC that is more than your tax liability is refunded to you, but ONLY if you file a tax return. For example, if you have no tax liability and qualify for a $600 EIC, you can get $600, but only if you file a tax return. If you have at least one qualifying child, you may get as much as $1,223 of the EIC in advance by completing Form W-5. The 1994 instructions for Forms 1040 and 1040A, and Pub. 596, explain the EIC in detail. You can get forms, instructions, and publications by calling toll-free 1-800-TAX-FORM (829-3676).

Corrections.– If your name, social security number, or address is incorrect, correct Copies B, C, and 2 and ask your employer to correct your employment record. Be sure to ask the employer to file **Form W-2c,** Statement of Corrected Income and Tax Amounts, with the Social Security Administration (SSA) to correct any name, amount, or number error reported to the SSA on Copy A of the Form W-2. If your name and number are correct but are not the same as shown on your social security card, you should ask for a new card at any Social Security office.

Credit for Excess Taxes.– If more than one employer paid you wages during 1994 and more than the maximum social security employee tax, railroad retirement (RRTA) tax, or combined social security and RRTA tax

was withheld, you may claim the excess as a credit against your Federal income tax. See your income tax return instructions.

Box 1.– Enter this amount on the wages line of your tax return.

Box 2.– Enter this amount on the Federal income tax withheld line of your tax return.

Box 8.– This amount is **not** included in boxes 1, 5, or 7. For information on how to report tips on your tax return, see the instructions for Form 1040, 1040A, or 1040EZ.

Box 9.– Enter this amount on the advance earned income credit payment line of your tax return.

Box 10.– This amount is the total dependent care benefits your employer paid to you (or incurred on your behalf). Any amount over $5,000 has been included in box 1. Part or all of this amount may be taxable unless you complete Schedule 2 of Form 1040A or Form 2441. See the instructions for Forms 1040 and 1040A.

Box 11.– Any amount in box 11 is a distribution made to you from a nonqualified deferred compensation or section 457 plan. This amount is included in box 1 and/or boxes 3 and 5.

Box 12.– This amount is included in box 1. If there is an amount in box 12, you may be able to deduct expenses that are related to fringe benefits; see the instructions for your tax return.

Box 13.– Any amount in box 13 should be coded (letter). The following list explains the codes. You may need this information to complete your tax return.

A– Uncollected social security tax on tips (see "Total tax" in Form 1040 instructions)

B– Uncollected Medicare tax on tips (see "Total tax" in Form 1040 instructions)

C– Cost of group-term life insurance coverage over $50,000

D– Elective deferrals to a section 401(k) cash or deferred arrangement

E– Elective deferrals to a section 403(b) salary reduction agreement

F– Elective deferrals to a section 408(k)(6) salary reduction SEP

G– Elective and nonelective deferrals to a section 457(b) deferred compensation plan

H– Elective deferrals to a section 501(c)(18)(D) tax-exempt organization plan (see Form 1040 instructions for how to deduct)

J– Sick pay not includible as income

K– Tax on excess golden parachute payments

L– Nontaxable part of employee business expense reimbursements

M– Uncollected social security tax on cost of group-term life insurance coverage over $50,000 (former employees only) (see Form 1040 instructions)

N– Uncollected Medicare tax on cost of group-term life insurance coverage over $50,000 (former employees only) (see Form 1040 instructions)

P– Excludable moving expense reimbursements

Box 15.– If the "Pension plan" box is marked, special limits may apply to the amount of IRA contributions you may deduct. If the "Deferred compensation" box is marked, the elective deferrals in box 13 (for all employers, and for all such plans to which you belong) are generally limited to $8,994. Elective deferrals for section 403(b) contracts are limited to $9,500 ($12,500 in limited circumstances, see Pub. 571). The limit for section 457(b) plans is $7,500. Amounts over that must be included in income. See instructions for Form 1040.

Caution: *The elective deferral dollar limitation of $8,994 is subject to change for 1994.*

▲ Exhibit B–2

Instructions for Recipient

Box 1.– Shows interest paid to you during the calendar year by the payer. This does not include interest shown in box 3.

If you receive a Form 1099-INT for interest paid on a tax-exempt obligation, please see the instructions for your income tax return.

Box 2.– Shows interest or principal forfeited because of early withdrawal of time savings. You may deduct this on your Federal income tax return only on the specific line of Form 1040 under "Adjustments to Income."

Box 3.– Shows interest on U.S. Savings Bonds, Treasury bills, Treasury bonds, and Treasury notes. This may or may not be all taxable. See **Pub. 550,** Investment Income and Expenses. This interest is exempt from state and local income taxes. **This interest is not included in box 1.**

Box 4.– Shows backup withholding. For example, persons not furnishing their taxpayer identification number to the payer become subject to backup withholding at a 31% rate. See **Form W-9,** Request for Taxpayer Identification Number

and Certification, for information on backup withholding. **Include this amount on your income tax return as tax withheld.**

Box 5.– Shows foreign tax paid. You may choose to claim this tax as a deduction or a credit on your Federal income tax return. See **Pub. 514,** Foreign Tax Credit for Individuals.

Nominees.– If your Federal identification number is shown on this form and the form includes amounts belonging to another person, you are considered a nominee recipient. You must file Form 1099-INT for each of the other owners showing the amounts allocable to each. You must also furnish a Form 1099-INT to each of the other owners. File Form(s) 1099-INT with **Form 1096,** Annual Summary and Transmittal of U.S. Information Returns, with the Internal Revenue Service Center for your area. On each Form 1099-INT, list yourself as the "payer" and the other owner as the "recipient." On Form 1096, list yourself as the "filer." A husband or wife is not required to file a nominee return to show amounts owned by the other.

☐ CORRECTED (if checked)

PAYER'S name, street address, city, state, and ZIP code	Payer's RTN (optional)	OMB No. 1545-0112	
Jefferson Trust 1 President Way Falmouth, RI 02458		19**94** Form **1099-INT**	**Interest Income**

PAYER'S Federal identification number 05-6771794	RECIPIENT'S identification number 150-52-0546	1 Interest income not included in box 3 $ 840.00		Copy B
RECIPIENT'S name Bill & Joyce Schnappauf		2 Early withdrawal penalty $ 67.00	3 Interest on U.S. Savings Bonds and Treas. obligations $	**For Recipient** This is important tax information and is being furnished to the Internal Revenue Service. If you are required to file a return, a negligence penalty or other sanction may be imposed on you if this income is taxable and the IRS determines that it has not been reported.
Street address (including apt. no.) 3242 Heights Drive		4 Federal income tax withheld $		
City, state, and ZIP code Barrington, RI 02806		5 Foreign tax paid	6 Foreign country or U.S. possession	
Account number (optional) 347681		$		

Form **1099-INT** (Keep for your records.) Department of the Treasury - Internal Revenue Service

▲ **Exhibit B–3**

☐ CORRECTED (if checked)

PAYER'S name, street address, city, state, and ZIP code	Payer's RTN (optional)	OMB No. 1545-0112	
U.S. Treasury 202 New Jersey Avenue Washington, D.C. 34862		**1994** Form **1099-INT**	**Interest Income**

PAYER'S Federal identification number 05-0000014	RECIPIENT'S identification number 371-42-5207	**1** Interest income not included in box 3 $	**Copy B** **For Recipient**
RECIPIENT'S name Joyce Schnappauf		**2** Early withdrawal penalty $	**3** Interest on U.S. Savings Bonds and Treas. obligations $ 347.00	This is important tax information and is being furnished to the Internal Revenue Service. If you are required to file a return, a negligence penalty or other sanction may be imposed on you if this income is taxable and the IRS determines that it has not been reported.
Street address (including apt. no.) 3242 Heights Drive		**4** Federal income tax withheld $		
City, state, and ZIP code Barrington, RI 02806		**5** Foreign tax paid	**6** Foreign country or U.S. possession	
Account number (optional) 54698479		$		

Form **1099-INT**   (Keep for your records.)   Department of the Treasury - Internal Revenue Service

▲ **Exhibit B–4**

☐ CORRECTED (if checked)

PAYER'S name, street address, city, state, and ZIP code	Payer's RTN (optional)	OMB No. 1545-0112	
Sanborn Savings Bank 11 Vespa Plaza Cranston, RI 02911		**1994** Form **1099-INT**	**Interest Income**

PAYER'S Federal identification number 05-8173693	RECIPIENT'S identification number 150-52-0546	**1** Interest income not included in box 3 $ 385.00	**Copy B** **For Recipient**
RECIPIENT'S name Bill & Joyce Schnappauf		**2** Early withdrawal penalty $	**3** Interest on U.S. Savings Bonds and Treas. obligations $	This is important tax information and is being furnished to the Internal Revenue Service. If you are required to file a return, a negligence penalty or other sanction may be imposed on you if this income is taxable and the IRS determines that it has not been reported.
Street address (including apt. no.) 3242 Heights Drive		**4** Federal income tax withheld $ 50.00		
City, state, and ZIP code Barrington, RI 02806		**5** Foreign tax paid	**6** Foreign country or U.S. possession	
Account number (optional) 471398		$		

Form **1099-INT**   (Keep for your records.)   Department of the Treasury - Internal Revenue Service

▲ Exhibit B–5

☐ CORRECTED (if checked)

PAYER'S name, street address, city, state, and ZIP code	Payer's RTN (optional)	OMB No. 1545-0112	
Wakefield Savings Bank 565 Main Street Wakefield, RI 02879		**1994** Form **1099-INT**	**Interest Income**

PAYER'S Federal identification number 05-2217118	RECIPIENT'S identification number 150-52-0546	**1** Interest income not included in box 3 $ 227.00	**Copy B** **For Recipient**
RECIPIENT'S name Bill & Joyce Schnappauf		**2** Early withdrawal penalty $	**3** Interest on U.S. Savings Bonds and Treas. obligations $	This is important tax information and is being furnished to the Internal Revenue Service. If you are required to file a return, a negligence penalty or other sanction may be imposed on you if this income is taxable and the IRS determines that it has not been reported.
Street address (including apt. no.) 3242 Heights Drive		**4** Federal income tax withheld $	
City, state, and ZIP code Barrington, RI 02806		**5** Foreign tax paid	**6** Foreign country or U.S. possession
Account number (optional) 120356		$	

Form **1099-INT**   (Keep for your records.)   Department of the Treasury - Internal Revenue Service

▲ Exhibit B–6

☐ CORRECTED (if checked)

PAYER'S name, street address, city, state, and ZIP code	Payer's RTN (optional)	OMB No. 1545-0112	
United Insurance Company 48 Center Street Arlington, VA 34787		**1994** Form **1099-INT**	**Interest Income**

PAYER'S Federal identification number 05-186230	RECIPIENT'S identification number 150-52-0546	**1** Interest income not included in box 3 $ 200.00	**Copy B** **For Recipient**
RECIPIENT'S name Bill Schnappauf		**2** Early withdrawal penalty $	**3** Interest on U.S. Savings Bonds and Treas. obligations $	This is important tax information and is being furnished to the Internal Revenue Service. If you are required to file a return, a negligence penalty or other sanction may be imposed on you if this income is taxable and the IRS determines that it has not been reported.
Street address (including apt. no.) 3242 Heights Drive		**4** Federal income tax withheld $	
City, state, and ZIP code Barrington, RI 02806		**5** Foreign tax paid	**6** Foreign country or U.S. possession
Account number (optional) L472280		$	

Form **1099-INT**   (Keep for your records.)   Department of the Treasury - Internal Revenue Service

▲ Exhibit B–7

Instructions for Recipient

Box 1a.– Gross dividends include any amounts shown in boxes 1b, 1c, 1d, and 1e. If an amount appears in box 1c or 1d or both, you must file **Form 1040.** If you file **Form 1040A,** report the amount in box 1a. If you file **Schedule 1 (Form 1040A)** or **Schedule B (Form 1040)** to report dividends, report the amount in box 1a. If you file Form 1040 without Schedule B, report the sum of boxes 1b and 1e on the "Dividend income" line and box 1c on **Schedule D (Form 1040)** or the "Capital gain or (loss)" line (write "CGD" on the dotted line).

The amount shown may be a distribution from an employee stock ownership plan (ESOP). Although you should report the ESOP distribution as a dividend on your income tax return, treat it as a plan distribution, not as investment income, for any other purpose.

Box 1b.– Ordinary dividends are fully taxable and are included in box 1a.

Box 1c.– Capital gain distributions are included in box 1a.

Box 1d.– This part of the distribution is nontaxable because it is a return of your cost (or other basis). You must reduce your cost (or other basis) by this amount for figuring gain or loss when you sell your stock. But if you get back all your cost (or other basis), you must report future nontaxable distributions as capital gains, even though this form shows them as nontaxable. This amount is included in box 1a. For more information, see **Pub. 550,** Investment Income and Expenses.

Box 1e.– Any amount shown is your share of the expenses of a nonpublicly offered regulated investment company, generally a nonpublicly offered mutual fund, which is included as a dividend in box 1a. The full amount shown in box 1a must be reported as income on your tax return. You can deduct the expenses shown in box 1e on the "Other expenses" line on **Schedule A (Form 1040)** subject to the 2% limit. Generally, the actual amount you should have received or had credited to you is the amount in box 1a less the amount in box 1e.

Box 2.– Shows backup withholding. For example, persons not furnishing their taxpayer identification number to the payer become subject to backup withholding at a 31% rate on certain payments. See **Form W-9,** Request for Taxpayer Identification Number and Certification, for information on backup withholding. **Include this amount on your income tax return as tax withheld.**

Box 3.– You may elect to claim the amount shown as a deduction or a credit. See **Pub. 514,** Foreign Tax Credit for Individuals.

Nominees.– If your Federal identification number is shown on this form and the form includes amounts belonging to another person, you are considered a nominee recipient. You must file Form 1099-DIV for each of the other owners showing the income allocable to each, and you must furnish a Form 1099-DIV to each. File Form(s) 1099-DIV with **Form 1096,** Information Returns, at the Internal Revenue Service Center for your area. On each Form 1099-DIV, list yourself as the "payer" and the other owner as the "recipient." On Form 1096, list yourself as the "filer." A husband or wife is not required to file a nominee return to show amounts owned by the other.

☐ CORRECTED (if checked)

PAYER'S name, street address, city, state, and ZIP code	1a Gross dividends and other distributions on stock (Total of 1b, 1c, 1d, and 1e) $ 505.00	OMB No. 1545-0110 **1994**	**Dividends and Distributions**
Lion Corporation 66 Roaring Way New York, NY 10017	1b Ordinary dividends $ 505.00		

PAYER'S Federal identification number 05-1473191	RECIPIENT'S identification number 371-42-5207	1c Capital gain distributions $	2 Federal income tax withheld $	**Copy B** **For Recipient**
RECIPIENT'S name Joyce Schnappauf		1d Nontaxable distributions $	3 Foreign tax paid $	This is important tax information and is being furnished to the Internal Revenue Service. If you are required to file a return, a negligence penalty or other sanction may be imposed on you if this income is taxable and the IRS determines that it has not been reported.
Street address (including apt. no.) 3242 Heights Drive		1e Investment expenses $	4 Foreign country or U.S. possession	
City, state, and ZIP code Barrington, RI 02806		**Liquidation Distributions**		
Account number (optional)		5 Cash $	6 Noncash (Fair market value) $	

Form **1099-DIV**   (Keep for your records.)   Department of the Treasury - Internal Revenue Service

▲ **Exhibit B–8**

☐ CORRECTED (if checked)

PAYER'S name, street address, city, state, and ZIP code	**1a** Gross dividends and other distributions on stock (Total of 1b, 1c, 1d, and 1e) $ 187.00	OMB No. 1545-0110 **1994**	**Dividends and Distributions**

Kangaroo Corporation
87 Proper Street
Providence, RI 02917

1b Ordinary dividends
$ 187.00   Form **1099-DIV**

PAYER'S Federal identification number 05-3789147	RECIPIENT'S identification number 150-52-0546	**1c** Capital gain distributions $	**2 Federal income tax withheld** $	**Copy B** **For Recipient**

RECIPIENT'S name

Bill & Joyce Schnappauf

Street address (including apt. no.)

3242 Heights Drive
City, state, and ZIP code
Barrington, RI 02806

1d Nontaxable distributions
$

3 Foreign tax paid
$

1e Investment expenses
$

4 Foreign country or U.S. possession

Liquidation Distributions

Account number (optional)

5 Cash
$

6 Noncash (Fair market value)
$

This is important tax information and is being furnished to the Internal Revenue Service. If you are required to file a return, a negligence penalty or other sanction may be imposed on you if this income is taxable and the IRS determines that it has not been reported.

Form **1099-DIV**   (Keep for your records.)   Department of the Treasury - Internal Revenue Service

---

▲ **Exhibit B–9**

☐ CORRECTED (if checked)

PAYER'S name, street address, city, state, and ZIP code	**1a** Gross dividends and other distributions on stock (Total of 1b, 1c, 1d, and 1e) $ 345.00	OMB No. 1545-0110 **1994**	**Dividends and Distributions**

West Publishing
457 Gorman Way
St. Paul, MN 54678

1b Ordinary dividends
$ 345.00   Form **1099-DIV**

PAYER'S Federal identification number 05-1919431	RECIPIENT'S identification number 150-52-0546	**1c** Capital gain distributions $	**2 Federal income tax withheld** $	**Copy B** **For Recipient**

RECIPIENT'S name

Bill Schnappauf

Street address (including apt. no.)

3242 Heights Drive
City, state, and ZIP code
Barrington, RI 02806

1d Nontaxable distributions
$

3 Foreign tax paid
$

1e Investment expenses
$

4 Foreign country or U.S. possession

Liquidation Distributions

Account number (optional)

5 Cash
$

6 Noncash (Fair market value)
$

This is important tax information and is being furnished to the Internal Revenue Service. If you are required to file a return, a negligence penalty or other sanction may be imposed on you if this income is taxable and the IRS determines that it has not been reported.

Form **1099-DIV**   (Keep for your records.)   Department of the Treasury - Internal Revenue Service

▲ **Exhibit B–10**

CORRECTED (if checked)

PAYER'S name, street address, city, state, and ZIP code	1a Gross dividends and other distributions on stock (Total of 1b, 1c, 1d, and 1e) $ 295.00	OMB No. 1545-0110 1994	**Dividends and Distributions**
Neway Mutual Fund 490 Majestic Way Fairfax, VA 34678	1b Ordinary dividends $ 205.00		

PAYER'S Federal identification number 05-1551739	RECIPIENT'S identification number 150-52-0546	1c Capital gain distributions $ 90.00	2 Federal income tax withheld $ 40.00	**Copy B** **For Recipient**
RECIPIENT'S name Bill & Joyce Schnappauf		1d Nontaxable distributions $	3 Foreign tax paid $	This is important tax information and is being furnished to the Internal Revenue Service. If you are required to file a return, a negligence penalty or other sanction may be imposed on you if this income is taxable and the IRS determines that it has not been reported.
Street address (including apt. no.) 3242 Heights Drive		1e Investment expenses $	4 Foreign country or U.S. possession	
City, state, and ZIP code Barrington, RI 02806		**Liquidation Distributions**		
Account number (optional)		5 Cash $	6 Noncash (Fair market value) $	

Form **1099-DIV**   (Keep for your records.)   Department of the Treasury - Internal Revenue Service

---

▲ **Exhibit B–11**

CORRECTED (if checked)

PAYER'S name, street address, city, state, and ZIP code	1a Gross dividends and other distributions on stock (Total of 1b, 1c, 1d, and 1e) $ 86.00	OMB No. 1545-0110 1994	**Dividends and Distributions**
Robins Industries 1150 Long Island Drive Jamica, NY 11749	1b Ordinary dividends $ 86.00		

PAYER'S Federal identification number 05-4443794	RECIPIENT'S identification number 150-52-0546	1c Capital gain distributions $	2 Federal income tax withheld $	**Copy B** **For Recipient**
RECIPIENT'S name Bill & Joyce Schnappauf		1d Nontaxable distributions $	3 Foreign tax paid $	This is important tax information and is being furnished to the Internal Revenue Service. If you are required to file a return, a negligence penalty or other sanction may be imposed on you if this income is taxable and the IRS determines that it has not been reported.
Street address (including apt. no.) 3242 Heights Drive		1e Investment expenses $	4 Foreign country or U.S. possession	
City, state, and ZIP code Barrington, RI 02806		**Liquidation Distributions**		
Account number (optional)		5 Cash $	6 Noncash (Fair market value) $	

Form **1099-DIV**   (Keep for your records.)   Department of the Treasury - Internal Revenue Service

▲ **Exhibit B–12**

Instructions for Recipient

Box 1.– Shows the total unemployment compensation paid to you this year. This amount is taxable income to you. For details, see the instructions for your Federal income tax return. If you expect to receive these benefits next year, see Form 1040-ES for estimated tax payments.

Box 2.– Shows refunds, credits, or offsets of state or local income tax you received. If there is an entry in this box, it may be taxable to you if you deducted the tax paid as an itemized deduction on your Federal income tax return. Even if you did not receive the amount shown, for example, because it was credited to your estimated tax, it is still taxable if it was deducted. Any interest received on this must be included as interest income on your return. See the instructions for Form 1040 or 1040A.

Box 3.– Identifies the tax year for which the refund, credit, or offset shown in box 2 was made. If there is no entry in this box, the refund is for 1994 taxes.

Box 4.– Shows backup withholding. For example, persons not furnishing their taxpayer identification number to the payer become subject to backup withholding at a 31% rate on certain payments. See **Form W-9,** Request for Taxpayer Identification Number and Certification, for information on backup withholding. **Include this on your income tax return as tax withheld.**

Box 6.– Shows the amount of taxable grants you received from the Federal, state, or local government.

Box 7.– Shows the amount of Department of Agriculture payments that are taxable to you. If the payer shown is anyone other than the Department of Agriculture, it means the payer has received a payment, as a nominee, that is taxable to you. This may represent the entire agricultural subsidy payment received on your behalf by the nominee, or it may be your pro rata share of the original payment. See **Pub. 225,** Farmer's Tax Guide, and the instructions for **Schedule F (Form 1040),** Profit or Loss From Farming, for information about where to report this income.

Box 8.– If this box is checked, the refund, credit, or offset in box 2 is attributable to an income tax that applies exclusively to income from a trade or business and is not a tax of general application. The amount, if taxable, should not be reported on page 1 of Form 1040, but should be reported on Schedule C, C-EZ, or F (Form 1040), as appropriate.

	☐ CORRECTED (if checked)	

PAYER'S name, street address, city, state, and ZIP code	**1** Unemployment compensation $	OMB No. 1545-0120 **1994**	**Certain Government Payments**
State of Rhode Island Taxation Office One Capital Hill Providence, RI 02908	**2** State or local income tax refunds, credits, or offsets $ 849.00		

PAYER'S Federal identification number 05-0000199	RECIPIENT'S identification number 150-52-0546	**3** Box 2 amount is for tax year 1993	**4** Federal income tax withheld $	**Copy B For Recipient**
RECIPIENT'S name Bill & Joyce Schnappauf		**5**	**6** Taxable grants $	This is important tax information and is being furnished to the Internal Revenue Service. If you are required to file a return, a negligence penalty or other sanction may be imposed on you if this income is taxable and the IRS determines that it has not been reported.
Street address (including apt. no.) 3242 Heights Drive		**7** Agriculture payments $	**8** The amount in box 2 applies to income from a trade or business ▶ ☐	
City, state, and ZIP code Barrington, RI 02806				
Account number (optional)				

Form **1099-G**   (Keep for your records.)   Department of the Treasury - Internal Revenue Service

▲ **Exhibit B–13**

☐ CORRECTED (if checked)

PAYER'S name, address, ZIP code, and Federal identification number	**1** Gross winnings $2,950.00	**2** Federal income tax withheld $590.00	OMB No. 1545-0238
Yardly Casino 435 Higgins Drive Groton, CT 03657	**3** Type of wager Blackjack	**4** Date won 03 : 13 : 94	19**94**
	5 Transaction	**6** Race	**Certain Gambling Winnings**
	7 Winnings from identical wagers	**8** Cashier	

WINNER'S name, address (including apt. no.), and ZIP code	**9** Winner's taxpayer identification no. 150-52-0546	**10** Window	This information is being furnished to the Internal Revenue Service.
Bill Schnappauf 3242 Heights Drive Barrington, RI 02806	**11** First I.D.	**12** Second I.D.	
	13 State/Payer's state identification no.	**14** State income tax withheld	**Copy B**

Under penalties of perjury, I declare that, to the best of my knowledge and belief, the name, address, and taxpayer identification number that I have furnished correctly identify me as the recipient of this payment and any payments from identical wagers, and that no other person is entitled to any part of these payments.

Signature ▶   Date ▶

Report this income on your Federal tax return. If this form shows Federal income tax withheld in box 2, attach this copy to your return.

Form **W-2G**   Department of the Treasury - Internal Revenue Service

Instructions to Winner

Box 1.—The payer must furnish a Form W-2G to you if you receive:

1. $600 or more in gambling winnings and the payout is at least 300 times the amount of the wager (except winnings from bingo, slot machines, and keno);

2. $1,200 or more in gambling winnings from bingo or slot machines;

3. $1,500 or more in proceeds (the amount of winnings less the amount of the wager) from keno; or

4. Any gambling winnings subject to Federal income tax withholding.

Generally, report all gambling winnings on the "Other income" line of Form 1040. You can deduct gambling losses as an itemized deduction, but you cannot deduct more than your winnings. Keep an accurate diary or similar record of your winnings and losses, and be able to prove those amounts by receipts, tickets, statements, or similar items.

Box 2.—Any Federal income tax withheld on these winnings is shown in this box. Federal income tax must be withheld at the rate of 28% on certain winnings less the wager. Whether Federal income tax must be withheld depends on the type and amount of the winnings, including winnings from identical wagers, and the odds.

If you did not provide your social security number to the payer, the amount in this box may be backup withholding at a 31% rate.

Include the amount shown in box 2 on your tax return as Federal income tax withheld.

Signature.—You must sign Form W-2G if you are the only person entitled to the winnings and the winnings are subject to regular gambling withholding.

Other Winners.—Prepare **Form 5754,** Statement by Person(s) Receiving Gambling Winnings, if another person is entitled to any part of these winnings.

▲ **Exhibit B–14**

☐ CORRECTED (if checked)

PAYER'S name, street address, city, state, and ZIP code	**1** Rents $	OMB No. 1545-0115	**Miscellaneous Income**
Good Learning Books 647 Fifth Avenue New York, NY 11140	**2** Royalties $ 6,500	**1994** Form **1099-MISC**	
	3 Other income $		

PAYER'S Federal identification number 05-1719274	RECIPIENT'S identification number 371-42-5207	**4** Federal income tax withheld $	**5** Fishing boat proceeds $	**Copy B** **For Recipient**
RECIPIENT'S name Joyce Schnappauf		**6** Medical and health care payments $	**7** Nonemployee compensation $	This is important tax information and is being furnished to the Internal Revenue Service. If you are required to file a return, a negligence penalty or other sanction may be imposed on you if this income is taxable and the IRS determines that it has not been reported.
Street address (including apt. no.) 3242 Heights Drive		**8** Substitute payments in lieu of dividends or interest $	**9** Payer made direct sales of $5,000 or more of consumer products to a buyer (recipient) for resale ▶ ☐	
City, state, and ZIP code Barrington, RI 02806		**10** Crop insurance proceeds $	**11** State income tax withheld $	
Account number (optional)		**12** State/Payer's state number		

Form **1099-MISC**   (Keep for your records.)   Department of the Treasury - Internal Revenue Service

Instructions for Recipient

Amounts shown on this form may be subject to self-employment tax computed on **Schedule SE (Form 1040)**. See **Pub. 533**, Self-Employment Tax, for information on self-employment income. If no income or social security and Medicare taxes were withheld by the payer, you may have to make estimated tax payments if you are still receiving these payments. See **Form 1040-ES**, Estimated Tax for Individuals.

If you are an individual, report the taxable amounts shown on this form on your tax return, as explained below. (Others, such as fiduciaries or partnerships, report the amounts on the corresponding lines of your tax return.)

Boxes 1 and 2.– Report rents from real estate on Schedule E (Form 1040). If you provided significant services to the tenant, sold real estate as a business, or rented personal property as a business, report on Schedule C or C-EZ (Form 1040). For royalties on timber, coal, and iron ore, see **Pub. 544**, Sales and Other Dispositions of Assets.

Box 3.– Report on the "Other income" line on Form 1040 and identify the payment. If it is trade or business income, report this amount on Schedule C, C-EZ, or F (Form 1040). The amount shown may be payments you received as the beneficiary of a deceased employee, prizes, awards, taxable damages, or other taxable income.

Box 4.– Shows backup withholding. For example, persons not furnishing their taxpayer identification number to the payer become subject to backup withholding at a 31% rate on certain payments. See **Form W-9**, Request for Taxpayer Identification Number and Certification, for information on backup withholding. **Include this on your income tax return as tax withheld.**

Box 5.– An amount in this box means the fishing boat operator considers you self-employed. Report this amount on Schedule C or C-EZ (Form 1040). See **Pub. 595**, Tax Guide for Commercial Fishermen.

Box 6.– Report on Schedule C or C-EZ (Form 1040).

Box 7.– Generally, payments for services reported in this box are income from self-employment. Since you received this form, rather than Form W-2, the payer may have considered you self-employed and did not withhold social security or Medicare taxes. Report self-employment income on Schedule C, C-EZ, or F (Form 1040), and **compute the self-employment tax on Schedule SE (Form 1040)**. However, if you are not self-employed, report this amount on Form 1040 on the "Wages, salaries, tips, etc." line. Call the IRS for information about how to report any social security and Medicare taxes.

If "EPP" is shown, this is excess golden parachute payments subject to a 20% excise tax. See your Form 1040 instructions for the "Total Tax" line. The unlabeled amount is your total compensation.

Box 8.– Report as "Other income" on your tax return. This amount is substitute payments in lieu of dividends or tax-exempt interest received by your broker on your behalf after transfer of your securities for use in a short sale.

Box 9.– An entry in the checkbox means sales to you of consumer products on a buy-sell, deposit-commission, or any other basis for resale have amounted to $5,000 or more. The person filing this return does not have to show a dollar amount in this box. Any income from your sale of these products should generally be reported on Schedule C or C-EZ (Form 1040).

Box 10.– Report on the "Crop insurance proceeds. . ." line on Schedule F (Form 1040).

▲ **Exhibit B–15**

☐ CORRECTED (if checked)

PAYER'S name, street address, city, state, and ZIP code	**1** Rents $	OMB No. 1545-0115	**Miscellaneous Income**
Mountain Publishing 480 Payton Lane Dallas, Texas 77689	**2** Royalties $ 7,250	**1994**	
	3 Other income $	Form **1099-MISC**	

PAYER'S Federal identification number	RECIPIENT'S identification number	**4 Federal income tax withheld** $	**5** Fishing boat proceeds $	**Copy B**
05-9765421	371-42-5207			**For Recipient**

RECIPIENT'S name	**6** Medical and health care payments $	**7** Nonemployee compensation $	This is important tax information and is being furnished to the Internal Revenue Service. If you are required to file a return, a negligence penalty or other sanction may be imposed on you if this income is taxable and the IRS determines that it has not been reported.
Joyce Schnappauf			
Street address (including apt. no.)	**8** Substitute payments in lieu of dividends or interest $	**9** Payer made direct sales of $5,000 or more of consumer products to a buyer (recipient) for resale ▶ ☐	
3242 Heights Drive			
City, state, and ZIP code	**10** Crop insurance proceeds $	**11** State income tax withheld $	
Barrington, RI 02806			
Account number (optional)	**12** State/Payer's state number		

Form **1099-MISC**   (Keep for your records.)   Department of the Treasury - Internal Revenue Service

---

▲ **Exhibit B–16**

☐ CORRECTED (if checked)

PAYER'S name, street address, city, state, and ZIP code	**1** Rents $	OMB No. 1545-0115	**Miscellaneous Income**
Melrose Publishing 150 Binder Lane Atlanta, GA 44142	**2** Royalties $ 10,300	**1994**	
	3 Other income $	Form **1099-MISC**	

PAYER'S Federal identification number	RECIPIENT'S identification number	**4 Federal income tax withheld** $ 2,100	**5** Fishing boat proceeds $	**Copy B**
05-8374165	371-42-5207			**For Recipient**

RECIPIENT'S name	**6** Medical and health care payments $	**7** Nonemployee compensation $	This is important tax information and is being furnished to the Internal Revenue Service. If you are required to file a return, a negligence penalty or other sanction may be imposed on you if this income is taxable and the IRS determines that it has not been reported.
Joyce Schnappauf			
Street address (including apt. no.)	**8** Substitute payments in lieu of dividends or interest $	**9** Payer made direct sales of $5,000 or more of consumer products to a buyer (recipient) for resale ▶ ☐	
3242 Heights Drive			
City, state, and ZIP code	**10** Crop insurance proceeds $	**11** State income tax withheld $	
Barrington, RI 02806			
Account number (optional)	**12** State/Payer's state number		

Form **1099-MISC**   (Keep for your records.)   Department of the Treasury - Internal Revenue Service

▲ **Exhibit B–17**

Instructions for Payer/Borrower

A person (including a financial institution, a governmental unit, and a cooperative housing corporation) who is engaged in a trade or business and, in the course of such trade or business, received from you at least $600 of mortgage interest (including certain points) on any one mortgage in the calendar year must furnish this statement to you.

If you received this statement as the payer of record on a mortgage on which there are other borrowers entitled to a deduction for the interest and points shown on this form, please furnish each of the other borrowers with information about the proper distribution of these amounts. Each borrower is entitled to deduct only the amount he or she paid and points paid by the seller that represent his or her share of the amount allowable as a deduction for mortgage interest and points.

If your mortgage payments were subsidized by a government agency, you may not be able to deduct the amount of the subsidy.

Box 1.—Shows the mortgage interest received by the interest recipient during the year. This amount includes interest on any obligation secured by real property, including a home equity, line of credit, or credit card loan. This amount does not include points, government subsidy payments, or seller payments on a "buy-down" mortgage. Such amounts are deductible by you only in certain circumstances. **Caution:** *If you prepaid interest in 1995 that accrued in full by January 15, 1996, this prepaid interest may be included in box 1. However, even though the prepaid amount may*

be included in box 1, you cannot deduct the prepaid amount in 1995. For more information, see **Pub. 936,** Home Mortgage Interest Deduction. If you are a mortgage credit certificate holder who can claim the mortgage interest credit, see **Form 8396,** Mortgage Interest Credit. If the interest was paid on a mortgage, home equity, line of credit, or credit card loan secured by your personal residence, you may be subject to a deduction limitation as explained in the instructions for **Schedule A (Form 1040).**

Box 2.—Not all points are reportable to you. This form shows points you or the seller paid this year for the purchase of your principal residence that are required to be reported to you. Generally, these points are fully deductible in the year paid, but you must subtract seller-paid points from the basis of your residence. Other points not reported in this box may be deductible. See Pub. 936. Also see your Form 1040 instructions.

Box 3.—Do not deduct this amount. It is a refund (or credit) from the interest recipient/lender for overpayment(s) of interest you made in a prior year or years. Generally, list the total amount shown in box 3 on the "Other income" line on your 1995 Form 1040. However, do not report the refund as income if you did not itemize deductions in the year(s) you paid the interest. No adjustment to your prior year(s) tax return(s) is necessary. For more information, see Pub. 936 and **Pub. 525,** Taxable and Nontaxable Income.

Box 4.—This box is for use by the interest recipient to furnish other information to you, such as real estate taxes or insurance paid from escrow.

☐ VOID ☐ CORRECTED

RECIPIENT'S/LENDER'S name, street address, city, state, and ZIP code		OMB No. 1545-0901	**Mortgage Interest Statement**
Jefferson Trust 1 President Way Falmouth, RI 02458		**1994** Form **1098**	

RECIPIENT'S Federal identification no. 05-6771794	PAYER'S social security number 150-52-0546	1 Mortgage interest received from payer(s)/borrower(s) $ 4,600	**Copy C** **For Recipient**
PAYER'S/BORROWER'S name Bill & Joyce Schnappauf		2 Points paid on purchase of principal residence $	For Paperwork Reduction Act Notice and instructions for completing this form, see **Instructions for Forms 1099, 1098, 5498, and W-2G.**
Street address (including apt. no.) 3242 Heights Drive		3 Refund of overpaid interest $	
City, state, and ZIP code Barrington, RI 02806		4	
Account number (optional) 4786102			

Form **1098**   Department of the Treasury - Internal Revenue Service

▲ **Exhibit B–18**

Personal

☐ VOID ☐ CORRECTED

RECIPIENT'S/LENDER'S name, street address, city, state, and ZIP code		OMB No. 1545-0901	Mortgage Interest Statement
Jefferson Trust 1 President Way Falmouth, RI 02458		**19 94** Form **1098**	

RECIPIENT'S Federal identification no. 05-6771794	PAYER'S social security number 150-52-0546	1 Mortgage interest received from payer(s)/borrower(s) $ 1,825	Copy C For Recipient
PAYER'S/BORROWER'S name Bill & Joyce Schnappauf		2 Points paid on purchase of principal residence $	For Paperwork Reduction Act Notice and instructions for completing this form, see **Instructions for Forms 1099, 1098, 5498, and W-2G.**
Street address (including apt. no.) 3242 Heights Drive		3 Refund of overpaid interest $	
City, state, and ZIP code Barrington, RI 02806		4	
Account number (optional) 4786102H			

Form **1098**   Department of the Treasury - Internal Revenue Service

▲ **Exhibit B–19**

Bus + Personal

☐ VOID ☐ CORRECTED

RECIPIENT'S/LENDER'S name, street address, city, state, and ZIP code		OMB No. 1545-0901	Mortgage Interest Statement
Narragansett Bay Bank 450 Laurel Lane Barrington, RI 02806		**19 94** Form **1098**	

RECIPIENT'S Federal identification no. 05-4249175	PAYER'S social security number 150-52-0546	1 Mortgage interest received from payer(s)/borrower(s) $ 3,200	Copy C For Recipient
PAYER'S/BORROWER'S name Bill & Joyce Schnappauf		2 Points paid on purchase of principal residence $ 3,600	For Paperwork Reduction Act Notice and instructions for completing this form, see **Instructions for Forms 1099, 1098, 5498, and W-2G.**
Street address (including apt. no.) 3242 Heights Drive		3 Refund of overpaid interest $	
City, state, and ZIP code Barrington, RI 02806		4	
Account number (optional) 5731025			

Form **1098**   Department of the Treasury - Internal Revenue Service

▲ Exhibit B–20

Instructions for Transferor

Generally, persons responsible for closing a real estate transaction must report the real estate proceeds to the Internal Revenue Service and must furnish this statement to you. If the real estate transferred was your main home, file **Form 2119,** Sale of Your Home, with your income tax return even if you sold at a loss or you did not replace your home. If the real estate transferred was not your main home, report the transaction in the applicable parts of **Form 4797,** Sales of Business Property, **Form 6252,** Installment Sale Income, and/or **Schedule D (Form 1040),** Capital Gains and Losses.

If you sold your home and (1) you did not own it for more than 9 years and (2) it was financed after 1990 under a Federally subsidized program (qualified mortgage bonds or mortgage credit certificates), you may have to recapture part of the subsidy. This will increase your tax. See **Form 8828,** Recapture of Federal Mortgage Subsidy, and **Pub. 523,** Selling Your Home.

Box 1.—Shows the date of closing.

Box 2.—Shows the gross proceeds from a real estate transaction, generally the sales price. Gross proceeds include cash and notes payable to you, notes assumed by the transferee (buyer), and any notes paid off at settlement. Box 2 does not include the value of other property or services you received or are to receive. See **Box 4.**

Box 3.—Shows the address of the property transferred or a legal description of the property.

Box 4.—If marked, shows that you received or will receive services or property (other than cash or notes) as part of the consideration for the property transferred. The value of any services or property (other than cash or notes) is not included in box 2.

Box 5.—Shows certain real estate tax on a residence charged to the buyer at settlement. If you have already paid the real estate tax for the period that includes the sale date, subtract this amount from the amount already paid to determine your deductible real estate tax. But if you have already deducted the real estate tax in a prior year, generally report this amount as income on the "Other income" line on Form 1040. For more information, see Pub. 523.

☐ CORRECTED (if checked)

FILER'S name, street address, city, state, and ZIP code	**1** Date of closing 8/10/1994	OMB No. 1545-0997	**Proceeds From Real Estate Transactions**
Home Mortgage Inc. 456 Kingstown Road Narragansett, RI 02882	**2** Gross proceeds $ 85,000	1994	

FILER'S Federal identification number 05-1010923	TRANSFEROR'S identification number 150-52-0546	**3** Address or legal description	**Copy B**
TRANSFEROR'S name Bill & Joyce Schnappauf		20 French Drive Kingston, RI 02881	**For Transferor** This is important tax information and is being furnished to the Internal Revenue Service. If you are required to file a return, a negligence penalty or other sanction may be imposed on you if this item is required to be reported and the IRS determines that it has not been reported.
Street address (including apt. no.) 3242 Heights Drive			
City, state, and ZIP code Barrington, RI 02806		**4** Transferor received or will receive property or services as part of the consideration (if checked) . . . ▶ ☐	
Account number (optional)		**5** Buyer's part of real estate tax (See **Box 5** on back.) $	

Form **1099-S**   (Keep for your records.)   Department of the Treasury - Internal Revenue Service

▲ **Exhibit B–21**

A. **Settlement Statement**

U.S. Department of Housing
and Urban Development

OMB No. 2502-0265

B. Type of Loan

1. [X] FHA	2. [ ] FmHA	3. [ ] Conv. Unins.	6. File Number SCH47682	7. Loan Number SCH47682	8. Mortgage Insurance Case Number MICN47682
4. [ ] VA	5. [ ] Conv. Ins.				

C. **NOTE:** *This form is furnished to give you a statement of actual settlement costs. Amounts paid to and by the settlement agent are shown. Items marked "(p.o.c.)" were paid outside the closing; they are shown here for informational purposes and are not included in the totals.*

D. NAME AND ADDRESS OF BORROWER: Henry & Claire Schwarzbach
14 Enterprise Street
South Kingstown, RI 02880

E. NAME AND ADDRESS OF SELLER: Bill & Joyce Schnappauf
27 Northup Street
Wakefield, RI 02879

F. NAME AND ADDRESS OF LENDER: Home Mortgage Inc.
456 Kingstown Road
Narragansett, RI 02882

G. PROPERTY
LOCATION: 20 French Street
Kingston, RI 02881

H. SETTLEMENT AGENT: Home Mortgage Inc.
PLACE OF SETTLEMENT: 456 Kingstown Road
Narragansett, RI 02882

I. SETTLEMENT DATE: August 10, 1994

J. SUMMARY OF BORROWER'S TRANSACTION		K. SUMMARY OF SELLER'S TRANSACTION	
100. GROSS AMOUNT DUE FROM BORROWER:		**400. GROSS AMOUNT DUE FROM SELLER:**	
101. Contract sales price	$85,000	401. Contract sales price	$85,000
102. Personal property		402. Personal property	
103. Settlement charges to borrower: *(from line 1400)*	4,819	403.	
104.		404.	
105.		405.	
ADJUSTMENTS FOR ITEMS PAID BY SELLER IN ADVANCE:		ADJUSTMENTS FOR ITEMS PAID BY SELLER IN ADVANCE:	
106. City/town taxes to		406. City/town taxes to	
107. County taxes to		407. County taxes to	
108. Assessments to		408. Assessments to	
109.		409.	
110.		410.	
111.		411.	
112.		412.	
120. GROSS AMOUNT DUE FROM BORROWER: ▶	$89,819	**420. GROSS AMOUNT DUE TO SELLER:** ▶	$85,000
200. AMOUNTS PAID BY OR IN BEHALF OF BORROWER:		**500. REDUCTIONS IN AMOUNT DUE TO SELLER:**	
201. Deposit or earnest money	850	501. Excess deposit *(see instructions)*	
202. Principal amount of new loan(s)	76,500	502. Settlement charges to seller *(line 1400)*	5,540
203. Existing loan(s) taken subject to		503. Existing loan(s) taken subject to	
204.		504. Payoff of first mortgage loan	39,240
205.		505. Payoff of second mortgage loan	
206.		506.	
207.		507.	
208.		508.	
209.		509.	
ADJUSTMENTS FOR ITEMS UNPAID BY SELLER:		ADJUSTMENTS FOR ITEMS UNPAID BY SELLER:	
210. City/town taxes 7/1/94 to 8/10/94	228	510. City/town taxes 7/1/94 to 8/10/94	228
211. County taxes to		511. County taxes to	
212. Assessments to		512. Assessments to	
213.		513.	
214.		514.	
215.		515.	
216.		516.	
217.		517.	
218.		518.	
219.		519.	
220. TOTAL PAID BY/FOR BORROWER: ▶	$77,578	**520. TOTAL REDUCTIONS IN AMOUNT DUE SELLER:** ▶	$45,008
300. CASH AT SETTLEMENT FROM/TO BORROWER:		**600. CASH AT SETTLEMENT TO/FROM SELLER:**	
301. Gross amount due from borrower *(line 120)*	$89,819	601. Gross amount due to seller *(line 420)*	$85,000
302. Less amount paid by/for borrower *(line 220)*	(77,578)	602. Less total reductions in amount due seller *(line 520)*	(45,008)
303. CASH ([X] FROM)([ ] TO) BORROWER: ▶	$12,241	**603. CASH ([X] TO) ([ ] FROM) SELLER:** ▶	$39,992

VMP -500 (9110)

VMP MORTGAGE FORMS • (313)293-8100 • (800)521-7291

HUD-1 (3-86)
RESPA, HB 4305.2

PAGE 1

▲ **Exhibit B–21**

(continued)

HUD-1 (Rev. 3/86)   OMB No. 2502-0265

L.	SETTLEMENT CHARGES	PAID FROM BORROWER'S FUNDS AT SETTLEMENT	PAID FROM SELLER'S FUNDS AT SETTLEMENT
700. TOTAL SALES / BROKER'S COMMISSION: BASED ON PRICE $ 85,000 @ 6 % = $5,100			
DIVISION OF COMMISSION (LINE 700) AS FOLLOWS:			
701. $ 2,550 to R.J. Hackett			
702. $ 2,550 to Sink & Associates			
703. Commission paid at settlement			$5,100
704.			
800. ITEMS PAYABLE IN CONNECTION WITH LOAN			
801. Loan origination fee 1 % of $85,000		$ 850	
802. Loan discount 1 % of $85,000		850	
803. Appraisal fee to:			
804. Credit report to:			
805. Lender's inspection fee			
806. Mortgage insurance application fee to			
807. Assumption fee			
808.			
809.			
810.			
811.			
900. ITEMS REQUIRED BY LENDER TO BE PAID IN ADVANCE:			
901. Interest from 8/11/94 to 8/31/94 @ $16.28 /day		342	
902. Mortgage insurance premium for mos. to			
903. Hazard insurance premium for yrs. to			
904. *Flood Insurance Premium for* yrs. to			
905.			
1000. RESERVES DEPOSITED WITH LENDER:			
1001. Hazard Insurance months @ $ per month			
1002. Mortgage insurance 4 months @ $ 35.00 per month		140	
1003. City property taxes 5 months @ $ 273.60 per month		1,368	
1004. County property taxes months @ $ per month			
1005. Annual assessments months @ $ per month			
1006. *Flood insurance* months @ $ per month			
1007. months @ $ per month			
1008. months @ $ per month			
1100. TITLE CHARGES:			
1101. Settlement or closing fee to			50
1102. Abstract or title search to		125	
1103. Title examination to		15	15
1104. Title insurance binder to		850	–
1105. Document preparation to			
1106. Notary fees to			
1107. Attorney's fees to		225	150
(includes above items Numbers:			
1108. Title insurance to			
(includes above items Numbers:			
1109. Lender's coverage $			
1110. Owner's coverage $			
1111.			
1112.			
1113.			
1200. GOVERNMENT RECORDING AND TRANSFER CHARGES:			
1201. Recording fees: Deed $; Mortgage $; Releases $		54	
1202. City/county tax / stamps: Deed $; Mortgage $			
1203. State tax / stamps Deed $; Mortgage $			
1204.			
1205.			
1300. ADDITIONAL SETTLEMENT CHARGES:			
1301. Survey to			225
1302. Pest inspection to			
1303.			
1304.			
1305.			
1306.			
1307.			
1400. TOTAL SETTLEMENT CHARGES *(Enter on line 103, Section J-and-line 502, Section K)* ▶		$4,819	$5,540

I have carefully reviewed the HUD-1 Settlement Statement and to the best of my knowledge and belief, it is a true and accurate statement of all receipts and disbursements made on my account or by me in this transaction. I further certify that I have received a copy of the HUD-1 Settlement Statement.

Borrower:_____ Date:_____ Seller:_____ Date:_____

Borrower:_____ Date:_____ Seller:_____ Date:_____

The HUD-1 Settlement Statement which I have prepared is a true and accurate account of this transaction. I have caused or will cause the funds to be disbursed in accordance with this statement.

_____ Date:_____ Settlement Agent:_____ Date:_____

WARNING: It is a crime to knowingly make false statements to the United States on this or any other similar form. Penalties upon conviction can include a fine and imprisonment. For details see: Title 18 U.S. Code Section 1001 and Section 1010.

▲ **Exhibit B–22**

Instructions for Transferor

Generally, persons responsible for closing a real estate transaction must report the real estate proceeds to the Internal Revenue Service and must furnish this statement to you. If the real estate transferred was your main home, file **Form 2119,** Sale of Your Home, with your income tax return even if you sold at a loss or you did not replace your home. If the real estate transferred was not your main home, report the transaction in the applicable parts of **Form 4797,** Sales of Business Property, **Form 6252,** Installment Sale Income, and/or **Schedule D (Form 1040),** Capital Gains and Losses.

If you sold your home and (1) you did not own it for more than 9 years and (2) it was financed after 1990 under a Federally subsidized program (qualified mortgage bonds or mortgage credit certificates), you may have to recapture part of the subsidy. This will increase your tax. See **Form 8828,** Recapture of Federal Mortgage Subsidy, and **Pub. 523,** Selling Your Home.

Box 1.—Shows the date of closing.

Box 2.—Shows the gross proceeds from a real estate transaction, generally the sales price. Gross proceeds include cash and notes payable to you, notes assumed by the transferee (buyer), and any notes paid off at settlement. Box 2 does not include the value of other property or services you received or are to receive. See **Box 4.**

Box 3.—Shows the address of the property transferred or a legal description of the property.

Box 4.—If marked, shows that you received or will receive services or property (other than cash or notes) as part of the consideration for the property transferred. The value of any services or property (other than cash or notes) is not included in box 2.

Box 5.—Shows certain real estate tax on a residence charged to the buyer at settlement. If you have already paid the real estate tax for the period that includes the sale date, subtract this amount from the amount already paid to determine your deductible real estate tax. But if you have already deducted the real estate tax in a prior year, generally report this amount as income on the "Other income" line on Form 1040. For more information, see Pub. 523.

☐ CORRECTED (if checked)

FILER'S name, street address, city, state, and ZIP code R. J. Hackett 1212 Main Street Wakefield, RI 02879	**1** Date of closing 9/16/94	OMB No. 1545-0997 **19 94**
	2 Gross proceeds $ 137,000	**Proceeds From Real Estate Transactions**

FILER'S Federal identification number 05-1023576	**TRANSFEROR'S identification number** 150-52-0546	**3** Address or legal description	**Copy B** **For Transferor**
TRANSFEROR'S name Bill & Joyce Schnappauf		27 Northup Street Wakefield, RI 02879	This is important tax information and is being furnished to the Internal Revenue Service. If you are required to file a return, a negligence
Street address (including apt. no.) 3242 Heights Drive			penalty or other sanction may be
City, state, and ZIP code Barrington, RI 02806		**4** Transferor received or will receive property or services as part of the consideration (if checked) . . . ▶ ☐	imposed on you if this item is required to be reported and the IRS
Account number (optional)		**5** Buyer's part of real estate tax (See **Box 5** on back.) $	determines that it has not been reported.

Form **1099-S** (Keep for your records.) Department of the Treasury - Internal Revenue Service

▲ **Exhibit B–23**

SCHEDULE K-1 (Form 1120S)	**Shareholder's Share of Income, Credits, Deductions, etc.**	OMB No. 1545-0130
Department of the Treasury Internal Revenue Service	▶ See separate instructions. **For calendar year 1994 or tax year** beginning January 1 , 1994, and ending December 31 , 19 94	19**94**

Shareholder's identifying number ▶ 371-42-5207	Corporation's identifying number ▶ 05 : 6176194
Shareholder's name, address, and ZIP code Joyce Schnappauf 3242 Heights Drive Barrington, RI 02806	Corporation's name, address, and ZIP code B & J Anitique Restoration 137 Weathervane Road Wakefield, RI 02879

A Shareholder's percentage of stock ownership for tax year (see Instructions for Schedule K-1) . . . . ▶ 30 %

B Internal Revenue Service Center where corporation filed its return ▶ Andover, MA 05501

C Tax shelter registration number (see Instructions for Schedule K-1) . . . . ▶

D Check applicable boxes: **(1)** ☐ Final K-1   **(2)** ☐ Amended K-1

	(a) Pro rata share items		(b) Amount	(c) Form 1040 filers enter the amount in column (b) on:
Income (Loss)	**1** Ordinary income (loss) from trade or business activities . .	**1**	775	See Shareholder's Instructions for Schedule K-1 (Form 1120S).
	2 Net income (loss) from rental real estate activities	**2**		
	3 Net income (loss) from other rental activities	**3**		
	4 Portfolio income (loss):			
	a Interest	**4a**	50	Sch. B, Part I, line 1
	b Dividends	**4b**		Sch. B, Part II, line 5
	c Royalties	**4c**		Sch. E, Part I, line 4
	d Net short-term capital gain (loss).	**4d**		Sch. D, line 5, col. (f) or (g)
	e Net long-term capital gain (loss)	**4e**		Sch. D, line 13, col. (f) or (g)
	f Other portfolio income (loss) (attach schedule)	**4f**		(Enter on applicable line of your return.)
	5 Net gain (loss) under section 1231 (other than due to casualty or theft)	**5**		See Shareholder's Instructions for Schedule K-1 (Form 1120S).
	6 Other income (loss) (attach schedule)	**6**		(Enter on applicable line of your return.)
Deductions	**7** Charitable contributions (see instructions) (attach schedule) .	**7**	80	Sch. A, line 15 or 16
	8 Section 179 expense deduction	**8**	525	See Shareholder's Instructions for Schedule K-1 (Form 1120S).
	9 Deductions related to portfolio income (loss) (attach schedule) .	**9**		
	10 Other deductions (attach schedule)	**10**		
Investment Interest	**11a** Interest expense on investment debts	**11a**		Form 4952, line 1
	b **(1)** Investment income included on lines 4a, 4b, 4c, and 4f above	**b(1)**		See Shareholder's Instructions for Schedule K-1 (Form 1120S).
	(2) Investment expenses included on line 9 above	**b(2)**		
Credits	**12a** Credit for alcohol used as fuel	**12a**		Form 6478, line 10
	b Low-income housing credit:			
	(1) From section 42(j)(5) partnerships for property placed in service before 1990	**b(1)**		Form 8586, line 5
	(2) Other than on line 12b(1) for property placed in service before 1990	**b(2)**		
	(3) From section 42(j)(5) partnerships for property placed in service after 1989	**b(3)**		
	(4) Other than on line 12b(3) for property placed in service after 1989	**b(4)**		
	c Qualified rehabilitation expenditures related to rental real estate activities (see instructions)	**12c**		See Shareholder's Instructions for Schedule K-1 (Form 1120S).
	d Credits (other than credits shown on lines 12b and 12c) related to rental real estate activities (see instructions)	**12d**		
	e Credits related to other rental activities (see instructions) . .	**12e**		
	13 Other credits (see instructions)	**13**		
Adjustments and Tax Preference Items	**14a** Depreciation adjustment on property placed in service after 1986	**14a**		See Shareholder's Instructions for Schedule K-1 (Form 1120S) and Instructions for Form 6251
	b Adjusted gain or loss	**14b**		
	c Depletion (other than oil and gas)	**14c**		
	d **(1)** Gross income from oil, gas, or geothermal properties . .	**d(1)**		
	(2) Deductions allocable to oil, gas, or geothermal properties .	**d(2)**		
	e Other adjustments and tax preference items (attach schedule) .	**14e**		

For Paperwork Reduction Act Notice, see page 1 of Instructions for Form 1120S.   Cat. No. 11520D   **Schedule K-1 (Form 1120S) 1994**

▲ Exhibit B–23
(continued)

Schedule K-1 (Form 1120S) (1994)   Page **2**

	(a) Pro rata share items		(b) Amount	(c) Form 1040 filers enter the amount in column (b) on:
Foreign Taxes	**15a** Type of income ▶ --			Form 1116, Check boxes
	b Name of foreign country or U.S. possession ▶ ---------------			
	c Total gross income from sources outside the United States *(attach schedule)*	15c		} Form 1116, Part I
	d Total applicable deductions and losses *(attach schedule)* . .	15d		
	e Total foreign taxes (check one): ▶ ☐ Paid ☐ Accrued .	15e		Form 1116, Part II
	f Reduction in taxes available for credit *(attach schedule)* . .	15f		Form 1116, Part III
	g Other foreign tax information *(attach schedule)*	15g		See Instructions for Form 1116
Other	**16a** Total expenditures to which a section 59(e) election may apply	16a		See Shareholder's Instructions for Schedule K-1 (Form 1120S).
	b Type of expenditures ▶ --			
	17 Tax-exempt interest income	17		Form 1040, line 8b
	18 Other tax-exempt income	18		
	19 Nondeductible expenses	19		See Shareholder's Instructions for Schedule K-1 (Form 1120S).
	20 Property distributions (including cash) other than dividend distributions reported to you on Form 1099-DIV	20	1,700	
	21 Amount of loan repayments for "Loans From Shareholders" .	21		
	22 Recapture of low-income housing credit:			
	a From section 42(j)(5) partnerships	22a		} Form 8611, line 8
	b Other than on line 22a	22b		

23 Supplemental information required to be reported separately to each shareholder *(attach additional schedules if more space is needed)*:

Supplemental Information

▲ Exhibit B–23
(continued)

Lines 1 Through 23

The amounts on lines 1 through 23 show your pro rata share of ordinary income, loss, deductions, credits, and other information from all corporate activities. These amounts do not take into account limitations on losses, credits, or other items that may have to be adjusted because of:

1. The adjusted basis of your stock and debt in the corporation,

2. The at-risk limitations,

3. The passive activity limitations, or

4. Any other limitations that must be taken into account at the shareholder level in figuring taxable income (e.g., the section 179 expense limitation).

The limitations of **1, 2,** and **3** are discussed above, and the limitations for **4** are discussed throughout these instructions and in other referenced forms and instructions.

If you are an individual, and your pro rata share items are not affected by any of the limitations, report the amounts shown in column (b) of Schedule K-1 as indicated in column (c). If any of the limitations apply, adjust the column (b) amounts for the limitations before you enter the amounts on your return. When applicable, the passive activity limitations on losses are applied after the limitations on losses for a shareholder's basis in stock and debt and the shareholder's at-risk amount.

Note: *The line number references in column (c) are to forms in use for tax years beginning in 1994. If you are a calendar year shareholder in a fiscal year 1994–95 corporation, enter these amounts on the corresponding lines of the tax form in use for 1995.*

Caution: *If you have losses, deductions, credits, etc., from a prior year that were not deductible or usable because of certain limitations, such as the basis rules or the at-risk limitations, take them into account in determining your income, loss, etc., for this year. However, except for passive activity losses and credits, do not combine the prior-year amounts with any amounts shown on this Schedule K-1 to get a net figure to report on your return. Instead, report the amounts on your return on a year-by-year basis.*

Income (Loss)

Line 1—Ordinary Income (Loss) From Trade or Business Activities

The amount reported on line 1 is your share of the ordinary income (loss) from trade or business activities of the corporation. Generally, where you report this amount on Form 1040 depends on whether the amount is from an activity that is a passive activity to you. If you are an individual shareholder, find your situation below and report your line 1 income (loss) as instructed after applying the basis and at-risk limitations on losses:

1. Report line 1 income (loss) from trade or business activities in which you materially participated on Schedule E (Form 1040), Part II, column (i) or (k).

2. Report line 1 income (loss) from trade or business activities in which you did not materially participate, as follows:

a. If income is reported on line 1, report the income on Schedule E, Part II, column (h).

b. If a loss is reported on line 1, follow the Instructions for Form 8582 to determine how much of the loss can be reported on Schedule E, Part II, column (g).

▲ **Exhibit B–23**
(continued)

Line 2—Net Income (Loss) From Rental Real Estate Activities

Generally, the income (loss) reported on line 2 is a passive activity amount for all shareholders. However, the income (loss) on line 2 is not from a passive activity if **(a)** you were a real estate professional (defined on page 2) and you materially participated in the activity, or **(b)** you held an interest in the activity as a qualified investor in a qualified low-income housing project. The corporation should have attached a schedule identifying any amounts you held as a qualified investor in a qualified low-income housing project.

If you are filing a 1994 Form 1040, use the following instructions to determine where to enter a line 2 amount:

1. If you have a loss from a passive activity on line 2 and you meet **all** of the following conditions, enter the loss on Schedule E (Form 1040), Part II, column (g):

a. You actively participated in the corporate rental real estate activities. (See **Active participation in a rental real estate activity** on page 3.)

b. Rental real estate activities with active participation were your only passive activities.

c. You have no prior year unallowed losses from these activities.

d. Your total loss from the rental real estate activities was not more than $25,000 (not more than $12,500 if married filing separately and you lived apart from your spouse all year).

e. If you are a married person filing separately, you lived apart from your spouse all year.

f. You have no current or prior year unallowed credits from a passive activity.

g. Your modified adjusted gross income was not more than $100,000 (not more than $50,000 if married filing separately and you lived apart from your spouse all year).

2. If you have a loss from a passive activity on line 2 and you **do not** meet all of the conditions in **1** above, follow the Instructions for Form 8582 to determine how much of the loss can be reported on Schedule E (Form 1040), Part II, column (g).

3. If **(a)** you were a real estate professional and you materially participated in the activity, or **(b)** you held an interest in the activity as a qualified investor in a qualified low-income housing project, report line 2 income (loss) on Schedule E, Part II, column (i) or (k).

4. If you have income from a passive activity on line 2, enter the income on Schedule E, Part II, column (h).

Line 3—Net Income (Loss) From Other Rental Activities

The amount on line 3 is a passive activity amount for all shareholders. Report the income or loss as follows:

1. If line 3 is a loss, report the loss following the Instructions for Form 8582.

2. If income is reported on line 3, report the income on Schedule E (Form 1040), Part II, column (h).

Line 4—Portfolio Income (Loss)

Portfolio income or loss is not subject to the passive activity limitations. Portfolio income includes income not derived in the ordinary course of a trade or business from interest, dividends, annuities, or royalties, and gain or loss on the sale of property that produces these types of income or is held for investment.

Column (c) of Schedule K-1 tells shareholders where to report this income on Form 1040 and related schedules. Line 4f of Schedule K-1 is used to report income other than that reported on lines 4a through 4e. The type and the amount of income reported on line 4f will be listed in the line 23 Supplemental Information space of Schedule K-1. An example of the type of income that is reported on line 4f is income from a real estate mortgage investment conduit (REMIC) in which the corporation is a residual interest holder. Report your share of any REMIC income on Schedule E (Form 1040), Part IV.

Line 5—Net Gain (Loss) Under Section 1231 (Other Than Due to Casualty or Theft)

Section 1231 gain or loss is reported on line 5. The corporation will identify in the line 23 Supplemental Information space the activity to which the section 1231 gain (loss) relates.

If the amount on line 5 is from a rental activity, the section 1231 gain (loss) is generally a passive activity amount. Likewise, if the amount relates to a trade or business activity and you did not materially participate in the activity, the section 1231 gain (loss) is a passive activity amount.

However, an amount on line 6 from a rental real estate activity is not from a passive activity if **(a)** you were a real estate professional (defined on page 2) and you materially participated in the activity, or **(b)** you held an interest in the activity as a qualified investor in a qualified low-income housing project. The corporation should have attached a schedule identifying any amounts you held as a qualified investor in a qualified low-income housing project.

● If the amount is **not** from a passive activity, report it on line 2, column (g) or (h), whichever is applicable, of **Form 4797,** Sales of Business Property. You

do not have to complete the information called for in columns (b) through (f), Form 4797. Write "From Schedule K-1 (Form 1120S)" across these columns.

● If gain from a passive activity is reported on line 5, report the gain on line 2, column (h) of Form 4797.

● If a loss from a passive activity is reported on line 5, see **Passive loss limitations** in the Instructions for Form 4797. You will need to report the loss following the Instructions for Form 8582 to determine how much of the loss is allowed on Form 4797.

Line 6—Other Income (Loss)

Amounts on this line are other items of income, gain, or loss not included on lines 1 through 5. The corporation should give you a description and the amount of your share for each of these items.

Report loss items that are passive activity amounts to you following the Instructions for Form 8582.

Report income or gain items that are passive activity amounts to you as instructed below.

The instructions below tell you where to report line 6 items if such items are **not** passive activity amounts.

Line 6 items include the following:

● Income from recoveries of tax benefit items. A tax benefit item is an amount you deducted in a prior tax year that reduced your income tax. Report this amount on Form 1040, line 21, to the extent it reduced your tax.

● Gambling gains and losses.

1. If the corporation was not engaged in the trade or business of gambling:

a. Report gambling winnings on Form 1040, line 21.

b. Deduct gambling losses to the extent of winnings on Schedule A, line 28.

2. If the corporation was engaged in the trade or business of gambling:

a. Report gambling winnings in Part II of Schedule E.

b. Deduct gambling losses to the extent of winnings in Part II of Schedule E.

● Net gain (loss) from involuntary conversions due to casualty or theft. The corporation will give you a schedule that shows the amounts to be reported on **Form 4684,** Casualties and Thefts, line 34, columns (b)(i), (b)(ii), and (c).

● Net short-term capital gain or loss and net long-term capital gain or loss from Schedule D (Form 1120S) that is **not** portfolio income (e.g., gain or loss from the disposition of nondepreciable personal property used in a trade or business activity of the corporation). Report a net short-term capital gain or loss on Schedule D (Form 1040), line 5, column (f) or (g), and a net long-term

▲ Exhibit B–23
(continued)

capital gain or loss on Schedule D (Form 1040), line 13, column (f) or (g).

• Any net gain or loss from section 1256 contracts. Report this amount on line 1 of **Form 6781,** Gains and Losses From Section 1256 Contracts and Straddles.

Deductions

Line 7—Charitable Contributions

The corporation will give you a schedule that shows the amount of contributions subject to the 50%, 30%, and 20% limitations. For more details, see the Form 1040 instructions.

If property other than cash is contributed, and the claimed deduction for one item or group of similar items of property exceeds $5,000, the corporation is required to give you a copy of **Form 8283,** Noncash Charitable Contributions, and you must attach it to your tax return. Do not deduct the amount shown on Form 8283. It is the corporation's contribution. You should deduct the amount shown on line 7, Schedule K-1.

If the corporation provides you with information that the contribution was property other than cash and does not give you a Form 8283, see the Instructions for Form 8283 for filing requirements. A Form 8283 does not have to be filed unless the total claimed deduction of all contributed items of property exceeds $500.

Charitable contribution deductions are not taken into account in figuring your passive activity loss for the year. Do not enter them on Form 8582.

Line 8—Section 179 Expense Deduction

Use this amount, along with the total cost of section 179 property placed in service during the year from other sources, to complete Part I of **Form 4562,** Depreciation and Amortization. Part I of Form 4562 is used to figure your allowable section 179 expense deduction from all sources. Report the amount on line 12 of Form 4562 allocable to a passive activity from the corporation following the Instructions for Form 8582. If the amount is not a passive activity deduction, report it on Schedule E (Form 1040), Part II, column (j).

Line 9—Deductions Related to Portfolio Income (Loss)

Amounts on line 9 are deductions that are clearly and directly allocable to portfolio income reported on lines 4a through 4f (other than investment interest expense and section 212 expenses from a REMIC). Generally, you should enter line 9 amounts on Schedule A (Form 1040), line 22. See the instructions for Schedule A, lines 22 and 28, for more information.

These deductions are not taken into account in figuring your passive activity loss for the year. Do not enter them on Form 8582.

Line 10—Other Deductions

Amounts on this line are other deductions not included on lines 7, 8, 9, 15e, and 16a, such as:

• Itemized deductions that Form 1040 filers enter on Schedule A (Form 1040).

Note: *If there was a gain (loss) from a casualty or theft to property* **not** *used in a trade or business or for income-producing purposes, you will be notified by the corporation. You will have to complete your own Form 4684.*

• Any penalty on early withdrawal of savings.

• Soil and water conservation expenditures. See section 175 for limitations on the amount you are allowed to deduct.

• Expenditures for the removal of architectural and transportation barriers to the elderly and disabled that the corporation elected to treat as a current expense. The deductions are limited by section 190(c) to $15,000 per year from all sources.

• Interest expense allocated to debt-financed distributions. The manner in which you report such interest expense depends on your use of the distributed debt proceeds. See Notice 89-35, 1989-1 C.B. 675, for details.

If the corporation has more than one corporate activity (line 1, 2, or 3 of Schedule K-1), it will identify the activity to which the expenses relate.

The corporation should also give you a description and your share of each of the expense items. Associate any passive activity deduction included on line 10 with the line 1, 2, or 3 activity to which it relates and report the deduction following the Instructions for Form 8582 (or only on Schedule E (Form 1040), if applicable).

Investment Interest

If the corporation paid or accrued interest on debts properly allocable to investment property, the amount of interest you are allowed to deduct may be limited.

For more information on the special provisions that apply to investment interest expense, get **Form 4952,** Investment Interest Expense Deduction, and **Pub. 550,** Investment Income and Expenses.

Line 11a—Interest Expense on Investment Debts

Enter this amount on Form 4952, line 1, along with investment interest expense from Schedule K-1, line 10, if any, and from other sources to determine how

much of your total investment interest is deductible.

Lines 11b(1) and (2)—Investment Income and Investment Expenses

Use the amounts on these lines to determine the amounts to enter in Part II of Form 4952.

Caution: *The amounts shown on lines 11b(1) and 11b(2) include only investment income and expenses reported on lines 4a, 4b, 4c, 4f, and 9 of this Schedule K-1. If applicable, the corporation will have listed in the line 23 Supplemental Information space any other items of investment income and expenses reported elsewhere on this Schedule K-1. Be sure to take these amounts into account, along with the amounts on lines 11b(1) and 11b(2) and your investment income and expenses from other sources, when figuring the amounts to enter in Part II of Form 4952.*

Credits

Caution: *If you have credits that are passive activity credits to you, you must complete Form 8582-CR in addition to the credit forms named below. See the Instructions for Form 8582-CR for more information.*

Also, if you are entitled to claim more than one general business credit (i.e., investment credit, jobs credit, credit for alcohol used as fuel, research credit, low-income housing credit, enhanced oil recovery credit, disabled access credit, renewable electricity production credit, Indian employment credit, credit for employer social security and Medicare taxes paid on certain employee tips, and credit for contributions to selected community development corporations), you must complete **Form 3800,** *General Business Credit, in addition to the credit forms named below. If you have more than one credit, see the instructions for Form 3800 for more information.*

Line 12a—Credit for Alcohol Used as Fuel

Your share of the corporation's credit for alcohol used as fuel from all trade or business activities is reported on line 12a. Enter this credit on **Form 6478,** Credit for Alcohol Used as Fuel, to determine your allowed credit for the year.

Line 12b—Low-Income Housing Credit

Your share of the corporation's low-income housing credit is shown on lines 12b(1) through (4). Your allowable credit is entered on **Form 8586,** Low-Income Housing Credit, to determine your allowed credit for the year.

If the corporation invested in a partnership to which the provisions of section 42(j)(5) apply, it will report separately on lines 12b(1) and 12b(3) your share of the credit it received from the partnership.

Your share of all other low-income housing credits of the corporation is reported on lines 12b(2) and 12b(4). You must keep a separate record of the amount of low-income housing credit from these lines so that you will be able to correctly compute any recapture of the credit that may result from the disposition of all or part of your stock in the corporation. For more information, see the instructions for **Form 8611,** Recapture of Low-Income Housing Credit.

Caution: *You cannot claim the low-income housing credit on any qualified low-income housing project if you, or any person, were allowed relief from the passive activity limitations on losses from the project (section 502 of the Tax Reform Act of 1986).*

Line 12c—Qualified Rehabilitation Expenditures Related to Rental Real Estate Activities

The corporation should identify your share of rehabilitation expenditures from each rental real estate activity. Enter the expenditures on the appropriate line of **Form 3468,** Investment Credit, to figure your allowable credit.

Line 12d—Credits (Other Than Credits Shown on Lines 12b and 12c) Related to Rental Real Estate Activities

The corporation will identify the type of credit and any other information you need to compute credits from rental real estate activities (other than the low-income housing credit and qualified rehabilitation expenditures).

Line 12e—Credits Related to Other Rental Activities

If applicable, your share of any credit from other rental activities will be reported on line 12e. Income or loss from these activities is reported on line 3 of Schedule K-1. If more than one credit is involved, the credits will be listed separately, each credit identified as a line 12e credit, and the activity to which the credit relates will be identified. This information will be shown on the line 23 Supplemental Information space. The credit may be limited by the passive activity limitations.

Line 13—Other Credits

If applicable, your pro rata share of any other credit (other than on lines 12a through 12e) will be shown on line 13. If more than one credit is reported, the credits will be shown and identified in the line 23 Supplemental Information space. Expenditures qualifying for the **(a)** rehabilitation credit from other than

rental real estate activities, **(b)** energy credit, or **(c)** reforestation credit will be reported to you on line 23.

Line 13 credits include the following:

● Nonconventional source fuel credit. Enter this credit on a schedule you prepare yourself to determine the allowed credit to take on your tax return. See section 29 for rules on how to figure the credit.

● Unused investment credit from cooperatives. Enter this credit on Form 3468 to figure your allowable investment credit.

● Credit for backup withholding on dividends, interest income, and other types of income. Include the amount the corporation reports to you in the total that you enter on line 54, page 2, Form 1040. Be sure to check the box on line 54 and write "From Schedule K-1."

● Credit for increasing research activities and orphan drug credit (Form 6765).

● Jobs credit (Form 5884).

● Disabled access credit (Form 8826).

● Enhanced oil recovery credit (Form 8830).

● Qualified electric vehicle credit (Form 8834).

● Renewable electricity production credit (Form 8835).

● Empowerment zone employment credit (Form 8844).

● Indian employment credit (Form 8845).

● Credit for employer social security and Medicare taxes paid on certain employee tips (Form 8846).

● Credit for contributions to selected community development corporations (Form 8847).

Adjustments and Tax Preference Items

Use the information reported on lines 14a through 14e (as well as adjustments and tax preference items from other sources) to prepare your **Form 6251,** Alternative Minimum Tax—Individuals, or Schedule H of **Form 1041,** U.S. Income Tax Return for Estates and Trusts.

Lines 14d(1) and 14d(2)—Gross Income From, and Deductions Allocable to, Oil, Gas, and Geothermal Properties

The amounts reported on these lines include only the gross income from, and deductions allocable to, oil, gas, and geothermal properties included on line 1 of Schedule K-1. The corporation should have reported separately any income from or deductions allocable to such properties that are included on lines 2 through 10. This separate information is reported in the line 23 Supplemental Information space. Use the amounts reported on lines 14d(1) and 14d(2) and any amounts reported separately to help

you determine the net amount to enter on line 14f of Form 6251.

Line 14e—Other Adjustments and Tax Preference Items

Enter the line 14e adjustments and tax preference items shown in the line 23 Supplemental Information space, with other items from other sources, on the applicable lines of Form 6251.

Foreign Taxes

Use the information on lines 15a through 15g, and attached schedules, to figure your foreign tax credit. For more information, get **Form 1116,** Foreign Tax Credit—Individual, Estate, Trust, or Nonresident Alien Individual, and its instructions.

Other

Lines 16a and 16b

The corporation will show on line 16a the total qualified expenditures to which an election under section 59(e) may apply. It will identify the type of expenditures on line 16b. If there is more than one type of expenditure, the amount of each type will be listed on an attachment. Generally, section 59(e) allows each shareholder to elect to deduct certain expenses ratably over the number of years in the applicable period rather than deduct the full amount in the current year. Under the election, you may deduct circulation expenditures ratably over a 3-year period. Research and experimental expenditures and mining exploration and development costs qualify for a writeoff period of 10 years. Intangible drilling and development costs may be deducted over a 60-month period, beginning with the month in which such costs were paid or incurred. If you make this election, these items are not treated as adjustments or tax preference items for purposes of the alternative minimum tax. Make the election on Form 4562.

Because each shareholder decides whether to make the election under section 59(e), the corporation cannot provide you with the amount of the adjustment or tax preference item related to the expenses listed on line 16a. You must decide both how to claim the expenses on your return and how to compute the resulting adjustment or tax preference item.

Line 17—Tax-Exempt Interest Income

You must report on your return, as an item of information, your share of the tax-exempt interest received or accrued by the corporation during the year. Individual shareholders should include this amount on Form 1040, line 8b. Generally, you must increase the basis

▲ Exhibit B–23
(continued)

of your stock in the corporation by this amount.

Line 18—Other Tax-Exempt Income

Generally, you must increase the basis of your stock in the corporation by the amount shown on line 18, but do not include it in income on your tax return.

Line 19—Nondeductible Expenses

The nondeductible expenses paid or incurred by the corporation are not deductible on your tax return. Generally, you must decrease the basis of your stock in the corporation by this amount.

Line 20

Reduce the basis of your stock in the corporation by the distributions on line 20. If these distributions exceed the basis of your stock, the excess is treated as gain from the sale or exchange of property and is reported on Schedule D (Form 1040).

Line 21

If the line 21 payments are made on indebtedness with a reduced basis, the repayments result in income to you to the extent the repayments are more than the adjusted basis of the loan. See Regulations section 1.1367-2 for information on reduction in basis of a loan and restoration in basis of a loan with a reduced basis. See Rev. Rul. 64-162, 1964-1 (Part 1) C.B. 304 and Rev. Rul. 68-537, 1968-2 C.B. 372, for other information.

Lines 22a and 22b—Recapture of Low-Income Housing Credit

The corporation will report separately on line 22a your share of any recapture of a low-income housing credit from its investment in partnerships to which the provisions of section 42(j)(5) apply. All other recapture of low-income housing credits will be reported on line 22b. You must keep a separate record of recapture from line 22a and 22b so that you will be able to correctly figure any credit recapture that may result from the disposition of all or part of your corporate stock. Use the line 22a and 22b amounts to compute the low-income housing credit recapture on Form 8611. See the instructions for Form 8611 and section 42(j) for additional information.

Supplemental Information

Line 23

If applicable, the corporation should have listed in line 23, Supplemental Information, or on an attached statement to Schedule K-1, your distributive share of the following:

1. Taxes paid on undistributed capital gains by a regulated investment company. (Form 1040 filers, enter your share of these taxes on line 59 of Form 1040, check the box for Form 2439, and add the words "Form 1120S." Also reduce the basis of your stock in the corporation by this tax.)

2. Gross income from the property, share of production for the tax year, etc., needed to figure your depletion deduction for oil and gas wells. The corporation should also allocate to you a proportionate share of the adjusted basis of each corporate oil or gas property. See Pub. 535 for how to figure your depletion deduction. Also, reduce the basis of your stock in the corporation by the amount of this deduction to the extent the deduction does not exceed your share of the adjusted basis of the property.

3. Recapture of the section 179 expense deduction. If the recapture was caused by a disposition of the property, include the amount on Form 4797, line 18. The recapture amount is limited to the amount you deducted in earlier years.

4. Recapture of certain mining exploration expenditures (section 617).

5. Any information or statements you need to comply with section 6111 (registration of tax shelters) or 6662(d)(2)(B)(ii) (regarding adequate disclosure of items that may cause an understatement of income tax).

6. Gross farming and fishing income. If you are an individual shareholder, enter this income, as an item of information, on Schedule E (Form 1040), Part V, line 41. Do not report this income elsewhere on Form 1040.

For a shareholder that is an estate or trust, report this income to the beneficiaries, as an item of information, on Schedule K-1 (Form 1041). Do not report it elsewhere on Form 1041.

7. Any information you need to figure the interest due under section 453(l)(3). If the corporation elected to report the dispositions of certain timeshares and residential lots on the installment method, your tax liability must be increased by the interest on tax attributable to your pro rata share of the installment payments received by the corporation during its tax year. If applicable, use the information provided by the corporation to figure your interest. Include the interest on Form 1040, line 53. Also write "453(l)(3)" and the amount of the interest on the dotted line to the left of line 53.

8. Any information you need to compute the interest due under section 453A(c) with respect to certain installment sales of property. If you are an individual, report the interest on Form 1040, line 53. Write "453A(c)" and the amount of the interest on the dotted line to the left of line 53. See the instructions

for **Form 6252,** Installment Sale Income, for more information. Also see section 453A(c) for details on making the computation.

9. Capitalization of interest under section 263A(f). To the extent certain production or construction expenditures of the corporation are made from proceeds associated with debt you incur as an owner-shareholder, you must capitalize the interest on this debt. If applicable, use the information on expenditures the corporation gives to you to determine the amount of interest you must capitalize. See Section XII of Notice 88-99, 1988-2 C.B. 422, for more information.

10. Any information you need to compute the interest due or to be refunded under the look-back method of section 460(b)(2) on certain long-term contracts. Use **Form 8697,** Interest Computation Under the Look-Back Method for Completed Long-Term Contracts, to report any such interest.

11. Your share of expenditures qualifying for the **(a)** rehabilitation credit from other than rental real estate activities, **(b)** energy credit, or **(c)** reforestation credit. Enter the expenditures on the appropriate line of Form 3468 to figure your allowable credit.

12. Investment credit properties subject to recapture. Any information you need to figure your recapture tax on **Form 4255,** Recapture of Investment Credit. See the Form 3468 on which you took the original credit for other information you need to complete Form 4255.

You may also need Form 4255 if you disposed of more than one-third of your stock in the corporation.

13. Preproductive period farm expenses. You may elect to deduct these expenses currently or capitalize them under section 263A. See **Pub. 225,** Farmer's Tax Guide, and Temporary Regulations section 1.263A-4T(c) for more information.

14. Any information you need to figure recapture of the qualified electric vehicle credit. See Pub 535 for details, including how to figure the recapture.

15. Any information you need to figure your recapture of the Indian employment credit. Generally, if the corporation terminated a qualified employee less than 1 year after the date of initial employment, any Indian employment credit allowed for a prior tax year by reason of wages paid or incurred to that employee must be recaptured. For details, see section 45A(d).

16. Any other information you may need to file with your individual tax return that is not shown elsewhere on Schedule K-1.

TAX FORMS

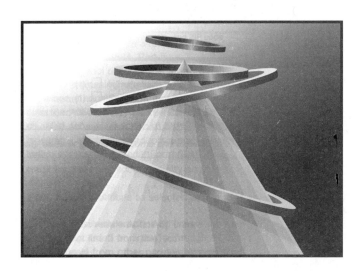

Form 1040EZ	Income Tax Return for Single and Joint Filers With No Dependents	C–3
Form 1040A	U.S. Individual Income Tax Return (Short Form)	C–4
Schedule 1	Interest and Dividend Income	C–6
Schedule 2	Child and Dependent Care Expenses	C–7
Schedule 3	Credit for the Elderly or the Disabled	C–9
Form 1040	U.S. Individual Income Tax Return	C–11
Schedule A	Itemized Deductions	C–13
Schedule B	Interest and Dividend Income	C–14
Schedule C	Profit or Loss From Business	C–15
Schedule C-EZ	Net Profit From Business	C–17
Schedule D	Capital Gains and Losses	C–18
Schedule E	Supplemental Income and Loss	C–20
Schedule EIC	Earned Income Credit	C–22
Table EIC	Earned Income Credit (EIC) Table	C–23
Schedule F	Profit or Loss From Farming	C–25
Schedule R	Credit for the Elderly or the Disabled	C–27
Schedule SE	Self-Employment Tax	C–29
Form 1040X	Amended U.S. Individual Income Tax Return	C–31
Form 1065	U.S. Partnership Return of Income	C–33
Schedule K–1	Partner's Share of Income, Credits, Deductions, etc.	C–37

Form 1116	Foreign Tax Credit	C–39
Form 1120	U.S. Corporation Income Tax Return	C–41
Form 1120S	U.S. Income Tax Return for an S Corporation	C–45
Schedule K–1	Shareholder's Share of Income, Credits, Deductions, etc.	C–49
Form 2106	Employee Business Expenses	C–51
Form 2119	Sale of Your Home	C–53
Form 2120	Multiple Support Declaration	C–54
Form 2210	Underpayment of Estimated Tax by Individuals, Estates, and Trusts	C–55
Form 2441	Child and Dependent Care Expenses	C–58
Form 2555	Foreign Earned Income	C–60
Form 2848	Power of Attorney and Declaration of Representative	C–63
Form 3800	General Business Credit	C–65
Form 3903	Moving Expenses	C–67
Form 4562	Depreciation and Amortization	C–69
Form 4684	Casualties and Thefts	C–71
Form 4797	Sales of Business Property	C–73
Form 4868	Application for Automatic Extension of Time To File U.S. Individual Income Tax Return	C–75
Form 4952	Investment Interest Expense Deduction	C–76
Form 5329	Additional Taxes Attributable to Qualified Retirement Plans (Including IRAs), Annuities, and Modified Endowment Contracts	C–77
Form 6251	Alternative Minimum Tax—Individuals	C–79
Form 7004	Application for Automatic Extension of Time To File Corporation Income Tax Return	C–80
Form 8283	Noncash Charitable Contributions	C–81
Form 8332	Release of Claim to Exemption for Child of Divorced or Separated Parents	C–83
Form 8453	U.S. Individual Income Tax Declaration for Electronic Filing	C–84
Form 8582	Passive Activity Loss Limitations	C–85
Form 8606	Nondeductible IRAs	C–88
Form 8615	Tax for Children Under Age 14 Who Have Investment Income of More Than $1,200	C–89
Form 8814	Parents' Election To Report Child's Interest and Dividends	C–90
Form 8829	Expenses for Business Use of Your Home	C–91

Form 1040EZ

Department of the Treasury–Internal Revenue Service

Income Tax Return for Single and Joint Filers With No Dependents **1994** (T)

OMB No. 1545-0675

Use the IRS label (See page 12.) Otherwise, please print.

LABEL HERE

Print your name (first, initial, last)

If a joint return, print spouse's name (first, initial, last)

Home address (number and street). If you have a P.O. box, see page 12.   Apt. no.

City, town or post office, state and ZIP code. If you have a foreign address, see page 12.

Your social security number

Spouse's social security number

See instructions on back and in Form 1040EZ booklet.

Presidential Election Campaign (See page 12.)

Note: *Checking "Yes" will not change your tax or reduce your refund.*

Do you want $3 to go to this fund? ▶

If a joint return, does your spouse want $3 to go to this fund? ▶

Yes   No

Income

Attach Copy B of Form(s) W-2 here. Enclose, but do not attach, any payment with your return.

Note: *You **must** check Yes or No.*

1 Total wages, salaries, and tips. This should be shown in box 1 of your W-2 form(s). Attach your W-2 form(s).   1

2 Taxable interest income of $400 or less. If the total is over $400, you cannot use Form 1040EZ.   2

3 Add lines 1 and 2. This is your **adjusted gross income.** If less than $9,000, see page 15 to find out if you can claim the earned income credit on line 7.   3

4 Can your parents (or someone else) claim you on their return?

☐ **Yes.** Do worksheet on back; enter amount from line G here.

☐ **No.** If **single,** enter 6,250.00. If **married,** enter 11,250.00. For an explanation of these amounts, see back of form.   4

5 Subtract line 4 from line 3. If line 4 is larger than line 3, enter 0. This is your **taxable income.** ▶ 5

Payments and tax

6 Enter your Federal income tax withheld from box 2 of your W-2 form(s).   6

7 **Earned income credit** (see page 15). Enter type and amount of nontaxable earned income below.

Type $ 7

8 Add lines 6 and 7 (don't include nontaxable earned income). These are your **total payments.**   8

9 **Tax.** Use the amount on **line 5** to find your tax in the tax table on pages 28–32 of the booklet. Then, enter the tax from the table on this line.   9

Refund or amount you owe

10 If line 8 is larger than line 9, subtract line 9 from line 8. This is your **refund.**   10

11 If line 9 is larger than line 8, subtract line 8 from line 9. This is the **amount you owe.** See page 20 for details on how to pay and what to write on your payment.   11

Dollars   Cents

Sign your return

Keep a copy of this form for your records.

I have read this return. Under penalties of perjury, I declare that to the best of my knowledge and belief, the return is true, correct, and accurately lists all amounts and sources of income I received during the tax year.

Your signature

Spouse's signature if joint return

Date   Your occupation

Date   Spouse's occupation

For IRS Use Only — Please do not write in boxes below.

Form
1040A

Department of the Treasury—Internal Revenue Service

U.S. Individual Income Tax Return (T) **1994** IRS Use Only—Do not write or staple in this space.

OMB No. 1545-0085

Label

(See page 16.)

Use the IRS label. Otherwise, please print or type.

L
A
B
E
L

H
E
R
E

Your first name and initial | Last name

If a joint return, spouse's first name and initial | Last name

Home address (number and street). If you have a P.O. box, see page 17. | Apt. no.

City, town or post office, state, and ZIP code. If you have a foreign address, see page 17.

Your social security number

Spouse's social security number

For Privacy Act and Paperwork Reduction Act Notice, see page 4.

Note: *Checking "Yes" will not change your tax or reduce your refund.*

Presidential Election Campaign Fund (See page 17.)
Do you want $3 to go to this fund? . . . .
If a joint return, does your spouse want $3 to go to this fund?

Yes | No

Check the box for your filing status

(See page 17.)

Check only one box.

1 ☐ Single
2 ☐ Married filing joint return (even if only one had income)
3 ☐ Married filing separate return. Enter spouse's social security number above and full name here. ▶
4 ☐ Head of household (with qualifying person). (See page 18.) If the qualifying person is a child but not your dependent, enter this child's name here. ▶
5 ☐ Qualifying widow(er) with dependent child (year spouse died ▶ 19 ____). (See page 19.)

Figure your exemptions

(See page 20.)

If more than seven dependents, see page 23.

6a ☐ **Yourself.** If your parent (or someone else) can claim you as a dependent on his or her tax return, **do not** check box 6a. But be sure to check the box on line 18b on page 2.

b ☐ **Spouse**

c **Dependents:**

(1) Name (first, initial, and last name)	(2) Check if under age 1	(3) If age 1 or older, dependent's social security number	(4) Dependent's relationship to you	(5) No. of months lived in your home in 1994

No. of boxes checked on 6a and 6b

No. of your children on 6c who:
• lived with you
• didn't live with you due to divorce or separation (see page 23)

Dependents on 6c not entered above

Add numbers entered on lines above

d If your child didn't live with you but is claimed as your dependent under a pre-1985 agreement, check here . . . . ▶ ☐

e Total number of exemptions claimed.

Figure your total income

Attach Copy B of your Forms W-2 and 1099-R here.

If you didn't get a W-2, see page 25.

Enclose, but do not attach, any payment with your return.

7 Wages, salaries, tips, etc. This should be shown in box 1 of your W-2 form(s). Attach Form(s) W-2. | 7

8a **Taxable** interest income (see page 25). If over $400, attach Schedule 1. | 8a

b **Tax-exempt** interest. DO NOT include on line 8a. | 8b

9 Dividends. If over $400, attach Schedule 1. | 9

10a Total IRA distributions. | 10a | 10b Taxable amount (see page 26). | 10b

11a Total pensions and annuities. | 11a | 11b Taxable amount (see page 27). | 11b

12 Unemployment compensation (see page 30). | 12

13a Social security benefits. | 13a | 13b Taxable amount (see page 31). | 13b

14 Add lines 7 through 13b (far right column). This is your **total income.** ▶ | 14

Figure your adjusted gross income

15a Your IRA deduction (see page 34). | 15a

b Spouse's IRA deduction (see page 34). | 15b

c Add lines 15a and 15b. These are your **total adjustments.** | 15c

16 Subtract line 15c from line 14. This is your **adjusted gross income.** If less than $25,296 and a child lived with you (less than $9,000 if a child didn't live with you), see "Earned income credit" on page 44. ▶ | 16

Cat. No. 11327A

1994 Form 1040A page 1

1994 Form 1040A page 2

Figure your standard deduction, exemption amount, and taxable income	**17**	Enter the amount from line 16.	**17**	

18a Check if: ☐ **You** were 65 or older ☐ Blind | **Spouse** was 65 or older ☐ Blind } Enter number of boxes checked ▶ **18a** ☐

b If your parent (or someone else) can claim you as a dependent, check here . . . . ▶ **18b** ☐

c If you are married filing separately and your spouse files Form 1040 and itemizes deductions, see page 38 and check here. ▶ **18c** ☐

19 Enter the **standard deduction** shown below for your filing status. **But if you checked any box on line 18a or b**, go to page 38 to find your standard deduction. **If you checked box 18c**, enter -0-.
- Single—$3,800 • Married filing jointly or Qualifying widow(er)—$6,350
- Head of household—$5,600 • Married filing separately—$3,175 | **19** |

20 Subtract line 19 from line 17. If line 19 is more than line 17, enter -0-. **20**

21 Multiply $2,450 by the total number of exemptions claimed on line 6e. **21**

22 Subtract line 21 from line 20. If line 21 is more than line 20, enter -0-. This is your **taxable income.** ▶ **22**

Figure your tax, credits, and payments

If you want the IRS to figure your tax, see the instructions for line 22 on page 39.

23 Find the tax on the amount on line 22. Check if from:
☐ Tax Table (pages 62–67) or ☐ Form 8615 (see page 40). **23**

24a Credit for child and dependent care expenses. Attach Schedule 2. **24a**

b Credit for the elderly or the disabled. Attach Schedule 3. **24b**

c Add lines 24a and 24b. These are your **total credits.** **24c**

25 Subtract line 24c from line 23. If line 24c is more than line 23, enter -0-. **25**

26 Advance earned income credit payments from Form W-2. **26**

27 Add lines 25 and 26. This is your **total tax.** ▶ **27**

28a Total Federal income tax withheld. If any tax is from Form(s) 1099, check here. ▶ ☐ **28a**

b 1994 estimated tax payments and amount applied from 1993 return. **28b**

c **Earned income credit.** If required, attach Schedule EIC (see page 44). **28c**
Nontaxable earned income:
amount ▶ _____ and type ▶ _____

d Add lines 28a, 28b, and 28c (don't include nontaxable earned income). These are your **total payments.** ▶ **28d**

Figure your refund or amount you owe

29 If line 28d is more than line 27, subtract line 27 from line 28d. This is the amount you **overpaid.** **29**

30 Amount of line 29 you want **refunded to you.** **30**

31 Amount of line 29 you want **applied to your 1995 estimated tax.** **31**

32 If line 27 is more than line 28d, subtract line 28d from line 27. This is the **amount you owe.** For details on how to pay, including what to write on your payment, see page 52. **32**

33 Estimated tax penalty (see page 52). Also, include on line 32. **33**

Sign your return

Keep a copy of this return for your records.

Under penalties of perjury, I declare that I have examined this return and accompanying schedules and statements, and to the best of my knowledge and belief, they are true, correct, and accurately list all amounts and sources of income I received during the tax year. Declaration of preparer (other than the taxpayer) is based on all information of which the preparer has any knowledge.

▶ Your signature	Date	Your occupation
▶ Spouse's signature. If joint return, BOTH must sign.	Date	Spouse's occupation

---

Paid preparer's use only

Preparer's signature ▶	Date	Check if self-employed ☐	Preparer's social security no.
Firm's name (or yours if self-employed) and address ▶		E.I. No.	
		ZIP code	

♲ *Printed on recycled paper*

1994 Form 1040A page 2

Schedule 1
(Form 1040A)

Department of the Treasury—Internal Revenue Service

Interest and Dividend Income
for Form 1040A Filers   (99)   **1994**

OMB No. 1545-0085

Name(s) shown on Form 1040A

Your social security number

Part I

Interest income

(See pages 25 and 68.)

Note: *If you received a Form 1099—INT, Form 1099—OID, or substitute statement from a brokerage firm, enter the firm's name and the total interest shown on that form.*

1 List name of payer. If any interest is from a seller-financed mortgage and the buyer used the property as a personal residence, see page 68 and list this interest first. Also, show that buyer's social security number and address.

	Amount
1	

2 Add the amounts on line 1.	2
3 Excludable interest on series EE U.S. savings bonds issued after 1989 from Form 8815, line 14. You MUST attach Form 8815 to Form 1040A.	3
4 Subtract line 3 from line 2. Enter the result here and on Form 1040A, line 8a.	4

Part II

Dividend income

(See pages 26 and 69.)

Note: *If you received a Form 1099—DIV or substitute statement from a brokerage firm, enter the firm's name and the total dividends shown on that form.*

5 List name of payer

	Amount
5	

6 Add the amounts on line 5. Enter the total here and on Form 1040A, line 9.	6

For Paperwork Reduction Act Notice, see Form 1040A instructions.   Cat. No. 12075R   **1994 Schedule 1 (Form 1040A) page 1**

Printed on recycled paper

Schedule 2
(Form 1040A)

Department of the Treasury—Internal Revenue Service
Child and Dependent Care
Expenses for Form 1040A Filers (T) **1994**

OMB No. 1545-0085

Name(s) shown on Form 1040A | **Your social security number**

You need to understand the following terms to complete this schedule: **Qualifying person(s), Dependent care benefits, Qualified expenses,** and **Earned income.** See **Important terms** on page 70.

Part I

Persons or organizations who provided the care

You MUST complete this part.

1

(a) Care provider's name	(b) Address (number, street, apt. no., city, state, and ZIP code)	(c) Identifying number (SSN or EIN)	(d) Amount paid (see page 72)

(If you need more space, use the bottom of page 2.)
2 Add the amounts in column (d) of line 1. | **2** |

3 Enter the number of **qualifying persons** cared for in 1994 . . . ▶ [ ]

| Did you receive **dependent care benefits?** | **NO** ──────▶ Complete only Part II below. |
| | **YES** ──────▶ Complete Part III on the back now. |

Part II

Credit for child and dependent care expenses

4 Enter the amount of **qualified expenses** you incurred and paid in 1994. DO NOT enter more than $2,400 for one qualifying person or $4,800 for two or more persons. If you completed Part III, enter the amount from line 25. | **4** |

5 Enter YOUR **earned income.** | **5** |

6 If married filing a joint return, enter YOUR SPOUSE'S earned income (if student or disabled, see page 73); **all others,** enter the amount from line 5. | **6** |

7 Enter the **smallest** of line 4, 5, or 6. | **7** |

8 Enter the amount from Form 1040A, line 17. | **8** |

9 Enter on line 9 the decimal amount shown below that applies to the amount on line 8.

If line 8 is—		Decimal amount is	If line 8 is—		Decimal amount is
Over	But not over		Over	But not over	
$0—10,000		.30	$20,000—22,000		.24
10,000—12,000		.29	22,000—24,000		.23
12,000—14,000		.28	24,000—26,000		.22
14,000—16,000		.27	26,000—28,000		.21
16,000—18,000		.26	28,000—No limit		.20
18,000—20,000		.25			

| **9** | × . |

10 Multiply **line 7** by the decimal amount on line 9. Enter the result. Then, see page 73 for the amount of credit to enter on Form 1040A, line 24a. | **10** | = |

Caution: *If you paid $50 or more in a calendar quarter to a person who worked in your home, you must file an employment tax return. Get **Form 942** for details.*

Name(s) shown on page 1	Your social security number

Part III

Dependent care benefits

Complete this part **only** if you received these benefits.

11 Enter the total amount of **dependent care benefits** you received for 1994. This amount should be shown in box 10 of your W-2 form(s). DO NOT include amounts that were reported to you as wages in box 1 of Form(s) W-2. **11**

12 Enter the amount forfeited, if any. See page 74. **12**

13 Subtract line 12 from line 11. **13**

14 Enter the total amount of **qualified expenses** incurred in 1994 for the care of the qualifying person(s). **14**

15 Enter the **smaller** of line 13 or 14. **15**

16 Enter YOUR **earned income.** **16**

17 If married filing a joint return, enter YOUR SPOUSE'S earned income (if student or disabled, see the line 6 instructions); if married filing a separate return, see the instructions for the amount to enter; **all others,** enter the amount from line 16. **17**

18 Enter the **smallest** of line 15, 16, or 17. **18**

19 **Excluded benefits.** Enter here the **smaller** of the following:
  ● The amount from line 18, or
  ● $5,000 ($2,500 if married filing a separate return **and** you were required to enter your spouse's earned income on line 17). **19**

20 **Taxable benefits.** Subtract line 19 from line 13. Also, include this amount on Form 1040A, line 7. In the space to the left of line 7, write "DCB." **20**

To claim the child and dependent care credit, complete lines 21—25 below, and lines 4—10 on the front of this schedule.

21 Enter the amount of qualified expenses you incurred and paid in 1994. DO NOT include on this line any excluded benefits shown on line 19. **21**

22 Enter $2,400 ($4,800 if two or more qualifying persons). **22**

23 Enter the amount from line 19. **23**

24 Subtract line 23 from line 22. If zero or less, **STOP.** You cannot take the credit. **Exception.** If you paid 1993 expenses in 1994, see the line 10 instructions. **24**

25 Enter the **smaller** of line 21 or 24 here **and** on line 4 on the front of this schedule. **25**

Schedule 3
(Form 1040A)

Department of the Treasury—Internal Revenue Service

**Credit for the Elderly or the Disabled
for Form 1040A Filers** (99) **1994**

OMB No. 1545-0085

Name(s) shown on Form 1040A

Your social security number

You may be able to take this credit and reduce your tax if by the end of 1994:

- You were age 65 or older, **OR** • You were under age 65, you retired on **permanent and total** disability, and you received taxable disability income.

But you must also meet other tests. See the separate instructions for Schedule 3.

Note: *In most cases, the IRS can figure the credit for you. See page 40 of the Form 1040A instructions.*

Part I Check the box for your filing status and age	If your filing status is:	And by the end of 1994:	Check only one box:
	Single, Head of household, or Qualifying widow(er) with dependent child	**1** You were 65 or older.	1 ☐
		2 You were under 65 and you retired on permanent and total disability	2 ☐
	Married filing a joint return	**3** Both spouses were 65 or older	3 ☐
		4 Both spouses were under 65, but only one spouse retired on permanent and total disability	4 ☐
		5 Both spouses were under 65, and both retired on permanent and total disability	5 ☐
		6 One spouse was 65 or older, and the other spouse was under 65 and retired on permanent and total disability	6 ☐
		7 One spouse was 65 or older, and the other spouse was under 65 and **NOT** retired on permanent and total disability	7 ☐
	Married filing a separate return	**8** You were 65 or older and you lived apart from your spouse for all of 1994	8 ☐
		9 You were under 65, you retired on permanent and total disability, and you lived apart from your spouse for all of 1994	9 ☐

If you checked box 1, 3, 7, or 8, skip Part II and complete Part III on the back. All others, complete Parts II and III.

Part II
Statement of permanent and total disability

Complete this part **only** if you checked box 2, 4, 5, 6, or 9 above.

IF: 1 You filed a physician's statement for this disability for 1983 or an earlier year, or you filed a statement for tax years after 1983 and your physician signed line B on the statement, **AND**

2 Due to your continued disabled condition, you were unable to engage in any substantial gainful activity in 1994, check this box ▶   ☐

- If you checked this box, you do not have to file another statement for 1994.
- If you **did not** check this box, have your physician complete the statement below.

Physician's statement (See instructions at bottom of page 2.)

I certify that _____
Name of disabled person

was permanently and totally disabled on January 1, 1976, or January 1, 1977, **OR** was permanently and totally disabled on the date he or she retired. If retired after December 31, 1976, enter the date retired ▶ _____

Physician: Sign your name on **either** line A or B below.

A The disability has lasted or can be expected to last continuously for at least a year . . . . .

B There is no reasonable probability that the disabled condition will ever improve . . . . .

Physician's signature   Date

Physician's signature   Date

Physician's name

Physician's address

1994 Schedule 3 (Form 1040A) page 2

Name(s) shown on page 1	Your social security number

Part III
Figure your credit

10 **If you checked (in Part I):**   **Enter:**
Box 1, 2, 4, or 7 . . . . $5,000
Box 3, 5, or 6 . . . . $7,500
Box 8 or 9 . . . . $3,750   **10**

Did you check box 2, 4, 5, 6, or 9 in Part I?	→ Yes → You **must** complete line 11.
	→ No → Enter the amount from line 10 on line 12 and go to line 13.

11
- If you checked box 6 in Part I, add $5,000 to the taxable disability income of the spouse who was under age 65. Enter the total.
- If you checked box 2, 4, or 9 in Part I, enter your taxable disability income.
- If you checked box 5 in Part I, add your taxable disability income to your spouse's taxable disability income. Enter the total.

TIP: For more details on what to include on line 11, see the instructions.   **11**

12 If you completed line 11, enter the **smaller** of line 10 or line 11; **all others,** enter the amount from line 10.   **12**

13 Enter the following pensions, annuities, or disability income that you (and your spouse if filing a joint return) received in 1994:

a Nontaxable part of social security benefits, and
Nontaxable part of railroad retirement benefits treated as social security. See instructions.   **13a**

b Nontaxable veterans' pensions and any other pension, annuity, or disability benefit that is excluded from income under any other provision of law. See instructions.   **13b**

c Add lines 13a and 13b. (Even though these income items are not taxable, they **must** be included here to figure your credit.) If you did not receive any of the types of nontaxable income listed on line 13a or 13b, enter -0- on line 13c.   **13c**

14 Enter the amount from Form 1040A, line 17.   **14**

15 **If you checked (in Part I):**   **Enter:**
Box 1 or 2 . . . . $7,500
Box 3, 4, 5, 6, or 7 . . . . $10,000
Box 8 or 9 . . . . $5,000   **15**

16 Subtract line 15 from line 14. If zero or less, enter -0-.   **16**

17 Divide line 16 above by 2.   **17**

18 Add lines 13c and 17.   **18**

19 Subtract line 18 from line 12. If zero or less, **stop;** you **cannot** take the credit. Otherwise, go to line 21.   **19**

20 Decimal amount used to figure the credit.   **20**   × .15

21 Multiply line 19 above by the decimal amount (.15) on line 20. Enter the result here and on Form 1040A, line 24b.   **21**

Instructions for physician's statement

Taxpayer.—If you retired after December 31, 1976, enter the date you retired in the space provided in Part II.

Physician.—A person is permanently and totally disabled if **both** of the following apply:
1. He or she cannot engage in any substantial gainful activity because of a physical or mental condition, and
2. A physician determines that the disability has lasted or can be expected to last continuously for at least a year or can lead to death.

1994 Schedule 3 (Form 1040A) page 2

♻ *Printed on recycled paper*

Form **1040**

Department of the Treasury—Internal Revenue Service
U.S. Individual Income Tax Return (T) **1994**

IRS Use Only—Do not write or staple in this space.

For the year Jan. 1–Dec. 31, 1994, or other tax year beginning ____ , 1994, ending ____ , 19 ___ | OMB No. 1545-0074

Label

(See instructions on page 12.)

Use the IRS label. Otherwise, please print or type.

L A B E L   H E R E

Your first name and initial | Last name | Your social security number

If a joint return, spouse's first name and initial | Last name | Spouse's social security number

Home address (number and street). If you have a P.O. box, see page 12. | Apt. no.

City, town or post office, state, and ZIP code. If you have a foreign address, see page 12.

For Privacy Act and Paperwork Reduction Act Notice, see page 4.

Presidential Election Campaign
(See page 12.)

▶ Do you want $3 to go to this fund? . . . .
If a joint return, does your spouse want $3 to go to this fund? . . . .

Yes | No | **Note:** *Checking "Yes" will not change your tax or reduce your refund.*

Filing Status

(See page 12.)

Check only one box.

1 ☐ Single
2 ☐ Married filing joint return (even if only one had income)
3 ☐ Married filing separate return. Enter spouse's social security no. above and full name here. ▶
4 ☐ Head of household (with qualifying person). (See page 13.) If the qualifying person is a child but not your dependent, enter this child's name here. ▶
5 ☐ Qualifying widow(er) with dependent child (year spouse died ▶ 19 ___). (See page 13.)

Exemptions

(See page 13.)

If more than six dependents, see page 14.

6a ☐ **Yourself.** If your parent (or someone else) can claim you as a dependent on his or her return, **do not** check box 6a. But be sure to check the box on line 33b on page 2

b ☐ **Spouse** . . . .

No. of boxes checked on 6a and 6b

c **Dependents:**

(1) Name (first, initial, and last name)	**(2)** Check if under age 1	**(3)** If age 1 or older, dependent's social security number	**(4)** Dependent's relationship to you	**(5)** No. of months lived in your home in 1994

No. of your children on 6c who:
• lived with you
• didn't live with you due to divorce or separation (see page 14)

Dependents on 6c not entered above

d If your child didn't live with you but is claimed as your dependent under a pre-1985 agreement, check here ▶ ☐

e Total number of exemptions claimed . . . .

Add numbers entered on lines above ▶

Income

Attach Copy B of your Forms W-2, W-2G, and 1099-R here.

If you did not get a W-2, see page 15.

Enclose, but do not attach, any payment with your return.

7 Wages, salaries, tips, etc. Attach Form(s) W-2 . . . . | 7 |
8a **Taxable** interest income (see page 15). Attach Schedule B if over $400 . . . . | 8a |
b **Tax-exempt** interest (see page 16). DON'T include on line 8a | 8b |
9 Dividend income. Attach Schedule B if over $400 . . . . | 9 |
10 Taxable refunds, credits, or offsets of state and local income taxes (see page 16) . . | 10 |
11 Alimony received . . . . | 11 |
12 Business income or (loss). Attach Schedule C or C-EZ . . . . | 12 |
13 Capital gain or (loss). If required, attach Schedule D (see page 16) . . . . . | 13 |
14 Other gains or (losses). Attach Form 4797 . . . . | 14 |
15a Total IRA distributions . | 15a | | b Taxable amount (see page 17) | 15b |
16a Total pensions and annuities | 16a | | b Taxable amount (see page 17) | 16b |
17 Rental real estate, royalties, partnerships, S corporations, trusts, etc. Attach Schedule E | 17 |
18 Farm income or (loss). Attach Schedule F . . . . | 18 |
19 Unemployment compensation (see page 18) . . . . | 19 |
20a Social security benefits | 20a | | b Taxable amount (see page 18) | 20b |
21 Other income. List type and amount—see page 18 _____ | 21 |
22 Add the amounts in the far right column for lines 7 through 21. This is your **total income** ▶ | 22 |

Adjustments to Income

Caution: See instructions . . ▶

23a Your IRA deduction (see page 19) . . . . . | 23a |
b Spouse's IRA deduction (see page 19) . . . . . | 23b |
24 Moving expenses. Attach Form 3903 or 3903-F . . . | 24 |
25 One-half of self-employment tax . . . . . | 25 |
26 Self-employed health insurance deduction (see page 21) | 26 |
27 Keogh retirement plan and self-employed SEP deduction | 27 |
28 Penalty on early withdrawal of savings . . . . . | 28 |
29 Alimony paid. Recipient's SSN ▶ | 29 |
30 Add lines 23a through 29. These are your **total adjustments** . . . . ▶ | 30 |

Adjusted Gross Income

31 Subtract line 30 from line 22. This is your **adjusted gross income**. If less than $25,296 and a child lived with you (less than $9,000 if a child didn't live with you), see "Earned Income Credit" on page 27 ▶ | 31 |

Cat. No. 11320B

Form **1040** (1994)

Form 1040 (1994)   Page **2**

Tax Compu-tation (See page 23.)	32	Amount from line 31 (adjusted gross income)	32	
	33a	Check if: ☐ **You** were 65 or older, ☐ Blind; ☐ **Spouse** was 65 or older, ☐ Blind. Add the number of boxes checked above and enter the total here . . . . ▶ 33a		
	b	If your parent (or someone else) can claim you as a dependent, check here . ▶ 33b ☐		
	c	If you are married filing separately and your spouse itemizes deductions or you are a dual-status alien, see page 23 and check here . . . . ▶ 33c ☐		
	34	Enter the larger of your: { **Itemized deductions** from Schedule A, line 29, **OR** **Standard deduction** shown below for your filing status. **But if you checked any box on line 33a or b,** go to page 23 to find your standard deduction. If you checked **box 33c,** your standard deduction is zero. • Single—$3,800 • Head of household—$5,600 • Married filing jointly or Qualifying widow(er)—$6,350 • Married filing separately—$3,175 }	34	
	35	Subtract line 34 from line 32	35	
	36	If line 32 is $83,850 or less, multiply $2,450 by the total number of exemptions claimed on line 6e. If line 32 is over $83,850, see the worksheet on page 24 for the amount to enter .	36	
If you want the IRS to figure your tax, see page 24.	37	**Taxable income.** Subtract line 36 from line 35. If line 36 is more than line 35, enter -0-	37	
	38	Tax. Check if from **a** ☐ Tax Table, **b** ☐ Tax Rate Schedules, **c** ☐ Capital Gain Tax Worksheet, or **d** ☐ Form 8615 (see page 24). Amount from Form(s) 8814 ▶ **e** _____	38	
	39	Additional taxes. Check if from **a** ☐ Form 4970 **b** ☐ Form 4972	39	
	40	Add lines 38 and 39 . . . . ▶	40	
Credits (See page 24.)	41	Credit for child and dependent care expenses. Attach Form 2441	41		
	42	Credit for the elderly or the disabled. Attach Schedule R .	42		
	43	Foreign tax credit. Attach Form 1116	43		
	44	Other credits (see page 25). Check if from **a** ☐ Form 3800 **b** ☐ Form 8396 **c** ☐ Form 8801 **d** ☐ Form (specify)___	44		
	45	Add lines 41 through 44	45	
	46	Subtract line 45 from line 40. If line 45 is more than line 40, enter -0- . . . . ▶	46	
Other Taxes (See page 25.)	47	Self-employment tax. Attach Schedule SE	47	
	48	Alternative minimum tax. Attach Form 6251	48	
	49	Recapture taxes. Check if from **a** ☐ Form 4255 **b** ☐ Form 8611 **c** ☐ Form 8828	49	
	50	Social security and Medicare tax on tip income not reported to employer. Attach Form 4137	50	
	51	Tax on qualified retirement plans, including IRAs. If required, attach Form 5329 .	51	
	52	Advance earned income credit payments from Form W-2	52	
	53	Add lines 46 through 52. This is your **total tax** . . . . ▶	53	
Payments Attach Forms W-2, W-2G, and 1099-R on the front.	54	Federal income tax withheld. If any is from Form(s) 1099, check ▶ ☐	54		
	55	1994 estimated tax payments and amount applied from 1993 return .	55		
	56	**Earned income credit.** If required, attach Schedule EIC (see page 27). Nontaxable earned income: amount ▶ ____ and type ▶ ____	56		
	57	Amount paid with Form 4868 (extension request)	57		
	58	Excess social security and RRTA tax withheld (see page 32)	58		
	59	Other payments. Check if from **a** ☐ Form 2439 **b** ☐ Form 4136	59		
	60	Add lines 54 through 59. These are your **total payments** . . . . . . ▶	60	
Refund or Amount You Owe	61	If line 60 is more than line 53, subtract line 53 from line 60. This is the amount you **OVERPAID** . ▶	61	
	62	Amount of line 61 you want **REFUNDED TO YOU** . . . . ▶	62	
	63	Amount of line 61 you want **APPLIED TO YOUR 1995 ESTIMATED TAX** ▶	63		
	64	If line 53 is more than line 60, subtract line 60 from line 53. This is the **AMOUNT YOU OWE.** For details on how to pay, including what to write on your payment, see page 32	64	
	65	Estimated tax penalty (see page 33). Also include on line 64	65		

Sign Here
Keep a copy of this return for your records.

Under penalties of perjury, I declare that I have examined this return and accompanying schedules and statements, and to the best of my knowledge and belief, they are true, correct, and complete. Declaration of preparer (other than taxpayer) is based on all information of which preparer has any knowledge.

▶ Your signature	Date	Your occupation
▶ Spouse's signature. If a joint return, BOTH must sign.	Date	Spouse's occupation

Paid Preparer's Use Only

Preparer's signature ▶	Date	Check if self-employed ☐	Preparer's social security no.
Firm's name (or yours if self-employed) and address ▶		E.I. No.	
		ZIP code	

♻ *Printed on recycled paper*

SCHEDULES A&B
(Form 1040)

Department of the Treasury
Internal Revenue Service (T)

Schedule A—Itemized Deductions

(Schedule B is on back)

► Attach to Form 1040. ► See Instructions for Schedules A and B (Form 1040).

OMB No. 1545-0074

1994

Attachment
Sequence No. **07**

Name(s) shown on Form 1040

Your social security number

Medical and Dental Expenses	**1** Medical and dental expenses (see page A-1)	**1**	
	2 Enter amount from Form 1040, line 32. ⌐**2** ┐		
	3 Multiply line 2 above by 7.5% (.075)	**3**	
	4 Subtract line 3 from line 1. If line 3 is more than line 1, enter -0-	**4**	
Taxes You Paid (See page A-1.)	**5** State and local income taxes	**5**	
	6 Real estate taxes (see page A-2)	**6**	
	7 Personal property taxes		
	8 Other taxes. List type and amount ► _____		
	_____	**8**	
	9 Add lines 5 through 8	**9**	
Interest You Paid (See page A-2.) **Note:** Personal interest is not deductible.	**10** Home mortgage interest and points reported to you on Form 1098	**10**	
	11 Home mortgage interest not reported to you on Form 1098. If paid to the person from whom you bought the home, see page A-3 and show that person's name, identifying no., and address ►		
	_____		
	_____		
	_____	**11**	
	12 Points not reported to you on Form 1098. See page A-3 for special rules	**12**	
	13 Investment interest. If required, attach Form 4952. (See page A-3.)	**13**	
	14 Add lines 10 through 13	**14**	
Gifts to Charity If you made a gift and got a benefit for it, see page A-3.	**15** Gifts by cash or check. If any gift of $250 or more, see page A-3	**15**	
	16 Other than by cash or check. If any gift of $250 or more, see page A-3. If over $500, you **MUST** attach Form 8283	**16**	
	17 Carryover from prior year	**17**	
	18 Add lines 15 through 17	**18**	
Casualty and Theft Losses	**19** Casualty or theft loss(es). Attach Form 4684. (See page A-4.)	**19**	
Job Expenses and Most Other Miscellaneous Deductions (See page A-5 for expenses to deduct here.)	**20** Unreimbursed employee expenses—job travel, union dues, job education, etc. If required, you **MUST** attach Form 2106 or 2106-EZ. (See page A-5.) ► _____		
	_____	**20**	
	21 Tax preparation fees _____	**21**	
	22 Other expenses—investment, safe deposit box, etc. List type and amount ► _____		
	_____	**22**	
	23 Add lines 20 through 22	**23**	
	24 Enter amount from Form 1040, line 32. ⌐**24** ┐		
	25 Multiply line 24 above by 2% (.02)	**25**	
	26 Subtract line 25 from line 23. If line 25 is more than line 23, enter -0-	**26**	
Other Miscellaneous Deductions	**27** Moving expenses incurred before 1994. Attach Form 3903 or 3903-F. (See page A-5.) . .	**27**	
	28 Other—from list on page A-5. List type and amount ► _____	**28**	
Total Itemized Deductions	**29** Is form 1040, line 32, over $111,800 (over $55,900 if married filing separately)?		
	NO. Your deduction is not limited. Add the amounts in the far right column for lines 4 through 28. Also, enter on Form 1040, line 34, the **larger** of this amount or your standard deduction. ⎫ ►	**29**	
	YES. Your deduction may be limited. See page A-5 for the amount to enter. ⎭		

Caution: *Do not include expenses reimbursed or paid by others.*

For Paperwork Reduction Act Notice, see Form 1040 instructions.   Cat. No. 11330X   Schedule A (Form 1040) 1994

Schedules A&B (Form 1040) 1994   OMB No. 1545-0074   Page **2**

Name(s) shown on Form 1040. Do not enter name and social security number if shown on other side. | **Your social security number**

Schedule B–Interest and Dividend Income

Attachment Sequence No. **08**

Part I
Interest Income

(See pages 15 and B-1.)

Note: If you received a Form 1099-INT, Form 1099-OID, or substitute statement from a brokerage firm, list the firm's name as the payer and enter the total interest shown on that form.

Note: If you had over $400 in taxable interest income, you must also complete Part III.

		Amount
1	List name of payer. If any interest is from a seller-financed mortgage and the buyer used the property as a personal residence, see page B-1 and list this interest first. Also show that buyer's social security number and address ▶	**1**

2 Add the amounts on line 1 . . . .   **2**

3 Excludable interest on series EE U.S. savings bonds issued after 1989 from Form 8815, line 14. You MUST attach Form 8815 to Form 1040 . . . . .   **3**

4 Subtract line 3 from line 2. Enter the result here and on Form 1040, line 8a ▶   **4**

Part II
Dividend Income

(See pages 16 and B-1.)

Note: If you received a Form 1099-DIV or substitute statement from a brokerage firm, list the firm's name as the payer and enter the total dividends shown on that form.

Note: If you had over $400 in gross dividends and/or other distributions on stock, you must also complete Part III.

		Amount
5	List name of payer. Include gross dividends and/or other distributions on stock here. Any capital gain distributions and nontaxable distributions will be deducted on lines 7 and 8 ▶	**5**

6 Add the amounts on line 5 . . . .   **6**

7 Capital gain distributions. Enter here and on Schedule D* .   **7**

8 Nontaxable distributions. (See the inst. for Form 1040, line 9.)   **8**

9 Add lines 7 and 8 . . . .   **9**

10 Subtract line 9 from line 6. Enter the result here and on Form 1040, line 9 . ▶   **10**

If you do not need Schedule D to report any other gains or losses, enter your capital gain distributions on Form 1040, line 13. Write "CGD" on the dotted line next to line 13.

Part III
Foreign Accounts and Trusts

(See page B-2.)

If you had over $400 of interest or dividends OR had a foreign account or were a grantor of, or a transferor to, a foreign trust, you must complete this part. | **Yes** | **No** |

11a At any time during 1994, did you have an interest in or a signature or other authority over a financial account in a foreign country, such as a bank account, securities account, or other financial account? See page B-2 for exceptions and filing requirements for Form TD F 90-22.1 . . . .

b If "Yes," enter the name of the foreign country ▶

12 Were you the grantor of, or transferor to, a foreign trust that existed during 1994, whether or not you have any beneficial interest in it? If "Yes," you may have to file Form 3520, 3520-A, or 926 .

For Paperwork Reduction Act Notice, see Form 1040 instructions.   *Printed on recycled paper*   Schedule B (Form 1040) 1994

SCHEDULE C
(Form 1040)

Department of the Treasury
Internal Revenue Service (T)

Profit or Loss From Business

(Sole Proprietorship)

▶ Partnerships, joint ventures, etc., must file Form 1065.

▶ Attach to Form 1040 or Form 1041. ▶ See Instructions for Schedule C (Form 1040).

OMB No. 1545-0074

1994

Attachment
Sequence No. **09**

Name of proprietor | Social security number (SSN)

A Principal business or profession, including product or service (see page C-1)

B Enter principal business code
(see page C-6) ▶

C Business name. If no separate business name, leave blank.

D Employer ID number (EIN), if any

E Business address (including suite or room no.) ▶ ....
City, town or post office, state, and ZIP code

F Accounting method: **(1)** ☐ Cash   **(2)** ☐ Accrual   **(3)** ☐ Other (specify) ▶ ....

G Method(s) used to
value closing inventory: **(1)** ☐ Cost   **(2)** ☐ Lower of cost or market   **(3)** ☐ Other (attach explanation)   **(4)** ☐ Does not apply (if checked, skip line H) | Yes | No

H Was there any change in determining quantities, costs, or valuations between opening and closing inventory? If "Yes," attach explanation . . . .

I Did you "materially participate" in the operation of this business during 1994? If "No," see page C-2 for limit on losses. . . .

J If you started or acquired this business during 1994, check here . . . . ▶ ☐

Part I   Income

1	Gross receipts or sales. **Caution:** *If this income was reported to you on Form W-2 and the "Statutory employee" box on that form was checked, see page C-2 and check here* . . . . ▶ ☐	**1**	
2	Returns and allowances	**2**	
3	Subtract line 2 from line 1	**3**	
4	Cost of goods sold (from line 40 on page 2)	**4**	
5	**Gross profit.** Subtract line 4 from line 3	**5**	
6	Other income, including Federal and state gasoline or fuel tax credit or refund (see page C-2) . .	**6**	
7	**Gross income.** Add lines 5 and 6 . . . . ▶	**7**	

Part II   Expenses. Enter expenses for business use of your home **only** on line 30.

8	Advertising	**8**		**19** Pension and profit-sharing plans	**19**	
9	Bad debts from sales or services (see page C-3) . .	**9**		**20** Rent or lease (see page C-4):		
				a Vehicles, machinery, and equipment .	**20a**	
10	Car and truck expenses (see page C-3)	**10**		**b** Other business property . .	**20b**	
11	Commissions and fees. . .	**11**		**21** Repairs and maintenance . .	**21**	
12	Depletion.	**12**		**22** Supplies (not included in Part III) .	**22**	
13	Depreciation and section 179 expense deduction (not included in Part III) (see page C-3) . .	**13**		**23** Taxes and licenses	**23**	
				24 Travel, meals, and entertainment:		
				a Travel	**24a**	
14	Employee benefit programs (other than on line 19) . . .	**14**		**b** Meals and entertainment . .		
15	Insurance (other than health) .	**15**		**c** Enter 50% of line 24b subject to limitations (see page C-4) .		
16	Interest:					
a	Mortgage (paid to banks, etc.) .	**16a**		**d** Subtract line 24c from line 24b	**24d**	
b	Other	**16b**		**25** Utilities	**25**	
17	Legal and professional services	**17**		**26** Wages (less employment credits) .	**26**	
18	Office expense	**18**		**27** Other expenses (from line 46 on page 2)	**27**	

28	**Total expenses** before expenses for business use of home. Add lines 8 through 27 in columns . ▶	**28**	
29	Tentative profit (loss). Subtract line 28 from line 7	**29**	
30	Expenses for business use of your home. Attach **Form 8829**	**30**	
31	**Net profit or (loss).** Subtract line 30 from line 29.		
	• If a profit, enter on **Form 1040, line 12,** and ALSO on **Schedule SE, line 2** (statutory employees, see page C-5). Estates and trusts, enter on Form 1041, line 3.	**31**	
	• If a loss, you MUST go on to line 32.		
32	If you have a loss, check the box that describes your investment in this activity (see page C-5).		
	• If you checked 32a, enter the loss on **Form 1040, line 12,** and ALSO on **Schedule SE, line 2** (statutory employees, see page C-5). Estates and trusts, enter on Form 1041, line 3.	**32a** ☐ All investment is at risk.	
	• If you checked 32b, you MUST attach **Form 6198.**	**32b** ☐ Some investment is not at risk.	

For Paperwork Reduction Act Notice, see Form 1040 instructions.   Cat. No. 11334P   **Schedule C (Form 1040) 1994**

Schedule C (Form 1040) 1994   Page **2**

Part III — Cost of Goods Sold (see page C-5)

33	Inventory at beginning of year. If different from last year's closing inventory, attach explanation . .	33		
34	Purchases less cost of items withdrawn for personal use	34		
35	Cost of labor. Do not include salary paid to yourself	35		
36	Materials and supplies	36		
37	Other costs	37		
38	Add lines 33 through 37	38		
39	Inventory at end of year	39		
40	**Cost of goods sold.** Subtract line 39 from line 38. Enter the result here and on page 1, line 4 . .	40		

Part IV — Information on Your Vehicle. Complete this part **ONLY** if you are claiming car or truck expenses on line 10 and are not required to file Form 4562 for this business. See the instructions for line 13 on page C-3 to find out if you must file.

41   When did you place your vehicle in service for business purposes? (month, day, year) ▶ _____ / _____ / _____ .

42   Of the total number of miles you drove your vehicle during 1994, enter the number of miles you used your vehicle for:

a Business _____   b Commuting _____   c Other _____

43   Do you (or your spouse) have another vehicle available for personal use? . . . . ☐ Yes   ☐ No

44   Was your vehicle available for use during off-duty hours? . . . . ☐ Yes   ☐ No

45a Do you have evidence to support your deduction? . . . . ☐ Yes   ☐ No
   b If "Yes," is the evidence written? . . . . ☐ Yes   ☐ No

Part V — Other Expenses. List below business expenses not included on lines 8—26 or line 30.

_____		
_____		
_____		
_____		
_____		
_____		
_____		
_____		
46 **Total other expenses.** Enter here and on page 1, line 27	46	

✪ *Printed on recycled paper*

SCHEDULE C-EZ
(Form 1040)

Department of the Treasury
Internal Revenue Service (T)

Net Profit From Business
(Sole Proprietorship)

▶ Partnerships, joint ventures, etc., must file Form 1065.

▶ Attach to Form 1040 or Form 1041. ▶ See instructions on back.

OMB No. 1545-0074

1994

Attachment
Sequence No. **09A**

Name of proprietor | Social security number (SSN)

Part I   **General Information**

You May Use This Schedule Only If You:

- Had gross receipts from your business of $25,000 or less.
- Had business expenses of $2,000 or less.
- Use the cash method of accounting.
- Did not have an inventory at any time during the year.
- Did not have a net loss from your business.
- Had only one business as a sole proprietor.

And You:

- Had no employees during the year.
- Are not required to file **Form 4562**, Depreciation and Amortization, for this business. See the instructions for Schedule C, line 13, on page C-3 to find out if you must file.
- Do not deduct expenses for business use of your home.
- Do not have prior year unallowed passive activity losses from this business.

A   Principal business or profession, including product or service   **B Enter principal business code** (see page C-6) ▶

C   Business name. If no separate business name, leave blank.   **D Employer ID number (EIN), if any**

E   Business address (including suite or room no.). Address not required if same as on Form 1040, page 1.

    City, town or post office, state, and ZIP code

Part II   **Figure Your Net Profit**

1   **Gross receipts.** If more than $25,000, you **must** use Schedule C.
Caution: *If this income was reported to you on Form W-2 and the "Statutory employee" box on that form was checked, see **Statutory Employees** in the instructions for Schedule C, line 1, on page C-2 and check here* . . . . ▶ ☐   **1**

2   **Total expenses.** If more than $2,000, you **must** use Schedule C. See instructions **2**

3   **Net profit.** Subtract line 2 from line 1. If less than zero, you **must** use Schedule C. Enter on **Form 1040, line 12,** and ALSO on **Schedule SE, line 2.** (Statutory employees **do not** report this amount on Schedule SE, line 2. Estates and trusts, enter on Form 1041, line 3.) **3**

Part III   **Information on Your Vehicle.** Complete this part **ONLY** if you are claiming car or truck expenses on line 2.

4   When did you place your vehicle in service for business purposes? (month, day, year) ▶ ..... / ..... / ....

5   Of the total number of miles you drove your vehicle during 1994, enter the number of miles you used your vehicle for:

a Business .... **b** Commuting .... **c** Other ....

6   Do you (or your spouse) have another vehicle available for personal use? . . . .   ☐ Yes   ☐ No

7   Was your vehicle available for use during off-duty hours? . . . .   ☐ Yes   ☐ No

8a Do you have evidence to support your deduction? . . . .   ☐ Yes   ☐ No

  b If "Yes," the evidence written? . . . .   ☐ Yes   ☐ No

For Paperwork Reduction Act Notice, see Form 1040 instructions.   Cat. No. 14374D   **Schedule C-EZ (Form 1040) 1994**

SCHEDULE D	Capital Gains and Losses	OMB No. 1545-0074
(Form 1040)	▶ **Attach to Form 1040.** ▶ **See Instructions for Schedule D (Form 1040).**	**1994**
Department of the Treasury Internal Revenue Service (T)	▶ **Use lines 20 and 22 for more space to list transactions for lines 1 and 9.**	Attachment Sequence No. **12**
Name(s) shown on Form 1040		Your social security number

Part I   Short-Term Capital Gains and Losses—Assets Held One Year or Less

(a) Description of property (Example: 100 sh. XYZ Co.)	(b) Date acquired (Mo., day, yr.)	(c) Date sold (Mo., day, yr.)	(d) Sales price (see page D-3)	(e) Cost or other basis (see page D-3)	(f) LOSS If (e) is more than (d), subtract (d) from (e)	(g) GAIN If (d) is more than (e), subtract (e) from (d)
1						

2	Enter your short-term totals, if any, from line 21	**2**	
3	**Total short-term sales price amounts.** Add column (d) of lines 1 and 2 . . .	**3**	
4	Short-term gain from Forms 2119 and 6252, and short-term gain or (loss) from Forms 4684, 6781, and 8824	**4**	
5	Net short-term gain or (loss) from partnerships, S corporations, estates, and trusts from Schedule(s) K-1	**5**	
6	Short-term capital loss carryover. Enter the amount, if any, from line 9 of your 1993 Capital Loss Carryover Worksheet	**6**	
7	Add lines 1, 2, and 4 through 6, in columns (f) and (g)	**7**	( )
8	**Net short-term capital gain or (loss).** Combine columns (f) and (g) of line 7 . . . . . ▶	**8**	

Part II   Long-Term Capital Gains and Losses—Assets Held More Than One Year

9						

10	Enter your long-term totals, if any, from line 23	**10**	
11	**Total long-term sales price amounts.** Add column (d) of lines 9 and 10 . . .	**11**	
12	Gain from Form 4797; long-term gain from Forms 2119, 2439, and 6252; and long-term gain or (loss) from Forms 4684, 6781, and 8824	**12**	
13	Net long-term gain or (loss) from partnerships, S corporations, estates, and trusts from Schedule(s) K-1	**13**	
14	Capital gain distributions	**14**	
15	Long-term capital loss carryover. Enter the amount, if any, from line 14 of your 1993 Capital Loss Carryover Worksheet	**15**	
16	Add lines 9, 10, and 12 through 15, in columns (f) and (g)	**16**	( )
17	**Net long-term capital gain or (loss).** Combine columns (f) and (g) of line 16 . . . . . ▶	**17**	

Part III   Summary of Parts I and II

18	Combine lines 8 and 17. If a loss, go to line 19. If a gain, enter the gain on Form 1040, line 13. **Note:** *If both lines 17 and 18 are gains, see the* **Capital Gain Tax Worksheet** *on page 25* . .	**18**	
19	If line 18 is a (loss), enter here and as a (loss) on Form 1040, line 13, the **smaller** of these losses:		
a	The (loss) on line 18; **or**		
b	($3,000) or, if married filing separately, ($1,500)	**19**	( )
	Note: *See the* **Capital Loss Carryover Worksheet** *on page D-3 if the loss on line 18 exceeds the loss on line 19* **or** *if Form 1040, line 35, is a loss.*		

For Paperwork Reduction Act Notice, see Form 1040 instructions.   Cat. No. 11338H   Schedule D (Form 1040) 1994

Schedule D (Form 1040) 1994   Attachment Sequence No. **12**   Page **2**

Name(s) shown on Form 1040. Do not enter name and social security number if shown on other side. | **Your social security number**

Part IV   Short-Term Capital Gains and Losses—Assets Held One Year or Less *(Continuation of Part I)*

(a) Description of property (Example: 100 sh. XYZ Co.)	(b) Date acquired (Mo., day, yr.)	(c) Date sold (Mo., day, yr.)	(d) Sales price (see page D-3)	(e) Cost or other basis (see page D-3)	(f) LOSS If (e) is more than (d), subtract (d) from (e)	(g) GAIN If (d) is more than (e), subtract (e) from (d)
20						

21 Short-term totals. Add columns (d), (f), and (g) of line 20. Enter here and on line 2   .   **21** | | | | | |

Part V   Long-Term Capital Gains and Losses—Assets Held More Than One Year *(Continuation of Part II)*

22						

23 Long-term totals. Add columns (d), (f), and (g) of line 22. Enter here and on line 10   .   **23** | | | | | |

Printed on recycled paper

SCHEDULE E
(Form 1040)

Department of the Treasury
Internal Revenue Service   (T)

Supplemental Income and Loss

(From rental real estate, royalties, partnerships,
S corporations, estates, trusts, REMICs, etc.)

► **Attach to Form 1040 or Form 1041.**   ► **See Instructions for Schedule E (Form 1040).**

OMB No. 1545-0074

1994

Attachment
Sequence No. **13**

Name(s) shown on return

Your social security number

Part I	**Income or Loss From Rental Real Estate and Royalties** Note: *Report income and expenses from your business of renting personal property on **Schedule C** or **C-EZ** (see page E-1). Report farm rental income or loss from **Form 4835** on page 2, line 39.*

1 Show the kind and location of each **rental real estate property:**

A ....

B ....

C ....

2 For each rental real estate property listed on line 1, did you or your family use it for personal purposes for more than the greater of 14 days or 10% of the total days rented at fair rental value during the tax year? (See page E-1.)

	Yes	No
A		
B		
C		

Income:

			Properties			Totals (Add columns A, B, and C.)
			A	B	C	
3	Rents received	3				3
4	Royalties received	4				4

Expenses:

5	Advertising	5				
6	Auto and travel (see page E-2)	6				
7	Cleaning and maintenance	7				
8	Commissions	8				
9	Insurance	9				
10	Legal and other professional fees	10				
11	Management fees	11				
12	Mortgage interest paid to banks, etc. (see page E-2)	12				12
13	Other interest	13				
14	Repairs	14				
15	Supplies	15				
16	Taxes	16				
17	Utilities	17				
18	Other (list) ►	18				
19	Add lines 5 through 18	19				19
20	Depreciation expense or depletion (see page E-2)	20				20
21	Total expenses. Add lines 19 and 20	21				
22	Income or (loss) from rental real estate or royalty properties. Subtract line 21 from line 3 (rents) or line 4 (royalties). If the result is a (loss), see page E-2 to find out if you must file **Form 6198**	22				
23	Deductible rental real estate loss. **Caution:** *Your rental real estate loss on line 22 may be limited. See page E-3 to find out if you must file **Form 8582**. Real estate professionals must complete line 42 on page 2*	23	( )	( )	( )	
24	**Income.** Add positive amounts shown on line 22. **Do not** include any losses					24
25	**Losses.** Add royalty losses from line 22 and rental real estate losses from line 23. Enter the total losses here					25 ( )
26	Total rental real estate and royalty income or (loss). Combine lines 24 and 25. Enter the result here. If Parts II, III, IV, and line 39 on page 2 do not apply to you, also enter this amount on Form 1040, line 17. Otherwise, include this amount in the total on line 40 on page 2					26

For Paperwork Reduction Act Notice, see Form 1040 instructions.   Cat. No. 11344L   **Schedule E (Form 1040) 1994**

Schedule E (Form 1040) 1994   Attachment Sequence No. **13**   Page **2**

Name(s) shown on return. Do not enter name and social security number if shown on other side.	**Your social security number**

Note: *If you report amounts from farming or fishing on Schedule E, you must enter your gross income from those activities on line 41 below. Real estate professionals must complete line 42 below.*

Part II   Income or Loss From Partnerships and S Corporations   Note: *If you report a loss from an at-risk activity, you MUST check either column (e) or (f) of line 27 to describe your investment in the activity. See page E-4. If you check column (f), you must attach Form 6198.*

27	(a) Name	(b) Enter **P** for partnership; **S** for S corporation	(c) Check if foreign partnership	(d) Employer identification number	**Investment At Risk?** (e) All is at risk	(f) Some is not at risk
A						
B						
C						
D						
E						

	Passive Income and Loss		Nonpassive Income and Loss		
	(g) Passive loss allowed (attach **Form 8582** if required)	**(h)** Passive income from **Schedule K-1**	**(i)** Nonpassive loss from **Schedule K-1**	**(j)** Section 179 expense deduction from **Form 4562**	**(k)** Nonpassive income from **Schedule K-1**
A					
B					
C					
D					
E					
28a Totals					
b Totals					

29	Add columns (h) and (k) of line 28a	29	
30	Add columns (g), (i), and (j) of line 28b	30 (	)
31	Total partnership and S corporation income or (loss). Combine lines 29 and 30. Enter the result here and include in the total on line 40 below	31	

Part III   Income or Loss From Estates and Trusts

32	(a) Name	(b) Employer identification number
A		
B		

	Passive Income and Loss		Nonpassive Income and Loss	
	(c) Passive deduction or loss allowed (attach **Form 8582** if required)	**(d)** Passive income from **Schedule K-1**	**(e)** Deduction or loss from **Schedule K-1**	**(f)** Other income from **Schedule K-1**
A				
B				
33a Totals				
b Totals				

34	Add columns (d) and (f) of line 33a	34	
35	Add columns (c) and (e) of line 33b	35 (	)
36	Total estate and trust income or (loss). Combine lines 34 and 35. Enter the result here and include in the total on line 40 below	36	

Part IV   Income or Loss From Real Estate Mortgage Investment Conduits (REMICs)—Residual Holder

37	(a) Name	(b) Employer identification number	(c) Excess inclusion from **Schedules Q**, line 2c (see page E-4)	(d) Taxable income (net loss) from **Schedules Q**, line 1b	(e) Income from **Schedules Q**, line 3b

38	Combine columns (d) and (e) only. Enter the result here and include in the total on line 40 below	38	

Part V   Summary

39	Net farm rental income or (loss) from **Form 4835**. Also, complete line 41 below . . . . ▶	39	
40	TOTAL income or (loss). Combine lines 26, 31, 36, 38, and 39. Enter the result here and on Form 1040, line 17 ▶	40	

41	**Reconciliation of Farming and Fishing Income.** Enter your **gross** farming and fishing income reported on Form 4835, line 7; Schedule K-1 (Form 1065), line 15b; Schedule K-1 (Form 1120S), line 23; and Schedule K-1 (Form 1041), line 13 (see page E-4)	41	
42	**Reconciliation for Real Estate Professionals.** If you were a real estate professional (see page E-3), enter the net income or (loss) you reported anywhere on Form 1040 from all rental real estate activities in which you materially participated under the passive activity loss rules . . .	42	

✲ *Printed on recycled paper*

SCHEDULE EIC
(Form 1040A or 1040)

Department of the Treasury
Internal Revenue Service   (T)

Earned Income Credit
(Qualifying Child Information)
▶ Attach to Form 1040A or 1040.
▶ See instructions on back.

OMB No. 1545-0074

19**94**

Attachment
Sequence No. **43**

Name(s) shown on return	Your social security number

Before You Begin . . .

- Answer the questions on page 44 (1040A) or page 27 (1040) to see if you can take this credit.

- If you can take the credit, fill in the worksheet on page 45 (1040A) or page 28 (1040) to figure your credit. **But if you want the IRS to figure it for you, see page 40 (1040A) or page 24 (1040).**

Then, complete and attach Schedule EIC only if you have a qualifying child (see boxes on back).

Information About Your Qualifying Child or Children

If you have more than two qualifying children, you only have to list two to get the maximum credit.

Caution: *If you don't fill in all the lines that apply, it will take us longer to process your return and issue your refund.*	**(a) Child 1**	**(b) Child 2**
1 Child's name (first, initial, and last name)		
2 Child's year of birth	19____	19____
3 If child was born **before 1976** AND–		
a was a student **under age 24** at the end of 1994, check the "Yes" box, **OR**	☐ Yes	☐ Yes
b was permanently and totally disabled (see back), check the "Yes" box	☐ Yes	☐ Yes
4 If child was born **before 1994,** enter the child's social security number		
5 Child's relationship to you (for example, son, grandchild, etc.)		
6 Number of months child lived with you in the U.S. in 1994	months	months

TIP: Do you want the earned income credit added to your take-home pay in 1995? To see if you qualify, get **Form W-5** from your employer or by calling the IRS at 1-800-TAX-FORM (1-800-829-3676).

For Paperwork Reduction Act Notice, see Form 1040A or 1040 instructions.   Cat. No. 13339M   **Schedule EIC (Form 1040A or 1040) 1994**

1994 Earned Income Credit (EIC) Table

Caution: This is **not** a tax table.

To find your credit: First, read down the "At least — But less than" columns and find the line that includes the amount you entered on line 6 or line 8 of the **Earned Income Credit Worksheet** on page 28. Next, read across to the column that includes the number of qualifying children you have. Then, enter the credit from that column on line 7 or line 9 of that worksheet, whichever applies.

If the amount on line 6 or line 8 of the worksheet on page 28 is—		And you have—		
At least	But less than	No children	One child	Two children
		Your credit is—		
$1	$50	$2	$7	$8
50	100	6	20	23
100	150	10	33	38
150	200	13	46	53
200	250	17	59	68
250	300	21	72	83
300	350	25	85	98
350	400	29	99	113
400	450	33	112	128
450	500	36	125	143
500	550	40	138	158
550	600	44	151	173
600	650	48	164	188
650	700	52	178	203
700	750	55	191	218
750	800	59	204	233
800	850	63	217	248
850	900	67	230	263
900	950	71	243	278
950	1,000	75	256	293
1,000	1,050	78	270	308
1,050	1,100	82	283	323
1,100	1,150	86	296	338
1,150	1,200	90	309	353
1,200	1,250	94	322	368
1,250	1,300	98	335	383
1,300	1,350	101	348	398
1,350	1,400	105	362	413
1,400	1,450	109	375	428
1,450	1,500	113	388	443
1,500	1,550	117	401	458
1,550	1,600	120	414	473
1,600	1,650	124	427	488
1,650	1,700	128	441	503
1,700	1,750	132	454	518
1,750	1,800	136	467	533
1,800	1,850	140	480	548
1,850	1,900	143	493	563
1,900	1,950	147	506	578
1,950	2,000	151	519	593
2,000	2,050	155	533	608
2,050	2,100	159	546	623
2,100	2,150	163	559	638
2,150	2,200	166	572	653
2,200	2,250	170	585	668
2,250	2,300	174	598	683
2,300	2,350	178	611	698
2,350	2,400	182	625	713
2,400	2,450	186	638	728
2,450	2,500	189	651	743
2,500	2,550	193	664	758
2,550	2,600	197	677	773
2,600	2,650	201	690	788
2,650	2,700	205	704	803
2,700	2,750	208	717	818
2,750	2,800	212	730	833
2,800	2,850	216	743	848
2,850	2,900	220	756	863
2,900	2,950	224	769	878
2,950	3,000	228	782	893

If the amount on line 6 or line 8 of the worksheet on page 28 is—		And you have—		
At least	But less than	No children	One child	Two children
		Your credit is—		
3,000	3,050	231	796	908
3,050	3,100	235	809	923
3,100	3,150	239	822	938
3,150	3,200	243	835	953
3,200	3,250	247	848	968
3,250	3,300	251	861	983
3,300	3,350	254	874	998
3,350	3,400	258	888	1,013
3,400	3,450	262	901	1,028
3,450	3,500	266	914	1,043
3,500	3,550	270	927	1,058
3,550	3,600	273	940	1,073
3,600	3,650	277	953	1,088
3,650	3,700	281	967	1,103
3,700	3,750	285	980	1,118
3,750	3,800	289	993	1,133
3,800	3,850	293	1,006	1,148
3,850	3,900	296	1,019	1,163
3,900	3,950	300	1,032	1,178
3,950	4,000	304	1,045	1,193
4,000	4,050	306	1,059	1,208
4,050	4,100	306	1,072	1,223
4,100	4,150	306	1,085	1,238
4,150	4,200	306	1,098	1,253
4,200	4,250	306	1,111	1,268
4,250	4,300	306	1,124	1,283
4,300	4,350	306	1,137	1,298
4,350	4,400	306	1,151	1,313
4,400	4,450	306	1,164	1,328
4,450	4,500	306	1,177	1,343
4,500	4,550	306	1,190	1,358
4,550	4,600	306	1,203	1,373
4,600	4,650	306	1,216	1,388
4,650	4,700	306	1,230	1,403
4,700	4,750	306	1,243	1,418
4,750	4,800	306	1,256	1,433
4,800	4,850	306	1,269	1,448
4,850	4,900	306	1,282	1,463
4,900	4,950	306	1,295	1,478
4,950	5,000	306	1,308	1,493
5,000	5,050	304	1,322	1,508
5,050	5,100	300	1,335	1,523
5,100	5,150	296	1,348	1,538
5,150	5,200	293	1,361	1,553
5,200	5,250	289	1,374	1,568
5,250	5,300	285	1,387	1,583
5,300	5,350	281	1,400	1,598
5,350	5,400	277	1,414	1,613
5,400	5,450	273	1,427	1,628
5,450	5,500	270	1,440	1,643
5,500	5,550	266	1,453	1,658
5,550	5,600	262	1,466	1,673
5,600	5,650	258	1,479	1,688
5,650	5,700	254	1,493	1,703
5,700	5,750	251	1,506	1,718
5,750	5,800	247	1,519	1,733
5,800	5,850	243	1,532	1,748
5,850	5,900	239	1,545	1,763
5,900	5,950	235	1,558	1,778
5,950	6,000	231	1,571	1,793

If the amount on line 6 or line 8 of the worksheet on page 28 is—		And you have—		
At least	But less than	No children	One child	Two children
		Your credit is—		
6,000	6,050	228	1,585	1,808
6,050	6,100	224	1,598	1,823
6,100	6,150	220	1,611	1,838
6,150	6,200	216	1,624	1,853
6,200	6,250	212	1,637	1,868
6,250	6,300	208	1,650	1,883
6,300	6,350	205	1,663	1,898
6,350	6,400	201	1,677	1,913
6,400	6,450	197	1,690	1,928
6,450	6,500	193	1,703	1,943
6,500	6,550	189	1,716	1,958
6,550	6,600	186	1,729	1,973
6,600	6,650	182	1,742	1,988
6,650	6,700	178	1,756	2,003
6,700	6,750	174	1,769	2,018
6,750	6,800	170	1,782	2,033
6,800	6,850	166	1,795	2,048
6,850	6,900	163	1,808	2,063
6,900	6,950	159	1,821	2,078
6,950	7,000	155	1,834	2,093
7,000	7,050	151	1,848	2,108
7,050	7,100	147	1,861	2,123
7,100	7,150	143	1,874	2,138
7,150	7,200	140	1,887	2,153
7,200	7,250	136	1,900	2,168
7,250	7,300	132	1,913	2,183
7,300	7,350	128	1,926	2,198
7,350	7,400	124	1,940	2,213
7,400	7,450	120	1,953	2,228
7,450	7,500	117	1,966	2,243
7,500	7,550	113	1,979	2,258
7,550	7,600	109	1,992	2,273
7,600	7,650	105	2,005	2,288
7,650	7,700	101	2,019	2,303
7,700	7,750	98	2,032	2,318
7,750	7,800	94	2,038	2,333
7,800	7,850	90	2,038	2,348
7,850	7,900	86	2,038	2,363
7,900	7,950	82	2,038	2,378
7,950	8,000	78	2,038	2,393
8,000	8,050	75	2,038	2,408
8,050	8,100	71	2,038	2,423
8,100	8,150	67	2,038	2,438
8,150	8,200	63	2,038	2,453
8,200	8,250	59	2,038	2,468
8,250	8,300	55	2,038	2,483
8,300	8,350	52	2,038	2,498
8,350	8,400	48	2,038	2,513
8,400	8,450	44	2,038	2,528
8,450	8,500	40	2,038	2,528
8,500	8,550	36	2,038	2,528
8,550	8,600	33	2,038	2,528
8,600	8,650	29	2,038	2,528
8,650	8,700	25	2,038	2,528
8,700	8,750	21	2,038	2,528
8,750	8,800	17	2,038	2,528
8,800	8,850	13	2,038	2,528
8,850	8,900	10	2,038	2,528
8,900	8,950	6	2,038	2,528
8,950	9,000	2	2,038	2,528

If the amount on line 6 or line 8 of the worksheet on page 28 is—		And you have—		
At least	But less than	No children	One child	Two children
		Your credit is—		
9,000	11,000	0	2,038	2,528
11,000	11,050	0	2,034	2,523
11,050	11,100	0	2,026	2,514
11,100	11,150	0	2,018	2,505
11,150	11,200	0	2,010	2,497
11,200	11,250	0	2,002	2,488
11,250	11,300	0	1,994	2,479
11,300	11,350	0	1,986	2,470
11,350	11,400	0	1,978	2,461
11,400	11,450	0	1,970	2,452
11,450	11,500	0	1,962	2,444
11,500	11,550	0	1,954	2,435
11,550	11,600	0	1,946	2,426
11,600	11,650	0	1,938	2,417
11,650	11,700	0	1,930	2,408
11,700	11,750	0	1,922	2,399
11,750	11,800	0	1,914	2,390
11,800	11,850	0	1,906	2,382
11,850	11,900	0	1,898	2,373
11,900	11,950	0	1,890	2,364
11,950	12,000	0	1,882	2,355
12,000	12,050	0	1,874	2,346
12,050	12,100	0	1,866	2,337
12,100	12,150	0	1,858	2,329
12,150	12,200	0	1,850	2,320
12,200	12,250	0	1,842	2,311
12,250	12,300	0	1,835	2,302
12,300	12,350	0	1,827	2,293
12,350	12,400	0	1,819	2,284
12,400	12,450	0	1,811	2,276
12,450	12,500	0	1,803	2,267
12,500	12,550	0	1,795	2,258
12,550	12,600	0	1,787	2,249
12,600	12,650	0	1,779	2,240
12,650	12,700	0	1,771	2,231
12,700	12,750	0	1,763	2,223
12,750	12,800	0	1,755	2,214
12,800	12,850	0	1,747	2,205
12,850	12,900	0	1,739	2,196
12,900	12,950	0	1,731	2,187
12,950	13,000	0	1,723	2,178
13,000	13,050	0	1,715	2,169
13,050	13,100	0	1,707	2,161
13,100	13,150	0	1,699	2,152
13,150	13,200	0	1,691	2,143
13,200	13,250	0	1,683	2,134
13,250	13,300	0	1,675	2,125
13,300	13,350	0	1,667	2,116
13,350	13,400	0	1,659	2,108
13,400	13,450	0	1,651	2,099
13,450	13,500	0	1,643	2,090
13,500	13,550	0	1,635	2,081
13,550	13,600	0	1,627	2,072
13,600	13,650	0	1,619	2,063
13,650	13,700	0	1,611	2,055
13,700	13,750	0	1,603	2,046
13,750	13,800	0	1,595	2,037
13,800	13,850	0	1,587	2,028
13,850	13,900	0	1,579	2,019
13,900	13,950	0	1,571	2,010

1994 Earned Income Credit (EIC) Table *Continued*

If the amount on line 6 or line 8 of the worksheet on page 28 is— At least	But less than	No children	One child	Two children
13,950	14,000	0	1,563	2,002
14,000	14,050	0	1,555	1,993
14,050	14,100	0	1,547	1,984
14,100	14,150	0	1,539	1,975
14,150	14,200	0	1,531	1,966
14,200	14,250	0	1,523	1,957
14,250	14,300	0	1,515	1,948
14,300	14,350	0	1,507	1,940
14,350	14,400	0	1,499	1,931
14,400	14,450	0	1,491	1,922
14,450	14,500	0	1,483	1,913
14,500	14,550	0	1,475	1,904
14,550	14,600	0	1,467	1,895
14,600	14,650	0	1,459	1,887
14,650	14,700	0	1,451	1,878
14,700	14,750	0	1,443	1,869
14,750	14,800	0	1,435	1,860
14,800	14,850	0	1,427	1,851
14,850	14,900	0	1,419	1,842
14,900	14,950	0	1,411	1,834
14,950	15,000	0	1,403	1,825
15,000	15,050	0	1,395	1,816
15,050	15,100	0	1,387	1,807
15,100	15,150	0	1,379	1,798
15,150	15,200	0	1,371	1,789
15,200	15,250	0	1,363	1,781
15,250	15,300	0	1,355	1,772
15,300	15,350	0	1,347	1,763
15,350	15,400	0	1,339	1,754
15,400	15,450	0	1,331	1,745
15,450	15,500	0	1,323	1,736
15,500	15,550	0	1,315	1,727
15,550	15,600	0	1,307	1,719
15,600	15,650	0	1,299	1,710
15,650	15,700	0	1,291	1,701
15,700	15,750	0	1,283	1,692
15,750	15,800	0	1,275	1,683
15,800	15,850	0	1,267	1,674
15,850	15,900	0	1,259	1,666
15,900	15,950	0	1,251	1,657
15,950	16,000	0	1,243	1,648
16,000	16,050	0	1,235	1,639
16,050	16,100	0	1,227	1,630
16,100	16,150	0	1,219	1,621
16,150	16,200	0	1,211	1,613
16,200	16,250	0	1,203	1,604
16,250	16,300	0	1,195	1,595
16,300	16,350	0	1,187	1,586
16,350	16,400	0	1,179	1,577
16,400	16,450	0	1,171	1,568
16,450	16,500	0	1,163	1,560
16,500	16,550	0	1,155	1,551
16,550	16,600	0	1,147	1,542
16,600	16,650	0	1,139	1,533
16,650	16,700	0	1,131	1,524
16,700	16,750	0	1,123	1,515
16,750	16,800	0	1,115	1,506
16,800	16,850	0	1,107	1,498
16,850	16,900	0	1,099	1,489
16,900	16,950	0	1,091	1,480
16,950	17,000	0	1,083	1,471
17,000	17,050	0	1,075	1,462
17,050	17,100	0	1,067	1,453
17,100	17,150	0	1,059	1,445

If the amount on line 6 or line 8 of the worksheet on page 28 is— At least	But less than	No children	One child	Two children
17,150	17,200	0	1,051	1,436
17,200	17,250	0	1,043	1,427
17,250	17,300	0	1,036	1,418
17,300	17,350	0	1,028	1,409
17,350	17,400	0	1,020	1,400
17,400	17,450	0	1,012	1,392
17,450	17,500	0	1,004	1,383
17,500	17,550	0	996	1,374
17,550	17,600	0	988	1,365
17,600	17,650	0	980	1,356
17,650	17,700	0	972	1,347
17,700	17,750	0	964	1,339
17,750	17,800	0	956	1,330
17,800	17,850	0	948	1,321
17,850	17,900	0	940	1,312
17,900	17,950	0	932	1,303
17,950	18,000	0	924	1,294
18,000	18,050	0	916	1,285
18,050	18,100	0	908	1,277
18,100	18,150	0	900	1,268
18,150	18,200	0	892	1,259
18,200	18,250	0	884	1,250
18,250	18,300	0	876	1,241
18,300	18,350	0	868	1,232
18,350	18,400	0	860	1,224
18,400	18,450	0	852	1,215
18,450	18,500	0	844	1,206
18,500	18,550	0	836	1,197
18,550	18,600	0	828	1,188
18,600	18,650	0	820	1,179
18,650	18,700	0	812	1,171
18,700	18,750	0	804	1,162
18,750	18,800	0	796	1,153
18,800	18,850	0	788	1,144
18,850	18,900	0	780	1,135
18,900	18,950	0	772	1,126
18,950	19,000	0	764	1,118
19,000	19,050	0	756	1,109
19,050	19,100	0	748	1,100
19,100	19,150	0	740	1,091
19,150	19,200	0	732	1,082
19,200	19,250	0	724	1,073
19,250	19,300	0	716	1,064
19,300	19,350	0	708	1,056
19,350	19,400	0	700	1,047
19,400	19,450	0	692	1,038
19,450	19,500	0	684	1,029
19,500	19,550	0	676	1,020
19,550	19,600	0	668	1,011
19,600	19,650	0	660	1,003
19,650	19,700	0	652	994
19,700	19,750	0	644	985
19,750	19,800	0	636	976
19,800	19,850	0	628	967
19,850	19,900	0	620	958
19,900	19,950	0	612	950
19,950	20,000	0	604	941
20,000	20,050	0	596	932
20,050	20,100	0	588	923
20,100	20,150	0	580	914
20,150	20,200	0	572	905
20,200	20,250	0	564	897
20,250	20,300	0	556	888
20,300	20,350	0	548	879

If the amount on line 6 or line 8 of the worksheet on page 28 is— At least	But less than	No children	One child	Two children
20,350	20,400	0	540	870
20,400	20,450	0	532	861
20,450	20,500	0	524	852
20,500	20,550	0	516	843
20,550	20,600	0	508	835
20,600	20,650	0	500	826
20,650	20,700	0	492	817
20,700	20,750	0	484	808
20,750	20,800	0	476	799
20,800	20,850	0	468	790
20,850	20,900	0	460	782
20,900	20,950	0	452	773
20,950	21,000	0	444	764
21,000	21,050	0	436	755
21,050	21,100	0	428	746
21,100	21,150	0	420	737
21,150	21,200	0	412	729
21,200	21,250	0	404	720
21,250	21,300	0	396	711
21,300	21,350	0	388	702
21,350	21,400	0	380	693
21,400	21,450	0	372	684
21,450	21,500	0	364	676
21,500	21,550	0	356	667
21,550	21,600	0	348	658
21,600	21,650	0	340	649
21,650	21,700	0	332	640
21,700	21,750	0	324	631
21,750	21,800	0	316	622
21,800	21,850	0	308	614
21,850	21,900	0	300	605
21,900	21,950	0	292	596
21,950	22,000	0	284	587
22,000	22,050	0	276	578
22,050	22,100	0	268	569
22,100	22,150	0	260	561
22,150	22,200	0	252	552
22,200	22,250	0	244	543
22,250	22,300	0	237	534
22,300	22,350	0	229	525
22,350	22,400	0	221	516
22,400	22,450	0	213	508
22,450	22,500	0	205	499
22,500	22,550	0	197	490
22,550	22,600	0	189	481
22,600	22,650	0	181	472
22,650	22,700	0	173	463
22,700	22,750	0	165	455
22,750	22,800	0	157	446
22,800	22,850	0	149	437
22,850	22,900	0	141	428
22,900	22,950	0	133	419
22,950	23,000	0	125	410
23,000	23,050	0	117	401
23,050	23,100	0	109	393
23,100	23,150	0	101	384
23,150	23,200	0	93	375
23,200	23,250	0	85	366
23,250	23,300	0	77	357
23,300	23,350	0	69	348
23,350	23,400	0	61	340
23,400	23,450	0	53	331
23,450	23,500	0	45	322
23,500	23,550	0	37	313

If the amount on line 6 or line 8 of the worksheet on page 28 is— At least	But less than	No children	One child	Two children
23,550	23,600	0	29	304
23,600	23,650	0	21	295
23,650	23,700	0	13	287
23,700	23,750	0	5	278
23,750	23,800	0	*	269
23,800	23,850	0	0	260
23,850	23,900	0	0	251
23,900	23,950	0	0	242
23,950	24,000	0	0	234
24,000	24,050	0	0	225
24,050	24,100	0	0	216
24,100	24,150	0	0	207
24,150	24,200	0	0	198
24,200	24,250	0	0	189
24,250	24,300	0	0	180
24,300	24,350	0	0	172
24,350	24,400	0	0	163
24,400	24,450	0	0	154
24,450	24,500	0	0	145
24,500	24,550	0	0	136
24,550	24,600	0	0	127
24,600	24,650	0	0	119
24,650	24,700	0	0	110
24,700	24,750	0	0	101
24,750	24,800	0	0	92
24,800	24,850	0	0	83
24,850	24,900	0	0	74
24,900	24,950	0	0	66
24,950	25,000	0	0	57
25,000	25,050	0	0	48
25,050	25,100	0	0	39
25,100	25,150	0	0	30
25,150	25,200	0	0	21
25,200	25,250	0	0	13
25,250	25,296	0	0	4
25,296 or more		0	0	0

* If the amount on line 6 or line 8 of the worksheet is at least $23,750 **but** less than $23,755, your credit is $1. Otherwise, you **cannot** take the credit.

SCHEDULE F
(Form 1040)

Department of the Treasury
Internal Revenue Service

Profit or Loss From Farming

▶ Attach to Form 1040, Form 1041, or Form 1065.

▶ See Instructions for Schedule F (Form 1040).

OMB No. 1545-0074

1994

Attachment
Sequence No. **14**

Name of proprietor | Social security number (SSN)

A Principal product. Describe in one or two words your principal crop or activity for the current tax year.

B Enter principal agricultural activity code (from page 2) ▶

D Employer ID number (EIN), if any

C Accounting method: **(1)** ☐ Cash   **(2)** ☐ Accrual

E Did you "materially participate" in the operation of this business during 1994? If "No," see page F-2 for limit on passive losses.   ☐ Yes   ☐ No

Part I Farm Income—Cash Method. Complete Parts I and II (Accrual method taxpayers complete Parts II and III, and line 11 of Part I.)
Do not include sales of livestock held for draft, breeding, sport, or dairy purposes; report these sales on Form 4797.

1	Sales of livestock and other items you bought for resale	**1**	
2	Cost or other basis of livestock and other items reported on line 1	**2**	
3	Subtract line 2 from line 1		**3**
4	Sales of livestock, produce, grains, and other products you raised		**4**
5a	Total cooperative distributions (Form(s) 1099-PATR) **5a**	**5b** Taxable amount	**5b**
6a	Agricultural program payments (see page F-2) **6a**	**6b** Taxable amount	**6b**
7	Commodity Credit Corporation (CCC) loans (see page F-2):		
a	CCC loans reported under election		**7a**
b	CCC loans forfeited or repaid with certificates **7b**	**7c** Taxable amount	**7c**
8	Crop insurance proceeds and certain disaster payments (see page F-2):		
a	Amount received in 1994 **8a**	**8b** Taxable amount	**8b**
c	If election to defer to 1995 is attached, check here ▶ ☐	**8d** Amount deferred from 1993	**8d**
9	Custom hire (machine work) income		**9**
10	Other income, including Federal and state gasoline or fuel tax credit or refund (see page F-3)		**10**
11	**Gross income.** Add amounts in the right column for lines 3 through 10. If accrual method taxpayer, enter the amount from page 2, line 51. ▶		**11**

Part II Farm Expenses—Cash and Accrual Method. Do not include personal or living expenses such as taxes, insurance, repairs, etc., on your home.

12	Car and truck expenses (see page F-3—also attach **Form 4562**)	**12**	**25**	Pension and profit-sharing plans	**25**	
13	Chemicals	**13**	**26**	Rent or lease (see page F-4):		
14	Conservation expenses. Attach **Form 8645**	**14**	**a**	Vehicles, machinery, and equipment	**26a**	
15	Custom hire (machine work)	**15**	**b**	Other (land, animals, etc.)	**26b**	
16	Depreciation and section 179 expense deduction not claimed elsewhere (see page F-4)	**16**	**27**	Repairs and maintenance	**27**	
			28	Seeds and plants purchased	**28**	
			29	Storage and warehousing	**29**	
17	Employee benefit programs other than on line 25	**17**	**30**	Supplies purchased	**30**	
18	Feed purchased	**18**	**31**	Taxes	**31**	
19	Fertilizers and lime	**19**	**32**	Utilities	**32**	
20	Freight and trucking	**20**	**33**	Veterinary, breeding, and medicine	**33**	
21	Gasoline, fuel, and oil	**21**	**34**	Other expenses (specify):		
22	Insurance (other than health)	**22**	**a**		**34a**	
23	Interest:		**b**		**34b**	
a	Mortgage (paid to banks, etc.)	**23a**	**c**		**34c**	
b	Other	**23b**	**d**		**34d**	
24	Labor hired (less employment credits)	**24**	**e**		**34e**	
			f		**34f**	

35	**Total expenses.** Add lines 12 through 34f ▶	**35**
36	**Net farm profit or (loss).** Subtract line 35 from line 11. If a profit, enter on **Form 1040, line 18,** and ALSO on **Schedule SE, line 1.** If a loss, you MUST go on to line 37 (estates, trusts, and partnerships, see page F-5)	**36**
37	If you have a loss, you MUST check the box that describes your investment in this activity (see page F-5). If you checked 37a, enter the loss on **Form 1040, line 18,** and ALSO on **Schedule SE, line 1.** If you checked 37b, you MUST attach **Form 6198.**	**37a** ☐ All investment is at risk. **37b** ☐ Some investment is not at risk.

For Paperwork Reduction Act Notice, see Form 1040 instructions.   Cat. No. 11346H   **Schedule F (Form 1040) 1994**

Schedule F (Form 1040) 1994

Part III Farm Income—Accrual Method (see page F-5)

Do not include sales of livestock held for draft, breeding, sport, or dairy purposes; report these sales on Form 4797 and do not include this livestock on line 46 below.

38	Sales of livestock, produce, grains, and other products during the year	38	
39a	Total cooperative distributions (Form(s) 1099-PATR)	39b Taxable amount	39b
40a	Agricultural program payments	40b Taxable amount	40b
41	Commodity Credit Corporation (CCC) loans:		
a	CCC loans reported under election		41a
b	CCC loans forfeited or repaid with certificates	41c Taxable amount	41c
42	Crop insurance proceeds		42
43	Custom hire (machine work) income		43
44	Other income, including Federal and state gasoline or fuel tax credit or refund		44
45	Add amounts in the right column for lines 38 through 44		45
46	Inventory of livestock, produce, grains, and other products at beginning of the year	46	
47	Cost of livestock, produce, grains, and other products purchased during the year	47	
48	Add lines 46 and 47	48	
49	Inventory of livestock, produce, grains, and other products at end of year	49	
50	Cost of livestock, produce, grains, and other products sold. Subtract line 49 from line 48*		50
51	**Gross income.** Subtract line 50 from line 45. Enter the result here and on page 1, line 11 ▶		51

*If you use the unit-livestock-price method or the farm-price method of valuing inventory and the amount on line 49 is larger than the amount on line 48, subtract line 48 from line 49. Enter the result on line 50. Add lines 45 and 50. Enter the total on line 51.

Part IV Principal Agricultural Activity Codes

Caution: File **Schedule C** (Form 1040), Profit or Loss From Business, or **Schedule C-EZ** (Form 1040), Net Profit From Business, instead of Schedule F if:

• Your principal source of income is from providing agricultural services such as soil preparation, veterinary, farm labor, horticultural, or management for a fee or on a contract basis, or

• You are engaged in the business of breeding, raising, and caring for dogs, cats, or other pet animals.

Select one of the following codes and write the 3-digit number on page 1, line B:

120 **Field crop,** including grains and nongrains such as cotton, peanuts, feed corn, wheat, tobacco, Irish potatoes, etc.

160 **Vegetables and melons,** garden-type vegetables and melons, such as sweet corn, tomatoes, squash, etc.

170 **Fruit and tree nuts,** including grapes, berries, olives, etc.

180 **Ornamental floriculture and nursery products**

185 **Food crops grown under cover,** including hydroponic crops

211 **Beefcattle feedlots**

212 **Beefcattle,** except feedlots

215 **Hogs, sheep, and goats**

240 **Dairy**

250 **Poultry and eggs,** including chickens, ducks, pigeons, quail, etc.

260 **General livestock,** not specializing in any one livestock category

270 **Animal specialty,** including bees, fur-bearing animals, horses, snakes, etc.

280 **Animal aquaculture,** including fish, shellfish, mollusks, frogs, etc., produced within confined space

290 **Forest products,** including forest nurseries and seed gathering, extraction of pine gum, and gathering of forest products

300 **Agricultural production,** not specified

Printed on recycled paper

Schedule R
(Form 1040)

Department of the Treasury
Internal Revenue Service   (T)

Credit for the Elderly or the Disabled

► **Attach to Form 1040.**   ► **See separate instructions for Schedule R.**

OMB No. 1545-0074

1994

Attachment
Sequence No. **16**

Name(s) shown on Form 1040	Your social security number

You may be able to take this credit and reduce your tax if by the end of 1994:

- You were age 65 or older, **OR** ● You were under age 65, you retired on **permanent and total** disability, and you received taxable disability income.

But you must also meet other tests. See the separate instructions for Schedule R.
Note: *In most cases, the IRS can figure the credit for you. See page 24 of the Form 1040 instructions.*

Part I   Check the Box for Your Filing Status and Age

If your filing status is:	And by the end of 1994:	Check only one box:
Single, Head of household, or Qualifying widow(er) with dependent child	**1** You were 65 or older **1**	☐
	2 You were under 65 and you retired on permanent and total disability . . . **2**	☐
	3 Both spouses were 65 or older **3**	☐
	4 Both spouses were under 65, but only one spouse retired on permanent and total disability **4**	☐
Married filing a joint return	**5** Both spouses were under 65, and both retired on permanent and total disability **5**	☐
	6 One spouse was 65 or older, and the other spouse was under 65 and retired on permanent and total disability **6**	☐
	7 One spouse was 65 or older, and the other spouse was under 65 and **NOT** retired on permanent and total disability **7**	☐
Married filing a separate return	**8** You were 65 or older and you lived apart from your spouse for all of 1994 . . **8**	☐
	9 You were under 65, you retired on permanent and total disability, and you lived apart from your spouse for all of 1994 . . . . **9**	☐

If you checked box 1, 3, 7, or 8, skip Part II and complete Part III on the back. All others, complete Parts II and III.

Part II   Statement of Permanent and Total Disability (Complete **only** if you checked box 2, 4, 5, 6, or 9 above.)

IF: 1 You filed a physician's statement for this disability for 1983 or an earlier year, or you filed a statement for tax years after 1983 and your physician signed line B on the statement, **AND**

2 Due to your continued disabled condition, you were unable to engage in any substantial gainful activity in 1994, check this box . . . . ► ☐

- If you checked this box, you do not have to file another statement for 1994.
- If you **did not** check this box, have your physician complete the statement below.

Physician's Statement (See instructions at bottom of page 2.)

I certify that _____
Name of disabled person

was permanently and totally disabled on January 1, 1976, or January 1, 1977, **OR** was permanently and totally disabled on the date he or she retired. If retired after December 31, 1976, enter the date retired. ► _____

Physician: Sign your name on **either** line A or B below.

A The disability has lasted or can be expected to last continuously for at least a year . . . . _____

Physician's signature	Date

B There is no reasonable probability that the disabled condition will ever improve . . . . . _____

Physician's signature	Date

Physician's name	Physician's address

For Paperwork Reduction Act Notice, see Form 1040 instructions.   Cat. No. 11359K   **Schedule R (Form 1040) 1994**

Schedule R (Form 1040) 1994   Page **2**

Part III   Figure Your Credit

10 If you checked (in Part I):   **Enter:**

   Box 1, 2, 4, or 7 . . . . $5,000 ⎫

   Box 3, 5, or 6 . . . . $7,500 ⎬ . . . . | **10** |

   Box 8 or 9 . . . . $3,750 ⎭

Did you check box 2, 4, 5, 6, or 9 in Part I?	——— Yes ———▶	You **must** complete line 11.
	——— No ———▶	Enter the amount from line 10 on line 12 and go to line 13.

11 If you checked:

   • Box 6 in Part I, add $5,000 to the taxable disability income of the spouse who was under age 65. Enter the total. ⎫

   • Box 2, 4, or 9 in Part I, enter your taxable disability income. ⎬ . . . . | **11** |

   • Box 5 in Part I, add your taxable disability income to your spouse's taxable disability income. Enter the total. ⎭

   TIP: For more details on what to include on line 11, see the instructions.

12 If you completed line 11, enter the **smaller** of line 10 or line 11; **all others,** enter the amount from line 10 . . . . | **12** |

13 Enter the following pensions, annuities, or disability income that you (and your spouse if filing a joint return) received in 1994:

   a Nontaxable part of social security benefits, and Nontaxable part of railroad retirement benefits treated as social security. See instructions. ⎬ . . . | **13a** |

   b Nontaxable veterans' pensions, and Any other pension, annuity, or disability benefit that is excluded from income under any other provision of law. See instructions. ⎬ . . . | **13b** |

   c Add lines 13a and 13b. (Even though these income items are not taxable, they **must** be included here to figure your credit.) If you did not receive any of the types of nontaxable income listed on line 13a or 13b, enter -0- on line 13c . . . . | **13c** |

14 Enter the amount from Form 1040, line 32 | **14** |

15 If you checked (in Part I):   **Enter:**

   Box 1 or 2 . . . . $7,500 ⎫

   Box 3, 4, 5, 6, or 7 . . . . $10,000 ⎬ | **15** |

   Box 8 or 9 . . . . $5,000 ⎭

16 Subtract line 15 from line 14. If zero or less, enter -0- . . . . | **16** |

17 Divide line 16 above by 2 . . . . | **17** |

18 Add lines 13c and 17 . . . . | **18** |

19 Subtract line 18 from line 12. If zero or less, **stop;** you **cannot** take the credit. Otherwise, go to line 21 . . . . | **19** |

20 Decimal amount used to figure the credit . . . . | **20** | × .15

21 Multiply line 19 above by the decimal amount (.15) on line 20. Enter the result here and on Form 1040, line 42. **Caution:** *If you file Schedule C, C-EZ, D, E, or F (Form 1040), your credit may be limited. See the instructions for line 21 for the amount of credit you can claim* . . . . . . | **21** |

Instructions for Physician's Statement

Taxpayer

If you retired after December 31, 1976, enter the date you retired in the space provided in Part II.

Physician

A person is permanently and totally disabled if **both** of the following apply:

   1. He or she cannot engage in any substantial gainful activity because of a physical or mental condition, and

   2. A physician determines that the disability has lasted or can be expected to last continuously for at least a year or can lead to death.

SCHEDULE SE
(Form 1040)

Department of the Treasury
Internal Revenue Service (T)

Self-Employment Tax

▶ **See Instructions for Schedule SE (Form 1040).**

▶ **Attach to Form 1040.**

OMB No. 1545-0074

19 94

Attachment
Sequence No. **17**

Name of person with **self-employment** income (as shown on Form 1040)	Social security number of person with **self-employment** income ▶

Who Must File Schedule SE

You must file Schedule SE if:

- You had net earnings from self-employment from other than church employee income (line 4 of Short Schedule SE or line 4c of Long Schedule SE) of $400 or more, **OR**
- You had church employee income of $108.28 or more. Income from services you performed as a minister or a member of a religious order **is not** church employee income. See page SE-1.

Note: *Even if you have a loss or a small amount of income from self-employment, it may be to your benefit to file Schedule SE and use either "optional method" in Part II of Long Schedule SE. See page SE-2.*

Exception. If your only self-employment income was from earnings as a minister, member of a religious order, or Christian Science practitioner, **and** you filed Form 4361 and received IRS approval not to be taxed on those earnings, **do not** file Schedule SE. Instead, write "Exempt—Form 4361" on Form 1040, line 47.

May I Use Short Schedule SE or MUST I Use Long Schedule SE?

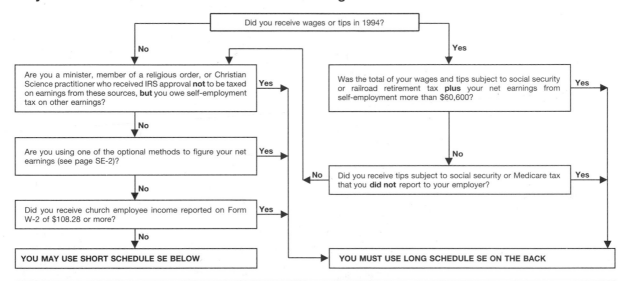

Section A—Short Schedule SE. Caution: *Read above to see if you can use Short Schedule SE.*

1	Net farm profit or (loss) from Schedule F, line 36, and farm partnerships, Schedule K-1 (Form 1065), line 15a	**1**
2	Net profit or (loss) from Schedule C, line 31; Schedule C-EZ, line 3; and Schedule K-1 (Form 1065), line 15a (other than farming). Ministers and members of religious orders see page SE-1 for amounts to report on this line. See page SE-2 for other income to report	**2**
3	Combine lines 1 and 2	**3**
4	**Net earnings from self-employment.** Multiply line 3 by 92.35% (.9235). If less than $400, **do not** file this schedule; you do not owe self-employment tax . . . . ▶	**4**
5	**Self-employment tax.** If the amount on line 4 is: • $60,600 or less, multiply line 4 by 15.3% (.153). Enter the result here and on **Form 1040, line 47.** • More than $60,600, multiply line 4 by 2.9% (.029). Then, add $7,514.40 to the result. Enter the total here and on **Form 1040, line 47.**	**5**
	Deduction for one-half of self-employment tax. Multiply line 5 by 50% (.5). Enter the result here and on **Form 1040, line 25**	**6**

For Paperwork Reduction Act Notice, see Form 1040 instructions.   Cat. No. 11358Z   **Schedule SE (Form 1040) 1994**

Schedule SE (Form 1040) 1994	Attachment Sequence No. **17**		Page **2**

Name of person with **self-employment** income (as shown on Form 1040)	Social security number of person with **self-employment** income ▶		

Section B—Long Schedule SE

Part I Self-Employment Tax

Note: *If your only income subject to self-employment tax is church employee income, skip lines 1 through 4b. Enter -0- on line 4c and go to line 5a. Income from services you performed as a minister or a member of a religious order is not church employee income. See page SE-1.*

A If you are a minister, member of a religious order, or Christian Science practitioner **and** you filed Form 4361, but you had $400 or more of **other** net earnings from self-employment, check here and continue with Part I . . . . . . ▶ ☐

1	Net farm profit or (loss) from Schedule F, line 36, and farm partnerships, Schedule K-1 (Form 1065), line 15a. **Note:** *Skip this line if you use the farm optional method. See page SE-3* . .	**1**	
2	Net profit or (loss) from Schedule C, line 31; Schedule C-EZ, line 3; and Schedule K-1 (Form 1065), line 15a (other than farming). Ministers and members of religious orders see page SE-1 for amounts to report on this line. See page SE-2 for other income to report. **Note:** *Skip this line if you use the nonfarm optional method. See page SE-3.*	**2**	
3	Combine lines 1 and 2	**3**	
4a	If line 3 is more than zero, multiply line 3 by 92.35% (.9235). Otherwise, enter amount from line 3	**4a**	
b	If you elected one or both of the optional methods, enter the total of lines 15 and 17 here . .	**4b**	
c	Combine lines 4a and 4b. If less than $400, **do not** file this schedule; you do not owe self-employment tax. **Exception.** If less than $400 and you had church employee income, enter -0- and continue . ▶	**4c**	
5a	Enter your church employee income from Form W-2. **Caution:** *See page SE-1 for definition of church employee income*	**5a**		
b	Multiply line 5a by 92.35% (.9235). If less than $100, enter -0-	**5b**	
6	**Net earnings from self-employment.** Add lines 4c and 5b	**6**	
7	Maximum amount of combined wages and self-employment earnings subject to social security tax or the 6.2% portion of the 7.65% railroad retirement (tier 1) tax for 1994	**7**	60,600 00
8a	Total social security wages and tips (total of boxes 3 and 7 on Form(s) W-2) and railroad retirement (tier 1) compensation	**8a**		
b	Unreported tips subject to social security tax (from Form 4137, line 9)	**8b**		
c	Add lines 8a and 8b	**8c**	
9	Subtract line 8c from line 7. If zero or less, enter -0- here and on line 10 and go to line 11 . ▶	**9**	
10	Multiply the **smaller** of line 6 or line 9 by 12.4% (.124)	**10**	
11	Multiply line 6 by 2.9% (.029)	**11**	
12	**Self-employment tax.** Add lines 10 and 11. Enter here and on **Form 1040, line 47**	**12**	
13	**Deduction for one-half of self-employment tax.** Multiply line 12 by 50% (.5). Enter the result here and on **Form 1040, line 25**	**13**		

Part II Optional Methods To Figure Net Earnings (See page SE-2.)

Farm Optional Method. You may use this method **only if:**
- Your gross farm income[1] was not more than $2,400, **or**
- Your gross farm income[1] was more than $2,400 and your net farm profits[2] were less than $1,733.

14	Maximum income for optional methods	**14**	1,600 00
15	Enter the **smaller** of: two-thirds (⅔) of gross farm income[1] (not less than zero) **or** $1,600. Also, include this amount on line 4b above	**15**	

Nonfarm Optional Method. You may use this method **only if:**
- Your net nonfarm profits[3] were less than $1,733 and also less than 72.189% of your gross nonfarm income,[4] **and**
- You had net earnings from self-employment of at least $400 in 2 of the prior 3 years.

Caution: *You may use this method no more than five times.*

16	Subtract line 15 from line 14	**16**	
17	Enter the **smaller** of: two-thirds (⅔) of gross nonfarm income[4] (not less than zero) **or** the amount on line 16. Also, include this amount on line 4b above	**17**	

[1]From Schedule F, line 11, and Schedule K-1 (Form 1065), line 15b.   [3]From Schedule C, line 31; Schedule C-EZ, line 3; and Schedule K-1 (Form 1065), line 15a.
[2]From Schedule F, line 36, and Schedule K-1 (Form 1065), line 15a.   [4]From Schedule C, line 7; Schedule C-EZ, line 1; and Schedule K-1 (Form 1065), line 15c.

 Printed on recycled paper

Form 1040X
(Rev. October 1994)

Department of the Treasury—Internal Revenue Service

Amended U.S. Individual Income Tax Return
▶ See separate instructions.

OMB No. 1545-0091

This return is for calendar year ▶ 19 , OR fiscal year ended ▶ , 19 .

Please print or type

Your first name and initial	Last name	Your social security number
If a joint return, spouse's first name and initial	Last name	Spouse's social security number
Home address (number and street). If you have a P.O. box, see instructions.	Apt. no.	Telephone number (optional) ( )
City, town or post office, state, and ZIP code. If you have a foreign address, see instructions.		For Paperwork Reduction Act Notice, see page 1 of separate instructions.

Enter name and address as shown on original return. If same as above, write "Same." If changing from separate to joint return, enter names and addresses from original returns.

A Service center where original return was filed

B Has original return been changed or audited by the IRS? ☐ Yes ☐ No
If "No," have you been notified that it will be? . . . . ☐ Yes ☐ No
If "Yes," identify the IRS office ▶

C If you are amending your return to include any item (loss, credit, deduction, other tax benefit, or income) relating to a tax shelter required to be registered, attach **Form 8271**, Investor Reporting of Tax Shelter Registration Number, and check here . . . . ▶ ☐

D Filing status claimed. **Note:** *You cannot change from joint to separate returns after the due date has passed.*

On original return ▶ ☐ Single ☐ Married filing joint return ☐ Married filing separate return ☐ Head of household ☐ Qualifying widow(er)
On this return ▶ ☐ Single ☐ Married filing joint return ☐ Married filing separate return ☐ Head of household ☐ Qualifying widow(er)

Income and Deductions (see instructions)
USE PART II ON PAGE 2 TO EXPLAIN ANY CHANGES

			A. As originally reported or as previously adjusted (see instructions)	**B.** Net change—Increase or (Decrease)—explain on page 2	**C.** Correct amount
1	Adjusted gross income (see instructions)	1			
2	Itemized deductions or standard deduction	2			
3	Subtract line 2 from line 1	3			
4	Exemptions. If changing, fill in Parts I and II on page 2 . .	4			
5	Taxable income. Subtract line 4 from line 3	5			
Tax Liability 6	Tax (see instructions). Method used in col. C _____	6			
7	Credits (see instructions)	7			
8	Subtract line 7 from line 6. Enter the result but not less than zero .	8			
9	Other taxes (such as self-employment tax, alternative minimum tax, etc.)	9			
10	Total tax. Add lines 8 and 9	10			
Payments 11	Federal income tax withheld and excess social security, Medicare, and RRTA taxes withheld. If changing, see instructions	11			
12	Estimated tax payments	12			
13	Earned income credit	13			
14	Credits for Federal tax paid on fuels, regulated investment company, etc.	14			
15	Amount paid with Form 4868, Form 2688, or Form 2350 (application for extension of time to file) .	15		
16	Amount of tax paid with original return plus additional tax paid after it was filed	16		
17	Total payments. Add lines 11 through 16 in column C	17		

Refund or Amount You Owe

18	Overpayment, if any, as shown on original return or as previously adjusted by the IRS . . .	18.	
19	Subtract line 18 from line 17 (see instructions)	19	
20	**AMOUNT YOU OWE.** If line 10, column C, is more than line 19, enter the difference and see instructions .	20	
21	If line 10, column C, is less than line 19, enter the difference	21	
22	Amount of line 21 you want **REFUNDED TO YOU**	22	
23	Amount of line 21 you want **APPLIED TO YOUR 19** __ **ESTIMATED TAX**	23	

Sign Here
Keep a copy of this return for your records.

Under penalties of perjury, I declare that I have filed an original return and that I have examined this amended return, including accompanying schedules and statements, and to the best of my knowledge and belief, this amended return is true, correct, and complete. Declaration of preparer (other than taxpayer) is based on all information of which the preparer has any knowledge.

▶ Your signature | Date
▶ Spouse's signature. If a joint return, BOTH must sign. | Date

Paid Preparer's Use Only

Preparer's signature ▶	Date	Check if self-employed ☐	Preparer's social security no.
Firm's name (or yours if self-employed) and address ▶		E.I. No.	
		ZIP code	

Cat. No. 11360L

Form **1040X** (Rev. 10-94)

Form 1040X (Rev. 10-94)   Page **2**

Part I   Exemptions. See Form 1040 or Form 1040A instructions.

If you are **not changing your exemptions,** do not complete this part.
If claiming **more exemptions,** complete lines 24–30 and, if applicable, line 31.
If claiming **fewer exemptions,** complete lines 24–29.

		A. Number originally reported	B. Net change	C. Correct number
24	Yourself and spouse **24**			
	Caution: *If your parents (or someone else) can claim you as a dependent (even if they chose not to), you cannot claim an exemption for yourself.*			
25	Your dependent children who lived with you **25**			
26	Your dependent children who did not live with you due to divorce or separation **26**			
27	Other dependents **27**			
28	Total number of exemptions. Add lines 24 through 27 . . . . . **28**			

29   Multiply the number of exemptions claimed on line 28 by the amount listed below for the tax year you are amending. Enter the result here and on line 4.

Tax Year	Exemption Amount	But see the instructions if the amount on line 1 is over:
1994	$2,450	$83,850
1993	2,350	81,350
1992	2,300	78,950
1991	2,150	75,000

29

30   Dependents (children and other) not claimed on original return:

(a) Name (first, initial, and last name)	(b) Check if under age 1	(c) If age 1 or older, enter dependent's social security number	(d) Dependent's relationship to you	(e) No. of months lived in your home

No. of your children on line 30 who lived with you . . ▶ ☐

No. of your children on line 30 who **didn't** live with you due to divorce or separation (see instructions) ▶ ☐

No. of dependents on line 30 not entered above . ▶ ☐

31   If your child listed on line 30 didn't live with you but is claimed as your dependent under a pre-1985 agreement, check here ▶ ☐

Part II   Explanation of Changes to Income, Deductions, and Credits

Enter the line number from page 1 for each item you are changing and give the reason for each change. Attach all supporting forms and schedules for items changed. If you don't, your Form 1040X may be returned. Be sure to include your name and social security number on any attachments.

If the change relates to a net operating loss carryback or a general business credit carryback, attach the schedule or form that shows the year in which the loss or credit occurred. See instructions. Also, check here . . . . ▶ ☐

_____

_____

_____

_____

_____

_____

_____

_____

Part III   Presidential Election Campaign Fund. Checking below will not increase your tax or reduce your refund.

If you did not previously want to have $3 go to the fund but now want to, check here . . . . ▶ ☐
If a joint return and your spouse did not previously want to have $3 go to the fund but now wants to, check here . . . ▶ ☐

✷ *Printed on recycled paper*

Form **1065**

Department of the Treasury
Internal Revenue Service

U.S. Partnership Return of Income

For calendar year 1994, or tax year beginning _ _ _ _ _ _ , 1994, and ending _ _ _ _ _ _ , 19 _ _ _ _
▶ **See separate instructions.**

OMB No. 1545-0099

1994

A Principal business activity	Use the IRS label. Other-wise, please print or type.	Name of partnership	**D** Employer identification number
B Principal product or service		Number, street, and room or suite no. (If a P.O. box, see page 9 of the instructions.)	**E** Date business started
C Business code number		City or town, state, and ZIP code	**F** Total assets (see **Specific Instructions**) $

G Check applicable boxes: **(1)** ☐ Initial return **(2)** ☐ Final return **(3)** ☐ Change in address **(4)** ☐ Amended return
H Check accounting method: **(1)** ☐ Cash **(2)** ☐ Accrual **(3)** ☐ Other (specify) ▶ -
I Number of Schedules K-1. Attach one for each person who was a partner at any time during the tax year ▶ - - - - - - - - - - - - -

Caution: *Include **only** trade or business income and expenses on lines 1a through 22 below. See the instructions for more information.*

Income

1a Gross receipts or sales	**1a**		
b Less returns and allowances	**1b**		**1c**
2 Cost of goods sold (Schedule A, line 8)			**2**
3 Gross profit. Subtract line 2 from line 1c			**3**
4 Ordinary income (loss) from other partnerships, estates, and trusts *(attach schedule)* .			**4**
5 Net farm profit (loss) *(attach Schedule F (Form 1040))*			**5**
6 Net gain (loss) from Form 4797, Part II, line 20 .			**6**
7 Other income (loss) (see instructions) *(attach schedule)*			**7**
8 **Total income (loss).** Combine lines 3 through 7			**8**

Deductions (see instructions for limitations)

9 Salaries and wages (other than to partners) (less employment credits) .			**9**
10 Guaranteed payments to partners			**10**
11 Repairs and maintenance			**11**
12 Bad debts			**12**
13 Rent			**13**
14 Taxes and licenses			**14**
15 Interest			**15**
16a Depreciation (see instructions)	**16a**		
b Less depreciation reported on Schedule A and elsewhere on return	**16b**		**16c**
17 Depletion **(Do not deduct oil and gas depletion.)**			**17**
18 Retirement plans, etc.			**18**
19 Employee benefit programs			**19**
20 Other deductions *(attach schedule)*			**20**
21 **Total deductions.** Add the amounts shown in the far right column for lines 9 through 20 .			**21**
22 **Ordinary income (loss)** from trade or business activities. Subtract line 21 from line 8 .			**22**

Please Sign Here

Under penalties of perjury, I declare that I have examined this return, including accompanying schedules and statements, and to the best of my knowledge and belief, it is true, correct, and complete. Declaration of preparer (other than general partner) is based on all information of which preparer has any knowledge.

▶ _____ ▶ _____
Signature of general partner or limited liability company member   Date

Paid Preparer's Use Only

Preparer's signature ▶	Date	Check if self-employed ▶ ☐	Preparer's social security no.
Firm's name (or yours if self-employed) and address ▶		E.I. No. ▶	
		ZIP code ▶	

For Paperwork Reduction Act Notice, see page 1 of separate instructions.   Cat. No. 11390Z   Form **1065** (1994)

Schedule A   Cost of Goods Sold

1 Inventory at beginning of year	**1**	
2 Purchases less cost of items withdrawn for personal use	**2**	
3 Cost of labor.	**3**	
4 Additional section 263A costs (see instructions) *(attach schedule)*	**4**	
5 Other costs *(attach schedule)*	**5**	
6 **Total.** Add lines 1 through 5	**6**	
7 Inventory at end of year	**7**	
8 **Cost of goods sold.** Subtract line 7 from line 6. Enter here and on page 1, line 2	**8**	

9a Check all methods used for valuing closing inventory:

   (i) ☐ Cost

   (ii) ☐ Lower of cost or market as described in Regulations section 1.471-4

   (iii) ☐ Writedown of "subnormal" goods as described in Regulations section 1.471-2(c)

   (iv) ☐ Other (specify method used and attach explanation) ▶ _____

   b Check this box if the LIFO inventory method was adopted this tax year for any goods *(if checked, attach Form 970)* . . ▶ ☐

   c Do the rules of section 263A (for property produced or acquired for resale) apply to the partnership? . . ☐ **Yes** ☐ **No**

   d Was there any change in determining quantities, cost, or valuations between opening and closing inventory? ☐ **Yes** ☐ **No**

   If "Yes," attach explanation.

Schedule B   Other Information

	Yes	No
1 What type of entity is filing this return?		
Check the applicable box ▶ ☐ General partnership ☐ Limited partnership ☐ Limited liability company		
2 Are any partners in this partnership also partnerships?.		
3 Is this partnership a partner in another partnership?		
4 Is this partnership subject to the consolidated audit procedures of sections 6221 through 6233? If "Yes," see **Designation of Tax Matters Partner** below		
5 Does this partnership meet **ALL THREE** of the following requirements?		
a The partnership's total receipts for the tax year were less than $250,000;		
b The partnership's total assets at the end of the tax year were less than $600,000; **AND**		
c Schedules K-1 are filed with the return and furnished to the partners on or before the due date (including extensions) for the partnership return.		
If "Yes," the partnership is not required to complete Schedules L, M-1, and M-2; Item F on page 1 of Form 1065; or Item J on Schedule K-1		
6 Does this partnership have any foreign partners?		
7 Is this partnership a publicly traded partnership as defined in section 469(k)(2)?		
8 Has this partnership filed, or is it required to file, **Form 8264,** Application for Registration of a Tax Shelter? .		
9 At any time during calendar year 1994, did the partnership have an interest in or a signature or other authority over a financial account in a foreign country (such as a bank account, securities account, or other financial account)? (See the instructions for exceptions and filing requirements for Form TD F 90-22.1.) If "Yes," enter the name of the foreign country. ▶ _____		
10 Was the partnership the grantor of, or transferor to, a foreign trust that existed during the current tax year, whether or not the partnership or any partner has any beneficial interest in it? If "Yes," you may have to file Forms 3520, 3520-A, or 926		
11 Was there a distribution of property or a transfer (e.g., by sale or death) of a partnership interest during the tax year? If "Yes," you may elect to adjust the basis of the partnership's assets under section 754 by attaching the statement described under **Elections Made By the Partnership**		

Designation of Tax Matters Partner (See instructions.)

Enter below the general partner designated as the tax matters partner (TMP) for the tax year of this return:

Name of designated TMP ▶ _____	Identifying number of TMP ▶ _____
Address of designated TMP ▶ _____	

Schedule K	Partners' Shares of Income, Credits, Deductions, etc.		
	(a) Distributive share items		(b) Total amount

Income (Loss)	**1** Ordinary income (loss) from trade or business activities (page 1, line 22)	**1**	
	2 Net income (loss) from rental real estate activities (attach Form 8825)	**2**	
	3a Gross income from other rental activities ⬚ **3a**		
	b Expenses from other rental activities (attach schedule) ⬚ **3b**		
	c Net income (loss) from other rental activities. Subtract line 3b from line 3a	**3c**	
	4 Portfolio income (loss) (see instructions): **a** Interest income	**4a**	
	b Dividend income	**4b**	
	c Royalty income	**4c**	
	d Net short-term capital gain (loss) (attach Schedule D (Form 1065))	**4d**	
	e Net long-term capital gain (loss) (attach Schedule D (Form 1065))	**4e**	
	f Other portfolio income (loss) (attach schedule)	**4f**	
	5 Guaranteed payments to partners	**5**	
	6 Net gain (loss) under section 1231 (other than due to casualty or theft) (attach Form 4797)	**6**	
	7 Other income (loss) (attach schedule)	**7**	
Deductions	**8** Charitable contributions (see instructions) (attach schedule)	**8**	
	9 Section 179 expense deduction (attach Form 4562)	**9**	
	10 Deductions related to portfolio income (see instructions) (itemize)	**10**	
	11 Other deductions (attach schedule)	**11**	
Invest-ment Interest	**12a** Interest expense on investment debts	**12a**	
	b (1) Investment income included on lines 4a, 4b, 4c, and 4f above	**12b(1)**	
	(2) Investment expenses included on line 10 above	**12b(2)**	
Credits	**13a** Credit for income tax withheld	**13a**	
	b Low-income housing credit (see instructions):		
	(1) From partnerships to which section 42(j)(5) applies for property placed in service before 1990	**13b(1)**	
	(2) Other than on line 13b(1) for property placed in service before 1990	**13b(2)**	
	(3) From partnerships to which section 42(j)(5) applies for property placed in service after 1989	**13b(3)**	
	(4) Other than on line 13b(3) for property placed in service after 1989	**13b(4)**	
	c Qualified rehabilitation expenditures related to rental real estate activities (attach Form 3468)	**13c**	
	d Credits (other than credits shown on lines 13b and 13c) related to rental real estate activities (see instructions)	**13d**	
	e Credits related to other rental activities (see instructions)	**13e**	
	14 Other credits (see instructions)	**14**	
Self-Employ-ment	**15a** Net earnings (loss) from self-employment	**15a**	
	b Gross farming or fishing income	**15b**	
	c Gross nonfarm income	**15c**	
Adjustments and Tax Preference Items	**16a** Depreciation adjustment on property placed in service after 1986	**16a**	
	b Adjusted gain or loss	**16b**	
	c Depletion (other than oil and gas)	**16c**	
	d (1) Gross income from oil, gas, and geothermal properties	**16d(1)**	
	(2) Deductions allocable to oil, gas, and geothermal properties	**16d(2)**	
	e Other adjustments and tax preference items (attach schedule)	**16e**	
Foreign Taxes	**17a** Type of income ▶ _____ **b** Foreign country or U.S. possession ▶ _____		
	c Total gross income from sources outside the United States (attach schedule)	**17c**	
	d Total applicable deductions and losses (attach schedule)	**17d**	
	e Total foreign taxes (check one): ▶ ☐ Paid ☐ Accrued	**17e**	
	f Reduction in taxes available for credit (attach schedule)	**17f**	
	g Other foreign tax information (attach schedule)	**17g**	
Other	**18a** Total expenditures to which a section 59(e) election may apply	**18a**	
	b Type of expenditures ▶ _____		
	19 Tax-exempt interest income	**19**	
	20 Other tax-exempt income	**20**	
	21 Nondeductible expenses	**21**	
	22 Other items and amounts required to be reported separately to partners (see instructions) (attach schedule)		
Analysis	**23a** Income (loss). Combine lines 1 through 7 in column (b). From the result, subtract the sum of lines 8 through 12a, 17e, and 18a	**23a**	

b Analysis by type of partner:	(a) Corporate	(b) Individual		(c) Partnership	(d) Exempt organization	(e) Nominee/Other
		i. Active	ii. Passive			
(1) General partners						
(2) Limited partners						

Note: If Question 5 of Schedule B is answered "Yes," the partnership is not required to complete Schedules L, M-1, and M-2.

Schedule L   Balance Sheets

Assets	Beginning of tax year		End of tax year	
	(a)	(b)	(c)	(d)
1 Cash				
2a Trade notes and accounts receivable				
b Less allowance for bad debts				
3 Inventories				
4 U.S. government obligations				
5 Tax-exempt securities				
6 Other current assets (attach schedule)				
7 Mortgage and real estate loans				
8 Other investments (attach schedule)				
9a Buildings and other depreciable assets				
b Less accumulated depreciation				
10a Depletable assets				
b Less accumulated depletion				
11 Land (net of any amortization)				
12a Intangible assets (amortizable only)				
b Less accumulated amortization				
13 Other assets (attach schedule)				
14 **Total** assets				
Liabilities and Capital				
15 Accounts payable				
16 Mortgages, notes, bonds payable in less than 1 year				
17 Other current liabilities (attach schedule)				
18 All nonrecourse loans				
19 Mortgages, notes, bonds payable in 1 year or more				
20 Other liabilities (attach schedule)				
21 Partners' capital accounts				
22 **Total** liabilities and capital				

Schedule M-1   Reconciliation of Income (Loss) per Books With Income (Loss) per Return (see instructions)

1 Net income (loss) per books

2 Income included on Schedule K, lines 1 through 4, 6, and 7, not recorded on books this year (itemize): ....

....

3 Guaranteed payments (other than health insurance)

4 Expenses recorded on books this year not included on Schedule K, lines 1 through 12a, 17e, and 18a (itemize):

a Depreciation $ ....

b Travel and entertainment $ ....

....

5 Add lines 1 through 4

6 Income recorded on books this year not included on Schedule K, lines 1 through 7 (itemize):

a Tax-exempt interest $ ....

....

7 Deductions included on Schedule K, lines 1 through 12a, 17e, and 18a, not charged against book income this year (itemize):

a Depreciation $ ....

....

....

8 Add lines 6 and 7

9 Income (loss) (Schedule K, line 23a). Subtract line 8 from line 5

Schedule M-2   Analysis of Partners' Capital Accounts

1 Balance at beginning of year

2 Capital contributed during year

3 Net income (loss) per books

4 Other increases (itemize): ....

....

5 Add lines 1 through 4

6 Distributions: a Cash

b Property

7 Other decreases (itemize): ....

....

8 Add lines 6 and 7

9 Balance at end of year. Subtract line 8 from line 5

Printed on recycled paper

SCHEDULE K-1
(Form 1065)
Department of the Treasury
Internal Revenue Service

Partner's Share of Income, Credits, Deductions, etc.

▶ See separate instructions.

For calendar year 1994 or tax year beginning   , 1994, and ending   , 19

OMB No. 1545-0099

1994

Partner's identifying number ▶

Partnership's identifying number ▶

Partner's name, address, and ZIP code

Partnership's name, address, and ZIP code

A   This partner is a ☐ general partner ☐ limited partner
    ☐ limited liability company member
B   What type of entity is this partner? ▶ ....
C   Is this partner a ☐ domestic or a ☐ foreign partner?
D   Enter partner's percentage of:
     (i) Before change or termination   **(ii)** End of year

Profit sharing . . . . % .... %
Loss sharing . . . . % .... %
Ownership of capital . . . . % .... %

E   IRS Center where partnership filed return:

F   Partner's share of liabilities (see instructions):
    Nonrecourse . . . . $ ....
    Qualified nonrecourse financing . $ ....
    Other . . . . $ ....
G   Tax shelter registration number . ▶ ....
H   Check here if this partnership is a publicly traded partnership as defined in section 469(k)(2) . . . . . ☐
I   Check applicable boxes: **(1)** ☐ Final K-1 **(2)** ☐ Amended K-1

J   **Analysis of partner's capital account:**

(a) Capital account at beginning of year	(b) Capital contributed during year	(c) Partner's share of lines 3, 4, and 7, Form 1065, Schedule M-2	(d) Withdrawals and distributions	(e) Capital account at end of year (combine columns (a) through (d))
			( )	

	(a) Distributive share item		(b) Amount	(c) 1040 filers enter the amount in column (b) on:
Income (Loss)	**1** Ordinary income (loss) from trade or business activities . .	**1**		See Partner's Instructions for Schedule K-1 (Form 1065).
	2 Net income (loss) from rental real estate activities	**2**		
	3 Net income (loss) from other rental activities	**3**		
	4 Portfolio income (loss):			
	a Interest	**4a**		Sch. B, Part I, line 1
	b Dividends	**4b**		Sch. B, Part II, line 5
	c Royalties	**4c**		Sch. E, Part I, line 4
	d Net short-term capital gain (loss)	**4d**		Sch. D, line 5, col. (f) or (g)
	e Net long-term capital gain (loss)	**4e**		Sch. D, line 13, col. (f) or (g)
	f Other portfolio income (loss) *(attach schedule)*	**4f**		Enter on applicable line of your return.
	5 Guaranteed payments to partner	**5**		See Partner's Instructions for Schedule K-1 (Form 1065).
	6 Net gain (loss) under section 1231 (other than due to casualty or theft)	**6**		
	7 Other income (loss) *(attach schedule)*	**7**		Enter on applicable line of your return.
Deductions	**8** Charitable contributions (see instructions) *(attach schedule)* .	**8**		Sch. A, line 15 or 16
	9 Section 179 expense deduction	**9**		See Partner's Instructions for Schedule K-1 (Form 1065).
	10 Deductions related to portfolio income *(attach schedule)* . .	**10**		
	11 Other deductions *(attach schedule)*	**11**		
Investment Interest	**12a** Interest expense on investment debts	**12a**		Form 4952, line 1
	b (1) Investment income included on lines 4a, 4b, 4c, and 4f above	**b(1)**		See Partner's Instructions for Schedule K-1 (Form 1065).
	(2) Investment expenses included on line 10 above . . .	**b(2)**		
Credits	**13a** Credit for income tax withheld	**13a**		See Partner's Instructions for Schedule K-1 (Form 1065).
	b Low-income housing credit:			
	(1) From section 42(j)(5) partnerships for property placed in service before 1990	**b(1)**		Form 8586, line 5
	(2) Other than on line 13b(1) for property placed in service before 1990	**b(2)**		
	(3) From section 42(j)(5) partnerships for property placed in service after 1989	**b(3)**		
	(4) Other than on line 13b(3) for property placed in service after 1989	**b(4)**		
	c Qualified rehabilitation expenditures related to rental real estate activities (see instructions)	**13c**		See Partner's Instructions for Schedule K-1 (Form 1065).
	d Credits (other than credits shown on lines 13b and 13c) related to rental real estate activities (see instructions) . .	**13d**		
	e Credits related to other rental activities (see instructions) . .	**13e**		
	14 Other credits (see instructions)	**14**		

For Paperwork Reduction Act Notice, see Instructions for Form 1065.   Cat. No. 11394R   **Schedule K-1 (Form 1065) 1994**

Schedule K-1 (Form 1065) 1994   Page **2**

	(a) Distributive share item		(b) Amount	(c) 1040 filers enter the amount in column (b) on:
Self-employment	**15a** Net earnings (loss) from self-employment	15a		Sch. SE, Section A or B
	b Gross farming or fishing income	15b		} See Partner's Instructions for
	c Gross nonfarm income	15c		Schedule K-1 (Form 1065).
Adjustments and Tax Preference Items	**16a** Depreciation adjustment on property placed in service after 1986	16a		
	b Adjusted gain or loss	16b		See Partner's Instructions
	c Depletion (other than oil and gas)	16c		for Schedule K-1
	d (1) Gross income from oil, gas, and geothermal properties	d(1)		(Form 1065) and
	(2) Deductions allocable to oil, gas, and geothermal properties	d(2)		Instructions for Form 6251.
	e Other adjustments and tax preference items *(attach schedule)*	16e		
Foreign Taxes	**17a** Type of income ▶			Form 1116, check boxes
	b Name of foreign country or U.S. possession ▶			
	c Total gross income from sources outside the United States *(attach schedule)*	17c		} Form 1116, Part I
	d Total applicable deductions and losses *(attach schedule)*	17d		
	e Total foreign taxes (check one): ▶ ☐ Paid ☐ Accrued	17e		Form 1116, Part II
	f Reduction in taxes available for credit *(attach schedule)*	17f		Form 1116, Part III
	g Other foreign tax information *(attach schedule)*	17g		See Instructions for Form 1116.
Other	**18a** Total expenditures to which a section 59(e) election may apply	18a		} See Partner's Instructions for Schedule K-1 (Form 1065).
	b Type of expenditures ▶			
	19 Tax-exempt interest income	19		Form 1040, line 8b
	20 Other tax-exempt income	20		} See Partner's Instructions for
	21 Nondeductible expenses	21		Schedule K-1 (Form 1065).
	22 Recapture of low-income housing credit:			
	a From section 42(j)(5) partnerships	22a		} Form 8611, line 8
	b Other than on line 22a	22b		

Supplemental Information

23 Supplemental information required to be reported separately to each partner *(attach additional schedules if more space is needed):*

Printed on recycled paper

Form 1116

Department of the Treasury
Internal Revenue Service

Foreign Tax Credit

(Individual, Fiduciary, or Nonresident Alien Individual)

▶ Attach to Form 1040, 1040NR, 1041, or 990-T.

▶ See separate instructions.

OMB No. 1545-0121

1994

Attachment
Sequence No. **19**

Name	Identifying number as shown on page 1 of your tax return

*Report all amounts in U.S. dollars except where specified in Part II. Use a separate Form 1116 for each category of income listed below. Check only **one** box. Before you check a box, read **Categories of Income** on page 3 of the instructions. Complete this form for credit for taxes on:*

a ☐ Passive income

b ☐ High withholding tax interest

c ☐ Financial services income

d ☐ Shipping income

e ☐ Dividends from a DISC or former DISC

f ☐ Certain distributions from a foreign sales corporation (FSC) or former FSC

g ☐ Lump-sum distributions (see instructions before completing form)

h ☐ General limitation income—all other income from sources outside the United States (including income from sources within U.S. possessions)

i Resident of (name of country) ▶

Note: *If you paid taxes to one foreign country or U.S. possession, use column A in Part I and line A in Part II. If you paid taxes to **more than one** foreign country or U.S. possession, use a separate column and line for each country or possession. However, see the exception under **How To Complete Form 1116** on page 1 of the Instructions.*

Part I **Taxable Income or Loss From Sources Outside the United States for Separate Category Checked Above**

		Foreign Country or U.S. Possession			Total
		A	**B**	**C**	(Add cols. A, B, and C.)
j	Enter the name of the foreign country or U.S. possession . . . . ▶				
1	Gross income from sources within country shown above and of the type checked above. See instructions:				**1**
	Applicable deductions and losses. (See instructions.):				
2	Expenses directly allocable to the income on line 1 (attach schedule)				
3	Pro rata share of other deductions not directly allocable:				
a	Certain itemized deductions or standard deduction. See instructions				
b	Other deductions (attach schedule)				
c	Add lines 3a and 3b				
d	Gross foreign source income. See instructions .				
e	Gross income from all sources. See instructions				
f	Divide line 3d by line 3e				
g	Multiply line 3c by line 3f				
4	Pro rata share of interest expense. See instructions:				
a	Home mortgage interest from line 5 of the worksheet on page 6 of the instructions . . .				
b	Other interest expense				
5	Losses from foreign sources.				
6	Add lines 2, 3g, 4a, 4b, and 5				**6**
7	Subtract line 6 from line 1. Enter the result here and on line 14. . . . . ▶				**7**

Part II **Foreign Taxes Paid or Accrued** (See instructions.)

Country	Credit is claimed for taxes (you must check one)		Foreign taxes paid or accrued								
			In foreign currency				In U.S. dollars				
	(k) ☐ Paid		Taxes withheld at source on:			(q) Other foreign taxes paid or accrued	Taxes withheld at source on:			(u) Other foreign taxes paid or accrued	(v) Total foreign taxes paid or accrued (add cols. (r) through (u))
	(l) ☐ Accrued	(m) Date paid or accrued	(n) Dividends	(o) Rents and royalties	(p) Interest		(r) Dividends	(s) Rents and royalties	(t) Interest		
A											
B											
C											

| **8** | Add lines A through C, column (v). Enter the total here and on line 9 . . . . ▶ | **8** | |

For Paperwork Reduction Act Notice, see page 1 of separate instructions.

Cat. No. 11440U

Form **1116** (1994)

| **Part III** | **Figuring the Credit** |

9   Enter amount from line 8. This is the total foreign taxes paid or accrued for the category of income checked above Part I. . . . . | **9** |

10 Carryback or carryover (attach detailed computation) . . . . . | **10** |

11 Add lines 9 and 10 . . . . | **11** |

12 Reduction in foreign taxes. See instructions . . . . | **12** |

13 Subtract line 12 from line 11. This is the total amount of foreign taxes available for credit . . . . | **13** |

14 Enter amount from line 7. This is your taxable income or (loss) from sources outside the United States (before adjustments) for the category of income checked above Part I. See instructions . . . | **14** |

15 Adjustments to line 14. See instructions . . . . | **15** |

16 Combine the amounts on lines 14 and 15. This is your net foreign source taxable income. (If the result is zero or less, you have no foreign tax credit for the category of income you checked above Part I. Skip lines 17 through 21.) . . . . | **16** |

17 **Individuals:** Enter amount from Form 1040, line 35. If you are a nonresident alien, enter amount from Form 1040NR, line 34. **Estates and trusts:** Enter your taxable income without the deduction for your exemption | **17** |

   Caution: *If you figured your tax using the maximum tax rate on capital gains, see instructions.*

18 Divide line 16 by line 17. If line 16 is more than line 17, enter the figure "1" . . . . | **18** |

19 **Individuals:** Enter amount from Form 1040, line 40, **less** any amounts on Form 1040, lines 41, 42, and any mortgage interest credit (from Form 8396) on line 44. If you are a nonresident alien, enter amount from Form 1040NR, line 39, less any amount on Form 1040NR, line 40 and any mortgage interest credit (from Form 8396) on line 42.
   Estates and trusts: Enter amount from Form 1041, Schedule G, line 1c, or Form 990-T, lines 36 and 37 . | **19** |

20 Multiply line 19 by line 18 (maximum amount of credit) . . . . | **20** |

21 Enter the amount from line 13 or line 20, whichever is smaller. (If this is the only Form 1116 you are completing, skip lines 22 through 29 and enter this amount on line 30. Otherwise, complete the appropriate lines in Part IV.) . . . . ▶ | **21** |

| **Part IV** | **Summary of Credits From Separate Parts III** (See instructions.) |

22 Credit for taxes on passive income . . . . | **22** |

23 Credit for taxes on high withholding tax interest . . . . | **23** |

24 Credit for taxes on financial services income . . . . | **24** |

25 Credit for taxes on shipping income . . . . | **25** |

26 Credit for taxes on dividends from a DISC or former DISC . . . . | **26** |

27 Credit for taxes on certain distributions from a FSC or former FSC | **27** |

28 Credit for taxes on lump-sum distributions . . . . | **28** |

29 Credit for taxes on general limitation income (all other income from sources outside the United States) . . . . | **29** |

30 Add lines 22 through 29. . . . . | **30** |

31 Reduction of credit for international boycott operations. See instructions for line 12 . . . . . . | **31** |

32 Subtract line 31 from line 30. This is your foreign tax credit. Enter here and on Form 1040, line 43; Form 1040NR, line 41; Form 1041, Schedule G, line 2a; or Form 990-T, line 38a. . . . . . . ▶ | **32** |

♻ *Printed on recycled paper*

Form **1120**	U.S. Corporation Income Tax Return	OMB No. 1545-0123
Department of the Treasury Internal Revenue Service	For calendar year 1994 or tax year beginning .... , 1994, ending .... , 19 ... ▶ Instructions are separate. See page 1 for Paperwork Reduction Act Notice.	**1994**

A Check if a:		**Use IRS label. Other-wise, please print or type.**	Name		**B** Employer identification number
1	Consolidated return (attach Form 851) ☐				
2	Personal holding co. (attach Sch. PH) ☐		Number, street, and room or suite no. (If a P.O. box, see page 6 of instructions.)		**C** Date incorporated
3	Personal service corp. (as defined in Temporary Regs. sec. 1.441-4T— see instructions) ☐		City or town, state, and ZIP code		**D** Total assets (see Specific Instructions)

E Check applicable boxes: (1) ☐ Initial return (2) ☐ Final return (3) ☐ Change of address $

Income	1a	Gross receipts or sales [____] **b** Less returns and allowances [____] **c** Bal ▶	1c	
	2	Cost of goods sold (Schedule A, line 8)	2	
	3	Gross profit. Subtract line 2 from line 1c	3	
	4	Dividends (Schedule C, line 19)	4	
	5	Interest	5	
	6	Gross rents	6	
	7	Gross royalties	7	
	8	Capital gain net income (attach Schedule D (Form 1120)) . .	8	
	9	Net gain or (loss) from Form 4797, Part II, line 20 (attach Form 4797) . .	9	
	10	Other income (see instructions—attach schedule)	10	
	11	**Total income.** Add lines 3 through 10 . . . . ▶	11	

Deductions (See instructions for limitations on deductions.)	12	Compensation of officers (Schedule E, line 4)	12	
	13	Salaries and wages (less employment credits)	13	
	14	Repairs and maintenance	14	
	15	Bad debts	15	
	16	Rents	16	
	17	Taxes and licenses	17	
	18	Interest	18	
	19	Charitable contributions (see instructions for 10% limitation) . .	19	
	20	Depreciation (attach Form 4562)	20	
	21	Less depreciation claimed on Schedule A and elsewhere on return . .	21a . . 21b	
	22	Depletion	22	
	23	Advertising	23	
	24	Pension, profit-sharing, etc., plans	24	
	25	Employee benefit programs	25	
	26	Other deductions (attach schedule)	26	
	27	**Total deductions.** Add lines 12 through 26 . . . . . ▶	27	
	28	Taxable income before net operating loss deduction and special deductions. Subtract line 27 from line 11	28	
	29	**Less: a** Net operating loss deduction (see instructions)	29a	
		b Special deductions (Schedule C, line 20)	29b . . 29c	

Tax and Payments	30	**Taxable income.** Subtract line 29c from line 28	30	
	31	**Total tax** (Schedule J, line 10)	31	
	32	**Payments: a** 1993 overpayment credited to 1994	32a	
	b	1994 estimated tax payments . .	32b	
	c	Less 1994 refund applied for on Form 4466	32c ( ) **d** Bal ▶ 32d	
	e	Tax deposited with Form 7004	32e	
	f	Credit from regulated investment companies (attach Form 2439) . . .	32f	
	g	Credit for Federal tax on fuels (attach Form 4136). See instructions . .	32g . . 32h	
	33	Estimated tax penalty (see instructions). Check if Form 2220 is attached . . . . . ▶ ☐	33	
	34	**Tax due.** If line 32h is smaller than the total of lines 31 and 33, enter amount owed . .	34	
	35	**Overpayment.** If line 32h is larger than the total of lines 31 and 33, enter amount overpaid . .	35	
	36	Enter amount of line 35 you want: **Credited to 1995 estimated tax** ▶ **Refunded** ▶	36	

Please Sign Here

Under penalties of perjury, I declare that I have examined this return, including accompanying schedules and statements, and to the best of my knowledge and belief, it is true, correct, and complete. Declaration of preparer (other than taxpayer) is based on all information of which preparer has any knowledge.

▶ _____   _____   ▶ _____
Signature of officer   Date   Title

Paid Preparer's Use Only

Preparer's signature ▶		Date	Check if self-employed ☐	Preparer's social security number
Firm's name (or yours if self-employed) and address ▶			E.I. No. ▶	
			ZIP code ▶	

Cat. No. 11450Q

Form 1120 (1994)　　　　　　　　　　　　　　　　　　　　　　　　　　　　Page **2**

Schedule A　Cost of Goods Sold (See instructions.)

1	Inventory at beginning of year	1
2	Purchases	2
3	Cost of labor	3
4	Additional section 263A costs (attach schedule)	4
5	Other costs (attach schedule)	5
6	**Total.** Add lines 1 through 5	6
7	Inventory at end of year	7
8	**Cost of goods sold.** Subtract line 7 from line 6. Enter here and on page 1, line 2	8

9a Check all methods used for valuing closing inventory:

☐ Cost　　　　☐ Lower of cost or market as described in Regulations section 1.471-4

☐ Writedown of subnormal goods as described in Regulations section 1.471-2(c)

☐ Other (Specify method used and attach explanation.) ▶ ------------------------------------

　b　Check if the LIFO inventory method was adopted this tax year for any goods (if checked, attach Form 970) . . . . . ▶ ☐

　c　If the LIFO inventory method was used for this tax year, enter percentage (or amounts) of closing
　　　inventory computed under LIFO . . . . | 9c |

　d　Do the rules of section 263A (for property produced or acquired for resale) apply to the corporation? . . . . . ☐ Yes ☐ No

　e　Was there any change in determining quantities, cost, or valuations between opening and closing inventory? If "Yes,"
　　　attach explanation . . . . ☐ Yes ☐ No

Schedule C　Dividends and Special Deductions (See instructions.)

		(a) Dividends received	(b) %	(c) Special deductions (a) × (b)
1	Dividends from less-than-20%-owned domestic corporations that are subject to the 70% deduction (other than debt-financed stock)		70	
2	Dividends from 20%-or-more-owned domestic corporations that are subject to the 80% deduction (other than debt-financed stock)		80	
3	Dividends on debt-financed stock of domestic and foreign corporations (section 246A)		see instructions	
4	Dividends on certain preferred stock of less-than-20%-owned public utilities . . .		42	
5	Dividends on certain preferred stock of 20%-or-more-owned public utilities . . .		48	
6	Dividends from less-than-20%-owned foreign corporations and certain FSCs that are subject to the 70% deduction		70	
7	Dividends from 20%-or-more-owned foreign corporations and certain FSCs that are subject to the 80% deduction		80	
8	Dividends from wholly owned foreign subsidiaries subject to the 100% deduction (section 245(b))		100	
9	**Total.** Add lines 1 through 8. See instructions for limitation			
10	Dividends from domestic corporations received by a small business investment company operating under the Small Business Investment Act of 1958		100	
11	Dividends from certain FSCs that are subject to the 100% deduction (section 245(c)(1))		100	
12	Dividends from affiliated group members subject to the 100% deduction (section 243(a)(3))		100	
13	Other dividends from foreign corporations not included on lines 3, 6, 7, 8, or 11 . . .			
14	Income from controlled foreign corporations under subpart F (attach Form(s) 5471) .			
15	Foreign dividend gross-up (section 78)			
16	IC-DISC and former DISC dividends not included on lines 1, 2, or 3 (section 246(d)) .			
17	Other dividends			
18	Deduction for dividends paid on certain preferred stock of public utilities			
19	**Total dividends.** Add lines 1 through 17. Enter here and on line 4, page 1 . . ▶			

20　**Total special deductions.** Add lines 9, 10, 11, 12, and 18. Enter here and on line 29b, page 1 . . . . . ▶

Schedule E　Compensation of Officers (See instructions for line 12, page 1.)

Complete Schedule E only if total receipts (line 1a plus lines 4 through 10 on page 1, Form 1120) are $500,000 or more.

(a) Name of officer	(b) Social security number	(c) Percent of time devoted to business	Percent of corporation stock owned		(f) Amount of compensation
			(d) Common	(e) Preferred	
1		%	%	%	
		%	%	%	
		%	%	%	
		%	%	%	
		%	%	%	

2　Total compensation of officers . . . .

3　Compensation of officers claimed on Schedule A and elsewhere on return . . . .

4　Subtract line 3 from line 2. Enter the result here and on line 12, page 1 . . . .

Form 1120 (1994)   Page **3**

Schedule J **Tax Computation** (See instructions.)

1 Check if the corporation is a member of a controlled group (see sections 1561 and 1563) . . . . ▶ ☐

2a If the box on line 1 is checked, enter the corporation's share of the $50,000, $25,000, and $9,925,000 taxable income brackets (in that order):

(1) $ _____ **(2)** $ _____ **(3)** $ _____

b Enter the corporation's share of:

(1) Additional 5% tax (not more than $11,750) $ _____

(2) Additional 3% tax (not more than $100,000) $ _____

3 Income tax. Check this box if the corporation is a qualified personal service corporation as defined in section 448(d)(2) (see instructions on page 14). . . . . ▶ ☐   **3**

4a Foreign tax credit (attach Form 1118) **4a**

b Possessions tax credit (attach Form 5735) **4b**

c Orphan drug credit (attach Form 6765) **4c**

d Check: ☐ Nonconventional source fuel credit ☐ QEV credit (attach Form 8834) **4d**

e General business credit. Enter here and check which forms are attached:

☐ 3800 ☐ 3468 ☐ 5884 ☐ 6478 ☐ 6765 ☐ 8586 ☐ 8830
☐ 8826 ☐ 8835 ☐ 8844 ☐ 8845 ☐ 8846 ☐ 8847 . . . . **4e**

f Credit for prior year minimum tax (attach Form 8827) **4f**

5 **Total credits.** Add lines 4a through 4f **5**

6 Subtract line 5 from line 3 . . . . **6**

7 Personal holding company tax (attach Schedule PH (Form 1120)) **7**

8 Recapture taxes. Check if from: ☐ Form 4255 ☐ Form 8611 . . . . **8**

9a Alternative minimum tax (attach Form 4626) **9a**

b Environmental tax (attach Form 4626) **9b**

10 **Total tax.** Add lines 6 through 9b. Enter here and on line 31, page 1 . . . . **10**

Schedule K **Other Information** (See pages 17 and 18 of instructions.)

	Yes	No

1 Check method of accounting: **a** ☐ Cash **b** ☐ Accrual **c** ☐ Other (specify) ▶ _____

2 Refer to page 19 of the instructions and state the principal:

a Business activity code no. ▶ _____

b Business activity ▶ _____

c Product or service ▶ _____

3 Did the corporation at the end of the tax year own, directly or indirectly, 50% or more of the voting stock of a domestic corporation? (For rules of attribution, see section 267(c).) . . . .

If "Yes," attach a schedule showing: (a) name and identifying number, (b) percentage owned, and (c) taxable income or (loss) before NOL and special deductions of such corporation for the tax year ending with or within your tax year.

4 Is the corporation a subsidiary in an affiliated group or a parent-subsidiary controlled group? . . . . . .

If "Yes," enter employer identification number and name of the parent corporation ▶ _____

5 Did any individual, partnership, corporation, estate or trust at the end of the tax year own, directly or indirectly, 50% or more of the corporation's voting stock? (For rules of attribution, see section 267(c).) . . . .

If "Yes," attach a schedule showing name and identifying number. (Do not include any information already entered in **4** above.) Enter percentage owned ▶ _____

6 During this tax year, did the corporation pay dividends (other than stock dividends and distributions in exchange for stock) in excess of the corporation's current and accumulated earnings and profits? (See secs. 301 and 316.) . . . .

If "Yes," file Form 5452. If this is a consolidated return, answer here for the parent corporation and on **Form 851,** Affiliations Schedule, for each subsidiary.

7 Was the corporation a U.S. shareholder of any controlled foreign corporation? (See sections 951 and 957.) . . .

If "Yes," attach Form 5471 for each such corporation. Enter number of Forms 5471 attached ▶ _____

8 At any time during the 1994 calendar year, did the corporation have an interest in or a signature or other authority over a financial account in a foreign country (such as a bank account, securities account, or other financial account)? .

If "Yes," the corporation may have to file Form TD F 90-22.1. If "Yes," enter name of foreign country ▶ _____

9 Was the corporation the grantor of, or transferor to, a foreign trust that existed during the current tax year, whether or not the corporation has any beneficial interest in it? If "Yes," the corporation may have to file Forms 926, 3520, or 3520-A

10 Did one foreign person at any time during the tax year own, directly or indirectly, at least 25% of: **(a)** the total voting power of all classes of stock of the corporation entitled to vote, or **(b)** the total value of all classes of stock of the corporation? If "Yes,"

a Enter percentage owned ▶ _____

b Enter owner's country ▶ _____

c The corporation may have to file Form 5472. Enter number of Forms 5472 attached ▶ _____

11 Check this box if the corporation issued publicly offered debt instruments with original issue discount . ▶ ☐

If so, the corporation may have to file Form 8281.

12 Enter the amount of tax-exempt interest received or accrued during the tax year ▶ $ _____

13 If there were 35 or fewer shareholders at the end of the tax year, enter the number ▶ _____

14 If the corporation has an NOL for the tax year and is electing to forego the carryback period, check here ▶ ☐

15 Enter the available NOL carryover from prior tax years (Do not reduce it by any deduction on line 29a.) ▶ $ _____

Form 1120 (1994)

Schedule L	Balance Sheets	Beginning of tax year		End of tax year	
	Assets	(a)	(b)	(c)	(d)
1	Cash				
2a	Trade notes and accounts receivable				
b	Less allowance for bad debts	( )		( )	
3	Inventories				
4	U.S. government obligations				
5	Tax-exempt securities (see instructions)				
6	Other current assets (attach schedule)				
7	Loans to stockholders				
8	Mortgage and real estate loans				
9	Other investments (attach schedule)				
10a	Buildings and other depreciable assets				
b	Less accumulated depreciation	( )		( )	
11a	Depletable assets				
b	Less accumulated depletion	( )		( )	
12	Land (net of any amortization)				
13a	Intangible assets (amortizable only)				
b	Less accumulated amortization	( )		( )	
14	Other assets (attach schedule)				
15	Total assets				
	Liabilities and Stockholders' Equity				
16	Accounts payable				
17	Mortgages, notes, bonds payable in less than 1 year				
18	Other current liabilities (attach schedule)				
19	Loans from stockholders				
20	Mortgages, notes, bonds payable in 1 year or more				
21	Other liabilities (attach schedule)				
22	Capital stock: a Preferred stock				
	b Common stock				
23	Paid-in or capital surplus				
24	Retained earnings—Appropriated (attach schedule)				
25	Retained earnings—Unappropriated				
26	Less cost of treasury stock		( )		( )
27	Total liabilities and stockholders' equity				

Note: *You are not required to complete Schedules M-1 and M-2 below if the total assets on line 15, column (d) of Schedule L are less than $25,000.*

Schedule M-1	Reconciliation of Income (Loss) per Books With Income per Return (See instructions.)

1	Net income (loss) per books		7	Income recorded on books this year not included on this return (itemize):	
2	Federal income tax				
3	Excess of capital losses over capital gains			Tax-exempt interest $	
4	Income subject to tax not recorded on books this year (itemize):			....	
	....		8	Deductions on this return not charged against book income this year (itemize):	
5	Expenses recorded on books this year not deducted on this return (itemize):				
			a	Depreciation $	
a	Depreciation $		b	Contributions carryover $	
b	Contributions carryover $			....	
c	Travel and entertainment $			....	
	....		9	Add lines 7 and 8	
6	Add lines 1 through 5		10	Income (line 28, page 1)—line 6 less line 9	

Schedule M-2	Analysis of Unappropriated Retained Earnings per Books (Line 25, Schedule L)

1	Balance at beginning of year		5	Distributions: a Cash	
2	Net income (loss) per books			b Stock	
3	Other increases (itemize):			c Property	
	....		6	Other decreases (itemize):	
	....			....	
	....		7	Add lines 5 and 6	
4	Add lines 1, 2, and 3		8	Balance at end of year (line 4 less line 7)	

Printed on recycled paper

Form **1120S**	**U.S. Income Tax Return for an S Corporation**
Department of the Treasury Internal Revenue Service	▶ Do not file this form unless the corporation has timely filed Form 2553 to elect to be an S corporation. ▶ See separate instructions.

OMB No. 1545-0130

1994

For calendar year 1994, or tax year beginning _____ , 1994, and ending _____ , 19 __

A Date of election as an S corporation

B Business code no. (see Specific Instructions)

Use IRS label. Otherwise, please print or type.

Name

Number, street, and room or suite no. (If a P.O. box, see page 9 of the instructions.)

City or town, state, and ZIP code

C Employer identification number

D Date incorporated

E Total assets (see Specific Instructions)

$

F Check applicable boxes: (1) ☐ Initial return (2) ☐ Final return (3) ☐ Change in address (4) ☐ Amended return

G Check this box if this S corporation is subject to the consolidated audit procedures of sections 6241 through 6245 (see instructions before checking this box) . ▶ ☐

H Enter number of shareholders in the corporation at end of the tax year . . . . ▶

Caution: *Include only trade or business income and expenses on lines 1a through 21. See the instructions for more information.*

Income

1a	Gross receipts or sales |_____| **b** Less returns and allowances |_____| **c** Bal ▶	**1c**	
2	Cost of goods sold (Schedule A, line 8)	**2**	
3	Gross profit. Subtract line 2 from line 1c	**3**	
4	Net gain (loss) from Form 4797, Part II, line 20 *(attach Form 4797)*	**4**	
5	Other income (loss) (see instructions) *(attach schedule)*	**5**	
6	**Total income (loss).** Combine lines 3 through 5 . . . . ▶	**6**	

Deductions (See instructions for limitations.)

7	Compensation of officers	**7**	
8	Salaries and wages (less employment credits)	**8**	
9	Repairs and maintenance	**9**	
10	Bad debts	**10**	
11	Rents	**11**	
12	Taxes and licenses	**12**	
13	Interest	**13**	
14a	Depreciation (see instructions)	**14a**		
b	Depreciation claimed on Schedule A and elsewhere on return .	**14b**		
c	Subtract line 14b from line 14a	**14c**	
15	Depletion **(Do not deduct oil and gas depletion.)**	**15**	
16	Advertising	**16**	
17	Pension, profit-sharing, etc., plans	**17**	
18	Employee benefit programs	**18**	
19	Other deductions (see instructions) *(attach schedule)*	**19**	
20	**Total deductions.** Add the amounts shown in the far right column for lines 7 through 19 ▶	**20**	
21	Ordinary income (loss) from trade or business activities. Subtract line 20 from line 6 . .	**21**	

Tax and Payments

22	**Tax: a** Excess net passive income tax *(attach schedule)*. . .	**22a**		
b	Tax from Schedule D (Form 1120S)	**22b**		
c	Add lines 22a and 22b (see instructions for additional taxes)	**22c**	
23	**Payments: a** 1994 estimated tax payments and amount applied from 1993 return	**23a**		
b	Tax deposited with Form 7004	**23b**		
c	Credit for Federal tax paid on fuels *(attach Form 4136)* . . .	**23c**		
d	Add lines 23a through 23c	**23d**	
24	Estimated tax penalty (see instructions). Check if Form 2220 is attached . . . . . ▶ ☐	**24**	
25	**Tax due.** If the total of lines 22c and 24 is larger than line 23d, enter amount owed. See instructions for depositary method of payment . . . . ▶	**25**	
26	**Overpayment.** If line 23d is larger than the total of lines 22c and 24, enter amount overpaid ▶	**26**	
27	Enter amount of line 26 you want: **Credited to 1995 estimated tax** ▶ |_____| **Refunded** ▶	**27**	

Please Sign Here

Under penalties of perjury, I declare that I have examined this return, including accompanying schedules and statements, and to the best of my knowledge and belief, it is true, correct, and complete. Declaration of preparer (other than taxpayer) is based on all information of which preparer has any knowledge.

▶ _____ _____ ▶ _____
Signature of officer   Date   Title

Paid Preparer's Use Only

Preparer's signature ▶		Date	Check if self-employed ▶ ☐	Preparer's social security number
Firm's name (or yours if self-employed) and address ▶		E.I. No. ▶	
		ZIP code ▶	

For Paperwork Reduction Act Notice, see page 1 of separate instructions. Cat. No. 11510H Form **1120S** (1994)

Form 1120S (1994)   Page **2**

Schedule A   Cost of Goods Sold (See instructions.)

1	Inventory at beginning of year	**1**	
2	Purchases	**2**	
3	Cost of labor	**3**	
4	Additional section 263A costs (see instructions) *(attach schedule)*	**4**	
5	Other costs *(attach schedule)*	**5**	
6	**Total.** Add lines 1 through 5	**6**	
7	Inventory at end of year	**7**	
8	**Cost of goods sold.** Subtract line 7 from line 6. Enter here and on page 1, line 2	**8**	

9a Check all methods used for valuing closing inventory:

  (i) ☐ Cost

  (ii) ☐ Lower of cost or market as described in Regulations section 1.471-4

  (iii) ☐ Writedown of "subnormal" goods as described in Regulations section 1.471-2(c)

  (iv) ☐ Other (specify method used and attach explanation) ▶ ----------------------------

  b Check if the LIFO inventory method was adopted this tax year for any goods *(if checked, attach Form 970)* . . . . . ▶ ☐

  c If the LIFO inventory method was used for this tax year, enter percentage (or amounts) of closing inventory computed under LIFO . . . . | **9c** | |

  d Do the rules of section 263A (for property produced or acquired for resale) apply to the corporation? . . . ☐ Yes ☐ No

  e Was there any change in determining quantities, cost, or valuations between opening and closing inventory? . ☐ Yes ☐ No
  If "Yes," attach explanation.

Schedule B   Other Information

		Yes	No
1	Check method of accounting: **(a)** ☐ Cash **(b)** ☐ Accrual **(c)** ☐ Other (specify) ▶ ----------------		
2	Refer to the list in the instructions and state the corporation's principal: **(a)** Business activity ▶ ---------------------- **(b)** Product or service ▶ ----------------------		
3	Did the corporation at the end of the tax year own, directly or indirectly, 50% or more of the voting stock of a domestic corporation? (For rules of attribution, see section 267(c).) If "Yes," attach a schedule showing: **(a)** name, address, and employer identification number and **(b)** percentage owned.		
4	Was the corporation a member of a controlled group subject to the provisions of section 1561?		
5	At any time during calendar year 1994, did the corporation have an interest in or a signature or other authority over a financial account in a foreign country (such as a bank account, securities account, or other financial account)? (See instructions for exceptions and filing requirements for Form TD F 90-22.1.) If "Yes," enter the name of the foreign country ▶ ----------------------		
6	Was the corporation the grantor of, or transferor to, a foreign trust that existed during the current tax year, whether or not the corporation has any beneficial interest in it? If "Yes," the corporation may have to file Forms 3520, 3520-A, or 926.		
7	Check this box if the corporation has filed or is required to file **Form 8264,** Application for Registration of a Tax Shelter . . . . ▶ ☐		
8	Check this box if the corporation issued publicly offered debt instruments with original issue discount . . ▶ ☐ If so, the corporation may have to file **Form 8281,** Information Return for Publicly Offered Original Issue Discount Instruments.		
9	If the corporation: **(a)** filed its election to be an S corporation after 1986, **(b)** was a C corporation before it elected to be an S corporation **or** the corporation acquired an asset with a basis determined by reference to its basis (or the basis of any other property) in the hands of a C corporation, and **(c)** has net unrealized built-in gain (defined in section 1374(d)(1)) in excess of the net recognized built-in gain from prior years, enter the net unrealized built-in gain reduced by net recognized built-in gain from prior years (see instructions) . . . . . . ▶ $ ----------------------		
10	Check this box if the corporation had subchapter C earnings and profits at the close of the tax year (see instructions) . . . . ▶ ☐		

Designation of Tax Matters Person (See instructions.)

Enter below the shareholder designated as the tax matters person (TMP) for the tax year of this return:

Name of
designated TMP ▶

Identifying
number of TMP ▶

Address of
designated TMP ▶

Schedule K | Shareholders' Shares of Income, Credits, Deductions, etc.

	(a) Pro rata share items		(b) Total amount	
	1 Ordinary income (loss) from trade or business activities (page 1, line 21)	**1**		
	2 Net income (loss) from rental real estate activities *(attach Form 8825)*	**2**		
	3a Gross income from other rental activities	3a			
	b Expenses from other rental activities *(attach schedule)*.	3b			
	c Net income (loss) from other rental activities. Subtract line 3b from line 3a	**3c**		
	4 Portfolio income (loss):			
	a Interest income	**4a**		
	b Dividend income	**4b**		
	c Royalty income	**4c**		
	d Net short-term capital gain (loss) *(attach Schedule D (Form 1120S))*	**4d**		
	e Net long-term capital gain (loss) *(attach Schedule D (Form 1120S))*.	**4e**		
	f Other portfolio income (loss) *(attach schedule)*	**4f**		
	5 Net gain (loss) under section 1231 (other than due to casualty or theft) *(attach Form 4797)*	**5**		
	6 Other income (loss) *(attach schedule)*	**6**		
	7 Charitable contributions (see instructions) *(attach schedule)*	**7**		
	8 Section 179 expense deduction *(attach Form 4562)*.	**8**		
	9 Deductions related to portfolio income (loss) (see instructions) (itemize)	**9**		
	10 Other deductions *(attach schedule)*	**10**		
	11a Interest expense on investment debts	**11a**		
	b (1) Investment income included on lines 4a, 4b, 4c, and 4f above	**11b(1)**		
	(2) Investment expenses included on line 9 above	**11b(2)**		
	12a Credit for alcohol used as a fuel *(attach Form 6478)*	**12a**		
	b Low-income housing credit (see instructions):			
	(1) From partnerships to which section 42(j)(5) applies for property placed in service before 1990	**12b(1)**		
	(2) Other than on line 12b(1) for property placed in service before 1990. . . .	**12b(2)**		
	(3) From partnerships to which section 42(j)(5) applies for property placed in service after 1989	**12b(3)**		
	(4) Other than on line 12b(3) for property placed in service after 1989	**12b(4)**		
	c Qualified rehabilitation expenditures related to rental real estate activities *(attach Form 3468)* .	**12c**		
	d Credits (other than credits shown on lines 12b and 12c) related to rental real estate activities (see instructions).	**12d**		
	e Credits related to other rental activities (see instructions)	**12e**		
	13 Other credits (see instructions)	**13**		
	14a Depreciation adjustment on property placed in service after 1986	**14a**		
	b Adjusted gain or loss	**14b**		
	c Depletion (other than oil and gas)	**14c**		
	d (1) Gross income from oil, gas, or geothermal properties	**14d(1)**		
	(2) Deductions allocable to oil, gas, or geothermal properties	**14d(2)**		
	e Other adjustments and tax preference items *(attach schedule)*	**14e**		
	15a Type of income ▶ ---------------------------			
	b Name of foreign country or U.S. possession ▶ ---------------------			
	c Total gross income from sources outside the United States *(attach schedule)* . . .	**15c**		
	d Total applicable deductions and losses *(attach schedule)*	**15d**		
	e Total foreign taxes (check one): ▶ ☐ Paid ☐ Accrued	**15e**		
	f Reduction in taxes available for credit *(attach schedule)*	**15f**		
	g Other foreign tax information *(attach schedule)*	**15g**		
	16a Total expenditures to which a section 59(e) election may apply	**16a**		
	b Type of expenditures ▶ -----------------------------			
	17 Tax-exempt interest income	**17**		
	18 Other tax-exempt income	**18**		
	19 Nondeductible expenses	**19**		
	20 Total property distributions (including cash) other than dividends reported on line 22 below	**20**		
	21 Other items and amounts required to be reported separately to shareholders (see instructions) *(attach schedule)*			
	22 Total dividend distributions paid from accumulated earnings and profits	**22**		
	23 **Income (loss).** (Required only if Schedule M-1 must be completed.) Combine lines 1 through 6 in column (b). From the result, subtract the sum of lines 7 through 11a, 15e, and 16a	**23**		

Row group labels (left margin, top to bottom): Income (Loss); Deductions; Investment Interest; Credits; Adjustments and Tax Preference Items; Foreign Taxes; Other

Form 1120S (1994) Page **4**

Schedule L — Balance Sheets

	Assets	Beginning of tax year (a)	(b)	End of tax year (c)	(d)
1	Cash				
2a	Trade notes and accounts receivable .				
b	Less allowance for bad debts . . .				
3	Inventories				
4	U.S. Government obligations				
5	Tax-exempt securities				
6	Other current assets (attach schedule) .				
7	Loans to shareholders				
8	Mortgage and real estate loans . . .				
9	Other investments (attach schedule) .				
10a	Buildings and other depreciable assets .				
b	Less accumulated depreciation . . .				
11a	Depletable assets				
b	Less accumulated depletion				
12	Land (net of any amortization) . . .				
13a	Intangible assets (amortizable only) . .				
b	Less accumulated amortization . . .				
14	Other assets (attach schedule) . . .				
15	Total assets				
	Liabilities and Shareholders' Equity				
16	Accounts payable				
17	Mortgages, notes, bonds payable in less than 1 year				
18	Other current liabilities (attach schedule)				
19	Loans from shareholders				
20	Mortgages, notes, bonds payable in 1 year or more				
21	Other liabilities (attach schedule) . .				
22	Capital stock				
23	Paid-in or capital surplus				
24	Retained earnings				
25	Less cost of treasury stock		( )		( )
26	Total liabilities and shareholders' equity .				

Schedule M-1 — Reconciliation of Income (Loss) per Books With Income (Loss) per Return (You are not required to complete this schedule if the total assets on line 15, column (d), of Schedule L are less than $25,000.)

1	Net income (loss) per books		5	Income recorded on books this year not included on Schedule K, lines 1 through 6 (itemize):	
2	Income included on Schedule K, lines 1 through 6, not recorded on books this year (itemize): _____				
	_____		a	Tax-exempt interest $ _____	
				_____	
3	Expenses recorded on books this year not included on Schedule K, lines 1 through 11a, 15e, and 16a (itemize):		6	Deductions included on Schedule K, lines 1 through 11a, 15e, and 16a, not charged against book income this year (itemize):	
a	Depreciation $ _____		a	Depreciation $ _____	
b	Travel and entertainment $ _____			_____	
	_____			_____	
	_____		7	Add lines 5 and 6	
4	Add lines 1 through 3		8	Income (loss) (Schedule K, line 23). Line 4 less line 7	

Schedule M-2 — Analysis of Accumulated Adjustments Account, Other Adjustments Account, and Shareholders' Undistributed Taxable Income Previously Taxed (See instructions.)

		(a) Accumulated adjustments account	(b) Other adjustments account	(c) Shareholders' undistributed taxable income previously taxed
1	Balance at beginning of tax year . .			
2	Ordinary income from page 1, line 21 .			
3	Other additions			
4	Loss from page 1, line 21	( )		
5	Other reductions	( )	( )	
6	Combine lines 1 through 5			
7	Distributions other than dividend distributions .			
8	Balance at end of tax year. Subtract line 7 from line 6			

SCHEDULE K-1
(Form 1120S)

Department of the Treasury
Internal Revenue Service

Shareholder's Share of Income, Credits, Deductions, etc.

▶ See separate instructions.

For calendar year 1994 or tax year
beginning _____ , 1994, and ending _____ , 19____

OMB No. 1545-0130

1994

Shareholder's identifying number ▶ _____

Corporation's identifying number ▶ _____

Shareholder's name, address, and ZIP code

Corporation's name, address, and ZIP code

A Shareholder's percentage of stock ownership for tax year (see Instructions for Schedule K-1) . . . . . . ▶ _____ %

B Internal Revenue Service Center where corporation filed its return ▶ _____

C Tax shelter registration number (see Instructions for Schedule K-1) . . . . ▶ _____

D Check applicable boxes: **(1)** ☐ Final K-1   **(2)** ☐ Amended K-1

		(a) Pro rata share items		(b) Amount	(c) Form 1040 filers enter the amount in column (b) on:
Income (Loss)	**1**	Ordinary income (loss) from trade or business activities . .	**1**		See Shareholder's Instructions for Schedule K-1 (Form 1120S).
	2	Net income (loss) from rental real estate activities	**2**		
	3	Net income (loss) from other rental activities	**3**		
	4	Portfolio income (loss):			
	a	Interest	**4a**		Sch. B, Part I, line 1
	b	Dividends	**4b**		Sch. B, Part II, line 5
	c	Royalties	**4c**		Sch. E, Part I, line 4
	d	Net short-term capital gain (loss)	**4d**		Sch. D, line 5, col. (f) or (g)
	e	Net long-term capital gain (loss)	**4e**		Sch. D, line 13, col. (f) or (g)
	f	Other portfolio income (loss) *(attach schedule)*	**4f**		(Enter on applicable line of your return.)
	5	Net gain (loss) under section 1231 (other than due to casualty or theft)	**5**		See Shareholder's Instructions for Schedule K-1 (Form 1120S).
	6	Other income (loss) *(attach schedule)*	**6**		(Enter on applicable line of your return.)
Deductions	**7**	Charitable contributions (see instructions) *(attach schedule)* .	**7**		Sch. A, line 15 or 16
	8	Section 179 expense deduction	**8**		See Shareholder's Instructions for Schedule K-1 (Form 1120S).
	9	Deductions related to portfolio income (loss) *(attach schedule)* .	**9**		
	10	Other deductions *(attach schedule)*	**10**		
Investment Interest	**11a**	Interest expense on investment debts	**11a**		Form 4952, line 1
	b	**(1)** Investment income included on lines 4a, 4b, 4c, and 4f above	**b(1)**		See Shareholder's Instructions for Schedule K-1 (Form 1120S).
		(2) Investment expenses included on line 9 above	**b(2)**		
Credits	**12a**	Credit for alcohol used as fuel	**12a**		Form 6478, line 10
	b	Low-income housing credit:			
		(1) From section 42(j)(5) partnerships for property placed in service before 1990	**b(1)**		Form 8586, line 5
		(2) Other than on line 12b(1) for property placed in service before 1990	**b(2)**		
		(3) From section 42(j)(5) partnerships for property placed in service after 1989	**b(3)**		
		(4) Other than on line 12b(3) for property placed in service after 1989	**b(4)**		
	c	Qualified rehabilitation expenditures related to rental real estate activities (see instructions)	**12c**		See Shareholder's Instructions for Schedule K-1 (Form 1120S).
	d	Credits (other than credits shown on lines 12b and 12c) related to rental real estate activities (see instructions)	**12d**		
	e	Credits related to other rental activities (see instructions) . .	**12e**		
	13	Other credits (see instructions)	**13**		
Adjustments and Tax Preference Items	**14a**	Depreciation adjustment on property placed in service after 1986	**14a**		See Shareholder's Instructions for Schedule K-1 (Form 1120S) and Instructions for Form 6251
	b	Adjusted gain or loss	**14b**		
	c	Depletion (other than oil and gas)	**14c**		
	d	**(1)** Gross income from oil, gas, or geothermal properties . .	**d(1)**		
		(2) Deductions allocable to oil, gas, or geothermal properties .	**d(2)**		
	e	Other adjustments and tax preference items *(attach schedule)* .	**14e**		

For Paperwork Reduction Act Notice, see page 1 of Instructions for Form 1120S.   Cat. No. 11520D   **Schedule K-1 (Form 1120S) 1994**

(a) Pro rata share items		(b) Amount	(c) Form 1040 filers enter the amount in column (b) on:
Foreign Taxes	**15a** Type of income ▶		Form 1116, Check boxes
	b Name of foreign country or U.S. possession ▶		
	c Total gross income from sources outside the United States *(attach schedule)*	**15c**	Form 1116, Part I
	d Total applicable deductions and losses *(attach schedule)* . .	**15d**	
	e Total foreign taxes (check one): ▶ ☐ Paid ☐ Accrued . .	**15e**	Form 1116, Part II
	f Reduction in taxes available for credit *(attach schedule)* . .	**15f**	Form 1116, Part III
	g Other foreign tax information *(attach schedule)*	**15g**	See Instructions for Form 1116
Other	**16a** Total expenditures to which a section 59(e) election may apply	**16a**	See Shareholder's Instructions for Schedule K-1 (Form 1120S).
	b Type of expenditures ▶		
	17 Tax-exempt interest income	**17**	Form 1040, line 8b
	18 Other tax-exempt income	**18**	
	19 Nondeductible expenses	**19**	See Shareholder's Instructions for Schedule K-1 (Form 1120S).
	20 Property distributions (including cash) other than dividend distributions reported to you on Form 1099-DIV	**20**	
	21 Amount of loan repayments for "Loans From Shareholders" .	**21**	
	22 Recapture of low-income housing credit:		
	a From section 42(j)(5) partnerships	**22a**	Form 8611, line 8
	b Other than on line 22a	**22b**	

23 Supplemental information required to be reported separately to each shareholder *(attach additional schedules if more space is needed)*:

Supplemental Information

Form **2106**

Department of the Treasury
Internal Revenue Service (T)

Employee Business Expenses

▶ **See separate instructions.**

▶ **Attach to Form 1040.**

OMB No. 1545-0139

1994

Attachment
Sequence No. **54**

Your name	Social security number	Occupation in which expenses were incurred

Part I Employee Business Expenses and Reimbursements

STEP 1 Enter Your Expenses

		Column A Other Than Meals and Entertainment		Column B Meals and Entertainment	
1	Vehicle expense from line 22 or line 29	**1**			
2	Parking fees, tolls, and transportation, including train, bus, etc., that **did not** involve overnight travel	**2**			
3	Travel expense while away from home overnight, including lodging, airplane, car rental, etc. **Do not** include meals and entertainment	**3**			
4	Business expenses not included on lines 1 through 3. **Do not** include meals and entertainment	**4**			
5	Meals and entertainment expenses (see instructions)	**5**			
6	**Total expenses.** In Column A, add lines 1 through 4 and enter the result. In Column B, enter the amount from line 5	**6**			

Note: *If you were not reimbursed for any expenses in Step 1, skip line 7 and enter the amount from line 6 on line 8.*

STEP 2 Enter Amounts Your Employer Gave You for Expenses Listed in STEP 1

7	Enter amounts your employer gave you that were **not** reported to you in box 1 of Form W-2. Include any amount reported under code "L" in box 13 of your Form W-2 (see instructions) . . .	**7**			

STEP 3 Figure Expenses To Deduct on Schedule A (Form 1040)

8	Subtract line 7 from line 6	**8**			
	Note: *If **both columns** of line 8 are zero, **stop here.** If Column A is less than zero, report the amount as income on Form 1040, line 7.*				
9	In Column A, enter the amount from line 8 (if zero or less, enter -0-). In Column B, multiply the amount on line 8 by 50% (.50) .	**9**			
10	Add the amounts on line 9 of both columns and enter the total here. **Also, enter the total on Schedule A (Form 1040), line 20.** (Qualified performing artists and individuals with disabilities, see the instructions for special rules on where to enter the total.) . . . . ▶	**10**			

For Paperwork Reduction Act Notice, see instructions.   Cat. No. 11700N   Form **2106** (1994)

Form 2106 (1994) Page **2**

Part II　Vehicle Expenses (See instructions to find out which sections to complete.)

Section A.—General Information

			(a) Vehicle 1	(b) Vehicle 2
11	Enter the date vehicle was placed in service	11	/ /	/ /
12	Total miles vehicle was driven during 1994	12	miles	miles
13	Business miles included on line 12	13	miles	miles
14	Percent of business use. Divide line 13 by line 12	14	%	%
15	Average daily round trip commuting distance	15	miles	miles
16	Commuting miles included on line 12	16	miles	miles
17	Other personal miles. Add lines 13 and 16 and subtract the total from line 12	17	miles	miles

18 Do you (or your spouse) have another vehicle available for personal purposes? ☐ Yes ☐ No

19 If your employer provided you with a vehicle, is personal use during off duty hours permitted? ☐ Yes ☐ No ☐ Not applicable

20 Do you have evidence to support your deduction? ☐ Yes ☐ No

21 If "Yes," is the evidence written? ☐ Yes ☐ No

Section B.—Standard Mileage Rate (Use this section only if you own the vehicle.)

22 Multiply line 13 by 29¢ (.29). Enter the result here and on line 1. (Rural mail carriers, see instructions.) ... 22

Section C.—Actual Expenses

			(a) Vehicle 1		(b) Vehicle 2	
23	Gasoline, oil, repairs, vehicle insurance, etc.	23				
24a	Vehicle rentals	24a				
b	Inclusion amount (see instructions)	24b				
c	Subtract line 24b from line 24a	24c				
25	Value of employer-provided vehicle (applies only if 100% of annual lease value was included on Form W-2—see instructions)	25				
26	Add lines 23, 24c, and 25	26				
27	Multiply line 26 by the percentage on line 14	27				
28	Depreciation. Enter amount from line 38 below	28				
29	Add lines 27 and 28. Enter total here and on line 1.	29				

Section D.—Depreciation of Vehicles (Use this section only if you own the vehicle.)

			(a) Vehicle 1		(b) Vehicle 2	
30	Enter cost or other basis (see instructions)	30				
31	Enter amount of section 179 deduction (see instructions)	31				
32	Multiply line 30 by line 14 (see instructions if you elected the section 179 deduction)	32				
33	Enter depreciation method and percentage (see instructions)	33				
34	Multiply line 32 by the percentage on line 33 (see instructions)	34				
35	Add lines 31 and 34	35				
36	Enter the limitation amount from the table in the line 36 instructions	36				
37	Multiply line 36 by the percentage on line 14	37				
38	Enter the **smaller** of line 35 or line 37. Also, enter this amount on line 28 above	38				

♲ *Printed on recycled paper*

Form **2119**

Department of the Treasury
Internal Revenue Service

Sale of Your Home

▶ **Attach to Form 1040 for year of sale.**

▶ **See separate instructions.** ▶ **Please print or type.**

OMB No. 1545-0072

1994

Attachment
Sequence No. **20**

Your first name and initial. If a joint return, also give spouse's name and initial. | Last name | **Your social security number**

Fill in Your Address Only If You Are Filing This Form by Itself and Not With Your Tax Return

Present address (no., street, and apt. no., rural route, or P.O. box no. if mail is not delivered to street address) | **Spouse's social security number**

City, town or post office, state, and ZIP code

Part I Gain on Sale

1	Date your former main home was sold (month, day, year) ▶	1	/ /
2	Have you bought or built a new main home?		☐ Yes ☐ No
3	If any part of either main home was ever rented out or used for business, check here ▶ ☐ and see instructions.		
4	Selling price of home. Do not include personal property items you sold with your home	4	
5	Expense of sale (see instructions)	5	
6	Subtract line 5 from line 4	6	
7	Adjusted basis of home sold (see instructions)	7	
8	**Gain on sale.** Subtract line 7 from line 6	8	

Is line 8 more than zero?

Yes ▶ If line 2 is "Yes," you **must** go to Part II or Part III, whichever applies. If line 2 is "No," go to line 9.

No ▶ **Stop** and attach this form to your return.

9 If you haven't replaced your home, do you plan to do so within the **replacement period** (see instructions)? ☐ Yes ☐ No
- If line 9 is "Yes," stop here, attach this form to your return, and see **Additional Filing Requirements** in the instructions.
- If line 9 is "No," you **must** go to Part II or Part III, whichever applies.

Part II One-Time Exclusion of Gain for People Age 55 or Older—By completing this part, you are electing to take the one-time exclusion (see instructions). If you are not electing to take the exclusion, go to Part III now.

10	Who was age 55 or older on the date of sale? ☐ You ☐ Your spouse ☐ Both of you		
11	Did the person who was age 55 or older own and use the property as his or her main home for a total of at least 3 years (except for short absences) of the 5-year period before the sale? If "No," go to Part III now		☐ Yes ☐ No
12	At the time of sale, who owned the home? ☐ You ☐ Your spouse ☐ Both of you		
13	Social security number of spouse at the time of sale if you had a different spouse from the one above. If you were not married at the time of sale, enter "None" ▶	13	
14	**Exclusion.** Enter the **smaller** of line 8 or $125,000 ($62,500 if married filing separate return). Then, go to line 15	14	

Part III Adjusted Sales Price, Taxable Gain, and Adjusted Basis of New Home

15	If line 14 is blank, enter the amount from line 8. Otherwise, subtract line 14 from line 8	15	

- If line 15 is zero, stop and attach this form to your return.
- If line 15 is more than zero and line 2 is "Yes," go to line 16 now.
- If you are reporting this sale on the installment method, stop and see the instructions.
- All others, stop and **enter the amount from line 15 on Schedule D, col. (g), line 4 or line 12.**

16	Fixing-up expenses (see instructions for time limits)	16	
17	If line 14 is blank, enter amount from line 16. Otherwise, add lines 14 and 16	17	
18	**Adjusted sales price.** Subtract line 17 from line 6	18	
19a	Date you moved into new home ▶ / / **b** Cost of new home (see instructions)	19b	
20	Subtract line 19b from line 18. If zero or less, enter -0-	20	
21	**Taxable gain.** Enter the **smaller** of line 15 or line 20	21	

- If line 21 is zero, go to line 22 and attach this form to your return.
- If you are reporting this sale on the installment method, see the line 15 instructions and go to line 22.
- All others, **enter the amount from line 21 on Schedule D, col. (g), line 4 or line 12,** and go to line 22.

22	**Postponed gain.** Subtract line 21 from line 15	22	
23	**Adjusted basis of new home.** Subtract line 22 from line 19b	23	

Sign Here Only If You Are Filing This Form by Itself and Not With Your Tax Return

Under penalties of perjury, I declare that I have examined this form, including attachments, and to the best of my knowledge and belief, it is true, correct, and complete.

Your signature | Date | Spouse's signature | Date

▶ _____ ▶ _____

If a joint return, both must sign.

For Paperwork Reduction Act Notice, see separate instructions. Cat. No. 11710J Form **2119** (1994)

♻ *Printed on recycled paper*

Form **2120**
(Rev. January 1994)

Department of the Treasury
Internal Revenue Service

Multiple Support Declaration

▶ **Attach to Form 1040 or Form 1040A of Person
Claiming the Dependent.**

OMB No. 1545-0071
Expires 1-31-97

Attachment
Sequence No. **50**

Name of person claiming the dependent

Social security number

During the calendar year 19 ...., I paid over 10% of the support of

----
Name of person

I could have claimed this person as a dependent except that I did not pay over 50% of his or her support. I understand that this person named above is being claimed as a dependent on the income tax return of

----
Name

Address

I agree not to claim this person as a dependent on my Federal income tax return for any tax year that began in this calendar year.

Your signature

Your social security number

Date

Address (number, street, apt. no.)

City, state, and ZIP code

Instructions

Paperwork Reduction Act Notice

We ask for the information on this form to carry out the Internal Revenue laws of the United States. You are required to give us the information. We need it to ensure that you are complying with these laws and to allow us to figure and collect the right amount of tax.

The time needed to complete and file this form will vary depending on individual circumstances. The estimated average time is: **Recordkeeping**, 7 minutes; **Learning about the law or the form**, 2 minutes; **Preparing the form**, 7 minutes; and **Copying, assembling, and sending the form to the IRS**, 10 minutes.

If you have comments concerning the accuracy of these time estimates or suggestions for making this form more simple, we would be happy to hear from you. You can write to both the IRS and the Office of Management and Budget at the addresses listed in the instructions of the tax return with which this form is filed.

Purpose of Form

When two or more individuals together pay over 50% of another person's support, Form 2120 or a similar statement is used to allow one of them to claim the person as a dependent for tax purposes.

The similar statement must contain the same information that is required by this form.

Who Can Claim the Dependent

To claim someone as a dependent, you must pay over 50% of that person's living expenses (support).

If no one meets this support test, but two or more of you together provide over 50% of a person's support, then one of you can claim that person as a dependent.

To claim the dependent, you must meet **all three** of the following requirements:

1. You paid over 10% of the support, and

2. All others who paid over 10% agree not to claim the person as a dependent, and

3. The other four dependency tests are met. See **Dependents** in the Form 1040 or Form 1040A instructions.

All contributors who provided over 10% support must choose which one of them will claim the dependent. If you will be claiming the dependent, see **How To File** below.

If you are a 10% contributor but **will not** be claiming the dependent, complete and sign a Form 2120 or similar statement. Give it to the person claiming the dependent.

How To File

If you are claiming the dependent, you must attach to your tax return a Form 2120 or similar statement that is completed and signed by each of the 10% contributors who are not claiming the dependent for the tax year. Be sure your name and social security number are at the top of each Form 2120 or similar statement.

Additional Information

See **Pub. 501,** Exemptions, Standard Deduction, and Filing Information, for more information.

Cat. No. 11712F

Form **2120** (Rev. 1-94)

Form 2210

Department of the Treasury
Internal Revenue Service

Underpayment of
Estimated Tax by Individuals, Estates, and Trusts
▶ See separate instructions.
▶ **Attach to Form 1040, Form 1040A, Form 1040NR, or Form 1041.**

OMB No. 1545-0140

1994

Attachment
Sequence No. **06**

Name(s) shown on tax return	Identifying number

Note: *In most cases, you* **do not** *need to file Form 2210. The IRS will figure any penalty you owe and send you a bill. File Form 2210* **only** *if one or more boxes in Part I apply to you. If you do not need to file Form 2210, you still may use it to figure your penalty. Enter the amount from line 20 or line 36 on the penalty line of your return, but do not attach Form 2210.*

Part I   **Reasons For Filing–** If 1a, b, or c below applies to you, you may be able to lower or eliminate your penalty. But you MUST check the boxes that apply and file Form 2210 with your tax return. If 1d below applies to you, check that box and file Form 2210 with your tax return.

1   Check whichever boxes apply (if none apply, see the **Note** above):

a ☐ You request a **waiver.** In certain circumstances, the IRS will waive all or part of the penalty. See **Waiver of Penalty** on page 1 of the instructions.

b ☐ You use the **annualized income installment method.** If your income varied during the year, this method may reduce the amount of one or more required installments. See page 4 of the instructions.

c ☐ You had Federal income tax withheld from wages and you treat it as paid for estimated tax purposes when it was **actually** withheld instead of in equal amounts on the payment due dates. See the instructions for line 22.

d ☐ Your required annual payment (line 13 below) is based on your 1993 tax and you filed or are filing a joint return for either 1993 or 1994 but not for both years.

Part II   **Required Annual Payment**

2	Enter your 1994 tax after credits (see instructions)	**2**
3	Other taxes (see instructions)	**3**
4	Add lines 2 and 3	**4**
5	Earned income credit **5**	
6	Credit for Federal tax paid on fuels **6**	
7	Add lines 5 and 6	**7**
8	Current year tax. Subtract line 7 from line 4	**8**
9	Multiply line 8 by 90% (.90) **9**	
10	Withholding taxes. **Do not** include any estimated tax payments on this line (see instructions) .	**10**
11	Subtract line 10 from line 8. If less than $500, stop here; **do not** complete or file this form. You do not owe the penalty	**11**
12	Enter the tax shown on your 1993 tax return (110% of that amount if the adjusted gross income shown on that return is more than $150,000, or if married filing separately for 1994, more than $75,000). **Caution:** *See instructions.*	**12**
13	**Required annual payment.** Enter the **smaller** of line 9 or line 12	**13**

Note: *If line 10 is equal to or more than line 13, stop here; you do not owe the penalty. Do not file Form 2210 unless you checked box 1d above.*

Part III   **Short Method (Caution:** *Read the instructions to see if you can use the short method. If you checked box* **1b** *or c in Part I, skip this part and go to Part IV.)*

14	Enter the amount, if any, from line 10 above **14**	
15	Enter the total amount, if any, of estimated tax payments you made **15**	
16	Add lines 14 and 15	**16**
17	**Total underpayment for year.** Subtract line 16 from line 13. If zero or less, stop here; you do not owe the penalty. Do not file Form 2210 unless you checked box 1d above	**17**
18	Multiply line 17 by .05725	**18**
19	● If the amount on line 17 was paid **on or after** 4/15/95, enter -0-. ● If the amount on line 17 was paid **before** 4/15/95, make the following computation to find the amount to enter on line 19. $$\begin{array}{ccc}\text{Amount on} & \text{Number of days paid} \\ \text{line 17} & \text{before 4/15/95}\end{array} \times \;\;\;\;\; \times \;\; .00025 \;\; . . . .$$	**19**
20	**PENALTY.** Subtract line 19 from line 18. Enter the result here and on Form 1040, line 65; Form 1040A, line 33; Form 1040NR, line 66; or Form 1041, line 26 . . . . ▶	**20**

For Paperwork Reduction Act Notice, see page 1 of separate instructions.   Cat. No. 11744P   Form **2210** (1994)

Form 2210 (1994)

| **Part IV** | Regular Method (See the instructions if you are filing Form 1040NR.) |

Section A—Figure Your Underpayment

		Payment Due Dates			
		(a) 4/15/94	**(b)** 6/15/94	**(c)** 9/15/94	**(d)** 1/15/95
21	Required installments. If box 1b applies, enter the amounts from Schedule AI, line 26. Otherwise, enter ¼ of line 13, Form 2210, in each column **21**				
22	Estimated tax paid and tax withheld (see instructions). For column (a) only, also enter the amount from line 22 on line 26. If line 22 is equal to or more than line 21 for all payment periods, stop here; you do not owe the penalty. Do not file Form 2210 unless you checked a box in Part I **22**				
	Complete lines 23 through 29 of one column before going to the next column.				
23	Enter amount, if any, from line 29 of previous column **23**				
24	Add lines 22 and 23 . . . . **24**				
25	Add amounts on lines 27 and 28 of the previous column **25**				
26	Subtract line 25 from line 24. If zero or less, enter -0-. For column (a) only, enter the amount from line 22 **26**				
27	If the amount on line 26 is zero, subtract line 24 from line 25. Otherwise, enter -0- **27**				
28	Underpayment. If line 21 is equal to or more than line 26, subtract line 26 from line 21. Then go to line 23 of next column. Otherwise, go to line 29 . . ▶ **28**				
29	Overpayment. If line 26 is more than line 21, subtract line 21 from line 26. Then go to line 23 of next column **29**				

Section B—Figure the Penalty (Complete lines 30 through 35 of one column before going to the next column.)

Rate Period 1	**April 16, 1994—June 30, 1994**	4/15/94	6/15/94		
	30 Number of days FROM the date shown above line 30 TO the date the amount on line 28 was paid **or** 6/30/94, whichever is earlier **30**	*Days:*	*Days:*		
	31 $\frac{\text{Underpayment on line 28 (see instructions)}} \times \frac{\text{Number of days on line 30}}{365} \times .07$ ▶ **31**	$	$		
Rate Period 2	**July 1, 1994—September 30, 1994**	6/30/94	6/30/94	9/15/94	
	32 Number of days FROM the date shown above line 32 TO the date the amount on line 28 was paid **or** 9/30/94, whichever is earlier **32**	*Days:*	*Days:*	*Days:*	
	33 $\frac{\text{Underpayment on line 28 (see instructions)}} \times \frac{\text{Number of days on line 32}}{365} \times .08$ ▶ **33**	$	$	$	
Rate Period 3	**October 1, 1994—April 15, 1995**	9/30/94	9/30/94	9/30/94	1/15/95
	34 Number of days FROM the date shown above line 34 TO the date the amount on line 28 was paid **or** 4/15/95, whichever is earlier **34**	*Days:*	*Days:*	*Days:*	*Days:*
	35 $\frac{\text{Underpayment on line 28 (see instructions)}} \times \frac{\text{Number of days on line 34}}{365} \times .09$ ▶ **35**	$	$	$	$

| 36 | PENALTY. Add all amounts on lines 31, 33, and 35 in all columns. Enter the total here and on Form 1040, line 65; Form 1040A, line 33; Form 1040NR, line 66; or Form 1041, line 26. . . . . . . ▶ **36** | $ |

Schedule AI—Annualized Income Installment Method (see instructions)

Estates and trusts, **do not** use the period ending dates shown to the right. Instead, use the following: 2/28/94, 4/30/94, 7/31/94, and 11/30/94.

		(a) 1/1/94–3/31/94	(b) 1/1/94–5/31/94	(c) 1/1/94–8/31/94	(d) 1/1/94–12/31/94

Part I   Annualized Income Installments   Caution: *Complete lines 20–26 of one column before going to the next column.*

		(a)	(b)	(c)	(d)
1	Enter your adjusted gross income for each period (see instructions). (Estates and trusts, enter your taxable income without your exemption for each period.)				
2	Annualization amounts. (Estates and trusts, see instructions.)	4	2.4	1.5	1
3	Annualized income. Multiply line 1 by line 2				
4	Enter your itemized deductions for the period shown in each column. If you do not itemize, enter -0- and skip to line 7. (Estates and trusts, enter -0-, skip to line 9, and enter the amount from line 3 on line 9.)				
5	Annualization amounts	4	2.4	1.5	1
6	Multiply line 4 by line 5 (see instructions if line 3 is more than $55,900)				
7	In each column, enter the full amount of your standard deduction from Form 1040, line 34; or Form 1040A, line 19 (Form 1040NR filers, enter -0-. **Exception:** Indian students and business apprentices, enter standard deduction from Form 1040NR, line 33.)				
8	Enter line 6 or line 7, whichever is **larger**				
9	Subtract line 8 from line 3				
10	In each column, multiply $2,450 by the total number of exemptions claimed (see instructions if line 3 is more than $83,850). (Estates and trusts and Form 1040NR filers, enter the exemption amount shown on your tax return.)				
11	Subtract line 10 from line 9				
12	Figure your tax on the amount on line 11 (see instructions)				
13	Form 1040 filers only, enter your self-employment tax from line 35 below				
14	Enter other taxes for each payment period (see instructions)				
15	Total tax. Add lines 12, 13, and 14				
16	For each period, enter the same type of credits as allowed on Form 2210, lines 2, 5, and 6 (see instructions)				
17	Subtract line 16 from line 15. If zero or less, enter -0-				
18	Applicable percentage	22.5%	45%	67.5%	90%
19	Multiply line 17 by line 18				
20	Add the amounts in all preceding columns of line 26				
21	Subtract line 20 from line 19. If zero or less, enter -0-				
22	Enter ¼ of line 13, Form 2210, in each column				
23	Enter amount from line 25 of the preceding column of this schedule				
24	Add lines 22 and 23 and enter the total				
25	Subtract line 21 from line 24. If zero or less, enter -0-				
26	Enter the **smaller** of line 21 or line 24 here and on Form 2210, line 21 ▶				

Part II   Annualized Self-Employment Tax

		(a)	(b)	(c)	(d)
27a	Net earnings from self-employment for the period (see instructions)				
b	Annualization amounts	4	2.4	1.5	1
c	Multiply line 27a by line 27b				
28	Social security tax limit	$60,600	$60,600	$60,600	$60,600
29	Enter actual wages subject to social security tax or the 6.2% portion of the 7.65% railroad retirement (tier 1) tax				
30	Annualization amounts	4	2.4	1.5	1
31	Multiply line 29 by line 30				
32	Subtract line 31 from line 28. If zero or less, enter -0-				
33	Multiply the smaller of line 27c or line 32 by .124				
34	Multiply line 27c by .029				
35	Add lines 33 and 34. Enter the result here and on line 13 above ▶				

Form **2441**	**Child and Dependent Care Expenses**	OMB No. 1545-0068
Department of the Treasury Internal Revenue Service (T)	▶ **Attach to Form 1040.** ▶ **See separate instructions.**	**19 94** Attachment Sequence No. **21**

Name(s) shown on Form 1040	Your social security number

You need to understand the following terms to complete this form: **Qualifying Person(s), Dependent Care Benefits, Qualified Expenses,** and **Earned Income.** See **Important Terms** on page 1 of the Form 2441 instructions.

Part I **Persons or Organizations Who Provided the Care—**You **must** complete this part. (If you need more space, use the bottom of page 2.)

1	**(a)** Care provider's name	**(b)** Address (number, street, apt. no., city, state, and ZIP code)	**(c)** Identifying number (SSN or EIN)	**(d)** Amount paid (see instructions)

2 Add the amounts in column (d) of line 1 . . . .   **2**

3 Enter the number of **qualifying persons** cared for in 1994 . . . . ▶ [ ]

Did you receive **dependent care benefits?**	**NO** ──────▶ Complete only Part II below.
	YES ─────▶ Complete Part III on the back now.

Part II **Credit for Child and Dependent Care Expenses**

4 Enter the amount of **qualified expenses** you incurred and paid in 1994. DO NOT enter more than $2,400 for one qualifying person or $4,800 for two or more persons. If you completed Part III, enter the amount from line 25 . . . .   **4**

5 Enter YOUR **earned income** **5**

6 If married filing a joint return, enter YOUR SPOUSE'S earned income (if student or disabled, see the instructions); **all others,** enter the amount from line 5 . . . .   **6**

7 Enter the **smallest** of line 4, 5, or 6 . . . .   **7**

8 Enter the amount from Form 1040, line 32 . . . .   **8**

9 Enter on line 9 the decimal amount shown below that applies to the amount on line 8

If line 8 is—		Decimal amount is		If line 8 is—		Decimal amount is
Over	But not over			Over	But not over	
$0	10,000	.30		$20,000	22,000	.24
10,000	12,000	.29		22,000	24,000	.23
12,000	14,000	.28		24,000	26,000	.22
14,000	16,000	.27		26,000	28,000	.21
16,000	18,000	.26		28,000	No limit	.20
18,000	20,000	.25				

9   × .

10 Multiply **line 7** by the decimal amount on line 9. Enter the result. Then, see the instructions for the amount of credit to enter on Form 1040, line 41 . . . .   **10**

Caution: *If you paid $50 or more in a calendar quarter to a person who worked in your home, you must file an employment tax return. Get **Form 942** for details.*

For Paperwork Reduction Act Notice, see separate instructions.   Cat. No. 11862M   Form **2441** (1994)

Part III Dependent Care Benefits—Complete this part **only** if you received these benefits.

11 Enter the total amount of **dependent care benefits** you received for 1994. This amount should be shown in box 10 of your W-2 form(s). DO NOT include amounts that were reported to you as wages in box 1 of Form(s) W-2 . . . . **11**

12 Enter the amount forfeited, if any. See the instructions **12**

13 Subtract line 12 from line 11 . . . . **13**

14 Enter the total amount of **qualified expenses** incurred in 1994 for the care of the qualifying person(s) **14**

15 Enter the **smaller** of line 13 or 14 . . . . **15**

16 Enter YOUR **earned income** **16**

17 If married filing a joint return, enter YOUR SPOUSE'S earned income (if student or disabled, see the line 6 instructions); if married filing a separate return, see the instructions for the amount to enter; **all others,** enter the amount from line 16 . . **17**

18 Enter the **smallest** of line 15, 16, or 17 . . . . **18**

19 **Excluded benefits.** Enter here the **smaller** of the following:

- The amount from line 18, or
- $5,000 ($2,500 if married filing a separate return **and** you were required to enter your spouse's earned income on line 17). **19**

20 **Taxable benefits.** Subtract line 19 from line 13. Also, include this amount on Form 1040, line 7. On the dotted line next to line 7, write "DCB" **20**

To claim the child and dependent care credit, complete
lines 21—25 below, and lines 4—10 on the front of this form.

21 Enter the amount of qualified expenses you incurred and paid in 1994. DO NOT include on this line any excluded benefits shown on line 19 . . . . **21**

22 Enter $2,400 ($4,800 if two or more qualifying persons) . . . **22**

23 Enter the amount from line 19 . . . . **23**

24 Subtract line 23 from line 22. If zero or less, **STOP**. You cannot take the credit. **Exception.** If you paid 1993 expenses in 1994, see the line 10 instructions **24**

25 Enter the **smaller** of line 21 or 24 here **and** on line 4 on the front of this form **25**

Printed on recycled paper

Form **2555**

Department of the Treasury
Internal Revenue Service

Foreign Earned Income

▶ See separate instructions.   ▶ Attach to front of Form 1040.

OMB No. 1545-0067

19**94**

Attachment
Sequence No. **34**

For Use by U.S. Citizens and Resident Aliens Only

Name shown on Form 1040	Your social security number

Part I   **General Information**

1 Your foreign address (including country) | **2** Your occupation

3 Employer's name ▶ ....

4a Employer's U.S. address ▶ ....

b Employer's foreign address ▶ ....

5 Employer is (check
any that apply):   ▶   **a** ☐ A foreign entity   **b** ☐ A U.S. company   **c** ☐ Self
                              d ☐ A foreign affiliate of a U.S. company   **e** ☐ Other (specify) ▶ ....

6a If, after 1981, you filed Form 2555 to claim either of the exclusions or Form 2555-EZ to claim the foreign earned income exclusion, enter the last year you filed the form. ▶ ....

b If you did not file Form 2555 or 2555-EZ after 1981 to claim either of the exclusions, check here ▶ ☐ and go to line 7 now.

c Have you ever revoked either of the exclusions? . . . .   ☐ Yes ☐ No

d If you answered "Yes," enter the type of exclusion and the tax year for which the revocation was effective. ▶ ....

7 Of what country are you a citizen/national? ▶ ....

8a Did you maintain a separate foreign residence for your family because of adverse living conditions at your tax home? See **Second foreign household** on page 3 of the instructions . . . .   ☐ Yes ☐ No

b If "Yes," enter city and country of the separate foreign residence. Also, enter the number of days during your tax year that you maintained a second household at that address. ▶ ....

9 List your tax home(s) during your tax year and date(s) established. ▶ ....

Next, complete either Part II or Part III. If an item does not apply, write "NA." If you do not give the information asked for, any exclusion or deduction you claim may be disallowed.

Part II   **Taxpayers Qualifying Under Bona Fide Residence Test** (See page 2 of the instructions.)

10 Date bona fide residence began ▶ ...., and ended ▶ ....

11 Kind of living quarters in foreign country ▶ **a** ☐ Purchased house **b** ☐ Rented house or apartment **c** ☐ Rented room
                              d ☐ Quarters furnished by employer

12a Did any of your family live with you abroad during any part of the tax year?. . . . .   ☐ Yes ☐ No

b If "Yes," who and for what period? ▶ ....

13a Have you submitted a statement to the authorities of the foreign country where you claim bona fide residence that you are not a resident of that country? (See instructions.) . . . .   ☐ Yes ☐ No

b Are you required to pay income tax to the country where you claim bona fide residence? (See instructions.)   ☐ Yes ☐ No

If you answered "Yes" to 13a and "No" to 13b, you do not qualify as a bona fide resident. Do not complete the rest of this part.

14 If you were present in the United States or its possessions during the tax year, complete columns **(a)-(d)** below. **Do not** include the income from column **(d)** in Part IV, but report it on Form 1040.

(a) Date arrived in U.S.	(b) Date left U.S.	(c) Number of days in U.S. on business	(d) Income earned in U.S. on business (attach computation)	(a) Date arrived in U.S.	(b) Date left U.S.	(c) Number of days in U.S. on business	(d) Income earned in U.S. on business (attach computation)

15a List any contractual terms or other conditions relating to the length of your employment abroad. ▶ ....

b Enter the type of visa under which you entered the foreign country. ▶ ....

c Did your visa limit the length of your stay or employment in a foreign country? If "Yes," attach explanation   ☐ Yes ☐ No

d Did you maintain a home in the United States while living abroad?. . . . .   ☐ Yes ☐ No

e If "Yes," enter address of your home, whether it was rented, the names of the occupants, and their relationship to you. ▶ ....

For Paperwork Reduction Act Notice, see page 1 of separate instructions.   Cat. No. 11900P   Form **2555** (1994)

Part III   **Taxpayers Qualifying Under Physical Presence Test** (See page 2 of the instructions.)

16   The physical presence test is based on the 12-month period from ▶ .... through ▶ ....

17   Enter your principal country of employment during your tax year. ▶ ....

18   If you traveled abroad during the 12-month period entered on line 16, complete columns **(a)–(f)** below. Exclude travel between foreign countries that did not involve travel on or over international waters, or in or over the United States, for 24 hours or more. If you have no travel to report during the period, enter "Physically present in a foreign country or countries for the entire 12-month period." **Do not** include the income from column **(f)** below in Part IV, but report it on Form 1040.

(a) Name of country (including U.S.)	**(b)** Date arrived	**(c)** Date left	**(d)** Full days present in country	**(e)** Number of days in U.S. on business	**(f)** Income earned in U.S. on business (attach computation)

Part IV   **All Taxpayers**

Note: *Enter on lines 19 through 23 all income, including noncash income, you earned and actually or constructively received during your 1994 tax year for services you performed in a foreign country. If any of the foreign earned income received this tax year was earned in a prior tax year, or will be earned in a later tax year (such as a bonus), see the instructions. **Do not** include income from line 14, column **(d),** or line 18, column **(f).** Report amounts in U.S. dollars, using the exchange rates in effect when you actually or constructively received the income.*

If you are a cash basis taxpayer, report on Form 1040 all income you received in 1994, no matter when you performed the service.

1994 Foreign Earned Income		Amount (in U.S. dollars)
19 Total wages, salaries, bonuses, commissions, etc..	**19**	
20 Allowable share of income for personal services performed (see instructions):		
a In a business (including farming) or profession	**20a**	
b In a partnership. List partnership's name and address and type of income. ▶	**20b**	
21 Noncash income (market value of property or facilities furnished by employer—attach statement showing how it was determined):		
a Home (lodging)	**21a**	
b Meals	**21b**	
c Car	**21c**	
d Other property or facilities. List type and amount. ▶	**21d**	
22 Allowances, reimbursements, or expenses paid on your behalf for services you performed:		
a Cost of living and overseas differential **22a**		
b Family **22b**		
c Education **22c**		
d Home leave **22d**		
e Quarters. **22e**		
f For any other purpose. List type and amount. ▶ **22f**		
g Add lines 22a through 22f	**22g**	
23 Other foreign earned income. List type and amount. ▶	**23**	
24 Add lines 19 through 21d, line 22g, and line 23	**24**	
25 Total amount of meals and lodging included on line 24 that is excludable (see instructions) . .	**25**	
26 Subtract line 25 from line 24. Enter the result here and on line 27 on page 3. This is your **foreign earned income** . . . . ▶	**26**	

Form 2555 (1994)   Page **3**

Part V   **All Taxpayers**

27	Enter the amount from line 26	**27**

- If you choose to claim the housing exclusion or are claiming the housing deduction, complete Part VI.
- All others, go to Part VII.

Part VI   **For Taxpayers Claiming the Housing Exclusion AND/OR Deduction**

28   Qualified housing expenses for the tax year (see instructions) **28**

29   Number of days in your qualifying period that fall within your 1994 tax year (see instructions) **29**

30   Multiply $24.82 by the number of days on line 29. If 365 entered on line 29, enter $9,060.00 here .   **30**

31   Subtract line 30 from line 28. If zero or less, do not complete the rest of this part or any of Part IX **31**

32   Enter employer-provided amounts (see instructions) **32**

33   Divide line 32 by line 27. Enter the result as a decimal (to two places), but do not enter more than "1.00" . . . .   **33**   × .

34   **Housing exclusion.** Multiply line 31 by line 33. Enter the result but do not enter more than the amount on line 32. Also, complete Part VIII . . . . ▶   **34**

    Note: *The housing deduction is figured in Part IX. If you choose to claim the foreign earned income exclusion, complete Parts VII and VIII before Part IX.*

Part VII   **For Taxpayers Claiming the Foreign Earned Income Exclusion**

35   Maximum foreign earned income exclusion . . . .   **35** $70,000 | 00

36
- If you completed Part VI, enter the number from line 29.
- All others, enter the number of days in your qualifying period that fall within your 1994 tax year (see the instructions for line 29).   **36**

37
- If line 36 and the number of days in your 1994 tax year (usually 365) are the same, enter "1.00."
- Otherwise, divide line 36 by the number of days in your 1994 tax year and enter the result as a decimal (to two places).   **37**   × .

38   Multiply line 35 by line 37 . . . .   **38**

39   Subtract line 34 from line 27 . . . .   **39**

40   **Foreign earned income exclusion.** Enter the **smaller** of line 38 or line 39. Also, complete Part VIII ▶   **40**

Part VIII   **For Taxpayers Claiming the Housing Exclusion, Foreign Earned Income Exclusion, or Both**

41   Add lines 34 and 40 . . . .   **41**

42   Deductions allowed in figuring your adjusted gross income (Form 1040, line 31) that are allocable to the excluded income. See instructions and attach computation **42**

43   Subtract line 42 from line 41. Enter the result here and in parentheses on Form 1040, line 21. Next to the amount write "Form 2555." On Form 1040, subtract this amount from your income to arrive at total income on Form 1040, line 22 . . . . ▶   **43**

Part IX   **For Taxpayers Claiming the Housing Deduction**—Complete this part only if (a) line 31 is more than line 34 and (b) line 27 is more than line 41.

44   Subtract line 34 from line 31 . . . .   **44**

45   Subtract line 41 from line 27 . . . .   **45**

46   Enter the **smaller** of line 44 or line 45 . . . .   **46**

    Note: *If line 45 is more than line 46 and you couldn't deduct all of your 1993 housing deduction because of the 1993 limit, use the worksheet on page 4 of the instructions to figure the amount to enter on line 47. Otherwise, go to line 48.*

47   Housing deduction carryover from 1993 (from worksheet on page 4 of the instructions) . . .   **47**

48   **Housing deduction.** Add lines 46 and 47. Enter the total here and on Form 1040 to the left of line 30. Next to the amount on Form 1040, write "Form 2555." Add it to the total adjustments reported on that line . . . . ▶   **48**

     ♻   *Printed on recycled paper*

Form **2848**
(Rev. February 1993)

Department of the Treasury
Internal Revenue Service

Power of Attorney
and Declaration of Representative

▶ **For Paperwork Reduction and Privacy Act Notice, see the instructions.**

OMB No. 1545-0150

Expires 2-29-96

Part I **Power of Attorney** (Please type or print.)

1 Taxpayer Information (Taxpayer(s) must sign and date this form on page 2, line 9.)

Taxpayer name(s) and address	Social security number(s)	Employer identification number
		Plan number (if applicable)
	Daytime telephone number ( )	

hereby appoint(s) the following representative(s) as attorney(s)-in-fact:

2 Representative(s) (Representative(s) must sign and date this form on page 2, Part II.)

Name and address	CAF No. .... Telephone No. ( ) .... Fax No. ( ) .... Check if new: Address ☐ Telephone No. ☐
Name and address	CAF No. .... Telephone No. ( ) .... Fax No. ( ) .... Check if new: Address ☐ Telephone No. ☐
Name and address	CAF No. .... Telephone No. ( ) .... Fax No. ( ) .... Check if new: Address ☐ Telephone No. ☐

to represent the taxpayer(s) before the Internal Revenue Service for the following tax matters:

3 Tax Matters

Type of Tax (Income, Employment, Excise, etc.)	Tax Form Number (1040, 941, 720, etc.)	Year(s) or Period(s)

4 Specific Use Not Recorded on Centralized Authorization File (CAF).— If the power of attorney is for a specific use not recorded on CAF, please check this box. (See **Line 4—Specific Uses Not Recorded on CAF** on page 3.). . . . . ▶ ☐

5 Acts Authorized.—The representatives are authorized to receive and inspect confidential tax information and to perform any and all acts that I (we) can perform with respect to the tax matters described in line 3, for example, the authority to sign any agreements, consents, or other documents. The authority does not include the power to receive refund checks (see line 6 below) or the power to sign certain returns (see **Line 5—Acts Authorized** on page 4).
List any specific additions or deletions to the acts otherwise authorized in this power of attorney: ....
....
....

Note: *In general, an unenrolled preparer of tax returns cannot sign any document for a taxpayer. See Revenue Procedure 81-38, printed as Pub. 470, for more information.*

Note: *The tax matters partner/person of a partnership or S corporation is not permitted to authorize representatives to perform certain acts. See the instructions for more information.*

6 Receipt of Refund Checks.—If you want to authorize a representative named in line 2 to receive, **BUT NOT TO ENDORSE OR CASH**, refund checks, initial here _____ and list the name of that representative below.

Name of representative to receive refund check(s) ▶

Form 2848 (Rev. 2-93)   Page **2**

7 **Notices and Communications.**—Notices and other written communications will be sent to the first representative listed in line 2.

  a If you also want the second representative listed to receive such notices and communications, check this box . . . ▶ ☐

  b If you do not want any notices or communications sent to your representative, check this box . . . . ▶ ☐

8 **Retention/Revocation of Prior Power(s) of Attorney.**—The filing of this power of attorney automatically revokes all earlier power(s) of attorney on file with the Internal Revenue Service for the same tax matters and years or periods covered by this document. If you do not want to revoke a prior power of attorney, check here . . . . ▶ ☐
    YOU MUST ATTACH A COPY OF ANY POWER OF ATTORNEY YOU WANT TO REMAIN IN EFFECT.

9 **Signature of Taxpayer(s).**—If a tax matter concerns a joint return, **both** husband and wife must sign if joint representation is requested, otherwise, see the instructions. If signed by a corporate officer, partner, guardian, tax matters partner/person, executor, receiver, administrator, or trustee on behalf of the taxpayer, I certify that I have the authority to execute this form on behalf of the taxpayer.

  ▶ **IF THIS POWER OF ATTORNEY IS NOT SIGNED AND DATED, IT WILL BE RETURNED.**

Signature	Date	Title (if applicable)

Print Name		

Signature	Date	Title (if applicable)

Print Name		

Part II   Declaration of Representative

Under penalties of perjury, I declare that:

- I am not currently under suspension or disbarment from practice before the Internal Revenue Service;
- I am aware of regulations contained in Treasury Department Circular No. 230 (31 CFR, Part 10), as amended, concerning the practice of attorneys, certified public accountants, enrolled agents, enrolled actuaries, and others;
- I am authorized to represent the taxpayer(s) identified in Part I for the tax matter(s) specified there; and
- I am one of the following:
  - **a** Attorney—a member in good standing of the bar of the highest court of the jurisdiction shown below.
  - **b** Certified Public Accountant—duly qualified to practice as a certified public accountant in the jurisdiction shown below.
  - **c** Enrolled Agent—enrolled as an agent under the requirements of Treasury Department Circular No. 230.
  - **d** Officer—a bona fide officer of the taxpayer organization.
  - **e** Full-Time Employee—a full-time employee of the taxpayer.
  - **f** Family Member—a member of the taxpayer's immediate family (i.e., spouse, parent, child, brother, or sister).
  - **g** Enrolled Actuary—enrolled as an actuary by the Joint Board for the Enrollment of Actuaries under 29 U.S.C. 1242 (the authority to practice before the Service is limited by section 10.3(d)(1) of Treasury Department Circular No. 230).
  - **h** Unenrolled Return Preparer—an unenrolled return preparer under section 10.7(a)(7) of Treasury Department Circular No. 230.

▶ **If this declaration of representative is not signed and dated, the power of attorney will be returned.**

Designation —Insert above letter **(a–h)**	Jurisdiction (state) or Enrollment Card No.	Signature	Date

Form **3800** Department of the Treasury Internal Revenue Service	**General Business Credit** ▶ Attach to your tax return. ▶ See separate instructions.	OMB No. 1545±0895 19**94** Attachment Sequence No. **22**

Name(s) shown on return | Identifying number

Part I Tentative Credit

1a	Current year investment credit (Form 3468, Part I)	**1a**	
b	Current year jobs credit (Form 5884, Part I)	**1b**	
c	Current year credit for alcohol used as fuel (Form 6478)	**1c**	
d	Current year credit for increasing research activities (Form 6765, Part III)	**1d**	
e	Current year low-income housing credit (Form 8586, Part I)	**1e**	
f	Current year enhanced oil recovery credit (Form 8830, Part I)	**1f**	
g	Current year disabled access credit (Form 8826, Part I)	**1g**	
h	Current year renewable electricity production credit (Form 8835, Part I)	**1h**	
i	Current year Indian employment credit (Form 8845, Part I)	**1i**	
j	Current year credit for employer social security and Medicare taxes paid on certain employee tips (Form 8846, Part I)	**1j**	
k	Current year credit for contributions to selected community development corporations (Form 8847, Part I)	**1k**	
l	**Current year general business credit.** Add lines 1a through 1k	**1l**	
2	Passive activity credits included on lines 1a through 1k (see instructions)	**2**	
3	Subtract line 2 from line 1l	**3**	
4	Passive activity credits allowed for 1994 (see instructions)	**4**	
5	Carryforward of general business, WIN, or ESOP credit to 1994 (see instructions for the schedule to attach)	**5**	
6	Carryback of general business credit to 1994 (see instructions)	**6**	
7	**Tentative general business credit.** Add lines 3 through 6	**7**	

Part II General Business Credit Limitation Based on Amount of Tax

8a	Individuals. Enter amount from Form 1040, line 40			
b	Corporations. Enter amount from Form 1120, Schedule J, line 3 (or Form 1120-A, Part I, line 1)	}	**8**	
c	Other filers. Enter regular tax before credits from your return (see instructions). . .			
9	Credits that reduce regular tax before the general business credit:			
a	Credit for child and dependent care expenses (Form 2441, line 10)	**9a**		
b	Credit for the elderly or the disabled (Schedule R (Form 1040), line 21)	**9b**		
c	Mortgage interest credit (Form 8396, line 11)	**9c**		
d	Foreign tax credit (Form 1116, line 32, or Form 1118, Sch. B, line 12) .	**9d**		
e	Possessions tax credit (Form 5735)	**9e**		
f	Orphan drug credit (Form 6765, line 10)	**9f**		
g	Credit for fuel from a nonconventional source	**9g**		
h	Qualified electric vehicle credit (Form 8834, line 19) . . .	**9h**		
i	Add lines 9a through 9h		**9i**	
10	Net regular tax. Subtract line 9i from line 8		**10**	
11	Tentative minimum tax (see instructions):			
a	Individuals. Enter amount from Form 6251, line 26			
b	Corporations. Enter amount from Form 4626, line 13	}	**11**	
c	Estates and trusts. Enter amount from Form 1041, Schedule H, line 37			
12	Net income tax:			
a	Individuals. Add line 10 above and line 28 of Form 6251			
b	Corporations. Add line 10 above and line 15 of Form 4626 . . .	}	**12**	
c	Estates and trusts. Add line 10 above and line 39 of Form 1041, Schedule H			
13	If line 10 is more than $25,000, enter 25% (.25) of the excess (see instructions) . . .		**13**	
14	Subtract line 11 or line 13, whichever is greater, from line 12. If less than zero, enter -0- .		**14**	
15	**General business credit allowed for current year.** Enter the **smaller** of line 7 or line 14. Enter here and on Form 1040, line 44; Form 1120, Schedule J, line 4e; Form 1120-A, Part I, line 2a; or the appropriate line of your tax return. (Individuals, estates, and trusts, see instructions if the credit for increasing research activities is claimed. C corporations, see instructions for Schedule A if any regular investment credit carryforward is claimed. See the instructions if the corporation has undergone a post-1986 "ownership change.")		**15**	

For Paperwork Reduction Act Notice, see page 2 of this form.   Cat. No. 12392F   Form **3800** (1994)

Schedule A— **Additional General Business Credit Allowed By Section 38(c)(2) (Before Repeal by the Revenue Reconciliation Act of 1990)—Only Applicable to C Corporations**

16	Enter the portion of the credit shown on line 5, page 1, that is attributable to the regular investment credit under section 46 (before amendment by the Revenue Reconciliation Act of 1990) . . .	**16**	
17	Tentative minimum tax (from line 11, page 1)	**17**	
18	Multiply line 17 by 25% (.25)	**18**	
19	Enter the amount from line 14, page 1.	**19**	
20	Enter the portion of the credit shown on line 7, page 1, that is NOT attributable to the regular investment credit under section 46 (before amendment by the Revenue Reconciliation Act of 1990).	**20**	
21	Subtract line 20 from line 19 (if less than zero, enter -0-)	**21**	
22	Subtract line 21 from line 16 (if less than zero, enter -0-)	**22**	
23	For purposes of this line only, refigure the amount on line 11, Form 4626, by using zero on line 6, Form 4626, and enter the result here .	**23**	
24	Multiply line 23 by 10% (.10)	**24**	
25	Net income tax (from line 12, page 1)	**25**	
26	General business credit (from line 15, page 1)	**26**	
27	Subtract line 26 from line 25	**27**	
28	Subtract line 24 from line 27	**28**	
29	Enter the smallest of line 18, line 22, or line 28	**29**	
30	Subtract line 29 from line 17	**30**	
31	Enter the greater of line 30 or line 13, page 1	**31**	
32	Subtract line 31 from line 25	**32**	
33	Enter the smaller of line 32 or line 10, page 1. Enter this amount also on line 15, page 1, instead of the amount previously figured on that line. Write "Sec. 38(c)(2)" in the margin next to your entry on line 15, page 1	**33**	
34	If line 32 is greater than line 33, enter the excess here (see instructions)	**34**	

Paperwork Reduction Act Notice

We ask for the information on this form to carry out the Internal Revenue laws of the United States. You are required to give us the information. We need it to ensure that you are complying with these laws and to allow us to figure and collect the right amount of tax.

The time needed to complete and file this form will vary depending on individual circumstances. The estimated average time is:

Recordkeeping . . . .11 hr., 43 min.

Learning about the law or the form . . . . 1 hr.

Preparing and sending the form to the IRS . 1 hr., 14 min.

If you have comments concerning the accuracy of these time estimates or suggestions for making this form simpler, we would be happy to hear from you. You can write to both the IRS and the Office of Management and Budget at the addresses listed in the instructions for the tax return with which this form is filed.

✸ *Printed on recycled paper*

Form 3903

Department of the Treasury
Internal Revenue Service

Moving Expenses

▶ **Attach to Form 1040.**

▶ **See separate instructions.**

OMB No. 1545-0062

1994

Attachment
Sequence No. **62**

Name(s) shown on Form 1040

Your social security number

Part I **Moving Expenses Incurred in 1994**

Caution: *If you are a member of the armed forces, see the instructions before completing this part.*

1 Enter the number of miles from your **old home** to your **new workplace** . | **1** | miles

2 Enter the number of miles from your **old home** to your **old workplace** . . | **2** | miles

3 Subtract line 2 from line 1. Enter the result but not less than zero . . . | **3** | miles

Is line 3 at least 50 miles?

Yes ▶   Go to line 4. Also **see Time Test** in the in the instructions.

No ▶   You **cannot** deduct your moving expenses incurred in 1994. Do not compete the rest of this part. See the **Note** below if you also incurred moving expenses before 1994.

4 Transportation and storage of household goods and personal effects . . . . | **4** |

5 Travel and lodging expenses of moving from your old home to your new home. **Do not** include meals | **5** |

6 Add lines 4 and 5 . . . . | **6** |

7 Enter the total amount your employer paid for your move (including the value of services furnished in kind) that is **not** included in the wages box (box 1) of your W-2 form. This amount should be identified with code **P** in box 13 of your W-2 form . . . . | **7** |

Is line 6 more than line 7?

Yes ▶   Go to line 8.

No ▶   You **cannot** deduct your moving expenses incurred in 1994. If line 6 is less than line 7, subtract line 6 from line 7 and include the result in income on form 1040, line 7.

8 Subtract line 7 from line 6. Enter the result here and on Form 1040, line 24. This is your **moving expense deduction for expenses incurred in 1994** . . . . | **8** |

Note: *If you incurred moving expenses **before 1994** and you did not deduct those expenses on a prior year's tax return, complete Parts II and III on the back to figure the amount, if any, you may deduct on **Schedule A,** Itemized Deductions.*

For Paperwork Reduction Act Notice, see separate instructions.   Cat. No. 12490K   Form **3903** (1994)

Form 3903 (1994)   Attachment Sequence No. **62**   page **2**

Name(s) shown on Form 1040. Do not enter name and social security number if shown on other side.	**Your social security number**

Caution: If you are a member of the armed forces, see the instructions before completing Parts II and III.

Part II Moving Expenses Incurred Before 1994

1	Enter the number of miles from your **old home** to your **new workplace**	**1**		miles
2	Enter the number of miles from your **old home** to your **old workplace**	**2**		miles
3	Subtract line 2 from line 1. Enter the result but not less than zero . . . . ▶	**3**		miles

If line 3 is 35 or more miles, complete the rest of this part and Part III. Also, see **Time Test** in the instructions. If line 3 is less than 35 miles, you **cannot** deduct your moving expenses incurred before 1994.

Note: *Any payments your employer made for your moving expenses incurred before 1994 (including the value of any services furnished in kind) should be included as wages on your W-2 form. Report that amount on* **Form 1040, line 7.**

Section A—Transportation of Household Goods

| **4** | Transportation and storage of household goods and personal effects. . . . . | **4** | |

Section B—Expenses of Moving From Old To New Home

5	Travel and lodging **not** including meals	**5**	
6	Total meals	**6**	
7	Multiply line 6 by 80% (.80)	**7**	
8	Add lines 5 and 7	**8**	

Section C—Pre-move Househunting Expenses and Temporary Quarters
(for any 30 days in a row after getting your job)

9	Pre-move travel and lodging **not** including meals	**9**	
10	Temporary quarters expenses **not** including meals	**10**	
11	Total meal expenses for both pre-move househunting and temporary quarters	**11**	
12	Multiply line 11 by 80% (.80)	**12**	
13	Add lines 9, 10, and 12	**13**	

Section D—Qualified Real Estate Expenses

| **14** | Expenses of (check one) **a** ☐ selling or exchanging your old home, or ⎫ **b** ☐ if renting, settling an unexpired lease. ⎬ | **14** | |
| **15** | Expenses of (check one) **a** ☐ buying your new home, or ⎫ . . . **b** ☐ if renting, getting a new lease. ⎭ | **15** | |

Part III Dollar Limits and Moving Expense Deduction For Expenses Incurred Before 1994

Note: *If you and your spouse moved to separate homes, see the instructions.*

16	Enter the **smaller** of: • The amount on line 13, or • $1,500 ($750 for certain married individuals filing a separate ⎬ . return—see instructions).	**16**	
17	Add lines 14, 15, and 16	**17**	
18	Enter the **smaller** of: • The amount on line 17, or • $3,000 ($1,500 for certain married individuals filing a separate ⎬ . . . . return—see instructions).	**18**	
19	Add lines 4, 8, and 18. Enter the total here and on Schedule A, line 27. This is your **moving expense deduction for expenses incurred before 1994**. . . . . ▶	**19**	

✱ *Printed on recycled paper*

Form **4562**	**Depreciation and Amortization**	OMB No. 1545-0172

(Including Information on Listed Property)

1994

Department of the Treasury
Internal Revenue Service (T)

▶ See separate instructions. ▶ Attach this form to your return.

Attachment
Sequence No. **67**

Name(s) shown on return

Identifying number

Business or activity to which this form relates

Part I **Election To Expense Certain Tangible Property (Section 179)** (**Note:** *If you have any "Listed Property," complete Part V before you complete Part I.*)

1	Maximum dollar limitation (If an enterprise zone business, see instructions.)	**1** $17,500
2	Total cost of section 179 property placed in service during the tax year (see instructions) . .	**2**
3	Threshold cost of section 179 property before reduction in limitation	**3** $200,000
4	Reduction in limitation. Subtract line 3 from line 2. If zero or less, enter -0-	**4**
5	Dollar limitation for tax year. Subtract line 4 from line 1. If zero or less, enter -0-. (If married filing separately, see instructions.).	**5**

(a) Description of property	(b) Cost	(c) Elected cost
6		

7	Listed property. Enter amount from line 26. . . . . **7**	
8	Total elected cost of section 179 property. Add amounts in column (c), lines 6 and 7 . . .	**8**
9	Tentative deduction. Enter the smaller of line 5 or line 8	**9**
10	Carryover of disallowed deduction from 1993 (see instructions).	**10**
11	Taxable income limitation. Enter the smaller of taxable income (not less than zero) or line 5 (see instructions)	**11**
12	Section 179 expense deduction. Add lines 9 and 10, but do not enter more than line 11 . .	**12**
13	Carryover of disallowed deduction to 1995. Add lines 9 and 10, less line 12 ▶ **13**	

Note: *Do not use Part II or Part III below for listed property (automobiles, certain other vehicles, cellular telephones, certain computers, or property used for entertainment, recreation, or amusement). Instead, use Part V for listed property.*

Part II **MACRS Depreciation For Assets Placed in Service ONLY During Your 1994 Tax Year (Do Not Include Listed Property)**

(a) Classification of property	(b) Month and year placed in service	(c) Basis for depreciation (business/investment use only—see instructions)	(d) Recovery period	(e) Convention	(f) Method	(g) Depreciation deduction
Section A—General Depreciation System (GDS) (see instructions)						
14a 3-year property						
b 5-year property						
c 7-year property						
d 10-year property						
e 15-year property						
f 20-year property						
g Residential rental property			27.5 yrs.	MM	S/L	
			27.5 yrs.	MM	S/L	
h Nonresidential real property				MM	S/L	
				MM	S/L	
Section B—Alternative Depreciation System (ADS) (see instructions)						
15a Class life					S/L	
b 12-year			12 yrs.		S/L	
c 40-year			40 yrs.	MM	S/L	

Part III **Other Depreciation (Do Not Include Listed Property)**

16	GDS and ADS deductions for assets placed in service in tax years beginning before 1994 (see instructions)	**16**
17	Property subject to section 168(f)(1) election (see instructions)	**17**
18	ACRS and other depreciation (see instructions)	**18**

Part IV **Summary**

19	Listed property. Enter amount from line 25.	**19**
20	**Total.** Add deductions on line 12, lines 14 and 15 in column (g), and lines 16 through 19. Enter here and on the appropriate lines of your return. (Partnerships and S corporations—see instructions)	**20**
21	For assets shown above and placed in service during the current year, enter the portion of the basis attributable to section 263A costs (see instructions) **21**	

For Paperwork Reduction Act Notice, see page 1 of the separate instructions. Cat. No. 12906N Form **4562** (1994)

Form 4562 (1994)   Page **2**

Part V	Listed Property–Automobiles, Certain Other Vehicles, Cellular Telephones, Certain Computers, and Property Used for Entertainment, Recreation, or Amusement

*For any vehicle for which you are using the standard mileage rate or deducting lease expense, complete **only** 22a, 22b, columns (a) through (c) of Section A, all of Section B, and Section C if applicable.*

Section A–Depreciation and Other Information *(Caution: See instructions for limitations for automobiles.)*

22a Do you have evidence to support the business/investment use claimed? ☐ **Yes** ☐ **No**   **22b** If "Yes," is the evidence written? ☐ **Yes** ☐ **No**

(a) Type of property (list vehicles first)	(b) Date placed in service	(c) Business/ investment use percentage	(d) Cost or other basis	(e) Basis for depreciation (business/investment use only)	(f) Recovery period	(g) Method/ Convention	(h) Depreciation deduction	(i) Elected section 179 cost
23 Property used more than 50% in a qualified business use (see instructions):								
		%						
		%						
		%						
24 Property used 50% or less in a qualified business use (see instructions):								
		%			S/L –			
		%			S/L –			
		%			S/L –			

25	Add amounts in column (h). Enter the total here and on line 19, page 1.	**25**	
26	Add amounts in column (i). Enter the total here and on line 7, page 1	**26**	

Section B–Information on Use of Vehicles– *If you deduct expenses for vehicles:*

- *Always complete this section for vehicles used by a sole proprietor, partner, or other "more than 5% owner," or related person.*
- *If you provided vehicles to your employees, first answer the questions in Section C to see if you meet an exception to completing this section for those vehicles.*

		(a) Vehicle 1	(b) Vehicle 2	(c) Vehicle 3	(d) Vehicle 4	(e) Vehicle 5	(f) Vehicle 6
27	Total business/investment miles driven during the year (DO NOT include commuting miles)						
28	Total commuting miles driven during the year						
29	Total other personal (noncommuting) miles driven						
30	Total miles driven during the year. Add lines 27 through 29. . . .						

		Yes	No	Yes	No	Yes	No	Yes	No	Yes	No	Yes	No
31	Was the vehicle available for personal use during off-duty hours? . . .												
32	Was the vehicle used primarily by a more than 5% owner or related person?												
33	Is another vehicle available for personal use?												

Section C–Questions for Employers Who Provide Vehicles for Use by Their Employees

Answer these questions to determine if you meet an exception to completing Section B. **Note:** *Section B must always be completed for vehicles used by sole proprietors, partners, or other more than 5% owners or related persons.*

		Yes	No
34	Do you maintain a written policy statement that prohibits all personal use of vehicles, including commuting, by your employees?		
35	Do you maintain a written policy statement that prohibits personal use of vehicles, except commuting, by your employees? (See instructions for vehicles used by corporate officers, directors, or 1% or more owners.)		
36	Do you treat all use of vehicles by employees as personal use?		
37	Do you provide more than five vehicles to your employees and retain the information received from your employees concerning the use of the vehicles?		
38	Do you meet the requirements concerning qualified automobile demonstration use (see instructions)? . . .		

Note: *If your answer to 34, 35, 36, 37, or 38 is "Yes," you need not complete Section B for the covered vehicles.*

Part VI	Amortization

(a) Description of costs	(b) Date amortization begins	(c) Amortizable amount	(d) Code section	(e) Amortization period or percentage	(f) Amortization for this year
39 Amortization of costs that begins during your 1994 tax year:					

40	Amortization of costs that began before 1994	**40**	
41	**Total.** Enter here and on "Other Deductions" or "Other Expenses" line of your return . .	**41**	

✿ *Printed on recycled paper*

Form **4684**

Department of the Treasury
Internal Revenue Service

Casualties and Thefts

▶ See separate instructions.
▶ Attach to your tax return.
▶ Use a separate Form 4684 for each different casualty or theft.

OMB No. 1545-0177

1994

Attachment
Sequence No. **26**

Name(s) shown on tax return	Identifying number

SECTION A—Personal Use Property (Use this section to report casualties and thefts of property **not** used in a trade or business or for income-producing purposes.)

1 Description of properties (show type, location, and date acquired for each):

Property **A** ....

Property **B** ....

Property **C** ....

Property **D** ....

Properties (Use a separate column for each property lost or damaged from one casualty or theft.)

		A	B	C	D
2	Cost or other basis of each property				
3	Insurance or other reimbursement (whether or not you filed a claim). See instructions **Note:** If line 2 is **more than** line 3, skip line 4.				
4	Gain from casualty or theft. If line 3 is **more than** line 2, enter the difference here and skip lines 5 through 9 for that column. See instructions if line 3 includes insurance or other reimbursement you did not claim, or you received payment for your loss in a later tax year				
5	Fair market value **before** casualty or theft				
6	Fair market value **after** casualty or theft				
7	Subtract line 6 from line 5				
8	Enter the **smaller** of line 2 or line 7				
9	Subtract line 3 from line 8. If zero or less, enter -0-				

10	Casualty or theft loss. Add the amounts on line 9. Enter the total	**10**
11	Enter the amount from line 10 or $100, whichever is **smaller**	**11**
12	Subtract line 11 from line 10	**12**
	Caution: Use only one Form 4684 for lines 13 through 18.	
13	Add the amounts on line 12 of all Forms 4684	**13**
14	Combine the amounts from line 4 of all Forms 4684	**14**
15	• If line 14 is **more than** line 13, enter the difference here and on Schedule D. Do not complete the rest of this section (see instructions). • If line 14 is **less than** line 13, enter -0- here and continue with the form. • If line 14 is **equal to** line 13, enter -0- here. Do not complete this section.	**15**
16	If line 14 is **less than** line 13, enter the difference	**16**
17	Enter 10% of your adjusted gross income (Form 1040, line 32). Estates and trusts, see instructions	**17**
18	Subtract line 17 from line 16. If zero or less, enter -0-. Also enter result on Schedule A (Form 1040), line 19. Estates and trusts, enter on the "Other deductions" line of your tax return	**18**

For Paperwork Reduction Act Notice, see page 1 of separate instructions.   Cat. No. 12997O   Form **4684** (1994)

Name(s) shown on tax return. Do not enter name and identifying number if shown on other side. | **Identifying number**

SECTION B—Business and Income-Producing Property (Use this section to report casualties and thefts of property used in a trade or business or for income-producing purposes.)

Part I Casualty or Theft Gain or Loss (Use a separate Part I for each casualty or theft.)

19 Description of properties (show type, location, and date acquired for each):

Property **A** ....

Property **B** ....

Property **C** ....

Property **D** ....

Properties (Use a separate column for each property lost or damaged from one casualty or theft.)

		A	**B**	**C**	**D**
20	Cost or adjusted basis of each property				
21	Insurance or other reimbursement (whether or not you filed a claim). See the instructions for line 3 . **Note:** *If line 20 is **more than** line 21, skip line 22.*				
22	Gain from casualty or theft. If line 21 is **more than** line 20, enter the difference here and on line 29 or line 34, column (c), except as provided in the instructions for line 33. Also, skip lines 23 through 27 for that column. See the instructions for line 4 if line 21 includes insurance or other reimbursement you did not claim, or you received payment for your loss in a later tax year				
23	Fair market value **before** casualty or theft . . .				
24	Fair market value **after** casualty or theft				
25	Subtract line 24 from line 23				
26	Enter the **smaller** of line 20 or line 25				
	Note: *If the property was totally destroyed by casualty or lost from theft, enter on line 26 the amount from line 20.*				
27	Subtract line 21 from line 26. If zero or less, enter -0-				
28	Casualty or theft loss. Add the amounts on line 27. Enter the total here and on line 29 **or** line 34 (see instructions).	**28**			

Part II Summary of Gains and Losses (from separate Parts I)

(a) Identify casualty or theft	(b) Losses from casualties or thefts		(c) Gains from casualties or thefts includible in income
	(i) Trade, business, rental or royalty property	(ii) Income-producing property	

Casualty or Theft of Property Held One Year or Less

		(i)	(ii)	(c)
29		( )	( )	
		( )	( )	
30	Totals. Add the amounts on line 29 . . . . **30**	( )	( )	
31	Combine line 30, columns (b)(i) and (c). Enter the net gain or (loss) here and on Form 4797, line 15. If Form 4797 is not otherwise required, see instructions **31**			
32	Enter the amount from line 30, column (b)(ii) here and on Schedule A (Form 1040), line 22. Partnerships, S corporations, estates and trusts, see instructions **32**			

Casualty or Theft of Property Held More Than One Year

		(i)	(ii)	(c)
33	Casualty or theft gains from Form 4797, line 34 . . . . **33**			
34		( )	( )	
		( )	( )	
35	Total losses. Add amounts on line 34, columns (b)(i) and (b)(ii) . . . **35**	( )	( )	
36	Total gains. Add lines 33 and 34, column (c) **36**			
37	Add amounts on line 35, columns (b)(i) and (b)(ii) **37**			
38	If the loss on line 37 is **more than** the gain on line 36:			
a	Combine line 35, column (b)(i) and line 36, and enter the net gain or (loss) here. Partnerships and S corporations see the note below. All others enter this amount on Form 4797, line 15. If Form 4797 is not otherwise required, see instructions **38a**			
b	Enter the amount from line 35, column (b)(ii) here. Partnerships and S corporations see the note below. Individuals enter this amount on Schedule A (Form 1040), line 22. Estates and trusts, enter on the "Other deductions" line of your tax return **38b**			
39	If the loss on line 37 is **equal to** or **less than** the gain on line 36, combine these lines and enter here. Partnerships, see the note below. All others, enter this amount on Form 4797, line 3 . . . . **39**			

Note: *Partnerships, enter the amount from line 38a, 38b, or line 39 on Form 1065, Schedule K, line 7. S corporations, enter the amount from line 38a or 38b on Form 1120S, Schedule K, line 6.*

Form **4797**

Department of the Treasury
Internal Revenue Service

Sales of Business Property

(Also Involuntary Conversions and Recapture Amounts
Under Sections 179 and 280F(b)(2))

▶ Attach to your tax return.   ▶ See separate instructions.

OMB No. 1545-0184

1994

Attachment
Sequence No. **27**

Name(s) shown on return

Identifying number

1 Enter here the gross proceeds from the sale or exchange of real estate reported to you for 1994 on Form(s) 1099-S (or a substitute statement) that you will be including on line 2, 11, or 22 . . . . | **1** |

Part I Sales or Exchanges of Property Used in a Trade or Business and Involuntary Conversions From Other Than Casualty or Theft—Property Held More Than 1 Year

(a) Description of property	(b) Date acquired (mo., day, yr.)	(c) Date sold (mo., day, yr.)	(d) Gross sales price	(e) Depreciation allowed or allowable since acquisition	(f) Cost or other basis, plus improvements and expense of sale	(g) LOSS ((f) minus the sum of (d) and (e))	(h) GAIN ((d) plus (e) minus (f))
2							

3 Gain, if any, from Form 4684, line 39 . . . . | **3** | | |

4 Section 1231 gain from installment sales from Form 6252, line 26 or 37 . . . . | **4** | | |

5 Section 1231 gain or (loss) from like-kind exchanges from Form 8824 . . . . | **5** | | |

6 Gain, if any, from line 34, from other than casualty or theft . . . . | **6** | | |

7 Add lines 2 through 6 in columns (g) and (h) . . . . | **7** | (|) | |

8 Combine columns (g) and (h) of line 7. Enter gain or (loss) here, and on the appropriate line as follows: . . . | **8** |

Partnerships—Enter the gain or (loss) on Form 1065, Schedule K, line 6. Skip lines 9, 10, 12, and 13 below.

S corporations—Report the gain or (loss) following the instructions for Form 1120S, Schedule K, lines 5 and 6. Skip lines 9, 10, 12, and 13 below, unless line 8 is a gain and the S corporation is subject to the capital gains tax.

All others—If line 8 is zero or a loss, enter the amount on line 12 below and skip lines 9 and 10. If line 8 is a gain and you did not have any prior year section 1231 losses, or they were recaptured in an earlier year, enter the gain as a long-term capital gain on Schedule D and skip lines 9, 10, and 13 below.

9 Nonrecaptured net section 1231 losses from prior years (see instructions) . . . . | **9** |

10 Subtract line 9 from line 8. If zero or less, enter -0-. Also enter on the appropriate line as follows (see instructions): | **10** |

S corporations—Enter this amount (if more than zero) on Schedule D (Form 1120S), line 13, and skip lines 12 and 13 below.

All others—If line 10 is zero, enter the amount from line 8 on line 13 below. If line 10 is more than zero, enter the amount from line 9 on line 13 below, and enter the amount from line 10 as a long-term capital gain on Schedule D.

Part II Ordinary Gains and Losses

11 Ordinary gains and losses not included on lines 12 through 18 (include property held 1 year or less):

12 Loss, if any, from line 8 . . . . | **12** | | |

13 Gain, if any, from line 8, or amount from line 9 if applicable . . . . | **13** | | |

14 Gain, if any, from line 33 . . . . | **14** | | |

15 Net gain or (loss) from Form 4684, lines 31 and 38a . . . . | **15** | | |

16 Ordinary gain from installment sales from Form 6252, line 25 or 36 . . . . | **16** | | |

17 Ordinary gain or (loss) from like-kind exchanges from Form 8824 . . . . | **17** | | |

18 Recapture of section 179 expense deduction for partners and S corporation shareholders from property dispositions by partnerships and S corporations (see instructions) . . . . . | **18** | | |

19 Add lines 11 through 18 in columns (g) and (h) . . . . | **19** | (|) | |

20 Combine columns (g) and (h) of line 19. Enter gain or (loss) here, and on the appropriate line as follows: . . | **20** |

a For all except individual returns: Enter the gain or (loss) from line 20 on the return being filed.

b For individual returns:

(1) If the loss on line 12 includes a loss from Form 4684, line 35, column (b)(ii), enter that part of the loss here and on line 22 of Schedule A (Form 1040). Identify as from "Form 4797, line 20b(1)." See instructions . . . | **20b(1)** | |

(2) Redetermine the gain or (loss) on line 20, excluding the loss, if any, on line 20b(1). Enter here and on Form 1040, line 14 . | **20b(2)** | |

For Paperwork Reduction Act Notice, see page 1 of separate instructions.   Cat. No. 13086I   Form **4797** (1994)

Form 4797 (1994)   Page **2**

Part III   Gain From Disposition of Property Under Sections 1245, 1250, 1252, 1254, and 1255

21	(a) Description of section 1245, 1250, 1252, 1254, or 1255 property:	(b) Date acquired (mo., day, yr.)	(c) Date sold (mo., day, yr.)
A			
B			
C			
D			

	Relate lines 21A through 21D to these columns ▶		Property A	Property B	Property C	Property D
22	Gross sales price (**Note:** *See line 1 before completing.*)	22				
23	Cost or other basis plus expense of sale	23				
24	Depreciation (or depletion) allowed or allowable	24				
25	Adjusted basis. Subtract line 24 from line 23	25				
26	Total gain. Subtract line 25 from line 22	26				
27	**If section 1245 property:**					
a	Depreciation allowed or allowable from line 24	27a				
b	Enter the **smaller** of line 26 or 27a	27b				
28	**If section 1250 property:** If straight line depreciation was used, enter -0- on line 28g, except for a corporation subject to section 291.					
a	Additional depreciation after 1975 (see instructions)	28a				
b	Applicable percentage multiplied by the **smaller** of line 26 or line 28a (see instructions)	28b				
c	Subtract line 28a from line 26. If residential rental property or line 26 is not more than line 28a, skip lines 28d and 28e	28c				
d	Additional depreciation after 1969 and before 1976	28d				
e	Enter the **smaller** of line 28c or 28d	28e				
f	Section 291 amount (corporations only)	28f				
g	Add lines 28b, 28e, and 28f	28g				
29	**If section 1252 property:** Skip this section if you did not dispose of farmland or if this form is being completed for a partnership.					
a	Soil, water, and land clearing expenses	29a				
b	Line 29a multiplied by applicable percentage (see instructions)	29b				
c	Enter the **smaller** of line 26 or 29b	29c				
30	**If section 1254 property:**					
a	Intangible drilling and development costs, expenditures for development of mines and other natural deposits, and mining exploration costs (see instructions)	30a				
b	Enter the **smaller** of line 26 or 30a	30b				
31	**If section 1255 property:**					
a	Applicable percentage of payments excluded from income under section 126 (see instructions)	31a				
b	Enter the **smaller** of line 26 or 31a	31b				

Summary of Part III Gains. Complete property columns A through D, through line 31b before going to line 32.

32	Total gains for all properties. Add columns A through D, line 26	32	
33	Add columns A through D, lines 27b, 28g, 29c, 30b, and 31b. Enter here and on line 14	33	
34	Subtract line 33 from line 32. Enter the portion from casualty or theft on Form 4684, line 33. Enter the portion from other than casualty or theft on Form 4797, line 6	34	

Part IV   Recapture Amounts Under Sections 179 and 280F(b)(2) When Business Use Drops to 50% or Less   See instructions.

			(a) Section 179	(b) Section 280F(b)(2)
35	Section 179 expense deduction or depreciation allowable in prior years	35		
36	Recomputed depreciation. See instructions	36		
37	Recapture amount. Subtract line 36 from line 35. See the instructions for where to report	37		

✹ *Printed on recycled paper*

Form 4868

Department of the Treasury
Internal Revenue Service

Application for Automatic Extension of Time To File U.S. Individual Income Tax Return

OMB No. 1545-0188

1994

Please Type or Print

Your first name and initial	Last name	Your social security number
If a joint return, spouse's first name and initial	Last name	Spouse's social security number
Home address (number, street, and apt. no. or rural route). If you have a P.O. box, see the instructions.		
City, town or post office, state, and ZIP code		

I request an automatic 4-month extension of time to August 15, 1995, to file Form 1040EZ, Form 1040A, or Form 1040 for the calendar year 1994 or to _____ , 19 ____ , for the fiscal tax year ending _____ , 19 ____ .

Part I Individual Income Tax—You must complete this part.

1 **Total tax liability for 1994.** This is the amount you expect to enter on Form 1040EZ, line 9; Form 1040A, line 27; or Form 1040, line 53. If you expect this amount to be zero, enter -0-. . . . **1**

Caution: *You MUST enter an amount on line 1 or your extension will be denied. You can estimate this amount, but be as exact as you can with the information you have. If we later find that your estimate was not reasonable, the extension will be null and void.*

2 **Total payments for 1994.** This is the amount you expect to enter on Form 1040EZ, line 8; Form 1040A, line 28d; or Form 1040, line 60 (excluding line 57) **2**

3 **BALANCE DUE.** Subtract line 2 from line 1. If line 2 is more than line 1, enter -0-. If you are making a payment, you must use the Form 4868-V at the bottom of page 3. For details on how to pay, including what to write on your payment, see the instructions . . . . ▶ **3**

Part II Gift or Generation-Skipping Transfer (GST) Tax—Complete this part if you expect to owe either tax.

Caution: *Do not include income tax on lines 5a and 5b. See the instructions.*

4 If you or your spouse plan to file a gift tax return (Form 709 or 709-A) for 1994, generally due by April 17, 1995, see the instructions and check here . . . } Yourself ▶ ☐ Spouse ▶ ☐

5a Enter the amount of gift or GST tax **you** are paying with this form. Also, you must use the Form 4868-V at the bottom of page 3 . . . . **5a**

b Enter the amount of gift or GST tax **your spouse** is paying with this form. Also, you must use the Form 4868-V at the bottom of page 3 . . . . **5b**

Signature and Verification

Under penalties of perjury, I declare that I have examined this form, including accompanying schedules and statements, and to the best of my knowledge and belief, it is true, correct, and complete; and, if prepared by someone other than the taxpayer, that I am authorized to prepare this form.

▶ _____ | _____ ▶ _____ | _____
  Your signature   Date   Spouse's signature, if filing jointly   Date

▶ _____ | _____
  Preparer's signature (other than taxpayer)   Date

If you want correspondence regarding this extension to be sent to you at an address other than that shown above or to an agent acting for you, please enter the name of the agent and/or the address where it should be sent.

Please Type or Print

Name
Number and street (include suite, room, or apt. no.) or P.O. box number if mail is not delivered to street address
City, town or post office, state, and ZIP code

For Paperwork Reduction Act Notice, see page 3.   Cat. No. 13141W   Form **4868** (1994)

Form **4952**	**Investment Interest Expense Deduction**	OMB No. 1545-0191 **1994**	
Department of the Treasury Internal Revenue Service	▶ **Attach to your tax return.**	Attachment Sequence No. **12A**	
Name(s) shown on return		Identifying number	

Part I   Total Investment Interest Expense

1	Investment interest expense paid or accrued in 1994. See instructions	**1**	
2	Disallowed investment interest expense from 1993 Form 4952, line 7	**2**	
3	**Total investment interest expense.** Add lines 1 and 2	**3**	

Part II   Net Investment Income

4a	Gross income from property held for investment (excluding any net gain from the disposition of property held for investment)	**4a**	
b	Net gain from the disposition of property held for investment . .	**4b**	
c	Net capital gain from the disposition of property held for investment	**4c**	
d	Subtract line 4c from line 4b. If zero or less, enter -0-	**4d**	
e	Enter all or part of the amount on line 4c that you elect to include in investment income. Do not enter more than the amount on line 4b. See instructions . . . . ▶	**4e**	
f	Investment income. Add lines 4a, 4d, and 4e. See instructions	**4f**	
5	Investment expenses. See instructions	**5**	
6	**Net investment income.** Subtract line 5 from line 4f. If zero or less, enter -0-	**6**	

Part III   Investment Interest Expense Deduction

7	Disallowed investment interest expense to be carried forward to 1995. Subtract line 6 from line 3. If zero or less, enter -0-	**7**	
8	**Investment interest expense deduction.** Enter the smaller of line 3 or 6. See instructions .	**8**	

Paperwork Reduction Act Notice

We ask for the information on this form to carry out the Internal Revenue laws of the United States. You are required to give us the information. We need it to ensure that you are complying with these laws and to allow us to figure and collect the right amount of tax.

The time needed to complete and file this form will vary depending on individual circumstances. The estimated average time is:

Recordkeeping . . . . . .13 min.
Learning about the law or the form . . . . . .15 min.
Preparing the form . . . . . 21 min.
Copying, assembling, and sending the form to the IRS . . 10 min.

If you have comments concerning the accuracy of these time estimates or suggestions for making this form simpler, we would be happy to hear from you. You can write to both the IRS and the Office of Management and Budget at the addresses listed in the instructions for the tax return with which this form is filed.

General Instructions

Section references are to the Internal Revenue Code unless otherwise noted.

Purpose of Form

Interest expense paid by an individual, estate, or a trust on a loan that is allocable to property held for investment may not be fully deductible in the current year. Form 4952 is used to figure the amount of investment interest expense deductible for the current

year and the amount, if any, to carry forward to future years.

For more details, get **Pub. 550,** Investment Income and Expenses.

Who Must File

If you are an individual, estate, or a trust, and you claim a deduction for investment interest expense, you must complete and attach Form 4952 to your tax return, unless **all** of the following apply:

● Your only investment income was from interest or dividends,

● You have no other deductible expenses connected with the production of interest or dividends,

● Your investment interest expense is not more than your investment income, and

● You have no disallowed investment interest expense from 1993.

Form **5329**

Department of the Treasury
Internal Revenue Service

Additional Taxes Attributable to Qualified Retirement Plans (Including IRAs), Annuities, and Modified Endowment Contracts
(Under Sections 72, 4973, 4974, and 4980A of the Internal Revenue Code)
▶ Attach to Form 1040. See separate instructions.

OMB No. 1545-0203

1994

Attachment
Sequence No. **29**

Name of individual subject to additional tax. (If married filing jointly, see instructions.)

Your social security number

Fill in Your Address Only If You Are Filing This Form by Itself and Not With Your Tax Return

Home address (number and street), or P.O. box if mail is not delivered to your home

Apt. no.

City, town or post office, state, and ZIP code

If this is an amended return, check here ▶ ☐

If you are subject to the 10% tax on early distributions **only,** see **Who Must File** in the instructions before continuing. You may be able to report this tax directly on Form 1040 without filing Form 5329.

Part I   **Tax on Early Distributions**

Complete this part if a taxable distribution was made from your qualified retirement plan (including an IRA), annuity contract, or modified endowment contract before you reached age 59½ (or was incorrectly indicated as such on your Form 1099-R—see instructions). **Note:** *You must include the amount of the distribution on line 15b or 16b of Form 1040 or on the appropriate line of Form 4972.*

1	Early distributions included in gross income (see instructions)	**1**	
2	Distributions excepted from additional tax (see instructions). Enter appropriate exception number from instructions ▶ _____	**2**	
3	Amount subject to additional tax. Subtract line 2 from line 1	**3**	
4	**Tax due.** Multiply line 3 by 10% (.10). Enter here and on Form 1040, line 51	**4**	

Part II   **Tax on Excess Contributions to Individual Retirement Arrangements**

Complete this part if, either in this year or in earlier years, you contributed more to your IRA than is or was allowable and you have an excess contribution subject to tax.

5	Excess contributions for 1994 (see instructions). Do not include this amount on Form 1040, line 23a or 23b		**5**	
6	Earlier year excess contributions not previously eliminated (see instructions)	**6**		
7	Contribution credit. If your actual contribution for 1994 is less than your maximum allowable contribution, see instructions; otherwise, enter -0-	**7**		
8	1994 distributions from your IRA account that are includible in taxable income	**8**		
9	1993 tax year excess contributions (if any) withdrawn after the due date (including extensions) of your 1993 income tax return, and 1992 and earlier tax year excess contributions withdrawn in 1994 . . .	**9**		
10	Add lines 7, 8, and 9	**10**		
11	Adjusted earlier year excess contributions. Subtract line 10 from line 6. Enter the result, but not less than zero		**11**	
12	Total excess contributions. Add lines 5 and 11		**12**	
13	**Tax due.** Enter the **smaller** of 6% (.06) of line 12 or 6% (.06) of the value of your IRA on the last day of 1994. Also enter this amount on Form 1040, line 51		**13**	

For Paperwork Reduction Act Notice, see page 1 of separate instructions.   Cat. No. 13329Q   Form **5329** (1994)

Form 5329 (1994)   Page **2**

Part III	**Tax on Excess Accumulation in Qualified Retirement Plans (Including IRAs)**		

14	Minimum required distribution (see instructions)	**14**	
15	Amount actually distributed to you	**15**	
16	Subtract line 15 from line 14. If line 15 is more than line 14, enter -0-	**16**	
17	**Tax due.** Multiply line 16 by 50% (.50). Enter here and on Form 1040, line 51	**17**	

Part IV	**Tax on Excess Distributions From Qualified Retirement Plans (Including IRAs)**		

		Column A **Regular Distributions**	Column B **Lump-Sum Distributions**
Complete Column A for regular distributions. Complete Column B for lump-sum distributions.			
18	Total amount of regular retirement or lump-sum distributions **18**		
19	Amount excluded from additional tax. Enter appropriate exception number from instructions ▶ _____ **19**		
20	Subtract line 19 from line 18 . **20**		
21	Enter the **greater** of the threshold amount or the 1994 recovery of the grandfather amount (from Worksheet 1 or 2). See instructions **21**		
22	Excess distributions. Subtract line 21 from line 20. If less than zero, enter -0- **22**		
23	Tentative tax. Multiply line 22 by 15% (.15) **23**		
24	Early distributions tax offset (see instructions) **24**		
25	Subtract line 24 from line 23. . . . . **25**		
26	**Tax due.** Combine columns (a) and (b) of line 25. Enter here and on Form 1040, line 51. . . **26**		

Acceleration Elections (see the instructions for Part IV)

1   If you elected the discretionary method in 1987 or 1988 and wish to make an acceleration election beginning in 1994
     under Temporary Regulations section 54.4981A-1T, Q&A b-12, check here ▶ ☐ .

2   If you previously made an acceleration election and wish to revoke that election, check here ▶ ☐ .

Signature. *Complete **ONLY** if you are filing this form by itself and not with your tax return.*

Please Sign Here	Under penalties of perjury, I declare that I have examined this form, including accompanying schedules and statements, and to the best of my knowledge and belief, it is true, correct, and complete. Declaration of preparer (other than taxpayer) is based on all information of which preparer has any knowledge.	
	▶ _____ Your signature	▶ _____ Date

Paid Preparer's Use Only	Preparer's ▶ signature		Date	Check if self- employed ▶ ☐	Preparer's social security no.
	Firm's name (or yours, if self-employed) and address	▶		E.I. No. ▶	
				ZIP code ▶	

✿ *Printed on recycled paper*

Form **6251**

Department of the Treasury
Internal Revenue Service

Alternative Minimum Tax–Individuals

▶ See separate instructions.

▶ Attach to Form 1040 or Form 1040NR.

OMB No. 1545-0227

1994

Attachment
Sequence No. **32**

Name(s) shown on Form 1040

Your social security number

Part I Adjustments and Preferences

1	If you itemized deductions on Schedule A (Form 1040), go to line 2. If you did not itemize deductions, enter your standard deduction from Form 1040, line 34, and skip to line 6	**1**		
2	Medical and dental. Enter the smaller of Schedule A, line 4, or 2½% of Form 1040, line 32	**2**		
3	Taxes. Enter the amount from Schedule A, line 9	**3**		
4	Certain interest on a home mortgage not used to buy, build, or improve your home	**4**		
5	Miscellaneous itemized deductions. Enter the amount from Schedule A, line 26	**5**		
6	Refund of taxes. Enter any tax refund from Form 1040, line 10 or 21	**6**	(	)
7	Investment interest. Enter difference between regular tax and AMT deduction	**7**		
8	Post-1986 depreciation. Enter difference between regular tax and AMT depreciation	**8**		
9	Adjusted gain or loss. Enter difference between AMT and regular tax gain or loss	**9**		
10	Incentive stock options. Enter excess of AMT income over regular tax income	**10**		
11	Passive activities. Enter difference between AMT and regular tax income or loss	**11**		
12	Beneficiaries of estates and trusts. Enter the amount from Schedule K-1 (Form 1041), line 8	**12**		
13	Tax-exempt interest from private activity bonds issued after 8/7/86	**13**		

14 Other. Enter the amount, if any, for each item and enter the total on line 14.

a Charitable contributions	**h** Loss limitations		
b Circulation expenditures	**i** Mining costs		
c Depletion			
d Depreciation (pre-1987)	**k** Pollution control facilities		
e Installment sales	**l** Research and experimental		
f Intangible drilling costs	**m** Tax shelter farm activities		
g Long-term contracts	**n** Related adjustments	**14**	

15	**Total Adjustments and Preferences.** Combine lines 1 through 14 ▶	**15**	

Part II Alternative Minimum Taxable Income

16	Enter the amount from **Form 1040, line 35.** If less than zero, enter as a (loss) ▶	**16**		
17	Net operating loss deduction, if any, from Form 1040, line 21. Enter as a positive amount	**17**		
18	If Form 1040, line 32, is over $111,800 (over $55,900 if married filing separately), and you itemized deductions, enter the amount, if any, from line 9 of the worksheet for Schedule A, line 29	**18**	(	)
19	Combine lines 15 through 18 ▶	**19**		
20	Alternative tax net operating loss deduction. See instructions	**20**		
21	**Alternative Minimum Taxable Income.** Subtract line 20 from line 19. (If married filing separately and line 21 is more than $165,000, see instructions.) ▶	**21**		

Part III Exemption Amount and Alternative Minimum Tax

22 **Exemption Amount.** (If this form is for a child under age 14, see instructions.)

If your filing status is:	And line 21 is not over:	Enter on line 22:		
Single or head of household	$112,500	$33,750		
Married filing jointly or qualifying widow(er)	150,000	45,000	**22**	
Married filing separately	75,000	22,500		

If line 21 is **over** the amount shown above for your filing status, see instructions.

23	Subtract line 22 from line 21. If zero or less, enter -0- here and on lines 26 and 28 ▶	**23**	
24	If line 23 is $175,000 or less ($87,500 or less if married filing separately), multiply line 23 by 26% (.26). Otherwise, multiply line 23 by 28% (.28) and subtract $3,500 ($1,750 if married filing separately) from the result	**24**	
25	Alternative minimum tax foreign tax credit. See instructions	**25**	
26	Tentative minimum tax. Subtract line 25 from line 24 ▶	**26**	
27	Enter your tax from Form 1040, line 38 (plus any amount from Form 4970 included on Form 1040, line 39), minus any foreign tax credit from Form 1040, line 43	**27**	
28	**Alternative Minimum Tax.** (If this form is for a child under age 14, see instructions.) Subtract line 27 from line 26. If zero or less, enter -0-. Enter here and on Form 1040, line 48 ▶	**28**	

For Paperwork Reduction Act Notice, see separate instructions.   Cat. No. 13600G   Form **6251** (1994)

Form **7004**
(Rev. May 1994)
Department of the Treasury
Internal Revenue Service

Application for Automatic Extension of Time To File Corporation Income Tax Return

OMB No. 1545-0233

Name of corporation

Employer identification number

Number, street, and room or suite no. (If a P.O. box, see instructions.)

City or town, state, and ZIP code

Check type of return to be filed:

☐ Form 1120 ☐ Form 1120-F ☐ Form 1120-L ☐ Form 1120-POL ☐ Form 1120S
☐ Form 1120-A ☐ Form 1120-FSC ☐ Form 1120-ND ☐ Form 1120-REIT ☐ Form 990-C
☐ Form 1120-SF ☐ Form 1120-H ☐ Form 1120-PC ☐ Form 1120-RIC ☐ Form 990-T

Form 1120-F filers: Check here if you do not have an office or place of business in the United States . . . . ▶ ☐

1a I request an automatic 6-month (or, for certain foreign corporations, 3-month) extension of time
until ...., 19......, to file the income tax return of the corporation named above for ▶ ☐ calendar
year 19 ......or ▶ ☐ tax year beginning ...., 19......, and ending ...., 19........

b If this tax year is for less than 12 months, check reason:
☐ Initial return ☐ Final return ☐ Change in accounting period ☐ Consolidated return to be filed

2 If this application also covers subsidiaries to be included in a consolidated return, complete the following:

Name and address of each member of the affiliated group	Employer identification number	Tax period

3	Tentative tax (see instructions).	**3**	
4	**Credits:**		
a	Overpayment credited from prior year.	**4a**	
b	Estimated tax payments for the tax year	**4b**	
c	Less refund for the tax year applied for on Form 4466	**4c** ( ) **Bal ▶** **4d**	
e	Credit from regulated investment companies	**4e**	
f	Credit for Federal tax on fuels	**4f**	
5	Total. Add lines 4d through 4f	**5**	
6	**Balance due.** Subtract line 5 from line 3. **Deposit this amount with a Federal Tax Deposit (FTD) Coupon** (see instructions)	**6**	

Signature.—Under penalties of perjury, I declare that I have been authorized by the above-named corporation to make this application, and to the best of my knowledge and belief, the statements made are true, correct, and complete.

....
(Signature of officer or agent)

....
(Title)

....
(Date)

For Paperwork Reduction Act Notice, see instructions.   Cat. No. 13804A   Form **7004** (Rev. 5-94)

Form **8283**	**Noncash Charitable Contributions**	OMB No. 1545-0908

Form 8283
(Rev. November 1992)

Department of the Treasury
Internal Revenue Service

Noncash Charitable Contributions

▶ **Attach to your tax return if the total deduction claimed
for all property contributed exceeds $500.**

▶ **See separate instructions.**

OMB No. 1545-0908
Expires 11-30-95

Attachment
Sequence No. **55**

Name(s) shown on your income tax return

Identifying number

Note: *Figure the amount of your contribution deduction before completing this form. See your tax return instructions.*

Section A—Include in this section **only** items (or groups of similar items) for which you claimed a deduction of $5,000 or less per item or group, and certain publicly traded securities (see instructions).

Part I **Information on Donated Property**—If you need more space, attach a statement.

1	(a) Name and address of the donee organization	(b) Description of donated property
A		
B		
C		
D		
E		

Note: *If the amount you claimed as a deduction for an item is $500 or less, you do not have to complete columns (d), (e), and (f).*

	(c) Date of the contribution	(d) Date acquired by donor (mo., yr.)	(e) How acquired by donor	(f) Donor's cost or adjusted basis	(g) Fair market value	(h) Method used to determine the fair market value
A						
B						
C						
D						
E						

Part II **Other Information**—If you gave less than an entire interest in property listed in Part I, complete lines 2a–2e. If restrictions were attached to a contribution listed in Part I, complete lines 3a–3c.

2 If less than the entire interest in the property is contributed during the year, complete the following:

a Enter letter from Part I that identifies the property _____. If Part II applies to more than one property, attach a separate statement.

b Total amount claimed as a deduction for the property listed in Part I: **(1)** For this tax year _____
(2) For any prior tax years _____.

c Name and address of each organization to which any such contribution was made in a prior year (complete only if different than the donee organization above). _____

Name of charitable organization (donee)

_____

Address (number, street, and room or suite no.)

_____

City or town, state, and ZIP code

d For tangible property, enter the place where the property is located or kept _____

e Name of any person, other than the donee organization, having actual possession of the property _____

3 If conditions were attached to any contribution listed in Part I, answer the following questions and attach the required statement (see instructions):

		Yes	No
a	Is there a restriction, either temporary or permanent, on the donee's right to use or dispose of the donated property?		
b	Did you give to anyone (other than the donee organization or another organization participating with the donee organization in cooperative fundraising) the right to the income from the donated property or to the possession of the property, including the right to vote donated securities, to acquire the property by purchase or otherwise, or to designate the person having such income, possession, or right to acquire?		
c	Is there a restriction limiting the donated property for a particular use?		

For Paperwork Reduction Act Notice, see separate instructions.   Cat. No. 62299J   Form **8283** (Rev. 11-92)

Form 8283 (Rev. 11-92)   Page **2**

Name(s) shown on your income tax return	Identifying number

Section B—Appraisal Summary—Include in this section only items (or groups of similar items) for which you claimed a deduction of more than $5,000 per item or group. Report contributions of certain publicly traded securities only in Section A.

If you donated art, you may have to attach the complete appraisal. See the **Note** in Part I below.

Part I   **Information on Donated Property**—To be completed by the taxpayer and/or appraiser.

4   Check type of property:

☐ Art* (contribution of $20,000 or more)   ☐ Real Estate   ☐ Gems/Jewelry   ☐ Stamp Collections

☐ Art* (contribution of less than $20,000)   ☐ Coin Collections   ☐ Books   ☐ Other

*Art includes paintings, sculptures, watercolors, prints, drawings, ceramics, antique furniture, decorative arts, textiles, carpets, silver, rare manuscripts, historical memorabilia, and other similar objects.

Note: *If your total art contribution deduction was $20,000 or more, you must attach a complete copy of the signed appraisal. See instructions.*

5	(a) Description of donated property (if you need more space, attach a separate statement)	(b) If tangible property was donated, give a brief summary of the overall physical condition at the time of the gift	(c) Appraised fair market value
A			
B			
C			
D			

	(d) Date acquired by donor (mo., yr.)	(e) How acquired by donor	(f) Donor's cost or adjusted basis	(g) For bargain sales, enter amount received	(h) Amount claimed as a deduction	(i) Average trading price of securities
A						
B						
C						
D						

(See instructions — over columns (h) and (i))

Part II   **Taxpayer (Donor) Statement**—List each item included in Part I above that is separately identified in the appraisal as having a value of $500 or less. See instructions.

I declare that the following item(s) included in Part I above has to the best of my knowledge and belief an appraised value of not more than $500 (per item). Enter identifying letter from Part I and describe the specific item: _____

Signature of taxpayer (donor) ▶   Date ▶

Part III   **Certification of Appraiser**

I declare that I am not the donor, the donee, a party to the transaction in which the donor acquired the property, employed by, married to, or related to any of the foregoing persons, or an appraiser regularly used by any of the foregoing persons and who does not perform a majority of appraisals during the taxable year for other persons.

Also, I declare that I hold myself out to the public as an appraiser or perform appraisals on a regular basis; and that because of my qualifications as described in the appraisal, I am qualified to make appraisals of the type of property being valued. I certify that the appraisal fees were not based upon a percentage of the appraised property value. Furthermore, I understand that a false or fraudulent overstatement of the property value as described in the qualified appraisal or this appraisal summary may subject me to the civil penalty under section 6701(a) (aiding and abetting the understatement of tax liability). I affirm that I have not been barred from presenting evidence or testimony by the Director of Practice.

Sign Here

Signature ▶   Title ▶   Date of appraisal ▶

Business address (including room or suite no.)	Identifying number

City or town, state, and ZIP code

Part IV   **Donee Acknowledgment**—To be completed by the charitable organization.

This charitable organization acknowledges that it is a qualified organization under section 170(c) and that it received the donated property as described in Section B, Part I, above on _____

(Date)

Furthermore, this organization affirms that in the event it sells, exchanges, or otherwise disposes of the property (or any portion thereof) within 2 years after the date of receipt, it will file an information return (**Form 8282,** Donee Information Return) with the IRS and furnish the donor a copy of that return. This acknowledgment does not represent concurrence in the claimed fair market value.

Name of charitable organization (donee)	Employer identification number
Address (number, street, and room or suite no.)	City or town, state, and ZIP code

Authorized signature	Title	Date

Form **8332**

(Rev. March 1993)

Department of the Treasury
Internal Revenue Service

Release of Claim to Exemption
for Child of Divorced or Separated Parents

ATTACH to noncustodial parent's return each year exemption claimed.

OMB No. 1545-0915
Expires 3-31-96

Attachment
Sequence No. **51**

Name(s) of parent claiming exemption

Social security number

Part I Release of Claim to Exemption for Current Year

I agree not to claim an exemption for _____
Name(s) of child (or children)

for the tax year 19_____ .

_____
Signature of parent releasing claim to exemption

_____
Social security number

_____
Date

If you choose not to claim an exemption for this child (or children) for future tax years, complete Part II.

Part II Release of Claim to Exemption for Future Years *(If completed, see **Noncustodial Parent** below.)*

I agree not to claim an exemption for _____
Name(s) of child (or children)

for the tax year(s) _____ .
(Specify. See instructions.)

_____
Signature of parent releasing claim to exemption

_____
Social security number

_____
Date

General Instructions

Paperwork Reduction Act Notice.—We ask for the information on this form to carry out the Internal Revenue laws of the United States. You are required to give us the information. We need it to ensure that you are complying with these laws and to allow us to figure and collect the right amount of tax.

The time needed to complete and file this form will vary depending on individual circumstances. The estimated average time is: **Recordkeeping,** 7 min.; **Learning about the law or the form,** 5 min.; **Preparing the form,** 7 min.; and **Copying, assembling, and sending the form to the IRS,** 14 min.

If you have comments concerning the accuracy of these time estimates or suggestions for making this form more simple, we would be happy to hear from you. You can write to both the IRS and the Office of Management and Budget at the addresses listed in the instructions for the return with which this form is filed.

Purpose of Form.—If you are a **custodial parent,** you may use this form to release your claim to your child's exemption. To do so, complete this form and give it to the **noncustodial parent** who will claim the child's exemption. Then, the noncustodial parent must attach this form or a similar statement to his or her tax return each year the exemption is claimed.

You are the **custodial parent** if you had custody of the child for most of the year. You are the **noncustodial parent** if you had custody for a shorter period of time or did not have custody at all.

Instead of using this form, you (the custodial parent) may use a similar

statement as long as it contains the same information required by this form.

Children of Divorced or Separated Parents.—Special rules apply to determine if the support test is met for children of parents who are divorced or legally separated under a decree of divorce or separate maintenance or separated under a written separation agreement. The rules also apply to children of parents who did not live together at any time during the last 6 months of the year, even if they do not have a separation agreement.

The general rule is that the custodial parent is treated as having provided over half of the child's support if:

1. The child received over half of his or her total support for the year from both of the parents, **AND**

2. The child was in the custody of one or both of his or her parents for more than half of the year.

Note: *Public assistance payments, such as Aid to Families with Dependent Children, are not support provided by the parents.*

If both **1** and **2** above apply, and the other four dependency tests in the instructions for Form 1040 or Form 1040A are also met, the custodial parent can claim the child's exemption.

Exception. The general rule does not apply if **any** of the following applies:

● The custodial parent agrees not to claim the child's exemption by signing this form or similar statement. The noncustodial parent **must** attach this form or similar statement to his or her tax return for the tax year. See **Custodial Parent** later.

● The child is treated as having received over half of his or her total support from a

person under a multiple support agreement **(Form 2120,** Multiple Support Declaration).

● A pre-1985 divorce decree or written separation agreement states that the noncustodial parent can claim the child as a dependent. But the noncustodial parent must provide at least $600 for the child's support during the year. The noncustodial parent must also check the box on line 6d of Form 1040 or Form 1040A. This rule does not apply if the decree or agreement was changed after 1984 to say that the noncustodial parent cannot claim the child as a dependent.

Additional Information.—For more details, get **Pub. 504,** Divorced or Separated Individuals.

Specific Instructions

Custodial Parent.—You may agree to release your claim to the child's exemption for the current tax year or for future years, or both.

● Complete **Part I** if you agree to release your claim to the child's exemption for the current tax year.

● Complete **Part II** if you agree to release your claim to the child's exemption for any or all future years. If you do, write the specific future year(s) or "all future years" in the space provided in Part II.

Noncustodial Parent.—Attach Form 8332 or a similar statement to your tax return for the tax year in which you claim the child's exemption. You may claim the exemption **only** if the other four dependency tests in the Form 1040 or Form 1040A instructions are met.

Note: *If the custodial parent completed Part II, you **must** attach a copy of this form to your tax return for each future year in which you claim the exemption.*

Cat. No. 13910F

Form **8332** (Rev. 3-93)

Declaration Control Number (DCN)

| 0 | 0 | – | | | | | | | – | | | | | | – | 5 |

IRS Use Only–Do not write or staple in this space.

Form **8453**

Department of the Treasury
Internal Revenue Service

U.S. Individual Income Tax Declaration for Electronic Filing
For the year January 1–December 31, 1994
▶ **See instructions on back.**

OMB No. 1545-0936

19**94**

Use the IRS label. Otherwise, please print or type.

L A B E L H E R E

Your first name and initial	Last name	Your social security number
If a joint return, spouse's first name and initial	Last name	Spouse's social security number
Home address (number and street). If a P.O. box, see instructions.	Apt. no.	Telephone number (optional) ( )
City, town or post office, state, and ZIP code		**For Paperwork Reduction Act Notice, see instructions.**

If the taxpayer's name changed during the past 3 years due to marriage, divorce, etc. and he or she filed a Federal income tax return for such years using the former name, enter the most recently used last name here. ▶

Part I   **Tax Return Information** (Whole dollars only)

1 Total income (Form 1040, line 22; Form 1040A, line 14; Form 1040EZ, line 3)	**1**	
2 Total tax (Form 1040, line 53; Form 1040A, line 27; Form 1040EZ, line 9)	**2**	
3 Federal income tax withheld (Form 1040, line 54; Form 1040A, line 28a; Form 1040EZ, line 6). If any is from Form(s) 1099, check here ▶ ☐	**3**	
4 Refund (Form 1040, line 62; Form 1040A, line 30; Form 1040EZ, line 10)	**4**	
5 Amount you owe (Form 1040, line 64; Form 1040A, line 32; Form 1040EZ, line 11)	**5**	

Part II   **Direct Deposit of Refund** (See instructions.)

Attach Copy B of your Forms W-2, W-2G, and 1099-R here.

6 Name of financial institution and, if applicable, branch name _____

7 Routing transit number (RTN)   The first two numbers of the RTN must be 01 through 12 or 21 through 32.

8 Depositor account number (DAN)

9 Type of account: ☐ Savings   ☐ Checking

10 Proof of account: ☐ Check   ☐ Other

11 Ownership of account: ☐ Self   ☐ Spouse   ☐ Self and Spouse

Part III   **Declaration of Taxpayer**

Under penalties of perjury, I declare that the information I have provided to my electronic return originator (ERO) and the amounts shown in Part I above agree with the amounts shown on the corresponding lines of my 1994 Federal income tax return. To the best of my knowledge and belief, my return is true, correct, and complete. I consent that my return, this declaration, and accompanying schedules and statements be sent to the IRS by my ERO. **I consent that my refund be directly deposited as designated in Part II above; I declare that the information shown on lines 6 through 11 in Part II above is correct; and I authorize the IRS to inform my ERO and/or transmitter whether my request**

for Direct Deposit will be honored. If I have filed a joint return and elected Direct Deposit, this is an irrevocable appointment of the other spouse as an agent to receive the refund. If I have filed a balance due return, I understand that if the IRS does not receive full and timely payment of my tax liability, I will remain liable for the tax liability and all applicable interest and penalties. If I have filed a joint Federal and state tax return and there is an error on my state return, I understand my Federal return will be rejected. **If the processing of my return or refund is delayed, I authorize the IRS to disclose to my ERO and/or the transmitter the reason(s) for the delay, or when the refund was sent.**

Sign Here

▶ _____ Your signature   Date

▶ _____ Spouse's signature. If a joint return, BOTH must sign.   Date

Part IV   **Declaration of Electronic Return Originator (ERO) and Paid Preparer** (See instructions.)

I declare that I have reviewed the above taxpayer's return and that the entries on Form 8453 are complete and correct to the best of my knowledge. If I am only a collector, I understand that I am not responsible for reviewing the taxpayer's return; I declare that Form 8453 accurately reflects the data on the return. If Part II is completed, I declare that I have verified the taxpayer's proof of account and it agrees with the name shown on this declaration. I have obtained the taxpayer's signature on Form 8453 before submitting this return to the IRS, have provided the taxpayer with a copy of all forms and information to be filed with the IRS,

and have followed all other requirements described in **Pub. 1345,** Handbook for Electronic Filers of Individual Income Tax Returns (Tax Year 1994). If I am also the Paid Preparer, under penalties of perjury I declare that I have examined the above taxpayer's return and accompanying schedules and statements, and to the best of my knowledge and belief, they are true, correct, and complete. This declaration of Paid Preparer is based on all information of which the preparer has any knowledge.

ERO's Use Only

ERO's signature ▶	Date	Check if also paid preparer ☐	Check if self-employed ☐	Your social security number
Firm's name (or yours if self-employed) and address ▶			E.I. No.	
			ZIP code	

Under penalties of perjury, I declare that I have examined the above taxpayer's return and accompanying schedules and statements, and to the best of my knowledge and belief, they are true, correct, and complete. Declaration of preparer is based on all information of which the preparer has any knowledge.

Paid Preparer's Use Only

Preparer's signature ▶	Date	Check if self-employed ☐	Preparer's social security no.
Firm's name (or yours if self-employed) and address ▶		E.I. No.	
		ZIP code	

Cat. No. 62766T

Form **8453** (1994)

Form **8582**

Department of the Treasury
Internal Revenue Service

Passive Activity Loss Limitations

► See separate instructions.

► Attach to Form 1040 or Form 1041.

OMB No. 1545-1008

1994

Attachment
Sequence No. **88**

Name(s) shown on return

Identifying number

Part I   **1994 Passive Activity Loss**

Caution: *See the instructions for Worksheets 1 and 2 on pages 7 and 8 before completing Part I.*

Rental Real Estate Activities With Active Participation (For the definition of active participation see **Active Participation in a Rental Real Estate Activity** on page 3 of the instructions.)

1a Activities with net income (from Worksheet 1, column (a)) . .	**1a**	
b Activities with net loss (from Worksheet 1, column (b)) . . .	**1b** ( )	
c Prior year unallowed losses (from Worksheet 1, column (c)) .	**1c** ( )	
d Combine lines 1a, 1b, and 1c	**1d**	

All Other Passive Activities

2a Activities with net income (from Worksheet 2, column (a)) . .	**2a**	
b Activities with net loss (from Worksheet 2, column (b)) . . .	**2b** ( )	
c Prior year unallowed losses (from Worksheet 2, column (c)) .	**2c** ( )	
d Combine lines 2a, 2b, and 2c	**2d**	

3 Combine lines 1d and 2d. If the result is net income or zero, see the instructions for line 3. If this line and line 1d are losses, go to line 4. Otherwise, enter -0- on line 9 and go to line 10 . | **3** |

Part II   **Special Allowance for Rental Real Estate With Active Participation**

Note: *Enter all numbers in Part II as positive amounts. (See instructions on page 8 for examples.)*

4 Enter the **smaller** of the loss on line 1d or the loss on line 3 . . . . | **4** |

5 Enter $150,000. If married filing separately, see the instructions . | **5** |

6 Enter modified adjusted gross income, but not less than zero (see instructions) . . . . | **6** |

Note: *If line 6 is equal to or greater than line 5, skip lines 7 and 8, enter -0- on line 9, and then go to line 10. Otherwise, go to line 7.*

7 Subtract line 6 from line 5 . . . . | **7** |

8 Multiply line 7 by 50% (.5). **Do not** enter more than $25,000. If married filing separately, see instructions . . . . | **8** |

9 Enter the **smaller** of line 4 or line 8 . . . . | **9** |

Part III   **Total Losses Allowed**

10 Add the income, if any, on lines 1a and 2a and enter the total . . . . | **10** |

11 **Total losses allowed from all passive activities for 1994.** Add lines 9 and 10. See the instructions to find out how to report the losses on your tax return . . . . | **11** |

For Paperwork Reduction Act Notice, see separate instructions.   Cat. No. 63704F   Form **8582** (1994)

Form 8582 (1994)   Page **2**

Caution: *The worksheets are not required to be filed with your tax return and may be detached before filing Form 8582. Keep a copy of the worksheets for your records.*

Worksheet 1—For Form 8582, Lines 1a, 1b, and 1c (See instructions on page 7.)

Name of activity	Current year		Prior year	Overall gain or loss	
	(a) Net income (line 1a)	(b) Net loss (line 1b)	(c) Unallowed loss (line 1c)	(d) Gain	(e) Loss
Total. Enter on Form 8582, lines 1a, 1b, and 1c. . . . . ▶					

Worksheet 2—For Form 8582, Lines 2a, 2b, and 2c (See instructions on page 8.)

Name of activity	Current year		Prior year	Overall gain or loss	
	(a) Net income (line 2a)	(b) Net loss (line 2b)	(c) Unallowed loss (line 2c)	(d) Gain	(e) Loss
Total. Enter on Form 8582, lines 2a, 2b, and 2c. . . . . ▶					

Worksheet 3—Use this worksheet if an amount is shown on Form 8582, line 9 (See instructions on page 8.)

Name of activity	Form or schedule to be reported on	(a) Loss (See instructions.)	(b) Ratio (See instructions.)	(c) Special allowance (See instructions.)	(d) Subtract column (c) from column (a) (See instructions.)
Total . . . . ▶			1.00		

Worksheet 4—Allocation of Unallowed Losses (See instructions on page 9.)

Name of activity	Form or schedule to be reported on	(a) Loss (See instructions.)	(b) Ratio (See instructions.)	(c) Unallowed loss (See instructions.)
Total . . . . ▶			1.00	

Worksheet 5—Allowed Losses (See instructions on page 9.)

Name of activity	Form or schedule to be reported on	(a) Loss (See instructions.)	(b) Unallowed loss (See instructions.)	(c) Allowed loss (See instructions.)
Total . . . . ▶				

Worksheet 6—Activities With Losses Reported on Two or More Different Forms or Schedules (See instructions on page 9.)

Name of Activity:	(a) (See instr.)	(b) (See instr.)	(c) Ratio (See instr.)	(d) Unallowed loss (See instr.)	(e) Allowed loss (See instr.)
Form or Schedule To Be Reported on:					
1a Net loss plus prior year unallowed loss from form or schedule . ▶					
b Net income from form or schedule . . . . . . ▶					
c Subtract line 1b from line 1a. If zero or less, enter -0- . . . . ▶					
Form or Schedule To Be Reported on:					
1a Net loss plus prior year unallowed loss from form or schedule . ▶					
b Net income from form or schedule . . . . . . ▶					
c Subtract line 1b from line 1a. If zero or less, enter -0- . . . . ▶					
Form or Schedule To Be Reported on:					
1a Net loss plus prior year unallowed loss from form or schedule . ▶					
b Net income from form or schedule . . . . . . ▶					
c Subtract line 1b from line 1a. If zero or less, enter -0- . . . . ▶					
Total . . . . ▶			1.00		

Form **8606**

Department of the Treasury
Internal Revenue Service

Nondeductible IRAs
(Contributions, Distributions, and Basis)
▶ **Please see What Records Must I Keep? on page 2.**
▶ **Attach to Form 1040, Form 1040A, or Form 1040NR.**

OMB No. 1545-1007

1994

Attachment
Sequence No. **47**

Name. If married, file a separate Form 8606 for each spouse. See instructions.

Your social security number

Fill in Your Address Only If You Are Filing This Form by Itself and Not With Your Tax Return

Home address (number and street, or P.O. box if mail is not delivered to your home)

Apt. no.

City, town or post office, state, and ZIP code

Contributions, Nontaxable Distributions, and Basis

1	Enter your IRA contributions for 1994 that you choose to be nondeductible. Include those made during 1/1/95–4/17/95 that were for 1994. See instructions	**1**
2	Enter your total IRA basis for 1993 and earlier years. See instructions	**2**
3	Add lines 1 and 2	**3**

Did you receive any IRA distributions (withdrawals) in 1994?

No ──────▶ Enter the amount from line 3 on line 12. Then, **stop** and read **When and Where To File** on page 2.

Yes ──────▶ Go to line 4.

4	Enter only those contributions included on line 1 that were made during 1/1/95–4/17/95. This amount will be the same as line 1 if all of your nondeductible contributions for 1994 were made in 1995 by 4/17/95. See instructions	**4**
5	Subtract line 4 from line 3	**5**
6	Enter the total value of **ALL** your IRAs as of 12/31/94 plus any outstanding rollovers. See instructions **6**	
7	Enter the total IRA distributions received during 1994. Do not include amounts rolled over before 1/1/95. See instructions **7**	
8	Add lines 6 and 7 . . . . **8**	
9	Divide line 5 by line 8 and enter the result as a decimal (to at least two places). Do not enter more than "1.00" . . . . **9** × .	
10	Multiply line 7 by line 9. This is the amount of your **nontaxable distributions for 1994**	**10**
11	Subtract line 10 from line 5. This is the **basis in your IRA(s) as of 12/31/94**	**11**
12	Add lines 4 and 11. This is your **total IRA basis for 1994 and earlier years**	**12**

Taxable Distributions for 1994

13	Subtract line 10 from line 7. Enter the result here and on Form 1040, line 15b; Form 1040A, line 10b; or Form 1040NR, line 16b, whichever applies	**13**

Sign Here Only If You Are Filing This Form by Itself and Not With Your Tax Return

Under penalties of perjury, I declare that I have examined this form, including accompanying attachments, and to the best of my knowledge and belief, it is true, correct, and complete.

▶ Your signature

▶ Date

Form **8615**	**Tax for Children Under Age 14**	OMB No. 1545-0998
	Who Have Investment Income of More Than $1,200	**1994**
Department of the Treasury Internal Revenue Service	▶ See instructions below and on back. ▶ **Attach ONLY to the child's Form 1040, Form 1040A, or Form 1040NR.**	Attachment Sequence No. **33**

Child's name shown on return	Child's social security number

A Parent's name (first, initial, and last). **Caution:** *See instructions on back before completing.*   **B** Parent's social security number

C Parent's filing status (check one):

☐ Single ☐ Married filing jointly ☐ Married filing separately ☐ Head of household ☐ Qualifying widow(er)

Step 1   Figure child's net investment income

1	Enter child's investment income, such as taxable interest and dividend income. See instructions. If this amount is $1,200 or less, **stop here;** do not file this form	**1**	
2	If the child DID NOT itemize deductions on Schedule A (Form 1040 or Form 1040NR), enter $1,200. If the child ITEMIZED deductions, see instructions	**2**	
3	Subtract line 2 from line 1. If the result is zero or less, **stop here;** do not complete the rest of this form but ATTACH it to the child's return	**3**	
4	Enter child's **taxable** income from Form 1040, line 37; Form 1040A, line 22; or Form 1040NR, line 36	**4**	
5	Enter the **smaller** of line 3 or line 4. . . . . ▶	**5**	

Step 2   Figure tentative tax based on the tax rate of the parent listed on line A

6	Enter parent's **taxable** income from Form 1040, line 37; Form 1040A, line 22; Form 1040EZ, line 5; or Form 1040NR, line 36. If the parent transferred property to a trust, see instructions .	**6**	
7	Enter the total net investment income, if any, from Forms 8615, line 5, of ALL OTHER children of the parent identified above. **Do not** include the amount from line 5 above	**7**	
8	Add lines 5, 6, and 7	**8**	
9	Tax on line 8 based on the **parent's** filing status. See instructions. If from Capital Gain Tax Worksheet, enter amount from line 4 of that worksheet here ▶ _____	**9**	
10	Enter parent's tax from Form 1040, line 38; Form 1040A, line 23; Form 1040EZ, line 9; or Form 1040NR, line 37. If from **Capital Gain Tax Worksheet,** enter amount from line 4 of that worksheet here ▶ _____	**10**	
11	Subtract line 10 from line 9. If line 7 is blank, enter on line 13 the amount from line 11; skip lines 12a and 12b	**11**	
12a	Add lines 5 and 7 . . . . **12a**		
b	Divide line 5 by line 12a. Enter the result as a decimal (rounded to two places)	**12b**	× .
13	Multiply line 11 by line 12b . . . . ▶	**13**	

Step 3   Figure child's tax—If lines 4 and 5 above are the same, enter -0- on line 15 and go to line 16.

14	Subtract line 5 from line 4 . . . . **14**		
15	Tax on line 14 based on the **child's** filing status. See instructions. If from Capital Gain Tax Worksheet, enter amount from line 4 of that worksheet here ▶ _____	**15**	
16	Add lines 13 and 15	**16**	
17	Tax on line 4 based on the **child's** filing status. See instructions. If from Capital Gain Tax Worksheet, check here . . . . ▶ ☐	**17**	
18	Enter the **larger** of line 16 or line 17 here and on Form 1040, line 38; Form 1040A, line 23; or Form 1040NR, line 37. Be sure to check the box for "Form 8615" even if line 17 is more than line 16 . ▶	**18**	

Form **8814**

Department of the Treasury
Internal Revenue Service

Parents' Election To Report
Child's Interest and Dividends
▶ See instructions below and on back.
▶ Attach to parents' Form 1040 or Form 1040NR.

OMB No. 1545-1128

1994

Attachment
Sequence No. **40**

Name(s) shown on your return

Your social security number

A Child's name (first, initial, and last)

B Child's social security number

C If more than one Form 8814 is attached, check here . . . . ▶ ☐

Step 1	**Figure amount of child's interest and dividend income to report on your return**		
1a	Enter your child's **taxable** interest income. If this amount is different from the amounts shown on the child's Forms 1099-INT and 1099-OID, see the instructions	**1a**	
b	Enter your child's **tax-exempt** interest income. **DO NOT** include this amount on line 1a **1b**		
2a	Enter your child's gross dividends, including any Alaska Permanent Fund dividends. If none, enter -0- on line 2c and go to line 3. If your child received any capital gain distributions or dividends as a nominee, see the instructions **2a**		
b	Enter your child's nontaxable distributions that are included on line 2a. These should be shown in box 1d of Form 1099-DIV . . . **2b**		
c	Subtract line 2b from line 2a	**2c**	
3	Add lines 1a and 2c. If the total is $1,000 or less, skip lines 4 and 5 and go to line 6. If the total is $5,000 or more, **do not** file this form. Your child **must** file his or her own return to report the income	**3**	
4	Base amount	**4**	1,000 00
5	Subtract line 4 from line 3. If you checked the box on line C above or if line 2a includes any capital gain distributions, see the instructions. Also, include this amount in the total on Form 1040, line 21, or Form 1040NR, line 21. In the space next to line 21, enter "Form 8814" and show the amount. Go to line 6 below . . . . ▶	**5**	
Step 2	**Figure your tax on the first $1,000 of child's interest and dividend income**		
6	Amount not taxed	**6**	500 00
7	Subtract line 6 from line 3. If the result is zero or less, enter -0-	**7**	
8	**Tax.** Is the amount on line 7 less than $500? **NO.** Enter $75 here and see the **Note** below. **YES.** Multiply line 7 by 15% (.15). Enter the result here and see the **Note** below.	**8**	

Note: *If you checked the box on line C above, see the instructions. Otherwise, include the amount from line 8 in the tax you enter on Form 1040, line 38, or Form 1040NR, line 37. Also, enter the amount from line 8 in the space provided next to line 38 on Form 1040, or next to line 37 on Form 1040NR.*

Form **8829**	**Expenses for Business Use of Your Home**	OMB No. 1545-1266
	▶ File only with Schedule C (Form 1040). Use a separate Form 8 829 for each home you used for business during the year.	19**94**
Department of the Treasury Internal Revenue Service	▶ See separate instructions.	Attachment Sequence No. **66**

Name(s) of proprietor(s)	Your social security number

Part I — Part of Your Home Used for Business

1	Area used regularly and exclusively for business, regularly for day care, or for inventory storage. See instructions	1	
2	Total area of home	2	
3	Divide line 1 by line 2. Enter the result as a percentage	3	%

• **For day-care facilities not used exclusively for business, also complete lines 4±6.**

• **All others, skip lines 4-6 and enter the amount from line 3 on line 7.**

4	Multiply days used for day care during year by hours used per day	4	hr.
5	Total hours available for use during the year (365 days × 24 hours). See instructions	5	8,760 hr.
6	Divide line 4 by line 5. Enter the result as a decimal amount	6	.
7	Business percentage. For day-care facilities not used exclusively for business, multiply line 6 by line 3 (enter the result as a percentage). All others, enter the amount from line 3 ▶	7	%

Part II — Figure Your Allowable Deduction

		(a) Direct expenses	(b) Indirect expenses		
8	Enter the amount from Schedule C, line 29, **plus** any net gain or (loss) derived from the business use of your home and shown on Schedule D or Form 4797. If more than one place of business, see instructions			8	
	See instructions for columns (a) and (b) before completing lines 9-20.				
9	Casualty losses. See instructions	9			
10	Deductible mortgage interest. See instructions	10			
11	Real estate taxes. See instructions	11			
12	Add lines 9, 10, and 11	12			
13	Multiply line 12, column (b) by line 7		13		
14	Add line 12, column (a) and line 13			14	
15	Subtract line 14 from line 8. If zero or less, enter -0-			15	
16	Excess mortgage interest. See instructions	16			
17	Insurance	17			
18	Repairs and maintenance	18			
19	Utilities	19			
20	Other expenses. See instructions	20			
21	Add lines 16 through 20	21			
22	Multiply line 21, column (b) by line 7	22			
23	Carryover of operating expenses from 1993 Form 8829, line 41	23			
24	Add line 21 in column (a), line 22, and line 23			24	
25	Allowable operating expenses. Enter the **smaller** of line 15 or line 24			25	
26	Limit on excess casualty losses and depreciation. Subtract line 25 from line 15			26	
27	Excess casualty losses. See instructions	27			
28	Depreciation of your home from Part III below	28			
29	Carryover of excess casualty losses and depreciation from 1993 Form 8829, line 42	29			
30	Add lines 27 through 29			30	
31	Allowable excess casualty losses and depreciation. Enter the **smaller** of line 26 or line 30			31	
32	Add lines 14, 25, and 31			32	
33	Casualty loss portion, if any, from lines 14 and 31. Carry amount to **Form 4684,** Section B			33	
34	Allowable expenses for business use of your home. Subtract line 33 from line 32. Enter here and on Schedule C, line 30. If your home was used for more than one business, see instructions ▶			34	

Part III — Depreciation of Your Home

35	Enter the **smaller** of your home's adjusted basis or its fair market value. See instructions	35	
36	Value of land included on line 35	36	
37	Basis of building. Subtract line 36 from line 35	37	
38	Business basis of building. Multiply line 37 by line 7	38	
39	Depreciation percentage. See instructions	39	%
40	Depreciation allowable. Multiply line 38 by line 39. Enter here and on line 28 above. See instructions	40	

Part IV — Carryover of Unallowed Expenses to 1995

41	Operating expenses. Subtract line 25 from line 24. If less than zero, enter -0-	41	
42	Excess casualty losses and depreciation. Subtract line 31 from line 30. If less than zero, enter -0-	42	

For Paperwork Reduction Act Notice, see page 1 of separate instructions. ✪ *Printed on recycled paper*   Cat. No. 13232M   Form **8829** (1994)

STATEMENTS ON RESPONSIBILITIES IN TAX PRACTICE

1991 Revision
Statements 1–8 and Interpretation 1–1

Issued by the Tax Executive Committee
of the American Institute of Certified Public Accountants

CONTENTS

Foreword   D-4

Introduction   D-5
  The Program   D-5
  The Significance of the Statements   D-5
  The Objectives   D-5
  The Program in Perspective   D-5
  The Scope and Purpose of the Statements   D-6
  Authority of the Tax Executive Committee   D-6
  The Procedures   D-6

Statement No. 1: Tax Return Positions   D-7
  Introduction   D-7
  Statement   D-7
  Explanation   D-7

Interpretation No. 1–1: Realistic Possibility Standard   D-9
  Background   D-9
  General Interpretation   D-9
  Specific Illustrations   D-10

Statement No. 2: Answers to Questions on Returns   D-14
  Introduction   D-14
  Statement   D-14
  Explanation   D-14

Statement No. 3: Certain Procedural Aspects of Preparing Returns   D-15
  Introduction   D-15
  Statement   D-15
  Explanation   D-15

Statement No. 4: Use of Estimates   D-17
  Introduction   D-17
  Statement   D-17
  Explanation   D-17

Statement No. 5: Departure from a Position Previously Concluded in an Administrative Proceeding or Court Decision   D-19
   Introduction   D-19
   Statement   D-19
   Explanation   D-19

Statement No. 6: Knowledge of Error: Return Preparation   D-21
   Introduction   D-21
   Statement   D-21
   Explanation   D-21

Statement No. 7: Knowledge of Error: Administrative Proceedings   D-23
   Introduction   D-23
   Statement   D-23
   Explanation   D-23

Statement No. 8: Form and Content of Advice to Clients   D-25
   Introduction   D-25
   Statement   D-25
   Explanation   D-25

Statements on Responsibilities in Tax Practice are published for the guidance of members of the Institute and do not constitute enforceable standards. The statements have been approved by at least two-thirds of the members of the Responsibilities in Tax Practice Committee and the Tax Executive Committee.

Statements containing recommended standards of responsibilities that are more restrictive than those established by the Internal Revenue Code, the Treasury Department, or the Institute's Code of Professional Conduct depend for their authority on the general acceptability of the opinions expressed. These statements are not intended to be retroactive.

FOREWORD

This booklet contains the current version of the Statements on Responsibilities in Tax Practice (SRTPs) plus Interpretation 1-1, "Realistic Possibility Standard." The original Statements on Responsibilities in Tax Practice were issued between 1964 and 1977 to provide a body of advisory opinions on good standards of tax practice, delineating the CPA's responsibilities to the client, the public, the government, and the profession. Statement Nos. 1 through 9 and the Introduction were codified in 1976 as *Statements on Responsibilities in Tax Practice.* Statement No. 10 was issued in 1977.

The original statements concerning the CPA's responsibility to sign the return (Statement Nos. 1 and 2, "Signature of Preparers" and "Signature of Reviewer: Assumption of Preparer's Responsibility") were withdrawn in 1982 after Treasury Department regulations were issued adopting substantially the same standards for all tax return preparers. Statement Nos. 6 and 7, concerning the responsibility of a CPA who becomes aware of an error, were revised in 1991. The first interpretation of the Statements on Responsibilities in Tax Practice, Interpretation 1-1, was approved in December 1990. The previously issued statements have been renumbered as indicated in the Appendix, and the current statements should be cited as "SRTP No. 1," "SRTP No. 2," etc.

This publication is intended to be part of an ongoing process that will require changes to and interpretations of current statements and additions of new statements in recognition of the accelerating rate of change in tax laws and the increasing importance of tax practice to CPAs.

Statements on Responsibilities in Tax Practice are developed by the Responsibilities in Tax Practice Committee and approved by the Tax Executive Committee. This revision was approved by the 1990–91 Responsibilities in Tax Practice Committee and the 1990–91 Tax Executive Committee, but acknowledgment is also due to the many members whose efforts over the years went into the development of these statements.

Donald H. Skadden
Vice President—Taxation

INTRODUCTION

The Program

.01   The program contemplates publication and dissemination of a numbered series of Statements on Responsibilities in Tax Practice by the Institute's Tax Executive Committee.

The Significance of the Statements

.02   The statements constitute a body of advisory opinion on what are appropriate standards of tax practice, outlining the extent of a CPA's responsibility to clients, the public, the government, and the profession. Each statement covers a particular aspect of tax practice. The statements, which are educational and advisory, take into account applicable legal requirements of tax practice as well as the Tax Division's opinions as to appropriate standards of responsibilities in tax practice.

The Objectives

.03   The principal objectives of the program are—

a.   To recommend appropriate standards of responsibilities in tax practice and to promote their uniform application by CPAs.

b.   To encourage the development of increased understanding of the responsibilities of CPAs by the Treasury Department and Internal Revenue Service and to urge their officials to promote the application of commensurate standards of responsibilities by their personnel.

c.   To foster increased public understanding of, compliance with, and confidence in our tax system through awareness of the recommended standards of responsibilities of CPAs in tax practice.

The Program in Perspective

.04   There are numerous guides to help determine practice responsibilities. The CPA is required to follow the statutes, regulations, and rules governing practice before the Internal Revenue Service (for example, Treasury Department Circular 230). The Institute's Code of Professional Conduct requires the observance of high ethical standards. These statements are published to clarify the CPA's dual responsibilities to the tax system and clients.

.05   Although the CPA has no separate enforceable statement of standards of conduct relating solely to tax practice, the Institute's Code of Professional Conduct requires attitudes and habits of truthfulness and integrity in all of a CPA's practice, including tax practice. Rule 102 of the Code of Professional Conduct states:

> In the performance of any professional service, a member shall maintain objectivity and integrity, shall be free of conflicts of interest, and shall not knowingly misrepresent facts or subordinate his or her judgment to others.

.06   The statements are not intended to establish a code of conduct in tax practice that is separate and apart from the general ethical precepts of the Institute's Code of Professional Conduct. That Code imposes upon individual members obligations to maintain high standards of technical competence and integrity in dealing with clients and the public in all phases of the professional activities of members, including tax practice.

.07   In this environment, the Tax Executive Committee concludes that while the Code of Professional Conduct is a major factor in molding the CPA's professional behavior, it is in the public interest and in the self-interest of the CPA to develop separate statements of recommended standards of responsibilities of CPAs in tax practice for the guidance of taxpayers and CPAs alike.

The Scope and Purpose of the Statements

.08   The statements generally are confined to discussions of the considerations relating to *federal income tax* practice, including the preparation of tax returns, tax planning, and representation before the Internal Revenue Service. The Tax Executive Committee will consider development of statements of responsibilities in other areas of tax practice in the future as part of its ongoing program to review, revise, and add statements as necessary or appropriate.

.09   The primary purpose of the program is educational. The statements do not have the force of authority, in contrast, for example, to the regulations contained in Treasury Department Circular 230, the Internal Revenue Code or its regulations, or the AICPA Code of Professional Conduct. Statements containing recommended standards of responsibilities that are more restrictive than those established by the Internal Revenue Code, the Treasury Department, or the AICPA Code of Professional Conduct are advisory opinions and CPAs should use them as guides.

Authority of the Tax Executive Committee

.10   By resolution of the Institute's Council, the Tax Executive Committee is authorized to express opinions on matters of broad policy related to taxation including the issuance of Statements on Responsibilities in Tax Practice.

The Procedures

.11   The statements present the opinion of at least two-thirds of the members of the Responsibilities in Tax Practice Committee and two-thirds of the Tax Executive Committee.

.12   Drafts of a proposed statement are given appropriate exposure before the Tax Executive Committee issues a statement.

.13   Details of the procedural aspects of issuing the statements can be found in the AICPA *Tax Division Administrative Manual*.

Statement on Responsibilities in Tax Practice No. 1
Issued August 1988

TAX RETURN POSITIONS

Introduction

.01   This statement sets forth the standards a CPA should follow in recommending tax return positions and in preparing or signing tax returns including claims for refunds. For this purpose, a "tax return position" is (1) a position reflected on the tax return as to which the client has been specifically advised by the CPA or (2) a position as to which the CPA has knowledge of all material facts and, on the basis of those facts, has concluded that the position is appropriate.

Statement

.02   With respect to tax return positions, a CPA should comply with the following standards:

a.   A CPA should not recommend to a client that a position be taken with respect to the tax treatment of any item on a return unless the CPA has a good faith belief that the position has a realistic possibility of being sustained administratively or judicially on its merits if challenged.

b.   A CPA should not prepare or sign a return as an income tax return preparer if the CPA knows that the return takes a position that the CPA could not recommend under the standard expressed in paragraph .02*a*.

c.   Notwithstanding paragraphs .02*a* and .02*b*, a CPA may recommend a position that the CPA concludes is not frivolous so long as the position is adequately disclosed on the return or claim for refund.

d.   In recommending certain tax return positions and in signing a return on which a tax return position is taken, a CPA should, where relevant, advise the client as to the potential penalty consequences of the recommended tax return position and the opportunity, if any, to avoid such penalties through disclosure.

.03   The CPA should not recommend a tax return position that—

a.   Exploits the Internal Revenue Service audit selection process; or

b.   Serves as a mere "arguing" position advanced solely to obtain leverage in the bargaining process of settlement negotiation with the Internal Revenue Service.

.04   A CPA has both the right and responsibility to be an advocate for the client with respect to any positions satisfying the aforementioned standards.

Explanation

.05   Our self-assessment tax system can only function effectively if taxpayers report their income on a tax return that is true, correct, and complete. A tax return is primarily a taxpayer's representation of facts, and the taxpayer has the final responsibility for positions taken on the return.

.06   CPAs have a duty to the tax system as well as to their clients. However, it is well-established that the taxpayer has no obligation to pay more taxes than are legally owed, and the CPA has a duty to the client to assist in achieving the result. The aforementioned standards will guide the CPA in meeting responsibilities to the tax system and to clients.

.07   The standards suggested herein require that a CPA in good faith believe that the position is warranted in existing law or can be supported by a good faith argument for an extension, modification, or reversal of existing law. For example, the CPA may reach such a conclusion on the basis of well-reasoned articles, treatises, IRS General Counsel Memoranda, a General Explanation of a Revenue Act prepared by the staff of the Joint Committee on Taxation and Internal Revenue Service written determinations (for example, private letter rulings), whether or not such sources are treated as "authority" under section 6661. A position would meet these standards even though, for example, it is later abandoned due to practical or procedural aspects of an IRS administrative hearing or in the litigation process.

.08   Where the CPA has a good faith belief that more than one position meets the standards suggested herein, the CPA's advice concerning alternative acceptable positions may include a discussion of the likelihood that each such position might or might not cause the client's tax return to be examined and whether the position would be challenged in an examination.

.09   In some cases, a CPA may conclude that a position is not warranted under the standard set forth in the preceding paragraph, .02*a*. A client may, however, still wish to take such a tax return position. Under such circumstances, the client should have the opportunity to make such an assertion, and the CPA should be able to prepare and sign the return provided the position is adequately disclosed on the return or claim for refund and the position is not frivolous. A "frivolous" position is one which is knowingly advanced in bad faith and is patently improper.

.10   The CPA's determination of whether information is adequately disclosed by the client is based on the facts and circumstances of the particular case. No detailed rules have been formulated, for purposes of this statement, to prescribe the manner in which information should be disclosed.

.11   Where particular facts and circumstances lead the CPA to believe that a taxpayer penalty might be asserted, the CPA should so advise the client and should discuss with the client issues related to disclosure on the tax return. Although disclosure is not required if the position meets the standard in paragraph .02*a*, the CPA may nevertheless recommend that a client disclose a position. Disclosure should be considered when the CPA believes it would mitigate the likelihood of claims of taxpayer penalties under the Internal Revenue Code or would avoid the possible application of the six-year statutory period for assessment under section 6501(e). Although the CPA should advise the client with respect to disclosure, it is the client's responsibility to decide whether and how to disclose.

Statement on Responsibilities in Tax Practice Interpretation No. 1-1
Issued December 1990

REALISTIC POSSIBILITY STANDARD

Background

.01   The AICPA Tax Division issues Statements on Responsibilities in Tax Practice (SRTPs). The primary purpose of these advisory statements on appropriate standards of tax practice is educational. This interpretation does not have the force of authority, in contrast, for example, to the regulations contained in Treasury Department Circular 230 or the preparer penalty provisions of the Internal Revenue Code.

.02   SRTP No. 1, "Tax Return Positions," contains the standards a CPA should follow in recommending tax return positions and in preparing or signing tax returns and claims for refunds. In general, a CPA should have "a good-faith belief that the [tax return] position [being recommended] has a realistic possibility of being sustained administratively or judicially on its merits if challenged" (see SRTP No. 1, paragraph .02*a*). This is referred to here as the "realistic possibility standard." If a CPA concludes that a tax return position does not meet the realistic possibility standard, the CPA may still recommend the position to the client or, if the position is not frivolous and is adequately disclosed on the tax return or claim for refund, the CPA may prepare and sign a return containing the position.

.03   A "frivolous" position is one which is knowingly advanced in bad faith and is patently improper (see SRTP No. 1, paragraph .09). The CPA's determination of whether information is adequately disclosed on the client's tax return or claim for refund is based on the facts and circumstances of the particular case (see SRTP No. 1, paragraph .10).

.04   If the CPA believes there is a possibility that a tax return position might result in penalties being asserted against the client, the CPA should so advise the client and should discuss with the client the opportunity, if any, of avoiding such penalties through disclosure (see SRTP No. 1, paragraph .11).

General Interpretation

.05   To meet the realistic possibility standard, a CPA should have a good-faith belief that the position is warranted by existing law or can be supported by a good-faith argument for an extension, modification, or reversal of existing law through the administrative or judicial process. The CPA should have an honest belief that the position meets the realistic possibility standard. Such a belief must be based on sound interpretations of the tax law. A CPA should not take into account the likelihood of audit or detection when determining whether this standard has been met (see SRTP No. 1, paragraph .03*a*).

.06   The realistic possibility standard cannot be expressed in terms of percentage odds. The realistic possibility standard is less stringent than the "substantial authority" and the "more likely than not" standards that apply under the Internal Revenue Code to substantial understatements of liability by taxpayers. It is more strict than the "reasonable basis" standard under regulations issued prior to the Revenue Reconciliation Act of 1989.

.07 In determining whether a tax return position meets the realistic possibility standard, a CPA may rely on authorities in addition to those evaluated when determining whether substantial authority exists. Accordingly, CPAs may rely on well-reasoned treatises, articles in recognized professional tax publications, and other reference tools and sources of tax analyses commonly used by tax advisors and preparers of returns.

.08 In determining whether a realistic possibility exists, the CPA should do all of the following:[1]

a. Establish relevant background facts.

b. Distill the appropriate questions from these facts.

c. Search for authoritative answers to those questions.

d. Resolve the questions by weighing the authorities uncovered by that search.

e. Arrive at a conclusion supported by the authorities.

.09 The CPA should consider the weight of each authority in order to conclude whether a position meets the realistic possibility standard. In determining the weight of an authority, the CPA should consider its persuasiveness, relevance, and source. Thus, the type of authority is a significant factor. Other important factors include whether the facts stated by the authority are distinguishable from those of the client and whether the authority contains an analysis of the issue or merely states a conclusion.

.10 The realistic possibility standard may be met despite the absence of certain types of authority. For example, a CPA may conclude that the realistic possibility standard has been met when the position is supported only by a well-reasoned construction of the applicable statutory provision.

.11 In determining whether the realistic possibility standard has been met, the extent of research required is left to the judgment of the CPA with respect to all the facts and circumstances known to the CPA. The CPA may conclude that more than one position meets the realistic possibility standard.

Specific Illustrations

.12 The following illustrations deal with general fact patterns. Accordingly, the application of the guidance discussed above to variances in such general facts or to particular facts or circumstances may lead to different conclusions. In each illustration there is no authority other than that indicated.

> *Illustration 1.* The CPA's client has engaged in a transaction that is adversely affected by a new statutory provision. Prior law supports a position favorable to the client. The client believes, and the CPA concurs, that the new statute is inequitable as applied to the client's situation. The statute is clearly drafted and unambiguous. The committee reports discussing the new statute contain general comments that do not specifically address the client's situation.

The CPA should recommend the return position supported by the new statute. A position contrary to a clear, unambiguous statute would ordinarily be considered a frivolous position.

---

1. See Ray M. Sommerfeld, et al., *Tax Research Techniques,* 3rd rev. ed. (New York: AICPA, 1989), for a discussion of this process.

Illustration 2. The facts are the same as in illustration 1 except that the committee reports discussing the new statute specifically address the client's situation and take a position favorable to the client.

In a case where the statute is clearly and unambiguously against the taxpayer's position but a contrary position exists based on committee reports specifically addressing the client's situation, a return position based on either the statutory language or the legislative history satisfies the realistic possibility standard.

Illustration 3. The facts are the same as in illustration 1 except that the committee reports can be interpreted to provide some evidence or authority in support of the taxpayer's position; however, the legislative history does not specifically address the situation.

In a case where the statute is clear and unambiguous, a contrary position based on an interpretation of committee reports that do not explicitly address the client's situation does not meet the realistic possibility standard. However, since the committee reports provide some support or evidence for the taxpayer's position, such a return position is not frivolous. The CPA may recommend the position to the client if it is adequately disclosed on the tax return.

Illustration 4. A client is faced with an issue involving the interpretation of a new statute. Following its passage, the statute was widely recognized to contain a drafting error, and a technical correction proposal has been introduced. The IRS issues an announcement indicating how it will administer the provision. The IRS pronouncement interprets the statute in accordance with the proposed technical correction.

Return positions based on either the existing statutory language or the IRS pronouncement satisfy the realistic possibility standard.

Illustration 5. The facts are the same as in illustration 4 except that no IRS pronouncement has been issued.

In the absence of an IRS pronouncement interpreting the statute in accordance with the technical correction, only a return position based on the existing statutory language will meet the realistic possibility standard. A return position based on the proposed technical correction may be recommended if it is adequately disclosed, since it is not frivolous.

Illustration 6. A client is seeking advice from a CPA regarding a recently amended Internal Revenue Code section. The CPA has reviewed the Code section, committee reports that specifically address the issue, and a recently published IRS Notice. The CPA has concluded in good faith that, based on the Code section and the committee reports, the IRS's position as stated in the Notice does not reflect congressional intent.

The CPA may recommend the position supported by the Internal Revenue Code section and the committee reports since it meets the realistic possibility standard.

Illustration 7. The facts are the same as in illustration 6 except that the IRS pronouncement is a temporary regulation.

In determining whether the position meets the realistic possibility standard, the CPA should determine the weight to be given the regulation by analyzing factors such as whether the regulation is legislative, interpretative, or inconsistent with the statute. If the CPA concludes that the position does not meet the realistic possibility standard, the position may nevertheless be recommended if it is adequately disclosed, since it is not frivolous.

Illustration 8. A tax form published by the IRS is incorrect, but completion of the form as published provides a benefit to the client. The CPA knows that the IRS has published an announcement acknowledging the error.

In these circumstances, a return position in accordance with the published form is a frivolous position.

Illustration 9. The client wants to take a position that the CPA has concluded is frivolous. The client maintains that even if the return is examined by the IRS, the issue will not be raised.

The CPA should not consider the likelihood of audit or detection when determining whether the realistic possibility standard has been met. The CPA should not prepare or sign a return that contains a frivolous position even if it is disclosed.

Illustration 10. Congress passes a statute requiring the capitalization of certain expenditures. The client believes, and the CPA concurs, that in order to comply fully, the client will need to acquire new computer hardware and software and implement a number of new accounting procedures. The client and the CPA agree that the costs of full compliance will be significantly greater than the resulting increase in tax due under the new provision. Because of these cost considerations, the client makes no effort to comply. The client wants the CPA to prepare and sign a return on which the new requirement is simply ignored.

The return position desired by the client is frivolous, and the CPA should neither prepare nor sign the return.

Illustration 11. The facts are the same as in illustration 10 except that the client has made a good-faith effort to comply with the law by calculating an estimate of expenditures to be capitalized under the new provision.

In this situation, the realistic possibility standard has been met. When using estimates in the preparation of a return, the CPA should refer to SRTP No. 4, "Use of Estimates."

Illustration 12. On a given issue, the CPA has located and weighed two authorities. The IRS has published its clearly enunciated position in a Revenue Ruling. A court opinion is favorable to the client. The CPA has considered the source of both authorities and has concluded that both are persuasive and relevant.

The realistic possibility standard is met by either position.

Illustration 13. A tax statute is silent on the treatment of an item under the statute. However, the committee reports explaining the statute direct the IRS to issue regulations that will require a specified treatment of the item. No regulations have been issued at the time the CPA must recommend a position on the tax treatment of the item.

The CPA may recommend the position supported by the committee reports, since it meets the realistic possibility standard.

Illustration 14. The client wants to take a position that the CPA concludes meets the realistic possibility standard based on an assumption regarding an underlying nontax legal issue. The CPA recommends that the client seek advice from its legal counsel, and the client's attorney gives an opinion on the nontax legal issue.

A legal opinion on a nontax legal issue may, in general, be relied upon by a CPA. The CPA must, however, use professional judgment when relying on a legal opinion. If, on its face, the opinion of the client's attorney appears to be unreasonable, unsubstantiated, or unwarranted, the CPA should consult his or her attorney before relying on the opinion.

> *Illustration 15.* The client has obtained from its attorney an opinion on the tax treatment of an item and requests that the CPA rely on the opinion.

The authorities on which a CPA may rely include well-reasoned sources of tax analysis. If the CPA is satisfied as to the source, relevance, and persuasiveness of the legal opinion, the CPA may rely on that opinion when determining whether the realistic possibility standard has been met.

Statement on Responsibilities in Tax Practice No. 2
Issued August 1988

ANSWERS TO QUESTIONS ON RETURNS

Introduction

.01   This statement considers whether a CPA may sign the preparer's declaration on a tax return where one or more questions on the return have not been answered. The term "questions" includes requests for information on the return, in the instructions, or in the regulations, whether or not stated in the form of a question.

Statement

.02   A CPA should make a reasonable effort to obtain from the client, and provide, appropriate answers to all questions on a tax return before signing as preparer.

Explanation

.03   It is recognized that the questions on tax returns are not of uniform importance, and often they are not applicable to the particular taxpayer. Nevertheless, aside from administrative convenience to the Internal Revenue Service, there are at least two considerations which dictate that a CPA should be satisfied that a reasonable effort has been made to provide appropriate answers to the questions on the return which are applicable to the taxpayer:

a.   A question may be of importance in determining taxable income or loss, or the tax liability shown on the return, in which circumstance the omission tends to detract from the quality of the return.

b.   The CPA must sign the preparer's declaration stating that the return is true, correct, and complete.

.04   While an effort should be made to provide an answer to each question on the return that is applicable to the taxpayer, reasonable grounds may exist for omitting an answer. For example, reasonable grounds may include the following:

a.   The information is not readily available and the answer is not significant in terms of taxable income or loss, or the tax liability shown on the return.

b.   Genuine uncertainty exists regarding the meaning of the question in relation to the particular return.

c.   The answer to the question is voluminous; in such cases, assurance should be given on the return that the data will be supplied upon examination.

.05   The fact that an answer to a question might prove disadvantageous to the client does not justify omitting an answer.

.06   Where reasonable grounds exist for omission of an answer to an applicable question, a CPA is not required to provide on the return an explanation of the reason for the omission. In this connection, the CPA should consider whether the omission of an answer to a question may cause the return to be deemed incomplete.

Statement on Responsibilities in Tax Practice No. 3
Issued August 1988

CERTAIN PROCEDURAL ASPECTS OF PREPARING RETURNS

Introduction

.01   This statement considers the responsibility of the CPA to examine or verify certain supporting data or to consider information related to another client when preparing a client's tax return.

Statement

.02   In preparing or signing a return, the CPA may in good faith rely without verification upon information furnished by the client or by third parties. However, the CPA should not ignore the implications of information furnished and should make reasonable inquiries if the information furnished appears to be incorrect, incomplete, or inconsistent either on its face or on the basis of other facts known to the CPA. In this connection, the CPA should refer to the client's returns for prior years whenever feasible.

.03   Where the Internal Revenue Code or income tax regulations impose a condition to deductibility or other tax treatment of an item (such as taxpayer maintenance of books and records or substantiating documentation to support the reported deduction or tax treatment), the CPA should make appropriate inquiries to determine to his or her satisfaction whether such condition has been met.

.04   The individual CPA who is required to sign the return should consider information actually known to that CPA from the tax return of another client when preparing a tax return if the information is relevant to that tax return, its consideration is necessary to properly prepare that tax return, and use of such information does not violate any law or rule relating to confidentiality.

Explanation

.05   The preparer's declaration on the income tax return states that the information contained therein is true, correct, and complete to the best of the preparer's knowledge and belief "based on all information of which preparer has any knowledge." This reference should be understood to relate to information furnished by the client or by third parties to the CPA in connection with the preparation of the return.

.06   The preparer's declaration does not require the CPA to examine or verify supporting data. However, a distinction should be made between (1) the need to either determine by inquiry that a specifically required condition (such as maintaining books and records or substantiating documentation) has been satisfied, or to obtain information when the material furnished appears to be incorrect or incomplete, and (2) the need for the CPA to examine underlying information. In fulfilling his or her obligation to exercise due diligence in preparing a return, the CPA ordinarily may rely on information furnished by the client unless it appears to be incorrect, incomplete, or inconsistent. Although the CPA has certain responsibilities in exercising due diligence in preparing a return, the client has ultimate responsibility for the contents of the return. Thus, where the client presents unsupported data in the form of lists of tax information, such as dividends and interest received, charitable contributions, and medical expenses, such information may be used in the preparation of a tax return without verification unless it appears to be incorrect, incomplete, or inconsistent either on its face or on the basis of other facts known to the CPA.

.07   Even though there is no requirement to examine underlying documentation, the CPA should encourage the client to provide supporting data where appropriate. For example, the CPA should encourage the client to submit underlying documents for use in tax return preparation to permit full consideration of income and deductions arising from security transactions and from pass-through entities such as estates, trusts, partnerships, and S corporations. This should reduce the possibility of misunderstanding, inadvertent errors, and administrative problems in the examination of returns by the Internal Revenue Service.

.08   The source of information provided to the CPA by a client for use in preparing the return is often a pass-through entity, such as a limited partnership, in which the client has an interest but is not involved in management. In some instances, it may be appropriate for the CPA to advise the client to ascertain the nature and amount of possible exposures to tax deficiencies, interest, and penalties, by contact with management of the pass-through entity. However, the CPA need not require the client to do so and may accept the information provided by the pass-through entity without further inquiry, unless there is reason to believe it is incorrect, incomplete, or inconsistent either on its face or on the basis of other facts known to the CPA.

.09   The CPA should make use of the client's prior years' returns in preparing the current return whenever feasible. Reference to prior returns and discussion with the client of prior year tax determinations should provide information as to the client's general tax status, avoid the omission or duplication of items, and afford a basis for the treatment of similar or related transactions. As with the examination of information supplied for the current year's return, the extent of comparison of the details of income and deduction between years depends upon the particular circumstances.

Statement on Responsibilities in Tax Practice No. 4
Issued August 1988

USE OF ESTIMATES

Introduction

.01   This statement considers the CPA's responsibility in connection with the CPA's use of the taxpayer's estimates in the preparation of a tax return. The CPA may advise on estimates used in the preparation of a tax return, but responsibility for estimated data is that of the client, who should provide the estimated data. Appraisals or valuations are not considered estimates for purposes of this statement.

Statement

.02   A CPA may prepare tax returns involving the use of the taxpayer's estimates if it is impracticable to obtain exact data and the estimated amounts are reasonable under the facts and circumstances known to the CPA. When the taxpayer's estimates are used, they should be presented in such a manner as to avoid the implication of greater accuracy than exists.

Explanation

.03   Accounting requires the exercise of judgment and in many instances the use of approximations based on judgment. The application of such accounting judgments, as long as not in conflict with methods set forth in the Internal Revenue Code, is acceptable and expected. These judgments are not estimates within the purview of this statement. For example, the income tax regulations provide that if all other conditions for accrual are met, the exact amount of income or expense need not be known or ascertained at year end if the amount can be determined with reasonable accuracy.

.04   In the case of transactions involving small expenditures, accuracy in recording some data may be difficult to achieve. Therefore, the use of estimates by the taxpayer in determining the amount to be deducted for such items may be appropriate.

.05   In other cases where all of the facts relating to a transaction are not accurately known, either because records are missing or because precise information is not available at the time the return must be filed, estimates of the missing data may be made by the taxpayer.

.06   Estimated amounts should not be presented in a manner which provides a misleading impression as to the degree of factual accuracy.

.07   Although specific disclosure that an estimate is used for an item in the return is not required in most instances, there are unusual circumstances where such disclosure is needed to avoid misleading the Internal Revenue Service regarding the degree of accuracy of the return. Some examples of unusual circumstances include the following:

a. The taxpayer has died or is ill at the time the return must be filed.

b. The taxpayer has not received a K-1 for a flow-through entity at the time the tax return is to be filed.

c. There is litigation pending (for example, a bankruptcy proceeding) which bears on the return.

d. Fire or computer failure destroyed the relevant records.

Statement on Responsibilities in Tax Practice No. 5
Issued August 1988

DEPARTURE FROM A POSITION PREVIOUSLY CONCLUDED IN AN ADMINISTRATIVE PROCEEDING OR COURT DECISION

Introduction

.01   This statement discusses whether a CPA may recommend a tax return position that departs from the treatment of an item as concluded in an administrative proceeding or a court decision with respect to a prior return of the taxpayer. For this purpose, a "tax return position" is (1) a position reflected on the tax return as to which the client has been specifically advised by the CPA, or (2) a position about which the CPA has knowledge of all material facts and, on the basis of those facts, has concluded that the position is appropriate.

.02   For purposes of this statement, "administrative proceeding" includes an examination by the Internal Revenue Service or an appeals conference relating to a return or a claim for refund.

.03   For purposes of this statement, "court decision" means a decision by any federal court having jurisdiction over tax matters.

Statement

.04   The recommendation of a position to be taken concerning the tax treatment of an item in the preparation or signing of a tax return should be based upon the facts and the law as they are evaluated at the time the return is prepared or signed by the CPA. Unless the taxpayer is bound to a specified treatment in the later year, such as by a formal closing agreement, the treatment of an item as part of concluding an administrative proceeding or as part of a court decision does not restrict the CPA from recommending a different tax treatment in a later year's return. Therefore, if the CPA follows the standards in SRTP No. 1, the CPA may recommend a tax return position, prepare, or sign a tax return that departs from the treatment of an item as concluded in an administrative proceeding or a court decision with respect to a prior return of the taxpayer.

Explanation

.05   A CPA usually will recommend a position with respect to the tax treatment of an item that is the same as was consented to by the taxpayer for a similar item as a result of an administrative proceeding or that was subject to a court decision concerning a prior year's return of the taxpayer. The question is whether the CPA is required to do so. Considerations include the following:

a.   The Internal Revenue Service tends to act consistently with the manner in which an item was disposed of in a prior administrative proceeding, but is not bound to do so. Similarly, a taxpayer is not bound to follow the tax treatment of an item as consented to in an earlier administrative proceeding.

    b. An unfavorable court decision does not prevent a taxpayer from taking a position contrary to the earlier court decision in a subsequent year.

    c. The consent in an earlier administrative proceeding and the existence of an unfavorable court decision are factors that the CPA should consider in evaluating whether the standards in SRTP No. 1 are met.

    d. The taxpayer's consent to the treatment in the administrative proceeding or the court's decision may have been caused by a lack of documentation, whereas supporting data for the later year is adequate.

    e. The taxpayer may have yielded in the administrative proceeding for settlement purposes or not appealed the court decision even though the position met the standards in SRTP No. 1.

    f. Court decisions, rulings, or other authorities that are more favorable to the taxpayer's current position may have developed since the prior administrative proceeding was concluded or the prior court decision was rendered.

Statement on Responsibilities in Tax Practice No. 6
Issued May 1991

KNOWLEDGE OF ERROR: RETURN PREPARATION

Introduction

.01 This statement considers the responsibility of a CPA who becomes aware of an error in a client's previously filed tax return or of the client's failure to file a required tax return. As used herein, the term "error" includes any position, omission, or method of accounting that, at the time the return is filed, fails to meet the standards set out in SRTP No. 1. The term "error" also includes a position taken on a prior year's return that no longer meets these standards due to legislation, judicial decisions, or administrative pronouncements having retroactive effect. However, an error does not include an item that has an insignificant effect on the client's tax liability.

.02 This statement applies whether or not the CPA prepared or signed the return that contains the error.

Statement

.03 The CPA should inform the client promptly upon becoming aware of an error in a previously filed return or upon becoming aware of a client's failure to file a required return. The CPA should recommend the measures to be taken. Such recommendation may be given orally. The CPA is not obligated to inform the Internal Revenue Service, and the CPA may not do so without the client's permission, except where required by law.

.04 If the CPA is requested to prepare the current year's return and the client has not taken appropriate action to correct an error in a prior year's return, the CPA should consider whether to withdraw from preparing the return and whether to continue a professional relationship with the client. If the CPA does prepare such current year's return, the CPA should take reasonable steps to ensure that the error is not repeated.

Explanation

.05 While performing services for a client, a CPA may become aware of an error in a previously filed return or may become aware that the client failed to file a required return. The CPA should advise the client of the error (as required by Treasury Department Circular 230) and the measures to be taken. It is the client's responsibility to decide whether to correct the error. In appropriate cases, particularly where it appears that the Internal Revenue Service might assert the charge of fraud or other criminal misconduct, the client should be advised to consult legal counsel before taking any action. In the event that the client does not correct an error, or agree to take the necessary steps to change from an erroneous method of accounting, the CPA should consider whether to continue a professional relationship with the client.[1]

.06   If the CPA decides to continue a professional relationship with the client and is requested to prepare a tax return for a year subsequent to that in which the error occurred, then the CPA should take reasonable steps to ensure that the error is not repeated. If a CPA learns the client is using an erroneous method of accounting, when it is past the due date to request IRS permission to change to a method meeting the standards of SRTP No. 1, the CPA may sign a return for the current year, providing the return includes appropriate disclosure of the use of the erroneous method.

.07   Whether an error has no more than an insignificant effect on the client's tax liability is left to the judgment of the individual CPA based on all the facts and circumstances known to the CPA. In judging whether an erroneous method of accounting has more than an insignificant effect, the CPA should consider the method's cumulative effect and its effect on the current year's return.

.08   Where the CPA becomes aware of the error during an engagement which does not involve tax return preparation, the responsibility of the CPA is to advise the client of the existence of the error and to recommend that the error be discussed with the client's tax return preparer.

---

1. The CPA should consider consulting his or her own legal counsel before deciding upon recommendations to the client and whether to continue a professional relationship with the client. The potential of violating Rule of Conduct 301 (relating to the CPA's confidential client relationship), the Internal Revenue Code and income tax regulations, or state laws on privileged communications and other considerations may create a conflict between the CPA's interests and those of the client.

Statement on Responsibilities in Tax Practice No. 7
Issued May 1991

KNOWLEDGE OF ERROR: ADMINISTRATIVE PROCEEDINGS

Introduction

.01   This statement considers the responsibility of a CPA who becomes aware of an error in a return that is the subject of an administrative proceeding, such as an examination by the IRS or an appeals conference relating to a return or a claim for refund. As used herein, the term "error" includes any position, omission, or method of accounting, which, at the time the return is filed, fails to meet the standards set out in SRTP No. 1. The term "error" also includes a position taken on a prior year's return that no longer meets these standards due to legislation, judicial decisions, or administrative pronouncements having retroactive effect. However, an error does not include an item that has an insignificant effect on the client's tax liability.

.02   This statement applies whether or not the CPA prepared or signed the return that contains the error; it does not apply where a CPA has been engaged by legal counsel to provide assistance in a matter relating to the counsel's client.

Statement

.03   When the CPA is representing a client in an administrative proceeding with respect to a return which contains an error of which the CPA is aware, the CPA should inform the client promptly upon becoming aware of the error. The CPA should recommend the measures to be taken. Such recommendation may be given orally. The CPA is neither obligated to inform the Internal Revenue Service nor may the CPA do so without the client's permission, except where required by law.

.04   The CPA should request the client's agreement to disclose the error to the Internal Revenue Service. Lacking such agreement, the CPA should consider whether to withdraw from representing the client in the administrative proceeding and whether to continue a professional relationship with the client.

Explanation

.05   When the CPA is engaged to represent the client before the Internal Revenue Service in an administrative proceeding with respect to a return containing an error of which the CPA is aware, the CPA should advise the client to disclose the error to the Internal Revenue Service. It is the client's responsibility to decide whether to disclose the error. In appropriate cases, particularly where it appears that the Internal Revenue Service might assert the charge of fraud or other criminal misconduct, the client should be advised to consult legal counsel before taking any action. If the client refuses to disclose or permit disclosure of an error, the CPA should consider whether to withdraw from representing the client in the administrative proceeding and whether to continue a professional relationship with the client.[1]

.06   Once disclosure is agreed upon, it should not be delayed to such a degree that the client or CPA might be considered to have failed to act in good faith or to have, in effect, provided misleading information. In any event, disclosure should be made before the conclusion of the administrative proceeding.

.07   Whether an error has an insignificant effect on the client's tax liability should be left to the judgment of the individual CPA based on all the facts and circumstances known to the CPA. In judging whether an erroneous method of accounting has more than an insignificant effect, the CPA should consider the method's cumulative effect and its effect on the return which is the subject of the administrative proceeding.

---

1. The CPA should consider consulting his or her own legal counsel before deciding upon recommendations to the client and whether to continue a professional relationship with the client. The potential of violating Rule of Conduct 301 (relating to the CPA's confidential client relationship), the Internal Revenue Code and income tax regulations, or state laws on privileged communications and other considerations may create a conflict between the CPA's interests and those of the client.

Statement on Responsibilities in Tax Practice No. 8
Issued August 1988

FORM AND CONTENT OF ADVICE TO CLIENTS

Introduction

.01   This statement discusses certain aspects of providing tax advice to a client and considers the circumstances in which the CPA has a responsibility to communicate with the client when subsequent developments affect advice previously provided. The statement does not, however, cover the CPA's responsibilities when it is expected that the advice rendered is likely to be relied upon by parties other than the CPA's client.[1]

Statement

.02   In providing tax advice to a client, the CPA should use judgment to ensure that the advice given reflects professional competence and appropriately serves the client's needs. The CPA is not required to follow a standard format or guidelines in communicating written or oral advice to a client.

.03   In advising or consulting with a client on tax matters, the CPA should assume that the advice will affect the manner in which the matters or transactions considered ultimately will be reported on the client's tax returns. Thus, for all tax advice the CPA gives to a client, the CPA should follow the standards in SRTP No. 1 relating to tax return positions.

.04   The CPA may choose to communicate with a client when subsequent developments affect advice previously provided with respect to significant matters. However, the CPA cannot be expected to have assumed responsibility for initiating such communication except while assisting a client in implementing procedures or plans associated with the advice provided or when the CPA undertakes this obligation by specific agreement with the client.

Explanation

.05   Tax advice is recognized as a valuable service provided by CPAs. The form of advice may be oral or written and the subject matter may range from routine to complex. Because the range of advice is so extensive and because advice should meet specific needs of a client, neither standard format nor guidelines for communicating advice to the client can be established to cover all situations.

.06   Although oral advice may serve a client's needs appropriately in routine matters or in well-defined areas, written communications are recommended in important, unusual, or complicated transactions. In the judgment of the CPA, oral advice may be followed by a written communication to the client.

---

1. The CPA's responsibilities when providing advice that will be relied upon by third parties will be addressed in a future statement.

.07   In deciding on the form of advice provided to a client, the CPA should exercise professional judgment and should consider such factors as the following:

a.   The importance of the transaction and amounts involved

b.   The specific or general nature of the client's inquiry

c.   The time available for development and submission of the advice

d.   The technical complications presented

e.   The existence of authorities and precedents

f.   The tax sophistication of the client and the client's staff

g.   The need to seek legal advice

.08   The CPA may assist a client in implementing procedures or plans associated with the advice offered. During this active participation, the CPA continues to advise and should review and revise such advise as warranted by new developments and factors affecting the transaction.

.09   Sometimes the CPA is requested to provide tax advice but does not assist in implementing the plans adopted. While developments such as legislative or administrative changes or further judicial interpretations may affect the advice previously provided, the CPA cannot be expected to communicate later developments that affect such advice unless the CPA undertakes this obligation by specific agreement with the client. Thus, the communication of significant developments affecting previous advice should be considered an additional service rather than an implied obligation in the normal CPA-client relationship.

.10   The client should be informed that advice reflects professional judgment based on an existing situation and that subsequent developments could affect previous professional advice. CPAs should use precautionary language to the effect that their advice is based on facts as stated and authorities that are subject to change.

AOD. Action on decision.

Abandoned spouse. See *filing status.*

Ability-to-pay concept. A tax should be based on the amount that the taxpayer can afford to pay, relative to other taxpayers.

Accelerated Cost Recovery System (ACRS). Applies to tangible property placed in service after 1980 and before 1987. ACRS was enacted to encourage investment that would lead to economic expansion by accelerating the capital recovery taxpayers received from depreciating property.

Accountable plan. See *employee reimbursement plan.*

Accounting method. The taxpayer must select an accounting method to determine the year(s) in which taxable transactions are to be reported. The two basic allowable methods are the *cash basis of accounting* and the *accrual basis of accounting.* Taxpayers using the cash basis are taxed on income as it is received and take deductions as they are paid. In contrast, accrual basis taxpayers report their income as it is earned and take deductions as they are incurred, without regard to the actual receipt or payment of cash.

Accrual basis of accounting. See *accounting method.*

Acquiescence. A pronouncement by the IRS that it will follow the decision of a regular Tax Court case to the extent that the decision favored the taxpayer.

Acquisition debt. See *qualified home mortgage interest.*

Active income. Income from a trade or business in which the taxpayer materially participates. This category includes wages and salaries, as well as income from a trade or business in which the taxpayer materially participates. Working interest in oil and gas deposits and certain low-income housing projects are always considered active income. Such activities may produce losses that are not subject to the passive loss rules.

Active investor. See *securities dealer.*

Active participant. See *active participation exception.*

Active participation exception. *Active participants* in rental real estate may use passive activity losses amounting to as much as $25,000 per year to offset portfolio and active sources of income. An active participant must own at least a 10% interest in the activity and have significant and bona-fide involvement in the activity, a standard less stringent than that for material participation. The $25,000 annual deduction amount is phased out when the individual's AGI exceeds $100,000.

Active trader. See *securities dealer.*

Actual cost method. See *auto expense.*

Adjusted basis. The original basis, plus or minus changes in the amount of unrecovered investment. It roughly corresponds to the book-value concept studied in financial accounting. At any point in time, the remaining capital investment to be recovered is represented by an asset's adjusted basis. An asset's adjusted basis may never be less than zero.

Adjusted gross income (AGI). Deductions of individuals are broken into two classes—deductions for AGI and deductions from AGI. This difference in deductions results in an intermediate income number called the AGI. It is used to provide limitations on the deductions from AGI of an individual taxpayer. *Deductions for adjusted gross income* include trade or business expenses, rental and royalty expenses, capital losses, and certain other expenditures that the tax law specifically allows. Once the allowable amount of an expenditure has been determined, it is not subject to further reduction based on the income of the taxpayer.

Adjusted sales price. Equal to the amount realized on the sale of a principal residence, less fixing up expenses. Fixing up expenses are noncapital expenditures that prepare the residence for sale, that are incurred within 90 days previous to the sale, and paid within 30 days after the sale.

Administrative convenience concept. Items may be omitted from the tax base whenever the cost of compliance would exceed the revenue generated. The cost is generally the time and effort for taxpayers to accumulate the information necessary to implement the concept as well as the cost to the government of ensuring compliance.

Ad valorem tax. Taxes that are based on the value of the property being taxed (e.g., property taxes). However, most property taxes are not based on the true fair market value of the property. Rather, the *assessed value* of the property is used to determine the tax. The assessed value of property is typically 50 to 75% of the estimated market value of the property.

Alimony. In a divorce situation, one spouse often makes payments to a former spouse. The payments may be to provide for the support of children (called *child support payments*), they may be simply a sharing of income between the two parties (called *alimony*), or they may constitute a division of marital property (*property settlement*). Payments that are a sharing of current income (alimony) are taxable to the recipient and deductible by the payer.

All-events test. An accrual basis taxpayer may deduct expenses in the year in which two tests are met: the all-events and economic performance tests. The all-events test is met when all events have occurred that determine that a liability exists and the amount of the liability can be determined with reasonable accuracy. The *economic performance test* requires economic performance to have occurred with regard to the liability. Economic performance occurs when services or property are provided to the taxpayer or when the taxpayer uses property.

All-inclusive income concept. All income received is taxable unless some specific provision can be found in the tax law that excludes the item in question from taxation or defers its recognition to a future tax year. The tax law always starts with the proposition that anything of value received is taxable.

Alternate valuation date. See *inherited property.*

Alternative Depreciation System (ADS). The ADS system must be used to calculate depreciation deductions for purposes of the alternative minimum tax. ADS depreciation is generally computed using the straight-line method during the specified longer alternative recovery period. An election to use ADS for regular tax purposes is made on a class-by-class, year-by-year basis for property other than real estate. For real estate, the ADS is elected on a property-by-property basis in the year of acquisition.

Alternative minimum tax (AMT). An alternative calculation of the tax liability that results in the minimum amount of tax that the taxpayer must pay. The AMT is a separate, parallel tax system. Within this system, many preference items allowed in the calculation of the regular tax liability are either not allowed or the amount of tax relief provided is greatly diminished.

Alternative minimum taxable income (AMTI). The tax base used to calculate the alternative minimum tax. AMTI is calculated by making modifications to regular taxable income for prescribed adjustment and preference items.

Alternative minimum tax adjustment. Accounts for the effect of items that must be determined using either alternative calculations or alternative methods for AMT purposes. In general, the use of the AMT calculation or method results in either accelerating income items or deferring deduction items. The net effect of either is a higher taxable income in the initial period(s) of difference. However, most adjustment items are not disallowed for AMT purposes; they are merely spread out (in the case of deductions) or accelerated (in the case of income items). The difference in the two calculations is temporary, not permanent.

AMT credit. A problem can arise if accelerated income is taxed first under the AMT and later, when the timing difference reverses, for regular tax purposes. To avoid double taxation of reversal items, Congress enacted a minimum tax credit that can only be used to reduce the regular tax liability in later years when the regular tax exceeds the alternative minimum tax. The credit is calculated each year in which the AMT applies.

Alternative minimum tax preferences. Preferences are different from adjustments in two distinct ways. First, the AMT preferences apply to all taxpayers. Second, preferences are always added in the computation of AMT income. Unlike adjustments, preference items will not reverse.

Amortization. Amortization is a tax accounting method used to recover the investment in assets. This provides a reasonable allocation of bases to the annual accounting periods benefited by the use of the assets. Intangible property with definite useful lives, such as patents, copyrights, or agreements not to compete, may be amortized.

Amount realized. Capital is recovered at disposition by offsetting the adjusted basis at the date of disposition with the amount realized from the *property disposition.* The amount realized from a disposition is the amount received from the disposition (generally the sales price of the property), less the expenses incurred to make the disposition. If the amount is greater than the adjusted basis, the taxpayer has a *realized gain* on the disposition. If the amount realized is less than the adjusted basis, capital investment is not fully recovered, resulting in a *realized loss.*

Annual accounting period concept. All entities must report the results of their operations on an annual basis (the tax year). Each tax year stands on its own, apart from other tax years.

Annual loss. See *loss.*

Annual personal casualty loss limitation. See *personal casualty loss.*

Annuity. An annuity is a string of payments received over equal time periods for a determinable period. The general formula for determining the amount of each payment that is a return of capital and therefore excluded from income is called the *annuity exclusion ratio.* The formula is the cost of the contract divided by the expected return (contract payment $\times$ expected number of payments) on the contract.

Annuity exclusion ratio. See *annuity.*

Arm's-length transaction concept. All parties to the transaction have bargained in good faith and for their individual benefit, not for the benefit of the transaction group. Transactions not made at arm's length are generally given no tax effect or are not given the intended tax effect.

Assessed value. See *ad valorem tax.*

Assessment for local benefits. Real estate taxes that are related to assessments for local benefits, such as sidewalks, streets, sewers, and other improvements, and are not deductible. The tax imposed for local benefits is deemed to increase the value of the taxpayer's property and is considered a capital expenditure. The tax is added to the improved asset's basis, which may be recoverable through depreciation, amortization, or upon its disposition.

Assignment-of-income doctrine. The tax entity that owns the income produced is resposible for the tax on the income,

regardless of which entity actually receives the income. Merely directing payment of income (assigning income) that has been earned by one entity to another, although legal, does not relieve the owner of the income from paying tax.

Associated with. See *meal and entertainment expense.*

At-risk rules. Taxpayers cannot deduct losses in excess of the amount they have at risk in an activity. The at-risk amount is equal to cash or other assets that have been contributed to the activity. In addition, any debts of the activity that the taxpayer would have to pay if the activity could not are also considered at risk. Thus, the amount at risk in an activity is the maximum amount of personal funds (assets) that could be lost if the activity failed. The amount at risk is also adjusted for the taxpayer's share of the income (loss) from the activity and reduced by withdrawals from the activity. Any current period losses that are not deductible beause they exceed the taxpayer's at-risk amount are carried forward and are deductible when the taxpayer has enough at risk to allow the deduction.

Auto expense. A taxpayer can choose one of two methods of computing a deduction for using an auto for business purposes, the standard mileage rate method or the actual cost method. Using the *standard mileage rate method,* a taxpayer deducts a certain amount for each business mile the car was driven during the tax year. The standard mileage rate is designed to be an estimate of the cost of operating the car. Because these costs change over time, the standard rate is set each year to reflect changes in the cost of operating a car (30 cents per mile for 1995). In addition to the standard mileage rate, the taxpayer can deduct direct out-of-pocket expenses unrelated to the operating costs of the car that are incurred while attending to business. Using the *actual cost method,* a taxpayer can deduct depreciation, gas and oil, repairs, insurance, interest, license, and other expenses of driving the car. If the car is used for both business and personal purposes, the expenses must be allocated according to the miles driven for each purpose.

Average tax rate. The average rate of tax on each dollar of income that is taxable. The total federal income tax divided by taxable income (tax base). See also *proportional rate structure.*

Bargain purchase. A true bargain purchase is taxable to the buyer. Such a purchase occurs when the difference between the purchase price and the fair market value represents an effort by the seller to confer an economic advantage to the buyer. Bargain purchases are typically found in employer/employee purchases and related party transactions.

Basis. The amount of unrecovered investment in an asset. As amounts are expended and/or recovered relative to an asset over time, the basis is adjusted in consideration of such changes. See also *adjusted basis.*

Boot. When properties of different values are exchanged, the party with the property of lower value must equalize the value being exchanged by transferring cash, securities, services, assumptions of debt, or other property not of like kind. This nonqualifying property is called *boot.*

Brother-sister relationship. See *controlled groups.*

Business bad debt. To be deductible, a bad debt must be related to a transaction that has a business purpose. If the bad debt arose from a transction in the taxpayer's trade or business, the bad debt is allowed as a business deduction; otherwise, the bad debt is considered a nonbusiness bad debt. A *nonbusiness bad debt* cannot be deducted if the debt was voluntarily forgiven or the forgiveness of the debt was intended as a gift. Nonbusiness bad debts are deducted as a short-term capital loss, using the specific charge-off method. See also *specific charge-off method.*

Business casualty loss. See *casualty.*

Business gift. A taxpayer can deduct up to $25 per year per donee for gifts to business customers. Gifts are not subject to the 50% limitation that applies to meals and entertainment expenses. To apply the $25 limitation, direct and indirect gifts given to a person must be counted. An indirect gift is one made to a related party, such as a taxpayer's spouse or child.

Business purpose concept. To be deductible, an expenditure or a loss must have a business or other economic purpose that exceeds any tax avoidance motive. The primary motive for the transaction must be to make a profit. Two general types of expense deductions in the tax law embody the profit motive requirement: expenses incurred in a trade or business and those related to the production of income (investment activity). These are commonly referred to as *trade or business expenses* and *investment expenses.*

Business purpose tax year. See *natural business year.*

Cafeteria plan. A menu of tax-free benefits that is offered at the employer's cost. Each employee is allowed to choose a certain dollar amount of benefits from the menu or may choose to take the cash cost of the benefit. Employees who choose the tax-free benefits are not taxed on the value of the benefit; however, those who elect to receive cash are taxed on the amount of cash received. The employer must make the benefits of the plan available to all employees on a nondiscriminatory basis.

Capital asset. Any asset that is *not* a receivable, inventory, real or depreciable property used in a trade or business, and certain intangible assets, such as copyrights. Common capital assets of individuals include stocks, bonds, and personal use assets.

Capital expenditure. Taxpayers cannot deduct capital expenditures in total in the period in which they are paid. The main characteristic of a capital expenditure is that its usefulness extends substantially beyond the end of the tax year in which the expenditure is made.

Capital gain (loss). The difference between the sales price of a capital asset and the adjusted basis of that asset.

Capital recovery concept. No income is realized until the taxpayer receives more than the amount invested to produce the income. The amount invested in an asset represents the maximum amount recoverable.

Carryback. See *net operating loss.*

Carryforward. See *net operating loss.*

Carryover basis. Indicates that all or part of an asset's basis transfers from one owner to another or from one asset to another. Transactions resulting in carryover basis are subject to special rules for determining holding period—an adding on of the holding period of the prior asset or of a prior owner.

Cash basis of accounting. See *accounting method.*

Cash-equivalent approach. Income does not have to be received in cash to be recognized. The receipt of anything with a fair market value triggers recognition of income.

Casualty. The result of some sudden, unexpected, and/or unusual event (i.e., fire, storms, earthquakes, and accidents). Thefts are treated as casualties. Actual physical damage to property must occur. When a business property is fully destroyed (or stolen), the measure of the *business casualty loss* for fully destroyed property is the property's basis. If the insurance proceeds received from a casualty exceed the adjusted basis of the property, the result would be a *casualty gain,* which is subject to a special election under which a casualty gain may be deferred. When a casualty occurs and property is not totally destroyed, an estmate must be made of the amount lost as a result of the casualty. In this case, a *casualty loss* is equal to the lower of the decline in the value of the property or the adjusted basis of the property.

Casualty gain (loss). See *casualty* and *involuntary conversion.*

Centralized management. See *corporation.*

Charitable contribution. Individuals are allowed an itemized deduction for donations to *charitable organizations*—those organized for religious, charitable, educational, scientific, or literary purposes. The deductible amount of charitable contributions has three major limitations. The overall amount of the deduction cannot exceed 50% of the taxpayer's AGI. Contributions of ordinary income property are limited to the lesser of the property's adjusted basis or its fair market value. Contributions of capital gain property that are deducted at fair market value cannot exceed 30% of AGI. But a taxpayer who is willing to give up the deduction related to the property's appreciation (i.e., use the adjusted basis as the deductible amount) is not subject to the 30% limit. Any contributions in excess of the limitations are carried forward for deduction for five years.

Charitable organization. See *charitable contribution.*

Child and dependent care credit. Taxpayers who incur expenses for child and dependent care that enable them to be employed are eligible for a nonrefundable credit based on the amount of their expenses and their earned income level. The taxpayer must incur employment-related expenses for the care of qualified individuals. A qualifying individual includes any dependent under the age of 13 or a dependent or a spouse of the taxpayer who is mentally or physically incapacitated. The expenditures qualifying for the credit cannot exceed the earned income of the taxpayer.

Child support payment. See *alimony.*

Citator. Primarily used to determine both the history of a judicial decision and how that decision has been criticized, approved, or otherwise commented upon in other court decisions. The most common citators are RIA's *Federal Tax Citator* and Commerce Clearing House's two-volume set, which is included in its tax service.

Cited case. Citators refer to the case being evaluated as the *cited case,* and any cases discussing that case are called the *citing cases.* Cited cases are listed alphabetically, followed by the citing cases and rulings.

Citing case. See *cited case.*

Citizen or residency test. See *dependent.*

Claim-of-right doctrine. A realization occurs whenever an amount is received without restriction as to its disposition. An item is received without restriction when the receiver has no definitive obligation to repay the amount received.

Class life. Both ACRS and MACRS require that assets be categorized in classes. The class life of an asset determines its cost-recovery period. In general, assets have longer class lives under MACRS than the same assets under ACRS.

Closely held corporation. For passive loss purposes, a corporation is closely held if five or fewer shareholders own 50% or more of the stock in the corporation during the last half of the tax year. Closely held corporations are allowed to use net passive losses to offset active income of the business. However, they cannot use passive losses to offset portfolio income.

Complex trust. See *trust.*

Computer-assisted tax research (CATR). Secondary source of tax information in which the computer is used to access a large database containing the full text of virtually all primary and secondary authorities. The major CATR systems are LEXIS and WESTLAW.

Conduit entity. A nontaxable reporting entity, the tax attributes of which (income, deductions, losses, credits) flow through to its owner(s) for tax purposes.

Constructive ownership rules. These rules are related to the related party provisions. Some individuals might attempt to reduce their direct ownership in a corporation or a partnership by distributing ownership among family members, other corporations, or partnerships that they control. This effort is stymied by the constructive ownership rules, which state the relationships within which an individual is deemed to indirectly own an interest actually owned by another person or entity.

Constructive receipt doctrine. Cash basis taxpayers are deemed to be in receipt of income when it is credited to their accounts or otherwise made unconditionally available to them. Physical possession of income is not required for it to be taxed.

Continuity of life. See *corporation.*

Controlled group. A controlled group is a group of two or more corporations that are owned directly or indirectly by the same shareholder(s). If a parent or subsidiary group in total owns 80% or more of the stock of another corporation, the other corporation is included in the *parent-subsidiary relationship.* Passing two tests creates a *brother-sister relationship.* The first test (the 80% test) requires that five or fewer persons own 80% or more of the stock of all corporations in the group. The second test (the 50% test) requires that five or fewer persons own more than 50% of the stock of two or more corporations (taking into account only the stock ownership that each person has that is identical with respect to each corporation). A shareholder's identical ownership is the percentage of stock the shareholder owns in common in each corporation. That percentage is the smallest amount owned in any single corporation.

Corporate distribution. See *earnings and profits.*

Corporation. An artificial entity created under the auspices of state law. As a separate legal entity, a corporation can enter into contracts in its name, own property, be sued for malfeasance, and is required to pay income tax based on its taxable income. Corporations provide limited liability to its owners such that the owner's liability extends only to the amount invested in the entity. The characteristics of free transferability of ownership, continuity of life, *limited liability,* and the characteristic of *centralized management* lend themselves to raising large amounts of money from many sources. *Free transferability of ownership* means that a corporate shareholder may sell or buy shares at any time without restriction. *Continuity of life* ensures that the business will not cease to exist, regardless of which shareholders trade their stock. The biggest disadvantage of a corporation is the double taxation of dividends. See *double taxation.*

Cost depletion. One of two methods used to compute depletion of natural resources. The cost depletion computation allocates the unrecovered basis over the number of mineral units of the natural resource (useful life of the resource) to which the investment relates. Because an estimate of the remaining recoverable units at the end of each year is used to make the computation, the cost depletion per unit will probably change each tax year. See also *percentage depletion (statutory depletion).*

Courts. See entries under U.S.

Cumulative Bulletin (C.B.). An official publication of the IRS, consolidating material that first was published in the *Internal Revenue Bulletin* in a hard-cover volume (usually semiannual).

DIF. *Discriminant Function System.*

Damage payments. Damage payments for personal injury or sickness are excluded from taxation. The courts have interpreted *personal injury* to include any personal wrong committed against the taxpayer, such as libel, slander, breach of promise to marry, invasion of privacy, assault, and battery. The exclusion also applies to loss-of-income payments that result from the personal injury. In addition to payments for pain and suffering (which are excluded as damages), the courts often award punitive damages and/or *loss-of-income damages* in personal injury actions. Damage payments made to replace lost income are generally taxable as a replacement of taxable income unless they are related to a personal injury. *Punitive damages* are meant to punish the offender in a personal injury case for gross negligence or the intentional infliction of harm to the other party. Punitive damages are included in gross income unless they are the result of a claim for physical injury or physical sickness.

Death benefit payment. The tax law allows one $5,000 exclusion for death benefits paid to a deceased employee's beneficiaries. In order to qualify for this exclusion, the payment must be made solely because of death and cannot represent payment for services performed before the employee died. If more than $5,000 is paid to more than one beneficiary, the $5,000 exclusion must be taken pro rata among the beneficiaries.

Deductions. Amounts that the tax law specifically allows as subtractions from gross income.

Deductions for adjusted gross income. See *adjusted gross income.*

Deductions from adjusted gross income. Certain personal expenditures and other specified nonpersonal expenditures are allowed to be deducted by individuals as deductions from AGI. These deductions are commonly referred to as *itemized deductions.*

Deferral. An item that does not affect the current period's taxable income but will affect taxable income in some future tax year.

Deferred (third-party) exchange. Allows a transaction to be structured as an exchange when the two parties to an exchange do not have property that they want to exchange directly. The property to be exchanged must be identified within 45 days of the date of the first property transfer. In addition, the exchange must be completed within 180 days of the first property transfer.

De minimis fringe benefit. Those items that are too small to permit a reasonable accounting (i.e., free coffee in break room, employee parties, and small holiday gifts). The exclusion is based on administrative convenience.

Dependency exemption. See *personal exemption.*

Dependent. In order to qualify as a dependent, five tests must be met. First, under the *gross income test,* the gross income of an individual must be less than the dependency exemption ($2,500 in 1995). The gross income test is waived for any child of the taxpayer who is either younger than 19 at the end of the tax year or a full-time student younger than 24 at the end of the tax year. Second, the *support test* requires that the taxpayer claiming the dependency exemption provide more than one-half of the support of the dependent. In the case of divorced parents, the custodial parent is entitled to the dependency exemption, regardless of actual support provided, unless the custodial parent agrees in writing to give up this right. Third, under the *relationship, or member of household, test,* a dependent must be either a relative of the taxpayer's or a member of the taxpayer's household for the entire year. Fourth, under the *citizen or residency test,* a dependent must be either a citizen of the United States or a resident of the United States, Canada, or Mexico. Fifth, under the *joint return test,* a dependent may not file a joint return with his or her spouse for the exemption year in question, unless they would not be required to file a tax return but file a return solely for the purpose of obtaining a refund.

Depletion.   A tax accounting method used to recover the investment in assets, such as oil or coal, that waste away through extraction. This provides a reasonable allocation of bases to the annual accounting periods benefited by the use of the assets.

Depreciable basis.   The amount of basis that is subject to depreciation and is the amount used to determine the annual depreciation deduction. The depreciable basis does not change during the asset's tax life unless additional capital expenditures are made in regard to the asset.

Depreciation.   A tax accounting method used to recover investment in long-lived assets. This provides a reasonable allocation of bases to the annual accounting periods benefited by the use of the assets. Tangible property, used in a trade or business or held for the purpose of investment, with definite useful lives, such as buildings and office equipment, are subject to depreciation.

Depreciation convention.   Both ACRS and MACRS use conventions to allocate depreciation to the first and last years. The conventions used in ACRS are referred to as the *half-year, full-month,* and *mid-month conventions.* Under a *half-year convention,* one-half year of depreciation is allowed in the year of acquisition and no depreciation is allowed in the year of disposition. The *full-month convention* bases the acquisition and disposition year deduction on the number of months the property was in service during the year, under the assumption that property is acquired and disposed of on the first day of the month. The *mid-month convention* also is based on the number of months in service, but the months of acquisition and disposition are counted only as half months. MACRS uses the mid-year, mid-quarter, and mid-month conventions to allocate depreciation in the first and last year of an asset's life. The mid-month convention is the same as used for ACRS. The *mid-year convention* assumes that all property is placed in service and disposed of in the

middle of the year. The *mid-quarter convention* assumes that all property is placed in service and disposed of in the middle of the quarter year of acquisition and disposition.

Depreciation recapture.   Depreciation recapture rules reclassify gains from depreciation as ordinary income. Recapture can be considered as giving back the ordinary deduction that created the gain. Only the gain in excess of the recapture amount is accorded capital gain or Section 1231 treatment. The depreciation recapture rules apply only to gains caused by depreciation; losses are not subject to recapture.

Direct construction costs.   Costs that are actually incurred to physically construct an asset. Examples of direct costs include materials, labor, supplies, and payments to subcontractors. See also *indirect construction costs.*

Directly related.   See *meal and entertainment expense.*

Disability payment.   Amounts received as disability payments (sick pay or wage-continuation plans) from an employer-provided health and accident plan are included in gross income. However, the same payments made from a plan purchased by the individual taxpayer are excluded from gross income.

Discharge of indebtedness.   If a lender forgives all or a portion of the debt of the borrower, the borrower realizes an increase in wealth from the reduction of the liability. The borrower who is relieved of a debt has obtained a claim of right to the amount of debt forgiven. The increase in wealth is generally taxable to the borrower. The tax law provides an exception to the general rule of taxability of a discharge of indebtedness when the borrower is insolvent (liabilities exceed assets), both before and after the forgiveness of the debt, and for discharges of qualified real property indebtedness.

Dividend.   See *earnings and profits* and *stock dividends.*

Dividends-received deduction (DRD).   Because of the double taxation effect, if one corporation is a shareholder in another corporation, triple taxation results. The dividends-received deduction generally provides only partial relief from triple taxation. The actual amount of the DRD depends upon the percentage of ownership the recipient shareholder holds in the distributing corporation. See also *double taxation.*

Dominant motive.   An expense frequently is incurred for both business and personal reasons. To be deductible, the expense must bear a proximate relationship to the income-producing activity. In addition, the primary or dominant motivation for incurring the expense must be the business purpose.

Double taxation.   Obtaining cash distributions is generally the ultimate objective of corporate owners. Cash is distributed to shareholders via dividends. Dividends are payments of already-taxed earnings of corporations. When shareholders receive dividends, taxation occurs again. The double taxation effect results because the corporation is recognized as a separate taxpaying entity. See also *dividends-received deduction*.

Earned income. Income derived from labor. The most common forms of earned income are wages, salaries, tips, bonuses, and commissions; income from the active conduct of a trade or business; income from the rendering of services; and income from the performance of illegal activities.

Earned income credit (EIC). Provides tax relief to low-income taxpayers. The credit is refundable (paid even if no tax is due). The amount of the credit is dependent on the taxpayer's earned income and phases out after income reaches a predetemined level. Married taxpayers are required to file a joint return to take the EIC.

Earnings and profits (E&P). Earnings and profits are a measure of a corporation's ability to pay dividends without impairing capital. The tax definition of a *dividend* is a distribution by a corporation from either its current-year or accumulated earnings and profits, referred to as a *corporate distribution*. If a corporate distribution exceeds both the current and accumulated earnings and profits, the capital recovery concept dictates that the excess distribution is tax free to shareholders.

Economic performance test. See *all-events test*.

Educational assistance program. Up to $5,250 in payments made by an employer to an employee for such costs as tuition and books are excludable if the payments are made from a nondiscriminatory educational assistance program.

Education expense. A taxpayer may deduct education expenses if it meets either of the following requirements: The education is a requirement—either by law or the taxpayer's employer—for the taxpayer's continued employment, or the education maintains or improves the skills required in the taxpayer's trade or business.

Effective tax rate. The total federal income tax divided by the taxpayer's economic income (the tax base plus nontaxable income).

Employee discount. In order to exclude employee discounts from taxation, the discount must be made available to all employees on a nondiscriminatory basis and the goods and/or services provided must be in the same line of business. The excludable discount on goods is limited to the gross profit percentage on the goods purchased. Excludable service discounts are limited to 20%.

Employer-provided lodging. In order for a taxpayer to exclude from taxable income the value of employer-provided lodging, the lodging must be on the employer's premises and must be for the convenience of the employer. In addition, the lodging must be a condition of employment—the employee has no choice but to live in the employer-provided housing.

Employer reimbursement plan. An employer reimbursement plan is an *accountable plan* if employees are required to file an adequate accounting (documentation) of their expenses with their employer and to return excess reimbursements to the employer. If reimbursement equals actual expenses (any excess reimbursement is returned to the employer), the employee does not report the reimbursement. If reimbursement is less than actual expenses, the reimbursement must be included in the employee's gross income and the portion of the expenses reimbursed is deductible for AGI. The excess actual expenses are deductible as miscellaneous itemized deductions, subject to the 2% of adjusted gross income limitation. If the reimbursement is greater than actual expenses, the employee must include the excess reimbursement in gross income. If an employer reimbursement plan is *nonaccountable,* the employee must include the reimbursement (if any) in gross income. No deductions for AGI are allowed. The employee can deduct expenses only as miscellaneous itemized deductions.

Employer's athletic facility. The value of the use of an employer's athletic facility may be excluded from taxation, provided that the facility is on the employer's premises and substantially all use of the facility is by employees and their families.

Employment taxes. Businesses are liable for the payment of Social Security taxes *(FICA)* and federal and state unemployment taxes *(FUTA and SUTA)* for all employees.

Entity concept. All items of income, deductions, and so on are traced to the tax unit responsible for the item.

Estate. Created upon the death of an individual. Generally, the estate is merely a temporary, transitional entity. It holds the deceased person's property until the property is distributed to beneficiaries. After all property is transferred from the estate, its purpose has ended and it ceases to exist. During the estate's life, the property held by the fiduciary may earn income. That income is taxed to the estate and taxes are paid from estate assets.

Estate tax. A tax that is paid on the fair market value of the assets of a deceased taxpayer. The tax is paid by the executor of the estate from the assets of the estate.

Exclusions. Increases in a taxpayer's wealth and recoveries of the taxpayer's capital investment that Congress has decided should not be subject to income tax. Thus, income exclusions are not counted as gross income. Common income exclusions include inheritances, gifts, and interest on certain municipal bonds.

Exemption. Individuals, trusts, and estates may subtract predetermined amounts to determine their taxable income. Congress recognizes that people need a minimum amount of income to provide for their basic living expenses. This minimum amount of income is deducted as an exemption and is not subject to tax. See also *personal exemption*.

Exemption deduction phase-out. High-income taxpayers must reduce their exemption deductions. The basic reduction is 2% of the allowable exemption amount for each $2,500 (or portion thereof) of AGI in excess of the threshold amount. The total exemption amount, not each individual exemption, is subject to the phase-out.

Expense.   A current period expenditure that is incurred in order to earn income. Deductions for expenses are limited to those incurred in a trade or business, in an income-producing activity (investment activity), and for certain specifically allowed personal expenses of individuals.

F.2d.   *Federal Reporter,* 2d series.

FICA.   Federal Insurance Contribution Act. See *Social Security* and *employment taxes.*

F. Supp.   *Federal Supplement.*

FUTA.   Federal Unemployment Tax Act. See *employment taxes.*

Fiduciary.   A person who occupies a position of special confidence, especially trustees, guardians, receivers, conservators, executors, and administrators. Such people have legal title to property, which they hold for the benefit of others, subject to strict duties under state law. Many, but not all, fiduciaries are required to file income tax returns on behalf of the entity (i.e., trust or estate) for which they are responsible.

Filing requirements.   Individuals are generally required to file a return when their gross income exceeds the sum of (1) their standard deduction amount (including the additional amount for age but not for blindness), and (2) their allowable personal (not dependency) exemptions. Three major exceptions are that individuals with net earnings from self-employment in excess of $400 must file a return, regardless of their gross income level; married taxpayers filing separate returns are required to file if their gross income exceeds $2,500, the personal exemption amount; and dependents with unearned income greater than $650. Taxpayers with gross income less than the required filing level will want to file a return when they are entitled to a refund.

Filing status.   All taxpayers must take deductions and pay taxes based on their filing status. Filing status indicates whether a taxpayer is married or unmarried. Married taxpayers may file jointly or separately. To qualify for *married, filing jointly* the taxpayers must be legally married on the last day of the tax year. In the case of a death of a spouse, a *surviving spouse* who has at least one dependent child or stepchild living at home may use the joint return tax rates to compute the tax for the two years after the year the spouse dies. Filing *married, filing separately* is primarily used when a husband and wife cannot agree to file together and are not divorced or legally separated by year end. A *single* taxpayer is a person who is not married on the last day of the tax year and who does not have any dependents to support. In order to qualify as a *head of household,* the unmarried taxpayer must pay more than half of the cost of maintaining a home that is the principal residence for more than half of the year for a qualified dependent (children, parents, and other relatives). The taxpayer's parents do not have to live

in the taxpayer's home if they meet the dependency tests. In addition, the principal residence may be for an unmarried child or other direct lineal descendent (i.e., parent, grandchild) who does not qualify as a dependent. The benefit of filing as a head of household is extended to an abandoned spouse. A married person is treated as an *abandoned spouse* if a dependent child lives in the taxpayer's home for more than half of the year and the taxpayer's spouse does not live in the home at any time during the last half of the year.

Final regulation.   The Treasury Department's official explanation of a related provision in the Internal Revenue Code. Also called a *Treasury regulation.*

Flexible benefits (salary reduction) plan.   The employee has an annual amount withheld from his or her salary that is used to pay medical expenses or child-care expenses. Amounts paid into the account by the employee are not included in the employee's gross income, thus the term *salary reduction plan.* These plans allow employees to pay for medical costs and child care with before-tax dollars rather than after-tax dollars.

Foreign earned income.   To provide relief from double taxation for U.S. citizens working in foreign countries, the tax law allows individuals two options. First, taxpayers may include the foreign earned income in their taxable income, calculate the U.S. tax on the income, and take a tax credit for any foreign taxes paid. The amount of the allowable *foreign tax credit* is the lesser of the actual foreign taxes paid and the U.S. tax that would have been paid on the foreign earned income. Under the second option, individuals may exclude up to $70,000 in foreign earned income for each full year they work in a foreign country. An individual must be either a bonafide resident of the foreign country or must be present in the foreign country for 330 days in any 12 consecutive months to obtain the tax relief.

Foreign tax credit.   See *foreign earned income.*

Free transferability of ownership.   See *corporation.*

Full-month convention.   See *depreciation convention.*

GCM.   General counsel's memoranda.

Gain.   The difference between the selling price of an asset and its basis; the result of disposing of the asset. Gains result in income.

General asset class.   See *like-kind property.*

Gift.   A gift in the statutory sense proceeds from a detached and disinterested generosity that originates from affection, respect, admiration, charity, or like impulses. What controls is the intention with which payment, however voluntary, has been made. A gift is a transfer of property from a donor to a donee that is not a profit-motivated arm's-length transaction. Neither the donor nor the donee recognizes any income or pays income tax on the transfer of gift property. A *gift tax* may be imposed on the donor for the fair market value of the gift at the date of transfer.

Gift tax. See *gift*.

Goodwill. In the purchase of a business, goodwill represents the difference between the purchase price and fair market value of the net assets acquired. If purchased after August 9, 1993, goodwill is amortized over 15 years.

Grantor. See *trust*.

Grantor trust. See *trust*.

Gross income. Gross income is income broadly defined, minus income items that are excluded from taxation. Items of gross income are included in the computation of taxable income. Generally, gross income is the starting point for reporting income items on a tax return.

Gross income test. See *dependent*.

Group term life insurance. Premiums paid by an employer on the first $50,000 face amount of group term life insurance are excluded from taxation. The exclusion is available only for term insurance that is provided to a group of employees on a nondiscriminatory basis.

Guaranteed payment. See *partners*.

Half-year convention. See *depreciation convention*.

Head of household. See *filing status*.

Health and accident insurance. Premiums paid by an employer to purchase health and accident insurance coverage for employees (and their dependents) are excluded from the employee's income.

Hobby. A taxpayer may engage in an income-earning activity primarily for personal reasons, such as recreation and personal enjoyment, which disqualify it as a trade or business or an investment activity; profitability is a secondary concern. Such an activity is classified as a hobby because it lacks a business purpose. A taxpayer's allowable hobby expenses cannot exceed the gross income from the hobby. Expenses in excess of hobby income are referred to as *hobby losses*, which are not deductible. Hobby expenses are reported as miscellaneous itemized deductions, which are subject to a limit of 2% of adjusted gross income.

Hobby loss. See *hobby*.

Holding period. The length of time an asset is owned. An asset's holding period normally begins on the day after it is acquired and ends on the day of its disposition.

Home equity debt. See *qualified home mortgage interest*.

Home office deduction. Taxpayers who operate a trade or business out of their home can claim a deduction for expenses related to its business use. To claim a deduction, strict tests must be satisfied. The exclusive use test states that a specific part of the home must be used exclusively for carrying on a trade or business. The home office area must also be regularly used as the principal place to conduct a trade or business belonging to the taxpayer, or as a place to meet or deal with patients, clients, or customers in the normal course of the trade or business. Employee use must be for the convenience of the employer and required as a condition of employment before any deductions for a home office may be taken. The home office deduction is limited to the income earned from the home office activity after deducting all other business expenses that are unrelated to the use of the home office.

Hybrid method of accounting. Allows the taxpayer to account for sales of merchandise and the related cost of goods sold on the accrual basis and to use the cash basis for all other items of income and expense; a mixture of the accrual and cash methods.

Improvements by a lessee. A property owner does not have income when a lessee makes improvements to the owner's property or when such improvements revert to the property owner at the termination of the lease. This allows the property owner to defer the gain in value that results from the improvements until the property is sold, at which time the owner will have the wherewithal to pay the tax on the increased value.

Imputed income. The three most common forms of imputed income subject to tax are below market-rate loans, payment of expenses by others, and bargain purchases. Most imputed income is not taxed.

Indirect construction costs. General costs of a business not directly related to a construction project but that support the project. Examples include interest on funds to finance the construction, taxes, general administrative costs, and depreciation on equipment used in the project. See also *direct construction costs*.

Individual accounting treatments. Individual treatments of specific items where the tax law allows the taxpayer options in the treatment of an item. Depreciation methods, accounting for inventories, installment sales accounting, and accounting for long-term contracts are all examples of individual accounting treatments.

Individual retirement account (IRA). All taxpayers are allowed to contribute up to $2,000 per year of their earned income to an IRA. A husband and wife who both have earned sources of income may each contribute up to the $2,000 limit to separate IRA accounts. An IRA can also be established for a nonworking spouse. However, the total amount paid into the two IRAs cannot exceed $2,250, and no one account can receive more than $2,000. If an individual and spouse are not covered by an employer-sponsored retirement plan, all allowable contributions made to the plan are deductible for adjusted gross income. The IRA deduction is reduced if one taxpayer is covered by an employer-provided retirement plan.

Inheritance. The value of property received by inheritance is excluded from taxation. Property held in an estate is subject to the estate tax. Thus, the income tax exclusion for inheritances avoids a double taxation of the property of a deceased taxpayer.

Inherited property. Property passing from a dead person to an heir. The general rule for determining the initial basis is the fair market value of the property on the date of death, called the *primary valuation date.* The executor of the estate may elect to use the *alternate valuation date,* which is six months after the date of death. If assets are distributed before the six-month valuation date and the alternate valuation date has been elected, the asset's basis is the fair market value on the date it is distributed.

Initial basis. Represents the taxpayer's total investment in an asset on its acquisition date. It is equal to the purchase price of the asset plus any cost incurred to get the asset ready for its intended use (i.e., commissions, legal fees, surveys).

Installment sale. Occurs whenever property is sold and at least one payment is received in the tax year subsequent to the year of sale. Taxpayers who are not dealers in the particular type of property must recognize income from the casual sale of property by using the installment method, unless they elect to recognize the entire gain in the year of the sale. The installment method is based on the wherewithal-to-pay concept and recognizes income proportionally as the selling price is received.

Intangible property. Property that lacks any physical characteristics and exists only because of economic rights the property possesses.

Internal Revenue Bulletin (I.R.B.) An official weekly publication of the IRS that includes announcements, Treasury regulations, revenue rulings, revenue procedures, and other information that is of interest to a tax researcher.

Interpretive regulation. Issued under the general authority given to the Treasury Department to provide official interpretations of Internal Revenue Code provisions.

Investment expense. See *business purpose concept.*

Investment interest. Interest paid on debt used to purchase portfolio investments is deductible as an itemized deduction. The deduction for investment interest is limited to *net investment income* (investment income less investment expense other than interest) of the taxpayer for the year. Any interest not currently deductible because of the limitation may be carried forward indefinitely and applied to future years.

Investment-related loss. A loss on the sale or other disposition of an investment asset.

Investment tax credit (ITC). A credit for a percentage of the cost of qualifying property (generally, only personal property has been allowed the ITC) that is granted by Congress. The ITC was repealed in 1986 and has not been reinstated.

Involuntary conversion. Occurs whenever a gain or loss is realized from a transaction that occurs against the taxpayer's will (beyond the control of the taxpayer). Involuntary conversions result when property is destroyed or damaged in a casualty or theft, when a government unit condemns property under its power of eminent domain, or when a foreign government seizes or nationalizes property. Losses on involuntary conversions of business or investment property are always recognized in full. When an involuntary conversion results in a *casualty gain,* the taxpayer may elect to defer the gain if a qualified replacement property is purchased.

Itemized deduction. See *deductions from adjusted gross income.*

Itemized deduction phase-out. High-income taxpayers must reduce the amount of their allowable itemized deductions. Allowable deductions for medical expenses, investment interest, gambling losses, and casualty and theft losses are not subject to reduction. In general, taxpayers with adjusted gross income in excess of $114,700 in 1995 must reduce their otherwise allowable itemized deductions by 3% of adjusted gross income in excess $114,700. In addition, itemized deductions may not be reduced by more than 80% of the otherwise allowable amount.

Joint return test. See *dependent.*

Kiddie tax. See *minor child.*

Least aggregate deferral tax year. See *partnership tax year.*

Legislative grace concept. Any tax relief provided to taxpayers is the result of specific acts of Congress that must be strictly applied and interpreted. All income received is taxable unless a specific provision can be found in the tax law that excludes the income from taxation. Deductions must be approached with the philosophy that nothing is deductible unless a provision in the tax law allows the deduction.

Legislative regulation. Issued when Congress specifically delegates authority to the Treasury Department to write specific rules for a designated Code section. Legislative regulations carry a higher level of authority than interpretative regulations.

Letter rulings. Private letter rulings and technical advice memoranda are generically referred to as *letter rulings* and, although they are not officially published by the government, they are unofficially made available to the public by many private publishers, such as Commerce Clearing House and Research Institute of America.

Life insurance proceeds. Payments from life insurance that are paid upon the death of the insured are generally excluded from income tax, although life insurance proceeds may be included in the dead person's gross estate, which is subject to estate tax. Life insurance proceeds are excluded even if the payments are received in installments, although any earnings included in the installment payments are taxable.

Like-kind exchange. The exchange of like-kind property. The tax law requires the deferral of the recognition of gain or loss until the property is disposed of, providing cash (or other assets) with which to pay the tax. A gain on a like-kind exchange is recognized to the extent of any boot received (but never more than the realized gain on the exchange). Losses on like-kind exchanges are never recognized, even when boot is received. Nonrecognition of gains and losses on exchanges of like-kind property is mandatory. See also *boot.*

Like-kind property. The like-kind exchange rules require that the property being transferred in an exchange be used in a trade or business or held as an investment. The property must be of like kind in the taxpayer's hands, not the prior owner's. Any real property may be exchanged for any other real property in a like-kind exchange. To qualify as like-kind property, personal property must be of like class—within the same *general asset class* as defined for cost-recovery purposes. If both properties being exchanged do not fall within one of the general asset classes, the properties are of like kind if they fall within the same product class. *Product class* is defined as the 4-digit product class of the *Standard Industrial Classification Manual (SIC Codes).*

Limited liability. See *corporation.*

Limited liability company (LLC). Combines the corporate characteristic of limited liability with the conduit tax treatment of partnerships. Whereas corporations are created by filing articles of incorporation, LLCs file articles of organization. The entity must have two or more members, have an objective to carry on a business, and establish a specific method for dividing the profits and losses from the business. An LLC is not subject to corporate taxation, unless it has more corporate characteristics than noncorporate characteristics.

Limited liability partnership (LLP). A general partnership with the added characteristic of limited liability for owners. An LLP permits the usual partnership conduit tax treatment but limits the liabilities of its owners (partners).

Limited partnership. A partnership in which at least one partner's liability is limited to the amount of her or his investment in the partnership. This attribute provides a measure of protection for the limited partners' personal assets. To obtain the limited liability attribute, limited partners give up any right to participate in the management of the business. Management is left to at least one general partner whose liability is not limited and who is responsible for the ongoing activities of the business.

Listed property. Listed property includes the following categories of property: passenger autos; other property used for transportation such as trucks, trains, buses or boats; property of a type that is generally used for purposes of entertainment, recreation, or amusement; any computer or peripheral equipment; any cellular telephone or similar communications equipment. The *listed property rules* require taxpayers to substantiate the extent of an asset's business use. If listed property is not used predominantly in a trade

or business, the business use portion of the asset must be depreciated using the Alternative Depreciation System (ADS). If more than 50% of an asset's total use for each year of its tax life is related to the taxpayer's trade or business, the asset is treated the same as any other business asset.

Listed property rules. See *listed property.*

Long-term capital gain (loss). A gain (loss) on the sale of a capital asset that is held for more than one year.

Lookback method. Pertains to the percentage-of-completed-contract method. To remove the incentive to overestimate costs, the taxpayer must use the lookback method at the completion of the contract to determine whether taxes have been underpaid or overpaid each year based on the actual total costs of the contract. If the taxpayer has underpaid (i.e., costs were overestimated) taxes, the taxpayer must pay interest on the income deferred by the underpayment. If an overpayment has been made, the taxpayer receives interest on the overpayment. See also *percentage-of-completed-contract method.*

Lookback recapture rule. See *Section 1231 netting procedure.*

Loss. Occurs when an asset is disposed of for a selling price that is less than its basis. Such a loss is referred to as a *transaction loss* and represents a loss of capital invested in the asset. An *annual loss* results from an excess of allowable deductions for a tax year over the reported income for the year.

Loss-of-income damages. See *damage payments.*

Lower of cost-or-market method. The lower of cost-or-market method requires a comparison of cost and market for each inventory item. Comparison of the total cost and total market value of dissimilar inventory items is not permitted. *Cost* refers to the amount determined under the cost method using the unicap rules. *Market for purchased merchandise* means the bid price for the particular inventory item in the volume in which it is normally purchased by the taxpayer. For manufactured goods, market is the total reproduction cost at current bid prices.

Majority-interest tax year. See *partnership tax year.*

Marginal tax rate. The rate of tax that will be paid on the next dollar of income or the rate of tax that will be saved by the next dollar of deduction. Used in tax planning to determine the effect of reporting additional income or deductions during a tax year. See also *proportional rate structure.*

Married, filing jointly (separately). See *filing status.*

Material participant. See *material participation* and *material participation exception.*

Material participation. Requires that the taxpayer be involved in the operations of the activity on a regular, continuous, and substantial basis. The basic test for material participation is that the individual (including the individual's spouse) participates in the activity for more than 500 hours per year. Six other tests qualify a taxpayer as a material participant based on lower levels of participation. See also *passive activity.*

Material participation exception. Rental activities of taxpayers meeting this exception are not passive activities. Losses from the rental activities are fully deductible against other active and portfolio income. To qualify for this exception, the taxpayer must materially participate in the rental activity, more than 50% of the taxpayer's total personal service time must be devoted to real property trades or businesses in which the taxpayer materially participates, and more than 750 hours of personal service time must be performed in real property trades or businesses in which the taxpayer materially participates.

Meal and entertainment expense. A taxpayer can deduct 50% of the cost of meals and entertainment incurred for a business purpose. The expense must be an ordinary and necessary expense of the business and not be lavish or extravagant under the circumstances. Also, to be deductible, the expense must be either directly related to or associated with the active conduct of an activity for which the taxpayer has a business purpose. The expense is *directly related* to the active conduct of the taxpayer's business if it meets all four of the following conditions: there is more than a general expectation of deriving income or a business benefit from the meal or entertainment; a bonafide business activity takes place during the meal or entertainment; the principal reason for providing the meal or entertainment is to conduct business; and the expenses are related to the taxpayer and persons involved in the business activity. The *associated with* test has two conditions: the meal or entertainment has a clear business purpose and the meal or entertainment directly precedes or follows a substantial and bonafide business discussion.

Meals provided by employer. The value of meals provided an employee free of charge may be excluded from the employee's income if the meals are provided on the employer's business premises and the provision of the meals is for the convenience of the employer. Cash meal allowances are generally taxable because they are not meals provided by the employer.

Medical expense. Individuals are allowed an itemized deduction for their unreimbursed medical costs. To be deductible, medical expenses must be incurred for the diagnosis, cure, mitigation, treatment or prevention of disease, or they must be incurred for the purpose of affecting a structure or function of the body. Unreimbursed medical costs are only deductible to the extent they exceed 7.5% of AGI.

Mid-month convention. See *depreciation convention.*

Mid-quarter convention. See *depreciation convention.*

Mid-year convention. See *depreciation convention.*

Minor child. Congress in 1986 enacted provisions that are designed to eliminate the tax rate advantage that could have been gained under prior law through shifting of unearned forms of income from parents to a minor child. The basic thrust is to tax the net unearned income of a child who has not attained the age of 14 (minor child) at the parent's mar-

ginal tax rate *(the kiddie tax). Net unearned income* is all unearned inome reduced by $650 and by the greater of the cost of producing the income or $650.

Miscellaneous itemized deductions. Category of deductions that includes amounts expended for unreimbursed employee business expenses, investment expenses (other than investment interest), hobby-related deductions, and gambling losses to the extent of gambling winnings. Some expenditures are subject to an annual limitation of 2% of AGI.

Mixed-use asset. See *mixed-use property.*

Mixed-use expenditure. Expenses that are incurred for both profit and personal reasons. These expenditures must be allocated between business and personal use and deducted according to the rules for each use.

Mixed-use property. A single property may be used in more than one use category. Proper accounting for mixed-use property requires a reasonable allocation of costs between the uses of the property. Also called *mixed-use asset.*

Modified Accelerated Cost Recovery System (MACRS). Applies to tangible property placed in service after 1986. Congress specified longer recovery periods for depreciable assets that would result in depreciation slower than allowed by ACRS.

Moving expenses. Moving expenses are deductible for adjusted gross income if two tests are met. The distance test requires that the commuting distance from the old residence to the new job be 50 miles farther than the distance was to the old job. The time test requires the taxpayer to be employed at the new location for 39 weeks in the 12-month period following the move. Self-employed individuals must work in the new location for 78 weeks during the succeeding 2-year period. The time requirement is waived for death, disability, or discharge or transfer that is not the fault of the employee.

Multiple asset purchase. When more than one asset is bought for a single price, the cost must be allocated to the individual assets in proportion to their fair market value on the date purchased. An appraisal of the individual assets usually provides a reasonable basis for allocating the purchase price. The buyer and seller can agree, at arm's length, on an allocation of the purchase price. The cost of real estate can also be allocated according to the values assessed for property tax purposes.

Multiple support agreement. In the case of two or more individuals who collectively provide more than 50% of the support of an individual who meets all of the other tests for depedency, any member of the support group who contributes more than 10% of the total support may claim the dependency exemption through a multiple support agreement. All members of the support group must agree in writing which person in the group is entitled to receive the exemption.

Municipal bond interest. The tax law provides an exclusion for interest earned on bonds issued by state and local governments (cities, counties, state agencies such as turnpike authorities) of the United States as well as those of U.S. possessions (Guam, Puerto Rico).

Natural business year. The annual accounting period encompassing all related income and expenses. An S corporation must generally use a calendar year. However, an alternate year can be used under the ownership tax year or the business purpose tax year exceptions. To qualify, an S corporation must have peak and off-peak business periods. The natural business year is the end of the peak business period. An annual accounting period qualifies as a *business purpose tax year* if the gross receipts from sales or services for the final two months of the current year and each of the two preceding years equals or exceeds 25% of the gross receipts for the entire 12-month period.

Necessary expense. To be deductible, an expense must be necessary—a reasonable and prudent businessperson would incur the expense in a similar situation. The expense need not be essential to the continued existence of the income-producing activity.

Net investment income. See *investment interest.*

Net operating loss (NOL). An annual loss incurred in a trade or business in which the taxpayer materially participates. It results from an excess of allowable deductions over income for the accounting period. For a taxable entity (i.e., individuals and corporations), a carryover system allows losses incurred in one year to be deducted against income in other years. A *carryback* means that the loss may be used to reduce income from prior years. A *carryforward* means that the loss is used to offset income in future periods. An NOL may be carried back three years. If taxable income in the three-year carryback period is not sufficient to fully absorb the NOL, any remaining loss may be carried forward for 15 years. A taxpayer may elect not to carry the loss back and only carry the loss forward for 15 years.

Net unearned income. See *minor child.*

No additional cost services. A service given to an employee by an employer free of charge. In order for a no additional cost service to be excluded from taxation, the service must be made available to employees on a nondiscriminatory basis and must also be in the same line of business in which the employee works.

Nonaccountable plan. See *employee reimbursement plan.*

Nonacquiescence. An announcement by the IRS that it will not follow the decision of a regular Tax Court decision that was adverse to the government.

Nonbusiness bad debt. See *business bad debt.*

Nonrecognition transaction. A transaction that is not given current effect. The initial realization is considered part of a continuing investment process. Under the substance-over-form doctrine, the new property acquired in the transaction (i.e., like-kind exchanges, involuntary conversions, and sale of principal residence) is viewed as a continuation of the original investment in the asset. Also, the taxpayer lacks the wherewithal to pay the tax on the realized gain, because the amount realized on the transaction is reinvested in the replacement asset. For total deferral of gain, any amounts realized from the disposition must be fully reinvested in a replacement asset.

Nonrecourse debt. A liability that is secured only by the underlying property; the borrower is not personally liable for the debt.

Nonrefundable tax credit. If the amount of the credit exceeds the tax liability, the taxpayer is not entitled to a refund of the excess. Although most business tax credits are nonrefundable, they generally provide that the amount of the credit not used in the current year may be carried forward and used in future years.

One-year rule for prepaid expenses. A cash basis taxpayer may deduct prepaid expenses in the year paid if the prepayment does not create an asset that extends substantially beyond the end of the year of payment. The courts have held that a prepayment of an expense that will be used up before the end of the tax year following the year of prepayment can be deducted when paid. The taxpayer must show that the payment is required by the creditor and that the payment does not distort income. Prepaid taxes are deductible in the year paid, even if the prepayment results in a refund in a later year. Prepaid interest is not generally deductible under the one-year rule.

One-year rule for services. Accrual basis taxpayers may continue to use the accrual method to account for prepaid service income, if the services will be performed before the end of the tax year following the year of receipt.

Ordinary expense. To be deductible, an expenditure must qualify as an ordinary expense. The expense must be of a kind commonly incurred in the particular income-earning activity. The expense may be said to be customary or usual for the activity. The expenditure must also be assignable to the current accounting period.

Ordinary income. Recurring income earned by a taxpayer for a tax year; the type of income that people and businesses expect to earn. Ordinary income typically includes business profits, rent from property, interest on investments, and wages. Ordinary income receives no special treatment under the tax laws.

Organizational costs. Because a corporation is a legal entity formed under state law, various expenditures (i.e., legal services, accounting services, and fees paid to the state of incorporation) must be incurred to accomplish the corporate creation. Most of the expenses benefit future periods of the corporation's life. A corporation may elect to amortize qualified organizational expenses over a period of 60 months or more. If the election to amortize these expenses is not made on the tax return for the first taxable year, the costs are not deductible until the corporation ceases business and liquidates.

Original issue discount security (OID). A debt instrument for which the interest is paid upon maturity of the debt rather than throughout the term of the debt.

Overall accounting methods. The method or system by which taxpayers determine the amount of their income, gains, losses, deductions, and credits, as well as the proper time to recognize these items. The three acceptable overall methods are the cash method, the accrual method, and the hybrid method. The method must be used consistently from period to period and must clearly reflect the income of the taxpayer.

Ownership tax year. The tax year of more than 50% of the owners of an S corporation.

Parent-subsidiary relationship. See *controlled group.*

Partners. Owners of a partnership. An employer/employee relationship cannot exist between a partnership and its partners. Compensation to a partner may be classified as a guaranteed payment or a compensatory payment. A partnership may offer a partner a *guaranteed payment*, which is determined without regard to the partnership's income. Such compensation is ordinary income for the partner and is a deductible compensation expense for the partnership. If a partner receives *compensatory payments* based in any way on the partnership's gross or net income, the payments are classified as the partner's share of partnership profits. The partnership records the payments as nondeductible withdrawals, and the partner recognizes the income in the year of receipt.

Partnership. A general partnership is characterized as follows for tax purposes: a partner's liability is not limited; the life of the partnership depends on the life of the partner(s); all partners share in the partnership management; partnership interests are not freely transferable. Although partnerships are considered conduits for the purpose of income taxation, they are treated as separate entities under local law. Partnerships can transact business and own property in their own names, separate from the partners.

Partnership debt. Initial basis in a partnership begins with a person's contribution of assets or services in exchange for a capital interest. Basis is increased by a partner's share of partnership liabilities. Partnership debt assumed by a partner and the partner's share of partnership debt are deemed to be additional cash contributions by the partner to the partnership. Decreases in partnership debt are deemed cash distributions to the partner and reduce the partner's basis in the partnership.

Partnership distribution. A partner's receipt of a cash or property distribution from a partnership is generally tax free. No gain is recognized (capital recovery concept) until after the basis in the capital investment is recovered. Any excess of cash (or the basis of property) over the basis in a partner's interest is a recognizable gain for the partner who receives it.

Partnership tax year. The selection of a taxable year for a partnership is done on a hierarchical basis that attempts to match the tax years of the partnership to the partners'. First, the partnership must use the same tax year as that used by those partners having a majority interest (more than 50%) in partnership profits and capital (*majority interest tax year).* If the majority interest partners do not have the same tax year, the partnership must use the tax year of its principal partners (a partner with at least a 5% interest), called the *principal partner tax year.* When the principal partners do not have the same tax year, the partnership must use the tax year that results in the least aggregate deferral of income of the partners. The deferral of each partner for each tax year is determined by the number of months from the end of the partnership's tax year forward to the end of the tax year of the partner. The aggregate deferral is determined by totaling the products of the number of months of deferral for each partner and multiplying the result by each partner's ownership interest. The tax year that produces the lowest deferral is the *least aggregate deferral tax year.*

Passive activity. The conduct of any trade or business in which the taxpayer does not materially participate. Limited partnership interests are always passive. Rental activities are generally passive unless the material participation exception applies. Working interests in oil and gas deposits and certain low-income housing projects are always active and not subject to the passive loss rules. See also *material participation exception.*

Passive activity loss rules. The purpose of the passive activity rules is to deny current loss deductions for tax shelter activities. The general rule is that passive losses may only be deducted to the extent of passive income, not against income from portfolio or active income. Any passive activity loss that is not deductible in the current year is suspended. A *suspended loss* is not permanently disallowed but is carried forward and may be deducted against passive income in subsequent years. Deductions of suspended losses are allowed when passive activities are disposed of by sale and because of death. Gifts of passive activities do not result in deduction of suspended losses from the activity.

Pay-as-you-go concept. A tax should be collected as close as possible to the time in which the income is earned.

Percentage depletion (statutory depletion). One of two methods used to compute depletion of natural resources. Percentage depletion is calculated by multiplying gross income from the sale of the natural resource by a statutory percentage. The statutory percentage is the depletion rate specified by the tax law. The maximum allowable percentage depletion deduction for the tax year is 50 percent of the taxable income from the natural resource before subtracting the depletion deduction. See also *cost depletion.*

Percentage-of-completed contract method. Most long-term construction contracts must be accounted for by using the percentage-of-completed contract method. Income is recognized according to the amount of work completed on the contract each year. The work completed must be based on costs incurred during the year in relation to the estimated total costs of the project. See also *lookback method*.

Personal casualty loss. The only personal use loss that the tax law allows as a deduction (itemized) is for losses from casualty and theft. Personal casualty and theft losses are always measured as the lower of the decline in the value of the property or the basis of the property. The amount of loss must be reduced by any insurance proceeds received. Personal use casualty losses are also reduced by a $100 *statutory floor* amount per occurrence. An *annual personal casualty loss limitation* is imposed that limits total personal casualty and theft loss deductions for the year to the extent that they exceed 10% of the taxpayer's adjusted gross income.

Personal exemption. Individuals are allowed to deduct a predetermined amount for each qualifying exemption. The intention is to exempt from tax a minimum amount of income that is used to support the taxpayer and those who are dependent on that taxpayer. Because support costs increase with inflation, the exemption amounts are increased each year to account for the prior year's inflation. Personal exemptions are allowed for the taxpayer and the taxpayer's spouse. *Dependency exemptions* are granted for individuals who are dependent on the taxpayer for support.

Personal injury. See *damage payments*.

Personal property (personalty). Any tangible property that is not real property. Personal property includes machines, equipment, furniture, computers, and autos.

Personal service corporation (PSC). A PSC is a corporation, the shareholder-employees of which provide personal services (e.g., medical, dental, legal, accounting, engineering, actuarial, consulting, or performing arts). PSCs do not enjoy the tax savings from the lower tax brackets assigned to regular corporations because they are taxed at a flat 35% on all income.

Personalty. See *personal property*.

Personal use property. Any property that is used by the taxpayer for purely personal purposes. *Personal use* applies to personal property, real property, and intangible property.

Points. Points are prepaid interest amounts that are required in order to acquire financing. They are expressed as a percentage of the value of the loan and paid at loan acquisition. They represent prepaid interest, which usually is capitalized and amortized over the term of the loan. In the year the points are paid, the tax law allows a deduction for points paid to acquire an initial mortgage on a taxpayer's principal residence. Points paid to refinance an existing mortgage must be capitalized and amortized as interest expense over the term of the loan.

Portfolio income. Consists of unearned income from dividends, interest, royalties, annuities, and other assets held as investments. In portfolio activities, the investor only receives income from the activity and does not share in the expenses related to the activity. Any losses on portfolio income generally occur at the point of sale of the asset producing the income.

Primary authorities. The legislative, administrative, and/or judicial sources. The legislative authorities include the Constitution, tax treaties, and law enacted by Congress. The administrative authorities are the official interpretations of the law prepared by the Treasury Department and the Internal Revenue Service. Decisions by the various trial and appellate courts represent the judicial authorities.

Primary valuation date. See *inherited property*.

Principal partner tax year. See *partnership tax year*.

Principal residence. To be eligible for gain deferral, both the old and new residences must be used as the principal residence (where the taxpayer lives most of the time) of the taxpayer. A taxpayer can have only one principal residence at a time. A principal residence can be a house, mobile home, cooperative apartment, condominium, or a houseboat. The old residence must be replaced by a new residence within a period beginning two years before the sale of the old residence and ending two years after the sale of the old residence. The taxpayer must occupy and use the new residence as a principal residence during this period.

Private activity bond. A bond issued by a government unit, the proceeds from which are used by anyone other than a government unit.

Private letter rulings (LTR). Issued by the National Office of the IRS in response to specific questions raised by taxpayers and typically deal with prospective transactions. An LTR applies only to the taxpayer requesting the ruling and does not bind the IRS to take the same position when dealing with a different taxpayer.

Product class. See *like-kind property*.

Progressive rate structure. A tax in which the average tax rate increases as the tax base increases. The marginal tax rate will be higher than the average tax rate as the tax base increases. The average tax rate, the marginal tax rate, and total tax all increase with increases in the tax base.

Property. Any long-lived asset that is owned by a taxpayer. The terms *asset* and *property* are used interchangeably to mean anything owned or possessed by a taxpayer. Property is classified by both its use and its type for tax purposes. The use of property determines whether deductions are allowed for current-year expenditures made in relation to the property and for capital recovery deductions for depreciation, depletion, or amortization. In order to take any deductions relating to property, there must be a business purpose (used in a trade or business or held for the production of income) for the property. All property is either tangible or intangible property. The type of property does not change from taxpayer to taxpayer.

Property disposition. See *amount realized.*

Property settlement. See *alimony.*

Proportional rate structure. A tax for which the average tax rate remains the same as the tax base increases (also referred to as a *flat tax*). The marginal tax rate and the average tax rate are the same at all levels of the tax base. As the tax base increases, the total tax paid will increase at a constant rate. Examples include sales taxes, real estate and personal property taxes, and certain excise taxes, such as the tax on gasoline.

Proposed regulation. Issued to let the public know what the IRS believes is the proper interpretation of a related Code provision and to provide an opportunity for the public to comment before a regulation is issued in final form.

Punitive damages. See *damage payments.*

Qualified home mortgage interest. Only interest on debt that is secured by the taxpayer's principal residence and one other residence is deductible. Qualified home mortgage interest includes both acquisition debt and home equity debt. *Acquisition debt* is any debt incurred to acquire, construct, or substantially improve a qualified residence of the taxpayer. *Home equity debt* is any debt that is secured by a personal residence and that is not acquisition debt. The proceeds of home equity debt can be used for any purpose. Interest paid on up to $1,000,000 of acquisition debt is deductible. Interest on debt in excess of $1,000,000 is considered personal interest and is not deductible. Interest paid on home equity debt up to $100,000 is also deductible.

Qualified pension plan. Payments made by an employer to an employee's account in a qualified pension plan are not taxable in the period in which the payments are made. The tax on such payments is deferred until the employee actually withdraws the payments from the plan. Earnings on amounts paid into such plans are not taxed until they are withdrawn by the employee.

Qualified real property business indebtedness. Debt that is incurred or assumed before 1993 in connection with real property used in a trade or business that is secured by that property. Debt that is a refinancing of previously incurred qualified debt or that is incurred after 1992 to acquire, construct, or substantially improve real property used in a trade or business is also qualified real property business indebtedness.

RAR. Revenue agent's report.

Real estate. See *real property.*

Realization concept. No income or loss is recognized for tax purposes (is included in taxable income) until it has been realized by the taxpayer. In most cases, a realization occurs when an arm's-length transaction takes place. A realization involves a change in the form and/or the substance of a

taxpayer's property rights that results from an arm's-length transaction.

Realized gain (loss). See *amount realized.*

Real property. In general, real property is land and any structures that are permanently attached to land, such as buildings.

Real property trade or business. A trade or business involving the development, redevelopment, construction, acquisition, conversion, rental operation, management, leasing, or brokerage of real property.

Reasonable compensation. Employee compensation is subject to two basic tests for deductibility. First, payments must be for services actually performed by the employee. Second, the total payment for services of the employee must be reasonable in amount. When the compensation paid to an employee is found to be excessive, only a reasonable salary deduction is allowed. Whether compensation paid an employee is reasonable is decided by considering several factors, including (1) the employee's duties, responsibilities, and pay history; (2) the volume and complexity of the business; (3) the time required to do the work; (4) the ability and accomplishments of the employee; (5) the general cost of living and the company pay policy; (6) the relationship of the compensation, the gross and net income of the business, and dividends paid to shareholders. Reasonable compensation issues generaly arise in connection with related parties.

Reasonable expense. To be deductible, an expense must be reasonable in amount. The reasonableness test most often becomes an issue in transactions involving related parties.

Recognized gain (loss). To recognize a gain or loss means to include the amount of the gain or loss in the current year's taxable income calculation.

Refundable tax credit. The taxpayer is entitled to a refund of any excess credit. This is a form of negative income tax. The taxpayer not only pays no tax but receives a payment from the government that is based on the taxpayer's income.

Regressive rate structure. A tax in which the average tax rate decreases as the tax base increases. The marginal tax rate will be less than the average tax rate as the tax base increases. Although the average tax rate and the marginal tax rate both decrease as the tax base increases, the total tax paid will increase.

Rehabilitation tax credit. In order to provide incentive for businesses to rehabilitate older buildings and certified historic structures, a 10% credit is allowed for the expenditures incurred in the rehabilitation of a building placed in service before 1936. Rehabilitation expenditures incurred on a certified historic structure are granted a 20% tax credit. The basis of the building or structure must be reduced by the amount of credit taken. In order to retain the full benefit of the tax credit, the property must be held for five full years.

Related party. Family members and corporations that are owned by family members are considered related parties, as are certain other relationships between entities in which the power to control the substance of a transaction is evidenced through majority ownership.

Relationship, or member of household, test. See *dependent*.

Remainderman. See *trust*.

Rental activity. A payment received primarily for the use of tangible property. Rental activities are generally considered passive activities, unless the material participation exception applies. Rental activities that also provide significant services (i.e., hotel rooms, car rentals, hospital rooms, and golf course fees) are exempt from the passive loss rules as long as the owner(s) of such activities meet the material participation standard. The most common forms of passive activity rentals involve the rental of real property (i.e., apartment buildings, rental houses, office building rentals, warehouse rentals, factory rentals, etc.).

Reporter. A series of books published by the federal government or by a private publishing company that provides the full text of court decisions. Different reporters are cited for each court that renders a decision.

Research and experimental (R&E) credit. Encourages research and development of new technologies and processes. The incremental credit is equal to 20% of the qualified research expenditures in the current year in excess of the base amount. The basic research credit is equal to 20% of qualified expenditures for research that is intended to advance scientific knowledge without a specific commercial objective. The payments must be made in cash under written agreement, and the research must be performed or controlled by a university, college, or other nonprofit scientific research organization.

Revenue procedure. Issued to explain internal IRS administrative practices and procedures.

Revenue ruling. Interpretation by the IRS of the Code and regulations as they apply to specific factual situations. A revenue ruling represents official policy of the IRS.

Reversionary interest. See *trust*.

S. Ct. *Supreme Court Reports.*

SIC Codes. See *like-kind property*.

SUTA. State Unemployment Tax Act. See *employment taxes*.

Salary reduction plan. See *flexible benefits plan*.

Scholarship. A college student who is a candidate for a degree may exclude the value of the scholarship, provided that the award does not require the student to perform any future services such as teaching, grading papers, or tutoring. The scholarship must be gratuitous in nature and not merely a form of compensation for past, present, or future services. The amount of the exclusion is limited to the direct costs of the student's college education. Direct costs consist of the student's tuition, fees, books, supplies, and other equipment required in the course of instruction. Amounts received in excess of the direct costs of the education are taxable.

Secondary authority. Serves primarily as a tool in locating the relevant primary authority and a source for better understanding, interpretation, and application of primary authorities. Secondary authorities include all statements, pronouncements, explanations, or interpretations of the law that are not primary and consist chiefly of tax services, citators, computer software systems that research tax databases, and tax journals and newsletters.

Section 179. Under this provision, taxpayers are allowed to expense up to $17,500 (per year) of the cost of tangible personal property used in a trade or business. Amounts expensed under this provision reduce the depreciable basis of the property. The amount of the annual deduction limit is reduced when purchases of qualifying property exceed $200,000. In addition, the deductible amount cannot exceed the taxable income from the active conduct of all the taxpayer's trade or business activities.

Section 1231 gain (loss). Results from the sale or other disposition of a Section 1231 property.

Section 1231 netting procedure. Tax treatments accorded Section 1231 assets apply to the net gain or loss on all Section 1231 transactions occurring during a tax year. The Section 1231 netting procedure nets together all casualty (theft) gains and losses on Section 1231 assets to produce a single net casualty gain or loss for the year. If the result is a loss, all casualty gains and losses for the year are considered ordinary losses. If the result of the netting is a gain, the net casualty gain is netted together with all other Section 1231 gains and losses occurring during the year. If the result is a loss, all gains and losses for the year are considered ordinary. When the result is a gain, another netting must take place *(lookback recapture rule)*. This nets the current year net Section 1231 gain against any Section 1231 ordinary loss deductions taken in the previous five years.

Section 1231 property. Property used in a trade or business, held for more than one year, that is used in a trade or business; timber, coal, and domestic iron ore; livestock that is held for more than one year and horses that are held for more than two years; and unharvested crops.

Section 1245 property. All depreciable tangible personal property is Section 1245 property (i.e., autos, trucks, equipment, machinery, computers, patents, copyrights, leaseholds, and livestock). Certain real property depreciated using ACRS is also classified as Section 1245 property.

Section 1245 recapture rule. Section 1245 assets are subject to a full recapture of all depreciation taken as ordinary income. No capital gain or Section 1231 treatment results from the sale of a Section 1245 asset unless it is sold for more than its original cost.

Section 1250 property. In general, depreciable real property is Section 1250 property (i.e., office buildings, apartment buildings, warehouses, factory buildings, and low-income housing). However, certain real property depreciated using ACRS is also classified as Section 1245 property.

Section 1250 recapture rule. Under Section 1250, only gains that are attributable to excess depreciation are recaptured as ordinary income. *Excess depreciation* is defined as the total depreciation taken to date, less the allowable straight-line depreciation on the asset.

Securities dealer. A person who transacts in securities may be an active investor, an active trader, or a dealer in securities. Unlike active traders and dealers, active investors are not considered to be in a trade or business. A securities dealer purchases a security expecting to realize a profit from selling it to a customer for a fee or commission. An *active investor* is a person who continuouly, regularly, and extensively manages his or her own portfolio with a view toward long-term appreciation in the portfolio's value and not short-term profit. An active investor's expenses are deductible only as miscellaneous itemized deductions. An *active trader* earns a livelihood buying and selling securities for personal profit. The active trader's expenses are deductible for adjusted gross income.

Self-employment tax. Self-employed individuals pay a Social Security tax equal to the sum of the employer's and employee's payments (15.3%). Because employees are not taxed on the Social Security contribution made on their behalf by their employees, self-employed taxpayers are allowed to deduct one-half of their self-employment tax as a business expense to equalize the tax treatments of employees and the self-employed.

Self-insured medical plan. A plan established by a company that chooses to self-insure by making payments to a fund that is used to pay employees' medical expenses. The payments are excluded from employees' income. However, if a self-insured medical plan discriminates in favor of highly compensated employees, the amounts paid for medical expenses of a highly compensated employee covered by the plan are included in the individual's taxable income.

Short sale. A technique for investing in a security that is expected to decline in value. Short sellers sell a security that they do not own and receive the net selling price from the buyer. Because short-sellers do not actually own the securities, they borrow them from their brokers, who give the actual shares of stock to the buyers. At a later date, the short seller purchases the shares previously sold on the open market and gives them back to the broker to repay the shares borrowed at the initial short-sale date (closing the short sale). The short seller's profit or loss is the net selling price of the shares in the first step minus the price that the short seller paid to purchase the shares back in the second step. Short sellers are betting that the shares sold short will decline in value and they will be able to buy them back for less than they initially sold for.

Short sale against the box. The taxpayer closes a short sale by giving shares the taxpayer already owned (rather than buying them on the market) to the broker in the next tax year. This allows the taxpayer to lock in a gain on the shares owned in the current tax year while deferring recognition of the gain until the next tax year.

Short-term capital gain (loss). A gain (loss) on the sale on a capital asset that is held for one year or less.

Simple trust. See *trust.*

Single. See *filing status.*

Small business stock. The tax law provides an exception to the $3,000 annual capital loss deduction limitation on losses incurred on qualifying small business stock. This allows an individual taxpayer to deduct up to $50,000 in losses on small business stock per year or $100,000 for a married couple filing a joint return. The stock must be purchased directly from the corporation at original issue. The corporation must satisfy several other requirements, the most important of which is that the contributed capital of the corporation at the time the stock is issued must be less than $1,000,000.

Social Security taxes. Under the Federal Insurance Contribution Act *(FICA)*, a tax is levied on wages and salaries earned. Social Security taxes are matched by employers. Employees are not taxed on the Social Security contribution made on their behalf by their employers. In 1995, a tax of 6.2% is levied on the first $61,200 of wages for Old Age, Survivors, and Disability Insurance (OASDI). A tax of 1.45% on all wages and salaries pays for Medical Health Insurance (MHI).

Specific charge-off method. Bad debts are deductible when the taxpayer determines that a particular debt is no longer collectible. *Business bad debts* are deductible in the accounting period in which the facts known to the taxpayer indicate that the account is fully or partially uncollectible. Nonbusiness bad debts are not deductible until the accounting period in which the actual amount of worthlessness of the debt is known to the taxpayer.

Split basis rule for gifts. If the fair market of the gift property at the date of the gift is less than the donor's basis, the property has one basis for determining gains and a separate basis for determining losses on dispositions (split basis). The basis for determining gains is the donor's adjusted basis. The basis for determining losses is the fair market value on the date of the gift. This effectively eliminates the transfer of unrealized losses from one taxpayer to another by gift.

Split basis rules for business property. When property held for personal use is changed to property held for a business purpose, the split basis rules kick in. If the fair market value of personal use property is more than its adjusted basis on the date business use begins, the asset's adjusted basis is used to compute depreciation and gain or loss on its disposition. If the fair market value of personal use property is less than its adjusted basis on the date it is changed to a business use, the initial basis for gain is the property's adjusted basis on the conversion date and the initial basis for loss and depreciation is the property's fair market value on the conversion date. If the property is later sold for an amount that falls between the adjusted basis for gain and the adjusted basis for loss, the adjusted basis for the sale is the sales price.

Standard deduction. An amount that Congress allows all taxpayers to deduct, regardless of their actual qualifying itemized deductions. Thus, taxpayers itemize their deductions only if their total allowable itemized deductions exceed the standard deduction.

Standard mileage rate method. See *auto expense.*

Start-up costs. Start-up costs are related to investigating and creating a new active trade or business. Start-up costs are the expenses incurred before the new business begins its activities. Start-up costs include surveys and analyses of markets, facilities, and labor force; travel to develop the business and locate potential customers and suppliers; advertising the new business; salaries to train employees; salaries for executives and consultants; and various other expenses such as legal and accounting fees.

Statute of limitations. The time period within which the IRS or the taxpayer must assert that a tax return is not correct. The general statute of limitations period is three years from the due date of the return. Several exceptions extend the statute of limitations beyond the general three-year period.

Statutory depletion. See *percentage depletion.*

Statutory floor. See *personal casualty loss.*

Stock dividend. A dividend in cash or other property distributed to a shareholder generally is taxable as income to the shareholders. Also, the distributing corporation may not take a deduction for the amount of dividends distributed for tax purposes. But the receipt of a stock dividend does not constitute a realization of income. The value of a shareholder's interest does not change; it is merely spread over more ownership units. However, if the recipient of the stock dividend has the option to receive cash in lieu of stock, the dividend is taxed as if the cash option had been selected. In this case, the shares of the stock are deemed to have a cash equivalent and thus are taxable.

Substance-over-form doctrine. Transactions are to be taxed according to their true intention rather than some form that may have been contrived.

Substantiation requirements. Entertainment, auto, travel, and gift expenses are subject to strict documentation requirements. The tax law requires the taxpayer to keep records that show the amount of the expense; the time and place of travel or entertainment or date and description of a gift; the business purpose of the travel, entertainment, or gift; and the business relationship to the person entertained or receiv-ing the gift. Failure to keep the records necessary to substantiate an expense can result in loss of the deduction.

Support test. See *dependent.*

Surviving spouse. See *filing status.*

Suspended loss. See *passive activity loss rules.*

T.C. *Reports of the United States Tax Court.*

TCM. *Tax Court Memorandum Decisions.* See also *tax court memorandum decision.*

TCMP. *Taxpayer Compliance Measurement Program.*

TM. Technical memorandum.

Tangible property. Any property that has a physical existence (form, shape, and substance).

Taxable entity. Entities that are liable for the payment of tax. The four entities responsible for the payment of income tax are individuals, regular (or C) corporations, estates, and some trusts.

Taxable income. The tax base for the federal income tax. The difference between the total income of a taxpayer and the deductions allowed that taxpayer.

Tax avoidance. The use of legal methods allowed by the tax law to minimize a tax liability. Tax avoidance generally involves planning an intended transaction to obtain a specific tax treatment.

Tax base. The value that is subject to tax. See also *proportional rate structure.*

Tax benefit rule. Any deduction taken in a prior year that is recovered in a subsequent year is reported as income in the year it is recovered, to the extent that a tax benefit is received from the deduction. The tax benefit received is the amount by which taxable income was actually reduced by the deduction recovered.

Tax Court memorandum decision. All decisions that are not Tax Court regular decisions. They are only published by Research Institute of America (RIA) in *Tax Court Reports* (TC Memo) and by Commerce Clearing House (CCH) under the title *Tax Court Memorandum Decisions* (TCM).

Tax Court regular decision. Presumed to have value as precedents or involve issues that have not previously been considered. Regular decisions are generally regarded as having a stronger authority than memorandum decisions. Published by the government in a reporter called *Reports of the United States Tax Court* (T.C.).

Tax credit. A direct reduction in the income tax liability. In effect, tax credits are treated like tax prepayments.

Taxes. Itemized deductions are allowed for amounts paid in for state and local income taxes, real estate taxes, and other personal property taxes. In order to be deductible, personal property taxes must be ad valorem (based on the value of the property being taxed).

Tax evasion. Occurs when a taxpayer uses fraudulent methods or deceptive behavior to hide the actual tax liability. Tax evasion usually involves three elements: a willfulness on the part of the taxpayer, an underpayment of tax, and an affirmative act by the taxpayer to evade the tax.

Tax home. See *travel expenses.*

Tax service. A type of secondary authority that principally serves as a tool in locating the primary authorities related to various factual circumstances. They generally consist of multivolume sets of loose-leaf binders that are constantly updated for new developments. One category of tax services consists of very limited editorial discussion and numerous brief interpretations and citations to the primary authorities other than the Code and regulations, which are provided in full text [i.e., *Standard Federal Tax Reporter* (CCH) and *United States Tax Reporter* (RIA)]. The other category of tax services contains extensive editorial discussion and interpretation of the law with citations to the primary authorities provided in footnotes [i.e., *Federal Tax Coordinator Second* (RIA), *Tax Management Portfolios* (Bureau of National Affairs), and *Mertens Law of Federal Income Taxation* (Callaghan and Co.)].

Tax shelter. Any investment activity that is designed to minimize the effect of the income tax on wealth accumulation. The term is generally applied to investments that produce significant tax losses as a result of the allowable deductions associated with the investment. The losses are then used to offset (shelter) taxable income from other income sources. Eventually, the taxpayer investing in such a shelter will have to pay a tax on the investment when it is sold. However, the deduction of losses from the shelter in tax years prior to the payment of tax on the gain presents a time value of money savings opportunity.

Technical advice memorandum (TAM). A private letter ruling on a completed transaction. A TAM is a request for assistance by the local office of the IRS and typically arises during an ongoing audit. The TAM is issued by the National Office of the IRS and is not binding on the IRS.

Temporary regulation. Issued to provide taxpayers with guidance until a final regulation is issued. All temporary regulations must be issued as proposed regulations; the regulation expires if not amended or issued as a final regulation within three years.

Testamentary trust. See *trust.*

Theft. Similar to a casualty in that it must be sudden and unexpected. A theft may occur as a result of a robbery, larceny, or an embezzlement. The damage caused by a theft is that the entire property is lost. A theft is treated as property fully destroyed (all value lost).

Theft loss. See *theft.*

Trade or business expense. See *business purpose concept.*

Trade or business loss. A general category that pertains to a transaction loss. These losses are treated as ordinary losses in the period they are incurred and deducted without limit against income from the trade or business. For an individual, a trade or business loss is deductible as a deduction for AGI. An exception to this rule is for losses on exchanges of business property that must be deferred to a future period.

Transaction loss. Results from a single disposition of property. The loss must be categorized by the activity producing the loss to determine its deductibility: trade or business losses, investment-related losses, and personal use losses. In general, transaction losses must have a business purpose to be deductible. See *loss.*

Travel expenses. A taxpayer can deduct travel expenses (i.e., transportation, lodging, 50% of the cost of meals, and incidental expenses—telephone calls, laundry, etc.) incurred while pursuing a business purpose. For an expense to qualify as travel, the taxpayer must be away from her or his tax home overnight. A *tax home* is the general area where the taxpayer conducts her or his principal business activity. Overnight is substantially longer than a normal workday and can be less than 24 hours. The taxpayer cannot deduct any of the transportation costs if the purpose of the trip is primarily personal. If more than 50% of the total time is related to personal activities, the primary purpose will be deemed to be personal.

Treasury regulation. The Treasury Department's official explanation of a related provision in the Internal Revenue Code. Also called a *final regulation.*

Trial courts. Courts of original jurisdiction that are used to initiate litigation. Taxpayers willing to pay the tax in dispute and then sue for a refund have the option of taking their case to a *U.S. District Court* or the *U.S. Claims Court.* In order to have a jury trial, taxpayers must file in district court. Taxpayers may choose not to pay the additional tax and file a petition in U.S. Tax Court for relief.

Trust. A legal entity created when a person transfers ownership of property to a *trustee* to be held for the benefit of another person. The person who transfers the corpus, or trust assets, to the trustee is called the *grantor.* The directions given the trustee by the grantor are included in the trust instrument, or indenture. The trustee's primary purpose is to preserve the trust assets for the benefit of the beneficiaries. If the trustee is required to distribute all annual income to the trust beneficiaries, the trust is called a *simple trust.* All other trusts are called *complex trusts.* In addition, there is a *remainderman,* the beneficiary who will receive the balance of the trust assets when the trust is terminated. For a trust to be recognized as a taxable entity, no more than 5% of the trust assets may revert to the grantor or spouse (*a reversionary interest*) upon the termination (if the trust was created or had additional assets transferred to it after March 1, 1986). If a trust does not meet this requirement, trust income is taxed to the grantor. This type of trust is called a *grantor trust.* A trust created at death and funded by the assets of an estate is called a *testamentary trust.*

Trustee. See *trust.*

U.S. *United States Reports.*

U.S. Claims Court. A trial-level court in which the taxpayer typically sues the government for a refund of overpaid tax liability, although it also hears certain nontax claims against the federal government. Its decisions must be appealed to the U.S. Court of Appeals for the Federal Circuit in Washington, D.C. See *trial courts.*

U.S. Court of Appeals. Federal appellate courts that hear appeals from U.S. Tax Court, U.S. District Court, and U.S. Claims Court. The courts are organized as 12 geographic circuits, each of which hears appeals from taxpayers living within its geographic area. The U.S. Court of Appeals for the Federal Circuit hears all appeals from U.S. Claims Court.

U.S. Court of Appeals for the Federal Circuit. An appellate court that reviews decisions of the U.S. Claims Court.

U.S. District Court. The trial-level federal court that hears cases only from taxpayers who live within the specific geographic area over which the court presides.

U.S. Supreme Court. The ultimate appellate court of the United States. The Court limits its review of tax cases to those of major importance or to those in which the decisions of the circuit courts conflict.

U.S. Tax Court. Often referred to as the "poor person's court" because taxpayers in dispute with the IRS may choose not to pay additional tax and file a petition for relief in Tax Court, which specializes in tax matters.

Unearned income. Unearned income constitutes a return on an investment and does not require any labor by the owner of the investment in order to produce the income. The most common forms of unearned income are interest income, dividend income, income from rental and royalty-producing activities, income from annuities, income from conduit entities, and gains from the sale of investments producing any of the five forms of unearned income.

Unified donative-transfers credit. A lifetime credit of $192,800 that taxpayers may use to reduce gift and estate taxes. The credit is equivalent to being able to exclude $600,000 in property from the gift and/or the estate tax.

Uniform capitalization (unicap) rules. Manufacturers and certain retailers and wholesalers are required to determine the cost of their inventories using the uniform capitalization (unicap) rules. Retailers and wholesalers with average annual gross revenue of less than $10 million are exempt from the unicap rules. The unicap rules require a reasonable allocation of all direct and indirect costs to the cost of inventory. Indirect costs include all costs other than selling and administrative costs that are not related to production.

Vacation home. A taxpayer who owns a vacation home that is used for family vacations and rented to unrelated persons during the remainder of the year is subject to special rules. The use of the vacation home for more than a minimal length of time as rental property and as a personal vacation home (i.e., personal use is more than 14 days) results in the deduction for expenses' being limited to the amount of the rental income. Vacation home expenses in excess of current income can be carried forward for use in a later year.

Wash sale. Occurs when a security is sold at a loss and is replaced within 30 days before or after the sales date with a substantially identical security. A loss from a wash sale is deferred until the taxpayer's interest in the replacement stock is disposed of in a taxable transaction. The wash sale rule applies on a first-in, first-out basis only to the extent the loss stock is replaced. As a result, a loss on shares of stock not replaced is deductible. The wash sale provisions do not apply to dispositions at a gain, to securities that are sold at a loss but not replaced, or to dealers in securities.

Wherewithal-to-pay concept. Income is recognized in the period in which the taxpayer has the means to pay the tax on the income.

Workers' compensation. Payments from a state workers' compensation fund are excluded from taxation. These payments are made to workers who become unable to work as a result of a work-related injury.

Working-condition fringe benefit. Any item provided to an employee that would have been deductible by the employee as an employee business expense if the employee had paid for the item. This class of fringe benefits includes dues to professional organizations, professional journals, and uniforms. Free parking is specifically included as a working-condition fringe benefit.

Working interest in oil and gas deposit. An outright ownership interest held by the operator of the property. A working interest has unlimited liability for all debts of the operation and is responsible for the costs of operating the property. A working interest in an oil and gas deposit is always considered an active business for purposes of the passive activity rules.

Worthless security. When a security becomes worthless, a technical disposition does not take place. However, the tax law gives recognition to the loss of investment suffered by the taxpayer in such situations by allowing a realization of the loss on the last day of the tax year in which the security is determined to be worthless. The loss realized is the basis of the worthless security. Using the last day of the tax year as the date of realization determines the holding period of the security for classification as a short-term or long-term loss.

A

Abandoned spouse, 323–324
Ability to pay concept, 5
Accelerated Cost Recovery System (ACRS),
    476, 479–480, 487–491
  basis subject to cost recovery, 480–481
  class lives, 481
  conventions, 490
  depreciation conventions, 481–482
  depreciation methods for, 489
  differences from MACRS, 491
  overview of, 488
  property subject to cost recovery, 480
  real property recovery periods, 488
  straight-line election, 490–491
  tables of,
      15 year real property, 530
      18 year real property, 531
      19 year real property percentage, 489
      19 year real property (19-year 175%
          declining balance, 532
      low-income housing, 530
  use of percentage tables, 489
Accident policies, payments from, 155–156
Accountable plan, 325–326
Accounting concept, 54–61
  annual accounting period concept, 58–61
  entity concept, 54–58
  summary of, 74
Accounting methods, 58–59, 632–641. See
    also Accrual basis accounting
    methods; Cash basis accounting
    methods
  accrual, 58–59
  cash basis, 58–59
  changing, 632
  conduit entities, 397
  corporations and, 388–389, 633
  defined, 202, 632
  effect of, on income, 117–122
  financial vs. tax, 20, 208–210
  hybrid, 121
  for individuals, 317
  installment sales and, 121–122
  for inventories, 637–641
  long-term construction contracts,
      634–637
    lookback method, 122
    percentage-of-completed contract
        method, 122
  overall accounting methods, 632
  partnerships, 633
  tax shelter activity, 633
  timing deductions and effect of, 202–210
Accounting periods, 627–632
  calendar year, 58, 627
  conduit entities, 396–397

corporations and, 388–389
  fiduciaries and, 395
  fiscal year, 58, 627–628
  taxable year, 627–632
    limitations on choice of, 629–632
Accrual basis accounting method, 58–59
  constructive receipt doctrine, 65–66
  effect of, on income, 119–121
  exception to income recognition, 120–122
  one-year rule for services, 120
  related party accrued expenses, 239–240
  timing of deductions and, 205–208
Acquiescence, 680–681
Acquisition debt, 338
ACRS. See Accelerated Cost Recovery
    System (ACRS)
Actions on decisions (AOD), 681
Active income, 282–283
Active investor, 187–188
Active participant, 290
Active participation exception, 290
Active trader, 188
Activity loss, 270
Actual cost method, automobile expense,
    229–230
Ad valorem taxes, 15
Add-on minimum tax, 651
Adjusted basis, 72, 428–432
  calculation of, 73, 430
  decreases in basis, 430–432
  increases in basis, 429–430
  property disposition and, 99–100
Adjusted gross income (AGI), 26, 182, 318
  deductions for, 26–27
  deductions from, 27–29
Adjusted sales price, 605
Administrative authorities, 673, 674,
    679–681
  acquiescence and nonacquiescence,
      680–681
  other pronouncements, 681
  revenue rulings and procedures, 680
  treasury regulations, 679–680
Administrative convenience concept, 51–52
Agreement not to compete, 505–507
Alimony, 61
  as income, 105–106
  recapture rules and, 106
All the facts and circumstances, 189–190
All-events test, 205–206
All-inclusive income concept, 61–62
Alternated valuation date, 445–446
Alternative Depreciation System (ADS),
    491–492, 496, 499, 500
  recovery class, 491
Alternative minimum tax (AMT), 650–661,
    627

adjustment items, 652–657
  basic computation of, 651–653
  credit against the regular tax, 659–660
  exemptions, 658
  history of, 650–651
  minimum tax credit, 660
  net operating loss deduction, 656–657
  preference items, 652, 657–658
  private activity bond, 657–658
  purpose of, 650–651
  tax credits, 658–659
  tax planning and, 660–661
  tentative minimum tax liability, 652
Alternative minimum tax rate, 651
Alternative minimum taxable income
    (AMTI), 651
American Federal Tax Reports, 686
American Institute of Certified Public
    Accountants (AICPA), 36
Amortization, 505–507
  capital recovery concept and, 72
  defined, 474
  introduction to, 472–474
  property subject to, 474–475
Amount realized, in property disposition,
    433–434
Annual accounting period concept,
    58–61
  accounting method, 58–59
  substance-over-form doctrine, 60–61
  tax benefit rule, 59
Annual basis accounting method,
    net operating losses and, 272–273
Annual losses, 21, 270
  net operating losses, 272–275
  passive activity losses, 272
  treatment of, 273
Annual personal casualty loss limitation,
    300
Annuities, 97–99
  annual accounting period concept, 99
  defined, 97
  exclusion formula, 142
  exclusion ratio, 97–98
  miscellaneous deduction for
      unrecovered investment because of
      death, 342–343
Appeal process, 697–698
Appellate courts, 683
Arm's length transaction concept, 52–53
  related party provisions, 52–53
Articles of incorporation, 375
Assessments for local benefits, 243
Assets. See also Property
  basis of replacement, 586–588
  business expense, 196–197

classification of, for property disposition, 542
defined, 425
determining amount invested, 435–437
general asset classes, 592
goodwill and, 438–439
intangible, 505–507
purchase of, 435–441
  bargain purchases, 437
  business, 438–440
  constructed assets, 440–441
  goodwill, 438–439
  multiple assets, 437–438
Section 1231, 557
Assignment-of-income doctrine, 58–59
earned income and, 95
Associated with,
  meal and entertainment expense,
  225–226
At-risk rules, 276–279
nonrecourse debt and, 278
Audit process, 695–698
administrative appeals, 697–698
Discriminant Function System, 696
document perfection program, 696
information-matching program, 696
settlement procedures, 697
special audit programs, 696
tax return selection processes, 696
taxpayer Compliance Measurement
  Program (TCMP), 696
types of examinations, 696–697
Automobile expenses, 228–230
actual cost method, 229–230
depreciation deduction, 230
passenger automobile limitation,
  501–502
Section 179 and, 485
standard mileage rate method, 227
Average cost method, 638, 640–641
Average tax rate, defined, 7–8
Awards, 101

B

Bad debts, 236–239
business, 236–239
nonbusiness, 236–239
specific charge-off method, 238
Bankruptcy, 159
Bargain purchases,
basis of, 437
vs. employee discounts, 150–151
as imputed income, 111–112
Basis, 71, 181
adjusted, 72, 73, 428–432
of bargain purchases, 437
carryover, 287, 434
in conduit entities, 432–433
decreases in, 430–432
defined, 63
depreciation, 476

increases in, 429–430
initial, 428, 435
in partnerships, 397–399, 402–403
of personal use property converted to
  business use, 449–451
of property,
  acquired by gift, 441–444
  acquired by inheritance, 444–448
  acquired from a spouse, 448–449
replacement asset, 586
in S corporations, 397–399
in securities, 451–455
split basis rule for business property,
  449–451
subject to capital recovery, 476
subject to cost recovery, 480–481
summary of rules, 456–457
unrecovered, 503
Below market-rate loans, 107–111
Betterments, 198
Boot,
defined, 589
effect of, on like-kind exchanges,
  594–598
Brother-sister relationship, 390–391
Business,
defined, 187
purchase of, 438–440
  assets of, 438–440
  corporate stock, 440
  goodwill, 438–439
Business bad debt, 236–239
Business casualty loss, 291–295
Business expenses, 68, 180–210, 223–252
auto expense, 228–230
bad debts, 236–239
business gifts, 232–233
compensation of employees, 234–236
dcfined, 68–69, 180, 187–188
education expenses, 233–234
hobby expenses, 245–247
home office expenses, 250–252
illegal expenses, 200
insurance, 241
introduction to, 179–181, 223–224
legal fees, 244–245
limited mixed-use expenses, 245–252
  hobby expenses, 245–247
  home office expenses, 250–252
  vacation home expenses, 247–250
lobbying expenses/other political
  activities, 200–201
meals and entertainment, 224–228
mixed-use assets, 191–192
mixed-use expenditures, 192–193
one-year rule for prepaid expenses, 204
production of income, 188–189
profit-motivated expenditures, 185–186
reimbursed employee, 325–328
related party accrued expenses, 239–240
rental activity and, 189–191
rental payments, 243–244

repair-and-maintenance expense, 198
reporting deductions, 182–185
  conduit entities, 183–185
start-up cost, 198–199
substantiation requirement, 233
taxes, 241–243
test for deductibility, 193–202
  must be for taxpayer's benefit, 202
  necessary expense, 194–195
  not a capital expenditure, 196–197
  not a personal expense, 195–196
  not frustrate public policy, 199–201
  not related to tax-exempt income,
    201–202
  ordinary expense, 193–194
  reasonable in amount, 195
timing of deductions, effect of
  accounting method, 202–210
travel expenses, 230–232
vacation home expenses, 247–250
Business gifts, 232–233
Business property,
split basis rules for, 449–451
Business purpose concept, 68–71
Business tax credit, 642–646
foreign tax credit, 642–644
investment tax credit, 642
purpose of, 642, 643
rehabilitation tax credit, 645–646
research and experimental (R & E) tax
  credit, 644–645
summary of, 643

C

C corporations, 55
Cafeteria plan, 152
Calendar years, 58
Capital asset, 542
defined, 62–63, 112, 295, 546
Capital expenditure, 425
business expenses and, 196–197
defined, 71–72
Capital gains, 21, 63, 286, 434
capital asset defined, 546
of conduit entities, 116–117
exclusion on qualified small business
  stock, 551–552
history of taxation of, 112, 545–546
holding period, 113
long-term, 113
netting procedure for, 113–115, 547–551
planning strategies, 552–557
  net capital gain position, 552–553
short sales, 553–555
short-term, 113
tax treatment of, 115
treatment of, 549
Capital losses, 63, 286, 295–296, 434
of conduit entities, 116–117
of corporations, 296, 384–385
history of taxation of, 545–546

holding period, 113
of individuals, 295–296
long-term, 113
vs. short-term classification, 546–547
netting procedure for, 113–115, 547–551
planning strategies, 552–557
basis of securities sold, 556–557
net capital loss position, 553
short sales, 553–555
worthless securities, 555–556
short-term, 113
tax treatment of, 115–116
treatment of, 549
Capital recovery concept, 63, 71–73, 181, 425. *See also* Amortization; Depletion; Depreciation
basis and, 430–431, 476
capital expenditure, 71–72
land and, 72–73
property subject to periodic, 474–475
stock, 72
Carryback, 273
Carryforward, 273
Carryover, 434
Carryover basis, 287
Carryover basis rule,
for divorce, 448
property acquired from spouse, 448
Cash basis accounting method, 58–59
constructive receipt doctrine, 65
effect of, on income, 117–119
exception to income recognition, 118–119, 121–122
original issue discount securities, 119–120
related party accrued expense, 239–240
restrictions on use of, 633–634
timing of deductions and, 203–205
Cash-equivalent approach, 95–96
Casualty (theft) gains/losses, 291, 293, 558
Centralized management, 375
Certainty, defined, 6
Charitable contributions, 28, 340–342
corporations and, 385–387
donated inventory, 386
fiduciaries and, 394
Chief counsel's memoranda, 681
Child and dependent care credit, 648–650
Child and dependent care services,
as income exclusion, 151
Child support payments, 61, 105–106
Children employees,
owner-employee status, 380–381
sole proprietorship and, 400
Cited case, 687
Citing cases, 687
Citizen or residency test, 320–321
Claim-of-right doctrine, 64–65
vs. constructive receipt, 66–67
Class Life Asset Depreciation Range (ADR), 476, 478–479
Class lives, 479, 481

defined, 521
for MACRS, 524–529
Closely held corporation,
defined, 284
passive activity losses and, 283–284
Closing the short sale, 553
Code. *See* Internal Revenue Code
Code of Professional Conduct, 36
Commerce Clearing House (CCH), 685
Compensation of employees, 234–236
covered employee, 235
reasonable compensation, 235
Complex trusts, 393
Computer-assisted tax research (CATR), 688–689
Concepts,
accounting, 54–61
constructs and, 50
deduction, 68–74
doctrines and, 50
general, 50–54
income, 61–68
summary of, 74
Condemnation gain or loss, 601
Condemned property, replacement requirements, 602
Conduit entities, 55–57, 396–410
accounting methods, 397
accounting periods for, 396–397
basis in, 432–433
partnerships and S corporations, 397–399
capital gains/losses of, 116–117
comparison of characteristics of, 409
defined, 55
income shifting and, 57
as income splitting strategy, 408–410
limited liability companies, 404–405
limited liability partnerships, 405
partnerships, 55, 374, 400–405
reporting deductions, 183–185
S corporations, 55, 405–408
sole proprietorship, 56, 399–400
unearned income and, 100
Constructed assets, 440–441
direct construction costs, 440–441
indirect construction costs, 440–441
Construction,
long-term contracts and accounting methods, 634–637
Constructive ownership rules, 53
Constructive receipt doctrine,
vs. claim of right, 66–67
Constructs, 50
Continuity of life, 375
Controlled groups, 390–391
brother-sister relationship, 390–391
parent-subsidiary relationship, 390–391
Convenience, defined, 6–7
Copyrights, 505–507
Corporate distributions, 389–390
Corporate tax, 377–379

vs. individual tax rate, 378–379
vs. sole proprietorship, 376–379
schedule of rate, 22
Corporations, 375–391
accounting methods and, 633–634
accounting periods and methods for, 388–389
advantages/disadvantages, 410
articles of incorporation, 375
calculation of taxable income, 387–388
centralized management, 375
change from C corporation to S corporation, 406–407
continuity of life, 375
controlled groups, 390–391
defined, 375
distributions for shareholders, 389–390
double taxation, 377
free transferability of ownership, 375
income tax considerations, 376–381
sole proprietorship vs. corporate tax rate, 376–379
tax rate differentials, 376–379
limited liability, 375
multiple corporations, 390–391
net-capital losses, 296
owner-employee status, 379–381
children as employees, 380–381
double taxation, 381
employment taxes, 381
fringe benefits, 380
unreasonable compensation, 381
personal service corporations (PSC), 379
S corporations, 405–408
special rules for, 381–387
capital loss limitations, 384–385
charitable contribution limitations, 385–387
dividends-received deduction, 381–383
organizational costs, 387
passive activity losses, 383–384
transfers of assets to controlled corporation, 453
Correspondence examinations, 696
Cost depletion, 503–504
Cost recovery. *See also* Depreciation
basis subject to, 480–481
class lives, 481
depreciation convention, 481–482
IRS percentage tables, 482
property subject to, 480
Court decisions,
all other courts except U. S. Supreme Court, 686
citations to, 685
Supreme Court, 686
tax court, 685–686
use of in tax research, 691–692
Covered employee, 235
Cumulative Bulletin, 685, 686

D

Daily Tax Report, 688
Damage payments, 154
De minimis fringes, 151
Death benefits payments,
 as income exclusion, 144
Debt,
 assumption and realized gain/loss,
  543–545
Declining balance depreciation, 478, 481,
 491
Deduction concepts, 68–74
 business purpose concept, 68–71
 capital recovery concept, 71–73
 legislative grace concept, 68
 summary of, 74
Deductions, 21. *See also* Business expenses
 all-events test, 205–206
 classification of business, 185–193
  production of income, 188–189
  profit-motivated expenditures, 185–186
  trade or business expenses, 187–188
 classification of individual, 185
 depreciation, 72
 economic performance test, 206–208
 entity reporting, 183–185
 exemptions, 21
 expense, 21
 investment expenses, 188–189
 itemized, 27–29, 70, 334–335
 loss, 21
 vs. losses, 270
 mixed-use assets, 191–192
 mixed-use expenditures, 192–193
 moving expenses, 331–332
 one-year rule for prepaid expenses, 204
 personal expenses, 191
 production of income, 188–189
 reimbursed employee business expenses,
  325–328
 rental activity and, 189–191
 reporting, 182–185
 restrictions on, 179
 retirement plan contribution deductions,
  329–331
 self-employed taxpayers, 328–329
 standard, 27, 51–52, 70–71, 332–333
 tests for business expenses, 193–202
 timing of and effect of accounting
  method, 202–210
Deductions for adjusted gross income,
 26–27, 182, 318, 324–332
 list of, 324
 moving expenses, 331–332
 reimbursed employee business expenses,
  325
 retirement plan contribution deductions,
  329–331
 for self-employed taxpayers, 328
Deductions from adjusted gross income,
 27–29, 182–183, 318, 332–345

 itemized deductions, 334–345
 standard deduction, 332–333
Deferral,
 defined, 20
 nonrecognition transactions, 583–586
Deferred (third-party) exchange, 590–591
Dependency exemption deduction, 29,
 318–321
 citizen or residency test, 320–321
 divorce and, 320
 gross income test, 319
 joint return test, 321
 multiple support agreement, 320
 relationship or member of household
  test, 320
 restrictions on, 346
 support test, 319–320
Depletion, 502–505
 defined, 474
 introduction to, 472–474
 methods,
  cost, 503–504
  percentage (statutory), 504–505
 property subject to, 474–475
Depreciable basis, 476
Depreciation. *See also* Cost recovery
 Alternative Depreciation System, 499
 before 1982, 477–479
 class life asset depreciation range,
  478–479
 declining balance, 478, 481
 deductions, 72, 432
 defined, 474
 excess, 563
 introduction to, 472–474, 476–477
 inventory, 475
 IRS percentage tables, 482
 property subject to, 474–475
 Section 179 of IRS code, 482–487
 straight line method, 478, 481
 sum-of-years digits, 478
Depreciation convention, 481–482
 Accelerated Cost Recovery System, 490
 full-month, 482
 half-year, 482
 mid-month, 482
 mid-quarter, 482
 mid-year, 482
Depreciation methods,
 Accelerated Cost Recovery System,
  479–480, 489
 Alternative Depreciation System,
  491–492
 fact and circumstances method, 477–478
 major changes in, 477
 Modified Accelerated Cost Recovery
  System, 479–480, 495–496
Depreciation recapture, 561–567
 classification of Section 1245/Section
  1250 properties, 566–567
 defined, 561–562

 installment sales of depreciable assets,
  565–566
 nonrecognition transaction, 588–589
 Section 1245 recapture rule, 563
 Section 1250 recapture rule, 563–565
Direct construction costs, 440–441
Directly related,
 meal and entertainment expense, 225
Disability payments, 155
Discharge of indebtedness,
 as income exclusion, 158–161
 qualified real property business
  indebtedness, 159–160
Discriminant Function System, 696
Distribution date, 446
Dividends, double taxation and, 377
Dividends-received deduction (DRD),
 381–383
 rates for, 382
Divorce,
 carryover basis rules for property, 448
 dependency exemption deduction and,
  320
Doctrine, 50
Document perfection program, 696
Dominant motive, 186
Donated inventory, 386
Donative items,
 gifts, 140–141
 as income exclusions, 139–144
Double taxation, 381

E

Earned income, 94–96
 assignment-of-income doctrine, 95
 cash-equivalent approach, 95–96
Earned income credit (EIC), 647–648
Earnings and profits (E & P), 389–390
Economic income, 8
Economic performance test, 206–208
Economic Recovery Act, 479
Economy, defined, 7
Education expenses, 233–234
Educational assistance program,
 as income exclusion, 151
Effective tax rate, defined, 7–8
Employee business expenses, 342–343
Employee discounts, 150
Employer benefit plans,
 as income exclusion, 151–152
Employer reimbursement plan, 325–326
Employer's athletic facility,
 as income exclusion, 151
Employer-provided lodging,
 as income exclusion, 149–150
Employment taxes, 12–15, 381
Employment-related exclusions,
 144–153
 cafeteria plan, 152
 employer benefit plans, 151–153
 flexible benefits plan, 152–153

foreign earned income, 145
fringe benefits, 150–151
group term life insurance, 147–148
health and accident insurance
    premiums, 148–149
meals and lodging provided by
    employer, 149–150
payments made on behalf of employee,
    145–153
qualified pension plans, 146–147
salary reduction plan, 152–153
Employment-related loans, 109
Entertainment expenses, 224–228
    reciprocal, 227
Entity concept, 54–58
    assignment-of-income doctrine, 58–59
    conduit entities, 55
    taxable entities, 55
Equality,
    defined, 5–6
    horizontal, 5
    vertical, 5
Estate Planning, 688
Estate tax, 16–18, 444
Estates, 55, 392
    defined, 392
Estimated tax payment requirements, 54
Excess depreciation, 563
Excise taxes, 16
Exclusions. See also Income exclusions
    defined, 20
    employment-related, 144–153
    one-time exclusion of gain, 607–608
Exemption deduction phase-out, 345
Exemptions, 21
    dependency, 29
    for fiduciaries, 395
    personal, 29
    restrictions on dependents, 346
Expense, 21

F

Facts and circumstances method, 477–478
Farming business,
    accounting method and, 634
Federal estate tax, 17–18
Federal gift tax, 17
Federal Insurance Contribution Act
    (FICA), 13–14
Federal Reporter, 686
Federal Supplement, 686
Federal Tax Citator, 688
Federal Tax Coordinator 2d, 687
Federal Unemployment Tax (FUTA), 14–15
Fiduciaries, 392–386
    accounting periods, 395
    charitable contributions, 394
    estates, 392
    exemption amounts, 395
    income tax calculation for, 395–396
    income taxation of, 393–394

tax rates for, 392
trusts, 392–393
Field examinations, 697
Filing requirements, 348
Filing status, 321–324
    head of household, 323–324
    married, filing jointly, 321–322
    married, filing separately, 322
    single, 322–323
Final regulations, 680
Financial accounting,
    vs. tax accounting, 20, 208–210
Financial conformity rule, 641
Fines, 5
First-in, first-out (FIFO) method, 556, 638,
    641
Fiscal years, 58
Flat tax, 8
Flexible benefits plan, 152–153
Foreign earned income, as income
    exclusion, 145
Foreign tax credit, 642–644
Franchises, 505–507
Free transferability of ownership, 375
Fringe benefits, 150–151
    child and dependent care services, 151
    de minimis fringe benefits, 151
    educational assistance program, 151
    employee discounts, 150–151
    employer's athletic facility, 151
    no additional cost services, 150
    for owner-employee status, 380
    working-condition fringes, 151
Full absorption costing method, 638
Full-month convention, 482, 490
Functional use test, 602

G

Gains,
    characterizing from property disposition,
        545
    deferral of, nonrecognition transaction,
        583–586
    defined, 20–21
    realized, 541–545
    recognized, 540–541
Gambling losses, 342–343
General asset classes, 592
General concepts, 50–54
    ability-to-pay concept, 50–51
    administrative convenience concept,
        51–52
    arm's length transaction concept, 52–53
    pay-as-you-go concept, 53–54
    summary of, 74
General counsel's memoranda (GCM), 681
Generally accepted accounting principles
    (GAAP), 20
Gift loans, 108–109
Gift taxes, 16–17
Gifts. See also Business gifts

business, 140–141, 232–233
    defined, 140
    holding period, 444
    as income exclusion, 140–141
    property acquired by, 441–444
    split basis rule for loss property,
        443–444
    unified donative-transfers credit, 17
Golsen rule, 683
Goodwill, 438–439
    amortization of, 505–506
Government Printing Office, 685
Grantor, 393
Grantor trust, 393
Gross income, 19–20
    defined, 90–91
    determining, 89
Gross income test, 319
Gross sales price, 542–543
Group term life insurance,
    as income exclusion, 147–148
Guaranteed payment, 401–402

H

H. R. 10 plan, 329
Half-month convention, 490
Half-year convention, 482
Hand, Learned, 34
Hazards of litigation, 697
Head of household, 323–324
Health and accident insurance premiums,
    as income exclusion, 148–149
Health and accident policy payments,
    as income exclusion, 155–156
Hobby expenses, 245–247
Hobby losses, 246
Hobby-related deductions, 342–343
Holding period, 113, 434, 547
    for gifts, 444
    like-kind exchanges, 599
    nonrecognition transaction, 588–589
Home equity debt, 338
Home mortgage interest, 338–339
Home office expenses, 250–252
Horizontal equity, 5
Hybrid accounting method
    defined, 121
    effect of, on income, 121

I

Illegal business expenses, 200
Impairment-related work expenses,
    342–343
Improvements, 198
    by lessee, as income exclusion, 161
Imputed income, 106–112
    bargain purchases, 111–112
    below market-rate loans, 107–111
    defined, 107
    payment of expenses by others, 111

Imputed interest rules, 108
  exceptions to, 110–111
Income,
  ability-to-pay concept, 50–51
  active, 282–283
  assignment-of-income doctrine, 95
  cash-equivalent approach, 95–96
  current view of, 93–94
  defined, 19–21
  derived from labor and capital, 91–92
  earned, 94–96
  effect of accounting method on, 117–122
  financial account vs. taxable, 20
  gross, 19–20, 89–91
  imputed, 106–112
  as increase in wealth, 92
  investment, 339
  ordinary, 20
  passive, 283
  portfolio, 282
  realization and, 90–94
  transfer, 100–106
  types of, 282–283
  unearned, 96–100
    annuities, 97–99
    rental and royalty income, 96–97
Income concepts, 61–68
  all-inclusive income concept, 61–62
  capital recovery concept, 63
  legislative grace concept, 62–63
  realization concept, 63–67
  summary of, 74
  wherewithal-to-pay concept, 67–68
Income deferral, 20
  vs. exclusion, 138–139
Income exclusions, 20, 138–161
  vs. deferral, 138–139
  donative items, 139–144
    death benefits, 144
    gifts, 140–141
    inheritances, 141
    life insurance proceeds, 141–143
    scholarships, 143–144
  employment-related, 144–153
    foreign earned income, 145
    payments made on behalf of
      employee, 145–153
  investment-related exclusions, 156–163
    discharge of indebtedness, 158–161
    improvement by lessee, 161
    municipal bond interest, 156–157
    stock dividends, 158
  IRS code and, 139
  returns of human capital, 153–156
    damage payments, for personal injury
      or sickness, 154
    payments from health and accident
      policies, 155–156
    workers' compensation, 153
Income shifting, 30, 33–34
  conduit entities and, 57
Income splitting,

conduit entities and, 408–410
Income tax,
  calculating individual, 25–29
  revenues of, 11–12
  as system, 49–50
Income tax credits. *See* Tax credits
Indirect construction costs, 440–441
Individual accounting treatments, 632
Individual retirement accounts (IRA),
  330–331
Individual tax credits, 646–650
  child and dependent care credit, 648–650
  earned income credit, 647–648
  purpose of, 646–647
Individuals, taxation of,
  calculating tax liability, 25–29, 346–348
  computing, 182
  deductions for adjusted gross income,
    324–332
    list of, 324
    moving expenses, 331–332
    reimbursed employee business
      expenses, 325
    retirement plan contribution
      deductions, 329–331
    for self-employed taxpayers, 328
  deductions from adjusted gross income,
    332–345
    itemized deductions, 334–345
    standard deduction, 332–333
  dependency exemption deduction, 318
  exemption and standard deduction
    restrictions on dependents, 346
  exemption deduction phase-out, 345
  filing requirements, 348
  filing status, 321–324
  itemized deduction phase-out, 344
  kiddie tax, 347–348
  personal exemption deduction, 318
  rate for, vs. corporate rate, 378–379
Individuals,
  accounting methods for, 317
  income calculation, 317
  taxation of, 317–348
Information-matching program, 696
Inherited property, 444–448
  alternate valuation date, 445–446
  distribution date, 446
  as income exclusion, 141
  other considerations, 446–447
  primary valuation date, 445
Initial basis, 435
Installment sales, 121–122
  of depreciable assets, 565–566
Insurance, as business expense, 241
Intangible assets,
  amortization of, 505–507
  specifically excluded from amortization,
    507
Intangible property, 427
Interest, 28
Interest expenses, as itemized deductions,

home mortgage interest, 338–339
  investment interest, 339–340
Interest-free loan, 107–111
Internal Revenue Bulletin, 685
Internal Revenue Code, 18, 675–679
  amendments to, 677–679
  citations to, 684
  income exclusions, 139
  Rev. Proc. 87–56, 521–523
  Section 61 gross income, 90–91
  Section 162, 187
  Section 170, 676–677
  Section 179, 18, 480, 482–487
  Section 197, 438, 505–506
  Section 212, 188–189
  Section 280A, 692–695
  Section 351 transfer, 453
  Section 1202, 551–552
  Section 1231, 434, 557–561
  structure of, 675–677
  subtitles of, 675
  use of in tax research, 690–691
Internal Revenue Service, 18–19
  appeals to, 19, 697
  examinations, 696–697
Interpretative regulations, 679–680
Inventories,
  accounting methods for, 637–641
  average cost method, 638, 640–641
  depreciation and, 475
  financial conformity rule, 641
  first-in, first-out method, 638, 641
  full absorption costing method, 638
  inventory cost, 638
  inventory flow assumptions, 640–641
  last-in, first-out (LIFO) method, 638, 641
  lower of cost-or-market valuation,
    639–640, 641
  market for purchased merchandise, 639
  specific identification method, 640
  uniform capitalization (unicap) rules,
    639
Investment expenses, 188–189, 339,
    342–343
  defined, 68–69
Investment income, 339
Investment interest, 339–340
Investment tax credit (ITC), 642
Investment-related exclusions,
  discharge of indebtedness, 158–161
  improvement by lessee, 161
  municipal bond interest, 156–157
  stock dividends, 158
Investment-related losses,
  capital losses,
    of corporations, 296
    of individuals, 295–296
  related party sales, 297–298
  small business stock, 296–297
  specially treated investment losses,
    296–299
  wash sales, 298–299

Involuntary conversions, 599–602
  capital gain, 601
  condemnation gain or loss, 601
  defined, 599–600
  direct conversion, 601
  functional use test, 602
  gains/losses, 600–602
  qualified replacement property, 602
  replacement period, 602
  Section 1231, 601
Itemized deduction phase-out, 344
Itemized deductions, 27–29, 70, 183, 334–345
  charitable contributions, 340–342
  interest expenses, 28, 338–340
  medical expenses deductions, 28, 334–336
  miscellaneous itemized deductions, 188, 342–344
  summary of categories and limitations of, 335
  taxes, 28, 337–338

J

Joint return test, 321
Journal of Taxation, 688
Judicial authorities, 673, 674, 681–683
  appellate courts, 683
  Supreme Court, 683
  trial courts, 682

K

Keogh plan, 329
Kiddie tax, 347–348

L

Land, capital recovery concept, 72–73
Last-in, first-out (LIFO) method, 638, 641
Least aggregate deferral tax year, 630
Legal fees, as business expenses, 244–245
Legislative authorities, 673–679
  internal revenue code, 675–679
  legislative process, 677–679
  tax treaties, 679
  U. S. Constitution, 673–675
Legislative grace concept, 62–63, 68
Legislative regulation, 680
Letter rulings, 681
LEXIS, 688
Life insurance,
  group term as income exclusion, 147–148
  proceeds, as income exclusion, 141–143
Like-kind exchanges, 67, 589–599
  boot, 589
  carryover of tax attributes, 599
  deferred (third-party) exchange, 590–591
  depreciation recapture, 599
  direct exchange of property requirement, 590

  effect of boot on, 594–598
  exchange requirement, 589–591
  exchanges that never qualify, 594
  holding period, 599
  losses and, 590, 597
  related party exchanges, 598
Like-kind property, 591–594
  general asset classes, 592
  IRS interpretation, 591
  product class, 592–594
  rules for, 591
Limited liability, 375
Limited liability companies (LLCs), 404–405
Limited liability partnerships (LLPs), 405
Limited mixed-use expenses, 245–252
  hobby expenses, 245–247
  home office expenses, 250–252
  vacation home expenses, 247–250
Limited partnerships, 401
  passive activity and, 281
  as tax shelter, 276
Listed property,
  adequate record keeping, 502
  defined, 500
  limitation on passenger autos, 501–502
  rules for, 499–502
Loans,
  below market-rate, 107–111
  employment-related, 109–110
  gift, 108–110
  interest-free, 107–111
  shareholder, 109–110
Lobbying expenses, 200–201
Lodging. *See* Employer-provided lodging
Long-term capital gains, 113
Long-term capital losses, 113
Long-term construction contracts, 122
  accounting methods,
    lookback method, 635–636
    percentage-of-completed-contract method, 634–635, 637
Lookback method, 635–636
Lookback recapture rule, 559–560
Loss-of-income damages, as income exclusion, 154
Losses, 21. *See also* specific losses
  activity, 270
  annual, 21, 270, 272–275
  characterizing from property disposition, 545
  vs. deductions, 270
  investment-related, 295–299
  net operating losses, 272–275
  passive activity, 272, 279–290
  personal casualty, 299–301
  realized, 541–545
  recognized, 540–541
  suspended, 284
  tax-shelter, 275–290
  trade or business, 291–295
  transaction, 21, 271, 290–301

  treatment of, 271
Low-income housing, 567
  depreciation of, 489
  passive activity and, 282
Lower of cost-or-market valuation, 639–640, 641
Luxury tax, 16

M

MACRS. *See* Modified Accelerated Cost Recovery
Majority-interest tax year, 629–630
Marginal tax rate,
  defined, 7–8
  tax planning and, 33
Market for purchased merchandise, 639
Marriage penalty tax, 322–323
Married, filing jointly, 321–322
Married, filing separately, 322
Material participant, 279–280
Material participation, 279
Material participation exception, 288–290
Meals and entertainment expense, 224–228
  associated with, 225–226
  club dues, 226
  directly related, 225
  reciprocal entertaining, 227
Meals provided by the employer,
  as income exclusion, 149
Medical expenses deductions, 28, 334–336
  defined, 334
  of dependent, 202
Medicare Health Insurance (MHI), 13, 329
Member of household test, 320
Mertens Law of Federal Income Taxation, 687
Mid-month convention, 482, 496–498
Mid-quarter convention, 482, 496–498
Mid-year convention, 482, 496–498
Miscellaneous itemized deductions, 28–29, 188, 342–344
  fully deductible expenditures, 342–343
  gambling losses, 342–343
  hobby-related deductions, 342–343
  impairment-related work expenses, 342–343
  investment expenses, 342–343
  partially deductible expenditures, 342–344
  tax advice and preparations, 342–343
Mixed-use assets, 191–192
Mixed-use expenditures, 192–193
Mixed-use property, 426–427
Modified Accelerated Cost Recovery (MACRS), 476–477, 479–480, 491–502
  adequate record keeping, 502
  Alternative Depreciation System, 499
  basis subject to cost recovery, 480–481
  class lives, 481
  depreciation conventions, 481–482, 496–499
  depreciation methods, 495–496

differences from ACRS, 491
limitation on passenger autos, 501–502
limitations on listed property, 499–501
overview of, 491–492
property subject to cost recovery, 480
recovery classes, 492–493
tables of,
  classes, 524–529
  depreciation for car placed in service
    in 1994 and 1995, 200% declining
    balance method, 537
  depreciation for optional straight-line,
    537
  depreciation for residential rental
    property, 535
  depreciation 200% or 150% declining
    balance, switching to straight-line,
    495, 532–534
  nonresidential real property, 496
  using percentage tables, 494–495
Moving expenses, 331–332
Multiple asset purchase, 437–438
Multiple corporations, 390–391
Municipal bond interest, as income
  exclusion, 156–157

N

Natural business year, 631
Natural resources, depletion and, 502–505
Necessary expense, 194–195
Net capital gain,
  planning strategies for, 552–553
Net capital loss,
  planning strategies for, 552–553
Net investment income, 339
Net long-term capital gain, 115, 549
Net long-term capital loss, 115–116, 549
Net operating losses (NOL), 272–275
  annual accounting and, 272
  carryback, 273–274
  carryforward, 273–274
  defined, 272
  personal casualty loss, 275
  purchases, 275
Net short-term capital gain, 549
Net short-term capital loss, 549
Netting procedure,
  for capital gain/loss, 113–115
  for capital gains or losses, 547–551
  Section 1231 gains/losses, 557–561
90-day letter, 697
No additional cost services, 150
Nonaccountable reimbursement plans,
  326–328
Nonacquiescence, 680–681
Nonbusiness bad debt, 236–239
Nonbusiness expenses, 188–189
Nonrecognition transactions, 583–609
  adjustment of replacement assets basis,
    586–588
  characteristics of, 610

classes of, 583
commonalities of, 584–589
  deferral of realized gain, 585–586
  depreciation recapture, 588–589
  holding period, 588–589
  replacement asset, 585
  summary of, 585
  tax attributes, 588–589
defined, 583
involuntary conversions, 599–602
like-kind exchanges, 589–599
rationale for, 584
  continuity of investment criteria, 584
  lack of wherewithal to pay, 584
sale of principal residence, 603–609
Nonrecourse debt, 278

O

Office examinations, 696
Old Age, Survivors and Disability
  Insurance (OASDI), 13, 329
Omnibus Budget Reconciliation Act,
  active participation exception, 290
  corporate tax rate, 377
  lobbying expenses, 201
  material participation exception, 288–290
  membership to clubs, 226
  moving expenses, 331–332
  passive activities, 280
  Social Security benefits and, 103
One-year rule for prepaid expenses, 204
One-year rule for services, 120
Ordinary expense, 193–194
Ordinary income, 20
Ordinary income assets, 542
Ordinary income loss, 62
Organizational costs, for corporations, 387
Original issue discount (OID) securities,
  118–119
Overall accounting methods, 632
Owner-employee status, 379–381
  children as employees, 380–381
  double taxation, 381
  employment taxes, 381
  fringe benefits, 380
  unreasonable compensation, 381
Ownership tax year, 631

P

Parent-subsidiary relationship, 390–391
Partnerships, 374, 400–405
  accounting methods and, 633–634
  advantages/disadvantages, 410
  basis in, 397–399
    of partnership interest, 402–403
  as conduit entity, 55
  distributions, 403–404
  guaranteed payment, 401–402
  legal characteristics, 401
  limited, 401

limited liability companies, 404–405
limited liability partnerships, 405
  partners are not employees, 401–402
  partnership debt, 402–403
  Section 179 and, 484–485
  taxable year, 397
    business purpose, 630–631
    least aggregate deferral, 630
    limitations on choice of, 629–631
    majority-interest, 629–630
    natural business, 631
    principal partner, 620
  terminations of, 404
Passive activity, defined, 279
Passive activity loss (PAL) rules, 276, 279
  active participation exception, 290
  disposition of passive activities, 284–287
    by gift, 287
    by sale, 285–286
    upon death, 286–287
  exception for rental real estate, 287–290
  general rules for, 284
  material participation exception, 288–290
  suspended loss, 284
  taxpayers subject to limits, 284–285
  types of income, 282–283
Passive activity losses, 272, 279–290,
  383–384
  limited partnerships and, 281
  low-income housing projects, 282
  personal service corporations and,
    383–384
  rental activities and, 280–281
  working interest in oil and gas, 282
Passive income, 283
Patents, 505–507
Pay-as-you-go concept, 7, 12, 53–54
Payment of expenses by others, as
  imputed income, 111
Payments made on behalf of employee,
  as income exclusion, 145–153
Penalties, 5
Pension plans, qualified, 99
Per-diem payments, 325
Percentage depletion, 504–505
Percentage-of-completed contract method,
  122, 634–635
  taxpayers exempt from, 637
Personal casualty and theft loss, 28,
  299–301
  annual limitations, 300
  limitation on, 300–301
  measuring, 300
  net operating losses and, 275
  statutory floor, 300
Personal exemption deduction, 29, 318
Personal expenses, defined, 68–69
Personal injury, 154
Personal property, 15
Personal service corporations (PSC), 379
  accounting methods for, 389
  passive activity losses, 383–384

Personal use assets, 542
Personal use property, 426
    converted to business use, 449–451
Personalty, 427
Points, 338
Portfolio income, 282
Prepaid expenses, 204
Prepaid interest, 205
Prepaid taxes, 204–205
Prepayments,
    one-year rule for services, 120–121
Present value tables, 31
Primary authorities, 673–686
    administrative authorities, 673, 674,
        679–681
    citations to,
        code and regulations, 684
        committee reports, 683–684
        court decisions, 685–686
        other IRS pronouncements, 685
    defined, 673
    judicial authorities, 673, 674, 681–683
    legislative authorities, 673–679
Primary valuation date, 445
Principal partner tax year, 630
Principal residence,
    adjusted sales price, 605
    deferral of gain, 605–606
    defined, 603
    gain exclusion requirements, 607
    interaction of deferral and exclusion
        provisions, 608–609
    one-time exclusion of gain, 607–608
    replacement period, 604–605
    sale of, 603–609
    taxpayers older than fifty-five, 607–609
Principal residence replacement period,
    604
Private activity bond, 657–658
Private letter ruling (LTR), 681
Prizes, 101
Product class. *See* Standard Industrial
    Classification Manual (SIC Codes)
Production of income expenses, 188–189
Profit-motivated expenditures, 185–186
Progressive tax rate structure,
    ability-to-pay concept and, 51
    defined, 10–11
Pronouncements, use of in tax research,
    691
Property, 425–455. *See also* Assets
    all the facts and circumstances test,
        189–190
    assessed value of, 15
    basis in,
        acquired by gift, 441–444
        acquired by inheritance, 444–448
        acquired from spouse, 448–449
        adjusted, 428–432
        initial, 428, 435
        personal use property converted to
            business use, 449–451

as charitable contribution, 340–341
    classes of, 426–427
        intangible property, 427
        mixed-use property, 426–427
        personal use property, 426
        personalty, 427
        real estate, 427
        summary of, 428
        tangible property, 427
    condemned, 602
    defined, 425
    depreciation recapture, 561–567
    determining amount invested, 435–437
    holding period, 434
    investment cycle of, 427–434
    personal, 15
    real, 15
    rental activity and, 189–191
    Section 179 and, 483–484
    Section 1231, 557
    Section, 1245, 566–567
    Section 1250, 566–567
    subject to capital recovery, 474–475
    subject to cost recovery, 480
    with no class life, 522
Property disposition, 190–191, 433–434,
    539–567
    amount realized, 433–434
    capital gains/losses, 99–100, 545–557
    character of gain or loss, 545
    classification of assets, 542
    gross sales price, 542–543
    introduction to, 539–541
    realized gain/loss, 433–434, 541–545
    recognized gain/loss, 540–541
    Section 1231 gains/losses, 557–561
    steps in analysis of, 539–541
    summary of, 568
Property settlements, 105–106
Property taxes, 15–16
Proportional rate structure, defined, 8–9
Proposed regulations, 680
Protest letter, 697
Punitive damages, as income exclusion,
    154

Q

Qualified home mortgage interest, 338–339
Qualified pension plans, 99
    as income deferral, 146–147
Qualified real property business
    indebtedness, 159–160

R

Real estate, 427
Real estate taxes, 242–243
Real property (real estate), 15, 427, 567
    Accelerated Cost Recovery System and,
        488
Real property tax year, 436

Real property trade or business, defined,
    289
Realistic possibility standard, 36
Realization concept, 63–67
    claim-of-right doctrine, 64–65
    constructive receipt doctrine, 65–66
    income and, 90–91
Realized gain/loss, 433–434, 541–545
    amount realized, 542–543
    effect of debt assumptions, 543–545
    gross sales price, 542
Reasonable compensation, 235
Reasonable expenses, 195
Recapture rules, 106
Reciprocal entertaining, 227
Recognized gain/loss
    categories of, 541
    defined, 540
Recovery classes,
    for Modified Accelerated Cost Recovery,
        493
Regressive rate structure, defined, 9–10
Regular corporations, 55
Rehabilitation tax credit, 645–646
Reimbursed employee business expenses,
    325–328
    accountable reimbursement plans,
        325–326
    nonaccountable reimbursement plans,
        326–328
Related party,
    accrued expenses, as business expense,
        239–240
    exchanges, 598
Related party provisions, 52–53
Related party sales, losses on, 297–298
Relationship or member of household test,
    320
Remainderman, 393
Rental activity, 189–191
    all the facts and circumstances test,
        189–190
    disposition of, 561
    passive activity and, 280–281
Rental income, 96–97
Rental payments, as business expense,
    243–244
Rental real estate,
    active participation exception, 290
    determining if active or passive, 288
    PAL rule exceptions for, 287–290
Repair-and-maintenance expense, 198
Replacement, 198
Replacement property, 602
Reporter, 685
Reports of the United States Tax Court, 685
Research and experimental (R & E) tax
    credit, 644–645
Research Institute of America (RIA), 681,
    685
Residency test, 320–321
Residential rental property, 522, 567

Retained earnings, 390
Retirement plan contribution deductions,
   individual retirement account, 329–331
Returns, tax,
   amended, 25
   filing, 24–25
   statute of limitations, 24–25
Returns of human capital,
   damage payments for personal injury or
      sickness, 154
   as income exclusion, 153–156
   payments from health and accident
      policies, 155–156
   workers' compensation, 153
Rev. Proc. 87–56, 521–523
Revenue agent's report, 697
Revenue procedures, 680
Revenue rulings, 18, 680
Reversionary interest, 393
Royalty income, 96–97

S

S corporations, 405–408
   accounting methods for, 389
   advantages/disadvantages, 410
   basis in, 397–399
   change from C corporation to S
      corporation, 406–407
   as conduit entity, 55
   distributions and basis adjustments,
      407–408
   employee status of stockholders, 407
   qualification requirements, 405–406
   revocation of S election, 406
   Section 179 and, 484–485
   taxable year, 397
      limitations on choice of, 631–632
      natural business, 631
      ownership, 631
Salary reduction plan, 152–153
Sale of principal residence,
   deferral of gain, 605–606
   gain exclusion requirements, 607
   interaction of deferral and exclusion
      provisions, 608–609
   one-time exclusion of gain, 607–608
   principal residence defined, 603
   replacement period, 604–605
   taxpayers older than fifty-five, 607–609
Sales tax, 15, 242
Salvage value, 477–478
Savings bonds, 119
Scholarships, as income exclusion, 143–144
Secondary authorities, 19, 686–689
   citators, 687–688
   computer-assisted tax research, 688–689
   defined, 673
   tax periodicals, 688
   tax services, 686–687
Section 61 of IRS Code, 90–91
Section 162 of IRS code, 187

Section 170 of IRS code,
   subdivisions of, 676–677
Section 179 of IRS code, 18, 480, 482–487
   limitations on deduction, 484–487
      active trade or business income limit,
         486–487
      annual deduction limit, 484–485
      annual investment limit, 486
   qualified property, 483–484
   qualified taxpayers, 483
Section 197 of IRS code, 438, 505–506
Section 212 of IRS code, 188–189
Section 280A of IRS code, 692–695
Section 351 transfer of IRS code, 453
Section 1202 of IRS code, 551–552
Section 1231 of IRS code, 557
   assets, 542, 557
   disposition of rental activities, 561
   gains/losses, 434, 557–561
   importance of capital gain relief,
      560–561
   lookback recapture rule, 559–560
   netting procedure, 557–561
   property defined, 557
Section 1245 properties, classification of,
      566–567
   recapture rule, 563
Section 1250 properties,
   classification of, 566–567
   recapture rule, 563–565
Securities,
   active investor, 187–188
   active trader, 188
   basis in, 451–455
      stock dividends, 452–453
      transfers of assets to controlled
         corporations, 453
      wash sale stock, 453–455
      when sold, 556–557
   commission paid, 197
   first-in, first-out order (FIFO), 556
   securities dealer, 188
   short sales, 553–555
   wash sales, 298–299
   worthless, 555–556
Securities dealer, 188
Self-assessment, 7
Self-employed taxpayers, deductions for,
      328–329
Self-employment tax, 12–14, 400
   deductions for, 328
Self-insured medical plan,
   as income exclusion, 148–149
Shareholder loans, 109–110
Short sale against the box, 553, 555
   vs. short sale, 555
Short sales, 553–555
   closing, 553
   process illustrated, 554
   vs. short sale against the box, 555
Short-term capital gain, 113
Short-term capital losses, 113

Sic codes. See Standard Industrial
   Classification Manual (SIC Codes)
Simple trusts, 393
Single, 322–323
Small business stock, losses on, 296–297
Smith, Adam, 5
Social Security benefits,
   Omnibus Budget Reconciliation Act,
      103–105
   as taxable income, 101–105
Social Security tax, 12–14
   revenues of, 11–12
Sole proprietorships, 56, 399–400
   children employees and, 400
   compared to corporate tax rate, 376–379
   self-employment tax, 400
Special audit programs, 696
Specific charge-off method, 238
Specific identification method, 640
Split basis rule for business property,
      449–451
Split basis rule for gifts, 443–444
Standard deduction, 27, 51–52, 70–71
   age and, 333
   amounts for, 333
   blindness and, 333
   restrictions on dependents, 346
Standard Federal Tax Reporter (CCH), 687
Standard Industrial Classification Manual
   (SIC Codes), 592–594
   construction machinery and equipment,
      593, 621–622
   farm machinery and equipment, 623–624
   industrial trucks, tractors, trailers,
      stackers, 623
   mobile homes, 622
   motor vehicles and passenger car
      bodies, 593, 621
   power-driven handtools, 622
   service industry machinery, not
      elsewhere classified, 622
   woodworking machinery, 624
Standard mileage rate method, automobile
   expense, 227
Start-up costs, 198–199
Statements on Responsibilities in Tax
   Practice (SRTP), 36–38
Statute of limitations, 24–25
Statutory authorities, 673
Statutory depletion, 504–505
Statutory floor, 300
Statutory notice of deficiency, 697
Stock,
   capital gain exclusion on qualified small
      business, 551–552
   capital recovery of, 72
   purchase of corporate, 440
Stock dividends,
   basis in, 451–453
   taxable, 452–453
   as income exclusions, 158
Straight line method of depreciation, 478,

481, 490–491, 496, 499
    recovery classes, 492
Substance-over-form doctrine, 60–61
    nonrecognition transactions, 584
Substantial rehabilitation, 645
Substantiation requirement, 233
Sum-of-years digits method of
    depreciation, 478
Support test, 319–320
    multiple support agreement, 320
Supreme Court, 683
    decisions by, 686
Supreme Court Reports, 686
Surviving spouse, 322

T

Tangible property, 427
Taxable entities, 55
    defined, 55
Taxable income, 7
Taxable year,
    business purpose tax year, 630–631
    calendar year, 627
    defined, 627
    fiscal year, 627
    least aggregate tax year, 630
    limitations on choice of, 629–630
    majority-interest tax year, 629–630
    natural business year, 631
    principal partner tax year, 630
    rationale for, 628
Tax accounting,
    vs. financial accounting, 208–210
Tax Advisor, 688
Tax avoidance, 34–35
Tax base, 7
Tax benefit rule, 59
Tax compliance,
    vs. tax planning, 689
Tax court, 682
    decisions by, 685–686
    memorandum decisions, 682
    regular decisions, 682
Tax Court Memorandum Decisions, 685
Tax Court Reporter, 685
Tax credits, 24
    business, 642–646
        foreign, 642–644
        investment, 642
        rehabilitation, 645–646
        research and experimental, 644–645
    defined, 642
    individual, 646–650
        child and dependent care credit,
            648–650
        earned income credit, 647–648
    nonrefundable, 642
    purpose of, 642
    refundable, 642
Taxes, 28
    alternative minimum, 650–661

as business expense, 241–243
calculating individual, 25–29
comprehensive tax return illustration,
    367–372
computed, 7
definition of, 3–5
employment, 12–14
estate, 16–18
evaluating,
    certainty, 6
    convenience, 6–7
    economy, 7
    equality, 5–6
excise, 16
filing returns, 24–25
flat, 8
gift, 16–17
income, 11–12
inflation and, 22–23
as itemized deductions, 337–338
as personal itemized deduction, 28
present value tables, 31
property, 15–16
purpose of, 3
sales, 15
self-employment, 12–14
Social Security, 12–14
types of, 11–18
unemployment, 14–15
wealth transfer, 16–18
TAXES—The Tax Magazine, 688
Tax evasion, 34–35
Tax-exempt income, deductions and,
    201–202
Tax guides, 687
Tax home, 230
Tax law,
    citations for, 18
    legislative process for, 677–679
    primary authorities, 18–19, 673–686
    secondary authorities, 19, 673
Tax liability, calculating, 346–348
Tax Management Portfolios, 687
Tax Notes, 688
Taxpayer Compliance Measurement
    Program (TCMP), 696
Tax periodicals, 688
Tax planning, 29–35
    income shifting, 33–34
    marginal tax rate, 33
    mechanics of, 29–34
    summary of rules for, 33
    tax avoidance vs. evasion, 34–35
    time value of money and, 32
    timing income and deductions, 30–33
    vs. tax compliance, 689
Tax practice,
    ethical considerations in, 35–38
    penalties for preparers, 36
    statements on Responsibilities in Tax
        Practice (SRTP), 36–38
Tax preference items, 650–651

Tax prepayments, 23–24
Tax rate schedules, 21–23
    corporate, 377
Tax rate structures,
    defined, 8–11
    progressive, 10–11
    proportional, 8–9
    regressive, 9–10
Tax rates,
    average, 7–8
    defined, 7–8
    effective, 7–8
    fiduciaries, 392
    individual vs. corporate, 378–379
    marginal, 7–8
Tax research, 689–695
    code and regulations, 690–691
    comprehensive research example,
        692–695
    computer-assisted, 688–689
    court decisions, 691–692
    primary authorities, 673–686
    pronouncements, 691
    secondary authorities, 673
    step 1: establish fact/determine issues,
        689–690
    step 2: locate relevant authorities, 690
    step 3: assess importance of authorities,
        690–692
    step 4: conclusions, recommendations
        and communication of results, 692
    tax compliance vs. tax planning, 689
Tax returns,
    comprehensive illustration of,
        367–372
Tax services, 686–687
Tax shelters,
    accounting methods and, 633–634
    at-risk rules, 277–279
    defined, 275
    history of, 275–276
    limited partnership, 276
    losses, 275–290
Tax treaties, 679
Technical advice memorandum (TAM),
    681
Technical memoranda (TM), 681
Temporary regulations, 680
Tentative minimum tax liability, 652
Testamentary trust, 393
Theft, 291
Theft gains/losses, 291, 299–301, 558
30-day letter, 697
Time value of money, tax planning and,
    32
Trade, defined, 187
Trade expenses, 68–69. *See also* Business
    expenses
    defined, 68–69, 187–188
Trade name, 506
Trade or business losses,
    business casualty, 291

business property fully destroyed, 291–293
business property partially destroyed, 293–295
theft losses, 291
Trademark, 506
Transaction losses, 21, 290–301
defined, 271
investment-related losses, 295–299
personal casualty, 299–301
trade or business losses, 291–295
treatment of, 271
Transfer income, 100–106
alimony received, 105–106
prizes and awards, 101
Social Security benefits, 101–105
unemployment compensation, 101
Travel expenses, 230–232
tax home and, 230–231
Treasury regulations, 18, 679–680
citation to, 684
final regulations, 680
interpretative regulations, 679–680
legislative regulation, 680
proposed regulations, 680
temporary regulations, 680
use of, in tax research, 691
Trial courts, 682
Trustee, 392

Trusts, 55, 392–393
complex, 393
reversionary interest, 393
simple, 393

U

U. S. Claims Court, 682
U. S. Constitution, 673–675
U. S. Court of Appeals for the Federal Circuit, 683
U. S. Courts of Appeals, 683
U. S. District court, 682
U. S. Supreme Court, 683
U. S. Tax Cases, 686
U. S. Tax Court, 682
Unearned income, 96–100
calculation of gain/loss on sale of investments, 99–100
conduit entities, 100
of minor child, 347–348
Unemployment compensation, as income, 101
Unemployment taxes, 14–15
Unified donative-transfers credit, 17
United States Reports, 686
United States Tax Reporter (RIA), 687
Units-of-production method, 503–504
University of Virginia Law Review, 688

V

Vacation home expenses, 247–250
Vertical equity, 5
Voluntary compliance, 7

W

Waiver of restrictions on assessment (Form 870), 697
Warranty repair allowances, 209
Wash sales, 298–299
Wealth of Nations, The (Smith), 5
Wealth transfer taxes, 16–18
WESTLAW, 688
Wherewithal to pay concept, 67–68
nonrecognition transaction, 584
Withholding provisions, 54
Workers' compensation, as income exclusion, 153
Working interest in oil and gas, passive activity and, 282
Working-condition fringe benefit, 151
Worthless securities, 555–556

Unreasonable compensation, 381
Unrecovered basis, 503
Unrecovered investment, 342–343